NEW PERSPECTIVES

SHELLMAN | VODNIK

Microsoft® Office 365®
Access® 2019

Comprehensive

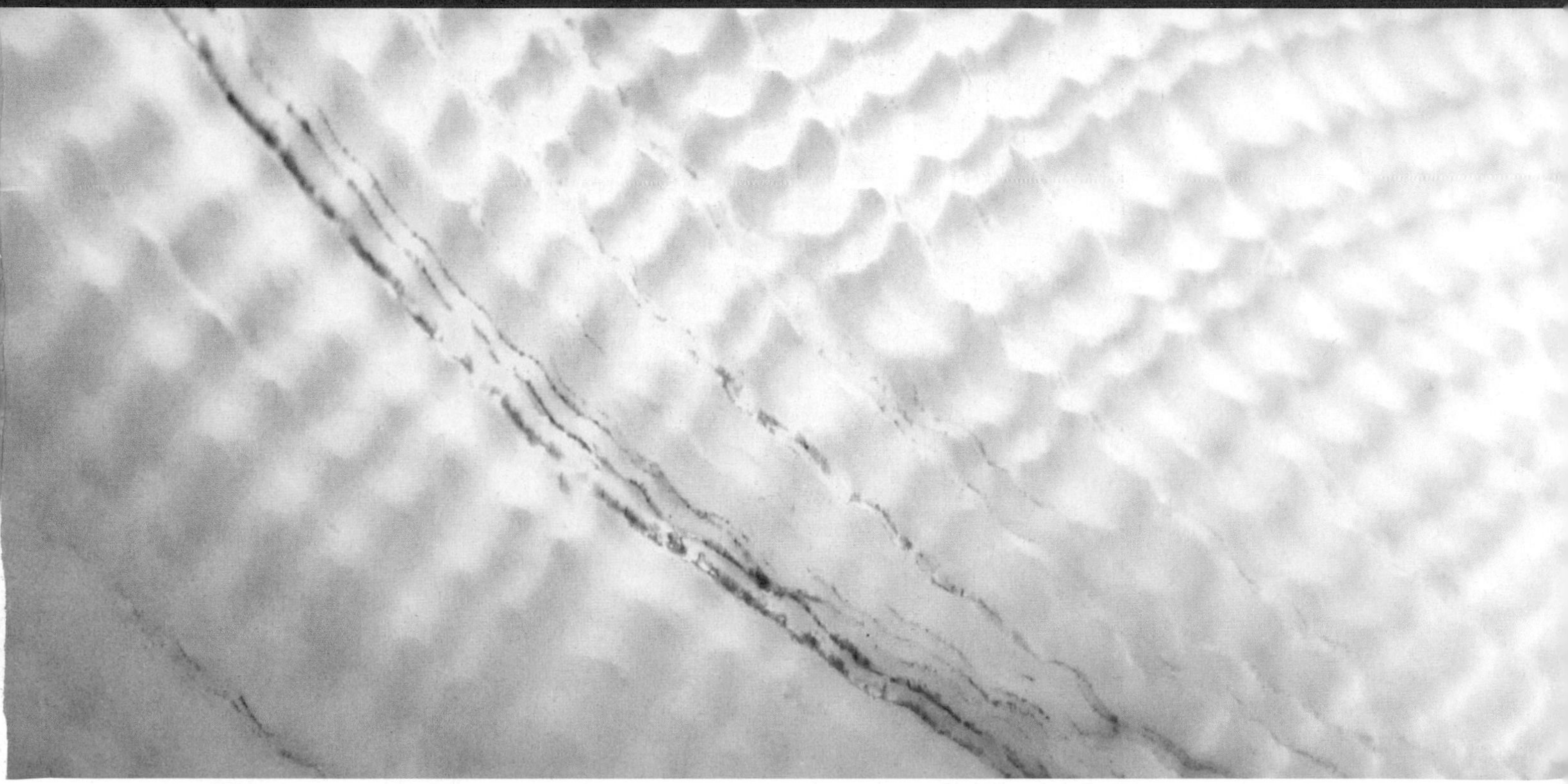

CENGAGE

Australia • Brazil • Mexico • Singapore • United Kingdom • United States

CENGAGE

New Perspectives Microsoft® Office 365® Access® 2019 Comprehensive
Mark Shellman and Sasha Vodnik

SVP, GM Skills & Global Product Management: Jonathan Lau

Product Director: Lauren Murphy

Product Assistant: Veronica Moreno-Nestojko

Executive Director, Content Design: Marah Bellegarde

Director, Learning Design: Leigh Hefferon

Learning Designer: Courtney Cozzy

Vice President, Marketing - Science, Technology, and Math: Jason R. Sakos

Senior Marketing Director: Michele McTighe

Marketing Manager: Timothy J. Cali

Director, Content Delivery: Patty Stephan

Content Manager: Christina Nyren

Digital Delivery Lead: Jim Vaughey

Designer: Lizz Anderson

Text Designer: Althea Chen

Cover Designer: Lizz Anderson

Cover Template Designer: Wing-Ip Ngan, Ink Design, Inc.

Cover Image: Krivosheev Vitaly/ShutterStock.com

Mac Users: If you're working through this product using a Mac, some of the steps may vary. Additional information for Mac users is included with the Data files for this product.

Disclaimer: This text is intended for instructional purposes only; data is fictional and does not belong to any real persons or companies.

Disclaimer: The material in this text was written using Microsoft Windows 10 and Office 365 Professional Plus and was Quality Assurance tested before the publication date. As Microsoft continually updates the Windows 10 operating system and Office 365, your software experience may vary slightly from what is presented in the printed text.

For product information and technology assistance, contact us at
Cengage Customer & Sales Support, 1-800-354-9706 or support.cengage.com.

For permission to use material from this text or product, submit all requests online at **www.cengage.com/permissions.**

Library of Congress Control Number: 2019936891

Student Edition ISBN: 978-0-357-02575-8
*Looseleaf available as part of a digital bundle

Cengage
20 Channel Center Street
Boston, MA 02210
USA

Cengage is a leading provider of customized learning solutions with employees residing in nearly 40 different countries and sales in more than 125 countries around the world. Find your local representative at **www.cengage.com.**

Cengage products are represented in Canada by Nelson Education, Ltd.

To learn more about Cengage platforms and services, visit **www.cengage.com.**

To register or access your online learning solution or purchase materials for your course, visit **www.cengage.com.**

Notice to the Reader

Publisher does not warrant or guarantee any of the products described herein or perform any independent analysis in connection with any of the product information contained herein. Publisher does not assume, and expressly disclaims, any obligation to obtain and include information other than that provided to it by the manufacturer. The reader is expressly warned to consider and adopt all safety precautions that might be indicated by the activities described herein and to avoid all potential hazards. By following the instructions contained herein, the reader willingly assumes all risks in connection with such instructions. The publisher makes no representations or warranties of any kind, including but not limited to, the warranties of fitness for particular purpose or merchantability, nor are any such representations implied with respect to the material set forth herein, and the publisher takes no responsibility with respect to such material. The publisher shall not be liable for any special, consequential, or exemplary damages resulting, in whole or part, from the readers' use of, or reliance upon, this material.

Printed in the United States of America
Print Number: 01 Print Year: 2019

BRIEF CONTENTS

TABLE OF CONTENTS

Getting to Know Microsoft Office Versions

Cengage is proud to bring you the next edition of Microsoft Office. This edition was designed to provide a robust learning experience that is not dependent upon a specific version of Office.

Microsoft supports several versions of Office:

- **Office 365:** A cloud-based subscription service that delivers Microsoft's most up-to-date, feature-rich, modern productivity tools direct to your device. There are variations of Office 365 for business, educational, and personal use. Office 365 offers extra online storage and cloud-connected features, as well as updates with the latest features, fixes, and security updates.
- **Office 2019:** Microsoft's "on-premises" version of the Office apps, available for both PCs and Macs, offered as a static, one-time purchase and outside of the subscription model.
- **Office Online:** A free, simplified version of Office web applications (Word, Excel, PowerPoint, and OneNote) that facilitates creating and editing files collaboratively.

Office 365 (the subscription model) and Office 2019 (the one-time purchase model) had only slight differences between them at the time this content was developed. Over time, Office 365's cloud interface will continuously update, offering new application features and functions, while Office 2019 will remain static. Therefore, your onscreen experience may differ from what you see in this product. For example, the more advanced features and functionalities covered in this product may not be available in Office Online or may have updated from what you see in Office 2019.

For more information on the differences between Office 365, Office 2019, and Office Online, please visit the Microsoft Support site.

Cengage is committed to providing high-quality learning solutions for you to gain the knowledge and skills that will empower you throughout your educational and professional careers.

Thank you for using our product, and we look forward to exploring the future of Microsoft Office with you!

Using SAM Projects and Textbook Projects

SAM and *MindTap* are interactive online platforms designed to transform students into Microsoft Office and Computer Concepts masters. Practice with simulated SAM Trainings and MindTap activities and actively apply the skills you learned live in Microsoft Word, Excel, PowerPoint, or Access. Become a more productive student and use these skills throughout your career.

If your instructor assigns SAM Projects:

1. Launch your SAM Project assignment from SAM or MindTap.
2. Click the links to download your **Instructions file**, **Start file**, and **Support files** (when available).
3. Open the Instructions file and follow the step-by-step instructions.
4. When you complete the project, upload your file to SAM or MindTap for immediate feedback.

To use SAM Textbook Projects:

1. Launch your SAM Project assignment from SAM or MindTap.
2. Click the links to download your **Start file** and **Support files** (when available).
3. Locate the module indicated in your book or eBook.
4. Read the module and complete the project.

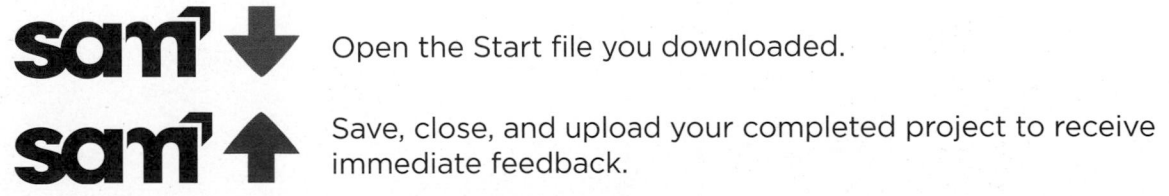

sam ↓ Open the Start file you downloaded.

sam ↑ Save, close, and upload your completed project to receive immediate feedback.

IMPORTANT: To receive full credit for your Textbook Project, you must complete the activity using the Start file you downloaded from SAM or MindTap.

MODULE 1

Creating a Database

Tracking Patient, Visit, and Billing Data

ACCESS

OBJECTIVES

Session 1.1
- Define basic database concepts and terms
- Start and exit Access
- Identify the Microsoft Access window and Backstage view
- Create a blank database
- Create and save a table in Datasheet view and Design view
- Add fields to a table in Datasheet view and Design view
- Set a table's primary key in Design view

Session 1.2
- Open an Access database
- Open a table using the Navigation Pane
- Copy and paste records from another Access database
- Navigate a table datasheet and enter records
- Create and navigate a simple query
- Create and navigate a simple form
- Create, preview, navigate, and print a simple report
- Use Help in Access
- Identify how to compact, back up, and restore a database

Case | *Lakewood Community Health Services*

Lakewood Community Health Services, a nonprofit health clinic located in the greater Atlanta, Georgia area, provides a range of medical services to patients of all ages. The clinic specializes in chronic disease management, cardiac care, and geriatrics. Donna Taylor, the office manager for Lakewood Community Health Services, oversees a small staff and is responsible for maintaining records for the clinic's patients.

In order to best manage the clinic, Donna and her staff rely on electronic medical records for patient information, billing, inventory control, purchasing, and accounts payable. Several months ago, the clinic upgraded to **Microsoft Access 2019** (or simply **Access**), a computer program used to enter, maintain, and retrieve related data in a format known as a database. Donna and her staff want to use Access to store information about patients, billing, vendors, and products. She asks for your help in creating the necessary Access database.

STARTING DATA FILES

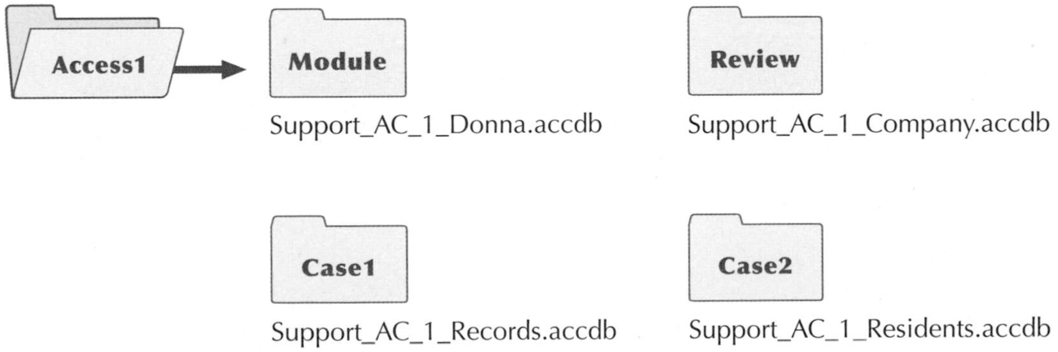

Access1
Module
Support_AC_1_Donna.accdb
Review
Support_AC_1_Company.accdb
Case1
Support_AC_1_Records.accdb
Case2
Support_AC_1_Residents.accdb

Session 1.1 Visual Overview:

The **Quick Access Toolbar** provides one-click access to commonly used commands, such as Save.

The **Table Tools Fields tab** provides options for adding, removing, and formatting the fields in a table.

The **Shutter Bar Open/Close Button** allows you to close and open the Navigation Pane; you might want to close the pane so that you have more room on the screen to view the object's contents.

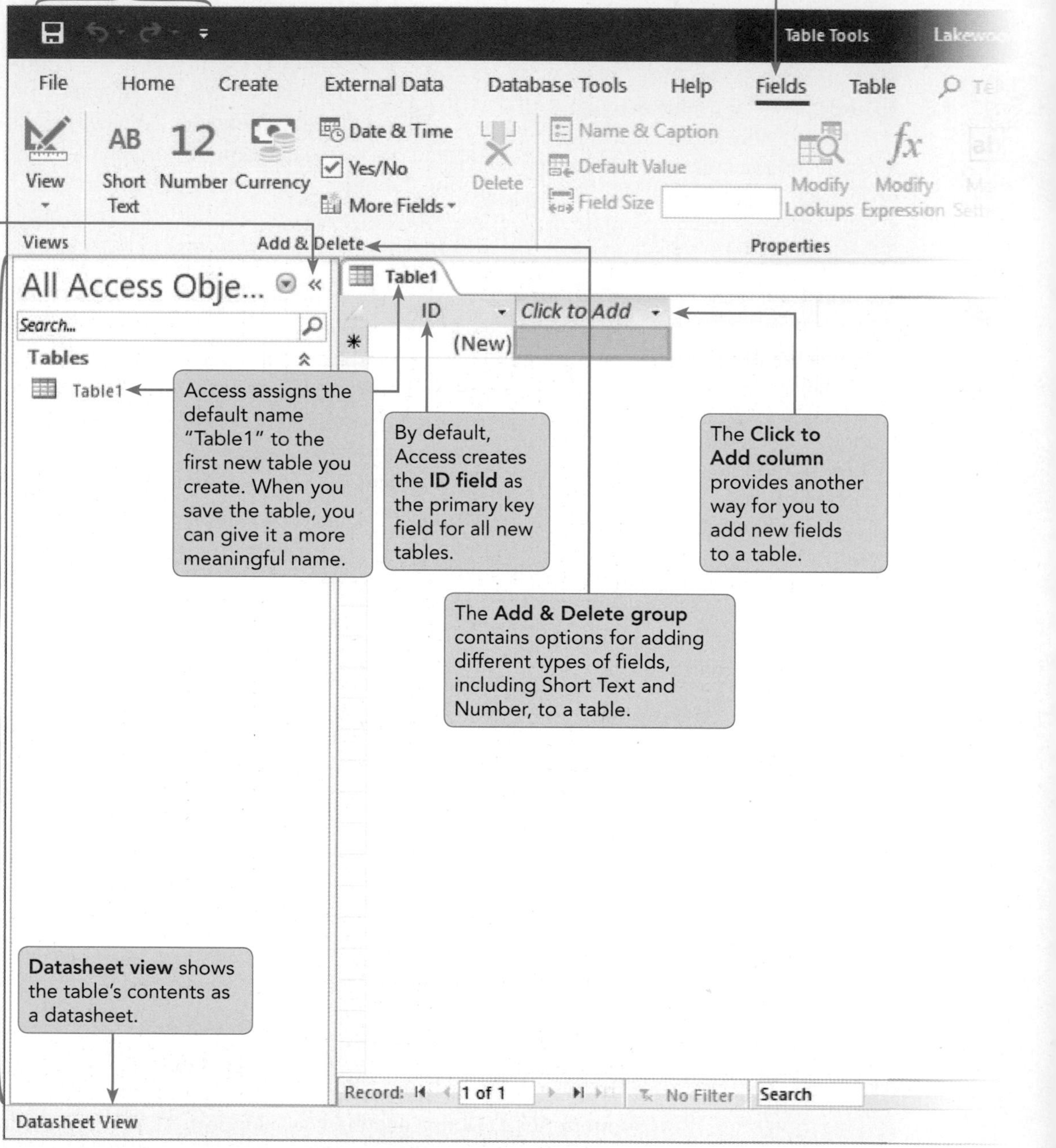
Table Tools
File
Home
Create
External Data
Database Tools
Help
Fields
Table
View
AB
Short Text
12
Number
Currency
Date & Time
Yes/No
More Fields
Delete
Name & Caption
Default Value
Field Size
Modify Lookups
Modify Expression
Views
Add & Delete
Properties
All Access Obje...
Search...
Tables
Table1
Table1
ID
Click to Add
(New)
Record: 1 of 1
No Filter
Search
Datasheet View

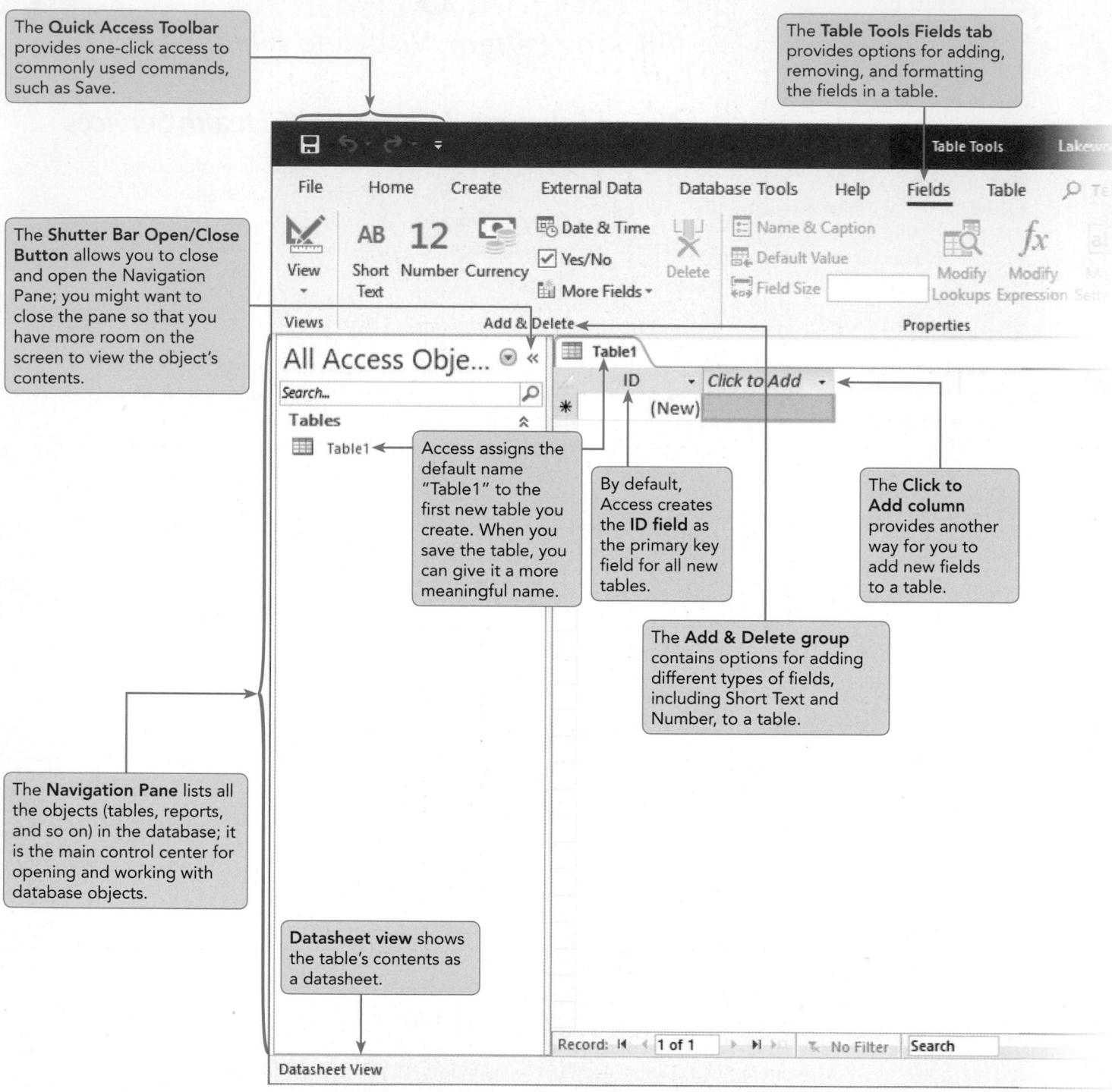

Access assigns the default name "Table1" to the first new table you create. When you save the table, you can give it a more meaningful name.

By default, Access creates the **ID field** as the primary key field for all new tables.

The **Click to Add column** provides another way for you to add new fields to a table.

The **Add & Delete group** contains options for adding different types of fields, including Short Text and Number, to a table.

The **Navigation Pane** lists all the objects (tables, reports, and so on) in the database; it is the main control center for opening and working with database objects.

Datasheet view shows the table's contents as a datasheet.

The Access Window

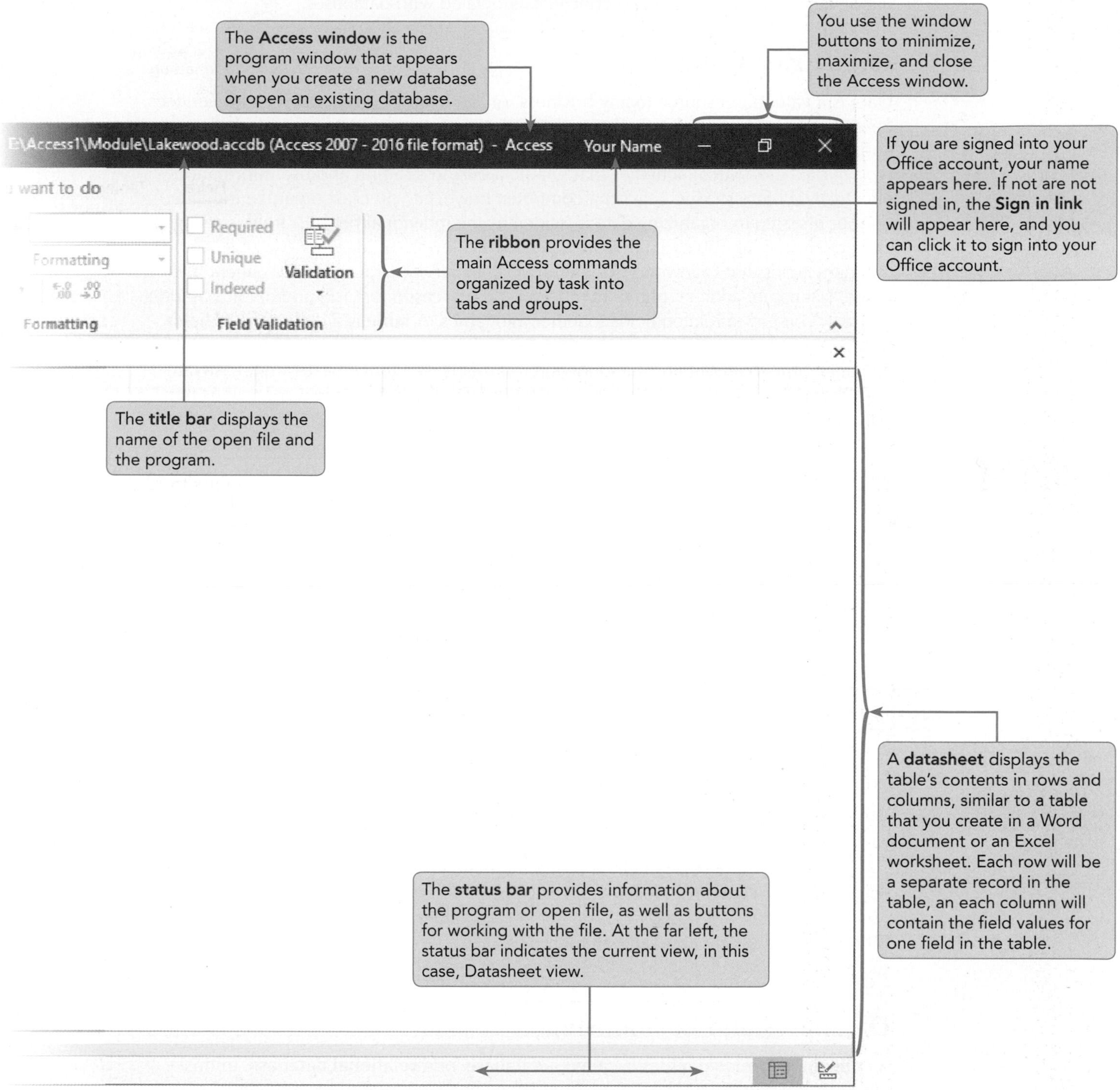
The **Access window** is the program window that appears when you create a new database or open an existing database.
You use the window buttons to minimize, maximize, and close the Access window.
E:\Access1\Module\Lakewood.accdb (Access 2007 - 2016 file format) - Access
Your Name
If you are signed into your Office account, your name appears here. If not are not signed in, the **Sign in link** will appear here, and you can click it to sign into your Office account.
want to do
Required
Unique
Indexed
Validation
Formatting
Formatting
Field Validation
The **ribbon** provides the main Access commands organized by task into tabs and groups.
The **title bar** displays the name of the open file and the program.
A **datasheet** displays the table's contents in rows and columns, similar to a table that you create in a Word document or an Excel worksheet. Each row will be a separate record in the table, an each column will contain the field values for one field in the table.
The **status bar** provides information about the program or open file, as well as buttons for working with the file. At the far left, the status bar indicates the current view, in this case, Datasheet view.

Introduction to Database Concepts

Before you begin using Access to create the database for Donna, you need to understand a few key terms and concepts associated with databases.

Organizing Data

Data is a valuable resource to any business. At Lakewood Community Health Services, for example, important data includes the patients' names and addresses, visit dates, and billing information. Organizing, storing, maintaining, retrieving, and sorting this type of data are critical activities that enable a business to find and use information effectively. Before storing data on a computer, however, you must organize the data.

Your first step in organizing data is to identify the individual fields. A **field** is a single characteristic or attribute of a person, place, object, event, or idea. For example, some of the many fields that Lakewood Community Health Services tracks are the patient ID, first name, last name, address, phone number, visit date, reason for visit, and invoice amount.

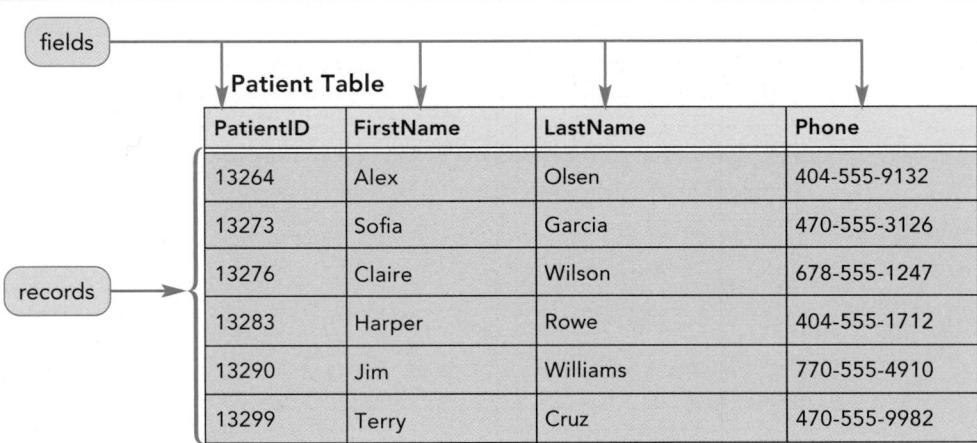

Next, you group related fields together into tables. A **table** is a collection of fields that describes a person, place, object, event, or idea. Figure 1–1 shows an example of a Patient table that contains the following four fields: PatientID, FirstName, LastName, and Phone. Each field is a column in the table, with the field name displayed as the column heading.

Figure 1–1 **Data organization for a table of patients**

Patient Table

PatientID	FirstName	LastName	Phone
13264	Alex	Olsen	404-555-9132
13273	Sofia	Garcia	470-555-3126
13276	Claire	Wilson	678-555-1247
13283	Harper	Rowe	404-555-1712
13290	Jim	Williams	770-555-4910
13299	Terry	Cruz	470-555-9982

The specific content of a field is called the **field value**. In Figure 1–1, the first set of field values for PatientID, FirstName, LastName, and Phone are, respectively: 13264, Alex, Olsen, and 404-555-9132. This set of field values is called a **record**. In the Patient table, the data for each patient is stored as a separate record. Figure 1–1 shows six records; each row of field values in the table is a record.

Databases and Relationships

A collection of related tables is called a **database**, or a **relational database**. In this module, you will create the database for Lakewood Community Health Services, and within that database, you'll create a table named Visit to store data about patient visits. Later on, you'll create two more tables, named Patient and Billing, to store related information about patients and their invoices.

As Donna and her staff use the database that you will create, they will need to access information about patients and their visits. To obtain this information, you must have a way to connect records in the Patient table to records in the Visit table. You connect the records in the separate tables through a **common field** that appears in both tables.

In the sample database shown in Figure 1–2, each record in the Patient table has a field named PatientID, which is also a field in the Visit table. For example, Jim Williams is the fifth patient in the Patient table and has a PatientID field value of 13290. This same PatientID field value, 13290, appears in two records in the Visit table. Therefore, Jim Williams is the patient that was seen at these two visits.

Figure 1–2 Database relationship between tables for patients and visits

Patient table

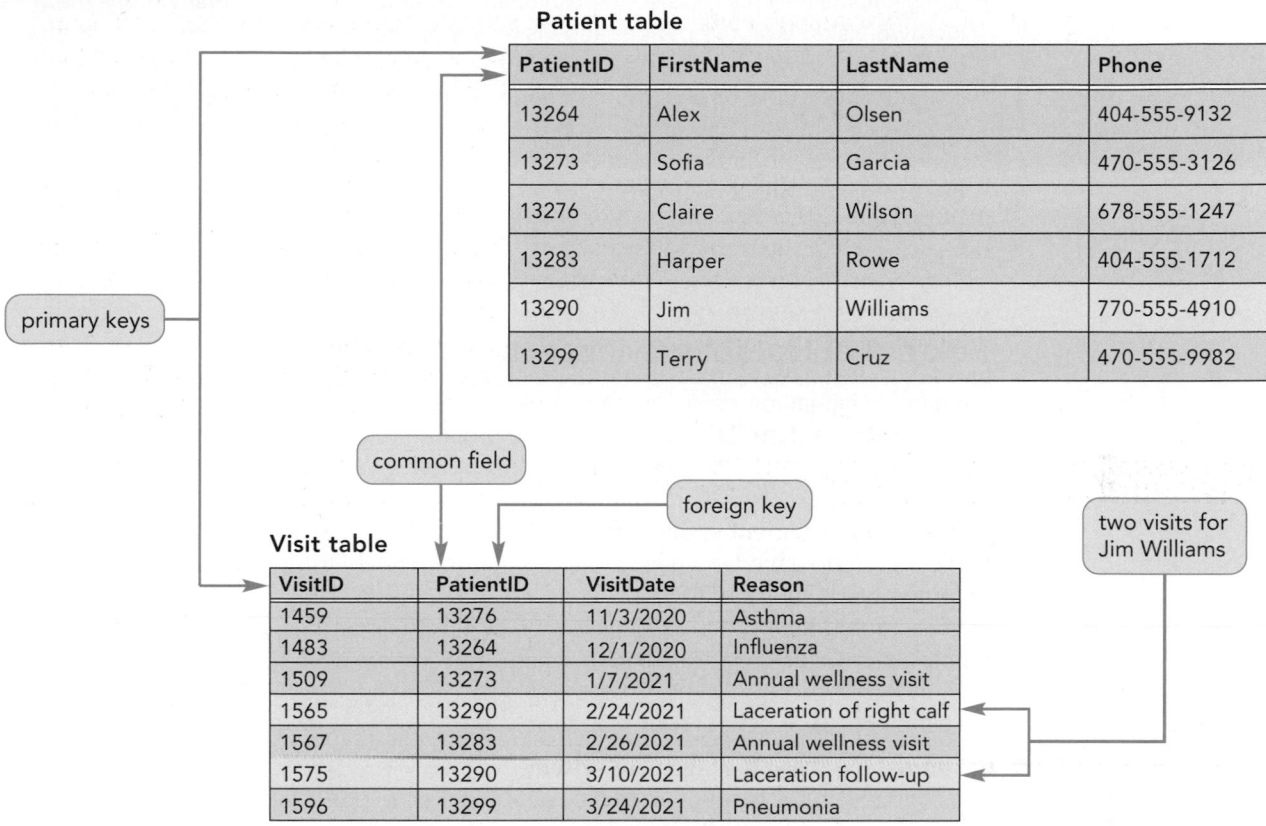

PatientID	FirstName	LastName	Phone
13264	Alex	Olsen	404-555-9132
13273	Sofia	Garcia	470-555-3126
13276	Claire	Wilson	678-555-1247
13283	Harper	Rowe	404-555-1712
13290	Jim	Williams	770-555-4910
13299	Terry	Cruz	470-555-9982

primary keys

common field

foreign key

two visits for Jim Williams

Visit table

VisitID	PatientID	VisitDate	Reason
1459	13276	11/3/2020	Asthma
1483	13264	12/1/2020	Influenza
1509	13273	1/7/2021	Annual wellness visit
1565	13290	2/24/2021	Laceration of right calf
1567	13283	2/26/2021	Annual wellness visit
1575	13290	3/10/2021	Laceration follow-up
1596	13299	3/24/2021	Pneumonia

Each ID value in the Patient table must be unique so that you can distinguish one patient from another. These unique PatientID values also identify each patient's specific visits in the Visit table. The PatientID field is referred to as the primary key of the Patient table. A **primary key** is a field, or a collection of fields, whose values uniquely identify each record in a table. No two records can contain the same value for the primary key field. In the Visit table, the VisitID field is the primary key because Lakewood Community Health Services assigns each visit a unique identification number.

When you include the primary key from one table as a field in a second table to form a relationship between the two tables, it is called a **foreign key** in the second table, as shown in Figure 1–2. For example, PatientID is the primary key in the Patient table and a foreign key in the Visit table.

The PatientID field must have the same characteristics in both tables. Although the primary key PatientID contains unique values in the Patient table, the same field as a foreign key in the Visit table does not necessarily contain unique values. The PatientID value 13290, for example, appears two times in the Visit table because Jim Williams made two visits to the clinic.

Each foreign key value, however, must match one of the field values for the primary key in the other table. In the example shown in Figure 1–2, each PatientID value in the Visit table must match a PatientID value in the Patient table. The two tables are related, enabling users to connect the facts about patients with the facts about their visits to the clinic.

INSIGHT

Storing Data in Separate Tables

When you create a database, you must create separate tables that contain only fields that are directly related to each other. For example, in the Lakewood database, the patient and visit data should not be stored in the same table because doing so would make the data difficult to update and prone to errors. Consider Jim Williams and his visits to the clinic, and assume that he has many more than just two visits. If all the patient and visit data was stored in the same table, so that each record (row) contained all the information about each visit and the patient, the patient data would appear multiple times in the table. This causes problems when the data changes. For example, if the phone number for Jim Williams changed, you would have to update the multiple occurrences of the phone number throughout the table. Not only would this be time-consuming, it would increase the likelihood of errors or inconsistent data.

Relational Database Management Systems

To manage its databases, a company uses a database management system. A **database management system (DBMS)** is a software program that lets you create databases, and then manipulate the data they contain. Most of today's database management systems, including Access, are called relational database management systems. In a **relational database management system**, data is organized as a collection of tables. As stated earlier, a relationship between two tables in a relational DBMS is formed through a common field.

A relational DBMS controls the storage of databases and facilitates the creation, manipulation, and reporting of data, as illustrated in Figure 1-3.

Figure 1-3 **Relational database management system**

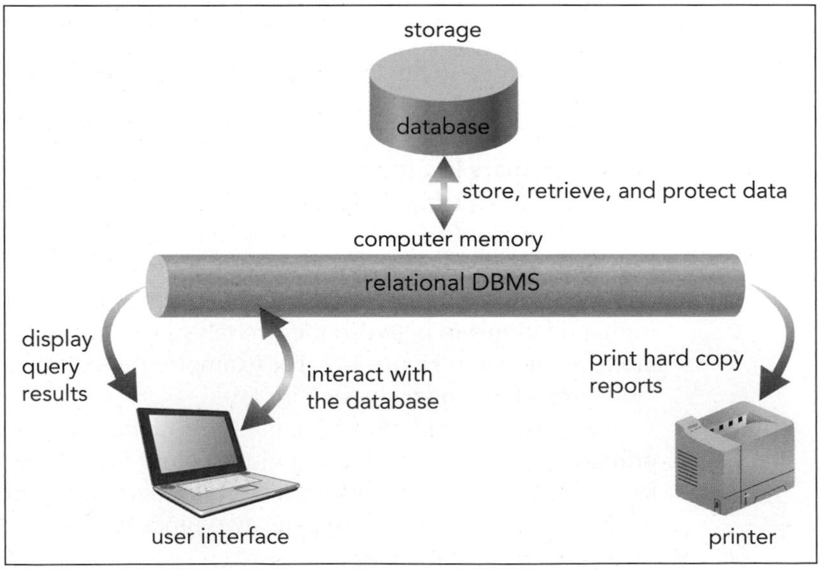
storage
database
store, retrieve, and protect data
computer memory
relational DBMS
display query results
interact with the database
print hard copy reports
user interface
printer

Specifically, a relational DBMS provides the following functions:

- It allows you to create database structures containing fields, tables, and table relationships.
- It lets you easily add new records, change field values in existing records, and delete records.
- It contains a built-in query language, which lets you obtain immediate answers to the questions (or queries) you ask about your data.
- It contains a built-in report generator, which lets you produce professional-looking, formatted reports from your data.
- It protects databases through security, control, and recovery facilities.

An organization such as Lakewood Community Health Services benefits from a relational DBMS because it allows users working in different groups to share the same data. More than one user can enter data into a database, and more than one user can retrieve and analyze data that other users have entered. For example, the database for Lakewood Community Health Services will contain only one copy of the Visit table, and all employees will use it to access visit information.

Finally, unlike other software programs, such as spreadsheet programs, a DBMS can handle massive amounts of data and allows relationships among multiple tables. Each Access database, for example, can be up to two gigabytes in size, can contain up to 32,768 objects (tables, reports, and so on), and can have up to 255 people using the database at the same time. For instructional purposes, the databases you will create and work with throughout this text contain a relatively small number of records compared to databases you would encounter outside the classroom, which would likely contain tables with very large numbers of records.

Starting Access and Creating a Database

Now that you've learned some database terms and concepts, you're ready to start Access and create the Lakewood database for Donna.

To start Access:

1. On the Windows taskbar, click the **Start** button. The Start menu opens.
2. On the Start menu, scroll down the list of apps, and then click **Access**. Access starts and displays the Recent screen in Backstage view. See Figure 1–4.

Figure 1–4 Recent screen in Backstage view

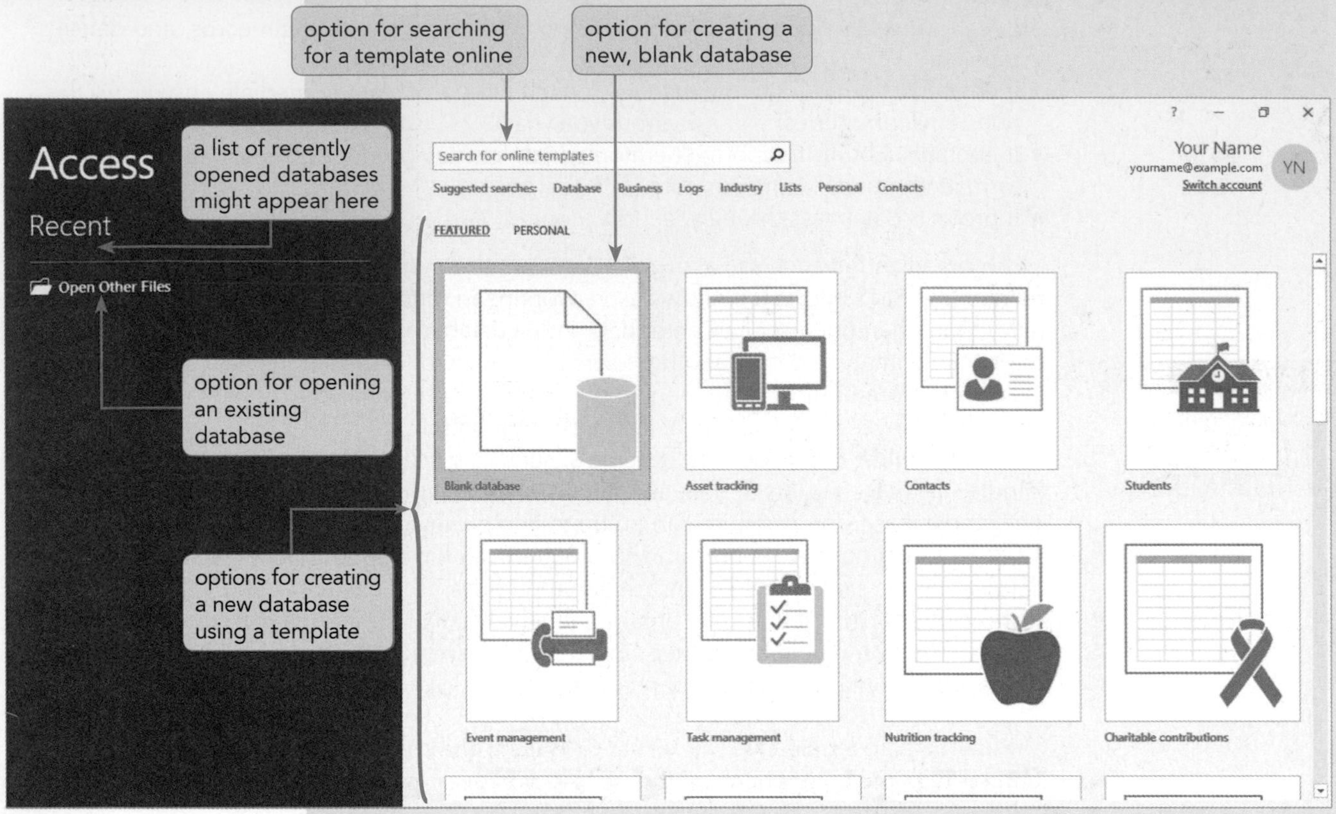
option for searching for a template online
option for creating a new, blank database
Access
Recent
a list of recently opened databases might appear here
Open Other Files
option for opening an existing database
options for creating a new database using a template
Search for online templates
Suggested searches: Database Business Logs Industry Lists Personal Contacts
FEATURED PERSONAL
Your Name
yourname@example.com
Switch account
YN
Blank database
Asset tracking
Contacts
Students
Event management
Task management
Nutrition tracking
Charitable contributions

When you start Access, the first screen that appears is Backstage view, which is the starting place for your work in Access. **Backstage view** contains commands that allow you to manage Access files and options. The Recent screen in Backstage view provides options for you to create a new database or open an existing database. To create a new database that does not contain any data or objects, you use the Blank database option. If the database you need to create contains objects that match those found in common databases, such as databases that store data about contacts or tasks, you can use one of the templates provided with Access. A **template** is a predesigned database that includes professionally designed tables, reports, and other database objects that can make it quick and easy for you to create a database. You can also search for a template online using the Search for online templates box.

In this case, the templates provided do not match Donna's needs for the clinic's database, so you need to create a new, blank database from scratch.

To create the new Lakewood database:

1. sam Make sure you have the Access starting Data Files on your computer.

   Trouble? If you don't have the starting Data Files, you need to get them before you can proceed. Your instructor will either give you the Data Files or ask you to obtain them from a specified location (such as a network drive). If you have any questions about the Data Files, see your instructor or technical support person for assistance.

2. On the Recent screen, click **Blank database** (see Figure 1–4). The Blank database screen opens.

Be sure to type **Lakewood** or you'll create a database named Database1.

3. In the File Name box, type **Lakewood** to replace the selected database name provided by Access, Database1. Next you need to specify the location for the file.
4. Click the **Browse** button to the right of the File Name box. The File New Database dialog box opens.
5. Navigate to the drive and folder where you are storing your files, as specified by your instructor.
6. Make sure the Save as type box displays "Microsoft Access 2007–2016 Databases."

   Trouble? If your computer is set up to show file name extensions, you will see the Access file name extension ".accdb" in the File name box.

TIP

If you don't type the filename extension, Access adds it automatically.

7. Click **OK**. You return to the Blank database screen, and the File Name box now shows the name Lakewood.accdb. The filename extension ".accdb" identifies the file as an Access 2007–2016 database.
8. Click **Create**. Access creates the new database, saves it to the specified location, and then opens an empty table named Table1.

   Trouble? If you see only ribbon tab names and no buttons, click the Home tab to expand the ribbon, and then in the lower-right corner of the ribbon, click the Pin this pane button to pin the ribbon.

Refer back to the Session 1.1 Visual Overview and spend some time becoming familiar with the components of the Access window.

INSIGHT

Understanding the Database File Type

Access 2019 uses the .accdb file extension, which is the same file extension used for databases created with Microsoft Access 2007, 2010, 2013, and 2016. To ensure compatibility between these earlier versions and the Access 2019 software, new databases created using Access 2019 have the same file extension and file format as Access 2007, Access 2010, Access 2013, and Access 2016 databases.

Working in Touch Mode

TIP

On a touch device, you *tap* instead of *click*.

If you are working on a touch device, such as a tablet, you can switch to Touch Mode in Access to make it easier for you to tap buttons on the ribbon and perform other touch actions. Your screens will not match those shown in the book exactly, but this will not cause any problems.

Note: The following steps assume that you are using a mouse. If you are instead using a touch device, please read these steps but don't complete them, so that you remain working in Touch Mode.

To switch to Touch Mode:

1. On the Quick Access Toolbar, click the **Customize Quick Access Toolbar** button. A menu opens listing buttons you can add to the Quick Access Toolbar as well as other options for customizing the toolbar.

   Trouble? If the Touch/Mouse Mode command on the menu has a checkmark next to it, press ESC to close the menu, and then skip to Step 3.

2. Click **Touch/Mouse Mode**. The Quick Access Toolbar now contains the Touch/Mouse Mode button, which you can use to switch between Mouse Mode, the default display, and Touch Mode.

3. On the Quick Access Toolbar, click the **Touch/Mouse Mode** button. A menu opens with two commands: Mouse, which shows the ribbon in the standard display and is optimized for use with the mouse; and Touch, which provides more space between the buttons and commands on the ribbon and is optimized for use with touch devices. The icon next to Mouse is shaded to indicate that it is selected.

   Trouble? If the icon next to Touch is shaded red, press ESC to close the menu and skip to Step 5.

4. Click **Touch**. The display switches to Touch Mode with more space between the commands and buttons on the ribbon. See Figure 1–5.

Figure 1–5 Ribbon displayed in Touch Mode

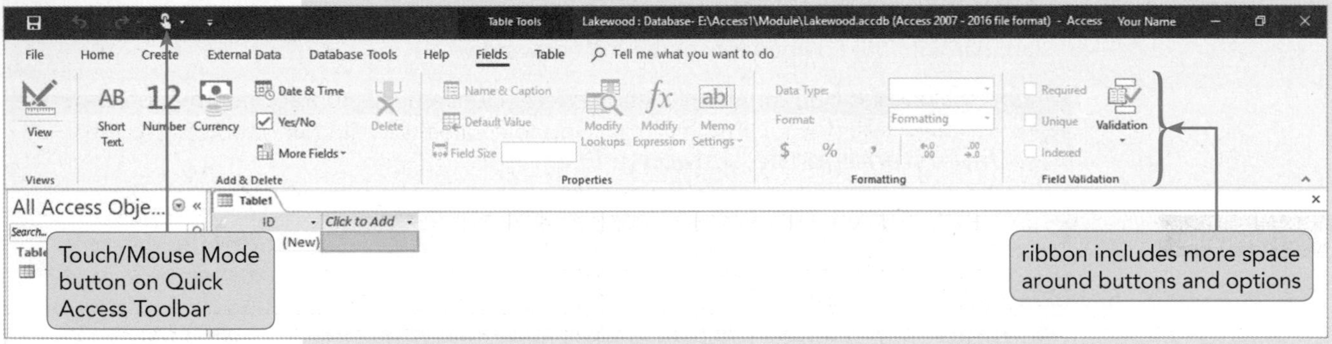
Table Tools
Lakewood : Database- E:\Access1\Module\Lakewood.accdb (Access 2007 - 2016 file format) - Access
Your Name
File
Home
Create
External Data
Database Tools
Help
Fields
Table
Tell me what you want to do
View
Short Text
Number
Currency
Date & Time
Yes/No
More Fields
Delete
Name & Caption
Default Value
Field Size
Modify Lookups
Modify Expression
Memo Settings
Data Type:
Format:
Formatting
Required
Unique
Indexed
Validation
Views
Add & Delete
Properties
Formatting
Field Validation
All Access Obje...
Table1
ID
Click to Add
(New)
Touch/Mouse Mode button on Quick Access Toolbar
ribbon includes more space around buttons and options

The figures in this text show the standard Mouse Mode display, and the instructions assume you are using a mouse to click and select options, so you'll switch back to Mouse Mode.

Trouble? If you are using a touch device and want to remain in Touch Mode, skip Steps 5 and 6.

5. On the Quick Access Toolbar, click the **Touch/Mouse Mode** button, and then click **Mouse**. The ribbon returns to the standard display, as shown in the Session 1.1 Visual Overview.

6. On the Quick Access Toolbar, click the **Customize Quick Access Toolbar** button, and then click **Touch/Mouse Mode** to deselect it. The Touch/Mouse Mode button is removed from the Quick Access Toolbar.

Creating a Table in Datasheet View

Tables contain all the data in a database and are the fundamental objects for your work in Access. You can create a table in Access in different ways, including entering the fields and records for the table directly in Datasheet view.

REFERENCE

Creating a Table in Datasheet View

- On the ribbon, click the Create tab.
- In the Tables group, click the Table button.
- Rename the default ID primary key field and change its data type, if necessary; or accept the default ID field with the AutoNumber data type.
- On the Fields tab in the Add & Delete group, click the button for the type of field you want to add to the table (for example, click the Short Text button), and then type the field name; or, in the table datasheet, click the Click to Add column heading, click the type of field you want to add from the list that opens, and then press TAB or ENTER to move to the next column in the datasheet. Repeat this step to add all the necessary fields to the table.
- In the first row below the field names, enter the value for each field in the first record, pressing TAB or ENTER to move from one field to the next.
- After entering the value for the last field in the first record, press TAB or ENTER to move to the next row, and then enter the values for the next record. Continue this process until you have entered all the records for the table.
- On the Quick Access Toolbar, click the Save button, enter a name for the table, and then click OK.

For Lakewood Community Health Services, Donna needs to track information about each patient visit at the clinic. She asks you to create the Visit table according to the plan shown in Figure 1–6.

Figure 1–6 **Plan for the Visit table**

Field	Purpose
VisitID	Unique number assigned to each visit; will serve as the table's primary key
PatientID	Unique number assigned to each patient; common field that will be a foreign key to connect to the Patient table
VisitDate	Date on which the patient visited the clinic
Reason	Reason/diagnosis for the patient visit
WalkIn	Whether the patient visit was a walk-in or scheduled appointment

As shown in Donna's plan, she wants to store data about visits in five fields, including fields to contain the date of each visit, the reason for the visit, and if the visit was a walk-in or scheduled appointment. These are the most important aspects of a visit and, therefore, must be tracked. Also, notice that the VisitID field will be the primary key for the table; each visit at Lakewood Community Health Services is assigned a unique number, so this field is the logical choice for the primary key. Finally, the PatientID field is needed in the Visit table as a foreign key to connect the information about visits to patients. The data about patients and their invoices will be stored in separate tables, which you will create later.

Notice the name of each field in Figure 1–6. You need to name each field, table, and object in an Access database.

PROSKILLS

Decision Making: Naming Fields in Access Tables

One of the most important tasks in creating a table is deciding what names to specify for the table's fields. Keep the following guidelines in mind when you assign field names:

- A field name can consist of up to 64 characters, including letters, numbers, spaces, and special characters, except for the period (.), exclamation mark (!), grave accent (`), and square brackets ([ ]).
- A field name cannot begin with a space.
- Capitalize the first letter of each word in a field name that combines multiple words, for example VisitDate.
- Use concise field names that are easy to remember and reference and that won't take up a lot of space in the table datasheet.
- Use standard abbreviations, such as Num for Number, Amt for Amount, and Qty for Quantity, and use them consistently throughout the database. For example, if you use Num for Number in one field name, do not use the number sign (#) for Number in another.
- Give fields descriptive names so that you can easily identify them when you view or edit records.
- Although Access supports the use of spaces in field names (and in other object names), experienced database developers avoid using spaces because they can cause errors when the objects are involved in programming tasks.

By spending time obtaining and analyzing information about the fields in a table, and understanding the rules for naming fields, you can create a well-designed table that will be easy for others to use.

Renaming the Default Primary Key Field

As noted earlier, Access provides the ID field as the default primary key for a new table you create in Datasheet view. Recall that a primary key is a field, or a collection of fields, whose values uniquely identify each record in a table. However, according to Donna's plan, the VisitID field should be the primary key for the Visit table. You'll begin by renaming the default ID field to create the VisitID field.

TIP

A shortcut menu opens when you right-click an object and provides options for working with that object.

To rename the ID field to the VisitID field:

1. Right-click the **ID** column heading to open the shortcut menu, and then click **Rename Field**. The column heading ID is selected, so that whatever text you type next will replace it.
2. Type **VisitID** and then click the row below the heading. The column heading changes to VisitID, and the insertion point moves to the row below the heading. The **insertion point** is a flashing cursor that shows where text you type will be inserted. In this case, it is hidden within the selected field value (New). See Figure 1–7.

   Trouble? If you make a mistake while typing the field name, use BACKSPACE to delete characters to the left of the insertion point or use DELETE to delete characters to the right of the insertion point. Then type the correct text. To correct a field name by replacing it entirely, press ESC, and then type the correct text.

Figure 1–7 **ID field renamed to VisitID**

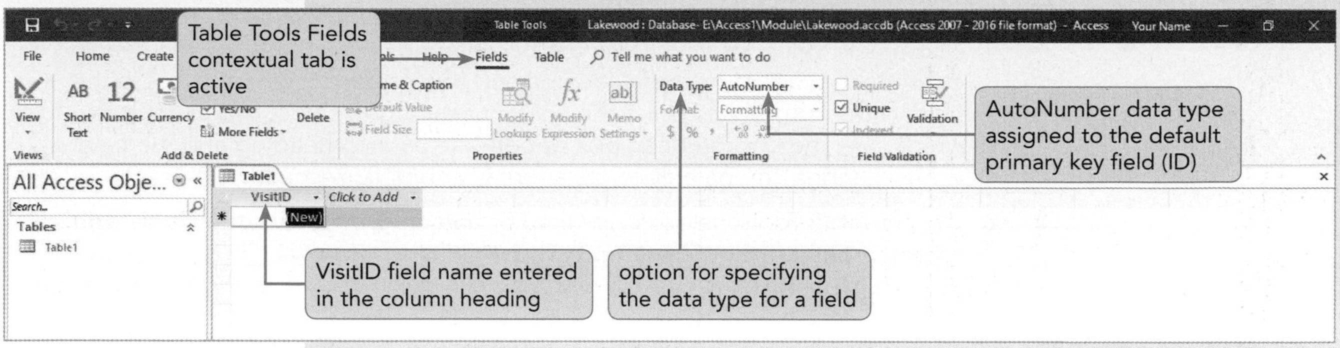
Table Tools Fields contextual tab is active
AutoNumber data type assigned to the default primary key field (ID)
VisitID field name entered in the column heading
option for specifying the data type for a field

Notice that the Table Tools Fields tab is active on the ribbon. This is an example of a **contextual tab**, which is a tab that appears and provides options for working with a specific object that is selected—in this case, the table you are creating. As you work with other objects in the database, other contextual tabs will appear with commands and options related to each selected object.

INSIGHT

Buttons and Labels on the Ribbon

Depending on the size of the monitor you are using and your screen resolution settings, you might see more or fewer buttons on the ribbon, and you might not see labels next to certain buttons. The screenshots in these modules were created using a screen resolution setting of 1366 x 768 with the program window maximized. If you are using a smaller monitor or a lower screen resolution, some buttons will appear only as icons, with no labels next to them, because there is not enough room on the ribbon to display the labels.

You have renamed the default primary key field, ID, to VisitID. However, the VisitID field still retains the characteristics of the ID field, including its data type. Your next task is to change the data type of this field.

Changing the Data Type of the Default Primary Key Field

Notice the Formatting group on the Table Tools Fields tab. One of the options available in this group is the Data Type option (see Figure 1–7). Each field in an Access table must be assigned a data type. The **data type** determines what field values you can enter for the field. In this case, the AutoNumber data type is displayed. Access assigns the AutoNumber data type to the default ID primary key field because the **AutoNumber** data type automatically inserts a unique number in this field for every record, beginning with the number 1 for the first record, the number 2 for the second record, and so on. Therefore, a field using the AutoNumber data type can serve as the primary key for any table you create.

Visit numbers at Lakewood Community Health Services are specific, four-digit numbers, so the AutoNumber data type is not appropriate for the VisitID field, which is the primary key field in the table you are creating. A better choice is the **Short Text** data type, which allows field values containing letters, digits, and other characters, and which is appropriate for identifying numbers, such as visit numbers, that are never used in calculations. So, Donna asks you to change the data type for the VisitID field from AutoNumber to Short Text.

To change the data type for the VisitID field:

1. Make sure that the VisitID column is selected. A column is selected when you click a field value, in which case the background color of the column heading changes to orange (the default color) and the insertion point appears in the field value. You can also click the column heading to select a column, in which case the background color of both the column heading and the field value changes (the default colors are gray and blue, respectively).
2. On the Table Tools Fields tab, in the Formatting group, click the **Data Type arrow**, and then click **Short Text**. The VisitID field is now a Short Text field. See Figure 1–8.

Figure 1–8 Short Text data type assigned to the VisitID field

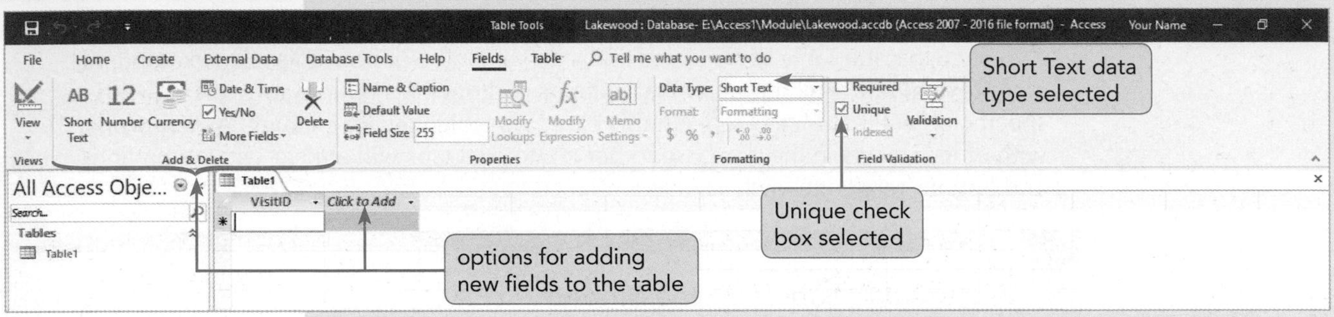
Short Text data type selected
Unique check box selected
options for adding new fields to the table

Note the Unique check box in the Field Validation group. This check box is selected because the VisitID field assumed the characteristics of the default primary key field, ID, including the fact that each value in the field must be unique. Because this check box is selected, no two records in the Visit table will be allowed to have the same value in the VisitID field.

With the VisitID field created and established as the primary key, you can now enter the rest of the fields in the Visit table.

Adding New Fields

When you create a table in Datasheet view, you can use the options in the Add & Delete group on the Table Tools Fields tab to add fields to your table. You can also use the Click to Add column in the table datasheet to add new fields. (See Figure 1–8.) You'll use both methods to add the four remaining fields to the Visit table. The next field you need to add is the PatientID field. Similar to the VisitID field, the PatientID field will contain numbers that will not be used in calculations, so it should be a Short Text field.

To add the rest of the fields to the Visit table:

1. On the Table Tools Fields tab, in the Add & Delete group, click the **Short Text** button. Access adds a new field named "Field1" to the right of the VisitID field. See Figure 1–9.

Figure 1–9 New Short Text field added to the table

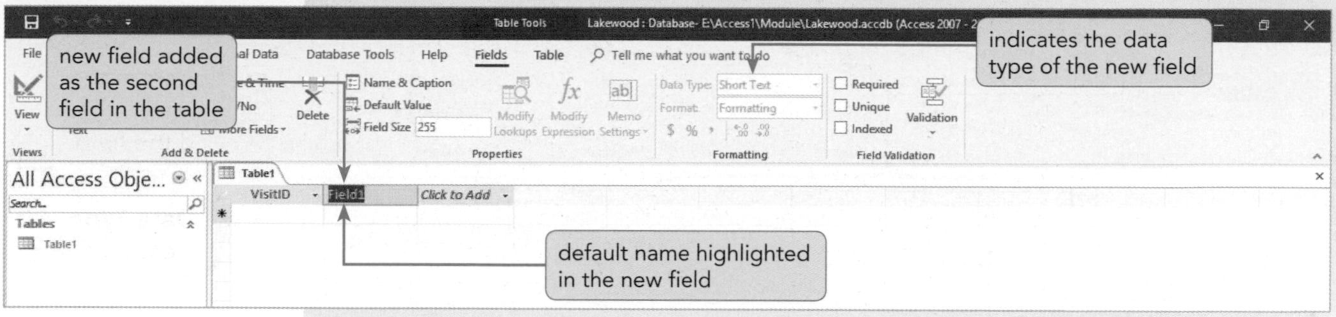
new field added as the second field in the table
indicates the data type of the new field
default name highlighted in the new field

The text "Field1" is selected, so you can simply type the new field name to replace it.

2. Type **PatientID**. Access adds the second field to the table. Next, you'll add the VisitDate field. Because this field will contain date values, you'll add a field with the **Date/Time** data type, which allows field values in a variety of date and time formats.
3. In the Add & Delete group, click the **Date & Time** button. Access adds a third field to the table, this time with the Date/Time data type.
4. Type **VisitDate** to replace the selected name "Field1." The fourth field in the Visit table is the Reason field, which will contain brief descriptions of the reason for the visit to the clinic. You'll add another Short Text field—this time using the Click to Add column.
5. Click the **Click to Add** column heading. Access displays a list of available data types for the new field.
6. Click **Short Text** in the list. Access adds a fourth field to the table.
7. Type **Reason** to replace the highlighted name "Field1," and then press **ENTER**. The Click to Add column becomes active and displays the list of field data types.

   The fifth and final field in the Visit table is the WalkIn field, which will indicate whether the patient had a scheduled appointment. The **Yes/No** data type is suitable for this field because it defines fields that store values representing one of two options—true/false, yes/no, or on/off.

TIP

You can also type the first letter of a data type to select it and close the Click to Add list.

8. Click **Yes/No** in the list, and then type **WalkIn** to replace the highlighted name "Field1."

   Trouble? If you pressed TAB or ENTER after typing the WalkIn field name, press ESC to close the Click to Add list.
9. Click in the row below the VisitID column heading. You have entered all five fields for the Visit table. See Figure 1–10.

Figure 1–10 **Table with all fields entered**

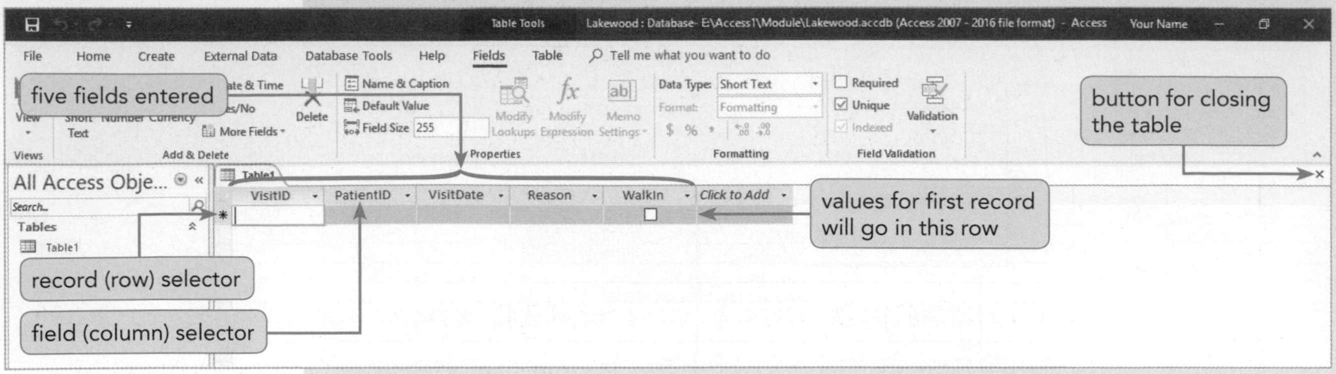
five fields entered
button for closing the table
values for first record will go in this row
record (row) selector
field (column) selector
VisitID
PatientID
VisitDate
Reason
WalkIn
Click to Add

The table contains three Short Text fields (VisitID, PatientID, and Reason), one Date/Time field (VisitDate), and one Yes/No field (WalkIn). You'll learn more about field data types in the next module.

As noted earlier, Datasheet view shows a table's contents in rows (records) and columns (fields). Each column is headed by a field name inside a field selector, and each row has a record selector to its left (see Figure 1–10). Clicking a **field selector** or a **record selector** selects that entire column or row (respectively), which you then can manipulate. A field selector is also called a **column selector**, and a record selector is also called a **row selector**.

Saving the Visit Table Structure

As you find out later, the records you enter are immediately stored in the database as soon as you enter them; however, the table's design—the field names and characteristics of the fields themselves, plus any layout changes to the datasheet—are not saved until you save the table. When you save a new table for the first time, you should give it a name that best identifies the information it contains. Like a field name, a table name can contain up to 64 characters, including spaces.

REFERENCE

Saving a Table

- Make sure the table you want to save is open.
- On the Quick Access Toolbar, click the Save button. The Save As dialog box opens.
- In the Table Name box, type the name for the table.
- Click OK.

According to Donna's plan, you need to save the table with the name "Visit."

To save, name, and close the Visit table:

TIP

You can also use the Save command in Backstage view to save and name a new table.

1. On the Quick Access Toolbar, click the **Save** button. The Save As dialog box opens.

2. With the default name Table1 selected in the Table Name box, type **Visit** and then click **OK**. The tab for the table now displays the name "Visit," and the Visit table design is saved in the Lakewood database.
3. Click the **Close 'Visit'** button [X] on the object tab (see Figure 1–10 for the location of this button). The Visit table closes, and the main portion of the Access window is now blank because no database object is currently open. The Lakewood database file is still open, as indicated by the filename in the Access window title bar.

Creating a Table in Design View

The Lakewood database also needs a table that will hold all of the invoices generated by each office visit. Donna has decided to call this new table the Billing table. You created the structure for the Visit table in Datasheet view. An alternate method of creating the structure of a table is by using Design view. You will create the new Billing table using Design view.

Creating a table in Design view involves entering the field names and defining the properties for the fields, specifying a primary key for the table, and then saving the table structure. Donna began documenting the design for the new Billing table by listing each field's name, data type, and purpose, and will continue to refine the design. See Figure 1–11.

Figure 1–11 **Initial design for the Billing table**

Field Name	Data Type	Purpose
InvoiceNum	Short Text	Unique number assigned to each invoice; will serve as the table's primary key
VisitID	Short Text	Unique number assigned to each visit; common field that will be a foreign key to connect to the Visit table
InvoiceAmount	Currency	Dollar amount of each invoice
InvoiceDate	Date/Time	Date the invoice was generated
InvoicePaid	Yes/No	Whether the invoice has been paid or not

You'll use Donna's design as a guide for creating the Billing table in the Lakewood database.

To begin creating the Billing table:

1. If the Navigation Pane is open, click the **Shutter Bar Open/Close Button** [«] to close it.
2. On the ribbon, click the **Create** tab.
3. In the Tables group, click the **Table Design** button. A new table named Table1 opens in Design view.

Defining Fields

When you first create a table in Design view, the insertion point is located in the first row's Field Name box, ready for you to begin defining the first field in the table. You enter values for the Field Name, Data Type, and Description field properties (optional), and then select values for all other field properties in the Field Properties pane. These other properties will appear when you move to the first row's Data Type box.

REFERENCE

Defining a Field in Design View

- In the Field Name box, type the name for the field, and then press TAB.
- Accept the default Short Text data type, or click the arrow and select a different data type for the field. Press TAB.
- Enter an optional description for the field, if necessary.
- Use the Field Properties pane to type or select other field properties, as appropriate.

The first field you need to define is the InvoiceNum field. This field will be the primary key for the Billing table. Each invoice at Lakewood Community Health Services is assigned a specific five-digit number. Although the InvoiceNum field will contain these number values, the numbers will never be used in calculations; therefore, you'll assign the Short Text data type to this field. Any time a field contains number values that will not be used in calculations—such as phone numbers, postal codes, and so on—you should use the Short Text data type instead of the Number data type.

To define the InvoiceNum field:

TIP

You can also press ENTER to move from one property to the next in the Table Design grid.

1. Type **InvoiceNum** in the first row's Field Name box, and then press **TAB** to advance to the Data Type box. The default data type, Short Text, appears highlighted in the Data Type box, which now also contains an arrow, and the field properties for a Short Text field appear in the Field Properties pane. See Figure 1–12.

Figure 1–12 Table window after entering the first field name

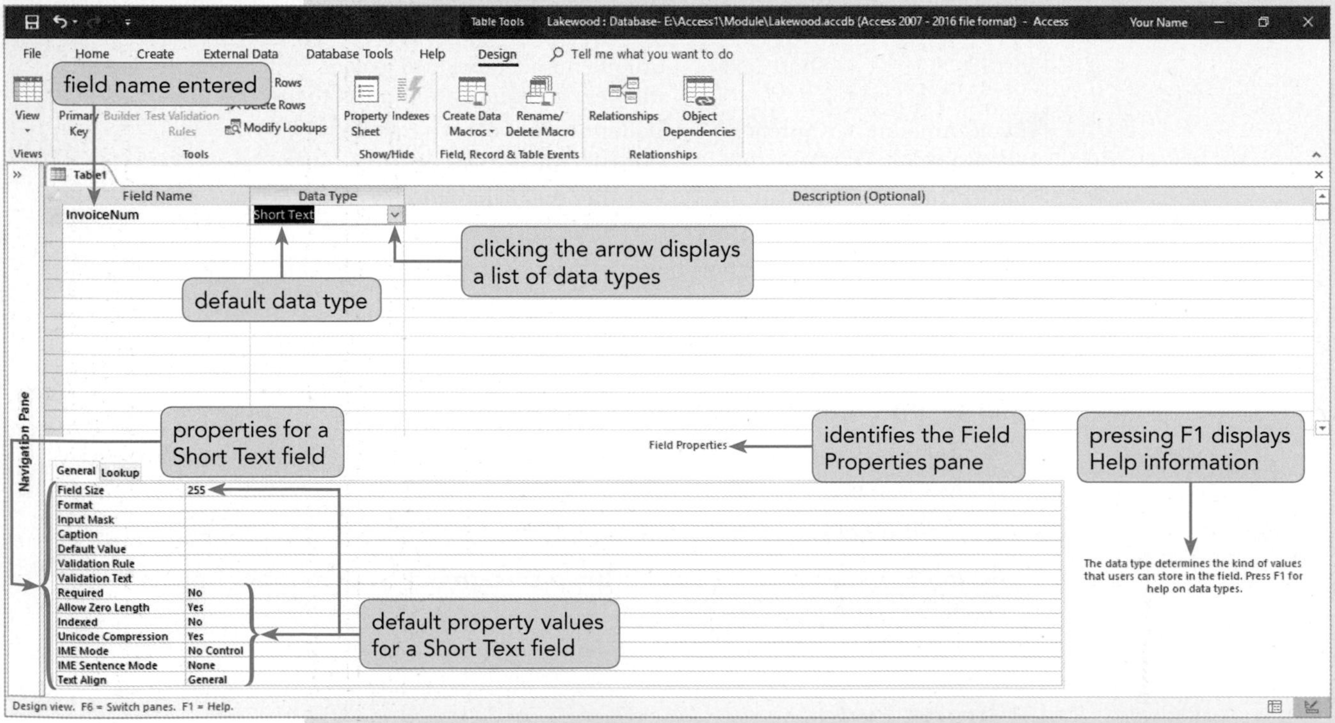
field name entered
clicking the arrow displays a list of data types
default data type
properties for a Short Text field
identifies the Field Properties pane
pressing F1 displays Help information
default property values for a Short Text field

The right side of the Field Properties pane now provides an explanation for the current property, Data Type.

Trouble? If you make a typing error, you can correct it by clicking to position the insertion point, and then using either BACKSPACE to delete characters to the left of the insertion point or DELETE to delete characters to the right of the insertion point. Then type the correct text.

Because the InvoiceNum field values will not be used in calculations, you will accept the default Short Text data type for the field.

2. Press **TAB** to accept Short Text as the data type and to advance to the Description (Optional) box.

   Next you'll enter the Description property value as "Primary key." The value you enter for the Description property will appear on the status bar when you view the table datasheet. Note that specifying "Primary key" for the Description property does *not* establish the current field as the primary key; you use a button on the ribbon to specify the primary key in Design view, which you will do later in this session.

TIP

You can also use TAB to advance to the second row's Field Name box.

3. Type **Primary key** in the Description (Optional) box and press **ENTER**.

   At this point, you have entered the first field (InvoiceNum) into the table and are ready to enter the remaining fields into the table.

Figure 1-13 **InvoiceNum field defined**

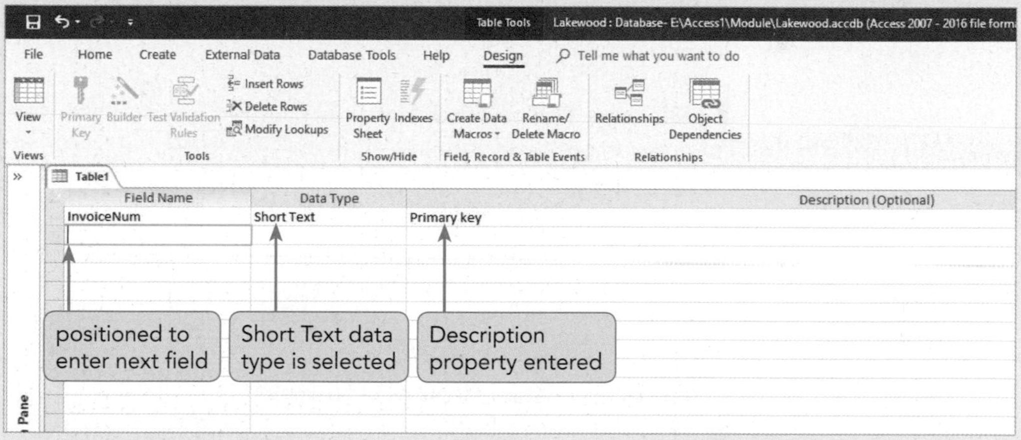
Table Tools
Lakewood : Database- E:\Access1\Module\Lakewood.accdb (Access 2007 - 2016 file form
File
Home
Create
External Data
Database Tools
Help
Design
Tell me what you want to do
View
Primary Key
Builder
Test Validation Rules
Insert Rows
Delete Rows
Modify Lookups
Property Sheet
Indexes
Create Data Macros
Rename/ Delete Macro
Relationships
Object Dependencies
Views
Tools
Show/Hide
Field, Record & Table Events
Relationships
Table1
Field Name
Data Type
Description (Optional)
InvoiceNum
Short Text
Primary key
positioned to enter next field
Short Text data type is selected
Description property entered

Donna's Billing table design (Figure 1-11) shows VisitID as the second field. Because Donna and other staff members need to relate information about invoices to the visit data in the Visit table, the Billing table must include the VisitID field, which is the Visit table's primary key. Recall that when you include the primary key from one table as a field in a second table to connect the two tables, the field is a foreign key in the second table.

To define the VisitID field:

1. If the insertion point is not already positioned in the second row's Field Name box, click the second row's Field Name box. Once properly positioned, type **VisitID** in the box, and then press **TAB** to advance to the Data Type box.

2. Press **TAB** to accept Short Text as the field's data type. Because the VisitID field is a foreign key to the Visit table, you'll enter "Foreign key" in the Description (Optional) box to help users of the database understand the purpose of this field.
3. Type **Foreign key** in the Description (Optional) box and press **ENTER**.

TIP

The quickest way to move back to the Table Design grid is to use the mouse.

The third field in the Billing table is the InvoiceAmt field, which will display the dollar amount of each invoice the clinic sends to the patients. The Currency data type is the appropriate choice for this field.

To define the InvoiceAmount field:

1. In the third row's Field Name box, type **InvoiceAmount** and then press **TAB** to advance to the Data Type box.
2. Click the **Data Type** arrow, click **Currency** in the list, and then press **TAB** to advance to the Description (Optional) box.

   The InvoiceAmount field is not a primary key, nor does it have a relationship with a field in another table, so you do not need to enter a description for this field. If you've assigned a descriptive field name and the field does not fulfill a special function (such as primary key), you usually do not enter a value for the optional Description property.
3. Press **TAB** to advance to the fourth row's Field Name box.

The fourth field in the Billing table is the InvoiceDate field. This field will contain the dates on which invoices are generated for the clinic's patients. You'll define the InvoiceDate field using the Date/Time data type.

To define the InvoiceDate field:

1. In the fourth row's Field Name box, type **InvoiceDate** and then press **TAB** to advance to the Data Type box.

   You can select a value from the Data Type list as you did for the InvoiceAmount field. Alternately, you can type the property value in the box or type just the first character of the property value.
2. Type **d**. The value in the fourth row's Data Type box changes to "date/Time," with the letters "ate/Time" highlighted. See Figure 1–14.

Figure 1–14 Selecting a value for the Data Type property

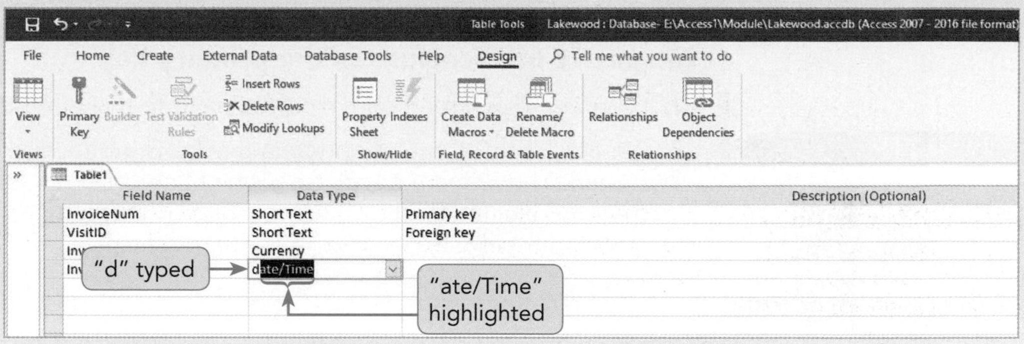
"d" typed
"ate/Time" highlighted

3. Press **TAB** to advance to the Description (Optional) box. Note that Access changes the value for the Data Type property to "Date/Time."
4. Because the InvoiceDate field does not need a special description, press **TAB**.

The fifth, and final, field to be defined in the Billing table is InvoicePaid. This field will be a Yes/No field to indicate the payment status of each invoice record stored in the Billing table. Recall that the Yes/No data type defines fields that store true/false, yes/no, and on/off field values. When you create a Yes/No field in a table, the default Format property is set to Yes/No.

To define the InvoicePaid field:

1. In the fifth row's Field Name box, type **InvoicePaid** and then press **TAB** to advance to the Data Type box.
2. Type **y**. Access completes the data type as "yes/No." Press **TAB** to select the Yes/No data type and move to the Description (Optional) box.
3. Because the InvoicePaid field does not need a special description, press **TAB**.

You've finished defining the fields for the Billing table. Next, you need to specify the primary key for the table.

Specifying the Primary Key

As you learned previously, the primary key for a table uniquely identifies each record in the table.

REFERENCE

Specifying a Primary Key in Design View

- Display the table in Design view.
- Click in the row for the field you've chosen to be the primary key to make it the active field. If the primary key will consist of two or more fields, click the row selector for the first field, press and hold down CTRL, and then click the row selector for each additional primary key field.
- On the Table Tools Design tab in the Tools group, click the Primary Key button.

According to Donna's design, you need to specify InvoiceNum as the primary key for the Billing table. You can do so while the table is in Design view.

To specify InvoiceNum as the primary key:

1. Click in the row for the InvoiceNum field to make it the current field.
2. On the Table Tools Design tab in the Tools group, click the **Primary Key** button. The Primary Key button is highlighted and a key symbol appears in the row selector for the first row, indicating that the InvoiceNum field is the table's primary key. See Figure 1–15.

TIP

The Primary Key button is a toggle; you can click it to remove the key symbol.

Figure 1–15 InvoiceNum field selected as the primary key

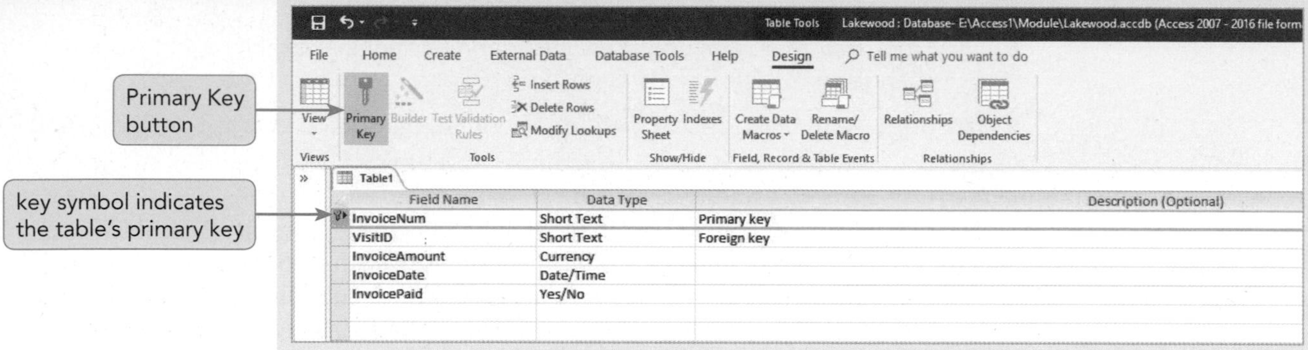
Primary Key button
key symbol indicates the table's primary key
Table Tools Lakewood : Database- E:\Access1\Module\Lakewood.accdb (Access 2007 - 2016 file form
File Home Create External Data Database Tools Help Design Tell me what you want to do
View Primary Key Builder Test Validation Rules Insert Rows Delete Rows Modify Lookups Property Sheet Indexes Create Data Macros Rename/ Delete Macro Relationships Object Dependencies
Views Tools Show/Hide Field, Record & Table Events Relationships
Table1
Field Name Data Type Description (Optional)
InvoiceNum Short Text Primary key
VisitID Short Text Foreign key
InvoiceAmount Currency
InvoiceDate Date/Time
InvoicePaid Yes/No

Renaming Fields in Design View

Donna has decided to rename the InvoiceAmount field in the Billing table to InvoiceAmt. Since Amt is an appropriate abbreviation for Amount, this new name will be just as readable, yet a little shorter.

To rename a field in Design view:

1. Click to position the insertion point to the right of the word "InvoiceAmount" in the third row's Field Name box, and then press **BACKSPACE** four times to delete the letters "ount." The name of the fourth field is now InvoiceAm. Now add the final letter by pressing the letter **t**. The name of the new field is now InvoiceAmt as Donna wants it to be. See Figure 1–16.
2. Click in the row for the InvoiceAmt field to make it the current field.

TIP

You can also select an entire field name and then type new text to replace it.

Figure 1–16 Billing table after renamed field

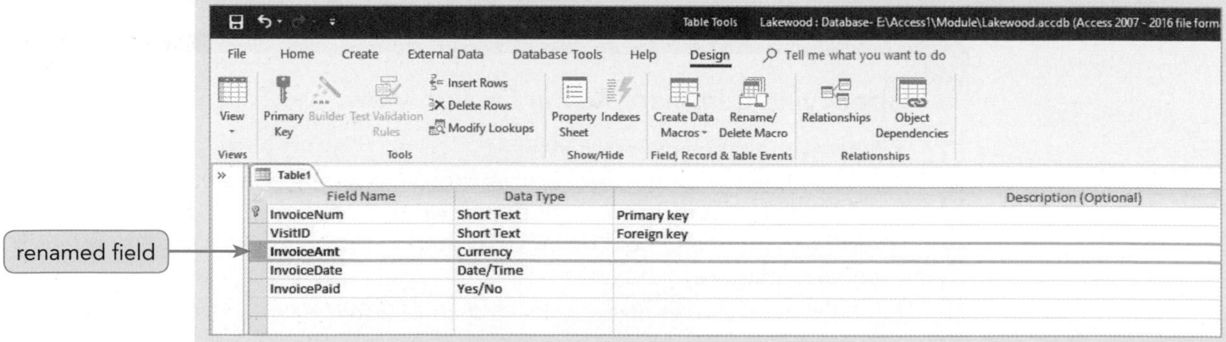
renamed field
Table Tools Lakewood : Database- E:\Access1\Module\Lakewood.accdb (Access 2007 - 2016 file form
File Home Create External Data Database Tools Help Design Tell me what you want to do
View Primary Key Builder Test Validation Rules Insert Rows Delete Rows Modify Lookups Property Sheet Indexes Create Data Macros Rename/ Delete Macro Relationships Object Dependencies
Views Tools Show/Hide Field, Record & Table Events Relationships
Table1
Field Name Data Type Description (Optional)
InvoiceNum Short Text Primary key
VisitID Short Text Foreign key
InvoiceAmt Currency
InvoiceDate Date/Time
InvoicePaid Yes/No

Saving the Billing Table Structure

As with the Visit table, the last step in creating a table is to name the table and save the table's structure. When you save a table structure, the table is stored in the database file (in this case, the Lakewood database file). After saving the table, you can enter data into it. According to Donna's plan, you need to save the table you've defined as "Billing."

To save, name, and close the Billing table:

1. On the Quick Access Toolbar, click the **Save** button. The Save As dialog box opens.
2. With the default name Table1 selected in the Table Name box, type **Billing**, and then click **OK**. The tab for the table now displays the name "Billing," and the Billing table design is saved in the Lakewood database.
3. Click the **Close 'Billing'** button on the object tab. The Billing table closes, and the main portion of the Access window is now blank because no database object is currently open. The Lakewood database file is still open, as indicated by the filename in the Access window title bar.

You have now successfully created and saved the structures for the Visit and Billing tables; however, you have not yet added any data to these tables. You can view and work with these objects in the Navigation Pane.

To view objects in the Lakewood database:

1. On the Navigation Pane, click the **Shutter Bar Open/Close Button** to open it. See Figure 1–17.

Figure 1–17 Visit and Billing tables (database objects) displayed in the Navigation Pane

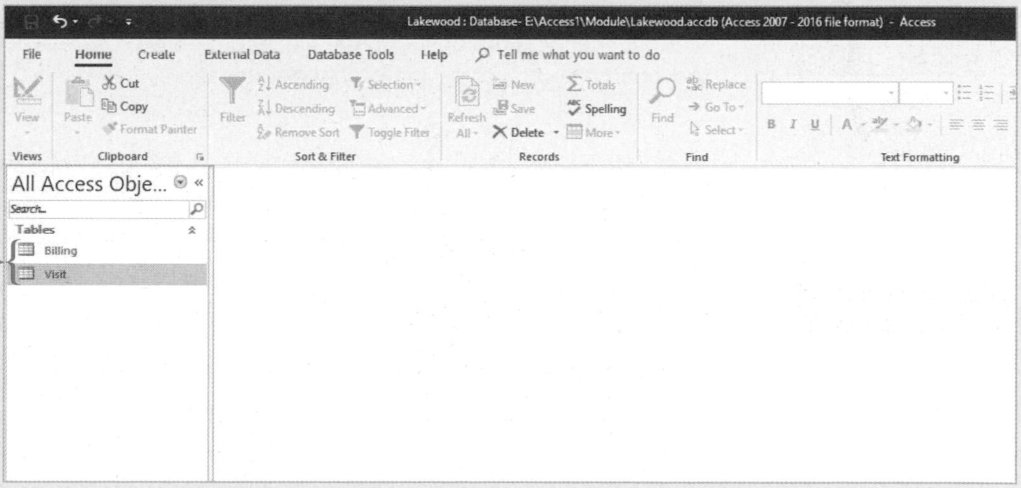
the Billing and Visit tables are now saved in the Lakewood database
Lakewood : Database- E:\Access1\Module\Lakewood.accdb (Access 2007 - 2016 file format) - Access
File
Home
Create
External Data
Database Tools
Help
Tell me what you want to do
All Access Obje...
Tables
Billing
Visit

Closing a Table and Exiting Access

When you are finished working in an Access table, it's a good idea to close the table so that you do not make unintended changes to the table data. You can close a table by clicking its Close button on the object tab, as you did earlier. Or, if you want to close the Access program as well, you can click the program's Close button. When you do, any open tables are closed, the active database is closed, and you exit the Access program.

To close any opened tables and exit Access:

1. Click the **Close** button on the program window title bar. Any opened tables would close, along with the Lakewood database, and then the Access program closes.

TIP

To close a database without exiting Access, click the File tab to display Backstage view, and then click Close.

INSIGHT

Saving a Database

Unlike the Save buttons in other Office programs, the Save button on the Quick Access Toolbar in Access does not save the active document (database). Instead, you use the Save button to save the design of an Access object, such as a table (as you saw earlier), or to save datasheet format changes, such as resizing columns. Access does not have or need a button or option you can use to save the active database.

Access saves changes to the active database automatically when you change or add a record or close the database. If your database is stored on a removable storage device, such as a USB drive, you should never remove the device while the database file is open. If you do, Access will encounter problems when it tries to save the database, which might damage the database. Make sure you close the database first before removing the storage device.

It is possible to save a database with a different name. To do so, you would click the File tab to open Backstage view, and then click the Save As option. You save the database in the default database format unless you select a different format, so click the Save As button to open the Save As dialog box. Enter the new name for the database, choose the location for saving the file, and then click Save. The database is saved with a new name and is stored in the specified location.

Now that you've become familiar with database concepts and Access, and created the Lakewood database and the structures for the Visit and Billing tables, Donna wants you to add records to the Visit table and work with the data stored in it to create database objects including a query, form, and report. You'll complete these tasks in the next session.

REVIEW

Session 1.1 Quick Check

1. A(n) ________ is a single characteristic of a person, place, object, event, or idea.
2. You connect the records in two separate tables through a(n) ________ that appears in both tables.
3. The ________, whose values uniquely identify each record in a table, is called a(n) ________ when it is placed in a second table to form a relationship between the two tables.
4. The ________ is the area of the Access window that lists all the objects in a database, and it is the main control center for opening and working with database objects.
5. What is the name of the field that Access creates, by default, as the primary key field for a new table in Datasheet view?
6. Which group on the Table Tools Fields tab contains the options you use to add new fields to a table?
7. What are the two views you can use to create a table in Access?
8. Explain how the saving process in Access is different from saving in other Office programs.

Session 1.2 Visual Overview:

The Microsoft Access Help button on the Help tab opens the **Access Help** window, where you can nd information about Access commands and features as well as instructions for using them.

The **Tell Me** feature allows you to search for specic help by typing what you would like to do.

The **Create tab** provides options for creating database objects including tables, forms, and reports. The options appear on the tab grouped by object type.

The **Query Wizard button** opens a dialog box listing types of wizards that guide you through the steps to create a query. One of these, the **Simple Query Wizard**, allows you to select records and elds to display in the query results.

You use the options in the Tables group to create a table in Datasheet view or in Design view.

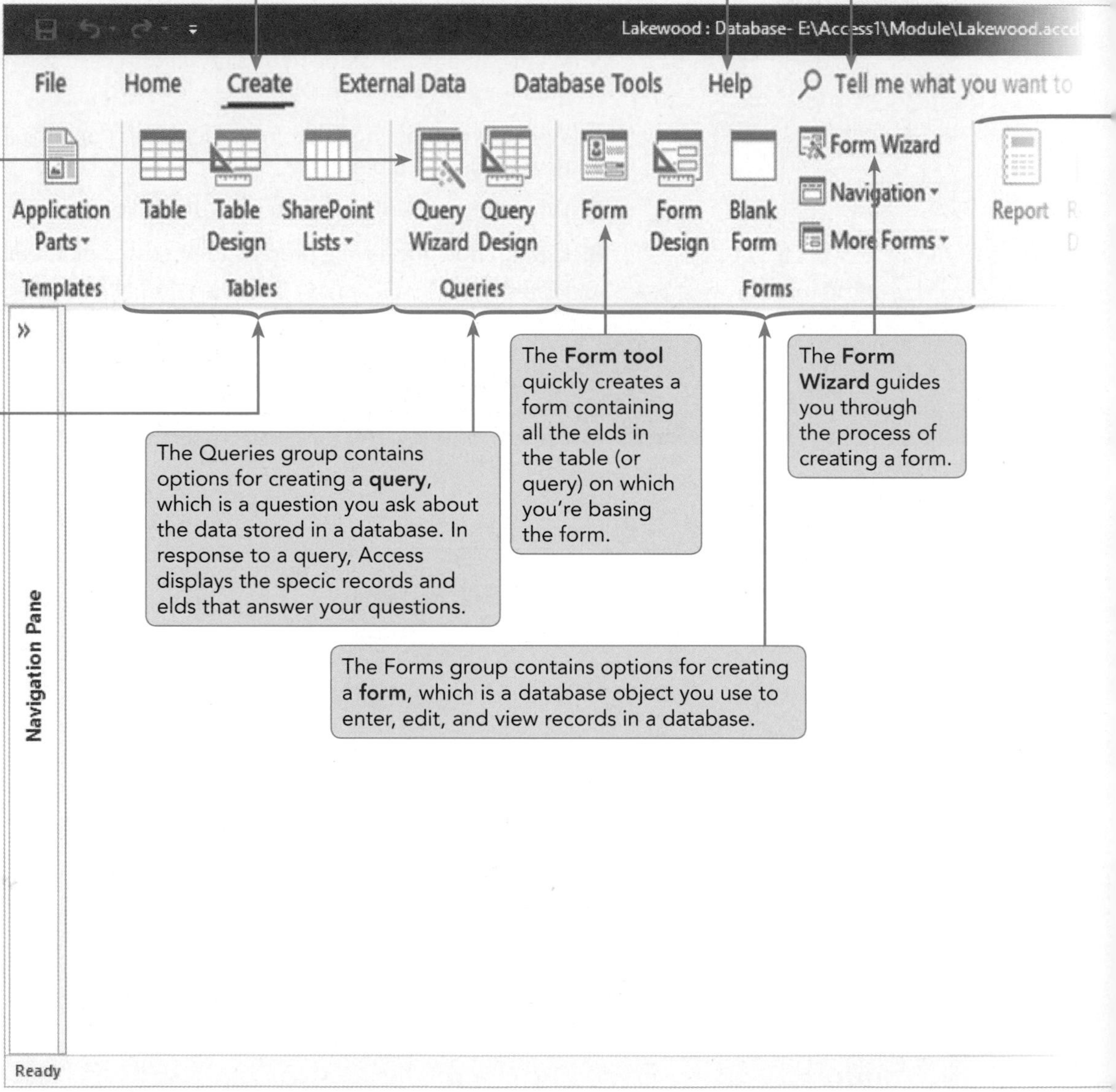

Lakewood : Database- E:\Access1\Module\Lakewood.acc
File
Home
Create
External Data
Database Tools
Help
Tell me what you want to
Application Parts
Table
Table Design
SharePoint Lists
Query Wizard
Query Design
Form
Form Design
Blank Form
Form Wizard
Navigation
More Forms
Report
Templates
Tables
Queries
Forms
Navigation Pane
Ready

The **Form tool** quickly creates a form containing all the elds in the table (or query) on which you're basing the form.

The **Form Wizard** guides you through the process of creating a form.

The Queries group contains options for creating a **query**, which is a question you ask about the data stored in a database. In response to a query, Access displays the specic records and elds that answer your questions.

The Forms group contains options for creating a **form**, which is a database object you use to enter, edit, and view records in a database.

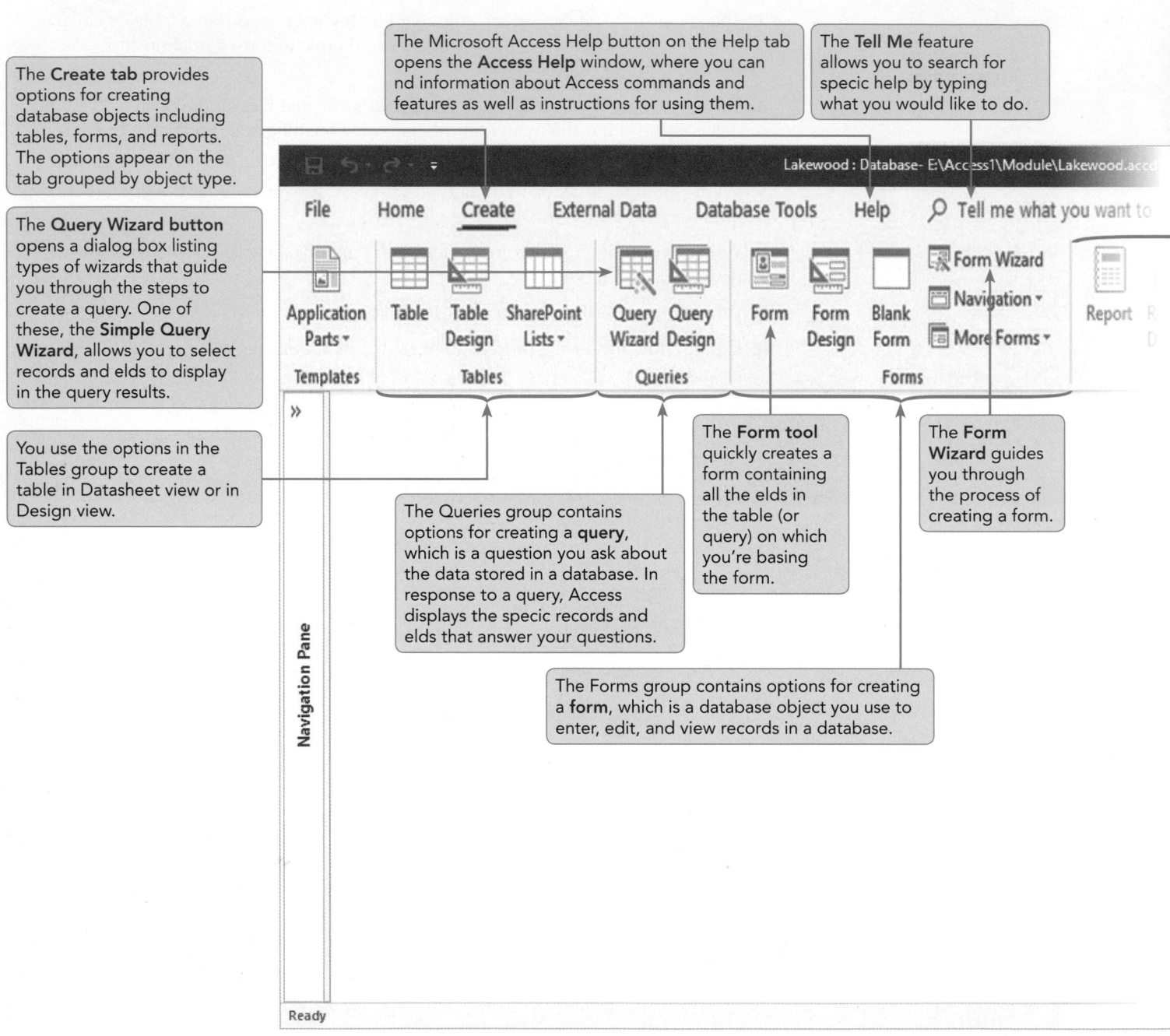

The Create Tab Options

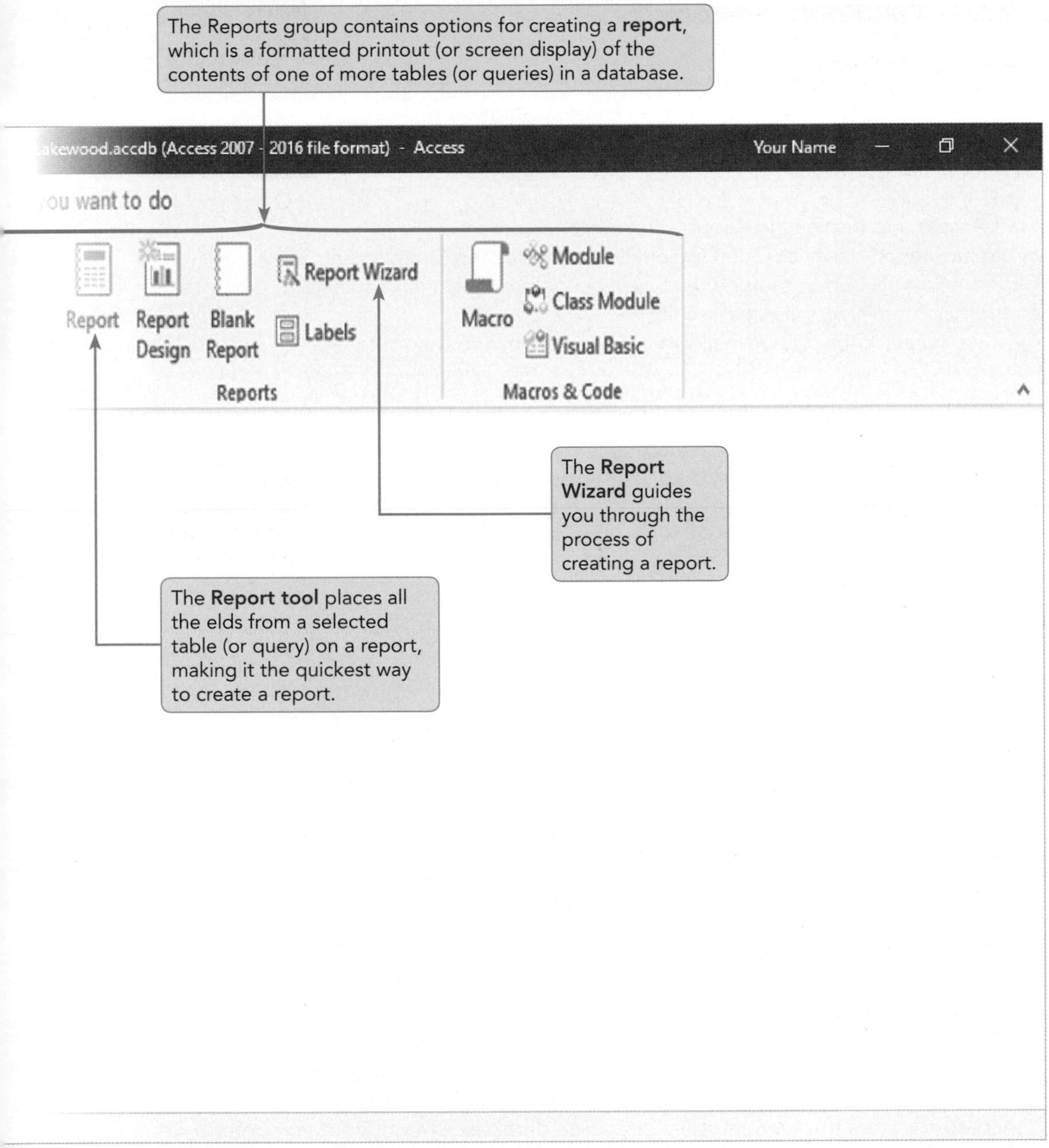

The Reports group contains options for creating a **report**, which is a formatted printout (or screen display) of the contents of one of more tables (or queries) in a database.
akewood.accdb (Access 2007 - 2016 file format) - Access
Your Name
ou want to do
Report
Report Design
Blank Report
Report Wizard
Labels
Reports
Macro
Module
Class Module
Visual Basic
Macros & Code
The **Report Wizard** guides you through the process of creating a report.
The **Report tool** places all the elds from a selected table (or query) on a report, making it the quickest way to create a report.

Entering Data into Tables

With the fields in place for the Visit table, you can now enter the field values for each record. However, if you closed Access, as instructed, after the previous session, you must first open Access and the Lakewood database to be able to work with the Visit table. If you did not close Access in the previous session and the Lakewood database is still open (see previous Figure 1–17), you may skip the steps below that open Access and the Lakewood database, and go directly to the steps to enter data into the Visit table.

REFERENCE

Opening a Database

- Start Access and display the Recent screen in Backstage view.
- Click the name of the database you want to open in the list of recently opened databases.

or

- Start Access and display the Recent screen in Backstage view.
- In the navigation bar, click Open Other Files to display the Open screen.
- Click the Browse button to open the Open dialog box, and then navigate to the drive and folder containing the database file you want to open.
- Click the name of the database file you want to open, and then click Open.

To open Access and Lakewood database:

1. On the Windows taskbar, click the **Start** button. The Start menu opens.
2. Click **Access**.
3. Access starts and displays the Recent screen in Backstage view. You may choose the **Lakewood** database from the Recent list (with its location listed below the database name), or click **Open Other Files** to display the Open screen in Backstage view and browse to your database and location. If you choose to open the Lakewood database from the Recent list, skip steps 4–6.
4. If you choose to open other files from step 3, on the Open screen, click **Browse**. The Open dialog box opens, showing folder information for your computer.

   Trouble? If you are storing your files on OneDrive, click OneDrive, and then sign in if necessary.
5. Navigate to the drive that contains your Data Files.
6. Navigate to the **Access1 > Module** folder, click the database file named **Lakewood**, and then click **Open**. The Lakewood database opens in the Access program window.

   Trouble? If a security warning appears below the ribbon indicating that some active content has been disabled, click the Enable Content button. Access provides this warning because some databases might contain content that could harm your computer. Because the Lakewood database does not contain objects that could be harmful, you can open it safely. If you are accessing the file over a network, you might also see a dialog box asking if you want to make the file a trusted document; click Yes.

Note that the Lakewood database contains two objects, the Billing and Visit tables you created at the end of the previous session (see Figure 1–17). The next step is for you to open the Visit table to begin adding records.

To open the Visit table:

1. In the Navigation Pane, double-click **Visit** to open the Visit table in Datasheet view.
2. On the Navigation Pane, click the **Shutter Bar Open/Close Button** « to close the pane.
3. Click the first row value for the VisitID field. See Figure 1–18.

Figure 1–18 Visit table opened and ready to enter data

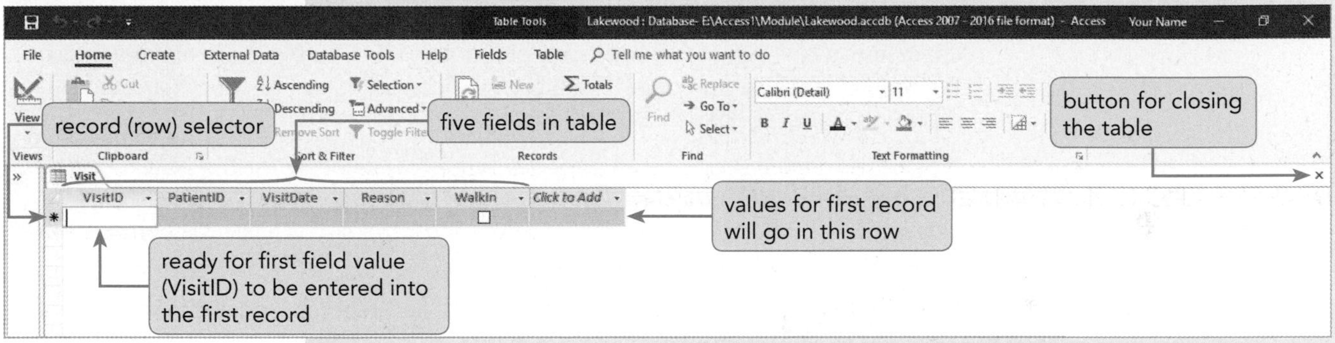
record (row) selector
five fields in table
button for closing the table
values for first record will go in this row
ready for first field value (VisitID) to be entered into the first record
VisitID
PatientID
VisitDate
Reason
WalkIn
Click to Add

You are now ready to begin adding records and are positioned in the first field (VisitID) of the first record. Donna requests that you enter eight records into the Visit table, as show in Figure 1–19.

Figure 1–19 Visit table records

VisitID	PatientID	VisitDate	Reason	WalkIn
1495	13310	12/23/2020	Rhinitis	Yes
1450	13272	10/26/2020	Influenza	Yes
1461	13250	11/3/2020	Dermatitis	Yes
1615	13308	4/1/2021	COPD management visit	No
1596	13299	3/24/2021	Pneumonia	Yes
1567	13283	2/26/2021	Annual wellness visit	No
1499	13264	12/28/2020	Hypotension	No
1475	13261	11/19/2020	Annual wellness visit	No

To enter the first record for the Visit table:

Be sure to type the numbers "0" and "1" and not the letters "O" and "l" when entering numeric values, even though the field is of the Short Text data type.

1. In the first row for the VisitID field, type **1495** (the VisitID field value for the first record), and then press **TAB**. Access adds the field value and moves the insertion point to the right, into the PatientID column. See Figure 1–20.

Figure 1–20 First field value entered

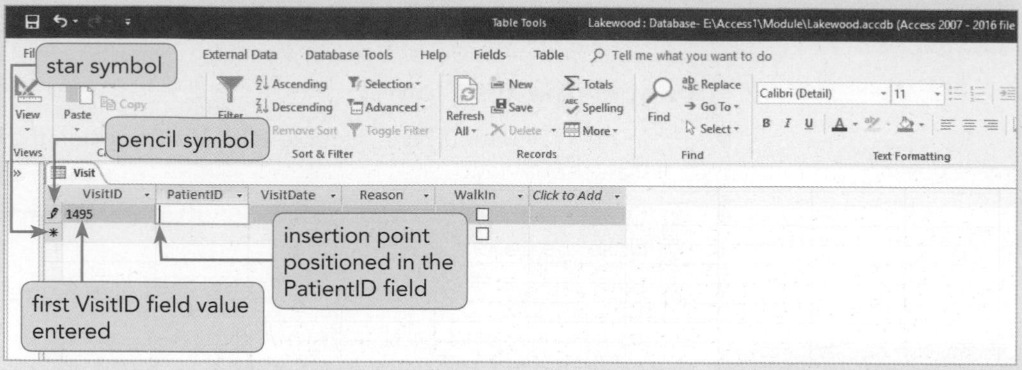
star symbol
pencil symbol
insertion point positioned in the PatientID field
first VisitID field value entered

Trouble? If you make a mistake when typing a value, use BACKSPACE to delete characters to the left of the insertion point or use DELETE to delete characters to the right of the insertion point. Then type the correct value. To correct a value by replacing it entirely, press ESC, and then type the correct value.

Notice the pencil symbol that appears in the row selector for the new record. The **pencil symbol** indicates that the record is being edited. Also notice the star symbol that appears in the row selector for the second row. The **star symbol** identifies the second row as the next row available for a new record.

2. Type **13310** (the PatientID field value for the first record), and then press **TAB**. Access enters the field value and moves the insertion point to the VisitDate column.
3. Type **12/23/20** (the VisitDate field value for the first record), and then press **TAB**. Access displays the year as "2020" even though you entered only the final two digits of the year. This is because the VisitDate field has the Date/Time data type, which automatically formats dates with four-digit years.
4. Type **Rhinitis** (the Reason field value for the first record), and then press **TAB** to move to the WalkIn column.

   Recall that the WalkIn field is a Yes/No field. Notice the check box displayed in the WalkIn column. By default, the value for any Yes/No field is "No"; therefore, the check box is initially empty. For Yes/No fields with check boxes, you press TAB to leave the check box unchecked, or you press SPACEBAR to insert a checkmark in the check box. The record you are entering in the table is for a walk-in visit, so you need to insert a checkmark in the check box to indicate "Yes."

TIP

You can also click a check box in a Yes/No field to insert or remove a checkmark.

5. Press **SPACEBAR** to insert a checkmark, and then press **TAB**. The first record is entered into the table, and the insertion point is positioned in the VisitID field for the second record. The pencil symbol is removed from the first row because the record in that row is no longer being edited. The table is now ready for you to enter the second record. See Figure 1–21.

Figure 1–21 **Datasheet with first record entered**

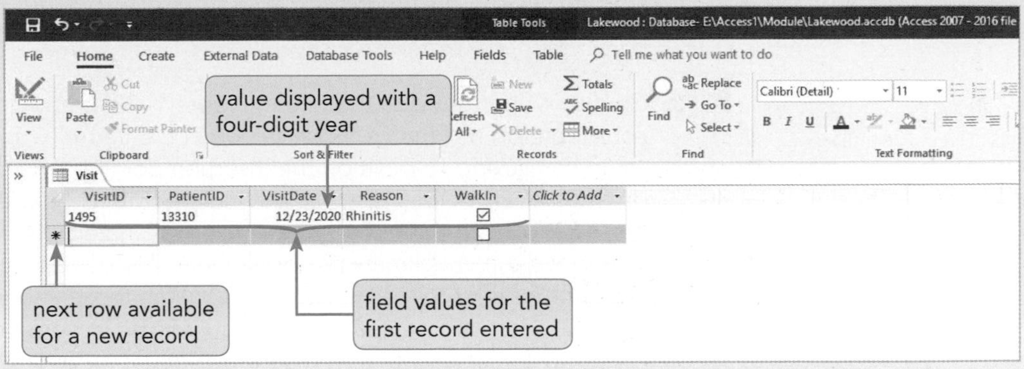
value displayed with a four-digit year
next row available for a new record
field values for the first record entered

Now you can enter the remaining seven records in the Visit table.

To enter the remaining records in the Visit table:

TIP

You can also press ENTER instead of TAB to move from one field to another and to the next row.

1. Referring to Figure 1–19, enter the values for records 2 through 8, pressing **TAB** to move from field to field and to the next row for a new record. Keep in mind that you do not have to type all four digits of the year in the VisitDate field values; you can enter only the final two digits, and Access will display all four. Also, for any WalkIn field values of "No," be sure to press TAB to leave the check box empty.

   Trouble? If you enter a value in the wrong field by mistake, such as entering a Reason field value in the VisitDate field, a menu might open with options for addressing the problem. If this happens, click the "Enter new value" option in the menu. You'll return to the field with the incorrect value selected, which you can then replace by typing the correct value.

   Notice that not all of the Reason field values are fully displayed. To see more of the table datasheet and the full field values, you'll resize the Reason column.

2. Place the pointer on the vertical line to the right of the Reason field name until the pointer changes to the column resizing pointer ↔, and then double-click the vertical line. All the Reason field values are now fully displayed. See Figure 1–22.

Figure 1–22 **Datasheet with eight records entered**

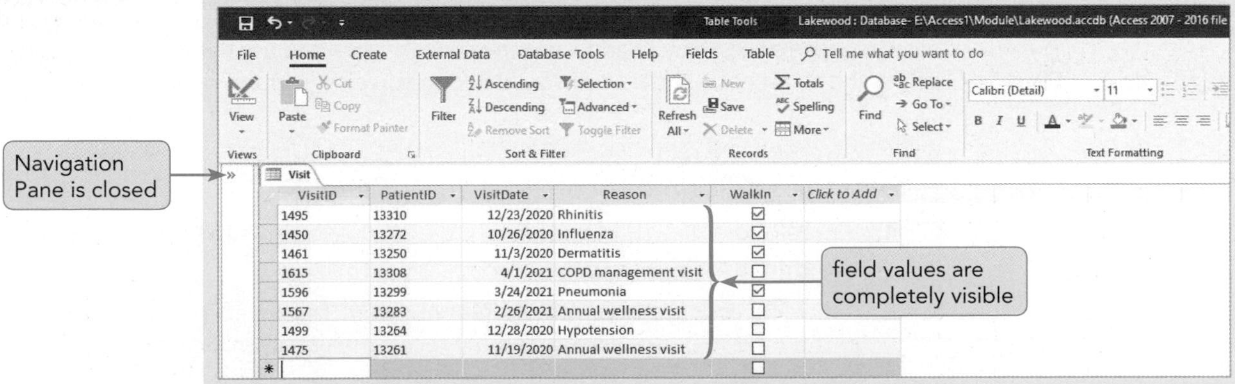
Navigation Pane is closed
field values are completely visible

When you resize a datasheet column by double-clicking the column dividing line, you are sizing the column to its **best fit**—that is, so the column is just wide enough to display the longest visible value in the column, including the field name.

Carefully compare your VisitID and PatientID values with those in the figure, and correct any errors before continuing.

3. Compare your table to the one in Figure 1–22. If any of the field values in your table do not match those shown in the figure, you can correct a field value by clicking to position the insertion point in the value, and then using BACKSPACE or DELETE to delete incorrect text. Type the correct text and press ENTER. To correct a value in the WalkIn field, click the check box to add or remove the checkmark as appropriate. Also, be sure the spelling and capitalization of field names in your table match those shown in the figure exactly and that there are no spaces between words. To correct a field name, double-click it to select it, and then type the correct name; or use the Rename Field option on the shortcut menu to rename a field with the correct name.

Remember that Access automatically saves the data stored in a table; however, you must save any new or modified structure to a table. Even though you have not clicked the Save button, your data has already been saved. To ensure this is the case, you can close the table and then reopen it.

To close and reopen Visit table:

1. Click the **Close 'Visit'** button [X] on the object tab for the Visit table. When asked if you would like to save the changes to the layout of the Visit table, click **Yes**. The Visit table closes.
2. On the Navigation Pane, click the **Shutter Bar Open/Close Button** [»] to open it.
3. In the Navigation Pane, double-click **Visit** to open the Visit table in Datasheet view.

Notice that after you closed and reopened the Visit table, Access sorted and displayed the records in order by the values in the VisitID field because it is the primary key. If you compare your screen to Figure 1–22, which shows the records in the order you entered them, you'll see that the current screen shows the records in order by the VisitID field values.

Donna asks you to add two more records to the Visit table. When you add a record to an existing table, you must enter the new record in the next row available for a new record; you cannot insert a row between existing records for the new record. In a table with just a few records, such as the Visit table, the next available row is visible on the screen. However, in a table with hundreds of records, you would need to scroll the datasheet to see the next row available. The easiest way to add a new record to a table is to use the New button, which scrolls the datasheet to the next row available so you can enter the new record.

To enter additional records in the Visit table:

1. If necessary, click the first record's VisitID field value (**1450**) to make it the current record.
2. In the Records group, click the **New** button. The insertion point is positioned in the next row available for a new record, which in this case is row 9. See Figure 1–23.

Figure 1–23 Entering a new record

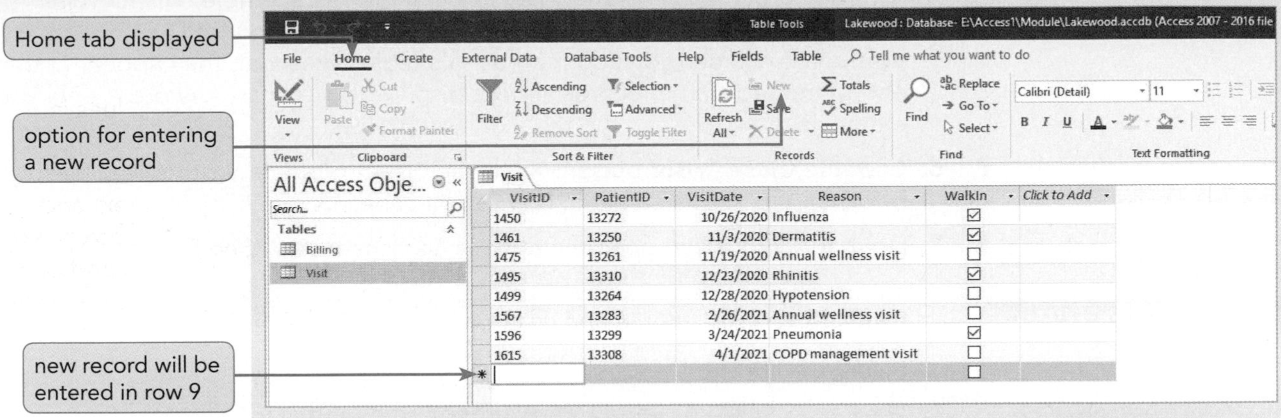
Home tab displayed
option for entering a new record
new record will be entered in row 9

3. With the insertion point in the VisitID field for the new record, type **1548** and then press **TAB**.
4. Complete the entry of this record by entering each value shown below, pressing **TAB** to move from field to field:

   PatientID = **13301**

   VisitDate = **2/10/2021**

   Reason = **Hypothyroidism**

   WalkIn = **No (unchecked)**
5. Enter the values for the next new record, as follows, and then press **TAB** after entering the WalkIn field value:

   VisitID = **1588**

   PatientID = **13268**

   VisitDate = **3/19/2021**

   Reason = **Cyst removal**

   WalkIn = **Yes (checked)**

   Your datasheet should look like the one shown in Figure 1–24.

Figure 1–24 Datasheet with additional records entered

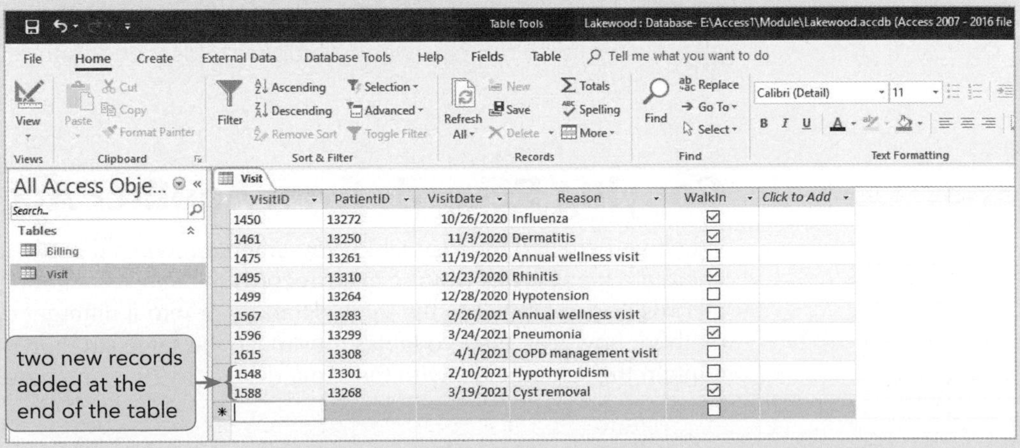
two new records added at the end of the table

The new records you added appear at the end of the table, and are not sorted in order by the primary key field values. For example, VisitID 1548 should be the sixth record in the table, placed between VisitID 1499 and VisitID 1567. When you add records to a table datasheet, they appear at the end of the table. The records are not displayed in primary key order until you either close and reopen the table or switch views.

6. Click the **Close 'Visit'** button ☒ on the object tab. The Visit table closes; however, it is still listed in the Navigation Pane.

7. Double-click **Visit** to open the table in Datasheet view. See Figure 1–25.

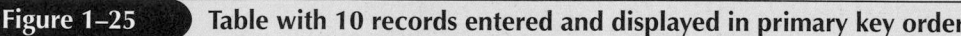

Figure 1–25 **Table with 10 records entered and displayed in primary key order**

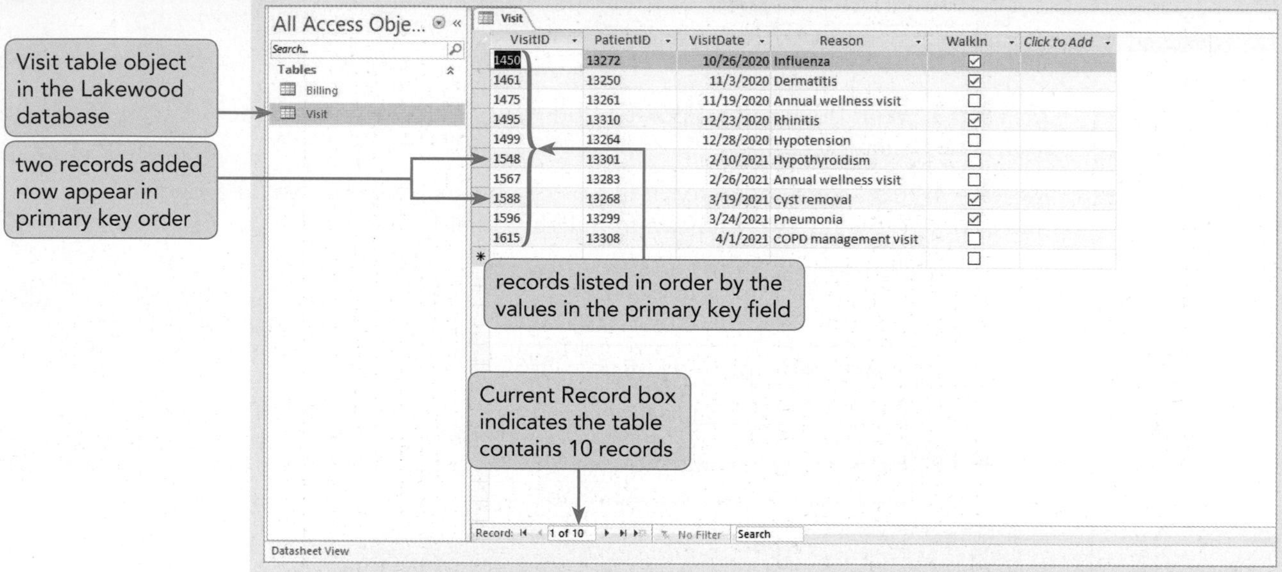
Visit table object in the Lakewood database
two records added now appear in primary key order
records listed in order by the values in the primary key field
Current Record box indicates the table contains 10 records
All Access Obje...
Tables
Billing
Visit
VisitID
PatientID
VisitDate
Reason
WalkIn
Click to Add
1450 13272 10/26/2020 Influenza
1461 13250 11/3/2020 Dermatitis
1475 13261 11/19/2020 Annual wellness visit
1495 13310 12/23/2020 Rhinitis
1499 13264 12/28/2020 Hypotension
1548 13301 2/10/2021 Hypothyroidism
1567 13283 2/26/2021 Annual wellness visit
1588 13268 3/19/2021 Cyst removal
1596 13299 3/24/2021 Pneumonia
1615 13308 4/1/2021 COPD management visit
Record: 1 of 10
No Filter
Search
Datasheet View

The two records you added, with VisitID field values of 1548 and 1588, now appear in the correct primary key order. The table contains a total of 10 records, as indicated by the **Current Record box** at the bottom of the datasheet. The Current Record box displays the number of the current record as well as the total number of records in the table.

Each record contains a unique VisitID value because this field is the primary key. Other fields, however, can contain the same value in multiple records; for example, the Reason field has two values of "Annual wellness visit."

8. Click the **Close** button ☒ on the program window title bar. The Visit table, along with the Lakewood database, close, and then the Access program closes.

Copying Records from Another Access Database

When you created the Visit table, you entered records directly into the table datasheet. There are many other ways to enter records in a table, including copying and pasting records from a table into the same database or into a different database. To use this method, however, the two tables must have the same structure—that is, the tables must contain the same fields, with the same design, in the same order.

Donna has already created a table named Appointment that contains additional records with visit data. The Appointment table is contained in a database named Support_AC_1_Donna.accdb located in the Access1 > Module folder included with your Data Files. The Appointment table has the same table structure as the Visit table you created.

Your next task is to copy the records from the Appointment table and paste them into your Visit table. To do so, you need to open the Support_AC_1_Donna.accdb database.

To copy the records from the Appointment table:

1. On the Windows taskbar, click the **Start** button. The Start menu opens.
2. Click **Access**.
3. Click **Open Other Files** to display the Open screen in Backstage view.
4. On the Open screen, click **Browse**. The Open dialog box opens, showing folder information for your computer.

   Trouble? If you are storing your files on OneDrive, click OneDrive, and then log in if necessary.
5. Navigate to the drive that contains your Data Files.
6. Navigate to the **Access1 > Module** folder, click the database file **Support_AC_1_Donna.accdb**, and then click **Open**. The Support_AC_1_Donna database opens in the Access program window. Note that the database contains only one object, the Appointment table.

   Trouble? If a security warning appears below the ribbon indicating that some active content has been disabled, click the Enable Content button. Access provides this warning because some databases might contain content that could harm your computer. Because the Support_AC_1_Donna.accdb database does not contain objects that could be harmful, you can open it safely. If you are accessing the file over a network, you might also see a dialog box asking if you want to make the file a trusted document; click Yes.
7. In the Navigation Pane, double-click **Appointment** to open the Appointment table in Datasheet view. The table contains 76 records and the same five fields, with the same characteristics, as the fields in the Visit table. See Figure 1–26.

Figure 1–26 **Appointment table in the Support_AC_1_Donna database**

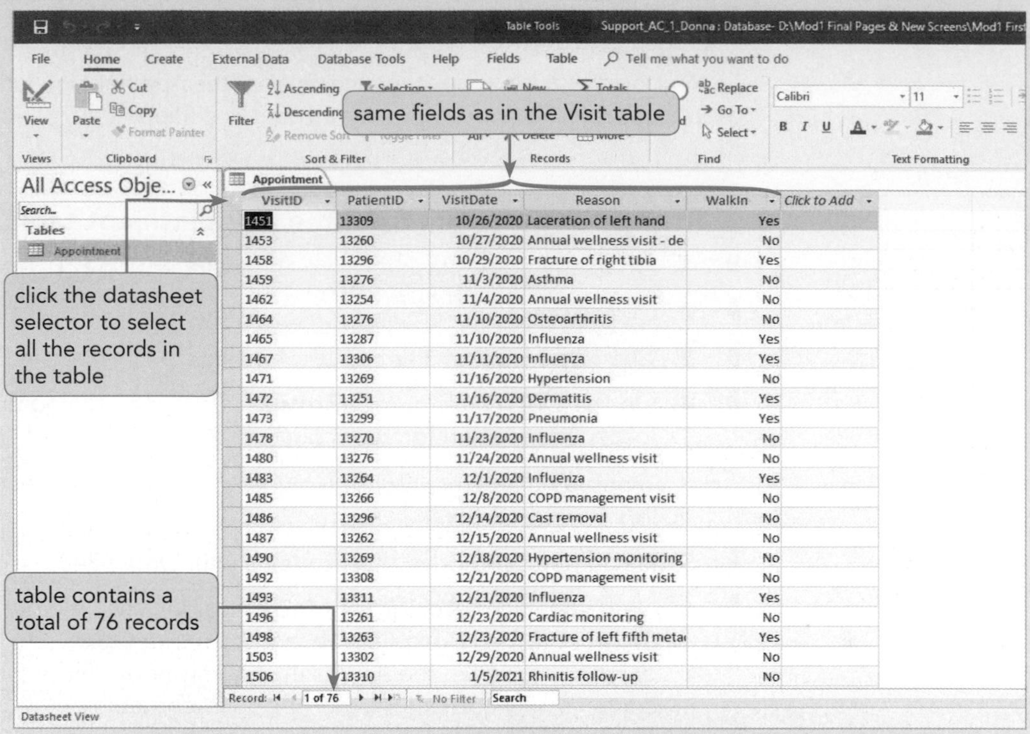
same fields as in the Visit table
click the datasheet selector to select all the records in the table
table contains a total of 76 records

Donna wants you to copy all the records in the Appointment table. You can select all the records by clicking the **datasheet selector**, which is the box to the left of the first field name in the table datasheet, as shown in Figure 1–26.

8. Click the **datasheet selector** to the left of the VisitID field. All the records in the table are selected.
9. In the Clipboard group, click the **Copy** button to copy all the records to the Clipboard.
10. Click the **Close 'Appointment'** button on the object tab. A dialog box may open asking if you want to save the data you copied to the Clipboard. This dialog box opens only when you copy a large amount of data to the Clipboard. If asked, click **Yes**. If opened, the dialog box closes, and then the Appointment table closes.

With the records copied to the Clipboard, you can now paste them into the Visit table. First you need to close the Support_AC_1_Donna.accdb database while keeping the Access program open, and then open the Lakewood database.

To close the Support_AC_1_Donna.accdb database and then paste the records into the Visit table:

1. Click the **File** tab to open Backstage view, and then click **Close** in the navigation bar to close the Support_AC_1_Donna.accdb database. You return to a blank Access program window, and the Home tab is the active tab on the ribbon.
2. Click the **File** tab to return to Backstage view, and then click **Open** in the navigation bar. Recent is selected on the Open screen, and the recently opened database files are listed. This list should include the Lakewood database.

3. Click **Lakewood** to open the Lakewood database file.

   Trouble? If the Lakewood database file is not in the list of recent files, click Browse. In the Open dialog box, navigate to the drive and folder where you are storing your files, and then open the Lakewood database file.

   Trouble? If the security warning appears below the ribbon, click the Enable Content button, and then, if necessary, click Yes to identify the file as a trusted document.

4. In the Navigation Pane, double-click **Visit** to open the Visit table in Datasheet view.
5. On the Navigation Pane, click the **Shutter Bar Open/Close Button** « to close the pane.
6. Position the pointer on the star symbol in the row selector for row 11 (the next row available for a new record) until the pointer changes to a right-pointing arrow ➡, and then click to select the row.
7. In the Clipboard group, click the **Paste** button. The pasted records are added to the table, and a dialog box opens asking you to confirm that you want to paste all the records (76 total).

   Trouble? If the Paste button isn't active, click the row selection ➡ pointer on the row selector for row 11, making sure the entire row is selected, and then repeat Step 7.

8. Click **Yes**. The dialog box closes, and the pasted records are selected. See Figure 1–27. Notice that the table now contains a total of 86 records—10 records that you entered previously and 76 records that you copied and pasted.

Figure 1–27 Visit table after copying and pasting records

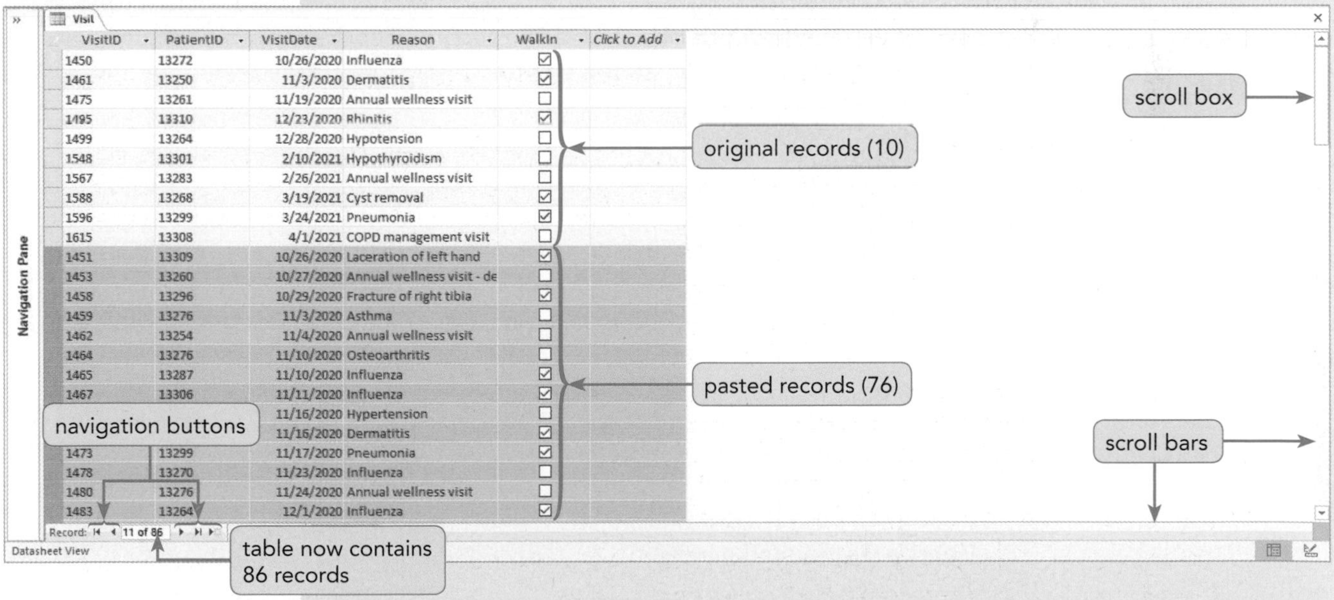
Visit
VisitID PatientID VisitDate Reason WalkIn Click to Add
Navigation Pane
Record: 11 of 86
Datasheet View
scroll box
original records (10)
pasted records (76)
navigation buttons
scroll bars
table now contains 86 records

Not all the Reason field values are completely visible, so you need to resize this column to its best fit.

9. Place the pointer on the column dividing line to the right of the Reason field name until the pointer changes to the column resizing pointer ✥, and then double-click the column dividing line. The Reason field values are now fully displayed.

Navigating a Datasheet

The Visit table now contains 86 records, but only some of the records are visible on the screen. To view fields or records not currently visible on the screen, you can use the horizontal and vertical scroll bars to navigate the data. The **navigation buttons**, shown in Figure 1–27 and also described in Figure 1–28, provide another way to move vertically through the records. The Current Record box appears between the two sets of navigation buttons and displays the number of the current record as well as the total number of records in the table. Figure 1–28 shows which record becomes the current record when you click each navigation button. The New (blank) record button works the same way as the New button on the Home tab, which you used earlier to enter a new record in the table.

Figure 1–28 Navigation buttons

Navigation Button	Record Selected	Navigation Button	Record Selected
⏮	First record	⏭	Last record
◀	Previous record	▶*	New (blank) record
▶	Next record		

Donna suggests that you use the various navigation techniques to move through the Visit table and become familiar with its contents.

TIP

You can make a field the current field by clicking anywhere within the column for that field.

To navigate the Visit datasheet:

1. Click the first record's VisitID field value (**1450**). The Current Record box shows that record 1 is the current record.
2. Click the **Next record** button ▶. The second record is now highlighted, which identifies it as the current record. The second record's value for the VisitID field is selected, and the Current Record box displays "2 of 86" to indicate that the second record is the current record.
3. Click the **Last record** button ⏭. The last record in the table, record 86, is now the current record.
4. Drag the scroll box in the vertical scroll bar up to the top of the bar. Record 86 is still the current record, as indicated in the Current Record box. Dragging the scroll box changes the display of the table datasheet, but does not change the current record.
5. Drag the scroll box in the vertical scroll bar back down until you can see the end of the table and the current record (record 86).
6. Click the **Previous record** button ◀. Record 85 is now the current record.
7. Click the **First record** button ⏮. The first record is now the current record and is visible on the screen.

   Earlier you resized the Reason column to its best fit, to ensure all the field values were visible. However, when you resize a column to its best fit, the column expands to fully display only the field values that are visible on the screen at that time. If you move through the complete datasheet and notice that not all of the field values are fully displayed after resizing the column, you need to resize the column again.

8. Scroll down through the records and observe if the field values for the Reason field are fully displayed. The Reason field values for visit 1595 and visit 1606 are not fully displayed. With these records displayed, place the pointer on the column dividing line to the right of the Reason field name until the pointer changes to the column resizing pointer ✛, and then double-click the column dividing line. The field values are now fully displayed.

The Visit table now contains all the data about patient visits for Lakewood Community Health Services. To better understand how to work with this data, Donna asks you to create simple objects for the other main types of database objects—queries, forms, and reports.

Creating a Simple Query

A query is a question you ask about the data stored in a database. When you create a query, you tell Access which fields you need and what criteria it should use to select the records that will answer your question. Then Access displays only the information you want, so you don't have to navigate through the entire database for the information. In the Visit table, for example, Donna might create a query to display only those records for visits that occurred in a specific month. Even though a query can display table information in a different way, the information still exists in the table as it was originally entered.

Donna wants to see a list of all the visit dates and reasons for visits in the Visit table. She doesn't want the list to include all the fields in the table, such as PatientID and WalkIn. To produce this list for Donna, you'll use the Simple Query Wizard to create a query based on the Visit table.

To start the Simple Query Wizard:

1. On the ribbon, click the **Create** tab.
2. In the Queries group, click the **Query Wizard** button. The New Query dialog box opens.
3. Make sure **Simple Query Wizard** is selected, and then click **OK**. The first Simple Query Wizard dialog box opens. See Figure 1–29.

Figure 1–29 **First Simple Query Wizard dialog box**

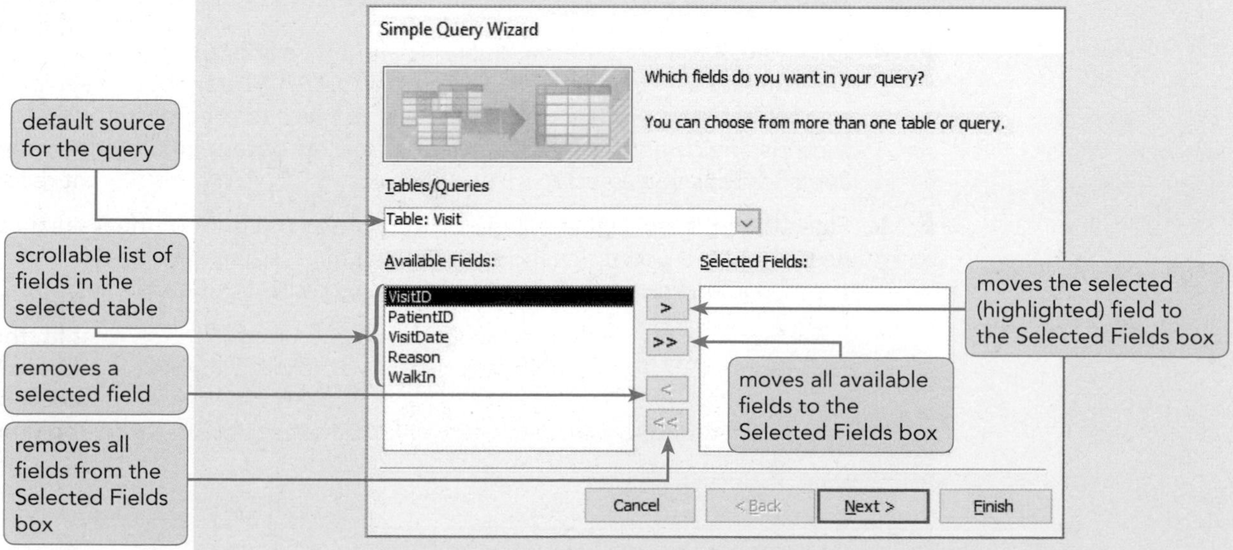
Simple Query Wizard
Which fields do you want in your query?
You can choose from more than one table or query.
Tables/Queries
Table: Visit
Available Fields:
Selected Fields:
VisitID
PatientID
VisitDate
Reason
WalkIn
>
>>
<
<<
Cancel
< Back
Next >
Finish
default source for the query
scrollable list of fields in the selected table
removes a selected field
removes all fields from the Selected Fields box
moves the selected (highlighted) field to the Selected Fields box
moves all available fields to the Selected Fields box

Because the Visit table is open in the Lakewood database, it is listed in the Tables/Queries box by default. If the database contained more objects, you could click the Tables/Queries arrow and choose another table or a query as the basis for the new query you are creating. In this case you could choose the Billing table; however, the Visit table contains the fields you need. The Available Fields box lists all the fields in the Visit table.

Trouble? If the Visit table is not the default source for the query, click the Tables/Queries arrow to choose the Visit table (Table: Visit) from the list.

You need to select fields from the Available Fields box to include them in the query. To select fields one at a time, click a field and then click the Select Single Field > button. The selected field moves from the Available Fields box on the left to the Selected Fields box on the right. To select all the fields, click the Select All Fields >> button. If you change your mind or make a mistake, you can remove a field by clicking it in the Selected Fields box and then clicking the Remove Single Field < button. To remove all fields from the Selected Fields box, click the Remove All Fields << button.

Each Simple Query Wizard dialog box contains buttons that allow you to move to the previous dialog box (Back button), move to the next dialog box (Next button), or cancel the creation process (Cancel button). You can also finish creating the object (Finish button) and accept the wizard's defaults for the remaining options.

Donna wants her query results list to include data from only the following fields: VisitID, VisitDate, and Reason. You need to select these fields to include them in the query.

To create the query using the Simple Query Wizard:

TIP

You can also double-click a field to move it from the Available Fields box to the Selected Fields box.

1. Click **VisitID** in the Available Fields box to select the field (if necessary), and then click the Select Single Field > button. The VisitID field moves to the Selected Fields box.
2. Repeat Step 1 for the fields **VisitDate** and **Reason**, and then click **Next**. The second, and final, Simple Query Wizard dialog box opens and asks you to choose a name (title) for your query. The suggested name is "Visit Query" because the query you are creating is based on the Visit table. You'll change the suggested name to "VisitList."
3. Click at the end of the suggested name, use **BACKSPACE** to delete the word "Query" and the space, and then type **List**. Now you can view the query results.
4. Click **Finish** to complete the query. The query results are displayed in Datasheet view, on a new tab named "VisitList." A query datasheet is similar to a table datasheet, showing fields in columns and records in rows—but only for those fields and records you want to see, as determined by the query specifications you select.
5. Place the pointer on the column divider line to the right of the Reason field name until the pointer changes to the column resizing pointer ✛, and then double-click the column divider line to resize the Reason field. See Figure 1–30.

Figure 1–30 Query results

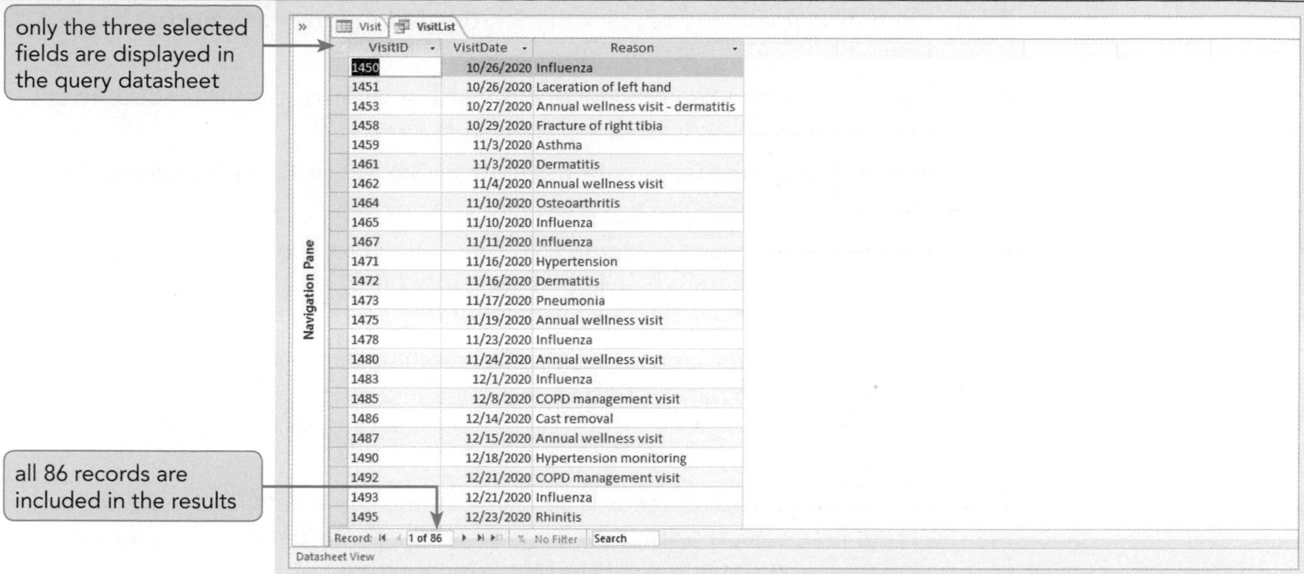
only the three selected fields are displayed in the query datasheet
all 86 records are included in the results
Visit
VisitList
VisitID
VisitDate
Reason
1450 10/26/2020 Influenza
1451 10/26/2020 Laceration of left hand
1453 10/27/2020 Annual wellness visit - dermatitis
1458 10/29/2020 Fracture of right tibia
1459 11/3/2020 Asthma
1461 11/3/2020 Dermatitis
1462 11/4/2020 Annual wellness visit
1464 11/10/2020 Osteoarthritis
1465 11/10/2020 Influenza
1467 11/11/2020 Influenza
1471 11/16/2020 Hypertension
1472 11/16/2020 Dermatitis
1473 11/17/2020 Pneumonia
1475 11/19/2020 Annual wellness visit
1478 11/23/2020 Influenza
1480 11/24/2020 Annual wellness visit
1483 12/1/2020 Influenza
1485 12/8/2020 COPD management visit
1486 12/14/2020 Cast removal
1487 12/15/2020 Annual wellness visit
1490 12/18/2020 Hypertension monitoring
1492 12/21/2020 COPD management visit
1493 12/21/2020 Influenza
1495 12/23/2020 Rhinitis
Navigation Pane
Record: 1 of 86
No Filter
Search
Datasheet View

The VisitList query datasheet displays the three fields in the order you selected them in the Simple Query Wizard, from left to right. The records are listed in order by the primary key field, VisitID. Even though the query datasheet displays only the three fields you chose for the query, the Visit table still includes all the fields for all records.

Navigation buttons are located at the bottom of the window. You navigate a query datasheet in the same way that you navigate a table datasheet.

6. Click the **Last record** button. The last record in the query datasheet is now the current record.
7. Click the **Previous record** button. Record 85 in the query datasheet is now the current record.
8. Click the **First record** button. The first record is now the current record.
9. Click the **Close 'VisitList'** button on the object tab. A dialog box opens asking if you want to save the changes to the layout of the query. This dialog box opens because you resized the Reason column.
10. Click **Yes** to save the query layout changes and close the query.

The query results are not stored in the database; however, the query design is stored as part of the database with the name you specified. You can re-create the query results at any time by opening the query again. When you open the query later, the results displayed will reflect up-to-date information to include any new records entered in the Visit table.

Donna asks you to display the query results again; however, this time she would like to list the records in descending order showing the most current VisitID first. The records are currently displayed in ascending order by VisitID, which is the primary key for the Visit table. In order to display the records in descending order, you can sort the records in Query Datasheet view.

To sort records in a query datasheet:

1. On the Navigation Pane, click the **Shutter Bar Open/Close Button** [»] to open it.
2. In the Navigation Pane, double-click **VisitList** to open the VisitList query in Datasheet view.
3. On the Navigation Pane, click the **Shutter Bar Open/Close Button** [«] to close it.
4. On the ribbon, click the **Home** tab. The first record value in the VisitID field is highlighted; therefore, VisitID is the current field. Also note the data in the first record (VisitID: 1450; VisitDate: 10/26/2020; and Reason: Influenza).
5. In the Sort & Filter group, click the **Descending** button. The records are sorted in descending order by the current field (VisitID). Because the list of records is now sorted in descending order, the original first record (VisitID 1450) should now be the last record.
6. Scroll down the list of records and see that the same data for VisitID 1450 is now in the last record. Donna has decided not to keep the data sorted in descending order and wants to return to ascending order.
7. In the Sort & Filter group, click the **Remove Sort** button. The data returns to its original state in ascending order with VisitID 1450 (and its corresponding data) listed in the first record.
8. Click the **Close 'VisitList'** button [X] on the object tab for the VisitList query. When asked if you would like to save the changes to the design of the VisitList query, click **No**. The VisitList query closes.

Next, Donna asks you to create a form for the Visit table so the staff at Lakewood Community Health Services can use the form to enter and work with data in the table easily.

Creating a Simple Form

As noted earlier, you use a form to enter, edit, and view records in a database. Although you can perform these same functions with tables and queries, forms can present data in many customized and useful ways.

Donna wants a form for the Visit table that shows all the fields for one record at a time, with fields listed one below another in a column. This type of form will make it easier for her staff to focus on all the data for a particular visit. You'll use the Form Wizard to create this form quickly and easily.

To create the form using the Form Wizard

1. Make sure the Visit table is still open in Datasheet view.

   Trouble? If the Visit table is not open, click the Shutter Bar Open/Close Button [»] to open the Navigation Pane. Double-click Visit to open the Visit table in Datasheet view. Click the Shutter Bar Open/Close Button [«] to close the pane.

2. On the ribbon, click the **Create** tab if necessary.

3. In the Forms group, click the **Form Wizard** button. The first Form Wizard dialog box opens. Make sure the Visit table is the default data source for the form.

   Trouble? If the Visit table is not the default source for the form, click the Tables/Queries arrow to choose the Visit table (Table: Visit) from the list.

   The first Form Wizard dialog box is very similar to the first Simple Query Wizard dialog box you used in creating a query.

4. Click the **Select All Fields** button >> to move all the fields to the Selected Fields box.
5. Click **Next** to display the second Form Wizard dialog box, in which you select a layout for the form. See Figure 1–31.

Figure 1–31 Choosing a layout for the form

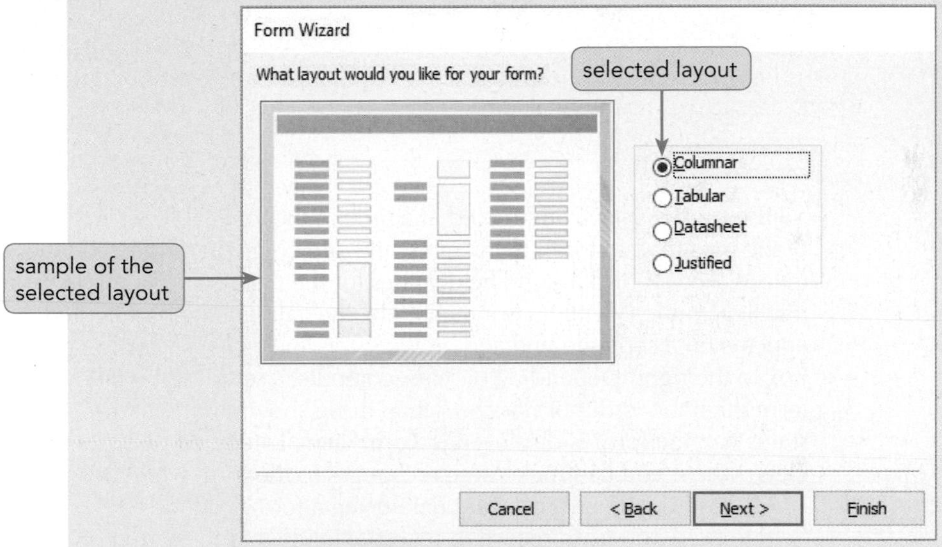
Form Wizard
What layout would you like for your form?
selected layout
Columnar
Tabular
Datasheet
Justified
sample of the selected layout
Cancel
< Back
Next >
Finish

   The layout choices are Columnar, Tabular, Datasheet, and Justified. A sample of the selected layout appears on the left side of the dialog box.

6. Click each option button and review the corresponding sample layout.
7. Because Donna wants to arrange the form data in a column with each field listed one below another, click the **Columnar** option button (if necessary), and then click **Next**.

   The third and final Form Wizard dialog box shows the Visit table's name as the default name for the form name. "Visit" is also the default title that will appear on the tab for the form.

   You'll use "VisitData" as the form name, and because you don't need to change the form's design at this point, you'll display the form.

8. Click to position the insertion point to the right of 'Visit' in the box, type **Data**, and then click the **Finish** button.

   The completed form opens in Form view, displaying the values for the first record in the Visit table. The Columnar layout places the field captions in labels on the left and the corresponding field values in boxes to the right, which vary in width depending on the size of the field. See Figure 1–32.

Figure 1–32 VisitData form in Form view

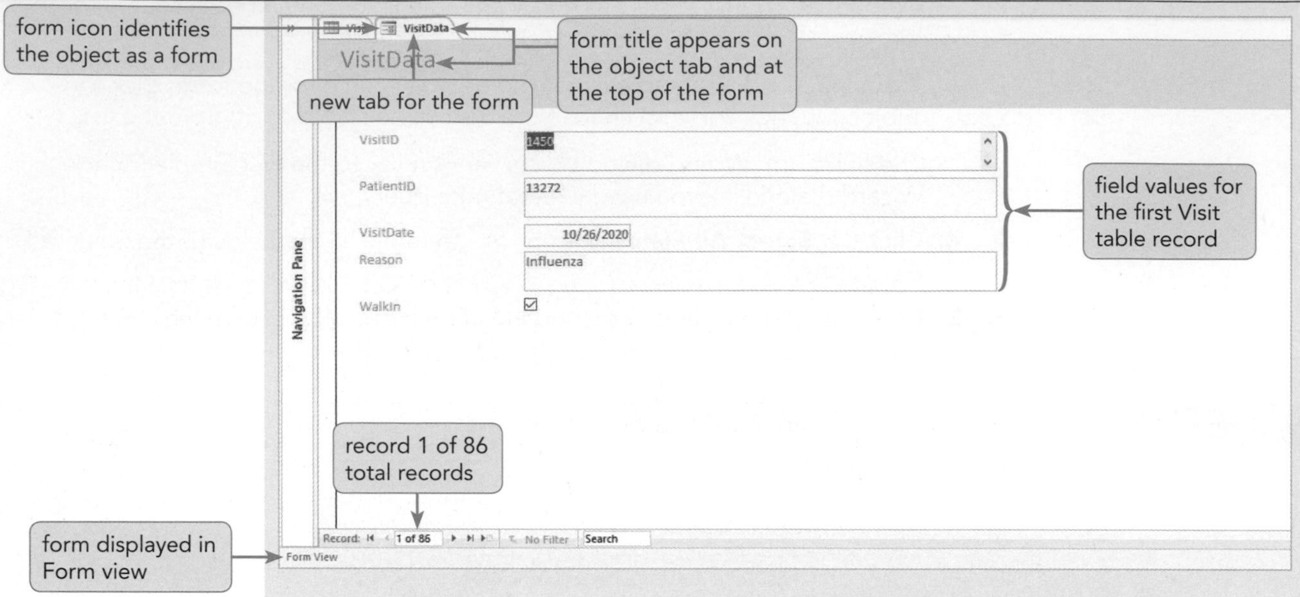
form icon identifies the object as a form
VisitData
form title appears on the object tab and at the top of the form
VisitData
new tab for the form
VisitID
1450
PatientID
13272
VisitDate
10/26/2020
Reason
Influenza
WalkIn
field values for the first Visit table record
Navigation Pane
record 1 of 86 total records
Record: 1 of 86
No Filter
Search
form displayed in Form view
Form View

The form displays one record at a time in the Visit table, providing another view of the data that is stored in the table and allowing you to focus on the values for one record. Access displays the field values for the first record in the table and selects the first field value (VisitID), as indicated by the value being highlighted. Each field name appears on a separate line and on the same line as its field value, which appears in a box to the right. Depending on your computer's settings, the field value boxes in your form might be wider or narrower than those shown in the figure. As indicated in the status bar, the form is displayed in **Form view**. Later, you will work with a form in **Layout view**, where you can make design changes to the form while it is displaying data.

To view, enter, and maintain data using a form, you must know how to move from field to field and from record to record. Notice that the form contains navigation buttons, similar to those available in Datasheet view, which you can use to display different records in the form. You'll use these now to navigate the form; then you'll save and close the form.

To navigate, save, and close the form:

1. Click the **Next record** button ▶. The form now displays the values for the second record in the Visit table.
2. Click the **Last record** button ▶| to move to the last record in the table. The form displays the information for VisitID 1623.
3. Click the **Previous record** button ◀ to move to record 85.
4. Click the **First record** button |◀ to return to the first record in the Visit table.
5. Click the **Close 'VisitData'** button ✕ on the object tab to close the form.

INSIGHT

Saving Database Objects

In general, it is best to save a database object—query, form, or report—only if you anticipate using the object frequently or if it is time-consuming to create, because all objects use storage space and increase the size of the database file. For example, you most likely would not save a form you created with the Form tool because you can re-create it easily with one click. (However, for the purposes of this text, you usually need to save the objects you create.)

Donna would like to see the information in the Visit table presented in a more readable and professional format. You'll help Donna by creating a report.

Creating a Simple Report

A report is a formatted printout (or screen display) of the contents of one or more tables or queries. You'll use the Report Wizard to guide you through producing a report based on the Visit table for Donna. The Report Wizard creates a report based on the selected table or query.

To create the report using the Report Wizard:

1. On the ribbon, click the **Create** tab.
2. In the Reports group, click the **Report Wizard** button. The first Report Wizard dialog box opens. Make sure the Visit table is the default data source for the report.

   Trouble? If the Visit table is not the default source for the report, click the Tables/Queries arrow to choose the Visit table (Table: Visit) from the list.

   The first Report Wizard dialog box is very similar to the first Simple Query Wizard dialog box you used in creating a query, and to the first Form Wizard dialog box you used in creating a form.

   You select fields in the order you want them to appear on the report. Donna wants to include only the VisitID, PatientID, and Reason fields (in that order) on the report.
3. Click **VisitID** in the Available Fields box (if necessary), and then click the **Select Single Field** button > to move the field to the Selected Fields box.
4. Repeat step 3 to add the **PatientID** and **Reason** fields to the Selected Fields box. The VisitID, PatientID, and Reason fields (in that order) are listed in the Selected Fields box to add to the report. See Figure 1–33.

Figure 1–33 First Report Wizard dialog box

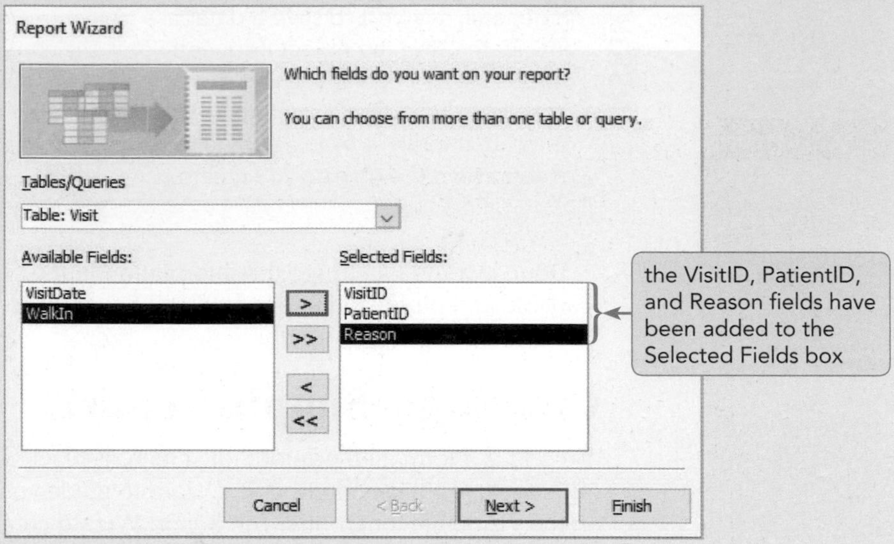
Report Wizard
Which fields do you want on your report?
You can choose from more than one table or query.
Tables/Queries
Table: Visit
Available Fields:
VisitDate
WalkIn
Selected Fields:
VisitID
PatientID
Reason
Cancel
< Back
Next >
Finish
the VisitID, PatientID, and Reason fields have been added to the Selected Fields box

5. Click **Next** to open the second Report Wizard dialog box, which asks whether you want to add grouping levels to your report. This concept will be discussed later; Donna's report does not have any grouping levels.
6. Click **Next** to proceed to the third Report Wizard dialog box, which asks whether to sort records in a certain order by a particular field on the report. Donna wants to list the records by the VisitID field in ascending order. Access allows up to four levels of sorting, although Donna wants only one.
7. Click the arrow in the first sort option box, and then click **VisitID**. See Figure 1-34. The default option for sorting on the VisitID field is ascending.

Figure 1–34 Third Report Wizard dialog box

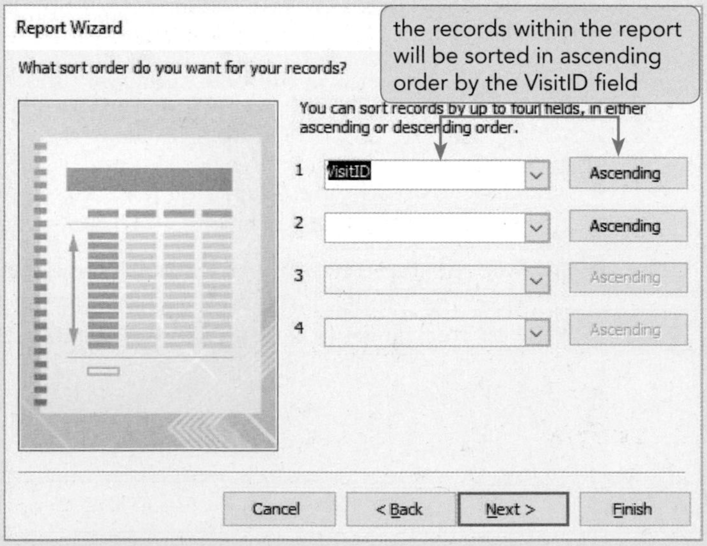
Report Wizard
What sort order do you want for your records?
the records within the report will be sorted in ascending order by the VisitID field
You can sort records by up to four fields, in either ascending or descending order.
1 VisitID Ascending
2 Ascending
3 Ascending
4 Ascending
Cancel
< Back
Next >
Finish

8. Click **Next** to proceed to the fourth Report Wizard dialog box, which asks you to select the layout for the report. You can click a Layout option to display an example of the layout.
9. Click the **Tabular** option button (if necessary). Later you can select other options for a report; however, this report uses the current default options.

10. Click **Next** to proceed to the final Report Wizard dialog box, in which you name the report. Donna wants to name the report "VisitDetails."
11. Click to position the insertion point to the right of 'Visit' in the box, and then type **Details**. Click **Finish** to preview the report. See Figure 1–35.

Figure 1–35 **Report in Print Preview**

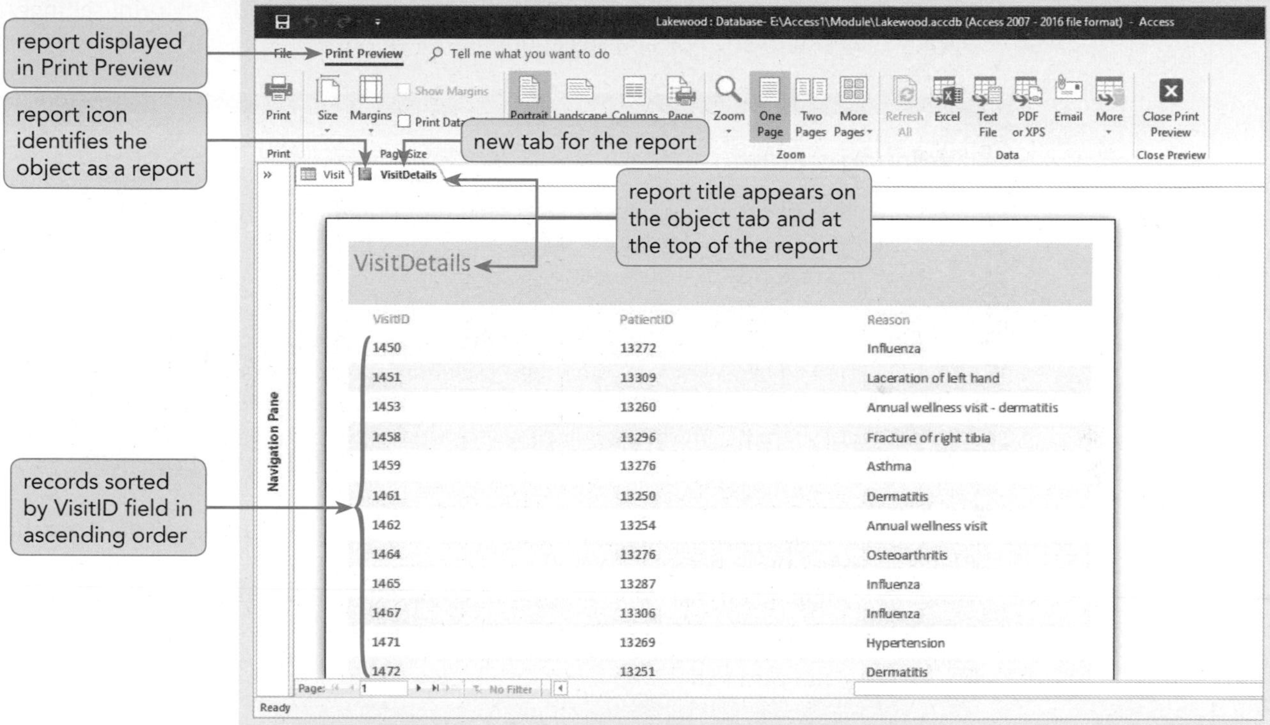
report displayed in Print Preview
report icon identifies the object as a report
new tab for the report
report title appears on the object tab and at the top of the report
records sorted by VisitID field in ascending order
Lakewood : Database- E:\Access1\Module\Lakewood.accdb (Access 2007 - 2016 file format) - Access
File
Print Preview
Tell me what you want to do
Print
Size
Margins
Show Margins
Print Data Only
Portrait
Landscape
Columns
Page Setup
Zoom
One Page
Two Pages
More Pages
Refresh All
Excel
Text File
PDF or XPS
Email
More
Close Print Preview
Page Size
Data
Close Preview
Visit
VisitDetails
Navigation Pane
VisitDetails
VisitID
PatientID
Reason
1450 13272 Influenza
1451 13309 Laceration of left hand
1453 13260 Annual wellness visit - dermatitis
1458 13296 Fracture of right tibia
1459 13276 Asthma
1461 13250 Dermatitis
1462 13254 Annual wellness visit
1464 13276 Osteoarthritis
1465 13287 Influenza
1467 13306 Influenza
1471 13269 Hypertension
1472 13251 Dermatitis
Page: 1
No Filter
Ready

The report shows each field in a column, with the field values for each record in a row, similar to a table or query datasheet. However, a report offers a more visually appealing format for the data. The report is currently shown in Print Preview. **Print Preview** shows exactly how the report will look when printed. Print Preview also provides page navigation buttons at the bottom of the window, similar to the navigation buttons you've used to move through records in a table, query, and form.

To navigate the report in Print Preview:

1. Click the **Next Page** button ▶. The second page of the report is displayed in Print Preview.
2. Click the **Last Page** button ▶| to move to the last page of the report.
3. Drag the scroll box in the vertical scroll bar down until the bottom of the report page is displayed. The current date is displayed at the bottom left of the page. The notation "Page 3 of 3" appears at the bottom right of the page, indicating that you are on page 3 out of a total of 3 pages in the report.

   Trouble? Depending on the printer you are using, your report might have more or fewer pages, and some of the pages might be blank. If so, don't worry. Different printers format reports in different ways, sometimes affecting the total number of pages and the number of records printed per page.

4. Click the **First Page** button [I◀] to return to the first page of the report, and then drag the scroll box in the vertical scroll bar up to display the top of the report.

Printing a Report

After creating a report, you might need to print it to distribute it to others who need to view the report's contents. You can print a report without changing any print settings, or display the Print dialog box and select options for printing.

REFERENCE

Printing a Report

- Open the report in any view, or select the report in the Navigation Pane.
- Click the File tab to display Backstage view, click Print, and then click Quick Print to print the report with the default print settings.

or

- Open the report in any view, or select the report in the Navigation Pane.
- Click the File tab, click Print, and then click Print; or, if the report is displayed in Print Preview, click the Print button in the Print group on the Print Preview tab. The Print dialog box opens, in which you can select the options you want for printing the report.

Donna asks you to print the entire report with the default settings, so you'll use the Quick Print option in Backstage view.

Note: To complete the following steps, your computer must be connected to a printer. Check with your instructor first to see if you should print the report.

To print the report and then close it:

1. On the ribbon, click the **File** tab to open Backstage view.
2. In the navigation bar, click **Print** to display the Print screen, and then click **Quick Print**. The report prints with the default print settings, and you return to the report in Print Preview.

   Trouble? If your report did not print, make sure that your computer is connected to a printer, and that the printer is turned on and ready to print. Then repeat Steps 1 and 2.
3. Click the **Close 'VisitDetails'** button [X] on the object tab to close the report.
4. Click the **Close 'Visit'** button [X] on the object tab to close the Visit table.

   Trouble? If you are asked to save changes to the layout of the table, click Yes.

You can also use the Print dialog box to print other database objects, such as table and query datasheets. Most often, these objects are used for viewing and entering data, and reports are used for printing the data in a database.

Viewing Objects in the Navigation Pane

The Lakewood database now contains five objects—the Billing table, the Visit table, the VisitList query, the VisitData form, and the VisitDetails report. When you work with the database file—such as closing it, opening it, or distributing it to others—the file includes all the objects you created and saved in the database. You can view and work with these objects in the Navigation Pane.

To view the objects in the Lakewood database:

1. On the Navigation Pane, click the **Shutter Bar Open/Close Button** » to open the pane. See Figure 1–36.

Figure 1–36 Lakewood database objects displayed in the Navigation Pane

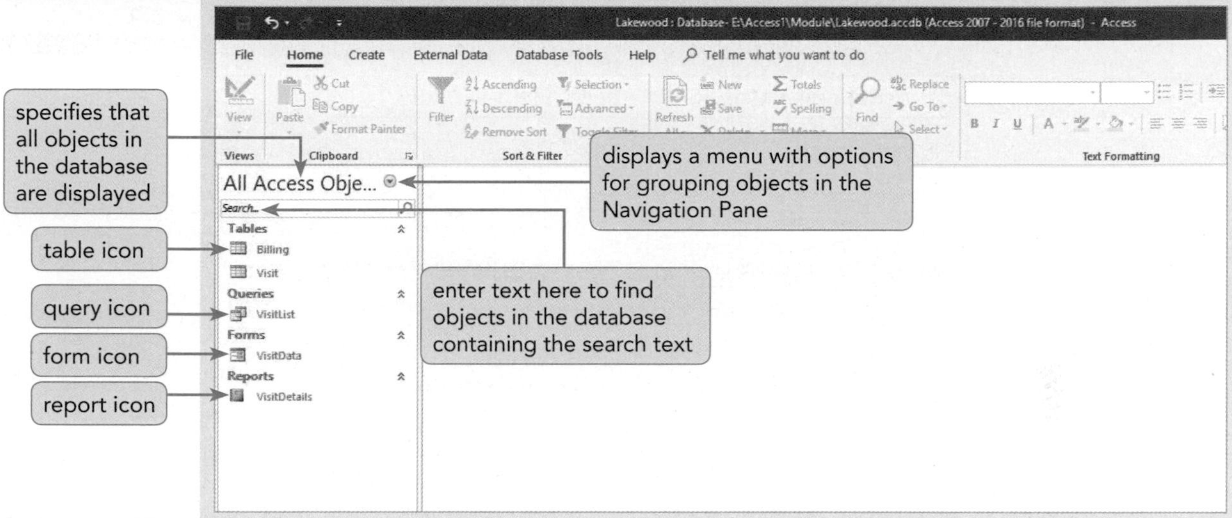
specifies that all objects in the database are displayed
table icon
query icon
form icon
report icon
displays a menu with options for grouping objects in the Navigation Pane
enter text here to find objects in the database containing the search text
All Access Obje...
Search...
Tables
Billing
Visit
Queries
VisitList
Forms
VisitData
Reports
VisitDetails

The Navigation Pane currently displays the default category, **All Access Objects**, which lists all the database objects in the pane. Each object type (Tables, Queries, Forms, and Reports) appears in its own group. Each database object (the Billing table, the Visit table, the VisitList query, the VisitData form, and the VisitDetails report) has a unique icon to its left to indicate the type of object. This makes it easy for you to identify the objects and choose which one you want to open and work with.

The arrow on the All Access Objects bar displays a menu with options for various ways to group and display objects in the Navigation Pane. The Search box enables you to enter text for Access to find; for example, you could search for all objects that contain the word "Visit" in their names. Note that Access searches for objects only in the categories and groups currently displayed in the Navigation Pane.

As you continue to build the Lakewood database and add more objects to it in later modules, you'll use the options in the Navigation Pane to manage those objects.

Using Microsoft Access Help

Access includes a Help system you can use to search for information about specific program features. You start Help by clicking the Microsoft Access Help tab on the ribbon, or by pressing F1.

You'll use Help now to learn more about the Navigation Pane.

To search for information about the Navigation Pane in Help:

TIP

You can also get help by typing keywords in the Tell Me box on the ribbon to access information about topics related to those words in the Access Help window.

1. On the ribbon, click the **Help** tab. Multiple buttons are displayed, with the first being the Help button. Click the **Help** button. The Access Help window opens.
2. Click in the **Search** box (if necessary), type **Navigation Pane**, and then press **ENTER**. The Access Help window displays a list of topics related to the Navigation Pane.
3. Click the topic **Show or hide the Navigation Pane in Access**. The Access Help window displays the article you selected. See Figure 1–37.

Figure 1–37 Article displayed in the Access Help window

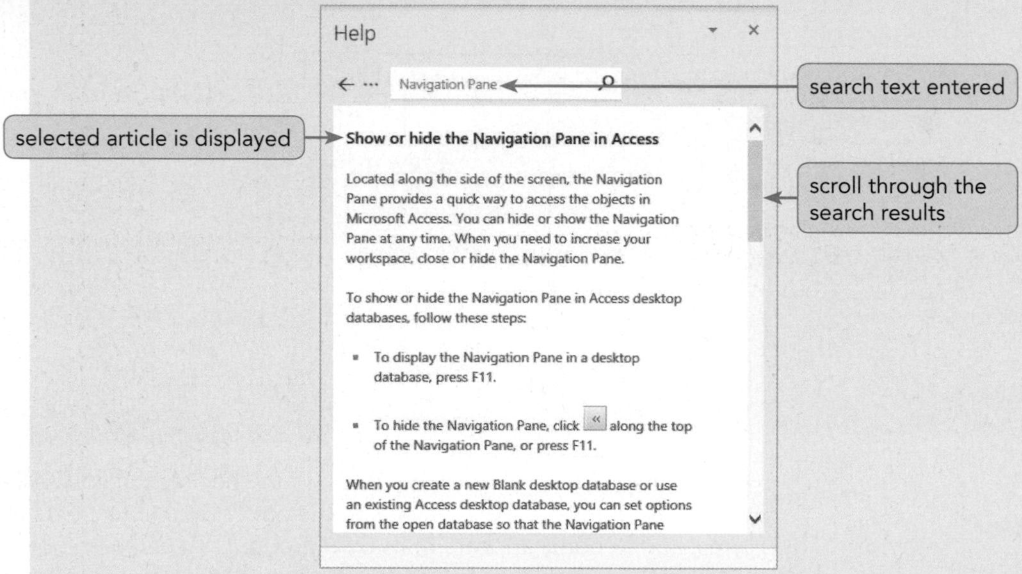
Help
Navigation Pane
search text entered
selected article is displayed
Show or hide the Navigation Pane in Access
Located along the side of the screen, the Navigation Pane provides a quick way to access the objects in Microsoft Access. You can hide or show the Navigation Pane at any time. When you need to increase your workspace, close or hide the Navigation Pane.
To show or hide the Navigation Pane in Access desktop databases, follow these steps:
To display the Navigation Pane in a desktop database, press F11.
To hide the Navigation Pane, click along the top of the Navigation Pane, or press F11.
When you create a new Blank desktop database or use an existing Access desktop database, you can set options from the open database so that the Navigation Pane
scroll through the search results

Trouble? If the article on managing database objects is not listed in your Help window, choose another article related to the Navigation Pane to read. Your Help window may also look different from the figure.

4. Scroll through the article to read detailed information about working with the Navigation Pane.
5. When finished, click the **Close** button [X] on the Access Help window to close it.

The Access Help system is an important reference tool for you to use if you need additional information about databases in general, details about specific Access features, or support with problems you might encounter.

Managing a Database

One of the main tasks involved in working with database software is managing your databases and the data they contain. Some of the activities involved in database management include compacting and repairing a database and backing up and restoring a database. By managing your databases, you can ensure that they operate in the most efficient way, that the data they contain is secure, and that you can work with the data effectively.

Compacting and Repairing a Database

Whenever you open an Access database and work in it, the size of the database increases. Further, when you delete records or when you delete or replace database objects—such as queries, forms, and reports—the storage space that had been occupied by the deleted or replaced records or objects does not automatically become available for other records or objects. To make the space available, and to increase the speed of data retrieval, you must compact the database. **Compacting** a database rearranges the data and objects in a database to decrease its file size, thereby making more storage space available and enhancing the performance of the database. Figure 1-38 illustrates the compacting process.

Figure 1-38 Compacting a database

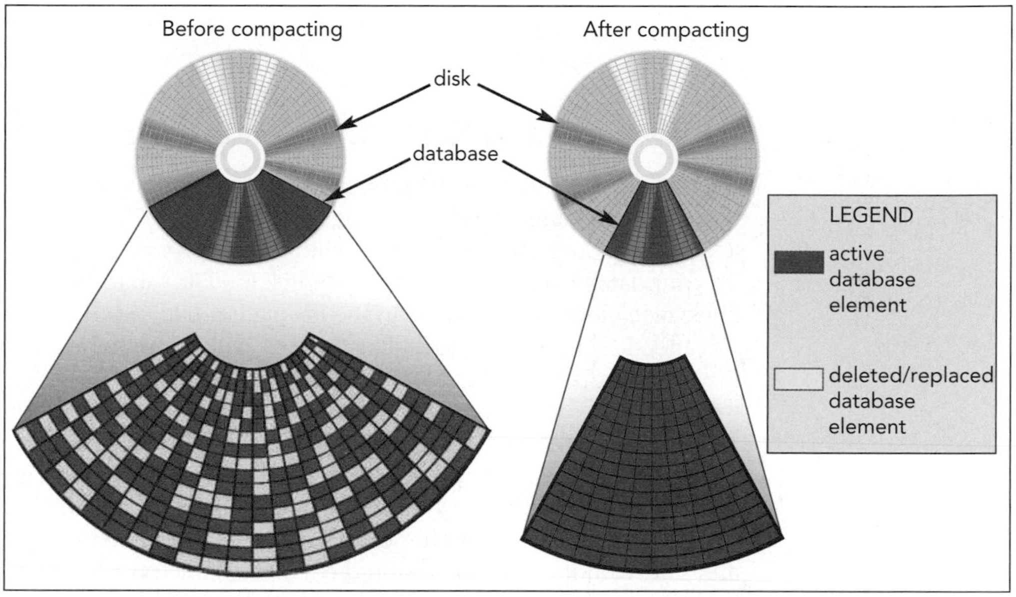
Before compacting
After compacting
disk
database
LEGEND
active database element
deleted/replaced database element

When you compact a database, Access repairs the database at the same time, if necessary. In some cases, Access detects that a database is damaged when you try to open it and gives you the option to compact and repair it at that time. For example, the data in your database might become damaged, or corrupted, if you exit the Access program suddenly by turning off your computer. If you think your database might be damaged because it is behaving unpredictably, you can use the Compact & Repair Database option to fix it.

REFERENCE

Compacting and Repairing a Database

- Make sure the database file you want to compact and repair is open.
- Click the File tab to display the Info screen in Backstage view.
- Click the Compact & Repair Database button.

Access also allows you to set an option to compact and repair a database file automatically every time you close it. The Compact on Close option is available in the Current Database section of the Access Options dialog box, which you open from Backstage view by clicking the Options command in the navigation bar. By default, the Compact on Close option is turned off.

Next, you'll compact the Lakewood database manually using the Compact & Repair Database option. This will make the database smaller and allow you to work with it more efficiently. After compacting the database, you'll close it.

To compact and repair the Lakewood database:

1. On the ribbon, click the **File** tab to open the Info screen in Backstage view.
2. Click the **Compact & Repair Database** button. Although nothing changes on the screen, Access compacts the Lakewood database, making it smaller, and repairs it at the same time. The Home tab is again the active tab on the ribbon.
3. sam Click the **File** tab to return to Backstage view, and then click **Close** in the navigation bar. The Lakewood database closes.

Backing Up and Restoring a Database

Backing up a database is the process of making a copy of the database file to protect your database against loss or damage. The Back Up Database command enables you to back up your database file from within the Access program while you are working on your database. To use this option, click the File tab to display the Info screen in Backstage view, click Save As in the navigation bar, click Back Up Database in the Advanced section of the Save Database As pane, and then click the Save As button. In the Save As dialog box that opens, a default filename is provided for the backup copy that consists of the same filename as the database you are backing up (for example, "Lakewood"), and an underscore character, plus the current date. This file naming system makes it easy for you to keep track of your database backups and when they were created. To restore a backup database file, you copy the backup from the location where it is stored to your hard drive, or whatever device you use to work in Access, and start working with the restored database file. (You will not actually back up the Lakewood database in this module unless directed by your instructor to do so.)

INSIGHT

Planning and Performing Database Backups

Experienced database users make it a habit to back up a database before they work with it for the first time, keeping the original data intact. They also make frequent backups while continuing to work with a database; these backups are generally on flash drives, recordable CDs or DVDs, external or network hard drives, or cloud-based storage (such as OneDrive). Also, it is recommended to store the backup copy in a different location from the original. For example, if the original database is stored on a flash drive, you should not store the backup copy on the same flash drive. If you lose the drive or the drive is damaged, you would lose both the original database and its backup copy.

If the original database file and the backup copy have the same name, restoring the backup copy might replace the original. If you want to save the original file, rename it before you restore the backup copy. To ensure that the restored database has the most current data, you should update the restored database with any changes made to the original between the time you created the backup copy and the time the original database became damaged or lost.

By properly planning for and performing backups, you can avoid losing data and prevent the time-consuming effort required to rebuild a lost or damaged database.

PROSKILLS

Decision Making: When to Use Access vs. Excel

Using a spreadsheet application like Microsoft Excel to manage lists or tables of information works well when the data is simple, such as a list of contacts or tasks. As soon as the data becomes complex enough to separate into tables that need to be related, you see the limitations of using a spreadsheet application. The strength of a database application such as Access is in its ability to easily relate one table of information to another. Consider a table of contacts that includes home addresses, with a separate row for each person living at the same address. When an address changes, it's too easy to make a mistake and not update the home address for each person who lives there. To ensure you have the most accurate data at all times, it's important to have only one instance of each piece of data. By creating separate tables that are related and keeping only one instance of each piece of data, you ensure the integrity of the data. Trying to accomplish this in Excel is complex, whereas Access is specifically designed for this functionality.

Another limitation of using Excel instead of Access to manage data has to do with the volume of data. Although a spreadsheet can hold thousands of records, a database can hold millions. A spreadsheet containing thousands of pieces of information is cumbersome to use. Think of large-scale commercial applications such as enrollment at a college or tracking customers for a large company. It's hard to imagine managing such information in an Excel spreadsheet. Instead, you'd use a database. Finally, with an Access database, multiple users can access the information it contains at the same time. Although an Excel spreadsheet can be shared, there can be problems when users try to open and edit the same spreadsheet at the same time.

When you're trying to decide whether to use Excel or Access, ask yourself the following questions.

1. Do you need to store data in separate tables that are related to each other?
2. Do you have a very large amount of data to store?
3. Will more than one person need to access the data at the same time?

If you answer "yes" to any of these questions, an Access database is most likely the appropriate application to use.

In the following modules, you'll help Donna complete and maintain the Lakewood database, and you'll use it to meet the specific information needs of the employees of the clinic.

REVIEW

Session 1.2 Quick Check

1. To copy the records from a table in one database to another table in a different database, the two tables must have the same ________.
2. A(n) ____________ is a question you ask about the data stored in a database.
3. The quickest way to create a form is to use the ________.
4. Which view enables you to see the total number of pages in a report and navigate through the report pages?
5. In the Navigation Pane, each database object has a unique ________ to its left that identifies the object's type.
6. ________ a database rearranges the data and objects in a database to decrease its file size and enhance the speed and performance of the database.
7. ________ a database is the process of making a copy of the database file to protect the database against loss or damage.

PRACTICE

Review Assignments

Data File needed for the Review Assignments: Support_AC_1_Company.accdb

For Lakewood Community Health Services, Donna asks you to create a new database to contain information about the vendors that the clinic works with to obtain medical supplies and equipment, and the vendors who service and maintain the equipment. Complete the following steps:

1. Create a new, blank database named **Vendor** and save it in the folder where you are storing your files, as specified by your instructor.
2. In Datasheet view, begin creating a table. Rename the default ID primary key field to **SupplierID**. Change the data type of the SupplierID field to Short Text.
3. Add the following 10 fields to the new table in the order shown; all of them are Short Text fields *except* InitialContact, which is a Date/Time field: **Company**, **Category**, **Address**, **City**, **State**, **Zip**, **Phone**, **ContactFirst**, **ContactLast**, and **InitialContact**. Resize the columns as necessary so that the complete field names are displayed.
4. Save the table as **Supplier** and close the table.
5. In Design view, begin creating a second table containing the following three Short Text fields in the order shown: **ProductID**, **SupplierID**, and **ProductName**.
6. Make ProductID the primary key and use **Primary key** as its description. Use **Foreign key** as the description for the SupplierID field.
7. Add a field called **Price** to the table, which is of the Currency data type.
8. Add the following two fields to the table in the order shown: **TempControl** and **Sterile**. Both are of the Yes/No data type.
9. Add the final field called **Units** to the table, which is of the Number data type.
10. Save the table as **Product** and close the table.
11. Use the Navigation Pane to open the Supplier table.
12. Enter the records shown in Figure 1–39 into the Supplier table. For the first record, enter your first name in the ContactFirst field and your last name in the ContactLast field.
    Note: When entering field values that are shown on multiple lines in the figure, do not try to enter the values on multiple lines. The values are shown on multiple lines in the figure for page spacing purposes only.

Figure 1–39 Supplier table records

SupplierID	Company	Category	Address	City	State	Zip	Phone	Contact First	Contact Last	Initial Contact
ABC123	ABC Pharmaceuticals	Supplies	123 Hopson Ave	Manchester	NH	03102	603-555-8125	*Student First*	*Student Last*	9/22/2020
HAR912	Harper Surgical, LLC	Supplies	912 Huntington Pl	Knoxville	TN	37909	865-555-4239	Betty	Harper	10/26/2020
DUR725	Durham Medical Equipment	Equipment	725 Pike Dr	Durham	NC	27705	919-555-4226	Katherine	Wayles	12/14/2020
TEN247	Tenneka Labs, LLC	Service	247 Asland Dr	Norcross	GA	30071	678-555-5392	Thomas	Tenneka	11/30/2020
BAZ412	Bazarrack Enterprises	Supplies	412 Harper Dr	Alpharetta	GA	30004	678-555-2201	Adrian	Bazarrack	9/3/2020

13. Donna created a database named Support_AC_1_Company.accdb that contains a Business table with supplier data. The Supplier table you created has the same design as the Business table. Copy all the records from the **Business** table in the **Support_AC_1_Company.accdb** database (located in the Access1 > Review folder provided with your Data Files) and then paste them at the end of the Supplier table in the Vendor database.
14. Resize all datasheet columns to their best fit, and then save the Supplier table.
15. Close the Supplier table, and then use the Navigation Pane to reopen it. Note that the records are displayed in primary key order by the values in the SupplierID field.
16. Use the Simple Query Wizard to create a query that includes the Company, Category, ContactFirst, ContactLast, and Phone fields (in that order) from the Supplier table. Name the query **SupplierList**, and then close the query.
17. Use the Form Wizard to create a form for the Supplier table. Include all fields from the Supplier table on the form and use the Columnar layout. Save the form as **SupplierInfo**, and then close it.
18. Use the Report Wizard to create a report based on the Supplier table. Include the SupplierID, Company, and Phone fields on the report (in that order), and sort the report by the SupplierID field in ascending order. Use a Tabular layout, save the report as **SupplierDetails**, and then close it.
19. Close the Supplier table, and then compact and repair the Vendor database.
20. Close the Vendor database.

APPLY

Case Problem 1

Data File needed for this Case Problem: Support_AC_1_Records.accdb

Great Giraffe Jeremiah Garver is the operations manager at Great Giraffe, a career school in Denver, Colorado. Great Giraffe offers part-time and full-time courses in areas of study that are in high demand by industries in the area, including data science, digital marketing, and bookkeeping. Jeremiah wants to use Access to maintain information about the courses offered by Great Giraffe, the students who enroll at the school, and the payment information for students. He needs your help in creating this database. Complete the following steps:

1. Create a new, blank database named **Career** and save it in the folder where you are storing your files, as specified by your instructor.
2. In Datasheet view, begin creating a table. Rename the default ID primary key field to **StudentID**. Change the data type of the StudentID field to Short Text.
3. Add the following eight fields to the new table in the order shown; all of them are Short Text fields: **FirstName**, **LastName**, **Address**, **City**, **State**, **Zip**, **Phone**, and **Email**. Resize the columns as necessary so that the complete field names are displayed.
4. Add a field called **BirthDate** to the table, which is of the Date/Time data type.
5. Add a final field called **Assessment** to the table, which is of the Yes/No data type.
6. Save the table as **Student** and close the table.
7. In Design view, begin creating a second table containing the following three Short Text fields in the following order: **SignupID**, **StudentID**, and **InstanceID**.
8. Make SignupID the primary key and use **Primary key** as its description. Use **Foreign key** as the descriptions for the StudentID and InstanceID fields.
9. Add the following two fields to the table in the following order: **TotalCost** and **BalanceDue**. Both are of the Currency data type.
10. Add the final field called **PaymentPlan** to the table. It is of the Yes/No data type.
11. Save the table as **Registration** and close the table.
12. Use the Navigation Pane to open the Student table.
13. Enter the records shown in Figure 1–40 into the Student table.

Figure 1–40 **Student table records**

StudentID	First Name	LastName	Address	City	State	Zip	Phone	Email	BirthDate	Assessment
ALB7426	*Student First*	*Student Last*	378 North River Avenue	Denver	CO	80227	(303) 555-8364	student @example. com	3/28/1980	Yes
MAR4120	Jennifer	Marshall	185 St Clair Way	Denver	CO	80223	(303) 555-1434	j.marshall75 @example. com	4/7/1967	Yes
WAL5737	Michael	Walker	367 Lawler Avenue	Englewood	CO	80110	(303) 555-6369	m.walker61 @example. com	1/17/1971	No
PER4083	Richard	Perry	923 Charles Avenue	Denver	CO	80211	(303) 555-8773	r.perry15 @example. com	2/14/1987	Yes
DRE9559	Angelina	Dressler	370 Dower Street	Denver	CO	80233	(303) 555-7491	a.dressler80 @example. com	8/6/2000	No

14. Jeremiah created a database named Support_AC_1_Records.accdb that contains a MoreStudents table with additional student data. The Student table you created has the same design as the MoreStudents table. Copy all the records from the **MoreStudents** table in the **Support_AC_1_Records.accdb** database (located in the Access1 > Case1 folder provided with your Data Files), and then paste them at the end of the Student table in the Career database.
15. Resize all datasheet columns to their best fit, and then save the Student table.
16. Close the Student table, and then use the Navigation Pane to reopen it. Note that the records are displayed in primary key order by the values in the StudentID field.
17. Use the Simple Query Wizard to create a query that includes the StudentID, FirstName, LastName, and Email fields (in that order) from the Student table. Save the query as **StudentData**, and then close the query.
18. Use the Form Wizard to create a form for the Student table. Include only the StudentID, FirstName, LastName, Phone, and Email fields (in that order) from the Student table on the form and use the Columnar layout. Save the form as **StudentInfo**, and then close it.
19. Use the Report Wizard to create a report based on the Student table. Include the StudentID, FirstName, and Email fields on the report (in that order), and sort the report by the StudentID field in ascending order. Use a Tabular layout, save the report as **StudentList**, and then close it.
20. Close the Student table, and then compact and repair the Career database.
21. Close the Career database.

CHALLENGE

Case Problem 2

Data File needed for this Case Problem: Support_AC_1_Residents.accdb

Drain Adopter Tandrea Austin manages the Drain Adopter program for the Department of Water and Power in Bellingham, Washington. The program recruits volunteers to regularly monitor and clear storm drains near their homes to ensure the drains are clear and unobstructed when large rainstorms are predicted. The program has been a hit with residents, and has increased the capacity of department staff to deal with other issues that arise during major storms. Tandrea wants to use Access to maintain information about the residents who have signed up for the program, the locations of selected storm drains throughout the city, and the inventory of supplies given to program participants, such as safety vests and gloves. She needs your help in creating this database. Complete the following steps:

1. Create a new, blank database named **DrainAdopter** and save it in the folder where you are storing your files, as specified by your instructor.
2. In Datasheet view, begin creating a table. Rename the default ID primary key field to **VolunteerID**. Change the data type of the VolunteerID field to Short Text.
3. Add the following eight fields to the new table in the order shown; all of them are Short Text fields: **FirstName**, **LastName**, **Street**, **City**, **State**, **Zip**, **Phone**, and **Email**. Resize the columns as necessary so that the complete field names are displayed.
4. Add a field called **SignupDate** to the table, which is of the Date/Time data type.
5. Add a final field called **Trained** to the table, which is of the Yes/No data type.
6. Save the table as **Volunteer** and close the table.
7. In Design view, begin creating a second table containing the following five Short Text fields in the following order: **DrainID**, **MainStreet**, **CrossStreet**, **Direction**, and **VolunteerID**.
8. Make DrainID the primary key and use **Primary key** as its description. Use **Foreign key** as the description for the VolunteerID field.
9. Add the final field called **MaintReq** to the table. It is of the Yes/No data type.
10. Save the table as **Drain** and close the table.
11. Use the Navigation Pane to open the Volunteer table.
12. Enter the records shown in Figure 1–41 into the Volunteer table.

Figure 1–41 Volunteer table records

VolunteerID	First Name	Last Name	Street	City	State	Zip	Phone	Email	SignupDate	Trained
ABE2300	*Student First*	*Student Last*	734 Abbott Street	Bellingham	WA	98225	360-555-6202	student @example.com	3/12/2021	Yes
MUR1125	Tiffany	Murphy	308 Pollock Street	Bellingham	WA	98225	360-555-9025	t.murphy18 @example.com	11/16/2021	Yes
WIL2190	John	Wills	947 Quincy Street	Bellingham	WA	98225	360-555-9396	j.wills81 @example. com	3/9/2021	No
SER8504	Joyce	Serrano	857 Kenta Avenue	Bellingham	WA	98229	360-555-2965	j.serrano28 @example. com	7/13/2022	Yes
HAR6150	Mario	Harris	915 Oriole Street	Bellingham	WA	98226	360-555-8705	m.harris41 @example. com	12/31/2022	No

13. Tandrea created a database named Support_AC_1_Residents.accdb that contains a MoreVolunteers table with additional volunteer data. The Volunteer table you created has the same design as the MoreVolunteers table. Copy all the records from the **MoreVolunteers** table in the **Support_AC_1_Residents.accdb** database (located in the Access1 > Case2 folder provided with your Data Files), and then paste them at the end of the Volunteer table in the DrainAdopter database.
14. Resize all datasheet columns to their best fit, and then save the Volunteer table.
15. Close the Volunteer table, and then use the Navigation Pane to reopen it. Note that the records are displayed in primary key order by the values in the VolunteerID field.
16. Use the Simple Query Wizard to create a query that includes the VolunteerID, FirstName, LastName, SignupDate, Email, and Trained fields (in that order) from the Volunteer table. Choose the Detail option. Save the query as **VolunteerData**, and then close the query.

Explore 17. The results of the VolunteerData query are displayed in order by the VolunteerID value. Sort the query results so that they are displayed in ascending order by the SignupDate. Close the query and save the query changes.

Explore 18. Use the Form Wizard to create a form using the VolunteerData query results as the data source, not the Volunteer table. The fields to include on the report are the VolunteerID, FirstName, SignupDate, and Email (in that order). Use the Columnar layout and save the form as **VolunteerInfo**, and then close it.

Explore 19. Use the Report Wizard to create a report based on the VolunteerData query. Include the VolunteerID, Email, and FirstName fields (in that order) on the report, and sort the report by the VolunteerID field in ascending order. The results of the VolunteerData query are sorted by the SignupDate field; however, when you sort the report by the VolunteerID field, the results will also be in order by the VolunteerID field (the primary key for the Volunteer table). Use a Tabular layout, save the report as **VolunteerList**, print the report, and then close it.

20. Close the Volunteer table, and then compact and repair the DrainAdopter database.
21. Close the DrainAdopter database.

MODULE 2

Building a Database and Defining Table Relationships

Creating the Billing and Patient Tables

ACCESS

OBJECTIVES

Session 2.1
- Identify the guidelines for designing databases and setting field properties
- Define fields and set field properties
- Modify the structure of a table
- Change the order of fields in Design view
- Add new fields in Design view
- Change the Format property for a field in Datasheet view
- Modify field properties in Design view

Session 2.2
- Import data from Excel
- Import an existing table structure
- Add fields to a table with the Data Type gallery
- Delete fields
- Change the data type for a field in Design view
- Set the Default Value property for a field
- Import a text file
- Define a relationship between two tables

Case | *Lakewood Community Health Services*

The Lakewood database currently contains one table with data, the Visit table, and the basic structure of an additional table, the Billing table. Donna would like to further refine the structure of the Billing table, which will be used to track information about the invoices sent to patients. In addition, Donna would like to track information about each patient the clinic serves, including their name and contact information.

In this module, you'll modify the existing Billing table and create a new table in the Lakewood database—named Patient—to contain the additional data Donna wants to track. After adding records to the tables, you will define the necessary relationships between the tables in the Lakewood database to relate the tables, enabling Donna and her staff to work with the data more efficiently.

STARTING DATA FILES

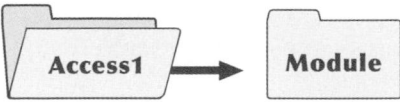

Access1 → Module

Module
Lakewood.accdb (cont.)
Support_AC_2_Invoices.xlsx
Support_AC_2_Patient.txt
Support_AC_2_Taylor.accdb

Review
Vendor.accdb (cont.)
Support_AC_2_Products.xlsx

Case1
Career.accdb (cont.)
Support_AC_2_Course.txt
Support_AC_2_Registration.xlsx

Case2
DrainAdopter.accdb (cont.)
Support_AC_2_Drain.xlsx
Support_AC_2_Supplies.xlsx

Session 2.1 Visual Overview:

Design view allows you to define or modify a table structure or the properties of the fields in a table.

The default name for a new table you create in Design view is Table1. This name appears on the tab for the new table.

The top portion of the Table window in Design view is called the **Table Design grid**. Here, you enter values for the Field Name, Data Type, and Description field properties.

After you assign a data type to a field, the General tab displays additional field properties for that data type. Initially, most field properties are assigned default values.

When defining the fields in a table, you can move from the Table Design grid to the Field Properties pane by pressing the **F6 key**.

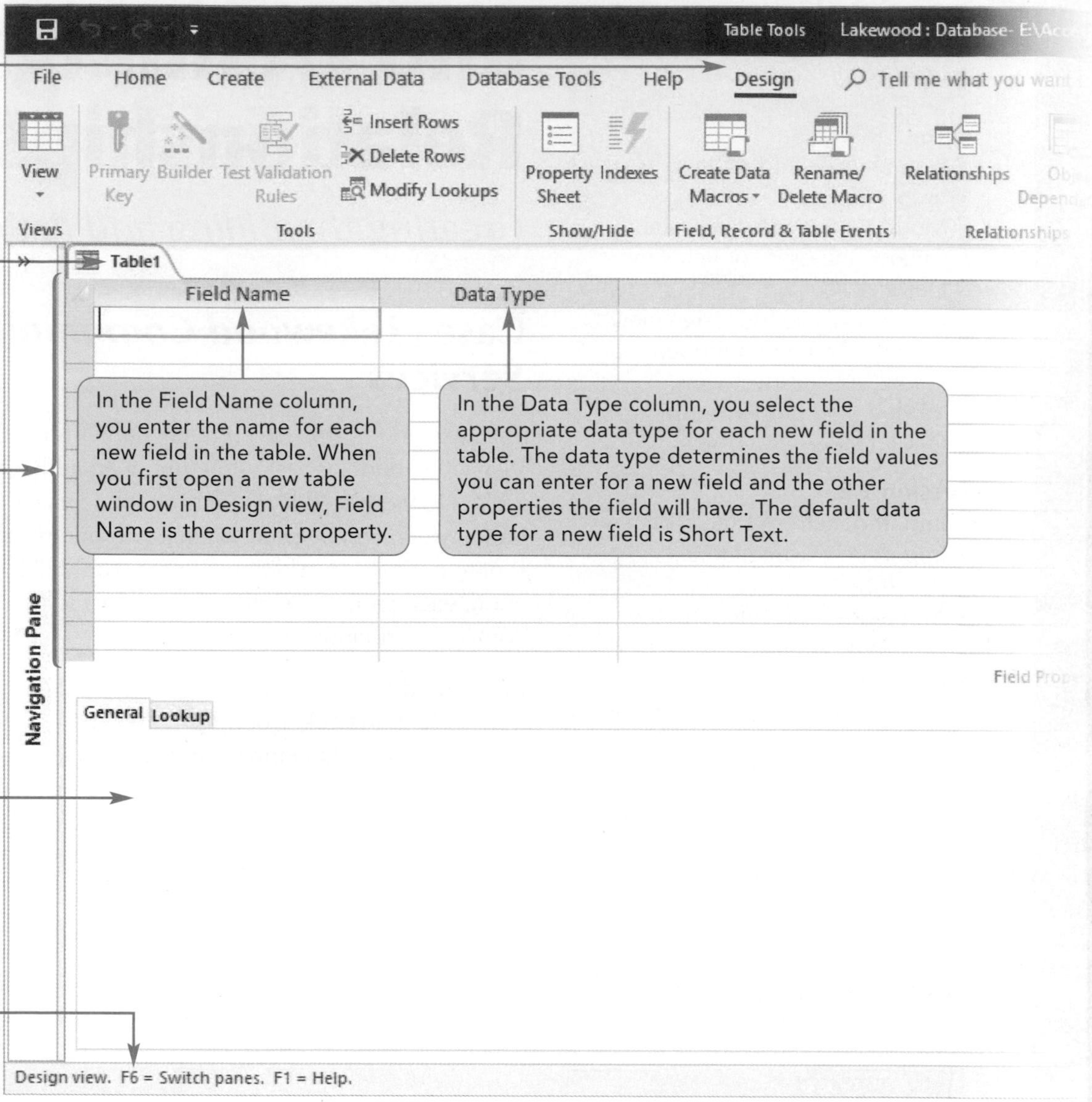

Table Tools
Lakewood : Database- E:\Acc
File
Home
Create
External Data
Database Tools
Help
Design
Tell me what you want
View
Primary Key
Builder
Test Validation Rules
Insert Rows
Delete Rows
Modify Lookups
Property Sheet
Indexes
Create Data Macros
Rename/ Delete Macro
Relationships
Views
Tools
Show/Hide
Field, Record & Table Events
Relationships
Table1
Field Name
Data Type
Navigation Pane
Field Prop
General
Lookup
Design view. F6 = Switch panes. F1 = Help.

In the Field Name column, you enter the name for each new field in the table. When you first open a new table window in Design view, Field Name is the current property.

In the Data Type column, you select the appropriate data type for each new field in the table. The data type determines the field values you can enter for a new field and the other properties the field will have. The default data type for a new field is Short Text.

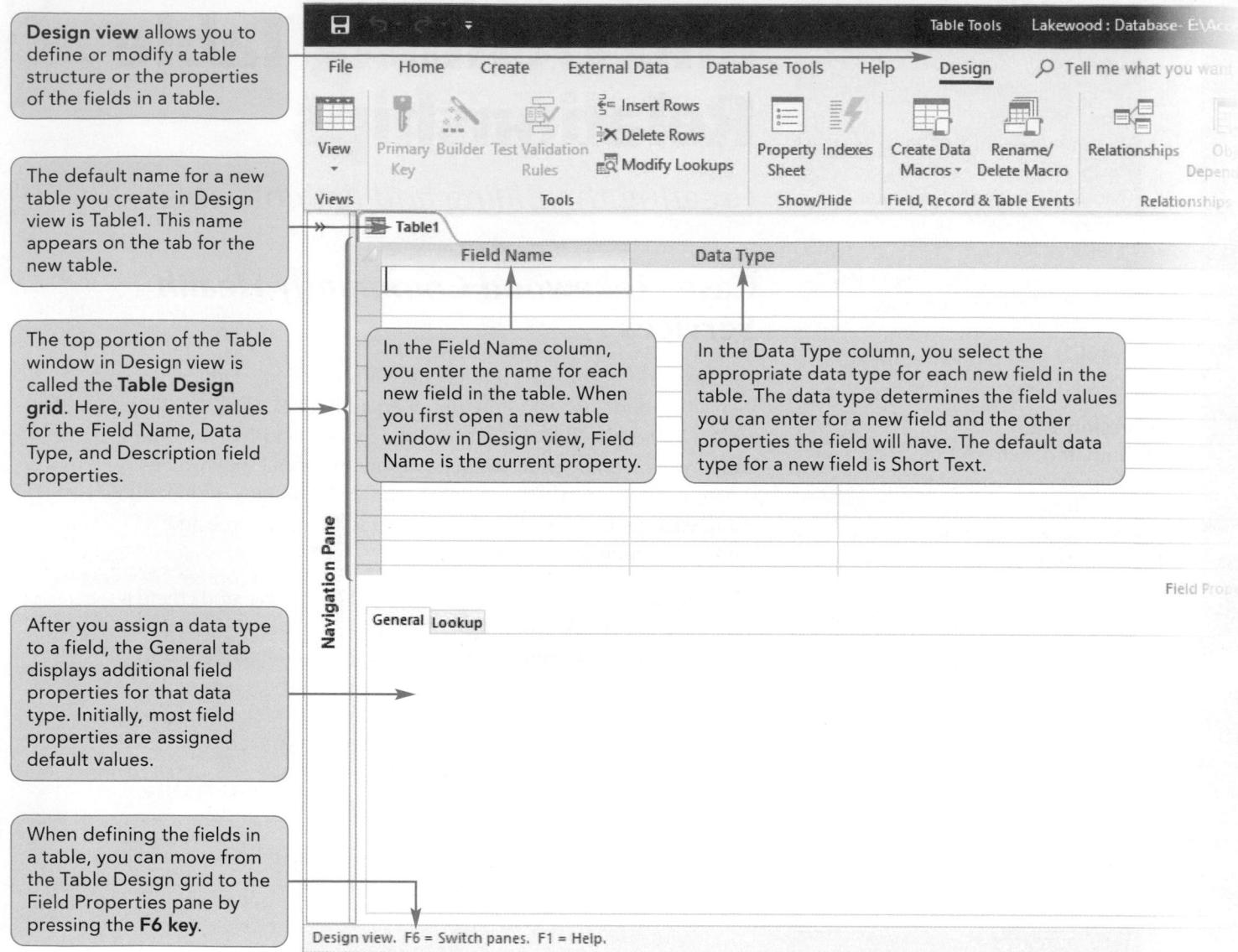

Table Window in Design View

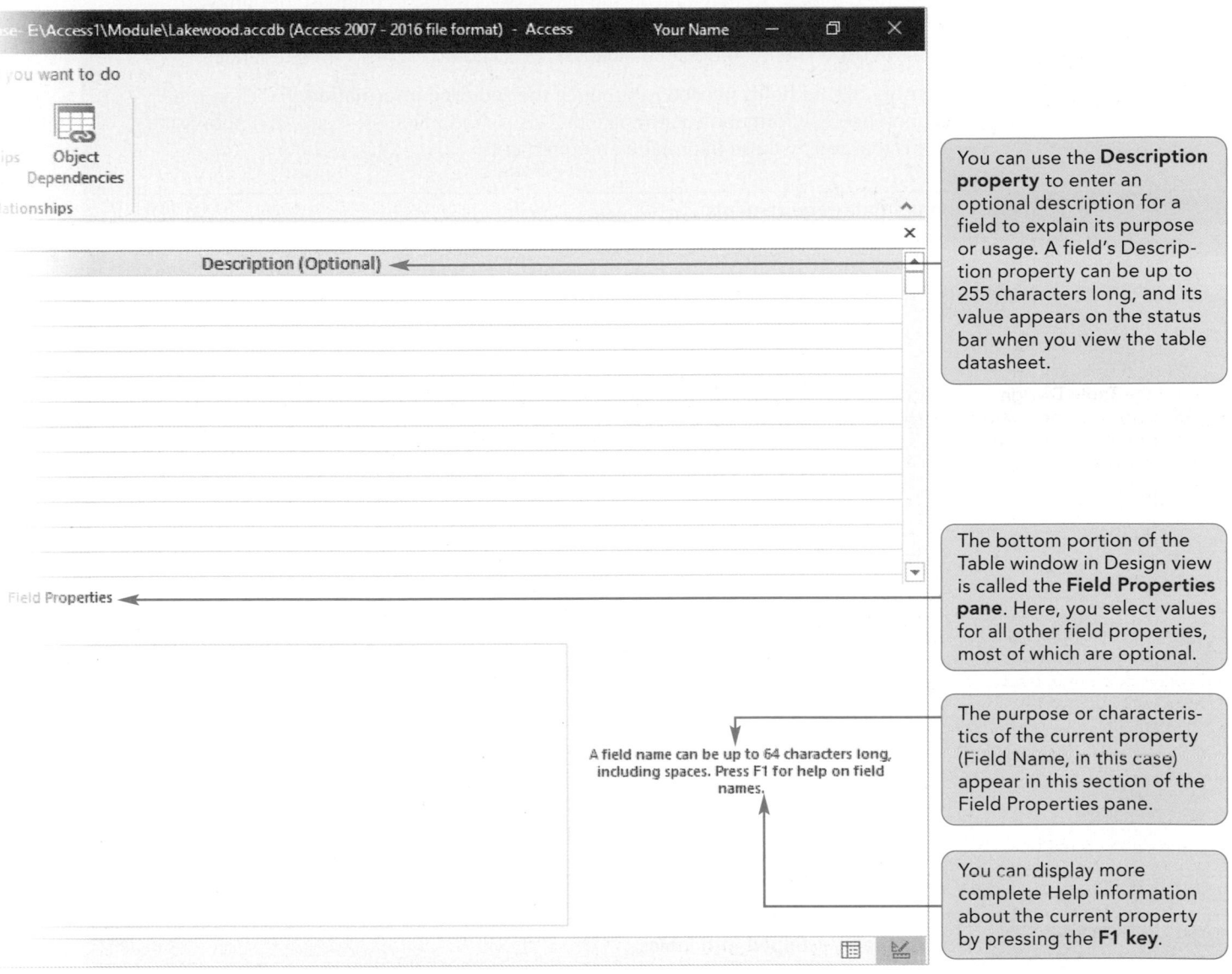

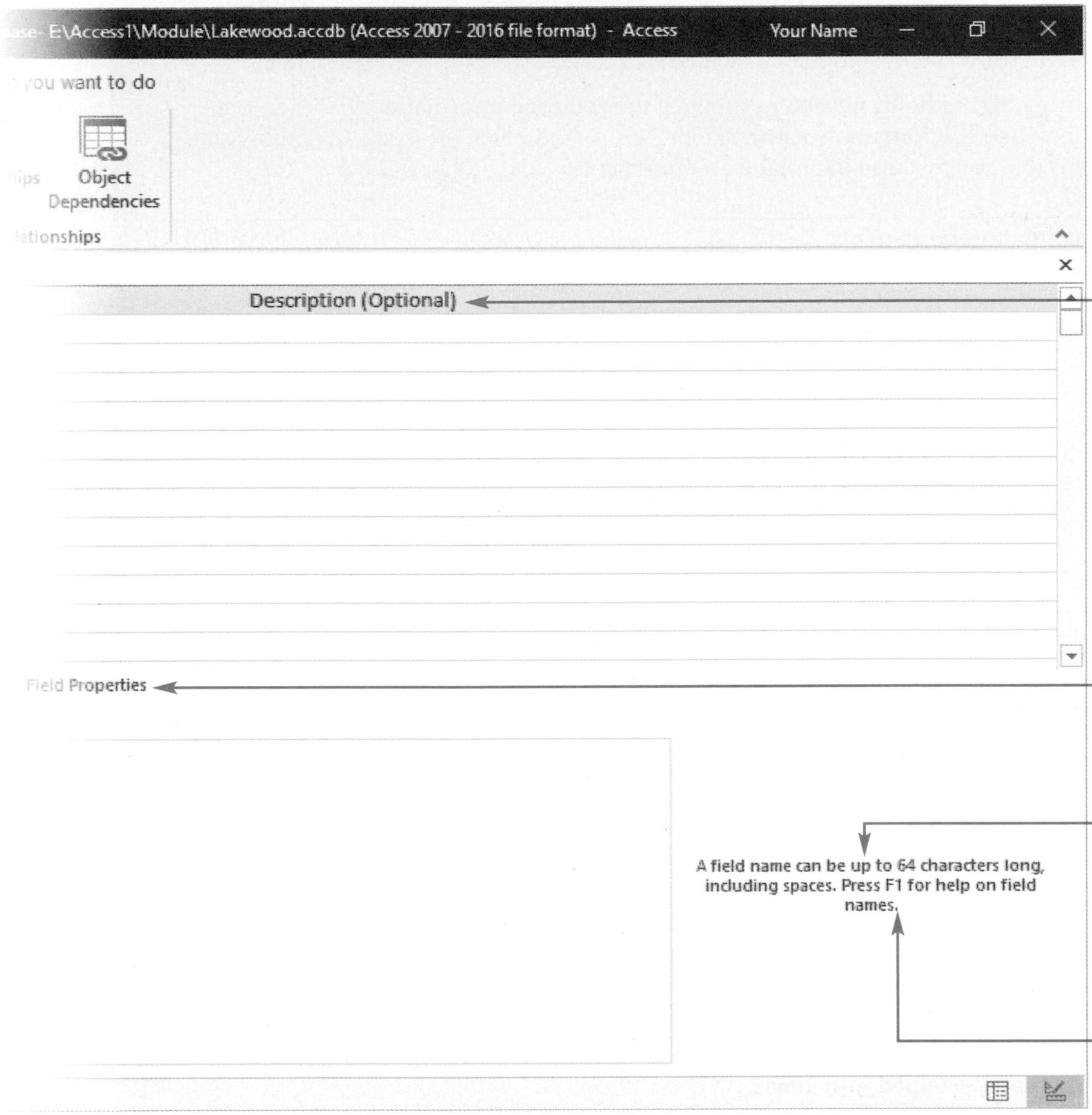
E:\Access1\Module\Lakewood.accdb (Access 2007 - 2016 file format) - Access
Your Name
you want to do
Object Dependencies
lationships
Description (Optional)
Field Properties
A field name can be up to 64 characters long, including spaces. Press F1 for help on field names.

You can use the **Description property** to enter an optional description for a field to explain its purpose or usage. A field's Description property can be up to 255 characters long, and its value appears on the status bar when you view the table datasheet.

The bottom portion of the Table window in Design view is called the **Field Properties pane**. Here, you select values for all other field properties, most of which are optional.

The purpose or characteristics of the current property (Field Name, in this case) appear in this section of the Field Properties pane.

You can display more complete Help information about the current property by pressing the **F1 key**.

Guidelines for Designing Databases

A database management system can be a useful tool, but only if you first carefully design the database so that it meets the needs of its users. In database design, you determine the fields, tables, and relationships needed to satisfy the data and processing requirements. When you design a database, you should follow these guidelines:

- **Identify all the fields needed to produce the required information.** For example, Donna needs information about patients, visits, and invoices. Figure 2–1 shows the fields that satisfy these information requirements.

Figure 2–1 Donna's data requirements

VisitID	InvoiceDate
PatientID	Reason
InvoiceAmt	Phone
FirstName	WalkIn
LastName	Email
Address	VisitDate
City	InvoiceNum
State	InvoicePaid
Zip	BirthDate

- **Organize each piece of data into its smallest useful part.** For example, Donna could store each patient's complete name in one field called PatientName instead of using two fields called FirstName and LastName, as shown in Figure 2–1. However, doing so would make it more difficult to work with the data. If Donna wanted to view the records in alphabetical order by last name, she wouldn't be able to do so with field values such as "Tom Chang" and "Keisha Miller" stored in a Name field. She could do so with field values such as "Chang" and "Miller" stored separately in a LastName field.
- **Group related fields into tables.** For example, Donna grouped the fields related to visits into the Visit table, which you created and populated in the previous module. The fields related to invoices are grouped into the Billing table, which you created the basic structure for in the previous module. The fields related to patients are grouped into the Patient table. Figure 2–2 shows the fields grouped into all three tables for the Lakewood database.

Figure 2–2 Donna's fields grouped into tables

Visit table	Billing table	Patient table
VisitID	InvoiceNum	PatientID
PatientID	VisitID	LastName
VisitDate	InvoiceDate	FirstName
Reason	InvoiceAmt	BirthDate
WalkIn	InvoicePaid	Phone
		Address
		City
		State
		Zip
		Email

- **Determine each table's primary key.** Recall that a primary key uniquely identifies each record in a table. For some tables, one of the fields, such as a credit card number, naturally serves as a primary key. For other tables, two or more fields might be needed to function as the primary key. In these cases, the primary key is called a

composite key. For example, a school grade table might use a combination of student number, term, and course code to serve as the primary key. For a third category of tables, no single field or combination of fields can uniquely identify a record in a table. In these cases, you need to add a field whose sole purpose is to serve as the table's primary key. For Donna's tables, VisitID is the primary key for the Visit table, InvoiceNum is the primary key for the Billing table, and PatientID is the primary key for the Patient table.

- **Include a common field in related tables.** You use the common field to connect one table logically with another table. In the Lakewood database, the Visit and Patient tables include the PatientID field as a common field. Recall that when you include the primary key from one table as a field in a second table to form a relationship, the field in the second table is called a foreign key; therefore, the PatientID field is a foreign key in the Visit table. With this common field, Donna can find all visits to the clinic made by a particular patient; she can use the PatientID value for a patient and search the Visit table for all records with that PatientID value. Likewise, she can determine which patient made a particular visit by searching the Patient table to find the one record with the same PatientID value as the corresponding value in the Visit table. Similarly, the VisitID field is a common field, serving as the primary key in the Visit table and a foreign key in the Billing table.
- **Avoid data redundancy.** When you store the same data in more than one place, **data redundancy** occurs. With the exception of common fields to connect tables, you should avoid data redundancy because it wastes storage space and can cause inconsistencies. Data would be inconsistent, for example, if you type a field value one way in one table and a different way in the same table or in a second table. Figure 2–3, which contains portions of potential data stored in the Patient and Visit tables, shows an example of incorrect database design that has data redundancy in the Visit table. In Figure 2–3, the LastName field in the Visit table is redundant, and one value for this field was entered incorrectly, in three different ways.

Figure 2–3 Incorrect database design with data redundancy

PatientID	LastName	FirstName	Address
13254	Brown	Gayle	452 Canipe St
13270	Li	Chen	85 Peach St
13283	Rowe	Harper	14 Long Ave
13291	Taylor	Bailey	847 Grace Ave
13300	Miller	Marjorie	90 Baxter Dr

data redundancy

VisitID	PatientID	LastName	VisitDate	WalkIn
1462	13254	Brown	11/4/2020	No
1478	13270	Lee	11/23/2020	No
1517	13283	Rowe	1/11/2021	Yes
1529	13270	Le	1/25/2021	Yes
1533	13291	Taylor	1/26/2021	Yes
1544	13300	Miller	2/4/2021	Yes
1546	13270	Leigh	2/8/2021	No

Inconsistent data

- **Determine the properties of each field.** You need to identify the **properties**, or characteristics, of each field so that the database knows how to store, display, and process the field values. These properties include the field's name, data type, maximum number of characters or digits, description, valid values, and other field characteristics. You will learn more about field properties later in this module.

The Billing table you need to modify, and the Patient table you need to create, will contain the fields shown in Figure 2–2. Before modifying and creating these new tables in the Lakewood database, you first need to learn some guidelines for setting field properties.

Guidelines for Setting Field Properties

As just noted, the last step of database design is to determine which values to assign to the properties, such as the name and data type, of each field. When you select or enter a value for a property, you **set** the property. Access has rules for naming fields and objects, assigning data types, and setting other field properties.

Naming Fields and Objects

You must name each field, table, and other object in an Access database. Access stores these items in the database, using the names you supply. Choose a field or object name that describes the purpose or contents of the field or object so that later you can easily remember what the name represents. For example, the three tables in the Lakewood database are named Visit, Billing, and Patient because these names suggest their contents. A table or query name must be unique within a database. A field name must be unique within a table, but it can be used again in another table.

Assigning Field Data Types

Each field must have a data type, which is either assigned automatically by Access or specifically by the table designer. The data type determines what field values you can enter for the field and what other properties the field will have. For example, the Patient table will include a BirthDate field, which will store date values, so you will assign the Date/Time data type to this field. Then Access will allow you to enter and manipulate only dates or times as values in the BirthDate field.

Figure 2–4 lists the most commonly used data types in Access, describes the field values allowed for each data type, explains when you should use each data type, and indicates the field size of each data type. You can find more complete information about all available data types in Access Help.

Figure 2–4 Common data types

Data Type	Description	Field Size
Short Text	Allows field values containing letters, digits, spaces, and special characters. Use for names, addresses, descriptions, and fields containing digits that are *not used in calculations*.	0 to 255 characters; default is 255
Long Text	Allows field values containing letters, digits, spaces, and special characters. Use for long comments and explanations.	1 to 65,535 characters; exact size is determined by entry
Number	Allows positive and negative numbers as field values. A number can contain digits, a decimal point, commas, a plus sign, and a minus sign. Use for fields that will be used in calculations, except those involving money.	1 to 15 digits
Date/Time	Allows field values containing valid dates and times from January 1, 100 to December 31, 9999. Dates can be entered in month/day/year format, several other date formats, or a variety of time formats, such as 10:35 PM. You can perform calculations on dates and times, and you can sort them. For example, you can determine the number of days between two dates.	8 bytes
Currency	Allows field values similar to those for the Number data type, but is used for storing monetary values. Unlike calculations with Number data type decimal values, calculations performed with the Currency data type are not subject to round-off error.	Accurate to 15 digits on the left side of the decimal point and to 4 digits on the right side
AutoNumber	Consists of integer values created automatically by Access each time you create a new record. You can specify sequential numbering or random numbering, which guarantees a unique field value, so that such a field can serve as a table's primary key.	9 digits
Yes/No	Limits field values to yes and no, on and off, or true and false. Use for fields that indicate the presence or absence of a condition, such as whether an order has been filled or whether an invoice has been paid.	1 character
Hyperlink	Consists of text used as a hyperlink address, which can have up to four parts: the text that appears in a field or control; the path to a file or page; a location within the file or page; and text displayed as a ScreenTip.	Up to 65,535 characters total for the four parts of the hyperlink

Setting Field Sizes

The **Field Size property** defines a field value's maximum storage size for Short Text, Number, and AutoNumber fields only. The other data types have no Field Size property because their storage size is either a fixed, predetermined amount or is determined automatically by the field value itself, as shown in Figure 2–4. A Short Text field has a default field size of 255 characters; you can also set its field size by entering a number from 0 to 255. For example, the FirstName and LastName fields in the Patient table will be Short Text fields with sizes of 20 characters and 25 characters, respectively. These field sizes will accommodate the values that will be entered in each of these fields.

PROSKILLS

Decision Making: Specifying the Field Size Property for Number Fields

When you use the Number data type to define a field, you need to decide what the Field Size setting should be for the field. You should set the Field Size property based on the largest value that you expect to store in that field. Access processes smaller data sizes faster, using less memory, so you can optimize your database's performance and its storage space by selecting the correct field size for each field. Field Size property settings for Number fields are as follows:

- **Byte**: Stores whole numbers (numbers with no fractions) from 0 to 255 in 1 byte
- **Integer**: Stores whole numbers from –32,768 to 32,767 in 2 bytes
- **Long Integer** (default): Stores whole numbers from –2,147,483,648 to 2,147,483,647 in 4 bytes
- **Single**: Stores positive and negative numbers to precisely 7 decimal places in 4 bytes
- **Double**: Stores positive and negative numbers to precisely 15 decimal places in 8 bytes
- **Replication ID**: Establishes a unique identifier for replication of tables, records, and other objects in databases created using Access 2003 and earlier versions in 16 bytes
- **Decimal**: Stores positive and negative numbers to precisely 28 decimal places in 12 bytes

Choosing an appropriate field size is important to optimize efficiency. For example, it would be wasteful to use the Long Integer field size for a Number field that will store only whole numbers ranging from 0 to 255 because the Long Integer field size uses 4 bytes of storage space. A better choice would be the Byte field size, which uses 1 byte of storage space to store the same values. By first gathering and analyzing information about the number values that will be stored in a Number field, you can make the best decision for the field's Field Size property and ensure the most efficient user experience for the database.

Setting the Caption Property for Fields

The **Caption property** for a field specifies how the field name is displayed in database objects, including table and query datasheets, forms, and reports. If you don't set the Caption property, Access displays the field name as the column heading or label for a field. However, field names such as InvoiceAmt and InvoiceDate in the Billing table can be difficult to read. Setting the Caption property for these fields to "Invoice Amt" and "Invoice Date" makes it easier for users to read the field names and work with the database.

INSIGHT

Setting the Caption Property vs. Naming Fields

Although Access allows you to include spaces in field names, this practice is not recommended because the spaces cause problems when you try to perform more complex tasks with the data in your database. Setting the Caption property allows you to follow best practices for naming fields, such as not including spaces in field names, while still providing users with more readable field names in datasheets, forms, and reports.

In the previous module, you created the Lakewood database file and, within that file, you created the Visit table working in Datasheet view. In addition, you created the Billing table working in Design view. Donna would like to further refine the design for the Billing table. So next, you'll modify the design for the Billing table for Donna in Design view.

Modifying a Table in Design View

In the previous module, you created the basic structure for the Billing table in Design view. To review, creating a basic table in Design view involves entering the field names, entering the data types for each field, entering an optional description for the fields, specifying a primary key for the table, and then saving the table structure. Creating a table in Design view can also involve defining properties for each field, which Donna would like you to do now. She has further refined the design for the Billing table by listing each field's name, data type, size, description (if applicable), and any other properties to set for each field. See Figure 2–5.

Figure 2–5 **Design for the Billing table**

Field Name	Data Type	Field Size	Description	Other
InvoiceNum	Short Text	5	Primary key	Caption = Invoice Num
VisitID	Short Text	4	Foreign key	Caption = Visit ID
InvoiceAmt	Currency			Format = Currency
				Decimal Places = 2
				Caption = Invoice Amt
InvoiceDate	Date/Time			Format = mm/dd/yyyy
				Caption = Invoice Date
InvoicePaid	Yes/No			Caption = Invoice Paid

You'll use Donna's design as a guide for modifying the Billing table in the Lakewood database.

Start Access and open the Billing table in Design view:

1. sam Start Access and open the **Lakewood** database you created in the previous module.

   Trouble? If the security warning is displayed below the ribbon, click the Enable Content button.

2. In the Navigation Pane, right-click the **Billing** table object and then click **Design View** on the shortcut menu.
3. Click the **Shutter Bar Open/Close Button** « to close the Navigation Pane.
4. Position the pointer in the row selector for row 1 (the InvoiceNum field) until the pointer changes to a right-pointing arrow ➡. Placing it over the key symbol is fine.
5. Click the **row selector** to select the entire InvoiceNum row. See Figure 2–6.

Figure 2–6 Billing table in Design view

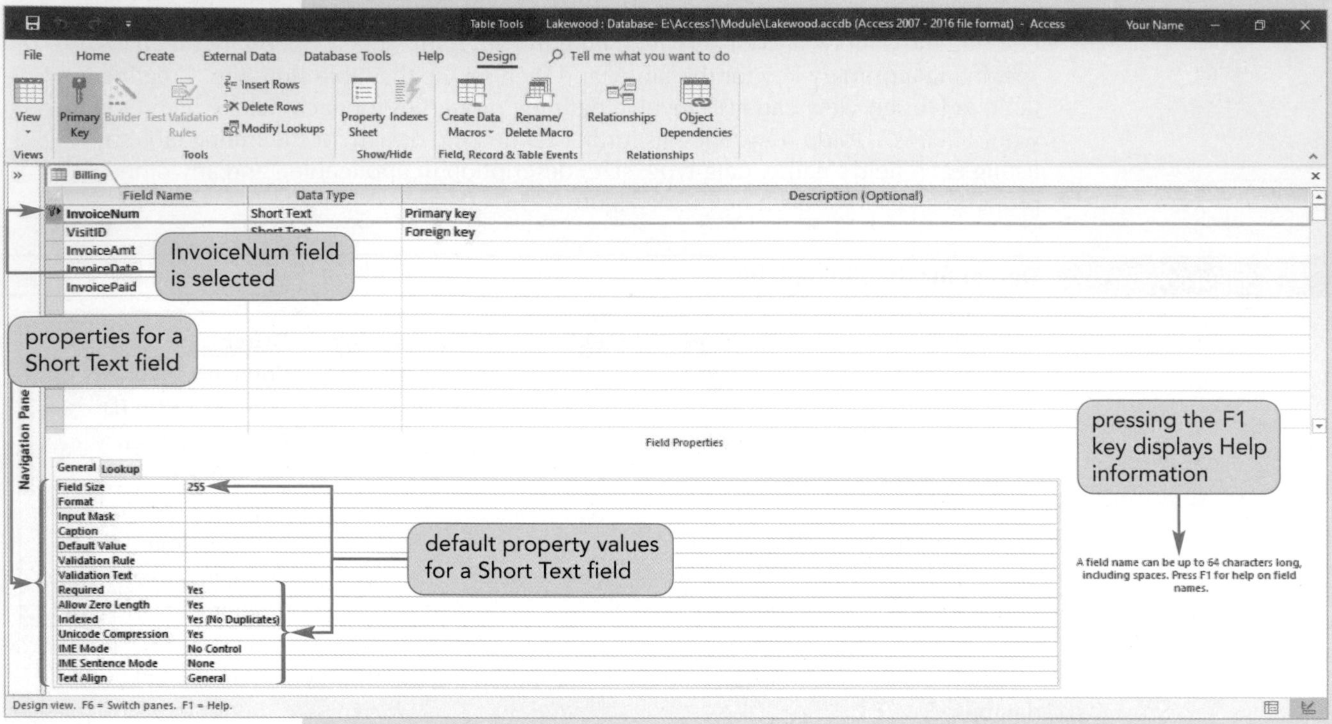
InvoiceNum field is selected
properties for a Short Text field
pressing the F1 key displays Help information
default property values for a Short Text field
A field name can be up to 64 characters long, including spaces. Press F1 for help on field names.

The Billing table contains the same fields as when you created it in the previous module. Donna wants you to continue to modify the fields in the table as listed in Figure 2–5. The first step is to add properties to the InvoiceNum field.

Because you have already defined the Field Name, Data Type, and Description properties for the InvoiceNum field, you will use the Field Properties Pane to set the additional properties Donna wants. When you created the InvoiceNum field, you gave it a data type of Short Text. Figure 2–6 shows that the default number of characters for a field of the Short Text data type is 255. In addition, a Short Text field by default has no Caption property, which specifies how the name appears. Updating the Caption property will make the field name more readable. Donna wants you to update the Field Size and Caption properties.

To add properties to the InvoiceNum field:

1. Double-click the number **255** in the Field Size property box to select it, and then type **5**.

   You also need to set the Caption property for the field so that its name appears with a space, as "Invoice Num."

2. Click the **Caption** property box, and then type **Invoice Num** (be sure to include a space between the two words). You have set properties for the InvoiceNum field. See Figure 2–7.

Figure 2–7 **InvoiceNum field properties updated**

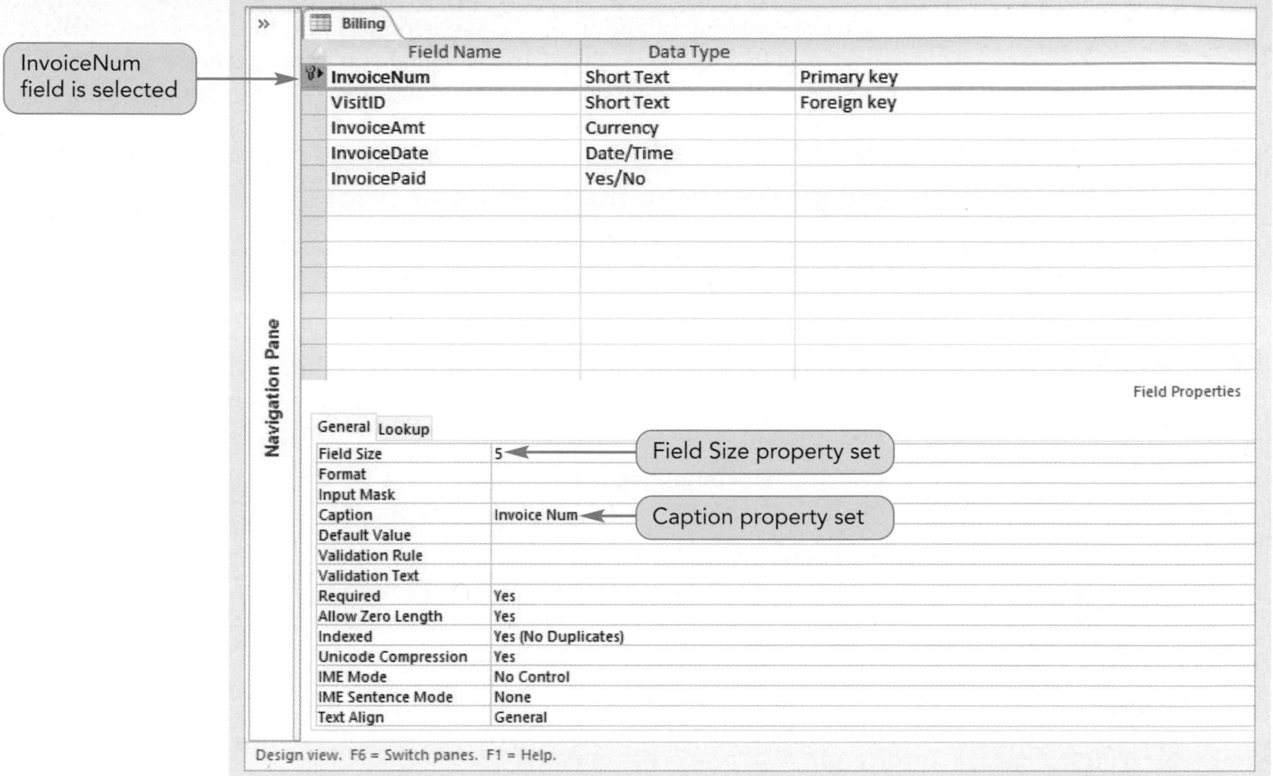
InvoiceNum field is selected
Billing
Field Name
Data Type
InvoiceNum
Short Text
Primary key
VisitID
Short Text
Foreign key
InvoiceAmt
Currency
InvoiceDate
Date/Time
InvoicePaid
Yes/No
Navigation Pane
Field Properties
General
Lookup
Field Size
5
Field Size property set
Format
Input Mask
Caption
Invoice Num
Caption property set
Default Value
Validation Rule
Validation Text
Required
Yes
Allow Zero Length
Yes
Indexed
Yes (No Duplicates)
Unicode Compression
Yes
IME Mode
No Control
IME Sentence Mode
None
Text Align
General
Design view. F6 = Switch panes. F1 = Help.

Next, you will add the properties Donna wants to the VisitID field. As with the InvoiceNum field, you will update the Field Size and Caption properties. Donna wants the field size of the VisitID field to be 4.

Recall that when you include the primary key from one table as a field in a second table to connect the two tables, the field is a foreign key in the second table. The field must be defined in the same way in both tables—that is, the field properties, including field size and data type, must match exactly. Later in this session, you'll change the Field Size property for the VisitID field in the Visit table to 4 so that the field definition is the same in both tables.

To add properties to the VisitID field:

1. Position the pointer in the row selector for row 2 (the VisitID field) until the pointer changes to a right-pointing arrow ➡.
2. Click the **row selector** to select the entire VisitID row.
3. Press **F6** to move to the Field Properties pane. The current entry for the Field Size property, 255, is selected.
4. Type **4** to set the Field Size property. Next, you need to set the Caption property for this field.
5. Press **TAB** three times to position the insertion point in the Caption box, and then type **Visit ID** (be sure to include a space between the two words). You have finished modifying the VisitID field.

The third field in the Billing table is the InvoiceAmt field, which has the Currency data type. Donna wants you to make a few modifications to the properties of this field.

In addition to adding a Caption field value, Donna wants to display the InvoiceAmt field values with two decimal places. The **Decimal Places property** specifies the number of decimal places that are displayed to the right of the decimal point.

To add properties to the InvoiceAmt field:

1. Position the pointer in the row selector for row 3 (the InvoiceAmt field) until the pointer changes to a right-pointing arrow ➡.
2. Click the **row selector** to select the entire InvoiceAmt row.
3. In the Field Properties pane, click the **Decimal Places** box to position the insertion point. An arrow appears on the right side of the Decimal Places box, which you can click to display a list of options.
4. Click the **Decimal Places** arrow, and then click **2** in the list to specify two decimal places for the InvoiceAmt field values.
5. Press **TAB** twice to position the insertion point in the Caption box, and then type **Invoice Amt** (be sure to include the space). The definition of the third field is now complete. Notice that the Format property is by default set to "Currency," which formats the values with dollar signs, and is what Donna wants. See Figure 2–8.

TIP

You can display the arrow and the list simultaneously by clicking the right side of a box.

Figure 2–8 InvoiceAmt field properties updated

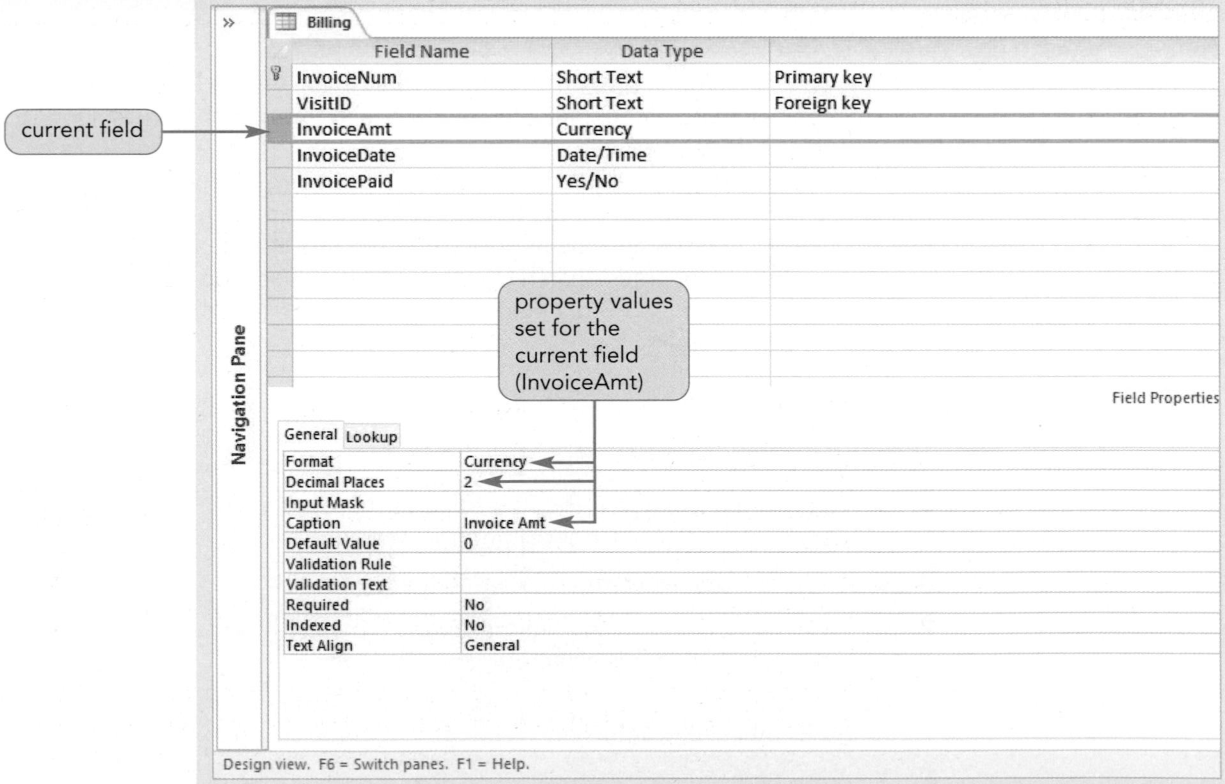
current field
property values set for the current field (InvoiceAmt)
Billing
Field Name
Data Type
InvoiceNum
Short Text
Primary key
VisitID
Short Text
Foreign key
InvoiceAmt
Currency
InvoiceDate
Date/Time
InvoicePaid
Yes/No
Navigation Pane
Field Properties
General
Lookup
Format
Currency
Decimal Places
2
Input Mask
Caption
Invoice Amt
Default Value
0
Validation Rule
Validation Text
Required
No
Indexed
No
Text Align
General
Design view. F6 = Switch panes. F1 = Help.

In these steps, you set the Decimal Places property for the InvoiceAmt field in Design view; however, it is also possible to change the number of decimal places for a field in Datasheet view. For fields of the Currency and Number data types, you can change the number of decimal places in either view. To change the number of decimal places in Datasheet view, you would first click a field to make it the active field. On the Table Tools Fields tab, in the Formatting group, use the Increase Decimals and Decrease Decimals buttons to add or remove decimal places in the field. When you do, Access makes the change in the corresponding Decimal Places property in Design view.

The fourth field in the Billing table is the InvoiceDate field. According to Donna's design (Figure 2–5), the date values should be displayed in the format mm/dd/yyyy, which is a two-digit month, a two-digit day, and a four-digit year. In addition, she wants you to update the Caption property.

To add properties to the InvoiceDate field:

1. Position the pointer in the row selector for row 4 (the InvoiceDate field) until the pointer changes to a right-pointing arrow ➡.
2. Click the **row selector** to select the entire InvoiceDate row.

   Donna wants to display the values in the InvoiceDate field in a format showing the month, the day, and a four-digit year, as in the following example: 05/24/2021. You use the Format property to control the display of a field value.
3. In the Field Properties pane, click the right side of the **Format** box to display the list of predefined formats for Date/Time fields. See Figure 2–9.

Figure 2–9 **Displaying available formats for Date/Time fields**

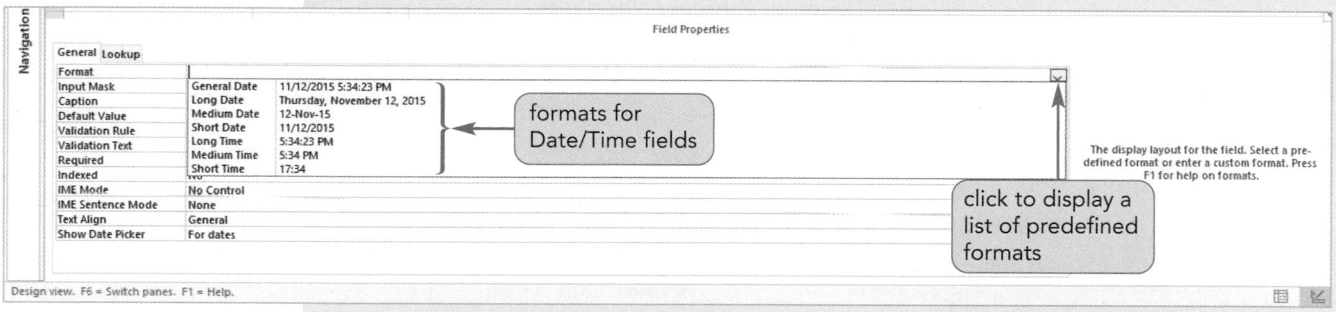
Navigation
Field Properties
General
Lookup
Format
Input Mask
Caption
Default Value
Validation Rule
Validation Text
Required
Indexed
IME Mode
IME Sentence Mode
Text Align
Show Date Picker
General Date 11/12/2015 5:34:23 PM
Long Date Thursday, November 12, 2015
Medium Date 12-Nov-15
Short Date 11/12/2015
Long Time 5:34:23 PM
Medium Time 5:34 PM
Short Time 17:34
No Control
None
General
For dates
formats for Date/Time fields
click to display a list of predefined formats
The display layout for the field. Select a pre-defined format or enter a custom format. Press F1 for help on formats.
Design view. F6 = Switch panes. F1 = Help.

Trouble? If you see an arrow instead of a list of predefined formats, click the arrow to display the list.

As noted in the right side of the Field Properties pane, you can choose a predefined format or enter a custom format. Even though the Short Date format seems to match the format Donna wants, it displays only one digit for January to September. For example, it would display the month of May with only the digit "5"—as in 5/24/2021—instead of displaying the month with two digits, as in 05/24/2021.

Because none of the predefined formats matches the exact layout Donna wants for the InvoiceDate values, you need to create a custom date format. Figure 2–10 shows some of the symbols available for custom date and time formats.

Figure 2–10 Symbols for some custom date formats

Symbol	Description
/	date separator
d	day of the month in one or two numeric digits, as needed (1 to 31)
dd	day of the month in two numeric digits (01 to 31)
ddd	first three letters of the weekday (Sun to Sat)
dddd	full name of the weekday (Sunday to Saturday)
w	day of the week (1 to 7)
ww	week of the year (1 to 53)
m	month of the year in one or two numeric digits, as needed (1 to 12)
mm	month of the year in two numeric digits (01 to 12)
mmm	first three letters of the month (Jan to Dec)
mmmm	full name of the month (January to December)
yy	last two digits of the year (01 to 99)
yyyy	full year (0100 to 9999)

Donna wants to display the dates with a two-digit month (mm), a two-digit day (dd), and a four-digit year (yyyy).

4. Click the **Format** arrow to close the list of predefined formats, and then type **mm/dd/yyyy** in the Format box.
5. Press **TAB** twice to position the insertion point in the Caption box, and then type **Invoice Date** (be sure to include a space between the words). See Figure 2–11.

Figure 2–11 Specifying the custom date format

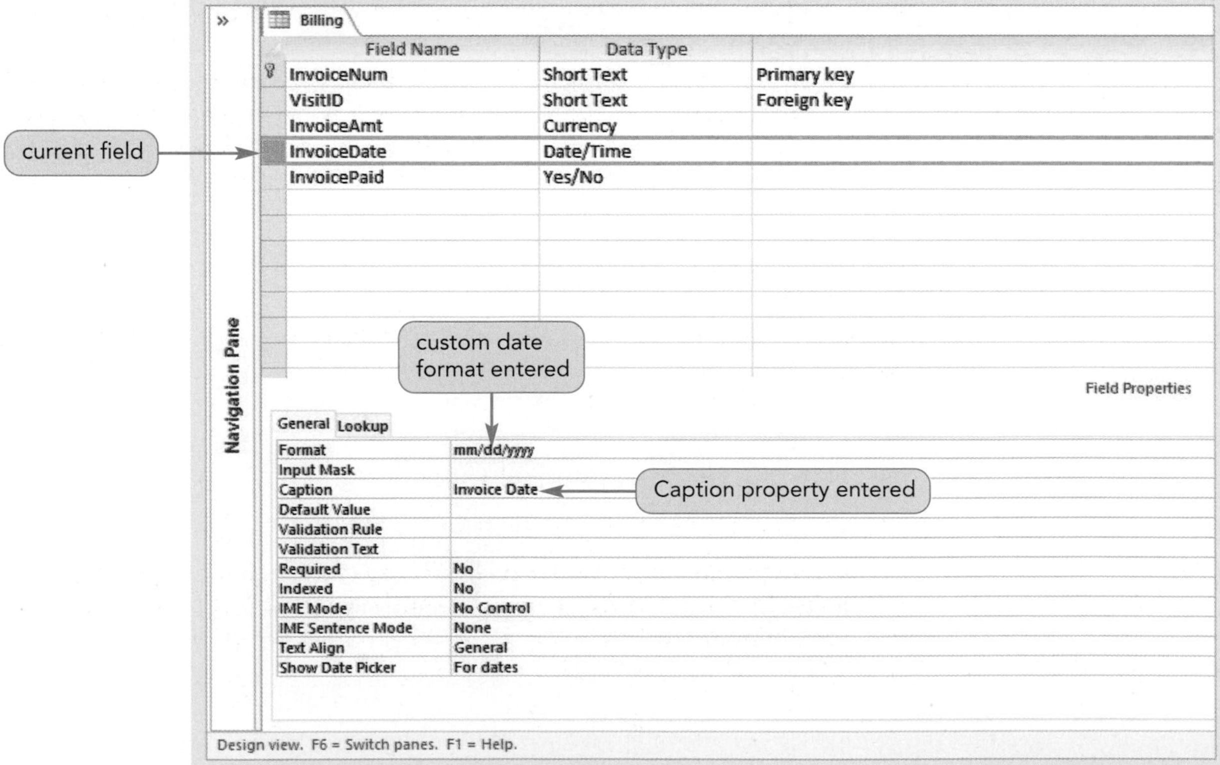
current field
Billing
Field Name
Data Type
InvoiceNum
Short Text
Primary key
VisitID
Short Text
Foreign key
InvoiceAmt
Currency
InvoiceDate
Date/Time
InvoicePaid
Yes/No
Navigation Pane
custom date format entered
Field Properties
General Lookup
Format mm/dd/yyyy
Input Mask
Caption Invoice Date
Caption property entered
Default Value
Validation Rule
Validation Text
Required No
Indexed No
IME Mode No Control
IME Sentence Mode None
Text Align General
Show Date Picker For dates
Design view. F6 = Switch panes. F1 = Help.

The fifth and final field to modify in the Billing table is the InvoicePaid field. The only property Donna wants to update for the InvoicePaid field is the Caption property.

To add property to the InvoicePaid field:

1. Position the pointer in the row selector for row 5 (the InvoicePaid field) until the pointer changes to a right-pointing arrow ➡.
2. Click the **row selector** to select the entire InvoicePaid row.
3. In the Field Properties pane, click the **Caption** box, and then type **Invoice Paid** (once again, be sure to include a space between the words).

You've finished adding properties to the fields for the Billing table. Normally after entering the fields and properties for a table in Design view, you would specify the primary key for the table; however, in the previous module you specified the primary key for the Billing table to be the InvoiceNum field.

INSIGHT

Understanding the Importance of the Primary Key

Although Access does not require a table to have a primary key, including a primary key offers several advantages:

- A primary key uniquely identifies each record in a table.
- Access does not allow duplicate values in the primary key field. For example, if the Visit table already has a record with a VisitID value of 1549, Access prevents you from adding another record with this same value in the VisitID field. Preventing duplicate values ensures the uniqueness of the primary key field.
- When a primary key has been specified, Access forces you to enter a value for the primary key field in every record in the table. This is known as **entity integrity**. If you do not enter a value for a field, you have actually given the field a **null value**. You cannot give a null value to the primary key field because entity integrity prevents Access from accepting and processing that record.
- You can enter records in any order, but Access displays them by default in order of the primary key's field values. If you enter records in no specific order, you will later be able to work with them in a more meaningful, primary key sequence.
- Access responds faster to your requests for specific records based on the primary key.

Saving the Table Structure

You have already given the table a name, Billing; however, because you added many property values, you should save the changes you made to the table structure.

To save the Billing table changes:

1. On the Quick Access Toolbar, click the **Save** button 💾.

   Unlike the first time you saved the Billing table, you are not prompted for a name for the table. Because the name has already been assigned, Access updates the structure of the table using the same name.

Modifying the Structure of an Access Table

Even a well-designed table might need to be modified. Some changes that you can make to a table's structure in Design view include changing the order of fields and adding new fields.

After meeting with her assistant, Taylor Bailey, and reviewing the structure of the Billing table, Donna asks you to make changes to the table. First, she wants to move the InvoiceAmt field so that it appears right before the InvoicePaid field. Then, she wants you to add a new Short Text field named InvoiceItem to include information about what the invoice is for, such as office visits, lab work, and so on. Donna would like to insert the InvoiceItem field between the InvoiceAmt and InvoicePaid fields.

Moving a Field in Design View

To move a field, you use the mouse to drag it to a new location in the Table Design grid. Although you can move a field in Datasheet view by dragging its column heading to a new location, doing so rearranges only the *display* of the table's fields; the table structure is not changed. To move a field permanently, you must move the field in Design view.

Next, you'll move the InvoiceAmt field so that it appears before the InvoicePaid field in the Billing table.

To move the InvoiceAmt field:

1. Position the pointer on the row selector for the InvoiceAmt field until the pointer changes to a right-pointing arrow.
2. Click the **row selector** to select the entire InvoiceAmt row.
3. Place the pointer on the row selector for the InvoiceAmt field until the pointer changes to a selection pointer, press and hold the mouse button, and then drag to the row selector for the InvoicePaid field. As you drag, the pointer changes to a move pointer. See Figure 2–12.

Figure 2–12 Moving the InvoiceAmt field in the table structure

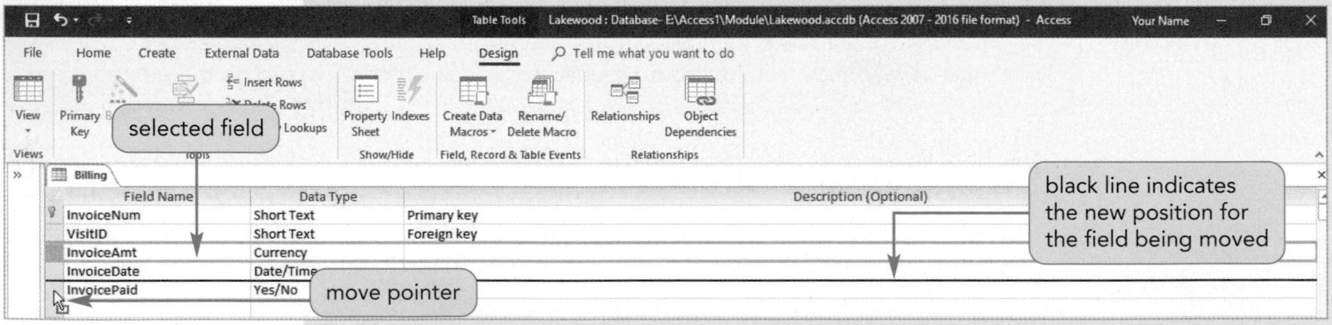

Table Tools
Lakewood : Database- E:\Access1\Module\Lakewood.accdb (Access 2007 - 2016 file format) - Access
Your Name
File
Home
Create
External Data
Database Tools
Help
Design
Tell me what you want to do
View
Primary Key
Insert Rows
Lookups
Property Sheet
Indexes
Create Data Macros
Rename/ Delete Macro
Relationships
Object Dependencies
Views
Show/Hide
Field, Record & Table Events
Relationships
Billing
Field Name
Data Type
Description (Optional)
InvoiceNum
Short Text
Primary key
VisitID
Short Text
Foreign key
InvoiceAmt
Currency
InvoiceDate
InvoicePaid
Yes/No
selected field
black line indicates the new position for the field being moved
move pointer

4. Release the mouse button. The InvoiceAmt field now appears between the InvoiceDate and InvoicePaid fields in the table structure.

   Trouble? If the InvoiceAmt field did not move, repeat Steps 1 through 4, making sure you hold down the mouse button while dragging.

Adding a Field in Design View

To add a new field between existing fields, you must insert a row. You begin by selecting the row below where you want to insert the new field.

REFERENCE

Adding a Field Between Two Existing Fields

- In the Table window in Design view, select the row below where you want to insert the new field.
- In the Tools group on the Table Tools Design tab, click the Insert Rows button.
- Define the new field by entering the field name, data type, optional description, and any property specifications.

Next, you need to add the InvoiceItem field to the Billing table structure between the InvoiceAmt and InvoicePaid fields.

To add the InvoiceItem field to the Billing table:

1. Click the **InvoicePaid** Field Name box. You need to establish this field as the current field to insert the row for the new field above this field.
2. On the Table Tools Design tab, in the Tools group, click **Insert Rows**. A new, blank row is added between the InvoiceAmt and InvoicePaid fields. The insertion point is positioned in the Field Name box for the new row, ready for you to type the name for the new field. See Figure 2–13.

Figure 2–13 Table structure after inserting a row

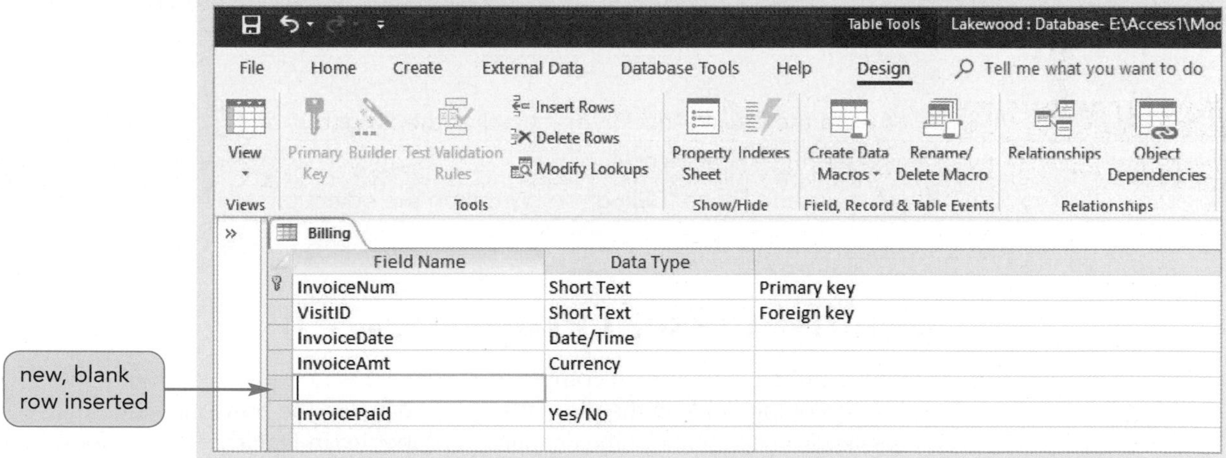
Table Tools
Lakewood : Database- E:\Access1\Moc
File
Home
Create
External Data
Database Tools
Help
Design
Tell me what you want to do
View
Primary Key
Builder
Test Validation Rules
Insert Rows
Delete Rows
Modify Lookups
Property Sheet
Indexes
Create Data Macros
Rename/ Delete Macro
Relationships
Object Dependencies
Views
Tools
Show/Hide
Field, Record & Table Events
Relationships
Billing
Field Name
Data Type
InvoiceNum
Short Text
Primary key
VisitID
Short Text
Foreign key
InvoiceDate
Date/Time
InvoiceAmt
Currency
InvoicePaid
Yes/No
new, blank row inserted

Trouble? If you selected the InvoicePaid field's row selector and then inserted the new row, you need to click the new row's Field Name box to position the insertion point in it.

You'll define the InvoiceItem field in the new row of the Billing table. This field will be a Short Text field with a field size of 40. You also need to set the Caption property to include a space between the words in the field name.

3. Type **InvoiceItem**, press **TAB** to move to the Data Type property, and then press **TAB** again to accept the default Short Text data type.

4. Press **F6** to select the default field size in the Field Size box, and then type **40**.
5. Press **TAB** three times to position the insertion point in the Caption box, and then type **Invoice Item**. The definition of the new field is complete. See Figure 2–14.

Figure 2–14 InvoiceItem field added to the Billing table

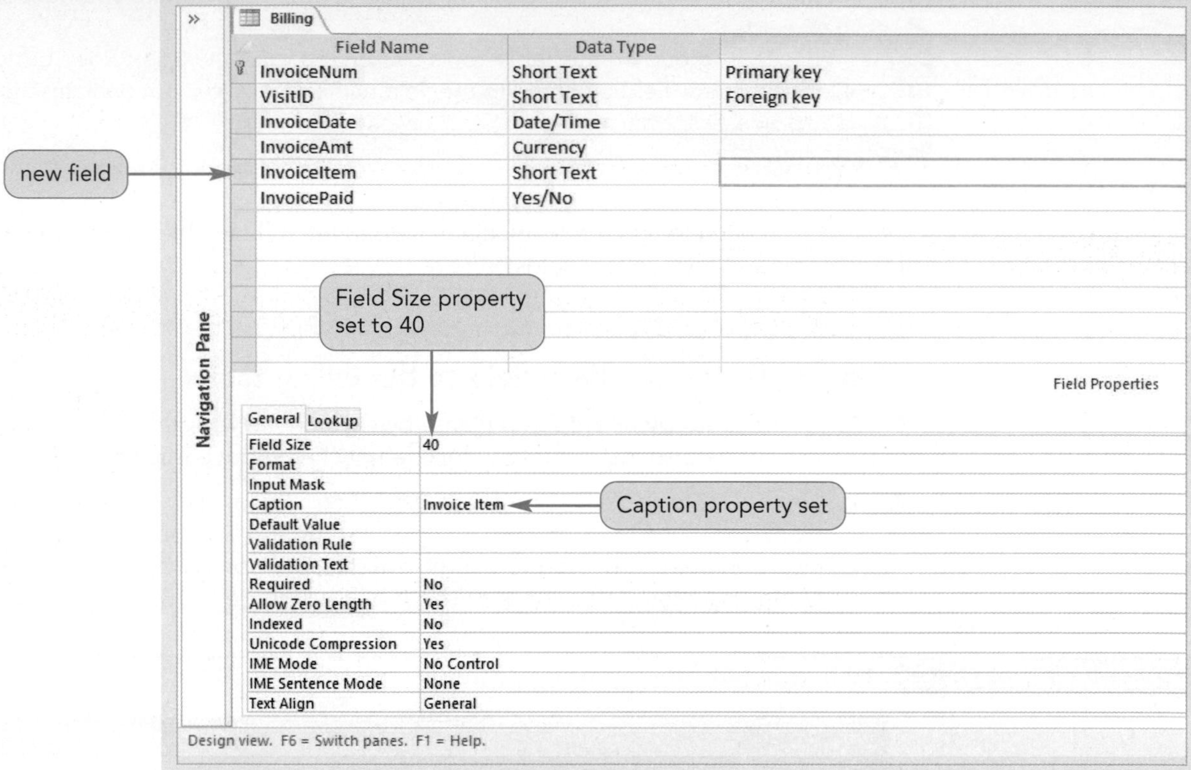
Billing
Field Name
Data Type
InvoiceNum
Short Text
Primary key
VisitID
Short Text
Foreign key
InvoiceDate
Date/Time
InvoiceAmt
Currency
InvoiceItem
Short Text
InvoicePaid
Yes/No
new field
Field Size property set to 40
Navigation Pane
Field Properties
General
Lookup
Field Size
40
Format
Input Mask
Caption
Invoice Item
Caption property set
Default Value
Validation Rule
Validation Text
Required
No
Allow Zero Length
Yes
Indexed
No
Unicode Compression
Yes
IME Mode
No Control
IME Sentence Mode
None
Text Align
General
Design view. F6 = Switch panes. F1 = Help.

6. On the Quick Access Toolbar, click the **Save** button to save the changes to the Billing table structure.
7. Click the **Close 'Billing'** button on the object tab to close the Billing table.

Modifying Field Properties

With the Billing table design complete, you can now go back and modify the properties of the fields in the Visit table you created in the previous module, as necessary. You can make some changes to properties in Datasheet view; for others, you'll work in Design view.

Changing the Format Property in Datasheet View

The Formatting group on the Table Tools Fields tab in Datasheet view allows you to modify some formatting properties for certain field types. When you format a field, you change the way data is displayed, but not the actual values stored in the table.

Next, you'll check the properties of the VisitDate field in the Visit table to see if any changes would improve the display of the date values.

To modify the VisitDate field's Format property:

1. In the Navigation Pane, click the **Shutter Bar Open/Close Button** » to open the pane. Notice that the Billing table is listed above the Visit table in the Tables section. By default, objects are listed in alphabetical order in the Navigation Pane.
2. Double-click **Visit** to open the Visit table in Datasheet view.
3. In the Navigation Pane, click the **Shutter Bar Open/Close Button** « to close the pane.
4. Position the pointer in the row selector for the first record (VisitID 1450) until the pointer changes to a right-pointing arrow ➡.
5. Click the **row selector** to select the entire first record. See Figure 2–15.

Figure 2–15 Visit table datasheet

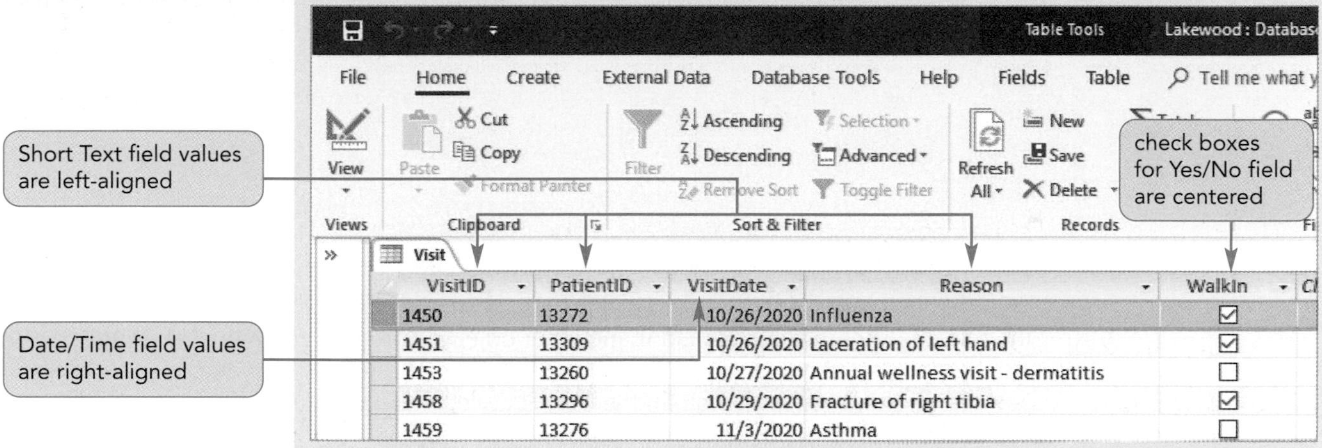
Short Text field values are left-aligned
Date/Time field values are right-aligned
check boxes for Yes/No field are centered
Table Tools
File
Home
Create
External Data
Database Tools
Help
Fields
Table
Tell me what y
Cut
Copy
Format Painter
Ascending
Descending
Remove Sort
Selection
Advanced
Toggle Filter
Refresh All
New
Save
Delete
Views
Clipboard
Sort & Filter
Records
Visit
VisitID
PatientID
VisitDate
Reason
WalkIn
1450 13272 10/26/2020 Influenza
1451 13309 10/26/2020 Laceration of left hand
1453 13260 10/27/2020 Annual wellness visit - dermatitis
1458 13296 10/29/2020 Fracture of right tibia
1459 13276 11/3/2020 Asthma

The values in the three Short Text fields—VisitID, PatientID, and Reason—appear left-aligned within their boxes, and the values in the Date/Time field (VisitDate) appear right-aligned. In Access, values for Short Text fields are left-aligned, and values for Number, Date/Time, and Currency fields are right-aligned. The WalkIn field is a Yes/No field, so its values appear in check boxes that are centered within the column.

6. On the ribbon, click the **Table Tools Fields** tab.
7. Click the **first field value** in the VisitDate column. The Data Type option shows that this field is a Date/Time field.

   By default, Access assigns the General Date format to Date/Time fields. Note the Format box in the Formatting group, which you use to set the Format property (similar to how you set the Format property in the Field Properties pane in Design view). Even though the Format box is empty, the VisitDate field has the General Date format applied to it. The General Date format includes settings for date or time values, or a combination of date and time values. However, Donna wants to display *only date values* in the VisitDate field, so she asks you to specify the Short Date format for the field.

8. In the Formatting group, click the **Format** arrow, and then click **Short Date**. See Figure 2–16.

Figure 2–16 VisitDate field after modifying the format

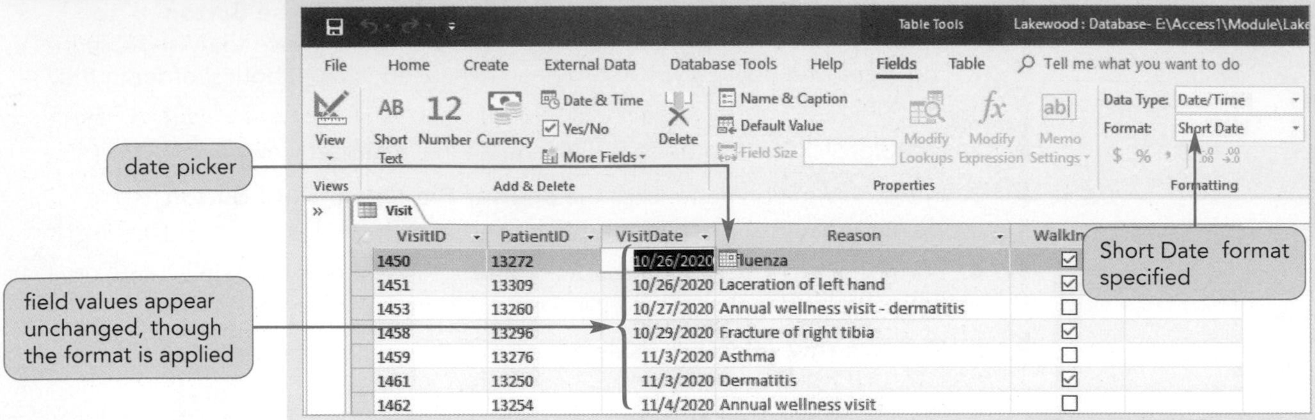
date picker
field values appear unchanged, though the format is applied
Short Date format specified
Table Tools
Lakewood : Database- E:\Access1\Module\Lake
File
Home
Create
External Data
Database Tools
Help
Fields
Table
Tell me what you want to do
View
Short Text
Number
Currency
Date & Time
Yes/No
More Fields
Delete
Name & Caption
Default Value
Field Size
Modify Lookups
Modify Expression
Memo Settings
Data Type: Date/Time
Format: Short Date
Views
Add & Delete
Properties
Formatting
Visit
VisitID
PatientID
VisitDate
Reason
WalkIn
1450 13272 10/26/2020 Influenza
1451 13309 10/26/2020 Laceration of left hand
1453 13260 10/27/2020 Annual wellness visit - dermatitis
1458 13296 10/29/2020 Fracture of right tibia
1459 13276 11/3/2020 Asthma
1461 13250 11/3/2020 Dermatitis
1462 13254 11/4/2020 Annual wellness visit

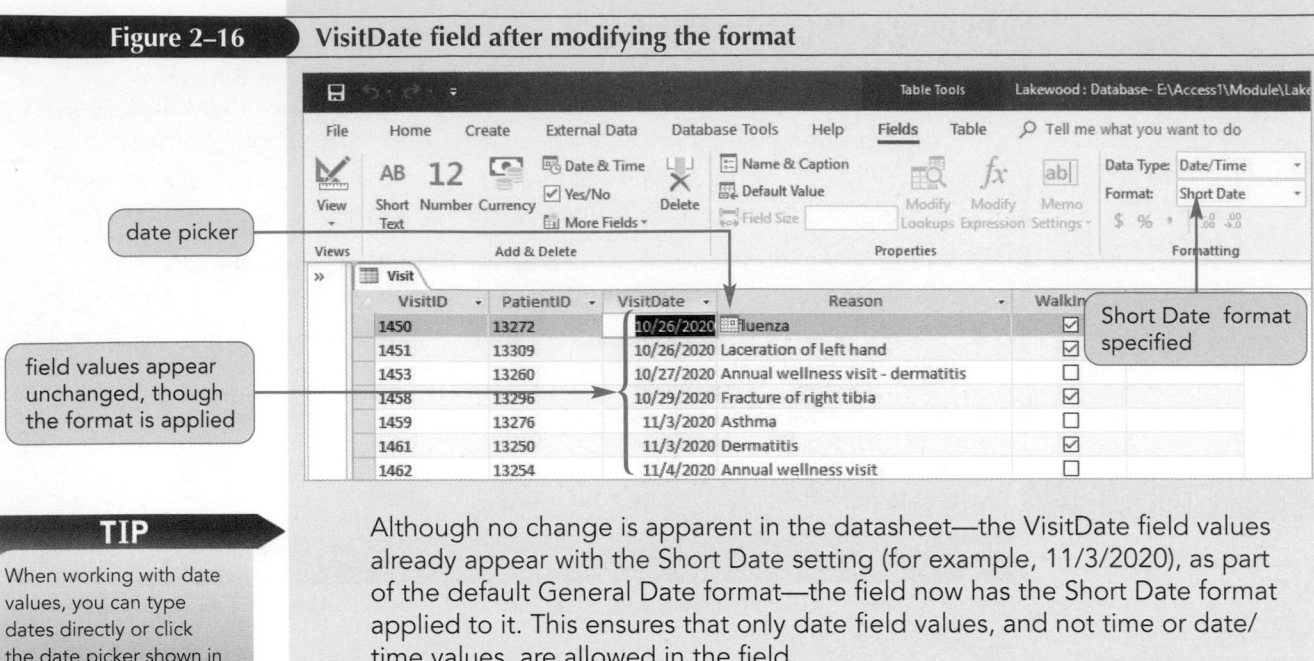

Although no change is apparent in the datasheet—the VisitDate field values already appear with the Short Date setting (for example, 11/3/2020), as part of the default General Date format—the field now has the Short Date format applied to it. This ensures that only date field values, and not time or date/time values, are allowed in the field.

> **TIP**
> When working with date values, you can type dates directly or click the date picker shown in Figure 2–16 to select a date from an interactive calendar.

When you change a field's property in Design view, you may see the Property Update Options button. This button appears when you modify a property for a field included in a query, form, or report in the database and asks if you want to update the related properties of the field in the other objects. For example, if the Lakewood database included a form or report that contained the PatientID field, and you modified a property of the PatientID field in the Patient table, you could choose to propagate, or update, the modified property by clicking the Property Update Options button, and then choosing the option to make the update everywhere the field is used. You are not required to update the related objects; however, in most cases, it is a good idea to perform the update.

Changing Properties in Design View

Recall that each of the Short Text fields in the Visit table—VisitID, PatientID, and Reason—still has the default field size of 255, which is too large for the data contained in these fields. Also, the VisitID and PatientID fields need descriptions to identify them as the primary and foreign keys, respectively, in the table. Finally, each of these fields needs a caption to include a space between the words in the field name or to make the name more descriptive. You can make all of these property changes more easily in Design view.

To modify the Field Size, Description, and Caption field properties:

> **TIP**
> You can also click the Design View button on the far right end of the status bar to switch to Design view.

1. On the Table Tools Fields tab, in the Views group, click the **View** button. The table is displayed in Design view with the VisitID field selected. You need to enter a Description property value for this field, the primary key in the table, and change its Field Size property to 4 because each visit number at Lakewood Community Health Services consists of four digits.

Trouble? If you clicked the arrow on the View button, a menu appears. Choose Design View from the menu.

2. Press **TAB** twice to position the insertion point in the Description (Optional) box, and then type **Primary key**.
3. Press **F6** to move to and select the default setting of 255 in the Field Size box in the Field Properties pane, and then type **4**. Next, you need to set the Caption property for this field.
4. Press **TAB** three times to position the insertion point in the Caption box, and then type **Visit ID**.
5. Click the **PatientID** Field Name box, press **TAB** twice to position the insertion point in the Description (Optional) box, and then type **Foreign key**.
6. Press **F6** to move to and select the default setting of 255 in the Field Size box in the Field Properties pane, and then type **5**.
7. Press **TAB** three times to position the insertion point in the Caption box, and then type **Patient ID**.
8. Click the **VisitDate** Field Name box, click the **Caption** box, and then type **Date of Visit**.

   For the Reason field, you will set the Field Size property to 60. This size can accommodate the longer values in the Reason field. You'll also set this field's Caption property to provide a more descriptive name.

9. Click the **Reason** Field Name box, press **F6**, type **60**, press **TAB** three times to position the insertion point in the Caption box, and then type **Reason/Diagnosis**.

   Finally, you'll set the Caption property for the WalkIn field.

10. Click the **WalkIn** Field Name box, click the **Caption** box, and then type **Walk-in?**. See Figure 2–17.

Figure 2–17 Visit table after modifying field properties

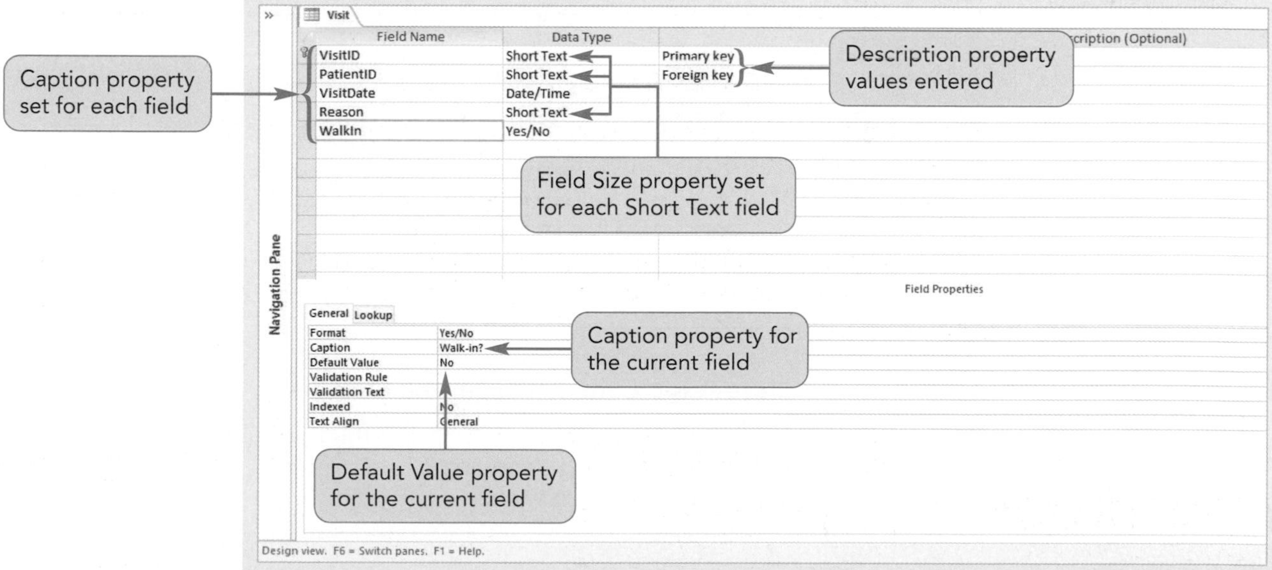
Caption property set for each field
Visit
Field Name
Data Type
Description (Optional)
VisitID
PatientID
VisitDate
Reason
WalkIn
Short Text
Short Text
Date/Time
Short Text
Yes/No
Primary key
Foreign key
Description property values entered
Field Size property set for each Short Text field
Navigation Pane
Field Properties
General
Lookup
Format
Caption
Default Value
Validation Rule
Validation Text
Indexed
Text Align
Yes/No
Walk-in?
No
No
General
Caption property for the current field
Default Value property for the current field
Design view. F6 = Switch panes. F1 = Help.

The WalkIn field's Default Value property is automatically set to "No," which means the check box for this field will be empty for each new record. This is the default for this property for any Yes/No field. You can set the Default Value property for other types of fields to make data entry easier. You'll learn more about setting this property in the next session.

The changes to the Visit table's properties are now complete, so you can save the table and view the results of your changes in Datasheet view.

To save and view the modified Visit table:

1. On the Quick Access Toolbar, click the **Save** button to save the modified table. A dialog box opens informing you that some data may be lost because you decreased the field sizes. Because all of the values in the VisitID, PatientID, and Reason fields contain the same number of or fewer characters than the new Field Size properties you set for each field, you can ignore this message.
2. Click the **Yes** button.
3. On the Table Tools Design tab, in the Views group, click the **View** button to display the Visit table in Datasheet view. Each column (field) heading now displays the text you specified in the Caption property for that field. See Figure 2–18.

Figure 2–18 **Modified Visit table in Datasheet view**

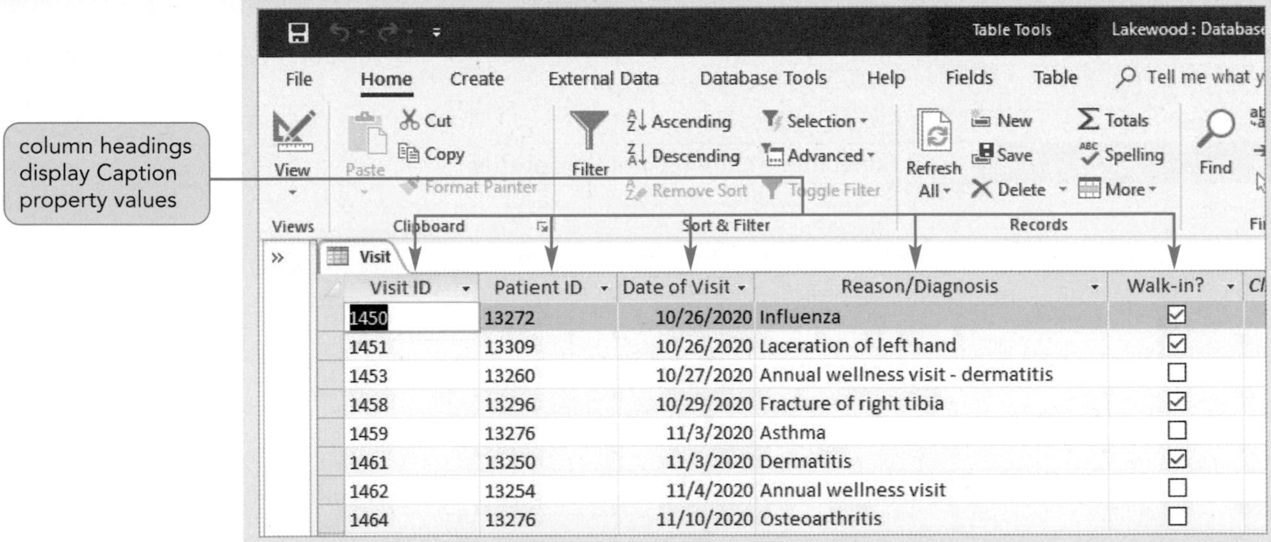
column headings display Caption property values
Table Tools
Lakewood : Databas
File
Home
Create
External Data
Database Tools
Help
Fields
Table
Tell me what y
View
Paste
Cut
Copy
Format Painter
Filter
Ascending
Descending
Remove Sort
Selection
Advanced
Toggle Filter
Refresh All
New
Save
Delete
Totals
Spelling
More
Find
Views
Clipboard
Sort & Filter
Records
Visit
Visit ID
Patient ID
Date of Visit
Reason/Diagnosis
Walk-in?
1450 13272 10/26/2020 Influenza
1451 13309 10/26/2020 Laceration of left hand
1453 13260 10/27/2020 Annual wellness visit - dermatitis
1458 13296 10/29/2020 Fracture of right tibia
1459 13276 11/3/2020 Asthma
1461 13250 11/3/2020 Dermatitis
1462 13254 11/4/2020 Annual wellness visit
1464 13276 11/10/2020 Osteoarthritis

4. Click the **Close 'Visit'** button on the object tab to close the Visit table.
5. If you are not continuing to Session 2.2, click the **File** tab, and then click **Close** to close the Lakewood database.

You have modified the design of the Billing table. In the next session, you'll add records to the Billing table and create the Patient table in the Lakewood database.

REVIEW

Session 2.1 Quick Check

1. What guidelines should you follow when designing a database?
2. What is the purpose of the Data Type property for a field?
3. The ________ property specifies how a field's name is displayed in database objects, including table and query datasheets, forms, and reports.
4. For which three types of fields can you assign a field size?
5. The default Field Size property setting for a Short Text field is ________.
6. In Design view, which key do you press to move from the Table Design grid to the Field Properties pane?
7. List three reasons you should specify a primary key for an Access table.

Session 2.2 Visual Overview:

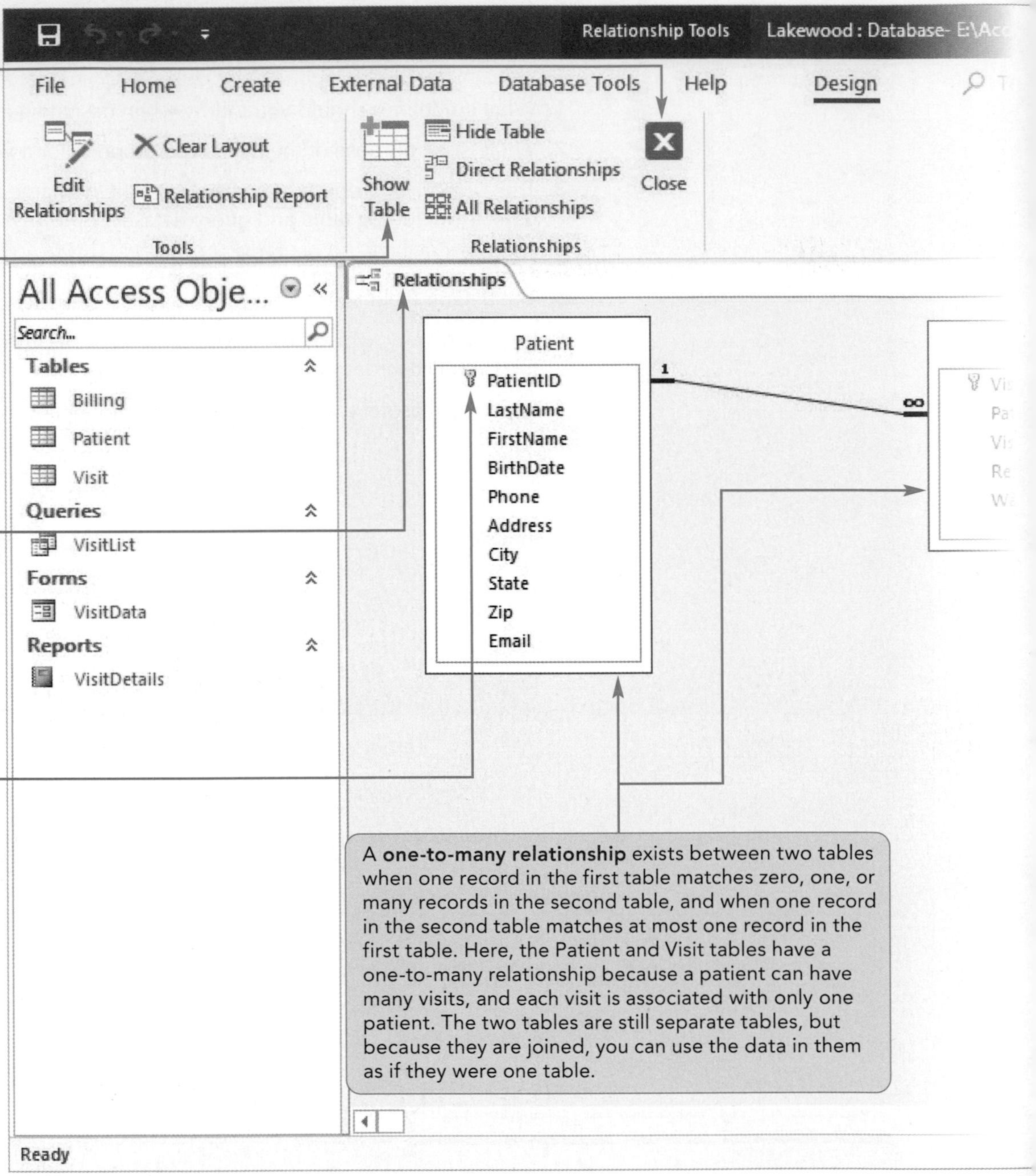
Relationship Tools
Lakewood : Database- E:\Ac
File
Home
Create
External Data
Database Tools
Help
Design
Edit Relationships
Clear Layout
Relationship Report
Tools
Show Table
Hide Table
Direct Relationships
All Relationships
Close
Relationships
All Access Obje...
Search...
Tables
Billing
Patient
Visit
Queries
VisitList
Forms
VisitData
Reports
VisitDetails
Relationships
Patient
PatientID
LastName
FirstName
BirthDate
Phone
Address
City
State
Zip
Email
1
Ready

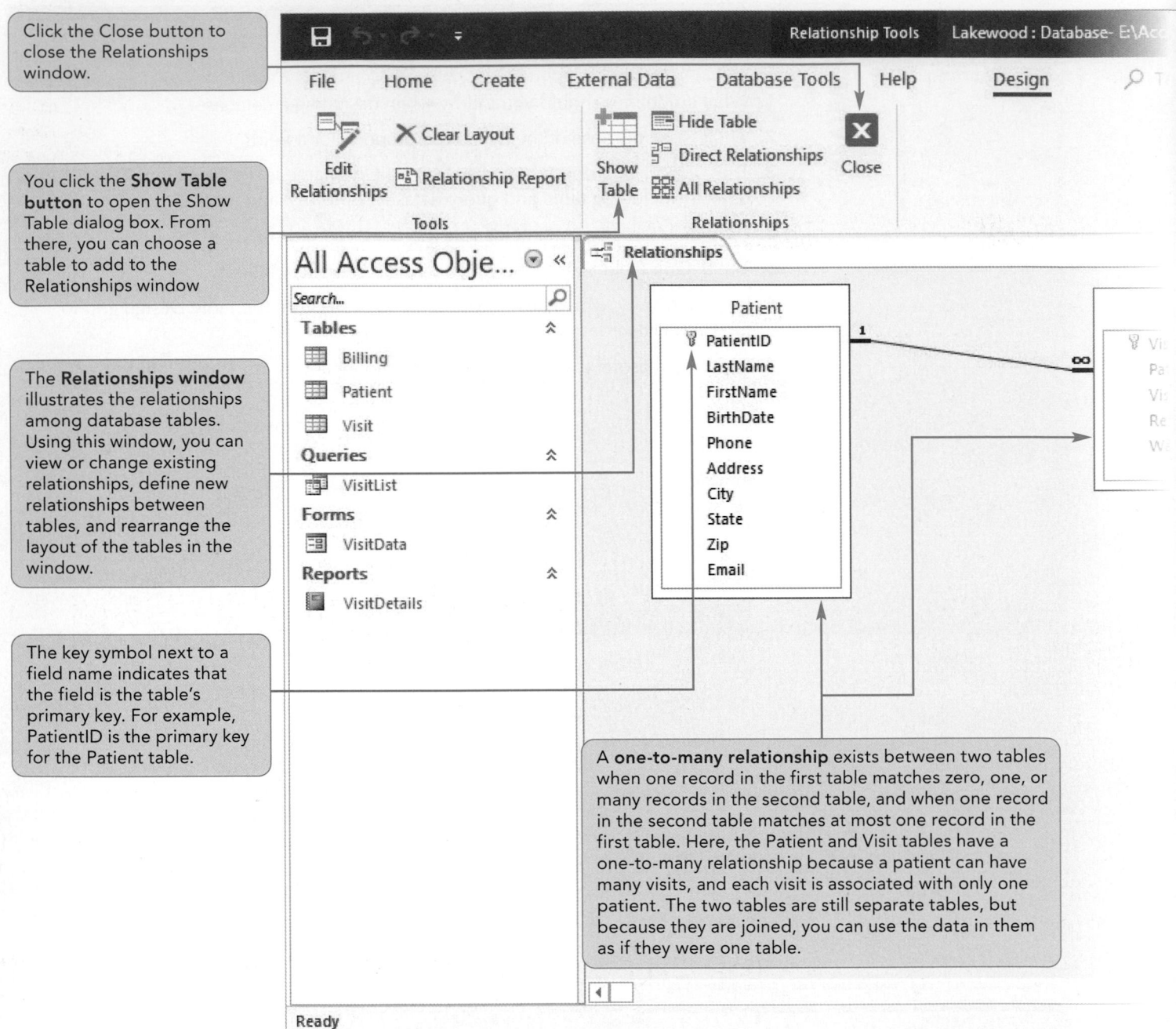

Click the Close button to close the Relationships window.

You click the **Show Table button** to open the Show Table dialog box. From there, you can choose a table to add to the Relationships window

The **Relationships window** illustrates the relationships among database tables. Using this window, you can view or change existing relationships, define new relationships between tables, and rearrange the layout of the tables in the window.

The key symbol next to a field name indicates that the field is the table's primary key. For example, PatientID is the primary key for the Patient table.

A **one-to-many relationship** exists between two tables when one record in the first table matches zero, one, or many records in the second table, and when one record in the second table matches at most one record in the first table. Here, the Patient and Visit tables have a one-to-many relationship because a patient can have many visits, and each visit is associated with only one patient. The two tables are still separate tables, but because they are joined, you can use the data in them as if they were one table.

Understanding Table Relationships

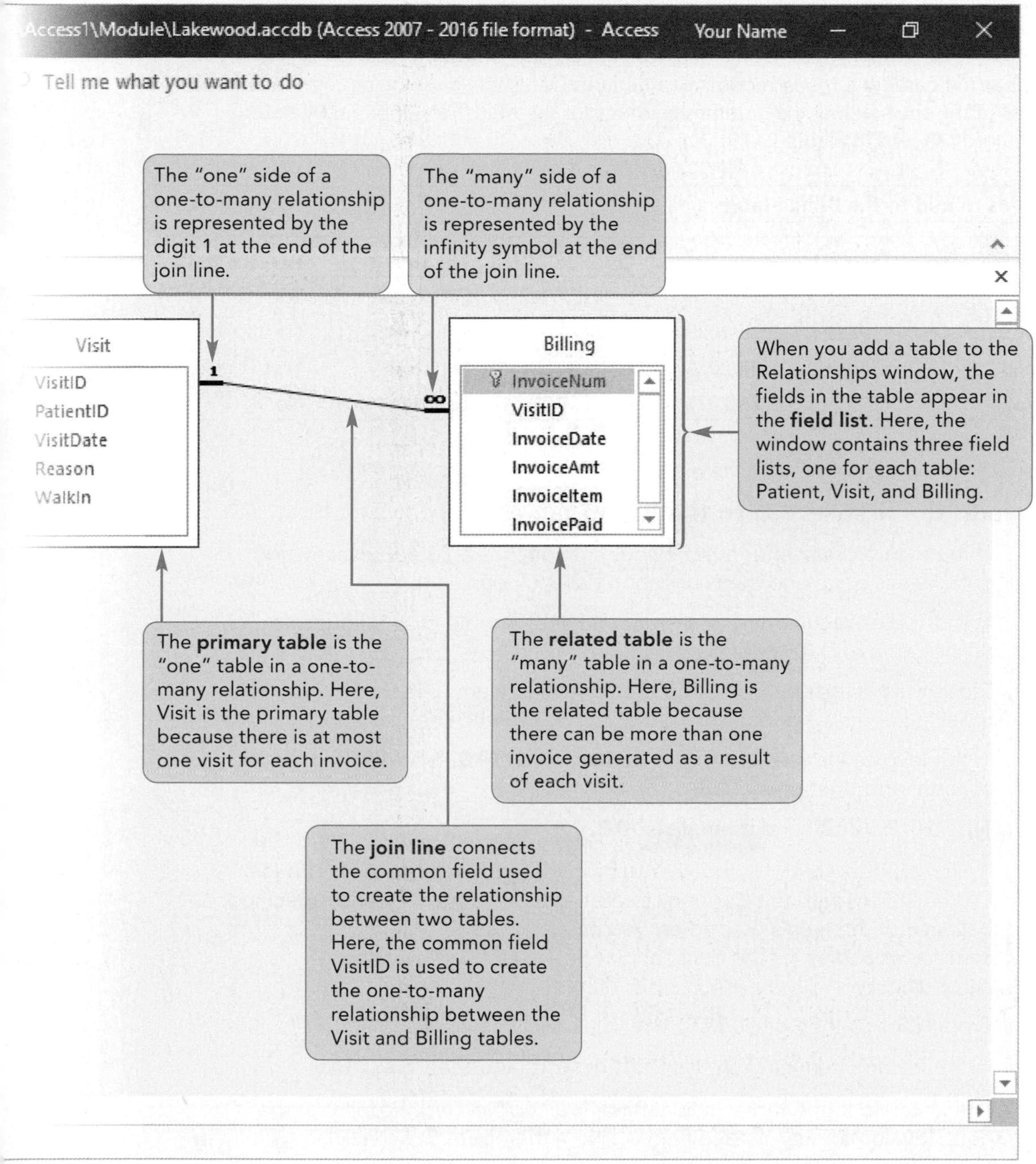
Access1\Module\Lakewood.accdb (Access 2007 - 2016 file format) - Access
Your Name
Tell me what you want to do
The "one" side of a one-to-many relationship is represented by the digit 1 at the end of the join line.
The "many" side of a one-to-many relationship is represented by the infinity symbol at the end of the join line.
Visit
VisitID
PatientID
VisitDate
Reason
WalkIn
1
Billing
InvoiceNum
VisitID
InvoiceDate
InvoiceAmt
InvoiceItem
InvoicePaid
When you add a table to the Relationships window, the fields in the table appear in the **field list**. Here, the window contains three field lists, one for each table: Patient, Visit, and Billing.
The **primary table** is the "one" table in a one-to-many relationship. Here, Visit is the primary table because there is at most one visit for each invoice.
The **related table** is the "many" table in a one-to-many relationship. Here, Billing is the related table because there can be more than one invoice generated as a result of each visit.
The **join line** connects the common field used to create the relationship between two tables. Here, the common field VisitID is used to create the one-to-many relationship between the Visit and Billing tables.

Adding Records to a New Table

Before you can begin to define the table relationships illustrated in the Session 2.2 Visual Overview, you need to finish creating the tables in the Lakewood database.

The Billing table design is complete. Now, Donna would like you to add records to the table so it contains the invoice data for Lakewood Community Health Services. As you learned earlier, you add records to a table in Datasheet view by typing the field values in the rows below the column headings for the fields. You'll begin by entering the records shown in Figure 2–19.

Figure 2–19 **Records to add to the Billing table**

Invoice Num	Visit ID	Invoice Date	Invoice Amt	Invoice Item	Invoice Paid
26501	1450	10/27/2020	$125.00	Office visit	Yes
26589	1495	12/28/2020	$125.00	Office visit	No
26655	1530	01/27/2021	$50.00	Lab work	Yes
26767	1598	03/26/2021	$50.00	Lab work	No

To add the first record to the Billing table:

1. If you took a break after the previous session, make sure the Lakewood database is open and the Navigation Pane is open.
2. In the Tables section of the Navigation Pane, double-click **Billing** to open the Billing table in Datasheet view.
3. Close the Navigation Pane, and then use the column resizing pointer ✛ to resize columns, as necessary, so that the field names are completely visible.
4. In the Invoice Num column, type **26501**, press **TAB**, type **1450** in the Visit ID column, and then press **TAB**.

Be sure to type the numbers "0" and "1" and *not* the letters "O" and "I" in the field values.

5. Type **10/27/2020** and then press **TAB**.

   Next, you need to enter the invoice amount for the first record. This is a Currency field with the Currency format and two decimal places specified. Because of the field's properties, you do not need to type the dollar sign, comma, or zeroes for the decimal places; Access displays these items automatically.

6. Type **125** and then press **TAB**. The value is displayed as "$125.00."
7. In the Invoice Item column, type **Office visit**, and then press **TAB**.

   The last field in the table, InvoicePaid, is a Yes/No field. Recall that the default value for any Yes/No field is "No"; therefore, the check box is initially empty. For the record you are entering in the Billing table, the invoice has been paid, so you need to insert a checkmark in the check box in the Invoice Paid column.

8. Press **SPACEBAR** to insert a checkmark, and then press **TAB**. The values for the first record are entered. See Figure 2–20.

Figure 2–20 First record entered in the Billing table

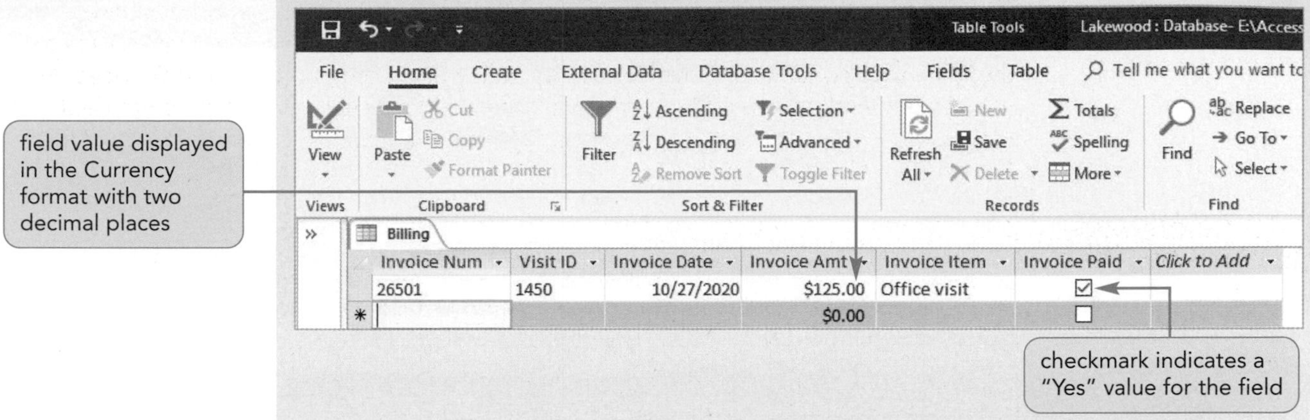
field value displayed in the Currency format with two decimal places
checkmark indicates a "Yes" value for the field
Invoice Num
Visit ID
Invoice Date
Invoice Amt
Invoice Item
Invoice Paid
Click to Add
26501
1450
10/27/2020
$125.00
Office visit
$0.00

Now you can add the remaining three records. As you do, you'll learn a keyboard shortcut for inserting the value from the same field in the previous record. A **keyboard shortcut** is a key or combination of keys you press to complete an action more efficiently.

To add the next three records to the Billing table:

1. Refer to Figure 2–19 and enter the values in the second record's Invoice Num, Visit ID, and Invoice Date columns.

   Notice that the value in the second record's Invoice Amt column is $125.00. This value is the exact same value as in the first record. You can quickly insert the value from the same column in the previous record using the CTRL+' (apostrophe) keyboard shortcut. To use this shortcut, you press and hold CTRL, press the ' key once, and then release both keys. (The plus sign in the keyboard shortcut indicates you are pressing two keys at once; you do not press the + key.)
2. With the insertion point in the Invoice Amt column, press **CTRL+'**. The value "$125.00" is inserted in the Invoice Amt column for the second record.
3. Press **TAB** to move to the Invoice Item column. Again, the value you need to enter in this column—Office visit—is the same as the value for this column in the previous record. So, you can use the keyboard shortcut again.
4. With the insertion point in the Invoice Item column, press **CTRL+'**. Access inserts the value "Office visit" in the Invoice Item column for the second record.
5. Press **TAB** to move to the Invoice Paid column, and then press **TAB** to leave the Invoice Paid check box unchecked to indicate the invoice has not been paid. The second record is entered in the Billing table.
6. Refer to Figure 2–19 to enter the values for the third and fourth records, using CTRL+' to enter the value in the fourth record's Invoice Amt and Invoice Item columns. Your table should look like the one in Figure 2–21.

Figure 2–21 Billing table with four records entered

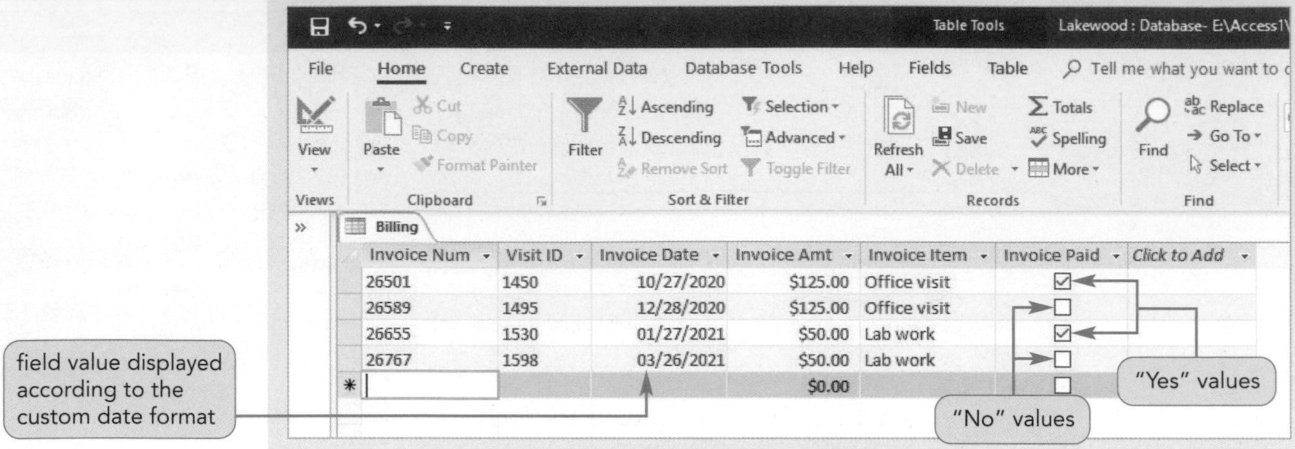
field value displayed according to the custom date format
"No" values
"Yes" values
Invoice Num
Visit ID
Invoice Date
Invoice Amt
Invoice Item
Invoice Paid
26501 1450 10/27/2020 $125.00 Office visit
26589 1495 12/28/2020 $125.00 Office visit
26655 1530 01/27/2021 $50.00 Lab work
26767 1598 03/26/2021 $50.00 Lab work

To finish entering records in the Billing table, you'll use a method that allows you to import the data.

Importing Data from an Excel Worksheet

Often, the data you want to add to an Access table is stored in another file, such as a Word document or an Excel workbook. You can add the data from other files to Access in different ways. For example, you can copy and paste the data from an open file, or you can **import** the data, which is a process that allows you to copy the data from a source without having to open the source file.

INSIGHT

Caption Property Values and the Import Process

When you import data from an Excel worksheet into an Access table, the import process does not consider any Caption property values set for the fields in the table. For example, the Access table could have fields such as InvoiceDate and InvoiceAmt with Caption property values of Invoice Date and Invoice Amt, respectively. If the Excel worksheet you are importing has the column headings Invoice Date and Invoice Amt, you might think that the data matches and you can proceed with the import. However, if the underlying field names in the Access table do not match the Excel worksheet column headings exactly, the import process will fail. It is a good idea to double-check to make sure that the actual Access field names—and not just the column headings displayed in a table datasheet (as specified by the Caption property)—match the Excel worksheet column headings. If there are differences, you can change the column headings in the Excel worksheet to match the Access table field names before you import the date, ensuring that the process will work correctly.

Donna had been using Excel to track invoice data for Lakewood Community Health Services and already created a workbook, named Support_AC_2_Invoices.xlsx, containing this data. You'll import the Billing worksheet from this Excel workbook into your Billing table to complete the entry of data in the table. To use the import method, the columns in the Excel worksheet must match the names and data types of the fields in the Access table.

The Billing worksheet contains the following columns: InvoiceNum, VisitID, InvoiceDate, InvoiceAmt, InvoiceItem, and InvoicePaid. These column headings match the field names in the Billing table exactly, so you can import the data. Before you import data into a table, you need to close the table.

To import the Excel data into the Billing table:

1. Click the **Close 'Billing'** button ✕ on the object tab to close the Billing table, and then click the **Yes** button in the dialog box asking if you want to save the changes to the table layout. This dialog box opens because you resized the table columns.
2. On the ribbon, click the **External Data** tab.
3. In the Import & Link group, click the **New Data Source** button.
4. In the New Data Source list, click the **From File** option. You may also point to the option.
5. In the From File list, click **Excel**. The Get External Data - Excel Spreadsheet dialog box opens. See Figure 2–22.

Figure 2–22 Get External Data – Excel Spreadsheet dialog box

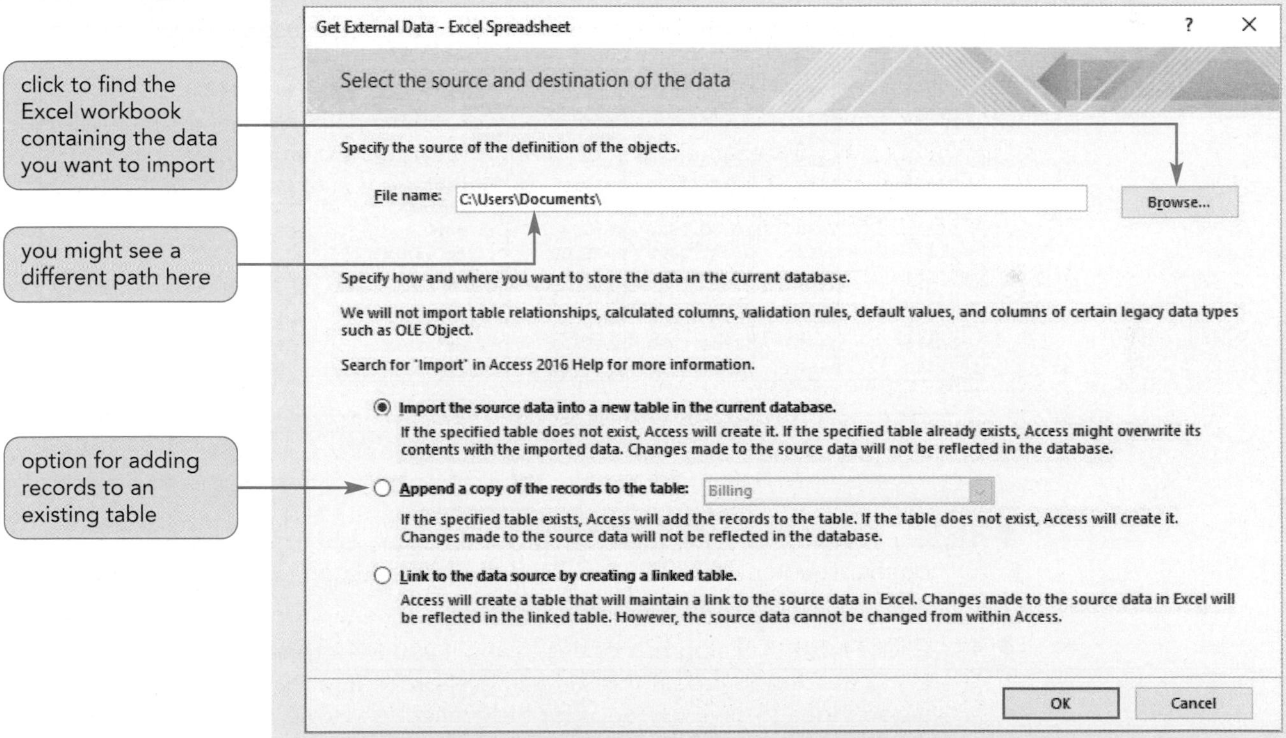
Get External Data - Excel Spreadsheet
Select the source and destination of the data
Specify the source of the definition of the objects.
File name: C:\Users\Documents\
Browse...
Specify how and where you want to store the data in the current database.
We will not import table relationships, calculated columns, validation rules, default values, and columns of certain legacy data types such as OLE Object.
Search for "Import" in Access 2016 Help for more information.
Import the source data into a new table in the current database.
If the specified table does not exist, Access will create it. If the specified table already exists, Access might overwrite its contents with the imported data. Changes made to the source data will not be reflected in the database.
Append a copy of the records to the table: Billing
If the specified table exists, Access will add the records to the table. If the table does not exist, Access will create it. Changes made to the source data will not be reflected in the database.
Link to the data source by creating a linked table.
Access will create a table that will maintain a link to the source data in Excel. Changes made to the source data in Excel will be reflected in the linked table. However, the source data cannot be changed from within Access.
OK
Cancel
click to find the Excel workbook containing the data you want to import
you might see a different path here
option for adding records to an existing table

The dialog box provides options for importing the entire worksheet as a new table in the current database, adding the data from the worksheet to an existing table, or linking the data in the worksheet to the table. You need to add, or append, the worksheet data to the Billing table.

6. Click the **Browse** button. The File Open dialog box opens. The Excel workbook file is named "Support_AC_2_Invoices.xlsx" and is located in the Access1 > Module folder provided with your Data Files.

7. Navigate to the **Access1 > Module** folder, where your Data Files are stored, and then double-click the **Support_AC_2_Invoices.xlsx** Excel file. You return to the dialog box.
8. Click the **Append a copy of the records to the table** option button. The box to the right of this option becomes active and displays the Billing table name because it is the first table listed in the Navigation Pane.
9. Click **OK**. The first Import Spreadsheet Wizard dialog box opens. The dialog box confirms that the first row of the worksheet you are importing contains column headings. The bottom section of the dialog box displays some of the data contained in the worksheet. See Figure 2–23.

Figure 2–23 First Import Spreadsheet Wizard dialog box

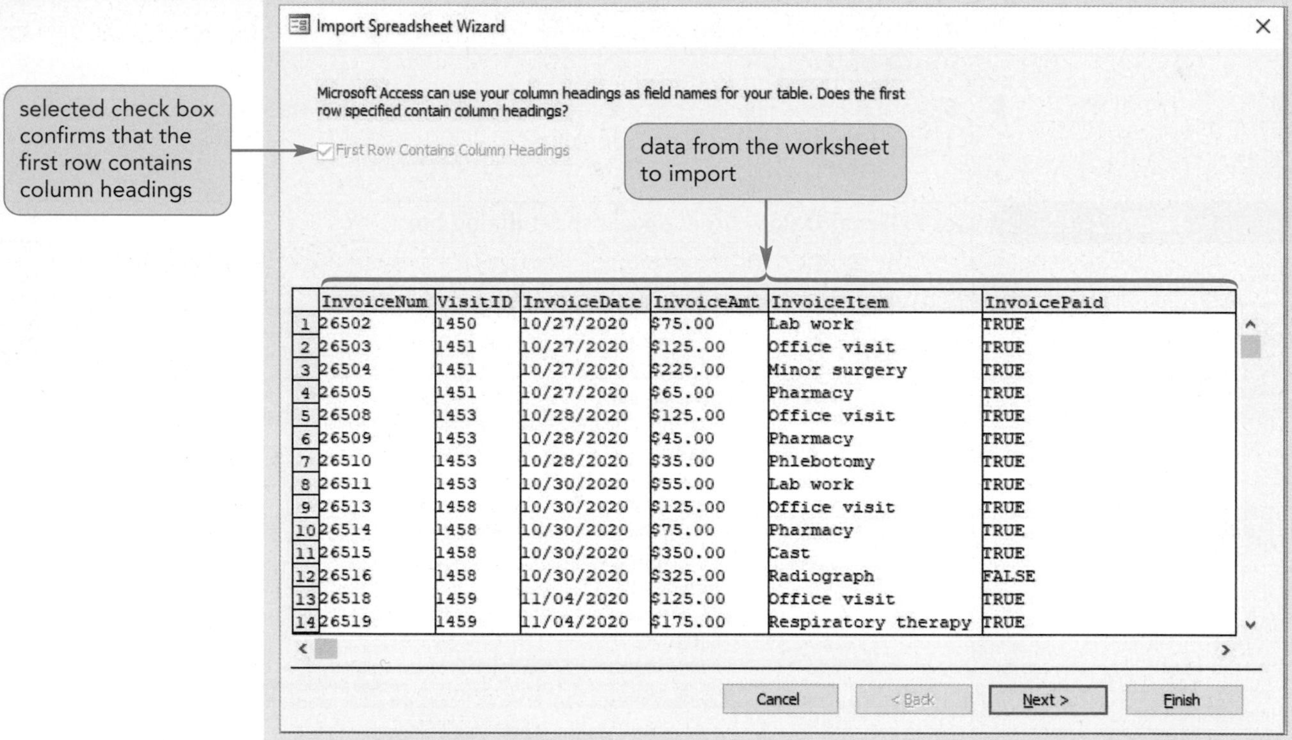
Import Spreadsheet Wizard
Microsoft Access can use your column headings as field names for your table. Does the first row specified contain column headings?
First Row Contains Column Headings
selected check box confirms that the first row contains column headings
data from the worksheet to import
InvoiceNum VisitID InvoiceDate InvoiceAmt InvoiceItem InvoicePaid
1 26502 1450 10/27/2020 $75.00 Lab work TRUE
2 26503 1451 10/27/2020 $125.00 Office visit TRUE
3 26504 1451 10/27/2020 $225.00 Minor surgery TRUE
4 26505 1451 10/27/2020 $65.00 Pharmacy TRUE
5 26508 1453 10/28/2020 $125.00 Office visit TRUE
6 26509 1453 10/28/2020 $45.00 Pharmacy TRUE
7 26510 1453 10/28/2020 $35.00 Phlebotomy TRUE
8 26511 1453 10/30/2020 $55.00 Lab work TRUE
9 26513 1458 10/30/2020 $125.00 Office visit TRUE
10 26514 1458 10/30/2020 $75.00 Pharmacy TRUE
11 26515 1458 10/30/2020 $350.00 Cast TRUE
12 26516 1458 10/30/2020 $325.00 Radiograph FALSE
13 26518 1459 11/04/2020 $125.00 Office visit TRUE
14 26519 1459 11/04/2020 $175.00 Respiratory therapy TRUE
Cancel
< Back
Next >
Finish

10. Click **Next**. The second, and final, Import Spreadsheet Wizard dialog box opens. The Import to Table box shows that the data from the spreadsheet will be imported into the Billing table.
11. Click **Finish**. A dialog box opens asking if you want to save the import steps. If you needed to repeat this same import procedure many times, it would be a good idea to save the steps for the procedure. However, you don't need to save these steps because you are importing the data only one time. After the data is in the Billing table, Donna will no longer use Excel to track invoice data.
12. Click **Close** in the dialog box to close it without saving the steps.

The data from the Billing worksheet in the Support_AC_2_Invoices.xlsx workbook has been added to the Billing table. Next, you'll open the table to view the new records.

To open the Billing table and view the imported data:

1. Open the Navigation Pane, and then double-click **Billing** in the Tables section to open the table in Datasheet view.
2. Resize the Invoice Item column to its best fit, scrolling the worksheet and resizing, as necessary.
3. Press **CTRL+HOME** to scroll to the top of the datasheet. The table now contains a total of 205 records—the four records you entered plus 201 records imported from the Invoices worksheet. The records are displayed in primary key order by the values in the Invoice Num column. See Figure 2–24.

Figure 2–24 Billing table after importing data from Excel

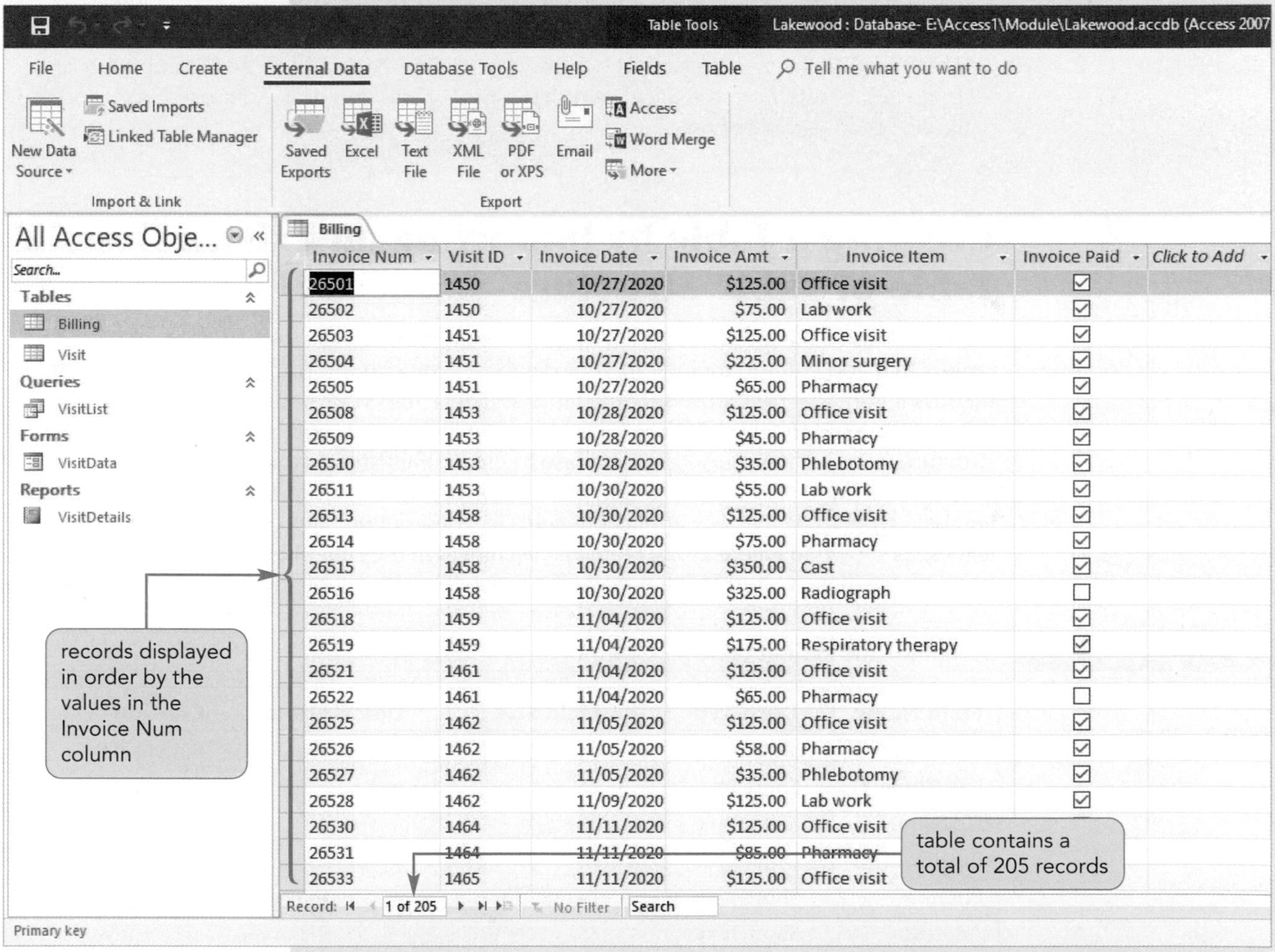
Table Tools
Lakewood : Database- E:\Access1\Module\Lakewood.accdb (Access 2007
File
Home
Create
External Data
Database Tools
Help
Fields
Table
Tell me what you want to do
New Data Source
Saved Imports
Linked Table Manager
Import & Link
Saved Exports
Excel
Text File
XML File
PDF or XPS
Email
Access
Word Merge
More
Export
All Access Obje...
Search...
Tables
Billing
Visit
Queries
VisitList
Forms
VisitData
Reports
VisitDetails
Invoice Num
Visit ID
Invoice Date
Invoice Amt
Invoice Item
Invoice Paid
Click to Add
26501 1450 10/27/2020 $125.00 Office visit
26502 1450 10/27/2020 $75.00 Lab work
26503 1451 10/27/2020 $125.00 Office visit
26504 1451 10/27/2020 $225.00 Minor surgery
26505 1451 10/27/2020 $65.00 Pharmacy
26508 1453 10/28/2020 $125.00 Office visit
26509 1453 10/28/2020 $45.00 Pharmacy
26510 1453 10/28/2020 $35.00 Phlebotomy
26511 1453 10/30/2020 $55.00 Lab work
26513 1458 10/30/2020 $125.00 Office visit
26514 1458 10/30/2020 $75.00 Pharmacy
26515 1458 10/30/2020 $350.00 Cast
26516 1458 10/30/2020 $325.00 Radiograph
26518 1459 11/04/2020 $125.00 Office visit
26519 1459 11/04/2020 $175.00 Respiratory therapy
26521 1461 11/04/2020 $125.00 Office visit
26522 1461 11/04/2020 $65.00 Pharmacy
26525 1462 11/05/2020 $125.00 Office visit
26526 1462 11/05/2020 $58.00 Pharmacy
26527 1462 11/05/2020 $35.00 Phlebotomy
26528 1462 11/09/2020 $125.00 Lab work
26530 1464 11/11/2020 $125.00 Office visit
26531 1464 11/11/2020 $85.00 Pharmacy
26533 1465 11/11/2020 $125.00 Office visit
records displayed in order by the values in the Invoice Num column
table contains a total of 205 records
Record: 1 of 205
No Filter
Search
Primary key

4. Save and close the Billing table, and then close the Navigation Pane.

Two of the tables—Visit and Billing—are now complete. According to Donna's plan for the Lakewood database, you still need to create the Patient table. You'll use a different method to create this table.

INSIGHT

Options for Importing Data from a Spreadsheet

Because you already created and added the initial four records to the Billing table, you chose the option to append the additional records from the Invoices worksheet to the Billing table. The Get External Data – Excel Spreadsheet dialog box also has two other options (see Figure 2–22).

The first option is to import the source data into a new table in the current database. If the Invoices worksheet contained all the records to add to the Billing table, you could have chosen this option to import all the records. If the specified table does not exist, Access creates it. If the specified table already exists, Access might overwrite its contents with the imported data. Changes made to the source data would not be reflected in the database.

The second option is to link to the data source by creating a linked table. With this option, Access creates a table that maintains a link to the source data in Excel. Changes made to the source data in Excel will be reflected in the linked table. However, the source data cannot be changed within Access. Because Donna wanted to move the data from the Excel worksheet into Access and no longer use Excel, you did not choose this option.

Creating a Table by Importing an Existing Table or Table Structure

If another Access database contains a table—or only the design, or structure, of a table—that you want to include in your database, you can import the table and any records it contains or import only the table structure into your database. To create the new Patient table per Donna's plan shown in Figure 2–2, you will import a table structure from a different Access database to create the Patient table.

Donna documented the design for the new Patient table by listing each field's name and data type, as well as any applicable field size, description, and caption property values, as shown in Figure 2–25. Note that each field in the Patient table, except BirthDate, will be a Short Text field, and the PatientID field will be the table's primary key.

Figure 2–25 Design for the Patient table

Field Name	Data Type	Field Size	Description	Caption
PatientID	Short Text	5	Primary key	Patient ID
LastName	Short Text	25		Last Name
FirstName	Short Text	20		First Name
BirthDate	Date/Time			Date of Birth
Phone	Short Text	14		
Address	Short Text	35		
City	Short Text	25		
State	Short Text	2		
Zip	Short Text	10		
Email	Short Text	50		

Donna's assistant Taylor already created an Access database containing a Patient table design; however, she hasn't entered any records into the table. After reviewing the table design, both Taylor and Donna agree that it contains some of the fields they want, but that some changes are needed. You will import the table structure in Taylor's database to create the Patient table in the Lakewood database, and later in this session, you will modify the imported table to produce the final table structure according to Donna's design.

To create the Patient table by importing the structure of another table:

1. Make sure the External Data tab is the active tab on the ribbon.
2. In the Import & Link group, click the **New Data Source** button.
3. In the New Data Source list, click the **From Database** option. You may also point to the option.
4. In the From Database list, click **Access**. The Get External Data – Access Database dialog box opens. This dialog box is similar to the one you used earlier when importing the Excel spreadsheet.
5. Click the **Browse** button. The File Open dialog box opens. The Access database file from which you need to import the table structure is named "Support_AC_2_Taylor.accdb" and is located in the Access1 > Module folder provided with your Data Files.
6. Navigate to the **Access1 > Module** folder, where your Data Files are stored, and then double-click the **Support_AC_2_Taylor.accdb** database file. You return to the dialog box.
7. Make sure the **Import tables, queries, forms, reports, macros, and modules into the current database** option button is selected, and then click **OK**. The Import Objects dialog box opens. The dialog box contains tabs for importing all types of Access database objects—tables, queries, forms, and so on. The Tables tab is the current tab.
8. Click the **Options** button in the dialog box to see all the options for importing tables. See Figure 2–26.

Figure 2–26 Import Objects dialog box

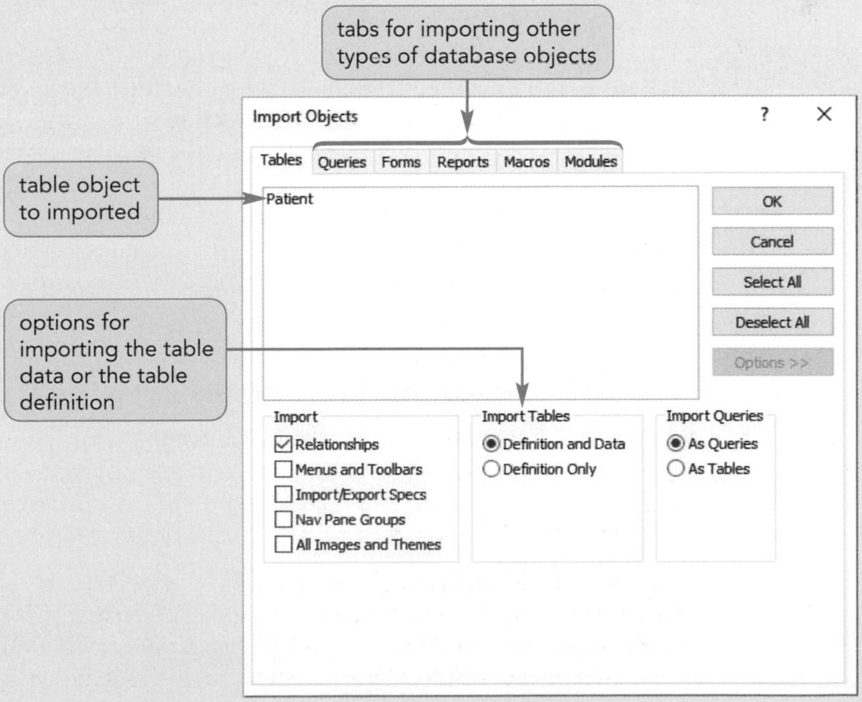
tabs for importing other types of database objects
table object to imported
options for importing the table data or the table definition
Import Objects
Tables
Queries
Forms
Reports
Macros
Modules
Patient
OK
Cancel
Select All
Deselect All
Options >>
Import
Relationships
Menus and Toolbars
Import/Export Specs
Nav Pane Groups
All Images and Themes
Import Tables
Definition and Data
Definition Only
Import Queries
As Queries
As Tables

9. On the Tables tab, click **Patient** to select this table.
10. In the Import Tables section of the dialog box, click the **Definition Only** option button, and then click **OK**. Access creates the Patient table in the Lakewood database using the structure of the Patient table in the Support_AC_2_Taylor.accdb database, and opens a dialog box asking if you want to save the import steps.
11. Click **Close** to close the dialog box without saving the import steps.
12. Open the Navigation Pane, double-click **Patient** in the Tables section to open the table, and then close the Navigation Pane. The Patient table opens in Datasheet view. The table contains no records. See Figure 2–27.

Figure 2–27 Imported Patient table in Datasheet view

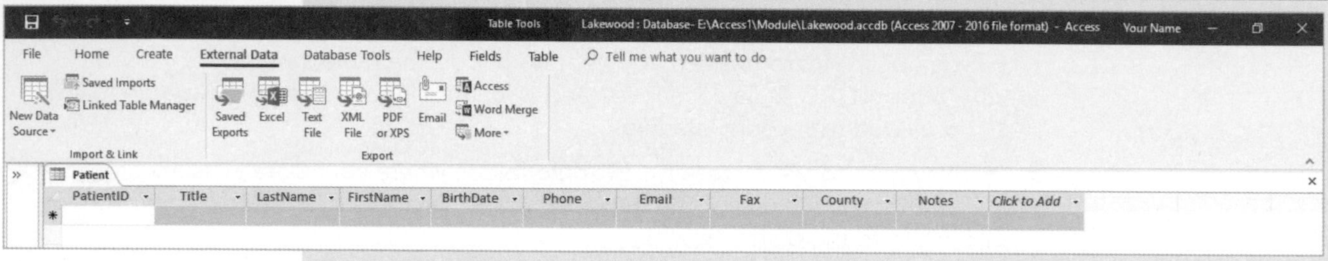
Table Tools
Lakewood : Database- E:\Access1\Module\Lakewood.accdb (Access 2007 - 2016 file format) - Access
Your Name
File
Home
Create
External Data
Database Tools
Help
Fields
Table
Tell me what you want to do
Saved Imports
Linked Table Manager
New Data Source
Import & Link
Saved Exports
Excel
Text File
XML File
PDF or XPS
Email
Access
Word Merge
More
Export
Patient
PatientID
Title
LastName
FirstName
BirthDate
Phone
Email
Fax
County
Notes
Click to Add

The table structure you imported contains some of the fields Donna wants, but not all (see Figure 2–25); it also contains some fields Donna does not want in the Patient table. You can add the missing fields using the Data Type gallery.

Adding Fields to a Table Using the Data Type Gallery

The **Data Type gallery**, available from the More Fields button in the Add & Delete group on the Table Tools Fields tab, allows you to add a group of related fields to a table at the same time, rather than adding each field to the table individually. The group of fields you add is called a **Quick Start selection**. For example, the **Address Quick Start selection** adds a collection of fields related to an address, such as Address, City, State, and so on, to the table at one time. When you use a Quick Start selection, the fields you add already have properties set. However, you need to review and possibly modify the properties to ensure the fields match your design needs for the database.

Next, you'll use the Data Type gallery to add the missing fields to the Patient table.

To add fields to the Patient table using the Data Type gallery:

1. On the ribbon, click the **Table Tools Fields** tab. Note the More Fields button in the Add & Delete group; you use this button to display the Data Type gallery. Before inserting fields from the Data Type gallery, you need to place the insertion point in the field to the right of where you want to insert the new fields. According to Donna's design, the Address field should come after the Phone field, so you need to make the next field, Email, the active field.

Make sure the correct field is active before adding new fields.

2. Click the **first row** in the Email field to make it the active field.

3. In the Add & Delete group, click the **More Fields** button. The Data Type gallery opens and displays options for types of fields you can add to your table.
4. Scroll down the gallery until the Quick Start section is visible. See Figure 2–28.

Figure 2–28 **Patient table with the Data Type gallery displayed**

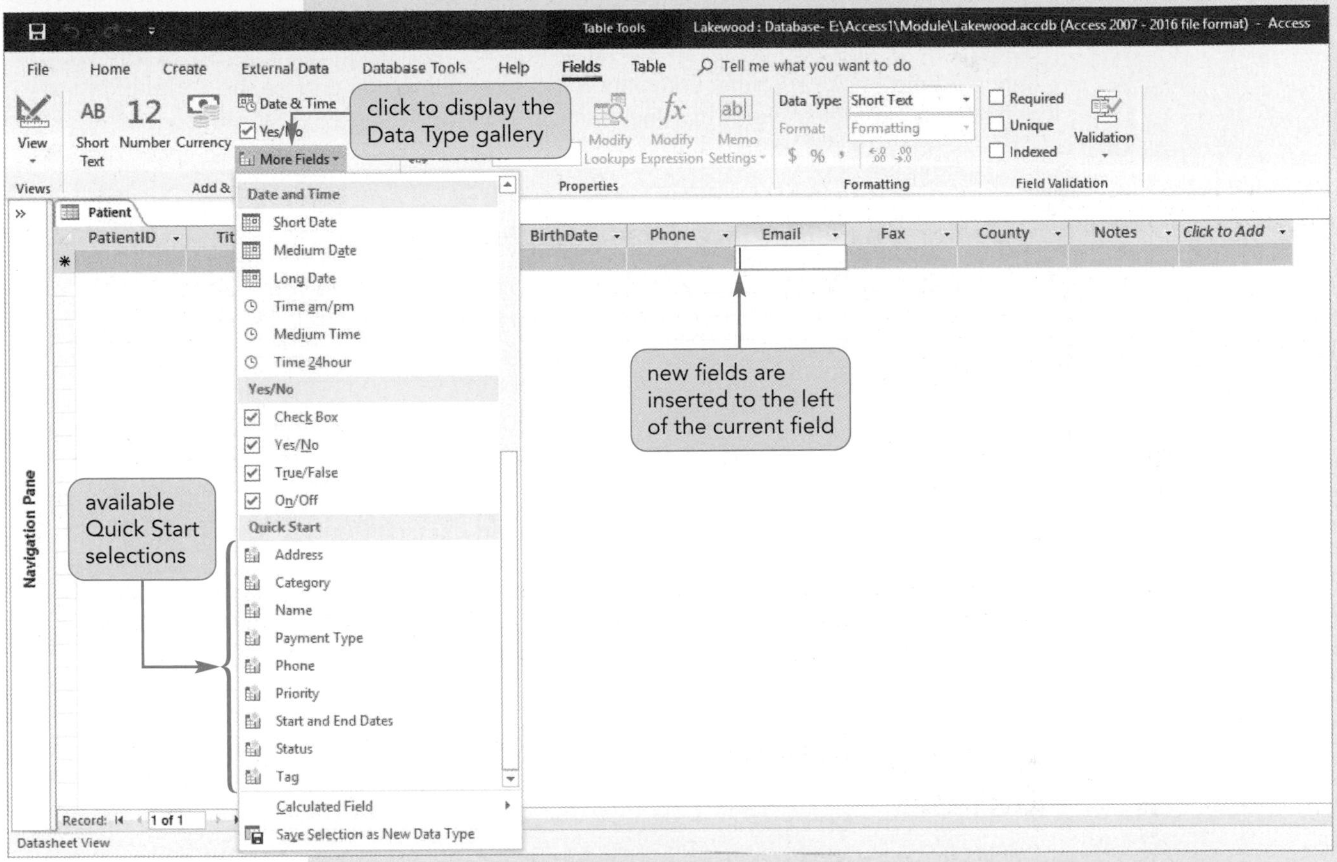
click to display the Data Type gallery
new fields are inserted to the left of the current field
available Quick Start selections
Date and Time
Short Date
Medium Date
Long Date
Time am/pm
Medium Time
Time 24hour
Yes/No
Check Box
Yes/No
True/False
On/Off
Quick Start
Address
Category
Name
Payment Type
Phone
Priority
Start and End Dates
Status
Tag
Calculated Field
Save Selection as New Data Type

The Quick Start section provides options that add related fields to the table at one time. The new fields will be inserted to the left of the current field.

5. In the Quick Start section, click **Address**. Five fields are added to the table: Address, City, State Province, ZIP Postal, and Country Region. See Figure 2–29.

Figure 2–29 **Patient table after adding fields from the Data Type gallery**

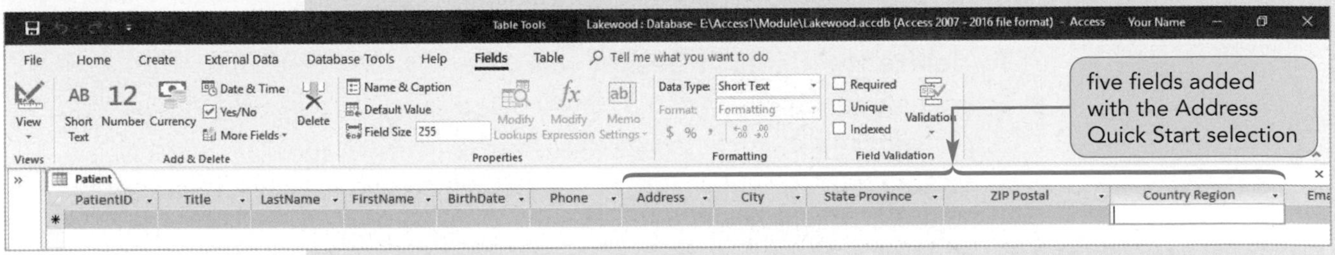
five fields added with the Address Quick Start selection
PatientID
Title
LastName
FirstName
BirthDate
Phone
Address
City
State Province
ZIP Postal
Country Region

Modifying the Structure of an Imported Table

Refer back to Donna's design for the Patient table (Figure 2–25). To finalize the table design, you need to modify the imported table by deleting fields, renaming fields, and changing field data types. You'll begin by deleting fields.

Deleting Fields from a Table Structure

After you've created a table, you might need to delete one or more fields. When you delete a field, you also delete all the values for that field from the table. So, before you delete a field, make sure that you want to do so and that you choose the correct field to delete. You can delete fields in either Datasheet view or Design view.

REFERENCE

Deleting a Field from a Table Structure

- In Datasheet view, click anywhere in the column for the field you want to delete.
- On the Table Tools Fields tab in the Add & Delete group, click the Delete button.

or

- In Design view, click the Field Name box for the field you want to delete.
- On the Table Tools Design tab in the Tools group, click the Delete Rows button.

The Address Quick Start selection added a field named "Country Region" to the Patient table. Donna doesn't need a field to store country data because all of the patients of Lakewood Community Health Services are located in the United States. You'll begin to modify the Patient table structure by deleting the Country Region field.

To delete the Country Region field from the table in Datasheet view:

1. Click the **first row** in the Country Region field (if necessary).
2. On the Table Tools Fields tab, in the Add & Delete group, click the **Delete** button. The Country Region field is removed and the first field, PatientID, is now the active field.

You can also delete fields from a table structure in Design view. You'll switch to Design view to delete the other unnecessary fields.

To delete the fields in Design view:

1. On the Table Tools Fields tab, in the Views group, click the **View** button. The Patient table opens in Design view. See Figure 2–30.

   Trouble? If you clicked the arrow on the View button, a menu appears. Choose Design View from the menu.

Figure 2–30 Patient table in Design view

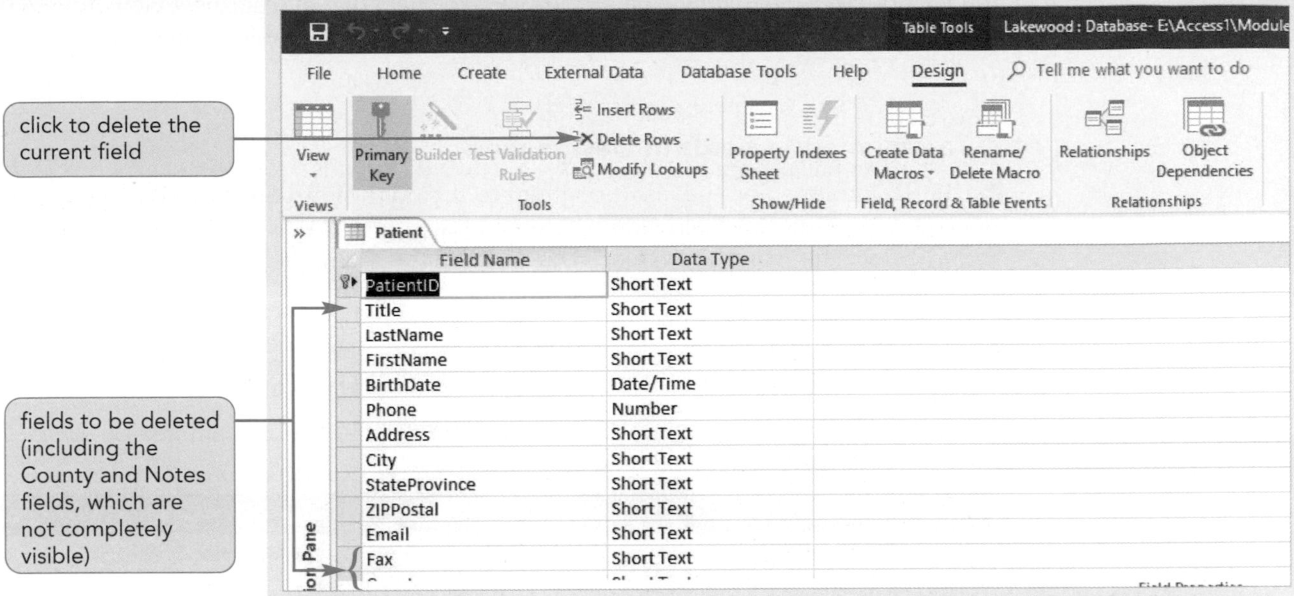
click to delete the current field
fields to be deleted (including the County and Notes fields, which are not completely visible)
Table Tools
Lakewood : Database- E:\Access1\Module
File
Home
Create
External Data
Database Tools
Help
Design
Tell me what you want to do
Insert Rows
Delete Rows
Modify Lookups
View
Primary Key
Builder
Test Validation Rules
Property Sheet
Indexes
Create Data Macros
Rename/ Delete Macro
Relationships
Object Dependencies
Views
Tools
Show/Hide
Field, Record & Table Events
Relationships
Patient
Field Name
Data Type
PatientID
Short Text
Title
Short Text
LastName
Short Text
FirstName
Short Text
BirthDate
Date/Time
Phone
Number
Address
Short Text
City
Short Text
StateProvince
Short Text
ZIPPostal
Short Text
Email
Short Text
Fax
Short Text

2. Click the **Title** Field Name box to make it the current field.
3. On the Table Tools Design tab, in the Tools group, click the **Delete Rows** button. The Title field is removed from the Patient table structure. You'll delete the Fax, County, and Notes fields next. Instead of deleting these fields individually, you'll select and delete them at the same time.
4. On the row selector for the **Fax** field, press and hold the mouse button and then drag the mouse to select the **County** and **Notes** fields.
5. Release the mouse button. The rows for the three fields are outlined in red, indicating all three fields are selected.

   You may not be able to see the Notes field; however, you can scroll down to view the selection.
6. In the Tools group, click the **Delete Rows** button. See Figure 2–31.

Figure 2–31 Patient table after deleting fields

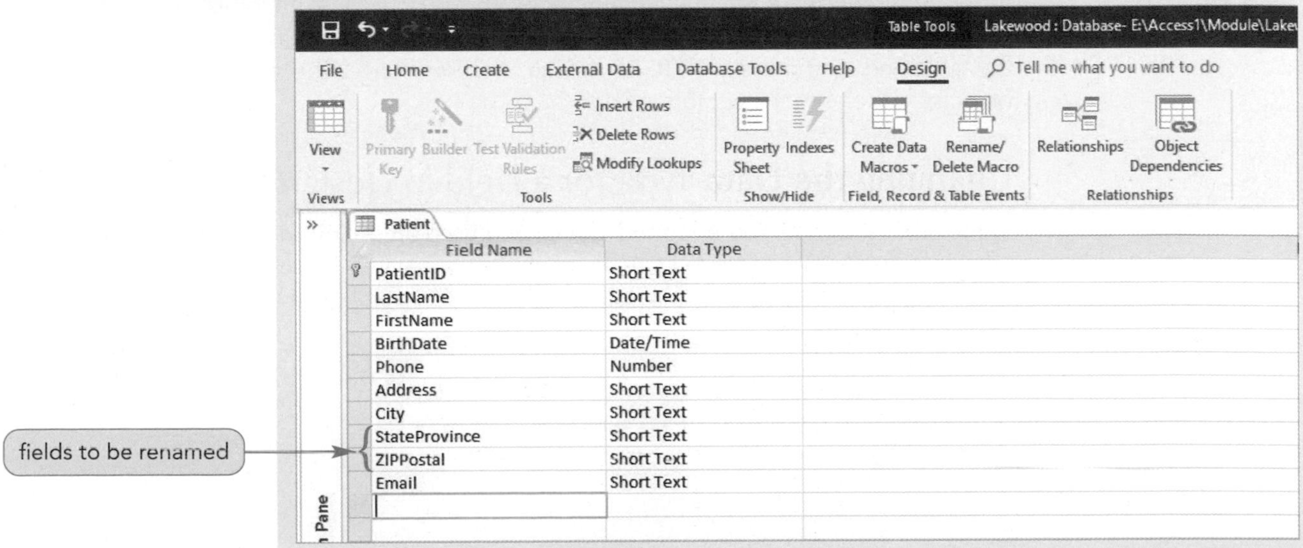
fields to be renamed
Table Tools
Lakewood : Database- E:\Access1\Module\Lake
File
Home
Create
External Data
Database Tools
Help
Design
Tell me what you want to do
Insert Rows
Delete Rows
Modify Lookups
View
Primary Key
Builder
Test Validation Rules
Property Sheet
Indexes
Create Data Macros
Rename/ Delete Macro
Relationships
Object Dependencies
Views
Tools
Show/Hide
Field, Record & Table Events
Relationships
Patient
Field Name
Data Type
PatientID
Short Text
LastName
Short Text
FirstName
Short Text
BirthDate
Date/Time
Phone
Number
Address
Short Text
City
Short Text
StateProvince
Short Text
ZIPPostal
Short Text
Email
Short Text

Renaming Fields in Design View

To match Donna's design for the Patient table, you need to rename some of the fields. You already have renamed the default primary key field (ID) in Datasheet view. You can also rename fields in Design view by editing the names in the Table Design grid.

To rename the fields in Design view:

1. Click to position the insertion point to the right of the text StateProvince in the eighth row's Field Name box, and then press **BACKSPACE** eight times to delete the word "Province." The name of the eighth field is now State.

   You can also select an entire field name and then type new text to replace it.

2. In the ninth row's Field Name box, drag to select the text **ZIPPostal**, and then type **Zip**. The text you type replaces the original text. See Figure 2–32.

Figure 2–32 **Patient table after renaming fields**

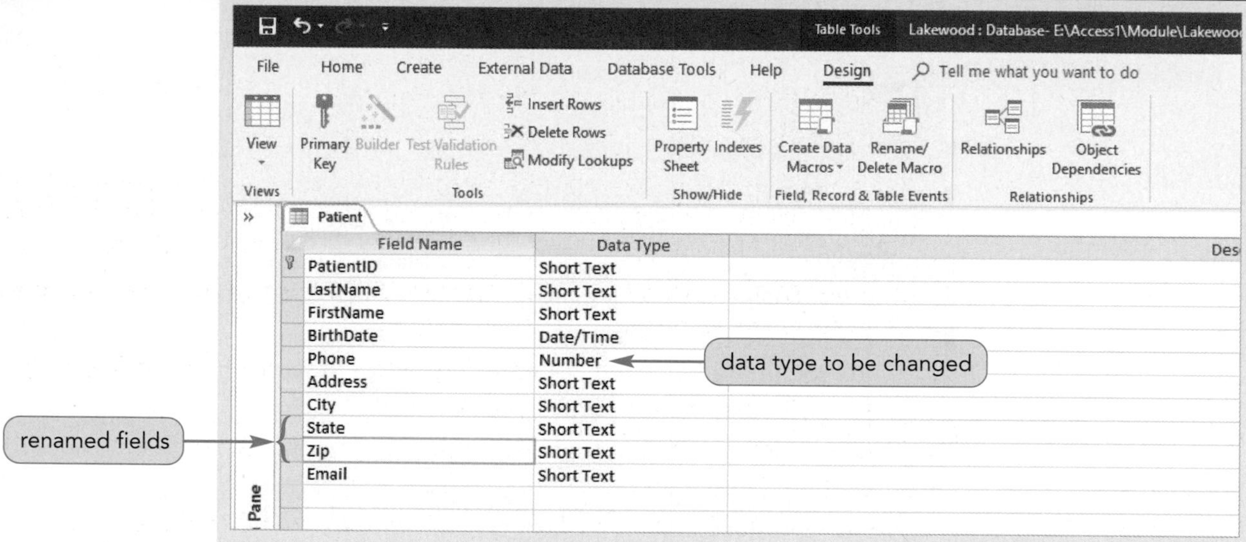

Table Tools
Lakewood : Database- E:\Access1\Module\Lakewoo
File
Home
Create
External Data
Database Tools
Help
Design
Tell me what you want to do
View
Primary Key
Builder
Test Validation Rules
Insert Rows
Delete Rows
Modify Lookups
Property Sheet
Indexes
Create Data Macros
Rename/ Delete Macro
Relationships
Object Dependencies
Views
Tools
Show/Hide
Field, Record & Table Events
Relationships
Patient
Field Name
Data Type
Des
PatientID
Short Text
LastName
Short Text
FirstName
Short Text
BirthDate
Date/Time
Phone
Number
Address
Short Text
City
Short Text
State
Short Text
Zip
Short Text
Email
Short Text
data type to be changed
renamed fields
Pane

Besides renaming fields, you can rename Access objects such as tables, queries, forms, and reports. To rename a table, for example, right-click the table object in the Navigation Pane, and then click Rename on the shortcut menu. Type the new name for the table and then press ENTER. By default, Access changes the table name in any other objects that reference the table.

Changing the Data Type for a Field in Design View

In the table structure you imported earlier, you used an option in Datasheet view to change a field's data type. You can also change the data type for a field in Design view. According to Donna's plan, all the fields in the Patient table should be Short Text fields, except for BirthDate.

To change the data type of the Phone field in Design view:

1. Click the right side of the Data Type box for the Phone field to display the list of data types.
2. Click **Short Text** in the list. The Phone field is now a Short Text field. By default, the Field Size property is set to 255. According to Donna's plan, the Phone field should have a Field Size property of 14. You'll make this change next.
3. Press **F6** to move to and select the default Field Size property, and then type **14**.

Each of the remaining fields you added using the Address Quick Start selection—Address, City, State, and Zip—also has the default field size of 255. You need to change the Field Size property for these fields to match Donna's design. You'll also delete any Caption property values for these fields because the field names match how Donna wants them displayed, so captions are unnecessary.

To change the Field Size and Caption properties for the fields:

1. Click the **Address** Field Name box to make it the current field.
2. Press **F6** to move to and select the default Field Size property, and then type **35**. Because the Caption property setting for this field is the same as the field name, the field doesn't need a caption, so you can delete this value.
3. Press **TAB** three times to select Address in the Caption box, and then press **Delete**. The Caption property value is removed.
4. Repeat Steps 1 through 3 for the City field to change the Field Size property to **25** and delete its Caption property value.
5. Change the Field Size property for the State field to **2**, and then delete its Caption property value.
6. Change the Field Size property for the Zip field to **10**, and then delete its Caption property value.
7. On the Quick Access Toolbar, click the **Save** button to save your changes to the Patient table.

Finally, Donna would like you to set the Description property for the PatientID field and the Caption property for the PatientID, LastName, and FirstName fields. You'll make these changes now.

To enter the Description and Caption property values:

1. Click the **Description (Optional)** box for the PatientID field, and then type **Primary key**.
2. In the Field Properties pane, click the **Caption** box.
3. In the Caption box for the PatientID field, type **Patient ID**.
4. Click the **LastName** Field Name box to make it the current field, click the **Caption** box, and then type **Last Name**.

5. Click the **FirstName** Field Name box to make it the current field, click the **Caption** box, and then type **First Name**.
6. Click the **BirthDate** Field Name box to make it the current field, click the **Caption** box, and then type **Date of Birth**. See Figure 2–33.

Figure 2–33 **Patient table after entering descriptions and captions**

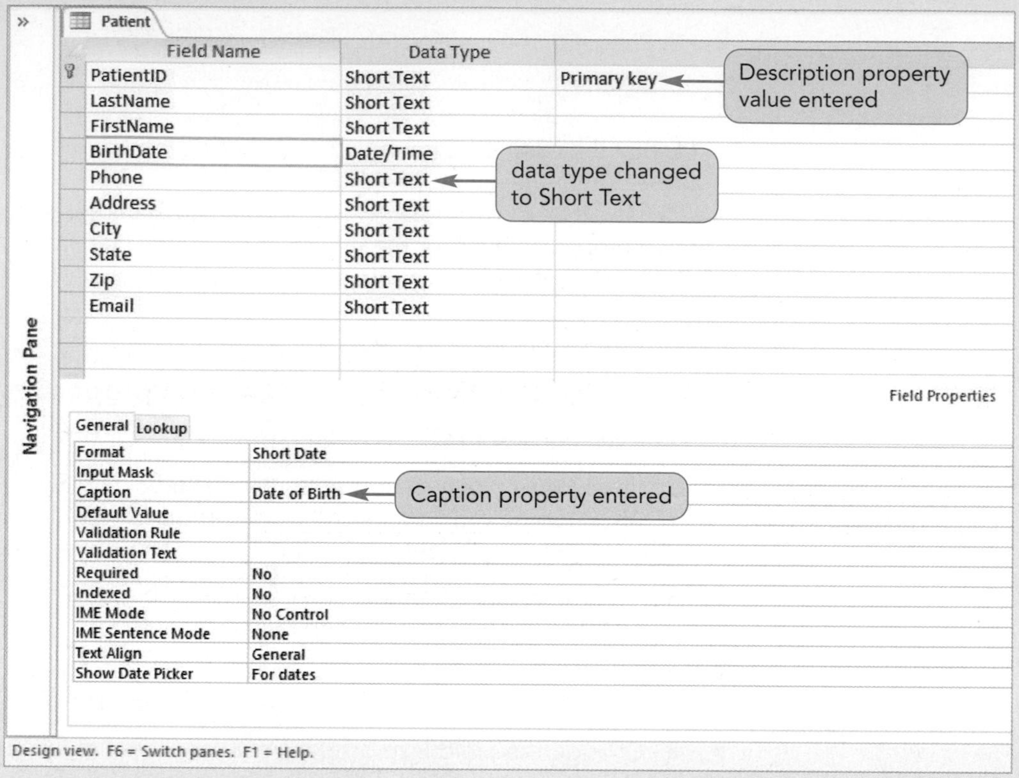
Patient
Field Name
Data Type
PatientID
LastName
FirstName
BirthDate
Phone
Address
City
State
Zip
Email
Short Text
Date/Time
Primary key
Description property value entered
data type changed to Short Text
Navigation Pane
Field Properties
General
Lookup
Format
Short Date
Input Mask
Caption
Date of Birth
Caption property entered
Default Value
Validation Rule
Validation Text
Required
No
Indexed
No
IME Mode
No Control
IME Sentence Mode
None
Text Align
General
Show Date Picker
For dates
Design view. F6 = Switch panes. F1 = Help.

7. On the Quick Access Toolbar, click the **Save** button to save your changes to the Patient table.
8. On the Table Tools Design tab, in the Views group, click the **View** button to display the table in Datasheet view.
9. Resize each column to its best fit, and then click in the first row for the **Patient ID** column. See Figure 2–34.

Figure 2–34 **Modified Patient table in Datasheet view**

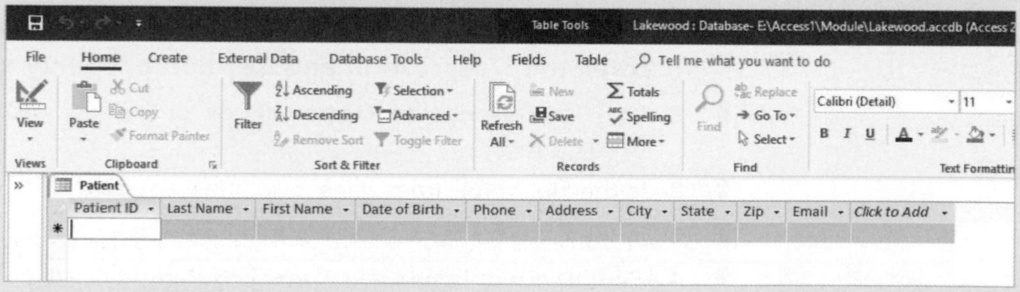
Table Tools
Lakewood : Database- E:\Access1\Module\Lakewood.accdb
File
Home
Create
External Data
Database Tools
Help
Fields
Table
Tell me what you want to do
View
Paste
Cut
Copy
Format Painter
Filter
Ascending
Descending
Remove Sort
Selection
Advanced
Toggle Filter
Refresh All
New
Save
Delete
Totals
Spelling
More
Find
Replace
Go To
Select
Calibri (Detail)
11
Views
Clipboard
Sort & Filter
Records
Find
Patient
Patient ID
Last Name
First Name
Date of Birth
Phone
Address
City
State
Zip
Email
Click to Add

Donna mentions that data entry would be easier if the State field had the value of "GA" for each new record added to the table, because all of the patients live in Georgia. You can accomplish this by setting the Default Value property for the field.

Setting the Default Value Property for a Field

The **Default Value property** for a field specifies what value will appear, by default, for the field in each new record you add to a table.

Because all the patients at Lakewood Community Health Services live in Georgia, you'll specify a default value of "GA" for the State field in the Patient table. With this setting, each new record in the Patient table will have the correct State field value entered automatically.

To set the Default Value property for the State field:

1. In the Views group, click the **View** button to display the Patient table in Design view.
2. Click the **State** Field Name box to make it the current field.
3. In the Field Properties pane, click the **Default Value** box, type **GA**, and then press **TAB**. See Figure 2–35.

Figure 2–35 **Specifying the Default Value property for the State field**

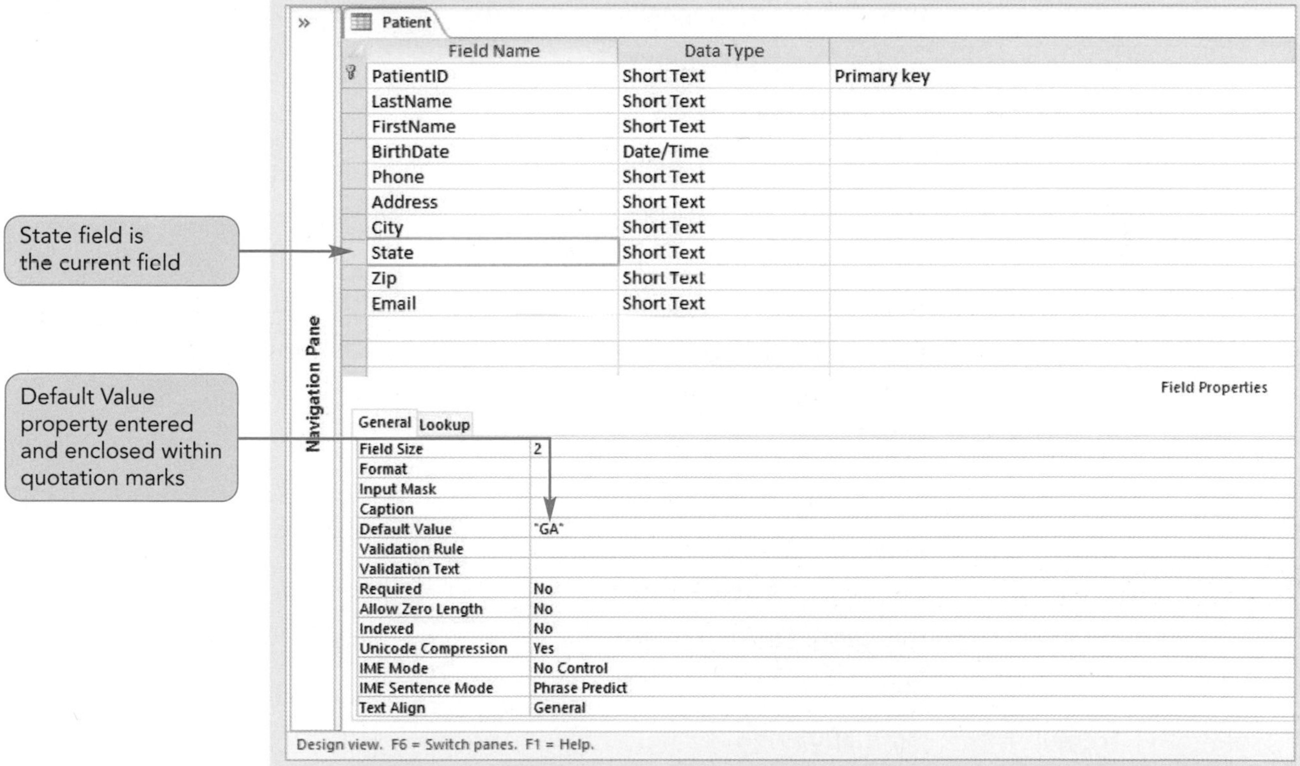
State field is the current field
Default Value property entered and enclosed within quotation marks
Patient
Navigation Pane
Field Name
Data Type
PatientID
Short Text
Primary key
LastName
FirstName
BirthDate
Date/Time
Phone
Address
City
State
Zip
Email
Field Properties
General
Lookup
Field Size
2
Format
Input Mask
Caption
Default Value
"GA"
Validation Rule
Validation Text
Required
No
Allow Zero Length
Indexed
Unicode Compression
Yes
IME Mode
No Control
IME Sentence Mode
Phrase Predict
Text Align
General
Design view. F6 = Switch panes. F1 = Help.

Note that a text entry in the Default Value property must be enclosed within quotation marks. If you do not type the quotation marks, Access adds them for you. However, for some entries, such as those that include punctuation, you would receive an error message indicating invalid syntax if you omitted the quotation marks. In such cases, you have to enter the quotation marks yourself.

4. On the Quick Access Toolbar, click the **Save** button to save your changes to the Patient table.

5. Display the table in Datasheet view. Note that the State field for the first row now displays the default value "GA" as specified by the Default Value property. Each new record entered in the table will automatically have this State field value entered.

TIP

You can change the value in a record from the default value to another value, if necessary.

With the Patient table design set, you can now enter records in it. You'll begin by entering two records in the datasheet, and then use a different method to add the remaining records.

To add two records to the Patient table:

Be sure to enter your last name and first name where indicated.

1. Enter the following values in the columns in the first record; press **TAB** to move past the default State field value:

   Patient ID = **13250**

   Last Name = **[student's last name]**

   First Name = **[student's first name]**

   Date of Birth = **4/9/1995**

   Phone = **404-555-8445**

   Address = **123 Harbor Rd**

   City = **Atlanta**

   State = **GA**

   Zip = **30303**

   Email = **student@example.com**

2. Enter the following values in the columns in the second record:

   Patient ID = **13287**

   Last Name = **Perez**

   First Name = **Luis**

   Date of Birth = **11/30/1988**

   Phone = **404-555-5903**

   Address = **78 Wynborne Dr**

   City = **Decatur**

   State = **GA**

   Zip = **30030**

   Email = **l.perez12@example.com**

3. Resize columns to their best fit, as necessary, and then save and close the Patient table.

Before Donna decided to store data using Access, Taylor managed the patient data for the clinic in a different system. She exported that data into a text file and now asks you to import it into the new Patient table. You can import the data contained in this text file to add the remaining records to the Patient table.

Adding Data to a Table by Importing a Text File

So far, you've learned how to add data to an Access table by importing an Excel spreadsheet, and you've created a new table by importing the structure of an existing table. You can also import data contained in text files.

To finish entering records in the Patient table, you'll import the data contained in Taylor's text file. The file is named "Support_AC_2_Patient.txt" and is located in the Access1 > Module folder provided with your Data Files.

To import the data contained in the Patient text file:

1. On the ribbon, click the **External Data** tab.
2. In the Import & Link group, click the **New Data Source** button.
3. In the New Data Source list, click the **From File** option. You may also point to the option.
4. In the From File list, click **Text File**. The Get External Data – Text File dialog box opens. This dialog box is similar to the one you used earlier when importing the Excel spreadsheet.
5. Click the **Browse** button. The File Open dialog box opens.
6. Navigate to the **Access1 > Module** folder, where your Data Files are stored, and then double-click the **Support_AC_2_Patient.txt** file. You return to the Get External Data – Text File dialog box.
7. Click the **Append a copy of the records to the table** option button. The box to the right of this option becomes active. Next, you need to select the table to which you want to add the data.
8. Click the arrow in the box, and then click **Patient**.
9. Click **OK**. The first Import Text Wizard dialog box opens. The dialog box indicates that the data to import is in a delimited format. In a **delimited text file**, fields of data are separated by a character such as a comma or a tab. In this case, the dialog box shows that data is separated by the comma character in the text file.
10. Make sure the **Delimited** option button is selected in the dialog box, and then click **Next**. The second Import Text Wizard dialog box opens. See Figure 2–36.

Figure 2–36 Second Import Text Wizard dialog box

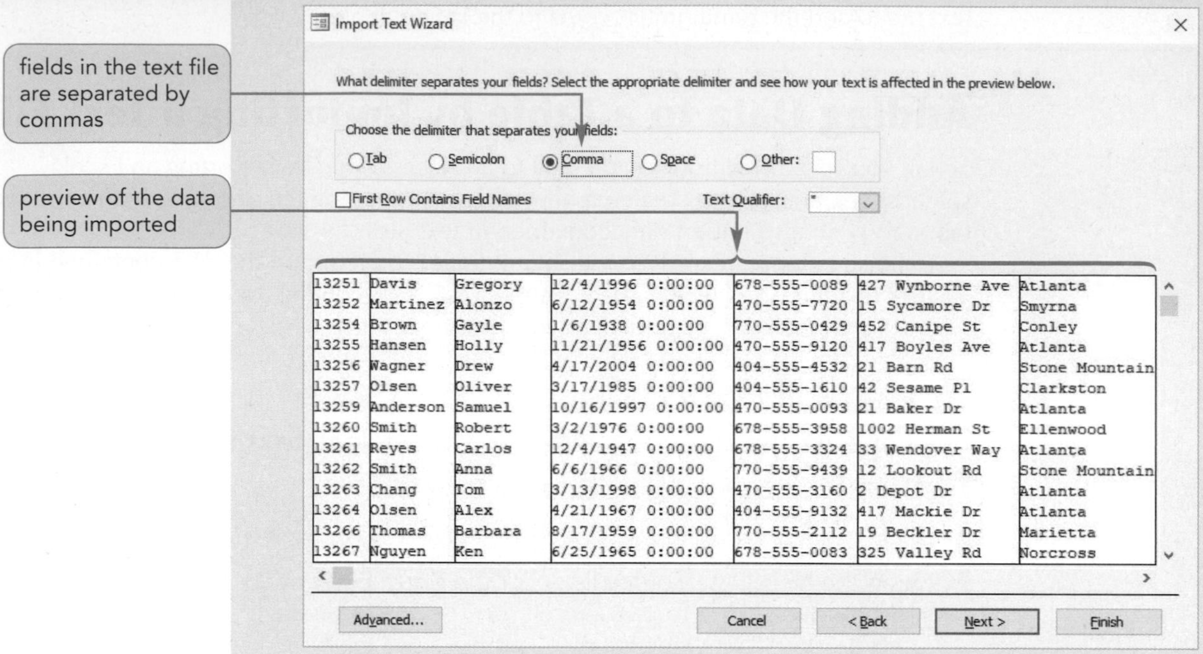
fields in the text file are separated by commas
preview of the data being imported
Import Text Wizard
What delimiter separates your fields? Select the appropriate delimiter and see how your text is affected in the preview below.
Choose the delimiter that separates your fields:
Tab
Semicolon
Comma
Space
Other:
First Row Contains Field Names
Text Qualifier:
13251 Davis Gregory 12/4/1996 0:00:00 678-555-0089 427 Wynborne Ave Atlanta
13252 Martinez Alonzo 6/12/1954 0:00:00 470-555-7720 15 Sycamore Dr Smyrna
13254 Brown Gayle 1/6/1938 0:00:00 770-555-0429 452 Canipe St Conley
13255 Hansen Holly 11/21/1956 0:00:00 470-555-9120 417 Boyles Ave Atlanta
13256 Wagner Drew 4/17/2004 0:00:00 404-555-4532 21 Barn Rd Stone Mountain
13257 Olsen Oliver 3/17/1985 0:00:00 404-555-1610 42 Sesame Pl Clarkston
13259 Anderson Samuel 10/16/1997 0:00:00 470-555-0093 21 Baker Dr Atlanta
13260 Smith Robert 3/2/1976 0:00:00 678-555-3958 1002 Herman St Ellenwood
13261 Reyes Carlos 12/4/1947 0:00:00 678-555-3324 33 Wendover Way Atlanta
13262 Smith Anna 6/6/1966 0:00:00 770-555-9439 12 Lookout Rd Stone Mountain
13263 Chang Tom 3/13/1998 0:00:00 470-555-3160 2 Depot Dr Atlanta
13264 Olsen Alex 4/21/1967 0:00:00 404-555-9132 417 Mackie Dr Atlanta
13266 Thomas Barbara 8/17/1959 0:00:00 770-555-2112 19 Beckler Dr Marietta
13267 Nguyen Ken 6/25/1965 0:00:00 678-555-0083 325 Valley Rd Norcross
Advanced...
Cancel
< Back
Next >
Finish

This dialog box asks you to confirm the delimiter character that separates the fields in the text file you're importing. Access detects that the comma character is used in the Patient text file and selects this option. The bottom area of the dialog box provides a preview of the data you're importing.

11. Make sure the **Comma** option button is selected, and then click **Next**. The third and final Import Text Wizard dialog box opens. The Import to Table box shows that the data will be imported into the Patient table.
12. Click **Finish**, and then click **Close** in the dialog box that opens to close it without saving the import steps.

Donna asks you to open the Patient table in Datasheet view so she can see the results of importing the text file.

To view the Patient table datasheet:

1. Open the Navigation Pane (if necessary), and then double-click **Patient** to open the Patient table in Datasheet view. The Patient table contains a total of 51 records.
2. Close the Navigation Pane, and then resize columns to their best fit, scrolling the table datasheet as necessary, so that all field values are displayed. Scroll back to display the first fields in the table, and then click the first row's **Patient ID** field, if necessary. See Figure 2–37.

Figure 2–37 **Patient table after importing data from the text file**

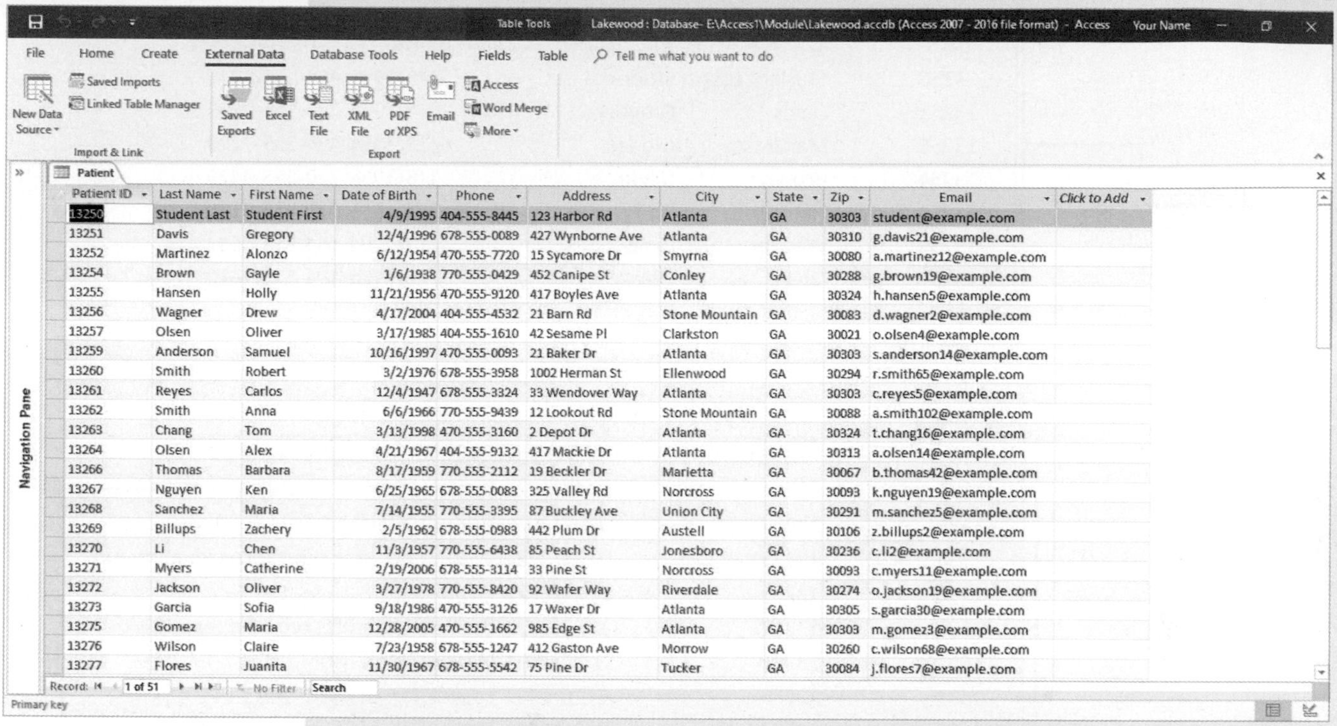

Patient ID	Last Name	First Name	Date of Birth	Phone	Address	City	State	Zip	Email	Click to Add
13250	Student Last	Student First	4/9/1995	404-555-8445	123 Harbor Rd	Atlanta	GA	30303	student@example.com	
13251	Davis	Gregory	12/4/1996	678-555-0089	427 Wynborne Ave	Atlanta	GA	30310	g.davis21@example.com	
13252	Martinez	Alonzo	6/12/1954	470-555-7720	15 Sycamore Dr	Smyrna	GA	30080	a.martinez12@example.com	
13254	Brown	Gayle	1/6/1938	770-555-0429	452 Canipe St	Conley	GA	30288	g.brown19@example.com	
13255	Hansen	Holly	11/21/1956	470-555-9120	417 Boyles Ave	Atlanta	GA	30324	h.hansen5@example.com	
13256	Wagner	Drew	4/17/2004	404-555-4532	21 Barn Rd	Stone Mountain	GA	30083	d.wagner2@example.com	
13257	Olsen	Oliver	3/17/1985	404-555-1610	42 Sesame Pl	Clarkston	GA	30021	o.olsen4@example.com	
13259	Anderson	Samuel	10/16/1997	470-555-0093	21 Baker Dr	Atlanta	GA	30303	s.anderson14@example.com	
13260	Smith	Robert	3/2/1976	678-555-3958	1002 Herman St	Ellenwood	GA	30294	r.smith65@example.com	
13261	Reyes	Carlos	12/4/1947	678-555-3324	33 Wendover Way	Atlanta	GA	30303	c.reyes5@example.com	
13262	Smith	Anna	6/6/1966	770-555-9439	12 Lookout Rd	Stone Mountain	GA	30088	a.smith102@example.com	
13263	Chang	Tom	3/13/1998	470-555-3160	2 Depot Dr	Atlanta	GA	30324	t.chang16@example.com	
13264	Olsen	Alex	4/21/1967	404-555-9132	417 Mackie Dr	Atlanta	GA	30313	a.olsen14@example.com	
13266	Thomas	Barbara	8/17/1959	770-555-2112	19 Beckler Dr	Marietta	GA	30067	b.thomas42@example.com	
13267	Nguyen	Ken	6/25/1965	678-555-0083	325 Valley Rd	Norcross	GA	30093	k.nguyen19@example.com	
13268	Sanchez	Maria	7/14/1955	770-555-3395	87 Buckley Ave	Union City	GA	30291	m.sanchez5@example.com	
13269	Billups	Zachery	2/5/1962	678-555-0983	442 Plum Dr	Austell	GA	30106	z.billups2@example.com	
13270	Li	Chen	11/3/1957	770-555-6438	85 Peach St	Jonesboro	GA	30236	c.li2@example.com	
13271	Myers	Catherine	2/19/2006	678-555-3114	33 Pine St	Norcross	GA	30093	c.myers11@example.com	
13272	Jackson	Oliver	3/27/1978	770-555-8420	92 Wafer Way	Riverdale	GA	30274	o.jackson19@example.com	
13273	Garcia	Sofia	9/18/1986	470-555-3126	17 Waxer Dr	Atlanta	GA	30305	s.garcia30@example.com	
13275	Gomez	Maria	12/28/2005	470-555-1662	985 Edge St	Atlanta	GA	30303	m.gomez3@example.com	
13276	Wilson	Claire	7/23/1958	678-555-1247	412 Gaston Ave	Morrow	GA	30260	c.wilson68@example.com	
13277	Flores	Juanita	11/30/1967	678-555-5542	75 Pine Dr	Tucker	GA	30084	j.flores7@example.com	

3. Save and close the Patient table, and then open the Navigation Pane.

The Lakewood database now contains three tables—Billing, Patient, and Visit—and the tables contain all the necessary records. Your final task is to complete the database design by defining the necessary relationship between its tables.

Defining Table Relationships

One of the most powerful features of a relational database management system is its ability to define relationships between tables. You use a common field to relate one table to another. The process of relating tables is often called performing a **join**. When you join tables that have a common field, you can extract data from them as if they were one larger table. For example, you can join the Patient and Visit tables by using the PatientID field in both tables as the common field. Then you can use a query, form, or report to extract selected data from each table, even though the data is contained in two separate tables, as shown in Figure 2–38. The PatientVisits query shown in Figure 2–38 includes the PatientID, LastName, and FirstName fields from the Patient table, and the VisitDate and Reason fields from the Visit table. The joining of records is based on the common field of PatientID. The Patient and Visit tables have a type of relationship called a one-to-many relationship.

Figure 2–38 One-to-many relationship and sample query

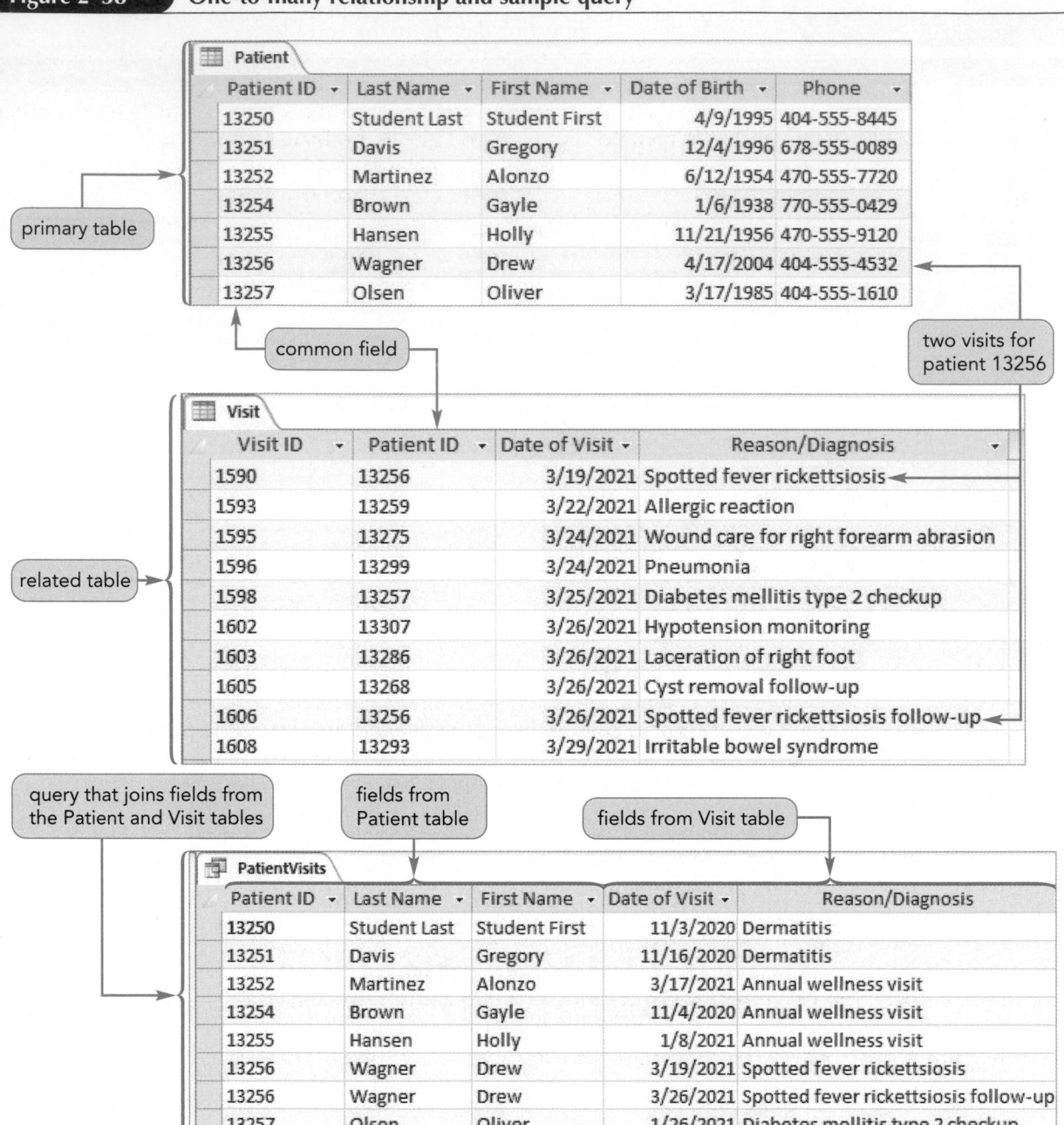

primary table

Patient

Patient ID	Last Name	First Name	Date of Birth	Phone
13250	Student Last	Student First	4/9/1995	404-555-8445
13251	Davis	Gregory	12/4/1996	678-555-0089
13252	Martinez	Alonzo	6/12/1954	470-555-7720
13254	Brown	Gayle	1/6/1938	770-555-0429
13255	Hansen	Holly	11/21/1956	470-555-9120
13256	Wagner	Drew	4/17/2004	404-555-4532
13257	Olsen	Oliver	3/17/1985	404-555-1610

common field

two visits for patient 13256

related table

Visit

Visit ID	Patient ID	Date of Visit	Reason/Diagnosis
1590	13256	3/19/2021	Spotted fever rickettsiosis
1593	13259	3/22/2021	Allergic reaction
1595	13275	3/24/2021	Wound care for right forearm abrasion
1596	13299	3/24/2021	Pneumonia
1598	13257	3/25/2021	Diabetes mellitis type 2 checkup
1602	13307	3/26/2021	Hypotension monitoring
1603	13286	3/26/2021	Laceration of right foot
1605	13268	3/26/2021	Cyst removal follow-up
1606	13256	3/26/2021	Spotted fever rickettsiosis follow-up
1608	13293	3/29/2021	Irritable bowel syndrome

query that joins fields from the Patient and Visit tables

fields from Patient table

fields from Visit table

PatientVisits

Patient ID	Last Name	First Name	Date of Visit	Reason/Diagnosis
13250	Student Last	Student First	11/3/2020	Dermatitis
13251	Davis	Gregory	11/16/2020	Dermatitis
13252	Martinez	Alonzo	3/17/2021	Annual wellness visit
13254	Brown	Gayle	11/4/2020	Annual wellness visit
13255	Hansen	Holly	1/8/2021	Annual wellness visit
13256	Wagner	Drew	3/19/2021	Spotted fever rickettsiosis
13256	Wagner	Drew	3/26/2021	Spotted fever rickettsiosis follow-up
13257	Olsen	Oliver	1/26/2021	Diabetes mellitis type 2 checkup

One-to-Many Relationships

As shown in the Session 2.2 Visual Overview, two tables have a one-to-many relationship when one record in the first table matches zero, one, or many records in the second table, and when one record in the second table matches at most one record in the first table. For example, as shown in Figure 2–38, patient 13256 has two visits in the Visit table. Other patients have one or more visits. Every visit has a single matching patient.

In Access, the two tables that form a relationship are referred to as the primary table and the related table. The primary table is the "one" table in a one-to-many relationship; in Figure 2–38, the Patient table is the primary table because there is only one patient for each visit. The related table is the "many" table; in Figure 2–38, the Visit table is the related table because a patient can have zero, one, or many visits.

Because related data is stored in two tables, inconsistencies between the tables can occur. Referring to Figure 2–38, consider the following three scenarios:

- Donna adds a record to the Visit table for a new patient, Edgar Faust, using Patient ID 13500. She did not first add the new patient's information to the Patient table, so this visit does not have a matching record in the Patient table. The data is inconsistent, and the visit record is considered to be an **orphaned record**.
- In another situation, Donna changes the PatientID in the Patient table for Drew Wagner from 13256 to 13510. Because the Patient table no longer has a patient with the PatientID 13256, this change creates two orphaned records in the Visit table, and the database is inconsistent.
- In a third scenario, Donna deletes the record for Drew Wagner, Patient 13256, from the Patient table because this patient has moved and no longer receives care from Lakewood. The database is again inconsistent; two records for Patient 13256 in the Visit table have no matching record in the Patient table.

You can avoid these types of problems and avoid having inconsistent data in your database by specifying referential integrity between tables when you define their relationships.

Referential Integrity

Referential integrity is a set of rules that Access enforces to maintain consistency between related tables when you update data in a database. Specifically, the referential integrity rules are as follows:

- When you add a record to a related table, a matching record must already exist in the primary table, thereby preventing the possibility of orphaned records.
- If you attempt to change the value of the primary key in the primary table, Access prevents this change if matching records exist in a related table. However, if you choose the **Cascade Update Related Fields option**, Access permits the change in value to the primary key and changes the appropriate foreign key values in the related table, thereby eliminating the possibility of inconsistent data.
- When you attempt to delete a record in the primary table, Access prevents the deletion if matching records exist in a related table. However, if you choose the **Cascade Delete Related Records option**, Access deletes the record in the primary table and also deletes all records in related tables that have matching foreign key values.

INSIGHT

Understanding the Cascade Delete Related Records Option

Although using the Cascade Delete Related Records option has some advantages for enforcing referential integrity, it presents risks as well. You should rarely select the Cascade Delete Related Records option because doing so might cause you to inadvertently delete records you did not intend to delete. It is best to use other methods that give you more control over deleting records.

Defining a Relationship Between Two Tables

When two tables have a common field, you can define a relationship between them in the Relationships window, as shown in the Session 2.2 Visual Overview. Next, you'll define a one-to-many relationship between the Patient and Visit tables, with Patient as the primary table and Visit as the related table, and with PatientID as the common field (the primary key in the Patient table and the foreign key in the Visit table). You'll also define a one-to-many relationship between the Visit and Billing tables, with Visit being the primary table and Billing being the related table, and with VisitID as the common field (the primary key in the Visit table and a foreign key in the Billing table).

To define the one-to-many relationship between the Patient and Visit tables:

1. On the ribbon, click the **Database Tools** tab.
2. In the Relationships group, click the **Relationships** button to display the Relationships window and then click the **Show Table** button to open the Show Table dialog box. See Figure 2–39.

Figure 2–39 Show Table dialog box

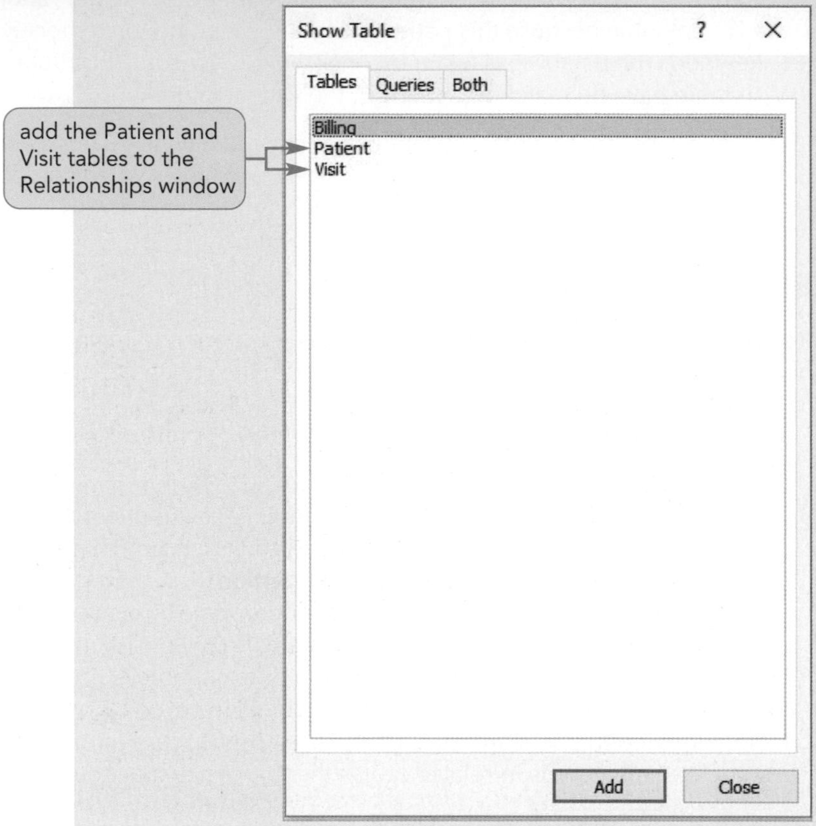
add the Patient and Visit tables to the Relationships window
Show Table
?
Tables
Queries
Both
Billing
Patient
Visit
Add
Close

You must add each table participating in a relationship to the Relationships window. Because the Patient table is the primary table in the relationship, you'll add it first.

TIP

You can also double-click a table in the Show Table dialog box to add it to the Relationships window.

3. Click **Patient**, and then click the **Add** button. The Patient table's field list is added to the Relationships window.
4. Click **Visit**, and then click the **Add** button. The Visit table's field list is added to the Relationships window.
5. Click the **Close** button in the Show Table dialog box to close it.

   So that you can view all the fields and complete field names, you'll resize the Patient table field list.

6. Position the pointer on the bottom border of the Patient table field list until it changes to a two-headed arrow ⇕, and then drag the bottom of the Patient table field list to lengthen it until the vertical scroll bar disappears and all the fields are visible.

   To form the relationship between the two tables, you drag the common PatientID field from the primary table to the related table. Access opens the Edit Relationships dialog box, in which you select the relationship options for the two tables.

7. Click **PatientID** in the Patient field list, and then drag it to **PatientID** in the Visit field list. When you release the mouse button, the Edit Relationships dialog box opens. See Figure 2–40.

Figure 2–40 Edit Relationships dialog box

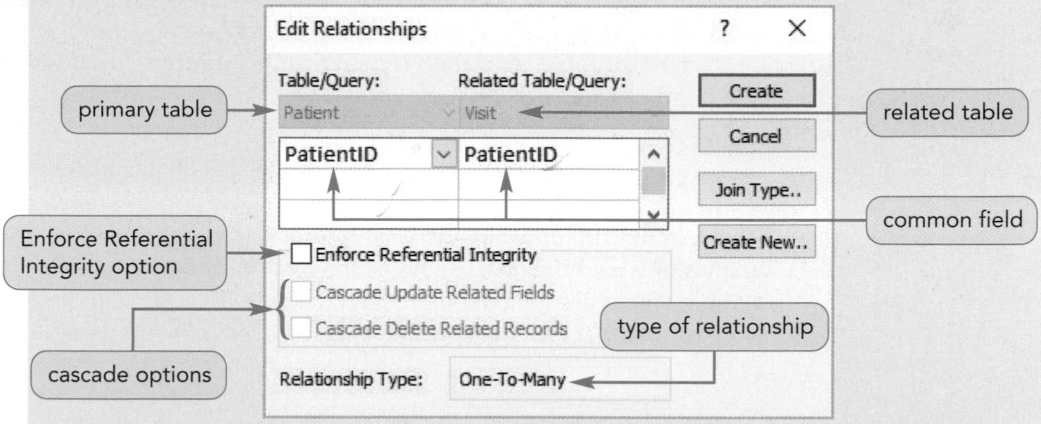
Edit Relationships
Table/Query:
Related Table/Query:
Patient
Visit
PatientID
PatientID
Create
Cancel
Join Type..
Create New..
Enforce Referential Integrity
Cascade Update Related Fields
Cascade Delete Related Records
Relationship Type:
One-To-Many
primary table
related table
common field
Enforce Referential Integrity option
cascade options
type of relationship

The primary table, related table, common field, and relationship type (One-To-Many) appear in the dialog box. Access correctly identifies the "One" side of the relationship and places the primary table Patient in the Table/Query section of the dialog box; similarly, Access correctly identifies the "Many" side of the relationship and places the related table Visit in the Related Table/Query section of the dialog box.

8. Click the **Enforce Referential Integrity** check box. The two cascade options become available. If you select the Cascade Update Related Fields option, Access will update the appropriate foreign key values in the related table when you change a primary key value in the primary table. You will *not* select the Cascade Delete Related Records option because doing so could cause you to delete records that you do not want to delete; this option is rarely selected.
9. Click the **Cascade Update Related Fields** check box.
10. Click the **Create** button to define the one-to-many relationship between the two tables and to close the dialog box. The completed relationship appears in the Relationships window, with the join line connecting the common field of PatientID in each table. See Figure 2–41.

Figure 2–41 Defined relationship in the Relationships window

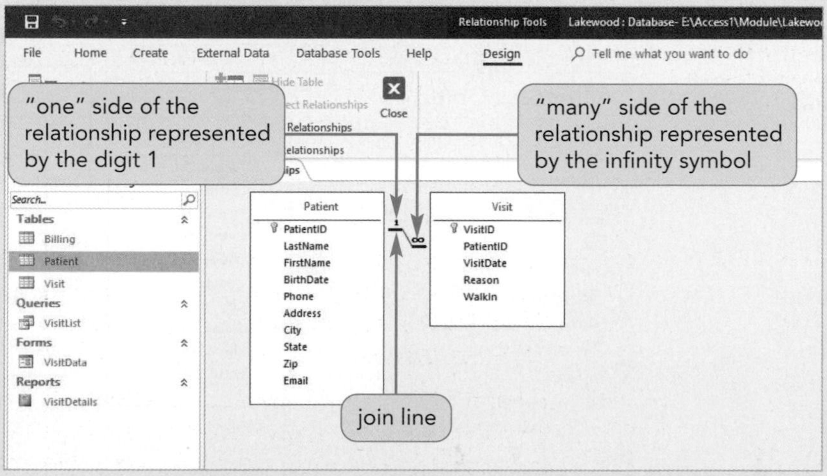
"one" side of the relationship represented by the digit 1
"many" side of the relationship represented by the infinity symbol
join line
File
Home
Create
External Data
Database Tools
Help
Design
Tell me what you want to do
Close
Patient
PatientID
LastName
FirstName
BirthDate
Phone
Address
City
State
Zip
Email
Visit
VisitID
PatientID
VisitDate
Reason
WalkIn
Tables
Billing
Patient
Visit
Queries
VisitList
Forms
VisitData
Reports
VisitDetails

Trouble? If a dialog box opens indicating a problem that prevents you from creating the relationship, you most likely made a typing error when entering the two records in the Patient table. If so, click OK in the dialog box and then click Cancel in the Edit Relationships dialog box. Refer back to the earlier steps instructing you to enter the two records in the Patient table and carefully compare your entries with those shown in the text, especially the PatientID field values. Make any necessary corrections to the data in the Patient table, and then repeat Steps 7 through 10. If you still receive an error message, ask your instructor for assistance.

The next step is to define the one-to-many relationship between the Visit and Billing tables. In this relationship, Visit is the primary ("one") table because there is at most one visit for each invoice. Billing is the related ("many") table because zero, one, or many invoices are generated for each patient visit. For example, some visits require lab work or pharmacy charges, which is invoiced separately.

To define the relationship between the Visit and Billing tables:

1. On the Relationship Tools Design tab, in the Relationships group, click the **Show Table** button to open the Show Table dialog box.
2. Click **Billing** on the Tables tab, click the **Add** button, and then click the **Close** button to close the Show Table dialog box. The Billing table's field list appears in the Relationships window to the right of the Visit table's field list.
3. Click and drag the **VisitID** field in the Visit field list to the **VisitID** field in the Billing field list. The Edit Relationships dialog box opens.
4. In the Edit Relationships dialog box, click the **Enforce Referential Integrity** check box, click the **Cascade Update Related Fields** check box, and then click the **Create** button to define the one-to-many relationship between the two tables and to close the dialog box. The completed relationships for the Lakewood database appear in the Relationships window. See Figure 2–42.

TIP

You can also use the mouse to drag a table from the Navigation Pane to add it to the Relationships window.

Figure 2–42 Two relationships defined

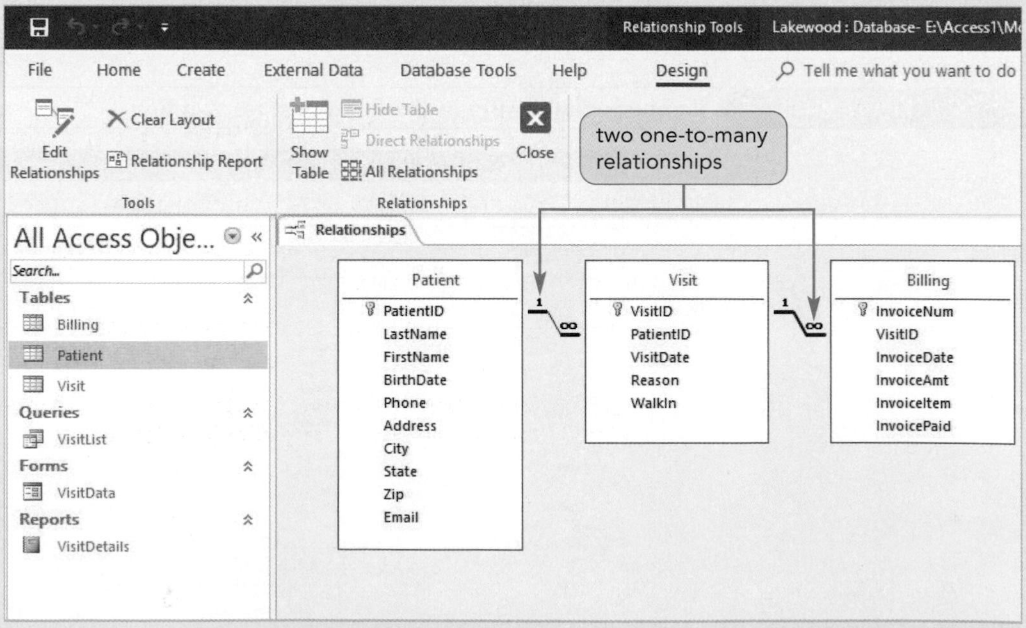
Relationship Tools
Lakewood : Database- E:\Access1\M
File
Home
Create
External Data
Database Tools
Help
Design
Tell me what you want to do
Edit Relationships
Clear Layout
Relationship Report
Tools
Show Table
Hide Table
Direct Relationships
All Relationships
Relationships
Close
two one-to-many relationships
All Access Obje...
Search...
Tables
Billing
Patient
Visit
Queries
VisitList
Forms
VisitData
Reports
VisitDetails
Relationships
Patient
PatientID
LastName
FirstName
BirthDate
Phone
Address
City
State
Zip
Email
Visit
VisitID
PatientID
VisitDate
Reason
WalkIn
Billing
InvoiceNum
VisitID
InvoiceDate
InvoiceAmt
InvoiceItem
InvoicePaid

5. On the Quick Access Toolbar, click the **Save** button to save the layout in the Relationships window.
6. On the Relationship Tools Design tab, in the Relationships group, click the **Close** button to close the Relationships window.
7. sam Compact and repair the Lakewood database, and then close the database.

PROSKILLS

Problem Solving: Creating a Larger Database

The Lakewood database is a relatively small database containing only a few tables, and the data and the reports you will generate from it are fairly simple. A larger database would most likely have many more tables and different types of relationships that can be quite complex. When creating a large database, follow this standard process:

- Consult people who will be using the data to gain an understanding of how it will be used. Gather sample reports and representative data if possible.
- Plan the tables, fields, data types, other properties, and the relationships between the tables.
- Create the tables and define the relationships between them.
- Populate the tables with sample data.
- Design some queries, forms, and reports that will be needed, and then test them.
- Modify the database structure, if necessary, based on the results of your tests.
- Enter the actual data into the database tables.

Testing is critical at every stage of creating a database. Once the database is finalized and implemented, it's not actually finished. The design of a database evolves as new functionality is required and as the data that is gathered changes.

REVIEW

Session 2.2 Quick Check

1. What is the keyboard shortcut for inserting the value from the same field in the previous record into the current record?
2. _________ data is a process that allows you to copy the data from a source without having to open the source file.
3. The _________ gallery allows you to add a group of related fields to a table at the same time, rather than adding each field to the table individually.
4. What is the effect of deleting a field from a table structure?
5. A(n) _________ text file is one in which fields of data are separated by a character such as a comma or a tab.
6. The _________ is the "one" table in a one-to-many relationship, and the _________ is the "many" table in the relationship.
7. _________ is a set of rules that Access enforces to maintain consistency between related tables when you update data in a database.

PRACTICE

Review Assignments

Data File needed for the Review Assignments: Vendor.accdb (*cont. from Module 1*) and Support_AC_2_Products.xlsx

In addition to tracking information about the vendors Lakewood Community Health Services works with, Donna also wants to track information about their products and services. First, Donna asks you to modify the necessary properties in the Supplier table in the Vendor database. Afterwards, Donna wants you to modify the structure and properties of the Product table in the Vendor database. Finally, Donna would like you to create the relationship between the tables. Complete the following:

1. Open the **Vendor** database you created in the previous module.
2. Open the **Supplier** table in Design view, and set the field properties shown in Figure 2–43.

Figure 2–43 Field properties for the Supplier table

Field Name	Data Type	Description	Field Size	Other
SupplierID	Short Text	Primary key	6	Caption = Supplier ID
Company	Short Text		50	
Category	Short Text		15	
Address	Short Text		35	
City	Short Text		25	
State	Short Text		2	
Zip	Short Text		10	
Phone	Short Text		14	Caption = Contact Phone
ContactFirst	Short Text		20	Caption = Contact First Name
ContactLast	Short Text		25	Caption = Contact Last Name
InitialContact	Date/Time			Format = Short Date
				Caption = Initial Contact

3. Save the Supplier table. Click the **Yes** button when a message appears, indicating some data might be lost. Switch to Datasheet view and resize columns, as necessary, to their best fit. Then save and close the Supplier table.
4. Open the **Product** table in Design view, and then set the field properties as shown in Figure 2–44.

Figure 2–44 Design for the Product table

Field Name	Data Type	Description	Field Size	Other
ProductID	Short Text	Primary key	5	Caption = Product ID
SupplierID	Short Text	Foreign key	6	Caption = Supplier ID
ProductName	Short Text		75	Caption = Product Name
Price	Currency			Format = Standard
				Decimal Places = 2
TempControl	Yes/No			Caption = Temp Controlled?
Sterile	Yes/No			Caption = Sterile?
Units	Number		Integer	Decimal Places = 0
				Caption = Units/Case
				Default Value = [no entry]

5. Modify the Product table structure by adding a new field between the Price and TempControl fields. Name the new field **Weight** (data type: **Number**; field size: **Single**; Decimal Places: **2**; Caption: **Weight in Lbs**; Default Value: [no entry]). Move the **Units** field between the Price and Weight fields.
6. In Datasheet view, resize the columns so all column headings are completely visible and then save the changes to the Product table.
7. Enter the records shown in Figure 2–45 in the Product table. Resize all datasheet columns to their best fit again. When finished, save and close the Product table.

Figure 2–45 Records for the Product table

Product ID	Supplier ID	Product Name	Price	Units/Case	Weight in Lbs	Temp Controlled?	Sterile?
TH930	GON470	Digital thermometer	35.00	1	1	Yes	No
EG397	TUR005	Non-latex exam gloves	5.50	100	2	No	No

8. Use the Import Spreadsheet Wizard to add data to the Product table. The data you need to import is contained in the Support_AC_2_Products.xlsx workbook, which is an Excel file located in the Access1 > Review folder provided with your Data Files.
   a. Specify the Support_AC_2_Products.xlsx workbook as the source of the data.
   b. Select the option for appending the data.
   c. Select Product as the table.
   d. In the Import Spreadsheet Wizard dialog boxes, make sure Access confirms that the first row contains column headings, and import to the Product table. Do not save the import steps.
9. Open the **Product** table in Datasheet view, and resize columns to their best fit, as necessary. Then save and close the Product table.
10. Define a one-to-many relationship between the primary Supplier table and the related Product table. Resize the table field lists so that all field names are visible. Select the referential integrity option and the cascade updates option for the relationship.
11. Save the changes to the Relationships window and close it, compact and repair the Vendor database, and then close the database.

APPLY

Case Problem 1

Data Files needed for this Case Problem: Career.accdb *(cont. from Module 1)*, **Support_AC_2_Course.txt, and Support_AC_2_Registration.xlsx**

Great Giraffe Jeremiah wants you to further refine the design of the existing tables (Student and Registration) in the Career database by modifying the field properties. Jeremiah would also like you to populate the Course and Registration tables. Complete the following:

1. Open the **Career** database you created in the previous module.
2. Open the **Student** table in Design view, and set the field properties shown in Figure 2–46.

Figure 2–46 **Field properties for the Student table**

Field Name	Data Type	Description	Field Size	Other
StudentID	Short Text	Primary key	7	Caption = Student ID
FirstName	Short Text		20	Caption = First Name
LastName	Short Text		25	Caption = Last Name
Address	Short Text		35	
City	Short Text		25	
State	Short Text		2	
Zip	Short Text		10	
Phone	Short Text		14	
Email	Short Text		50	
BirthDate	Date/Time			Format = Short Date Caption = Birth Date
Assessment	Yes/No			Default Value = No

3. Save the Student table. Click the **Yes** button when a message appears, indicating some data might be lost. Switch to Datasheet view and resize columns, as necessary, to their best fit. Then save and close the Student table.
4. Open the **Registration** table in Design view, and set the field properties as shown in the Figure 2–47.

Figure 2–47 **Field properties for the Registration table**

Field Name	Data Type	Description	Field Size	Other
SignupID	Short Text	Primary key	10	Caption = Signup ID
StudentID	Short Text	Foreign key	7	Caption = Student ID
InstanceID	Short Text	Foreign key	10	Caption = Instance ID
TotalCost	Currency			Format = Currency Decimal Places = 2 Caption = Total Cost Default Value = 0
BalanceDue	Currency			Format = Currency Decimal Places = 2 Caption = Balance Due Default Value = 0
PaymentPlan	Yes/No			Caption = Payment Plan Default Value = No

5. Switch to Datasheet view and resize columns, as necessary, to their best fit. Then save and close the Registration table.
6. Use the Import Spreadsheet Wizard to add data to the Registration table. The data you need to import is contained in the Support_AC_2_Registration.xlsx workbook, which is an Excel file located in the Access1 > Case1 folder provided with your Data Files.
   a. Specify the Support_AC_2_Registration.xlsx workbook as the source of the data.
   b. Select the option for appending the data.
   c. Select Registration as the table.
   d. In the Import Spreadsheet Wizard dialog boxes, make sure Access confirms that the first row contains column headings, and import to the Registration table. Do not save the import steps.

7. Open the **Registration** table in Datasheet view and resize columns to their best fit, as necessary. Then save and close the Registration table.
8. Create a new table in Design view, using the table design shown in Figure 2–48.

Figure 2–48 Field properties for the Course table

Field Name	Data Type	Description	Field Size	Other
InstanceID	Short Text	Primary key	10	Caption = Instance ID
StartDate	Date/Time	Date course begins		Format = Short Date Caption = Start Date
EndDate	Date/Time	Date course ends		Format = Short Date Caption = End Date
HoursPerWeek	Number		Integer	Decimal Places = 0 Caption = Hours Per Week Default Value = 40
Cost	Currency			Format = Currency Decimal Places = 0

9. Specify **InstanceID** as the primary key, and then save the table as **Course**.
10. Insert a new field named **Title** between the InstanceID and StartDate fields. The Title field is of the **Short Text** data type and has a field size of **25**. Save the changes to the Course table and close the table.
11. Use the Import Text File Wizard to add data to the Course table. The data you need to import is contained in the Support_AC_2_Course.txt text file, which is located in the Access1 > Case1 folder provided with your Data Files.
    a. Specify the Support_AC_2_Course.txt text file as the source of the data.
    b. Select the option for appending the data.
    c. Select Course as the table.
    d. In the Import Text File Wizard dialog boxes, choose the options to import delimited data, to use a comma delimiter, and to import the data into the Course table. Do not save the import steps.
12. Open the **Course** table in Datasheet view and resize columns to their best fit, as necessary. Then save and close the Course table.
13. Define a one-to-many relationship between the primary Student table and the related Registration table. Resize the Student table field list so that all field names are visible. Select the referential integrity option and the cascade updates option for this relationship.
14. Define a one-to-many relationship between the primary Course table and the related Registration table. Select the referential integrity option and the cascade updates option for this relationship. (*Hint*: The Registration table is positioned between the Student and Courses tables in the Relationships window.)
15. Save the changes to the Relationships window and close it, compact and repair the Career database, and then close the database.

CHALLENGE

Case Problem 2

Data Files needed for this Case Problem: DrainAdopter.accdb *(cont. from Module 1)*, **Support_AC_2_Drain.xlsx, and Support_AC_2_Supplies.xlsx**

Drain Adopter Tandrea wants you to further refine the design of the existing tables (Drain and Volunteer) in the DrainAdopter database by modifying the existing properties. Tandrea asks you to populate the Drain table. Finally, Tandrea would like you to create and populate a new table that will contain information on supplies needed for projects. Complete the following:

1. Open the **DrainAdopter** database you created in the previous module.
2. Open the **Volunteer** table in Design view, and set the field properties as shown in Figure 2–49.

Figure 2–49 Field properties for the Volunteer table

Field Name	Data Type	Description	Field Size	Other
VolunteerID	Short Text	Primary key	7	Caption = Volunteer ID
FirstName	Short Text		20	Caption = First Name
LastName	Short Text		25	Caption = Last Name
Street	Short Text		35	
City	Short Text		25	
State	Short Text		2	
Zip	Short Text		10	
Phone	Short Text		14	
Email	Short Text		50	
SignupDate	Date/Time			Format = Short Date Caption = Signup Date
Trained	Yes/No			Default Value = No

3. Save and close the Volunteer table. Click the Yes button when a message appears, indicating some data might be lost.
4. Open the **Drain** table in Design view, and set the field properties shown in Figure 2–50.

Figure 2–50 Field properties for the Drain table

Field Name	Data Type	Description	Field Size	Other
DrainID	Short Text	Primary key	7	Caption = Drain ID
MainStreet	Short Text		25	Caption = Main Street
CrossStreet	Short Text		20	Caption = Cross Street
Direction	Short Text		2	
VolunteerID	Short Text	Foreign key	7	Caption = Volunteer ID
MaintReq	Yes/No			Caption = Maint Req Default Value = No

5. Switch to Datasheet view and resize columns, as necessary, to their best fit. Then save and close the Drain table.

6. Use the Import Spreadsheet Wizard to add data to the Drain table. The data you need to import is contained in the Support_AC_2_Drain.xslx workbook, which is an Excel file located in the Access1 > Case2 folder provided with your Data Files.
   a. Specify the Support_AC_2_Drain.xslx workbook as the source of the data.
   b. Select the option for appending the data.
   c. Select Drain as the table.
   d. In the Import Spreadsheet Wizard dialog boxes, make sure Access confirms that the first row contains column headings, and import to the Drain table. Do not save the import steps.
7. Open the **Drain** table in Datasheet view and resize columns to their best fit, as necessary. Then save and close the Drain table.

Explore 8. Use the Import Spreadsheet Wizard to create a new table in the DrainAdopter database. As the source of the data, specify the Support_AC_2_Supplies.xlsx workbook, which is located in the Access1 > Case2 folder provided with your Data Files. Select the option to import the source data into a new table in the database.

Explore 9. Complete the Import Spreadsheet Wizard dialog boxes as follows:
   a. Select Support_AC_2_Supplies.xlsx as the worksheet you want to import.
   b. Specify that the first row contains column headings.
   c. Accept the field options suggested by the wizard, and do not skip any fields.
   d. Choose SupplyID as your primary key.
   e. Import the data to a table named Supply, and do not save the import steps.

10. Open the **Supply** table in Design view, and then modify the table so it matches the design shown in Figure 2–51, including changes to data types and field properties. For the Short Text fields, delete any formats specified in the Format property boxes.

Figure 2–51 **Field properties for the Supply table**

Field Name	Data Type	Description	Field Size	Other
SupplyID	Short Text	Primary key	12	Caption = Supply ID
Description	Short Text		30	
Cost	Currency			Format = Currency
				Decimal Places = 2
NumberOnHand	Number		Double	Caption = Number On Hand
				Format = Standard
				Decimal Places = 2
				Default Value = 0
LastOrderDate	Date/Time			Format = Short Date
				Caption = Last Order Date

11. Save your changes to the Supply table design, click Yes for the message about lost data, and then switch to Datasheet view.
12. Resize the columns in the Supply datasheet to their best fit. Then save the Supply table.

Explore 13. Tandrea realizes that the values in the NumberOnHand column would never need two decimal places. Make this field the current field in the datasheet. Then, on the Table Tools Fields tab, in the Formatting group, use the Decrease Decimals button to remove the two decimal places and the period from these values. Switch back to Design view, and note that the Decimal Places property for the NumberOnHand field is now set to 0.

14. Save and close the Supply table.
15. Define a one-to-many relationship between the primary Volunteer table and the related Drain table. Select the referential integrity option and the cascade updates option for this relationship.
16. Save the changes to the Relationships window and close it, compact and repair the DrainAdopter database, and then close the database.

MODULE 3

Maintaining and Querying a Database

Updating and Retrieving Information About Patients, Visits, and Invoices

ACCESS

OBJECTIVES

Session 3.1
- Find, modify, and delete records in a table
- Hide and unhide fields in a datasheet
- Work in the Query window in Design view
- Create, run, and save queries
- Update data using a query datasheet
- Create a query based on multiple tables
- Sort data in a query
- Filter data in a query

Session 3.2
- Specify an exact match condition in a query
- Use a comparison operator in a query to match a range of values
- Use the And and Or logical operators in queries
- Change the font size and alternate row color in a datasheet
- Create and format a calculated field in a query
- Perform calculations in a query using aggregate functions and record group calculations
- Change the display of database objects in the Navigation Pane

Case | ***Lakewood Community Health Services***

At a recent meeting, Donna Taylor and her staff discussed the importance of maintaining accurate information about the clinic's patients, visits, and invoices, and regularly monitoring the business activities of Lakewood Community Health Services. For example, Taylor Bailey, Donna's assistant, needs to make sure she has up-to-date contact information, such as phone numbers and email addresses, for all the clinic's patients. The office staff also must monitor billing activity to ensure that invoices are paid on time and in full. In addition, the staff handles marketing efforts for the clinic and tracks services provided to develop new strategies for promoting these services. Donna is also interested in analyzing other aspects of the business related to patient visits and finances. You can satisfy all these informational needs for Lakewood Community Health Services by updating data in the Lakewood database and by creating and using queries that retrieve information from the database.

STARTING DATA FILES

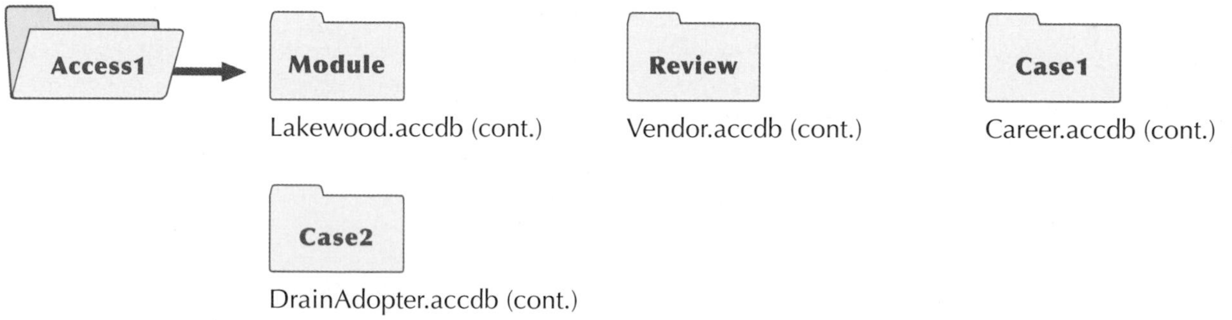

Access1
Module
Lakewood.accdb (cont.)
Review
Vendor.accdb (cont.)
Case1
Career.accdb (cont.)
Case2
DrainAdopter.accdb (cont.)

Session 3.1 Visual Overview:

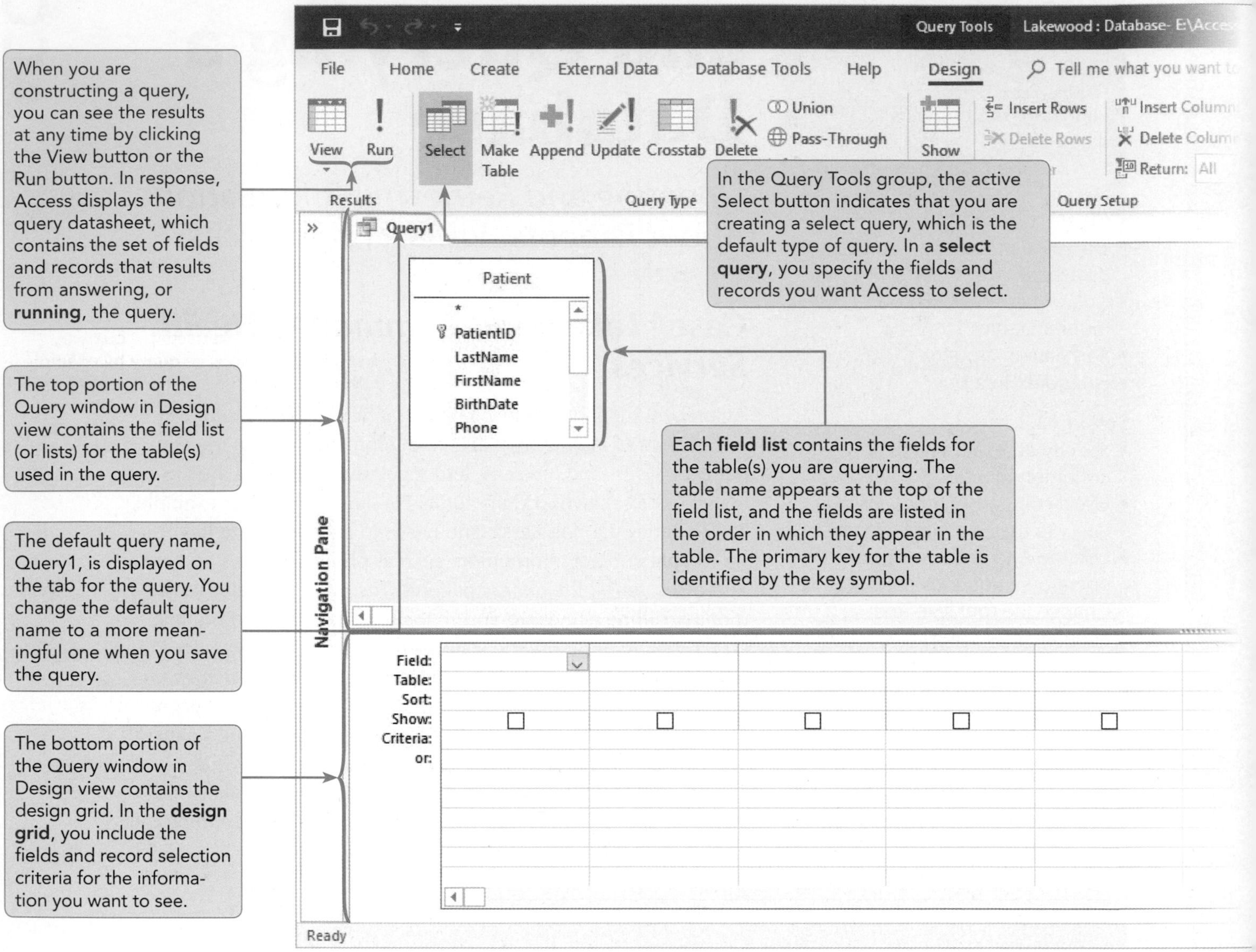
Query Tools
Lakewood : Database- E:\Acce
File
Home
Create
External Data
Database Tools
Help
Design
Tell me what you want
View
Run
Select
Make Table
Append
Update
Crosstab
Delete
Union
Pass-Through
Show
Insert Rows
Delete Rows
Insert Column
Delete Column
Return: All
Results
Query Type
Query Setup
Query1
Patient
*
PatientID
LastName
FirstName
BirthDate
Phone
Navigation Pane
Field:
Table:
Sort:
Show:
Criteria:
or:
Ready
When you are constructing a query, you can see the results at any time by clicking the View button or the Run button. In response, Access displays the query datasheet, which contains the set of fields and records that results from answering, or **running**, the query.
The top portion of the Query window in Design view contains the field list (or lists) for the table(s) used in the query.
The default query name, Query1, is displayed on the tab for the query. You change the default query name to a more meaningful one when you save the query.
The bottom portion of the Query window in Design view contains the design grid. In the **design grid**, you include the fields and record selection criteria for the information you want to see.
In the Query Tools group, the active Select button indicates that you are creating a select query, which is the default type of query. In a **select query**, you specify the fields and records you want Access to select.
Each **field list** contains the fields for the table(s) you are querying. The table name appears at the top of the field list, and the fields are listed in the order in which they appear in the table. The primary key for the table is identified by the key symbol.

Query Window in Design View

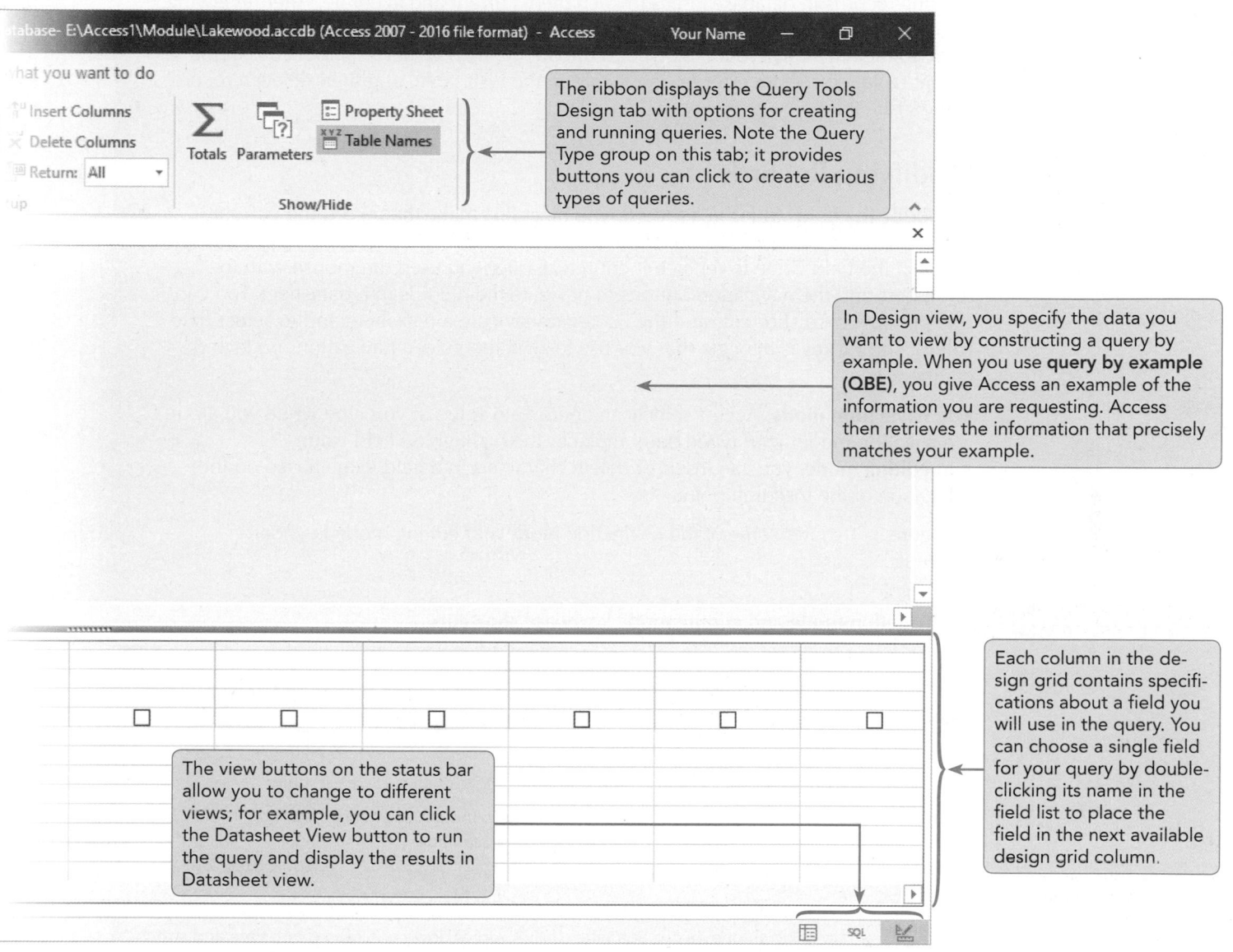

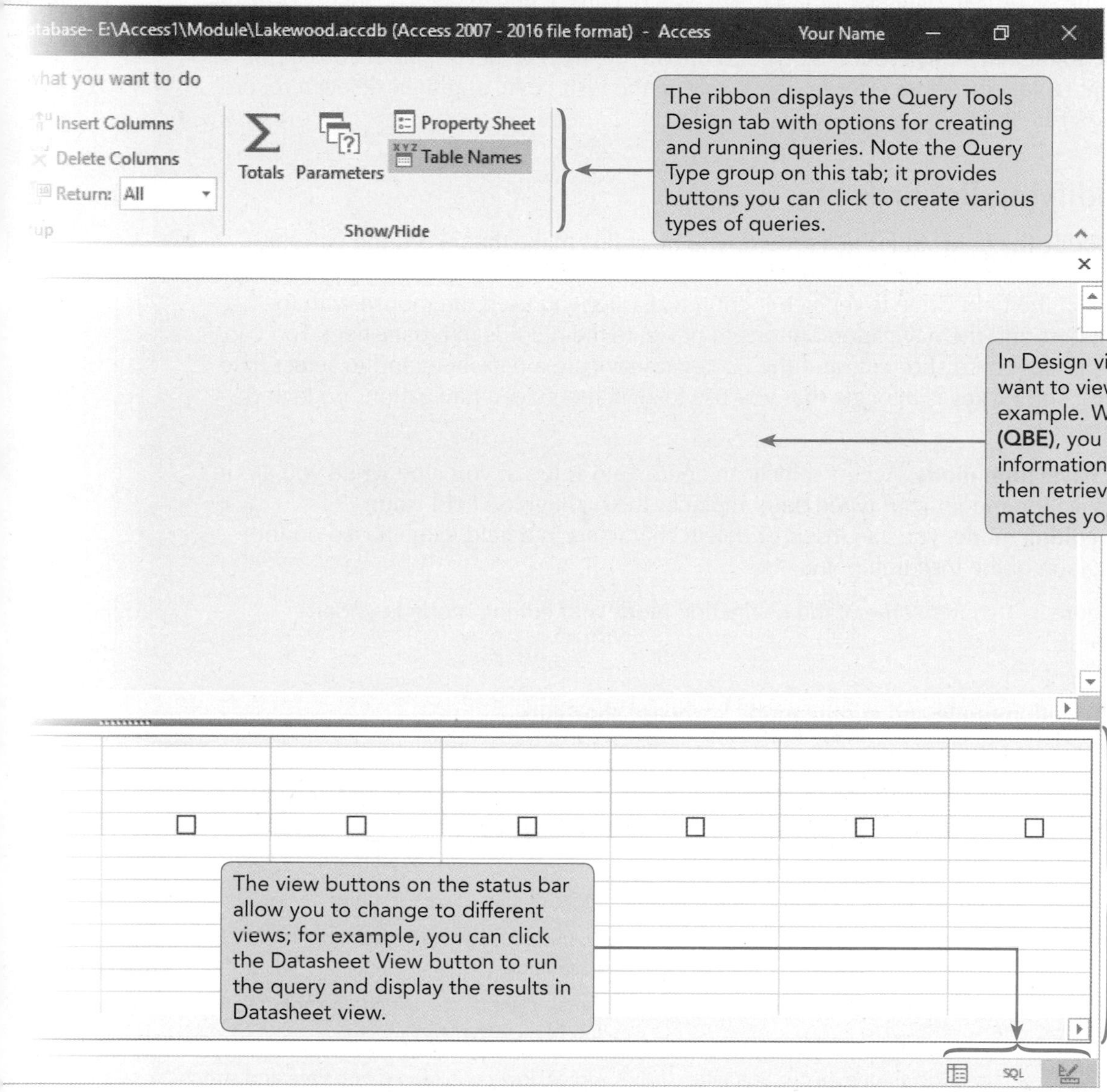
E:\Access1\Module\Lakewood.accdb (Access 2007 - 2016 file format) - Access
Your Name
Insert Columns
Delete Columns
Return: All
Totals
Parameters
Property Sheet
Table Names
Show/Hide
SQL

The ribbon displays the Query Tools Design tab with options for creating and running queries. Note the Query Type group on this tab; it provides buttons you can click to create various types of queries.

In Design view, you specify the data you want to view by constructing a query by example. When you use **query by example (QBE)**, you give Access an example of the information you are requesting. Access then retrieves the information that precisely matches your example.

Each column in the design grid contains specifications about a field you will use in the query. You can choose a single field for your query by double-clicking its name in the field list to place the field in the next available design grid column.

The view buttons on the status bar allow you to change to different views; for example, you can click the Datasheet View button to run the query and display the results in Datasheet view.

Updating a Database

Updating, or **maintaining**, a database is the process of adding, modifying, and deleting records in database tables to keep them current and accurate. After reviewing the data in the Lakewood database, Taylor identified some changes that need to be made to the data. She would like you to update the field values in one record in the Patient table, correct an error in one record in the Visit table, and then delete a record in the Visit table.

Modifying Records

To modify the field values in a record, you must first make the record the current record. Then you position the insertion point in the field value to make minor changes or select the field value to replace it entirely. Earlier you used the mouse with the scroll bars and the navigation buttons to navigate the records in a datasheet. You can also use keyboard shortcuts and the F2 key to navigate a datasheet and to select field values. The **F2 key** is a toggle that you use to switch between navigation mode and editing mode.

- In **navigation mode**, Access selects an entire field value. If you type while you are in navigation mode, your typed entry replaces the highlighted field value.
- In **editing mode**, you can insert or delete characters in a field value based on the location of the insertion point.

Figure 3–1 shows some of the navigation mode and editing mode keyboard shortcuts.

Figure 3–1 Navigation mode and editing mode keyboard shortcuts

Press	To Move the Selection in Navigation Mode	To Move the Insertion Point in Editing Mode
←	Left one field value at a time	Left one character at a time
→	Right one field value at a time	Right one character at a time
Home	Left to the first field value in the record	To the left of the first character in the field value
End	Right to the last field value in the record	To the right of the last character in the field value
↑ or ↓	Up or down one record at a time	Up or down one record at a time and switch to navigation mode
Tab or Enter	Right one field value at a time	Right one field value at a time and switch to navigation mode
Ctrl + Home	To the first field value in the first record	To the left of the first character in the field value
Ctrl + End	To the last field value in the last record	To the right of the last character in the field value

The Patient table record Taylor wants you to change is for 13309. This patient recently moved to another location in Atlanta and his zip code also changed, so you need to update the Patient table record with the new street address and zip code.

To open the Patient table in the Lakewood database:

1. Start Access and open the Lakewood database you created and worked with earlier.

   Trouble? If the security warning is displayed below the ribbon, click the Enable Content button.

2. Open the **Patient** table in Datasheet view.

The Patient table contains many fields. Sometimes, when updating data in a table, it can be helpful to remove the display of some fields on the screen.

Hiding and Unhiding Fields

> **TIP**
> Hiding a field removes it from the datasheet display only; the field and its contents are still part of the table.

When you are viewing a table or query datasheet in Datasheet view, you might want to temporarily remove certain fields from the displayed datasheet, making it easier to focus on the data you're interested in viewing. The **Hide Fields** command allows you to remove the display of one or more fields, and the **Unhide Fields** command allows you to redisplay any hidden fields.

To make it easier to modify the patient record, you'll first hide a couple of fields in the Patient table.

To hide fields in the Patient table and modify the patient record:

1. Right-click the **Date of Birth** field name to display the shortcut menu, and then click **Hide Fields**. The Date of Birth column is removed from the datasheet display.
2. Right-click the **Phone** field name, and then click **Hide Fields** on the shortcut menu. The Phone column is removed from the datasheet display.

   With the fields hidden, you can now update the patient record. The record you need to modify is near the end of the table and has a PatientID field value of 13309.

3. Scroll the datasheet until you see the last record in the table.
4. Click the PatientID field value **13309**, for Jose Rodriguez. The insertion point appears within the field value, indicating you are in editing mode.
5. Press **TAB** to move to the Last Name field value, Rodriguez. The field value is selected, indicating you are in navigation mode.
6. Press **TAB** two times to move to the Address field and select its field value, type **42 Ridge Rd**, and then press **TAB** three times to move to the Zip field.
7. Type **30305**, and then press **TAB** twice to move to the PatientID field of the next record. The changes to the record are complete. See Figure 3–2.

Figure 3–2 Table after changing field values in a record

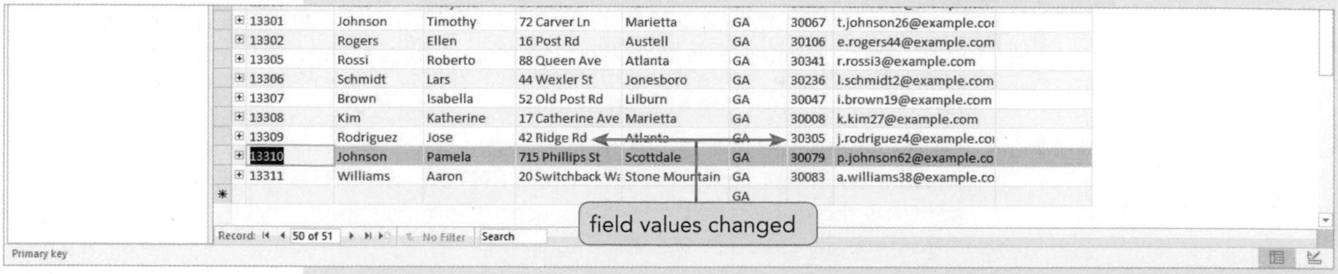
13301 Johnson Timothy 72 Carver Ln Marietta GA 30067 t.johnson26@example.cor
13302 Rogers Ellen 16 Post Rd Austell GA 30106 e.rogers44@example.com
13305 Rossi Roberto 88 Queen Ave Atlanta GA 30341 r.rossi3@example.com
13306 Schmidt Lars 44 Wexler St Jonesboro GA 30236 l.schmidt2@example.com
13307 Brown Isabella 52 Old Post Rd Lilburn GA 30047 i.brown19@example.com
13308 Kim Katherine 17 Catherine Ave Marietta GA 30008 k.kim27@example.com
13309 Rodriguez Jose 42 Ridge Rd Atlanta GA 30305 j.rodriguez4@example.coi
13310 Johnson Pamela 715 Phillips St Scottdale GA 30079 p.johnson62@example.co
13311 Williams Aaron 20 Switchback W Stone Mountain GA 30083 a.williams38@example.co
GA
Record: 50 of 51
No Filter
Search
field values changed
Primary key

Access saves changes to field values when you move to a new field or another record, or when you close the table. You don't have to click the Save button to save changes to field values or records.

8. Press **CTRL+HOME** to move to the first field value in the first record. With the changes to the record complete, you can unhide the hidden fields.
9. Right-click any field name to display the shortcut menu, and then click **Unhide Fields**. The Unhide Columns dialog box opens. See Figure 3–3.

Figure 3–3 **Unhide Columns dialog box**

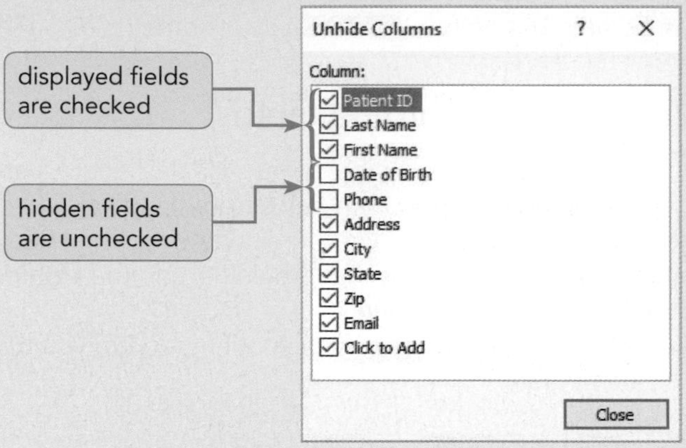
Unhide Columns
?
Column:
Patient ID
Last Name
First Name
Date of Birth
Phone
Address
City
State
Zip
Email
Click to Add
Close
displayed fields are checked
hidden fields are unchecked

All currently displayed fields are checked in this dialog box, and all hidden fields are unchecked. To redisplay them, you click their check boxes to select them.

10. In the Unhide Columns dialog box, click the **Date of Birth** check box to select it, click the **Phone** check box to select it, and then click **Close** to close the dialog box. The two hidden fields are now displayed in the datasheet.
11. Close the Patient table, and then click **No** in the dialog box that opens, asking if you want to save changes to the layout of the Patient table. This dialog box appears because you hid fields and redisplayed them.

    In this case, you can click either the Yes button or the No button, because no changes were actually made to the table layout or design.

Next you need to correct an error in the Visit table for a visit made by Mariana Salinas, Patient ID 13285. A staff member incorrectly entered "Hypertension monitoring" as the reason for the visit, when the patient actually came to the clinic that day for an annual wellness visit. Ensuring the accuracy of the data in a database is an important maintenance task.

To correct the record in the Visit table:

1. Open the **Visit** table in Datasheet view. The record containing the error is for Visit ID 1528.
2. Scroll the Visit table as necessary until you locate Visit ID **1528**, and then click at the end of the **Reason/Diagnosis** field value "Hypertension monitoring" for this record. You are in editing mode.
3. Delete **Hypertension monitoring** from the Reason/Diagnosis field, type **Annual wellness visit**, and then press **ENTER** twice. The record now contains the correct value in the Reason/Diagnosis field, and this change is automatically saved in the Visit table.

The next update Taylor asks you to make is to delete a record in the Visit table. One of the clinic's patients, Carlos Reyes, recently notified Taylor that he received an invoice for an annual wellness visit, but that he had canceled this scheduled appointment. Because this visit did not take place, the record for this visit needs to be deleted from the Visit table. Rather than scrolling through the table to locate the record to delete, you can use the Find command.

Finding Data in a Table

Access provides options you can use to locate specific field values in a table. Instead of scrolling the Visit table datasheet to find the visit that you need to delete—the record for Visit ID 1475—you can use the Find command to find the record. The **Find command** allows you to search a table or query datasheet, or a form, to locate a specific field value or part of a field value. This feature is particularly useful when searching a table that contains a large number of records.

To search for the record in the Visit table:

TIP

You can click any value in the column containing the field you want to search to make the field current.

1. Make sure the VisitID field value 1529 is still selected, and the Home tab is selected on the ribbon. You need to search the VisitID field to find the record containing the value 1475, so the insertion point is already correctly positioned in the field you want to search.
2. In the Find group, click **Find**. The Find and Replace dialog box opens. See Figure 3–4.

Figure 3–4 Find and Replace dialog box

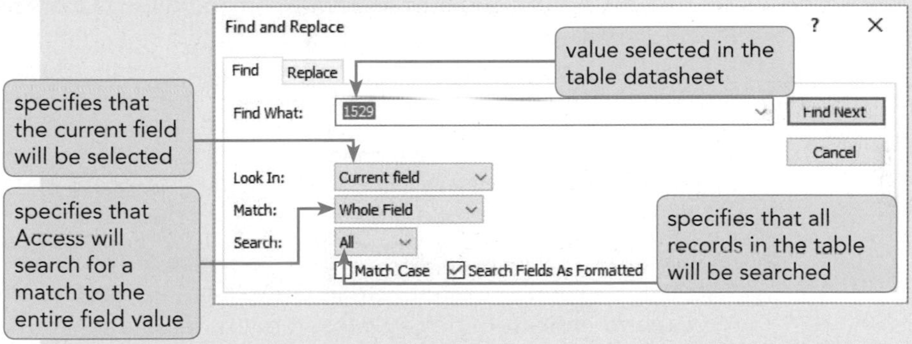
Find and Replace
?
Find
Replace
Find What:
1529
Find Next
Cancel
Look In:
Current field
Match:
Whole Field
Search:
All
Match Case
Search Fields As Formatted
value selected in the table datasheet
specifies that the current field will be selected
specifies that Access will search for a match to the entire field value
specifies that all records in the table will be searched

The field value 1529 appears in the Find What box because this value is selected in the table datasheet. You also can choose to search for only part of a field value, such as when you need to find all Visit IDs that start with a certain value. The Search box indicates that all the records in the table will be searched for the value you want to find. You also can choose to search up or down from the currently selected record.

Trouble? Some of the settings in your dialog box might be different from those shown in Figure 3–4 depending on the last search performed on the computer you're using. If so, change the settings so that they match those in the figure.

3. Make sure the value 1529 is selected in the Find What box, type **1475** to replace the selected value, and then click **Find Next**. Record 14 appears with the field value you specified selected.
4. Click **Cancel** to close the Find and Replace dialog box.

Deleting Records

To delete a record, you need to select the record in Datasheet view and then delete it using the Delete button in the Records group on the Home tab, or the Delete Record option on the shortcut menu.

REFERENCE

Deleting a Record

- With the table open in Datasheet view, click the row selector for the record you want to delete.
- In the Records group on the Home tab, click the Delete button; or right-click the row selector for the record, and then click Delete Record on the shortcut menu.
- In the dialog box asking you to confirm the deletion, click the Yes button.

Now that you have found the record with Visit ID 1475, you can delete it. To delete a record, you must first select the entire row for the record.

To delete the record:

1. Click the **row selector** ➡ for the record containing the VisitID field value **1475**, which should still be highlighted. The entire row is selected.
2. On the Home tab, in the Records group, click **Delete**. A dialog box opens indicating that you cannot delete the record because the Billing table contains records that related to VisitID 1475. Recall that you defined a one-to-many relationship between the Visit and Billing tables and you enforced referential integrity. When you try to delete a record in the primary table (Visit), the enforced referential integrity prevents the deletion if matching records exist in the related table (Billing). This protection helps to maintain the integrity of the data in the database.

   To delete the record in the Visit table, you first must delete the related record in the Billing table.
3. Click **OK** in the dialog box to close it. Notice the plus sign that appears at the beginning of each record in the Visit table. The plus sign, also called the **expand indicator**, indicates that the Visit table is the primary table related to another table—in this case, the Billing table. Clicking the expand indicator displays related records from other tables in the database in a **subdatasheet.**
4. Scroll down the datasheet until the selected record is near the top of the datasheet, so that you have room to view the related records for the visit record.
5. Click the **expand indicator** [+] next to VisitID 1475. One related record from the Billing table for this visit is displayed in the subdatasheet. See Figure 3–5.

Figure 3–5 Related records from the Billing table in the subdatasheet

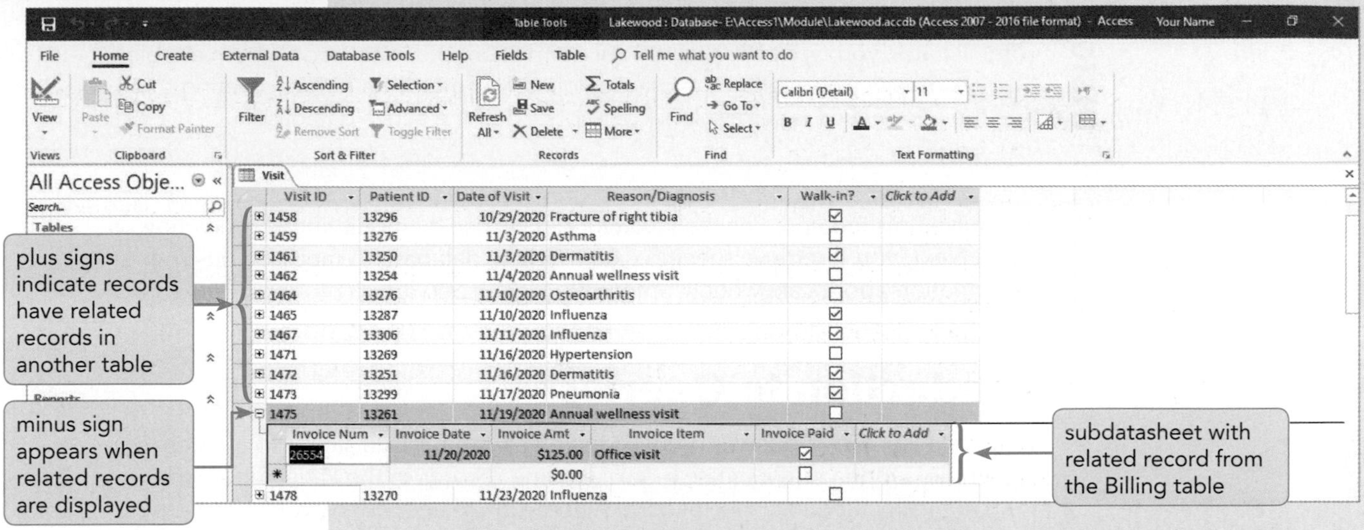
plus signs indicate records have related records in another table
minus sign appears when related records are displayed
subdatasheet with related record from the Billing table

When the subdatasheet is open, you can navigate and update it, just as you can using a table datasheet. The expand indicator for an open subdatasheet is replaced by a minus sign. Clicking the minus sign, or **collapse indicator**, hides the subdatasheet.

You need to delete the record in the Billing table that is related to Visit ID 1475 before you can delete this visit record. The record is for the invoice that was mistakenly sent to the patient, Carlos Reyes, who had canceled his annual wellness visit to the clinic. You could open the Billing table and find the related record. However, an easier way is to delete the record right in the subdatasheet. The record will be deleted from the Billing table automatically.

6. In the Billing table subdatasheet, click the **row selector** ➡ for invoice number **26554**. The entire row is selected.
7. On the Home tab, in the Records group, click **Delete**. Because the deletion of a record is permanent and cannot be undone, a dialog box opens asking you to confirm the deletion of the record.
8. Click **Yes** to confirm the deletion and close the dialog box. The record is removed from the Billing table, and the subdatasheet is now empty.
9. Click the **collapse indicator** ⊟ next to Visit ID 1475 to close the subdatasheet.

Now that you have deleted the related record in the Billing table, you can delete the record for Visit ID 1475. You'll use the shortcut menu to do so.

Be sure to select the correct record before deleting it.

10. Right-click the row selector ➡ for the record for Visit ID **1475** to select the record and open the shortcut menu.
11. Click **Delete Record** on the shortcut menu, and then click **Yes** in the dialog box to confirm the deletion. The record is deleted from the Visit table.
12. Close the Visit table.

INSIGHT

Process for Deleting Records

When working with more complex databases that are managed by a database administrator, you typically need special permission to delete records from a table. Many companies also follow the practice of archiving records before deleting them so that the information is still available but not part of the active database.

You have finished updating the Lakewood database by modifying and deleting records. Next, you'll retrieve specific data from the database to meet various requests for information about Lakewood Community Health Services.

Introduction to Queries

As you have learned, a query is a question you ask about data stored in a database. For example, Donna might create a query to find records in the Patient table for only those patients located in a specific city. When you create a query, you tell Access which fields you need and what criteria Access should use to select the records. Access provides powerful query capabilities that allow you to do the following:

- Display selected fields and records from a table
- Sort records
- Perform calculations
- Generate data for forms, reports, and other queries
- Update data in the tables in a database
- Find and display data from two or more tables

Most questions about data are generalized queries in which you specify the fields and records you want Access to select. These common requests for information, such as "Which patients are located in Atlanta?" or "How many invoices have been paid?" are select queries. The answer to a select query is returned in the form of a datasheet. The result of a query is also referred to as a **recordset** because the query produces a set of records that answers your question.

INSIGHT

Designing Queries vs. Using a Query Wizard

More specialized, technical queries, such as finding duplicate records in a table, are best formulated using a Query Wizard. A **Query Wizard** prompts you for information by asking a series of questions and then creates the appropriate query based on your answers. For example, earlier you used the Simple Query Wizard to display only some of the fields in the Visit table; Access provides other Query Wizards for more complex queries. For common, informational queries, designing your own query is more efficient than using a Query Wizard.

Taylor wants you to create a query to display the patient ID, last name, first name, city, and email address for each record in the Patient table. She needs this information to complete an email campaign advertising special services and screenings being offered to patients of Lakewood Community Health Services. You'll open the Query window in Design view to create the query for Taylor.

To open the Query window in Design view:

1. Close the Navigation Pane, and then, on the ribbon, click the **Create** tab.
2. In the Queries group, click the **Query Design** button to display the Query window in Design view, with the Show Table dialog box open and the Tables tab selected. See Figure 3–6.

Figure 3–6 Show Table dialog box

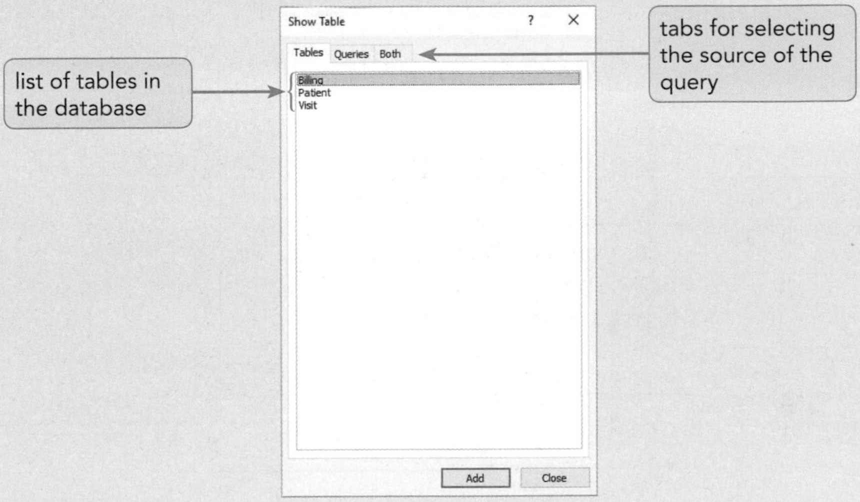
list of tables in the database
tabs for selecting the source of the query
Show Table
Tables
Queries
Both
Billing
Patient
Visit
Add
Close

The Show Table dialog box lists all the tables in the Lakewood database. You can choose to base a query on one or more tables, on other queries, or on a combination of tables and queries. The query you are creating will retrieve data from the Patient table, so you need to add this table to the Query window.

3. In the Tables list, click **Patient**, click **Add**, and then click **Close** to close the Show Table dialog box. The Patient table's field list appears in the Query window. Refer to the Session 3.1 Visual Overview to familiarize yourself with the Query window in Design view.

   Trouble? If you add the wrong table to the Query window, right-click the bar at the top of the field list containing the table name, and then click Remove Table on the shortcut menu. To add the correct table to the Query window, repeat Steps 2 and 3.

Now you'll create and run the query to display selected fields from the Patient table.

Creating and Running a Query

The default table datasheet displays all the fields in the table in the same order as they appear in the table. In contrast, a query datasheet can display selected fields from a table, and the order of the fields can be different from that of the table, enabling those viewing the query results to see only the information they need and in the order they want.

You need the PatientID, LastName, FirstName, City, and Email fields from the Patient table to appear in the query results. You'll add each of these fields to the design grid. First you'll resize the Patient table field list to display all of the fields.

To select the fields for the query, and then run the query:

1. Drag the bottom border of the Patient field list to resize the field list so that all the fields in the Patient table are visible.
2. In the Patient field list, double-click **PatientID** to place the field in the design grid's first column Field box. See Figure 3–7.

Figure 3–7 Field added to the design grid

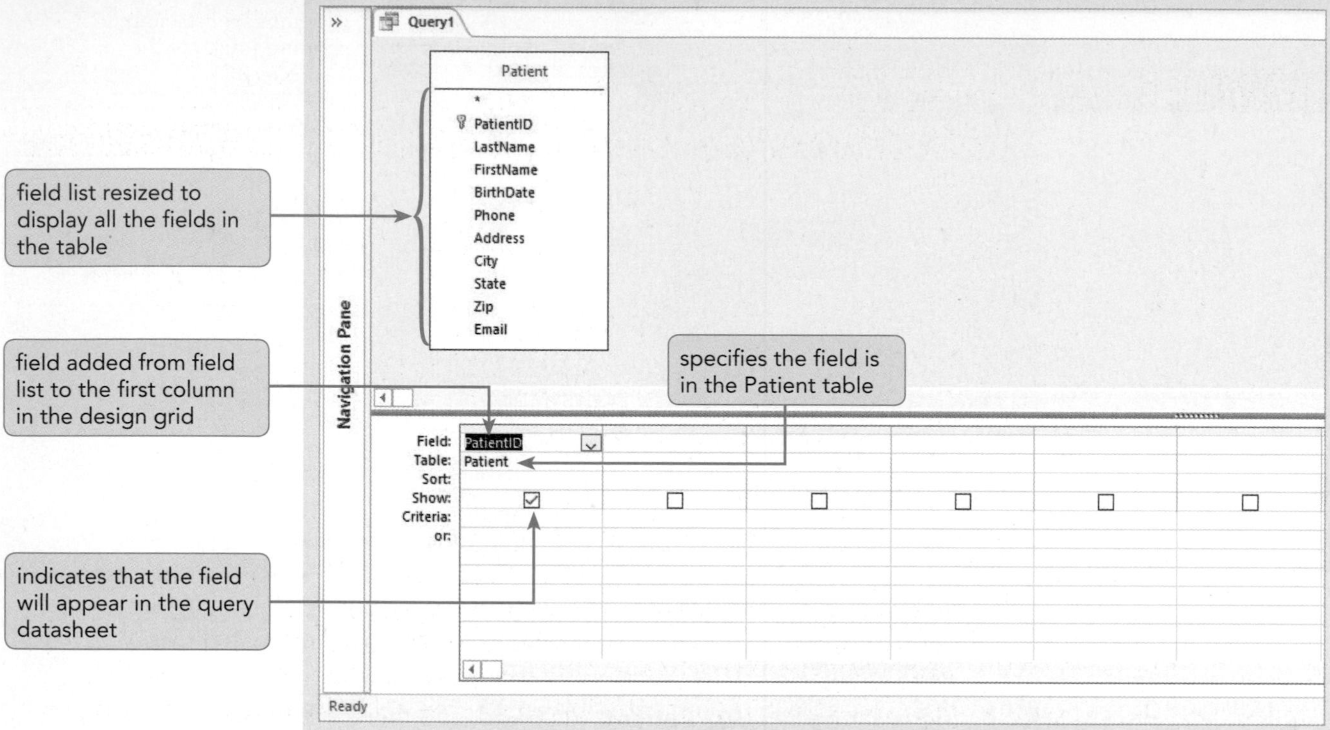
Query1
Patient
PatientID
LastName
FirstName
BirthDate
Phone
Address
City
State
Zip
Email
field list resized to display all the fields in the table
field added from field list to the first column in the design grid
specifies the field is in the Patient table
indicates that the field will appear in the query datasheet
Navigation Pane
Field:
Table:
Sort:
Show:
Criteria:
or:
PatientID
Patient
Ready

In the design grid's first column, the field name PatientID appears in the Field box, the table name Patient appears in the Table box, and the checkmark in the Show check box indicates that the field will be displayed in the datasheet when you run the query. Sometimes you might not want to display a field and its values in the query results. For example, if you are creating a query to list all patients located in Atlanta, and you assign the name "AtlantaPatients" to the query, you do not need to include the City field value for each record in the query results—the query design lists only patients with the City field value of "Atlanta." Even if you choose not to display a field in the query results, you can still use the field as part of the query to select specific records or to specify a particular sequence for the records in the datasheet. You can also add a field to the design grid using the arrow on the Field box; this arrow appears when you click the Field box, and if you click the arrow or the right side of an empty Field box, a menu of available fields opens.

TIP

You can also use the mouse to drag a field from the field list to a column in the design grid.

3. In the design grid, click the right side of the second column's Field box to display a menu listing all the fields in the Patient table, and then click **LastName** to add this field to the second column in the design grid.
4. Add the **FirstName**, **City**, and **Email** fields to the design grid in that order.

Trouble? If you accidentally add the wrong field to the design grid, select the field's column by clicking the selection pointer ⬇ on the field selector, which is the thin bar above the Field box, for the field you want to delete, and then press DELETE (or in the Query Setup group on the Query Tools Design tab, click the Delete Columns button).

Now that the five fields for the query have been selected, you can run the query.

5. On the Query Tools Design tab, in the Results group, click the **Run** button. Access runs the query and displays the results in Datasheet view. See Figure 3–8.

Figure 3–8 **Datasheet displayed after running the query**

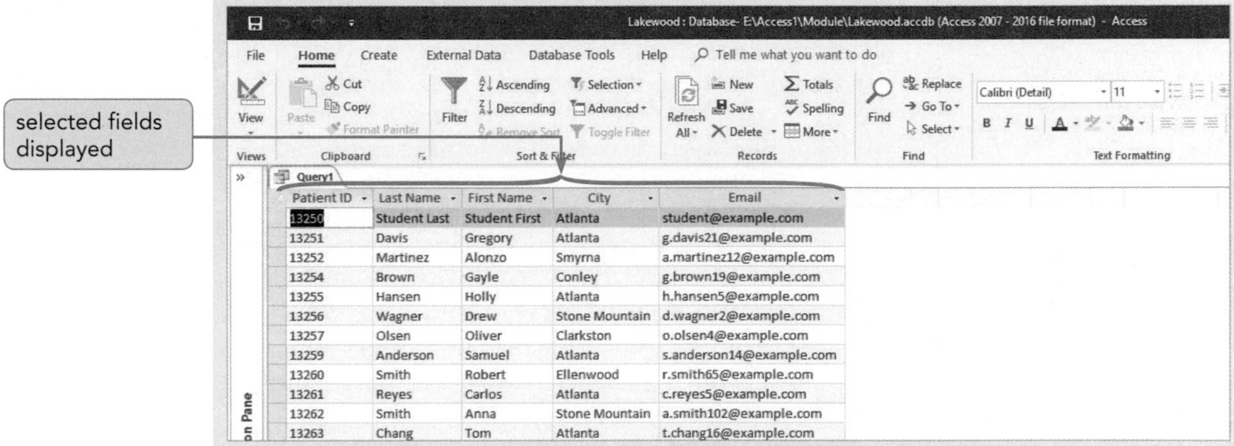
selected fields displayed
Lakewood : Database- E:\Access1\Module\Lakewood.accdb (Access 2007 - 2016 file format) - Access
Query1
Patient ID
Last Name
First Name
City
Email

The five fields you added to the design grid appear in the datasheet in the same order as they appear in the design grid. The records are displayed in primary key sequence by PatientID. The query selected all 51 records from the Patient table for display in the query datasheet. You will save the query as "PatientEmail" so that you can easily retrieve the same data again.

6. On the Quick Access Toolbar, click the **Save** button 🖫. The Save As dialog box opens.

7. In the Query Name box, type **PatientEmail** and then press **ENTER**. The query is saved with the specified name in the Lakewood database, and its name appears on the tab for the query.

PROSKILLS

Decision Making: Comparing Methods for Adding All Fields to the Design Grid

If the query you are creating includes every field from the specified table, you can use one of the following three methods to transfer all the fields from the field list to the design grid:

- Double-click (or click and drag) each field individually from the field list to the design grid. Use this method if you want the fields in your query to appear in an order that is different from the order in the field list.
- Double-click the asterisk at the top of the field list. The table name, followed by a period and an asterisk (as in "Patient.*"), appears in the Field box of the first column in the design grid, which signifies that the order of the fields is the same in the query as it is in the field list. Use this method if you don't need to sort the query or specify conditions based on the fields in the table you added in this way (for example, in a query based on more than one table). The advantage of using this method is that you do not need to change the query if you add or delete fields from the underlying table structure. Such changes are reflected automatically in the query.
- Double-click the field list title bar to select all the fields, and then click and drag one of the selected fields to the first column in the design grid. Each field appears in a separate column, and the fields are arranged in the order in which they appear in the field list. Use this method when you need to sort your query or include record selection criteria.

By choosing the most appropriate method to add all the table fields to the query design grid, you can work more efficiently and ensure that the query produces the results you want.

The record for one of the patients in the query results contains information that is not up to date. This patient, Drew Wagner, had informed the clinic that he now prefers to go by the name Andrew; he also provided a new email address. You need to update the record with the new first name and email address for this patient.

Updating Data Using a Query

A query datasheet is temporary, and its contents are based on the criteria in the query design grid; however, you can still update the data in a table using a query datasheet. In this case, you want to make changes to a record in the Patient table. Instead of making the changes in the table datasheet, you can make them in the PatientEmail query datasheet because the query is based on the Patient table. The underlying Patient table will be updated with the changes you make.

To update data using the PatientEmail query datasheet:

1. Locate the record with PatientID 13256, Drew Wagner (record 6 in the query datasheet).
2. In the First Name column for this record, double-click **Drew** to select the name, and then type **Andrew**.
3. Press **TAB** twice to move to the Email column, type **a.wagner6@example.com**, and then press **TAB**.

4. Close the PatientEmail query, and then open the Navigation Pane. Note that the PatientEmail query is listed in the Queries section of the Navigation Pane. Now you'll check the Patient table to verify that the changes you made in the query datasheet are reflected in the Patient table.
5. Open the **Patient** table in Datasheet view, and then close the Navigation Pane.
6. Locate the record for PatientID 13256 (record 6). Notice that the changes you made in the query datasheet to the First Name and Email field values were made to the record in the Patient table.
7. Close the Patient table.

Taylor also wants to view specific information in the Lakewood database. She would like to review the visit data for patients while also viewing certain contact information about them. So, she needs to see data from both the Patient table and the Visit table at the same time.

Creating a Multitable Query

A multitable query is a query based on more than one table. If you want to create a query that retrieves data from multiple tables, the tables must have a common field. Earlier, you established a relationship between the Patient (primary) and Visit (related) tables based on the common PatientID field that exists in both tables, so you can now create a query to display data from both tables at the same time. Specifically, Taylor wants to view the values in the City, FirstName, and LastName fields from the Patient table and the VisitDate and Reason fields from the Visit table.

To create the query using the Patient and Visit tables:

1. On the ribbon, click the **Create** tab.
2. In the Queries group, click the **Query Design** button. The Show Table dialog box opens in the Query window. You need to add the Patient and Visit tables to the Query window.
3. Click **Patient** in the Tables list, click the **Add** button, click **Visit**, click the **Add** button, and then click the **Close** button to close the Show Table dialog box. The Patient and Visit field lists appear in the Query window.
4. Resize the Patient and Visit field lists if necessary so that all the fields in each list are displayed.

   The one-to-many relationship between the two tables is shown in the Query window in the same way that a relationship between two tables is shown in the Relationships window. Note that the join line is thick at both ends; this signifies that you selected the option to enforce referential integrity. If you had not selected this option, the join line would be thin at both ends, and neither the "1" nor the infinity symbol would appear, even though the tables have a one-to-many relationship.

   You need to place the City, FirstName, and LastName fields (in that order) from the Patient field list into the design grid and then place the VisitDate and Reason fields from the Visit field list into the design grid. This is the order in which Taylor wants to view the fields in the query results.
5. In the Patient field list, double-click **City** to place this field in the design grid's first column Field box.

6. Repeat Step 5 to add the **FirstName** and **LastName** fields from the Patient table to the second and third columns of the design grid.
7. Repeat Step 5 to add the **VisitDate** and **Reason** fields (in that order) from the Visit table to the fourth and fifth columns of the design grid. The query specifications are complete, so you can now run the query.
8. In the Results group on the Query Tools Design tab, click **Run**. After the query runs, the results are displayed in Datasheet view. See Figure 3–9.

Figure 3–9 Datasheet for query based on the Patient and Visit tables

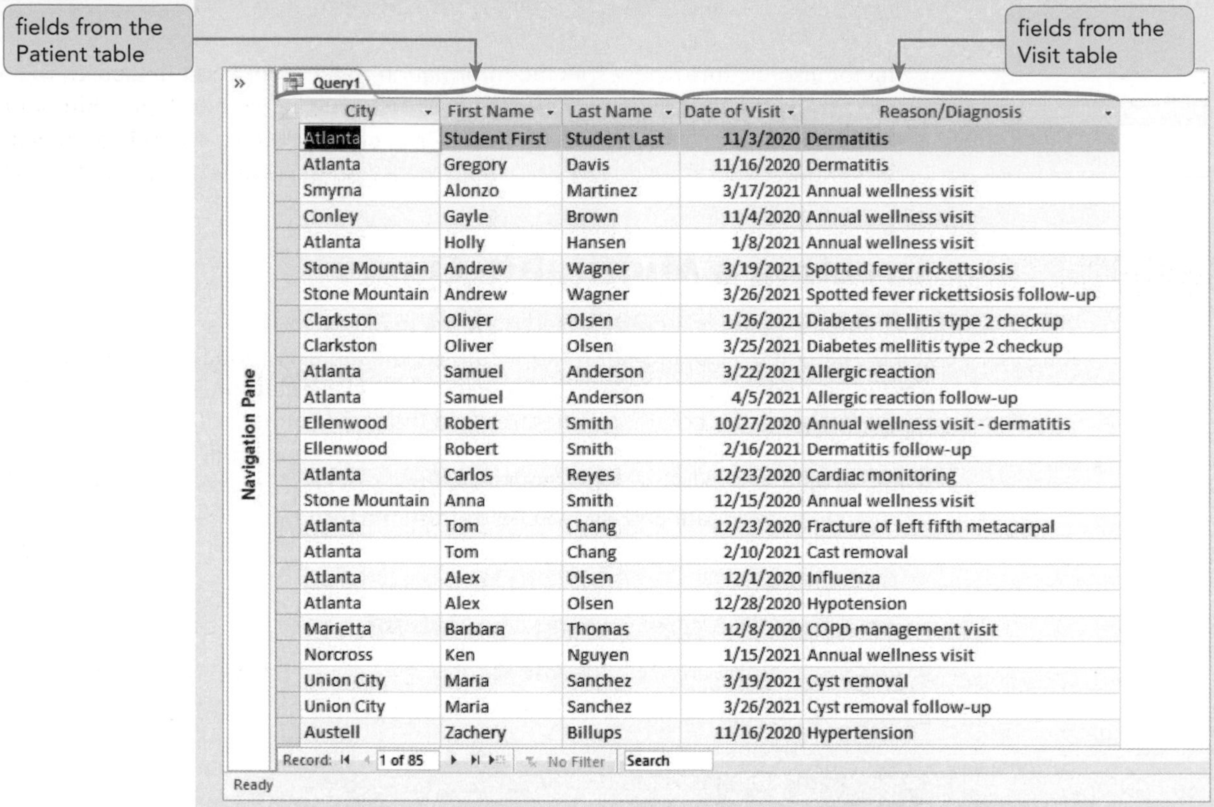
fields from the Patient table
fields from the Visit table
Query1
Navigation Pane
Record: 1 of 85
No Filter
Search
Ready

City	First Name	Last Name	Date of Visit	Reason/Diagnosis
Atlanta	Student First	Student Last	11/3/2020	Dermatitis
Atlanta	Gregory	Davis	11/16/2020	Dermatitis
Smyrna	Alonzo	Martinez	3/17/2021	Annual wellness visit
Conley	Gayle	Brown	11/4/2020	Annual wellness visit
Atlanta	Holly	Hansen	1/8/2021	Annual wellness visit
Stone Mountain	Andrew	Wagner	3/19/2021	Spotted fever rickettsiosis
Stone Mountain	Andrew	Wagner	3/26/2021	Spotted fever rickettsiosis follow-up
Clarkston	Oliver	Olsen	1/26/2021	Diabetes mellitis type 2 checkup
Clarkston	Oliver	Olsen	3/25/2021	Diabetes mellitis type 2 checkup
Atlanta	Samuel	Anderson	3/22/2021	Allergic reaction
Atlanta	Samuel	Anderson	4/5/2021	Allergic reaction follow-up
Ellenwood	Robert	Smith	10/27/2020	Annual wellness visit - dermatitis
Ellenwood	Robert	Smith	2/16/2021	Dermatitis follow-up
Atlanta	Carlos	Reyes	12/23/2020	Cardiac monitoring
Stone Mountain	Anna	Smith	12/15/2020	Annual wellness visit
Atlanta	Tom	Chang	12/23/2020	Fracture of left fifth metacarpal
Atlanta	Tom	Chang	2/10/2021	Cast removal
Atlanta	Alex	Olsen	12/1/2020	Influenza
Atlanta	Alex	Olsen	12/28/2020	Hypotension
Marietta	Barbara	Thomas	12/8/2020	COPD management visit
Norcross	Ken	Nguyen	1/15/2021	Annual wellness visit
Union City	Maria	Sanchez	3/19/2021	Cyst removal
Union City	Maria	Sanchez	3/26/2021	Cyst removal follow-up
Austell	Zachery	Billups	11/16/2020	Hypertension

Only the five selected fields from the Patient and Visit tables appear in the datasheet. The records are displayed in order according to the values in the PatientID field because it is the primary key field in the primary table, even though this field is not included in the query datasheet.

Taylor plans on frequently tracking the data retrieved by the query, so she asks you to save it as "PatientVisits."

9. On the Quick Access Toolbar, click the **Save** button. The Save As dialog box opens.
10. In the Query Name box, type **PatientVisits** and then press **ENTER**. The query is saved, and its name appears on the object tab.

Taylor decides she wants the records displayed in alphabetical order by city. Because the query displays data in order by the field values in the PatientID field, which is the primary key for the Patient table, you need to sort the records by the City field to display the data in the order Taylor wants.

Sorting Data in a Query

Sorting is the process of rearranging records in a specified order or sequence. Sometimes you might need to sort data before displaying or printing it to meet a specific request. For example, Taylor might want to review visit information arranged by the VisitDate field because she needs to know which months are the busiest for Lakewood Community Health Services in terms of patient visits. Donna might want to view billing information arranged by the InvoiceAmt field because she monitors the finances of the clinic.

When you sort data in a query, you do not change the sequence of the records in the underlying tables. Only the records in the query datasheet are rearranged according to your specifications.

To sort records, you must select the **sort field**, which is the field used to determine the order of records in the datasheet. In this case, Taylor wants the data sorted alphabetically by city, so you need to specify City as the sort field. Sort fields can be Short Text, Number, Date/Time, Currency, AutoNumber, or Yes/No fields, but not Long Text, Hyperlink, or Attachment fields. You sort records in either ascending (increasing) or descending (decreasing) order. Figure 3–10 shows the results of each type of sort for these data types.

Figure 3–10 **Sorting results for different data types**

Data Type	Ascending Sort Results	Descending Sort Results
Short Text	A to Z (alphabetical)	Z to A (reverse alphabetical)
Number	lowest to highest numeric value	highest to lowest numeric value
Date/Time	oldest to most recent date	most recent to oldest date
Currency	lowest to highest numeric value	highest to lowest numeric value
AutoNumber	lowest to highest numeric value	highest to lowest numeric value
Yes/No	yes (checkmark in check box) then no values	no then yes values

Access provides several methods for sorting data in a table or query datasheet and in a form. One of the easiest ways is to use the AutoFilter feature for a field.

Using an AutoFilter to Sort Data

TIP

You can also use the Ascending and Descending buttons in the Sort & Filter group on the Home tab to quickly sort records based on the currently selected field in a datasheet.

As you've probably noticed when working in Datasheet view for a table or query, each column heading has an arrow to the right of the field name. This arrow gives you access to the **AutoFilter** feature, which enables you to quickly sort and display field values in various ways. When you click this arrow, a menu opens with options for sorting and displaying field values. The first two options on the menu enable you to sort the values in the current field in ascending or descending order. Unless you save the datasheet or form after you've sorted the records, the rearrangement of records is temporary.

Next, you'll use an AutoFilter to sort the PatientVisits query results by the City field.

To sort the records using an AutoFilter:

1. Click the **arrow** on the City column heading to display the AutoFilter menu. See Figure 3–11.

Figure 3–11 Using AutoFilter to sort records in the datasheet

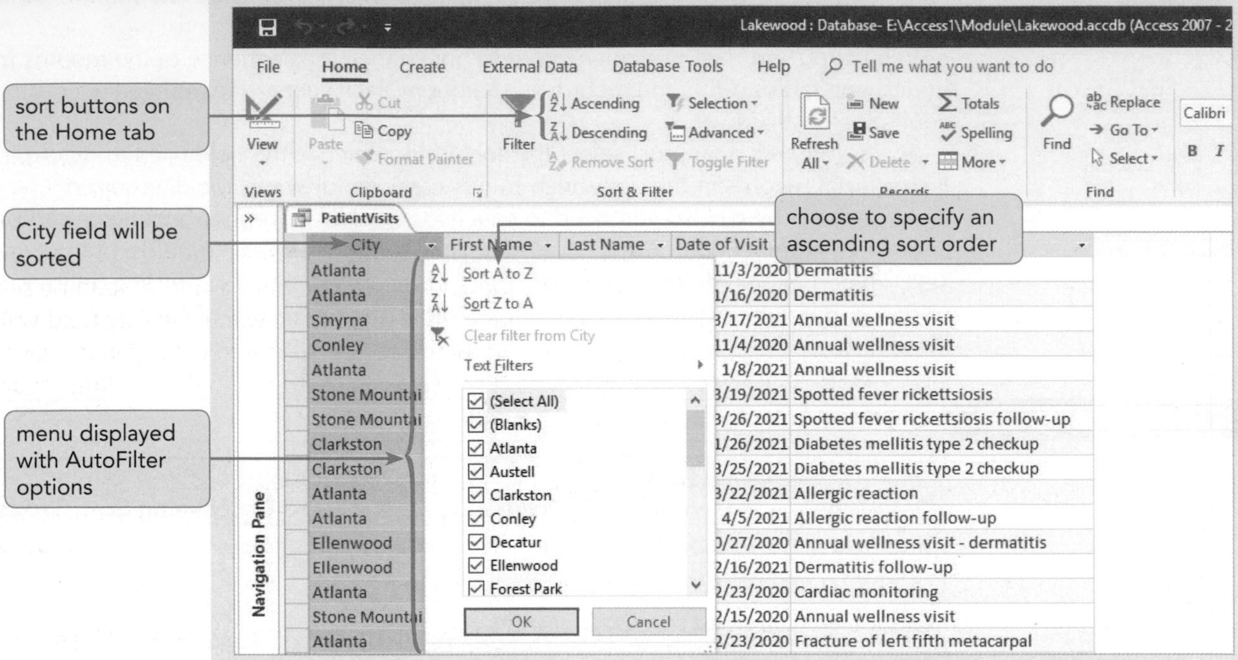
sort buttons on the Home tab
City field will be sorted
menu displayed with AutoFilter options
choose to specify an ascending sort order

Taylor wants the data sorted in ascending (alphabetical) order by the values in the City field, so you need to select the first option in the menu.

2. Click **Sort A to Z**. The records are rearranged in ascending alphabetical order by city. A small, upward-pointing arrow appears on the right side of the City column heading. This arrow indicates that the values in the field have been sorted in ascending order. If you used the same method to sort the field values in descending order, a small downward-pointing arrow would appear there instead.

After viewing the query results, Taylor decides that she would also like to see the records arranged by the values in the VisitDate field, so that the data is presented in chronological order. She still wants the records to be arranged by the City field values as well. To produce the results Taylor wants, you need to sort using two fields.

Sorting on Multiple Fields in Design View

Sort fields can be unique or nonunique. A sort field is **unique** if the value in the sort field for each record is different. The PatientID field in the Patient table is an example of a unique sort field because each patient record has a different value in this primary key field. A sort field is **nonunique** if more than one record can have the same value for the sort field. For example, the City field in the Patient table is a nonunique sort field because more than one record can have the same City value.

TIP

The primary sort field is not the same as a table's primary key. A table has at most one primary key, which must be unique, whereas any field in a table can serve as a primary sort field.

When the sort field is nonunique, records with the same sort field value are grouped together, but they are not sorted in a specific order within the group. To arrange these grouped records in a specific order, you can specify a **secondary sort field**, which is a second field that determines the order of records that are already sorted by the **primary sort field** (the first sort field specified).

In Access, you can select up to 10 different sort fields. When you use the buttons on the ribbon to sort by more than one field, the sort fields must be in adjacent columns in the datasheet. (Note that you cannot use an AutoFilter to sort on more than one field. This method works for a single field only.) You can specify only one type of sort—either ascending or descending—for the selected columns in the datasheet. You select the adjacent columns, and Access sorts first by the first column and then by each remaining selected column in order from left to right.

Taylor wants the records sorted first by the City field values, as they currently are, and then by the VisitDate values. The two fields are in the correct left-to-right order in the query datasheet, but they are not adjacent, so you cannot use the Ascending and Descending buttons on the ribbon to sort them. You could move the City field to the left of the VisitDate field in the query datasheet, but both columns would have to be sorted with the same sort order. This is not what Taylor wants—she wants the City field values sorted in ascending order so that they are in the correct alphabetical order, for ease of reference; and she wants the VisitDate field values to be sorted in descending order, so that she can focus on the most recent patient visits first. To sort the City and VisitDate fields with different sort orders, you must specify the sort fields in Design view.

In the Query window in Design view, you must arrange the fields you want to sort from left to right in the design grid, with the primary sort field being the leftmost. In Design view, multiple sort fields do not have to be adjacent to each other, as they do in Datasheet view; however, they must be in the correct left-to-right order.

REFERENCE

Sorting a Query Datasheet

- In the query datasheet, click the arrow on the column heading for the field you want to sort.
- In the menu that opens, click Sort A to Z for an ascending sort, or click Sort Z to A for a descending sort.

or

- In the query datasheet, select the column or adjacent columns on which you want to sort.
- In the Sort & Filter group on the Home tab, click the Ascending button or the Descending button.

or

- In Design view, position the fields serving as sort fields from left to right.
- Click the right side of the Sort box for each field you want to sort, and then click Ascending or Descending for the sort order.

To achieve the results Taylor wants, you need to modify the query in Design view to specify the sort order for the two fields.

TIP

In Design view, the sort fields do not have to be adjacent, and fields that are not sorted can appear between the sort fields.

To select the two sort fields in Design view:

1. On the Home tab, in the Views group, click the **View** button to open the query in Design view. The fields are currently in the correct left-to-right order in the design grid, so you only need to specify the sort order for the two fields.

   First, you need to specify an ascending sort order for the City field. Even though the records are already sorted by the values in this field, you need to modify the query so that this sort order, and the sort order you will specify for the VisitDate field, are part of the query's design. Any time the query is run, the records will be sorted according to these specifications.

2. Click the right side of the **City Sort** box to display the arrow and the sort options, and then click **Ascending**. You've selected an ascending sort order for the City field, which will be the primary sort field. The City field is a Short Text field, and an ascending sort order will display the field values in alphabetical order.

3. Click the right side of the **VisitDate Sort** box, click **Descending**, and then click in one of the empty boxes below the VisitDate field to deselect the setting. You've selected a descending sort order for the VisitDate field, which will be the secondary sort field because it appears to the right of the primary sort field (City) in the design grid. The VisitDate field is a Date/Time field, and a descending sort order will display the field values with the most recent dates first. See Figure 3–12.

Figure 3–12 Selecting two sort fields in Design view

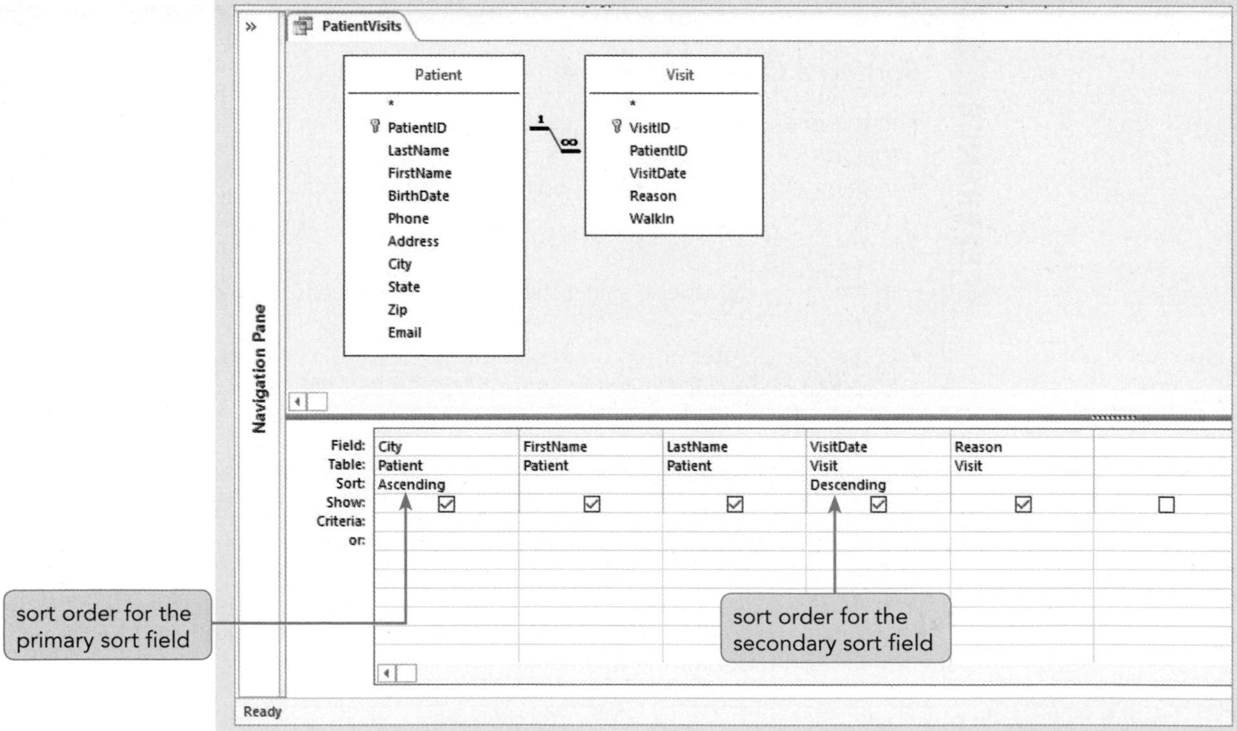
PatientVisits
Patient
*
PatientID
LastName
FirstName
BirthDate
Phone
Address
City
State
Zip
Email
Visit
*
VisitID
PatientID
VisitDate
Reason
WalkIn
Navigation Pane
Field: City | FirstName | LastName | VisitDate | Reason
Table: Patient | Patient | Patient | Visit | Visit
Sort: Ascending | | | Descending |
Show:
Criteria:
or:
sort order for the primary sort field
sort order for the secondary sort field
Ready

You have finished your query changes, so now you can run the query and then save the modified query with the same name.

4. On the Query Tools Design tab, in the Results group, click **Run**. After the query runs, the records appear in the query datasheet in ascending order based on the values in the City field. Within groups of records with the same City field value, the records appear in descending order by the values of the VisitDate field. See Figure 3–13.

Figure 3–13 **Datasheet sorted on two fields**

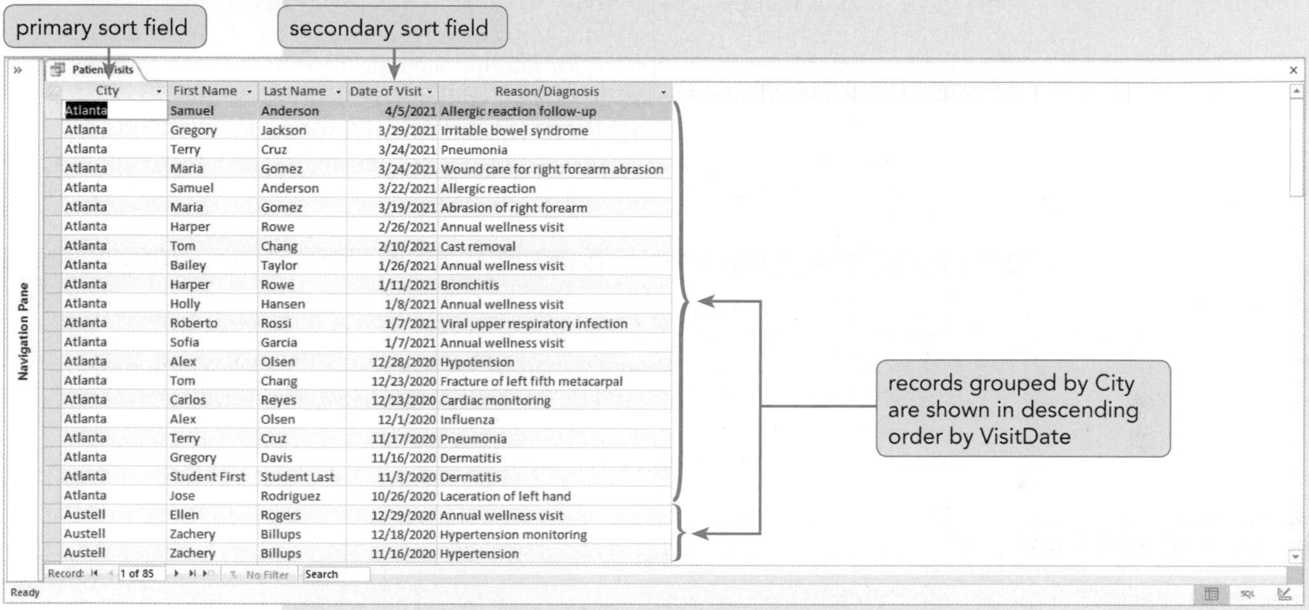
primary sort field
secondary sort field
records grouped by City are shown in descending order by VisitDate
PatientVisits
Navigation Pane
Record: 1 of 85
No Filter
Search
Ready

City	First Name	Last Name	Date of Visit	Reason/Diagnosis
Atlanta	Samuel	Anderson	4/5/2021	Allergic reaction follow-up
Atlanta	Gregory	Jackson	3/29/2021	Irritable bowel syndrome
Atlanta	Terry	Cruz	3/24/2021	Pneumonia
Atlanta	Maria	Gomez	3/24/2021	Wound care for right forearm abrasion
Atlanta	Samuel	Anderson	3/22/2021	Allergic reaction
Atlanta	Maria	Gomez	3/19/2021	Abrasion of right forearm
Atlanta	Harper	Rowe	2/26/2021	Annual wellness visit
Atlanta	Tom	Chang	2/10/2021	Cast removal
Atlanta	Bailey	Taylor	1/26/2021	Annual wellness visit
Atlanta	Harper	Rowe	1/11/2021	Bronchitis
Atlanta	Holly	Hansen	1/8/2021	Annual wellness visit
Atlanta	Roberto	Rossi	1/7/2021	Viral upper respiratory infection
Atlanta	Sofia	Garcia	1/7/2021	Annual wellness visit
Atlanta	Alex	Olsen	12/28/2020	Hypotension
Atlanta	Tom	Chang	12/23/2020	Fracture of left fifth metacarpal
Atlanta	Carlos	Reyes	12/23/2020	Cardiac monitoring
Atlanta	Alex	Olsen	12/1/2020	Influenza
Atlanta	Terry	Cruz	11/17/2020	Pneumonia
Atlanta	Gregory	Davis	11/16/2020	Dermatitis
Atlanta	Student First	Student Last	11/3/2020	Dermatitis
Atlanta	Jose	Rodriguez	10/26/2020	Laceration of left hand
Austell	Ellen	Rogers	12/29/2020	Annual wellness visit
Austell	Zachery	Billups	12/18/2020	Hypertension monitoring
Austell	Zachery	Billups	11/16/2020	Hypertension

When you save the query, all of your design changes—including the selection of the sort fields—are saved with the query. The next time Taylor runs the query, the records will appear sorted by the primary and secondary sort fields.

5. On the Quick Access Toolbar, click the **Save** button to save the revised PatientVisits query.

Taylor knows that Lakewood Community Health Services has seen an increase in the number of patients from Atlanta. She would like to focus briefly on the information for patients in that city only. Also, she is interested in knowing how many patients from Atlanta have had annual wellness visits. She is concerned that, although more patients are coming to the clinic from this city, not enough of them are scheduling wellness visits. Selecting only the records with a City field value of "Atlanta" and a Reason field value beginning with "Annual" is a temporary change that Taylor wants in the query datasheet, so you do not need to switch to Design view and change the query. Instead, you can apply a filter.

Filtering Data

A **filter** is a set of restrictions you place on the records in an open datasheet or form to *temporarily* isolate a subset of the records. A filter lets you view different subsets of displayed records so that you can focus on only the data you need. Unless you save a query or form with a filter applied, an applied filter is not available the next time you run the query or open the form.

The simplest technique for filtering records is Filter By Selection. **Filter By Selection** lets you select all or part of a field value in a datasheet or form and then display only those records that contain the selected value in the field. You can also use the AutoFilter feature to filter records. When you click the arrow on a column heading, the menu that opens provides options for filtering the datasheet based on a field value or the selected part of a field value. Another technique for filtering records is to use **Filter By Form**, which changes your datasheet to display blank fields. Then you can select a value using the arrow that appears when you click any blank field to apply a filter that selects only those records containing that value.

REFERENCE

Using Filter By Selection

- In the datasheet or form, select the part of the field value that will be the basis for the filter; or, if the filter will be based on the entire field value, click anywhere within the field value.
- On the Home tab, in the Sort & Filter group, click the Selection button.
- Click the type of filter you want to apply.

For Taylor's request, you need to select a City field value of Atlanta and then use Filter By Selection to display only those records with this value. Then you will filter the records further by selecting only those records with a Reason value that begins with "Annual" (for Annual wellness visit).

To display the records using Filter By Selection:

1. In the query datasheet, locate the first occurrence of a City field containing the value **Atlanta**, and then click anywhere within that field value.
2. On the Home tab, in the Sort & Filter group, click the **Selection** button. A menu opens with options for the type of filter to apply. See Figure 3–14.

Figure 3–14 Using Filter By Selection

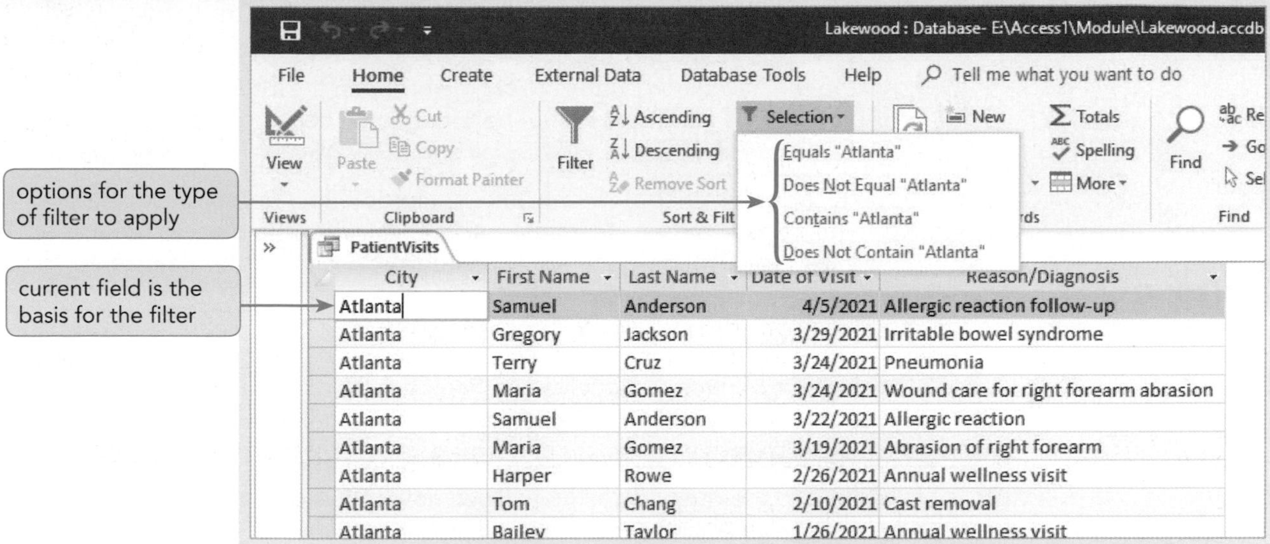
options for the type of filter to apply
current field is the basis for the filter
Equals "Atlanta"
Does Not Equal "Atlanta"
Contains "Atlanta"
Does Not Contain "Atlanta"
PatientVisits
City | First Name | Last Name | Date of Visit | Reason/Diagnosis
Atlanta | Samuel | Anderson | 4/5/2021 | Allergic reaction follow-up
Atlanta | Gregory | Jackson | 3/29/2021 | Irritable bowel syndrome
Atlanta | Terry | Cruz | 3/24/2021 | Pneumonia
Atlanta | Maria | Gomez | 3/24/2021 | Wound care for right forearm abrasion
Atlanta | Samuel | Anderson | 3/22/2021 | Allergic reaction
Atlanta | Maria | Gomez | 3/19/2021 | Abrasion of right forearm
Atlanta | Harper | Rowe | 2/26/2021 | Annual wellness visit
Atlanta | Tom | Chang | 2/10/2021 | Cast removal

The menu provides options for displaying only those records with a City field value that equals the selected value (in this case, Atlanta); does not equal the value; contains the value somewhere within the field; or does not contain the value somewhere within the field. You want to display all the records whose City field value equals Atlanta.

3. In the Selection menu, click **Equals "Atlanta"**. Only the 21 records that have a City field value of Atlanta appear in the datasheet. See Figure 3–15.

Figure 3–15 Datasheet after applying filter

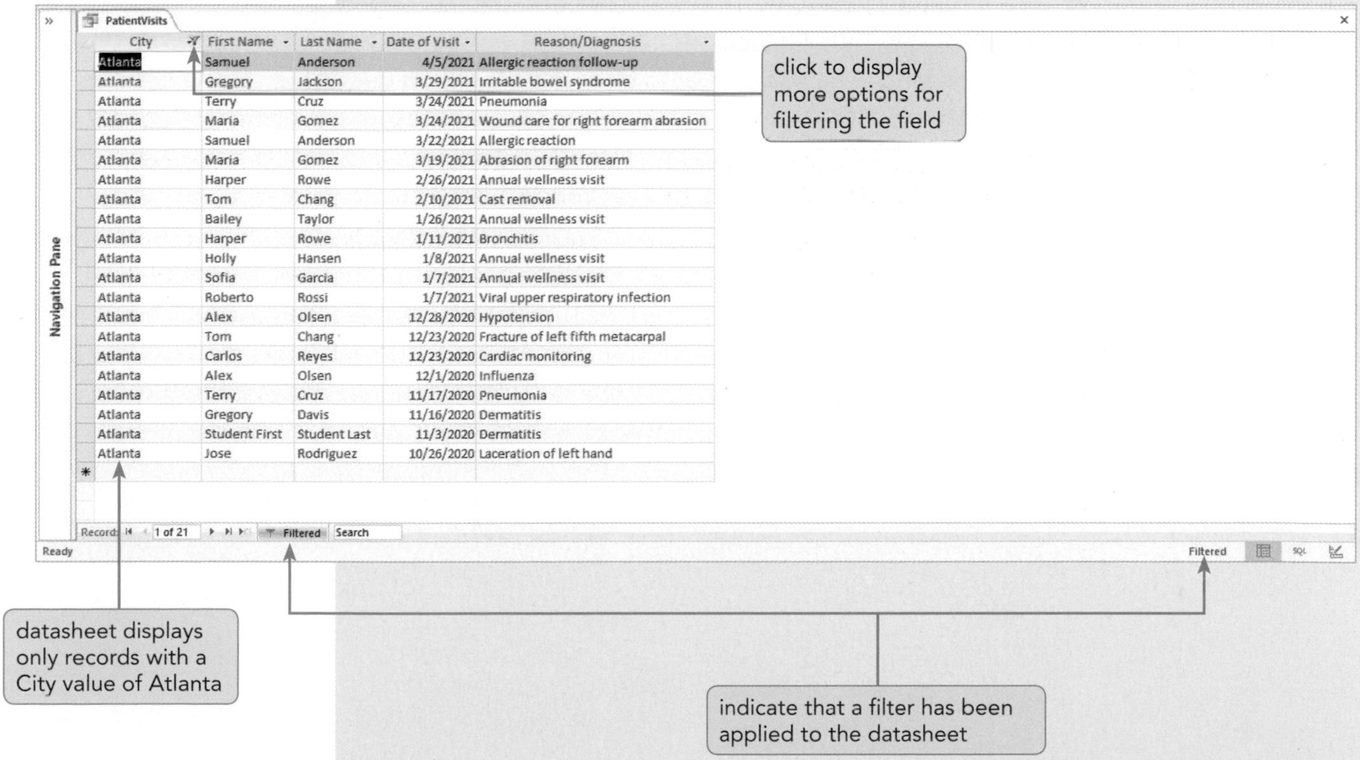
click to display more options for filtering the field
datasheet displays only records with a City value of Atlanta
indicate that a filter has been applied to the datasheet
PatientVisits
City | First Name | Last Name | Date of Visit | Reason/Diagnosis
Atlanta | Samuel | Anderson | 4/5/2021 | Allergic reaction follow-up
Atlanta | Gregory | Jackson | 3/29/2021 | Irritable bowel syndrome
Atlanta | Terry | Cruz | 3/24/2021 | Pneumonia
Atlanta | Maria | Gomez | 3/24/2021 | Wound care for right forearm abrasion
Atlanta | Samuel | Anderson | 3/22/2021 | Allergic reaction
Atlanta | Maria | Gomez | 3/19/2021 | Abrasion of right forearm
Atlanta | Harper | Rowe | 2/26/2021 | Annual wellness visit
Atlanta | Tom | Chang | 2/10/2021 | Cast removal
Atlanta | Bailey | Taylor | 1/26/2021 | Annual wellness visit
Atlanta | Harper | Rowe | 1/11/2021 | Bronchitis
Atlanta | Holly | Hansen | 1/8/2021 | Annual wellness visit
Atlanta | Sofia | Garcia | 1/7/2021 | Annual wellness visit
Atlanta | Roberto | Rossi | 1/7/2021 | Viral upper respiratory infection
Atlanta | Alex | Olsen | 12/28/2020 | Hypotension
Atlanta | Tom | Chang | 12/23/2020 | Fracture of left fifth metacarpal
Atlanta | Carlos | Reyes | 12/23/2020 | Cardiac monitoring
Atlanta | Alex | Olsen | 12/1/2020 | Influenza
Atlanta | Terry | Cruz | 11/17/2020 | Pneumonia
Atlanta | Gregory | Davis | 11/16/2020 | Dermatitis
Atlanta | Student First | Student Last | 11/3/2020 | Dermatitis
Atlanta | Jose | Rodriguez | 10/26/2020 | Laceration of left hand
Record: 1 of 21
Filtered
Search
Ready
Filtered

The button labeled "Filtered" to the right of the navigation buttons and the notation "Filtered" on the status bar both indicate a filter has been applied to the datasheet. Also, notice that the Toggle Filter button in the Sort & Filter group on the Home tab is active; you can click this button or the Filtered button next to the navigation buttons to toggle between the filtered and unfiltered displays of the query datasheet. The City column heading also has a filter icon on it; you can click this icon to display additional options for filtering the field.

Next, Taylor wants to view only those records with a Reason field value beginning with the word "Annual" so she can view the records for annual wellness visits. You need to apply an additional filter to the datasheet.

4. In any Reason field value beginning with the word "Annual", select only the text **Annual**.
5. In the Sort & Filter group, click the **Selection** button. The same four filter types are available for this selection as when you filtered the City field.
6. On the Selection menu, click **Begins With "Annual"**. The second filter is applied to the query datasheet, which now shows only the four records for patients from Atlanta who have had an annual wellness visit at the clinic.

   Now you can redisplay all the query records by clicking the Toggle Filter button, which you use to switch between the filtered and unfiltered displays.

TIP

The ScreenTip for this button is Remove Filter.

7. In the Sort & Filter group, click the **Toggle Filter** button. The filter is removed, and all 85 records appear in the query datasheet.
8. Close the PatientVisits query. A dialog box opens, asking if you want to save your changes to the design of the query—in this case, the filtered display, which is still available through the Toggle Filter button. Taylor does not want the query saved with the filter because she doesn't need to view the filtered information on a regular basis.
9. Click **No** to close the query without saving the changes.
10. If you are not continuing to Session 3.2, click the **File** tab, and then click **Close** in the navigation bar to close the Lakewood database.

REVIEW

Session 3.1 Quick Check

1. In Datasheet view, what is the difference between navigation mode and editing mode?
2. What command can you use in Datasheet view to remove the display of one or more fields from the datasheet?
3. What is a select query?
4. Describe the field list and the design grid in the Query window in Design view.
5. How are a table datasheet and a query datasheet similar? How are they different?
6. For a Date/Time field, how do the records appear when sorted in ascending order?
7. When you define multiple sort fields in Design view, describe how the sort fields must be positioned in the design grid.
8. A(n) ____________ is a set of restrictions you place on the records in an open datasheet or form to isolate a subset of records temporarily.

Session 3.2 Visual Overview:

When creating queries in Design view, you can enter criteria so that Access will display only selected records in the query results.

Field:	PatientID	LastName	FirstName	BirthDate	City
Table:	Patient	Patient	Patient	Patient	Patient
Sort:					
Show:	☑	☑	☑	☑	☑
Criteria:					"Marietta"
or:					

To define a condition for a field, you place the condition in the field's Criteria box in the design grid.

To tell Access which records you want to select, you must specify a condition as part of the query. A **condition** is a criterion, or rule, that determines which records are selected.

Field:	InvoiceNum	InvoiceDate	InvoiceAmt		
Table:	Billing	Billing	Billing		
Sort:					
Show:	☑	☑	☑	☐	☐
Criteria:			>325		
or:					

A condition usually consists of an operator, often a comparison operator, and a value. A **comparison operator** asks Access to compare the value to the condition value and to select all the records for which the condition is true.

Field:	VisitID	PatientID	VisitDate	Reason
Table:	Visit	Visit	Visit	Visit
Sort:				
Show:	☑	☑	☑	☑
Criteria:			Between #10/1/2020# And #10/31/2020#	
or:				

Most comparison operators (such as Between … And …) ask Access to select records that match a range of values for the condition—in this case, all records with dates that fall within the range shown.

Selection Criteria in Queries

The results of a query containing selection criteria include only the records that meet the specified criteria.

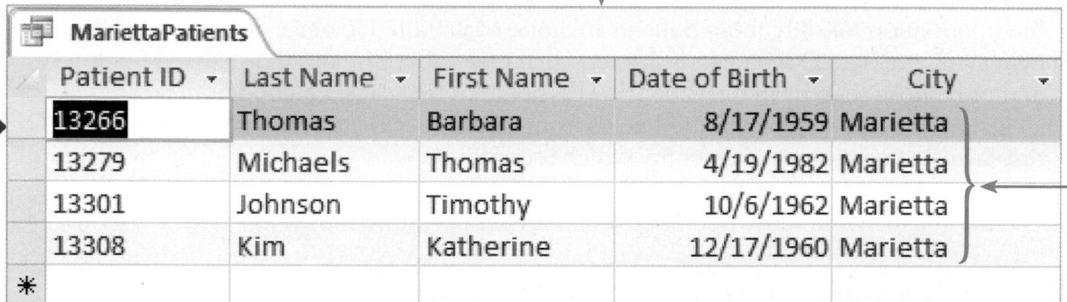

MariettaPatients

Patient ID	Last Name	First Name	Date of Birth	City
13266	Thomas	Barbara	8/17/1959	Marietta
13279	Michaels	Thomas	4/19/1982	Marietta
13301	Johnson	Timothy	10/6/1962	Marietta
13308	Kim	Katherine	12/17/1960	Marietta
*				

The results of this query show only patients from Marietta because the condition "Marietta" in the City field's Criteria box specifies that Access should select records only with City field values of Marietta. This type of condition is called an **exact match** because the value in the specified field must match the condition exactly in order for the record to be included in the query results.

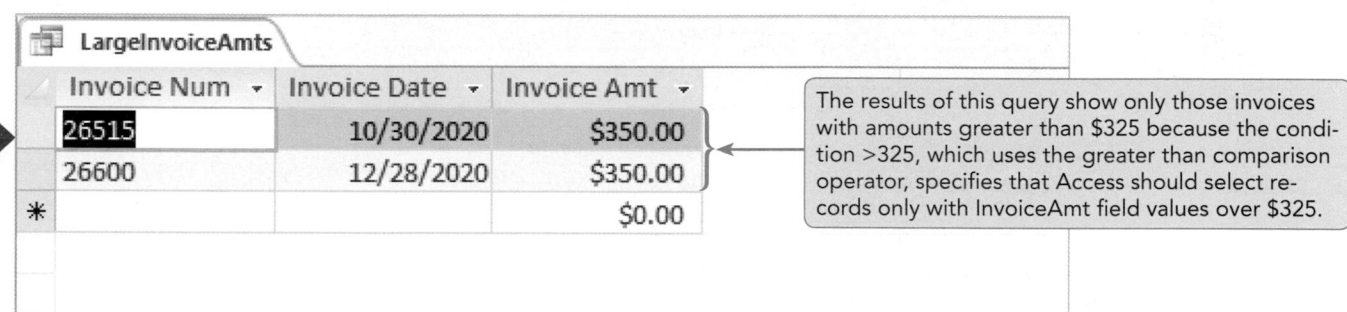

LargeInvoiceAmts

Invoice Num	Invoice Date	Invoice Amt
26515	10/30/2020	$350.00
26600	12/28/2020	$350.00
*		$0.00

The results of this query show only those invoices with amounts greater than $325 because the condition >325, which uses the greater than comparison operator, specifies that Access should select records only with InvoiceAmt field values over $325.

OctoberVisits

Visit ID	Patient ID	Date of Visit	Reason/Diagnosis
1450	13272	10/26/2020	Influenza
1451	13309	10/26/2020	Laceration of left hand
1453	13260	10/27/2020	Annual wellness visit - dermatitis
1458	13296	10/29/2020	Fracture of right tibia
*			

The results of this query show only those patient visits that took place in October 2020 because the condition in the VisitDate's Criteria box specifies that Access should select only records with a visit date between 10/1/2020 and 10/31/2020.

Defining Record Selection Criteria for Queries

Donna wants to display patient and visit information for all patients who live in Stone Mountain. She is considering having the clinic hold a health fair in Stone Mountain, so she is interested in knowing more about patients from this city. For this request, you could create a query to select the correct fields and all records in the Patient and Visit tables, select a City field value of Stone Mountain in the query datasheet, and then click the Selection button and choose the appropriate filter option to display the information for only those patients in Stone Mountain. However, a faster way of displaying the data Donna needs is to create a query that displays the selected fields and only those records in the Patient and Visit tables that satisfy a condition.

Just as you can display selected fields from a database in a query datasheet, you can display selected records. To identify which records you want to select, you must specify a condition as part of the query, as illustrated in the Session 3.2 Visual Overview. A condition usually includes one of the comparison operators shown in Figure 3–16.

Figure 3–16 Access comparison operators

Operator	Meaning	Example
=	equal to (optional; default operator)	="Hall"
<>	not equal to	<>"Hall"
<	less than	<#1/1/99#
<=	less than or equal to	<=100
>	greater than	>"C400"
>=	greater than or equal to	>=18.75
Between … And …	between two values (inclusive)	Between 50 And 325
In ()	in a list of values	In ("Hall", "Seeger")
Like	matches a pattern that includes wildcards	Like "706*"

Specifying an Exact Match

For Donna's request, you need to first create a query that will display only those records in the Patient table with the value Stone Mountain in the City field. This type of condition is an exact match because the value in the specified field must match the condition exactly in order for the record to be included in the query results. You'll create the query in Design view.

To create the query in Design view:

1. If you took a break after the previous session, make sure that the Lakewood database is open and the Navigation Pane is closed, and then on the ribbon, click the **Create** tab.
2. In the Queries group, click the **Query Design** button. The Show Table dialog box opens. You need to add the Patient and Visit tables to the Query window.
3. Click **Patient** in the Tables list, click **Add**, click **Visit**, click **Add**, and then click the **Close** button. The field lists for the Patient and Visit tables appear in the top portion of the window, and join lines indicating one-to-many relationships connect the tables.

4. Resize both field lists so that all the fields are displayed.
5. Add the following fields from the Patient table to the design grid in this order: **LastName**, **FirstName**, **Phone**, **Address**, **City**, and **Email**.

   Donna also wants information from the Visit table included in the query results.
6. Add the following fields from the Visit table to the design grid in this order: **VisitID**, **VisitDate**, and **Reason**. See Figure 3–17.

Figure 3–17 Design grid after adding fields from both tables

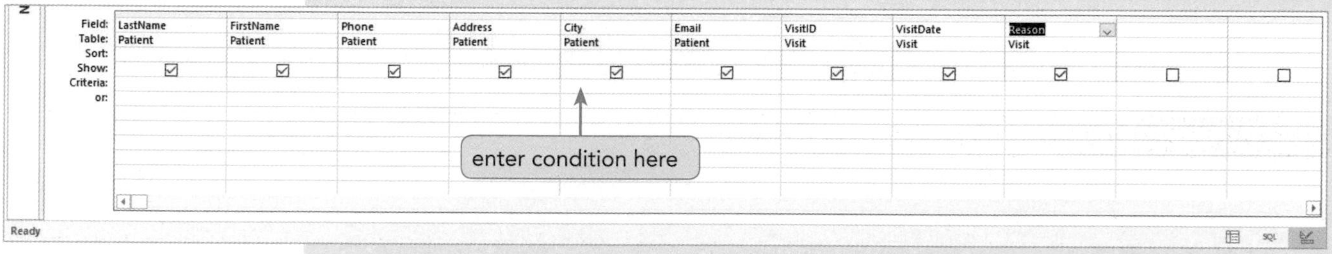
Field:
Table:
Sort:
Show:
Criteria:
or:
LastName
Patient
FirstName
Patient
Phone
Patient
Address
Patient
City
Patient
Email
Patient
VisitID
Visit
VisitDate
Visit
Reason
Visit
enter condition here
Ready

To display the information Donna wants, you need to enter the condition for the City field in its Criteria box, as shown in Figure 3–17. Donna wants to display only those records with a City field value of Stone Mountain.

To enter the exact match condition, and then save and run the query:

1. Click the **City Criteria** box, type **Stone Mountain**, and then press **ENTER**. The condition changes to "Stone Mountain".

   Access automatically enclosed the condition you typed in quotation marks. You must enclose text values in quotation marks when using them as selection criteria. If you omit the quotation marks, however, Access will include them automatically in most cases. Some words—including "in" and "select"—are special keywords in Access that are reserved for functions and commands. If you want to enter one of these keywords as the condition, you must type the quotation marks around the text or an error message will appear indicating the condition cannot be entered.
2. Save the query with the name **StoneMountainPatients**. The query is saved, and its name is displayed on the object tab.
3. Run the query. After the query runs, the selected field values for only those records with a City field value of Stone Mountain are shown. A total of 10 records is selected and displayed in the datasheet. See Figure 3–18.

Figure 3–18 **Datasheet displaying selected fields and records**

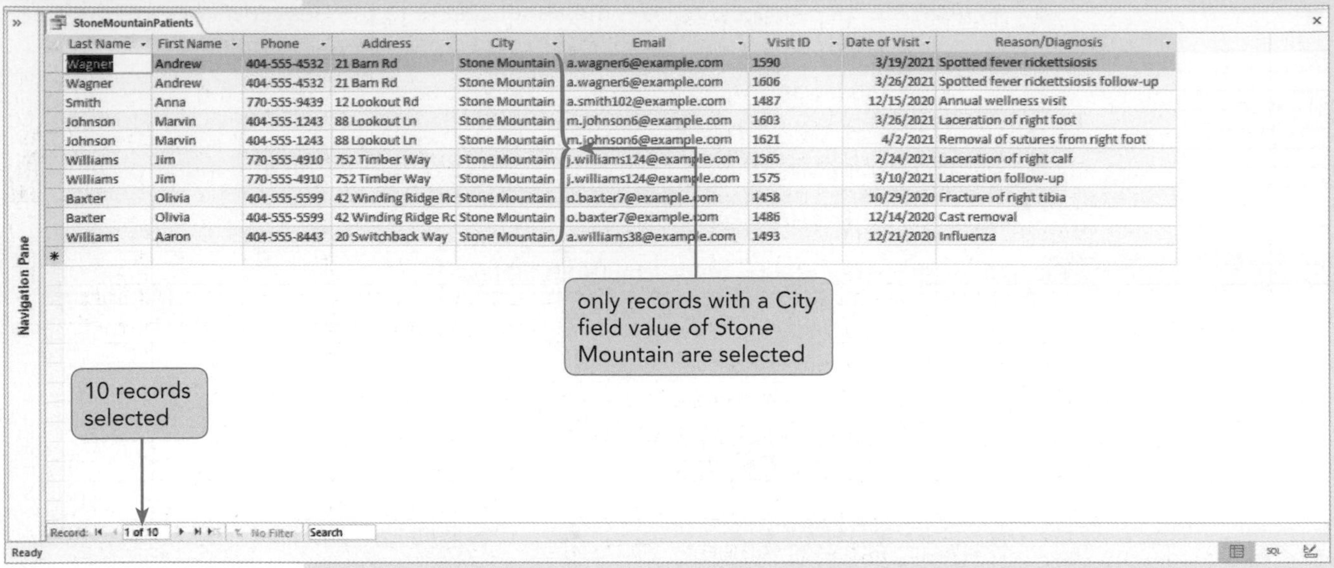
StoneMountainPatients
Navigation Pane
only records with a City field value of Stone Mountain are selected
10 records selected
Record: 1 of 10
No Filter
Search
Ready

Last Name	First Name	Phone	Address	City	Email	Visit ID	Date of Visit	Reason/Diagnosis
Wagner	Andrew	404-555-4532	21 Barn Rd	Stone Mountain	a.wagner6@example.com	1590	3/19/2021	Spotted fever rickettsiosis
Wagner	Andrew	404-555-4532	21 Barn Rd	Stone Mountain	a.wagner6@example.com	1606	3/26/2021	Spotted fever rickettsiosis follow-up
Smith	Anna	770-555-9439	12 Lookout Rd	Stone Mountain	a.smith102@example.com	1487	12/15/2020	Annual wellness visit
Johnson	Marvin	404-555-1243	88 Lookout Ln	Stone Mountain	m.johnson6@example.com	1603	3/26/2021	Laceration of right foot
Johnson	Marvin	404-555-1243	88 Lookout Ln	Stone Mountain	m.johnson6@example.com	1621	4/2/2021	Removal of sutures from right foot
Williams	Jim	770-555-4910	752 Timber Way	Stone Mountain	j.williams124@example.com	1565	2/24/2021	Laceration of right calf
Williams	Jim	770-555-4910	752 Timber Way	Stone Mountain	j.williams124@example.com	1575	3/10/2021	Laceration follow-up
Baxter	Olivia	404-555-5599	42 Winding Ridge Rc	Stone Mountain	o.baxter7@example.com	1458	10/29/2020	Fracture of right tibia
Baxter	Olivia	404-555-5599	42 Winding Ridge Rc	Stone Mountain	o.baxter7@example.com	1486	12/14/2020	Cast removal
Williams	Aaron	404-555-8443	20 Switchback Way	Stone Mountain	a.williams38@example.com	1493	12/21/2020	Influenza

Donna realizes that it's not necessary to include the City field values in the query results. The name of the query, StoneMountainPatients, indicates that the query design includes all patients who live in Stone Mountain, so the City field values are unnecessary and repetitive in the query results. Also, she decides that she would prefer the query datasheet to show the fields from the Visit table first, followed by the Patient table fields. You need to modify the query to produce the results Donna wants.

Modifying a Query

After you create a query and view the results, you might need to make changes to the query if the results are not what you expected or require. First, Donna asks you to modify the StoneMountainPatients query so that it does not display the City field values in the query results.

To remove the display of the City field values:

1. On the Home tab, in the Views group, click the **View** button. The StoneMountainPatients query opens in Design view.

   You need to keep the City field as part of the query design because it contains the defined condition for the query. You only need to remove the display of the field's values from the query results.

2. Click the **City Show** check box to remove the checkmark. The query will still find only those records with the value Stone Mountain in the City field, but the query results will not display these field values.

Next, you need to change the order of the fields in the query so that the visit information is listed first.

To move the Visit table fields to precede the Patient table fields:

1. Position the pointer on the VisitID field selector until the selection pointer appears ⬇, and then click to select the field. See Figure 3–19.

Figure 3–19 Selected VisitID field

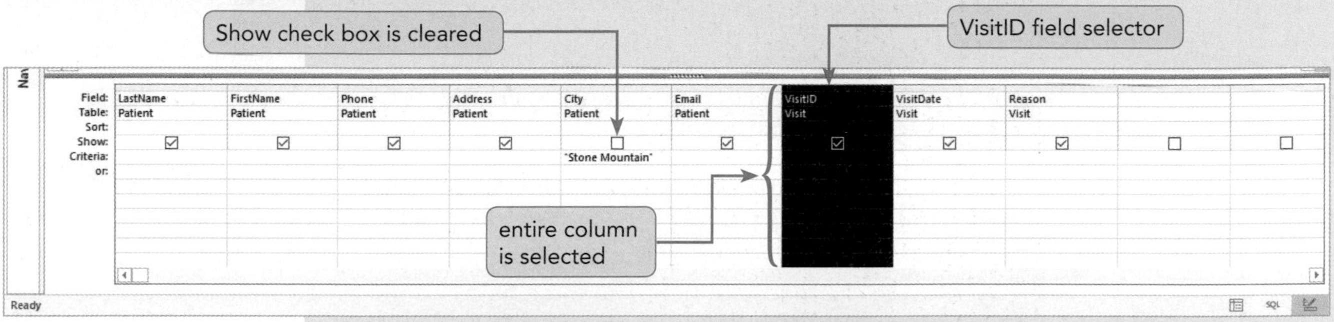
Show check box is cleared
VisitID field selector
entire column is selected
Field:
Table:
Sort:
Show:
Criteria:
or:
LastName
Patient
FirstName
Patient
Phone
Patient
Address
Patient
City
Patient
"Stone Mountain"
Email
Patient
VisitID
Visit
VisitDate
Visit
Reason
Visit
Ready

2. Position the pointer on the VisitID field selector, and then press and hold the mouse button; notice that the pointer changes to the move pointer, and a black vertical line appears to the left of the selected field. This line represents the selected field when you drag the mouse to move it.
3. Drag the pointer to the left until the vertical line representing the selected field is positioned to the left of the LastName field. See Figure 3–20.

Figure 3–20 Dragging the field in the design grid

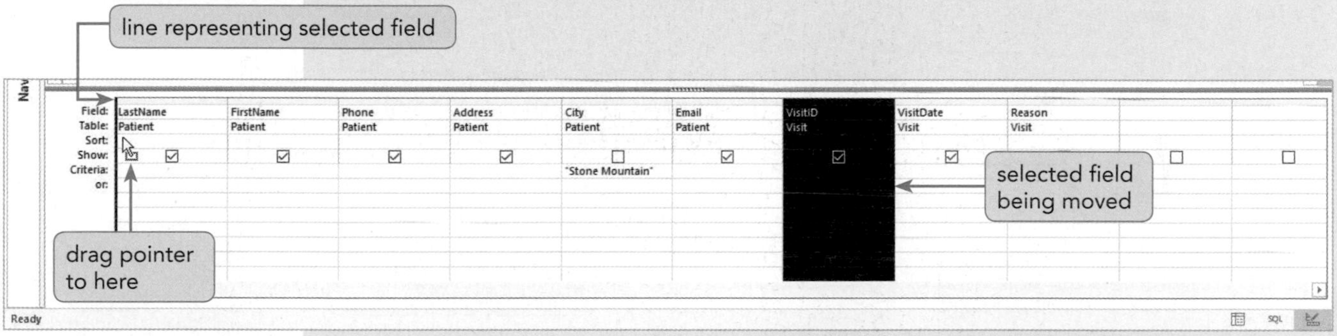
line representing selected field
drag pointer to here
selected field being moved
Field:
Table:
Sort:
Show:
Criteria:
or:
LastName
Patient
FirstName
Patient
Phone
Patient
Address
Patient
City
Patient
"Stone Mountain"
Email
Patient
VisitID
Visit
VisitDate
Visit
Reason
Visit
Ready

TIP

Instead of moving a field by dragging, you can also delete the field and then add it back to the design grid in the location you want.

4. Release the mouse button. The VisitID field moves to the left of the LastName field.

   You can also select and move multiple fields at once. You need to select and move the VisitDate and Reason fields so that they follow the VisitID field in the query design. To select multiple fields, you click and drag the mouse over the field selectors for the fields you want.

5. Click and hold the selection pointer ⬇ on the VisitDate field selector, drag the pointer to the right to select the Reason field, and then release the mouse button. Both fields are now selected. See Figure 3–21.

Figure 3–21 **Multiple fields selected to be moved**

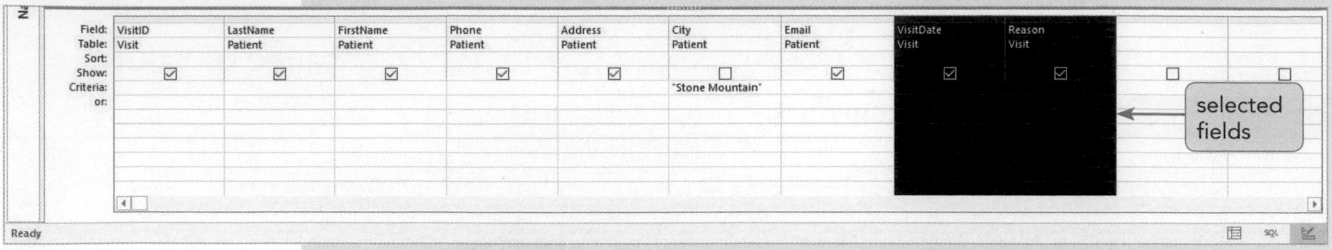

Field: VisitID | LastName | FirstName | Phone | Address | City | Email | VisitDate | Reason
Table: Visit | Patient | Patient | Patient | Patient | Patient | Patient | Visit | Visit
Sort:
Show:
Criteria: "Stone Mountain"
or:
selected fields
Ready

6. Position the selection pointer on the field selector for any of the two selected fields, press and hold the mouse button, and then drag to the left until the vertical line representing the selected fields is positioned to the left of the LastName field.
7. Release the mouse button. The three fields from the Visit table are now the first three fields in the query design.

   You have finished making the modifications to the query Donna requested, so you can now run the query.
8. Run the query. The results of the modified query are displayed. See Figure 3-22.

Figure 3–22 **Results of the modified query**

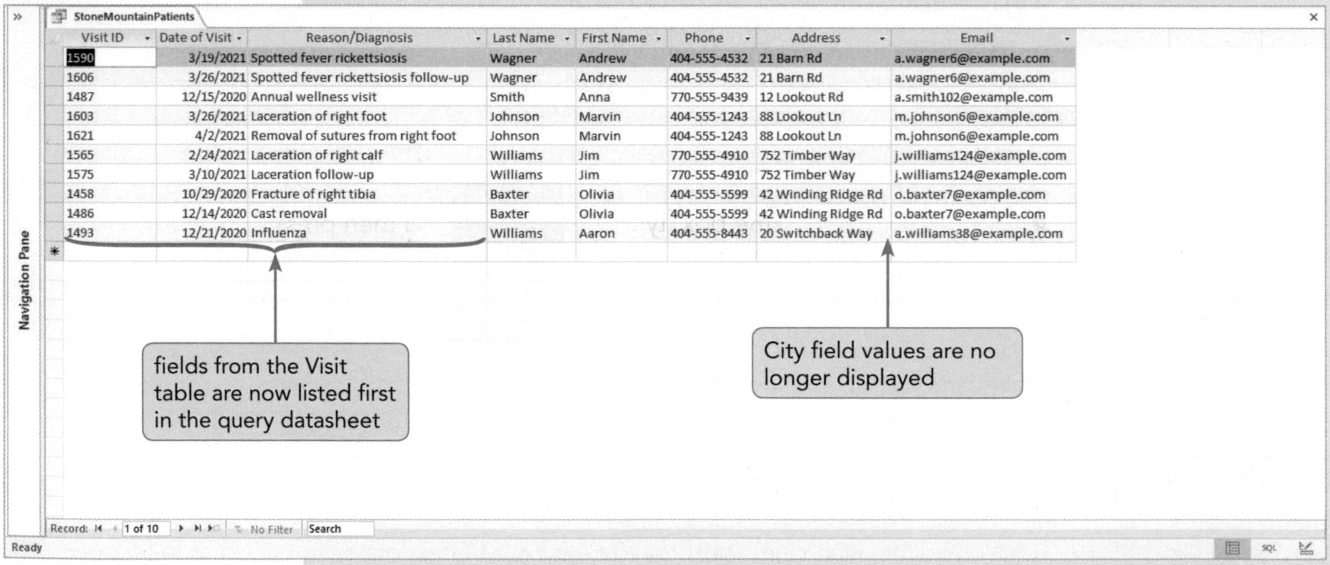

StoneMountainPatients

Visit ID	Date of Visit	Reason/Diagnosis	Last Name	First Name	Phone	Address	Email
1590	3/19/2021	Spotted fever rickettsiosis	Wagner	Andrew	404-555-4532	21 Barn Rd	a.wagner6@example.com
1606	3/26/2021	Spotted fever rickettsiosis follow-up	Wagner	Andrew	404-555-4532	21 Barn Rd	a.wagner6@example.com
1487	12/15/2020	Annual wellness visit	Smith	Anna	770-555-9439	12 Lookout Rd	a.smith102@example.com
1603	3/26/2021	Laceration of right foot	Johnson	Marvin	404-555-1243	88 Lookout Ln	m.johnson6@example.com
1621	4/2/2021	Removal of sutures from right foot	Johnson	Marvin	404-555-1243	88 Lookout Ln	m.johnson6@example.com
1565	2/24/2021	Laceration of right calf	Williams	Jim	770-555-4910	752 Timber Way	j.williams124@example.com
1575	3/10/2021	Laceration follow-up	Williams	Jim	770-555-4910	752 Timber Way	j.williams124@example.com
1458	10/29/2020	Fracture of right tibia	Baxter	Olivia	404-555-5599	42 Winding Ridge Rd	o.baxter7@example.com
1486	12/14/2020	Cast removal	Baxter	Olivia	404-555-5599	42 Winding Ridge Rd	o.baxter7@example.com
1493	12/21/2020	Influenza	Williams	Aaron	404-555-8443	20 Switchback Way	a.williams38@example.com

Navigation Pane
fields from the Visit table are now listed first in the query datasheet
City field values are no longer displayed
Record: 1 of 10
No Filter
Search
Ready

Note that the City field values are no longer displayed in the query results.

9. Save and close the StoneMountainPatients query.

After viewing the query results, Donna decides that she would like to see the same fields, but only for those records with a VisitDate field value before 1/1/2021. She is interested to know which patients of Lakewood Community Health Services in all cities have not been to the clinic recently, so that her staff can follow up with the patients by sending them reminder notes or emails. To create the query that will produce the results Donna wants, you need to use a comparison operator to match a range of values—in this case, any VisitDate value less than 1/1/2021. Because this new query will include information from several of the same fields as the StoneMountainPatients query, you can use that query as a starting point in designing this new query.

Using a Comparison Operator to Match a Range of Values

After you create and save a query, you can double-click the query name in the Navigation Pane to run the query again. You can then click the View button to change its design. You can also use an existing query as the basis for creating another query. Because the design of the query you need to create next is similar to the StoneMountainPatients query, you will copy, paste, and rename this query to create the new query. Using this approach keeps the StoneMountainPatients query intact.

To create the new query by copying the StoneMountainPatients query:

1. Open the Navigation Pane. Note that the StoneMountainPatients query is listed in the Queries section.

   You need to use the shortcut menu to copy the StoneMountainPatients query and paste it in the Navigation Pane; then you'll give the copied query a different name.

2. In the Queries section of the Navigation Pane, right-click **StoneMountainPatients** to select it and display the shortcut menu.
3. Click **Copy** on the shortcut menu.
4. Right-click the empty area near the bottom of the Navigation Pane, and then click **Paste** on the shortcut menu. The Paste As dialog box opens with the text "Copy Of StoneMountainPatients" in the Query Name box. Because Donna wants the new query to show data for patients that have not visited the clinic recently, you'll name the new query "EarlierVisits".
5. In the Query Name box, type **EarlierVisits** and then press **ENTER**. The new query appears in the Queries section of the Navigation Pane.
6. Double-click the **EarlierVisits** query to open, or run, the query. The design of this query is currently the same as the original StoneMountainPatients query.
7. Close the Navigation Pane.

Next, you need to open the query in Design view and modify its design to produce the results Donna wants—to display records for all patients and only those records with VisitDate field values that are earlier than, or less than, 1/1/2021.

To modify the design of the new query:

1. Display the query in Design view.
2. Click the **VisitDate Criteria** box, type **<1/1/2021** and then press **TAB**. Note that Access automatically encloses the date criteria with number signs. The condition specifies that a record will be selected only if its VisitDate field value is less than (earlier than) 1/1/2021. See Figure 3–23.

Figure 3–23 Criteria entered for the VisitDate field

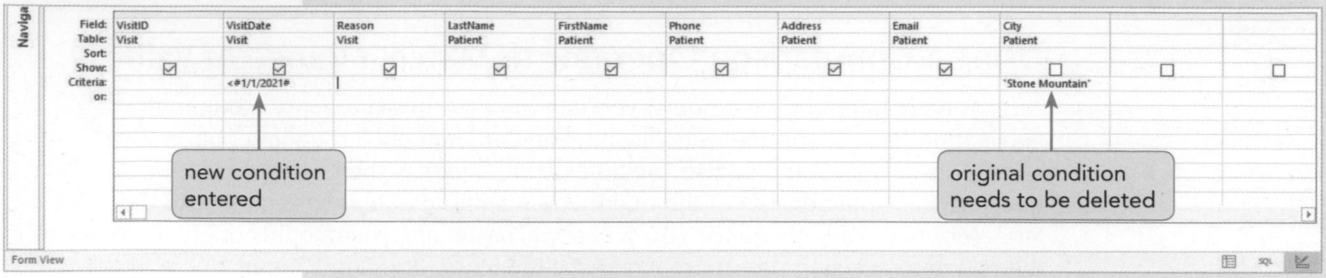
new condition entered
original condition needs to be deleted

Note that Access automatically encloses the date criteria with number signs. The condition specifies that a record will be selected only if its VisitDate field value is less than (earlier than) 1/1/2021.

Before you run the query, you need to delete the condition for the City field. Recall that the City field is part of the query, but its values are not displayed in the query results. When you modified the query to remove the City field values from the query results, Access moved the field to the end of the design grid. You need to delete the City field's condition, specify that the City field values should be included in the query results, and then move the field back to its original position following the Address field.

3. Press **TAB** six times to select the condition for the City field, and then press **DELETE**. The condition for the City field is removed.
4. Click the **Show** check box for the City field to insert a checkmark so that the field values will be displayed in the query results.
5. Use the pointer to select the City field, drag the selected field to position it to the left of the Email field, and then click in an empty box to deselect the City field. See Figure 3–24.

Figure 3–24 Design grid after moving the City field

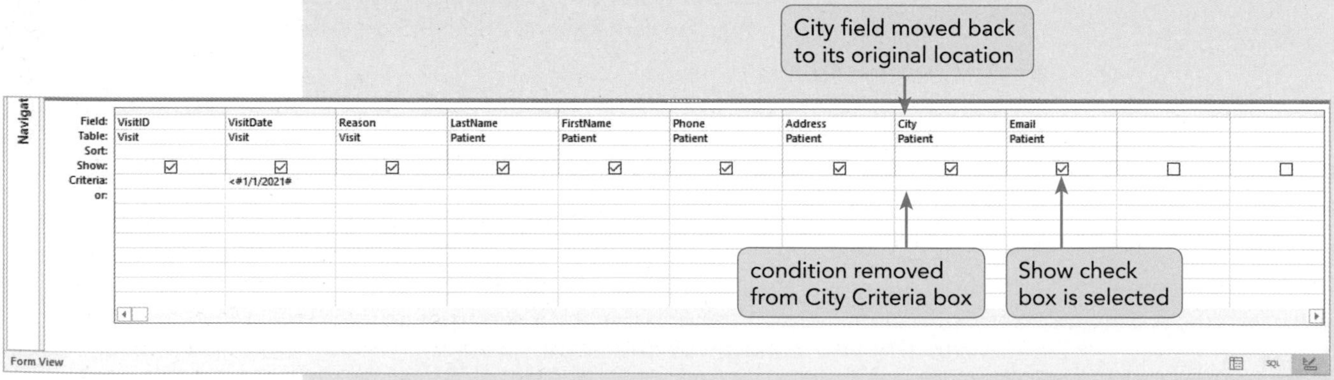
City field moved back to its original location
condition removed from City Criteria box
Show check box is selected

6. Run the query. The query datasheet displays the selected fields for only those records with a VisitDate field value less than 1/1/2021, a total of 27 records. See Figure 3–25.

Figure 3–25 **Running the modified query**

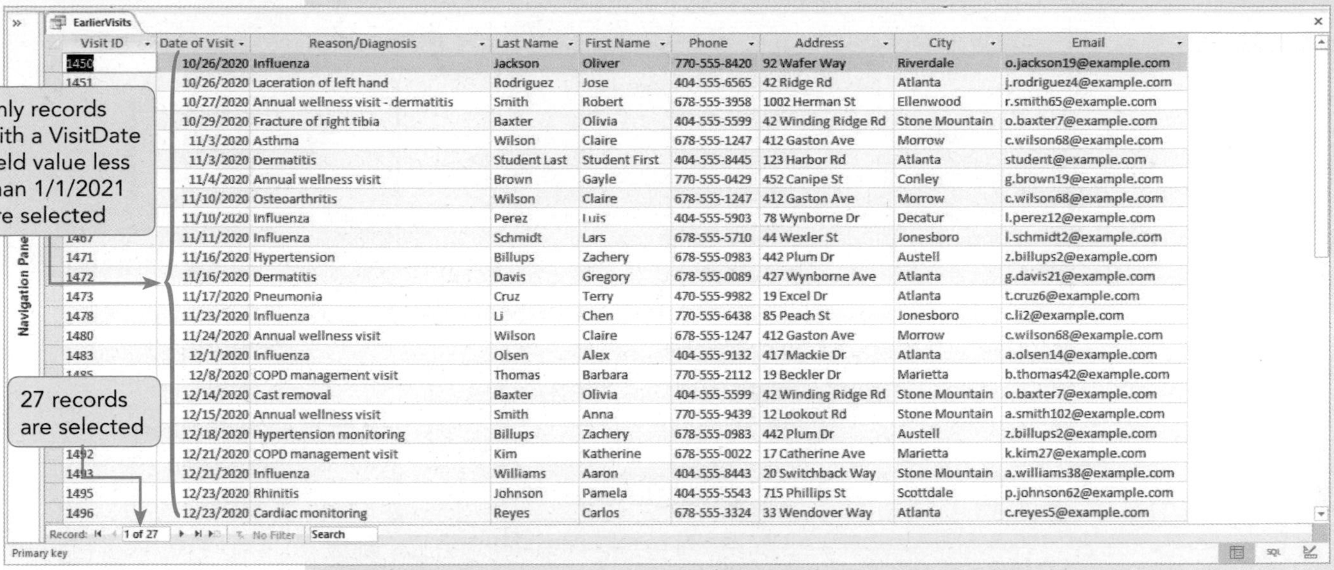
EarlierVisits
Visit ID | Date of Visit | Reason/Diagnosis | Last Name | First Name | Phone | Address | City | Email
1450 | 10/26/2020 | Influenza | Jackson | Oliver | 770-555-8420 | 92 Wafer Way | Riverdale | o.jackson19@example.com
1451 | 10/26/2020 | Laceration of left hand | Rodriguez | Jose | 404-555-6565 | 42 Ridge Rd | Atlanta | j.rodriguez4@example.com
10/27/2020 | Annual wellness visit - dermatitis | Smith | Robert | 678-555-3958 | 1002 Herman St | Ellenwood | r.smith65@example.com
10/29/2020 | Fracture of right tibia | Baxter | Olivia | 404-555-5599 | 42 Winding Ridge Rd | Stone Mountain | o.baxter7@example.com
11/3/2020 | Asthma | Wilson | Claire | 678-555-1247 | 412 Gaston Ave | Morrow | c.wilson68@example.com
11/3/2020 | Dermatitis | Student Last | Student First | 404-555-8445 | 123 Harbor Rd | Atlanta | student@example.com
11/4/2020 | Annual wellness visit | Brown | Gayle | 770-555-0429 | 452 Canipe St | Conley | g.brown19@example.com
11/10/2020 | Osteoarthritis | Wilson | Claire | 678-555-1247 | 412 Gaston Ave | Morrow | c.wilson68@example.com
11/10/2020 | Influenza | Perez | Luis | 404-555-5903 | 78 Wynborne Dr | Decatur | l.perez12@example.com
11/11/2020 | Influenza | Schmidt | Lars | 678-555-5710 | 44 Wexler St | Jonesboro | l.schmidt2@example.com
1471 | 11/16/2020 | Hypertension | Billups | Zachery | 678-555-0983 | 442 Plum Dr | Austell | z.billups2@example.com
1472 | 11/16/2020 | Dermatitis | Davis | Gregory | 678-555-0089 | 427 Wynborne Ave | Atlanta | g.davis21@example.com
1473 | 11/17/2020 | Pneumonia | Cruz | Terry | 470-555-9982 | 19 Excel Dr | Atlanta | t.cruz6@example.com
1478 | 11/23/2020 | Influenza | Li | Chen | 770-555-6438 | 85 Peach St | Jonesboro | c.li2@example.com
1480 | 11/24/2020 | Annual wellness visit | Wilson | Claire | 678-555-1247 | 412 Gaston Ave | Morrow | c.wilson68@example.com
1483 | 12/1/2020 | Influenza | Olsen | Alex | 404-555-9132 | 417 Mackie Dr | Atlanta | a.olsen14@example.com
12/8/2020 | COPD management visit | Thomas | Barbara | 770-555-2112 | 19 Beckler Dr | Marietta | b.thomas42@example.com
12/14/2020 | Cast removal | Baxter | Olivia | 404-555-5599 | 42 Winding Ridge Rd | Stone Mountain | o.baxter7@example.com
12/15/2020 | Annual wellness visit | Smith | Anna | 770-555-9439 | 12 Lookout Rd | Stone Mountain | a.smith102@example.com
12/18/2020 | Hypertension monitoring | Billups | Zachery | 678-555-0983 | 442 Plum Dr | Austell | z.billups2@example.com
12/21/2020 | COPD management visit | Kim | Katherine | 678-555-0022 | 17 Catherine Ave | Marietta | k.kim27@example.com
12/21/2020 | Influenza | Williams | Aaron | 404-555-8443 | 20 Switchback Way | Stone Mountain | a.williams38@example.com
1495 | 12/23/2020 | Rhinitis | Johnson | Pamela | 404-555-5543 | 715 Phillips St | Scottdale | p.johnson62@example.com
1496 | 12/23/2020 | Cardiac monitoring | Reyes | Carlos | 678-555-3324 | 33 Wendover Way | Atlanta | c.reyes5@example.com
Record: 1 of 27
No Filter
Search
Primary key
Navigation Pane
only records with a VisitDate field value less than 1/1/2021 are selected
27 records are selected

7. Save and close the EarlierVisits query.

Donna continues to analyze patient visits to Lakewood Community Health Services. She is especially concerned about being proactive and reaching out to older patients well in advance of flu season. With this in mind, she would like to see a list of all patients who are age 50 or older and who have visited the clinic suffering from influenza. She wants to track these patients in particular so that her staff can contact them early for flu shots. To produce this list, you need to create a query containing two conditions—one for the patient's date of birth and another for the reason/diagnosis for each patient visit.

Defining Multiple Selection Criteria for Queries

Multiple conditions require you to use **logical operators** to combine two or more conditions. When you want a record selected only if two or more conditions are met, you need to use the **And logical operator**. In this case, Donna wants to see only those records with a BirthDate field value less than or equal to 12/31/1970 *and* a Reason field value of "Influenza." If you place conditions in separate fields in the *same* Criteria row of the design grid, all conditions in that row must be met in order for a record to be included in the query results. However, if you place conditions in *different* Criteria rows, a record will be selected if at least one of the conditions is met. If none of the conditions are met, Access does not select the record. When you place conditions in different Criteria rows, you are using the **Or logical operator**. Figure 3–26 illustrates the difference between the And and Or logical operators.

Figure 3–26 Logical operators And and Or for multiple selection criteria

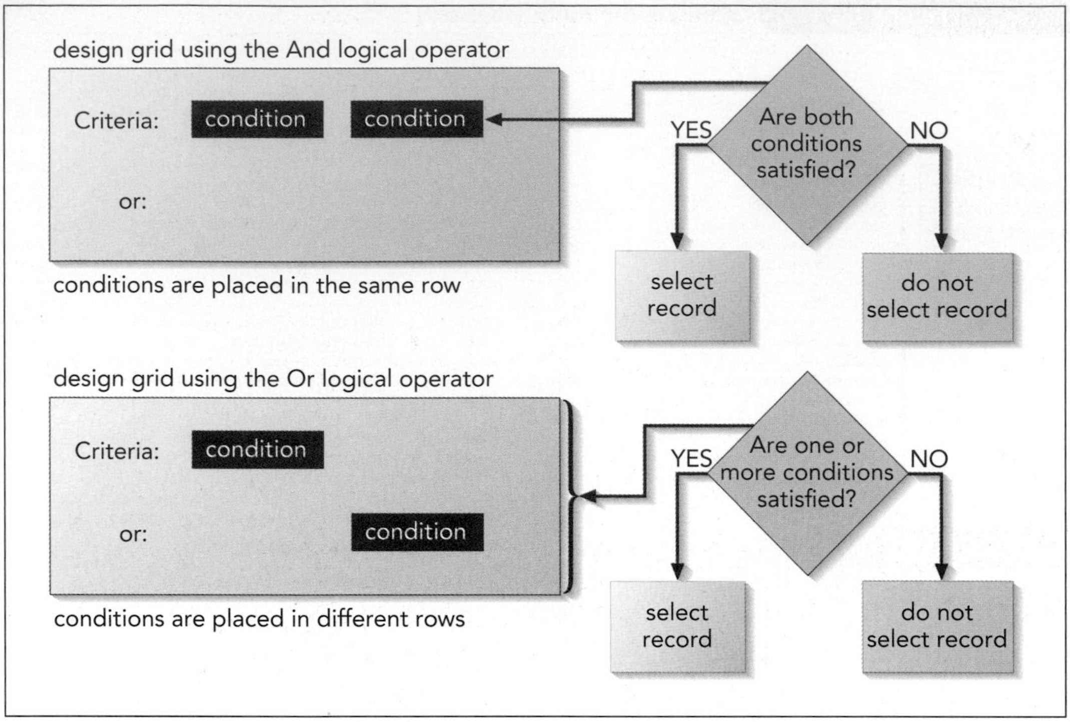
design grid using the And logical operator
Criteria:
condition
condition
or:
conditions are placed in the same row
Are both conditions satisfied?
YES
NO
select record
do not select record
design grid using the Or logical operator
Criteria:
condition
or:
condition
conditions are placed in different rows
Are one or more conditions satisfied?
YES
NO
select record
do not select record

The And Logical Operator

To create the query for Donna, you need to use the And logical operator to show only the records for patients that were born on or after 12/31/1970 *and* who have visited the clinic because of influenza. You'll create a new query based on the Patient and Visit tables to produce the necessary results. In the query design, both conditions you specify will appear in the same Criteria row; therefore, the query will select records only if both conditions are met.

To create a new query using the And logical operator:

1. On the ribbon, click the **Create** tab.
2. In the Queries group, click the **Query Design** button.
3. Add the **Patient** and **Visit** tables to the Query window, and then close the Show Table dialog box. Resize both field lists to display all the field names.
4. Add the following fields from the Patient field list to the design grid in the order shown: **FirstName**, **LastName**, **BirthDate**, **Phone**, and **City**.
5. Add the **VisitDate** and **Reason** fields from the Visit table to the design grid. Now you need to enter the two conditions for the query.
6. Click the **BirthDate Criteria** box, and then type **<=12/31/1970**.
7. Press **TAB** four times to move to the **Reason Criteria** box, type **Influenza**, and then press **TAB**. See Figure 3–27.

Figure 3–27 **Query to find older patients who have had influenza**

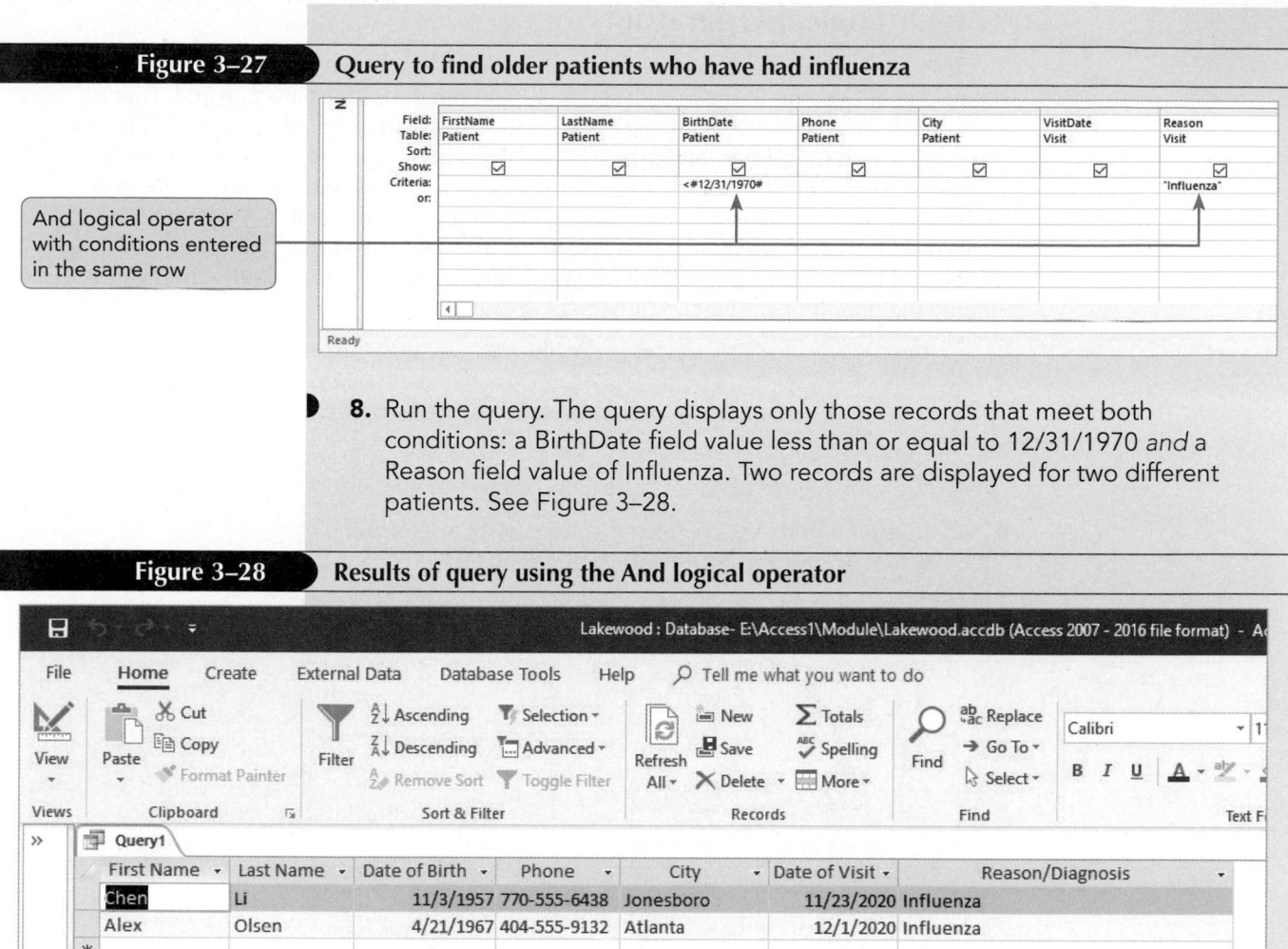

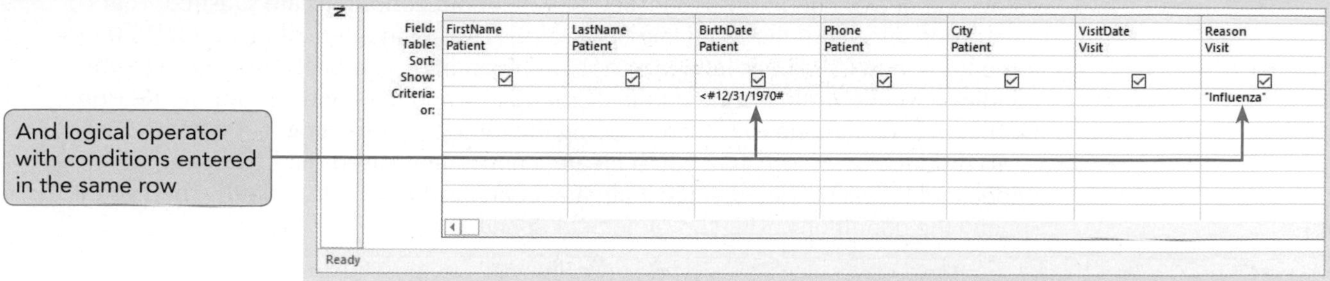
And logical operator with conditions entered in the same row
Field: FirstName LastName BirthDate Phone City VisitDate Reason
Table: Patient Patient Patient Patient Patient Visit Visit
Sort:
Show:
Criteria: <=#12/31/1970# "Influenza"
or:
Ready

8. Run the query. The query displays only those records that meet both conditions: a BirthDate field value less than or equal to 12/31/1970 *and* a Reason field value of Influenza. Two records are displayed for two different patients. See Figure 3–28.

Figure 3–28 **Results of query using the And logical operator**

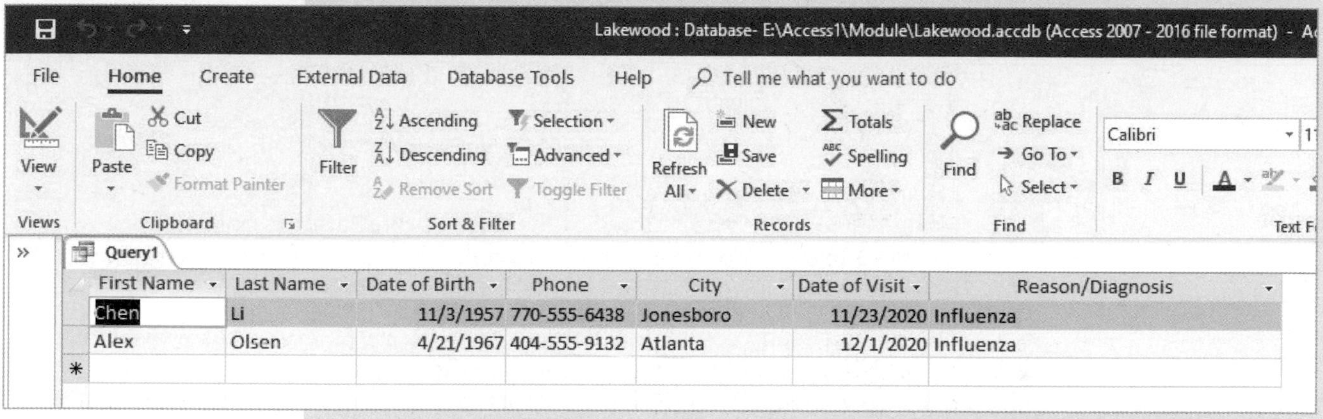
Lakewood : Database- E:\Access1\Module\Lakewood.accdb (Access 2007 - 2016 file format)
File Home Create External Data Database Tools Help Tell me what you want to do
Query1
First Name | Last Name | Date of Birth | Phone | City | Date of Visit | Reason/Diagnosis
Chen | Li | 11/3/1957 | 770-555-6438 | Jonesboro | 11/23/2020 | Influenza
Alex | Olsen | 4/21/1967 | 404-555-9132 | Atlanta | 12/1/2020 | Influenza

9. On the Quick Access Toolbar, click the **Save** button, and then save the query as **OlderAndFluPatients**.

10. Close the query.

Donna meets with staff members to discuss the issue of influenza and patients being informed about receiving flu shots at the clinic. After viewing the results of the OlderAndFluPatients query, the group agrees that the clinic should reach out to older patients regarding flu shots, because this segment of the population is particularly susceptible to the flu. In addition, the group feels the clinic should contact patients who have visited the clinic suffering from influenza to keep these patients informed about flu shots well in advance of flu season. To help with their planning, Donna asks you to produce a list of all patients that were born on or before 12/31/1970 or who visited the clinic because of influenza. To create this query, you need to use the Or logical operator.

The Or Logical Operator

To create the query that Donna requested, your query must select a record when either one of two conditions is satisfied or when both conditions are satisfied. That is, a record is selected if the BirthDate field value is less than or equal to 12/31/1970 *or* if the Reason field value is Influenza *or* if both conditions are met. You will enter the condition for the BirthDate field in the Criteria row and the condition for the Reason field in the "or" criteria row, thereby using the Or logical operator.

To display the information, you'll create a new query based on the existing OlderAndFluPatients query, since it already contains the necessary fields. Then you'll specify the conditions using the Or logical operator.

To create a new query using the Or logical operator:

1. Open the Navigation Pane. You'll use the shortcut menu to copy and paste the OlderAndFluPatients query to create the new query.
2. In the Queries section of the Navigation Pane, right-click **OlderAndFluPatients**, and then click **Copy** on the shortcut menu.
3. Right-click the empty area near the bottom of the Navigation Pane, and then click **Paste** on the shortcut menu. The Paste As dialog box opens with the text "Copy Of OlderAndFluPatients" in the Query Name box. You'll name the new query "OlderOrFluPatients".
4. In the Query Name box, type **OlderOrFluPatients** and then press **ENTER**. The new query appears in the Queries section of the Navigation Pane.
5. In the Navigation Pane, right-click the **OlderOrFluPatients** query, click **Design View** on the shortcut menu to open the query in Design view, and then close the Navigation Pane.

   The query already contains all the fields Donna wants to view, as well as the first condition—a BirthDate field value less than or equal to 12/31/1970. Because you want records selected if either the condition for the BirthDate field or the condition for the Reason field is satisfied, you must delete the existing condition for the Reason field in the Criteria row and then enter this same condition in the "or" row of the design grid for the Reason field.
6. In the design grid, delete **"Influenza"** in the Reason Criteria box.
7. Press **DOWN ARROW ↓** to move to the "or" row for the Reason field, type **Influenza**, and then press **TAB**. See Figure 3–29.

Figure 3–29 Query window with the Or logical operator

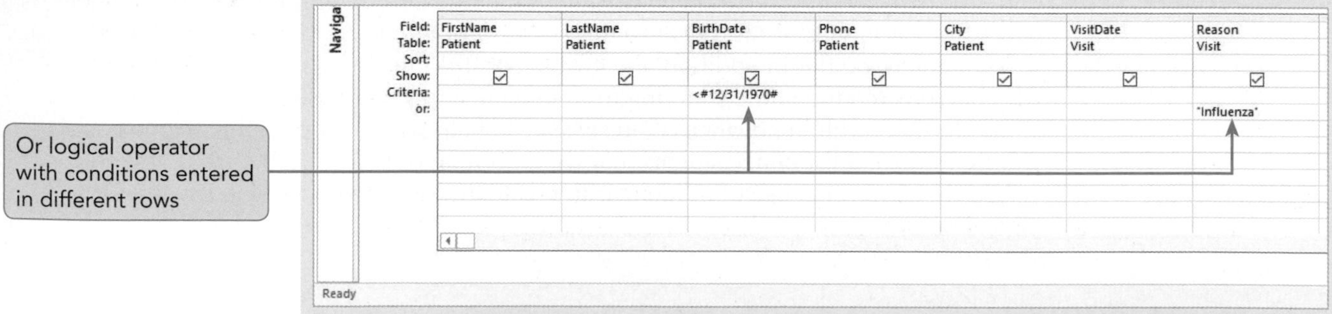
Naviga
Field: FirstName LastName BirthDate Phone City VisitDate Reason
Table: Patient Patient Patient Patient Patient Visit Visit
Sort:
Show:
Criteria: <#12/31/1970#
or: "Influenza"
Ready
Or logical operator with conditions entered in different rows

To better analyze the data, Donna wants the list displayed in descending order by BirthDate.

8. Click the right side of the **BirthDate Sort** box, and then click **Descending**.

9. Run the query. The query datasheet displays only those records that meet either condition: a BirthDate field value less than or equal to 12/31/1970 *or* a Reason field value of Influenza. The query also returns records that meet both conditions. The query displays a total of 43 records. The records in the query datasheet appear in descending order based on the values in the BirthDate field. See Figure 3–30.

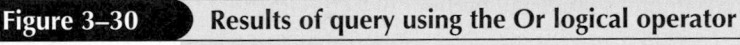

Figure 3–30 **Results of query using the Or logical operator**

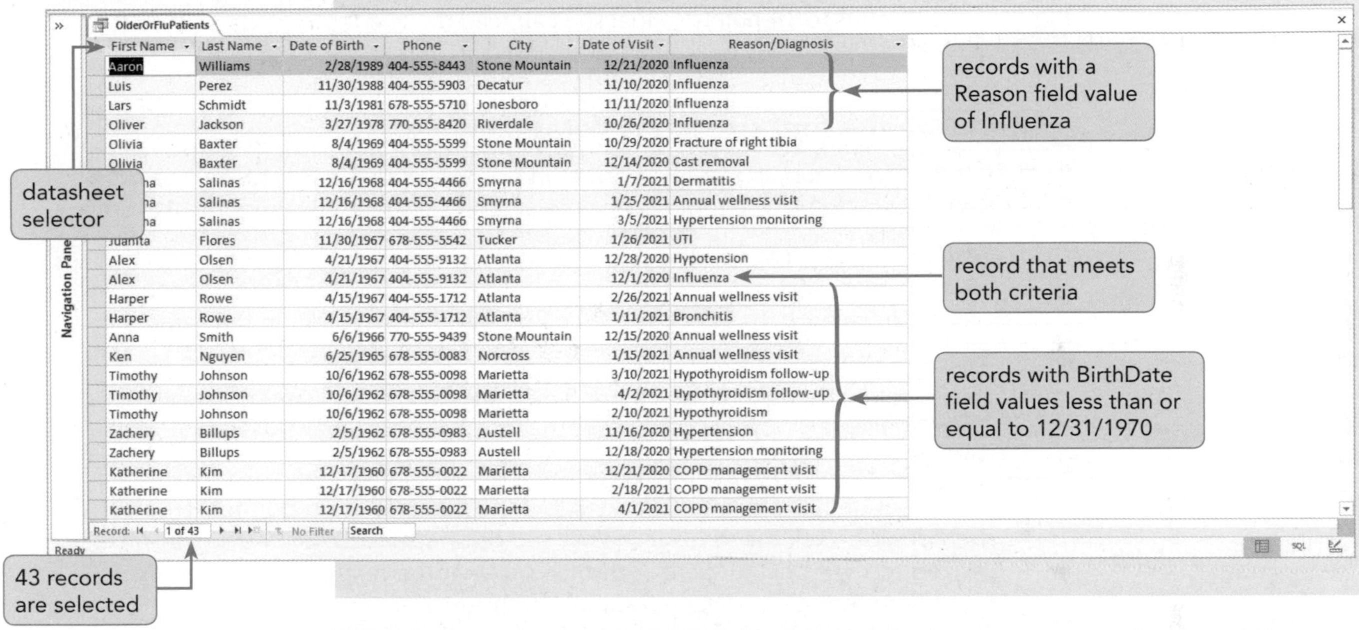
OlderOrFluPatients
records with a Reason field value of Influenza
datasheet selector
record that meets both criteria
records with BirthDate field values less than or equal to 12/31/1970
43 records are selected

Understanding the Results of Using And vs. Or

INSIGHT

When you use the And logical operator to define multiple selection criteria in a query, you *narrow* the results produced by the query because a record must meet more than one condition to be included in the results. For example, the OlderAndFluPatients query you created resulted in only 2 records. When you use the Or logical operator, you *broaden* the results produced by the query because a record must meet only one of the conditions to be included in the results. For example, the OlderOrFluPatients query you created resulted in 43 records. This is an important distinction to keep in mind when you include multiple selection criteria in queries, so that the queries you create will produce the results you want.

Donna would like to spend some time reviewing the results of the OlderOrFluPatients query. To make this task easier, she asks you to change how the datasheet is displayed.

Changing a Datasheet's Appearance

You can make many formatting changes to a datasheet to improve its appearance or readability. Many of these modifications are familiar types of changes you can also make in Word documents or Excel spreadsheets, such as modifying the font type, size, color, and the alignment of text. You can also remove gridlines to improve the appearance of the datasheet, and apply different colors to the rows and columns in a datasheet to make it easier to read.

Modifying the Font Size

Depending on the size of the monitor you are using or the screen resolution, you might need to increase or decrease the size of the font in a datasheet to view more or fewer columns of data. Donna asks you to change the font size in the query datasheet from the default 11 points to 14 points so that she can read the text more easily.

To change the font size in the datasheet:

1. On the Home tab, in the Text Formatting group, click the **Font Size** arrow, and then click **14**. The font size for the entire datasheet increases to 14 points.

   Next, you need to resize the columns to their best fit, so that all field values are displayed. Instead of resizing each column individually, you'll use the datasheet selector to select all the columns and resize them at the same time.

2. Click the **datasheet selector** ☐, which is the box to the left of the First Name column heading (see Figure 3–30). All the columns in the datasheet are selected.

3. Move the pointer to one of the vertical lines separating two columns in the datasheet until the pointer changes to the column resizing pointer ✛, and then double-click the vertical line. All the columns visible on the screen are resized to their best fit. Scroll down and repeat the resizing, as necessary, to make sure that all field values are fully displayed.

   Trouble? If all the columns are not visible on your screen, you need to scroll the datasheet to the right to make sure all field values for all columns are fully displayed. If you need to resize any columns, click a field value first to deselect the columns before resizing an individual column.

4. Click any value in the First Name column to make it the current field and to deselect the columns in the datasheet.

Changing the Alternate Row Color in a Datasheet

TIP

When choosing a row color, be sure not to select a color that is too dark because it might obscure the data rather than enhance it.

Access uses themes to format the objects in a database. A **theme** is a predefined set of formats including colors, fonts, and other effects that enhance an object's appearance and usability. When you create a database, Access applies the Office theme to objects as you create them. By default, the Office theme formats every other row in a datasheet with a gray background color to distinguish one row from another, making it easier to view and read the contents of a datasheet. The gray alternate row color provides a subtle difference compared to the rows that have the default white color. You can change the alternate row color in a datasheet to something more noticeable using the Alternate Row Color button in the Text Formatting group on the Home tab. Donna suggests that you change the alternate row color in the datasheet to see the effect of using this feature.

To change the alternate row color in the datasheet:

1. On the Home tab, in the Text Formatting group, click the **Alternate Row Color arrow** to display the gallery of color choices. See Figure 3-31.

Figure 3–31 Gallery of color choices for alternate row color

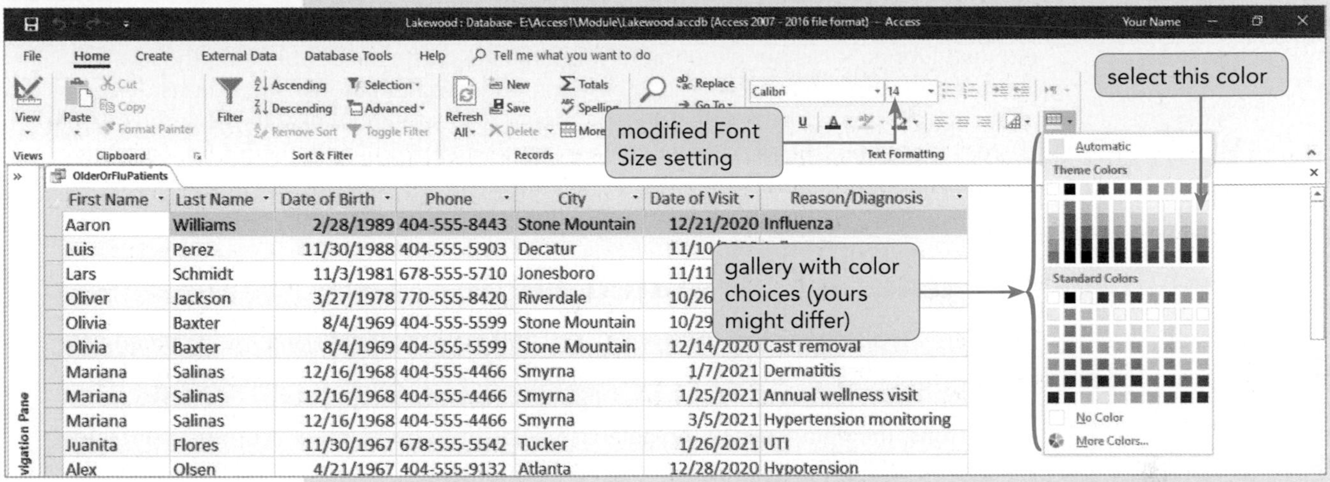
select this color
modified Font Size setting
gallery with color choices (yours might differ)

TIP

The name of the color appears in a ScreenTip when you point to a color in the gallery.

The Theme Colors section provides colors from the default Office theme, so that your datasheet's color scheme matches the one in use for the database. The Standard Colors section provides many standard color choices. You might also see a Recent Colors section, with colors that you have recently used in a datasheet. The No Color option, which appears at the bottom of the gallery, sets each row's background color to white. If you want to create a custom color, you can do so using the More Colors option. You'll use one of the theme colors.

2. In the Theme Colors section, click the **Green, Accent 6, Lighter 60%** color (third row, tenth color). The alternate row color is applied to the query datasheet. See Figure 3–32.

Figure 3–32 Datasheet formatted with alternate row color

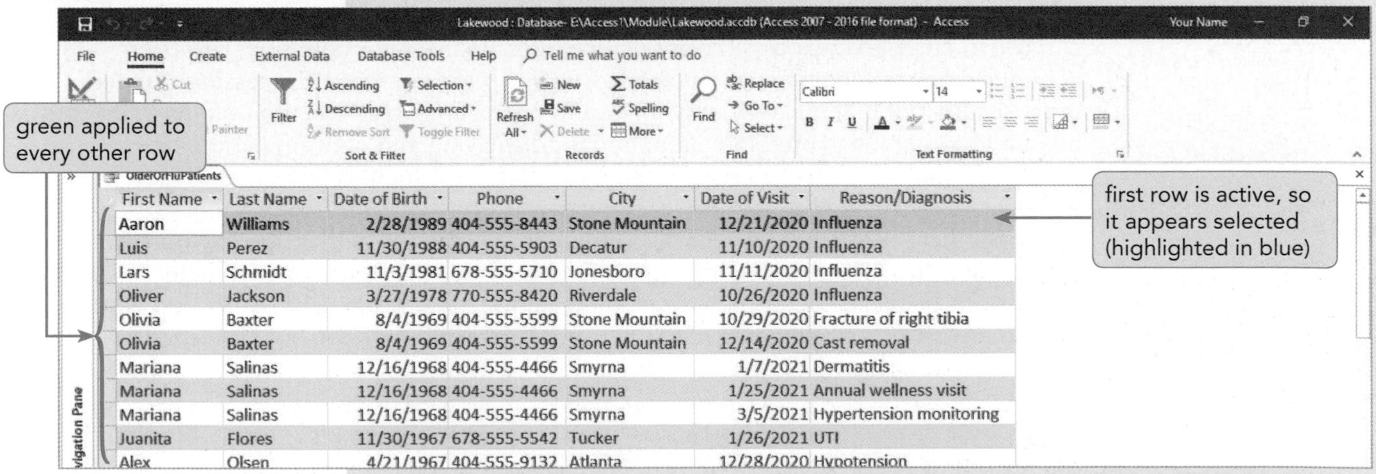
green applied to every other row
first row is active, so it appears selected (highlighted in blue)

Every other row in the datasheet uses the selected theme color. Donna likes how the datasheet looks with this color scheme, so she asks you to save the query.

3. Save and close the OlderOrFluPatients query. The query is saved with both the increased font size and the green alternate row color.

Next, Donna turns her attention to some financial aspects of operating the clinic. She wants to use the Lakewood database to perform calculations. She is considering imposing a 2% late fee on unpaid invoices and wants to know exactly what the late fee charges would be, should she decide to institute such a policy in the future. To produce the information for Donna, you need to create a calculated field.

Creating a Calculated Field

In addition to using queries to retrieve, sort, and filter data in a database, you can use a query to perform calculations. To perform a calculation, you define an **expression** containing a combination of database fields, constants, and operators. For numeric expressions, the data types of the database fields must be Number, Currency, or Date/Time; the constants are numbers such as .02 (for the 2% late fee); and the operators can be arithmetic operators (+ – * /) or other specialized operators. In complex expressions, you can enclose calculations in parentheses to indicate which one should be performed first; any calculation within parentheses is completed before calculations outside the parentheses. In expressions without parentheses, Access performs basic calculations using the following order of precedence: multiplication and division before addition and subtraction. When operators have equal precedence, Access calculates them in order from left to right.

To perform a calculation in a query, you add a calculated field to the query. A **calculated field** is a field that displays the results of an expression. A calculated field that you create with an expression appears in a query datasheet or in a form or report; however, it does not exist in a database. When you run a query that contains a calculated field, Access evaluates the expression defined by the calculated field and displays the resulting value in the query datasheet, form, or report.

To enter an expression for a calculated field, you can type it directly in a Field box in the design grid. Alternately, you can open the Zoom box or Expression Builder and use either one to enter the expression. The **Zoom box** is a dialog box that you can use to enter text, expressions, or other values. To use the Zoom box, however, you must know all the parts of the expression you want to create. **Expression Builder** is an Access tool that makes it easy for you to create an expression; it contains a box for entering the expression, an option for displaying and choosing common operators, and one or more lists of expression elements, such as table and field names. Unlike a Field box, which is too narrow to show an entire expression at one time, the Zoom box and Expression Builder are large enough to display longer expressions. In most cases, Expression Builder provides the easiest way to enter expressions because you don't have to know all the parts of the expression; you can choose the necessary elements from the Expression Builder dialog box, which also helps to prevent typing errors.

REFERENCE

Creating a Calculated Field Using Expression Builder

- Create and save the query in which you want to include a calculated field.
- Open the query in Design view.
- In the design grid, click the Field box in which you want to create an expression.
- In the Query Setup group on the Query Tools Design tab, click the Builder button.
- Use the expression elements and common operators to build the expression, or type the expression directly in the expression box.
- Click the OK button.

To produce the information Donna wants, you need to create a new query based on the Billing and Visit tables and, in the query, create a calculated field that will multiply each InvoiceAmt field value by .02 to calculate the proposed 2% late fee.

To create the new query:

1. On the ribbon, click the **Create** tab.
2. In the Queries group, click the **Query Design** button. The Show Table dialog box opens.

   Donna wants to see data from both the Visit and Billing tables, so you need to add these two tables to the Query window.
3. Add the **Visit** and **Billing** tables to the Query window, and resize the field lists as necessary so that all the field names are visible. The field lists appear in the Query window, and the one-to-many relationship between the Visit (primary) and Billing (related) tables is displayed.
4. Add the following fields to the design grid in the order given: **VisitID**, **PatientID**, and **VisitDate** from the Visit table; and **InvoiceItem**, **InvoicePaid**, and **InvoiceAmt** from the Billing table.

   Donna is interested in viewing data only for unpaid invoices because a late fee would apply only to them, so you need to enter the necessary condition for the InvoicePaid field. Recall that InvoicePaid is a Yes/No field. The condition you need to enter is the word "No" in the Criteria box for this field, so that Access will retrieve the records for unpaid invoices only.
5. In the **InvoicePaid Criteria box**, type **No**. As soon as you type the letter "N," a menu appears with options for entering various functions for the criteria. You don't need to enter a function, so you can close this menu.
6. Press **ESC** to close the menu.
7. Press **TAB**. The query name you'll use will indicate that the data is for unpaid invoices, so you don't need to include the InvoicePaid values in the query results.
8. Click the **InvoicePaid Show** check box to remove the checkmark.
9. Save the query with the name **UnpaidInvoiceLateFee**.

You must close the menu or you'll enter a function, which will cause an error.

Now you can use Expression Builder to create the calculated field for the InvoiceAmt field.

To create the calculated field:

1. Click the blank Field box to the right of the InvoiceAmt field. This field will contain the expression.
2. On the Query Tools Design tab, in the Query Setup group, click the **Builder** button. The Expression Builder dialog box opens.

   The insertion point is positioned in the large box at the top of the dialog box, ready for you to enter the expression. The Expression Categories section of the dialog box lists the fields from the query so you can include them in the expression. The Expression Elements section contains options for including other elements in the expression, including functions, constants, and operators. If the expression you're entering is a simple one, you can type it in the box; if it's more complex, you can use the options in the Expression Elements section to help you build the expression.

   The expression for the calculated field will multiply the InvoiceAmt field values by the numeric constant .02 (which represents a 2% late fee).
3. In the Expression Categories section of the dialog box, double-click **InvoiceAmt**. The field name is added to the expression box, within brackets and with a space following it. In an expression, all field names must be enclosed in brackets.

   Next you need to enter the multiplication operator, which is the asterisk (*), followed by the constant.
4. Type ***** (an asterisk) and then type **.02**. You have finished entering the expression. See Figure 3–33.

TIP

You must first save and name a query in order for its fields to be listed in the Expression Categories section.

Figure 3–33 Completed expression for the calculated field

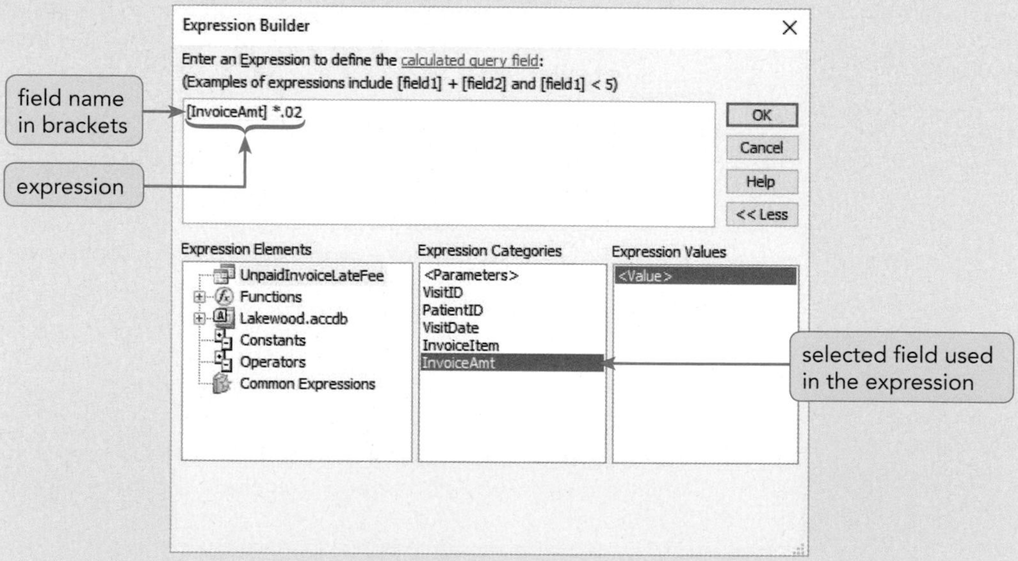
Expression Builder
Enter an Expression to define the calculated query field:
(Examples of expressions include [field1] + [field2] and [field1] < 5)
[InvoiceAmt] *.02
OK
Cancel
Help
<< Less
Expression Elements
UnpaidInvoiceLateFee
Functions
Lakewood.accdb
Constants
Operators
Common Expressions
Expression Categories
<Parameters>
VisitID
PatientID
VisitDate
InvoiceItem
InvoiceAmt
Expression Values
<Value>
field name in brackets
expression
selected field used in the expression

If you're not sure which operator to use, you can click Operators in the Expression Elements section to display a list of available operators in the center section of the dialog box.

5. Click **OK**. The Expression Builder dialog box closes, and the expression is added to the design grid in the Field box for the calculated field. When you

create a calculated field, Access uses the default name "Expr1" for the field. You need to specify a more meaningful field name so it will appear in the query results. You'll enter the name "LateFee," which better describes the field's contents.

6. Click to the left of the text "Expr1:" at the beginning of the expression, and then press **DELETE** five times to delete the text **Expr1**. *Do not delete the colon*; it is needed to separate the calculated field name from the expression.
7. Type **LateFee**. Next, you'll set this field's Caption property so that the field name will appear as "Late Fee" in the query datasheet.
8. On the Query Tools Design tab, in the Show/Hide group, click the **Property Sheet** button. The Property Sheet for the current field, LateFee, opens on the right side of the window. See Figure 3–34.

Figure 3–34 Property Sheet for the calculated field

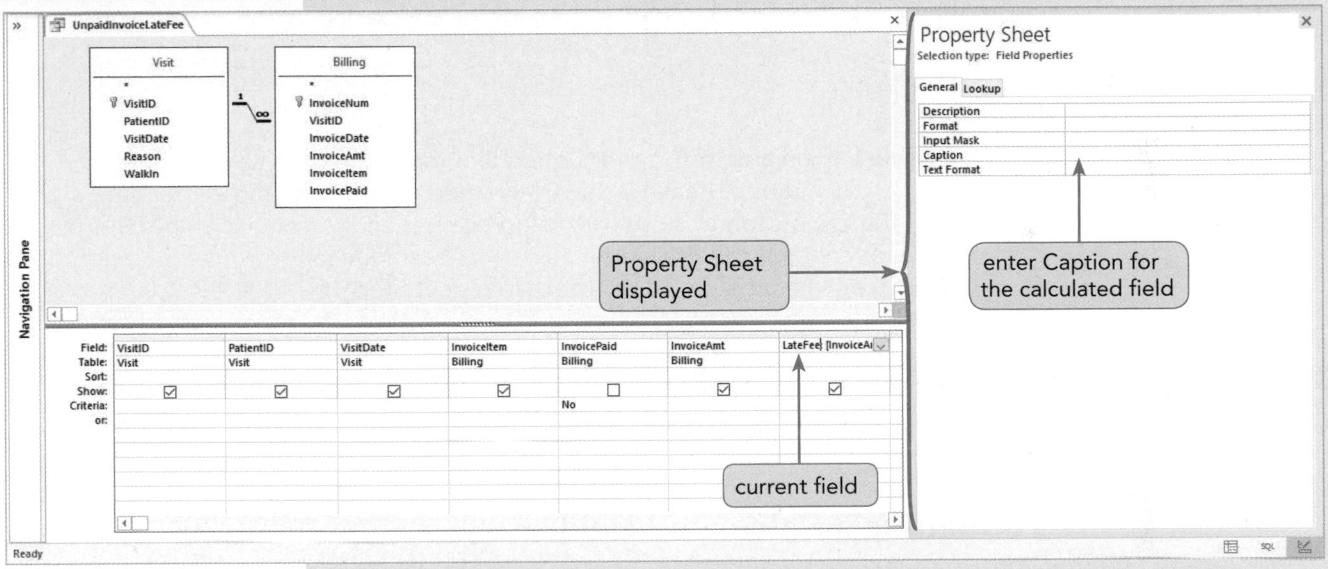
Property Sheet displayed
enter Caption for the calculated field
current field

9. In the Property Sheet, click in the Caption box, type **Late Fee** and then close the Property Sheet.
10. Run the query. The query datasheet is displayed and contains the specified fields and the calculated field with the caption "Late Fee." See Figure 3–35.

Figure 3–35 Datasheet displaying the calculated field

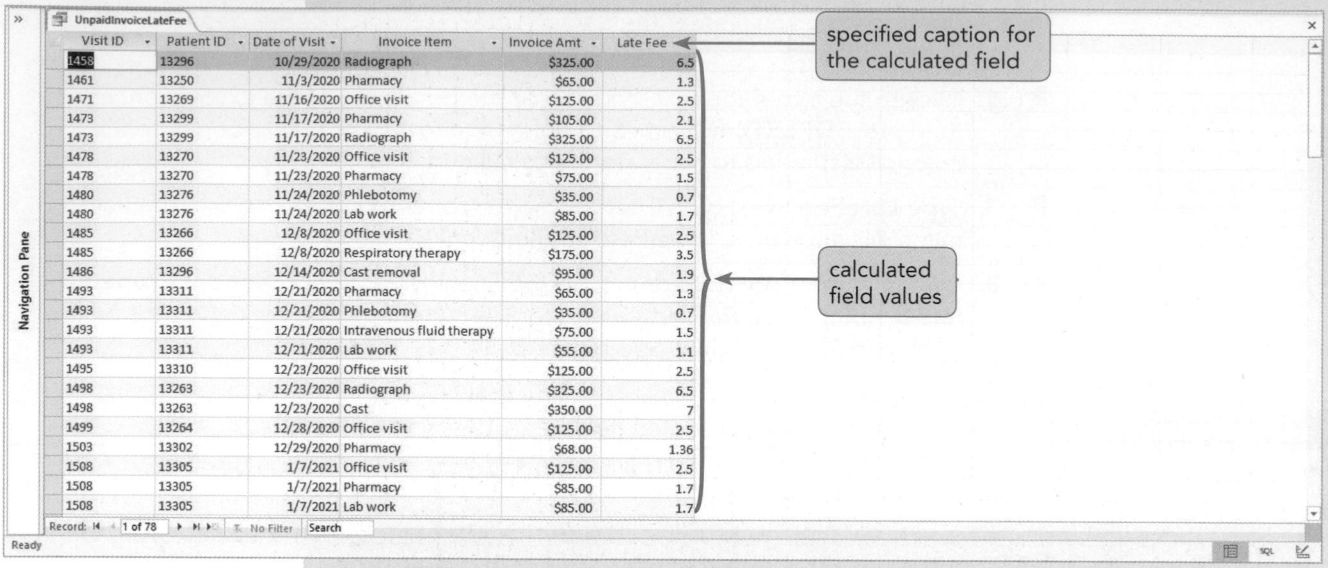
UnpaidInvoiceLateFee
specified caption for the calculated field
calculated field values
Navigation Pane
Record: 1 of 78
No Filter
Search
Ready

Visit ID	Patient ID	Date of Visit	Invoice Item	Invoice Amt	Late Fee
1458	13296	10/29/2020	Radiograph	$325.00	6.5
1461	13250	11/3/2020	Pharmacy	$65.00	1.3
1471	13269	11/16/2020	Office visit	$125.00	2.5
1473	13299	11/17/2020	Pharmacy	$105.00	2.1
1473	13299	11/17/2020	Radiograph	$325.00	6.5
1478	13270	11/23/2020	Office visit	$125.00	2.5
1478	13270	11/23/2020	Pharmacy	$75.00	1.5
1480	13276	11/24/2020	Phlebotomy	$35.00	0.7
1480	13276	11/24/2020	Lab work	$85.00	1.7
1485	13266	12/8/2020	Office visit	$125.00	2.5
1485	13266	12/8/2020	Respiratory therapy	$175.00	3.5
1486	13296	12/14/2020	Cast removal	$95.00	1.9
1493	13311	12/21/2020	Pharmacy	$65.00	1.3
1493	13311	12/21/2020	Phlebotomy	$35.00	0.7
1493	13311	12/21/2020	Intravenous fluid therapy	$75.00	1.5
1493	13311	12/21/2020	Lab work	$55.00	1.1
1495	13310	12/23/2020	Office visit	$125.00	2.5
1498	13263	12/23/2020	Radiograph	$325.00	6.5
1498	13263	12/23/2020	Cast	$350.00	7
1499	13264	12/28/2020	Office visit	$125.00	2.5
1503	13302	12/29/2020	Pharmacy	$68.00	1.36
1508	13305	1/7/2021	Office visit	$125.00	2.5
1508	13305	1/7/2021	Pharmacy	$85.00	1.7
1508	13305	1/7/2021	Lab work	$85.00	1.7

Trouble? If a dialog box opens noting that the expression contains invalid syntax, you might not have included the required colon in the expression. Click the OK button to close the dialog box, resize the column in the design grid that contains the calculated field to its best fit, change your expression to LateFee: [InvoiceAmt]*0.02 and then repeat Step 10.

The LateFee field values are currently displayed without dollar signs and decimal places. Donna wants these values to be displayed in the same format as the InvoiceAmt field values for consistency.

Formatting a Calculated Field

You can specify a particular format for a calculated field, just as you can for any field, by modifying its properties. Next, you'll change the format of the LateFee calculated field so that all values appear in the Currency format.

To format the calculated field:

1. Switch to Design view.
2. In the design grid, click in the **LateFee** calculated field to make it the current field, if necessary.
3. On the Query Tools Design tab, in the Show/Hide group, click the **Property Sheet** button to open the Property Sheet for the calculated field, if necessary.

   You need to change the Format property to Currency, which displays values with a dollar sign and two decimal places.
4. In the Property Sheet, click the right side of the **Format** box to display the list of formats, and then click **Currency**.
5. Close the Property Sheet, and then run the query. The amounts in the LateFee calculated field are now displayed with dollar signs and two decimal places.
6. Save and close the UnpaidInvoiceLateFee query.

PROSKILLS

Problem Solving: Creating a Calculated Field vs. Using the Calculated Field Data Type

You can also create a calculated field using the Calculated Field data type, which lets you store the result of an expression as a field in a table. However, database experts caution users against storing calculations in a table for several reasons. First, storing calculated data in a table consumes valuable space and increases the size of the database. The preferred approach is to use a calculated field in a query; with this approach, the result of the calculation is not stored in the database—it is produced only when you run the query—and it is always current. Second, the Calculated Field data type provides limited options for creating a calculation, whereas a calculated field in a query provides more functions and options for creating expressions. Third, including a field in a table using the Calculated Field data type limits your options if you need to upgrade the database at some point to a more robust DBMS, such as Oracle or SQL Server, that doesn't support this data type; you would need to redesign your database to eliminate this data type. Finally, most database experts agree that including a field in a table whose value is dependent on other fields in the table violates database design principles. To avoid such problems, it's best to create a query that includes a calculated field to perform the calculation you want, instead of creating a field in a table that uses the Calculated Field data type.

To better analyze costs at Lakewood Community Health Services, Donna wants to view more detailed information about invoices for patient care. Specifically, she would like to know the minimum, average, and maximum invoice amounts. She asks you to determine these statistics from data in the Billing table.

Using Aggregate Functions

You can calculate statistical information, such as totals and averages, on the records displayed in a table datasheet or selected by a query. To do this, you use the Access aggregate functions. **Aggregate functions** perform arithmetic operations on selected records in a database. Figure 3–36 lists the most frequently used aggregate functions.

Figure 3–36 Frequently used aggregate functions

Aggregate Function	Determines	Data Types Supported
Average	Average of the field values for the selected records	AutoNumber, Currency, Date/Time, Number
Count	Number of records selected	AutoNumber, Currency, Date/Time, Long Text, Number, OLE Object, Short Text, Yes/No
Maximum	Highest field value for the selected records	AutoNumber, Currency, Date/Time, Number, Short Text
Minimum	Lowest field value for the selected records	AutoNumber, Currency, Date/Time, Number, Short Text
Sum	Total of the field values for the selected records	AutoNumber, Currency, Date/Time, Number

Working with Aggregate Functions Using the Total Row

If you want to quickly perform a calculation using an aggregate function in a table or query datasheet, you can use the Totals button in the Records group on the Home tab. When you click this button, a row labeled "Total" appears at the bottom of the datasheet. You can then choose one of the aggregate functions for a field in the datasheet, and the results of the calculation will be displayed in the Total row for that field.

Donna wants to know the total amount of all invoices for the clinic. You can quickly display this amount using the Sum function in the Total row in the Billing table datasheet.

To display the total amount of all invoices in the Billing table:

1. Open the Navigation Pane, open the **Billing** table in Datasheet view, and then close the Navigation Pane.
2. Make sure the Home tab is displayed.
3. In the Records group, click the **Totals** button. A row with the label "Total" is added to the bottom of the datasheet.
4. Scroll to the bottom of the datasheet to view the Total row. You want to display the sum of all the values in the Invoice Amt column.
5. In the Total row, click the **Invoice Amt** field. An arrow appears on the left side of the field.
6. Click the **arrow** to display the menu of aggregate functions. The functions displayed depend on the data type of the current field; in this case, the menu provides functions for a Currency field. See Figure 3–37.

Figure 3–37 Using aggregate functions in the Total row

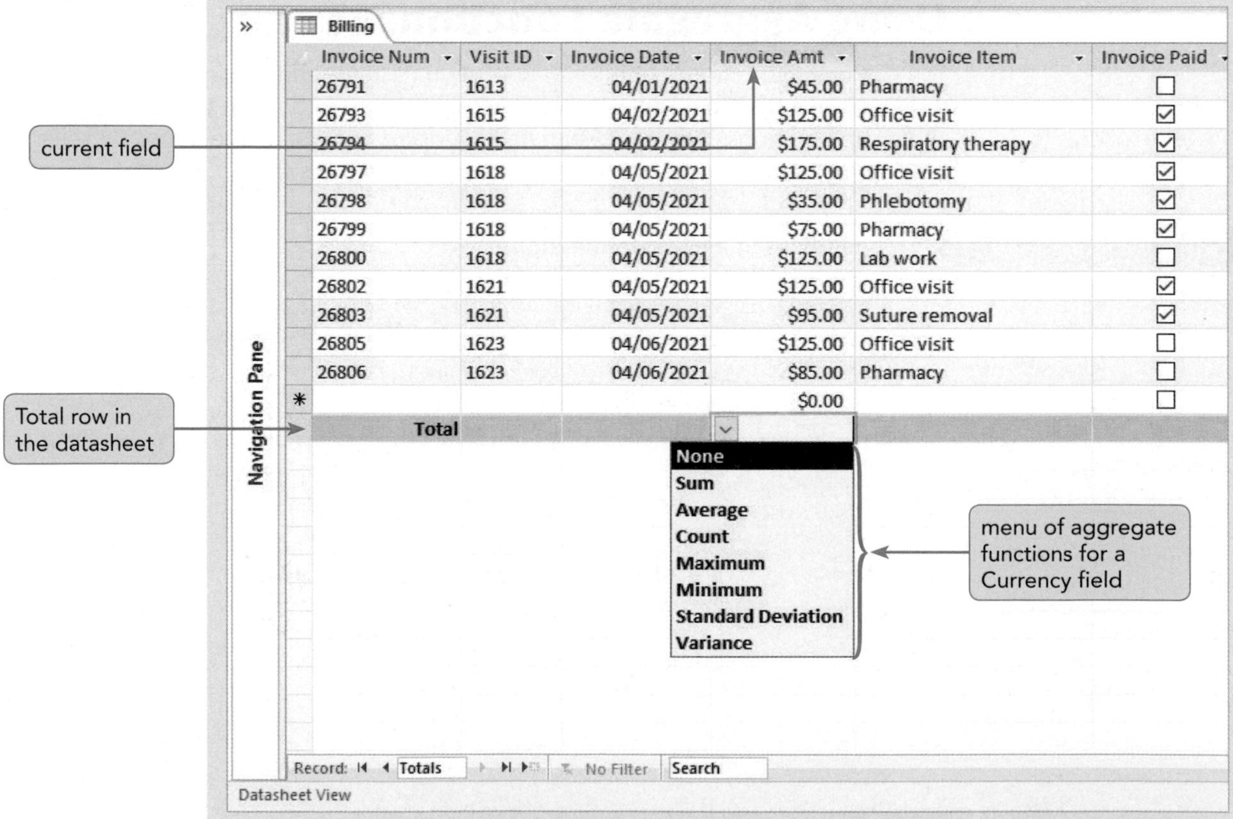
current field
Total row in the datasheet
menu of aggregate functions for a Currency field
Billing
Navigation Pane
Invoice Num
Visit ID
Invoice Date
Invoice Amt
Invoice Item
Invoice Paid
Total
None
Sum
Average
Count
Maximum
Minimum
Standard Deviation
Variance
Record: Totals
No Filter
Search
Datasheet View

7. Click **Sum** on the menu. All the values in the Invoice Amt column are added, and the total $22,223.00 appears in the Total row for the column.

   Donna doesn't want to change the Billing table to always display this total. You can remove the Total row by clicking the Totals button again; this button works as a toggle to switch between the display of the Total row with the results of any calculations in the row, and the display of the datasheet without this row.

8. In the Records group, click the **Totals** button. The Total row is removed from the datasheet.
9. Close the Billing table without saving the changes.

Donna wants to know the minimum, average, and maximum invoice amounts for Lakewood Community Health Services. To produce this information for Donna, you need to use aggregate functions in a query.

Creating Queries with Aggregate Functions

Aggregate functions operate on the records that meet a query's selection criteria. You specify an aggregate function for a specific field, and the appropriate operation applies to that field's values for the selected records.

To display the minimum, average, and maximum of all the invoice amounts in the Billing table, you will use the Minimum, Average, and Maximum aggregate functions for the InvoiceAmt field.

To calculate the minimum of all invoice amounts:

1. Create a new query in Design view, add the **Billing** table to the Query window, and then resize the Billing field list to display all fields.

   To perform the three calculations on the InvoiceAmt field, you need to add the field to the design grid three times.

2. In the Billing field list, double-click **InvoiceAmt** three times to add three copies of the field to the design grid.

   You need to select an aggregate function for each InvoiceAmt field. When you click the Totals button in the Show/Hide group on the Design tab, a row labeled "Total" is added to the design grid. The Total row provides a list of the aggregate functions that you can select.

3. On the Query Tools Design tab, in the Show/Hide group, click the **Totals** button. A new row labeled "Total" appears between the Table and Sort rows in the design grid. The default entry for each field in the Total row is the Group By operator, which you will learn about later in this module. See Figure 3–38.

Figure 3–38 Total row inserted in the design grid

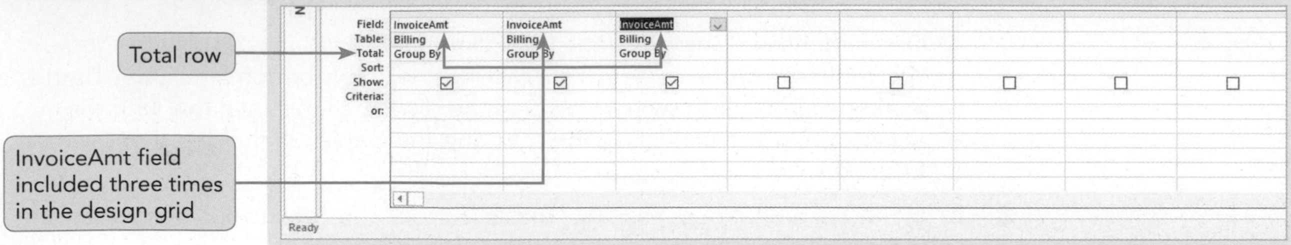
Total row
InvoiceAmt field included three times in the design grid
Field:
Table:
Total:
Sort:
Show:
Criteria:
or:
InvoiceAmt
Billing
Group By
InvoiceAmt
Billing
Group By
InvoiceAmt
Billing
Group By
Ready

In the Total row, you specify the aggregate function you want to use for a field.

4. Click the right side of the first column's **Total** box, and then click **Min**. This field will calculate the minimum amount of all the InvoiceAmt field values.

   When you run the query, Access automatically will assign a datasheet column name of "MinOfInvoiceAmt" for this field. You can change the datasheet column name to a more descriptive or readable name by entering the name you want in the Field box. However, you must also keep the InvoiceAmt field name in the Field box because it identifies the field to use in the calculation. The Field box will contain the datasheet column name you specify followed by the field name (InvoiceAmt) with a colon separating the two names.

TIP

Be sure to type the colon following the name or the query will not work correctly.

5. In the first column's Field box, click to the left of InvoiceAmt, and then type **MinimumInvoiceAmt:** (including the colon).
6. Resize the column so that you can see the complete field name, MinimumInvoiceAmt:InvoiceAmt.

   Next, you need to set the Caption property for this field so that the field name appears with spaces between words in the query datasheet.

7. On the Query Tools Design tab, in the Show/Hide group, click the **Property Sheet** button to open the Property Sheet for the current field.
8. In the Caption box, type **Minimum Invoice Amt**, and then close the Property Sheet.

You'll follow the same process to complete the query by calculating the average and maximum invoice amounts.

To calculate the average and maximum of all invoice amounts:

1. Click the right side of the second column's **Total** box, and then click **Avg**. This field will calculate the average of all the InvoiceAmt field values.
2. In the second column's Field box, click to the left of InvoiceAmt, and then type **AverageInvoiceAmt**.
3. Resize the second column to fully display the field name, AverageInvoiceAmt:InvoiceAmt.
4. Open the Property Sheet for the current field, and then set its Caption property to **Average Invoice Amt**. Leave the Property Sheet open.
5. Click the right side of the third column's **Total** box, and then click **Max**. This field will calculate the maximum amount of all the InvoiceAmt field values.

6. In the third column's Field box, click to the left of InvoiceAmt, and then type **MaximumInvoiceAmt**.
7. Resize the third column to fully display the field name, MaximumInvoiceAmt:InvoiceAmt.
8. In the Property Sheet, set the Caption property to **Maximum Invoice Amt**, and then close the Property Sheet. See Figure 3–39.

Figure 3–39 **Query with aggregate functions entered**

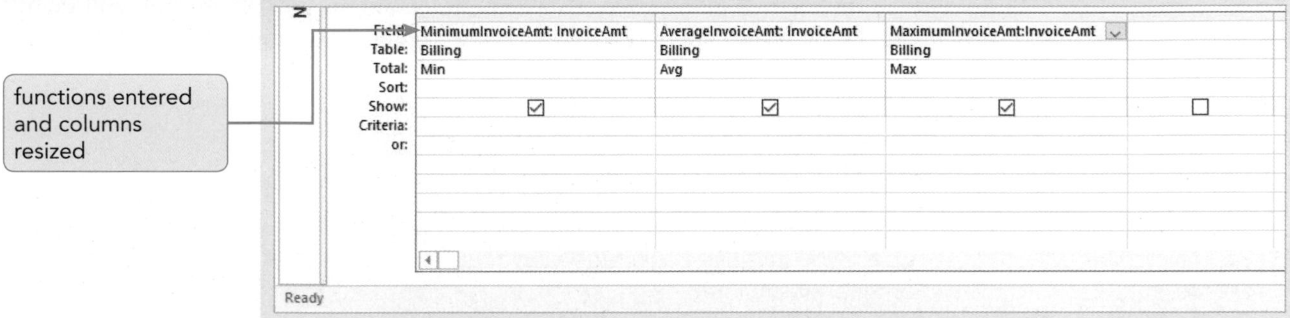
functions entered and columns resized
Field:
Table:
Total:
Sort:
Show:
Criteria:
or:
MinimumInvoiceAmt: InvoiceAmt
Billing
Min
AverageInvoiceAmt: InvoiceAmt
Billing
Avg
MaximumInvoiceAmt:InvoiceAmt
Billing
Max
Ready

Trouble? Carefully compare your field names to those shown in the figure to make sure they match exactly; otherwise the query will not work correctly.

9. Run the query. One record is displayed containing the three aggregate function results. The single row of summary statistics represents calculations based on all the records selected for the query—in this case, all 204 records in the Billing table.
10. Resize all columns to their best fit so that the column names are fully displayed, and then click the field value in the first column to deselect the value and view the results. See Figure 3–40.

Figure 3–40 **Result of the query using aggregate functions**

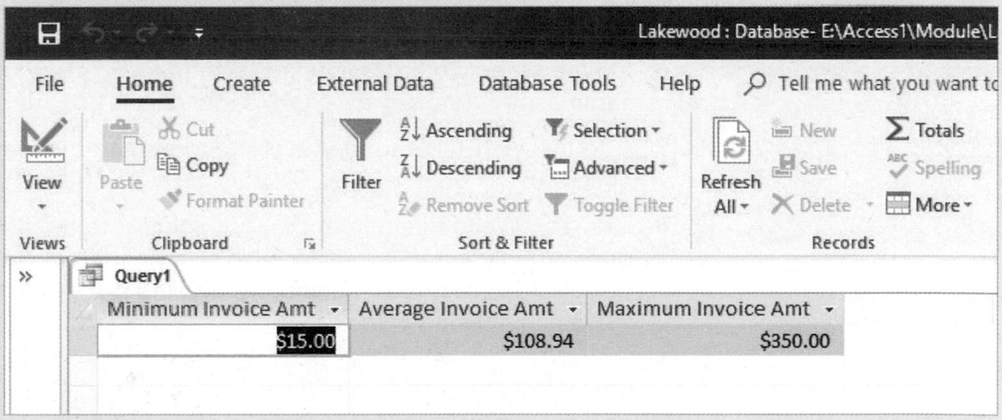
Lakewood : Database- E:\Access1\Module\L
File
Home
Create
External Data
Database Tools
Help
Tell me what you want to
View
Paste
Cut
Copy
Format Painter
Filter
Ascending
Descending
Remove Sort
Selection
Advanced
Toggle Filter
Refresh All
New
Save
Delete
Totals
Spelling
More
Views
Clipboard
Sort & Filter
Records
Query1
Minimum Invoice Amt
Average Invoice Amt
Maximum Invoice Amt
$15.00
$108.94
$350.00

11. Save the query as **InvoiceAmtStatistics**.

Donna would like to view the same invoice amount statistics (minimum, average, and maximum) as they relate to both appointments at the clinic and walk-in visits.

Using Record Group Calculations

In addition to calculating statistical information on all or selected records in selected tables, you can calculate statistics for groups of records. The **Group By operator** divides the selected records into groups based on the values in the specified field. Those records with the same value for the field are grouped together, and the datasheet displays one record for each group. Aggregate functions, which appear in the other columns of the design grid, provide statistical information for each group.

To create a query for Donna's latest request, you will modify the current query by adding the WalkIn field and assigning the Group By operator to it. The Group By operator will display the statistical information grouped by the values of the WalkIn field for all the records in the query datasheet. To create the new query, you will save the InvoiceAmtStatistics query with a new name, keeping the original query intact, and then modify the new query.

To create a new query with the Group By operator:

1. Display the InvoiceAmtStatistics query in Design view. Because the query is open, you can use Backstage view to save it with a new name, keeping the original query intact.
2. Click the **File** tab to display Backstage view, and then click **Save As** in the navigation bar. The Save As screen opens.
3. In the File Types section on the left, click **Save Object As**. The right side of the screen changes to display options for saving the current database object as a new object.
4. Click **Save As**. The Save As dialog box opens, indicating that you are saving a copy of the InvoiceAmtStatistics query.
5. Type **InvoiceAmtStatisticsByWalkIn** to replace the selected name, and then press **ENTER**. The new query is saved with the name you specified and appears in Design view.

   You need to add the WalkIn field to the query. This field is in the Visit table. To include another table in an existing query, you open the Show Table dialog box.

6. On the Query Tools Design tab, in the Query Setup group, click the **Show Table** button to open the Show Table dialog box.
7. Add the **Visit** table to the Query window, and then resize the Visit field list if necessary.
8. Drag the **WalkIn** field from the Visit field list to the first column in the design grid. When you release the mouse button, the WalkIn field appears in the design grid's first column, and the existing fields shift to the right. Group By, the default option in the Total row, appears for the WalkIn field.
9. Run the query. The query displays two records—one for each WalkIn group, Yes and No. Each record contains the WalkIn field value for the group and the three aggregate function values. The summary statistics represent calculations based on the 204 records in the Billing table. See Figure 3–41.

TIP

You could also open the Navigation Pane and drag the Visit table from the pane to the Query window.

Figure 3–41 Aggregate functions grouped by WalkIn

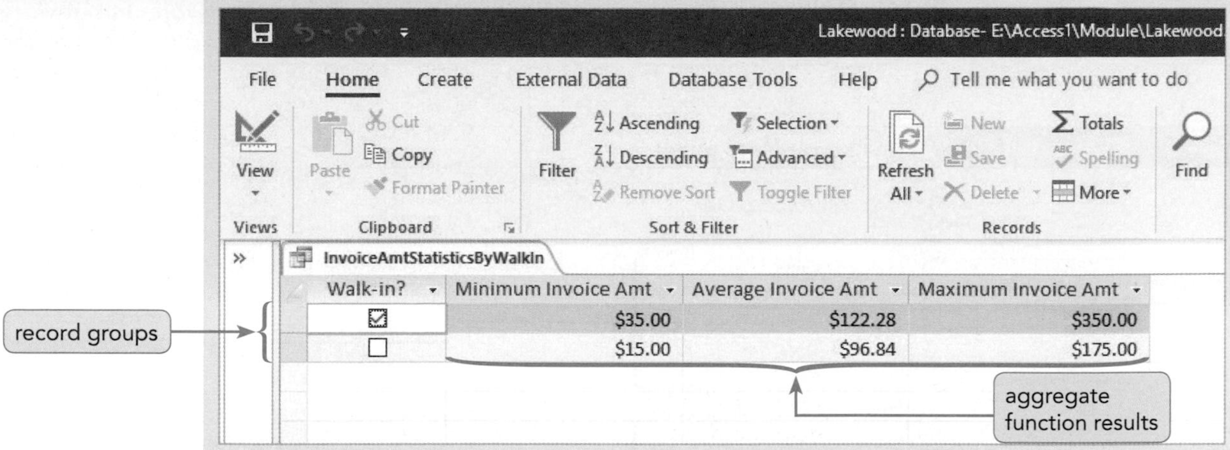
Lakewood : Database- E:\Access1\Module\Lakewood
File
Home
Create
External Data
Database Tools
Help
Tell me what you want to do
View
Paste
Cut
Copy
Format Painter
Filter
Ascending
Descending
Remove Sort
Selection
Advanced
Toggle Filter
Refresh All
New
Save
Delete
Totals
Spelling
More
Find
Views
Clipboard
Sort & Filter
Records
InvoiceAmtStatisticsByWalkIn
Walk-in?
Minimum Invoice Amt
Average Invoice Amt
Maximum Invoice Amt
$35.00
$122.28
$350.00
$15.00
$96.84
$175.00
record groups
aggregate function results

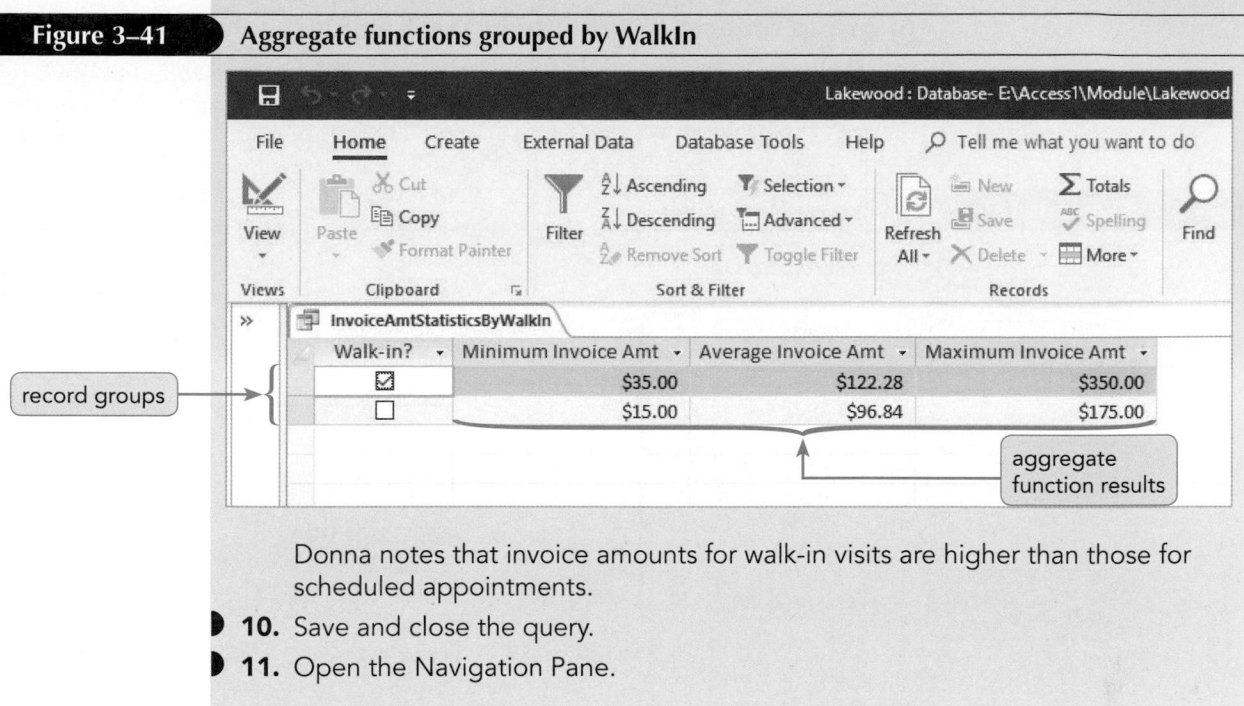

Donna notes that invoice amounts for walk-in visits are higher than those for scheduled appointments.

10. Save and close the query.

11. Open the Navigation Pane.

You have created and saved many queries in the Lakewood database. The Navigation Pane provides options for opening and managing the queries you've created, as well as the other objects in the database, such as tables, forms, and reports.

Working with the Navigation Pane

As noted earlier, the Navigation Pane is the main area for working with the objects in a database. As you continue to create objects in your database, you might want to display and work with them in different ways. The Navigation Pane provides options for grouping database objects in various ways to suit your needs. For example, you might want to view only the queries created for a certain table or all the query objects in the database.

INSIGHT

Hiding and Displaying Objects in the Navigation Pane

You can hide the display of a group's objects by clicking the button to the right of the group name; click the button again to expand the group and display its objects. You can also hide an object within a group, such as an individual query or report. To hide an object within a group, right-click the object and then click Hide in this Group. To display hidden objects without providing access to them, right-click the Navigation Pane menu and then click Navigation Options. In the Navigation Options dialog box, select the Show Hidden Objects check box, and then click OK. To fully enable the object, right-click the object, and then click Unhide in this Group.

As you know, the Navigation Pane divides database objects into categories. Each category contains groups, and each group contains one or more objects. The default category is **Object Type**, which arranges objects by type—tables, queries, forms, and reports. The default group is **All Access Objects**, which displays all objects in the database. You can also choose to display only one type of object, such as tables.

The default group name, All Access Objects, appears at the top of the Navigation Pane. Currently, each object type—Tables, Queries, Forms, and Reports—is displayed as a heading, and the objects related to each type are listed below the heading. To group objects differently, you can select another category by using the Navigation Pane menu. You'll try this next.

To group objects differently in the Navigation Pane:

1. At the top of the Navigation Pane, click the **All Access Objects** button. A menu opens with options for choosing different categories and groups. See Figure 3–42.

Figure 3–42 Navigation Pane menu

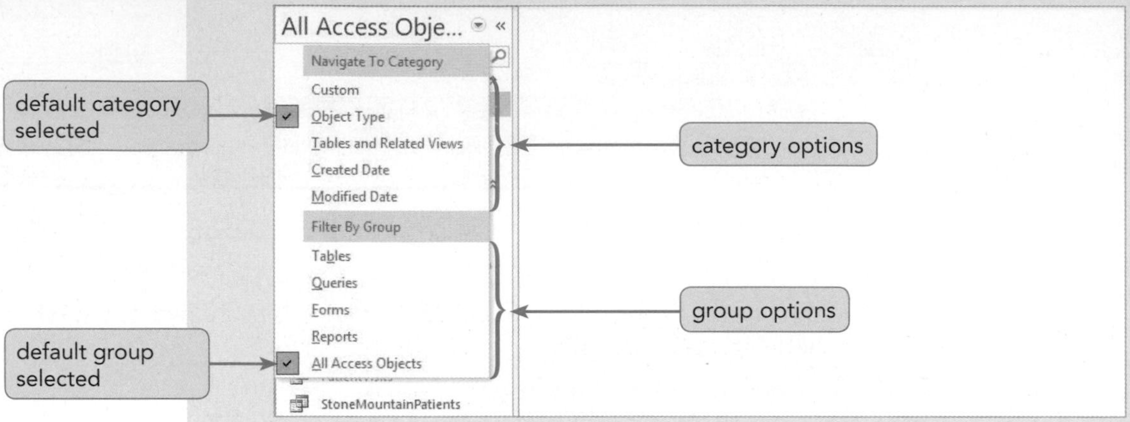
All Access Obje...
Navigate To Category
Custom
Object Type
Tables and Related Views
Created Date
Modified Date
Filter By Group
Tables
Queries
Forms
Reports
All Access Objects
StoneMountainPatients
default category selected
category options
group options
default group selected

The top section of the menu provides the options for choosing a different category. The Object Type category has a checkmark next to it, signifying that it is the currently selected category. The lower section of the menu provides options for choosing a different group; these options might change depending on the selected category.

2. In the Navigate To Category section, click **Tables and Related Views**. The Navigation Pane is now grouped into categories of tables, and each table in the database—Visit, Billing, and Patient—is its own group. All database objects related to a table are listed below the table's name. Use the scroll bar to scroll to the bottom of the objects list. (Notice the Visit heading has scrolled out of the Navigation Pane.) See Figure 3–43.

Figure 3–43 Database objects grouped by table in the Navigation Pane

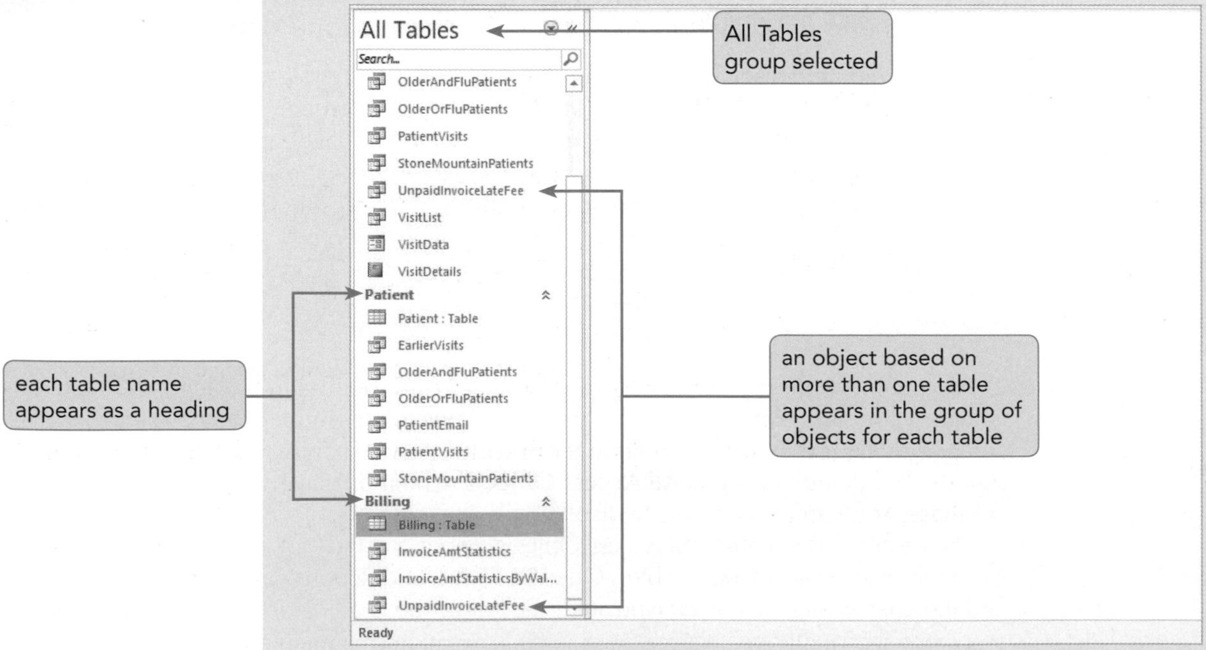
All Tables
Search...
OlderAndFluPatients
OlderOrFluPatients
PatientVisits
StoneMountainPatients
UnpaidInvoiceLateFee
VisitList
VisitData
VisitDetails
Patient
Patient : Table
EarlierVisits
OlderAndFluPatients
OlderOrFluPatients
PatientEmail
PatientVisits
StoneMountainPatients
Billing
Billing : Table
InvoiceAmtStatistics
InvoiceAmtStatisticsByWal...
UnpaidInvoiceLateFee
Ready
All Tables group selected
each table name appears as a heading
an object based on more than one table appears in the group of objects for each table

Some objects appear more than once. When an object is based on more than one table, that object appears in the group for each table. For example, the UnpaidInvoiceLateFee query is based on both the Visit and Billing tables, so it is listed in the group for both tables.

You can also choose to display the objects for only one table to better focus on that table.

3. At the top of the Navigation Pane, click the **All Tables** button to display the Navigation Pane menu, and then click **Patient**. The Navigation Pane now shows only the objects related to the Patient table—the table itself plus the six queries you created that include fields from the Patient table.
4. At the top of the Navigation Pane, click the **Patient** button, and then click **Object Type** to return to the default display of the Navigation Pane.
5. **sam** Compact and repair the Lakewood database, and then close the database.

Trouble? If a dialog box opens and warns that this action will cause Microsoft Access to empty the Clipboard, click the Yes button to continue.

The default All Access Objects category is a predefined category. You can also create custom categories to group objects in the way that best suits how you want to manage your database objects. As you continue to build a database and the list of objects grows, creating a custom category can help you to work more efficiently with the objects in the database.

The queries you've created and saved will help Donna and her staff to monitor and analyze the business activity of Lakewood Community Health Services and its patients. Now any staff member can run the queries at any time, modify them as needed, or use them as the basis for designing new queries to meet additional information requirements.

REVIEW

Session 3.2 Quick Check

1. A(n) ______________ is a criterion, or rule, that determines which records are selected for a query datasheet.
2. In the design grid, where do you place the conditions for two different fields when you use the And logical operator, and where do you place them when you use the Or logical operator?
3. To perform a calculation in a query, you define a(n) ______________ containing a combination of database fields, constants, and operators.
4. Which Access tool do you use to create an expression for a calculated field in a query?
5. What is an aggregate function?
6. The ______________ operator divides selected records into groups based on the values in a field.
7. What is the default category for the display of objects in the Navigation Pane?

PRACTICE

Review Assignments

Data File needed for the Review Assignments: Vendor.accdb ***(cont. from Module 2)***

Donna asks you to update some information in the Vendor database and to retrieve specific information from the database. Complete the following:

1. Open the **Vendor** database you created and worked with in previous modules, and then click the Enable Content button next to the security warning, if necessary.
2. Open the **Supplier** table in Datasheet view, and then change the following field values for the record with the Supplier ID HAR912: Address to **912 Medical Dr**, Contact Phone to **865-555-1226**, Contact First Name to **Isabella**, and Contact Last Name to **Lopez**. Close the table.
3. Create a query based on the Supplier table. Include the following fields in the query, in the order shown: Company, Category, ContactFirst, ContactLast, Phone, and City. Sort the query in ascending order based on the Category field values. Save the query as **ContactList**, and then run the query.
4. Use the ContactList query datasheet to update the Supplier table by changing the Phone field value for Killington Medical to **762-555-9811**.
5. Change the size of the text in the ContactList query datasheet to use a 12-point font size. Resize columns, as necessary, so that all field values and column headings are visible.
6. Change the alternate row color in the ContactList query datasheet to the Theme Color named Blue, Accent 5, Lighter 60%, and then save and close the query.
7. Create a query based on the Supplier and Product tables. Select the Company, Category, and State fields from the Supplier table, and the ProductName, Price, Units, and Weight fields from the Product table. Sort the query results in descending order based on price. Select only those records with a Category field value of Supplies, but do not display the Category field values in the query results. Save the query as **SupplyProducts**, run the query, and then close it.
8. Create a query that lists all products that cost more than $50 and are temperature controlled. Display the following fields from the Product table in the query results: ProductID, ProductName, Price, Units, and Sterile. (*Hint*: The TempControl field is a Yes/No field that should not appear in the query results.) Save the query as **HighPriceAndTempControl**, run the query, and then close it.
9. Create a query that lists information about suppliers who sell equipment or sterile products. Include the Company, Category, ContactFirst, and ContactLast fields from the Supplier table; and the ProductName, Price, TempControl, and Sterile fields from the Product table. Save the query as **EquipmentOrSterile**, run the query, and then close it.
10. Create a query that lists all resale products, along with a 10% markup amount based on the price of the product. Include the Company field from the Supplier table and the following fields from the Product table in the query: ProductID, ProductName, and Price. Save the query as **ResaleProductsWithMarkup**. Display the markup amount in a calculated field named **Markup** that determines a 10% markup based on the Price field values. Set the Caption property to **MarkUp** for the calculated field. Display the query results in descending order by Price. Save and run the query.
11. Modify the format of the Markup field in the ResaleProductsWithMarkup query so that it uses the Standard format and two decimal places. Run the query, resize all columns in the datasheet to their best fit, and then save and close the query.
12. Create a query that calculates the lowest, highest, and average prices for all products using the field names **MinimumPrice**, **MaximumPrice**, and **AveragePrice**, respectively. Set the Caption property for each field to include a space between the two words in the field name. Run the query, resize all columns in the datasheet to their best fit, save the query as **PriceStatistics**, and then close it.

13. In the Navigation Pane, copy the PriceStatistics query, and then rename the copied query as **PriceStatisticsBySupplier**.
14. Modify the PriceStatisticsBySupplier query so that the records are grouped by the Company field in the Supplier table. The Company field should appear first in the query datasheet. Save and run the query, and then close it.
15. Compact and repair the Vendor database, and then close it.

APPLY

Case Problem 1

Data File needed for this Case Problem: Career.accdb *(cont. from Module 2)*

Great Giraffe Jeremiah needs to modify a few records in the Career database and analyze the data within the database. To help Jeremiah, you'll update the Career database and create queries to answer his questions. Complete the following:

1. Open the **Career** database you created and worked with in previous modules, and then click the Enable Content button next to the security warning, if necessary.
2. In the **Student** table, find the record for StudentID ART5210, and then change the Street value to **417 Barclay Avenue** and the Zip to **80202**.
3. In the **Student** table, find the record for StudentID ESP1734, and then delete the record. (*Hint*: Delete the related records in the Registration subdatasheet first.) Close the Student table.
4. Create a query that lists students who are on a payment plan for any of the courses offered by Great Giraffe. List only the StudentID, FirstName, and LastName fields for the students in your results, and sort the results in ascending order by the LastName field. Save the query as **AllPaymentPlanStudents**, run the query, and then close it.
5. In the Navigation Pane, copy the AllPaymentPlanStudents query, and then rename the copied query as **LittletonPaymentPlanStudents**.
6. Modify the LittletonPaymentPlanStudents query so that it only displays those students from the city of Littleton. (*Hint*: When you are entering the criteria for a Short Text field, Access usually places the quotation marks around the text; however, you may also type the quotation marks if you are having trouble entering the text properly.) The City field should not appear in the query datasheet. Save and run the query, and then close it.
7. Create a query that lists students who are taking one of the Computer Science courses offered. (*Hint*: Instead of looking at the individual sections, look at the Title of the courses.) In the query results, display only the StudentID, FirstName, LastName, and Phone of the students in the courses. Sort the results by StudentID in ascending order. Save the query as **CompSciStudents** and run the query.
8. Use the CompSciStudents query datasheet to update the Student table by using **(303) 555-0042** for the Phone value for Wendy Bradshaw.
9. Change the size of the text in the CompSciStudents query datasheet to use a 14-point font size. Resize columns, as necessary, so that all field values and column headings are visible.
10. Change the alternate row color in the CompSciStudents query datasheet to the Theme Color named Green, Accent 6, Lighter 80%, and then save and close the query.
11. Create a query that lists the InstanceID, Title, StartDate, HoursPerWeek, and Cost fields for courses that begin anytime in the first three months of 2021. Save the query as **FirstQuarterClassOptions**, run the query, and then close it.
12. Create a query that lists the total outstanding balances for students on a payment plan and for those students that are not on a payment plan. Show in the query results only the sum of the balance due, grouped by PaymentPlan. Name the summation column **Balances**. Run the query, resize all columns in the datasheet to their best fit, save the query as **TotalBalancesByPlan**, and then close it.
13. Compact and repair the Career database, and then close it.

CHALLENGE

Case Problem 2

Data File needed for this Case Problem: DrainAdopter.accdb *(cont. from Module 2)*

Drain Adopter Tandrea needs to modify some records in the Center database, and then she wants to find specific information about the program. Tandrea asks you to help her update the database and create queries to find the information she needs. Complete the following:

1. Open the **DrainAdopter** database you created and worked with in previous modules, and then click the Enable Content button next to the security warning, if necessary.
2. Create a query based on the Volunteer table that includes the VolunteerID, FirstName, LastName, and SignupDate fields, in that order. Display only those records whose SignupDate is in the first three months of the program, which began in January 2021. Save the query as **FirstVolunteers**, and then run it.
3. Modify the FirstVolunteers query design so that it sorts records in ascending order by SignupDate. Save and run the query.
4. Create a query to count the number of volunteers that have completed training, and those that did not complete training. Show in the query results only the count of each category, grouped by the Trained field. Name the summation column **Total**. Run the query, resize all columns in the datasheet to their best fit, save the query as **NumberTrainedAndNotTrained**.
5. Create a query to count the number of drains that need maintenance, and those that do not need maintenance. Show in the query results only the count of each category, grouped by the MaintReq field. Name the summation column **Total**. Run the query, resize all columns in the datasheet to their best fit, and save the query as **NumberMaintRequired**.
6. **Explore** Create a query that includes all the fields from the Supply table in the order they appear in the table and creates a calculated field called **Value** to determine the dollar amount of each supply item on hand. (*Hint*: Place brackets around each field in the calculation and multiply the Cost field by the NumberOnHand field.) Save the query as **InventoryCosts** and run the query.
7. Modify the InventoryCosts query to use the Currency format for the new Value field and to give the field a Caption property of **Inventory Value**. Run the query, and then resize the columns to display the complete field names and values. Save and close the query.
8. **Explore** Create a query to total the inventory amounts from the InventoryCosts query. (*Hint*: The data source for a query can be a table or another query. To choose a query, click the Queries tab in the Show Table dialog box.) Just as with any other aggregate function, sum the value of the calculated field (Value) from the InventoryCosts query. Name the summation column **Total Inventory** and display the total using a Currency format. Run the query, resize all columns in the datasheet to their best fit, save the query as **TotalInventoryValue**, and then close it.
9. **Explore** Format the datasheet of the FirstVolunteers query so that it does not display gridlines, uses an alternate row Standard Color of Maroon 2, and displays a font size of 12. (*Hint*: Use the Gridlines button in the Text Formatting group on the Home tab to select the appropriate gridlines option.) Resize the columns to display the complete field names and values, if necessary. Save and close the query.
10. **Explore** In the Volunteer table, each VolunteerID value has a plus sign (expand indicator) next to it indicating a relationship to another table. To view each corresponding relationship, you could scroll and click each expand indictor to show the relationship; however, since there are 150 volunteers, this would take a while. Instead, click the Datasheet Selector button to the left of the VolunteerID field, and then click one of the expand indicators to expand all of the records. You can now see all of the records expanded and scroll through them much more efficiently. To close all of the expanded records, click the Datasheet Selector button again, and then click one of the minus signs (collapse indicators). The records are now collapsed. To deselect the entire form, click a field value within the datasheet. Close the datasheet. Since there were no changes to the structure of the table, you will not be prompted about whether to save your changes.
11. Compact and repair the DrainAdopter database, and then close it.

MODULE 4

Creating Forms and Reports

Using Forms and Reports to Display Patient and Visit Data

ACCESS

OBJECTIVES

Session 4.1
- Create a form using the Form Wizard
- Apply a theme to a form
- Add a picture to a form
- Change the color of text on a form
- Find and maintain data using a form
- Preview and print selected form records
- Create a form with a main form and a subform

Session 4.2
- Create a report using the Report Wizard
- Apply a theme to a report
- Change the alignment of field values on a report
- Move and resize fields in a report
- Insert a picture in a report
- Change the color of text on a report
- Apply conditional formatting in a report
- Preview and print a report

Case | *Lakewood Community Health Services*

Donna Taylor wants to continue enhancing the Lakewood database to make it easier for her staff to enter, locate, and maintain data. In particular, she wants the database to include a form based on the Patient table that staff can use to enter and change data about the clinic's patients. She also wants the database to include a form that shows data from both the Patient and Visit tables at the same time. This form will show the visit information for each patient along with the corresponding patient data, providing a complete picture of Lakewood Community Health Services patients and their visits to the clinic.

In addition, she would like the database to include a report of patient and visit data so that she and other staff members will have printed output when completing analyses and planning strategies for community outreach efforts. She wants the report to be formatted professionally and easy to use.

In this module, you will create the forms and reports in the Lakewood database for Donna and her staff.

STARTING DATA FILES

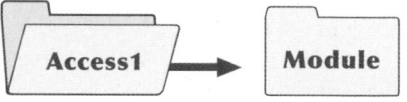

Access1 → **Module**
Lakewood.accdb (cont.)
Support_AC_4_Medical.png

Review
Support_AC_4_Items.png
Support_AC_4_Supplies.png
Vendor.accdb (cont.)

Case1
Career.accdb (cont.)
Support_AC_4_Giraffe.png

Case2
Support_AC_4_Drain.png
DrainAdopter.accdb (cont.)

Session 4.1 Visual Overview:

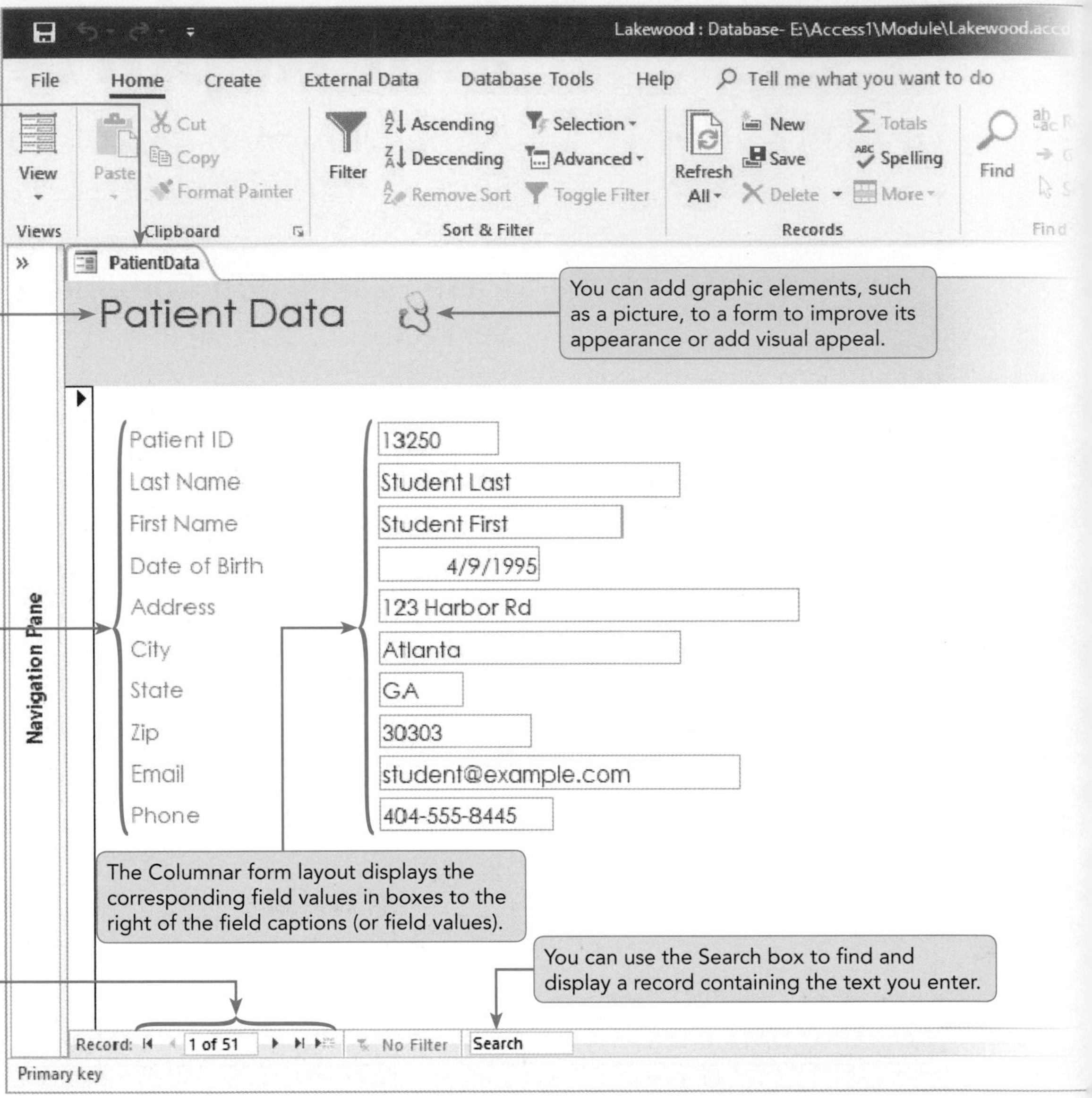
Lakewood : Database- E:\Access1\Module\Lakewood.accdb
File
Home
Create
External Data
Database Tools
Help
Tell me what you want to do
View
Paste
Cut
Copy
Format Painter
Views
Clipboard
Filter
Ascending
Descending
Remove Sort
Selection
Advanced
Toggle Filter
Sort & Filter
Refresh All
New
Save
Delete
Totals
Spelling
More
Records
Find
Navigation Pane
PatientData
Patient Data
Patient ID
13250
Last Name
Student Last
First Name
Student First
Date of Birth
4/9/1995
Address
123 Harbor Rd
City
Atlanta
State
GA
Zip
30303
Email
student@example.com
Phone
404-555-8445
Record: 1 of 51
No Filter
Search
Primary key

The form object's name is displayed on the tab for the form.

The form title appears at the top of the form. By default, the form object name is used as the form title, but you can edit the title to display the text you want, as done here—a space was added between the two words for readability.

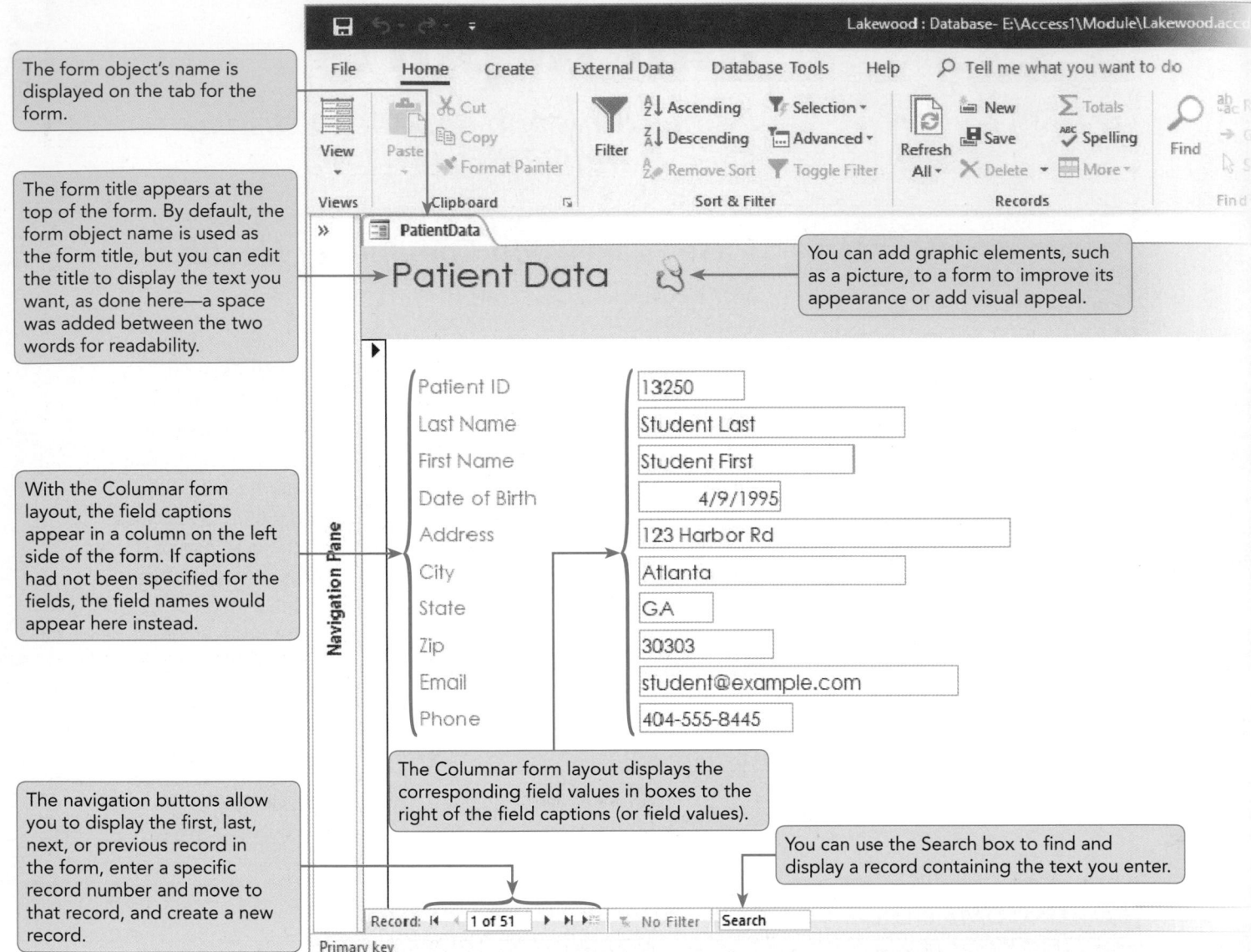

You can add graphic elements, such as a picture, to a form to improve its appearance or add visual appeal.

With the Columnar form layout, the field captions appear in a column on the left side of the form. If captions had not been specified for the fields, the field names would appear here instead.

The Columnar form layout displays the corresponding field values in boxes to the right of the field captions (or field values).

The navigation buttons allow you to display the first, last, next, or previous record in the form, enter a specific record number and move to that record, and create a new record.

You can use the Search box to find and display a record containing the text you enter.

Form Displayed in Form View

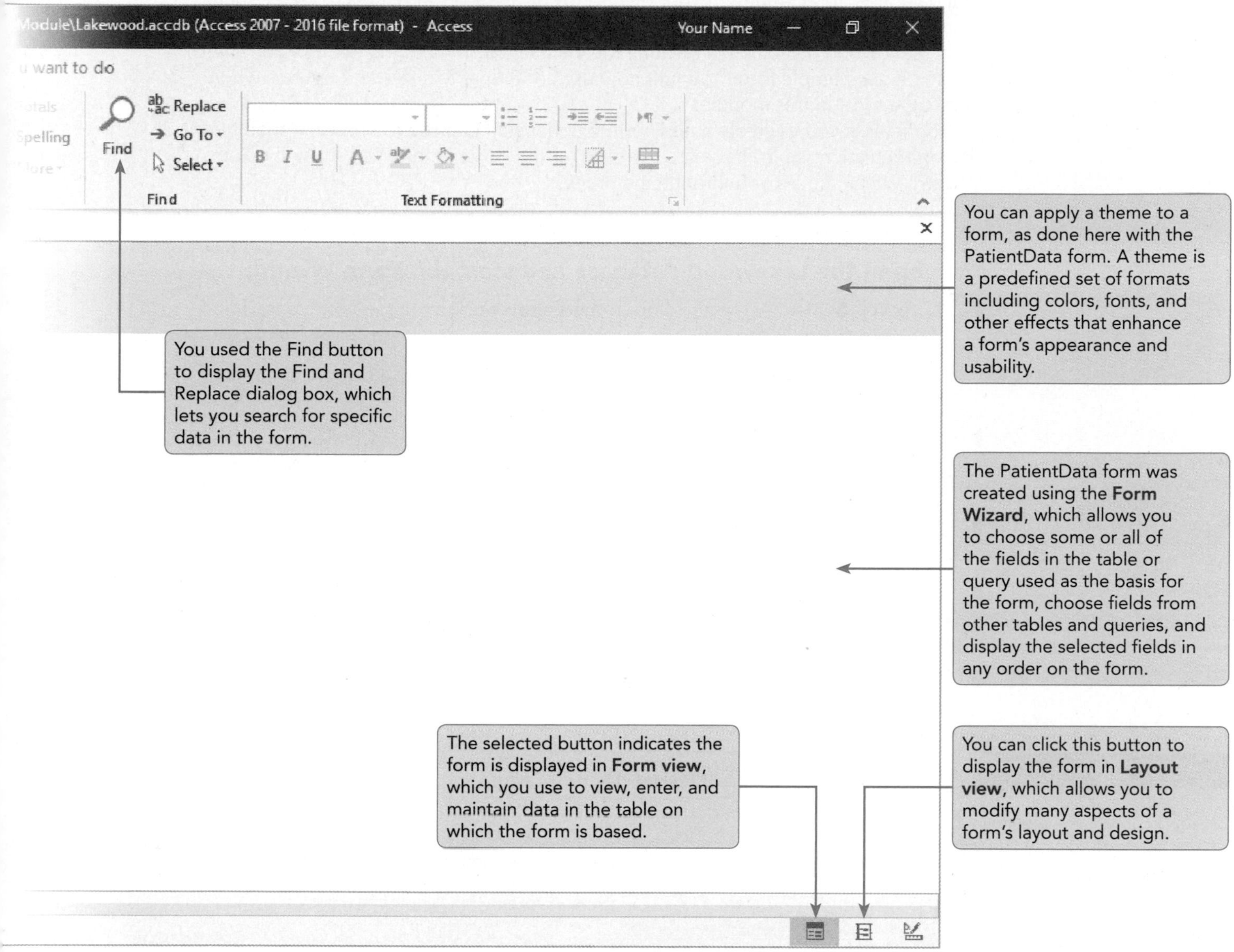
odule\Lakewood.accdb (Access 2007 - 2016 file Format) - Access
Your Name
u want to do
Replace
Go To
Select
Find
Find
Text Formatting
Spelling
You can apply a theme to a form, as done here with the PatientData form. A theme is a predefined set of formats including colors, fonts, and other effects that enhance a form's appearance and usability.
You used the Find button to display the Find and Replace dialog box, which lets you search for specific data in the form.
The PatientData form was created using the **Form Wizard**, which allows you to choose some or all of the fields in the table or query used as the basis for the form, choose fields from other tables and queries, and display the selected fields in any order on the form.
The selected button indicates the form is displayed in **Form view**, which you use to view, enter, and maintain data in the table on which the form is based.
You can click this button to display the form in **Layout view**, which allows you to modify many aspects of a form's layout and design.

Creating a Form Using the Form Wizard

As you learned earlier, a form is an object you use to enter, edit, and view records in a database. You can design your own forms or use tools in Access to create them automatically. You have already used the Form Wizard to create the VisitData form in the Lakewood database. In creating the VisitData form with the Form Wizard, you created a very simple form. You will now use additional features and options when creating a form in this module.

Donna asks you to create a new form that her staff can use to view and maintain data in the Patient table. To create the form for the Patient table, you'll use the Form Wizard, which guides you through the process.

To open the Lakewood database and start the Form Wizard:

1. Start Access and open the **Lakewood** database you created and worked with in the previous modules.

   Trouble? If the security warning is displayed below the ribbon, click the Enable Content button.

2. Open the Navigation Pane, if necessary. To create a form based on a table or query, you can select the table or query in the Navigation Pane first, or you can select it using the Form Wizard.
3. In the Tables section of the Navigation Pane, click **Patient** to select the Patient table as the basis for the new form.
4. On the ribbon, click the **Create** tab. The Forms group on the Create tab provides options for creating various types of forms and designing your own forms.
5. In the Forms group, click the **Form Wizard** button. The first Form Wizard dialog box opens. See Figure 4–1.

Figure 4–1 First Form Wizard dialog box

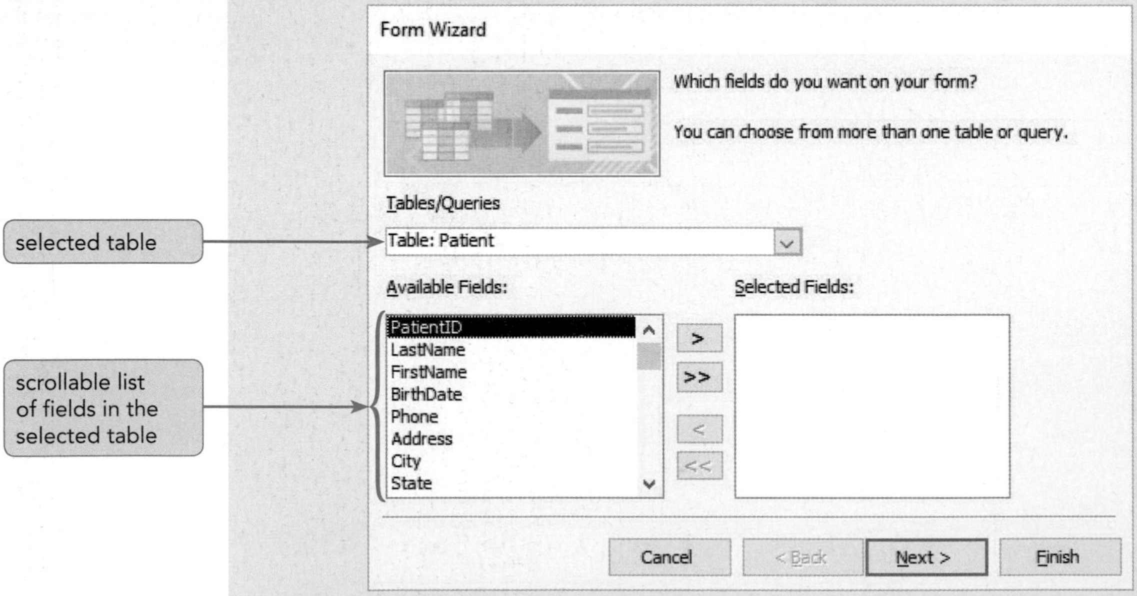
Form Wizard
Which fields do you want on your form?
You can choose from more than one table or query.
Tables/Queries
Table: Patient
Available Fields:
Selected Fields:
PatientID
LastName
FirstName
BirthDate
Phone
Address
City
State
>
>>
<
<<
Cancel
< Back
Next >
Finish
selected table
scrollable list of fields in the selected table

Because you selected the Patient table in the Navigation Pane before starting the Form Wizard, this table is selected in the Tables/Queries box, and the fields for the Patient table are listed in the Available Fields box.

Donna wants the form to display all the fields in the Patient table, but in a different order. She would like the Phone field to appear at the bottom of the form so that it stands out, making it easier for someone who needs to call patients to use the form to quickly locate the phone number for a patient.

To create the form using the Form Wizard:

1. Click the **Select All Fields** button >> to move all the fields to the Selected Fields box. Next, you need to position the Phone field so it will appear as the bottom-most field on the form. To accomplish this, you will first remove the Phone field and then add it back as the last selected field.
2. In the Selected Fields box, click the **Phone** field, and then click the **Remove Single Field** button < to move the field back to the Available Fields box.

   Because a new field is always added after the selected field in the Selected Fields box, you need to first select the last field in the list and then move the Phone field back to the Selected Fields box so it will be the last field on the form.
3. In the Selected Fields box, click the **Email** field.
4. With the Phone field selected in the Available Fields box, click the **Select Single Field** button > to move the Phone field to the end of the list in the Selected Fields box.
5. Click the **Next** button to display the second Form Wizard dialog box, in which you select a layout for the form. See Figure 4–2.

Figure 4–2 **Choosing a layout for the form**

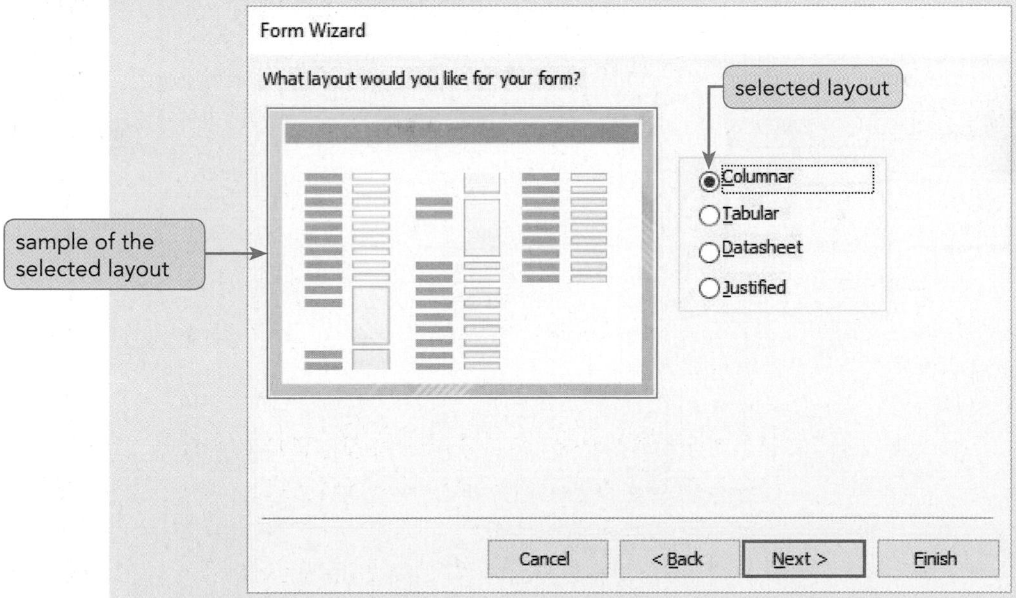
Form Wizard
What layout would you like for your form?
selected layout
Columnar
Tabular
Datasheet
Justified
sample of the selected layout
Cancel
< Back
Next >
Finish

   The layout choices are Columnar, Tabular, Datasheet, and Justified. A sample of the selected layout appears on the left side of the dialog box.
6. Click each of the option buttons and review the corresponding sample layout.

   The Tabular and Datasheet layouts display the fields from multiple records at one time, whereas the Columnar and Justified layouts display the fields from one record at a time. Donna thinks the Columnar layout is the appropriate arrangement for displaying and updating data in the table, so that anyone using the form can focus on just one patient record at a time.

7. Click the **Columnar** option button (if necessary), and then click the **Next** button.

The third and final Form Wizard dialog box shows the Patient table's name as the default form name. "Patient" is also the default title that will appear on the tab for the form.

You'll use "PatientData" as the form name, and, because you don't need to change the form's design at this point, you'll display the form.

8. Click to position the insertion point to the right of Patient in the box, type **Data**, and then click the **Finish** button.

Close the Navigation Pane to display only the Form window. The completed form opens in Form view, displaying the values for the first record in the Patient table. The Columnar layout you selected places the field captions in labels on the left and the corresponding field values in boxes on the right, which vary in width depending on the size of the field. See Figure 4–3.

Figure 4–3 **PatientData form in Form view**

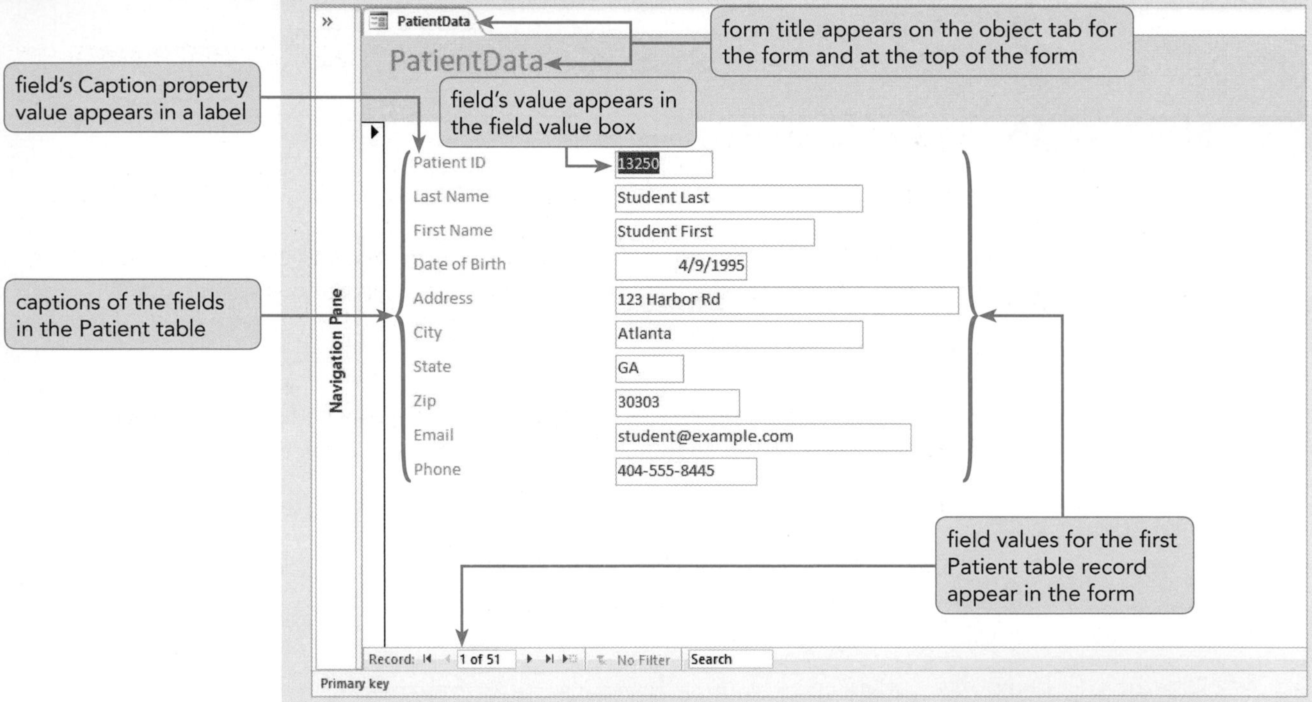
PatientData
PatientData
form title appears on the object tab for the form and at the top of the form
field's Caption property value appears in a label
field's value appears in the field value box
captions of the fields in the Patient table
Navigation Pane
Patient ID
13250
Last Name
Student Last
First Name
Student First
Date of Birth
4/9/1995
Address
123 Harbor Rd
City
Atlanta
State
GA
Zip
30303
Email
student@example.com
Phone
404-555-8445
field values for the first Patient table record appear in the form
Record: 1 of 51
No Filter
Search
Primary key

After viewing the form, Donna makes suggestions for improving the form's readability and appearance. The font used in the labels on the left is light in color and small, making them difficult to read. Also, she thinks inserting a graphic on the form would add visual interest, and modifying other form elements—such as the color of the title text—would improve the look of the form. You can make all of these changes working with the form in Layout view.

Modifying a Form's Design in Layout View

TIP

Some form design changes require you to switch to Design view, which gives you a more detailed view of the form's structure.

After you create a form, you might need to modify its design to improve its appearance or to make the form easier to use. You cannot make any design changes in Form view. However, Layout view displays the form as it appears in Form view while allowing you to modify the form's design. Because you can see the form and its data while you are modifying the form, Layout view makes it easy for you to see the results of any design changes you make.

The first modification you'll make to the PatientData form is to change its appearance by applying a theme.

Applying a Theme to a Database Object

By default, the objects you create in a database are formatted with the Office theme. A theme provides a design scheme for the colors and fonts used in the database objects. Access, like other Microsoft Office programs, provides many built-in themes, including the Office theme, making it easy for you to create objects with a unified look. You can also create a customized theme if none of the built-in themes suit your needs.

Sometimes a theme works well for one database object but is not as suitable for other objects in that database. Therefore, when applying a theme to an object, you can choose to apply the theme just to the open object, to objects of a particular type, or to all the existing objects in the database and set it as the default theme for any new objects that might be created.

To change a form's appearance, you can easily apply a new theme to it.

REFERENCE

Applying a Theme to Database Objects

- Display the object in Layout view.
- In the Themes group on the Form Layout Tools Design tab or Report Layout Tools Design tab, click the Themes button.
- In the Themes gallery, click the theme you want to apply to all objects; or, right-click the theme to display the shortcut menu, and then choose to apply the theme to the current object only or to all matching objects.

Donna would like to see if the PatientData form's appearance can be improved with a different theme. To apply a theme, you first need to switch to Layout view.

To apply a theme to the PatientData form:

1. On the ribbon, make sure the Home tab is displayed.
2. In the Views group, click **View**. The form is displayed in Layout view. See Figure 4–4.

Figure 4–4 Form displayed in Layout view

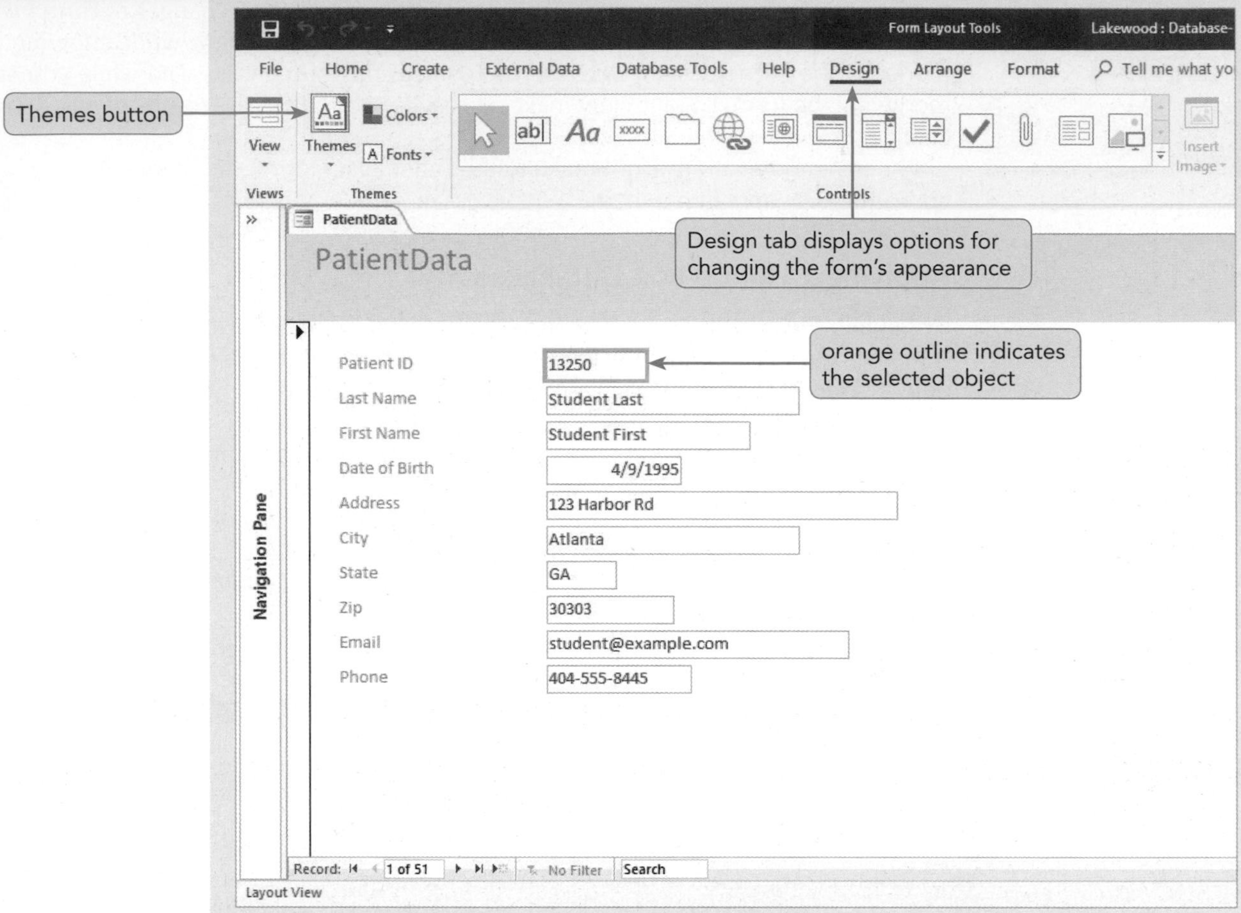
Themes button
Design tab displays options for changing the form's appearance
orange outline indicates the selected object
Form Layout Tools
Lakewood : Database-
File
Home
Create
External Data
Database Tools
Help
Design
Arrange
Format
Tell me what yo
View
Themes
Colors
Fonts
Views
Controls
Insert Image
PatientData
Navigation Pane
Patient ID
13250
Last Name
Student Last
First Name
Student First
Date of Birth
4/9/1995
Address
123 Harbor Rd
City
Atlanta
State
GA
Zip
30303
Email
student@example.com
Phone
404-555-8445
Record: 1 of 51
No Filter
Search
Layout View

Trouble? If the Field List or Property Sheet opens on the right side of the program window, close it before continuing.

In Layout view, an orange border identifies the currently selected element on the form. In this case, the field value for the PatientID field, 13250, is selected. You need to apply a theme to the PatientData form.

3. On the Form Layout Tools Design tab, in the Themes group, click **Themes**. A gallery opens showing the available themes for the form. See Figure 4–5.

Figure 4–5 Themes gallery displayed

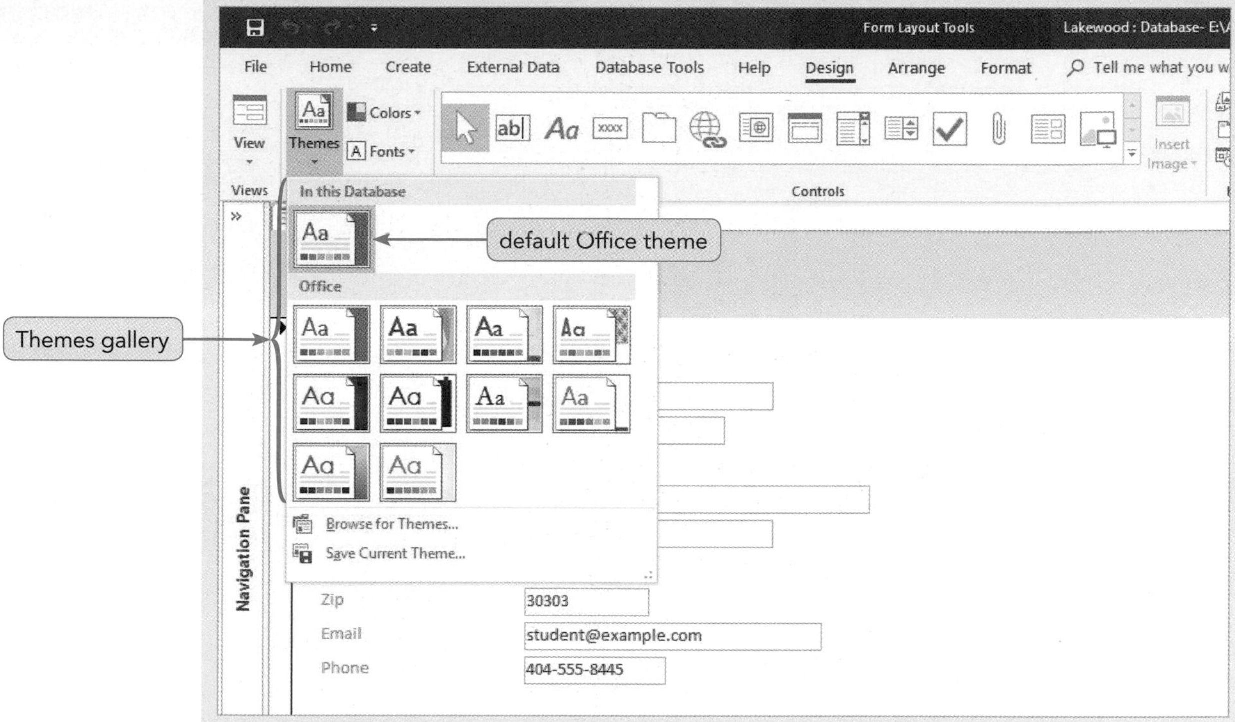
Form Layout Tools
Lakewood : Database- E:\
File
Home
Create
External Data
Database Tools
Help
Design
Arrange
Format
Tell me what you w
View
Themes
Colors
Fonts
Views
Controls
Insert Image
In this Database
default Office theme
Office
Themes gallery
Browse for Themes...
Save Current Theme...
Navigation Pane
Zip
30303
Email
student@example.com
Phone
404-555-8445

TIP

Themes other than the Office theme are listed in alphabetical order in the gallery.

The Office theme, the default theme currently applied in the database, is listed in the "In this Database" section and is also the first theme listed in the section containing other themes. You can point to each theme in the gallery to see its name in a ScreenTip. Also, when you point to a theme, the Live Preview feature shows the effect of applying the theme to the open object.

4. In the gallery, point to each of the themes to see how they would format the PatientData form. Notice the changes in color and font type of the text, for example.

   Donna likes the Slice theme because of its bright blue color in the title area at the top and its larger font size, which makes the text in the form easier to read. She asks you to apply this theme to the form.

5. Right-click the **Slice** theme. A shortcut menu opens with options for applying the theme. See Figure 4–6.

Figure 4–6 Shortcut menu for applying the theme

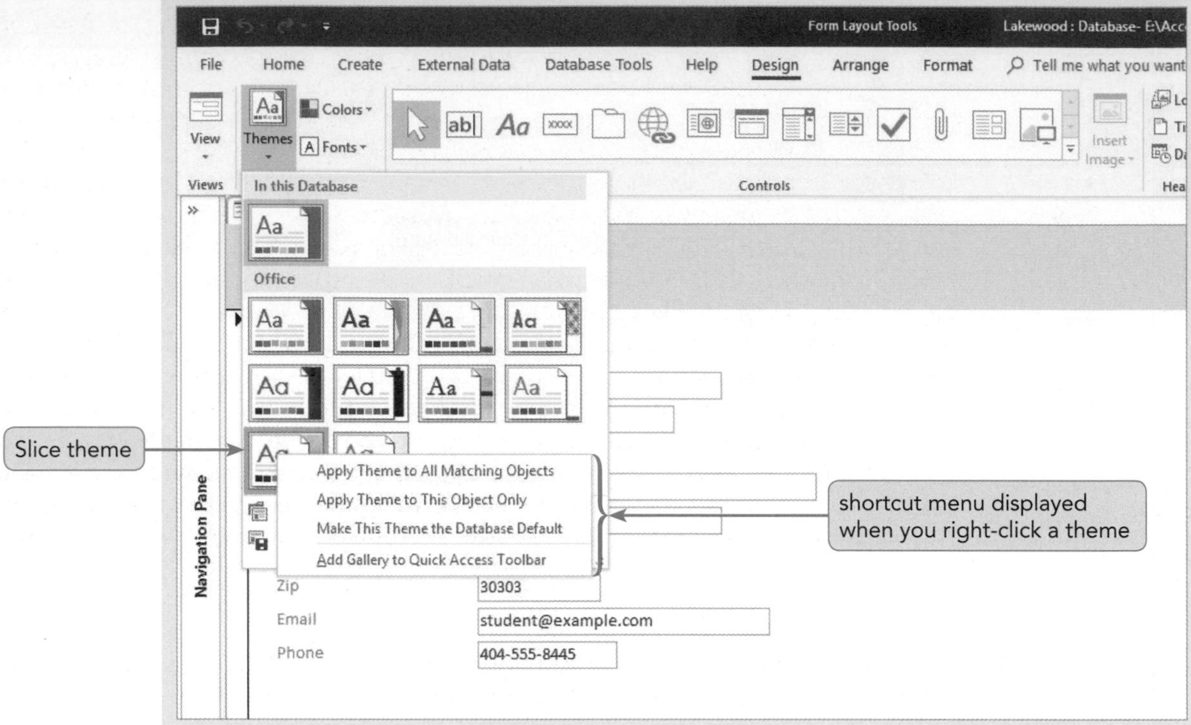
Form Layout Tools
Lakewood : Database- E:\Acc
File
Home
Create
External Data
Database Tools
Help
Design
Arrange
Format
Tell me what you want
View
Themes
Colors
Fonts
Views
In this Database
Office
Controls
Insert Image
Slice theme
Apply Theme to All Matching Objects
Apply Theme to This Object Only
Make This Theme the Database Default
Add Gallery to Quick Access Toolbar
shortcut menu displayed when you right-click a theme
Navigation Pane
Zip
30303
Email
student@example.com
Phone
404-555-8445

The menu provides options for applying the theme to all matching objects—for example, all the forms in the database—or to the current object only. You can also choose to make the theme the default theme in the database, which means any new objects you create will be formatted with the selected theme. Because Donna is not sure if all forms in the Lakewood database will look better with the Slice theme, she asks you to apply it only to the PatientData form.

Choose this option to avoid applying the theme to other forms in the database.

6. On the shortcut menu, click **Apply Theme to This Object Only**.

The gallery closes, and the Slice theme's colors and fonts are applied to the form.

Trouble? If you choose the wrong option by mistake, you might have applied the selected theme to other forms and reports in the database. Repeat Steps 3 through 6 to apply the Slice theme to the PatientData form. You can also follow the same process to reapply the default Office theme to the other forms and reports in the Lakewood database, as directed by your instructor.

INSIGHT

Working with Themes

Themes provide a quick and easy way for you to format the objects in a database with a consistent look, which is a good design principle to follow. In general, all objects of a type in a database—for example, all forms—should have a consistent design. However, keep in mind that when you select a theme in the Themes gallery and choose the option to apply the theme to all matching objects or to make the theme the default for the database, it might be applied to all the existing forms and reports in the database as well as to new forms and reports you create. Although this approach ensures a consistent design, it can cause problems. For example, if you have already created a form or report and its design is suitable, applying a theme that includes a larger font size could cause the text in labels and field value boxes to be cut off or to extend into other objects on the form or report. The colors applied by the theme could also interfere with elements on existing forms and reports. To handle these unintended results, you would have to spend time checking the existing forms and reports and fixing any problems introduced by applying the theme. A better approach is to select the option "Apply Theme to This Object Only," available on the shortcut menu for a theme in the Themes gallery, for each existing form and report. If the newly applied theme causes problems for any individual form or report, you can then reapply the original theme to return the object to its original design.

Next, you will add a picture to the form for visual interest. The picture, which is included on various flyers and other patient correspondence for Lakewood Community Health Services, is a small graphic of a stethoscope.

Adding a Picture to a Form

A picture is one of many controls you can add and modify on a form. A **control** is an item on a form, report, or other database object that you can manipulate to modify the object's appearance. The controls you can add and modify in Layout view for a form are available in the Controls group and the Header/Footer group on the Form Layout Tools Design tab. The picture you need to add is contained in a file named Support_AC_4_Medical.png, which is located in the Access1 > Module folder provided with your Data Files.

To add the picture to the form:

1. Make sure the form is still displayed in Layout view and that the Form Layout Tools Design tab is active.
2. In the Header/Footer group, click **Logo**. The Insert Picture dialog box opens.
3. Navigate to the **Access1 > Module** folder provided with your Data Files, click the **Support_AC_4_Medical.png** file, and then click **OK**. The picture appears on top of the form's title. See Figure 4–7.

Figure 4–7 Form with picture added

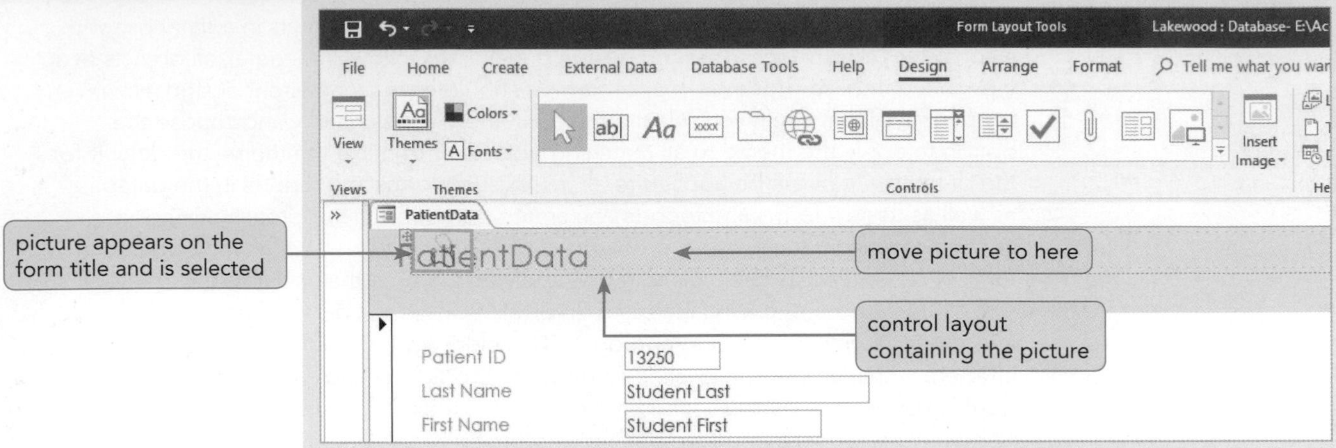

picture appears on the form title and is selected
move picture to here
control layout containing the picture
Form Layout Tools
PatientData
Patient ID
13250
Last Name
Student Last
First Name
Student First

A solid orange border surrounds the picture, indicating it is selected. The picture is placed in a **control layout**, which is a set of controls grouped together in a form or report so that you can manipulate the set as a single control. The dotted blue outline indicates the control layout. The easiest way to move the picture off the form title is to first remove it from the control layout. Doing so allows you to move the picture independently.

4. Right-click the picture to open the shortcut menu, point to **Layout**, and then click **Remove Layout**. The dotted blue outline no longer appears, and the picture is removed from the control layout. Now you can move the picture to the right of the form title.
5. Position the pointer on the picture, and then drag to the right of the form title. Although the image may not be visible while dragging, you can use the position of the pointer as a guide to where the image will be placed.
6. When the pointer is roughly one-half inch to the right of the form's title, release the mouse button. The picture is positioned to the right of the form title.
7. Click in a blank area to the right of the field values in the form to deselect the picture. See Figure 4–8.

Trouble? Don't be concerned if the picture is not in the exact location as the one shown in Figure 4–8. Just make sure the picture is not blocking any part of the form title and that it appears to the right of the form title and within the gray shaded area at the top of the form.

TIP

You can resize a selected image by dragging a corner of the orange selection border.

Figure 4–8 **Form with theme applied and picture repositioned**

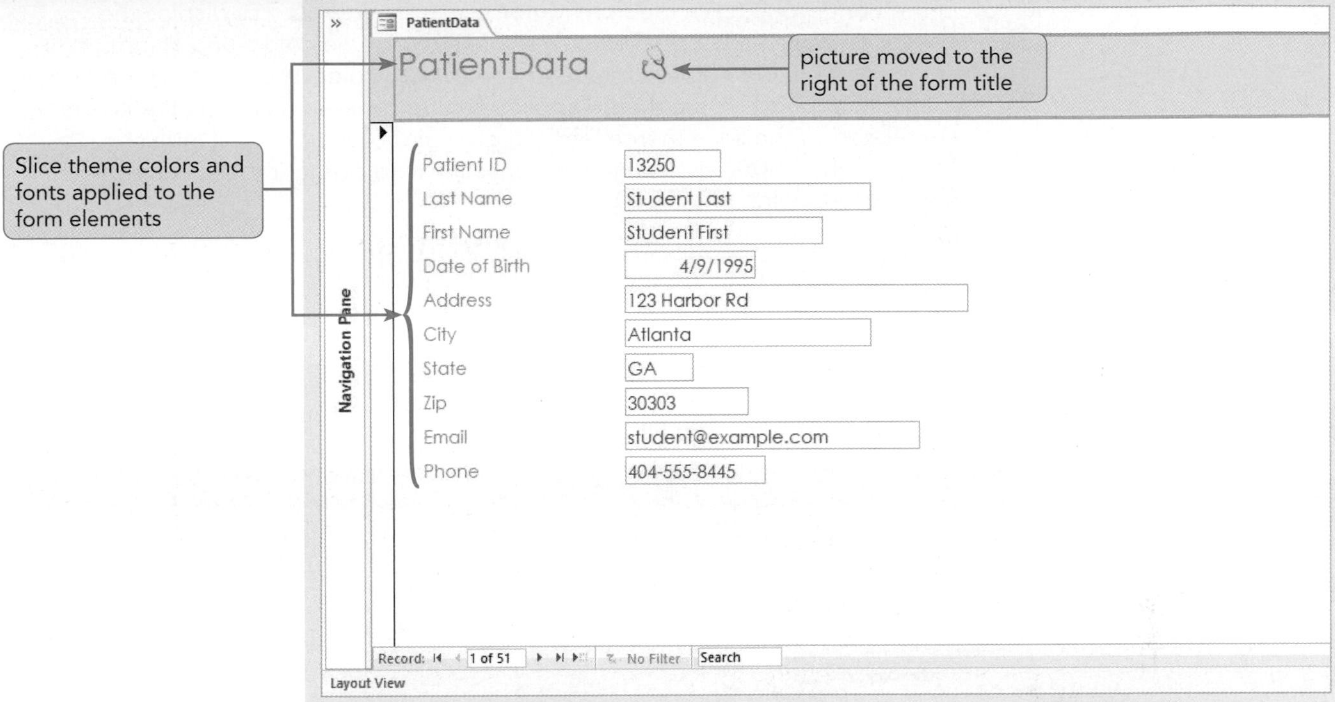
Slice theme colors and fonts applied to the form elements
picture moved to the right of the form title
PatientData
Patient ID
13250
Last Name
Student Last
First Name
Student First
Date of Birth
4/9/1995
Address
123 Harbor Rd
City
Atlanta
State
GA
Zip
30303
Email
student@example.com
Phone
404-555-8445
Navigation Pane
Record: 1 of 51
No Filter
Search
Layout View

Next, Donna asks you to change the color of the form title to a darker color so that it will stand out more on the form.

Changing the Color of Text on a Form

The Font group on the Form Layout Tools Format tab provides many options you can use to change the appearance of text on a form. For example, you can bold, italicize, and underline text; change the font, font color, and font size; and change the alignment of text. Before you change the color of the "PatientData" title on the form, you'll change the title to two words so it is easier to read.

To change the form title's text and color:

1. Click the **PatientData** form title. An orange border surrounds the title, indicating it is selected.
2. Click between the letters "t" and "D" to position the insertion point, and press **SPACEBAR**. The title on the form is now "Patient Data," but the added space caused the words to appear on two lines. You can fix this by resizing the box containing the title.
3. Position the pointer on the right edge of the box containing the form title until the pointer changes to the width change pointer ↔, and then drag to the right until the word "Data" appears on the same line as the word "Patient."

   Trouble? You might need to repeat Step 3 until the title appears on one line. Also, you might have to move the picture farther to the right to make room for the title.

   Next you will change the title's font color.

TIP

Changing the form's title does not affect the form object name; it is still PatientData, as shown on the object tab.

4. On the ribbon, click the **Form Layout Tools Format** tab.
5. In the Font group, click the **Font Color button arrow** to display the gallery of available colors. The gallery provides theme colors and standard colors, as well as an option for creating a custom color. The theme colors available depend on the theme applied to the form—in this case, the colors are related to the Slice theme. The current color of the title text—Black, Text 1, Lighter 50%—is outlined in the gallery, indicating it is the currently applied font color.
6. In the Theme Colors palette, click the **Black, Text 1, Lighter 25%** color, which is the fourth color down in the second column.
7. Click a blank area of the form to deselect the title. The darker color is applied to the form title text, making it stand out more. See Figure 4–9.

Figure 4–9 **Form title with new color applied**

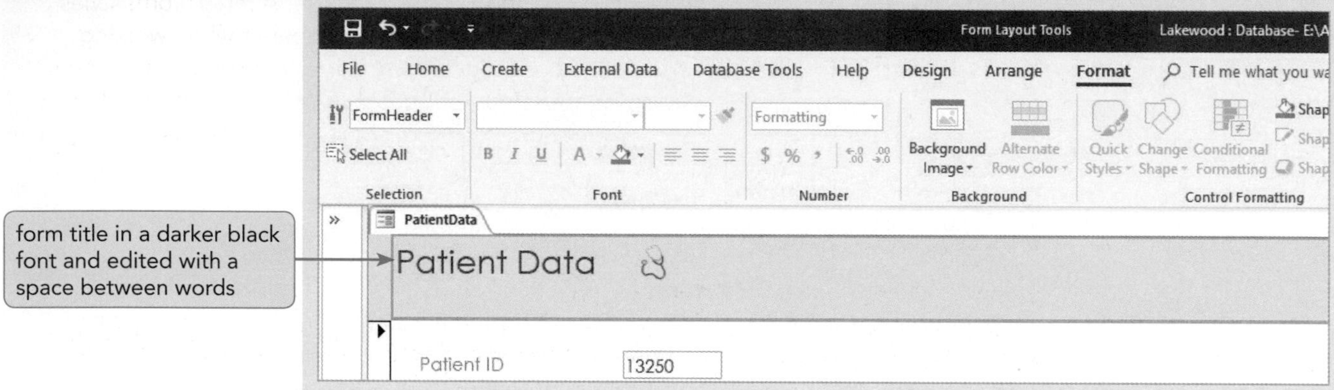
form title in a darker black font and edited with a space between words
Form Layout Tools
Lakewood : Database- E:\A
File
Home
Create
External Data
Database Tools
Help
Design
Arrange
Format
Tell me what you wa
FormHeader
Select All
Selection
Font
Formatting
Number
Background Image
Alternate Row Color
Background
Quick Styles
Change Shape
Conditional Formatting
Control Formatting
PatientData
Patient Data
Patient ID
13250

8. On the Quick Access Toolbar, click the **Save** button to save the modified form.
9. On the status bar, click the **Form View** button to display the form in Form view.

Donna is pleased with the modified appearance of the form.

PROSKILLS

Written Communication: Understanding the Importance of Form Design

Similar to any document, a form must convey written information clearly and effectively. When you create a form, it's important to consider how the form will be used, so that its design will accommodate the needs of people using the form to view, enter, and maintain data. For example, if a form in a database is meant to mimic a paper form that users will enter data from, the form in the database should have the same fields in the same order as on the paper form. This will enable users to easily tab from one field to the next in the database form to enter the necessary information from the paper form. Also, include a meaningful title on the form to identify its purpose and to enhance the appearance of the form. A form that is visually appealing makes working with the database more user-friendly and can improve the readability of the form, thereby helping to prevent errors in data entry. Also, be sure to use a consistent design for the forms in your database whenever possible. Users will expect to see similar elements—titles, pictures, fonts, and so on—in each form contained in a database. A mix of form styles and elements among the forms in a database could lead to problems when working with the forms. Finally, make sure the text on your form does not contain any spelling or grammatical errors. By producing a well-designed and well-written form, you can help to ensure that users will be able to work with the form in a productive and efficient manner.

Navigating a Form

To view, navigate, and change data using a form, you need to display the form in Form view. As you learned earlier, you navigate a form in the same way that you navigate a table datasheet. Also, the same navigation mode and editing mode keyboard shortcuts you have used working with datasheets can also be used when working with a form.

Donna wants to view data in the Patient table. Before using the PatientData form to display the specific information Donna wants to view, you will practice navigating between the fields in a record and navigating between records in the form. The PatientData form is already displayed in Form view, so you can use it to navigate through the fields and records of the Patient table.

To navigate the PatientData form:

1. If necessary, click in the **Patient ID** field value box to make it current.
2. Press **TAB** once to move to the Last Name field value box, and then press **END** to move to the Phone field value box.
3. Press **HOME** to move back to the Patient ID field value box. The first record in the Patient table still appears in the form.
4. Press **CTRL+END** to move to the Phone field value box for record 51, which is the last record in the table. The record number for the current record appears in the Current Record box between the navigation buttons at the bottom of the form.
5. Click the **Previous record** button ◄ to move to the Phone field value box in record 50.
6. Press ↑ twice to move to the Zip field value box in record 50.
7. Click to position the insertion point within the word "Phillips" in the Address field value to switch to editing mode, press **HOME** to move the insertion point to the beginning of the field value, and then press **END** to move the insertion point to the end of the field value.

8. Click the **First record** button [⏮] to move to the Address field value box in the first record. The entire field value is highlighted because you switched from editing mode to navigation mode.
9. Click the **Next record** button [▶] to move to the Address field value box in record 2, the next record.

Donna wants to find the record for a patient named Hansen. The paper form containing all the original contact information for this patient was damaged. Other than the patient's last name, Donna knows only the street the patient lives on. You will use the PatientData form to locate and view the complete record for this patient.

Finding Data Using a Form

As you learned earlier, the Find command lets you search for data in a datasheet so you can display only those records you want to view. You can also use the Find command to search for data in a form. You first choose a field to serve as the basis for the search by making that field the current field, and then you enter the value you want Access to match in the Find and Replace dialog box.

REFERENCE

Finding Data in a Form or Datasheet

- Open the form or datasheet, and then make the field you want to search the current field.
- On the Home tab, in the Find group, click the Find button to open the Find and Replace dialog box.
- In the Find What box, type the field value you want to find.
- Complete the remaining options, as necessary, to specify the type of search to conduct.
- Click the Find Next button to begin the search.
- Click the Find Next button to continue searching for the next match.
- Click the Cancel button to stop the search operation.

You need to find the record for the patient Donna wants to contact. The patient whose record she needs to find is named Hansen and lives on Boyles Ave. You'll search for this record using the Address field.

To find the record using the PatientData form:

1. Make sure the Address field value is still selected for the current record. This is the field you need to search.

   You can search for a record that contains part of the address anywhere in the Address field value. Performing a partial search such as this is often easier than matching the entire field value and is useful when you don't know or can't remember the entire field value.

2. On the Home tab, in the Find group, click the **Find** button. The Find and Replace dialog box opens. The Look In box indicates that the current field (in this case, Address) will be searched. You'll search for records that contain the word "boyles" in the address.

3. In the Find What box, type **boyles**. Note that you do not have to enter the word as "Boyles" with a capital letter "B" because the Match Case check box is not selected in the Find and Replace dialog box. The search will find any record containing the word "boyles" with any combination of uppercase and lowercase letters.

4. Click the **Match** arrow to display the list of matching options, and then click **Any Part of Field**. The search will find any record that contains the word "boyles" in any part of the Address field. See Figure 4–10.

Figure 4–10 Completed Find and Replace dialog box

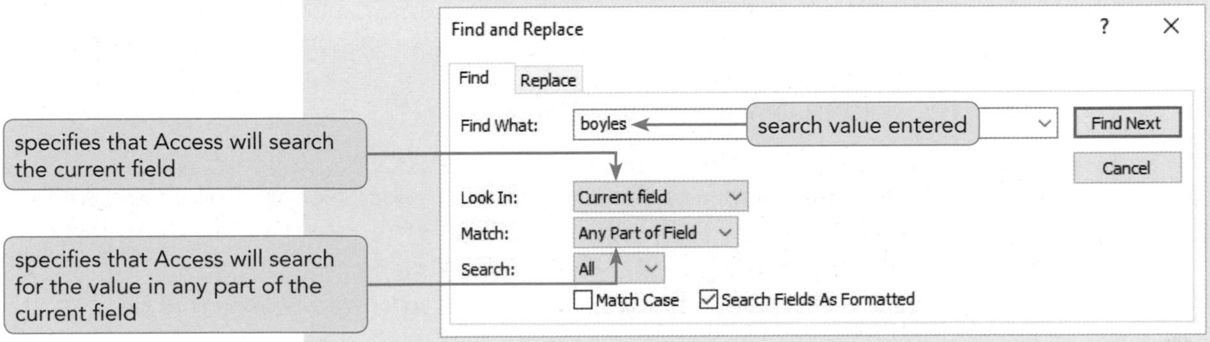
Find and Replace
?
Find
Replace
Find What:
boyles
search value entered
Find Next
Cancel
specifies that Access will search the current field
Look In:
Current field
Match:
Any Part of Field
Search:
All
specifies that Access will search for the value in any part of the current field
Match Case
Search Fields As Formatted

5. Click the **Find Next** button. The Find and Replace dialog box remains open, and the PatientData form now displays record 5, which is the record for Holly Hansen (PatientID 13255). The word "Boyles" is selected in the Address field value box because you searched for this word.

The search value you enter can be an exact value or it can include wildcard characters. A **wildcard character** is a placeholder you use when you know only part of a value or when you want to start or end with a specific character or match a certain pattern. Figure 4–11 shows the wildcard characters you can use when searching for data.

Figure 4–11 Wildcard characters

Wildcard Character	Purpose	Example
*	Match any number of characters it can be used as the first and/or last character in the character string	th* *finds* the, that, this, therefore, *and so on*
?	Match any single alphabetic character	a?t *finds* act, aft, ant, apt, *and* art
[]	Match any single character within the brackets	a[fr]t *finds* aft *and* art *but not* act, ant, *or* apt
!	Match any character not within brackets	a[!fr]t *finds* act, ant, *and* apt *but not* aft *or* art
-	Match any one of a range of characters the range must be in ascending order (a to z, not z to a)	a[d-p]t *finds* aft, ant, *and* apt *but not* act *or* art
#	Match any single numeric character	#72 *finds* 072, 172, 272, 372, *and so on*

Next, to see how a wildcard works, you'll view the records for any patients with zip codes that begin with 302. You could search for any record containing the digits 302 in any part of the Zip field, but this search may also find records with the digits 302 in any part of the zip code. To find only those records with the digits 302 at the beginning of the zip code, you'll use the * wildcard character.

To find the records using the * wildcard character:

1. Make sure the Find and Replace dialog box is still open.
2. Click anywhere in the PatientData form to make it active, and then press **TAB** until you reach the Zip field value box. This is the field you want to search.
3. Click the title bar of the Find and Replace dialog box to make it active, and then drag the Find and Replace dialog box to the right so you can see the Phone field on the form, if necessary. "Current field" is still selected in the Look In box, meaning now the Zip field is the field that will be searched.
4. Double-click **boyles** in the Find What box to select the entire value, and then type **302***.
5. Click the **Match** arrow, and then click **Whole Field**. Because you're using a wildcard character in the search value, you want the whole field to be searched.

   With the settings you've entered, the search will find records in which any field value in the Zip field begins with the value 302.
6. Click the **Find Next** button. Record 9 is displayed in the form, which is the first record found for a patient with a zip code that begins with 302. Notice that the search process started from the point of the previously displayed record in the form, which was record 5.
7. Click the **Find Next** button. Record 16 is displayed in the form, which is the next record found for a patient with a zip code that begins with 302.
8. Click the **Find Next** button to display record 18, and then click the **Find Next** button again. Record 20 is displayed, the fourth record found.
9. Click the **Find Next** button seven more times to display records 23, 26, 27, 33, 40, 42, and 46.
10. Click the **Find Next** button again. Record 4 is displayed. Notice that the search process cycles back through the beginning of the records in the underlying table.
11. Click the **Find Next** button. A dialog box opens, informing you that the search is finished.
12. Click the **OK** button to close the dialog box, and then click the **Cancel** button to close the Find and Replace dialog box.

Donna has identified some patient updates she wants you to make. You'll use the PatientData form to update the data in the Patient table.

Maintaining Table Data Using a Form

Maintaining data using a form is often easier than using a datasheet because you can focus on all the changes for a single record at one time. In Form view, you can edit the field values for a record, delete a record from the underlying table, or add a new record to the table.

Now you'll use the PatientData form to make the changes Donna wants to the Patient table. First, you'll update the record for patient Mariana Salinas, who recently moved from Smyrna to Marietta and provided a new mailing address. In addition to using the Find and Replace dialog box to locate a specific record, you can use the Search box to the right of the navigation buttons. You'll use the Search box to search for the patient's last name, Salinas, and display the patient record in the form.

To change the record using the PatientData form:

1. To the right of the navigation buttons, click the **Search** box and then type **Salinas**. As soon as you start to type, Access begins searching through all fields in the records to match your entry. Record 30 (Mariana Salinas) is now current.

   You will first update the address in this record.

2. Select the current entry in the Address field value box, and then type **17 Wyndmere Rd** to replace it.
3. Press **TAB** to select the city in the City field value box, and then type **Marietta**.
4. Press **TAB** twice to move to and select the Zip field value, and then type **30067**. The updates to the record are complete. See Figure 4–12.

TIP

The pencil symbol appears in the upper-left corner of the form when the form is in editing mode.

Figure 4–12 Patient record after changing field values

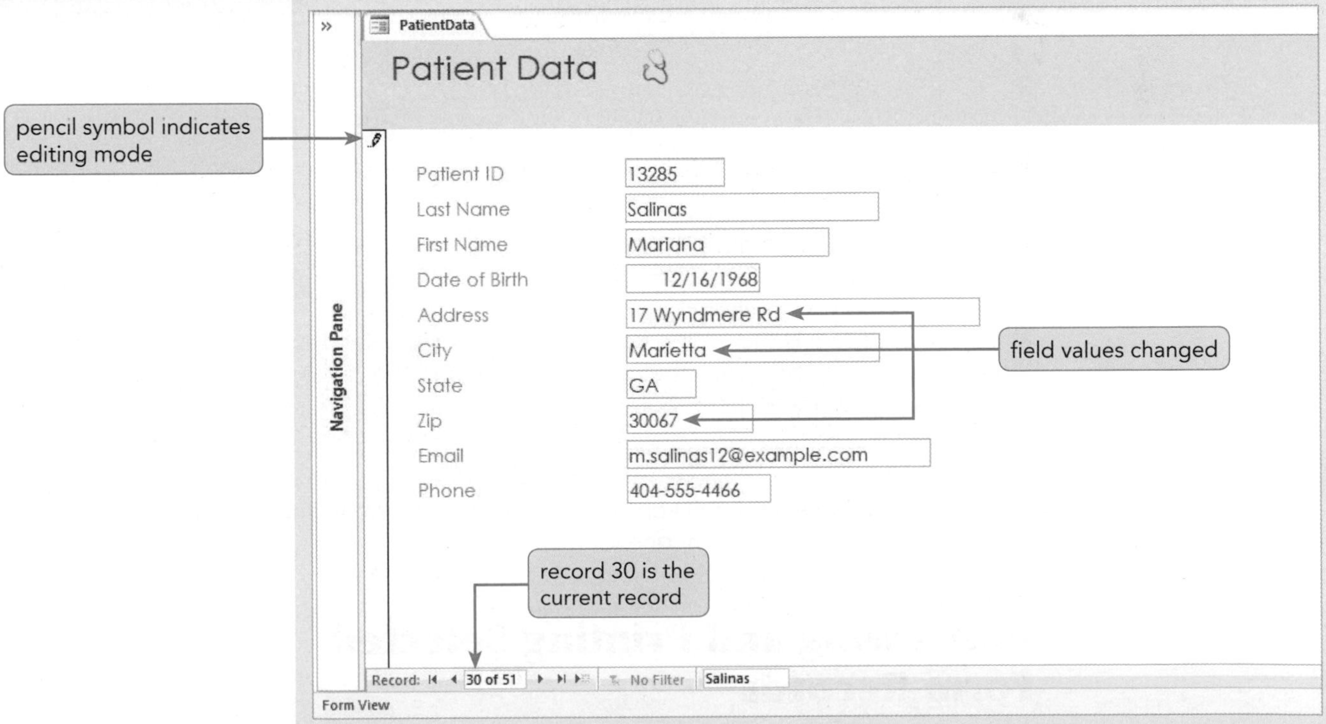
PatientData
Patient Data
pencil symbol indicates editing mode
Patient ID 13285
Last Name Salinas
First Name Mariana
Date of Birth 12/16/1968
Address 17 Wyndmere Rd
City Marietta
State GA
Zip 30067
Email m.salinas12@example.com
Phone 404-555-4466
field values changed
Navigation Pane
record 30 is the current record
Record: 30 of 51
No Filter
Salinas
Form View

Next, Donna asks you to add a record for a new patient. This person signed up to be a patient of the clinic at a recent health fair held by Lakewood Community Health Services, but has not yet visited the clinic. You'll use the PatientData form to add the new record.

To add the new record using the PatientData form:

1. On the Home tab, in the Records group, click the **New** button. Record 52, the next available new record, becomes the current record. All field value boxes are empty (except the State field, which displays the default value of GA), and the insertion point is positioned in the Patient ID field value box.
2. Refer to Figure 4–13 and enter the value shown for each field, pressing **TAB** to move from field to field.

Figure 4–13 Completed form for the new record

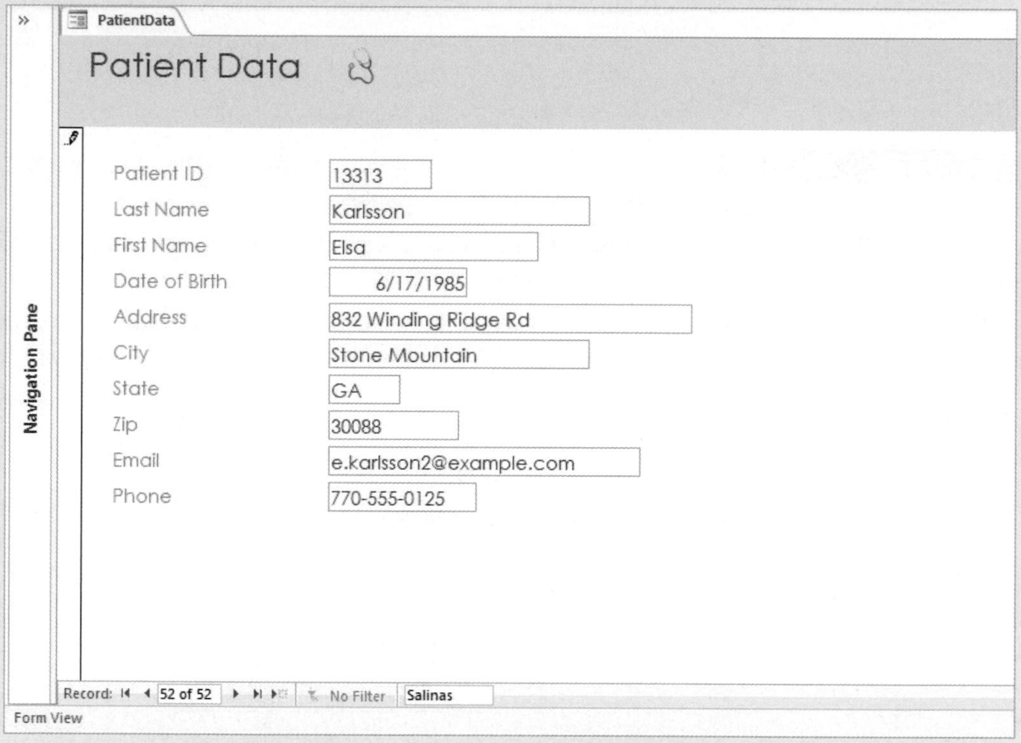
PatientData
Patient Data
Patient ID
13313
Last Name
Karlsson
First Name
Elsa
Date of Birth
6/17/1985
Address
832 Winding Ridge Rd
City
Stone Mountain
State
GA
Zip
30088
Email
e.karlsson2@example.com
Phone
770-555-0125
Navigation Pane
Record: 52 of 52
No Filter
Salinas
Form View

3. After entering the Phone field value, press **TAB**. Record 53, the next available new record, becomes the current record, and the record for PatientID 13313 is saved in the Patient table.

Donna would like a printed copy of the PatientData form to show to her staff members. She asks you to print one form record.

Previewing and Printing Selected Form Records

You can print as many form records as can fit on a printed page. If only part of a form record fits on the bottom of a page, the remainder of the record prints on the next page. You can print all pages or a range of pages. In addition, you can print just the currently selected form record.

Donna asks you to use the PatientData form to print the first record in the Patient table. Before you do, you'll preview the form record to see how it will look when printed.

To preview the form and print the data for record 1:

1. Click the **First record** button to display record 1 in the form. This is the record in which you have entered your first and last names.
2. Click the **File** tab to open Backstage view, click **Print** in the navigation bar, and then click **Print Preview**. The Print Preview window opens, showing the form records for the Patient table. Notice that each record appears in its own form and that shading is used to distinguish one record from another. See Figure 4–14.

Figure 4–14 Form records displayed in Print Preview

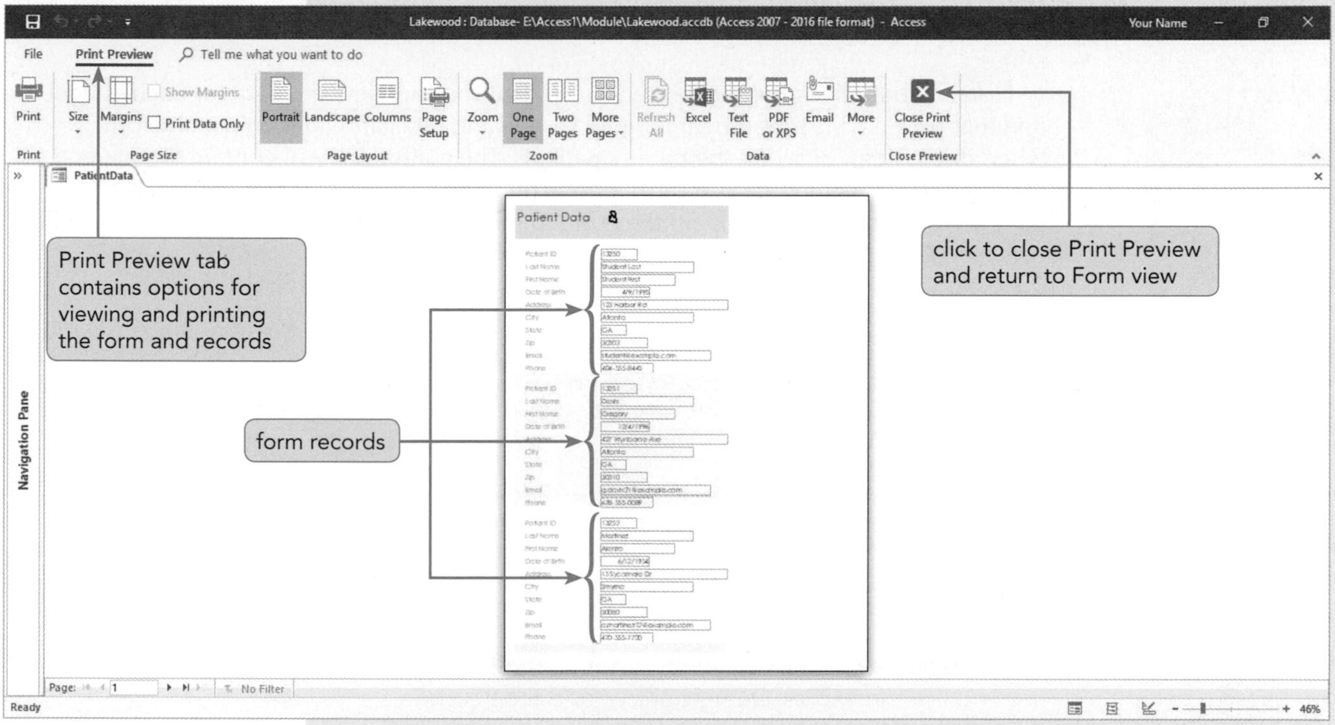
Print Preview tab contains options for viewing and printing the form and records
form records
click to close Print Preview and return to Form view

To print one selected record on a page by itself, you need to use the Print dialog box.

3. On the Print Preview tab, in the Close Preview group, click the **Close Print Preview** button. You return to Form view with the first record still displayed.
4. Click the **File** tab to open Backstage view again, click **Print** in the navigation bar, and then click **Print**. The **Print** dialog box opens.
5. Click the **Selected Record(s)** option button to print the current form record (record 1).

   Trouble? Check with your instructor to be sure you should print the form, then continue to the next step. If you should not print the form, click the Cancel button, and then skip to Step 7.
6. Click the **OK** button to close the dialog box and print the selected record.
7. Close the PatientData form.

After reviewing the printed PatientData form with her staff, Donna realizes that it would be helpful for staff members to also have a form showing information about both patients and their visits. Because this form will need to display information from two different tables, the type of form you need to create will include a main form and a subform.

Creating a Form with a Main Form and a Subform

To create a form based on two tables, you must first define a relationship between the two tables. Earlier, you defined a one-to-many relationship between the Patient (primary) and Visit (related) tables, so you can now create a form based on both tables.

When you create a form containing data from two tables that have a one-to-many relationship, you actually create a **main form** for data from the primary table and a **subform** for data from the related table. Access uses the defined relationship between the tables to join them automatically through the common field that exists in both tables.

Donna would like you to create a form so that she can view the data for each patient and that patient's visits at the same time. Donna and her staff will then use the form when discussing visits with the clinic's patients. The main form will contain the patient ID, first and last names, date of birth, phone number, and email address for each patient. The subform will contain the information about the visits for each patient. You'll use the Form Wizard to create the form.

To create the form using the Form Wizard:

1. On the ribbon, click the **Create** tab, and then in the Forms group, click the **Form Wizard** button. The first Form Wizard dialog box opens.

   When creating a form based on two tables, you first choose the primary table and select the fields you want to include in the main form; then you choose the related table and select fields from it for the subform. In this case, the correct primary table, Table: Patient, is already selected in the Tables/Queries box.

   Trouble? If Table: Patient is not currently selected in the Tables/Queries box, click the Tables/Queries arrow, and then click Table: Patient.

   The form needs to include only the PatientID, FirstName, LastName, BirthDate, Phone, and Email fields from the Patient table.

2. Click **PatientID** in the Available Fields box if necessary, and then click the **Select Single Field** button [>] to move the field to the Selected Fields box.
3. Repeat Step 2 for the **FirstName**, **LastName**, **BirthDate, Phone**, and **Email** fields, in that order.

   The subform needs to include all the fields from the Visit table, with the exception of the PatientID field, as that field has been added in the main form.

4. Click the **Tables/Queries** arrow, and then click **Table: Visit**. The fields from the Visit table appear in the Available Fields box. The quickest way to add the fields you want to include is to move all the fields to the Selected Fields box, and then remove the only field you don't want to include (PatientID).

TIP

The table name (Visit) is included in the PatientID field name to distinguish it from the same field in the Patient table.

5. Click the **Select All Fields** button >> to move all the fields in the Visit table to the Selected Fields box.
6. Click **Visit.PatientID** in the Selected Fields box, and then click the **Remove Single Field** button < to move the field back to the Available Fields box.
7. Click the **Next** button. The next Form Wizard dialog box opens. See Figure 4–15.

Figure 4–15 **Choosing a format for the main form and subform**

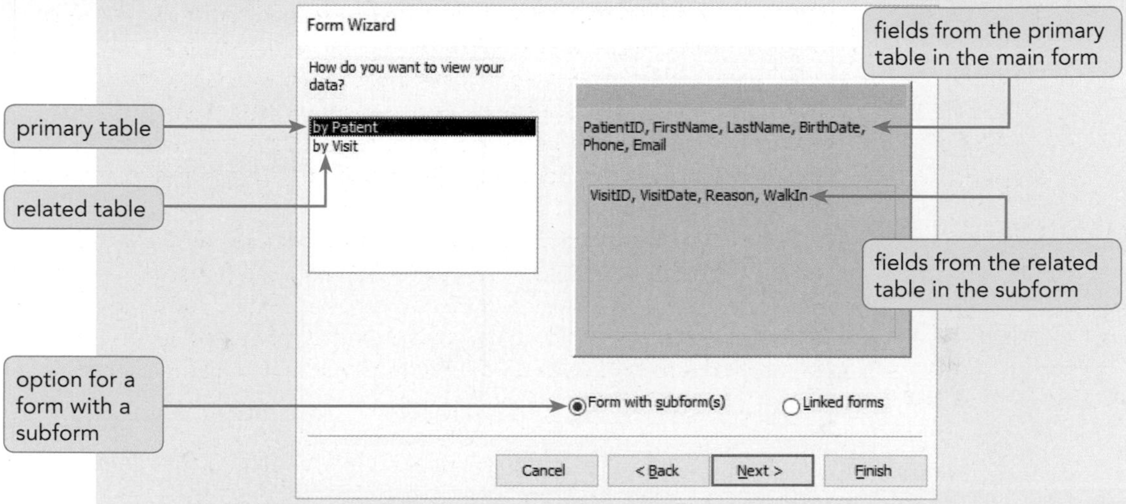
Form Wizard
How do you want to view your data?
by Patient
by Visit
PatientID, FirstName, LastName, BirthDate, Phone, Email
VisitID, VisitDate, Reason, WalkIn
Form with subform(s)
Linked forms
Cancel
< Back
Next >
Finish
primary table
related table
option for a form with a subform
fields from the primary table in the main form
fields from the related table in the subform

In this dialog box, the section on the left shows the order in which you will view the selected data: first by data from the primary Patient table, and then by data from the related Visit table. The form will be displayed as shown on the right side of the dialog box, with the fields from the Patient table at the top in the main form, and the fields from the Visit table at the bottom in the subform.

The default options shown in Figure 4–15 are correct for creating a form with Patient data in the main form and Visit data in the subform.

8. Click the **Next** button. The next Form Wizard dialog box opens, in which you choose the subform layout.

   The Tabular layout displays subform fields as a table, whereas the Datasheet layout displays subform fields as a table datasheet. The layout choice is a matter of personal preference. You'll use the Datasheet layout.

9. Click the **Datasheet** option button to select it if necessary, and then click the **Next** button. The next Form Wizard dialog box opens, in which you specify titles for the main form and the subform. You'll use the title "PatientVisits" for the main form and the title "VisitSubform" for the subform. These titles will also be the names for the form objects.
10. In the Form box, click to position the insertion point to the right of the last letter, and then type **Visits**. The main form name is now PatientVisits.
11. In the Subform box, delete the space between the two words so that the subform name appears as **VisitSubform**, and then click the **Finish** button. The completed form opens in Form view. See Figure 4–16.

Figure 4–16 Main form with subform in Form view

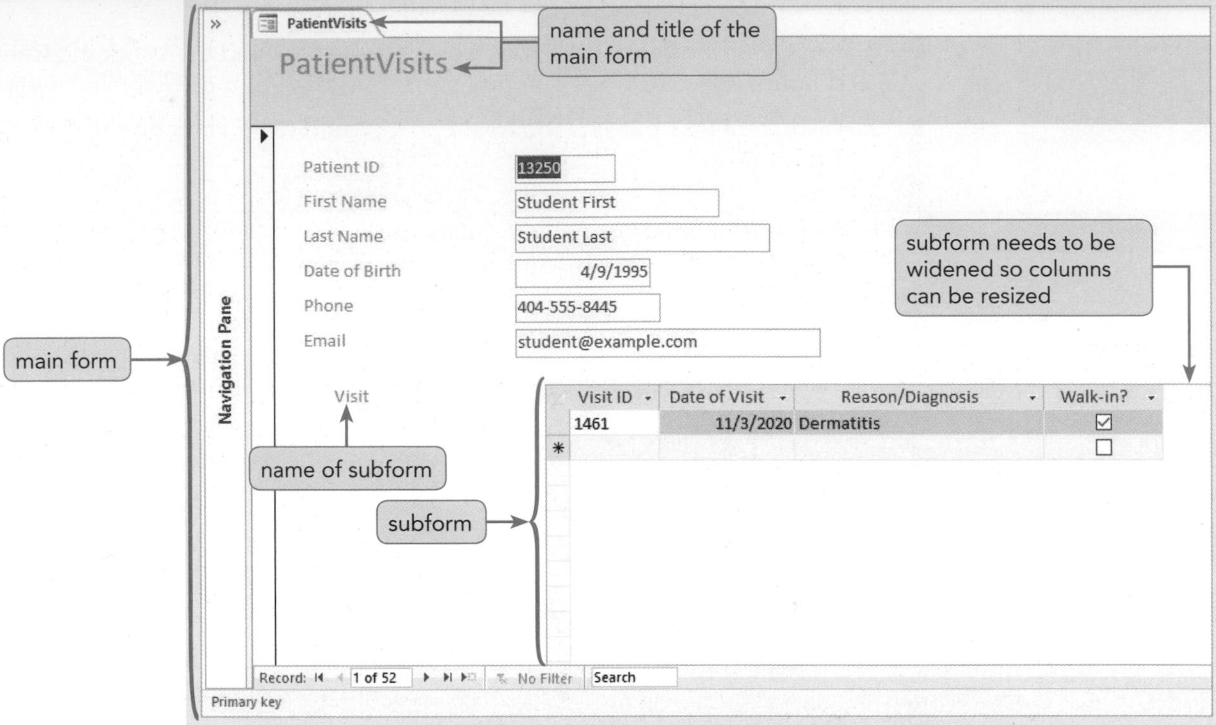
PatientVisits
PatientVisits
name and title of the main form
Patient ID
13250
First Name
Student First
Last Name
Student Last
Date of Birth
4/9/1995
Phone
404-555-8445
Email
student@example.com
subform needs to be widened so columns can be resized
main form
Navigation Pane
Visit
Visit ID
Date of Visit
Reason/Diagnosis
Walk-in?
1461
11/3/2020
Dermatitis
name of subform
subform
Record: 1 of 52
No Filter
Search
Primary key

TIP

The PatientVisits form is formatted with the default Office theme because you applied the Slice theme only to the PatientData form.

The main form displays the fields from the first record in the Patient table in a columnar format. The records in the main form appear in primary key order by PatientID. PatientID 13250 has one related record in the Visit table; this record, for VisitID 1461, is shown in the subform, which uses the datasheet format. The main form name, "PatientVisits," appears on the object tab and as the form title. The name of the table "Visit" appears to the left of the subform indicating the underlying table for the subform. Note that only the word "Visit" and not the complete name "VisitSubform" appears on the form. Only the table name is displayed for the subform itself, but the complete name of the object, "VisitSubform," is displayed when you view and work with objects in the Navigation Pane. The subform designation is necessary in a list of database objects so that you can distinguish the Visit subform from other objects, such as the Visit table, but the subform designation is not needed in the PatientVisits form. Only the table name is required to identify the table containing the records in the subform.

Next, you need to make some changes to the form. First, you'll edit the form title to add a space between the words so that it appears as "Patient Visits." Then, you'll resize the subform so that it is wide enough to allow for all the columns to be fully displayed. To make these changes, you need to switch to Layout view.

To modify the PatientVisits form in Layout view:

1. Switch to Layout view.

   Trouble? If the Field List or Property Sheet opens on the right side of the program window, close it before continuing.

2. Click **PatientVisits** in the gray area at the top of the form. The form title is selected.

3. Click between the letters "t" and "V" to place the insertion point, and then press **SPACEBAR**. The title on the form is now "Patient Visits."
4. Click in a blank area of the form to the right of the field value boxes to deselect the title. Next, you'll increase the width of the subform.
5. Click the **subform**. An orange border surrounds the subform, indicating it is selected.
6. Position the pointer on the right border of the selected subform until the pointer changes to the width change pointer ↔, and then drag to the right approximately three inches. The wider subform makes all the columns visible, even when the Reason field contains a long entry. See Figure 4–17.

Figure 4–17 Modified form in Layout view

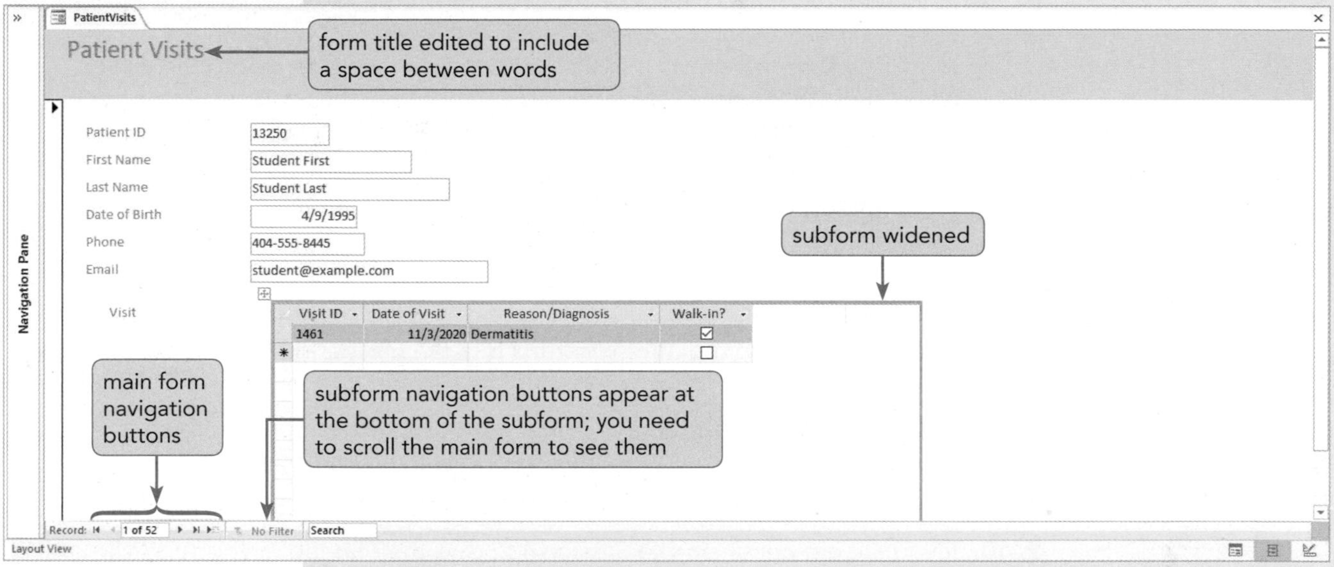
PatientVisits
Patient Visits
form title edited to include a space between words
Patient ID
13250
First Name
Student First
Last Name
Student Last
Date of Birth
4/9/1995
Phone
404-555-8445
Email
student@example.com
Visit
Visit ID
Date of Visit
Reason/Diagnosis
Walk-in?
1461
11/3/2020
Dermatitis
subform widened
main form navigation buttons
subform navigation buttons appear at the bottom of the subform; you need to scroll the main form to see them
Record: 1 of 52
No Filter
Search
Navigation Pane
Layout View

7. On the Quick Access Toolbar, click the **Save** button to save both the main form and the subform.
8. Switch to Form view, and then if necessary, scroll up to view all the fields in the main form.

The form includes two sets of navigation buttons. You use the set of navigation buttons at the bottom of the Form window to select records from the primary table in the main form (see Figure 4–17). The second set of navigation buttons is currently not visible; you need to scroll down the main form to see these buttons, which appear at the bottom of the subform. You use the subform navigation buttons to select records from the related table in the subform.

You'll use the navigation buttons to view different records.

To navigate to different main form and subform records:

1. In the main form, click the **Next record** button five times. Record 6 of 52 total records in the Patient table (for Andrew Wagner) becomes the current record in the main form. The subform shows that this patient made two visits to the clinic. Note that the field values in the Reason/Diagnosis columns are not fully displayed.

2. Double-click the column resizing pointer ✛ on the right column divider of the Reason/Diagnosis column in the subform to resize this field to its best fit and display the complete field values.
3. Use the main form navigation buttons to view each record, resizing any subform column to fully display any field values that are not completely visible.
4. In the main form, click the **Last record** button ▶|. Record 52 in the Patient table (for Elsa Karlsson) becomes the current record in the main form. The subform shows that this patient currently has made no visits to the clinic; recall that you just entered this record using the PatientData form. Donna could use the subform to enter the information on this patient's visits to the clinic, and that information will be updated in the Visit table.
5. In the main form, click the **Previous record** button ◀. Record 51 in the Patient table (for Aaron Williams) becomes the current record in the main form. The subform shows that this patient has made one visit to the clinic. If you know the number of the record you want to view, you can enter the number in the Current Record box to move to that record.
6. In the main form, select **51** in the Current Record box, type **18**, and then press **ENTER**. Record 18 in the Patient table (for Chen Li) becomes the current record in the main form. The subform shows that this patient has made three visits to the clinic.
7. If necessary, use the vertical scroll bar for the main form to scroll down and view the bottom of the subform. Note the navigation buttons for the subform.
8. At the bottom of the subform, click the **Last record** button ▶|. Record 3 in the Visit subform, for Visit ID 1546, becomes the current record.
9. Save and close the PatientVisits form.
10. If you are not continuing to Session 4.2, click the **File** tab, and then click **Close** in the navigation bar to close the Lakewood database.

Both the PatientData form and the PatientVisits form you created will enable Donna and her staff to view, enter, and maintain data easily in the Patient and Visit tables in the Lakewood database.

REVIEW

Session 4.1 Quick Check

1. Describe the difference between creating a form using the Form tool and creating a form using the Form Wizard.
2. What is a theme, and how do you apply one to an existing form?
3. A(n) ____________ is an item on a form, report, or other database object that you can manipulate to modify the object's appearance.
4. Which table record is displayed in a form when you press the CTRL+END keys while you are in navigation mode?
5. Which wildcard character matches any single alphabetic character?
6. To print only the current record displayed in a form, you need to select the ____________ option button in the Print dialog box.
7. In a form that contains a main form and a subform, what data is displayed in the main form and what data is displayed in the subform?

Session 4.2 Visual Overview:

The report object's name is displayed on the tab for the report.

The title appears at the top of the report. By default, the report object name is used as the report title, but you can edit the title to display the text you want, as done here, with spaces added between words for readability.

Fields from the primary Patient table appear first in the report.

Fields from the related Visit table appear below the fields from the primary table.

For a **grouped report**, the data from a record in the primary table (the Patient table in this report) appears as a group, followed on subsequent lines of the report by the joined records from the related table (the Visit table in this report.)

The navigation buttons allow you to display the first, last, next, or previous pages in the report, or to enter a specific page number and move to that page.

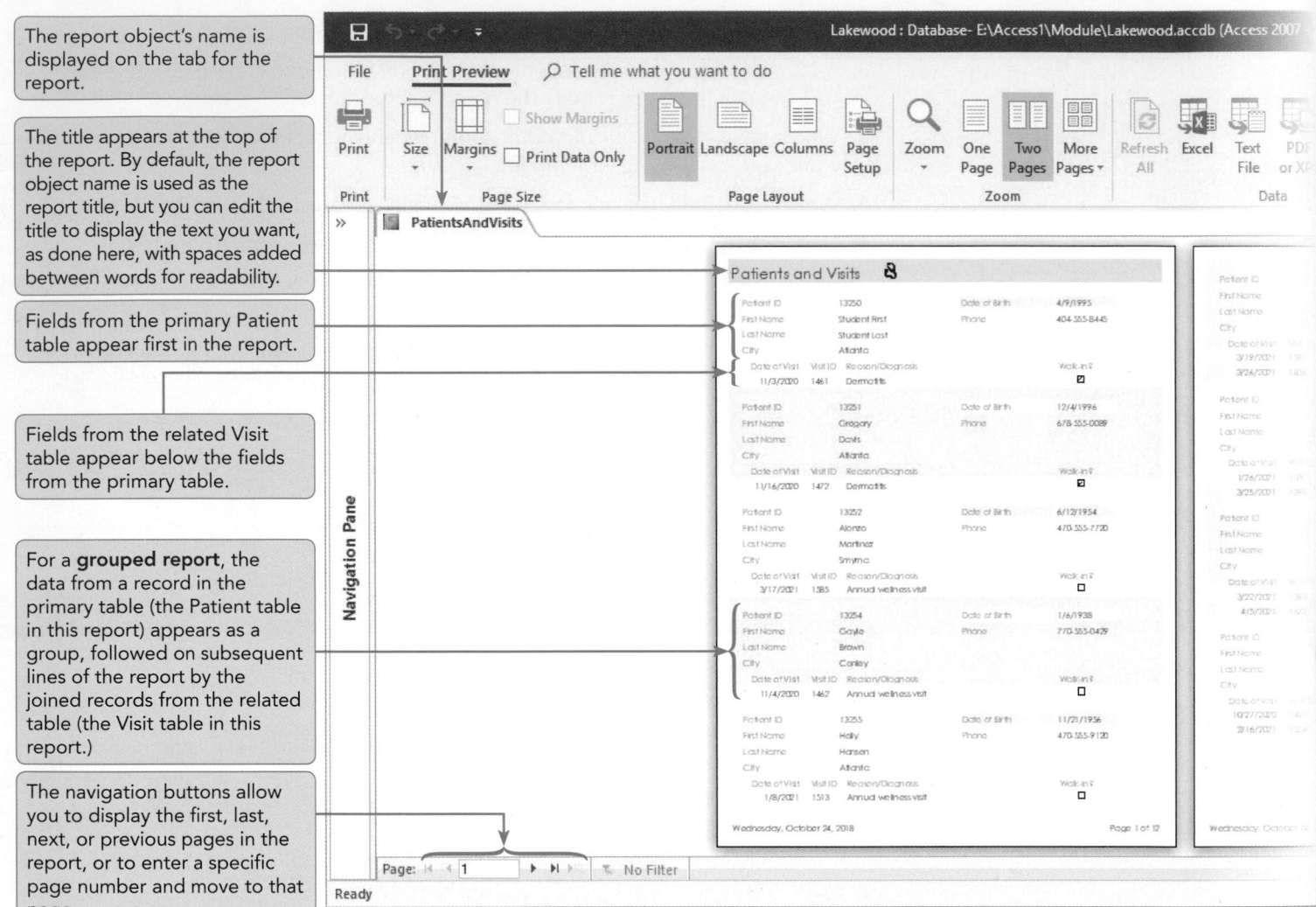

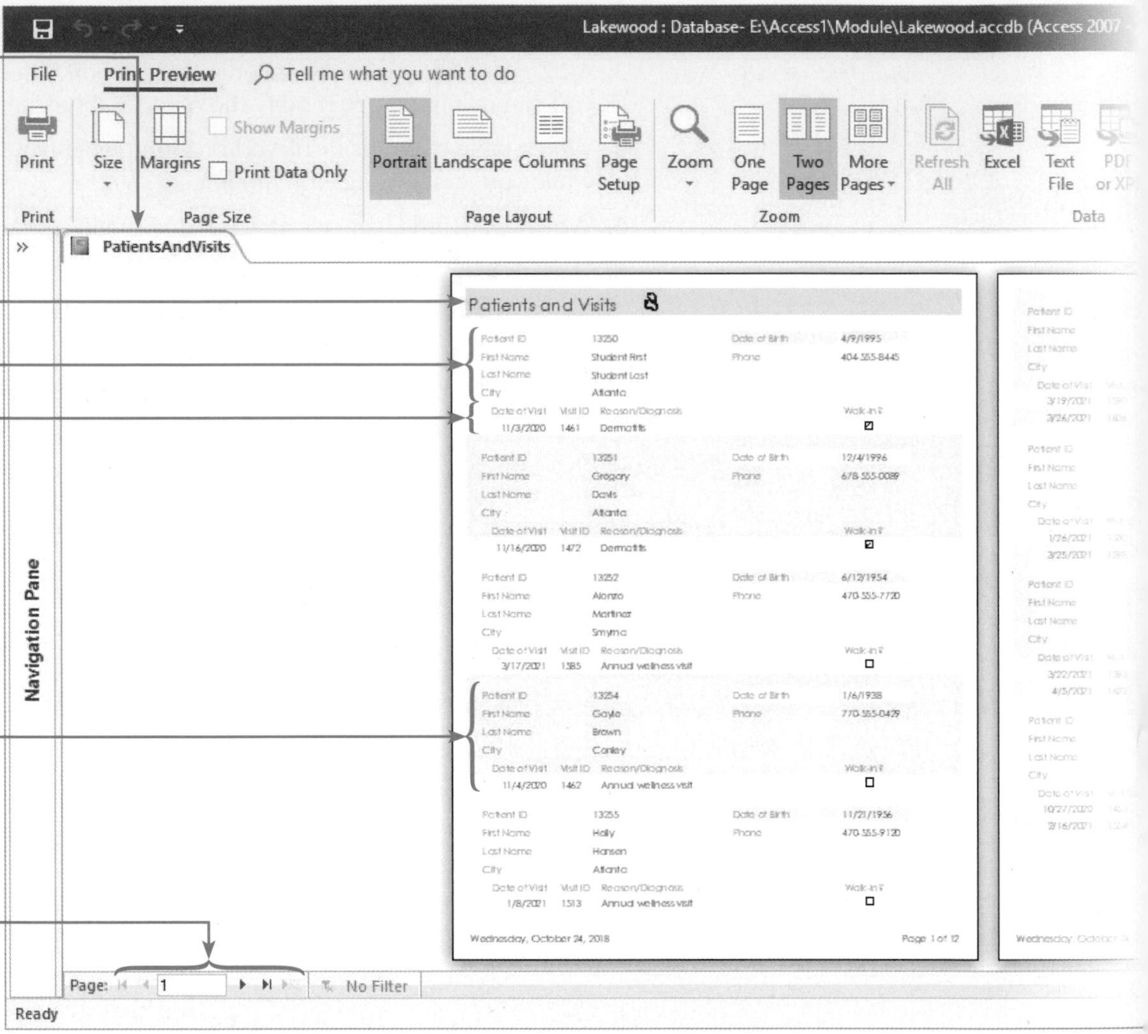

Lakewood : Database- E:\Access1\Module\Lakewood.accdb (Access 2007
File
Print Preview
Tell me what you want to do
Print
Size
Margins
Show Margins
Print Data Only
Portrait
Landscape
Columns
Page Setup
Zoom
One Page
Two Pages
More Pages
Refresh All
Excel
Text File
Print
Page Size
Page Layout
Zoom
Data
PatientsAndVisits
Navigation Pane
Patients and Visits
Patient ID
First Name
Last Name
City
Date of Birth
Phone
Date of Visit
Visit ID
Reason/Diagnosis
Walk-in?
Wednesday, October 24, 2018
Page 1 of 12
Page: 1
No Filter
Ready

Report Displayed in Print Preview

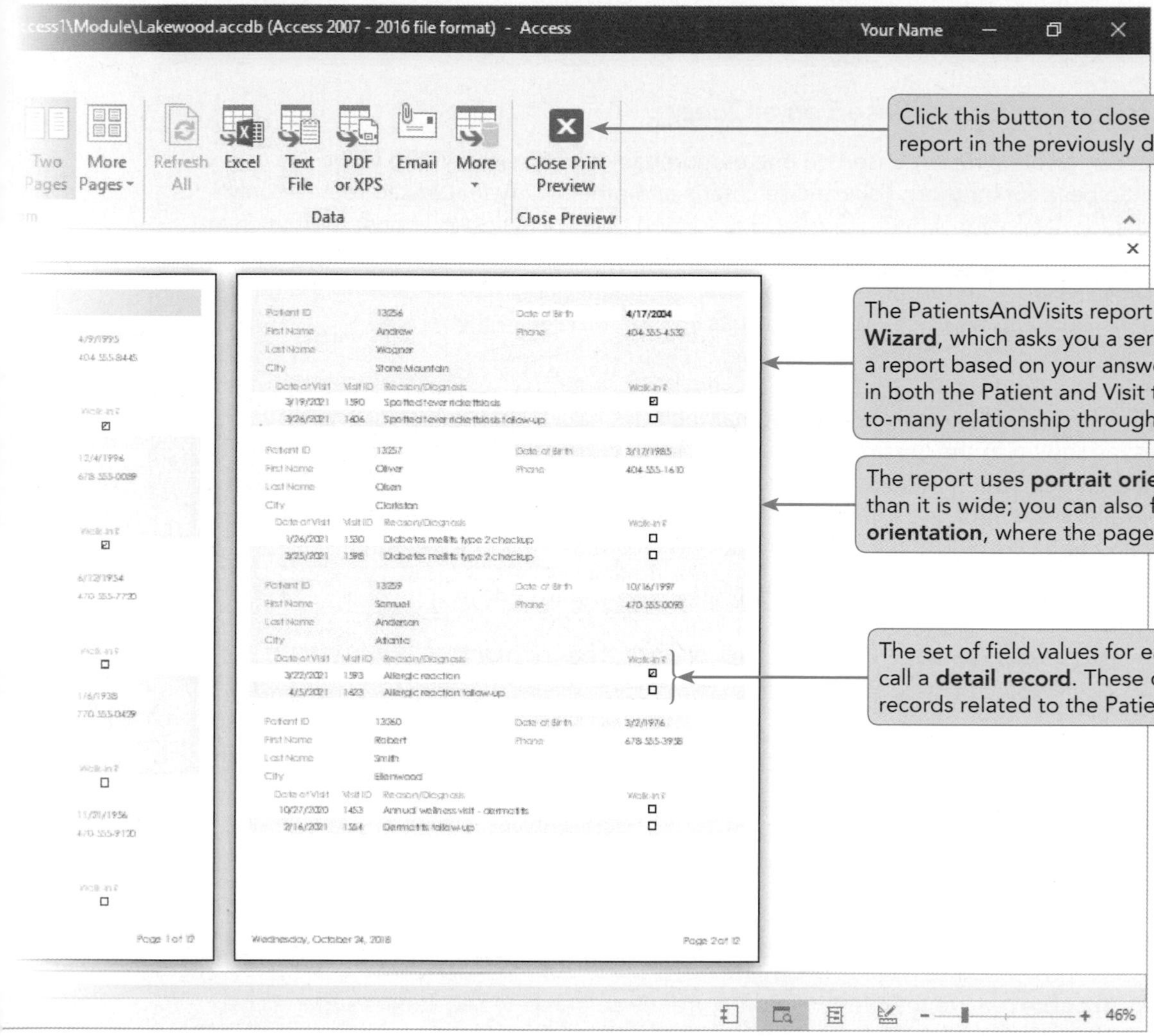
ccess1\Module\Lakewood.accdb (Access 2007 - 2016 file format) - Access
Your Name
Two Pages
More Pages
Refresh All
Excel
Text File
PDF or XPS
Email
More
Close Print Preview
Data
Close Preview
46%

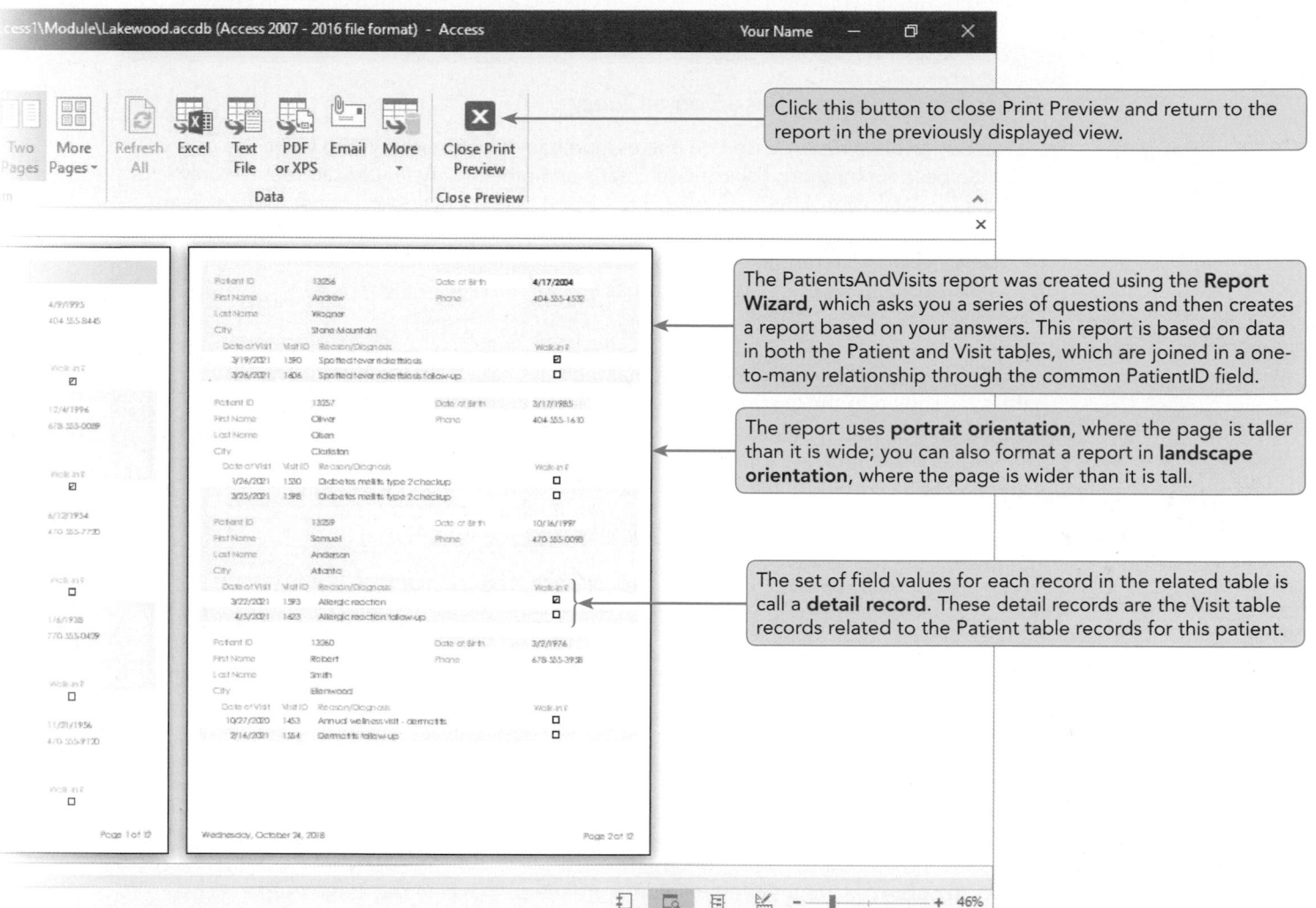

Click this button to close Print Preview and return to the report in the previously displayed view.

The PatientsAndVisits report was created using the **Report Wizard**, which asks you a series of questions and then creates a report based on your answers. This report is based on data in both the Patient and Visit tables, which are joined in a one-to-many relationship through the common PatientID field.

The report uses **portrait orientation**, where the page is taller than it is wide; you can also format a report in **landscape orientation**, where the page is wider than it is tall.

The set of field values for each record in the related table is call a **detail record**. These detail records are the Visit table records related to the Patient table records for this patient.

Creating a Report Using the Report Wizard

As you learned earlier, a report is a formatted printout or screen display of the contents of one or more tables or queries in a database. In Access, you can create your own reports or use the Report Wizard to create them for you. Whether you use the Report Wizard or design your own report, you can change a report's design after you create it.

INSIGHT

Creating a Report Based on a Query

You can create a report based on one or more tables or queries. When you use a query as the basis for a report, you can use criteria and other query features to retrieve only the information you want to display in the report. Experienced Access users often create a query just so they can create a report based on that query. When thinking about the type of report you want to create, consider creating a query first and basing the report on the query, to produce the exact results you want to see in the report.

Donna wants you to create a report that includes data from the Patient and Visit tables, as shown in the Session 4.2 Visual Overview. Like the PatientVisits form you created earlier, which includes a main form and a subform, the report will be based on both tables, which are joined in a one-to-many relationship through a common PatientID field. You'll use the Report Wizard to create the report for Donna.

To start the Report Wizard and create the report:

1. If you took a break after the previous session, make sure that the Lakewood database is open and the Navigation Pane is closed.
2. Click the **Create** tab, and then in the Reports group, click the **Report Wizard** button. The first Report Wizard dialog box opens.

   As was the case when you created the form with a subform, initially you can choose only one table or query to be the data source for the report. Then you can include data from other tables or queries. In this case, the correct primary table, Table: Patient, is already selected in the Tables/Queries box.

   Trouble? If Table: Patient is not currently selected in the Tables/Queries box, click the Tables/Queries arrow, and then click Table: Patient.

   You select fields in the order you want them to appear on the report. Donna wants the PatientID, FirstName, LastName, City, BirthDate, and Phone fields from the Patient table to appear on the report, in that order.
3. Click **PatientID** in the Available Fields box (if necessary), and then click the **Select Single Field** button [>]. The field moves to the Selected Fields box.
4. Repeat Step 3 to add the **FirstName**, **LastName**, **City**, **BirthDate**, and **Phone** fields to the report.
5. Click the **Tables/Queries** arrow, and then click **Table: Visit**. The fields from the Visit table appear in the Available Fields box.

   Donna wants all the fields from the Visit table to be included in the report.
6. Click the **Select All Fields** button [>>] to move all the fields from the Available Fields box to the Selected Fields box.
7. Click **Visit.PatientID** in the Selected Fields box, click the **Remove Single Field** button [<] to move the field back to the Available Fields box, and then click the **Next** button. The second Report Wizard dialog box opens. See Figure 4–18.

Figure 4–18 **Choosing a grouped or ungrouped report**

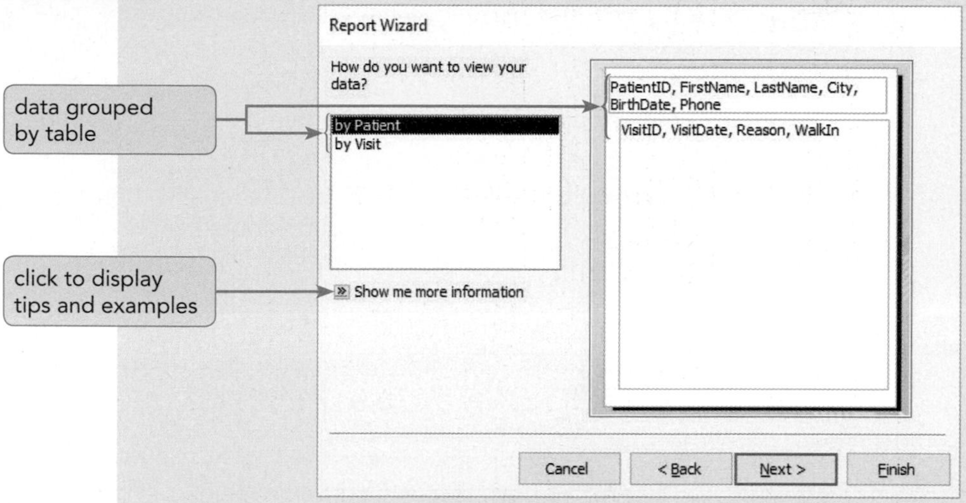
Report Wizard
How do you want to view your data?
by Patient
by Visit
PatientID, FirstName, LastName, City, BirthDate, Phone
VisitID, VisitDate, Reason, WalkIn
Show me more information
Cancel
< Back
Next >
Finish
data grouped by table
click to display tips and examples

You can choose to arrange the selected data grouped by table, which is the default, or ungrouped. You're creating a grouped report; the data from each record in the Patient table will appear in a group, followed by the related records for that patient from the Visit table.

8. Click the **Next** button. The next Report Wizard dialog box opens, in which you choose additional grouping levels.

   Currently the report contains only one grouping level, which is for the patient's data. Grouping levels are useful for reports with multiple levels, such as those containing monthly, quarterly, and annual totals, or for those containing city and country groups. The report requires no further grouping levels, so you can accept the default options.

9. Click the **Next** button. The next Report Wizard dialog box opens, in which you choose the sort order for the detail records. See Figure 4–19.

Figure 4–19 **Choosing the sort order for detail records**

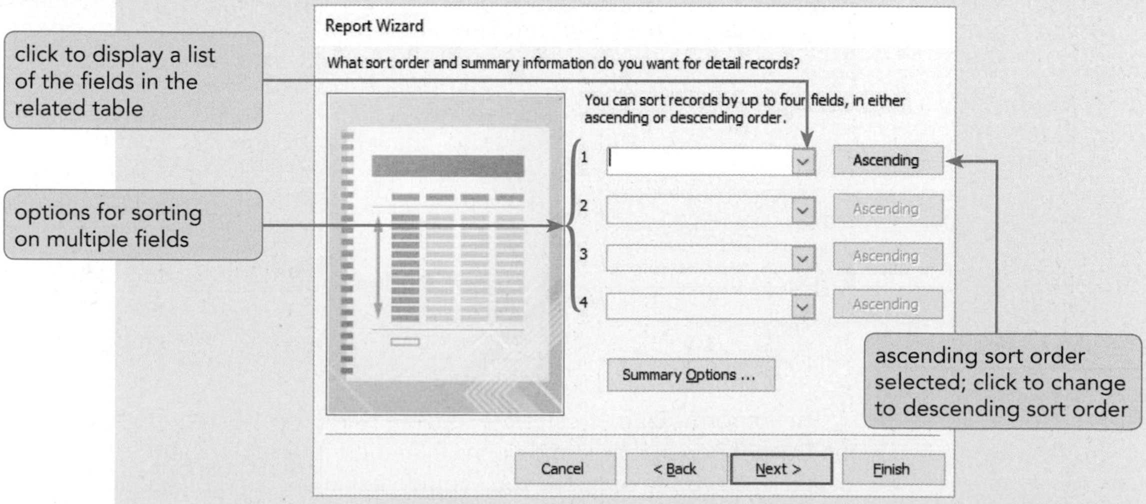
Report Wizard
What sort order and summary information do you want for detail records?
You can sort records by up to four fields, in either ascending or descending order.
1
2
3
4
Ascending
Ascending
Ascending
Ascending
Summary Options ...
Cancel
< Back
Next >
Finish
click to display a list of the fields in the related table
options for sorting on multiple fields
ascending sort order selected; click to change to descending sort order

The records from the Visit table for a patient represent the detail records for Donna's report. She wants these records to appear in ascending order by the value in the VisitDate field, so that the visits will be shown in chronological order. The Ascending option is already selected by default. To change to descending order, you click this same button, which acts as a toggle between the two sort orders. Also, you can sort on multiple fields, as you can with queries.

10. Click the **arrow** on the first box, click **VisitDate**, and then click the **Next** button. The next Report Wizard dialog box opens, in which you choose a layout and page orientation for the report. See Figure 4–20.

Figure 4–20 Choosing the report layout

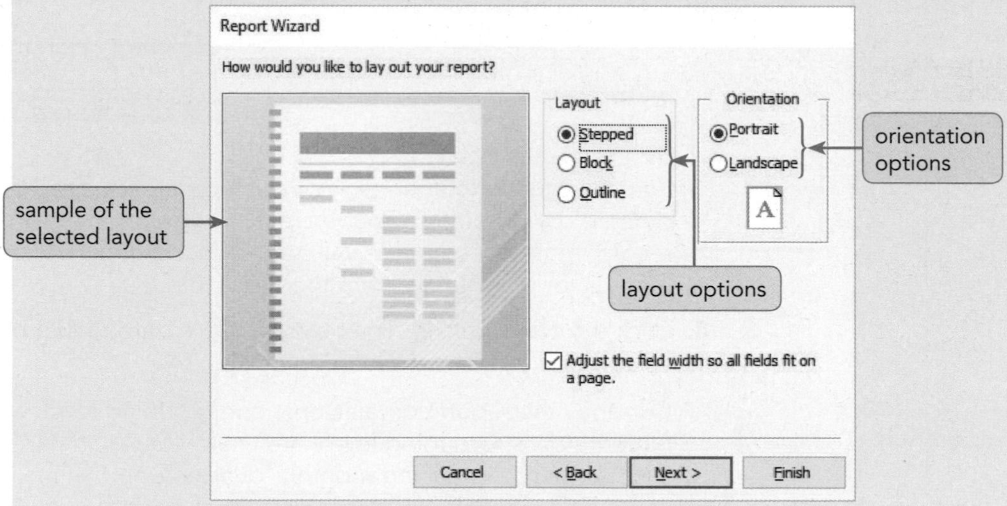
Report Wizard
How would you like to lay out your report?
Layout
Stepped
Block
Outline
Orientation
Portrait
Landscape
A
Adjust the field width so all fields fit on a page.
Cancel
< Back
Next >
Finish
sample of the selected layout
orientation options
layout options

11. Click each layout option to view each sample that appears, and then click the **Outline** option button to select that layout for the report.

    Because most of the fields in both the Patient and Visit tables contain relatively short field values, the portrait page orientation should provide enough space across the page to display all the field values.

12. Click the **Next** button. The final Report Wizard dialog box opens, in which you choose a report title, which also serves as the name for the report object in the database.

    Donna wants the report title "Patients and Visits" at the top of the report. Because the name you enter in this dialog box is also the name of the report object, you'll enter the report name as one word and edit the title on the report later.

13. In the box for the title, enter **PatientsAndVisits** and then click the **Finish** button.

The Report Wizard creates the report based on your answers, saves it as an object in the Lakewood database, and opens the report in Print Preview.

After you create a report, you should view it in Print Preview to see if you need to make any formatting or design changes. To view the entire page, you need to change the Zoom setting.

To view the report in Print Preview:

1. On the Print Preview tab, in the Zoom group, click the **Zoom arrow**, and then click **Fit to Window**. The first page of the report is displayed in Print Preview.
2. At the bottom of the window, click the **Next Page** button to display the second page of the report.

   When a report is displayed in Print Preview, you can zoom in for a close-up view of a section of the report.
3. Move the pointer to the center of the report, and then click the **Zoom In** pointer at the center of the report. The display changes to show a close-up view of the report. See Figure 4–21.

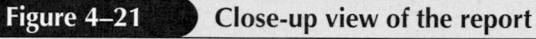

Figure 4–21 Close-up view of the report

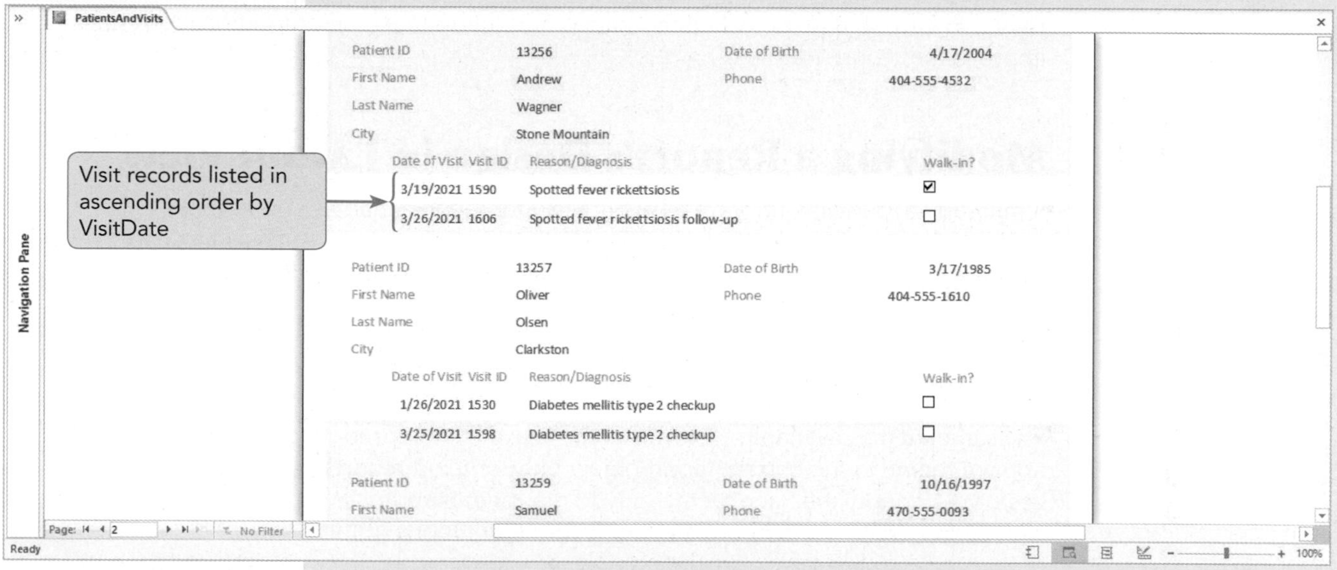

PatientsAndVisits
Navigation Pane
Patient ID 13256 Date of Birth 4/17/2004
First Name Andrew Phone 404-555-4532
Last Name Wagner
City Stone Mountain
Date of Visit Visit ID Reason/Diagnosis Walk-in?
3/19/2021 1590 Spotted fever rickettsiosis
3/26/2021 1606 Spotted fever rickettsiosis follow-up
Visit records listed in ascending order by VisitDate
Patient ID 13257 Date of Birth 3/17/1985
First Name Oliver Phone 404-555-1610
Last Name Olsen
City Clarkston
Date of Visit Visit ID Reason/Diagnosis Walk-in?
1/26/2021 1530 Diabetes mellitis type 2 checkup
3/25/2021 1598 Diabetes mellitis type 2 checkup
Patient ID 13259 Date of Birth 10/16/1997
First Name Samuel Phone 470-555-0093
Page: 2
No Filter
Ready
100%

TIP

Clicking a report in Print Preview toggles between a full-page display and a close-up display of the report.

The detail records for the Visit table fields appear in ascending order based on the values in the VisitDate field. Because the VisitDate field is used as the basis for sorting records, it appears as the first field in this section, even though you selected the fields in the order in which they appear in the Visit table.

4. Scroll to the bottom of the second page, checking the text in the report as you scroll. Notice the current date and page number at the bottom of the page; the Report Wizard included these elements as part of the report's design.
5. Move the pointer onto the report, click the **Zoom Out** pointer to zoom back out, and then click the **Next Page** button to move to page 3 of the report.
6. Continue to move through the pages of the report, and then click the **First Page** button to return to the first page.

INSIGHT

Changing a Report's Page Orientation and Margins

When you display a report in Print Preview, you can easily change the report layout using options on the Print Preview tab (refer to the Session 4.2 Visual Overview). For example, sometimes fields with longer values cause the report content to overflow onto the next page. You can fix this problem by clicking the Landscape button in the Page Layout group on the Print Preview tab to switch the report orientation to landscape, where the page is wider than it is tall. Landscape orientation allows more space for content to fit across the width of the report page. You can also use the Margins button in the Page Size group to change the margins of the report, choosing from commonly used margin formats or creating your own custom margins. Click the Margins arrow to display the menu of available margin options and select the one that works best for your report.

When you created the PatientData form, you applied the Slice theme. Donna would like the PatientsAndVisits report to be formatted with the same theme. You need to switch to Layout view to make this change. You'll also make other modifications to improve the report's design.

Modifying a Report's Design in Layout View

Similar to Layout view for forms, Layout view for reports enables you to make modifications to the report's design. Many of the same options—such as those for applying a theme and changing the color of text—are provided in Layout view for reports.

Applying a Theme to a Report

The same themes available for forms are also available for reports. You can choose to apply a theme to the current report object only, or to all reports in the database. In this case, you'll apply the Slice theme only to the PatientsAndVisits report because Donna isn't certain if it is the appropriate theme for other reports in the Lakewood database.

To apply the Slice theme to the report and edit the report name:

1. On the status bar, click the **Layout View** button. The report is displayed in Layout view and the Report Layout Tools Design tab is the active tab on the ribbon.

   Trouble? If the Field List or Property Sheet opens on the right side of the program window, close it before continuing.

2. In the Themes group, click the **Themes** button. The "In this Database" section at the top of the gallery shows both the default Office theme and the Slice theme. The Slice theme is included here because you applied it earlier to the PatientData form.

   TIP
   When you point to the Slice theme, a ScreenTip displays the names of the database objects that use the theme—in this case, the PatientData form.

3. At the top of the gallery, right-click the **Slice** theme to display the shortcut menu, and then click **Apply Theme to This Object Only**. The gallery closes and the theme is applied to the report.

   The larger font used by the Slice theme has caused the report title text to be cut off on the right. You'll fix this problem and edit the title text as well.

4. Click the **PatientsAndVisits** title at the top of the report to select it.
5. Position the pointer on the right border of the title's selection box until it changes to the width change pointer ↔, and then drag to the right until the title is fully displayed.
6. Click between the letters "s" and "A" in the title, press **SPACEBAR**, change the capital letter "A" to **a**, place the insertion point between the letters "d" and "V," and then press **SPACEBAR**. The title is now "Patients and Visits."
7. Click to the right of the report title in the shaded area to deselect the title.

Donna views the report and notices some other formatting changes she would like you to make. First, she doesn't like how the VisitDate field values are aligned compared to the other field values from the Visit table. You'll fix this next.

Changing the Alignment of Field Values

The Report Layout Tools Format tab provides options for you to easily modify the format of various report objects. For example, you can change the alignment of the text in a field value. Recall that Date/Time fields, like VisitDate, automatically right-align their field values, whereas Short Text fields, like VisitID, automatically left-align their field values. Donna asks you to change the alignment of the BirthDate field so its values appear left-aligned, which will improve the format of the report.

To change the alignment of the VisitDate field values:

1. On the ribbon, click the **Report Layout Tools Format** tab. The ribbon changes to display options for formatting the report. The options for modifying the format of a report are the same as those available for forms.
2. In the report, click the **first BirthDate** field value box, which contains the date 4/9/1995. The field value box has an orange border, indicating it is selected. Note that the other BirthDate field value boxes have a lighter orange border, indicating they are selected as well. Any changes you make will be applied to all BirthDate field values throughout the report.
3. On the Report Layout Tools Format tab, in the Font group, click the **Align Left** button. The text in the BirthDate field value boxes is now left-aligned. See Figure 4–22.

Figure 4–22 Report after applying a theme and changing field alignment

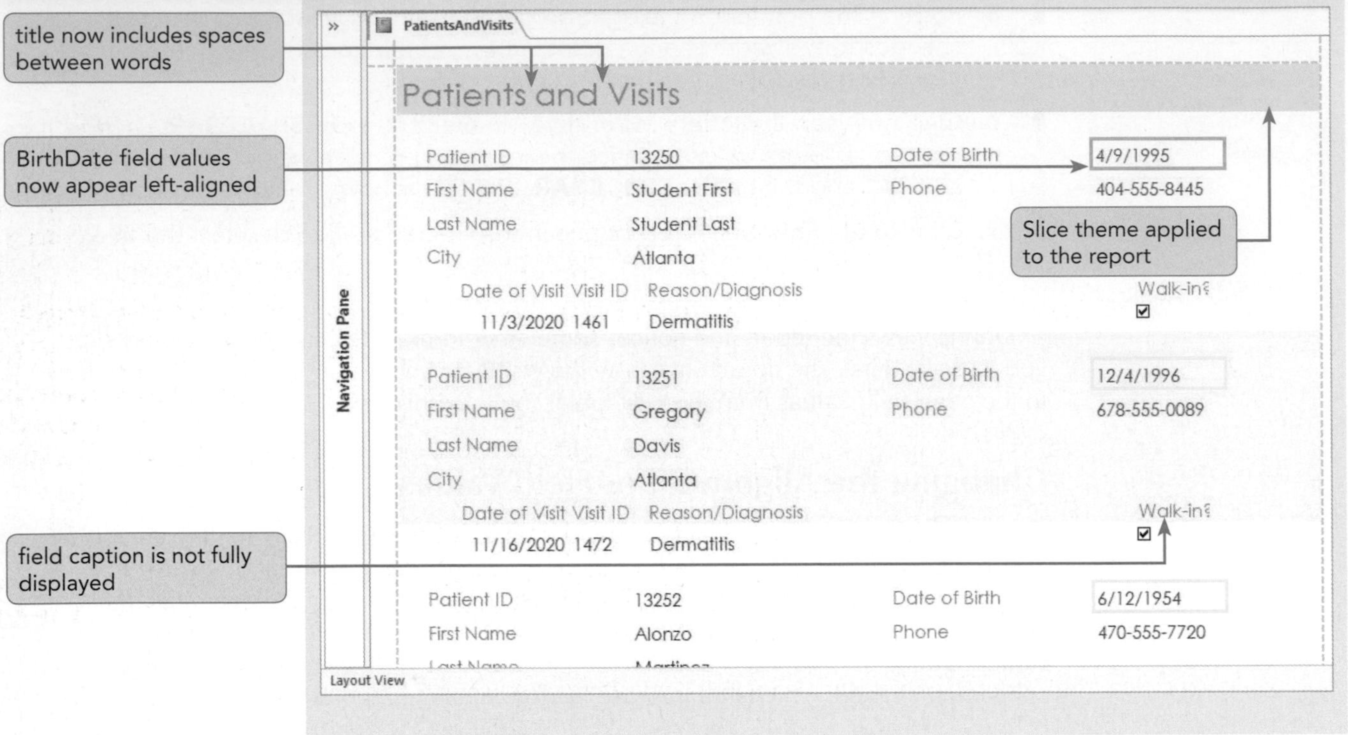
title now includes spaces between words
BirthDate field values now appear left-aligned
field caption is not fully displayed
Slice theme applied to the report
PatientsAndVisits
Patients and Visits
Patient ID
13250
Date of Birth
4/9/1995
First Name
Student First
Phone
404-555-8445
Last Name
Student Last
City
Atlanta
Date of Visit Visit ID Reason/Diagnosis
Walk-in?
11/3/2020 1461 Dermatitis
Patient ID
13251
Date of Birth
12/4/1996
First Name
Gregory
Phone
678-555-0089
Last Name
Davis
City
Atlanta
Date of Visit Visit ID Reason/Diagnosis
Walk-in?
11/16/2020 1472 Dermatitis
Patient ID
13252
Date of Birth
6/12/1954
First Name
Alonzo
Phone
470-555-7720
Navigation Pane
Layout View

Moving and Resizing Fields on a Report

Working in Layout view, you can resize and reposition fields and field value boxes to improve the appearance and readability of a report. You resize field value boxes by dragging their borders to the desired size. You can also move field labels and field value boxes by selecting one or more of them and then dragging them to a new location; or, for more precise control over the move, you can use the keyboard arrow keys to move selected objects.

In the PatientsAndVisits report, you need to move and resize the WalkIn field label so that the complete caption, Walk-In?, is displayed. Donna also thinks the report would look better with more room between the VisitDate and VisitID fields, so you'll move the VisitDate field label and associated field value box to the left. First, you will move the WalkIn field label so it appears centered over its check box.

To move and resize the WalkIn field label:

1. In the report, click the first occurrence of the **WalkIn?** field label. All instances of the label are selected throughout the report.
2. Press ← repeatedly until the label is centered (roughly) over its check box.
3. Position the pointer on the right border of the field label's selection box until the pointer changes to the width change pointer ↔, and then drag to the right until the label text is fully displayed.

Next, you need to move the VisitDate field label (Date of Visit) and field value box to the left, to provide more space between the VisitDate field and the VisitID field in the report. You can select both objects and modify them at the same time.

To move the VisitDate field label and field value box:

1. In the report, click the first occurrence of the **Date of Visit** field label, press and hold **SHIFT**, click the first occurrence of the associated field value box, which contains the date 11/3/2020. Both the field label and its associated field value box are selected and can be moved. See Figure 4–23.

Figure 4–23 **Report after selecting field label and field value box**

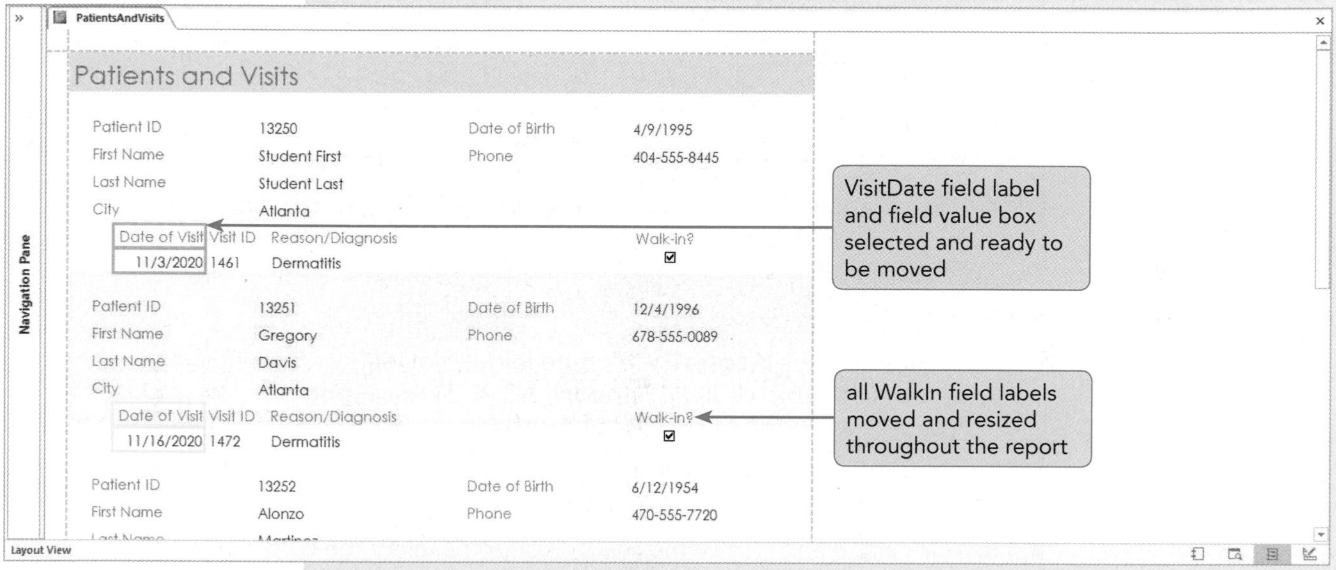
PatientsAndVisits
Patients and Visits
Patient ID 13250 Date of Birth 4/9/1995
First Name Student First Phone 404-555-8445
Last Name Student Last
City Atlanta
Date of Visit Visit ID Reason/Diagnosis Walk-in?
11/3/2020 1461 Dermatitis
Patient ID 13251 Date of Birth 12/4/1996
First Name Gregory Phone 678-555-0089
Last Name Davis
City Atlanta
Date of Visit Visit ID Reason/Diagnosis Walk-in?
11/16/2020 1472 Dermatitis
Patient ID 13252 Date of Birth 6/12/1954
First Name Alonzo Phone 470-555-7720
Navigation Pane
Layout View
VisitDate field label and field value box selected and ready to be moved
all WalkIn field labels moved and resized throughout the report

2. Press ← four times to move the field label and field value box to the left.

   Trouble? Once you press LEFT ARROW, the report might jump to display the end of the report. Just continue to press LEFT ARROW to move the labels and values. Then scroll the window back up to display the beginning of the report.

3. On the Quick Access Toolbar, click the **Save** button to save the modified report.

4. Click to the right of the report title in the shaded area to deselect the VisitDate field label and field value box.

5. Scroll through the report, checking the field labels and field values as you go to make sure all text is fully displayed. When finished, scroll back up to display the top of the report.

Next, Donna asks you to enhance the report's appearance to make it more consistent with the PatientData form.

Changing the Font Color and Inserting a Picture in a Report

You can change the color of text on a report to enhance its appearance. You can also add a picture to a report for visual interest or to identify a particular section of the report.

Before you print the report for Donna, she asks you to change the report title color to the darker black you applied earlier to the PatientData form and to include the Medical picture to the right of the report title.

Make sure the title is selected so the picture is inserted in the correct location.

To change the color of the report title and insert the picture:

1. At the top of the report, click the **Patients and Visits** title to select it.
2. Make sure the Report Layout Tools Format tab is still active on the ribbon.
3. In the Font group, click the **Font Color arrow**, and then in the Theme Colors section, click the **Black, Text 1, Lighter 25%** color (fourth color in the second column). The color is applied to the report title.

   Now you'll insert the picture to the right of the report title text.
4. On the ribbon, click the **Report Layout Tools Design** tab. The options provided on this tab for reports are the same as those you worked with for forms.
5. In the Header/Footer group, click the **Logo** button.
6. Navigate to the **Access1 > Module** folder provided with your Data Files, and then double-click the **Support_AC_4_Medical.png** file. The picture is inserted in the top-left corner of the report, partially covering the report title.
7. Position the **layout selector** pointer on the selected picture, and then drag it to the right of the report title.
8. Click in a blank area of the shaded bar to deselect the picture. See Figure 4–24.

Figure 4–24 Report after changing the title font color and inserting the picture

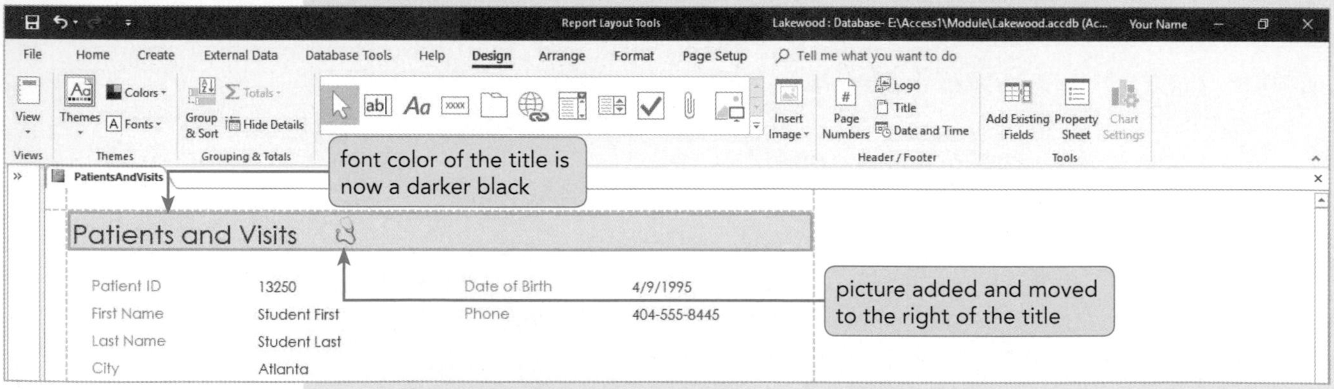
font color of the title is now a darker black
picture added and moved to the right of the title
Patients and Visits
Patient ID
13250
Date of Birth
4/9/1995
First Name
Student First
Phone
404-555-8445
Last Name
Student Last
City
Atlanta

Trouble? Don't be concerned if the picture in your report is not in the exact same location as the one shown in the figure. Just make sure it is to the right of the title text and within the shaded area.

Donna approves of the report's contents and design, but has one final suggestion for the report. She'd like to draw attention to patient records for children and teenagers by formatting their birth date with a bold, red font. Lakewood Community Health Services is planning a special event specifically geared to children and teenagers regarding healthy diets, so this format will make it easier to find these patient records in the report. Because Donna does not want all the birth dates to appear in this font, you need to use conditional formatting.

Using Conditional Formatting in a Report

Conditional formatting in a report (or form) is special formatting applied to certain field values depending on one or more conditions—similar to criteria you establish for queries. If a field value meets the condition or conditions you specify, the formatting is applied to the value.

Donna would like the PatientsAndVisits report to show any birth date that is greater than 1/1/1999 in a bold, dark red font. This formatting will help to highlight the patient records for children and teenagers. Donna plans to review this report in a planning meeting for the upcoming special event.

TIP

You must select a field value box, and not the field label, before applying a conditional format.

To apply conditional formatting to the BirthDate field in the report:

1. Make sure the report is still displayed in Layout view, and then click the **Report Layout Tools Format** tab on the ribbon.

   To apply conditional formatting to a field, you must first make it the active field by clicking any field value in the field's column.

2. Click the first BirthDate field value, **4/9/1995**, for PatientID 13250 to select the BirthDate field values in the report. The conditional formatting you specify will affect all the values for the field.
3. In the Control Formatting group, click the **Conditional Formatting** button. The Conditional Formatting Rules Manager dialog box opens. Because you selected a BirthDate field value box, the name of this field is displayed in the "Show formatting rules for" box. Currently, there are no conditional formatting rules set for the selected field. You need to create a new rule.
4. Click the **New Rule** button. The New Formatting Rule dialog box opens. See Figure 4–25.

Figure 4–25 New Formatting Rule dialog box

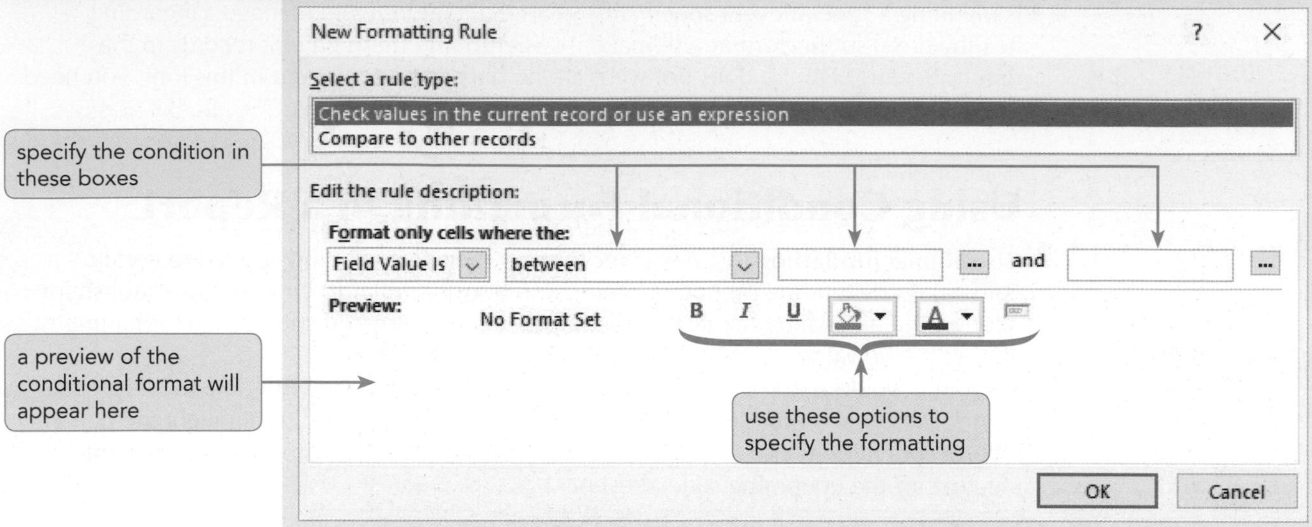
New Formatting Rule
Select a rule type:
Check values in the current record or use an expression
Compare to other records
Edit the rule description:
Format only cells where the:
Field Value Is
between
and
Preview:
No Format Set
OK
Cancel
specify the condition in these boxes
a preview of the conditional format will appear here
use these options to specify the formatting

The default setting for "Select a rule type" specifies that Access will check field values and determine if they meet the condition. This is the setting you want. You need to enter the condition in the "Edit the rule description" section of the dialog box. The setting "Field Value Is" means that the conditional format you specify will be applied only when the value for the selected field, City, meets the condition.

5. Click the **arrow** for the box containing the word "between," and then click **greater than**. You want only the birth dates greater than 1/1/1999 to be formatted.
6. Click in the next box, and then type **1/1/1999**.
7. In the Preview section, click the **Font color arrow** A, and then click the **Dark Red** color (first color in the last row in the Standard Colors section).
8. In the Preview section, click the **Bold** button B. The specifications for the conditional formatting are complete. See Figure 4–26.

Figure 4–26 Conditional formatting set for the BirthDate field

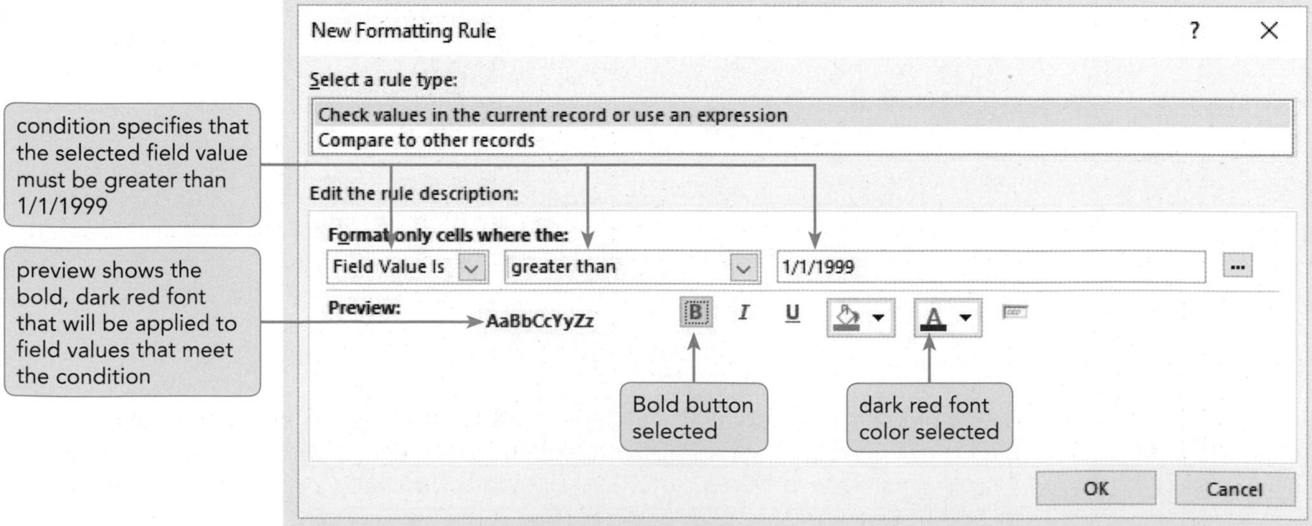
New Formatting Rule
Select a rule type:
Check values in the current record or use an expression
Compare to other records
Edit the rule description:
Format only cells where the:
Field Value Is
greater than
1/1/1999
Preview:
AaBbCcYyZz
OK
Cancel
condition specifies that the selected field value must be greater than 1/1/1999
preview shows the bold, dark red font that will be applied to field values that meet the condition
Bold button selected
dark red font color selected

9. Click **OK**. The new rule you specified appears in the Rule section of the Conditional Formatting Rules Manager dialog box as Value > 1/1/1999; the Format section on the right shows the conditional formatting (dark red, bold font) that will be applied based on this rule.
10. Click **OK**. The conditional format is applied to the BirthDate field values. To get a better view of the report and the formatting, you'll switch to Print Preview.
11. On the status bar, click the **Print Preview** button.
12. Move to page 2 of the report. Notice that the conditional formatting is applied only to BirthDate field values greater than 1/1/1999. See Figure 4–27.

Figure 4–27 **Viewing the finished report in Print Preview**

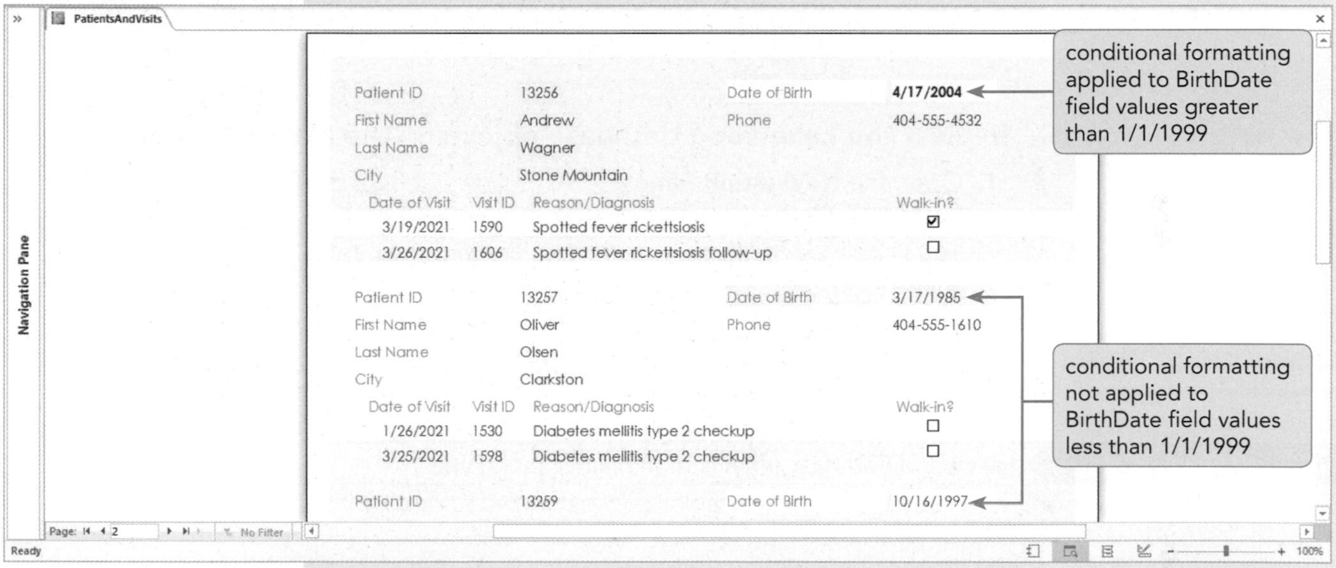
PatientsAndVisits
Navigation Pane
Patient ID 13256 Date of Birth 4/17/2004
First Name Andrew Phone 404-555-4532
Last Name Wagner
City Stone Mountain
Date of Visit Visit ID Reason/Diagnosis Walk-in?
3/19/2021 1590 Spotted fever rickettsiosis
3/26/2021 1606 Spotted fever rickettsiosis follow-up
Patient ID 13257 Date of Birth 3/17/1985
First Name Oliver Phone 404-555-1610
Last Name Olsen
City Clarkston
Date of Visit Visit ID Reason/Diagnosis Walk-in?
1/26/2021 1530 Diabetes mellitis type 2 checkup
3/25/2021 1598 Diabetes mellitis type 2 checkup
Patient ID 13259 Date of Birth 10/16/1997
conditional formatting applied to BirthDate field values greater than 1/1/1999
conditional formatting not applied to BirthDate field values less than 1/1/1999
Page: 2
No Filter
Ready
100%

PROSKILLS

Problem Solving: Understanding the Importance of Previewing Reports

When you create a report, it is a good idea to display the report in Print Preview occasionally as you develop it. Doing so will give you a chance to identify any formatting problems or other issues so that you can make any necessary corrections before printing the report. It is particularly important to preview a report after you've made changes to its design to ensure that the changes you made have not created new problems with the report's format. Before printing any report, you should preview it so you can determine where the pages will break and make any necessary adjustments. Following this problem-solving approach not only will ensure that the final report looks exactly the way you want it to, but will also save you time and help to avoid wasting paper if you print the report.

The report is now complete. You'll print just the first page of the report so that Donna can view the final results and share the report design with other staff members before printing the entire report. (*Note*: Ask your instructor if you should complete the following printing steps.)

To print page 1 of the report:

1. On the Print Preview tab, in the Print group, click the **Print** button. The Print dialog box opens.
2. In the Print Range section, click the **Pages** option button. The insertion point now appears in the From box so that you can specify the range of pages to print.
3. Type **1** in the From box, press **TAB** to move to the To box, and then type **1**. These settings specify that only page 1 of the report will be printed.
4. Click **OK**. The Print dialog box closes, and the first page of the report is printed.
5. Save and close the PatientsAndVisits report.

You've created many different objects in the Lakewood database. Before you close it, you'll open the Navigation Pane to view all the objects in the database.

To view the Lakewood database objects in the Navigation Pane:

1. Open the **Navigation Pane** and scroll down, if necessary, to display the bottom of the pane.

   The Navigation Pane now includes the PatientsAndVisits report in the Reports section of the pane. Also notice the PatientVisits form in the Forms section. This is the form you created containing a main form based on the Patient table and a subform based on the Visit table. The VisitSubform object is also listed; you can open it separately from the main form. See Figure 4–28.

Figure 4–28 Lakewood database objects in the Navigation Pane

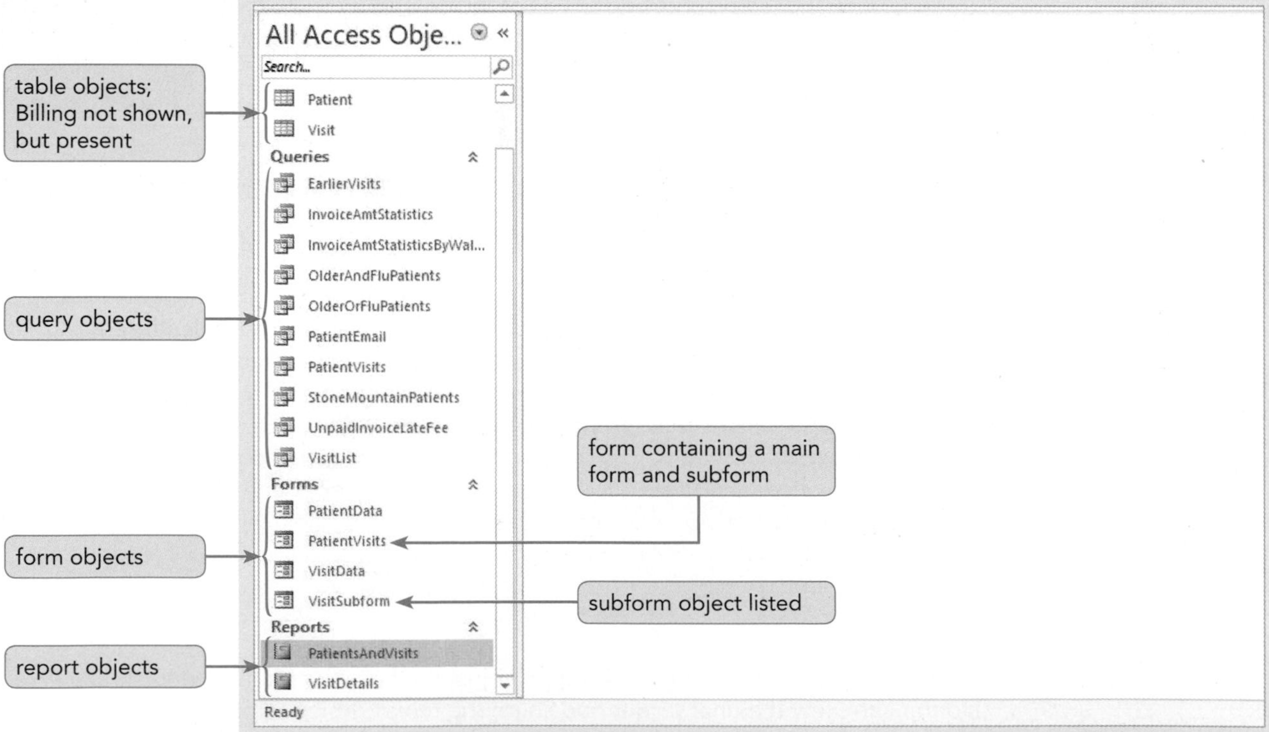
All Access Obje...
Search...
Patient
Visit
Queries
EarlierVisits
InvoiceAmtStatistics
InvoiceAmtStatisticsByWal...
OlderAndFluPatients
OlderOrFluPatients
PatientEmail
PatientVisits
StoneMountainPatients
UnpaidInvoiceLateFee
VisitList
Forms
PatientData
PatientVisits
VisitData
VisitSubform
Reports
PatientsAndVisits
VisitDetails
Ready
table objects; Billing not shown, but present
query objects
form objects
report objects
form containing a main form and subform
subform object listed

2. sam Compact and repair the Lakewood database, and then close the database.

Donna is satisfied that the forms you created—the PatientData form and the PatientVisits form—will make it easier to enter, view, and update data in the Lakewood database. The PatientsAndVisits report presents important information about the patients the clinic treats in an attractive and professional format, which will help Donna and other staff members in their work.

REVIEW

Session 4.2 Quick Check

1. In a(n) ________ report, the data from a record in the primary table appears together, followed on subsequent lines by the joined records from the related table.
2. When you create a report based on two tables that are joined in a one-to-many relationship, the field values for the records from the related table are called the ________ records.
3. Identify three types of modifications you can make to a report in Layout view.
4. Describe the process for moving a control to another location on a report in Layout view.
5. When working in Layout view for a report, which key do you press and hold down so that you can click to select multiple controls (field labels, field value boxes, and so on)?
6. ________ in a report (or form) is special formatting applied to certain field values depending on one or more conditions.

PRACTICE

Review Assignments

Data Files needed for the Review Assignments: Support_AC_4_Items.png, Support_AC_4_Supplies.png, and Vendor.accdb *(cont. from Module 3)*

Donna asks you to enhance the Vendor database with forms and reports. Complete the following steps:

1. Open the **Vendor** database you created and worked with in previous modules, and then click the Enable Content button next to the security warning, if necessary.
2. Use the Form Wizard to create a form based on the Product table. Select all fields for the form and the Columnar layout; specify the title **ProductData** for the form.
3. Apply the Integral theme to the ProductData form *only*.
4. Insert the **Support_AC_4_Supplies.png** picture, which is located in the Access1 > Review folder provided with your Data Files, in the ProductData form. Remove the picture from the control layout, and then move the picture to the right of the form title.
5. Edit the form title so that it appears as "Product Data" (two words), resize the title box as necessary so the title appears on a single line, and then change the font color of the form title to the Ice Blue, Background 2, Darker 50% theme color.
6. Resize the Weight in Lbs field value box so it is the same width (approximately) as the Units/Case field value box above it.
7. Change the alignment of the Price, Units/Case, and Weight in Lbs fields so that their values appear left-aligned in the field value boxes.
8. Save your changes to the form design.
9. Use the ProductData form to update the Product table as follows:
   a. Use the Find command to search for the word "penicillin" anywhere in the ProductName field, and then display the record for the Penicillin injections (ProductID PN284). Change the Price in this record to **262.00**.
   b. Add a new record with the following field values:
      Product ID: **GA606**
      Supplier ID: **CRO063**
      Product Name: **Gauze pads, 6x6"**
      Price: **124.00**
      Units/Case: **1000**
      Weight in Lbs: **19**
      Temp Controlled?: **no**
      Sterile?: **yes**
   c. Use the form to view each record with a ProductID value that starts with "XR".
   d. Save and close the form.
10. Use the Form Wizard to create a form containing a main form and a subform. Select all fields from the Supplier table for the main form, and select ProductID, ProductName, Price, TempControl, and Sterile—in that order—from the Product table for the subform. Use the Datasheet layout. Specify the title **SuppliersAndProducts** for the main form and **ProductSubform** for the subform.
11. Change the form title text to **Suppliers and Products**.
12. Resize the subform by widening it from its right side, increasing its width by approximately one inch, and then resize all columns in the subform to their best fit, working left to right. Navigate through each record in the main form to make sure all the field values in the subform are completely displayed, resizing subform columns and the subform itself, as necessary. Save and close the SuppliersAndProducts form.

13. Use the Report Wizard to create a report based on the primary Supplier table and the related Product table. Select the SupplierID, Company, City, Category, ContactFirst, ContactLast, and Phone fields—in that order—from the Supplier table, and the ProductID, ProductName, Price, and Units fields from the Product table. Do not specify any additional grouping levels, and sort the detail records in ascending order by ProductID. Choose the Outline layout and Portrait orientation. Specify the title **ProductsBySupplier** for the report.
14. Change the report title text to **Products by Supplier**.
15. Apply the Ion theme to the ProductsBySupplier report *only*.
16. Resize and reposition the following objects in the report in Layout view, and then scroll through the report to make sure all field labels and field values are fully displayed:
    a. Resize the report title so that the text of the title, Products by Supplier, is fully displayed.
    b. Move the ProductName field label and field value box to the right a bit (be sure not to move them too far so that the longest product name will still be completely visible).
    c. Resize the Product ID field label from its right side, increasing its width slightly so the label is fully displayed.
    d. Move the Units/Case field label and field value box to the right a bit; then resize the label on its left side, increasing its width slightly so the label is fully displayed.
17. Change the color of the report title text to the Light Gray, Background 2, Darker 75% theme color.
18. Insert the **Support_AC_4_Items.png** picture, which is located in the Access1 > Review folder provided with your Data Files, in the report. Move the picture to the right of the report title.
19. Apply conditional formatting so that the Category field values equal to **Supplies** appear as dark red and bold.
20. Preview each page of the report, verifying that all the fields fit on the page. If necessary, return to Layout view and make changes so the report prints within the margins of the page and so that all field names and values are completely displayed.
21. Save the report, print its first page (only if asked by your instructor to do so), and then close the report.
22. Compact and repair the Vendor database, and then close it.

APPLY

Case Problem 1

Data File needed for this Case Problem: Career.accdb *(cont. from Module 3)* and Support_AC_4_Giraffe.png

Great Giraffe Jeremiah uses the Career database to track and view information about the courses his business offers. He asks you to create the necessary forms and a report to help him work with this data more efficiently. Complete the following:

1. Open the **Career** database you created and worked with in previous modules, and then click the Enable Content button next to the security warning, if necessary.
2. Use the Form Wizard to create a form based on the Course table. Select all the fields for the form and the Columnar layout. Specify the title **CourseData** for the form.
3. Apply the Slice theme to the CourseData form *only*.
4. Edit the form title so that it appears as "Course Data" (two words); resize the title so that both words fit on the same line; and then change the font color of the form title to the Orange, Accent 5, Darker 25% theme color.

5. Use the CourseData form to add a new record to the Course table with the following field values:
   Instance ID: **DGTSCRF002**
   Title: **Digital Security**
   Start Date: **5/24/2021**
   End Date: **6/25/2021**
   Hours Per Week: **40**
   Cost: **24500**
6. Save and close the CourseData form.
7. Use the Form Wizard to create a form containing a main form and a subform. Select all the fields from the Course table for the main form, and select the StudentID, FirstName, LastName, and Phone fields from the Student table for the subform. Use the Datasheet layout. Specify the title **StudentsByCourse** for the main form and the title **StudentSubform** for the subform.
8. Change the form title text for the main form to **Students by Course**.
9. Resize all columns in the subform to their best fit, working from left to right; then move through all the records in the main form and check to make sure that all subform field values are fully displayed, resizing the columns as necessary.
10. Save and close the StudentsByCourse form.
11. Use the Report Wizard to create a report based on the primary Course table and the related Student table. Select all the fields from the Course table, and then select the StudentID, FirstName, LastName, Phone, and Email fields from the Student table. Do not select any additional grouping levels, and sort the detail records in ascending order by StudentID. Choose the Outline layout and Landscape orientation. Specify the title **CourseRosters** for the report.
12. Apply the Slice theme to the CourseRosters report *only*.
13. Resize the report title so that the text is fully displayed; edit the report title so that it appears as "Course Rosters" (two words); and change the font color of the title to the Orange, Accent 5, Darker 25% theme color.
14. Change the alignment of the Start Date and End Date fields so that their values appear left-aligned in the field value boxes.
15. Change the alignment of the Cost and Hours Per Week fields field so that their values appear left-aligned in the field value boxes.
16. Resize and reposition the following objects in the report in Layout view, and then scroll through the report to make sure all field labels and field values are fully displayed:
    a. Move the Email label and field value box to the right approximately 10 spaces.
    b. Move the Phone label and field value box to the right approximately 5 spaces.
    c. Move the LastName label and field value box to the right approximately 5 spaces.
    d. Move the FirstName label and field value box to the right approximately 5 spaces.
    e. Scroll to the bottom of the report; note that the page number might not be completely within the page border (the dotted vertical line). If necessary, select and move the box containing the text "Page 1 of 1" until the entire text is positioned to the left of the dotted vertical line marking the right page border by approximately 5 spaces.
17. Insert the **Support_AC_4_Giraffe.png** picture, which is located in the Access1 > Case1 folder provided with your Data Files, in the report. Move the picture to the right of the report title.
18. Apply conditional formatting so that any Hours Per Week field value equal to 40 appears as bold and with the Red color applied.
19. Preview the entire report to confirm that it is formatted correctly. If necessary, return to Layout view and make changes so that all field labels and field values are completely displayed.
20. Save the report, print its first page (only if asked by your instructor to do so), and then close the report.
21. Compact and repair the Career database, and then close it.

CHALLENGE

Case Problem 2

Data File needed for this Case Problem: DrainAdopter.accdb *(cont. from Module 2)* and Support_AC_4_Drain.png

Drain Adopter Tandrea uses the DrainAdopter database to track, maintain, and analyze data about the drains and volunteers. You'll help Tandrea by creating a form and a report based on this data. Complete the following:

1. Open the **DrainAdopter** database you created and worked with in previous modules, and then click the Enable Content button next to the security warning, if necessary.
2. Use the Form Wizard to create a form based on the Volunteer table. Select all the fields for the form and the Columnar layout. Specify the title **VolunteerMasterData** for the form.
3. Apply the Retrospect theme to the VolunteerMasterData form *only*.
4. Edit the form title so that it appears as "Volunteer Master Data" (three words) on one line, and change the font color of the form title to the Brown, Accent 3, Darker 25% theme color.

Explore 5. Use the appropriate button in the Font group on the Form Layout Tools Format tab to italicize the form title. Save the form.

6. Use the VolunteerMasterData form to update the Volunteer table as follows:
   a. Use the Find command to search for the record that contains the value "BUC5101" for the VolunteerID field, and then change the Phone field value for this record to **360-555-8502**.
   b. Add a new record with the following values:
   Volunteer ID: **BAR1730**
   First Name: **Mikala**
   Last Name: **Barnes**
   Street: **342 Sycamore Court**
   City: **Bellingham**
   State: **WA**
   Zip: **98226**
   Phone: **360-555-0028**
   Email: **m.barnes19@example.com**
   Signup Date: **5/25/2021**
   Trained: **[leave blank]**

   Explore c. Find the record with VolunteerID MIT8951, and then delete the record. (*Hint*: After displaying the record in the form, you need to select it by clicking the right-pointing triangle in the bar to the left of the field labels. Then use the appropriate button on the Home tab in the Records group to delete the record. When asked to confirm the deletion, click the Yes button.) Close the form.

7. Use the Form Wizard to create a form containing a main form and a subform. Select all the fields from the Volunteer table for the main form, and select all fields except VolunteerID from the Drain table for the subform. Use the Datasheet layout. Specify the name **VolunteersAndDrains** for the main form and the title **DrainSubform** for the subform.
8. Make sure the default Office theme is applied to the VolunteersAndDrains form.
9. Edit the form title so that it appears as "Volunteers and Drains." Resize the form title so that the text fits on one line. Change the font color of the title to the Blue, Accent 5, Darker 25% theme color.
10. Insert the **Support_AC_4_Drain.png** picture, which is located in the Access1 > Case2 folder provided with your Data Files, in the VolunteersAndDrains form. Remove the picture from the control layout, and then move the picture to the right of the form title. Resize the picture so it is approximately double the original size.

Explore 11. Use the appropriate button in the Font group on the Form Layout Tools Format tab to apply the theme color Tan, Accent 5, Lighter 60% as a background color for all the field value boxes in the main form. Then use the appropriate button in the Control Formatting group to change the outline of all the main form field value boxes to have a line thickness of 1 pt. (*Hint*: Select all the field value boxes before making these changes.)

12. Resize the subform by extending it to the right, and then resize all columns in the subform to their best fit. Navigate through the records in the main form to make sure all the field values in the subform are completely displayed, resizing subform columns as necessary. Save and close the form.
13. Use the Report Wizard to create a report based on the primary Volunteer table and the related Drain table. Select all the fields from the Volunteer table, and select all fields except VolunteerID from the Drain table. Sort the detail records in *descending* order by DrainID. Choose the Outline layout and Landscape orientation. Specify the name **VolunteersAndDrains** for the report.
14. Apply the Retrospect theme to the VolunteersAndDrains report *only*.
15. Resize the report title so that the text is fully displayed; edit the report title so that it appears as "Volunteers and Drains"; and change the font color of the title to the Brown, Accent 3, Darker 25% theme color.
16. Move the Email field value box to the left approximately 10 spaces. Then resize the Email field value box on the right, expanding its size to the edge of the report. Left-justify the field value box for Signup Date. Save the report.
17. Insert the **Support_AC_4_Drain.png** picture, which is located in the Access1 > Case2 folder provided with your Data Files, in the VolunteersAndDrains report. Move the picture to the right of the report title.
18. Apply conditional formatting so that any Signup Date in the first three months of 2021 is formatted as bold and with the Brown 5 font color.

Explore 19. Preview the report so you can see two pages at once. (*Hint*: Use a button on the Print Preview tab.) Check the report to confirm that it is formatted correctly and all field labels and field values are fully displayed. Save the report, print its first page (only if asked by your instructor to do so), and then close the report.

20. Compact and repair the DrainAdopter database, and then close it.

MODULE 5

Creating Advanced Queries and Enhancing Table Design

Making the Clinic Database Easier to Use

OBJECTIVES

Session 5.1
- Review object naming standards
- Use the Like, In, Not, and & operators in queries
- Filter data using an AutoFilter
- Use the IIf function to assign a conditional value to a calculated field in a query
- Create a parameter query

Session 5.2
- Use query wizards to create a crosstab query, a find duplicates query, and a find unmatched query
- Create a top values query

Session 5.3
- Modify table designs using lookup fields, input masks, and data validation rules
- Identify object dependencies
- Review a Long Text field's properties
- Designate a trusted folder

Case | ***Lakewood Community Health Services***

Lakewood Community Health Services, a nonprofit health clinic located in the greater Atlanta, Georgia area, provides a range of medical services to patients of all ages. The clinic specializes in chronic disease management, cardiac care, and geriatrics. Donna Taylor, the office manager for Lakewood Community Health Services, oversees a small staff and is responsible for maintaining records for the clinic's patients.

In order to best manage the clinic, Donna and her staff rely on electronic medical records for patient information, billing, inventory control, purchasing, and accounts payable. The Lakewood staff developed the Clinic database, which contains tables, queries, forms, and reports that Donna and other staff members use to track patient, visit, and billing information.

Donna is interested in taking better advantage of the power of Access to make the database easier to use and to create more sophisticated queries. For example, Donna wants to obtain lists of patients in certain cities. She also needs a summarized list of invoice amounts by city. In this module, you'll modify and customize the Clinic database to satisfy these and other requirements.

STARTING DATA FILES

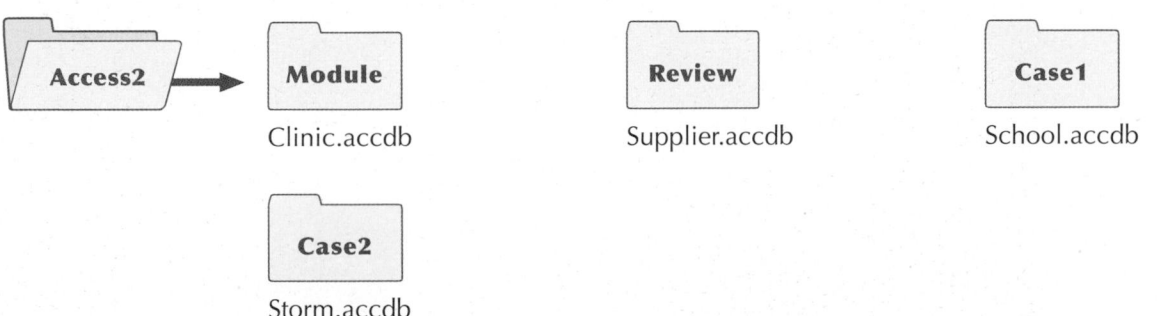

Access2 → Module: Clinic.accdb

Review: Supplier.accdb

Case1: School.accdb

Case2: Storm.accdb

Session 5.1 Visual Overview:

A Select query selects the records in the fields that satisfy the criteria.

The tbl prefix tag identifies a table object.

The qry prefix tag identifies a query object.

The frm prefix tag identifies a form object.

The rpt prefix tag identifies a report object.

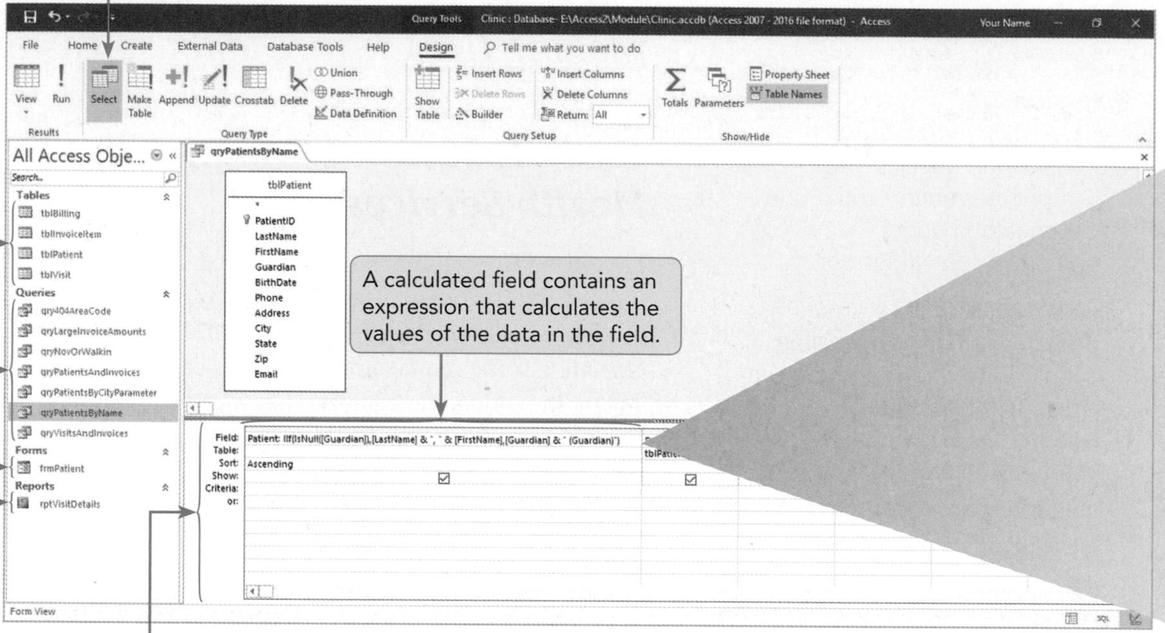

Query Tools
File
Home
Create
External Data
Database Tools
Help
Design
Tell me what you want to do
View
Run
Select
Make Table
Append
Update
Crosstab
Delete
Union
Pass-Through
Data Definition
Show Table
Insert Rows
Delete Rows
Builder
Insert Columns
Delete Columns
Return: All
Totals
Parameters
Property Sheet
Table Names
Results
Query Type
Query Setup
Show/Hide
All Access Obje...
Search...
Tables
tblBilling
tblInvoiceItem
tblPatient
tblVisit
Queries
qry404AreaCode
qryLargeInvoiceAmounts
qryNovOrWalkin
qryPatientsAndInvoices
qryPatientsByCityParameter
qryPatientsByName
qryVisitsAndInvoices
Forms
frmPatient
Reports
rptVisitDetails
qryPatientsByName
tblPatient
PatientID
LastName
FirstName
Guardian
BirthDate
Phone
Address
City
State
Zip
Email
Field:
Table:
Sort:
Show:
Criteria:
or:
Ascending
Form View

A calculated field contains an expression that calculates the values of the data in the field.

The design grid contains the fields and criteria that will be used in the query.

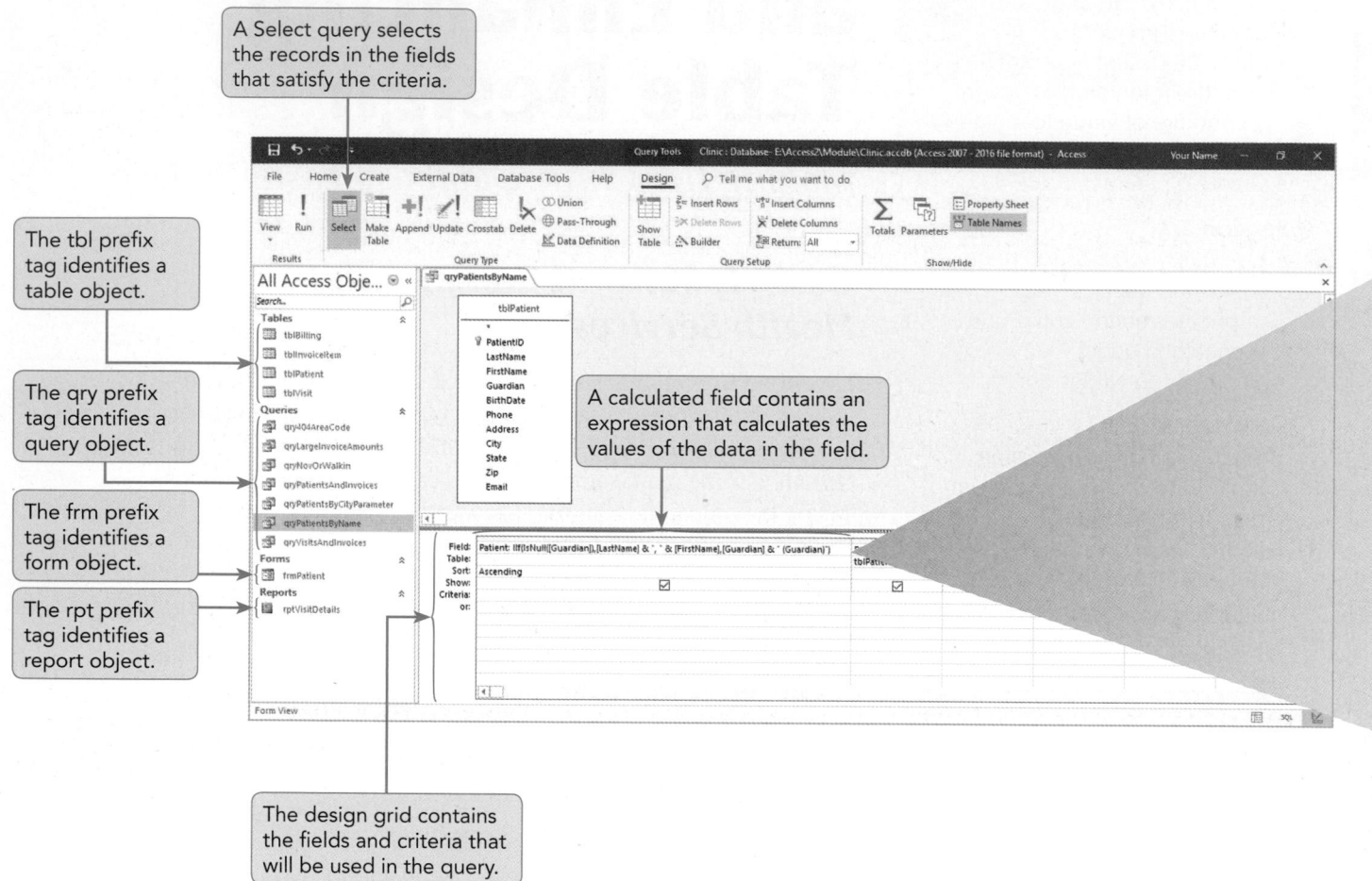

Calculated Field

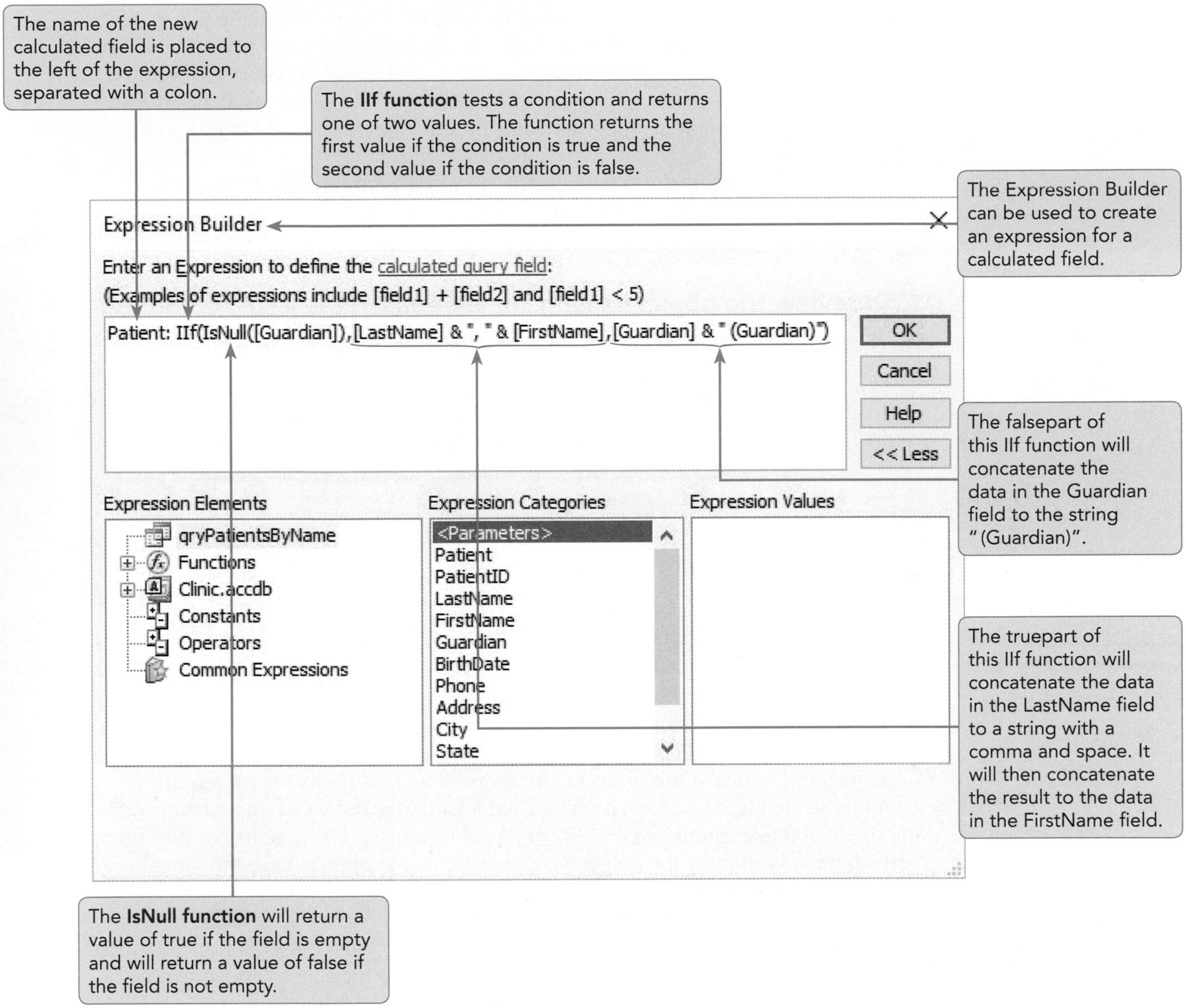
The name of the new calculated field is placed to the left of the expression, separated with a colon.
The **IIf function** tests a condition and returns one of two values. The function returns the first value if the condition is true and the second value if the condition is false.
The Expression Builder can be used to create an expression for a calculated field.
Expression Builder
Enter an Expression to define the calculated query field:
(Examples of expressions include [field1] + [field2] and [field1] < 5)
Patient: IIf(IsNull([Guardian]),[LastName] & ", " & [FirstName],[Guardian] & " (Guardian)")
OK
Cancel
Help
<< Less
The falsepart of this IIf function will concatenate the data in the Guardian field to the string " (Guardian)".
Expression Elements
qryPatientsByName
Functions
Clinic.accdb
Constants
Operators
Common Expressions
Expression Categories
<Parameters>
Patient
PatientID
LastName
FirstName
Guardian
BirthDate
Phone
Address
City
State
Expression Values
The truepart of this IIf function will concatenate the data in the LastName field to a string with a comma and space. It will then concatenate the result to the data in the FirstName field.
The **IsNull function** will return a value of true if the field is empty and will return a value of false if the field is not empty.

Reviewing the Clinic Database

Donna and her staff had no previous database experience when they created the Clinic database; they simply used the wizards and other easy-to-use Access tools. As business continued to grow at Lakewood Community Health Services, Donna realized she needed an expert to further enhance the database. She hired Reginald Morales, who has a business information systems degree and nine years of experience developing database systems. Reginald spent a few days reviewing the Clinic database, making sure it adhered to simple naming standards for the objects and field names to make his future work easier.

Before implementing the enhancements for Donna, you'll review the naming conventions for the object names in the Clinic database.

To review the object naming conventions in the Clinic database:

1. Make sure you have the Access starting Data Files on your computer.

   Trouble? If you don't have the starting Data Files, you need to get them before you can proceed. Your instructor will either give you the Data Files or ask you to obtain them from a specified location (such as a network drive). If you have any questions about the Data Files, see your instructor or technical support person for assistance.

2. **sam** Start Access, and then open the **Clinic** database from the Access2 > Module folder where your starting Data Files are stored.

   Trouble? If the security warning is displayed below the ribbon, click the Enable Content button.

As shown in Visual Overview 5.1, the Navigation Pane displays the objects grouped by object type. Each object name has a prefix tag—a tbl prefix tag for tables, a qry prefix tag for queries, a frm prefix tag for forms, and a rpt prefix tag for reports.

All three characters in each prefix tag are lowercase. The word immediately after the three-character prefix begins with an uppercase letter. Using object prefix tags, you can readily identify the object type, even when the objects have the same base name—for instance, tblPatient, frmPatient, and rptPatient. In addition, object names have no spaces, because other database management systems, such as SQL Server and Oracle, do not permit spaces in object and field names. It is important to adhere to industry standard naming conventions, both to make it easier to convert your database to another DBMS in the future, if necessary, and to develop personal habits that enable you to work seamlessly with other major DBMSs. If Lakewood Community Health Services needs to scale up to one of these other systems, using standard naming conventions means that Reginald will have to do less work to make the transition.

PROSKILLS

Teamwork: Following Naming Conventions

Most Access databases have hundreds of fields, objects, and controls. You'll find it easier to identify the type and purpose of these database items when you use a naming convention or standard. Most companies adopt a standard naming convention, such as the one used for the Clinic database, so that multiple people can develop a database, troubleshoot database problems, and enhance and improve existing databases. When working on a database, a team's tasks are difficult, if not impossible, to perform if a standard naming convention isn't used. In addition, most databases and database samples on websites and in training books use standard naming conventions that are similar to the ones used for the Clinic database. By following the standard naming convention established by your company or organization, you'll help to ensure smooth collaboration among all team members.

Now you'll create the queries that Donna needs.

Using a Pattern Match in a Query

You are already familiar with queries that use an exact match or a range of values (for example, queries that use the > or < comparison operators) to select records. Many other operators are available for creating select queries. These operators let you build more complicated queries that are difficult to create with exact-match or range-of-values selection criteria.

Donna created a list of questions she wants to answer using the Clinic database:

- Which patients have the 404 area code?
- What is the patient information for patients located in Decatur, Smyrna, or Stone Mountain?
- What is the patient information for all patients except those located in Decatur, Smyrna, or Stone Mountain?
- What is the patient and visit information for patients in Decatur or Stone Mountain who either walked in without an appointment or who visited during November?
- What are the first and last names of Lakewood Community Health Services patients, or the guardian name if it is listed? Patients with guardians should not be contacted directly.
- What is the patient information for patients in a particular city? This query needs to be flexible to allow the user to specify the city.

Next, you will create the queries necessary to answer these questions. Donna wants to view the records for all patients whose area code is 404. To answer Donna's question, you can create a query that uses a pattern match. A **pattern match** selects records with a value for the designated field that matches the pattern of a simple condition value—in this case, patients with the 404 area code. You do this using the Like comparison operator.

The **Like comparison operator** selects records by matching field values to a specific pattern that includes one or more of these wildcard characters: asterisk (*), question mark (?), and number symbol (#). The asterisk represents any string of characters, the question mark represents any single character, and the number symbol represents any single digit. Using a pattern match is similar to using an exact match, except that a pattern match includes wildcard characters.

To create the new query, you must first place the tblPatient table field list in the Query window in Design view.

To create the new query in Design view:

1. If necessary, click the **Shutter Bar Open/Close Button** « at the top of the Navigation Pane to close it.
2. On the ribbon, click the **Create** tab.
3. In the Queries group, click the **Query Design** button. The Show Table dialog box opens in front of the Query window in Design view.
4. Click **tblPatient** in the Tables box, click the **Add** button, and then click the **Close** button. The tblPatient table field list is added to the Query window, and the Show Table dialog box closes.
5. Drag the bottom border of the tblPatient field list down until you can see the full list of fields.
6. Double-click the **title bar** of the tblPatient field list to highlight all the fields, and then drag the highlighted fields to the first column's Field box in the design grid. Each field is placed in a separate column in the design grid, in the same order that the fields appear in the table. See Figure 5–1.

TIP

You can also double-click a table name to add the table's field list to the Query window.

Figure 5–1 Adding the fields for the pattern match query

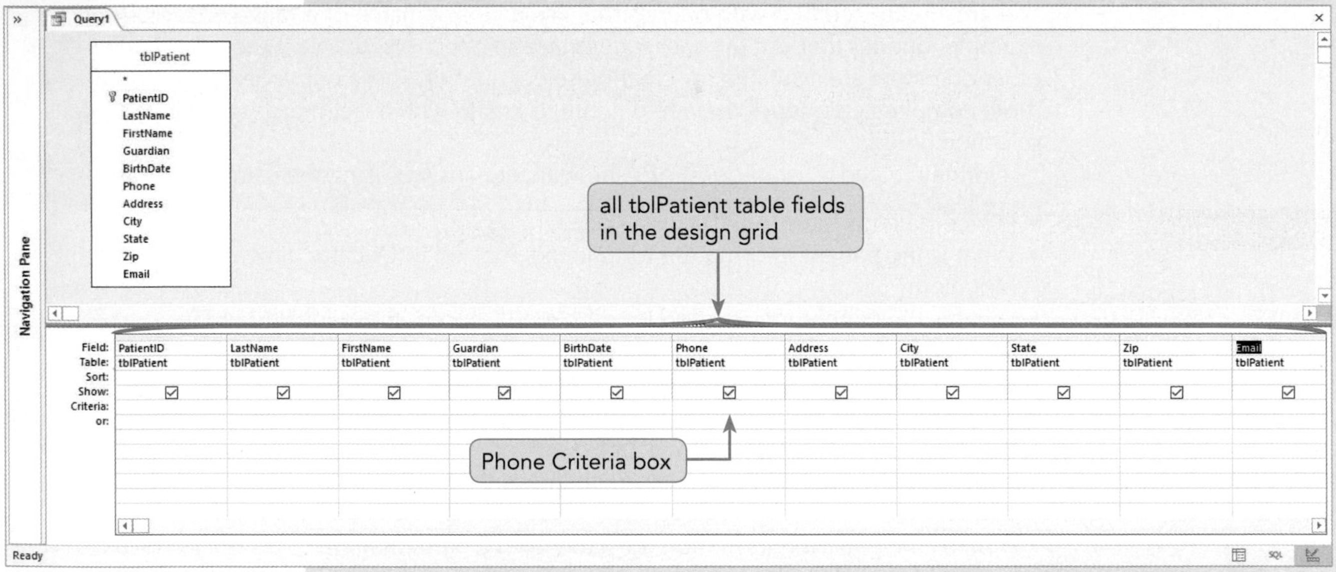
Query1
tblPatient
PatientID
LastName
FirstName
Guardian
BirthDate
Phone
Address
City
State
Zip
Email
all tblPatient table fields in the design grid
Navigation Pane
Field:
Table:
Sort:
Show:
Criteria:
or:
Phone Criteria box
Ready

Trouble? If tblPatient.* appears in the first column's Field box, you dragged the * from the field list instead of the highlighted fields. Press DELETE, and then repeat Step 6.

Now you will enter the pattern match condition Like "404*" for the Phone field. The query will select records with a Phone field value of 404 in positions one through three. The asterisk wildcard character specifies that any characters can appear in the remaining positions of the field value.

To specify records that match the indicated pattern:

TIP

If you omit the Like operator, it is automatically added when you run the query.

1. Click the **Phone Criteria** box, and then type **L**. The Formula AutoComplete menu displays a list of functions beginning with the letter L, but the Like operator is not one of the choices in the list. You'll finish typing the condition.
2. Type **ike "404*"**. See Figure 5–2.

Figure 5–2 Record selection based on matching a specific pattern

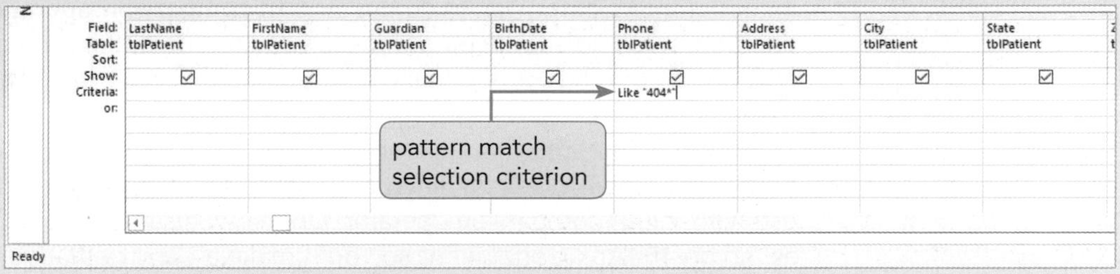
Field: LastName FirstName Guardian BirthDate Phone Address City State
Table: tblPatient tblPatient tblPatient tblPatient tblPatient tblPatient tblPatient tblPatient
Sort:
Show:
Criteria: Like "404*"
or:
pattern match selection criterion
Ready

3. Click the **Save** button on the Quick Access Toolbar to open the Save As dialog box.
4. Type **qry404AreaCode** in the Query Name box, and then press **ENTER**. The query is saved, and the name is displayed on the object tab.
5. On the Query Tools Design tab, in the Results group, click the **Run** button. The query results are displayed in the query window. Seventeen records have the area code 404. See Figure 5–3.

Figure 5–3 tblPatient table records for phone numbers starting with 404

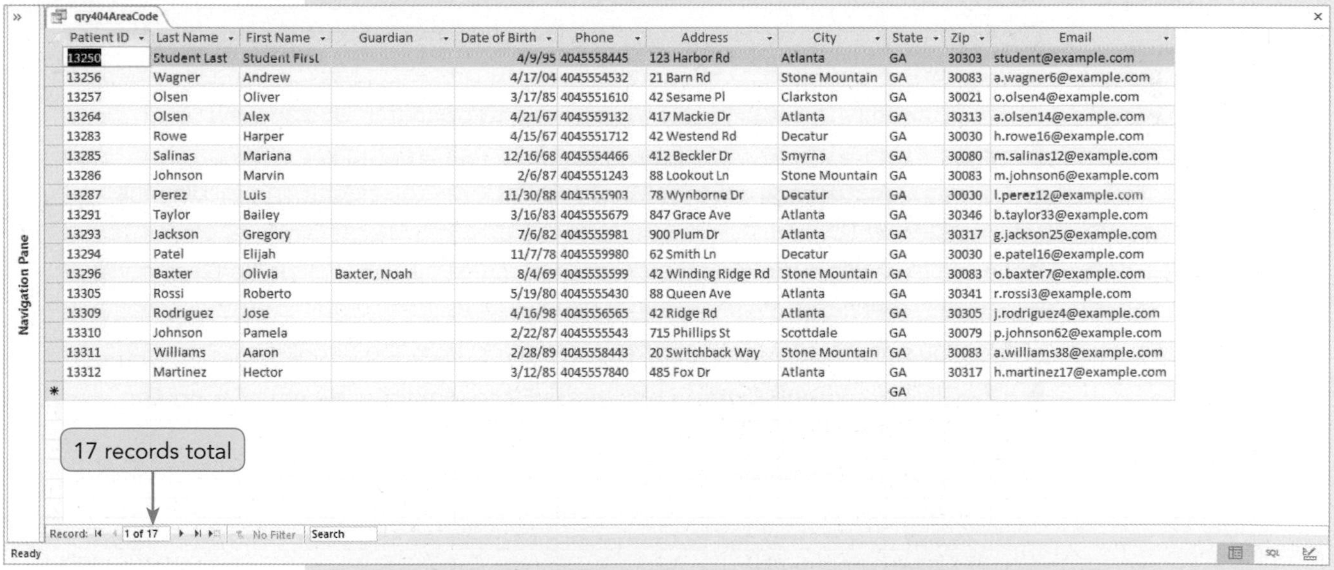
qry404AreaCode
Navigation Pane
17 records total
Record: 1 of 17 No Filter Search
Ready

Patient ID	Last Name	First Name	Guardian	Date of Birth	Phone	Address	City	State	Zip	Email
13250	Student Last	Student First		4/9/95	4045558445	123 Harbor Rd	Atlanta	GA	30303	student@example.com
13256	Wagner	Andrew		4/17/04	4045554532	21 Barn Rd	Stone Mountain	GA	30083	a.wagner6@example.com
13257	Olsen	Oliver		3/17/85	4045551610	42 Sesame Pl	Clarkston	GA	30021	o.olsen4@example.com
13264	Olsen	Alex		4/21/67	4045559132	417 Mackie Dr	Atlanta	GA	30313	a.olsen14@example.com
13283	Rowe	Harper		4/15/67	4045551712	42 Westend Rd	Decatur	GA	30030	h.rowe16@example.com
13285	Salinas	Mariana		12/16/68	4045554466	412 Beckler Dr	Smyrna	GA	30080	m.salinas12@example.com
13286	Johnson	Marvin		2/6/87	4045551243	88 Lookout Ln	Stone Mountain	GA	30083	m.johnson6@example.com
13287	Perez	Luis		11/30/88	4045555903	78 Wynborne Dr	Decatur	GA	30030	l.perez12@example.com
13291	Taylor	Bailey		3/16/83	4045555679	847 Grace Ave	Atlanta	GA	30346	b.taylor33@example.com
13293	Jackson	Gregory		7/6/82	4045555981	900 Plum Dr	Atlanta	GA	30317	g.jackson25@example.com
13294	Patel	Elijah		11/7/78	4045559980	62 Smith Ln	Decatur	GA	30030	e.patel16@example.com
13296	Baxter	Olivia	Baxter, Noah	8/4/69	4045555599	42 Winding Ridge Rd	Stone Mountain	GA	30083	o.baxter7@example.com
13305	Rossi	Roberto		5/19/80	4045555430	88 Queen Ave	Atlanta	GA	30341	r.rossi3@example.com
13309	Rodriguez	Jose		4/16/98	4045556565	42 Ridge Rd	Atlanta	GA	30305	j.rodriguez4@example.com
13310	Johnson	Pamela		2/22/87	4045555543	715 Phillips St	Scottdale	GA	30079	p.johnson62@example.com
13311	Williams	Aaron		2/28/89	4045558443	20 Switchback Way	Stone Mountain	GA	30083	a.williams38@example.com
13312	Martinez	Hector		3/12/85	4045557840	485 Fox Dr	Atlanta	GA	30317	h.martinez17@example.com
*								GA		

Note that Reginald removed the hyphens from the Phone field values; for example, 4045558445 in the first record used to be 404-555-8445. You'll modify the Phone field later in this module to format its values with hyphens.

6. If necessary, change the first record in the table, with Patient ID 13250, so the Last Name and First Name columns contain your last and first names, respectively, as shown in Figure 5–3.
7. Close the qry404AreaCode query.

Next, Donna asks you to create a query that displays information about patients who live in Decatur, Smyrna, or Stone Mountain. To produce the results Donna wants, you'll create a query using a list-of-values match.

Using a List-of-Values Match in a Query

A **list-of-values match** selects records whose value for the designated field matches one of two or more simple condition values. You could accomplish this by including several Or conditions in the design grid, but the In comparison operator provides an easier and clearer way to do this. The **In comparison operator** lets you define a condition with a list of two or more values for a field. If a record's field value matches one value from the list of defined values, then that record is selected and included in the query results.

To display the information Donna requested, you want to select records if their City field value equals Decatur, Smyrna, or Stone Mountain. These are the values you will use with the In comparison operator. Donna wants the query to contain the same fields as the qry404AreaCode query, so you'll make a copy of that query and modify it.

To create the query using a list-of-values match:

1. Open the Navigation Pane.
2. In the Queries group on the Navigation Pane, right-click **qry404AreaCode**, and then click **Copy** on the shortcut menu.

   Trouble? If you don't see the qry404AreaCode query in the Queries group, press F5 to refresh the object listings in the Navigation Pane.
3. Right-click the empty area in the Navigation Pane below the report and then click **Paste**.
4. In the Query Name box, type **qryDecaturSmyrnaStoneMountainPatients**, and then press **ENTER**.

   To modify the copied query, you need to open it in Design view.
5. In the Queries group on the Navigation Pane, right-click **qryDecaturSmyrnaStoneMountainPatients** to select it and display the shortcut menu.
6. Click **Design View** on the shortcut menu to open the query in Design view, and then close the Navigation Pane.

   You need to delete the existing condition from the Phone field.
7. Click the **Phone Criteria** box, press **F2** to highlight the entire condition, and then press **DELETE** to remove the condition.

   Now you can enter the criterion for the new query using the In comparison operator. When you use this operator, you must enclose the list of values you want to match within parentheses and separate the values with commas. In addition, for fields defined using the Short Text data type, you enclose each value in quotation marks, although the quotation marks are automatically added if you omit them. For fields defined using the Number or Currency data type, you don't enclose the values in quotation marks.
8. Right-click the **City Criteria** box to open the shortcut menu, click **Zoom** to open the Zoom dialog box, and then type **In ("Decatur","Smyrna","Stone Mountain")**, as shown in Figure 5–4.

Figure 5–4 **Record selection based on matching field values to a list of values**

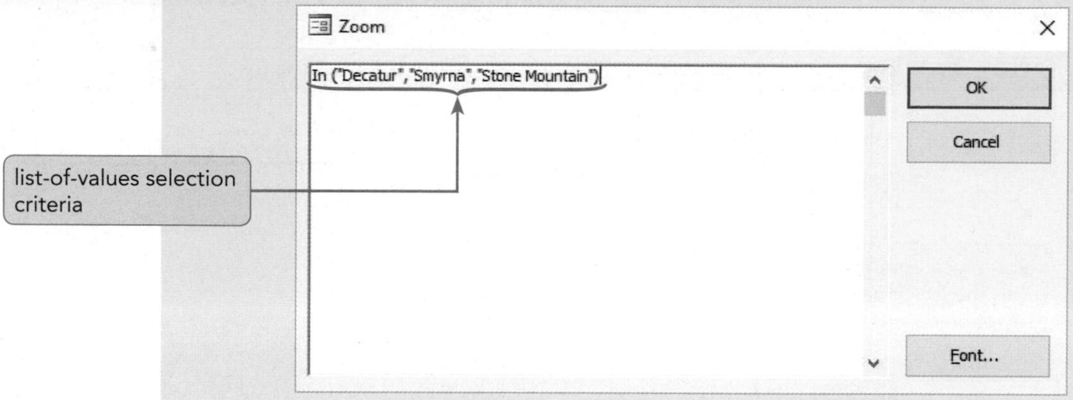
Zoom
In ("Decatur","Smyrna","Stone Mountain")
OK
Cancel
Font...
list-of-values selection criteria

TIP

After clicking in a box, you can also open its Zoom dialog box by holding down SHIFT and pressing F2.

9. Click the **OK** button to close the Zoom dialog box, and then save and run the query. The recordset is displayed, which shows the 11 records with Decatur, Smyrna, or Stone Mountain in the City field.
10. Close the query.

Donna would also like a list of patients who do not live in Decatur, Smyrna, or Stone Mountain. You can provide her with this information by creating a query with the Not logical operator.

Using the Not Logical Operator in a Query

The **Not logical operator** negates a criterion or selects records for which the designated field does not match the criterion. For example, if you enter *Not "Decatur"* in the Criteria box for the City field, the query results show records that do not have the City field value Decatur—that is, records of all patients not located in Decatur.

To create Donna's query, you will combine the Not logical operator with the In comparison operator to select patients whose City field value is not in the list *("Decatur","Smyrna","Stone Mountain")*. The qryDecaturSmyrnaStoneMountainPatients query has the fields that Donna needs to see in the query results. Donna doesn't need to keep the qryDecaturSmyrnaStoneMountainPatients query, so you'll rename and then modify the query.

To create the query using the Not logical operator:

TIP

You can rename any type of object, including a table, in the Navigation Pane using the Rename command on the shortcut menu.

1. Open the Navigation Pane.
2. In the Queries group, right-click **qryDecaturSmyrnaStoneMountainPatients**, and then on the shortcut menu, click **Rename**.
3. Position the insertion point after "qry," type **Non**, and then press **ENTER**. The query name is now qryNonDecaturSmyrnaStoneMountainPatients.
4. Open the **qryNonDecaturSmyrnaStoneMountainPatients** query in Design view, and then close the Navigation Pane.

   You need to change the existing condition in the City field to add the Not logical operator.

5. Click the **City Criteria** box, open the Zoom dialog box, click at the beginning of the expression, type **Not**, and then press **SPACEBAR**. See Figure 5–5.

Figure 5–5 **Record selection based on not matching a list of values**

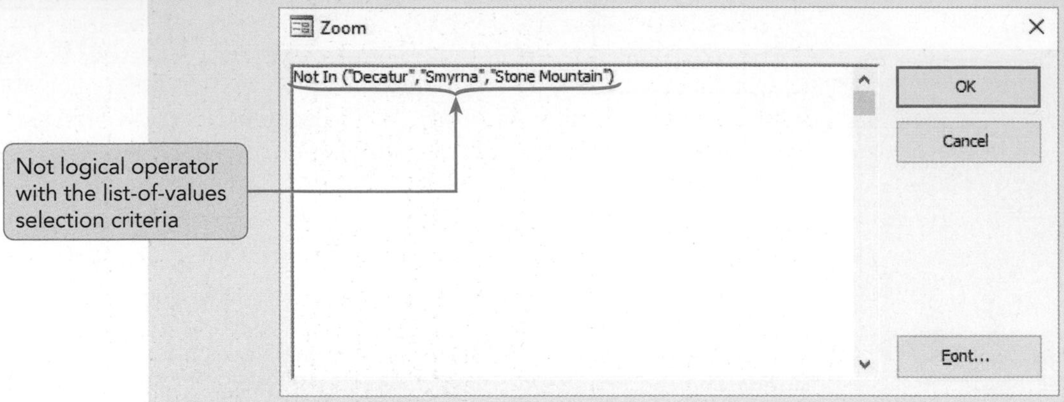
Zoom
Not In ("Decatur","Smyrna","Stone Mountain")
OK
Cancel
Font...
Not logical operator with the list-of-values selection criteria

6. Click the **OK** button, and then save and run the query. The recordset displays only those records with a City field value that is not Decatur, Smyrna, or Stone Mountain. The recordset includes a total of 41 patient records.
7. Scroll down the datasheet if necessary to make sure that no Decatur, Smyrna, or Stone Mountain patients appear in your results.

   Now you can close and delete the query, because Donna does not need to run this query again.

8. Close the query, and then open the Navigation Pane.
9. Right-click **qryNonDecaturSmyrnaStoneMountainPatients**, click **Delete** on the shortcut menu, and then click **Yes** in the dialog box warning that deleting this object will remove it from all groups.

TIP

You can delete any type of object, including a table, in the Navigation Pane using the Delete command on the shortcut menu.

You now are ready to answer Donna's question about patients in Decatur or Stone Mountain who walked in without an appointment or who visited during the month of November.

Using an AutoFilter to Filter Data

Donna wants to view the first and last names, cities, visit dates, walk-in statuses, and visit reasons for patients in Decatur or Stone Mountain who either walked in without an appointment or who visited during the month of November. The qryNovOrWalkin query contains the same fields Donna wants to view. This query also uses the Or logical operator to select records if the WalkIn field has a value of true or if the VisitDate field value is between 11/1/2020 and 11/30/2020. These are two of the conditions needed to answer Donna's question. You could modify the qryNovOrWalkin query in Design view to further restrict the records selected to patients located only in Decatur or Stone Mountain. However, you can use the AutoFilter feature to choose the city restrictions faster and with more flexibility. You previously used the AutoFilter feature to sort records, and you used Filter By Selection to filter records. Now you'll use the AutoFilter feature to filter records.

To filter the records using an AutoFilter:

1. Open the **qryNovOrWalkin** query in Design view, and then close the Navigation Pane.

   The true condition for the WalkIn field selects records for patients who walked in without an appointment, and the Between #11/1/2020# And #11/30/2020# condition for the VisitDate field selects records for patients whose visit date was in the month of November 2020. Although the WalkIn field is a yes/no field, these values are represented by true (yes) and false (no). Because the conditions are in two different rows, the query uses the Or logical operator.

   If you wanted to answer Donna's question in Design view, you would add a condition for the City field, using either the Or logical operator—"Decatur" Or "Stone Mountain"—or the In comparison operator—In ("Decatur","Stone Mountain"). You'd place the condition for the City field in both the Criteria row and in the Or row. The query recordset would include a record only if both conditions in either row are satisfied. Instead of changing the conditions in Design view, though, you'll choose the information Donna wants using an AutoFilter.

2. Run the query, and then click the **arrow** on the City column heading to display the AutoFilter menu. See Figure 5–6.

Figure 5–6 **Using an AutoFilter to filter records in the query recordset**

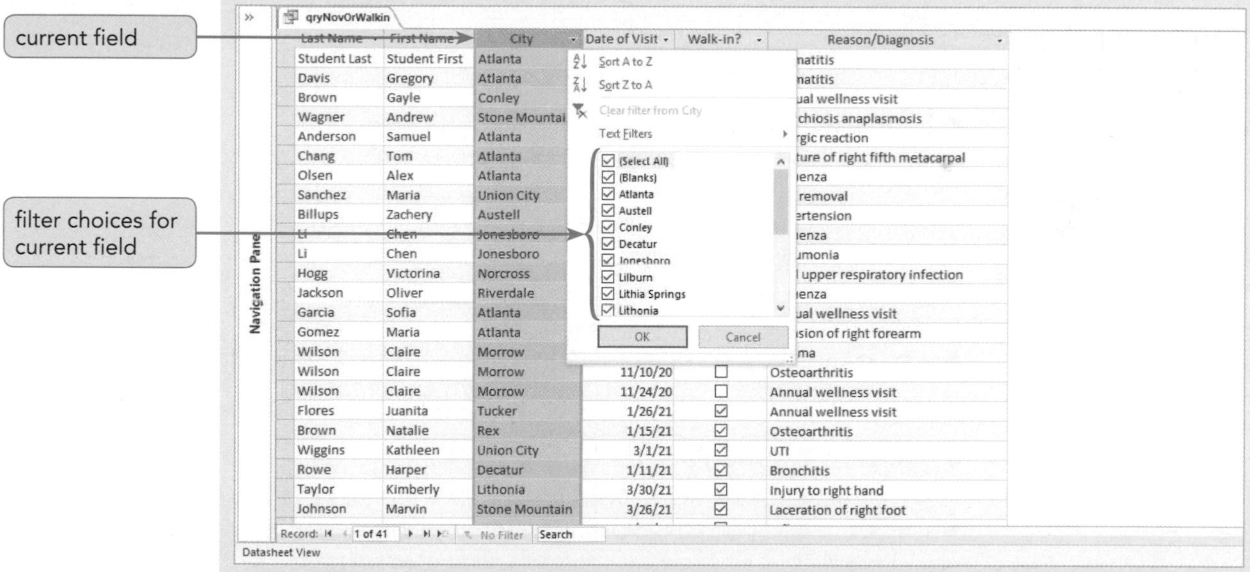
current field
filter choices for current field
qryNovOrWalkin
Sort A to Z
Sort Z to A
Clear filter from City
Text Filters
(Select All)
(Blanks)
Atlanta
Austell
Conley
Decatur
Lilburn
Lithia Springs
Lithonia
OK
Cancel
Navigation Pane
Datasheet View

The AutoFilter menu lists all City field values that appear in the recordset. A checkmark next to an entry indicates that records with that City field value appear in the recordset. To filter for selected City field values, you uncheck the cities you don't want selected and leave checked the cities you do want selected. You can click the "(Select All)" check box to select or deselect all field values. The "(Blanks)" option includes null values when checked and excludes null values when unchecked. (Recall that a null field value is the absence of a value for the field.)

3. Click the **(Select All)** check box to deselect all check boxes, click the **Decatur** check box, scroll down the list, and then click the **Stone Mountain** check box.

   The two check boxes indicate that the AutoFilter will include only Decatur and Stone Mountain City field values.

4. Click the **OK** button. The AutoFilter displays the 8 records for patients in Decatur and Stone Mountain who walked in without an appointment or who had a visit in November. See Figure 5–7.

Figure 5–7 **Recordset showing results of an AutoFilter**

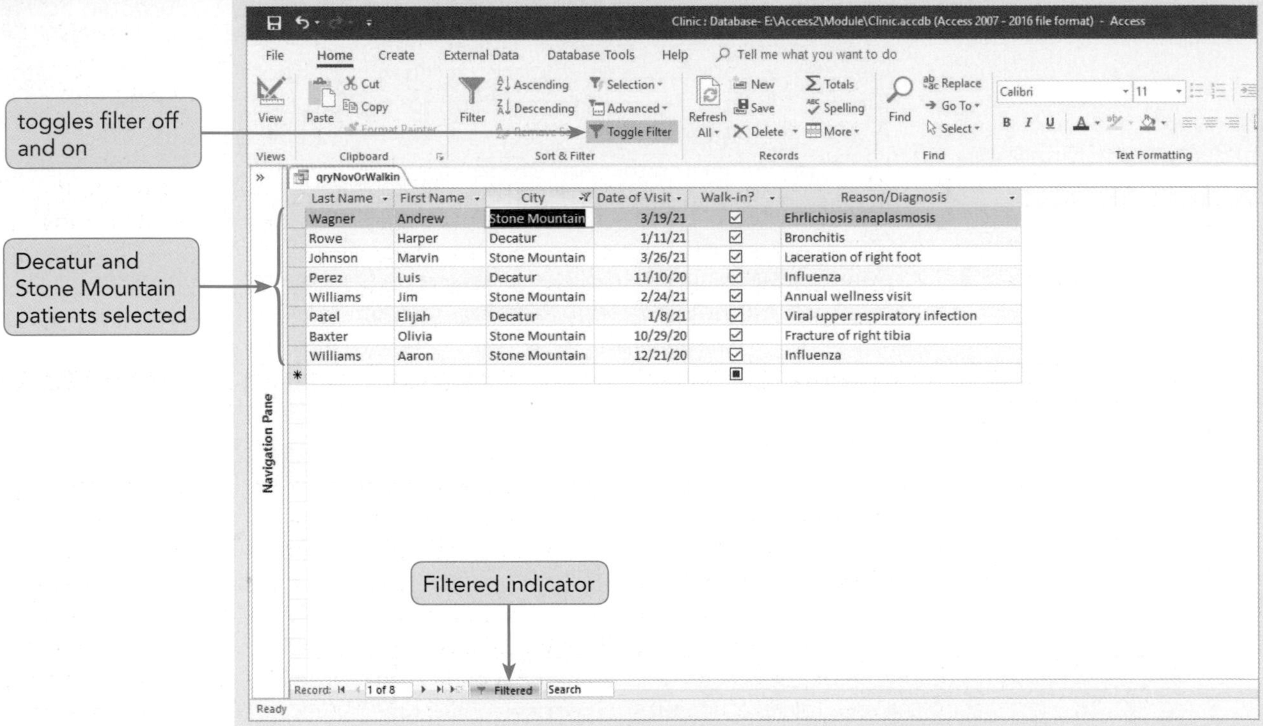

toggles filter off and on
Decatur and Stone Mountain patients selected
Filtered indicator
Toggle Filter
qryNovOrWalkin

5. On the Home tab, in the Sort & Filter group, click the **Toggle Filter** button.

   The filter is removed, and all 41 records appear in the recordset.

6. Click the **Toggle Filter** button. The City filter is applied, displaying the 8 records for patients in Decatur and Stone Mountain.

7. Save the query and close it.

Next, Donna wants to view all fields from the tblPatient table, along with the patient name or the guardian name if the patient has a guardian.

Assigning a Conditional Value to a Calculated Field

If a field in a record does not contain any information at all, it has a null value. Such a field is also referred to as a null field. A field in a record that contains any data at all—even a single space—is nonnull. Records for patients who do not have guardians have nonnull FirstName and LastName field values and null Guardian field values in the tblPatient table, while records for patients with guardians have nonnull values for all three fields. Donna wants to view records from the tblPatient table in order by the Guardian value, if it's nonnull, and at the same time in order by the LastName and then FirstName field values, if the Guardian field value is null. To produce this information for Donna, you need to create a query that includes all fields from the tblPatient table and then add a calculated field that will display the patient name—either the Guardian field value, which is entered using the format LastName, FirstName, or the LastName and FirstName field values, separated by a command and a space.

To combine the LastName and FirstName fields, you'll use the expression *LastName & ", " & FirstName*. The **& (ampersand) operator** is a concatenation operator that joins text expressions. **Concatenation** refers to joining two or more text fields or characters encapsulated in quotes. When you join the LastName field value to the string that contains the comma and space, you are concatenating these two strings. If the LastName field value is Trung and the FirstName field value is Grace, for example, the result of the expression *LastName & ", " & FirstName* is *Trung & ", " & Grace* which results in *Trung, Grace*.

INSIGHT

Using Concatenation

IT professionals generally refer to a piece of text data as a string. Most programming languages include the ability to join two or more strings using concatenation.

Imagine you're working with a database table that contains Title, FirstName, and LastName values for people who have made donations, and you've been asked to add their names to a report. You could add each individual field separately, but the data would look awkward, with each field in a separate column. Alternatively, you could create a calculated field with an expression that combines the fields with spaces into a more readable format, such as "Mr. Jim Sullivan." To do this, you would concatenate the fields with a space separator. The expression to perform this task might look like *=Title & " " & FirstName & " " & LastName*.

To display the correct patient value, you'll use the IIf function. The IIf (Immediate If) function assigns one value to a calculated field or control if a condition is true and a second value if the condition is false. The IIf function has three parts: a condition that is true or false, the result when the condition is true, and the result when the condition is false. Each part of the IIf function is separated by a comma. The condition you'll use is *IsNull(Guardian)*. The IsNull function tests a field value or an expression for a null value. If the field value or expression is null, the result is true; otherwise, the result is false. The expression *IsNull(Guardian)* is true when the Guardian field value is null and is false when the Guardian field value is not null.

For the calculated field, you'll enter *IIf(IsNull(Guardian),LastName & ", " & FirstName,Guardian & " (Guardian)")*. You interpret this expression as follows: If the Guardian field value is null, then set the calculated field value to the concatenation of the LastName field value, the text string ", " and the FirstName field value, which displays the patient's name. If the Guardian field value is not null, then set the calculated field value to the Guardian field value and the text string "(Guardian)" to indicate the displayed name is a patient's guardian.

Now you're ready to create Donna's query to display the patient name.

To create the query to display the patient name:

1. Click the **Create** tab, and then in the Queries group, click the **Query Design** button. The Show Table dialog box opens on top of the Query window in Design View.
2. Click **tblPatient** in the Tables box, click the **Add** button, and then click the **Close** button. The tblPatient table field list is placed in the Query window, and the Show Table dialog box closes.

   Donna wants all fields from the tblPatient table to appear in the query recordset, with the new calculated field in the first column.

3. Drag the bottom border of the tblPatient field list down until all fields are visible, double-click the title bar of the tblPatient field list to highlight all the fields, and then drag the highlighted fields to the second column's Field box in the design grid. Each field is placed in a separate column in the design grid starting with the second column, in the same order that the fields appear in the table.

   Trouble? If you accidentally drag the highlighted fields to the first column in the design grid, click the PatientID Field box, and then in the Query Setup group, click the Insert Columns button. Continue with Step 4.

TIP

After clicking in a box, you can also open its Expression Builder dialog box by holding down CTRL and pressing F2.

4. Right-click the blank Field box to the left of the PatientID field, and then click **Build** on the shortcut menu. The Expression Builder dialog box opens.

   Donna wants to use "Patient" as the name of the calculated field, so you'll type that name, followed by a colon, and then you'll choose the IIf function.

5. Type **Patient:** and then press **SPACEBAR**.
6. Double-click **Functions** in the Expression Elements (left) column, and then click **Built-In Functions**.

Make sure you double-click instead of single-click the IIf function.

7. Scroll down the Expression Categories (middle) column, click **Program Flow**, and then in the Expression Values (right) column, double-click **IIf**. The IIf function is added with four placeholders to the right of the calculated field name in the expression box. See Figure 5–8.

Figure 5–8 IIf function inserted for the calculated field

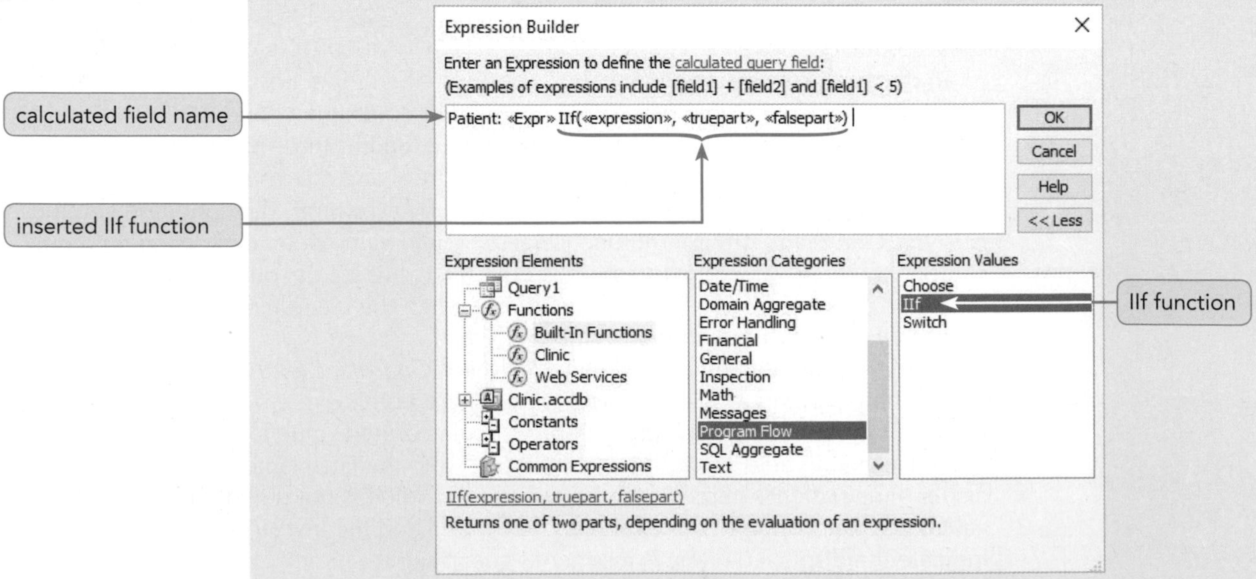
Expression Builder
Enter an Expression to define the calculated query field:
(Examples of expressions include [field1] + [field2] and [field1] < 5)
Patient: «Expr» IIf(«expression», «truepart», «falsepart»)
OK
Cancel
Help
<< Less
Expression Elements
Query1
Functions
Built-In Functions
Clinic
Web Services
Clinic.accdb
Constants
Operators
Common Expressions
Expression Categories
Date/Time
Domain Aggregate
Error Handling
Financial
General
Inspection
Math
Messages
Program Flow
SQL Aggregate
Text
Expression Values
Choose
IIf
Switch
IIf(expression, truepart, falsepart)
Returns one of two parts, depending on the evaluation of an expression.
calculated field name
inserted IIf function
IIf function

The expression you will create does not need the leftmost placeholder (<<Expr>>), so you'll delete it. You'll replace the second placeholder (<<expression>>) with the condition using the IsNull function, the third placeholder (<<truepart>>) with the expression using the & operator and the FirstName and LastName fields, and the fourth placeholder (<<falsepart>>) with the expression using the & operator and the Nickname and LastName fields.

8. Click **<<Expr>>** in the expression box, and then press **DELETE**. The first placeholder is deleted.
9. Click **<<expression>>** in the expression box, and then click **Inspection** in the Expression Categories (middle) column.
10. Double-click **IsNull** in the Expression Values (right) column, click **<<expression>>** in the expression box, and then type **Guardian**. You've completed the entry of the condition in the IIf function. See Figure 5–9.

Figure 5–9 After entering the condition for the calculated field's IIf function

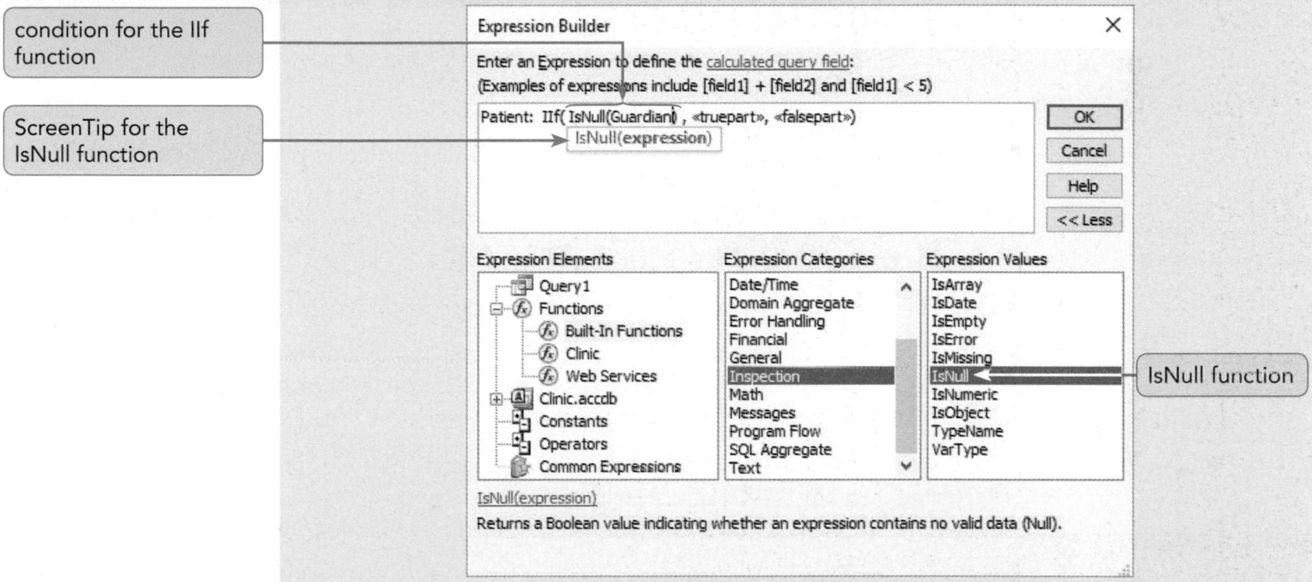
condition for the IIf function
ScreenTip for the IsNull function
IsNull function
Expression Builder
Enter an Expression to define the calculated query field:
(Examples of expressions include [field1] + [field2] and [field1] < 5)
Patient: IIf(IsNull(Guardian) , «truepart», «falsepart»)
IsNull(expression)
OK
Cancel
Help
<< Less
Expression Elements
Expression Categories
Expression Values
Query1
Functions
Built-In Functions
Clinic
Web Services
Clinic.accdb
Constants
Operators
Common Expressions
Date/Time
Domain Aggregate
Error Handling
Financial
General
Inspection
Math
Messages
Program Flow
SQL Aggregate
Text
IsArray
IsDate
IsEmpty
IsError
IsMissing
IsNull
IsNumeric
IsObject
TypeName
VarType
IsNull(expression)
Returns a Boolean value indicating whether an expression contains no valid data (Null).

After you typed the first letter of "Guardian," the Formula AutoComplete box displayed a list of functions beginning with the letter G, and a ScreenTip for the IsNull function was displayed above the box. The box closed after you typed the third letter, but the ScreenTip remains on the screen.

Instead of typing the field name of Guardian in the previous step, you could have double-clicked Clinic.accdb in the Expression Elements column, double-clicked Tables in the Expression Elements column, clicked tblPatient in the Expression Elements column, and then double-clicked Guardian in the Expression Categories column.

Now you'll replace the third placeholder and then the fourth placeholder.

11. Click **<<truepart>>**, and then type **LastName & ", " & FirstName**. Be sure you type a space after the comma within the quotation marks.
12. Click **<<falsepart>>**, and then type **Guardian & " (Guardian)"**. Be sure you type a space after the first quotation mark. See Figure 5–10.

Figure 5–10 Completed calculated field

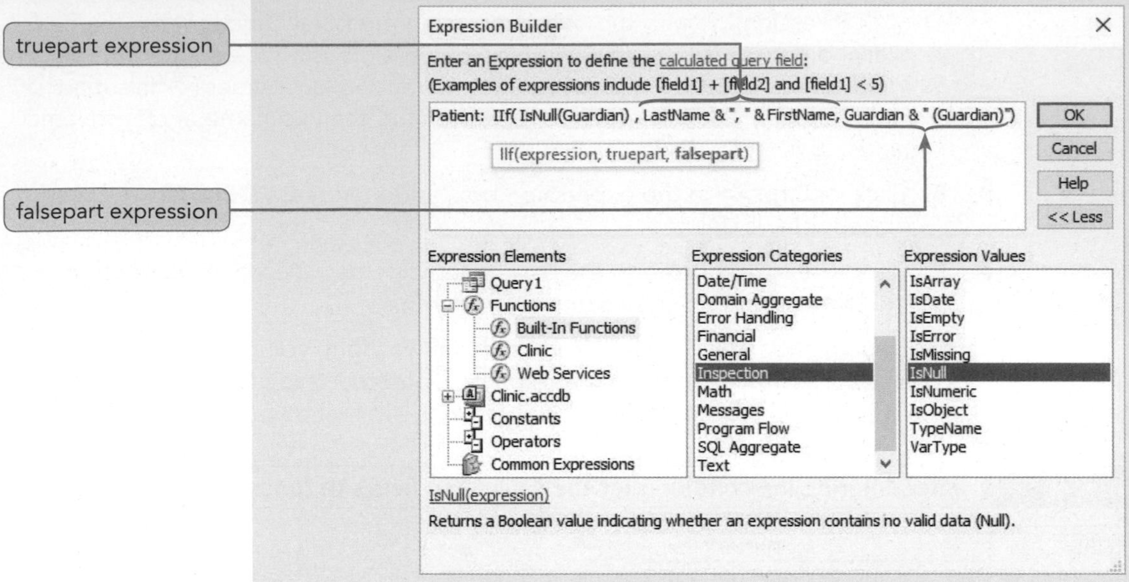
truepart expression
falsepart expression
Expression Builder
Enter an Expression to define the calculated query field:
(Examples of expressions include [field1] + [field2] and [field1] < 5)
Patient: IIf(IsNull(Guardian) , LastName & ", " & FirstName, Guardian & " (Guardian)")
IIf(expression, truepart, falsepart)
OK
Cancel
Help
<< Less
Expression Elements
Query1
Functions
Built-In Functions
Clinic
Web Services
Clinic.accdb
Constants
Operators
Common Expressions
Expression Categories
Date/Time
Domain Aggregate
Error Handling
Financial
General
Inspection
Math
Messages
Program Flow
SQL Aggregate
Text
Expression Values
IsArray
IsDate
IsEmpty
IsError
IsMissing
IsNull
IsNumeric
IsObject
TypeName
VarType
IsNull(expression)
Returns a Boolean value indicating whether an expression contains no valid data (Null).

Donna wants the query to sort records in ascending order by the Patient calculated field.

To sort, save, and run the query:

TIP

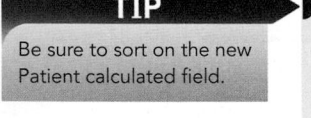

Be sure to sort on the new Patient calculated field.

1. Click the **OK** button in the Expression Builder dialog box to close it.
2. Click the right side of the Patient Sort box to display the sort order options, and then click **Ascending**. The query will display the records in alphabetical order based on the Patient field values.

   The calculated field name of Patient consists of a single word, so you do not need to set the Caption property for it. However, you'll review the properties for the calculated field by opening its property sheet.
3. On the Query Tools Design tab, in the Show/Hide group, click the **Property Sheet** button. The property sheet opens and displays the properties for the Patient calculated field. See Figure 5–11.

Figure 5–11 Property sheet for the Patient calculated field

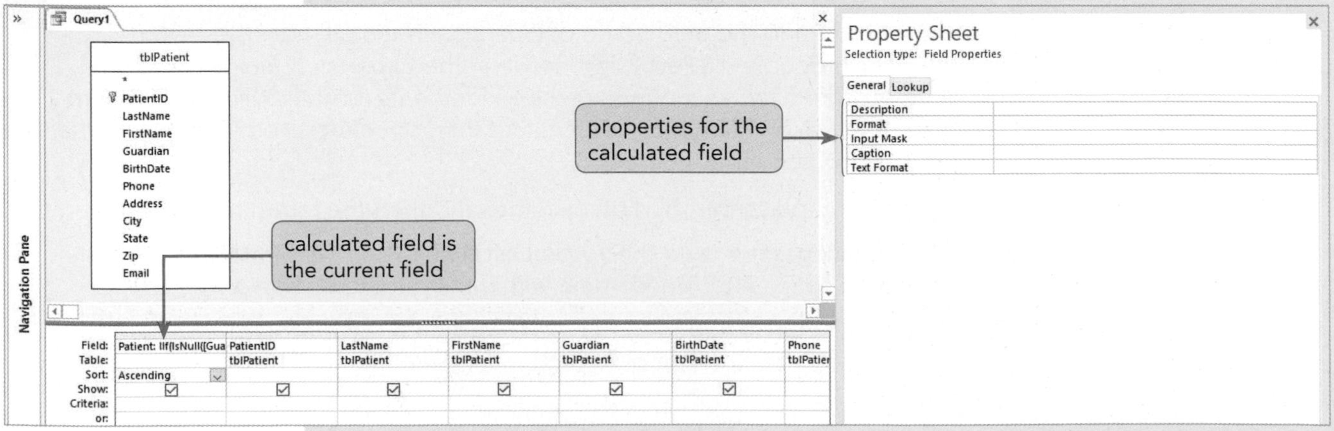
Query1
tblPatient
PatientID
LastName
FirstName
Guardian
BirthDate
Phone
Address
City
State
Zip
Email
Navigation Pane
properties for the calculated field
calculated field is the current field
Property Sheet
Selection type: Field Properties
General
Lookup
Description
Format
Input Mask
Caption
Text Format
Field:
Table:
Sort:
Show:
Criteria:
or:
Patient: IIf(IsNull([Gua
Ascending
PatientID
LastName
FirstName
Guardian
BirthDate
Phone

Among the properties for the calculated field, which is the current field, is the Caption property. Leaving the Caption property set to null means that the column name for the calculated field in the query recordset will be Patient, which is the calculated field name. The Property Sheet button is a toggle, so you'll click it again to close the property sheet.

4. Click the **Property Sheet** button again to close the property sheet.
5. Save the query as **qryPatientsByName**, run the query, and then resize the Patient column to its best fit. All records from the tblPatient table are displayed in alphabetical order by the Patient field. See Figure 5–12.

Figure 5–12 **Completed query displaying the Patient calculated field**

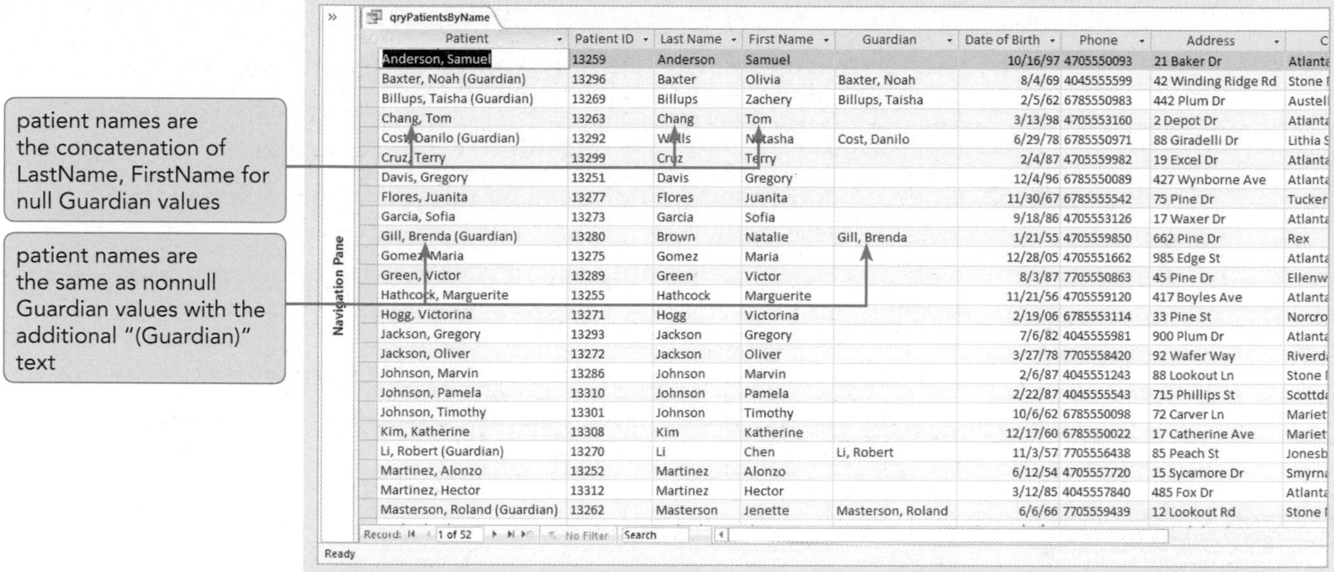
patient names are the concatenation of LastName, FirstName for null Guardian values
patient names are the same as nonnull Guardian values with the additional "(Guardian)" text
qryPatientsByName
Navigation Pane
Record: 1 of 52
No Filter
Search
Ready

Patient	Patient ID	Last Name	First Name	Guardian	Date of Birth	Phone	Address	C
Anderson, Samuel	13259	Anderson	Samuel		10/16/97	4705550093	21 Baker Dr	Atlanta
Baxter, Noah (Guardian)	13296	Baxter	Olivia	Baxter, Noah	8/4/69	4045555599	42 Winding Ridge Rd	Stone
Billups, Taisha (Guardian)	13269	Billups	Zachery	Billups, Taisha	2/5/62	6785550983	442 Plum Dr	Austell
Chang, Tom	13263	Chang	Tom		3/13/98	4705553160	2 Depot Dr	Atlanta
Cost, Danilo (Guardian)	13292	Wells	Natasha	Cost, Danilo	6/29/78	6785550971	88 Giradelli Dr	Lithia S
Cruz, Terry	13299	Cruz	Terry		2/4/87	4705559982	19 Excel Dr	Atlanta
Davis, Gregory	13251	Davis	Gregory		12/4/96	6785550089	427 Wynborne Ave	Atlanta
Flores, Juanita	13277	Flores	Juanita		11/30/67	6785555542	75 Pine Dr	Tucker
Garcia, Sofia	13273	Garcia	Sofia		9/18/86	4705553126	17 Waxer Dr	Atlanta
Gill, Brenda (Guardian)	13280	Brown	Natalie	Gill, Brenda	1/21/55	4705559850	662 Pine Dr	Rex
Gomez, Maria	13275	Gomez	Maria		12/28/05	4705551662	985 Edge St	Atlanta
Green, Victor	13289	Green	Victor		8/3/87	7705550863	45 Pine Dr	Ellenw
Hathcock, Marguerite	13255	Hathcock	Marguerite		11/21/56	4705559120	417 Boyles Ave	Atlanta
Hogg, Victorina	13271	Hogg	Victorina		2/19/06	6785553114	33 Pine St	Norcro
Jackson, Gregory	13293	Jackson	Gregory		7/6/82	4045555981	900 Plum Dr	Atlanta
Jackson, Oliver	13272	Jackson	Oliver		3/27/78	7705558420	92 Wafer Way	Riverd
Johnson, Marvin	13286	Johnson	Marvin		2/6/87	4045551243	88 Lookout Ln	Stone
Johnson, Pamela	13310	Johnson	Pamela		2/22/87	4045555543	715 Phillips St	Scottd
Johnson, Timothy	13301	Johnson	Timothy		10/6/62	6785550098	72 Carver Ln	Mariet
Kim, Katherine	13308	Kim	Katherine		12/17/60	6785550022	17 Catherine Ave	Mariet
Li, Robert (Guardian)	13270	Li	Chen	Li, Robert	11/3/57	7705556438	85 Peach St	Jonesb
Martinez, Alonzo	13252	Martinez	Alonzo		6/12/54	4705557720	15 Sycamore Dr	Smyrn
Martinez, Hector	13312	Martinez	Hector		3/12/85	4045557840	485 Fox Dr	Atlanta
Masterson, Roland (Guardian)	13262	Masterson	Jenette	Masterson, Roland	6/6/66	7705559439	12 Lookout Rd	Stone

6. Save and close the query.

You're now ready to create the query to satisfy Donna's request for information about patients in a particular city.

Creating a Parameter Query

Donna's next request is for records in the qryPatientsByName query for patients in a particular city. For this query, she wants to specify a city, such as Decatur or Stone Mountain, each time she runs the query.

To create this query, you will copy, rename, and modify the qryPatientsByName query. You could create a simple condition using an exact match for the City field, but you would need to change it in Design view every time you run the query. Alternatively, Donna or a member of her staff could filter the qryPatientsByName query for the city records they want to view. Instead, you will create a parameter query. A **parameter query** displays a dialog box that prompts the user to enter one or more criteria values when the query is run. In this case, you want to create a query that prompts for the city and selects only those patient records with that City field value from the table. You will enter the prompt in the Criteria box for the City field. When the query runs, it will open a dialog box and prompt you to enter the city. The query results will then be created, just as if you had changed the criteria in Design view.

REFERENCE

Creating a Parameter Query

- Create a select query that includes all fields to appear in the query results.
- Choose the sort fields, and set the criteria that do not change when you run the query.
- Decide which fields to use as prompts when the query runs. In the Criteria box for each of these fields, type the prompt you want to appear in a dialog box when you run the query, and enclose the prompt in brackets.

You'll copy and rename the qryPatientsByName query now, and then you'll change its design to create the parameter query.

To create the parameter query based on an existing query:

1. Open the Navigation Pane, copy and paste the qryPatientsByName query, and then name the new copy **qryPatientsByCityParameter**.
2. Open the **qryPatientsByCityParameter** query in Design view, and then close the Navigation Pane.

   Next, you must enter the criterion for the parameter query. In this case, Donna wants the query to prompt users to enter the city for the patient records they want to view. You need to enter the prompt in the Criteria box for the City field. Brackets must enclose the text of the prompt.
3. Click the **City Criteria** box, type **[Type the city:]** and then press **ENTER**. See Figure 5–13.

Figure 5–13 **Specifying the prompt for the parameter query**

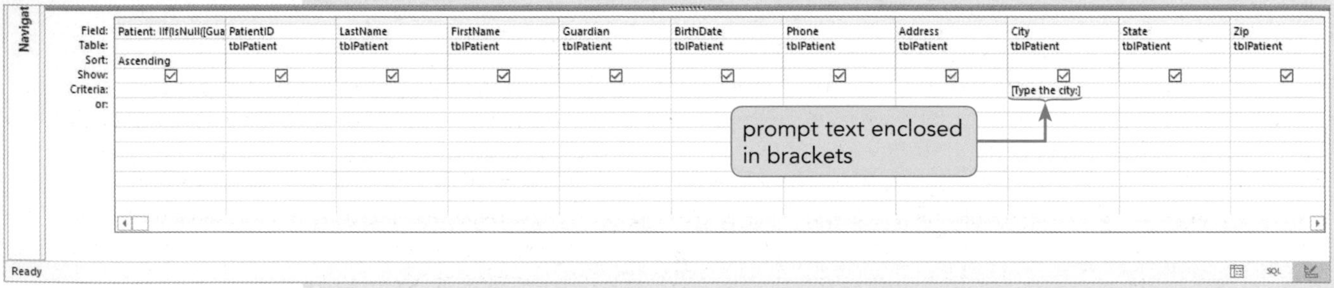
Navigat
Field:
Table:
Sort:
Show:
Criteria:
or:
Patient: IIf(IsNull([Gua
Ascending
PatientID
tblPatient
LastName
tblPatient
FirstName
tblPatient
Guardian
tblPatient
BirthDate
tblPatient
Phone
tblPatient
Address
tblPatient
City
tblPatient
[Type the city:]
State
tblPatient
Zip
tblPatient
prompt text enclosed in brackets
Ready

4. Save and run the query. A dialog box is displayed, prompting you for the name of the city. See Figure 5–14.

Figure 5–14 **Enter Parameter Value dialog box**

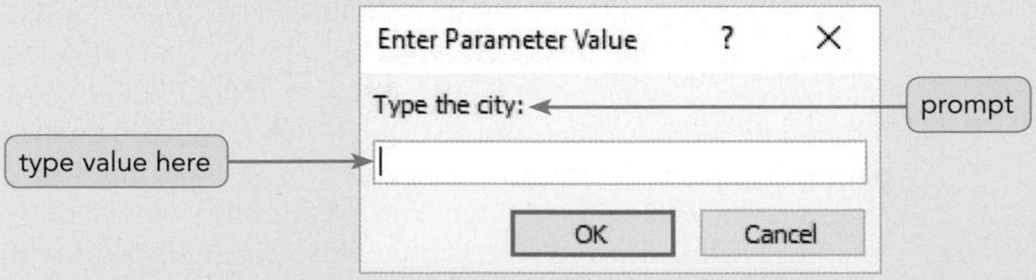
Enter Parameter Value
?
Type the city:
prompt
type value here
OK
Cancel

TIP

You must enter a value that matches the spelling of a City field value, but you can use either lowercase or uppercase letters.

The bracketed text you specified in the Criteria box of the City field appears above a box, in which you must type a City field value. Donna wants to see all patients in Decatur.

5. Type **Decatur**, press **ENTER**, and then scroll the datasheet to the right, if necessary, to display the City field values. The recordset displays the data for the three patients in Decatur. See Figure 5–15.

Figure 5–15 **Results of the parameter query**

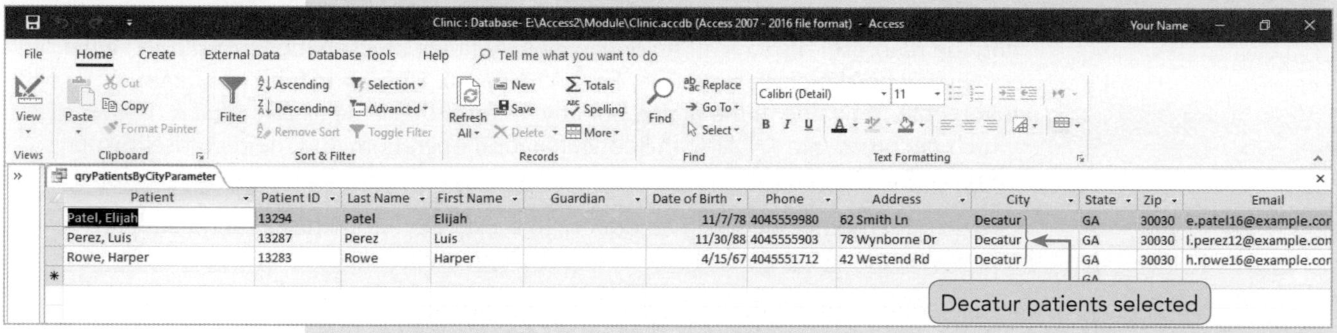
Clinic : Database- E:\Access2\Module\Clinic.accdb (Access 2007 - 2016 file format) - Access
Your Name
File
Home
Create
External Data
Database Tools
Help
Tell me what you want to do
qryPatientsByCityParameter
Patient
Patient ID
Last Name
First Name
Guardian
Date of Birth
Phone
Address
City
State
Zip
Email
Patel, Elijah 13294 Patel Elijah 11/7/78 4045559980 62 Smith Ln Decatur GA 30030 e.patel16@example.com
Perez, Luis 13287 Perez Luis 11/30/88 4045555903 78 Wynborne Dr Decatur GA 30030 l.perez12@example.com
Rowe, Harper 13283 Rowe Harper 4/15/67 4045551712 42 Westend Rd Decatur GA 30030 h.rowe16@example.com
Decatur patients selected

Donna asks what happens if she doesn't enter a value in the dialog box when she runs the qryPatientsByCityParameter query. You can run the query again to show Donna the answer to her question.

6. Switch to Design view, and then run the query. The Enter Parameter Value dialog box opens.

   If you click the OK button or press ENTER, you'll run the parameter query without entering a value for the City field criterion.

7. Click the **OK** button. No records are displayed in the query results.

When you run the parameter query and enter "Decatur" in the dialog box, the query runs just as if you had entered "Decatur" in the City Criteria box in the design grid and displays all Decatur patient records. When you do not enter a value in the dialog box, the query runs as if you had entered "null" in the City Criteria box. Because none of the records has a null City field value, no records are displayed. Donna asks if there's a way to display records for a selected City field value when she enters its value in the dialog box and to display all records when she doesn't enter a value.

Creating a More Flexible Parameter Query

Most users want a parameter query to display the records that match the parameter value the user enters or to display all records when the user doesn't enter a parameter value. To provide this functionality, you can change the value in the Criteria box in the design grid for the specified column. For example, you could change an entry for a City field from *[Type the city:]* to *Like [Type the city:] & "*"*. That is, you can prefix the Like operator to the original criterion and concatenate the criterion to a wildcard character. When you run the parameter query with this new entry, one of the following recordsets will be displayed:

- If you enter a specific City field value in the dialog box, such as *Smyrna*, the entry is the same as *Like "Smyrna" & "*"*, which becomes *Like "Smyrna*"* after the concatenation operation. That is, all records are selected whose City field values have Smyrna in the first six positions and any characters in the remaining positions. If the table on which the query is based contains records with City field values of Smyrna, only those records are displayed. However, if the table on which the query is based also contains records with City field values of Smyrna City, then both the Smyrna and the Smyrna City records would be displayed.
- If you enter a letter in the dialog box, such as *S*, the entry is the same as *Like "S*"*, and the recordset displays all records with City field values that begin with the letter S, which would include Scottdale, Smyrna, Smyrna City, and Stone Mountain.
- If you enter no value in the dialog box, the entry is the same as *Like Null & "*"*, which becomes *Like "*"* after the concatenation operation, and the recordset displays all records.

Now you'll modify the parameter query to satisfy Donna's request, and you'll test the new version of the query.

To modify and test the parameter query:

1. Switch to Design view.
2. Click the **City Criteria** box, and then open the **Zoom** dialog box.

   You'll use the Zoom dialog box to modify the value in the City Criteria box.
3. Click to the left of the expression in the Zoom dialog box, type **Like**, press **SPACEBAR**, and then press **END**.
4. Press **SPACEBAR**, type **&**, press **SPACEBAR**, and then type **"*"** as shown in Figure 5–16.

   Be sure you type "*" at the end of the expression.

Figure 5–16 Modified City Criteria value in the Zoom dialog box

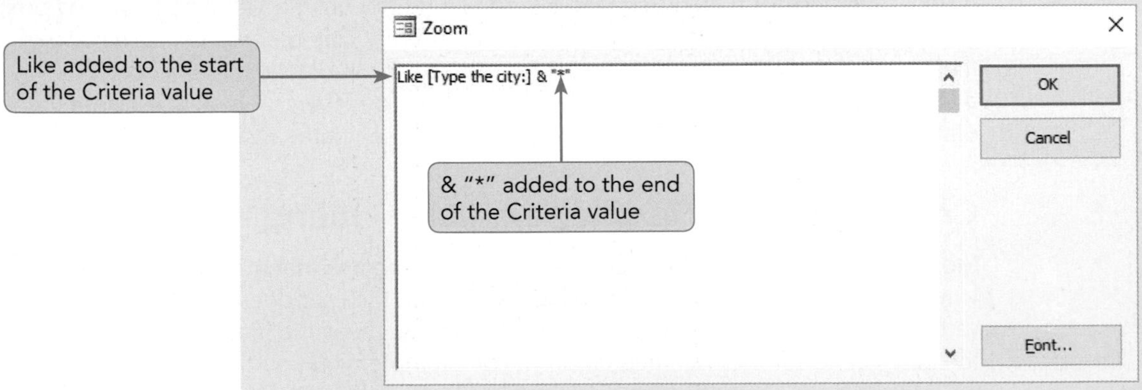
Like added to the start of the Criteria value
Zoom
Like [Type the city:] & "*"
OK
Cancel
& "*" added to the end of the Criteria value
Font...

Now you can test the modified parameter query.

5. Click the **OK** button to close the Zoom dialog box, save your query design changes, and then run the query.

   First, you'll test the query to display patients in Decatur.

6. Type **Decatur**, and then press **ENTER**. The recordset displays the data for the three patients in Decatur.

   Now you'll test the query without entering a value when prompted.

7. Switch to Design view, run the query, and then click the **OK** button. The recordset displays all 52 original records from the tblPatient table.

   Finally, you'll test how the query performs when you enter S in the dialog box.

8. On the Home tab, in the Records group, click the **Refresh All** button to open the Enter Parameter Value dialog box.

9. Type **S**, press **ENTER**, and then scroll to the right, if necessary, to display the City field values. The recordset displays the nine records for patients in Scottdale, Smyrna, and Stone Mountain.

10. Close the query.

11. If you are not continuing on to the next session, close the Clinic database, and then click the **Yes** button if necessary to empty the Clipboard.

The queries you created will make the Clinic database easier to use. In the next session, you'll use query wizards to create three different types of queries, and you'll use Design view to create a top values query.

REVIEW

Session 5.1 Quick Check

1. According to the naming conventions used in this session, you use the __________ prefix tag to identify queries.
2. Which comparison operator selects records based on a specific pattern?
3. What is the purpose of the asterisk (*) in a pattern match query?
4. When do you use the In comparison operator?
5. How do you negate a selection criterion?
6. The ___________ function returns one of two values based on whether the condition being tested is true or false.
7. When do you use a parameter query?

Session 5.2 Visual Overview:

A **crosstab query** uses aggregate functions such as Sum and Count to perform arithmetic operations on selected records.

A simple query selects records from one or more tables that satisfy criteria.

A **find duplicates query** is a select query that finds duplicate records in a table or query.

A **find unmatched query** is a select query that finds all records in a table or query that have no related records in a second table or query.

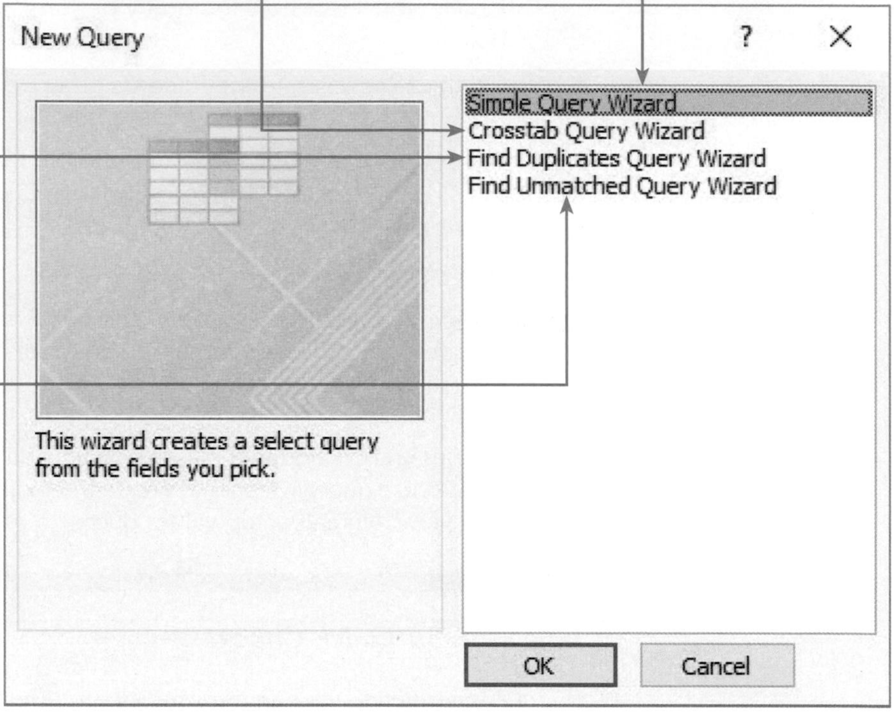
New Query
?
Simple Query Wizard
Crosstab Query Wizard
Find Duplicates Query Wizard
Find Unmatched Query Wizard
This wizard creates a select query from the fields you pick.
OK
Cancel

Each column and row intersection will display the sum of the InvoiceAmt values.

The selected field (InvoiceAmt) is used in the calculations for each column and row intersection.

This option determines whether to display an overall totals column in the crosstab query.

The crosstab query will display one column for the paid invoices and a second column for the unpaid invoices.

The crosstab query will display one row for each unique City field value.

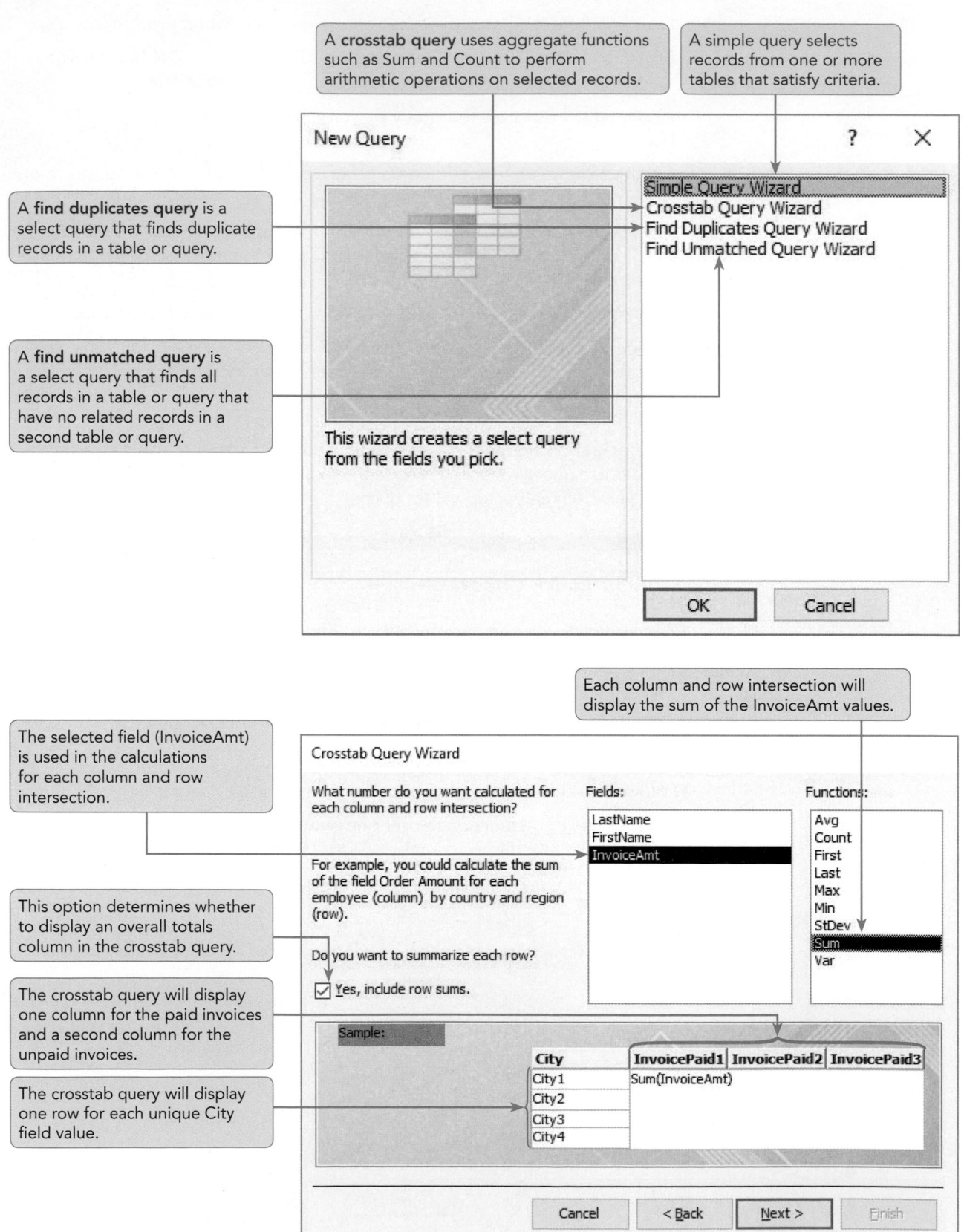

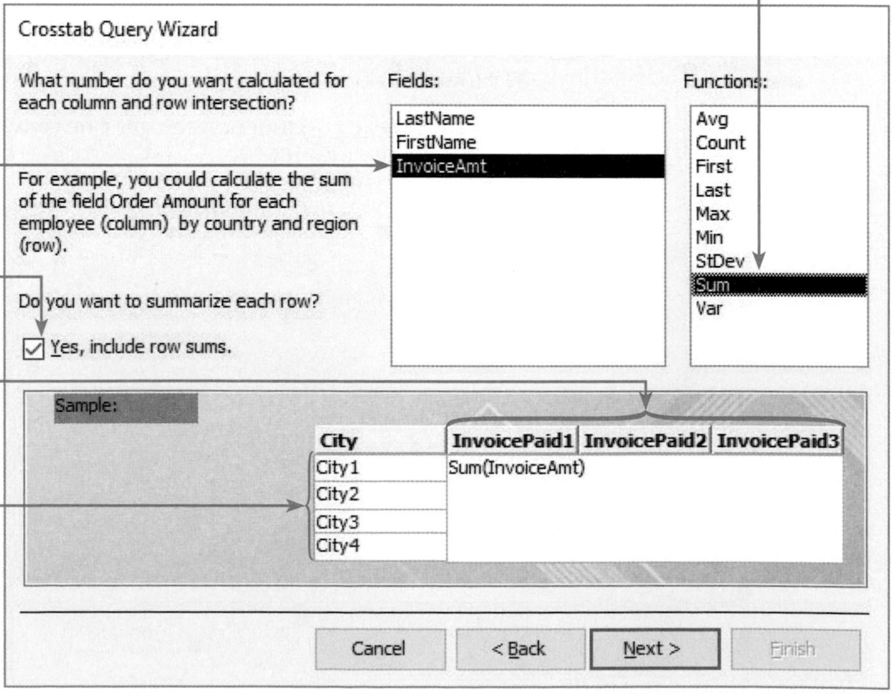
Crosstab Query Wizard
What number do you want calculated for each column and row intersection?
Fields:
Functions:
LastName
FirstName
InvoiceAmt
Avg
Count
First
Last
Max
Min
StDev
Sum
Var
For example, you could calculate the sum of the field Order Amount for each employee (column) by country and region (row).
Do you want to summarize each row?
Yes, include row sums.
Sample:
City
InvoicePaid1
InvoicePaid2
InvoicePaid3
City1
City2
City3
City4
Sum(InvoiceAmt)
Cancel
< Back
Next >
Finish

Advanced Query Wizards

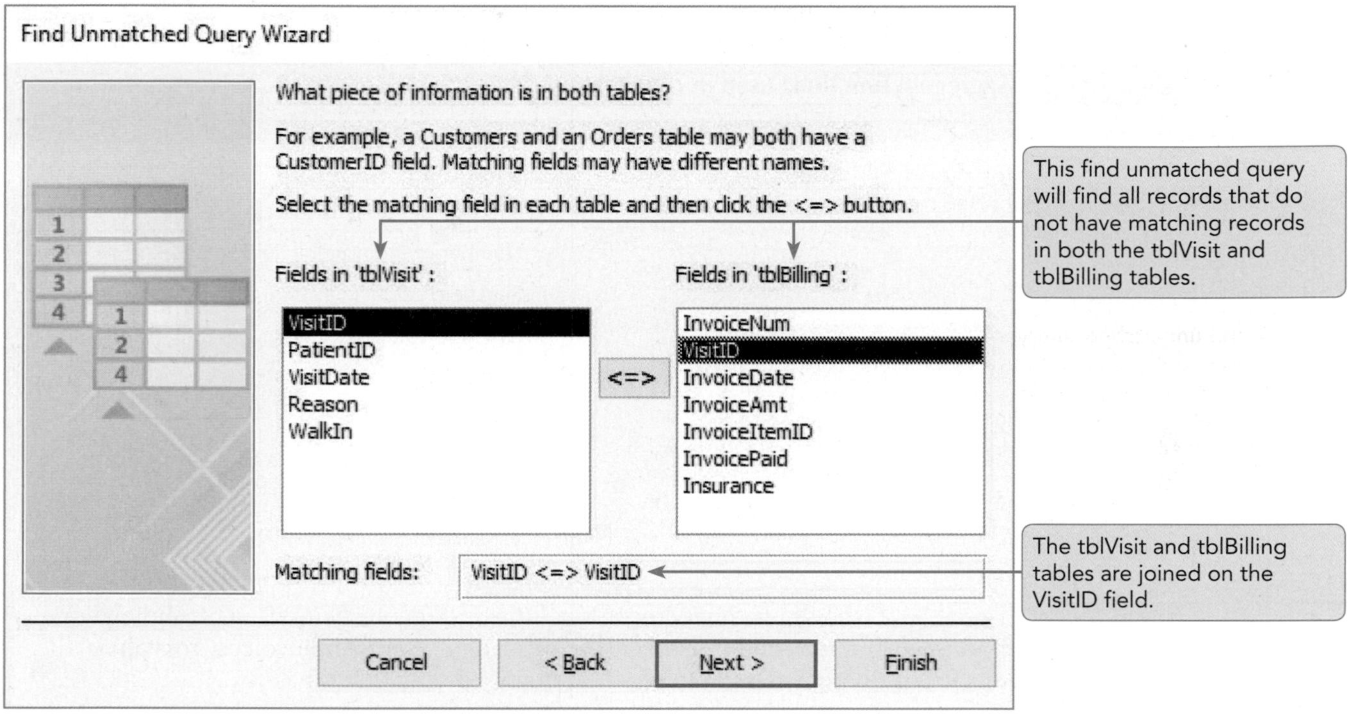
Find Unmatched Query Wizard
What piece of information is in both tables?
For example, a Customers and an Orders table may both have a CustomerID field. Matching fields may have different names.
Select the matching field in each table and then click the <=> button.
Fields in 'tblVisit' :
VisitID
PatientID
VisitDate
Reason
WalkIn
Fields in 'tblBilling' :
InvoiceNum
VisitID
InvoiceDate
InvoiceAmt
InvoiceItemID
InvoicePaid
Insurance
<=>
Matching fields:
VisitID <=> VisitID
Cancel
< Back
Next >
Finish
This find unmatched query will find all records that do not have matching records in both the tblVisit and tblBilling tables.
The tblVisit and tblBilling tables are joined on the VisitID field.

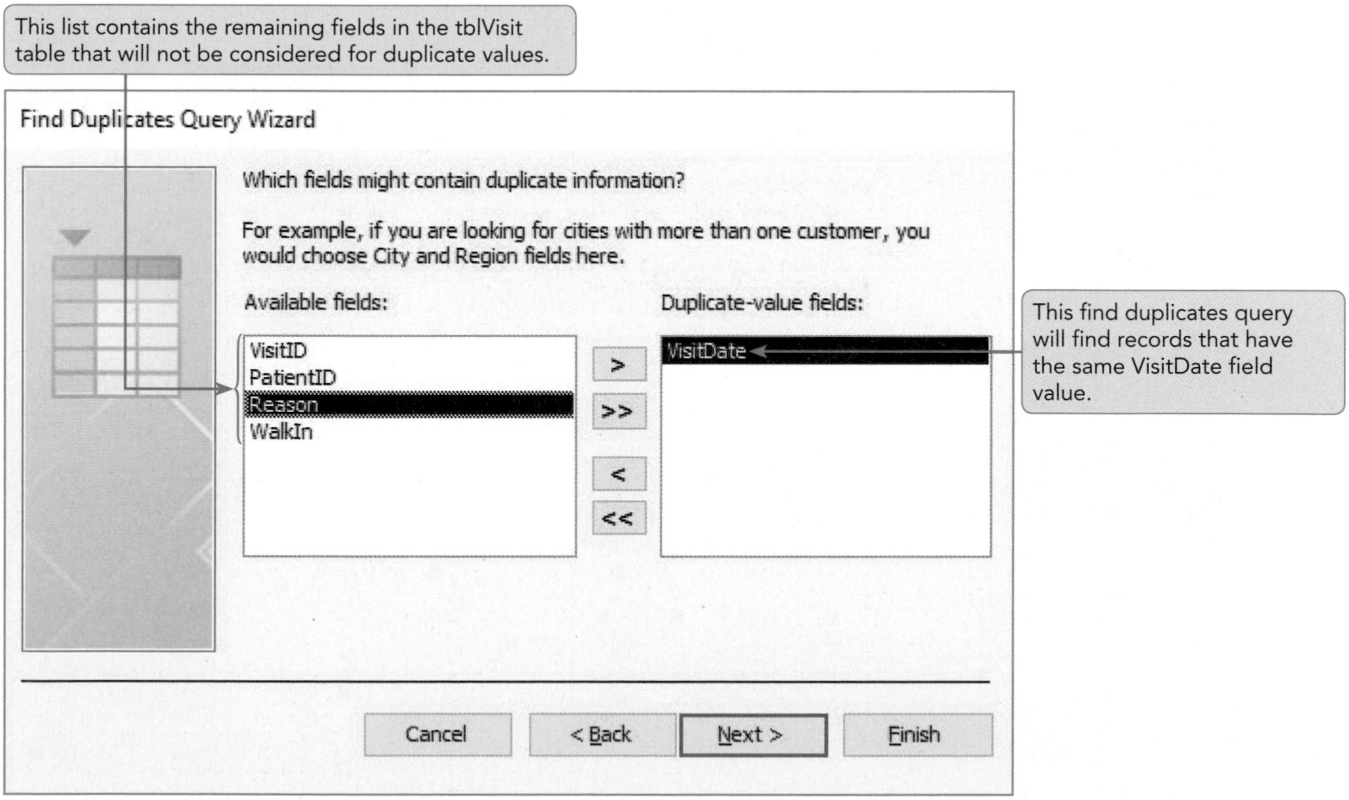
This list contains the remaining fields in the tblVisit table that will not be considered for duplicate values.
Find Duplicates Query Wizard
Which fields might contain duplicate information?
For example, if you are looking for cities with more than one customer, you would choose City and Region fields here.
Available fields:
VisitID
PatientID
Reason
WalkIn
Duplicate-value fields:
VisitDate
>
>>
<
<<
Cancel
< Back
Next >
Finish
This find duplicates query will find records that have the same VisitDate field value.

Creating a Crosstab Query

Donna wants to analyze the Lakewood Community Health Services invoices by city, so she can view the paid and unpaid invoice amounts for all patients located in each city. Crosstab queries use the aggregate functions shown in Figure 5–17 to perform arithmetic operations on selected records. A crosstab query can also display one additional aggregate function value that summarizes the set of values in each row. The crosstab query uses one or more fields for the row headings on the left and one field for the column headings at the top.

Figure 5–17 Aggregate functions used in crosstab queries

Aggregate Function	Definition
Avg	Average of the field values
Count	Number of the nonnull field values
First	First field value
Last	Last field value
Max	Highest field value
Min	Lowest field value
StDev	Standard deviation of the field values
Sum	Total of the field values
Var	Variance of the field values

Figure 5–18 shows two query recordsets—the first recordset (qryPatientsAndInvoices) is from a select query, and the second recordset (qryPatientsAndInvoicesCrosstab) is from a crosstab query based on the select query.

Figure 5–18 **Comparing a select query to a crosstab query**

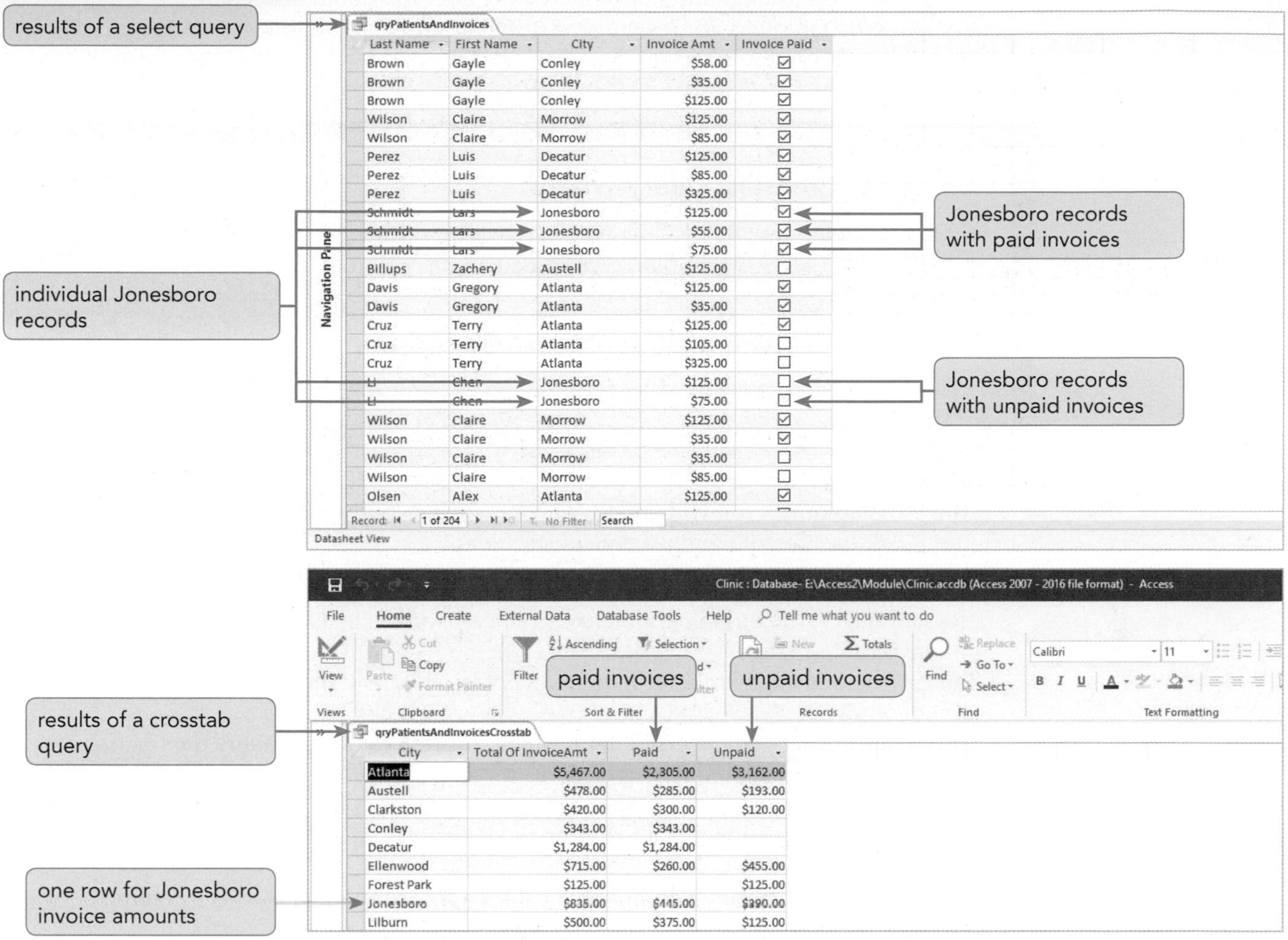
results of a select query
individual Jonesboro records
Jonesboro records with paid invoices
Jonesboro records with unpaid invoices
results of a crosstab query
paid invoices
unpaid invoices
one row for Jonesboro invoice amounts
qryPatientsAndInvoices
qryPatientsAndInvoicesCrosstab

The qryPatientsAndInvoices query, a select query, joins the tblPatient, tblVisit, and tblBilling tables to display selected data from those tables for all invoices. The qryPatientsAndInvoicesCrosstab query, a crosstab query, uses the qryPatientsAndInvoices query as its source query and displays one row for each unique City field value. The City column in the crosstab query identifies each row. The crosstab query uses the Sum aggregate function on the InvoiceAmt field to produce the displayed values in the Paid and Unpaid columns for each City row. An entry in the Total Of InvoiceAmt column represents the sum of the Paid and Unpaid values for the City field value in that row.

PROSKILLS

Decision Making: Using Select Queries and Crosstab Queries

Companies use both select queries and crosstab queries in their decision making. A select query displays several records—one for each row selected by the select query—while a crosstab query displays only one summarized record for each unique field value. When managers want to analyze data at a high level to see the big picture, they might start with a crosstab query, identify which field values to analyze further, and then look in detail at specific field values using select queries. Both select and crosstab queries serve as valuable tools in tracking and analyzing a company's business, and companies use both types of queries in the appropriate situations. By understanding how managers and other employees use the information in a database to make decisions, you can create the correct type of query to provide the information they need.

TIP

Microsoft Access Help provides more information on creating a crosstab query without using a wizard.

The quickest way to create a crosstab query is to use the **Crosstab Query Wizard**, which guides you through the steps for creating one. You could also change a select query to a crosstab query in Design view using the Crosstab button in the Query Type group on the Query Tools Design tab.

REFERENCE

Using the Crosstab Query Wizard

- On the Create tab, in the Queries group, click the Query Wizard button.
- In the New Query dialog box, click Crosstab Query Wizard, and then click the OK button.
- Complete the Wizard dialog boxes to select the table or query on which to base the crosstab query, select the row heading field (or fields), select the column heading field, select the calculation field and its aggregate function, and enter a name for the crosstab query.

The crosstab query you will create, which is similar to the one shown in Figure 5–18, has the following characteristics:

- The qryPatientsAndInvoices query in the Clinic database is the basis for the new crosstab query. The base query includes the LastName, FirstName, City, InvoiceAmt, and InvoicePaid fields.
- The City field is the leftmost column in the crosstab query and identifies each crosstab query row.
- The values from the InvoicePaid field, which is a Yes/No field, identify the rightmost columns of the crosstab query.
- The crosstab query applies the Sum aggregate function to the InvoiceAmt field values and displays the resulting total values in the Paid and Unpaid columns of the query results.
- The grand total of the InvoiceAmt field values appears for each row in a column with the heading Total Of InvoiceAmt.

Next you will create the crosstab query based on the qryPatientsAndInvoices query.

To start the Crosstab Query Wizard:

1. If you took a break after the previous session, make sure that the Clinic database is open and the Navigation Pane is closed.

   Trouble? If the security warning is displayed below the ribbon, click the Enable Content button next to the security warning.

2. Click the **Create** tab on the ribbon.
3. In the Queries group, click the **Query Wizard** button. The New Query dialog box opens.
4. Click **Crosstab Query Wizard**, and then click the **OK** button. The first Crosstab Query Wizard dialog box opens.

You'll now use the Crosstab Query Wizard to create the crosstab query for Donna.

To finish the Crosstab Query Wizard:

1. In the View section, click the **Queries** option button to display the list of queries in the Clinic database, and then click **Query: qryPatientsAndInvoices**. See Figure 5–19.

Figure 5–19 **Choosing the query for the crosstab query**

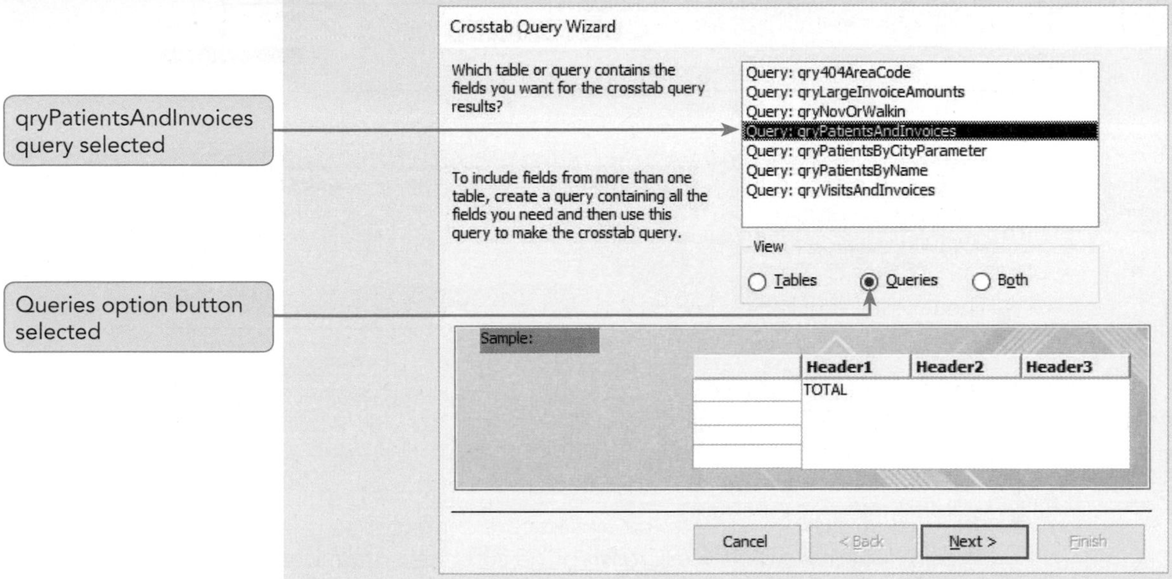

qryPatientsAndInvoices query selected
Queries option button selected
Crosstab Query Wizard
Which table or query contains the fields you want for the crosstab query results?
To include fields from more than one table, create a query containing all the fields you need and then use this query to make the crosstab query.
Query: qry404AreaCode
Query: qryLargeInvoiceAmounts
Query: qryNovOrWalkin
Query: qryPatientsAndInvoices
Query: qryPatientsByCityParameter
Query: qryPatientsByName
Query: qryVisitsAndInvoices
View
Tables
Queries
Both
Sample:
Header1
Header2
Header3
TOTAL
Cancel
< Back
Next >
Finish

2. Click the **Next** button to open the next Crosstab Query Wizard dialog box. This is the dialog box where you choose the field (or fields) for the *row* headings. Because Donna wants the crosstab query to display one row for each unique City field value, you will select that field for the row headings.

TIP

When you select a field, the sample crosstab query in the dialog box changes to illustrate your choice.

3. In the Available Fields box, click **City**, and then click the **Select Single Field** button > to move the City field to the Selected Fields box.
4. Click the **Next** button to open the next Crosstab Query Wizard dialog box, in which you select the field values that will serve as column headings. Donna wants to see the paid and unpaid total invoice amounts, so you need to select the InvoicePaid field for the column headings.
5. Click **InvoicePaid** in the box, and then click the **Next** button.

   In the next Crosstab Query Wizard dialog box, you choose the field that will be calculated for each row and column intersection and the function to use for the calculation. The results of the calculation will appear in the row and column intersections in the query results. Donna needs to calculate the sum of the InvoiceAmt field value for each row and column intersection.
6. Click **InvoiceAmt** in the Fields box, click **Sum** in the Functions box, and then make sure that the "Yes, include row sums" check box is checked. The "Yes, include row sums" option creates a column showing the overall totals for the values in each row of the query recordset. See Figure 5–20.

Figure 5–20 Completed crosstab query design

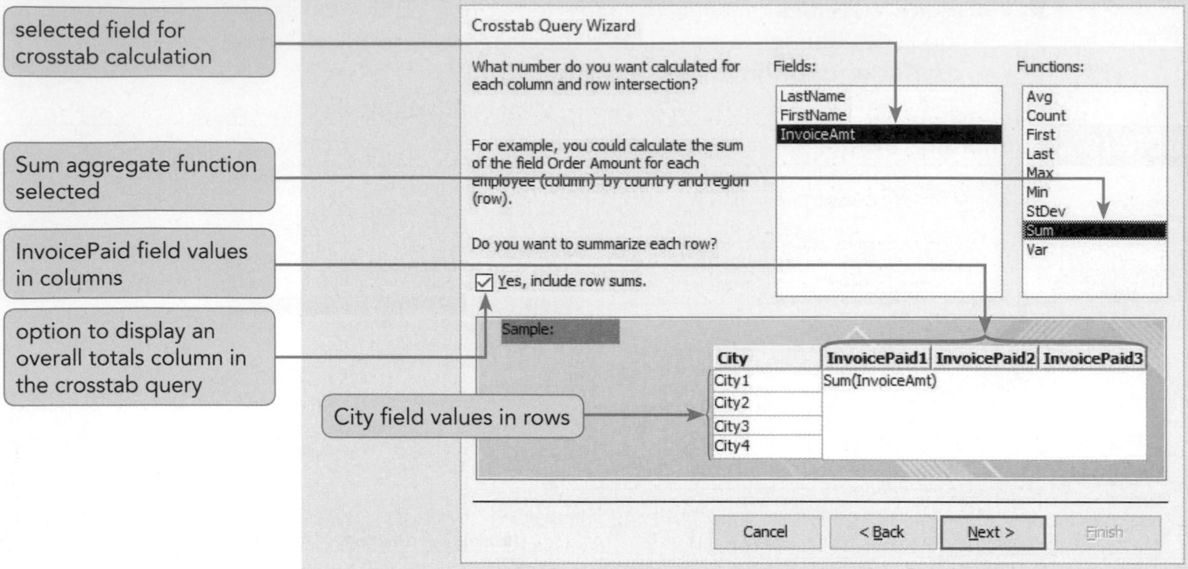
selected field for crosstab calculation
Sum aggregate function selected
InvoicePaid field values in columns
option to display an overall totals column in the crosstab query
City field values in rows
Crosstab Query Wizard
What number do you want calculated for each column and row intersection?
For example, you could calculate the sum of the field Order Amount for each employee (column) by country and region (row).
Do you want to summarize each row?
Yes, include row sums.
Fields:
LastName
FirstName
InvoiceAmt
Functions:
Avg
Count
First
Last
Max
Min
StDev
Sum
Var
Sample:
City
InvoicePaid1
InvoicePaid2
InvoicePaid3
City1
City2
City3
City4
Sum(InvoiceAmt)
Cancel
< Back
Next >
Finish

7. Click the **Next** button to open the final Crosstab Query Wizard dialog box, in which you choose the query name.
8. Click in the box, delete the underscore character so that the query name is qryPatientsAndInvoicesCrosstab, be sure the option button for viewing the query is selected, and then click the **Finish** button. The crosstab query is saved, and then the query recordset is displayed.
9. Resize all the columns in the query recordset to their best fit, and then click the City field value in the first row (**Atlanta**). See Figure 5–21.

Figure 5–21 Crosstab query recordset

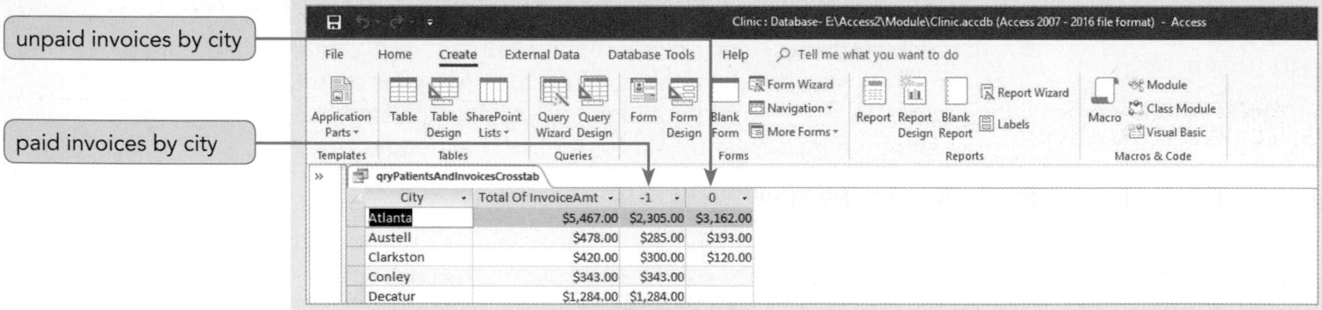
unpaid invoices by city
paid invoices by city
Clinic : Database- E:\Access2\Module\Clinic.accdb (Access 2007 - 2016 file format) - Access
qryPatientsAndInvoicesCrosstab
City
Total Of InvoiceAmt
-1
0
Atlanta $5,467.00 $2,305.00 $3,162.00
Austell $478.00 $285.00 $193.00
Clarkston $420.00 $300.00 $120.00
Conley $343.00 $343.00
Decatur $1,284.00 $1,284.00

The query recordset contains only one row for each City field value. The Total Of InvoiceAmt column shows the total invoice amount for the patients in each city. The columns labeled -1 and 0 show the sum total paid (-1 column) and sum total unpaid (0 column) invoice amounts for patients in each city. Because the InvoicePaid field is a Yes/No field, by default, field values in datasheets, forms, and reports are displayed in a check box (either checked or unchecked), but a checked value is stored in the database as a -1 and an unchecked value as a 0. Instead of displaying check boxes, the crosstab query displays the stored values as column headings.

Donna wants you to change the column headings of -1 to Paid and 0 to Unpaid. You'll use the IIf function to change the column headings, using the expression *IIf(InvoicePaid,"Paid","Unpaid")*—if the InvoicePaid field value is true (because it's a Yes/No field or a True/False field), or is checked, use "Paid" as the column heading;

otherwise, use "Unpaid" as the column heading. Because the InvoicePaid field is a Yes/No field, the condition *InvoicePaid* is the same as the condition *InvoicePaid* = *-1*, which uses a comparison operator and a value. For all data types except Yes/No fields, you must use a comparison operator in a condition.

To change the crosstab query column headings:

1. Click the **Home** tab on the ribbon, and then switch to Design view. The design grid has four entries. See Figure 5–22.

Figure 5–22 Crosstab query in the design grid

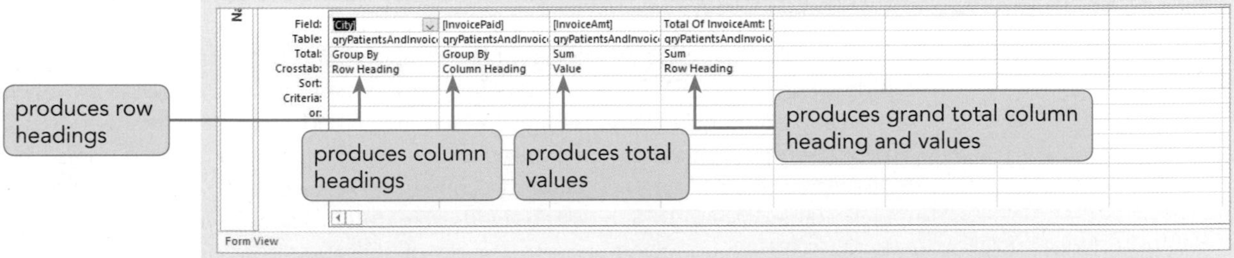
Field:
Table:
Total:
Crosstab:
Sort:
Criteria:
or:
[City]
qryPatientsAndInvoic
Group By
Row Heading
[InvoicePaid]
qryPatientsAndInvoic
Group By
Column Heading
[InvoiceAmt]
qryPatientsAndInvoic
Sum
Value
Total Of InvoiceAmt: [
qryPatientsAndInvoic
Sum
Row Heading
produces row headings
produces column headings
produces total values
produces grand total column heading and values
Form View

From left to right, the [City] entry produces the row headings, the [InvoicePaid] entry produces the column headings, the [InvoiceAmt] entry produces the totals in each row/column intersection, and the Total Of InvoiceAmt entry produces the row total column heading and total values. The field names are enclosed in brackets; the Total Of InvoiceAmt entry is the name of this calculated field, which displays the sum of the InvoiceAmt field values for each row.

You need to replace the Field box value in the second column with the IIf function expression to change the -1 and 0 column headings to Paid and Unpaid. You can type the expression in the box, use Expression Builder to create the expression, or type the expression in the Zoom dialog box. You'll use the last method.

2. Right-click the **InvoicePaid Field** box, and then open the Zoom dialog box.
3. Delete the InvoicePaid expression, and then type **IIf (InvoicePaid,"Paid","Unpaid")** in the Zoom dialog box. See Figure 5–23.

Figure 5–23 IIf function for the crosstab query column headings

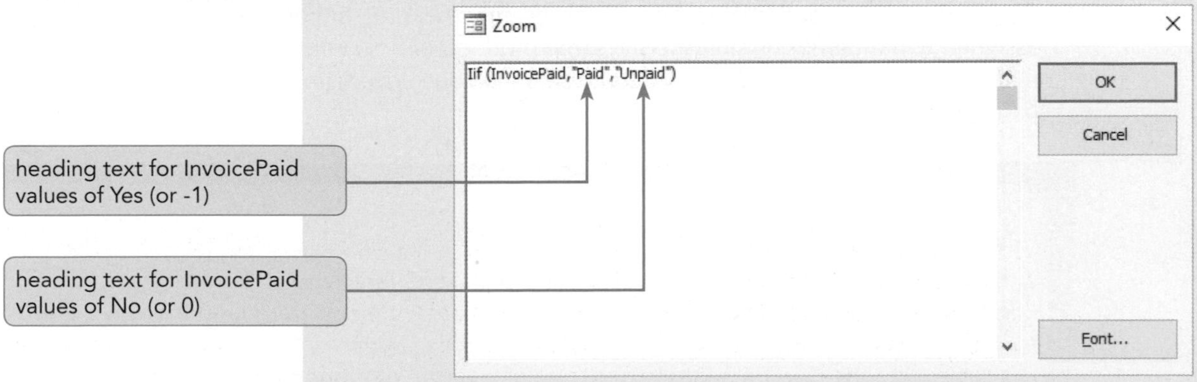
Zoom
IIf (InvoicePaid,"Paid","Unpaid")
OK
Cancel
Font...
heading text for InvoicePaid values of Yes (or -1)
heading text for InvoicePaid values of No (or 0)

4. Click the **OK** button, and then save and run the query. The completed crosstab query is displayed with Paid and Unpaid as the last two column headings, in alphabetical order, as shown in Figure 5–18.
5. Close the query, and then open the Navigation Pane.

TIP

Point to an object in the Navigation Pane to display the full object name in a ScreenTip.

In the Navigation Pane, unique icons represent different types of queries. The crosstab query icon appears in the Queries list to the left of the qryPatientsAndInvoicesCrosstab query. This icon looks different from the icon that appears to the left of the other queries, which are all select queries.

INSIGHT

Using Special Database Features Cautiously

When you create a query in Design view or with a wizard, an equivalent SQL statement is constructed, and only the SQL statement version of the query is saved. **SQL (Structured Query Language)** is a language that provides a standardized way to request information from a relational database system. If you learn SQL for one relational DBMS, it's a relatively easy task to begin using SQL for other relational DBMSs. However, DBMSs can have differences in their versions of SQL—somewhat like having different dialects in English—and in what additions they make to SQL. The SQL-equivalent statement created for a crosstab query in Access is one such SQL-language addition. If you need to convert an Access database to SQL Server, Oracle, or another DBMS, crosstab queries created in Access will not work in these other DBMSs. You'd have to construct a set of SQL statements in the other DBMS to replace the SQL statement automatically created by Access. Constructing this replacement set of statements is a highly technical process that only an experienced programmer can complete, so you should use special features of a DBMS judiciously.

Next, Donna wants to identify any visit dates that have the same visit dates as other patients because they might have potential scheduling difficulties.

To find the information Donna needs, you'll create a find duplicates query.

Creating a Find Duplicates Query

A find duplicates query is a select query that finds duplicate records in a table or query. The **Find Duplicates Query Wizard** guides you through the steps for creating this type of query. A find duplicates query searches for duplicate values based on the fields you select when answering the Wizard's questions. For example, you might want to display all employers that have the same name, all students who have the same phone number, or all products that have the same description. Using this type of query, you can locate duplicates to avert potential problems (for example, you might have inadvertently assigned two different numbers to the same product), or you can eliminate duplicates that cost money (for example, you could send just one advertising brochure to all patients having the same address).

REFERENCE

Using the Find Duplicates Query Wizard

- On the Create tab, in the Queries group, click the Query Wizard button.
- In the New Query dialog box, click Find Duplicates Query Wizard, and then click the OK button.
- Complete the Wizard dialog boxes to select the table or query on which to base the query, select the field (or fields) to check for duplicate values, select the additional fields to include in the query results, enter a name for the query, and then click the Finish button.

You'll use the Find Duplicates Query Wizard to create and run a new query to display duplicate visit dates in the tblVisit table.

To create the query using the Find Duplicates Query Wizard:

1. Close the Navigation Pane, click the **Create** tab on the ribbon, and then, in the Queries group, click the **Query Wizard** button to open the New Query dialog box.
2. Click **Find Duplicates Query Wizard**, and then click the **OK** button. The first Find Duplicates Query Wizard dialog box opens. In this dialog box, you select the table or query on which to base the new query. You'll use the tblVisit table.
3. Click **Table: tblVisit**, and then click the **Next** button. The next Find Duplicates Query Wizard dialog box opens, in which you choose the fields you want to check for duplicate values.
4. In the Available fields box, click **VisitDate**, click the **Select Single Field** button > to select the VisitDate field as the field to check for duplicate values, and then click the **Next** button. In the next Find Duplicates Query Wizard dialog box, you select the additional fields to display in the query results.

   Donna wants all remaining fields to be included in the query results.
5. Click the **Select All Fields** button >> to move all fields from the Available fields box to the Additional query fields box, and then click the **Next** button. The final Find Duplicates Query Wizard dialog box opens, in which you enter a name for the query. You'll use qryDuplicateVisitDates as the query name.
6. Type **qryDuplicateVisitDates** in the box, be sure the option button for viewing the results is selected, and then click the **Finish** button. The query is saved, and then the 50 records for visits with duplicate visit dates are displayed. See Figure 5–24.

Figure 5–24 Query recordset for duplicate visit dates

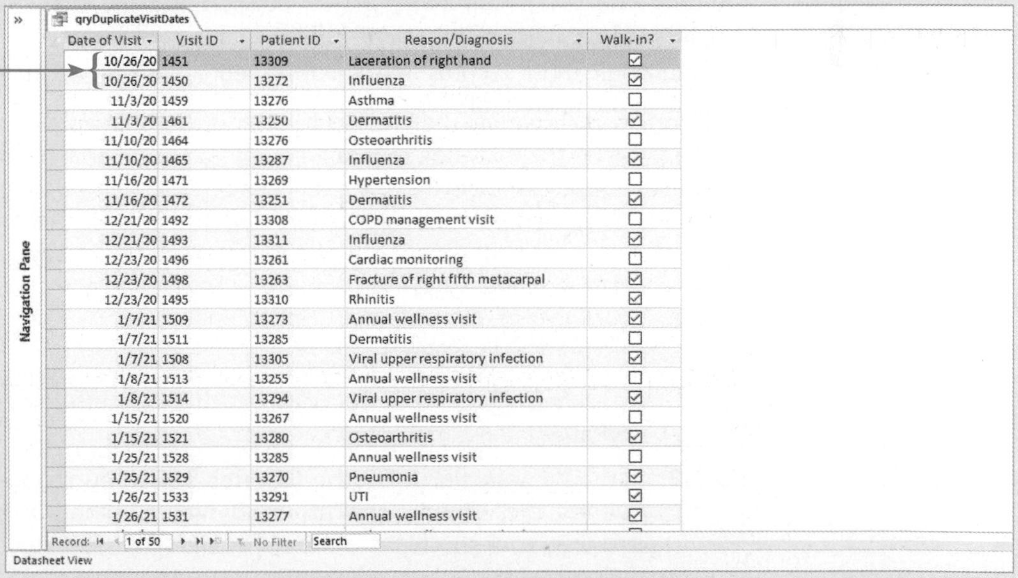
all records returned by the query share a visit date with other records
qryDuplicateVisitDates
Navigation Pane
Record: 1 of 50
No Filter
Search
Datasheet View

Date of Visit	Visit ID	Patient ID	Reason/Diagnosis	Walk-in?
10/26/20	1451	13309	Laceration of right hand	☑
10/26/20	1450	13272	Influenza	☑
11/3/20	1459	13276	Asthma	☐
11/3/20	1461	13250	Dermatitis	☑
11/10/20	1464	13276	Osteoarthritis	☐
11/10/20	1465	13287	Influenza	☑
11/16/20	1471	13269	Hypertension	☐
11/16/20	1472	13251	Dermatitis	☑
12/21/20	1492	13308	COPD management visit	☐
12/21/20	1493	13311	Influenza	☑
12/23/20	1496	13261	Cardiac monitoring	☐
12/23/20	1498	13263	Fracture of right fifth metacarpal	☑
12/23/20	1495	13310	Rhinitis	☑
1/7/21	1509	13273	Annual wellness visit	☑
1/7/21	1511	13285	Dermatitis	☐
1/7/21	1508	13305	Viral upper respiratory infection	☑
1/8/21	1513	13255	Annual wellness visit	☐
1/8/21	1514	13294	Viral upper respiratory infection	☑
1/15/21	1520	13267	Annual wellness visit	☐
1/15/21	1521	13280	Osteoarthritis	☑
1/25/21	1528	13285	Annual wellness visit	☐
1/25/21	1529	13270	Pneumonia	☑
1/26/21	1533	13291	UTI	☑
1/26/21	1531	13277	Annual wellness visit	☑

7. Close the query.

Donna now asks you to find the records for patients with no visits. These are patients who have been referred to Lakewood Community Health Services but have not had a first visit. Donna wants to contact these patients to see if they would like to book initial appointments. To provide Donna with this information, you need to create a find unmatched query.

Creating a Find Unmatched Query

A find unmatched query is a select query that finds all records in a table or query that have no related records in a second table or query. For example, you could display all patients who have had an appointment but have never been invoiced or all students who are not currently enrolled in classes. Such a query provides information for a medical office to ensure all patients who have received services have also been billed for those services and for a school administrator to contact the students to find out their future educational plans. The **Find Unmatched Query Wizard** guides you through the steps for creating this type of query.

REFERENCE

Using the Find Unmatched Query Wizard

- On the Create tab, in the Queries group, click the Query Wizard button.
- In the New Query dialog box, click Find Unmatched Query Wizard, and then click the OK button.
- Complete the Wizard dialog boxes to select the table or query on which to base the new query, select the table or query that contains the related records, specify the common field in each table or query, select the additional fields to include in the query results, enter a name for the query, and then click the Finish button.

Donna wants to know which patients have no visits. She will contact them to determine if they will be visiting Lakewood Community Health Services or whether they are receiving their medical services elsewhere. To create a list of patients who have not had a visit to the clinic, you'll use the Find Unmatched Query Wizard to display only those records from the tblPatient table with no matching PatientID field value in the related tblVisit table.

To create the query using the Find Unmatched Query Wizard:

1. On the Create tab, in the Queries group, click the **Query Wizard** button to open the New Query dialog box.
2. Click **Find Unmatched Query Wizard**, and then click the **OK** button. The first Find Unmatched Query Wizard dialog box opens. In this dialog box, you select the table or query on which to base the new query. You'll use the qryPatientsByName query.
3. In the View section, click the **Queries** option button to display the list of queries, click **Query: qryPatientsByName** in the box to select this query, and then click the **Next** button. The next Find Unmatched Query Wizard dialog box opens, in which you choose the table that contains the related records. You'll select the tblVisit table.
4. Click **Table: tblVisit** in the box, and then click the **Next** button. The next dialog box opens, in which you choose the common field for both tables. See Figure 5–25.

Figure 5–25 Selecting the common field

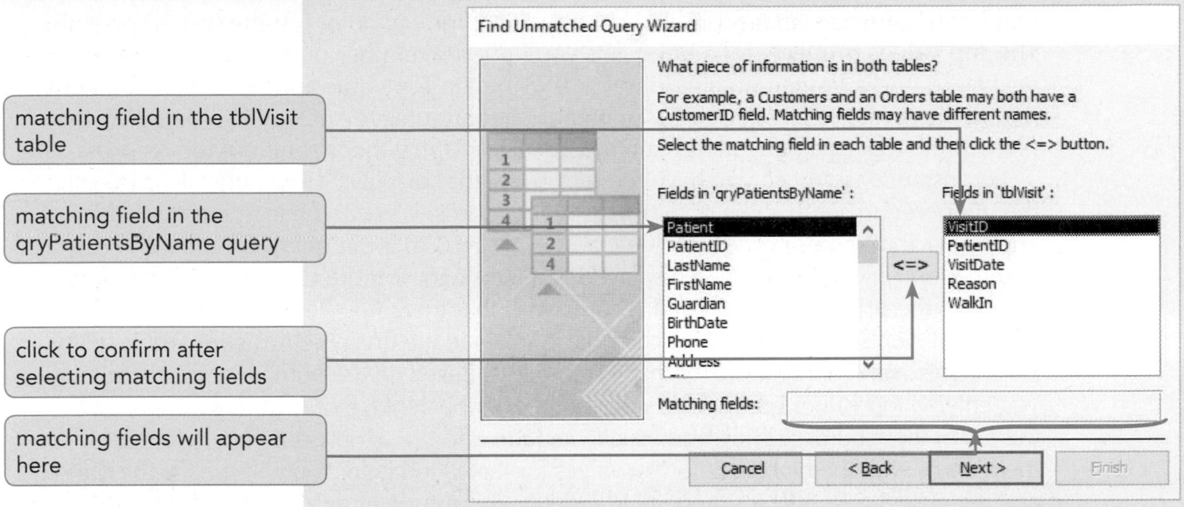
matching field in the tblVisit table
matching field in the qryPatientsByName query
click to confirm after selecting matching fields
matching fields will appear here
Find Unmatched Query Wizard
What piece of information is in both tables?
For example, a Customers and an Orders table may both have a CustomerID field. Matching fields may have different names.
Select the matching field in each table and then click the <=> button.
Fields in 'qryPatientsByName' :
Fields in 'tblVisit' :
Patient
PatientID
LastName
FirstName
Guardian
BirthDate
Phone
Address
VisitID
PatientID
VisitDate
Reason
WalkIn
<=>
Matching fields:
Cancel
< Back
Next >
Finish

The common field between the query and the table is the PatientID field. You need to click the common field in each box and then click the double-headed arrow button <=> between the two boxes to join the two objects. The Matching fields box then will display PatientID <=> PatientID to indicate the joining of the two matching fields. If the two selected objects already have a one-to-many relationship defined in the Relationships window, the Matching fields box will join the correct fields automatically.

Be sure you click the PatientID field in both boxes.

5. In the Fields in 'qryPatientsByName' box, click **PatientID**, in the Fields in 'tblVisit' box, click **PatientID**, click the double-headed arrow button <=> to connect the two selected fields, and then click the **Next** button. The next Find Unmatched Query Wizard dialog box opens, in which you choose the fields you want to see in the query recordset. Donna wants the query recordset to display all available fields.
6. Click the **Select All Fields** button >> to move all fields from the Available fields box to the Selected fields box, and then click the **Next** button. The final dialog box opens, in which you enter the query name.
7. Type **qryInactivePatients**, be sure the option button for viewing the results is selected, and then click the **Finish** button. The query is saved, and then one record is displayed in the query recordset. See Figure 5–26.

Figure 5–26 Query recordset displaying one patient without a visit

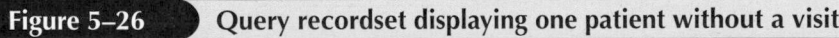

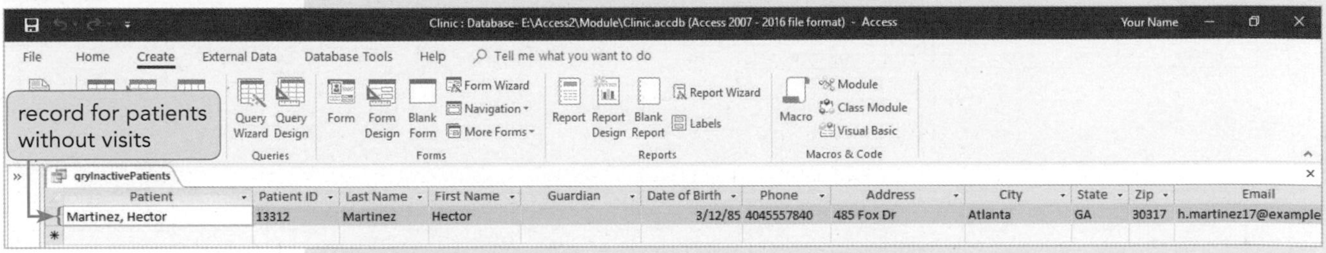
Clinic : Database- E:\Access2\Module\Clinic.accdb (Access 2007 - 2016 file format) - Access
Your Name
File Home Create External Data Database Tools Help Tell me what you want to do
record for patients without visits
qryInactivePatients
Patient | Patient ID | Last Name | First Name | Guardian | Date of Birth | Phone | Address | City | State | Zip | Email
Martinez, Hector | 13312 | Martinez | Hector | 3/12/85 | 4045557840 | 485 Fox Dr | Atlanta | GA | 30317 | h.martinez17@example

8. Close the query.

Next, Donna wants to contact those patients who have the highest invoice amounts to make sure that Lakewood Community Health Services is providing satisfactory service. To display the information Donna needs, you will create a top values query.

Creating a Top Values Query

Whenever a query displays a large group of records, you might want to limit the number to a more manageable size by displaying, for example, just the first 10 records. The **Top Values property** for a query lets you limit the number of records in the query results. To find a limited number of records using the Top Values property, you can click one of the preset values from a list or enter either an integer (such as 15, to display the first 15 records) or a percentage (such as 20%, to display the first fifth of the records).

For instance, suppose you have a select query that displays 45 records. If you want the query recordset to show only the first five records, you can change the query by entering a Top Values property value of either 5 or 10%. If the query contains a sort, and the last record that can be displayed is one of two or more records with the same value for the primary sort field, all records with that matching key value are displayed.

Donna wants to view the same data that appears in the qryLargeInvoiceAmounts query for patients with the highest 25% invoice amounts. Based on the number or percentage you enter, a top values query selects that number or percentage of records starting from the top of the recordset. Thus, you usually include a sort in a top values query to display the records with the highest or lowest values for the sorted field. You will modify the query and then use the Top Values property to produce this information for Donna.

To set the Top Values property for the query:

1. Open the Navigation Pane, open the **qryLargeInvoiceAmounts** query in Datasheet view, and then close the Navigation Pane. Nineteen records are displayed, all with InvoiceAmt field values greater than or equal to $150, in descending order by InvoiceAmt.
2. Switch to Design view.
3. On the Query Tools Design tab, in the Query Setup group, click the **Return** arrow (with the ScreenTip "Top Values"), and then click **25%**. See Figure 5–27.

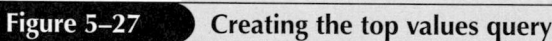

Figure 5–27 Creating the top values query

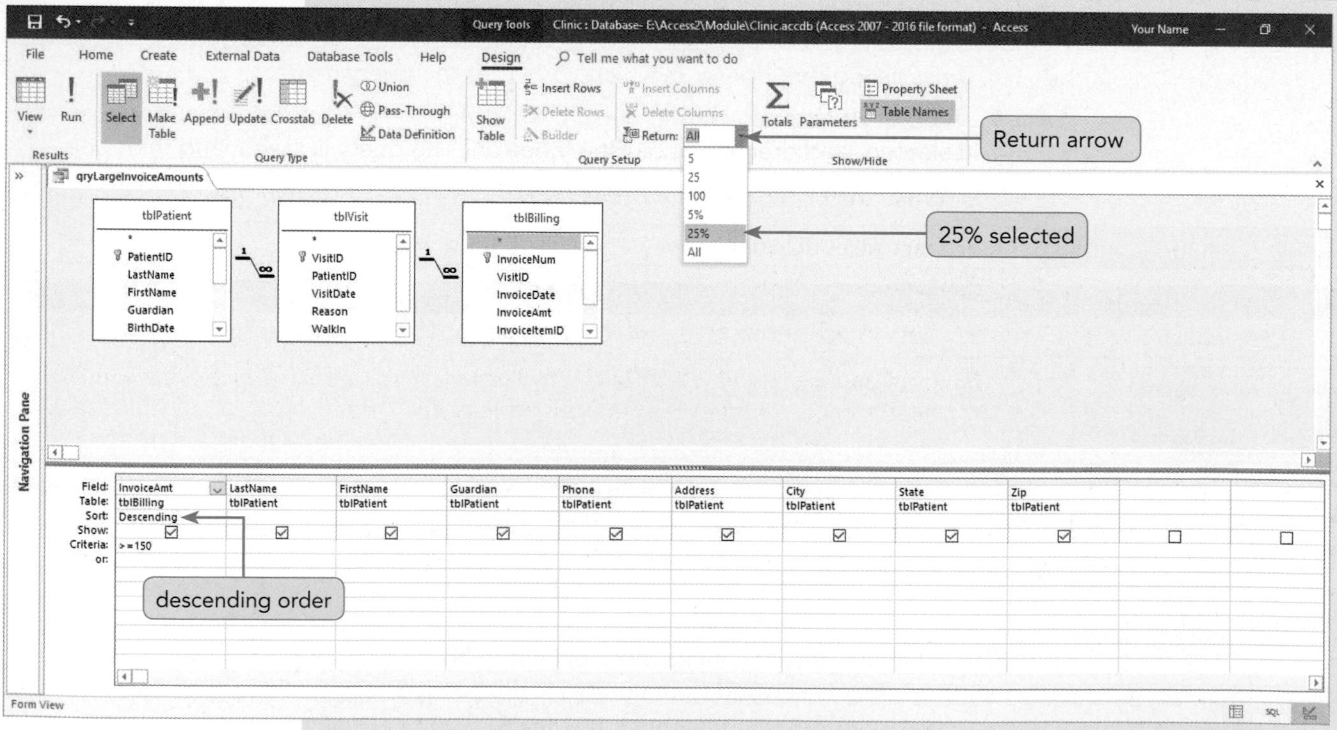
Return arrow
25% selected
descending order

If the number or percentage of records you want to select, such as 15 or 20%, doesn't appear in the Top Values list, you can type the number or percentage in the Return box.

4. Run the query. Nine records are displayed in the query recordset; these records represent the highest 25% of invoice amounts (25% of the original 19 records). See Figure 5–28.

Figure 5–28 Top values query recordset

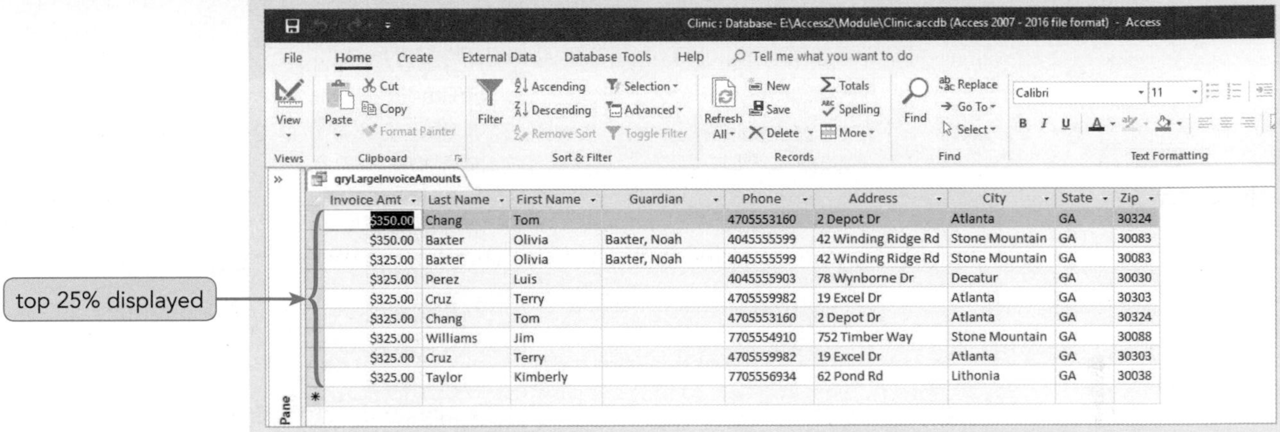
top 25% displayed
Clinic : Database- E:\Access2\Module\Clinic.accdb (Access 2007 - 2016 file format) - Access
File Home Create External Data Database Tools Help Tell me what you want to do
qryLargeInvoiceAmounts
Invoice Amt Last Name First Name Guardian Phone Address City State Zip
$350.00 Chang Tom 4705553160 2 Depot Dr Atlanta GA 30324
$350.00 Baxter Olivia Baxter, Noah 4045555599 42 Winding Ridge Rd Stone Mountain GA 30083
$325.00 Baxter Olivia Baxter, Noah 4045555599 42 Winding Ridge Rd Stone Mountain GA 30083
$325.00 Perez Luis 4045555903 78 Wynborne Dr Decatur GA 30030
$325.00 Cruz Terry 4705559982 19 Excel Dr Atlanta GA 30303
$325.00 Chang Tom 4705553160 2 Depot Dr Atlanta GA 30324
$325.00 Williams Jim 7705554910 752 Timber Way Stone Mountain GA 30088
$325.00 Cruz Terry 4705559982 19 Excel Dr Atlanta GA 30303
$325.00 Taylor Kimberly 7705556934 62 Pond Rd Lithonia GA 30038

5. Save and close the query.

6. If you are not continuing on to the next session, close the Clinic database.

Donna will use the information provided by the queries you created to analyze the Lakewood Community Health Services business and to contact patients. In the next session, you will enhance the tblPatient and tblVisit tables.

REVIEW

Session 5.2 Quick Check

1. What is the purpose of a crosstab query?
2. What are the four query wizards you can use to create a new query?
3. What is a find duplicates query?
4. What does a find unmatched query do?
5. What happens when you set a query's Top Values property?
6. What happens if you set a query's Top Values property to 2, and the first five records have the same value for the primary sort field?

Session 5.3 Visual Overview:

The tblInvoiceItem table supplies the field values for the lookup field in the tblBilling table. A **lookup field** lets the user select a value from a list of possible values to enter data into the field.

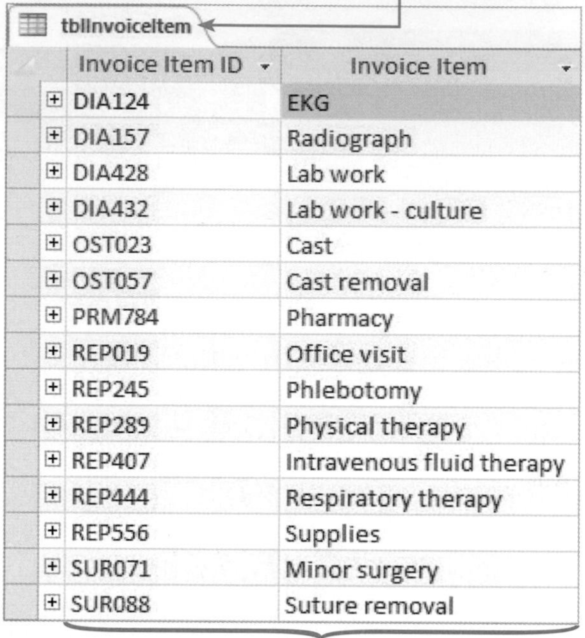

tblInvoiceItem

Invoice Item ID	Invoice Item
DIA124	EKG
DIA157	Radiograph
DIA428	Lab work
DIA432	Lab work - culture
OST023	Cast
OST057	Cast removal
PRM784	Pharmacy
REP019	Office visit
REP245	Phlebotomy
REP289	Physical therapy
REP407	Intravenous fluid therapy
REP444	Respiratory therapy
REP556	Supplies
SUR071	Minor surgery
SUR088	Suture removal

The InvoiceItemID and InvoiceItem fields from the tblInvoiceItem table are used to look up InvoiceItemID values in the tblBilling table.

The tblBilling table contains the lookup field.

tblBilling

Invoice Num	VisitID	Invoice Date	Invoice Amt	Invoice Item ID	Invoice Paid	Insurance	Click to Add
26501	1450	10/27/2020	$125.00	Office visit	☑	$0.00	
26502	1450	10/27/2020	$75.00			$0.00	
26503	1451	10/27/2020	$125.00			$100.00	
26504	1451	10/27/2020	$225.00			$0.00	
26505	1451	10/27/2020	$65.00			$0.00	
26508	1453	10/28/2020	$125.00			$100.00	
26509	1453	10/28/2020	$45.00			$0.00	
26510	1453	10/30/2020	$35.00			$0.00	
26511	1453	10/30/2020	$55.00			$0.00	
26513	1458	10/30/2020	$125.00			$0.00	
26514	1458	10/30/2020	$75.00			$0.00	
26515	1458	10/30/2020	$350.00			$0.00	
26516	1458	10/30/2020	$325.00			$0.00	
26518	1459	11/04/2020	$125.00			$100.00	
26519	1459	11/04/2020	$175.00			$0.00	
26521	1461	11/04/2020	$125.00	Phlebotomy	☑	$0.00	
26522	1461	11/04/2020	$65.00	Pharmacy	☐	$0.00	

EKG	DIA124
Radiograph	DIA157
Lab work	DIA428
Lab work - culture	DIA432
Cast	OST023
Cast removal	OST057
Pharmacy	PRM784
Office visit	REP019
Phlebotomy	REP245
Physical therapy	REP289
Intravenous fluid the	REP407
Respiratory therapy	REP444
Supplies	REP556
Minor surgery	SUR071
Suture removal	SUR088

Values in the lookup field appear in alphabetical order, sorted by Invoice Item ID.

Only the InvoiceItemID values are stored in the InvoiceItemID field in the tblBilling table even though the user also sees the InvoiceItem values in the datasheet.

Lookup Fields and Input Masks

The tblPatient table contains the field that displays values with an input mask. An **input mask** is a predefined format that is used to enter and display data in a field.

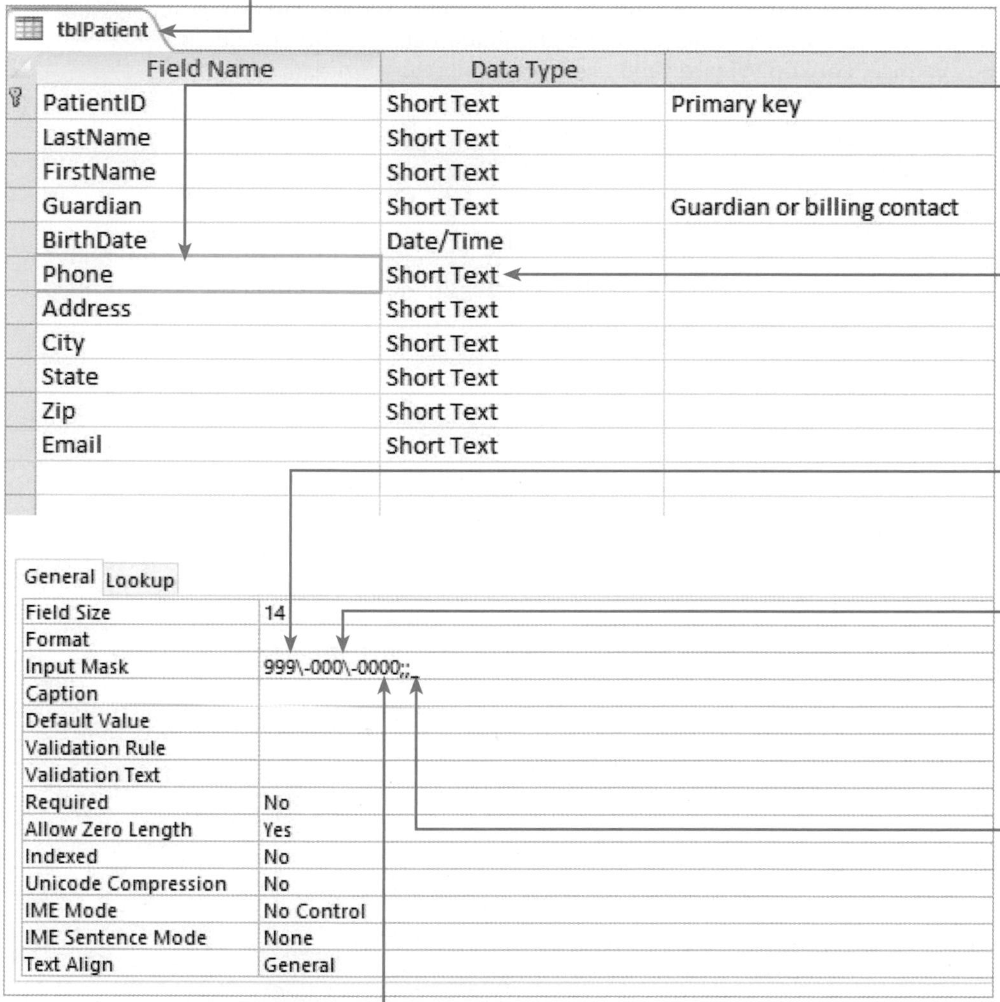
tblPatient
Field Name
Data Type
PatientID
Short Text
Primary key
LastName
Short Text
FirstName
Short Text
Guardian
Short Text
Guardian or billing contact
BirthDate
Date/Time
Phone
Short Text
Address
Short Text
City
Short Text
State
Short Text
Zip
Short Text
Email
Short Text
General
Lookup
Field Size
14
Format
Input Mask
999\-000\-0000;;_
Caption
Default Value
Validation Rule
Validation Text
Required
No
Allow Zero Length
Yes
Indexed
No
Unicode Compression
No
IME Mode
No Control
IME Sentence Mode
None
Text Align
General

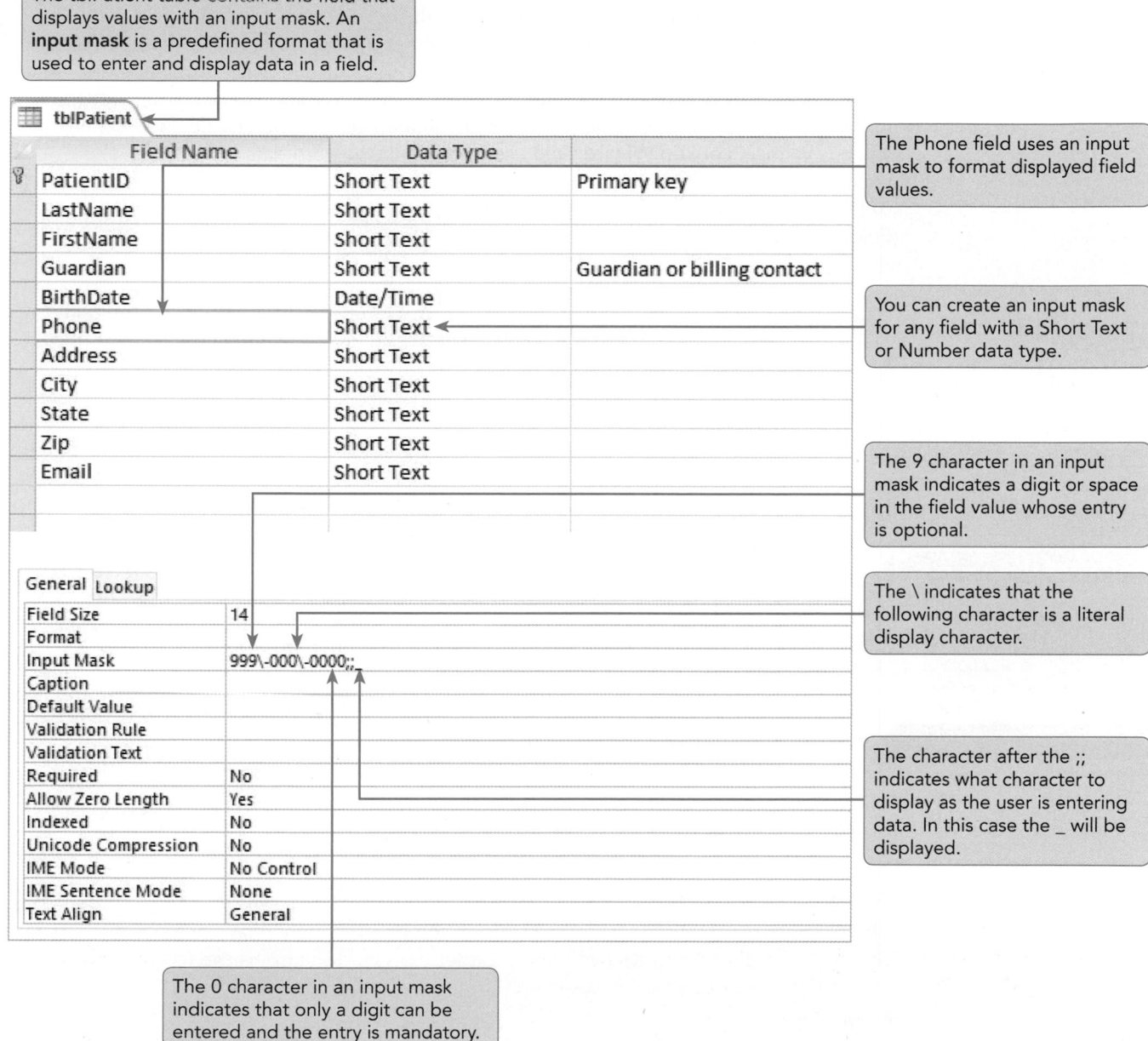

The Phone field uses an input mask to format displayed field values.

You can create an input mask for any field with a Short Text or Number data type.

The 9 character in an input mask indicates a digit or space in the field value whose entry is optional.

The \ indicates that the following character is a literal display character.

The character after the ;; indicates what character to display as the user is entering data. In this case the _ will be displayed.

The 0 character in an input mask indicates that only a digit can be entered and the entry is mandatory.

Creating a Lookup Field

The tblBilling table in the Clinic database contains information about patient invoices. Donna wants to make entering data in the table easier for her staff. In particular, data entry is easier if they do not need to remember the correct InvoiceItemID field value for each treatment. Because the tblInvoiceItem and tblBilling tables have a one-to-many relationship, Donna asks you to change the tblBilling table's InvoiceItemID field, which is a foreign key to the tblInvoiceItem table, to a lookup field. A lookup field lets the user select a value from a list of possible values. For the InvoiceItemID field, a user will be able to select an invoice item's ID number from the list of invoice item names in the tblBilling table rather than having to remember the correct InvoiceItemID field value. The InvoiceItemID field value will be stored in the tblBilling table, but both the invoice item and the InvoiceItemID field value will appear in Datasheet view when entering or changing an InvoiceItemID field value. This arrangement makes entering and changing InvoiceItemID field values easier for users and guarantees that the InvoiceItemID field value is valid. A **Lookup Wizard field** uses the Lookup Wizard data type, which lets you create a lookup field in a table.

Donna asks you to change the InvoiceItemID field in the tblBilling table to a lookup field. You'll begin by opening the tblBilling table in Design view.

To change the InvoiceItemID field to a lookup field:

1. If you took a break after the previous session, make sure that the Clinic database is open.

   Trouble? If the security warning is displayed below the ribbon, click the Enable Content button next to the warning.

2. If necessary, open the Navigation Pane, open the **tblBilling** table in Design view, and then close the Navigation Pane.

TIP

You can display the arrow and the menu simultaneously if you click the box near its right side.

3. Click the **Data Type** box for the InvoiceItemID field, click the arrow to display the list of data types, and then click **Lookup Wizard**. A message box appears, instructing you to delete the relationship between the tblBilling and tblInvoiceItem tables if you want to make the InvoiceItemID field a lookup field. See Figure 5–29.

Figure 5–29 Warning message for an existing table relationship

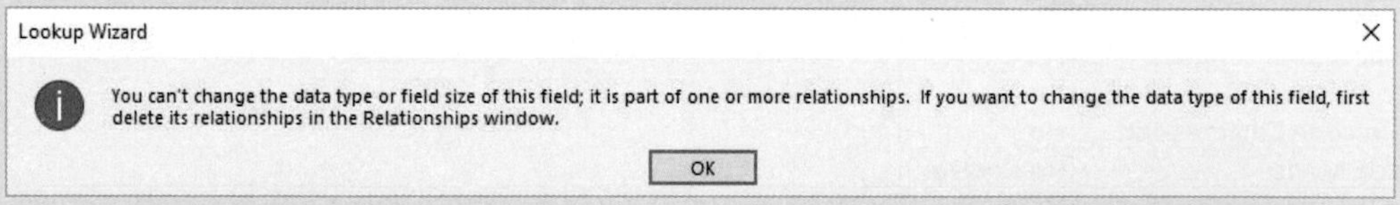
Lookup Wizard
You can't change the data type or field size of this field; it is part of one or more relationships. If you want to change the data type of this field, first delete its relationships in the Relationships window.
OK

The lookup field will be used to form the one-to-many relationship between the tblBilling and tblInvoiceItem tables, so you don't need the relationship that previously existed between the two tables.

4. Click the **OK** button and then close the tblBilling table, clicking the **No** button when asked if you want to save the table design changes.

5. Click the **Database Tools** tab on the ribbon, and then in the Relationships group, click the **Relationships** button to open the Relationships window.

6. Right-click the join line between the tblBilling and tblInvoiceItem tables, click **Delete**, and then click the **Yes** button to confirm the deletion.

   Trouble? If the Delete command does not appear on the shortcut menu, click a blank area in the Relationships window to close the shortcut menu, and then repeat Step 6, ensuring you right-click the relationship line.

7. Close the Relationships window.

Now you can resume changing the InvoiceItemID field to a lookup field.

To finish changing the InvoiceItemID field to a lookup field:

1. Open the **tblBilling** table in Design view, and then close the Navigation Pane.
2. Click the right side of the **Data Type** box for the InvoiceItemID field, if necessary click the arrow, and then click **Lookup Wizard**. The first Lookup Wizard dialog box opens.

   This dialog box lets you specify a list of allowed values for the InvoiceItemID field in a record in the tblBilling table. You can specify a table or query from which users select the value, or you can enter a new list of values. You want the InvoiceItemID values to come from the tblInvoiceItem table.
3. Make sure the option for "I want the lookup field to get the values from another table or query" is selected, and then click the **Next** button to display the next Lookup Wizard dialog box.
4. In the View section, click the **Tables** option button, if necessary, to display the list of tables, click **Table: tblInvoiceItem**, and then click the **Next** button to display the next Lookup Wizard dialog box. See Figure 5–30.

Figure 5–30 Selecting the lookup fields

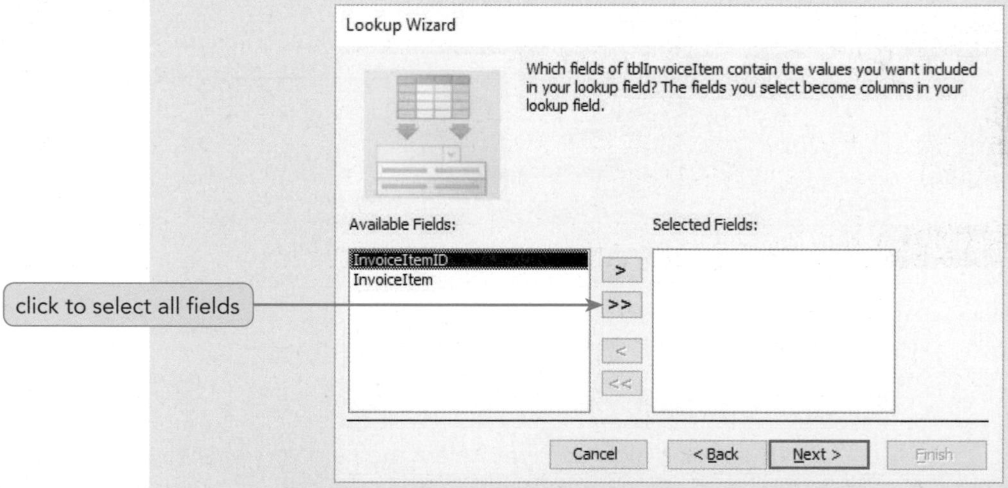

click to select all fields
Lookup Wizard
Which fields of tblInvoiceItem contain the values you want included in your lookup field? The fields you select become columns in your lookup field.
Available Fields:
Selected Fields:
InvoiceItemID
InvoiceItem
>
>>
<
<<
Cancel
< Back
Next >
Finish

   This dialog box lets you select the lookup fields from the tblInvoiceItem table. You need to select the InvoiceItemID field because it's the common field that links the tblInvoiceItem table and the tblBilling table. You must also select the InvoiceItem field because Donna wants the user to be able to select from a list of invoice item names when entering a new contract record or changing an existing InvoiceItemID field value.
5. Click the **Select All Fields** button >> to move the InvoiceItemID and InvoiceItem fields to the Selected Fields box, and then click the **Next** button to display the next Lookup Wizard dialog box. This dialog box lets you choose a sort order for the box entries. Donna wants the entries to appear in ascending Invoice Item Description order. Note that ascending is the default sort order.

6. Click the **arrow** for the first box, click **InvoiceItem**, and then click the **Next** button to open the next dialog box.

   In this dialog box, you can adjust the widths of the lookup columns. Note that when you resize a column to its best fit, the column is resized so that the widest column heading and the visible field values fit the column width. However, some field values that aren't visible in this dialog box might be wider than the column width, so you must scroll down the column to make sure you don't have to repeat the column resizing.

7. Click the **Hide key column** check box to remove the checkmark and display the InvoiceItemID field.

8. Click the Invoice Item ID column heading to select it. With the mouse pointer on the Invoice Item ID heading, drag it to the right of the Invoice Item column to reposition it.

9. Place the pointer on the right edge of the Invoice Item field column heading, and then when the pointer changes to the column resize pointer ✛, double-click to resize the column to its best fit.

10. Scroll down the columns, and repeat Step 9 as necessary until the Invoice Item column accommodates all contents, and then press **CTRL+HOME** to scroll back to the top of the columns. See Figure 5–31.

Figure 5–31 **Adjusting the width of the lookup column**

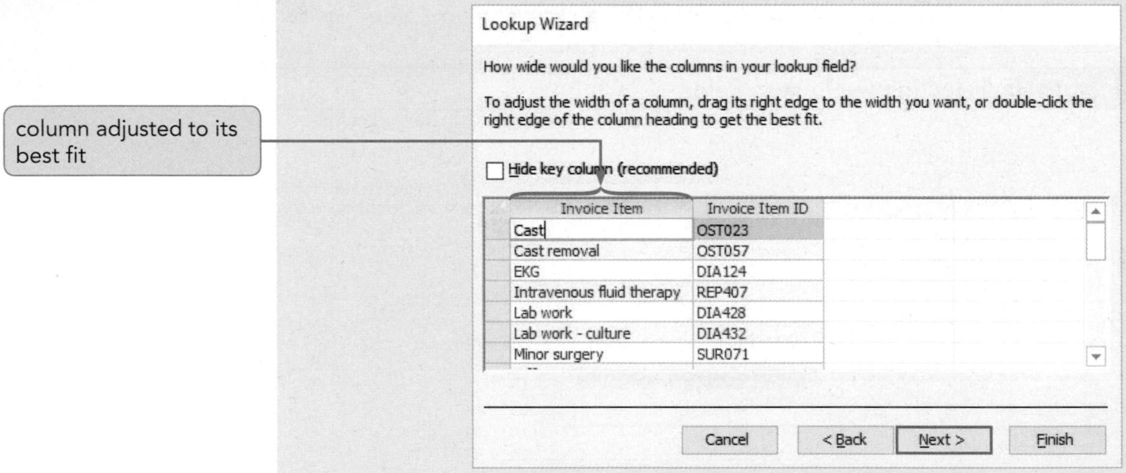
column adjusted to its best fit
Lookup Wizard
How wide would you like the columns in your lookup field?
To adjust the width of a column, drag its right edge to the width you want, or double-click the right edge of the column heading to get the best fit.
Hide key column (recommended)
Invoice Item
Invoice Item ID
Cast
OST023
Cast removal
OST057
EKG
DIA124
Intravenous fluid therapy
REP407
Lab work
DIA428
Lab work - culture
DIA432
Minor surgery
SUR071
Cancel
< Back
Next >
Finish

11. Click the **Next** button.

    In the next dialog box, you select the field you want to store in the table. You'll store the InvoiceItemID field in the tblBilling table because it's the foreign key to the tblInvoiceItem table.

12. Click **InvoiceItemID** in the Available Fields box if it's not already selected, and then click the **Next** button.

    In the next dialog box, you specify the field name for the lookup field. Because you'll be storing the InvoiceItemID field in the table, you'll accept the default field name, InvoiceItemID.

13. Click the **Finish** button, and then click **Yes** to save the table.

The Data Type value for the InvoiceItemID field is still Short Text because this field contains text data. However, when you update the field, the InvoiceItemID field value will be used to look up and display in the tblBilling table datasheet both the InvoiceItem and InvoiceItemID field values from the tblInvoiceItem table.

In reviewing patient visits recently, Donna noticed that the InvoiceItemID field value stored in the tblBilling table for visit number 26521 is incorrect. She asks you to test the new lookup field to select the correct field value. To do so, you need to switch to Datasheet view.

To change the InvoiceItemID field value:

1. Switch to Datasheet view, and then resize the Invoice Item ID column to its best fit.

   Notice that the Invoice Item ID column displays InvoiceItem field values, even though the InvoiceItemID field values are stored in the table.

2. For Invoice Num 26521, click **Phlebotomy** in the Invoice Item ID column, and then click the **arrow** to display the list of InvoiceItem and InvoiceItemID field values from the tblInvoiceItems table. See Figure 5–32.

Figure 5–32 **List of InvoiceItem and InvoiceItemID field values**

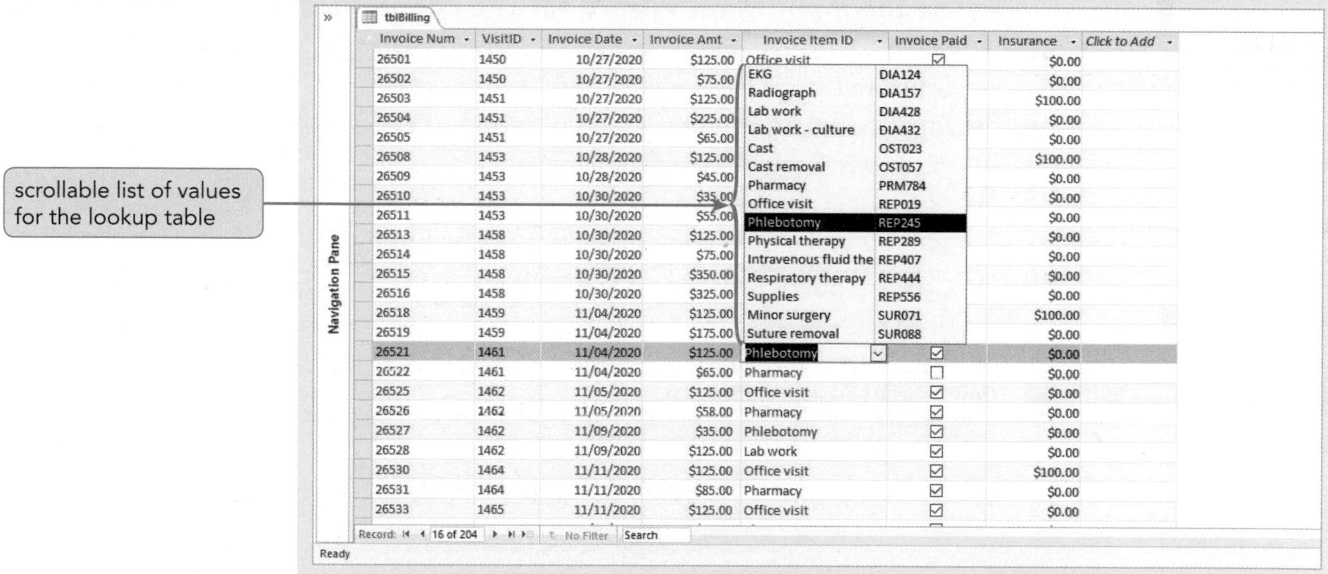
scrollable list of values for the lookup table
tblBilling
Navigation Pane
Invoice Num VisitID Invoice Date Invoice Amt Invoice Item ID Invoice Paid Insurance Click to Add
EKG DIA124
Radiograph DIA157
Lab work DIA428
Lab work - culture DIA432
Cast OST023
Cast removal OST057
Pharmacy PRM784
Office visit REP019
Phlebotomy REP245
Physical therapy REP289
Intravenous fluid the REP407
Respiratory therapy REP444
Supplies REP556
Minor surgery SUR071
Suture removal SUR088
Record: 16 of 204
No Filter
Search
Ready

   Note that the column displaying InvoiceItem values in your list may be narrower than the values themselves, even though you resized the column. This bug should be fixed in a future version of Access.

   The invoice item for visit 26521 should be Office Visit, so you need to select this entry in the list to change the InvoiceItemID field value.

3. Scroll through the list if necessary, and then click **Office visit** to select that value to display in the datasheet and to store the InvoiceItemID field value of REP019 in the table. The list closes, and "Office visit" appears in the Invoice Item ID column.

4. Save and close the tblBilling table.

Next, Donna asks you to change the appearance of the Phone field in the tblPatient table to a standard telephone number format.

Using the Input Mask Wizard

The Phone field in the tblPatient table is a 10-digit number that's difficult to read because it appears with none of the special formatting characters usually associated with a telephone number. For example, the Phone field value for Gregory Davis, which appears as 6785550089, would be more readable in any of the following formats: 678-555-0089, 678.555.0089, 678/555-0089, or (678) 555-0089. Donna asks you to use the (678) 555-0089 style for the Phone field.

Donna wants the parentheses and hyphens to appear as literal display characters whenever users enter Phone field values. A literal display character is a special character that automatically appears in specific positions of a field value; users don't need to type literal display characters. To include these characters, you need to create an input mask, which is a predefined format used to enter and display data in a field. An easy way to create an input mask is to use the **Input Mask Wizard**, an Access tool that guides you in creating a predefined format for a field. You must be in Design view to use the Input Mask Wizard.

To use the Input Mask Wizard for the Phone field:

1. Open the **tblPatient** table, close the Navigation Pane, and then, if necessary, switch to Design view.
2. Click the **Phone Field Name** box to make that row the current row and to display its Field Properties options.
3. Click the **Input Mask** box in the Field Properties pane. The Build button [...] appears at the right edge of the Input Mask box.
4. Click the **Build** button [...] in the Input Mask box. The first Input Mask Wizard dialog box opens. See Figure 5–33.

Figure 5–33 Input Mask Wizard dialog box

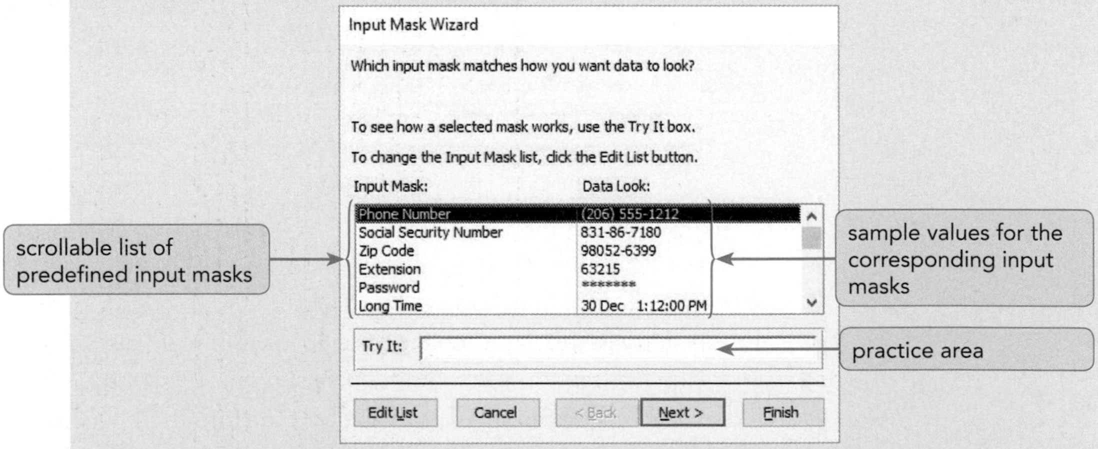
Input Mask Wizard
Which input mask matches how you want data to look?
To see how a selected mask works, use the Try It box.
To change the Input Mask list, click the Edit List button.
Input Mask:
Data Look:
Phone Number
(206) 555-1212
Social Security Number
831-86-7180
Zip Code
98052-6399
Extension
63215
Password
****
Long Time
30 Dec 1:12:00 PM
Try It:
Edit List
Cancel
< Back
Next >
Finish
scrollable list of predefined input masks
sample values for the corresponding input masks
practice area

You can scroll the Input Mask box, select the input mask you want, and then enter representative values to practice using the input mask.

5. If necessary, click **Phone Number** in the Input Mask box to select it.

6. Click the far left side of the **Try It** box. (___) ___-___ appears in the Try It box. As you type a phone number, the underscores, which are placeholder characters, are replaced.

   Trouble? If your insertion point is not immediately to the right of the left parenthesis, press ← until it is.

7. Type **6785550089** to practice entering a sample phone number. The input mask formats the typed value as (678) 555-0089.

8. Click the **Next** button. The next Input Mask Wizard dialog box opens. In it, you can change the input mask and the placeholder character. Because you can change an input mask easily after the Input Mask Wizard finishes, you'll accept all wizard defaults.

9. Click the **Finish** button, and then click to the right of the value in the Input Mask box to deselect the characters. The Input Mask Wizard creates the phone number input mask, placing it in the Input Mask box for the Phone field. See Figure 5–34.

Figure 5–34 **Phone number input mask created by the Input Mask Wizard**

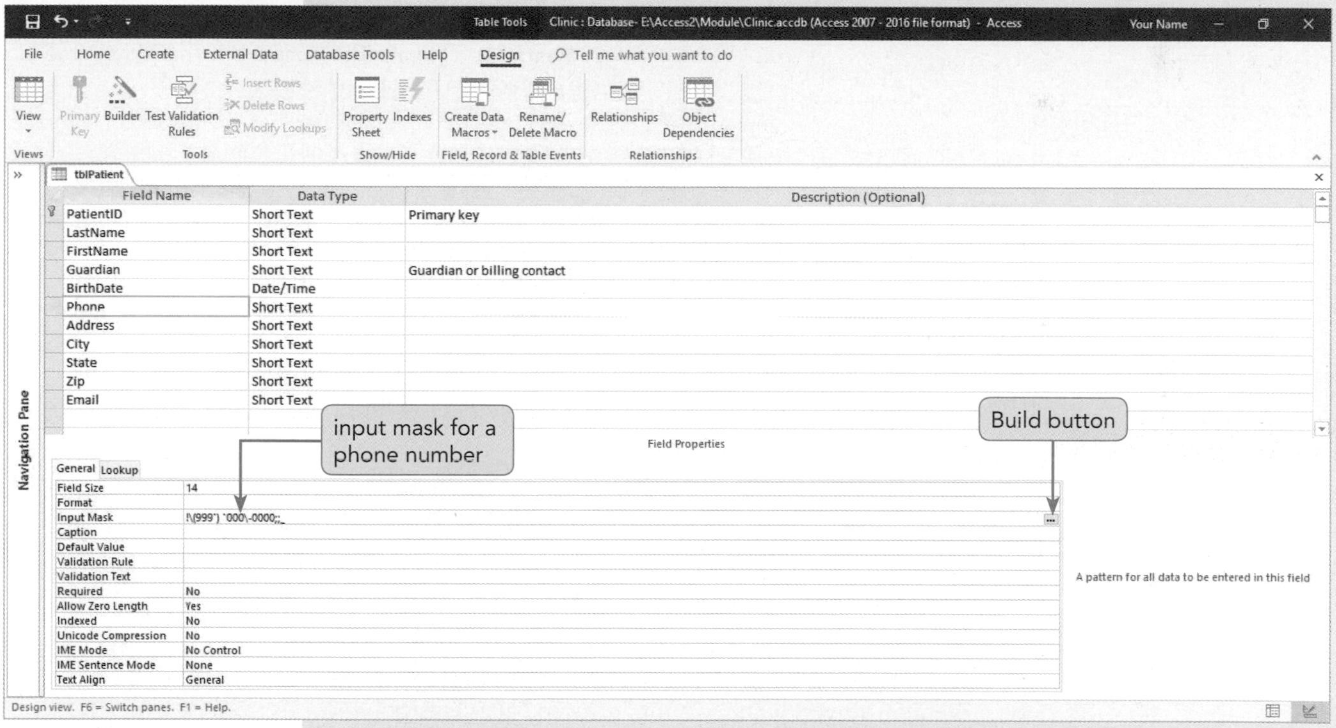
input mask for a phone number
Build button

The characters used in a field's input mask restrict the data you can enter in the field, as shown in Figure 5–35. Other characters that appear in an input mask, such as the left and right parentheses in the phone number input mask, are literal display characters.

Figure 5–35 Input mask characters

Input Mask Character	Description
0	Digit only must be entered. Entry is required.
9	Digit or space can be entered. Entry is optional.
#	Digit, space, or a plus or minus sign can be entered. Entry is optional.
L	Letter only must be entered. Entry is required.
?	Letter only can be entered. Entry is optional.
A	Letter or digit must be entered. Entry is required.
a	Letter or digit can be entered. Entry is optional.
&	Any character or a space must be entered. Entry is required.
C	Any character or a space can be entered. Entry is optional.
>	All characters that follow are displayed in uppercase.
<	All characters that follow are displayed in lowercase.
"	Enclosed characters treated as literal display characters.
\	Following character treated as a literal display character. This is the same as enclosing a single character in quotation marks.
!	Input mask is displayed from right to left, rather than the default of left to right. Characters typed into the mask always fill in from left to right.
;;	The character between the first and second semicolons determines whether to store the literal display characters in the database. If the value is 1 or if no value is provided, the literal display characters are not stored. If the value is 0, the literal display characters are stored. The character following the second semicolon is the placeholder character that appears in the displayed input mask.

Donna wants to view the Phone field with the default input mask.

To view and change the input mask for the Phone field:

1. Save the table, and then switch to Datasheet view. The Phone field values now have the format specified by the input mask.

   Donna decides that she would prefer to omit the parentheses around the area codes and use only hyphens as separators in the displayed Phone field values, so you'll change the input mask in Design view.

2. Switch to Design view.

   The input mask is set to !\(999") "000\-0000;;_. The backslash character (\) causes the character that follows it to appear as a literal display character. Characters enclosed in quotation marks also appear as literal display characters. (See Figure 5–35.) The exclamation mark (!) forces the existing data to fill the input mask from right to left instead of left to right. This does not affect new data. This applies only when data has already been entered in the table and a new input mask is applied. For instance, if the existing data is 5551234 and the input mask fills from left to right, the data with the input mask would look like (555) 123-4. If the input mask fills from right to left, the data with the input mask applied would look like ( ) 555-1234.

If you omit the backslashes preceding the hyphens, Access inserts them when you press TAB. However, Access does not add backslashes for other literal display characters, such as periods and slashes, so it's always best to type the backslashes. Since all of the existing data includes the area code, it will not make a difference whether the input mask applied to the data fills the data from left to right or from right to left, so you'll omit the ! symbol.

3. In the Input Mask box for the Phone field, change the input mask to **999\-000\-0000;;_** and then press **TAB**.

   Because you've modified a field property, the Property Update Options button appears to the left of the Input Mask property.

4. Click the **Property Update Options** button. A menu opens below the button, as shown in Figure 5–36.

Figure 5–36 Property Update Options button menu

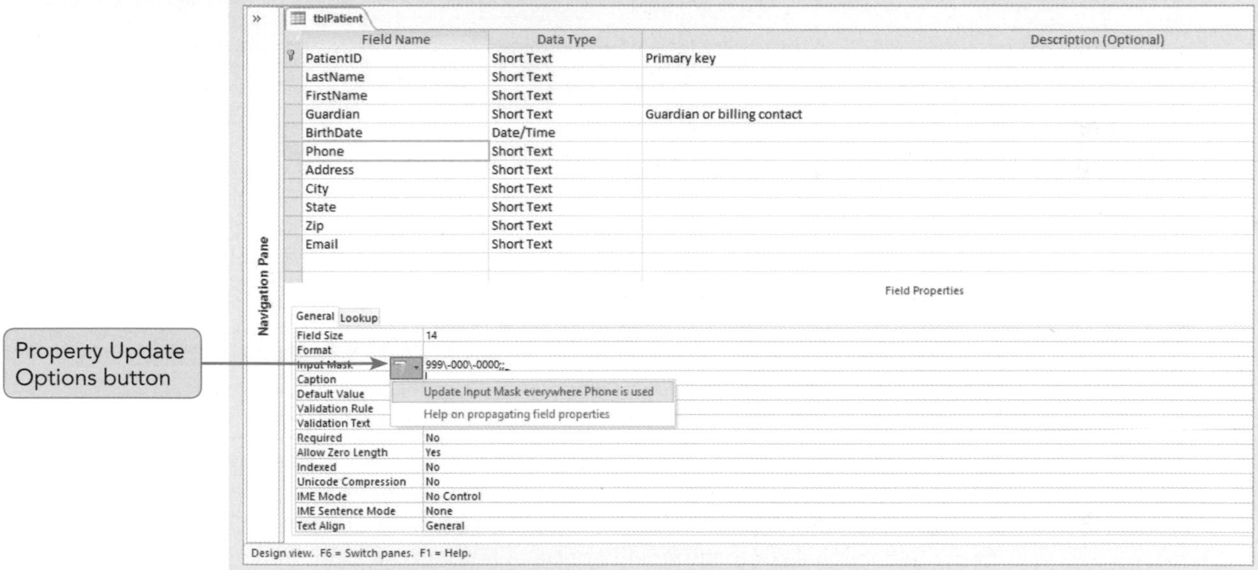
Property Update Options button
tblPatient
Field Name
Data Type
Description (Optional)
PatientID
Short Text
Primary key
LastName
FirstName
Guardian
Guardian or billing contact
BirthDate
Date/Time
Phone
Address
City
State
Zip
Email
Navigation Pane
Field Properties
General
Lookup
Field Size
14
Format
Input Mask
999\-000\-0000;;_
Caption
Default Value
Update Input Mask everywhere Phone is used
Validation Rule
Help on propagating field properties
Validation Text
Required
No
Allow Zero Length
Yes
Indexed
No
Unicode Compression
No
IME Mode
No Control
IME Sentence Mode
None
Text Align
General
Design view. F6 = Switch panes. F1 = Help.

5. Click **Update Input Mask everywhere Phone is used**. The Update Properties dialog box opens. See Figure 5–37.

Figure 5–37 Update Properties dialog box

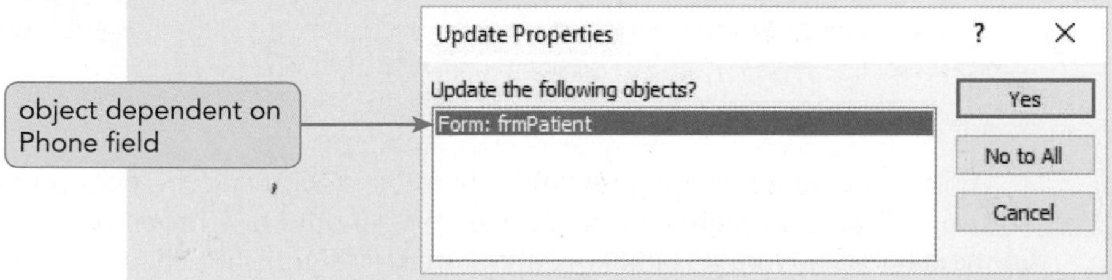
object dependent on Phone field
Update Properties
Update the following objects?
Form: frmPatient
Yes
No to All
Cancel

Because the frmPatient form displays the Phone field values from the tblPatient table, the Phone field's Input Mask property in this object will automatically be changed to your new input mask. If other form objects included the Phone field from the tblPatient table, they would be included in this dialog box as well. This capability to update control properties in objects when you modify a table field property is called **property propagation**.

Although the Update Properties dialog box displays no queries, property propagation also occurs with queries automatically. Property propagation is limited to field properties such as the Decimal Places, Description, Format, and Input Mask properties.

6. Click the **Yes** button, save the table, switch to Datasheet view, and then if necessary, resize the Phone column to its best fit. The Phone field values now have the format Donna requested. See Figure 5–38.

Figure 5–38 After changing the Phone field input mask

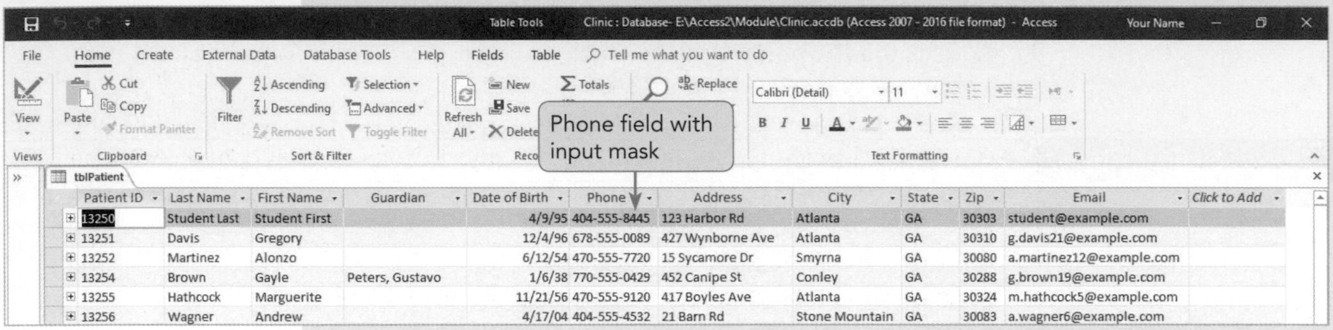
Clinic : Database- E:\Access2\Module\Clinic.accdb (Access 2007 - 2016 file format) - Access
Phone field with input mask
tblPatient
Patient ID Last Name First Name Guardian Date of Birth Phone Address City State Zip Email
13250 Student Last Student First 4/9/95 404-555-8445 123 Harbor Rd Atlanta GA 30303 student@example.com
13251 Davis Gregory 12/4/96 678-555-0089 427 Wynborne Ave Atlanta GA 30310 g.davis21@example.com
13252 Martinez Alonzo 6/12/54 470-555-7720 15 Sycamore Dr Smyrna GA 30080 a.martinez12@example.com
13254 Brown Gayle Peters, Gustavo 1/6/38 770-555-0429 452 Canipe St Conley GA 30288 g.brown19@example.com
13255 Hathcock Marguerite 11/21/56 470-555-9120 417 Boyles Ave Atlanta GA 30324 m.hathcock5@example.com
13256 Wagner Andrew 4/17/04 404-555-4532 21 Barn Rd Stone Mountain GA 30083 a.wagner6@example.com

Because Donna wants her staff to store only standard 10-digit U.S. phone numbers for patients, the input mask you've created will enforce the standard entry and display format that Donna desires.

INSIGHT

Understanding When to Use Input Masks

An input mask is appropriate for a field only if all field values have a consistent format. For example, you can use an input mask with hyphens as literal display characters to store U.S. phone numbers in a consistent format of 987-654-3210. However, a multinational company would not be able to use an input mask to store phone numbers from all countries because international phone numbers do not have a consistent format. In the same way, U.S. zip codes have a consistent format, and you could use an input mask of 00000#9999 to enter and display U.S. zip codes such as 98765 and 98765-4321, but you could not use an input mask if you need to store and display foreign postal codes in the same field. If you need to store and display phone numbers, zip/postal codes, and other fields in a variety of formats, it's best to define them as Short Text fields without an input mask so users can enter the correct literal display characters.

After you changed the Phone field's input mask, you had the option to update, selectively and automatically, the Phone field's Input Mask property in other objects in the database. Donna is thinking about making significant changes to the way data is stored in the tblPatient table and wants to understand which other elements those changes might impact. To determine the dependencies among objects in an Access database, you'll open the Object Dependencies pane.

Identifying Object Dependencies

An **object dependency** exists between two objects when a change to the properties of data in one object affects the properties of data in the other object. Dependencies between Access objects, such as tables, queries, and forms, can occur in various ways. For example, the tblVisit and tblBilling tables are dependent on each other because they have a one-to-many relationship. In the same way, the tblPatient table uses the qryPatientsByName query to obtain the Patient field to display along with the PatientID field, and this creates a dependency between these two objects. Any query, form, or other object that uses fields from a given table is dependent on that table. Any form or report that uses fields from a query is directly dependent on the query and is indirectly dependent on the tables that provide the data to the query. Large databases contain hundreds of objects, so it is useful to have a way to easily view the dependencies among objects before you attempt to delete or modify an object. The **Object Dependencies pane** displays a collapsible list of the dependencies among the objects in an Access database; you click the list's expand indicators to show or hide different levels of dependencies. Next, you'll open the Object Dependencies pane to examine the object dependencies in the Clinic database.

To open and use the Object Dependencies pane:

1. Click the **Database Tools** tab on the ribbon.
2. In the Relationships group, click the **Object Dependencies** button to open the Object Dependencies pane, and then drag the left edge of the pane to the left until none of the items in the list are cut off.
3. If necessary, click the **Objects that depend on me** option button to select it, then click the **Refresh** link to display the list of objects. See Figure 5–39.

Figure 5–39 The Object Dependencies pane for the tblPatient table

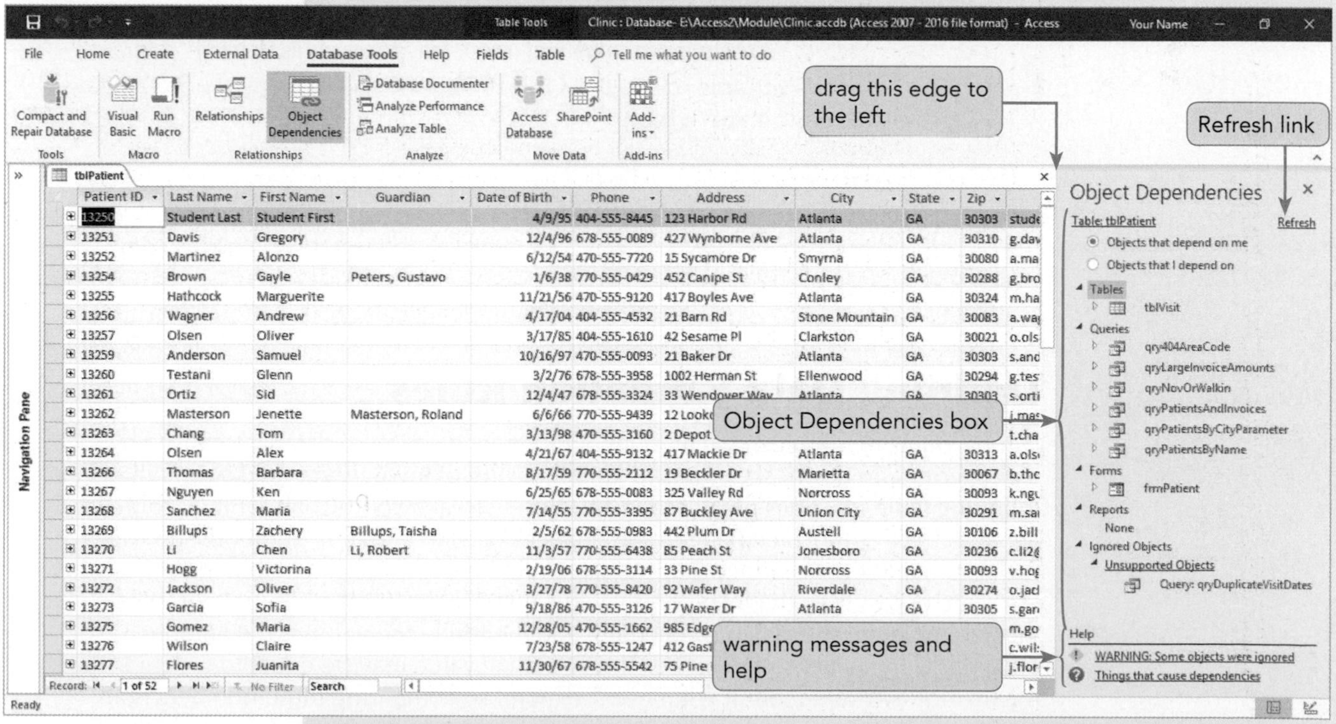
drag this edge to the left
Refresh link
Object Dependencies box
warning messages and help

The Object Dependencies pane displays the objects that depend on the tblPatient table, the object name that appears at the top of the pane. If you change the design of the tblPatient table, the change might affect objects in the pane. Changing a property for a field in the tblPatient table that's also used by a listed object affects that listed object. If a listed object does not use the field you are changing, that listed object is not affected.

Objects listed in the Ignored Objects section of the box might have an object dependency with the tblPatient table, and you'd have to review them individually to determine if a dependency exists. The Help section at the bottom of the pane displays links for further information about object dependencies.

4. Click the **frmPatient** link in the Object Dependencies pane. The frmPatient form opens in Design view. All the fields in the form are fields from the tblPatient table, which is why the form has an object dependency with the table.
5. Switch to Form view for the frmPatient form. Note that the Phone field value is displayed using the input mask you applied to the field in the tblPatient table. This change was propagated from the table to the form.
6. Close the frmPatient form, open the Navigation Pane, open the **tblVisit** table in Datasheet view, and then click the **Refresh** link near the top of the Object Dependencies pane. The Object Dependencies box now displays the objects that depend on the tblVisit table.
7. Click the **Objects that I depend on** option button near the top of the pane to view the objects that affect the tblPatient table.
8. Click the **Objects that depend on me** option button, and then click the right-pointing triangle expand indicator ▷ for the qryPatientsAndInvoices query in the Object Dependencies pane. The list expands to display the qryPatientsAndInvoicesCrosstab query, which is another query that depends on the tblVisit table.
9. Close the tblVisit table, close the Object Dependencies pane, and then save and close the tblPatient table.

You let Donna know about the object dependencies for the tblPatient table. She decides to leave the tblPatient table the way it is for the moment to avoid making changes to forms or queries.

Defining Data Validation Rules

Donna wants to minimize the amount of incorrect data in the database caused by typing errors. To do so, she wants to limit the entry of InvoiceAmt field values in the tblBilling table to values greater than $10 because Lakewood Community Health Services does not invoice patients for balances of $10 or less. In addition, she wants to make sure that the Insurance field value entered in each tblBilling table record is either the same or less than the InvoiceAmt field value. The InvoiceAmt value represents the total price for the visit or procedure, and the Insurance value is the amount covered by the patient's insurance. The Insurance value may be equal to or less than the InvoiceAmt value, but it will never be more, so comparing these numbers is an additional test to ensure the data entered in a record makes sense. To provide these checks on entered data, you'll set field validation properties for the InvoiceAmt field in the tblBilling table and set table validation properties in the tblBilling table.

Defining Field Validation Rules

To prevent a user from entering an unacceptable value in the InvoiceAmt field, you can create a **field validation rule** that verifies a field value by comparing it to a constant or to a set of constants. You create a field validation rule by setting the Validation Rule and the Validation Text field properties. The **Validation Rule property** value specifies the valid values that users can enter in a field. The **Validation Text property** value will be displayed in a dialog box if a user enters an invalid value (in this case, an InvoiceAmt field value of $10 or less). After you set these two InvoiceAmt field properties in the tblBilling table, users will be prevented from entering an invalid InvoiceAmt field value in the tblBilling table and in all current and future queries and future forms that include the InvoiceAmt field.

You'll now set the Validation Rule and Validation Text properties for the InvoiceAmt field in the tblBilling table.

To create and test a field validation rule for the InvoiceAmt field:

1. Open the **tblBilling** table in Design view, close the Navigation Pane, and then click the **InvoiceAmt Field Name** box to make that row the current row.

   To make sure that all values entered in the InvoiceAmt field are greater than 10, you'll use the > comparison operator in the Validation Rule box.

2. In the Field Properties pane, click the **Validation Rule** box, type **>10**, and then press **TAB**.

   You can set the Validation Text property to a value that appears in a dialog box that opens if a user enters a value not listed in the Validation Rule box.

3. In the Validation Text box, type **Invoice amounts must be greater than 10** as the message. See Figure 5–40.

Figure 5–40 Validation properties for the InvoiceAmt field

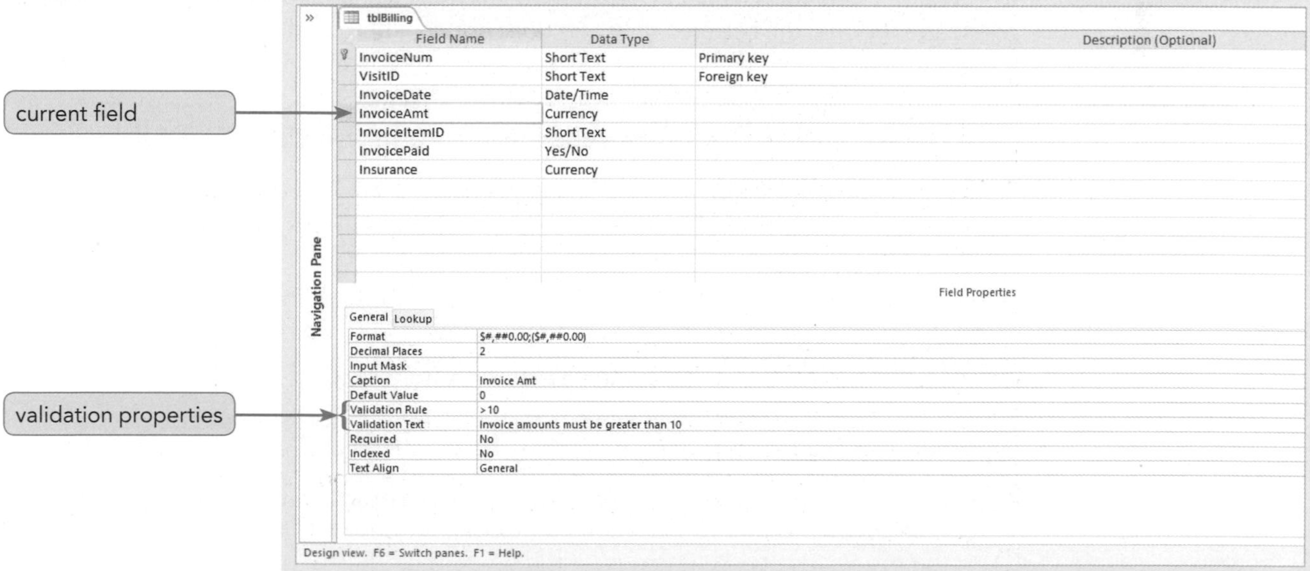
current field
validation properties
tblBilling
Field Name
Data Type
Description (Optional)
InvoiceNum
Short Text
Primary key
VisitID
Short Text
Foreign key
InvoiceDate
Date/Time
InvoiceAmt
Currency
InvoiceItemID
Short Text
InvoicePaid
Yes/No
Insurance
Currency
Navigation Pane
Field Properties
General
Lookup
Format
$#,##0.00;($#,##0.00)
Decimal Places
2
Input Mask
Caption
Invoice Amt
Default Value
0
Validation Rule
>10
Validation Text
Invoice amounts must be greater than 10
Required
No
Indexed
No
Text Align
General
Design view. F6 = Switch panes. F1 = Help.

You can now save the table design changes and then test the validation properties.

4. Save the table, and then click the **Yes** button when asked if you want to test the existing InvoiceAmt field values in the tblBilling table against the new validation rule.

   The existing records in the tblBilling table are tested against the validation rule. If any existing record violated the rule, you would be prompted to continue testing or to revert to the previous Validation Rule property setting. Next, you'll test the validation rule.

5. Switch to Datasheet view, select **$125.00** in the first row's InvoiceAmt field box, type **5**, and then press **TAB**. A dialog box opens containing the message "Invoice amounts must be greater than 10", which is the Validation Text property setting you created in Step 3.
6. Click the **OK** button, and then press **ESC**. The first row's InvoiceAmt field reverts to its original value, $125.00.
7. Close the tblBilling table.

Now that you've finished entering the field validation rule for the InvoiceAmt field in the tblBilling table, you'll enter the table validation rule for the date fields in the tblVisit table.

Defining Table Validation Rules

To make sure that the Insurance field value that a user enters in the tblBilling table is not larger than the InvoiceAmt field value, you can create a **table validation rule**, which compares one field value in a table record to another field value in the same record to verify their relative accuracy. Once again, you'll use the Validation Rule and Validation Text properties, but this time you'll set these properties for the table instead of for an individual field. You'll use a table validation rule because this validation involves multiple fields. A field validation rule is used when the validation involves a restriction for only the selected field and does not depend on other fields.

To create and test a table validation rule in the tblBilling table:

Be sure "Table Properties" is listed as the selection type in the property sheet.

1. Open the **tblBilling** table in Design view, close the Navigation Pane, and then on the Table Tools Design tab, in the Show/Hide group, click the **Property Sheet** button to open the property sheet for the table.

   To make sure that each Insurance field value is less than or equal to the InvoiceAmt field value, you use the Validation Rule box for the table.

2. In the property sheet, click the **Validation Rule** box.
3. Type **Insur**, press **TAB** to select Insurance in the AutoComplete box, type **<= InvoiceAm**, and then press **TAB**.
4. In the Validation Text box, type **Insurance coverage cannot be larger than the invoice amount** and then, if necessary, widen the Property Sheet pane so the Validation Rule text is visible. See Figure 5–41.

Figure 5–41 Setting table validation properties

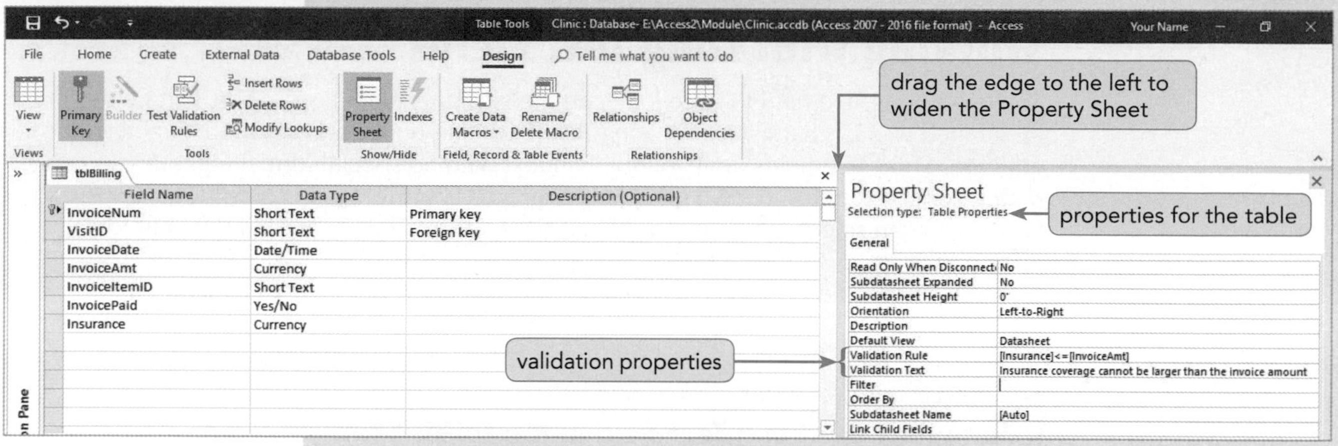
drag the edge to the left to widen the Property Sheet
properties for the table
validation properties
Property Sheet
Selection type: Table Properties
Validation Rule
[Insurance]<=[InvoiceAmt]
Validation Text
Insurance coverage cannot be larger than the invoice amount

5. Close the property sheet, save the table, and then click the **Yes** button when asked if you want to test the existing dates in the tblBilling table against the new validation rule.
6. Switch to Datasheet view, and then click the Insurance column value in the first record.
7. Edit the Insurance value to change it to $150.00, and then press **TAB** to complete your changes to the record. A dialog box opens containing the message "Insurance coverage cannot be larger than the invoice amount," which is the Validation Text property setting you entered in Step 4.

   Unlike field validation rule violations, which are detected immediately after you finish a field entry and advance to another field, table validation rule violations are detected only when you finish all changes to the current record and advance to another record.
8. Click the **OK** button, and then press **ESC** to undo your change to the Insurance column value.
9. Close the tblBilling table.

PROSKILLS

Problem Solving: Perfecting Data Quality

It's important that you design useful queries, forms, and reports and that you test them thoroughly. But the key to any database is the accuracy of the data stored in its tables. The data must be as error-free as possible. Most companies employ people who spend many hours tracking down and correcting errors and discrepancies in their data, and you can greatly assist and minimize their problem solving by using as many database features as possible to ensure the data is correct from the start. Among these features for fields are selecting the proper data type, setting default values whenever possible, restricting the permitted values by using field and table validation rules, enforcing referential integrity, and forcing users to select values from lists instead of typing the values. Likewise, having an arsenal of queries—such as find duplicates and top values queries—available to users will expedite the work they do to find and correct data errors.

Based on a request from Donna, Reginald added a Long Text field to the tblVisit table. Next you'll review Reginald's work.

Working with Long Text Fields

You use a Long Text field to store long comments and explanations. Short Text fields are limited to 255 characters, but Long Text fields can hold up to 65,535 characters. In addition, Short Text fields limit you to plain text with no special formatting, but you can define Long Text fields to store plain text similar to Short Text fields or to store rich text, which you can selectively format with options such as bold, italic, and different fonts and colors.

You'll review the Long Text field, named Comments, that Reginald added to the tblVisit table.

To review the Long Text field in the tblVisit table:

1. Open the Navigation Pane, open the **tblVisit** table in Datasheet view, and then close the Navigation Pane.
2. Increase the width of the Comments field so most of the comments fit in the column.

   Although everything fits on the screen when using a screen of average size and resolution, on some computer systems, you need to freeze panes to view everything at once. On a smaller screen, if you scroll to the right to view the Comments field, you'll no longer be able to identify which patient applies to a row because the Patient ID column will be hidden. You may also see this effect if you shrink the size of the Access window. You'll freeze the Visit ID, Patient ID, and Date of Visit columns so they remain visible in the datasheet as you scroll to the right.
3. Click the **Visit ID column** selector, press and hold down **SHIFT**, click the **Date of Visit** column selector, and then release **SHIFT**. The Visit ID, Patient ID, and Date of Visit columns are selected.
4. On the Home tab, in the Records group, click the **More** button, and then click **Freeze Fields**.
5. If necessary, reduce the size of the Access window so not all columns are visible, and then scroll to the right until you see the Comments column. Notice that the Visit ID, Patient ID, and Date of Visit columns, the three leftmost columns, remain visible when you scroll. See Figure 5–42.

Figure 5–42 **Freezing three datasheet columns**

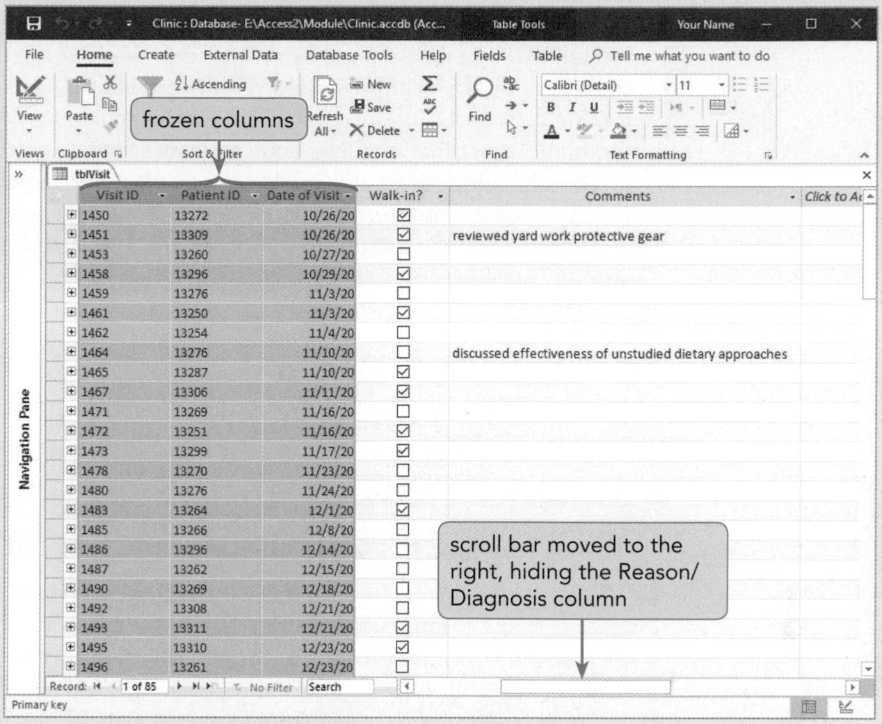
frozen columns
scroll bar moved to the right, hiding the Reason/ Diagnosis column

The Comments column is a Long Text field that Lakewood Community Health Services clinicians use to store observations and other commentary about each patient visit.

6. Scroll down if necessary so Visit ID 1557 is visible.

   Note that the Comment for Visit ID 1557 displays rich text using a bold and green font. The Comments field values are partially hidden because the datasheet column is not wide enough. You'll view a record's Comments field value in the Zoom dialog box.

7. Click the **Comments** box for the record for Visit ID 1557, hold down **SHIFT**, press **F2**, and then release **SHIFT**. The Zoom dialog box displays the entire Comments field value.

8. Click the **OK** button to close the Zoom dialog box.

INSIGHT

Viewing Long Text Fields with Large Contents in Datasheet View

For a Long Text field that contains many characters, you can widen the field's column to view more of its contents by dragging the right edge of the field's column selector to the right or by using the Field Width command when you click the More button in the Records group on the Home tab. However, increasing the column width reduces the number of other columns you can view at the same time. Further, for Long Text fields containing thousands of characters, you can't widen the column enough to be able to view the entire contents of the field at one time across the width of the screen. Therefore, increasing the column width of a Long Text field isn't necessarily the best strategy for viewing table contents. Instead, you should use the Zoom dialog box in a datasheet or use a large scrollable box on a form.

Now you'll review the property settings for the Comments field Reginald added to the tblVisit table.

To review the property settings of the Long Text field:

1. Save the table, switch to Design view, click the **Comments Field Name** box to make that row the current row, and then, if necessary, scroll to the bottom of the list of properties in the Field Properties pane.
2. Click the **Text Format** box in the Field Properties pane, and then click its arrow. The list of available text formats appears in the box. See Figure 5–43.

Figure 5–43 **Viewing the properties for a Long Text field**

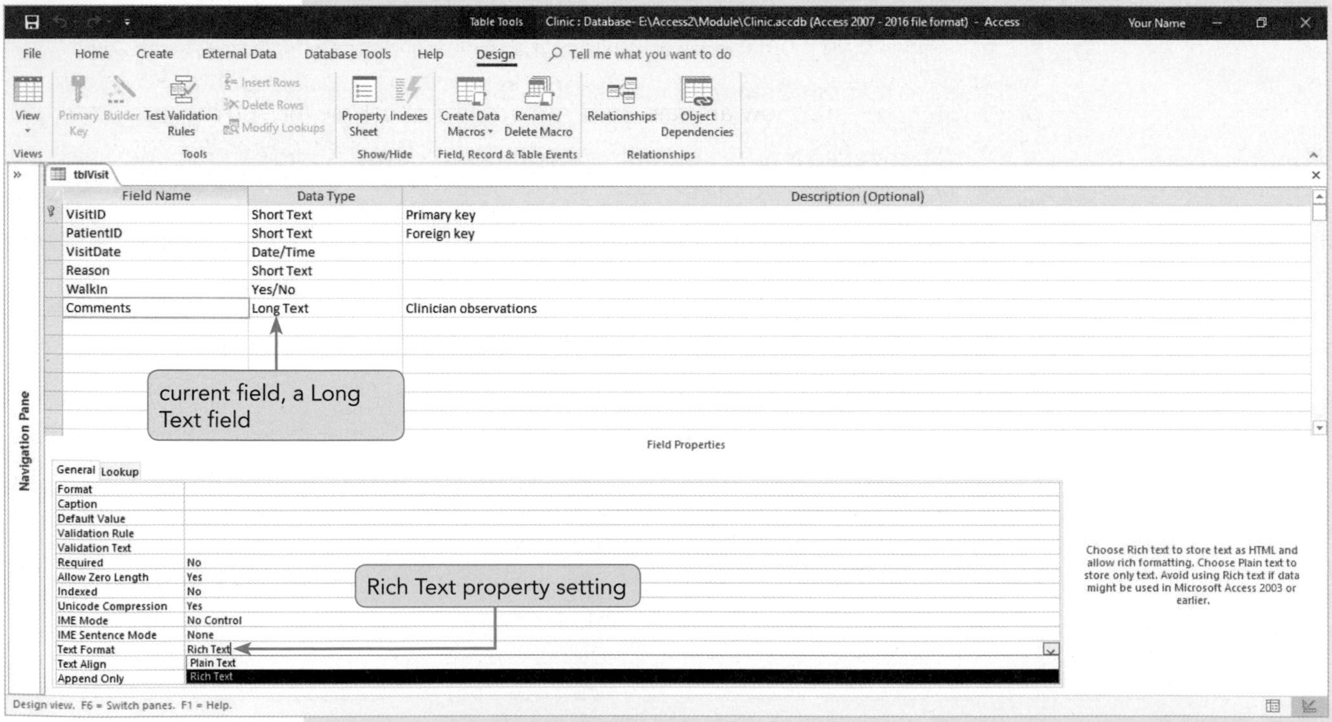
current field, a Long Text field
Rich Text property setting

Reginald set the **Text Format property** for the Comments field to Rich Text, which lets you format the field contents using the options in the Font group on the Home tab. The default Text Format property setting for a Long Text field is Plain Text, which doesn't allow text formatting.

3. Click the **arrow** on the Text Format box to close the list, and then click the **Append Only** box.

   The **Append Only property**, which appears at the bottom of the list of properties, enables you to track the changes that you make to a Long Text field. Setting this property to Yes causes a historical record of all versions of the Long Text field value to be maintained. You can view each version of the field value, along with a date and time stamp of when each version change occurred.

   You've finished your review of the Long Text field, so you can close the table.

4. Close the tblVisit table.

When employees at Lakewood Community Health Services open the Clinic database, a security warning might appear below the ribbon, and they must enable the content of the database before beginning their work. Donna asks if you can eliminate this extra step when employees open the database.

Designating a Trusted Folder

A database is a file, and files can contain malicious instructions that can damage other files on your computer or files on other computers on your network. Unless you take special steps, every database is treated as a potential threat to your computer. One special step that you can take is to designate a folder as a trusted folder. A **trusted folder** is a folder on a drive or network that you designate as trusted and where you place databases you know are safe. When you open a database located in a trusted folder, Access no longer displays a security warning. You can also place files used with other Microsoft Office programs, such as Word documents and Excel workbooks, in a trusted folder to eliminate warnings when you open them.

Because the Clinic database is from a trusted source, you'll specify its location as a trusted folder to eliminate the security warning when a user opens the database.

To designate a trusted folder:

1. Click the **File** tab, and then click **Options** in the navigation bar. The Access Options dialog box opens.
2. In the left section of the dialog box, click **Trust Center**. The Trust Center options are displayed in the dialog box.
3. In the right section of the dialog box, click the **Trust Center Settings** button to open the Trust Center dialog box.
4. In the left section of the Trust Center dialog box, click **Trusted Locations**. The trusted locations for your installation of Access and other trust options are displayed on the right. See Figure 5–44.

Figure 5–44 Designating a trusted folder

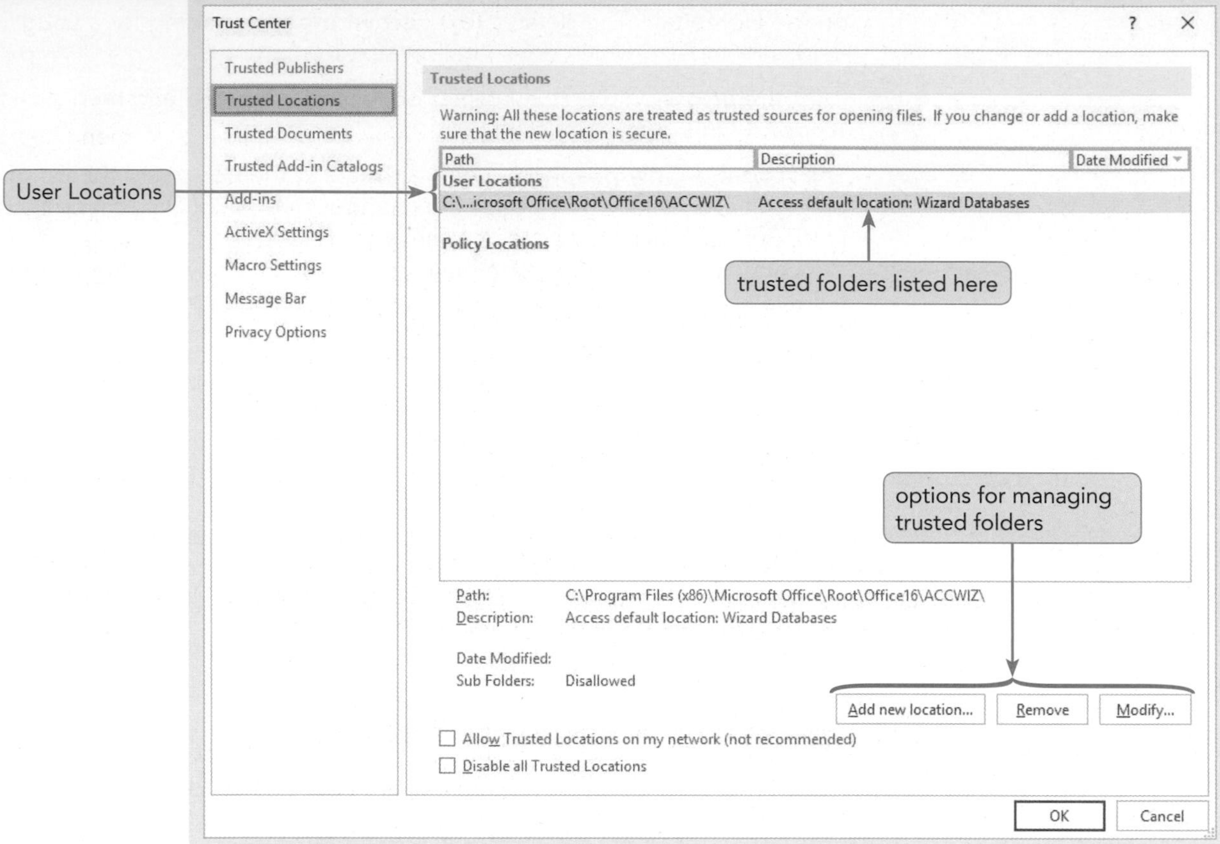
Trust Center
Trusted Publishers
Trusted Locations
Trusted Documents
Trusted Add-in Catalogs
Add-ins
ActiveX Settings
Macro Settings
Message Bar
Privacy Options
Trusted Locations
Warning: All these locations are treated as trusted sources for opening files. If you change or add a location, make sure that the new location is secure.
Path
Description
Date Modified
User Locations
C:\...icrosoft Office\Root\Office16\ACCWIZ\
Access default location: Wizard Databases
Policy Locations
User Locations
trusted folders listed here
options for managing trusted folders
Path: C:\Program Files (x86)\Microsoft Office\Root\Office16\ACCWIZ\
Description: Access default location: Wizard Databases
Date Modified:
Sub Folders: Disallowed
Add new location...
Remove
Modify...
Allow Trusted Locations on my network (not recommended)
Disable all Trusted Locations
OK
Cancel

Existing trusted locations appear in the list at the top, and options to add, remove, and modify trusted locations appear at the bottom.

Trouble? Check with your instructor before adding a new trusted location. If your instructor tells you not to create a new trusted location, skip to Step 8.

5. Click the **Add new location** button to open the Microsoft Office Trusted Location dialog box.
6. In the Microsoft Office Trusted Location dialog box, click the **Browse** button, navigate to the Access2 > Module folder where your Data Files are stored, and then click the **OK** button.

   You can also choose to designate subfolders of the selected location as trusted locations, but you won't select this option. By default, files in subfolders are not trusted.
7. Click the **OK** button. The Access2 > Module folder is added to the list of trusted locations.
8. Click the **OK** button to close the Trust Center dialog box, and then click the **OK** button to close the Access Options dialog box.

You've created several queries and completed several table design changes, so you should compact and repair the Clinic database. Reginald doesn't use the Compact on Close option with the Clinic database because it's possible to lose the database if there's a computer malfunction when the Compact on Close operation runs.

As a precaution, you'll make a backup copy of the database before you compact and repair it. Making frequent backup copies of your critical files safeguards your data from hardware and software malfunctions, which can occur at any time.

To back up, compact, and repair the Clinic database:

1. Click the **File** tab on the ribbon, and then click the **Save As** menu item.
2. Click the **Back Up Database** option, and then click the **Save As** button. The Save As dialog box opens with a suggested filename of Clinic_date in the File name box, where date is the current date in the format year-month-day. For instance, if you made a backup on April 22, 2021, the suggested filename would be Clinic_2021-04-22.
3. Navigate to the location of a USB drive or other external medium, if available, and then click the **Save** button to save the backup file.

   Next, you'll verify that the trusted location is working.
4. Click the **File** tab on the ribbon, and then click the **Close** command to close the Clinic database.
5. Click the **File** tab on the ribbon, click **Open** on the navigation bar, and then click **Clinic.accdb** in the Recent list. The database opens, and no security warning appears below the ribbon because the database is located in the trusted location you designated.

   Next, you'll compact and repair the database.
6. Click the **File** tab on the ribbon, and then click the **Compact & Repair Database** button.
7. sam Close the Clinic database.

You've completed the table design changes to the Clinic database, which will make working with it easier and more accurate.

REVIEW

Session 5.3 Quick Check

1. What is a lookup field?
2. A(n) ________ is a predefined format you use to enter and display data in a field.
3. What is property propagation?
4. Define the Validation Rule property, and give an example of when you would use it.
5. Define the Validation Text property, and give an example of when you would use it.
6. Setting a Long Text field's Text Format property to ________ lets you format its contents.
7. A(n) ________ folder is a location where you can place databases that you know are safe.

PRACTICE

Review Assignments

Data File needed for the Review Assignments: Supplier.accdb

Donna asks you to create several new queries and enhance the table design for the Supplier database. This database contains information about the vendors that Lakewood Community Health Services works with to obtain medical supplies and equipment for the center, as well as the vendors who service and maintain the equipment. Complete the following steps:

1. Open the **Supplier** database located in the Access2 > Review folder provided with your Data Files.
2. Modify the first record in the tblSupplier table datasheet by changing the ContactFirst and ContactLast Name field values to your first and last names, if necessary. Close the table.
3. Create a query called **qrySupplierNameAndAddress** that lists the following fields from the tblSupplier table: SupplierID, Company, City, State, and Zip. After you have created the query, use the AutoFilter feature of Access to list the suppliers in MD, PA, and VA only. Use the Toggle Filter button to remove and reapply the filter. Save and close the query.
4. Create a query to find all records in the tblSupplier table in which the City field value starts with the letter R. Display all fields in the query recordset, and sort in ascending order by the company name. Save the query as **qryRSelectedCities**, run the query, and then close it.
5. Make a copy of the qryRSelectedCities query using the new name **qryOtherSelectedCities**.
6. Modify the new query to find all records in the tblSupplier table in which the City field values are not Durham, Pittsburgh, or Richmond. Save and run the query, and then close it.
7. Create a query to find all records from the tblSupplier table in which the State value is GA, NC, or SC. Use a list-of-values match for the selection criteria. Display all fields in the query recordset, and sort in descending order by the company name. Save the query as **qrySelectedStates**, run the query, and then close it.
8. Create a query to display all records from the tblSupplier table, selecting the Company, City, and Phone fields, and sorting in ascending order by Company. Add a calculated field named **ContactName** as the last column that concatenates the ContactFirst value, a space, and the ContactLast value. If the contact has a nickname, use the nickname in place of the first name in the calculated field. Set the Caption property for the ContactName field to **Contact Name**. Save the query as **qryCompanyContacts**, run the query, resize the Contact Name column to its best fit, and then save and close the query.
9. Create a parameter query to select the tblSupplier table records for a State field value that the user specifies, using **Type the state**: as the prompt text. If the user doesn't enter a State field value, select all records from the table. Display the Company, Category, City, State, ContactFirst, ContactLast, and Phone fields in the query recordset, sorting in ascending order by City. Save the query as **qryStateParameter**. Run the query and enter no value as the State field value, and then run the query again and enter **WI** as the State field value. Close the query.
10. Create a crosstab query based on the tblSupplier table. Use the Category field values for the row headings, the SupplierID field values for the column headings, and the count of the Company field values as the summarized value. Include row sums. Save the query as **qrySupplierCategoryCrosstab**. Change the column heading for the total of each category to **Total of Companies**. Resize the Total of Companies column in the query recordset to its best fit, and then save and close the query.
11. Create a find duplicates query based on the tblProduct table. Select ProductName as the field that might contain duplicates, and select the ProductID, SupplierID, Price, and Units fields as additional fields in the query recordset. Save the query as **qryDuplicateProductTypes**, run the query, and then close it. Because the tblProduct table does not have any duplicate ProductName values, running this query should show that no duplicate records are found.
12. Create a find unmatched query that finds all records in the tblSupplier table that do not have a matching record in the tblProduct table. Select SupplierID as the information in both tables and choose Company, Phone, ContactFirst, ContactNickname, ContactLast, InitialContact, and

LatestContact as the fields for the query results. Specify **qryUnusedSuppliers** as the query name, view the results, and verify that one supplier is listed.

13. Create a query to display all records from the tblProduct table, selecting the ProductID, SupplierID, ProductName, and Price fields, and sorting in descending order by Price. Use the Top Values property to select the top 25 percent of records. Save the query as **qryTop25Price**, run the query, and then close it.
14. In the tblProduct table, change the SupplierID field to a lookup field. Select the Company field and then the SupplierID field from the tblSupplier table. Sort in ascending order by the Company field, do not hide the key column, make sure the Company column is the leftmost column, resize the lookup columns to their best fit, select SupplierID as the field to store in the table, and accept the default label for the lookup column. View the tblProduct table datasheet, resize the Supplier ID column to its best fit, test the lookup field without changing a value permanently, and then save and close the table.
15. Use the Input Mask Wizard to add an input mask to the Phone field in the tblSupplier table. The ending input mask should use periods as separators, as in 987.654.3210 with only the last seven digits required; do not store the literal display characters, if you are asked to do so. Update the Input Mask property everywhere the Phone field is used. Resize all columns in the datasheet to their best fit, and then test the input mask by typing over an existing Phone field value, being sure not to change the value by pressing ESC after you type the last digit in the Phone field.
16. Set a field validation rule on the Price field in the tblProduct table. Ensure that each product entered will have a price greater than zero. Should a user attempt to enter a value of zero, or less than zero, the following message should be displayed: **All prices must be greater than zero**. Test the field validation rule by modifying the price of the first item in the recordset to 0, and verify that the error message is displayed. Reset the value of the record to its original value. Save and close the tblProduct table.
17. Open the tblSupplier table, and then set a table validation rule on the tblSupplier table to ensure the initial contact date is prior to, or equal to, the latest contact date. If an invalid value is entered, the following message should be displayed: "Latest contact date cannot be prior to the initial contact date." Test the table validation rule by changing the latest contact date prior to the initial contact date in the first record. Advance to the next record, then verify that the error message is displayed. Reset the values of the first record to their original values. Save your changes to the tblSupplier table.
18. Open the tblProduct table, and then open the Object Dependencies pane for the tblProduct object. Click the Objects that depend on me option button, and then click the Refresh link if necessary to see the list of objects that depend upon the tblProduct table. Verify that the tblSupplier table depends upon the tblProduct table, as well as the following queries: qryEquipmentOrTempControl, qryFLSuppliers, qryHighPriceAndSterile, qryHighPriceWithDiscount, qryPriceStatistics, qryPriceStatisticsBySupplier, qryTop25Price, and qryUnusedSuppliers. (Note that various forms and reports will depend on the tblProduct table as well.) Close the Object Dependencies pane.
19. In the tblSupplier table, examine the Field Properties pane for the CompanyComments field. Verify that the Text Format property is set to Rich Text, and that the Append Only property is set to Yes. Close the tblSupplier table without saving changes.
20. Designate the Access2 > Review folder as a trusted folder. (*Note:* Check with your instructor before adding a new trusted location.)
21. Make a backup copy of the database, compact and repair the database, and then close it.

APPLY

Case Problem 1

Data File needed for this Case Problem: School.accdb

Great Giraffe Jeremiah Garver is the operations manager at Great Giraffe, a career school in Denver, Colorado. Great Giraffe offers part-time and full-time courses in areas of study that are in high demand by industries in the area, including data science, digital marketing, and bookkeeping. Jeremiah created an Access database named School to store data about courses, registrations, and students. He wants to create several new queries and make design changes to the tables. Complete the following steps:

1. Open the **School** database located in the Access2 > Case1 folder provided with your Data Files.
2. Modify the first record in the tblStudent table datasheet by changing the First Name and Last Name column values to your first and last names, if necessary. Close the table.
3. Create a query to find all records in the tblStudent table in which the LastName field begins with H. Display the FirstName, LastName, City, and Phone fields in the query recordset, and sort in ascending order by LastName. Save the query as **qryLastNameH**, run the query, and then close it.
4. Create a query that finds all records in the tblCourse table with a Title value of Computer Science or Data Science. Use a list-of-values criterion and include the fields Title, StartDate, and HoursPerWeek in the query recordset, sorted in ascending order by StartDate. Save the query as **qryCompOrDataSci**, run the query, and then close it.
5. Create a query that finds all records in the tblStudent table in which the City field value is not equal to Denver. Display the FirstName, LastName, City, and Email fields in the query recordset, and sort in ascending order by City. Save the query as **qryNonDenver**, run the query, and then close it.
6. Create a query to display the InstanceID, TotalCost, and BalanceDue fields from the tblRegistration table and the Phone and Email fields from the tblStudent table. Find all records for which the BalanceDue value is greater than 0. Add a calculated field named **Payer** as the first column that concatenates FirstName, a space, LastName, and (student) if the BillingLastName field is null. Otherwise, the calculated field should concatenate BillingFirstName, a space, BillingLastName, and (billing). Sort the results on the calculated field in ascending order. Save the query as **qryBalanceContacts**, run the query, resize all columns to their best fit, and then save and close the query.
7. Create a parameter query to select the tblStudent table records for a City field value that the user specifies, using **Enter the city**: as the prompt text. If the user doesn't enter a City field value, select all records from the table. Display all fields from the tblStudent table in the query recordset. Save the query as **qryStudentCityParameter**. Run the query and enter no value as the City field value, and then run the query again and enter **Littleton** as the City field value. Close the query.
8. Create a find duplicates query based on the tblRegistration table. Select StudentID as the field that might contain duplicates, and select all other fields in the table as additional fields in the query recordset. Save the query as **qryDuplicateStudentRegistrations**, run the query, and then close it. Because the tblRegistration contains one student registered for two different courses, running this query should show that two records are found containing a duplicate StudentID.
9. Create a find unmatched query that finds all records in the tblStudent table for which there is no matching record in the tblRegistration table. Select the FirstName, LastName, Phone, and Email fields from the tblStudents table. Save the query as **qryUnregisteredStudents**, run the query, and then close it. Running this query should find five unmatched records.
10. Create a new query based on the tblStudent and tblRegistration tables. In the query recordset, display the FirstName, LastName, BillingFirstName, BillingLastName, Phone, and Email fields from the tblStudent table and the TotalCost and BalanceDue fields from the tblRegistration table. Sort in descending order by the BalanceDue field, and then use the Top Values property to select the top 5% of records. Save the query as **qryTopOutstandingBalances**, run the query, and then close it.
11. Use the Input Mask Wizard to add an input mask to the Phone field in the tblStudent table. The input mask should use periods as separators, as in 987.654.3210, with only the last seven digits required. Do not store the literal display characters if you are asked to do so, and apply the updated image mask everywhere it is used within the database. Resize the Phone column to its best fit, and then test the input mask by typing over an existing Phone column value, being certain not to change the value by pressing ESC after you type the last digit in the Phone column. Save and close the table.
12. Create a crosstab query based on the tblCourse table. Specify the HoursPerWeek values as the row headings and the Title field values as the column headings, calculate the InstanceID count, and include row sums. Save the query as **qryFullPartTimeCrosstab**, view the results, resize the columns as necessary, then save and close the query.

13. In the tblRegistration table, change the InstanceID field data type to Lookup Wizard. Select the Title, StartDate, and HoursPerWeek fields from the tblCourse table, sort in ascending order by Title, do not show the key column, resize the lookup columns to their best fit, select InstanceID as the field to store in the table, and accept the default label for the lookup column. View the tblRegistration datasheet, resize the InstanceID column to its best fit, test the lookup field without changing a field value permanently, and then close the table.
14. Define a field validation rule for the HoursPerWeek field in the tblCourse table. Acceptable field values for the HoursPerWeek field are values less than or equal to 40. Enter the message **Hours per week cannot be greater than 40** so it appears if a user enters an invalid HoursPerWeek field value. Save your table changes, and then test the field validation rule for the HoursPerWeek field; be certain the field values are the same as they were before your testing, and then close the table.
15. Define a table validation rule for the tblCourse table to verify that StartDate field values precede EndDate field values in time. Use **The course start date must come before the course end date** as the validation message. Save your table changes, and then test the table validation rule, making sure any tested field values are the same as they were before your testing.
16. Designate the Access2 > Case1 folder as a trusted folder. (*Note:* Check with your instructor before adding a new trusted location.)
17. Make a backup copy of the database, compact and repair the database, and then close it.

TROUBLESHOOT

Case Problem 2

Data File needed for this Case Problem: Storm.accdb

Drain Adopter Tandrea Austin manages the Drain Adopter program for the Department of Water and Power in Bellingham, Washington. The program recruits volunteers to regularly monitor and clear storm drains near their homes to ensure the drains are clear and unobstructed when large rainstorms are predicted. The program has been a hit with residents, and has increased the capacity of department staff to deal with other issues that arise during major storms.

Tandrea created an Access database to maintain information about the residents who have signed up for the program, the locations of selected storm drains throughout the city, and the inventory of supplies given to program participants, such as safety vests and gloves. To make the database easier to use, Tandrea wants you to create several queries and modify its table design. Complete the following steps:

1. Open the **Storm** database located in the Access2 > Case2 folder provided with your Data Files.
2. Change the first record in the tblVolunteer table datasheet so the FirstName and LastName field values contain your first and last names.

Troubleshoot 3. In the tblVolunteer table datasheet, examine the Phone field values. The input mask for this field displays an incorrect parenthesis character, and allows entry of a phone number with only seven digits. Change the input mask so it displays phone numbers using the format (987) 654-3210 and requires users to enter all 10 digits. Apply the updated image mask everywhere it is used within the database. Resize the Phone column to its best fit, and then test the input mask by typing over an existing Phone column value, being certain not to change the value by pressing ESC after you type the last digit in the Phone column. Save and close the table.

Troubleshoot 4. Open the qryNewestVolunteers query, and then examine the results in the datasheet. Tandrea wants the query to use the Top Values property to show only the five most recently signed up volunteers, but the datasheet currently displays eight results. Make changes to the query design so it shows only the top five results for this query, then save and close the query.

Troubleshoot 5. Open the qryTrainedOrSignupDate query, then examine the results in the datasheet. The third column, Expr1, is a calculated column. Tandrea wants this to show the word "trained" if the Trained field value is yes; otherwise, she wants to show the text "Signed up" followed by a space and the value of the SignupDate field. Currently the values are reversed, with dates showing for trained volunteers, and "trained" showing for untrained volunteers. Tandrea would also like the field to display the caption Status. Edit the calculated column to make the requested changes, then save and close the query.

6. Create a find duplicates query based on the tblDrain table. Select VolunteerID as the field that might contain duplicates, and select DrainID, MainStreet, and CrossStreet as additional fields in the query recordset. Save the query as **qryMultipleAdopters**, run the query, and then close it.
7. Create a find unmatched query that finds all records in the tblVolunteers table for which there is no matching record in the tblDrain table. Display the FirstName, LastName, Phone, Email, SignupDate, and Trained fields from the tblVolunteer table in the query recordset. Save the query as **qryVolunteersWithoutDrains**, run the query, and then close it.
8. Create a parameter query to select the tblDrain table records for a CrossStreet field value that the user specifies the starting characters for. If the user doesn't enter a CrossStreet field value, select all records from the table. Include the DrainID, MainStreet, CrossStreet, and Direction fields from the tblDrain table in the query recordset. Save the query as **qryCrossStreetParameter**. Run the query and enter no value as the start of the CrossStreet field value, and then run the query again and enter **44** as the start of the CrossStreet field value. Close the query.
9. Create a crosstab query based on the tblVolunteer table. Use the Trained field values for the row headings, the Zip field values for the column headings, and the count of the VolunteerID field values as the summarized value, and include row sums. Save the query as **qryTrainedVolunteersCrosstab**. Resize the columns in the query recordset to their best fit, and then save and close the query.
10. Create a query to find all records in the tblSupply table in which the SupplyID field value is Gloves01, Vest01LG, Vest01MD, or Vest01XL. Use a list-of-values criterion, and display all fields in the query recordset, sorted in ascending order by Description. Save the query as **qryClothingSupplies**, run the query, and then close it.
11. Create a query to find all records in the tblVolunteer table in which the Zip field value is not equal to 98225. Display the FirstName, LastName, Zip, Phone, and Email fields in the query recordset, and sort in ascending order by LastName. Save the query as **qryNon98225Volunteers**, run the query, and then close it.
12. In the tblDrain table, change the VolunteerID field data type to Lookup Wizard. Select the FirstName, LastName, and VolunteerID fields from the tblVolunteer table, sort in ascending order by VolunteerID, show the key column and move it to the right of the other two columns, resize the lookup columns to their best fit, select VolunteerID as the field to store in the table, and accept the default label for the lookup column. In Datasheet view, change the VolunteerID value for the first record to verify that the lookup functions correctly, then restore the original VolunteerID value for the first record. Save and close the table.
13. Define a field validation rule for the Direction field in the tblDrain table. Acceptable field values for the Direction field are NE, NW, SE, or SW. Use the message **Direction must be NE, NW, SE, or SW** to notify a user who enters an invalid Direction field value. Save your table changes, test the field validation rule for the Direction field, making sure any tested field values are the same as they were before your testing, and then close the table.
14. Designate the Access2 > Case2 folder as a trusted folder. (*Note:* Check with your instructor before adding a new trusted location.)
15. Make a backup copy of the database, compact and repair the database, and then close it.

MODULE 6

Using Form Tools and Creating Custom Forms

Creating Forms for Lakewood Community Health Services

OBJECTIVES

Session 6.1
- Change a lookup field to a Short Text field
- View and print database documentation
- Create datasheet, multiple item, and split forms
- Modify a form and anchor form controls in Layout view

Session 6.2
- Plan, design, and create a custom form in Design view and in Layout view
- Select, move, align, resize, delete, and rename controls in a form
- Add a combo box to a form
- Add headers and footers to a form

Session 6.3
- Use a combo box in a form to find records
- Add a subform to a form
- Add calculated controls to a form and a subform
- Change the tab order in a form
- Improve the appearance of a form

Case | *Lakewood Community Health Services*

Donna Taylor hired Reginald Morales to enhance the Clinic database, and he initially concentrated on standardizing the table design and creating queries for Lakewood Community Health Services. Donna and her staff created a few forms before Reginald came onboard, and Reginald's next priority is to work with Donna to create new forms that will be more functional and easier to use.

In this module, you will create new forms for Lakewood Community Health Services. In creating the forms, you will use many Access form customization features, such as adding controls and a subform to a form, using combo boxes and calculated controls, and adding color and special effects. These features make it easier for database users like Donna and her staff to interact with a database.

STARTING DATA FILES

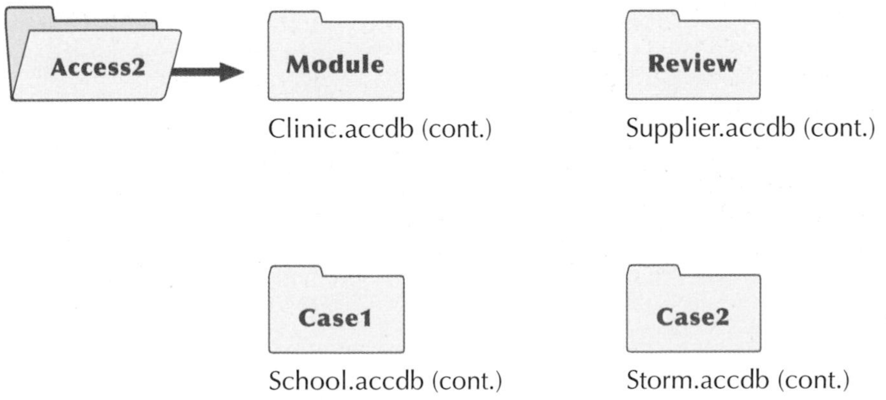
Access2
Module
Clinic.accdb (cont.)
Review
Supplier.accdb (cont.)
Case1
School.accdb (cont.)
Case2
Storm.accdb (cont.)

Session 6.1 Visual Overview:

A **tabular layout** arranges field value box controls in a datasheet format with a label above each column.

A **stacked layout** arranges field value box controls vertically with a label control to the left of each field value box control.

This form was created using the **Split Form Tool**, which creates a customizable form that simultaneously displays the data in both Form view and Datasheet view.

These text box controls are anchored to the top left of the form.

The WalkIn field value is displayed in a check box control. The control and its label have been removed from the stacked layout and are anchored to the bottom left of the form.

This form is displayed in Layout view

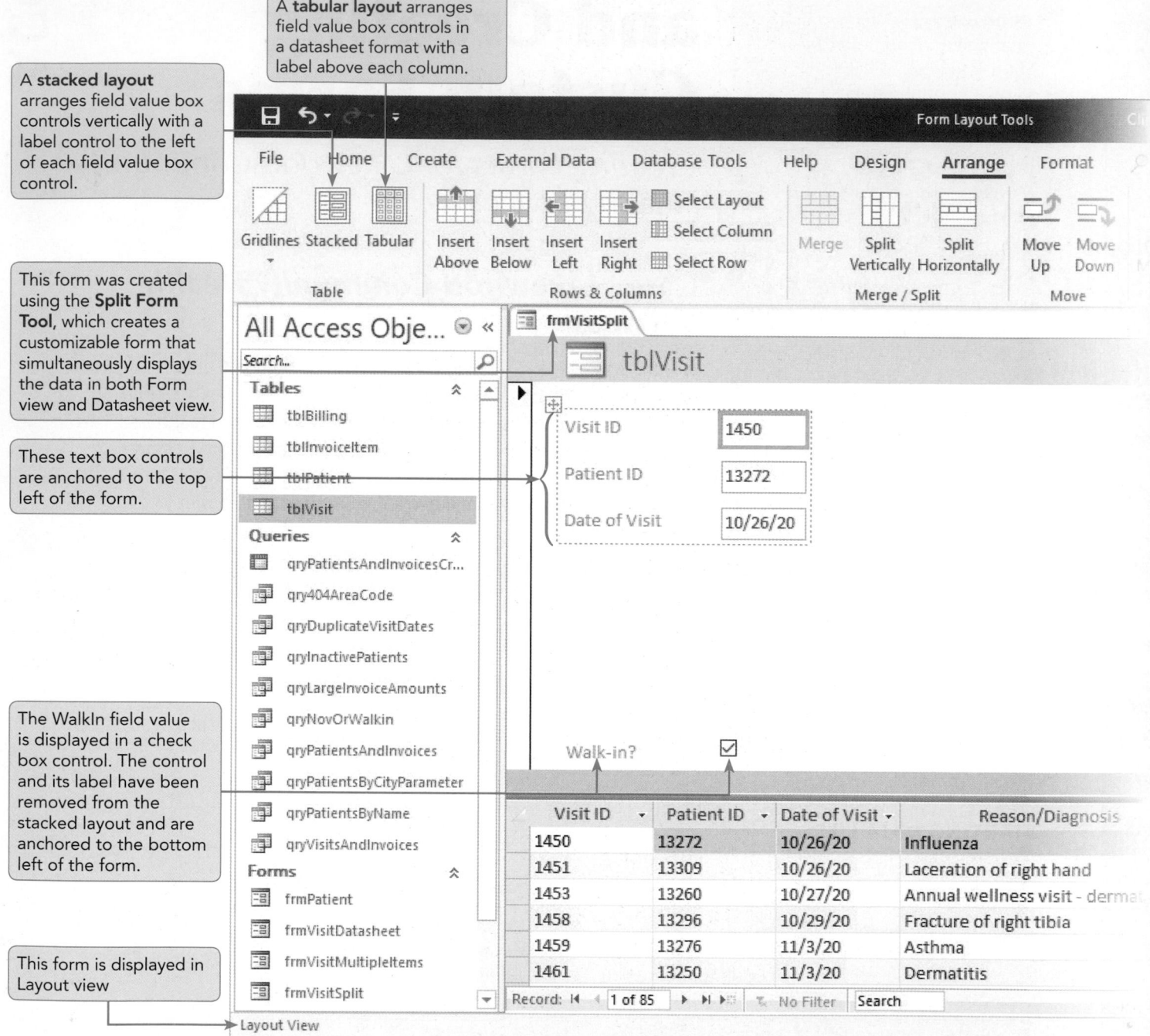

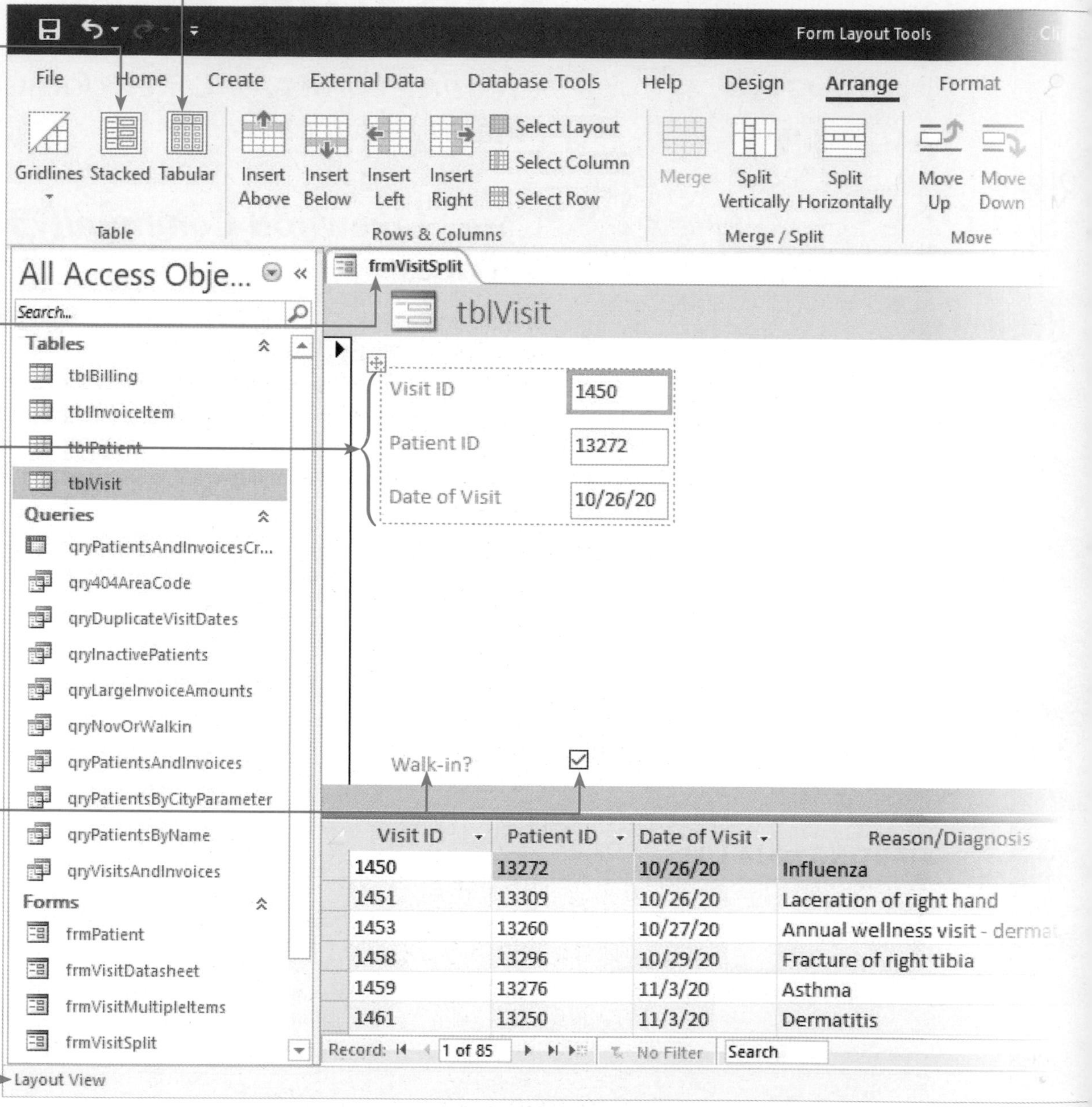

Form Layout Tools
File
Home
Create
External Data
Database Tools
Help
Design
Arrange
Format
Gridlines
Stacked
Tabular
Table
Insert Above
Insert Below
Insert Left
Insert Right
Select Layout
Select Column
Select Row
Rows & Columns
Merge
Split Vertically
Split Horizontally
Merge / Split
Move Up
Move Down
Move
All Access Obje...
Search...
Tables
tblBilling
tblInvoiceItem
tblPatient
tblVisit
Queries
qryPatientsAndInvoicesCr...
qry404AreaCode
qryDuplicateVisitDates
qryInactivePatients
qryLargeInvoiceAmounts
qryNovOrWalkin
qryPatientsAndInvoices
qryPatientsByCityParameter
qryPatientsByName
qryVisitsAndInvoices
Forms
frmPatient
frmVisitDatasheet
frmVisitMultipleItems
frmVisitSplit
frmVisitSplit
tblVisit
Visit ID
1450
Patient ID
13272
Date of Visit
10/26/20
Walk-in?
Visit ID
Patient ID
Date of Visit
Reason/Diagnosis
1450
13272
10/26/20
Influenza
1451
13309
10/26/20
Laceration of right hand
1453
13260
10/27/20
Annual wellness visit - derma
1458
13296
10/29/20
Fracture of right tibia
1459
13276
11/3/20
Asthma
1461
13250
11/3/20
Dermatitis
Record: 1 of 85
No Filter
Search
Layout View

Anchoring Controls

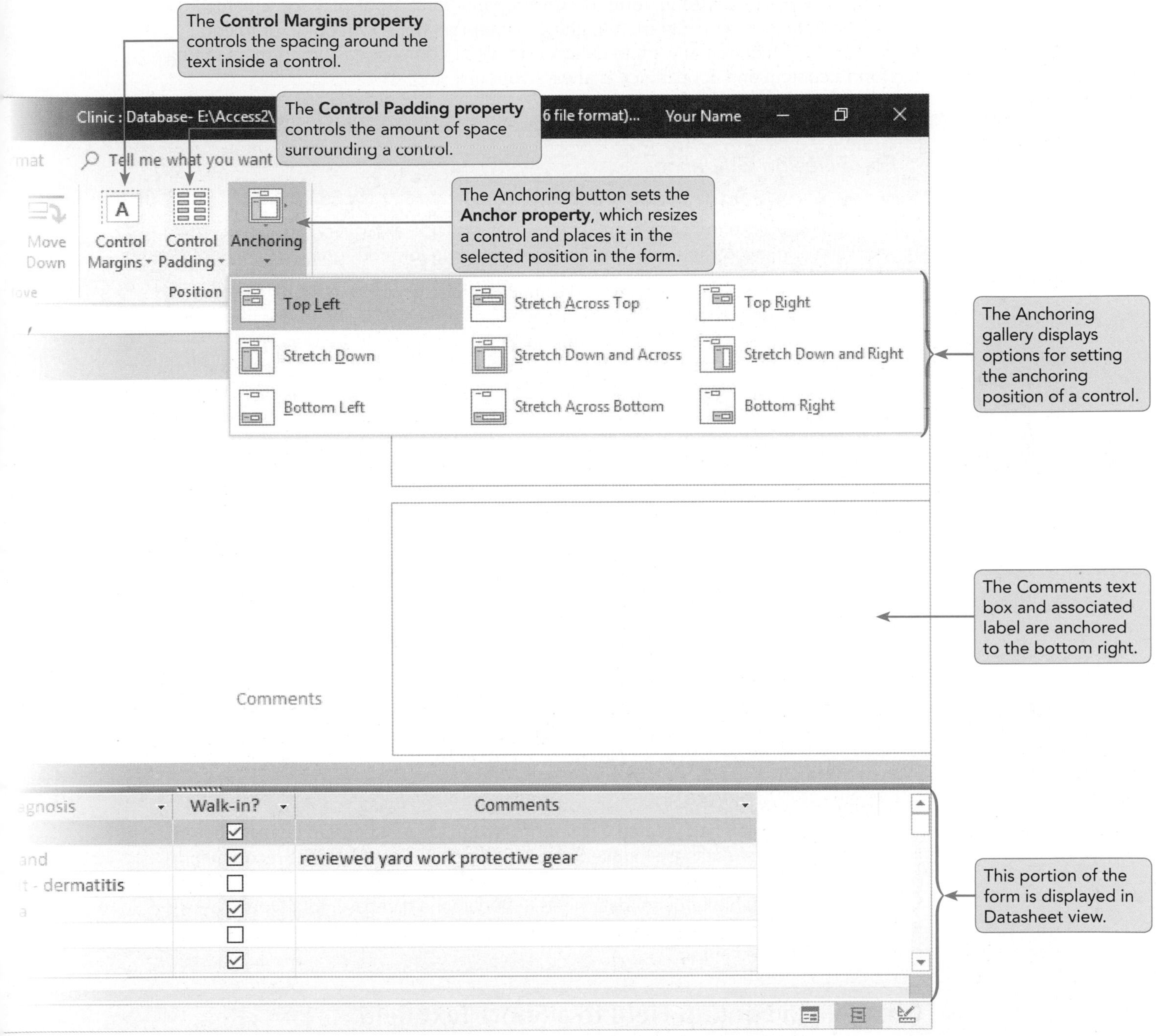
The Control Margins property controls the spacing around the text inside a control.
The Control Padding property controls the amount of space surrounding a control.
The Anchoring button sets the Anchor property, which resizes a control and places it in the selected position in the form.
The Anchoring gallery displays options for setting the anchoring position of a control.
The Comments text box and associated label are anchored to the bottom right.
This portion of the form is displayed in Datasheet view.
Clinic : Database- E:\Access2\
6 file format)...
Your Name
Tell me what you want
Move Down
Control Margins
Control Padding
Anchoring
Position
Top Left
Stretch Across Top
Top Right
Stretch Down
Stretch Down and Across
Stretch Down and Right
Bottom Left
Stretch Across Bottom
Bottom Right
Comments
Walk-in?
Comments
reviewed yard work protective gear
dermatitis

Designing Forms

To create a **custom form**, you can modify an existing form in Layout view or in Design view, or you can design and create a form from scratch in Layout view or in Design view. You can design a custom form to match a paper form, to display some fields side by side and others top to bottom, to highlight certain sections with color, or to add visual effects. Whether you want to create a simple or complex custom form, planning the form's content and appearance is always your first step.

INSIGHT

Form Design Guidelines

The users of your database should use forms to perform all database updates because forms provide better readability and control than do table and query recordsets. When you plan a form, you should keep in mind the following form design guidelines:

- Determine the fields and record source needed for each form. A form's **Record Source property** specifies the table or query that provides the fields for the form.
- Group related fields and position them in a meaningful, logical order.
- If users will refer to a source document while working with the form, design the form to closely match the source document.
- Identify each field value with a label that names the field, and align field values and labels for readability.
- Set the width of each field value box to fully display the values it contains and to provide a visual cue to users about the length of those values.
- Display calculated fields in a distinctive way, and prevent users from changing and updating them.
- Use default values, list boxes, and other form controls whenever possible to reduce user errors by minimizing keystrokes and limiting entries. A control is an item, such as a text box or command button, that you place in a form or report.
- Use colors, fonts, and graphics sparingly to keep the form uncluttered and to keep the focus on the data. Use white space to separate the form controls so that they are easier to find and read.
- Use a consistent style for all forms in a database. When forms are formatted differently, with form controls in different locations from one form to another, users must spend extra time looking for the form controls.

Donna and her staff had created a few forms and made table design changes before implementing proper database maintenance guidelines. These guidelines recommend performing all database updates using forms. As a result, Lakewood Community Health Services won't use table or query datasheets to update the database, and Donna asks if she should reconsider any of the table design changes she previously asked you to make to the Clinic database.

Changing a Lookup Field to a Short Text field

The input mask and validation rule changes are important table design modifications, but setting the InvoiceItemID field to a lookup field in the tblBilling table is an unnecessary change. A form combo box provides the same capability in a clearer, more flexible way. Many default forms use text boxes. A **text box** is a control that lets users type an entry. A **combo box** is a control that combines the features of a text box and a list box; it lets users either choose a value from a list or type an entry. A text box should be used when users must enter data, while a combo box should be used when there is a finite number of choices. Before creating the new forms for Donna, you'll change the data type of the InvoiceItemID field in the tblBilling table from a Lookup Wizard field to a Short Text field, so that you can create the relationship with referential integrity between the tblBilling and tblInvoiceItems tables.

To change the data type of the InvoiceItemID field:

1. **sam** Start Access, and then open the **Clinic** database you worked with in the previous module.

   Trouble? If the security warning is displayed below the ribbon, click the Enable Content button.

> **TIP**
>
> You can press F11 to open or close the Navigation Pane.

2. Open the Navigation Pane, if necessary, open the **tblBilling** table in Design view, and then close the Navigation Pane.
3. Click the **InvoiceItemID** Field Name box, and then in the Field Properties pane, click the **Lookup** tab. The Field Properties pane displays the lookup properties for the InvoiceItemID field. See Figure 6–1.

Figure 6–1 **Lookup properties for the InvoiceItemID field**

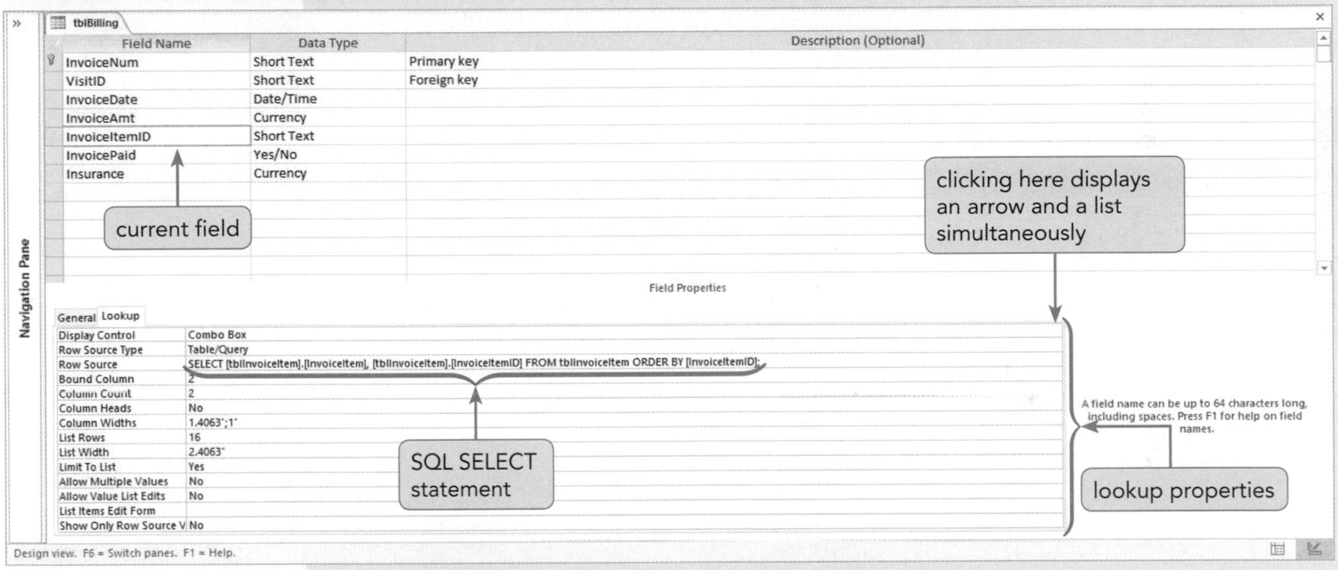
tblBilling
Field Name
Data Type
Description (Optional)
InvoiceNum
Short Text
Primary key
VisitID
Short Text
Foreign key
InvoiceDate
Date/Time
InvoiceAmt
Currency
InvoiceItemID
Short Text
InvoicePaid
Yes/No
Insurance
Currency
current field
clicking here displays an arrow and a list simultaneously
Navigation Pane
Field Properties
General
Lookup
Display Control
Combo Box
Row Source Type
Table/Query
Row Source
SELECT [tblInvoiceItem].[InvoiceItem], [tblInvoiceItem].[InvoiceItemID] FROM tblInvoiceItem ORDER BY [InvoiceItemID];
Bound Column
2
Column Count
2
Column Heads
No
Column Widths
1.4063";1"
List Rows
16
List Width
2.4063"
Limit To List
Yes
Allow Multiple Values
No
Allow Value List Edits
No
List Items Edit Form
Show Only Row Source V
No
SQL SELECT statement
A field name can be up to 64 characters long, including spaces. Press F1 for help on field names.
lookup properties
Design view. F6 = Switch panes. F1 = Help.

Notice the **Row Source property**, which specifies the data source for a control in a form or report or for a field in a table or query. The Row Source property is usually set to a table name, a query name, or a SQL statement. For the InvoiceItemID field, the Row Source property is set to a SQL SELECT statement.

To remove the lookup feature for the InvoiceItemID field, you need to change the **Display Control property**, which specifies the default control used to display a field, from Combo Box to Text Box.

4. Click the right end of the **Display Control** box, and then click **Text Box** in the list. All the lookup properties in the Field Properties pane disappear, and the InvoiceItemID field changes back to a standard Short Text field without lookup properties.
5. Click the **General** tab in the Field Properties pane, and notice that the properties for a Short Text field still apply to the InvoiceItemID field.

6. Save the table, switch to Datasheet view, resize the Invoice Item ID column to its best fit, and then click one of the Invoice Item ID boxes. An arrow does not appear in the Invoice Item ID box because the InvoiceItemID field is no longer a lookup field.
7. Save the table, and then close the tblBilling table.

Before you could change the InvoiceItemID field in the tblBilling table to a lookup field, you had to delete the one-to-many relationship between the tblInvoiceItem and tblBilling tables. Now that you've changed the data type of the InvoiceItemID field back to a Short Text field, you'll view the table relationships to make sure that the tables in the Clinic database are related correctly.

To view the table relationships in the Relationships window:

1. Click the **Database Tools** tab, and then in the Relationships group, click the **Relationships** button to open the Relationships window. See Figure 6–2.

Figure 6–2 Clinic database tables in the Relationships window

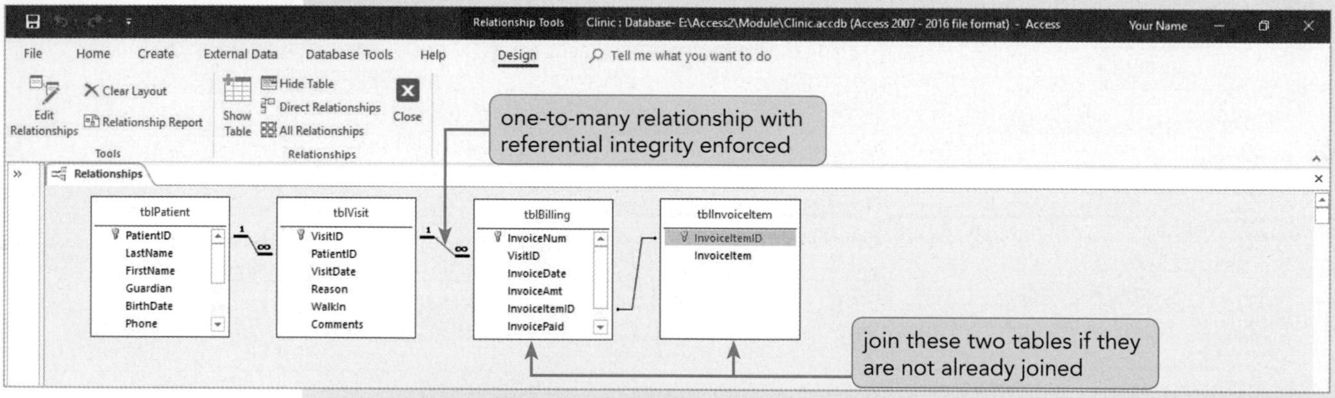
one-to-many relationship with referential integrity enforced
join these two tables if they are not already joined
tblPatient
tblVisit
tblBilling
tblInvoiceItem

Trouble? If the order of the table field lists in your Relationships window do not match Figure 6–2, drag the table field lists to rearrange them so that they appear in the same left-to-right order shown in the figure.

The tblVisit table and the related tblBilling table have a one-to-many relationship with referential integrity enforced. You need to establish a similar one-to-many relationship between the tblInvoiceItem and tblBilling tables.

2. Double-click the **relationship line** between the tblBilling and tblInvoiceItem tables to open the Edit Relationships dialog box.
3. Click the **Enforce Referential Integrity** check box, click the **Cascade Update Related Fields** check box, and then click the **OK** button to close the dialog box. The join line connecting the tblInvoiceItem and tblBilling tables now indicates a one-to-many relationship with referential integrity enforced.

Donna is interested in documenting information on the objects and relationships between objects in the database in a form that she and her staff can use as a reference. In Access, you can create a report of the database relationships. You can also give Donna information on all the objects in the database using the Documenter.

Creating a Relationship Report and Using the Documenter

From the Relationships window, you can create a Relationship report to document the fields, tables, and relationships in a database. You can also use the **Documenter**, another Access tool, to create detailed documentation of all, or selected, objects in a database. For each selected object, the Documenter lets you print documentation, such as the object's properties and relationships, and the names and properties of fields used by the object. You can use the documentation on an object, referred to as an Object Definition Report, to help you understand the object and to help you plan changes to that object.

PROSKILLS

Written Communication: Satisfying User Documentation Requirements

The Documenter produces object documentation that is useful to the technical designers, analysts, and programmers who develop and maintain Access databases and who need to understand the intricate details of a database's design. However, users who interact with databases generally have little interest in the documentation produced by the Documenter. Users need to know how to enter and maintain data using forms and how to obtain information using forms and reports, so they require special documentation that matches these needs; this documentation isn't produced by the Documenter, though. Many companies assign one or more users the task of creating the documentation needed by users based on the idea that users themselves are the most familiar with their company's procedures and understand most clearly the specific documentation that they and other users require. Databases with dozens of tables and with hundreds of other objects are complicated structures, so be sure you provide documentation that satisfies the needs of users separate from the documentation for database developers.

Next, you will create a Relationship report and use the Documenter to create documentation for the tblVisit table.

To create the Relationship report:

1. On the Relationship Tools Design tab, in the Tools group, click the **Relationship Report** button to open the Relationships for Clinic report in Print Preview. See Figure 6–3.

Figure 6–3 Relationships for Clinic report

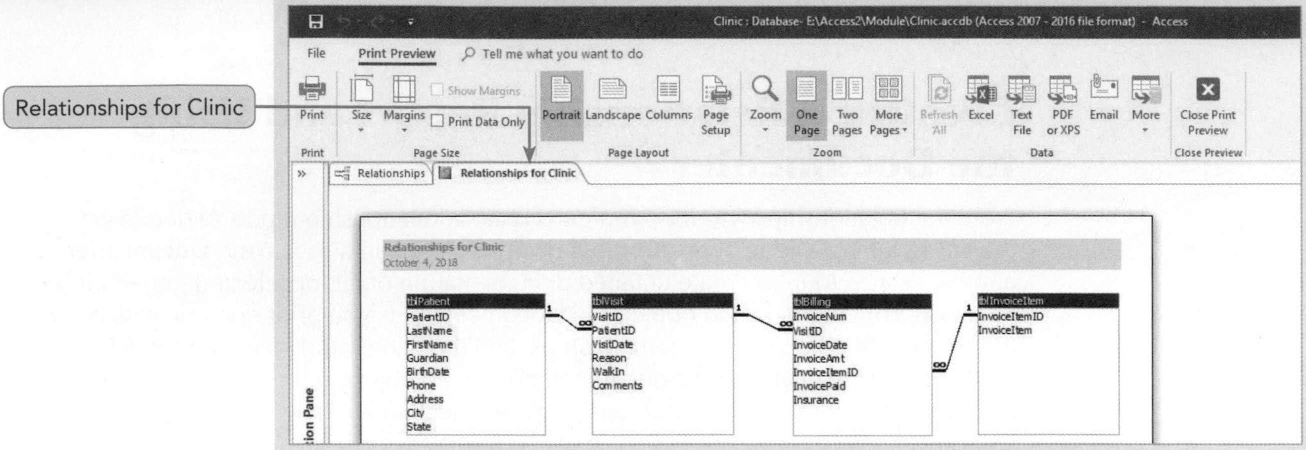
Relationships for Clinic
Clinic : Database- E:\Access2\Module\Clinic.accdb (Access 2007 - 2016 file format) - Access
File
Print Preview
Tell me what you want to do
Print
Size
Margins
Show Margins
Print Data Only
Portrait
Landscape
Columns
Page Setup
Zoom
One Page
Two Pages
More Pages
Refresh All
Excel
Text File
PDF or XPS
Email
More
Close Print Preview
Page Size
Page Layout
Data
Close Preview
Relationships
Relationships for Clinic
Relationships for Clinic
October 4, 2018
tblPatient
PatientID
LastName
FirstName
Guardian
BirthDate
Phone
Address
City
State
tblVisit
VisitID
PatientID
VisitDate
Reason
WalkIn
Comments
tblBilling
InvoiceNum
VisitID
InvoiceDate
InvoiceAmt
InvoiceItemID
InvoicePaid
Insurance
tblInvoiceItem
InvoiceItemID
InvoiceItem

2. Right-click the **Relationships for Clinic** tab, and then click **Close** to close the tab. A dialog box opens and asks if you want to save the design of the report.
3. Click the **Yes** button to save the report, click the **OK** button to use the default report name Relationships for Clinic, and then close the Relationships window.

Donna wants to show her staff a sample of the information the Documenter provides.

REFERENCE

Using the Documenter

- In the Analyze group on the Database Tools tab, click the Database Documenter button.
- In the Documenter dialog box, select the object(s) you want to document.
- If necessary, click the Options button to open the Print Table Definition dialog box, select specific documentation options for the selected object(s), and then click the OK button.
- Click the OK button to close the Documenter dialog box and open the Object Definition window in Print Preview.
- Print the documentation if desired, and then close the Object Definition window.

You will use the Documenter to create an Object Definition Report on the tblVisit table.

To use the Documenter to create, save, and print an Object Definition report:

1. On the ribbon, click the **Database Tools** tab.
2. In the Analyze group, click the **Database Documenter** button to open the Documenter dialog box, and then click the **Tables** tab (if necessary). See Figure 6–4.

Figure 6–4 Documenter dialog box

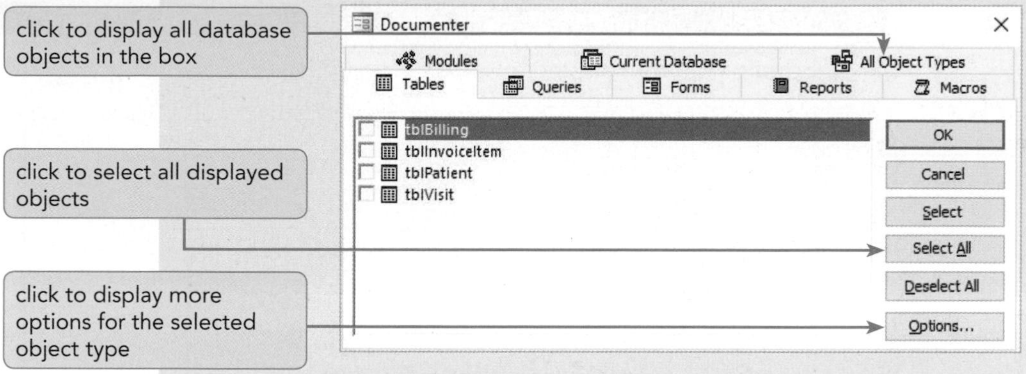
click to display all database objects in the box
click to select all displayed objects
click to display more options for the selected object type
Documenter
Modules
Current Database
All Object Types
Tables
Queries
Forms
Reports
Macros
tblBilling
tblInvoiceItem
tblPatient
tblVisit
OK
Cancel
Select
Select All
Deselect All
Options...

3. Click the **tblVisit** check box, and then click the **Options** button. The Print Table Definition dialog box opens. In this dialog box, you select which documentation you want the Documenter to include for the selected table, its fields, and its indexes.
4. In the Include for Table section, make sure the **Properties**, **Relationships**, and **Permissions by User and Group** check boxes are all checked.
5. In the Include for Fields section, click the **Names, Data Types, and Sizes** option button (if necessary), then in the Include for Indexes section, click the **Names and Fields** option button (if necessary). See Figure 6–5.

Figure 6–5 Print Table Definition dialog box

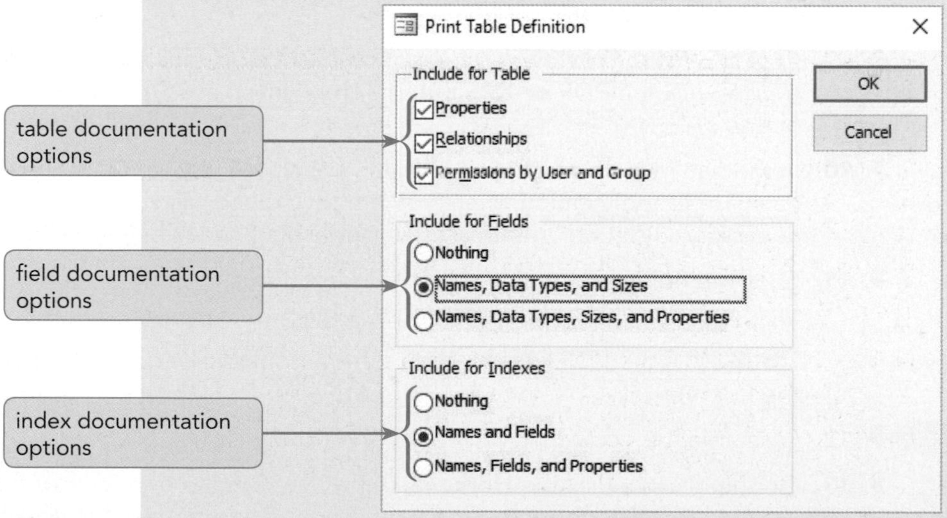
table documentation options
field documentation options
index documentation options
Print Table Definition
Include for Table
Properties
Relationships
Permissions by User and Group
OK
Cancel
Include for Fields
Nothing
Names, Data Types, and Sizes
Names, Data Types, Sizes, and Properties
Include for Indexes
Nothing
Names and Fields
Names, Fields, and Properties

TIP

In the Print Preview window, the Print Preview tab on the ribbon provides options for setting various printing options, such as page margins, page orientation, and number of columns to print for a form or report.

6. Click the **OK** button to close the Print Table Definition dialog box, and then click the **OK** button to close the Documenter dialog box. The Object Definition report opens in Print Preview.
7. On the Print Preview tab, in the Zoom group, click the **Zoom arrow**, and then click **Zoom 100%**. To display more of the report, you will collapse the ribbon.
8. On the right end of the ribbon, click the **Collapse the Ribbon** button, and then scroll down the report and examine its contents. See Figure 6–6.

Figure 6–6 **Print Preview of the Object Definition report**

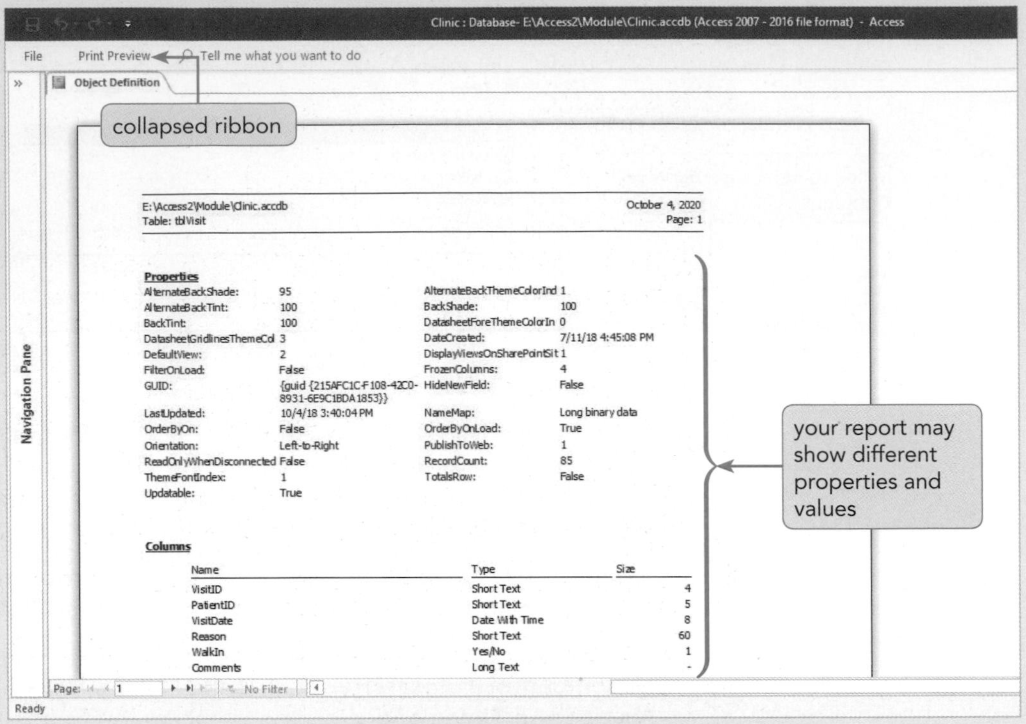
collapsed ribbon
your report may show different properties and values

The Object Definition report displays table, field, and relationship documentation for the tblVisit table. Next, you'll export the report and save it as a PDF document.

9. Click the **Print Preview** tab to expand the ribbon, and then in the Data group, click the **PDF or XPS** button. The Publish as PDF or XPS dialog box opens.
10. In the File name box, change the filename to **NP_AC_6_ClinicDocumenter**, navigate to the location where you are saving your files, and then if necessary, click the **Open file after publishing** check box to unselect it.
11. Click the **Publish** button and then click the **Close** button in the Export – PDF dialog box to close without saving the steps.

    Trouble? If the PDF you created opens automatically during Step 11, close the PDF viewer.

12. Close the Object Definition report. The ribbon is still collapsed.
13. On the ribbon, click the **Home** tab, and then, on the right end of the ribbon, click the **Pin the ribbon** button to expand and pin the ribbon again.

TIP

You can also collapse the ribbon by double-clicking any ribbon tab or by right-clicking a blank area of the ribbon and clicking Collapse the Ribbon on the shortcut menu.

The Clinic database currently contains the frmPatient form. The frmPatient form was created using the Form Wizard with some design changes that were made in Layout view including changing the theme, changing the form title color and line type, adding a picture, and moving a field. Next Donna would like you to create a form that allows her and her staff to see and modify the relevant data for patient visits. You will create this form using other form tools.

Creating Forms Using Form Tools

You can create forms with and without subforms using the Form Wizard. You can create other types of forms using different form tools, namely the Datasheet tool, the Multiple Items tool, and the Split Form tool.

PROSKILLS

Decision Making: Creating Multiple Forms and Reports

When developing a larger database application, it's not uncommon for the users of the database to be unsure as to what they want with respect to forms and reports. You may obtain some sample data and sample reports during the requirements-gathering phase that give you some ideas, but in the end, it is a good idea to have the users approve the final versions.

While you are actively developing the application, you might design different versions of forms and reports that you think will meet users' needs; later in the process, you might narrow the selection to a few forms and reports. Ultimately, you should ask the users to make the final choices of which forms and reports to incorporate into the database. By involving the users in the planning phase for forms and reports, the database is more likely to meet everyone's needs.

Donna has requested a form that her staff can use to work with information from the tblVisit table. Because her requirements at this point are vague, you'll create a selection of form designs for Donna to choose from. You'll create two simple forms that show the contents of the tblVisit table in a layout that resembles a table, and you'll create a custom form that Donna's staff may find a bit more user-friendly. First, you'll create the simple forms for Donna and her staff.

Creating a Form Using the Datasheet Tool

You can create a simple form using the Datasheet Tool. The **Datasheet tool** creates a form in a datasheet format that contains all the fields in the source table or query. Donna might prefer this if she and her staff are very comfortable entering data in an Access table in Datasheet view. You'll use the Datasheet tool to create a form based on the tblVisit table. When you use the Datasheet tool, the record source (either a table or query) for the form must be open or selected in the Navigation Pane.

To create the form using the Datasheet tool:

1. Open the Navigation Pane, and then click **tblVisit**.
2. On the ribbon, click the **Create** tab.
3. In the Forms group, click the **More Forms** button, click **Datasheet**, and then, if necessary, close the Property Sheet. The Datasheet tool creates a form showing every field in the tblVisit table in a datasheet format. See Figure 6–7.

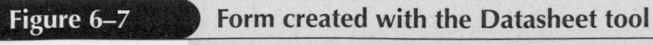

Figure 6–7 Form created with the Datasheet tool

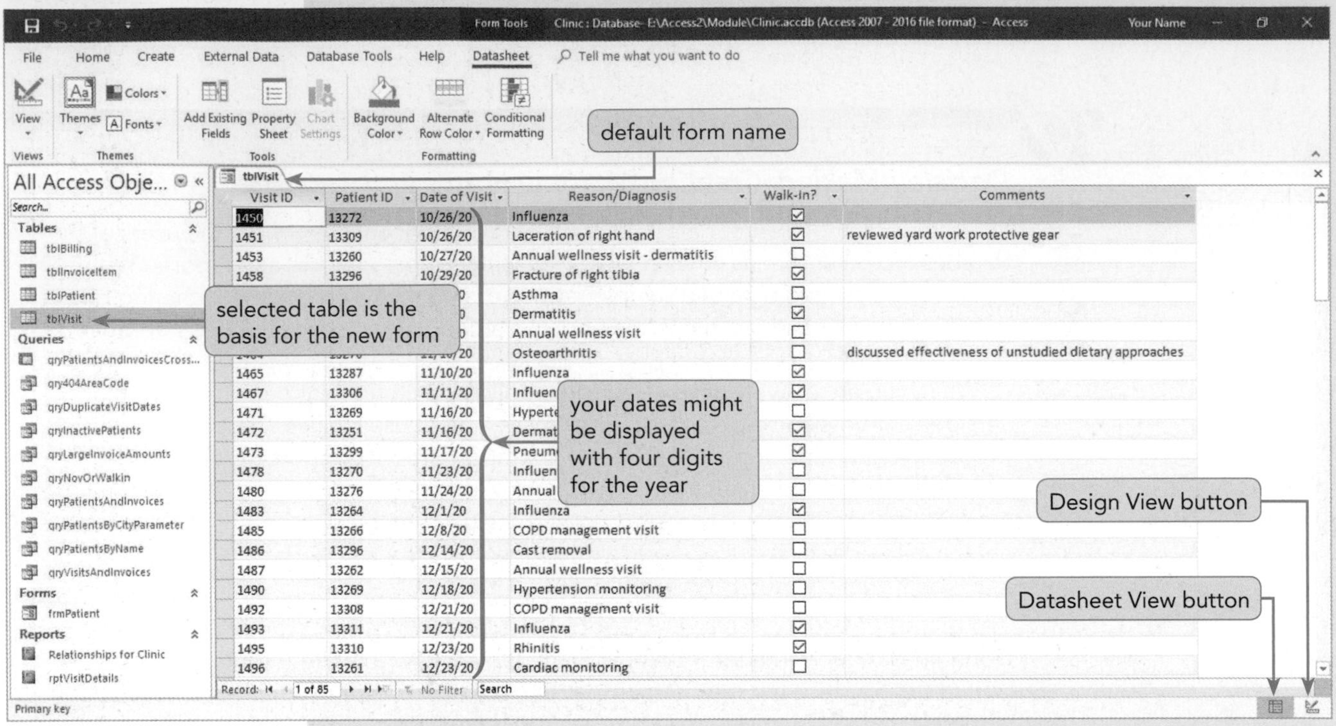
default form name
selected table is the basis for the new form
your dates might be displayed with four digits for the year
Design View button
Datasheet View button

Trouble? Depending on your computer's settings, the dates in the Date of Visit column may be displayed with either two or four digits for the year. If your date format is different from that shown in the figures, it will not cause a problem.

The form resembles the Datasheet view for the table except that it does not include the expand buttons at the beginning of each row. The form name, tblVisit, is the same name as the table used as the basis for the form. Recall that each table and query in a database must have a unique name. Although you could give a form or report the same name as a table or query, doing so would likely cause confusion. Fortunately, using object name prefixes prevents this confusing practice, and you will change the name when you save the form.

As you know, when working with forms, you view and update data in Form view, you view and make simple design changes in Layout view, and you make simple and complex design changes in Design view. However, not all of these views are available for every type of form. For the form created with the Datasheet tool, you'll check the available view options.

4. On the Form Tools Datasheet tab, in the Views group, click the **View arrow**. See Figure 6–8.

Figure 6–8 View options for a form created with the Datasheet tool

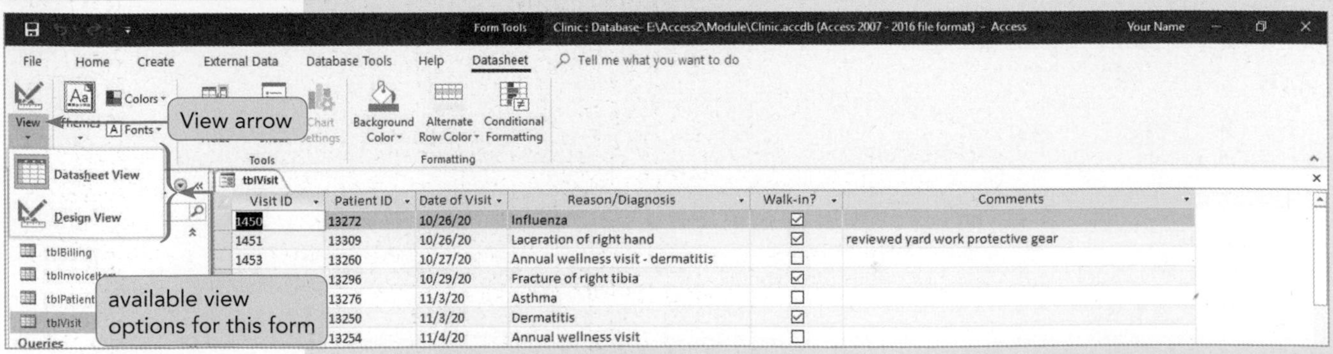
View arrow
available view options for this form

Notice Form view and Layout view are not options on the menu, which means that they are unavailable for this form type. Datasheet view allows you to view and update data, and Design view allows you to modify the form's layout and design. The buttons for accessing these two available views are also on the status bar.

You'll save this form to show Donna as one of the options for the forms for patient visits.

5. Save the form as **frmVisitDatasheet**, and then close the form.

Donna might prefer a form created using the Multiple Items tool because it will provide a form with larger text boxes for displaying a record's field values.

Creating a Form Using the Multiple Items Tool

The **Multiple Items tool** creates a customizable form that displays multiple records from a source table or query in a datasheet format. You'll use the Multiple Items tool to create a form based on the tblVisit table.

To create the form using the Multiple Items tool:

1. Make sure that the tblVisit table is selected in the Navigation Pane, and then click the **Create** tab.
2. In the Forms group, click the **More Forms** button, and then click **Multiple Items**. The Multiple Items tool creates a form showing every field in the tblVisit table and opens the form in Layout view. See Figure 6–9.

Figure 6–9 Form created with the Multiple Items tool

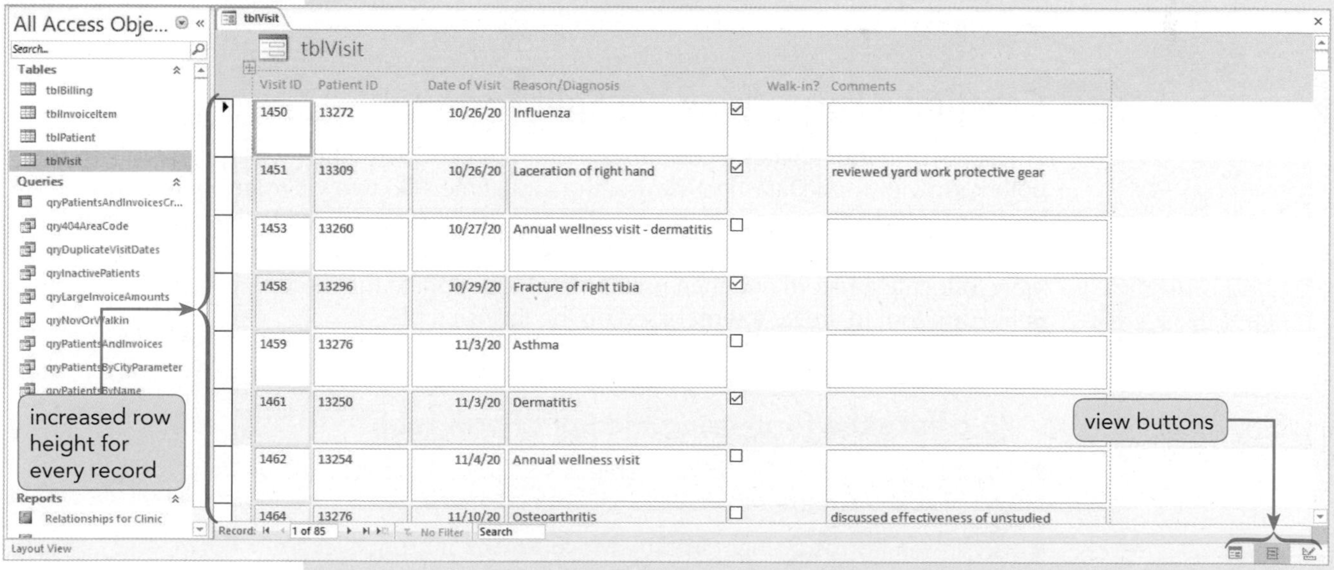
increased row height for every record
view buttons
tblVisit
Visit ID
Patient ID
Date of Visit
Reason/Diagnosis
Walk-in?
Comments

The new form displays all the records and fields from the tblVisit table in a format similar to a datasheet, but the row height for every record is increased compared to a standard datasheet. Unlike a form created with the Datasheet tool, which has only Datasheet view and Design view available, a Multiple Items form is a standard form that can be displayed in Form view, Layout view, and Design view, as indicated by the buttons on the right end of the status bar. You can also access these views for the forms created with the Multiple Items tool from the ribbon.

3. On the Form Layout Tools Design tab, in the Views group, click the **View arrow**. See Figure 6–10.

Figure 6–10 View options for a form created with the Multiple Items tool

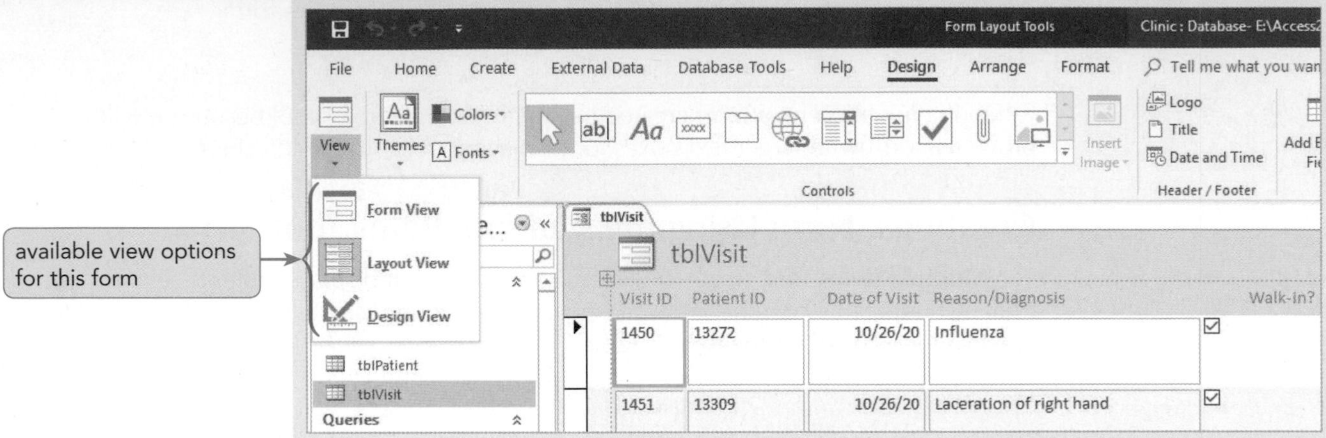
available view options for this form
Form Layout Tools
Form View
Layout View
Design View
tblVisit

You'll want to show this form to Donna as one of the options, so you'll save it.

4. Save the form as **frmVisitMultipleItems**, and then close the form.

The final form you'll create to show Donna will include two sections, one providing the standard form inputs of field value boxes and the other section showing the table in Datasheet view. She might like this to satisfy both the staff that are more technical and the staff that would like a more user-friendly form. The tool you'll use to create this is the Split Form tool.

Creating a Form Using the Split Form Tool

The Split Form tool creates a customizable form that displays the records in a table in both Form view and Datasheet view at the same time. The two views are synchronized at all times. Selecting a record in one view selects the same record in the other view. You can add, change, or delete data from either view. Typically, you'd use Datasheet view to locate a record and then use Form view to update the record. You'll use the Split Form tool to create a form based on the tblVisit table.

To create the form using the Split Form tool:

1. Make sure that the tblVisit table is selected in the Navigation Pane, and then click the **Create** tab.

2. In the Forms group, click the **More Forms** button, click **Split Form**, and then close the Navigation Pane. The Split Form tool creates a split form that opens in Layout view and displays a form with the contents of the first record in the tblVisit table in the top section and a datasheet showing the first several records in the tblVisit table in the bottom section. In Layout view,

the form on top presents a record's fields in either a single column or in two columns, depending on the size of the Access window when the form was created. If you have a two-column layout, that won't affect your ability to complete the steps that follow. Figure 6–11 shows the single-column layout.

Figure 6–11 Form created with the Split Form tool

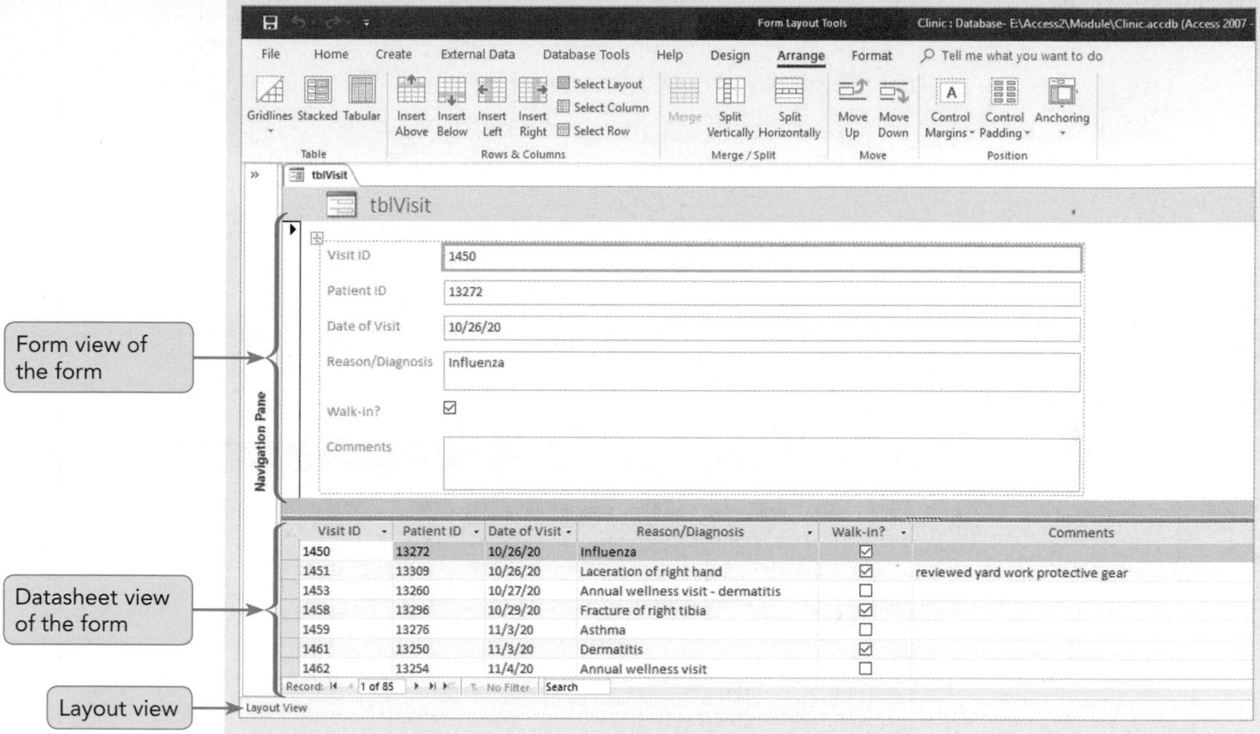
Form view of the form
Datasheet view of the form
Layout view

In Layout view, you can make layout and design changes to the form section and layout changes to the datasheet section of the split form.

Modifying a Split Form in Layout View

In previous modules, you've modified forms using options on the Form Layout Tools Format tab. Additional options for modifying forms are available on the Form Layout Tools Arrange tab. When working with a split form, you use the options on the Form Layout Tools Design tab to add controls and make other modifications to the form section but not to the datasheet section. Also in this case, the options on the Arrange tab apply only to the form section and do not apply to the datasheet section.

Donna notices that first three field value boxes in the form, Visit ID, Patient ID, and Date of Visit, are much wider than necessary. You will resize these field value boxes, and you will also move and resize the Reason/Diagnosis field label and field value box.

To resize field value boxes in the split form in Layout view:

1. On the ribbon, click the **Form Layout Tools Arrange** tab. The form's field label and field value boxes from the tblVisit table are grouped in a control layout. Recall that a control layout is a set of controls grouped together in a form or report so that you can manipulate the set as a single control. The control layout is a stacked layout, which arranges field value box controls vertically with a label control to the left of each field value box control in one or more vertical columns. You can also choose a tabular layout, which arranges field value box controls in a datasheet format with labels above each column.

   As you know, if you reduce the width of any field value box in a control layout, all the value boxes in the control layout are also resized. Donna wants you to reduce the width of the first three field value boxes only.

2. In the form, click the **Visit ID** label to select it, and then click the **layout selector** in the upper-left corner of the control layout. An orange selection border, which identifies the controls that you've selected, appears around the labels and field value boxes in the form. See Figure 6–12.

Figure 6–12 Control layout selected in the form

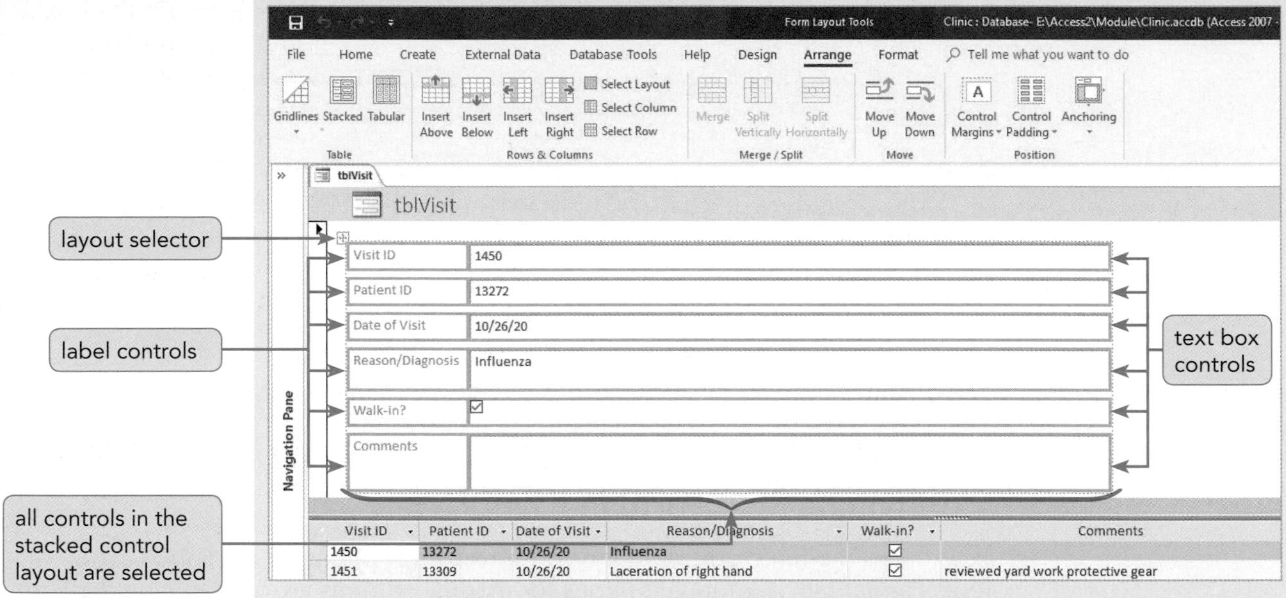
layout selector
label controls
all controls in the stacked control layout are selected
text box controls
Form Layout Tools
tblVisit
Visit ID
Patient ID
Date of Visit
Reason/Diagnosis
Walk-in?
Comments

Next, you'll resize the field value boxes in the control layout.

3. Click the **VisitDate** field value box (containing the value 10/26/20) to deselect the control layout and select only the VisitDate field value box.

4. Position the pointer on the right border of the VisitDate field value box until the pointer changes to a horizontal resize pointer ↔, click and drag to the left until the right edge is just to the right of the VisitDate field value, and then release the mouse button. If you have a one-column layout, you've resized all five field value boxes. If you have a two-column layout, you've resized the three field value boxes on the left. Figure 6–13 shows the single-column layout.

Figure 6–13 Resized field value boxes in the control layout

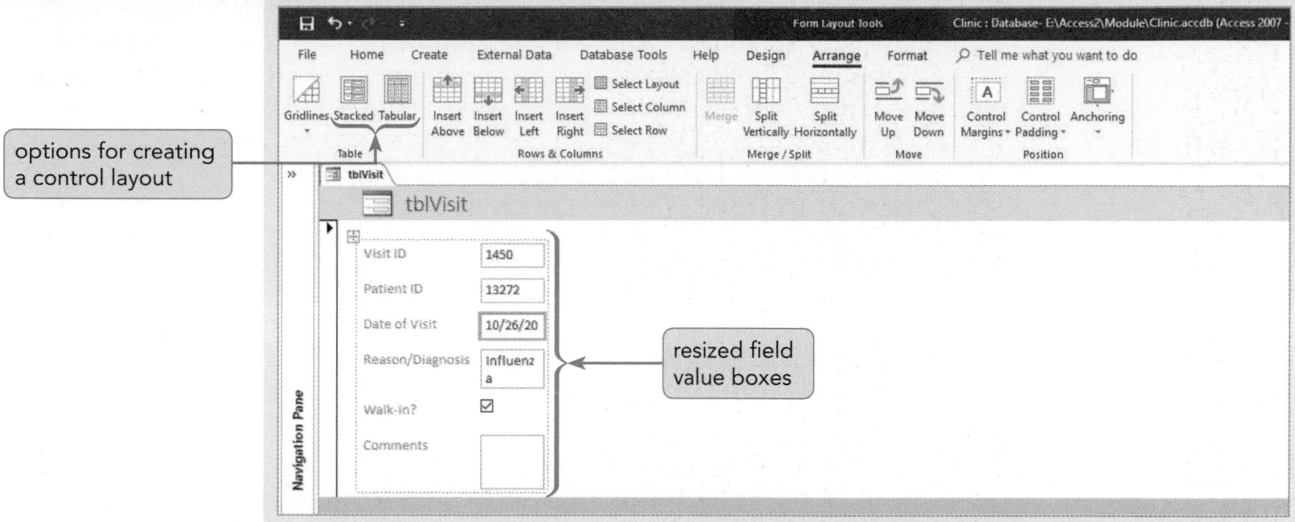
options for creating a control layout
resized field value boxes
tblVisit
Visit ID
1450
Patient ID
13272
Date of Visit
10/26/20
Reason/Diagnosis
Influenza
Walk-in?
Comments
Navigation Pane

Trouble? If you resize the field value boxes too far to the left, number signs appear inside the PatientID and VisitDate value boxes, indicating the boxes are too small to display the full values. Repeat Step 4, this time dragging the right border of the field value box to the right until the values are visible inside these boxes.

With the one-column layout shown in Figure 6–13, the form has too much white space. To better balance the elements in the form, Donna suggests you move and resize the Reason/Diagnosis, Walk-in?, and Comments labels and field value boxes to a second column so that they fill this available space. To do this, you first need to remove these items from the stacked layout control.

To remove field value labels and boxes from the layout control, and then move and resize them on the form:

1. Click the **Reason/Diagnosis** label, press and hold **CTRL**, click the **Reason** field value box, click the **Walk-in?** label, click the **WalkIn** check box, click the **Comments** label, and then click the **Comments** field value box to select all six controls, and then release **CTRL**.
2. Right-click the **Reason** field value box, point to **Layout** on the shortcut menu, and then click **Remove Layout**. You've removed the six selected controls from the stacked layout.
3. If your form has the single-column layout shown in Figure 6–13, make sure that the six controls are still selected, and then use the move pointer to drag them up and to the right until the tops of the Reason label and field value box align with the tops of the VisitID label and field value box.

   Trouble? If your form already has a two-column layout, skip Step 3.
4. Click the **Walk-in?** label, press and hold **CTRL**, click the **WalkIn** check box, and then release **CTRL**. The Walk-in? label and the WalkIn check box are selected.

5. Drag the **Walk-in?** label and **WalkIn** check box to the left and position them below the Date of Visit label and VisitDate field value box.
6. Select the **Comments** label and the **Comments** field value box, and then drag the selected controls up until they are top-aligned with the Date of Visit label and VisitDate field value box.
7. Click the **Comments** field value box to select it, and then drag the right border of the control to the right until the field value box is about four inches wide.
8. Click the **Reason** field value box so that it's the only selected control, drag the right border of the control to the right until it is the same width as the Comments field value box, and then drag the bottom border down until it aligns with the bottom of the PatientID field value box. Compare your screen with Figure 6–14, making any necessary adjustments.

Figure 6–14 **Moved and resized controls in the form**

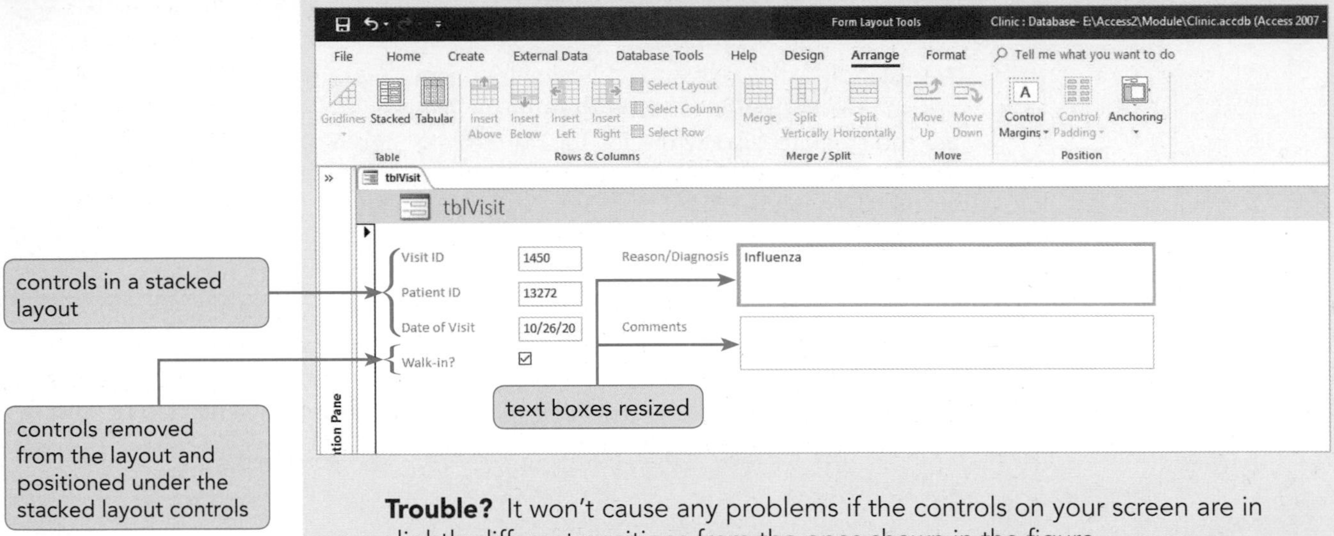
controls in a stacked layout
controls removed from the layout and positioned under the stacked layout controls
text boxes resized
Form Layout Tools
Clinic : Database- E:\Access2\Module\Clinic.accdb (Access 2007 -
File
Home
Create
External Data
Database Tools
Help
Design
Arrange
Format
Tell me what you want to do
Gridlines
Stacked
Tabular
Insert Above
Insert Below
Insert Left
Insert Right
Select Layout
Select Column
Select Row
Merge
Split Vertically
Split Horizontally
Move Up
Move Down
Control Margins
Control Padding
Anchoring
Table
Rows & Columns
Merge / Split
Move
Position
tblVisit
Visit ID
1450
Patient ID
13272
Date of Visit
10/26/20
Walk-in?
Reason/Diagnosis
Influenza
Comments

Trouble? It won't cause any problems if the controls on your screen are in slightly different positions from the ones shown in the figure.

You do not usually need to change the default settings for the Control Margins property, which controls the spacing around the text inside a control, or the Control Padding property, which controls the spacing around the outside of a control. However, you'll explore the effects of changing these properties.

9. In the form, click the **Visit ID** label to select it, and then click the **layout selector** to select the six controls that are still grouped in the stacked layout.
10. On the Arrange tab, in the Position group, click the **Control Margins** button, and then click **Medium**. The text inside the stacked layout controls moves down slightly.
11. Click the **Control Margins** button, click **Wide**, and observe the effect of this setting on the text inside the controls.
12. Click the **Control Margins** button again, and then click **Narrow**. Narrow is the default setting for the Control Margins property. Narrow is also the default setting for the Control Padding property.

    Now that the form is complete and the controls are sized appropriately, you will save the form.
13. Save the form as **frmVisitSplit**.

Next, you'll anchor the controls on the form.

Anchoring Controls in a Form

You can design forms that use the screen dimensions effectively when all the users of a database have the same-sized monitors and use the same screen resolution. How do you design forms when users have a variety of monitor sizes and screen resolutions? If you design a form to fit on large monitors using high screen resolutions, then only a portion of the controls in the form fit on smaller monitors with lower resolutions, forcing users to scroll the form. If you design a form to fit on smaller monitors with low screen resolutions, then the form is displayed on larger monitors in a small area in the upper-left corner of the screen, making the form look unattractively cramped. As a compromise, you can anchor the controls in the form. As shown in the Visual Overview for this session, as the screen size and resolution change, the Anchor property for a control automatically resizes the control and places it in the same relative position on the screen. Unfortunately, when you use the Anchor property, the control's font size is not scaled to match the screen size and resolution. Sometimes the results of anchoring controls work well, but sometimes the controls are spaced across a large screen, and the form may seem unorganized with controls moved to the corners of the screen.

Next, you'll anchor controls in the frmVisitSplit form. You can't anchor individual controls in a control layout; you can only anchor the entire control layout as a group. You've already removed the Reason/Diagnosis, Walk-in?, and Comments controls from the stacked layout so that you can anchor them separately from the stacked layout. Therefore, you'll have four sets of controls to anchor—the stacked layout is one set, the Reason/Diagnosis controls are the second set, the Comments controls are the third set, and the Walk-in? controls make up the fourth set.

To anchor controls in the form:

1. Click the **Walk-in?** label, press and hold **CTRL**, and then click the **WalkIn** check box.
2. On the Arrange tab, in the Position group, click the **Anchoring** button to open the Anchoring gallery. See Figure 6–15.

Figure 6–15 The Anchoring gallery

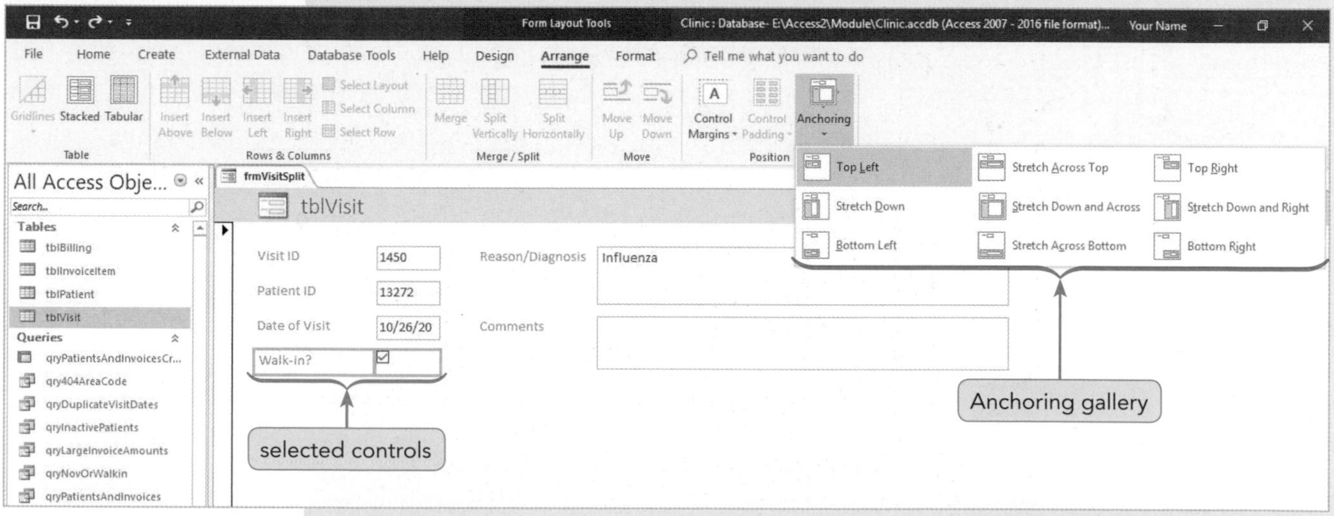
Top Left
Stretch Across Top
Top Right
Stretch Down
Stretch Down and Across
Stretch Down and Right
Bottom Left
Stretch Across Bottom
Bottom Right
Anchoring gallery
selected controls
tblVisit
Visit ID
1450
Patient ID
13272
Date of Visit
10/26/20
Walk-in?
Reason/Diagnosis
Influenza
Comments

Four of the nine options in the Anchoring gallery fix the position of the selected controls in the top-left (the default setting), bottom-left, top-right, or bottom-right positions in the form. If other controls block the corner positions for controls you're anchoring for the first time, the new controls are positioned in relation to the blocking controls. The other five anchoring options resize (or stretch) and position the selected controls.

You'll anchor the Walk-in? controls in the bottom left, the Reason/Diagnosis controls in the top right, and the Comments controls in the bottom right.

3. Click **Bottom Left** in the Anchoring gallery. The gallery closes, and the Walk-in? label and field value box move to the bottom-left corner of the form.
4. Click the **Reason** field value box, in the Position group, click the **Anchoring** button, and then click **Top Right**. The Reason label and field value box move to the upper-right corner of the form.
5. Anchor the Comments label and field value box to the Bottom Right.

Next, you'll increase the height of the form to simulate the effect of a larger screen for the form.

6. Open the Navigation Pane. The four sets of controls on the left shift to the right because the horizontal dimensions of the form decreased from the left, and these four sets of controls are anchored to the left in the form. The Reason and Comments controls remain in the same position in the form.
7. Position the pointer on the border between the form and the datasheet until the pointer changes to the vertical resize pointer ‡, and then drag down until only the column headings and the first row in the datasheet are visible. The bottom sets of controls shift down, because they are anchored to the bottom of the form, and the two sets of controls at the top remain in the same positions in the form. See Figure 6–16.

Figure 6–16 Anchored controls in a resized form

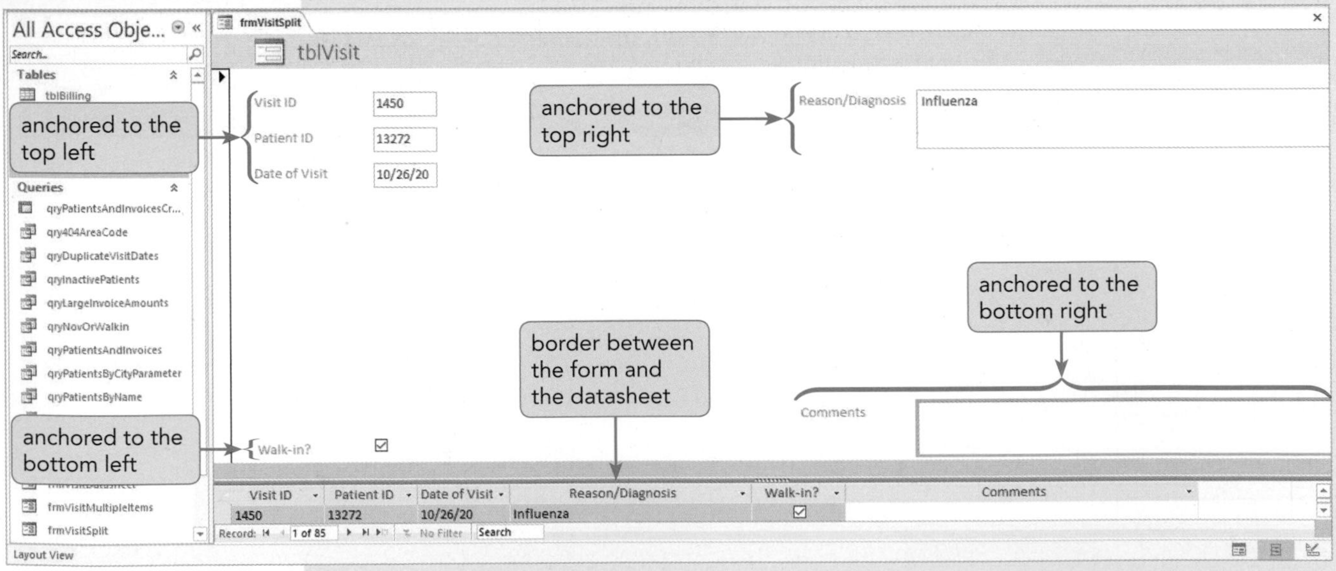
All Access Obje...
Tables
tblBilling
anchored to the top left
Queries
qryPatientsAndInvoicesCr...
qry404AreaCode
qryDuplicateVisitDates
qryInactivePatients
qryLargeInvoiceAmounts
qryNovOrWalkin
qryPatientsAndInvoices
qryPatientsByCityParameter
qryPatientsByName
anchored to the bottom left
frmVisitMultipleItems
frmVisitSplit
Layout View
frmVisitSplit
tblVisit
Visit ID 1450
Patient ID 13272
Date of Visit 10/26/20
anchored to the top right
Reason/Diagnosis Influenza
anchored to the bottom right
border between the form and the datasheet
Comments
Walk-in?
Visit ID | Patient ID | Date of Visit | Reason/Diagnosis | Walk-in? | Comments
1450 | 13272 | 10/26/20 | Influenza
Record: 1 of 85 No Filter Search

Finally, you'll use another anchoring option to resize the Comments text box as the form dimensions change.

8. Click the **Comments** field value box (if necessary), in the Position group, click the **Anchoring** button, and then click **Stretch Down and Right**. Because the Comments field value box is already anchored to the bottom right, it can't stretch any more to the right, but it does stretch up while leaving the label in place, to increase the height of the box.
9. Position the pointer on the border between the form and the datasheet until the pointer changes to the vertical resize pointer ‡, and then drag up to display several rows in the datasheet. The bottom set of controls shifts up, the bottom edge of the Comments field value box shifts up, and its height is reduced.
10. Save the changes you've made to the form's design, close the form, and then, if you are not continuing on to the next session, close the Clinic database.

You've used form tools to create forms, and you've modified forms in Layout view. In the next session, you will continue your work with forms.

REVIEW

Session 6.1 Quick Check

1. Which object(s) should you use to perform all database updates?
2. The __________ property specifies the data source for a control in a form or report or for a field in a table or query.
3. What is the Documenter?
4. What is the Multiple Items tool?
5. What is a split form?
6. As the screen's size and resolution change, the ________ property for a control automatically resizes the control.

Session 6.2 Visual Overview:

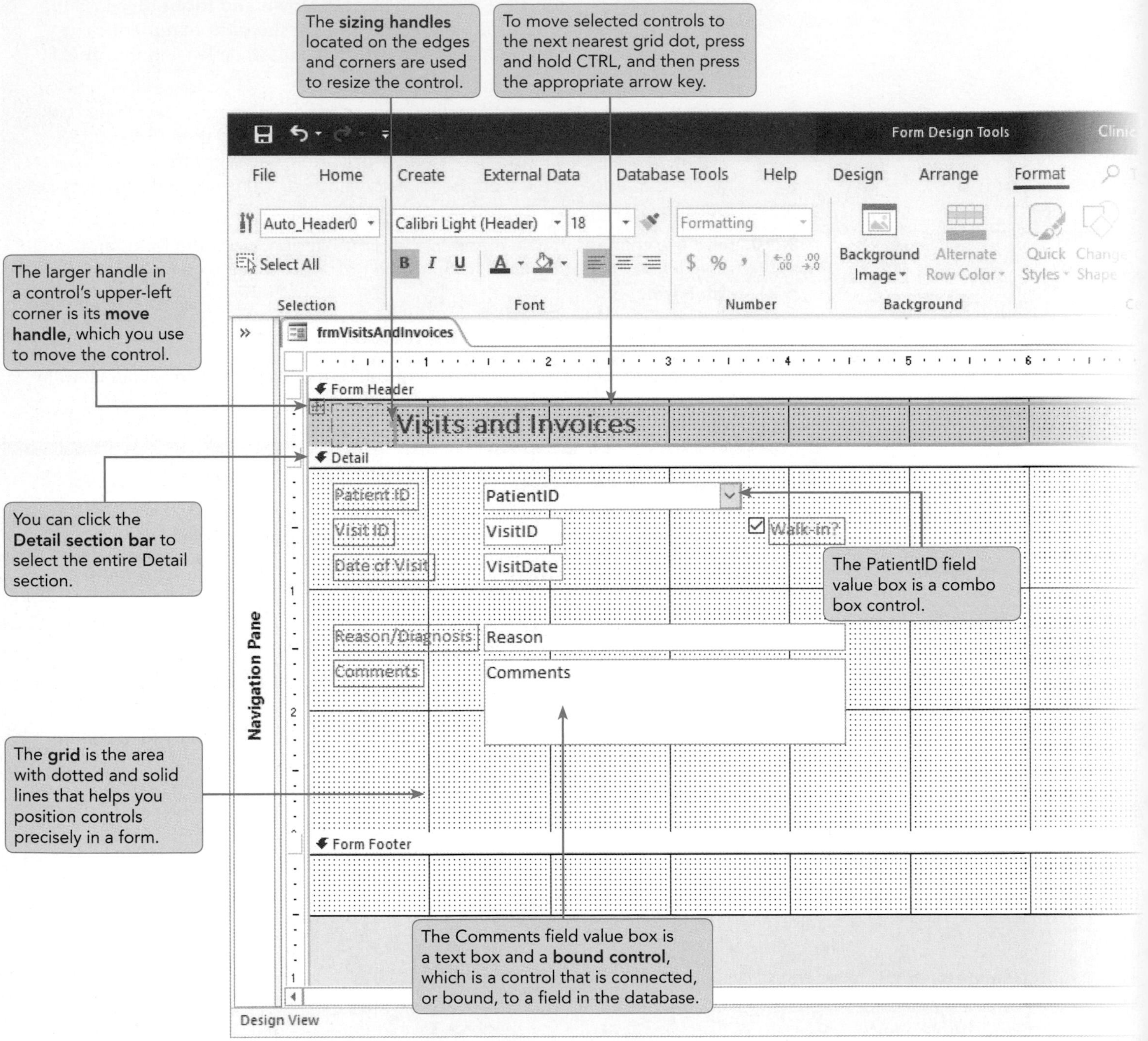
The **sizing handles** located on the edges and corners are used to resize the control.
To move selected controls to the next nearest grid dot, press and hold CTRL, and then press the appropriate arrow key.
The larger handle in a control's upper-left corner is its **move handle**, which you use to move the control.
You can click the **Detail section bar** to select the entire Detail section.
The PatientID field value box is a combo box control.
The **grid** is the area with dotted and solid lines that helps you position controls precisely in a form.
The Comments field value box is a text box and a **bound control**, which is a control that is connected, or bound, to a field in the database.
Form Design Tools
File
Home
Create
External Data
Database Tools
Help
Design
Arrange
Format
Auto_Header0
Select All
Selection
Calibri Light (Header)
18
Font
Formatting
Number
Background Image
Alternate Row Color
Background
Quick Styles
frmVisitsAndInvoices
Form Header
Visits and Invoices
Detail
Patient ID
PatientID
Visit ID
VisitID
Walk-in?
Date of Visit
VisitDate
Reason/Diagnosis
Reason
Comments
Comments
Form Footer
Navigation Pane
Design View

Custom Form in Design View

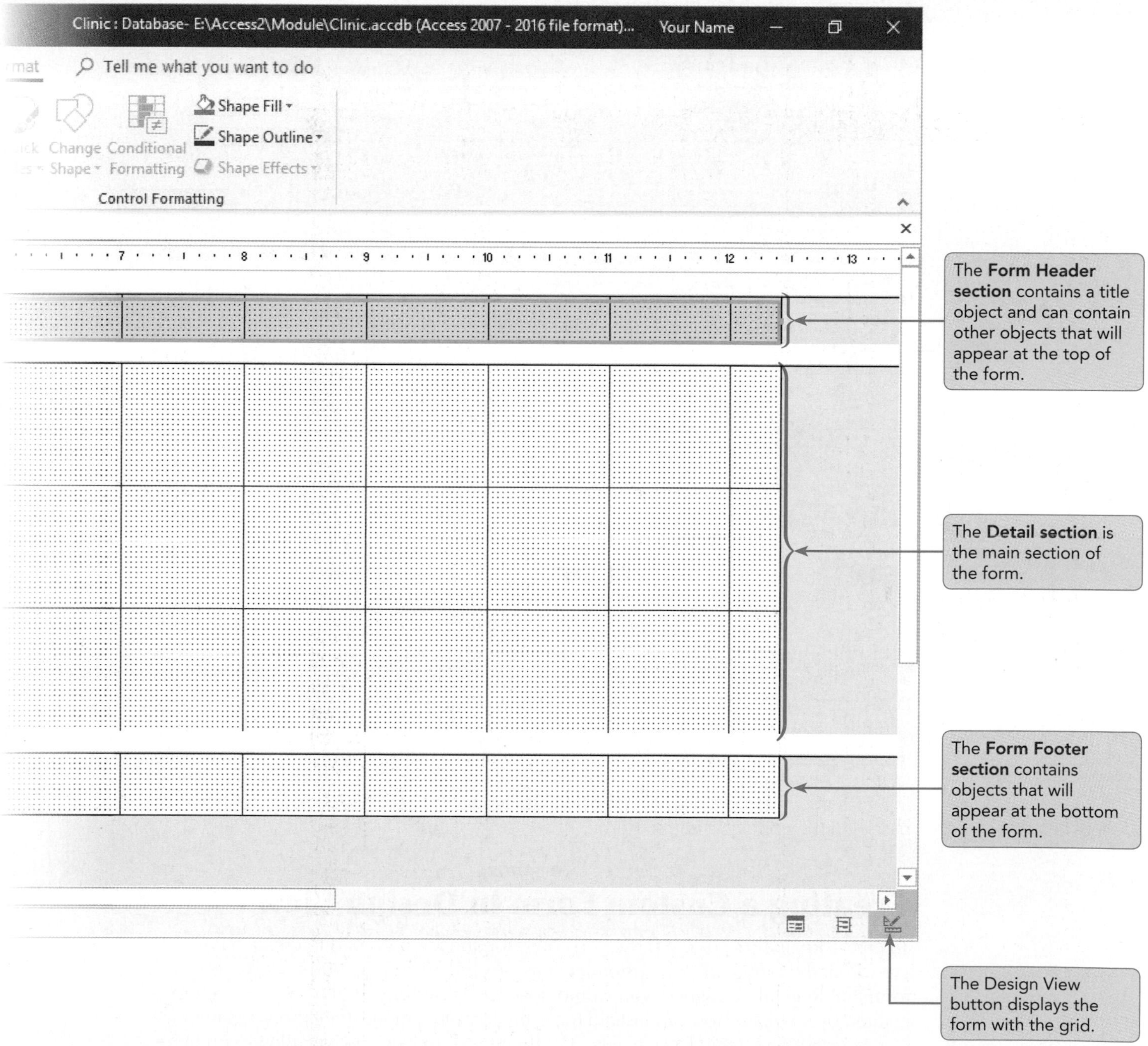

Clinic : Database- E:\Access2\Module\Clinic.accdb (Access 2007 - 2016 file format)...
Your Name
Tell me what you want to do
Shape Fill
Shape Outline
Shape Effects
Change Shape
Conditional Formatting
Control Formatting
The **Form Header section** contains a title object and can contain other objects that will appear at the top of the form.
The **Detail section** is the main section of the form.
The **Form Footer section** contains objects that will appear at the bottom of the form.
The Design View button displays the form with the grid.

Planning and Designing a Custom Form

Donna needs a form to enter and view information about Lakewood Community Health Services visits and their related invoices. She wants the information in a single form, and she asks Reginald to design a form for her review.

After several discussions with Donna and her staff, Reginald prepared a sketch for a custom form to display a patient visit and its related invoices. Reginald then used his paper design to create the form shown in Figure 6–17.

Figure 6–17 **Reginald's design for the custom form**

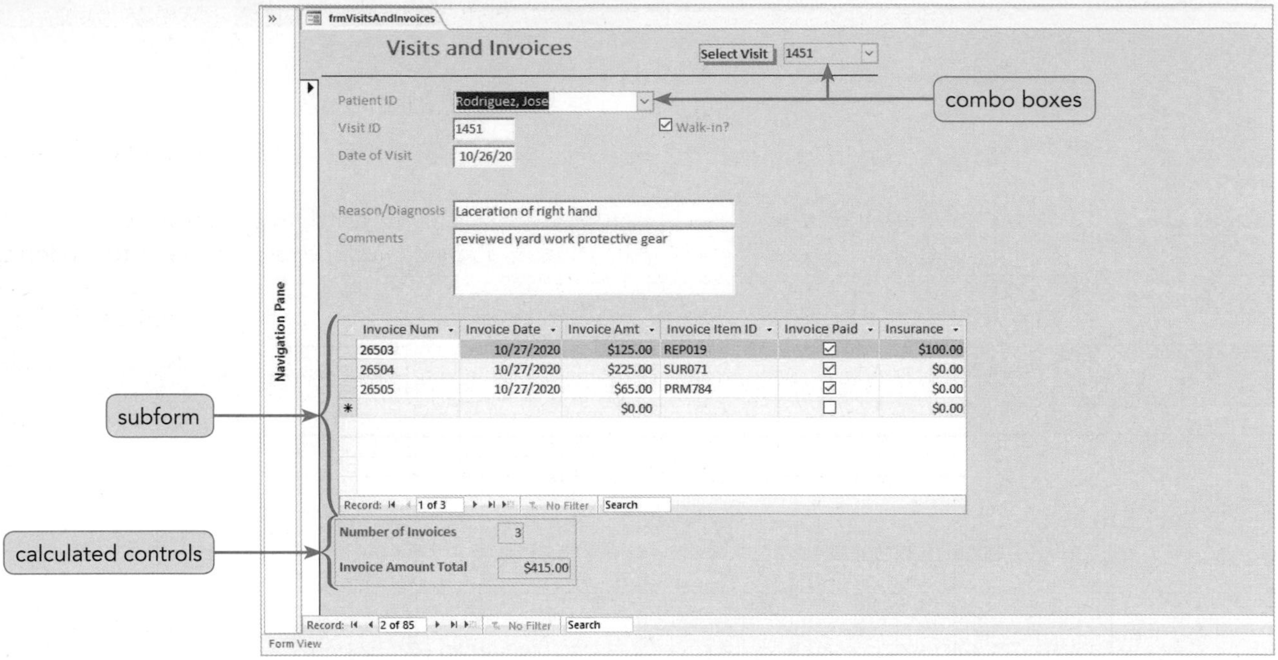

frmVisitsAndInvoices
Visits and Invoices
Select Visit
1451
combo boxes
Patient ID
Rodriguez, Jose
Visit ID
1451
Walk-in?
Date of Visit
10/26/20
Reason/Diagnosis
Laceration of right hand
Comments
reviewed yard work protective gear
Navigation Pane
Invoice Num
Invoice Date
Invoice Amt
Invoice Item ID
Invoice Paid
Insurance
26503 10/27/2020 $125.00 REP019 $100.00
26504 10/27/2020 $225.00 SUR071 $0.00
26505 10/27/2020 $65.00 PRM784 $0.00
$0.00 $0.00
subform
Record: 1 of 3 No Filter Search
calculated controls
Number of Invoices 3
Invoice Amount Total $415.00
Record: 2 of 85 No Filter Search
Form View

Notice that the top of the form displays a title and a combo box to select a visit record. Below these items are six field values with identifying labels from the tblVisit table; these fields are the PatientID, VisitID, WalkIn, VisitDate, Reason, and Comments fields. The PatientID field is displayed in a combo box, the WalkIn field is displayed as a check box, and the other field values are displayed in text boxes. The tblBilling table fields appear in a subform, which, as you know, is a separate form contained within another form. Unlike the tblVisit table data, which displays identifying labels to the left of the field values in text boxes, the tblBilling table data is displayed in datasheet format with identifying column headings above the field values. Finally, the Number of Invoices and Invoice Amount Total calculated controls in the main form display values based on the content of the subform.

Creating a Custom Form in Design View

To create Reginald's custom form, you could use the Form Wizard to create a basic version of the form and then customize it in Layout and Design views. However, for the form that Reginald designed, you would need to make many modifications to a form created by a wizard. You can instead build the form in a more straightforward manner by creating it directly in Design view. Creating forms in Design view allows you more control and precision and provides more options than creating forms in Layout view. You'll also find that you'll create forms more productively if you switch between Design view and Layout view because some design modifications are easier to make in one view than in the other view.

Working in the Form Window in Design View

You can use the Form window in Design view to create and modify forms. To create the custom form based on Reginald's design, you'll create a blank form, add the fields from the tblVisit and tblBilling tables, and then add other controls and make other modifications to the form.

The form you'll create will be a bound form. A **bound form** is a form that has a table or query as its record source. You use bound forms for maintaining and displaying table data. **Unbound forms** are forms that do not have a record source and are usually forms that help users navigate among the objects in a database.

REFERENCE

Creating a Form in Design View

- On the ribbon, click the Create tab.
- In the Forms group, click the Blank Form button to open the Form window in Layout view.
- Click the Design View button on the status bar to switch to Design view.
- Make sure the Field List pane is open, and then add the required fields to the form.
- Add other required controls to the form.
- Modify the size, position, and other properties as necessary for the fields and other controls in the form.
- Save the form.

Now you'll create a blank bound form based on the tblVisit table.

To create a blank bound form in Design view:

1. If you took a break after the previous session, make sure that the Clinic database is open and the Navigation Pane is open.
2. On the ribbon, click the **Create** tab, and then, in the Forms group, click the **Blank Form** button. The Form window opens in Layout view.
3. Click the **Design View** button on the status bar to switch to Design view, and then close the Navigation Pane.
4. If the Field List pane displays the "No fields available to be added to the current view" message, click **Show all tables** to display the tables in the Clinic database, and then click the **plus sign** next to tblVisit in the Field List pane to display the fields in the tblVisit table. See Figure 6–18.

Figure 6–18 **Blank form in Design view**

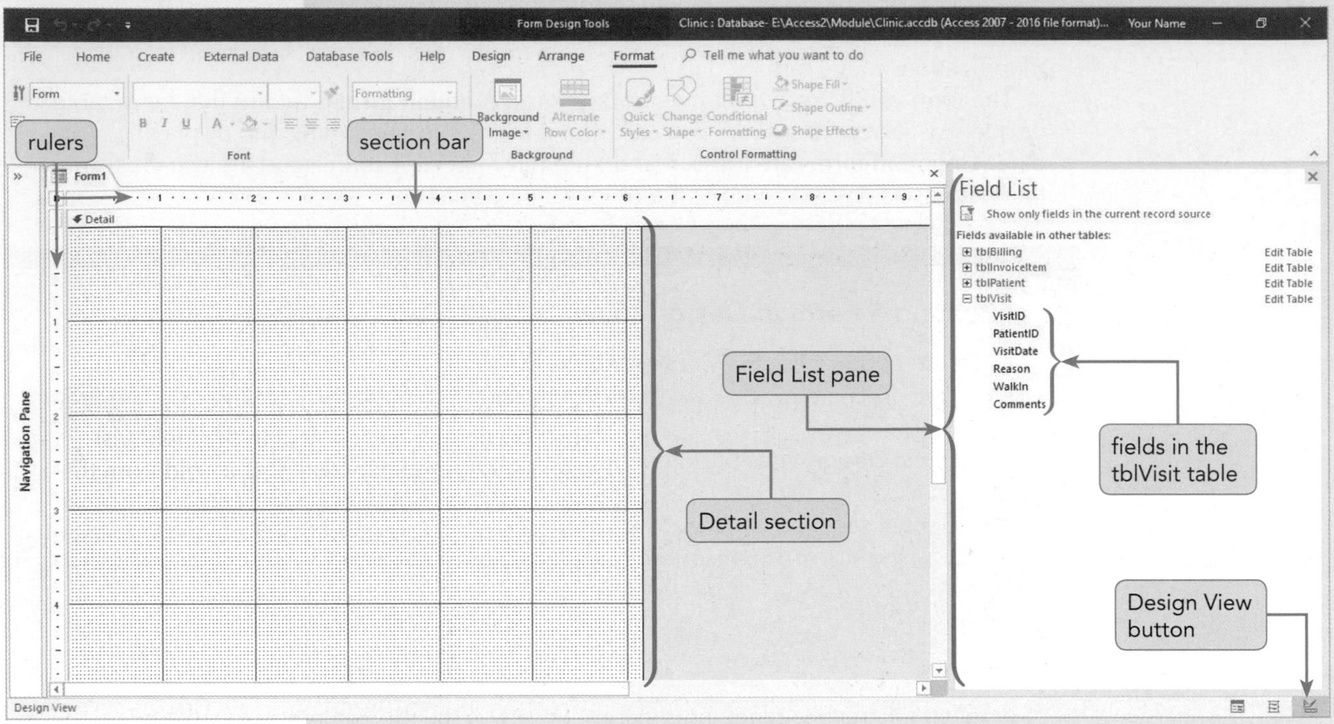
rulers
section bar
Field List pane
Detail section
fields in the tblVisit table
Design View button
Field List
Show only fields in the current record source
Fields available in other tables:
tblBilling
tblInvoiceItem
tblPatient
tblVisit
VisitID
PatientID
VisitDate
Reason
WalkIn
Comments
Edit Table
Form1
Detail
Navigation Pane
Design View

Trouble? If the tblVisit table in the Field List pane is not expanded to show the fields in the table, click the plus sign [+] next to tblVisit to display the fields.

Design view contains the tools necessary to create a custom form. You create the form by placing controls in the blank form. You can place three kinds of controls in a form:

- A bound control is connected, or bound, to a field in the database. The field could be selected from the fields in a table or query that are used as the record source. You use bound controls to display and maintain table field values.
- An **unbound control** is not connected to a field in the database. You use unbound controls to display text, such as a form title or instructions; to display lines, rect-angles, and other objects; or to display graphics and pictures created using other software programs. An unbound control that displays text is called a **label**.
- A **calculated control** displays a value that is the result of an expression. The expres-sion usually contains one or more fields, and the calculated control is recalculated each time any value in the expression changes.

To create bound controls, you add fields from the Field List pane to the Form window, and then position the bound controls where you want them to appear in the form. To place other controls in a form or a report, you use the tools in the Controls and Header/Footer groups on the Form Design Tools Design tab. The tools in the Controls group let you add controls such as lines, rectangles, images, buttons, check boxes, and list boxes to a form.

Design view for a form contains a Detail section, which is a rectangular area consisting of a grid with a section bar above the grid. You click the section bar to select the section in preparation for setting properties for the entire section. Some forms use Header, Detail, and Footer sections, but a simple form might have only a Detail section. The grid consists of dotted and solid lines that you use to position controls precisely in a form. In the Detail section, you place bound controls, unbound controls, and calculated controls in your form. You can change the size of the Detail section by dragging its borders. Rulers at the top and left edges of the Detail section define the horizontal and vertical dimensions of the form and serve as guides for placing controls in a form.

Your first task is to add bound controls to the Detail section for the six fields from the tblVisit table.

Adding Fields to a Form

When you add a bound control to a form, Access adds a field value box and, to its left, an attached label. The field value box displays a field value from the record source. The attached label displays either the Caption property value for the field, if the Caption property value has been set, or the field name. To create a bound control, you first display the Field List pane by clicking the Add Existing Fields button in the Tools group on the Form Design Tools Design tab. Then you double-click a field in the Field List pane to add the bound control to the Detail section. You can also drag a field from the Field List pane to the Detail section.

The Field List pane displays the four tables in the Clinic database and the six fields in the tblVisit table. Next, you'll add bound controls to the Detail section for the tblVisit table's six fields.

To add bound controls from the tblVisit table to the Detail section:

1. Double-click **VisitID** in the Field List pane. A bound text box control appears in the Detail section of the form. The Field List pane also lists the tblVisit table in the "Fields available for this view" section and the tblPatient and tblBilling tables in the "Fields available in related tables" section.
2. Repeat Step 1 for the **VisitDate**, **PatientID**, **Reason**, **Comments**, and **WalkIn** fields, in this order, in the Field List pane. Six bound controls—one for each of the six fields in the Field List pane—are added in the Detail section of the form. See Figure 6–19.

Figure 6–19 Bound controls added to the form

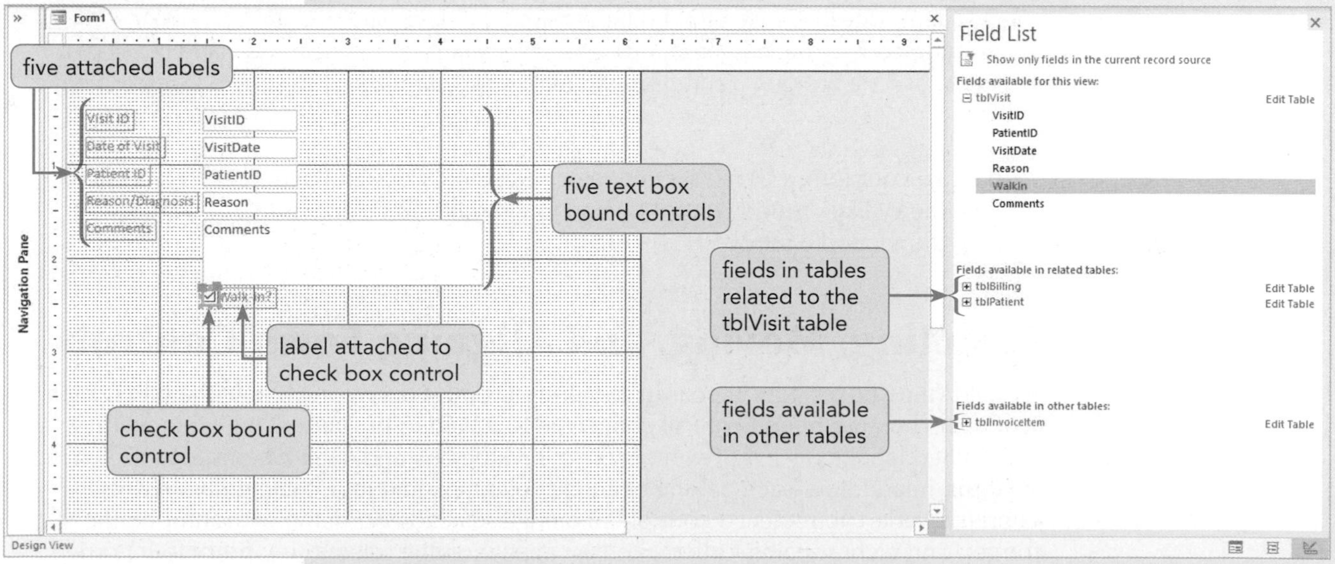
Form1
five attached labels
VisitID
VisitDate
PatientID
Reason
Comments
five text box bound controls
fields in tables related to the tblVisit table
label attached to check box control
check box bound control
fields available in other tables
Navigation Pane
Design View
Field List
Show only fields in the current record source
Fields available for this view:
tblVisit
Edit Table
VisitID
PatientID
VisitDate
Reason
WalkIn
Comments
Fields available in related tables:
tblBilling
tblPatient
Edit Table
Edit Table
Fields available in other tables:
tblInvoiceItem
Edit Table

You should periodically save your work as you create a form, so you'll save the form now.

3. Click the **Save** button on the Quick Access Toolbar. The Save As dialog box opens.
4. With the default name selected in the Form Name box, type **frmVisitsAndInvoices**, and then press **ENTER**. The tab for the form now displays the form name, and the form design is saved in the Clinic database.

You've added the fields you need to the grid, so you can close the Field List pane.

5. Click the **Form Design Tools Design** tab, and then, in the Tools group, click the **Add Existing Fields** button to close the Field List pane.

INSIGHT

Strategies for Building Forms

To help prevent common problems and more easily recover from errors while building forms, you should keep in mind the following suggestions:

- You can click the Undo button one or more times immediately after you make one or more errors or make form adjustments you don't want to keep.
- You should back up your database frequently, especially before you create new objects or customize existing objects. If you run into difficulty, you can revert to your most recent backup copy of the database.
- You should save your form after you've completed a portion of your work successfully and before you need to perform steps you've never done before. If you're not satisfied with subsequent steps, close the form without saving the changes you made since your last save, and then open the form and perform the steps again.
- You can always close the form, make a copy of the form in the Navigation Pane, and practice with the copy.
- Adding controls, setting properties, and performing other tasks correctly in Access should work all the time with consistent results, but in rare instances, you might find that a feature doesn't work properly. If a feature you've previously used successfully suddenly doesn't work, you should save your work, close the database, make a backup copy of the database, open the database, and then compact and repair the database. Performing a compact and repair resolves most of these types of problems.

To make your form's Detail section match Reginald's design (Figure 6–17), you need to move the WalkIn bound control up and to the right. To do so, you must start by selecting the bound control.

Selecting, Moving, and Aligning Form Controls

Six field value boxes now appear in the form's Detail section, one below the other. Each field value box is a bound control connected to a field in the underlying table, with an attached label to its left or right. Each field value box and each label is a control in the form; in addition, each pairing of a field value box and its associated label is itself a control. When you select a control, an orange selection border appears around the control, and eight squares, called handles, appear on the selection border's four corners and at the midpoints of its four edges. The larger handle in a control's upper-left corner is its move handle, which you use to move the control. You use the other seven handles, called sizing handles, to resize the control. When you work in Design view, controls you place in the form do not become part of a control layout, so you can individually select, move, resize, and otherwise manipulate one control without also changing the other controls. However, at any time you can select a group of controls and place them in a control layout—either a stacked layout or a tabular layout.

Based on Reginald's design for the custom form, shown in Figure 6–17, you need to move the WalkIn bound control up and to the right in the Detail section. The WalkIn bound control consists of a check box and an attached label, displaying the text "Walk-in?" to its right.

You can move a field value box and its attached label together. To move them, you place the pointer anywhere on the selection border of the field value box, but not on a move handle or a sizing handle. When the pointer changes to the move pointer, you drag the field value box and its attached label to the new location. As you move a control, an outline of the control moves on the rulers to indicate the current position of the control as you drag it. To move a group of selected controls, point to any selected control until the pointer changes to the move pointer, and then drag the group of selected controls to the new position. As you know, you can move controls with more precision by pressing the appropriate arrow key on the keyboard to move the selected control in small increments. To move selected controls to the next nearest grid dot, press and hold CTRL and then press the appropriate arrow key on the keyboard.

You can also move either a field value box or its label individually. If you want to move the field value box but not its label, for example, place the pointer on the field value box's move handle. When the pointer changes to the move pointer, drag the field value box to the new location. You use the label's move handle in a similar way to move only the label.

You'll now arrange the controls in the form to match Reginald's design.

To move the WalkIn bound control:

1. If necessary, click the **Walk-in?** label box to select it. Move handles, which are the larger handles, appear on the upper-left corners of the selected label box and its associated bound control. Sizing handles also appear but only on the label box. See Figure 6–20.

Figure 6–20 Selected WalkIn bound control and label

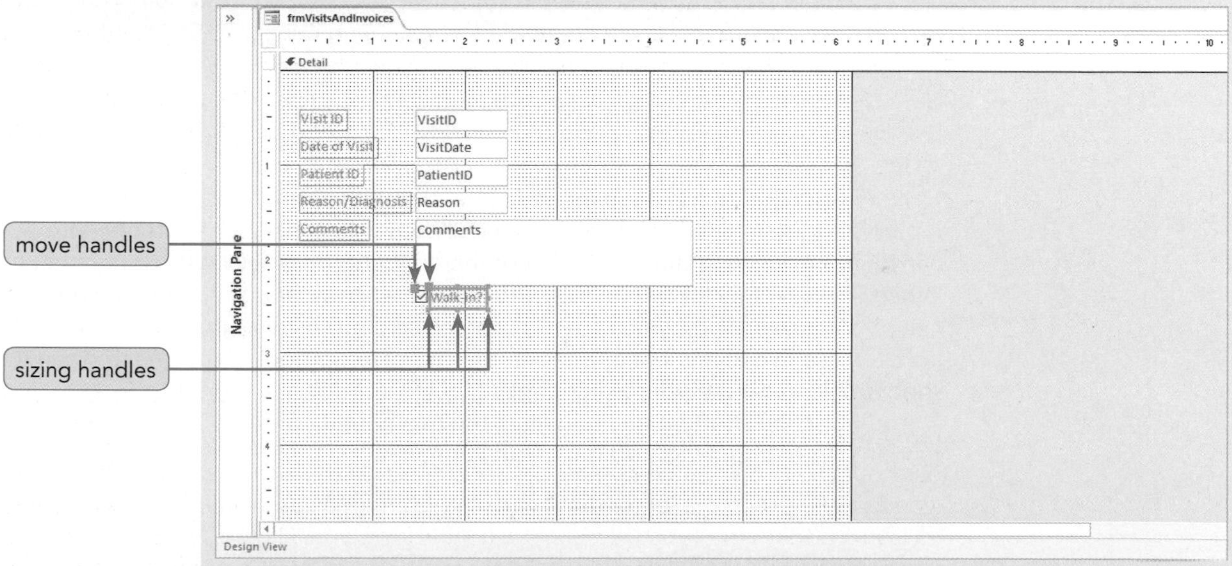
move handles
sizing handles
frmVisitsAndInvoices
Detail
Visit ID
VisitID
Date of Visit
VisitDate
Patient ID
PatientID
Reason/Diagnosis
Reason
Comments
Comments
Walk-in?
Navigation Pane
Design View

Be sure to position the pointer on one of the edges but not on a move handle or a sizing handle.

2. Position the pointer on the Walk-in? label box's orange selection border, but not on a move handle or a sizing handle, until the pointer changes to a move pointer, drag the control up and to the right of the VisitID field value box, and then release the mouse button.
3. Press ↓ twice. The selected label box and its associated bound control move one grid dot in the direction of the arrow key with each key press. You can move a selected control using ↑, ←, and → as well.
4. Click the Undo button on the Quick Access Toolbar. The selected label box and bound control move back up one grid dot.
5. Click the Undo button two more times. The selected label box and bound control move back up one grid dot, and then move back to their original position.
6. Click the Redo button. The label box and bound control return to the position where you dragged them.
7. Use any combination of dragging and arrow keys to position the WalkIn? label box and bound control as shown in Figure 6–21.

Figure 6–21 **Repositioned Walk-in? label and associated bound control**

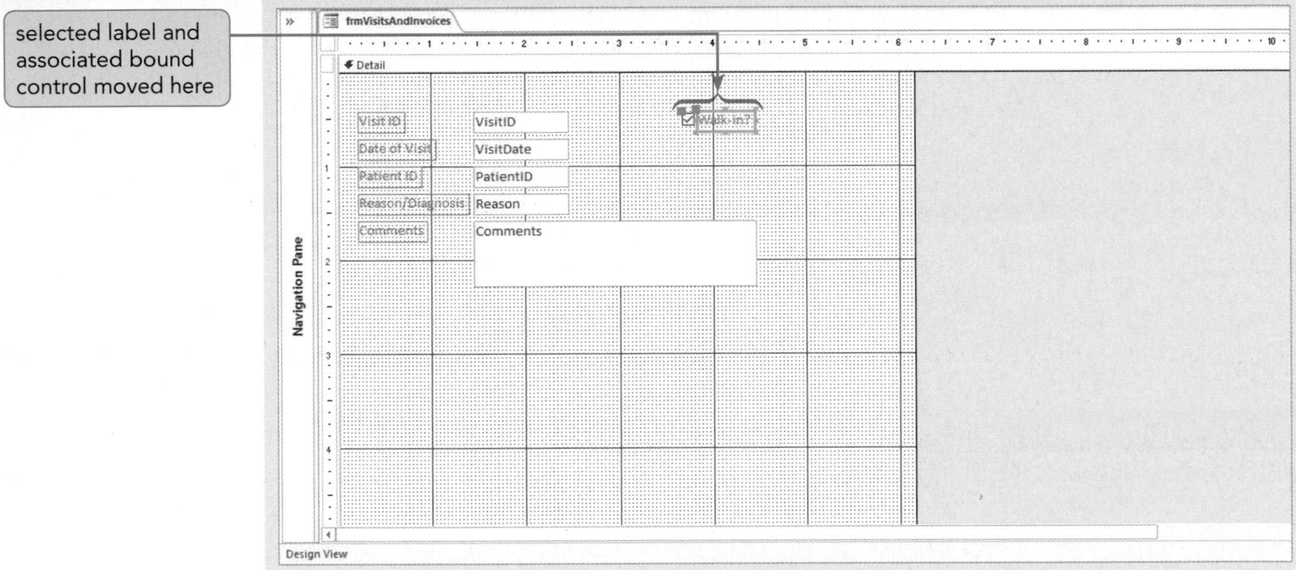
selected label and associated bound control moved here
frmVisitsAndInvoices
Detail
Visit ID
VisitID
Date of Visit
VisitDate
Patient ID
PatientID
Reason/Diagnosis
Reason
Comments
Comments
Walk-in?
Navigation Pane
Design View

Now you need to top-align the WalkIn and VisitID bound controls (meaning their top borders are aligned with one another). When you select a column of controls, you can align the controls along their left or their right borders (left-align or right-align). When you select a row of controls, you can top-align or bottom-align the controls. You can also align To Grid, which aligns the selected controls with the dots in the grid. You access these five alignment options on the Form Design Tools Arrange tab or on the shortcut menu for the selected controls.

You'll use the shortcut menu to align the two bound controls. Then you'll save the modified form and review your work in Form view.

To align the WalkIn and VisitID bound controls:

1. Make sure the Walk-in? label box is selected.

2. Press and hold **SHIFT**, click the **WalkIn** check box, click the **VisitID** field value box, click the **Visit ID** label, and then release **SHIFT**. The four controls are selected, and each selected control has an orange selection border.
3. Right-click one of the selected controls, point to **Align** on the shortcut menu, and then click **Top**. The four selected controls are top-aligned. See Figure 6–22.

Figure 6–22 Aligned controls in the Detail section

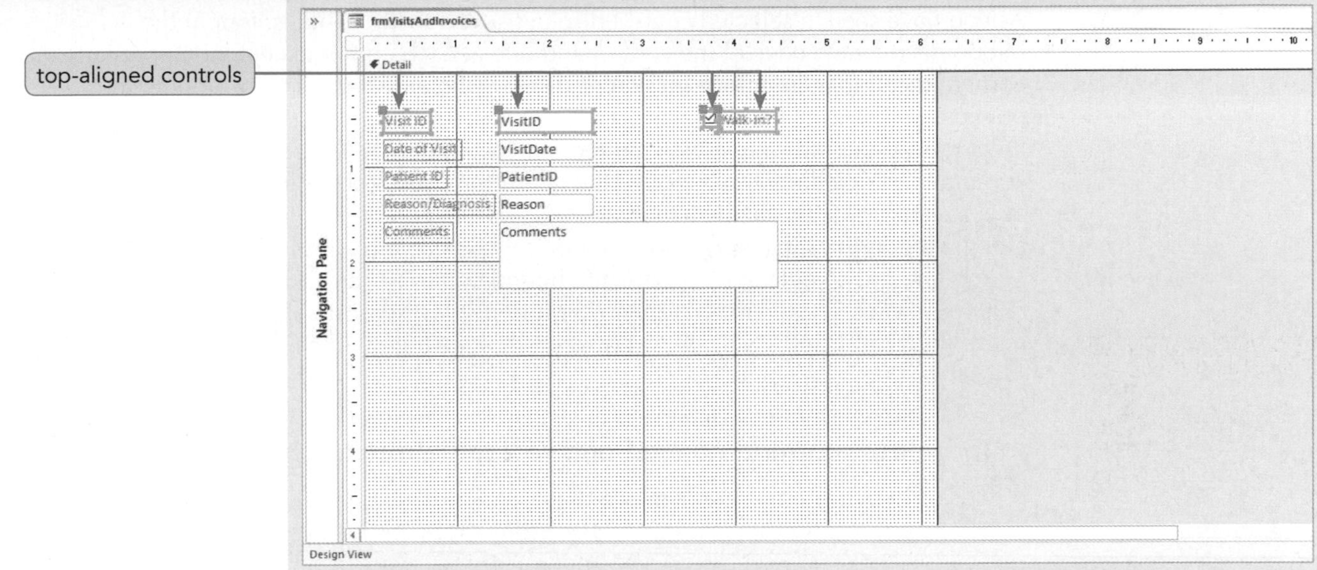
top-aligned controls
frmVisitsAndInvoices
Detail
Visit ID
VisitID
Walk-in?
Date of Visit
VisitDate
Patient ID
PatientID
Reason/Diagnosis
Reason
Comments
Comments
Navigation Pane
Design View

As you create a form, you should periodically save your modifications to the form and review your progress in Form view.

4. Save your form design changes, and then switch to Form view.
5. Click the **Next record** button ▶ to display the second record in the dataset (Visit ID #1451) in the form. See Figure 6–23.

Figure 6–23 Form displayed in Form view

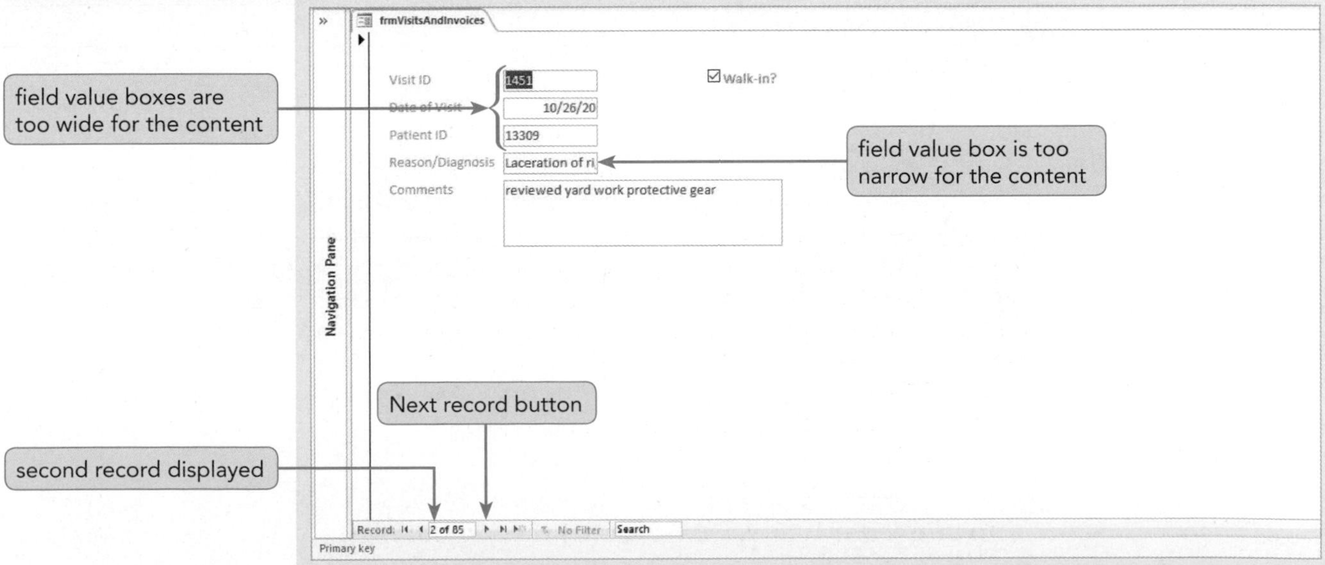
field value boxes are too wide for the content
field value box is too narrow for the content
Next record button
second record displayed
frmVisitsAndInvoices
Visit ID
1451
Walk-in?
Date of Visit
10/26/20
Patient ID
13309
Reason/Diagnosis
Laceration of ri
Comments
reviewed yard work protective gear
Navigation Pane
Record: 2 of 85
No Filter
Search
Primary key

The value in the Reason field value box is not fully displayed, so you need to increase the width of the text box control. The VisitID and VisitDate text boxes are wider than necessary, so you'll reduce their widths. Also, the PatientID bound control consists of a label and a text box, but the plan for the form shows a combo box for the PatientID positioned below the WalkIn bound control. You'll delete the PatientID bound control, and then add it back to the form, this time as a combo box.

Resizing and Deleting Controls

As you have seen, a selected control displays seven sizing handles: four at the midpoints on each edge of the control and one at each corner except the upper-left corner. Recall that the upper-left corner displays the move handle. Positioning the pointer over a sizing handle changes the pointer to a two-headed arrow; the directions the arrows point indicate in which direction you can resize the selected control. When you drag a sizing handle, you resize the control. As you resize the control, a thin line appears alongside the sizing handle to guide you in completing the task accurately, along with outlines that appear on the horizontal and vertical rulers.

You'll begin by deleting the PatientID bound control. Then you'll resize the Reason text box, which is too narrow and too short to display Reason field values. Next you'll resize the VisitID and VisitDate text boxes to reduce their widths.

To delete a bound control and resize field value boxes:

1. Switch to Design view, click a blank area of the window to deselect all controls, and then click the **PatientID** text box control to select it.
2. Right-click the **PatientID** text box to open the shortcut menu, and then click **Delete**. The label and the bound text box control for the PatientID field are deleted.
3. Click the **Reason** text box to select it.
4. Place the pointer on the middle-right handle of the Reason text box until it changes to a horizontal resize pointer ↔, and then drag the right border to the right until it is approximately the same width as the Comments text box. See Figure 6–24.

TIP

If you want to delete a label but not its associated field value box, right-click the label, and then click Delete on the shortcut menu.

Figure 6–24 Resized Reason text box

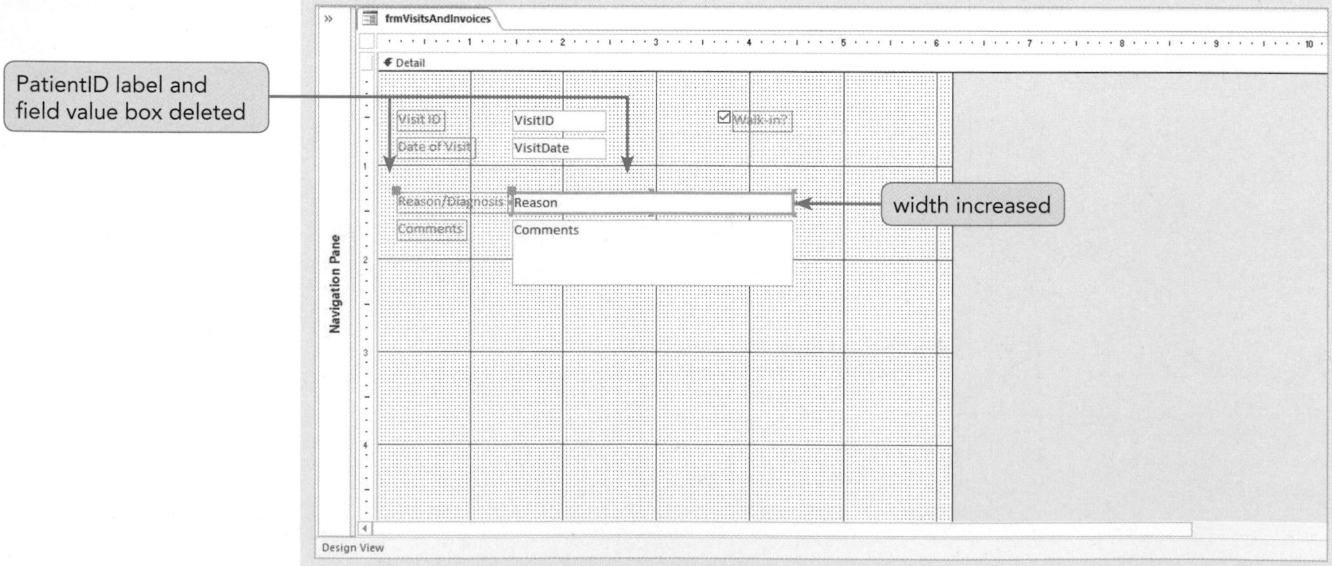
PatientID label and field value box deleted
width increased
frmVisitsAndInvoices
Detail
Visit ID
VisitID
Walk-in?
Date of Visit
VisitDate
Reason/Diagnosis
Reason
Comments
Comments
Navigation Pane
Design View

Resizing controls in Design view is a trial-and-error process, in which you resize a control in Design view, switch to Form view to observe the effect of the resizing, switch back to Design view to make further refinements to the control's size, and continue until the control is sized correctly. It's easier to resize controls in Layout view because you can see actual field values while you resize the controls. You'll resize the other two text box controls in Layout view. The sizes of the VisitID and VisitDate controls will look fine if you reduce them to the same widths, so you'll select both boxes and resize them with one action.

5. Switch to Layout view, and then click the **VisitID** field value box (if necessary) to select it.
6. Press and hold **SHIFT**, click the **VisitDate** field value box (next to the label "Date of Visit") to select it, and then release the mouse button.
7. Position the pointer on the right border of the **VisitDate** field value box until the pointer changes to a horizontal resize pointer ↔, drag the border to the left until the field box is slightly wider than the field value it contains, and the value in the VisitID field is also visible, and then release the mouse button. See Figure 6–25.

Figure 6–25 Resized field value boxes in Layout view

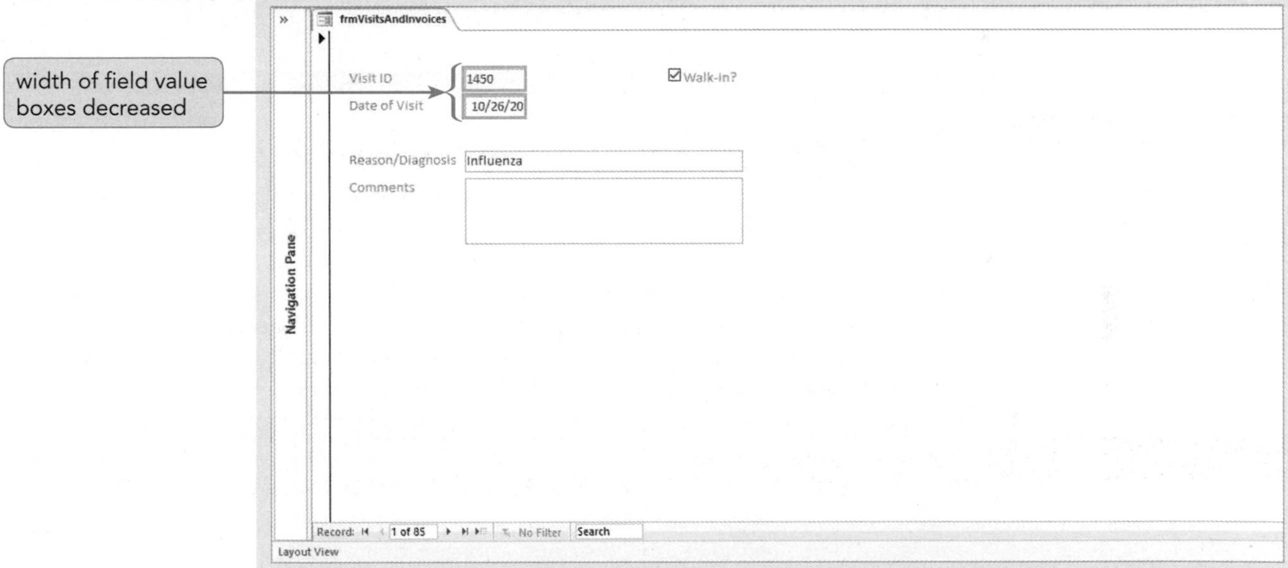

width of field value boxes decreased
frmVisitsAndInvoices
Visit ID
1450
Date of Visit
10/26/20
Walk-in?
Reason/Diagnosis
Influenza
Comments
Navigation Pane
Record: 1 of 85
No Filter
Search
Layout View

Trouble? If you resized the field value boxes too far to the left, number signs will be displayed inside the VisitDate field value box. Drag the right border to the right slightly until the date value is visible.

8. Navigate through the first several records to make sure the first three field value boxes are sized properly and display the full field values. If any field value box is too small, select it, and then resize it as appropriate.
9. Save your form design changes, switch to Design view, and then deselect all controls by clicking a blank area of the window.

INSIGHT

Making Form Design Modifications

When you design forms and other objects, you'll find it helpful to switch frequently between Design view and Layout view. Some form modifications are easier to make in Layout view, other form modifications are easier to make in Design view, and still other form modifications can be made only in Design view. You should check your progress frequently in either Layout view or Form view, and you should save your modifications after completing a set of changes successfully.

Recall that you removed the lookup feature from the PatientID field because a combo box provides the same lookup capability in a form. Next, you'll add a combo box control for the PatientID field to the custom form.

Adding a Combo Box Control to a Form

The tblPatient and tblVisit tables are related in a one-to-many relationship. The PatientID field in the tblVisit table is a foreign key to the tblVisit table, and you can use a combo box control in the custom form to view and maintain PatientID field values more easily and accurately than using a text box. Recall that a combo box is a control that provides the features of a text box and a list box; you can choose a value from the list or type an entry.

PROSKILLS

Problem Solving: Using Combo Boxes for Foreign Keys

When you design forms, combo box controls are a natural choice for foreign keys because foreign key values must match one of the primary key values in the related primary table. If you do not use a combo box control for a foreign key, you force users to type values in the text box control. When they make typing mistakes, Access rejects the values and displays nonmatching error messages, which can be frustrating and make the form less efficient for users. Combo box controls allow users to select only from a list of valid foreign key values so that nonmatching errors are eliminated. At the same time, combo boxes allow users who are skilled at data entry to more rapidly type the values, instead of using the more time-consuming technique of choosing a value from the list the combo box control provides. Whenever you use an Access feature such as combo boxes for foreign keys, it takes extra time during development to add the feature, but you save users time and improve their accuracy for the many months or years they use the database.

You use the **Combo Box tool** in Design view to add a combo box control to a form. If you want help when adding the combo box, you can select one of the Control Wizards. A **Control Wizard** asks a series of questions and then, based on your answers, creates a control in a form or report. Access offers Control Wizards for the Combo Box, List Box, Option Group, Command Button, Subform/Subreport, and other control tools.

You will use the Combo Box Wizard to add a combo box control to the form for the PatientID field.

To add a combo box control to the form:

1. Click the **Form Design Tools Design** tab, and then in the Controls group, click the **More** button to open the Controls gallery. See Figure 6–26.

Figure 6–26 Controls gallery

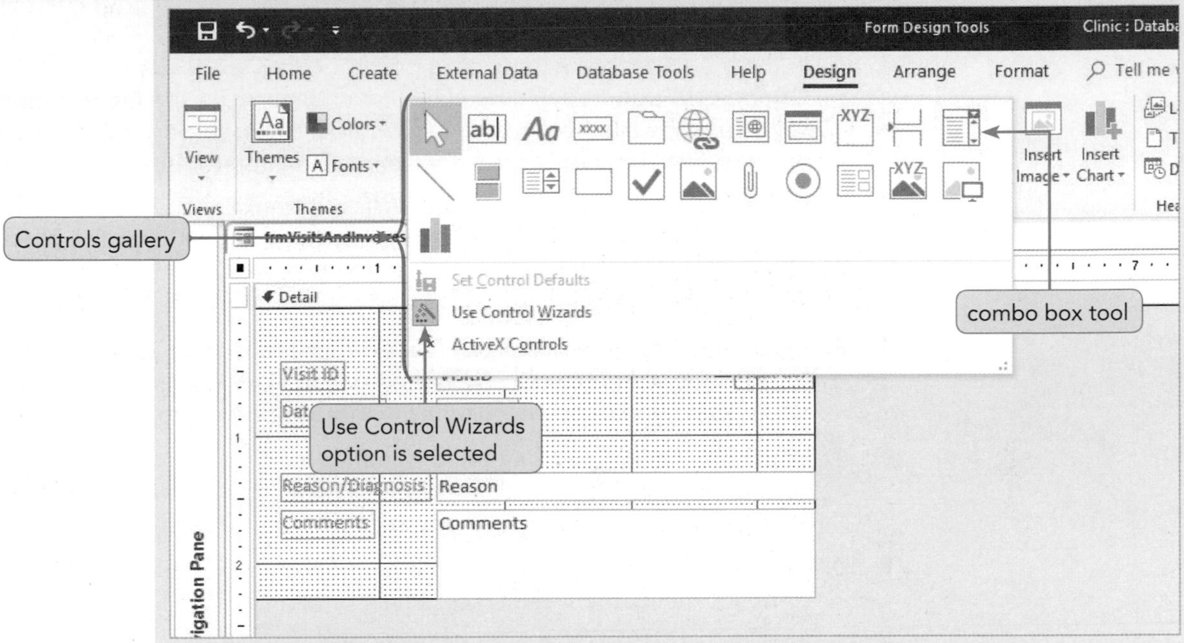

Form Design Tools
Clinic : Datab
File
Home
Create
External Data
Database Tools
Help
Design
Arrange
Format
Tell me
View
Themes
Colors
Fonts
Views
Themes
Insert Image
Insert Chart
Set Control Defaults
Use Control Wizards
ActiveX Controls
Controls gallery
combo box tool
Use Control Wizards option is selected
frmVisitsAndInvoices
Detail
Visit ID
Reason/Diagnosis
Reason
Comments
Comments
Navigation Pane

The Controls gallery contains tools that allow you to add controls (such as text boxes, lines, charts, and labels) to a form. You drag a control from the Controls gallery and place it in position in the grid. If you want to use the Combo Box Wizard to add a control, you need to select that option below the gallery.

2. In the gallery, make sure the Use Control Wizards option is selected (its icon should appear with a gray background) at the bottom of the Controls gallery.

   Trouble? If the Use Control Wizards option is not selected, click Use Control Wizards to select it, and then click the More button again to open the Controls gallery.

3. In the Controls gallery, click the **Combo Box** tool. The Controls gallery closes.

   Once you select the Combo Box tool (or most other tools in the Controls gallery) and move the mouse pointer into the Detail section of the form, the pointer changes to a shape that is unique for the control with a plus symbol in its upper-left corner. You position the plus symbol in the location where you want to place the upper-left corner of the control.

   You'll place the combo box near the top of the form, below the WalkIn bound control, and then position it more precisely after you've completed the steps in the wizard.

4. Position the plus symbol of the pointer shape below the WalkIn bound control and at the 3.5-inch mark on the horizontal ruler, and then click the mouse button. A combo box control appears in the form, and the first Combo Box Wizard dialog box opens.

You can use an existing table or query as the source for a new combo box or type the values for the combo box. In this case, you'll use the qryPatientsByName query as the basis for the new combo box.

5. Click the **I want the combo box to get the values from another table or query** option button (if necessary), and then click the **Next** button to open the next Combo Box Wizard dialog box, in which you specify the source of information for the combo box.
6. In the View section of the dialog box, click the **Queries** option button, click **Query: qryPatientsByName** in the list, and then click the **Next** button. The next dialog box in the Combo Box Wizard lets you select the fields from the query to appear as columns in the combo box. You will select the first two fields.
7. In the Available Fields box, double-click **Patient** to move this field to the Selected Fields box, double-click **PatientID**, and then click the **Next** button. The next dialog box lets you choose a sort order for the combo box entries. Reginald wants the entries to appear in ascending order on the Patient field.
8. Click the **arrow** in the first box, click **Patient**, and then click the **Next** button to open the next Combo Box Wizard dialog box, in which you specify the appropriate width for the columns in the combo box control.
9. Resize the Patient and Patient ID columns to fit their content, scroll the list in the dialog box to ensure all the Patient values are visible, and if any are not, resize the Patient column as necessary.
10. Click the **Next** button to open the next dialog box in the Combo Box Wizard. Here you select the foreign key, which is the PatientID field.
11. In the Available Fields list, click **PatientID**, and then click the **Next** button. In this dialog box, you specify the field in the tblVisit table where the selected PatientID value from the combo box will be stored. You'll store the value in the PatientID field in the tblVisit table.
12. Click the **Store that value in this field** option button, click the arrow to display a list of fields, click **PatientID**, and then click the **Next** button.

    Trouble? If PatientID doesn't appear in the list, click the Cancel button, press DELETE to delete the combo box, click the Add Existing Fields button in the Tools group on the Form Design Tools Design tab, double-click PatientID in the Field List pane, press DELETE to delete PatientID, close the Field List pane, and then repeat Steps 1–12.

    In the final Combo Box Wizard dialog box, you specify the name for the combo box control. You'll use the field name of PatientID.

13. With the current text selected in the "What label would you like for your combo box?" box, type **PatientID** and then click the **Finish** button. The completed PatientID combo box control appears in the form.

You need to position and resize the combo box control, but first you will change the Caption property for the PatientID combo box label control so that it matches the format used by the other label controls in the form.

REFERENCE

Changing a Label's Caption

- Right-click the label to select it and to display the shortcut menu, and then click Properties to display the Property Sheet.
- If necessary, click the All tab to display the All page in the Property Sheet.
- Edit the existing text in the Caption box; or click the Caption box, press F2 to select the current value, and then type a new caption.

You want the label control attached to the combo box control to display "Patient ID" instead of "PatientID". You will change the Caption property for the label control next.

TIP

After selecting a control, you can press F4 to open and close the Property Sheet for the control.

To set the Caption property for the PatientID combo box's label control:

1. Right-click the **PatientID** label, which is the control to the left of the PatientID combo box control, and then click **Properties** on the shortcut menu. The Property Sheet for the PatientID label control opens.

   Trouble? If the Selection type entry below the Property Sheet title bar is not "Label," then you selected the wrong control in Step 1. Click the PatientID label in the form to change to the Property Sheet for this control.

2. If necessary, in the Property Sheet, click the **All** tab to display all properties for the selected PatientID label control.

   The Selection type entry, which appears below the Property Sheet title bar, displays the control type (Label in this case) for the selected control. Below the Selection type entry in the Property Sheet is the Control box, which you can use to select another control in the form and list its properties in the Property Sheet. Alternately, you can click a control in the form and modify its properties in the Property Sheet. The first property in the Property Sheet, the **Name property**, specifies the name of a control, section, or object (PatientID_Label in this case). The Name property value is the same as the value displayed in the Control box, unless the Caption property has been set. For bound controls, the Name property value matches the field name. For unbound controls, an underscore and a suffix of the control type (for example, Label) is added to the Name property setting. For unbound controls, you can set the Name property to another, more meaningful value at any time.

3. In the Caption box, click before "ID", press **SPACEBAR**, and then press **TAB** to move to the next property in the Property Sheet. The Caption property value changes to Patient ID, and the label for the PatientID bound label control displays Patient ID. See Figure 6–27.

Figure 6–27 PatientID combo box and updated label added to the form

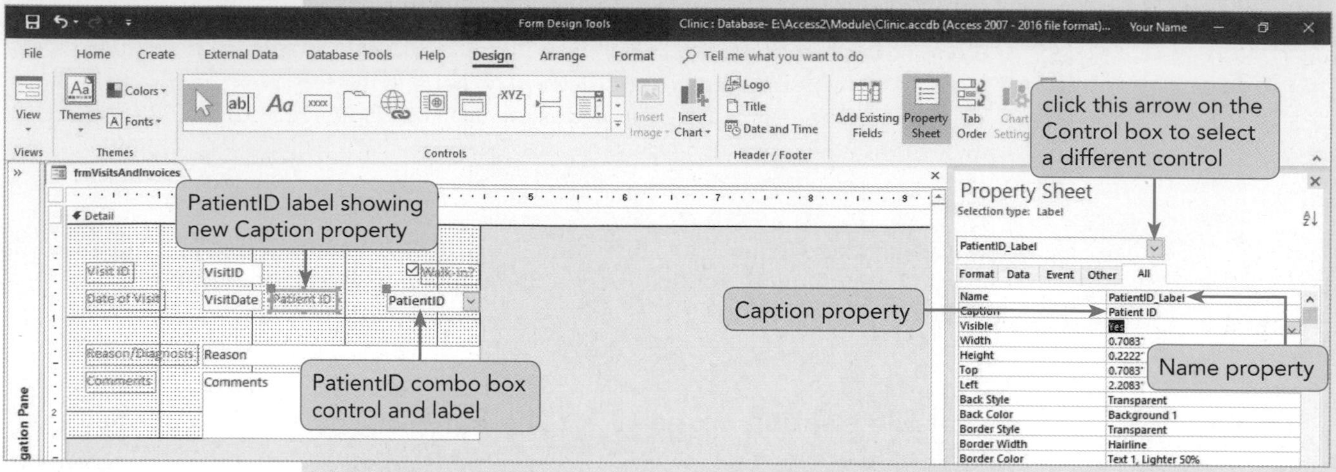
click this arrow on the Control box to select a different control
PatientID label showing new Caption property
Caption property
Name property
PatientID combo box control and label

Trouble? Some property values in your Property Sheet, such as the Width and Top property values, might differ if your label's position differs slightly from the label position used as the basis for Figure 6–27. These differences cause no problems.

TIP

You won't see the effects of the new property setting until you select another property, select another control, or close the Property Sheet.

4. Close the Property Sheet, and then save your design changes to the form.

Now that you've added the combo box control to the form, you can position and resize it appropriately. You'll need to view the form in Form view to determine any fine-tuning necessary for the width of the combo box.

To modify the combo box in Design and Layout views:

1. Click the **PatientID** combo box control, press and hold **SHIFT**, click the **Patient ID** label control, and then release **SHIFT** to select both controls.

   First, you'll move the selected controls above the VisitID controls. Then you'll left-align the PatientID, VisitID, VisitDate, Reason, and Comments labels; left-align the PatientID combo box control with the VisitID, VisitDate, Reason, and Comments text box controls; and then right-align the WalkIn label and check box control with the right edges of the Reason and Comments text box controls.

2. Drag the selected controls to a position above the VisitID controls. Do not try to align them.
3. Click in a blank area of the window to deselect the selected controls.
4. Press and hold **SHIFT** while you click the **Patient ID** label, the **Visit ID** label, **Date of Visit** label, **Reason/Diagnosis** label, and the **Comments** label, and then release **SHIFT**.
5. Click the **Form Design Tools Arrange** tab, in the Sizing & Ordering group, click the **Align** button, and then click **Left**. The selected controls are left-aligned.
6. Repeat Steps 4 and 5 to left-align the PatientID combo box, VisitID text box, VisitDate text box, Reason text box, and the Comments text box.

7. Click the **Walk-In?** label, press and hold **SHIFT**, click the **Reason** text box and **Comments** text box, and then release **SHIFT**.
8. In the Sizing & Ordering group, click the **Align** button, and then click **Right**. The selected controls are right-aligned.
9. Switch to Form view, and then click the **PatientID** arrow to open the combo box control's list box. Note that the column is not wide enough to show the full data values. See Figure 6–28.

Figure 6–28 PatientID combo box and updated label in Form view

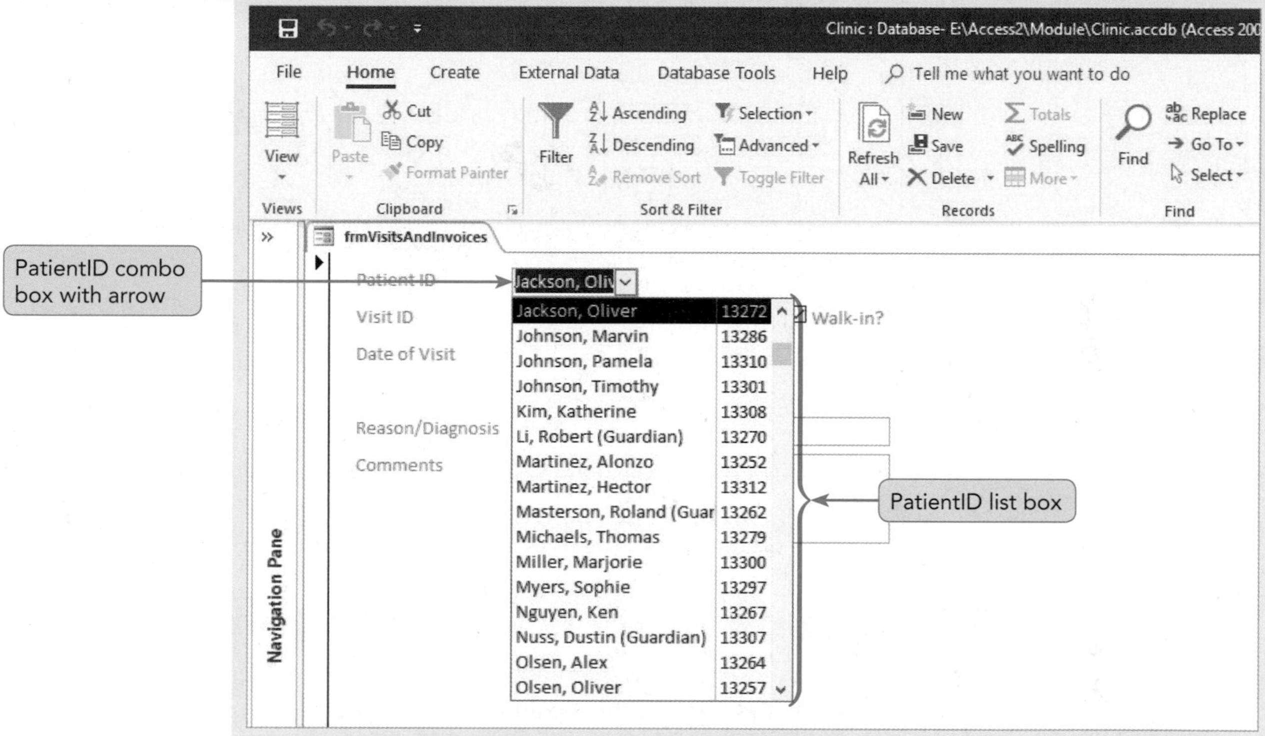
Clinic : Database- E:\Access2\Module\Clinic.accdb (Access 200
File
Home
Create
External Data
Database Tools
Help
Tell me what you want to do
View
Paste
Cut
Copy
Format Painter
Filter
Ascending
Descending
Remove Sort
Selection
Advanced
Toggle Filter
Refresh All
New
Save
Delete
Totals
Spelling
More
Find
Replace
Go To
Select
Views
Clipboard
Sort & Filter
Records
Find
frmVisitsAndInvoices
PatientID combo box with arrow
Patient ID
Jackson, Oliv
Visit ID
Date of Visit
Reason/Diagnosis
Comments
Walk-in?
Jackson, Oliver 13272
Johnson, Marvin 13286
Johnson, Pamela 13310
Johnson, Timothy 13301
Kim, Katherine 13308
Li, Robert (Guardian) 13270
Martinez, Alonzo 13252
Martinez, Hector 13312
Masterson, Roland (Guar 13262
Michaels, Thomas 13279
Miller, Marjorie 13300
Myers, Sophie 13297
Nguyen, Ken 13267
Nuss, Dustin (Guardian) 13307
Olsen, Alex 13264
Olsen, Oliver 13257
PatientID list box
Navigation Pane

You need to widen the PatientID combo box so that that the widest value in the list is displayed in the combo box. You can widen the combo box in Layout view or in Design view. Because Form view and Layout view display actual data from the table rather than placeholder text in each bound control, these views let you immediately see the effects of your layout changes. You'll use Layout view instead of Design view to make this change because you can determine the proper width more accurately in Layout view.

10. Switch to Layout view, and then navigate to record 19. Masterson, Roland (Guardian), which is the patient name for this record, is one of the widest values that is displayed in the combo box. You want to widen the combo box so that it is a little bit wider than the value in record 19.
11. Make sure that only the combo box is selected, and then drag the right border to widen the combo box until the entire name of the patient is visible. See Figure 6–29.

Figure 6–29 Resized PatientID combo box in Layout view

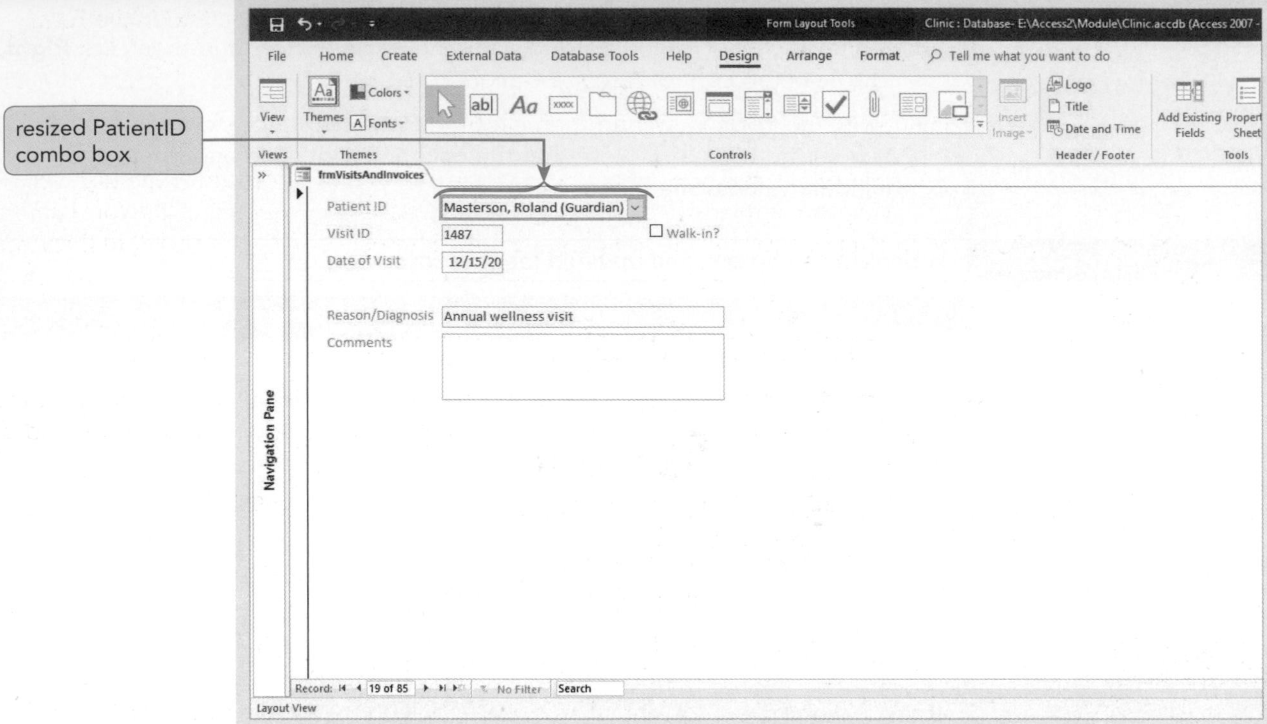
resized PatientID combo box
File
Home
Create
External Data
Database Tools
Help
Design
Arrange
Format
Tell me what you want to do
Form Layout Tools
Logo
Title
Date and Time
Add Existing Fields
Views
Themes
Controls
Header / Footer
Tools
frmVisitsAndInvoices
Patient ID
Masterson, Roland (Guardian)
Visit ID
1487
Walk-in?
Date of Visit
12/15/20
Reason/Diagnosis
Annual wellness visit
Comments
Navigation Pane
Record: 19 of 85
No Filter
Search
Layout View

Now you'll add the title to the top of the form by adding a Form Header section.

Using Form Headers and Form Footers

The Form Header and Form Footer sections let you add titles, instructions, command buttons, and other controls to the top and bottom of your form, respectively. Controls placed in the Form Header or Form Footer sections remain on the screen whenever the form is displayed in Form view or Layout view; they do not change when the contents of the Detail section change as you navigate from one record to another record.

To add either a form header or footer to your form, you must first add both the Form Header and Form Footer sections as a pair to the form. If your form needs one of these sections but not the other, you can remove a section by setting its height to zero, which is the same method you would use to remove any form section. You can also prevent a section from appearing in Form view or in Print Preview by setting its Visible property to "No." The **Visible property** determines if a control or section appears in Form view, in Print Preview, or when printed. You set the Visible property to Yes to display the control or section, and set the Visible property to No to hide it.

If you've set the Form Footer section's height to zero or set its Visible property to No and a future form design change makes adding controls to the Form Footer section necessary, you can restore the section by using the pointer to drag its bottom border back down or by setting its Visible property to Yes.

In Design view, you can add the Form Header and Form Footer sections as a pair to a form by right-clicking the Detail section selector, and then clicking Form Header/ Footer. You also can click the Logo button, the Title button, or the Date and Time button in the Header/Footer group on the Form Design Tools Design tab or the Form Layout Tools Design tab. Clicking any of these three buttons adds the Form Header and Form Footer sections to the form and places an appropriate control in the Form Header section only. A footer section is added to the form, but with a height set to zero to one-quarter inch.

Reginald's design includes a title at the top of the form. Because the title will not change as you navigate through the form records, you will add the title to the Form Header section in the form.

Adding a Title to a Form

You'll add the title to Reginald's form in Layout view. When you add a title to a form in Layout view, a Form Header section is added to the form and contains the form title. At the same time, a Page Footer section with a height setting of zero is added to the form.

To add a title to the form:

1. On the Form Layout Tools Design tab, in the Header/Footer group, click the **Title** button. A title consisting of the form name is added to the form and is selected.

   You need to change the title.

2. Type **Visits and Invoices** to replace the selected default title text. See Figure 6–30.

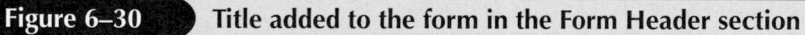

Figure 6–30 **Title added to the form in the Form Header section**

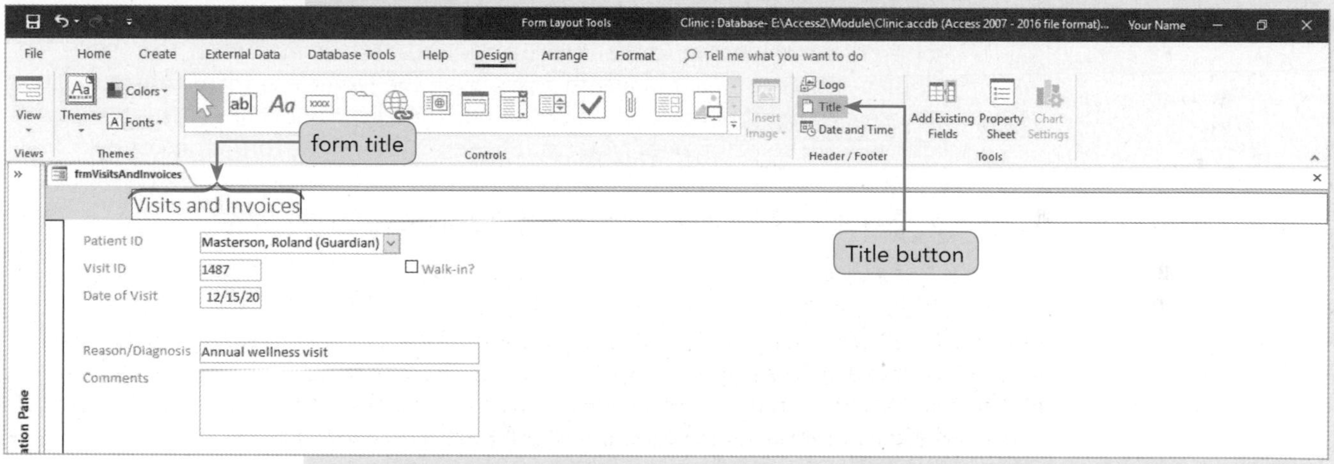
form title
Title button
Visits and Invoices
frmVisitsAndInvoices
Patient ID
Visit ID
Date of Visit
Reason/Diagnosis
Comments
Masterson, Roland (Guardian)
1487
12/15/20
Walk-in?
Annual wellness visit

The title has a larger font size than the font used for the form's labels and field value boxes, but Reginald would like you to apply bold to increase its prominence.

3. Click a blank area of the window, click the title control to select it, click the **Form Layout Tools Format** tab, and then in the Font group, click the **Bold** button B. The title is displayed in 18-point, bold text.

   It is not obvious in Layout view that the title is displayed in the Form Header section, so you'll view the form design in Design view.

4. Switch to Design view, and then click a blank area of the window to deselect all controls. The title is displayed in the Form Header section. See Figure 6–31.

Figure 6–31 Form Header, Detail, and Form Footer sections in Design view

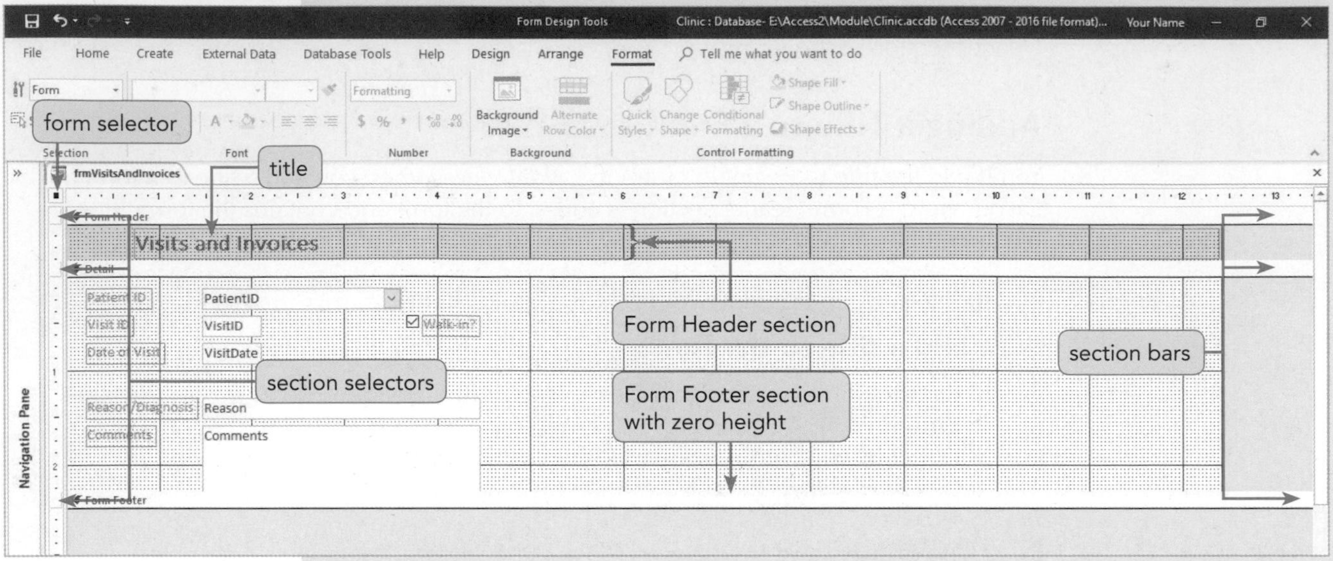
form selector
title
Form Header section
section bars
section selectors
Form Footer section with zero height
Visits and Invoices
PatientID
VisitID
VisitDate
Reason
Comments
Walk-in?
frmVisitsAndInvoices
Navigation Pane

The form now contains a Form Header section that displays the title, a Detail section that displays the bound controls and labels, and a Form Footer section that is set to a height of zero. Each section consists of a **section selector** and a section bar, either of which you can click to select and set properties for the entire section, and a grid or background, which is where you place controls that you want to display in the form. The **form selector** is the selector at the intersection of the horizontal and vertical rulers; you click the form selector when you want to select the entire form and set its properties. The vertical ruler is segmented into sections for the Form Header section, the Detail section, and the Form Footer section.

A form's total height includes the heights of the Form Header, Detail, and Form Footer sections. If you set a form's total height to more than the screen size, users will need to use scroll bars to view the content of your form, which is less productive for users and isn't good form design.

5. Save the design changes to the form, and then, if you are not continuing on to the next session, close the Clinic database.

So far, you've added controls to the form and modified the controls by selecting, moving, aligning, resizing, and deleting them. You've added and modified a combo box and added a title in the Form Header section. In the next session, you will continue your work with the custom form by adding a combo box control for use in finding records, adding a subform, adding calculated controls, changing form and section properties, and changing control properties.

REVIEW

Session 6.2 Quick Check

1. What is a bound form, and when do you use bound forms?
2. What is the difference between a bound control and an unbound control?
3. The ________ consists of the dotted and solid lines that appear in the Header, Detail, and Footer sections in Design view to help you position controls precisely in a form.
4. The larger handle in a selected object's upper-left corner is the ________ handle.
5. How do you move a selected field value box and its label at the same time?
6. How do you resize a control?
7. A(n) ________ control provides the features of a text box and a list box.
8. How do you change a label's caption?
9. What is the purpose of the Form Header section?

Session 6.3 Visual Overview:

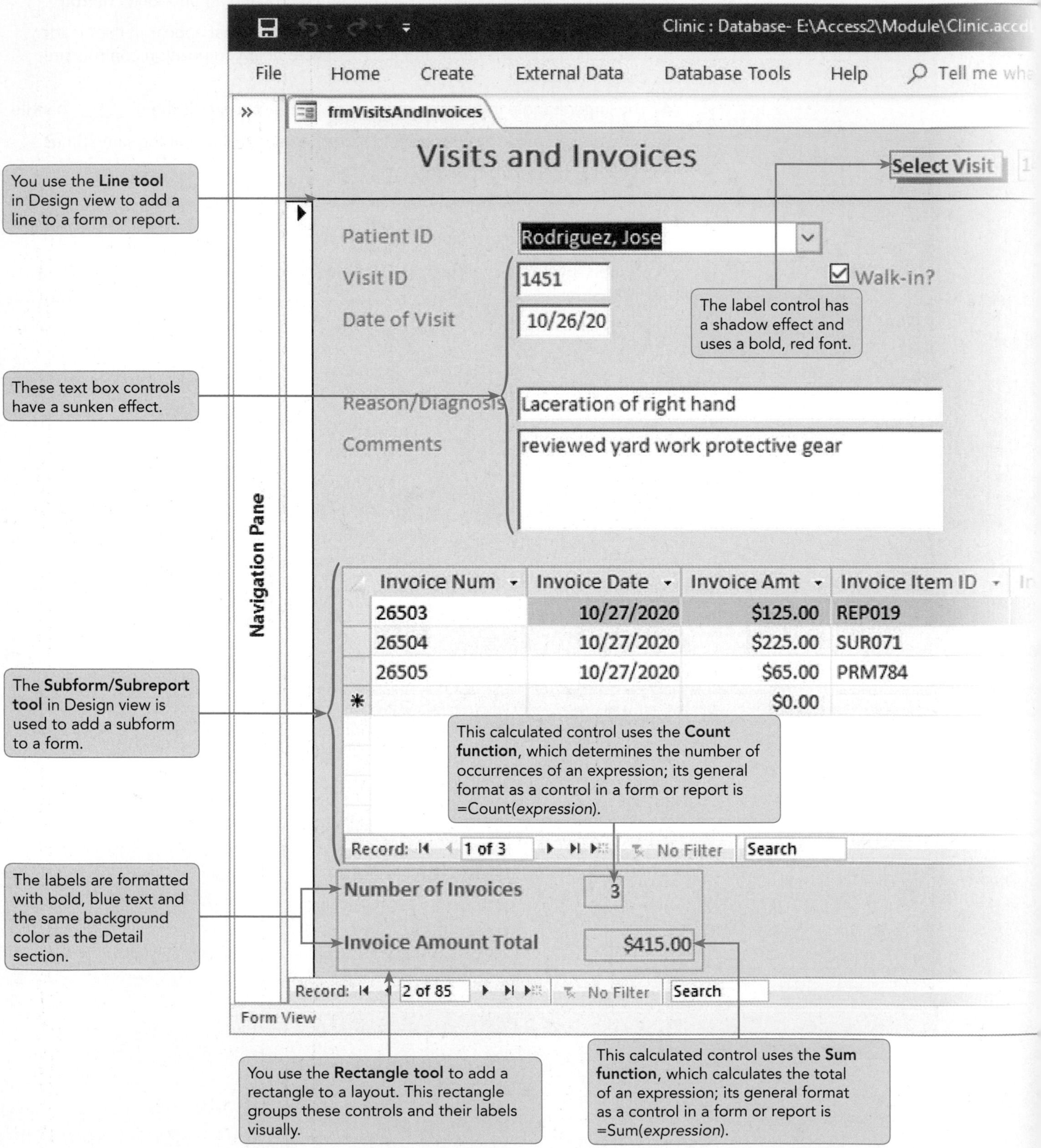

Clinic : Database- E:\Access2\Module\Clinic.accd
File
Home
Create
External Data
Database Tools
Help
Tell me wha
frmVisitsAndInvoices
Visits and Invoices
Select Visit
Navigation Pane
Patient ID
Rodriguez, Jose
Visit ID
1451
Walk-in?
Date of Visit
10/26/20
Reason/Diagnosis
Laceration of right hand
Comments
reviewed yard work protective gear
Invoice Num
Invoice Date
Invoice Amt
Invoice Item ID
26503 10/27/2020 $125.00 REP019
26504 10/27/2020 $225.00 SUR071
26505 10/27/2020 $65.00 PRM784
$0.00
Record: 1 of 3 No Filter Search
Number of Invoices 3
Invoice Amount Total $415.00
Record: 2 of 85 No Filter Search
Form View
You use the **Line tool** in Design view to add a line to a form or report.
These text box controls have a sunken effect.
The label control has a shadow effect and uses a bold, red font.
The **Subform/Subreport tool** in Design view is used to add a subform to a form.
This calculated control uses the **Count function**, which determines the number of occurrences of an expression; its general format as a control in a form or report is =Count(*expression*).
The labels are formatted with bold, blue text and the same background color as the Detail section.
You use the **Rectangle tool** to add a rectangle to a layout. This rectangle groups these controls and their labels visually.
This calculated control uses the **Sum function**, which calculates the total of an expression; its general format as a control in a form or report is =Sum(*expression*).

Custom Form in Form View

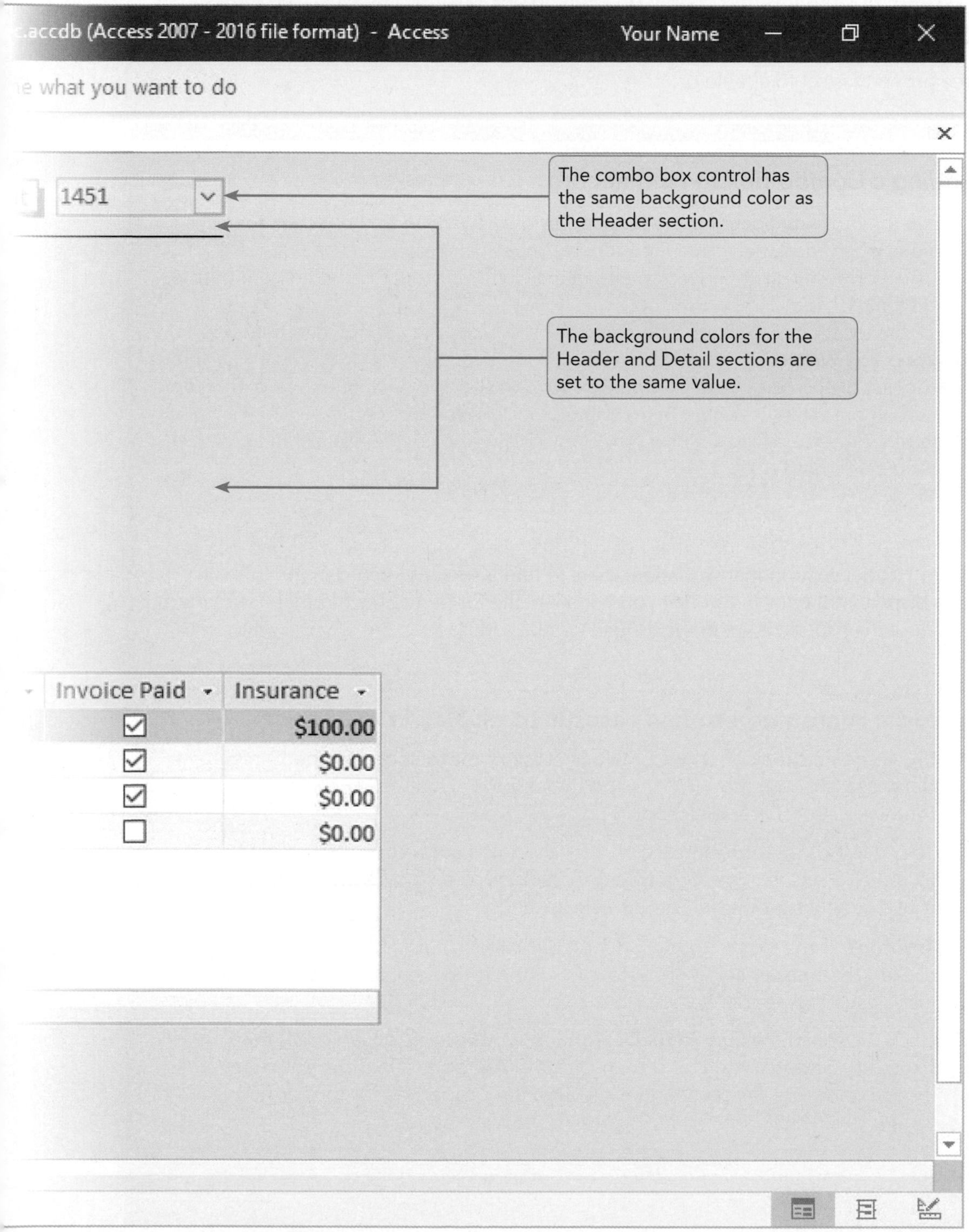
.accdb (Access 2007 - 2016 file format) - Access
Your Name
e what you want to do
1451
The combo box control has the same background color as the Header section.
The background colors for the Header and Detail sections are set to the same value.
Invoice Paid
Insurance
$100.00
$0.00
$0.00
$0.00

Adding a Combo Box to Find Records

As you know, a combo box control is used to display and update data in a form. You can also use a combo box control to allow users to find records. You can use the Combo Box Wizard to create this type of combo box control. However, the Combo Box Wizard provides this find option for a combo box control only when the form's record source is a table or query. Before creating a combo box control to be used to find records, you should view the Property Sheet for the form to confirm the Record Source property is set to a table or query.

REFERENCE

Adding a Combo Box to Find Records

- Open the Property Sheet for the form in Design view, confirm the record source is a table or query, and then close the Property Sheet.
- On the Form Design Tools Design tab, in the Controls group, click the More button, and then click the Combo Box tool.
- Click the location in the form where you want to place the control, and then open the Combo Box Wizard.
- In the first dialog box of the Combo Box Wizard, click the "Find a record on my form based on the value I selected in my combo box" option button.
- Complete the remaining Combo Box Wizard dialog boxes to finish creating the combo box control.

To continue creating the form that Reginald sketched, you will add a combo box to the Form Header section that will allow users to find a specific record in the tblVisit table to display in the form. But first you will view the Property Sheet to make sure the Record Source property is set to the tblVisit table.

To add a combo box to find records to display in the form:

1. If you took a break after the previous session, make sure that the Clinic database is open, the frmVisitsAndInvoices form is open in Design view, and the Navigation Pane is closed.
2. To the left of the horizontal ruler, click the **form selector** ☐ to select the form, if necessary. The form selector changes to display a black square inside it ▣, indicating that the form is selected.

   Trouble? If the Form Header section bar instead turns black, you might have clicked the header selector button. Click the form selector button, which is just above the header selector button.
3. Click the **Form Design Tools Design** tab, in the Tools group, click the **Property Sheet** button, and then click the **All** tab in the Property Sheet, if necessary. The Property Sheet displays the properties for the form. See Figure 6–32.

Figure 6–32 Property Sheet for the form

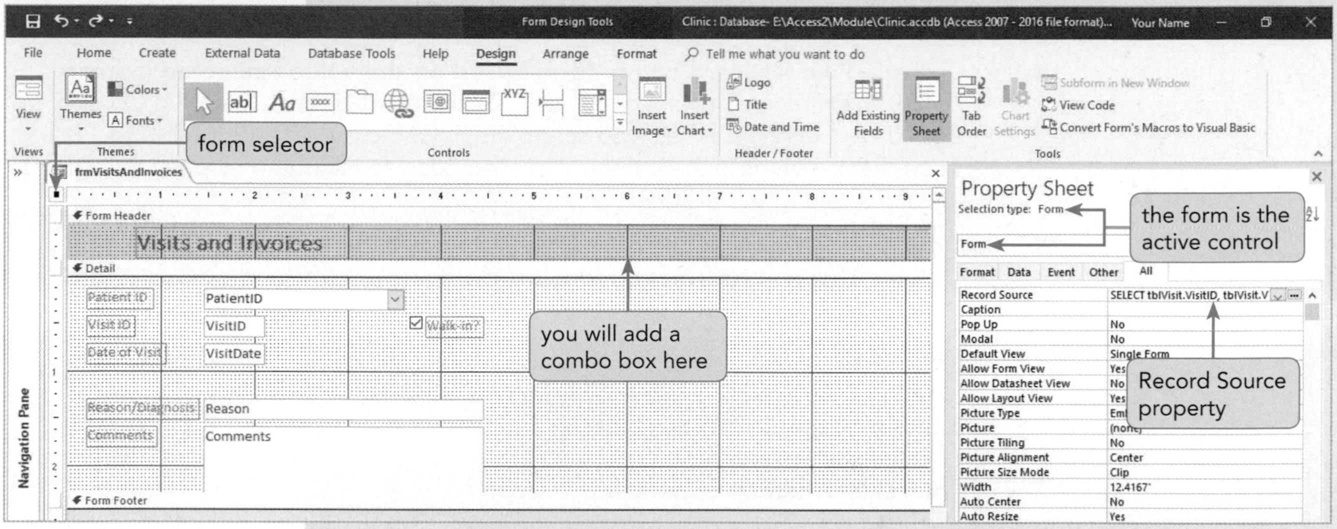
form selector
the form is the active control
you will add a combo box here
Record Source property

The Record Source property is set to a SQL SELECT statement, which is code that references a table. You need to change the Record Source property to a table or query, or the Combo Box Wizard will not present you with the option to find records in a form. You'll change the Record Source property to the tblVisit table because this table is the record source for all the bound controls you have added to the Detail section of the form.

4. In the Record Source box, click the **Record Source** arrow, click **tblVisit** in the list, and then close the Property Sheet.

   You'll now use the Combo Box Wizard to add a combo box to the form's Form Header section, which will enable a user to find a record in the tblVisit table to display in the form.

5. On the Form Design Tools Design tab, in the Controls group, click the **More** button to open the Controls gallery, and then click the **Combo Box** tool.

6. Position the plus symbol pointer at the top of the Form Header section at the 5-inch mark on the horizontal ruler (see Figure 6–32), and then click the mouse button. A combo box control appears in the Form Header section of the form, and the first Combo Box Wizard dialog box opens.

   Trouble? If the Combo Box Wizard dialog box does not open, delete the new controls and try again, ensuring the plus symbol pointer is very near the top of the Form Header grid.

   You will recall seeing this dialog box when you used the Combo Box Wizard in the previous session. The first dialog box in the Combo Box Wizard this time displays an additional option than what was available previously. This additional option, "Find a record on my form based on the value I selected in my combo box," is what you need to use for this combo box. (Recall in the last session you selected the first option, "I want the combo box to get the values from another table or query" when you used the Combo Box Wizard to create the PatientID combo box, allowing the user to select a value from a list of foreign key values from an existing table or query.) You would choose the second option if you wanted users to select a value from a short fixed list of values that don't change. For example, if Lakewood Community Health

Services wanted to include a field in the tblPatient table to identify the state in which the patient resides, you could use a combo box with this second option to display a list of states.

7. Click the **Find a record on my form based on the value I selected in my combo box** option button, and then click the **Next** button. The next Combo Box Wizard dialog box lets you select the fields from the tblVisit table to appear as columns in the combo box. You need to include only one column of values, listing the VisitID values.
8. Double-click **VisitID** to move this field to the Selected Fields box, and then click the **Next** button to open the next dialog box in the Combo Box Wizard.
9. In the dialog box, resize the VisitID column to its best fit, and then click the **Next** button.

   In the last dialog box in the Combo Box Wizard, you specify the name for the combo box's label. You'll use "Select Visit" as the label.
10. Type **Select Visit** and then click the **Finish** button. The completed unbound combo box control and its corresponding Select Visit label appear in the form. See Figure 6–33.

Figure 6–33 Unbound combo box added to the form

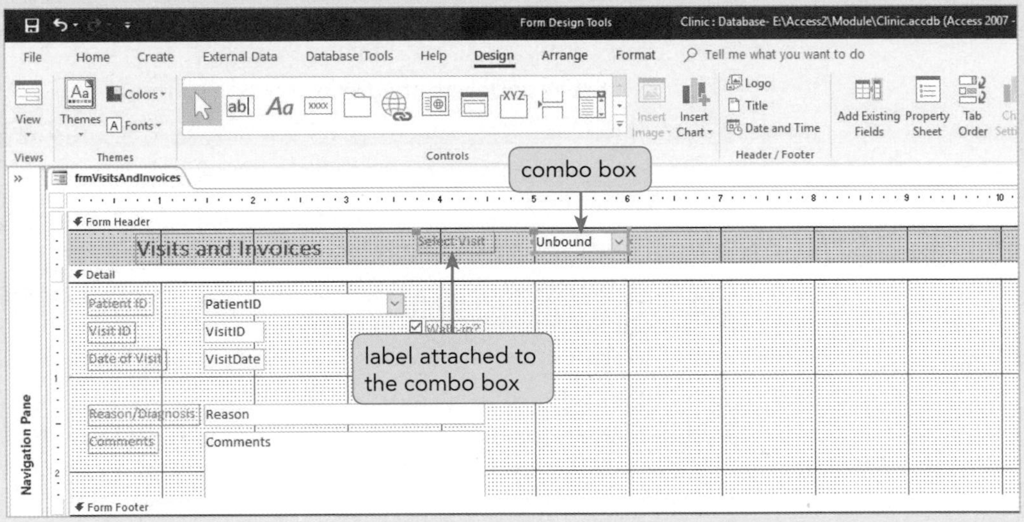
combo box
label attached to the combo box
Visits and Invoices
Unbound
PatientID
VisitID
VisitDate
Reason
Comments

You'll move the attached label closer to the combo box control, and then you'll align the bottoms of the combo box control and its attached label with the bottom of the title in the Form Header section.

11. Click the **Select Visit** label, point to the label's move handle on the upper-left corner of the orange selection border, and then drag the label to the right until its right edge is two grid dots to the left of the combo box.
12. With the Select Visit label still selected, press and hold **SHIFT**, click the **combo box**, and then click the **Visit and Invoices** form title.
13. Right-click the selected controls, point to **Align** on the shortcut menu, and then click **Bottom**. The three selected controls are bottom-aligned. See Figure 6–34.

Figure 6–34 Aligned combo box control and form title

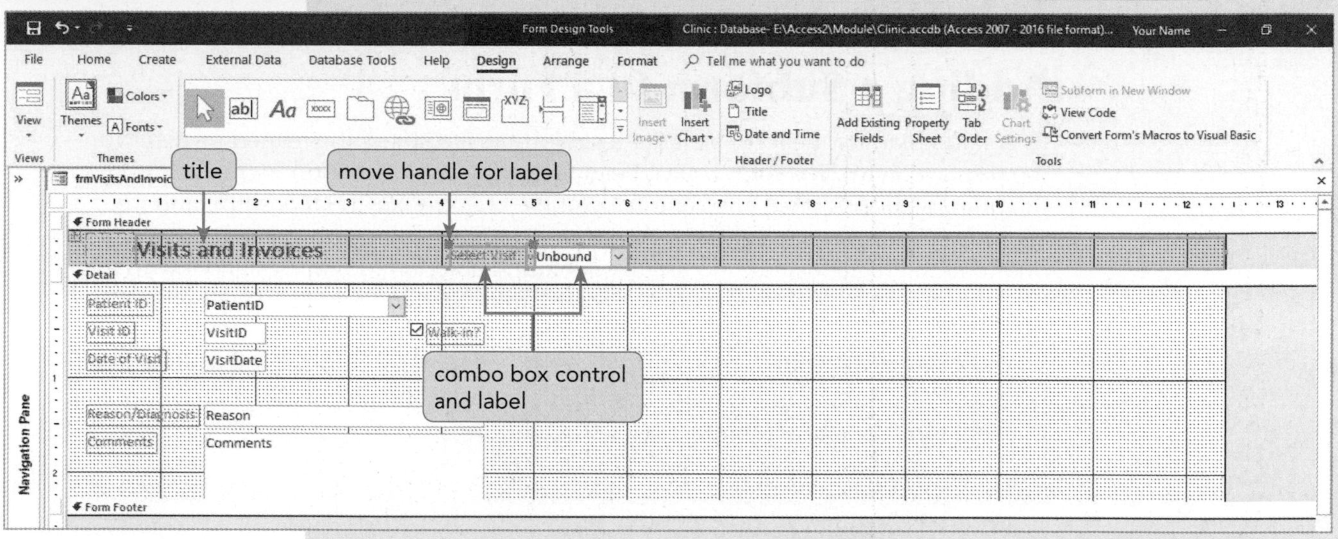
title
move handle for label
combo box control and label

You'll save your form changes and view the new combo box control in Form view.

To save the form and view the Select Visit combo box control:

1. Save the form design changes, and then switch to Form view.
2. Click the **Select Visit** arrow to display the list of Visit ID numbers. See Figure 6–35.

Figure 6–35 List of Visit IDs in the combo box

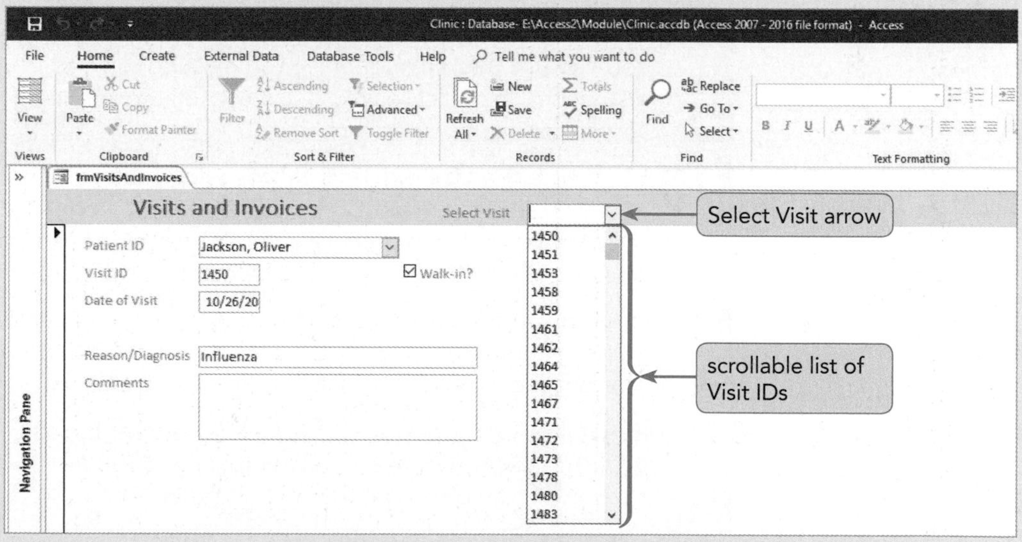
Select Visit arrow
scrollable list of Visit IDs

3. Scroll down the list, and then click **1467**. The current record changes from record 1 to record 10, which is the record for visit ID 1467.

   Trouble? If you see the data for record 1, the navigation combo box is not working correctly. Delete the combo box, check to ensure that you have set the Record Source for the form object correctly, and then repeat the previous set of steps to re-create the combo box.

The form design currently is very plain, with no color, formatting effects, or visual contrast among the controls. Before making the form more attractive and useful, though, you'll add the remaining controls: a subform and two calculated controls.

Adding a Subform to a Form

Reginald's plan for the form includes a subform that displays the related invoices for the displayed visit. The form you've been creating is the main form for records from the primary tblVisit table (the "one" side of the one-to-many relationship), and the subform will display records from the related tblBilling table (the "many" side of the one-to-many relationship). You use the Subform/Subreport tool in Design view to add a subform to a form. You can create a subform from scratch, or you can get help adding the subform by using the SubForm Wizard.

You will use the SubForm Wizard to add the subform for displaying tblBilling table records to the bottom of the form. First, you'll increase the height of the Detail section to make room for the subform.

TIP

Drag slightly beyond the desired ending position to expose the vertical ruler measurement, and then decrease the height back to the correct position.

To add the subform to the form:

1. Switch to Design view.
2. Position the pointer on the bottom border of the Detail section until the pointer changes to the vertical resize pointer ✛, and then drag the border down to the 5-inch mark on the vertical ruler.
3. On the Form Design Tools Design tab, in the Controls group, click the **More** button to open the Controls gallery, and then click the **Subform/Subreport** tool.
4. Position the plus symbol of the pointer in the Detail section at the 2.5-inch mark on the vertical ruler and at the 1-inch mark on the horizontal ruler, and then click the mouse button. A subform control appears in the form's Detail section, and the first SubForm Wizard dialog box opens.

   You can use a table, a query, or an existing form as the record source for a subform. In this case, you'll use the related tblBilling table as the record source for the new subform.
5. Make sure the **Use existing Tables and Queries** option button is selected, and then click the **Next** button. The next SubForm Wizard dialog box opens, in which you select a table or query as the record source for the subform and select the fields to use from the selected table or query.
6. Click the **Tables/Queries arrow** to display the list of tables and queries in the Clinic database, scroll to the top of the list, and then click **Table: tblBilling**. The Available Fields box lists the fields in the tblBilling table.

   Reginald's form design includes all fields from the tblBilling table in the subform, except for the VisitID field, which you already placed in the Detail section of the form from the tblVisit table.
7. Click the **Select All Fields** button >> to move all available fields to the Selected Fields box, click **VisitID** in the Selected Fields box, click the **Remove Field** button <, and then click the **Next** button to open the next SubForm Wizard dialog box. See Figure 6–36.

Figure 6–36 **Selecting the linking field**

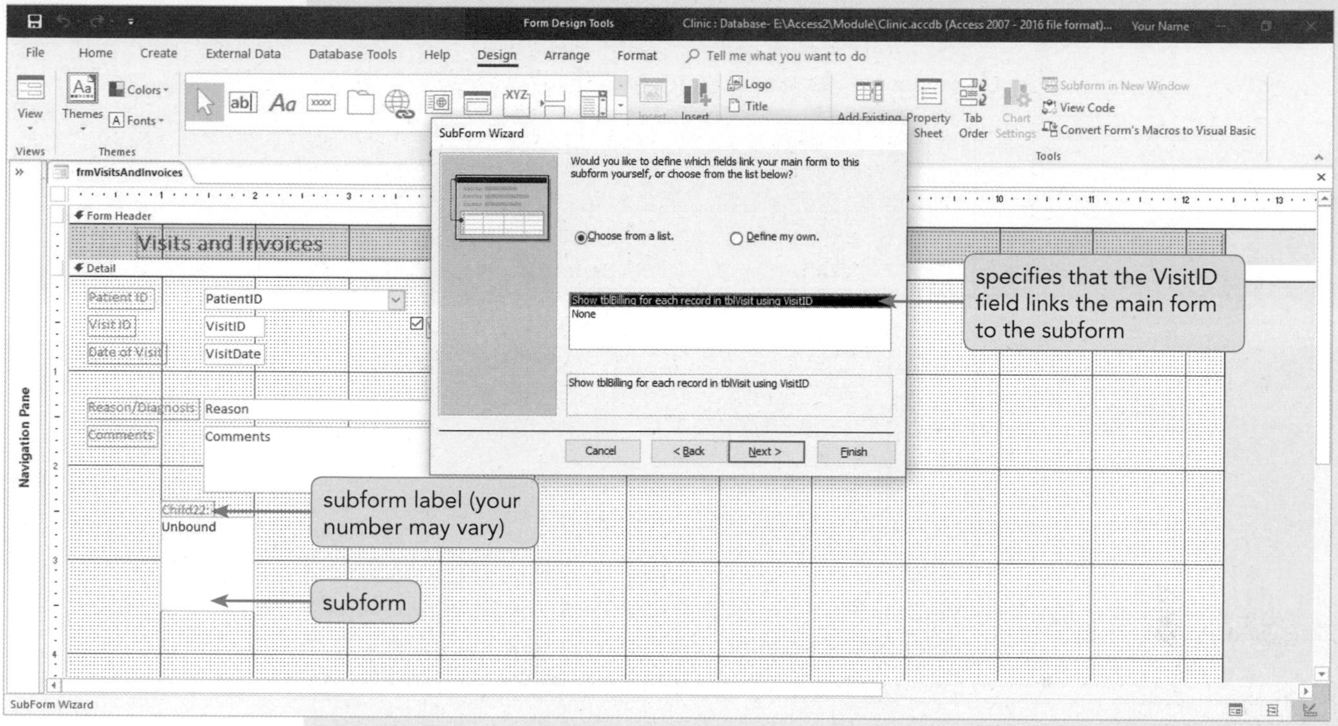
SubForm Wizard
Would you like to define which fields link your main form to this subform yourself, or choose from the list below?
Choose from a list.
Define my own.
Show tblBilling for each record in tblVisit using VisitID
None
Cancel
< Back
Next >
Finish
specifies that the VisitID field links the main form to the subform
subform label (your number may vary)
subform
Visits and Invoices
Unbound

In this dialog box, you select the link between the primary tblVisit table and the related tblBilling table. The common field in the two tables, VisitID, links the tables. The form will use the VisitID field to display a record in the main form, which displays data from the primary tblVisit table, and to select and display the related records for that contract in the subform, which displays data from the related tblBilling table.

8. Make sure the **Choose from a list** option button is selected, make sure **"Show tblBilling for each record in tblVisit using VisitID"** is selected in the list, and then click the **Next** button. In the last SubForm Wizard dialog box, you specify a name for the subform.
9. Type **frmBillingSubform** and then click the **Finish** button. The completed subform appears in the Details section of the Form window; its label appears above the subform and displays the subform name.
10. Click a blank area of the window, and then save the form.
11. Switch to Form view, click the **Select Visit** arrow, and then click **1453**. The subform displays the four invoices related to visit ID 1453. See Figure 6–37.

Figure 6–37 The subform in Form view

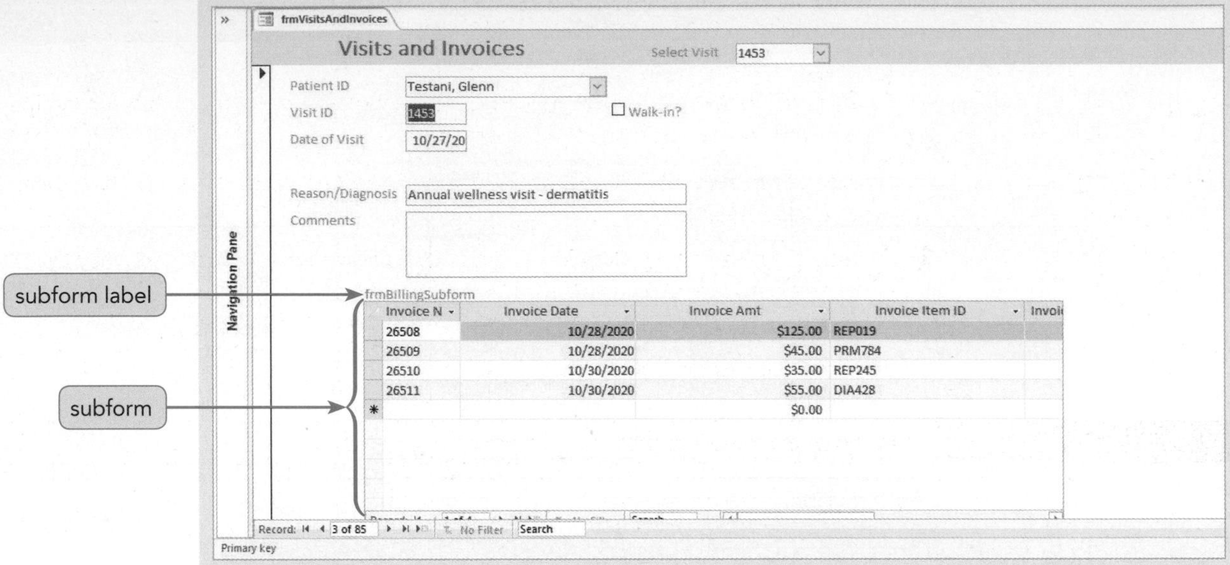
frmVisitsAndInvoices
Visits and Invoices
Select Visit
1453
Patient ID
Testani, Glenn
Visit ID
1453
Walk-in?
Date of Visit
10/27/20
Reason/Diagnosis
Annual wellness visit - dermatitis
Comments
Navigation Pane
subform label
frmBillingSubform
subform
Invoice N
Invoice Date
Invoice Amt
Invoice Item ID
26508 10/28/2020 $125.00 REP019
26509 10/28/2020 $45.00 PRM784
26510 10/30/2020 $35.00 REP245
26511 10/30/2020 $55.00 DIA428
$0.00
Record: 3 of 85
No Filter
Search
Primary key

Trouble? It is not a problem if the widths of the columns in your datasheet differ or the position of your subform is not exactly as shown in Figure 6–37. You will resize columns and position the subform in the next set of steps.

After viewing the form, Reginald identifies some modifications he wants you to make. He wants you to resize the subform and its columns so that all columns in the subform are entirely visible and the columns are sized to best fit. Also, he asks you to delete the subform label, because the label is unnecessary for identifying the subform contents. You'll use Design view and Layout view to make these changes.

To modify the subform's design and adjust its position in the form:

1. Switch to Design view. Notice that in Design view, the data in the subform control does not appear in a datasheet format as it does in Form view. That difference causes no problem; you can ignore it.

   First, you'll delete the subform label control.

2. Deselect all controls (if necessary), right-click the **frmBillingSubform** subform label control to open the shortcut menu, and then click **Delete**.

   Next, you'll align the subform control with the Comments label control.

3. Click the border of the subform control to select it, press and hold **SHIFT**, click the **Comments** label control, and then release **SHIFT**. The subform control and the Comments label control are selected. Next you'll left-align the two controls.

4. Right-click the **Comments** label control, point to **Align** on the shortcut menu, and then click **Left**. The two controls are left-aligned. Next, you'll resize the subform control in Layout view so that you can observe the effects of your changes as you make them.

5. Switch to Layout view, click the border of the subform to select it, and then drag the right border of the subform to the right until the Insurance column arrow is fully visible.

Before resizing the columns in the subform to best fit, you'll display record 22 in the main form. The subform for this record contains the related records in the tblBilling table with one of the longest field values.

6. Use the record navigation bar for the main form (at the bottom left of the form window) to display record 3, for visit number 1453, and then resize each column in the subform to its best fit.

Next, you'll resize the subform again so that its width matches the width of the resized columns.

7. Resize the subform so that its right border is aligned with the right border of the Insurance column, and then if necessary scroll down and resize the subform so it displays rows for eight records. See Figure 6–38.

8. Save your form design changes.

Figure 6–38 Moved and resized subform

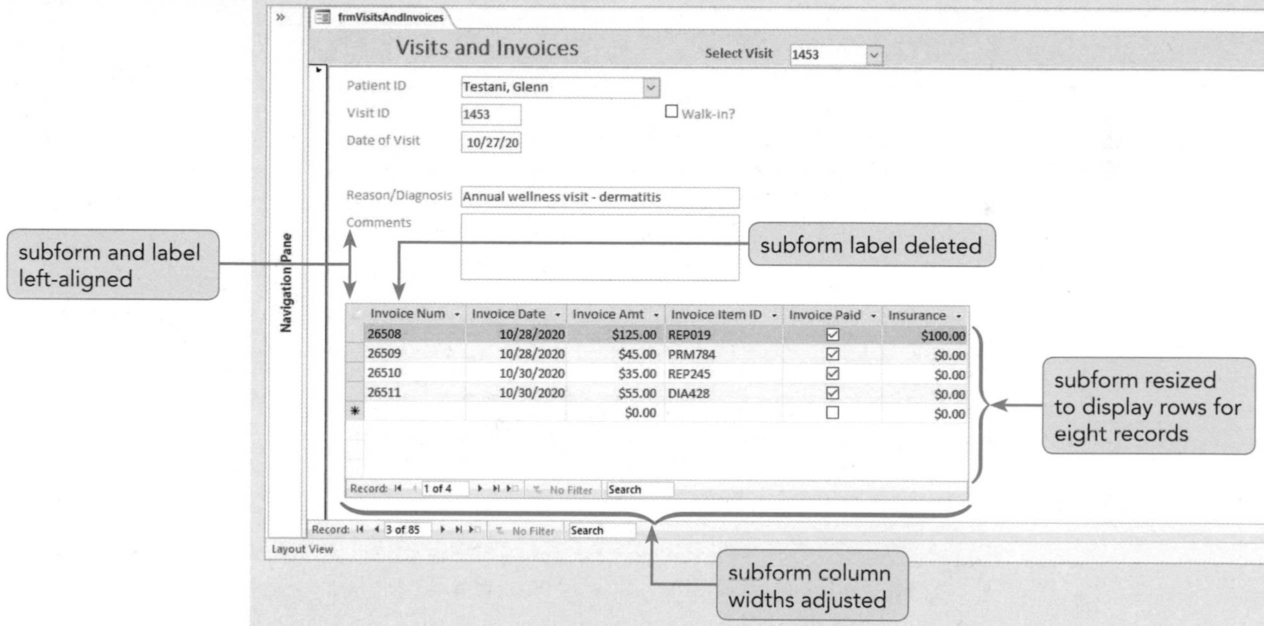
frmVisitsAndInvoices
Visits and Invoices
Select Visit
1453
Patient ID
Testani, Glenn
Visit ID
1453
Walk-in?
Date of Visit
10/27/20
Reason/Diagnosis
Annual wellness visit - dermatitis
Comments
subform and label left-aligned
subform label deleted
Navigation Pane
Invoice Num
Invoice Date
Invoice Amt
Invoice Item ID
Invoice Paid
Insurance
26508 10/28/2020 $125.00 REP019 $100.00
26509 10/28/2020 $45.00 PRM784 $0.00
26510 10/30/2020 $35.00 REP245 $0.00
26511 10/30/2020 $55.00 DIA428 $0.00
$0.00 $0.00
subform resized to display rows for eight records
Record: 1 of 4 No Filter Search
Record: 3 of 85 No Filter Search
Layout View
subform column widths adjusted

You've finished your work with the subform. Now you need to add two calculated controls to the main form.

Displaying a Subform's Calculated Controls in the Main Form

TIP

You precede expressions with an equal sign to distinguish them from field names, which do not have an equal sign.

Reginald's form design includes the display of calculated controls in the main form that tally the number of invoices and the total of the invoice amounts for the related records displayed in the subform. To display these calculated controls in a form or report, you use the Count and Sum functions. The Count function determines the number of occurrences of an expression; its general format as a control in a form or report is =Count(*expression*). The Sum function calculates the total of an expression, and its general format as a control in a form or report is =Sum(*expression*). The number of invoices and total of invoice amounts are displayed in the subform's Detail section, so you'll need to place the calculated controls in the subform's Form Footer section.

Adding Calculated Controls to a Subform's Form Footer Section

First, you'll open the subform in Design view in another window and add the calculated controls to the subform's Form Footer section.

To add calculated controls to the subform's Form Footer section:

1. Switch to Design view, click a blank area of the window to deselect any selected controls, right-click the subform's border, and then click **Subform in New Window** on the shortcut menu. The subform opens in its own tab in Design view. See Figure 6–39.

Figure 6–39 Subform in Design view

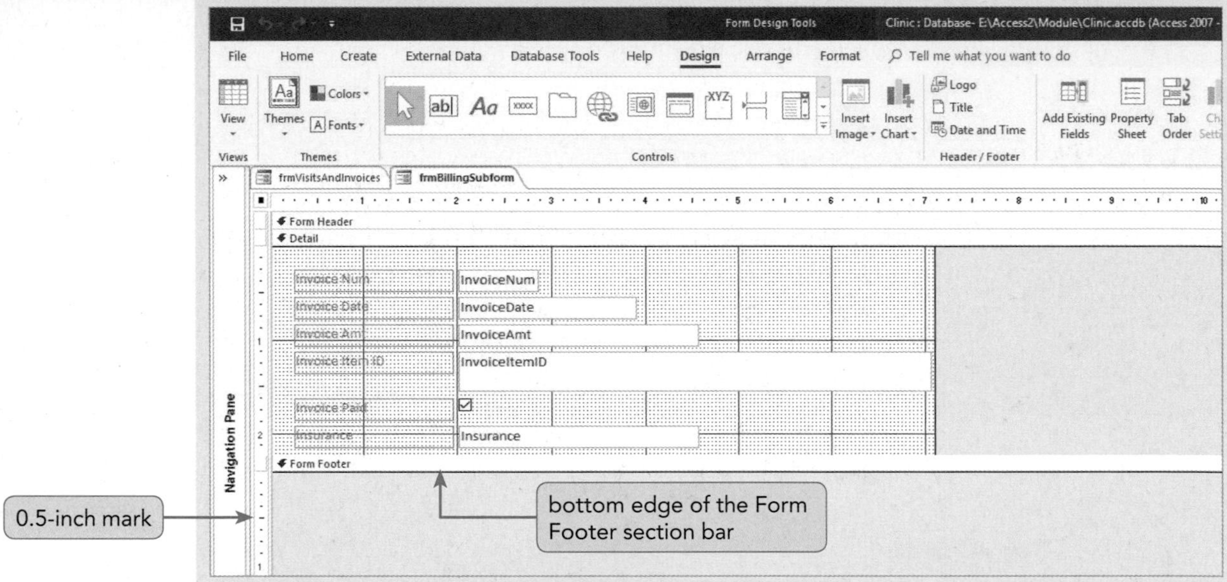
0.5-inch mark
bottom edge of the Form Footer section bar

The subform's Detail section contains the tblBilling table fields. As a subform in the main form, the fields appear in a datasheet even though the fields do not appear that way in Design view. The heights of the subform's Form Header and Form Footer sections are zero, meaning that these sections have been removed from the subform. You'll increase the height of the Form Footer section so that you can add the two calculated controls to the section.

2. Click the **Form Footer** section bar, position the pointer on the bottom border of the Form Footer section bar until the pointer changes to the vertical resize pointer ✛, and then drag the bottom border of the section down to the 0.5-inch mark on the vertical ruler.

   Now you'll add the first calculated control to the Form Footer section. To create the text box for the calculated control, you use the Text Box tool in the Controls group on the Form Design Tools Design tab. Because the Form Footer section is not displayed in a datasheet, you do not need to position the control precisely.

3. On the Form Design Tools Design tab, in the Controls group, click the **Text Box** tool ab|.

4. Position the plus symbol of the pointer near the top of the Form Footer section and aligned with the 1-inch mark on the horizontal ruler, and then

click the mouse button. A text box control and an attached label control appear in the Form Footer section. The text "Unbound" appears in the text box, indicating it is an unbound control.

Next, you'll set the Name and Control Source properties for the text box. Recall that the Name property specifies the name of an object or control. Later, when you add the calculated control in the main form, you'll reference the subform's calculated control value by using its Name property value. The **Control Source property** specifies the source of the data that appears in the control; the Control Source property setting can be either a field name or an expression.

5. Open the Property Sheet for the text box in the Form Footer section, click the **All** tab (if necessary), select the value in the Name box, type **txtInvoiceAmtSum** in the Name box, and then press **TAB** twice to move to the Control Source box.
6. In the Control Source box, type **=Sum(Inv**, press **TAB** to accept the rest of the field name of InvoiceAmt suggested by Formula AutoComplete, type **)** (a right parenthesis), and then press **TAB**. InvoiceAmt is enclosed in brackets in the expression because it's a field name. See Figure 6–40.

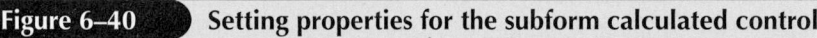

Figure 6–40 Setting properties for the subform calculated control

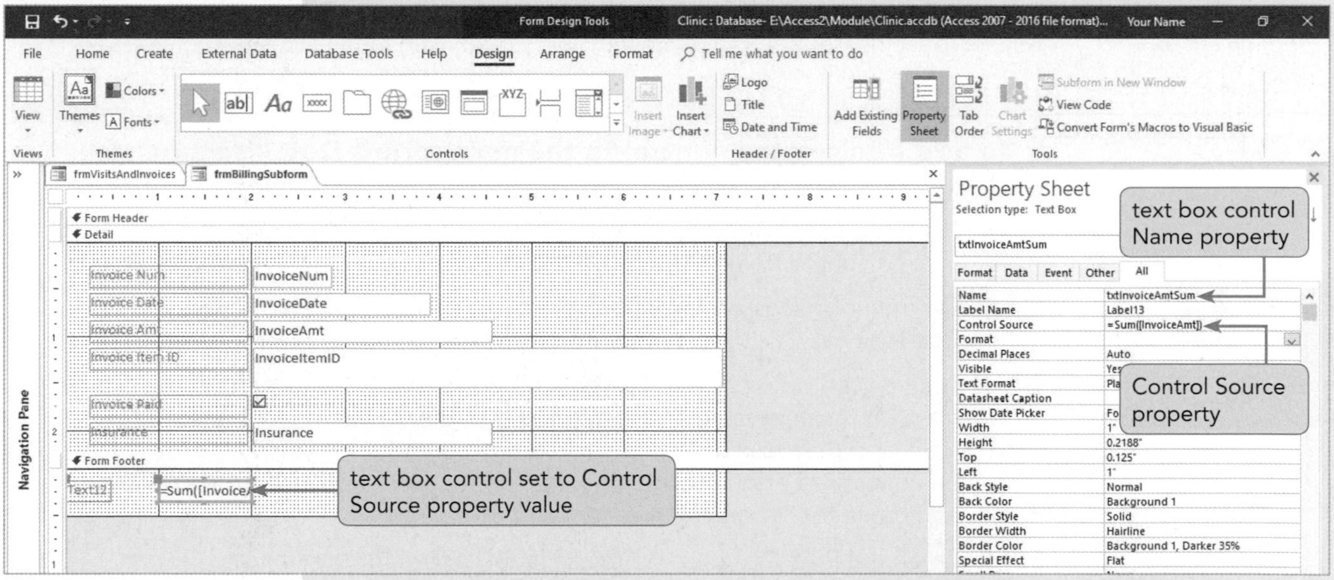
text box control Name property
Control Source property
text box control set to Control Source property value

You've finished creating the first calculated control; now you'll create the other calculated control.

TIP

In the Name property, txtInvoiceNumCount, txt identifies the control type (a text box), InvoiceNum is the related field name, and Count identifies the control as a count control.

7. Repeat Steps 3 through 6, positioning the calculated field text box near the top of the Form Footer section aligned to the 3.5-inch mark on the horizontal ruler, setting the Name property value to **txtInvoiceNumCount**, and setting the Control Source property value to **=Count([InvoiceNum])**.

When you use the Count function, you are counting the number of displayed records—in this case, the number of records displayed in the subform. Instead of using InvoiceNum as the expression for the Count function, you could use any of the other fields displayed in the subform.

You've finished creating the subform's calculated controls.

8. Close the Property Sheet, save your subform changes, and then close the subform. The active object is now the main form in Design view.

   Trouble? The subform in the frmContractsAndInvoices form might appear to be blank after you close the frmInvoiceSubform form. This is a temporary effect; the subform's controls do still exist. Switch to Form view and then back to Design view to display the subform's controls.

9. Switch to Form view. The calculated controls you added in the subform's Form Footer section are *not* displayed in the subform.

10. Switch to Design view.

Next, you'll add two calculated controls in the main form to display the two calculated controls from the subform.

Adding Calculated Controls to a Main Form

The subform's calculated controls now contain a count of the number of invoices and a total of the invoice amounts. However, notice that Reginald's design has the two calculated controls displayed in the main form, *not* in the subform. You need to add two calculated controls in the main form that reference the values in the subform's calculated controls. Because it's easy to make a typing mistake with these references, you'll use Expression Builder to set the Control Source property for the two main form calculated controls.

To add a calculated control to the main form's Detail section:

1. Adjust the length of the Detail section if necessary so that there is approximately 0.5 inch below the frmBillingSubform control. The Detail section should be approximately 5.5 inches.

2. On the Form Design Tools Design tab, in the Controls group, click the **Text Box** tool [ab|].

3. Position the pointer's plus symbol below the frmBillingSubform at the 5-inch mark on the vertical ruler and aligned with the 1-inch mark on the horizontal ruler, and then click to insert the text box control and label in the form. Don't be concerned about positioning the control precisely because you'll resize and move the label and text box later.

4. Open the Property Sheet, click the label control for the text box, set its Caption property to **Number of Invoices**, right-click the border of the label control, point to **Size** on the shortcut menu, and then click **To Fit**. Don't worry if the label control now overlaps the text box control.

   You'll use Expression Builder to set a Control Source property for the text box control.

5. Click the unbound text box control to select it, click the **Control Source** box in the Property Sheet, and then click the property's **Build** button [...] to open Expression Builder.

6. In the Expression Elements box, click the **expand indicator** [+] next to frmVisitsAndInvoices, and then click **frmBillingSubform** in the Expression Elements box.

7. Scroll down the Expression Categories box, and then double-click **txtInvoiceNumCount** in the Expression Categories box. See Figure 6–41.

Figure 6–41 **Text box control's expression in the Expression Builder dialog box**

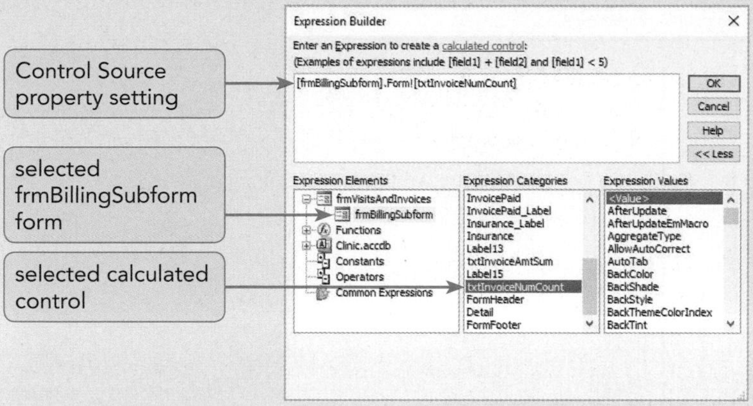
Control Source property setting
selected frmBillingSubform form
selected calculated control
Expression Builder
Enter an Expression to create a calculated control:
(Examples of expressions include [field1] + [field2] and [field1] < 5)
[frmBillingSubform].Form![txtInvoiceNumCount]
OK
Cancel
Help
<< Less
Expression Elements
Expression Categories
Expression Values

Instead of adding txtInvoiceNumCount to the expression box at the top, the Expression Builder changed it to [frmBillingSubform].Form![txtInvoiceNumCount]. This expression displays the value of the txtInvoiceNumCount control that is located in the frmBillingSubform form, which is a form object.

You need to add an equal sign to the beginning of the expression.

8. Press **HOME**, type **=** (an equal sign), and then click the **OK** button. The Expression Builder dialog box closes, and the Control Source property is set.

Next, you'll add a second text box control to the main form, set the Caption property for the label control, and use Expression Builder to set the text box's Control Source property.

Be sure you resize the label to its best fit.

9. Repeat Steps 2 through 4 to add a text box to the main form, positioning the text box at the 3.5-inch mark on the horizontal ruler and approximately the 5-inch mark on the vertical ruler, and setting the label's Caption property to **Invoice Amount Total**.
10. Click the unbound text box control to select it, click the **Control Source** box in the Property Sheet, and then click the property's **Build** button [...] to open Expression Builder.
11. In the Expression Builder dialog box, type **=** (an equal sign), in the Expression Elements box, click the **expand indicator** [+] next to frmVisitsAndInvoices, click **frmBillingSubform** in the Expression Elements box, scroll down the Expression Categories box, and then double-click **txtInvoiceAmtSum** in the Expression Categories box.
12. Click the **OK** button to accept the expression and close the Expression Builder dialog box, close the Property Sheet, and save the form.
13. Click the **Collapse the Ribbon** button [^], switch to Form view, and then display the record for VisitID 1453. See Figure 6–42.

Figure 6–42 Form with calculated controls

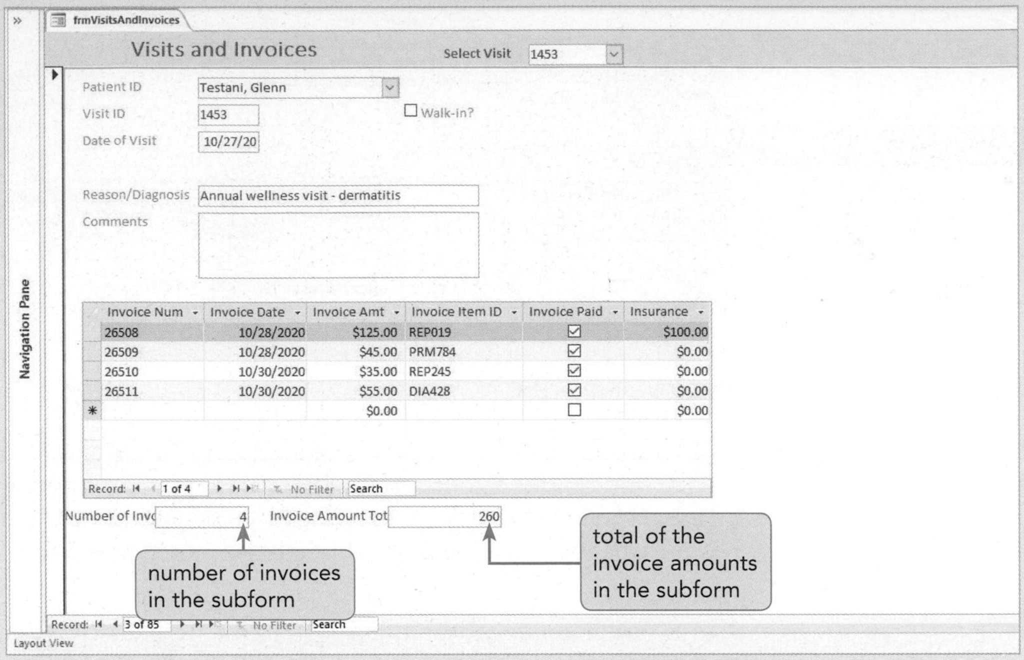
frmVisitsAndInvoices
Visits and Invoices
Select Visit
1453
Patient ID
Testani, Glenn
Visit ID
1453
Walk-in?
Date of Visit
10/27/20
Reason/Diagnosis
Annual wellness visit - dermatitis
Comments
Navigation Pane
Invoice Num
Invoice Date
Invoice Amt
Invoice Item ID
Invoice Paid
Insurance
26508
10/28/2020
$125.00
REP019
$100.00
26509
10/28/2020
$45.00
PRM784
$0.00
26510
10/30/2020
$35.00
REP245
$0.00
26511
10/30/2020
$55.00
DIA428
$0.00
$0.00
$0.00
Record: 1 of 4
No Filter
Search
Number of Invo
4
Invoice Amount Tot
260
number of invoices in the subform
total of the invoice amounts in the subform
Record: 3 of 85
No Filter
Search
Layout View

Now that the calculated controls are in the form, you will modify their appearance. You also will set additional properties for the calculated controls.

Resizing, Moving, and Formatting Calculated Controls

In addition to resizing and repositioning the two calculated controls and their attached labels, you need to change the format of the rightmost calculated control to Currency and to set the following properties for both calculated controls.

- Set the Tab Stop property to a value of No. The **Tab Stop property** specifies whether users can use TAB to navigate to a control on a form. If the Tab Stop property is set to No, users can't tab to the control.
- Set the ControlTip Text property to a value of "Calculated total number of invoices for this patient visit" for the calculated control on the left and "Calculated invoice total for this patient visit" for the calculated control on the right. The **ControlTip Text property** specifies the text that appears in a ScreenTip when users position the mouse pointer over a control in a form.

Now you'll resize, move, and format the calculated controls and their attached labels.

To size, move, and format the calculated controls and their attached labels:

1. Switch to Layout view, right-click the **Invoice Amount Total** calculated control, and then click **Properties** on the shortcut menu to open the Property Sheet.
2. Click the **All** tab in the Property Sheet (if necessary), set the Format property to **Currency**, and then close the Property Sheet. The value displayed in the calculated control changes from 200 to $200.00.

Now you'll resize and move the controls into their final positions in the form.

3. Individually, reduce the widths of the two calculated controls by dragging the left border to the right to decrease the text box width so that they approximately match those shown in Figure 6–43.

Figure 6–43 **Resized calculated controls and labels**

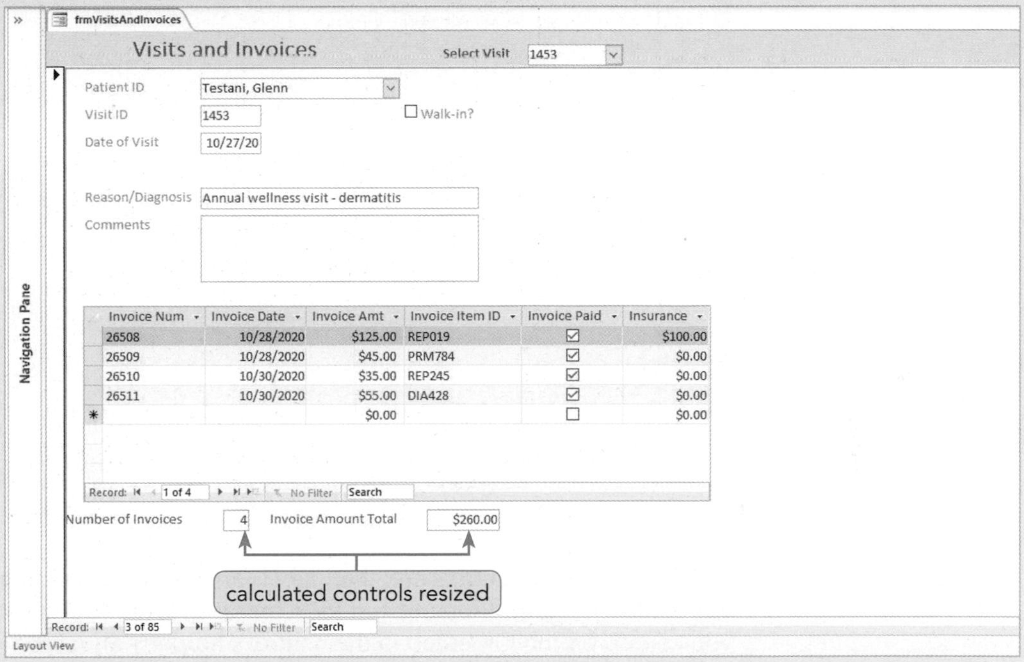

frmVisitsAndInvoices
Visits and Invoices
Select Visit
1453
Navigation Pane
Patient ID
Testani, Glenn
Visit ID
1453
Walk-in?
Date of Visit
10/27/20
Reason/Diagnosis
Annual wellness visit - dermatitis
Comments
Invoice Num
Invoice Date
Invoice Amt
Invoice Item ID
Invoice Paid
Insurance
26508 10/28/2020 $125.00 REP019 $100.00
26509 10/28/2020 $45.00 PRM784 $0.00
26510 10/30/2020 $35.00 REP245 $0.00
26511 10/30/2020 $55.00 DIA428 $0.00
$0.00 $0.00
Record: 1 of 4
No Filter
Search
Number of Invoices
4
Invoice Amount Total
$260.00
calculated controls resized
Record: 3 of 85
No Filter
Search
Layout View

4. Switch to Design view, select the **Number of Invoices** label and its related calculated control, and then use → to move the label and its related text box to the right, aligning the left edge of the label with the left edge of the Comments label as closely as possible.

5. Press ↑ to move the selected calculated control and its label until it is two grid dots from the bottom of the subform control.

6. Lengthen the Detail section to approximately the 6-inch marker on the vertical ruler.

7. Click the **Invoice Amount Total** label control, press **SHIFT**, click the corresponding calculated control text box, release **SHIFT**, and then drag the selected calculated control and its label to position them below and left-aligned with the Number of Invoices label control and its calculated control.

8. Switch to Layout view.

9. Click the **Invoice Amount Total** label control, and use the arrow keys to left-align the label control with the Number of Invoices label, select the **Invoice Amount Total** text box, and then use the arrows to left-align the calculated control text box with the Number of Invoices calculated control text box.

10. Deselect all controls, switch to Form view, and then select record 1453. See Figure 6–44.

TIP

In Design view you must use the move handle to move only a text box or its label, while in Layout view you can use either the move handle or the arrow keys.

Figure 6–44 **Calculated controls and labels aligned**

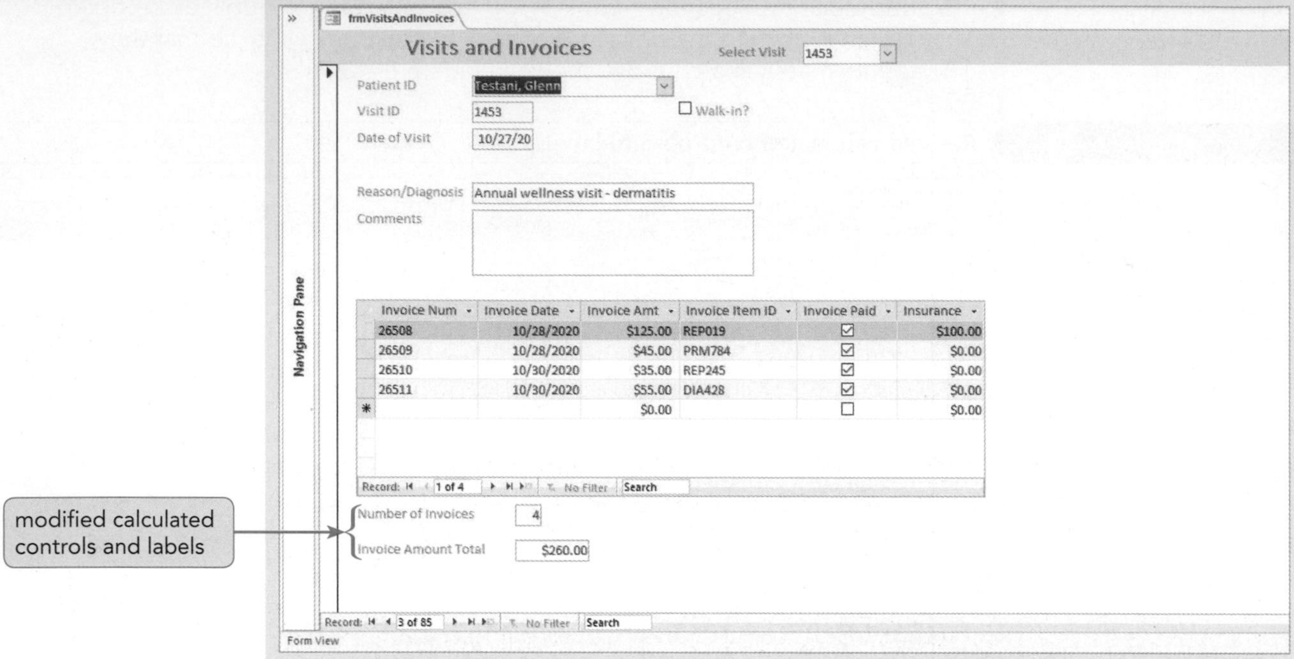
frmVisitsAndInvoices
Visits and Invoices
Select Visit 1453
Patient ID
Testani, Glenn
Visit ID 1453
Walk-in?
Date of Visit 10/27/20
Reason/Diagnosis Annual wellness visit - dermatitis
Comments
Navigation Pane
Invoice Num Invoice Date Invoice Amt Invoice Item ID Invoice Paid Insurance
26508 10/28/2020 $125.00 REP019 $100.00
26509 10/28/2020 $45.00 PRM784 $0.00
26510 10/30/2020 $35.00 REP245 $0.00
26511 10/30/2020 $55.00 DIA428 $0.00
$0.00 $0.00
Record: 1 of 4 No Filter Search
Number of Invoices 4
Invoice Amount Total $260.00
Record: 3 of 85 No Filter Search
Form View
modified calculated controls and labels

The calculated controls and their labels are properly placed in the form. Next you will set the Tab Stop Property and the ControlTip Text property for both controls, which you can do on the Other tab in the control's Property Sheet.

To set the Tab Stop Property and the ControlTipText property for the calculated controls:

1. Switch to Layout view, right-click the **Invoice Amount Total** calculated control, click **Properties** on the shortcut menu, and then click the **Other** tab in the Property Sheet.
2. Set the Tab Stop property to **No**, and then in the ControlTip Text box, specify **Calculated invoice total for this patient visit** as the value.
3. Click the **Number of Invoices** calculated control to display this control's properties in the Property Sheet, set the Tab Stop property to **No**, and then in the ControlTip Text box, specify **Calculated total number of invoices for this patient visit** as the value.
4. Close the Property Sheet, save your form design changes, switch to Form view, and then display visit 1453.
5. Position the pointer on the **Number of Invoices** box to display its ScreenTip, and then position the pointer on the **Invoice Amount Total** box to display its ScreenTip. You may have to pause while you position the pointer over the box, until the ScreenTip appears. See Figure 6–45.

Figure 6–45 ScreenTip for the calculated control

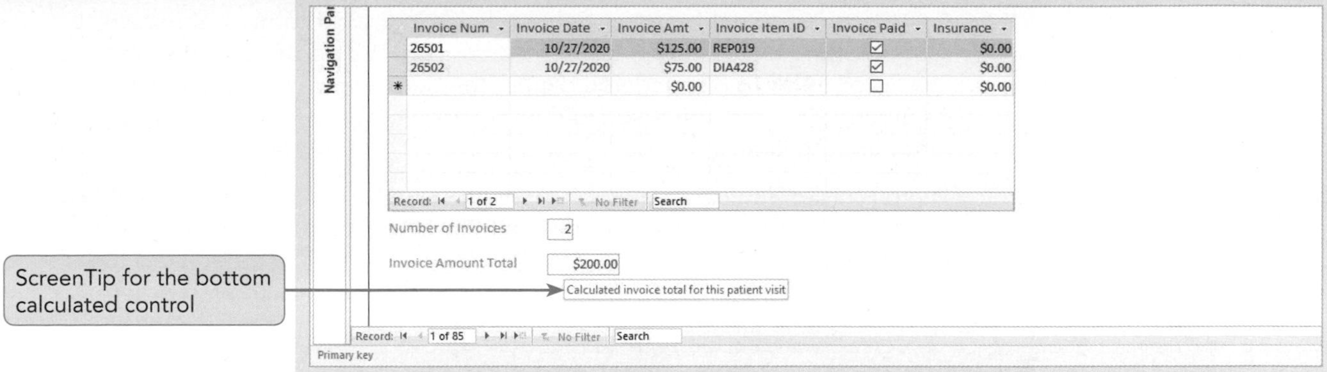
Invoice Num
Invoice Date
Invoice Amt
Invoice Item ID
Invoice Paid
Insurance
26501 10/27/2020 $125.00 REP019 $0.00
26502 10/27/2020 $75.00 DIA428 $0.00
$0.00 $0.00
Record: 1 of 2 No Filter Search
Number of Invoices 2
Invoice Amount Total $200.00
Calculated invoice total for this patient visit
Record: 1 of 85 No Filter Search
Primary key
Navigation Pa
ScreenTip for the bottom calculated control

Reginald asks you to verify that users can't update the calculated controls in the main form and that when users tab through the controls in the form, the controls are selected in the correct order.

Changing the Tab Order in a Form

Pressing TAB in Form view moves the focus from one control to another. A control is said to have **focus** when it is active and awaiting user action. The order in which the focus moves from control to control when a user presses TAB is called the **tab order**. Setting a logical tab order enables the user to keep his or her hands on the keyboard without reaching for the mouse, thereby speeding up the process of data entry in a form. Reginald wants to verify that the tab order in the main form is top-to-bottom, left-to-right. First, you'll verify that users can't update the calculated controls.

To test the calculated controls and modify the tab order:

1. Select the value in the Number of Invoices box, and then type **8**. The Number of Invoices value remains unchanged, and the message "Control can't be edited; it's bound to the expression '[frmBillingSubform].[Form]![txtInvoiceNumCount]'" is displayed on the status bar. The status bar message warns you that you can't update, or edit, the calculated control because it's bound to an expression. The calculated control in the main form changes in value only when the value of the expression changes in the subform.
2. Click the Invoice Amount Total box, and then type **8**. The value remains unchanged, and a message again is displayed on the status bar because you cannot edit a calculated control.

   Next, you'll determine the tab order of the fields in the main form. Reginald wants the tab order to be down and then across.
3. Select the value in the Visit ID box, press **TAB** to advance to the Date of Visit box, and then press **TAB** five more times to advance to the Reason/Diagnosis box, Comments text box, WalkIn check box, and PatientID combo box, in order, and then to the subform.

   Access sets the tab order in the same order in which you add controls to a form, so you should always check the form's tab order when you create a custom form in Layout or Design view. In this form you can see that the tab order is set such that the user will tab through the field value boxes in the main form before tabbing through the fields in the subform. In the main form, tabbing bypasses the two calculated controls because you set their Tab Stop properties to No, and you bypass the Select Visit combo box because it's an unbound control. Also, you tab through only the field value boxes in a form, not the labels.

The tab order Reginald wants for the field value boxes in the main form (top-to-bottom, left-to-right) should be the following: PatientID, VisitID, WalkIn, VisitDate, Reason, Comments, and then the subform. The default tab order doesn't match the order Reginald wants, so you'll change the tab order. You can change the tab order only in Design view.

4. Double-click the **Home** tab to restore the ribbon, switch to Design view, and then on the Form Design Tools Design tab, in the Tools group, click the **Tab Order** button. The Tab Order dialog box opens. See Figure 6–46.

Figure 6–46 **Tab Order dialog box**

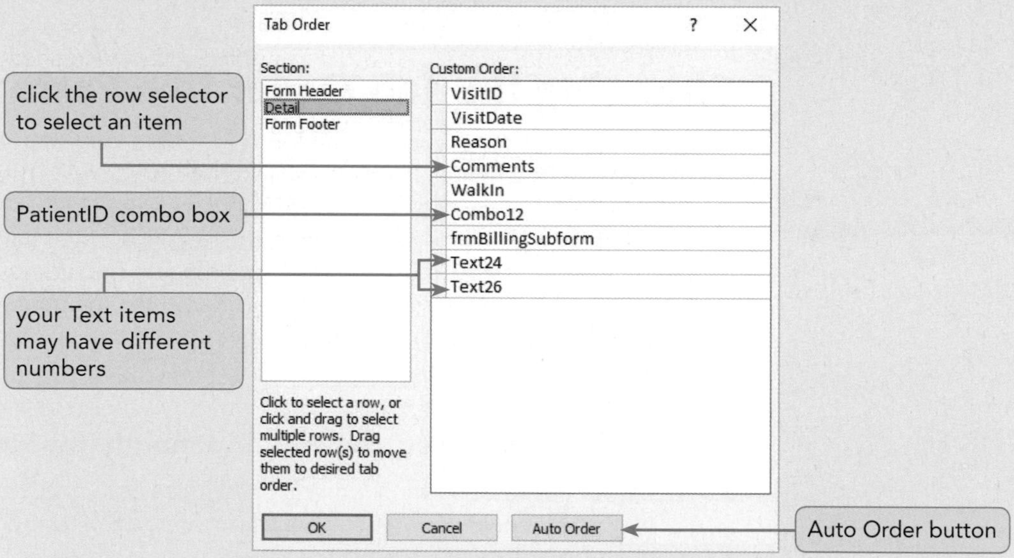
Tab Order
?
Section:
Form Header
Detail
Form Footer
Custom Order:
VisitID
VisitDate
Reason
Comments
WalkIn
Combo12
frmBillingSubform
Text24
Text26
Click to select a row, or click and drag to select multiple rows. Drag selected row(s) to move them to desired tab order.
OK
Cancel
Auto Order
click the row selector to select an item
PatientID combo box
your Text items may have different numbers
Auto Order button

Because you did not set the Name property for the combo box control and the calculated controls, Access assigned them names that consist of the type of control and number; for example Combo12 for the PatientID combo box, Text24 for the Number of Invoices calculated control, and Text26 for the Invoice Amount Total calculated control as shown in Figure 6–46. (The numbers assigned to your controls might differ.) The Auto Order button lets you create a left-to-right, top-to-bottom tab order automatically, which is not the order Reginald wants. You need to move the Combo12 entry above the VisitID entry.

TIP

Setting the Name property for all your controls to meaningful names avoids having to guess which control a name references in this and similar situations.

5. Click the **row selector** to the left of the Combo12 item (your number might differ), and then drag the row selector up to position it above the VisitID entry.

6. Click the row selector to the left of the WalkIn item, and then drag the row selector up to position it above VisitDate. The entries are now in the correct order. See Figure 6–47.

Figure 6–47 Tab Order dialog box with corrected order

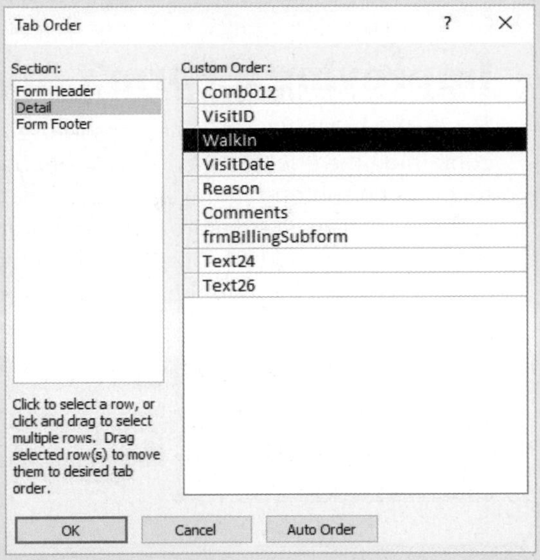
Tab Order
Section:
Form Header
Detail
Form Footer
Custom Order:
Combo12
VisitID
WalkIn
VisitDate
Reason
Comments
frmBillingSubform
Text24
Text26
Click to select a row, or click and drag to select multiple rows. Drag selected row(s) to move them to desired tab order.
OK
Cancel
Auto Order

7. Click the **OK** button to close the Tab Order dialog box, save your form design changes, and then switch to Form view.
8. Tab through the controls in the main form to make sure the tab order is correct, moving from the Patient ID box, to the Visit ID box, then to the Walk-in? check box, then to Date of Visit box, the Reason/Diagnosis box, the Comments box, and then finally to the subform.

   Trouble? If the tab order is incorrect, switch to Design view, click the Tab Order button in the Tools group, change your tab order in the Tab Order dialog box to match the order shown in Figure 6–47, and then repeat Steps 7 and 8.

PROSKILLS

Written Communication: Enhancing Information Using Calculated Controls

For a small number of records in a subform, it's easy for users to quickly count the number of records and to calculate numeric total amounts when the form doesn't display calculated controls. For instance, when students have completed few courses or when people have made few tax payments, it's easy for users to count the courses and calculate the student's GPA or to count and total the tax payments. But for subforms with dozens or hundreds of records—for instance, students with many courses, or people with many tax payments—displaying summary calculated controls is mandatory. By adding a few simple calculated controls to forms and reports, you can increase the usefulness of the information presented and improve the ability of users to process the information, spot trends, and be more productive in their jobs.

You've finished adding controls to the form, but the form is plain looking and lacks visual clues organizing the controls in the form. You'll complete the form by making it more attractive and easier for Donna and her staff to use.

Improving a Form's Appearance

The frmVisitsAndInvoices form has four distinct areas: the Form Header section containing the title and the Select Visit combo box, the six bound controls in the Detail section, the subform in the Detail section, and the two calculated controls in the Detail section. To visually separate these four areas, you'll increase the height of the Form Header section, add a horizontal line at the bottom of the Form Header section, and draw a rectangle around the calculated controls.

Adding a Line to a Form

You can use lines in a form to improve the form's readability, to group related information, or to underline important values. You use the Line tool in Design view to add a line to a form or report.

REFERENCE

Adding a Line to a Form or Report

- Display the form or report in Design view.
- On the Form Design Tools Design tab, in the Controls group, click the More button, and then click the Line tool.
- Position the pointer where you want the line to begin.
- Drag the pointer to the position for the end of the line, and then release the mouse button. If you want to ensure that you draw a straight horizontal or vertical line, press and hold SHIFT as you drag the pointer to draw the line.

You will add a horizontal line to the Form Header section to separate the controls in this section from the controls in the Detail section.

To add a line to the form:

1. Switch to Design view, and then drag the bottom border of the Form Header section down to the 1-inch mark on the vertical ruler to make room to draw a horizontal line at the bottom of the Form Header section.
2. On the Form Design Tools Design tab, in the Controls group, click the **More** button, and then click the **Line** tool.
3. Position the pointer's plus symbol at the left edge of the Form Header section just below the title.
4. Press and hold **SHIFT**, drag right to the 6-inch mark on the horizontal ruler, release the mouse button, and then release **SHIFT**. See Figure 6-48.

Figure 6–48 **Line added to the form**

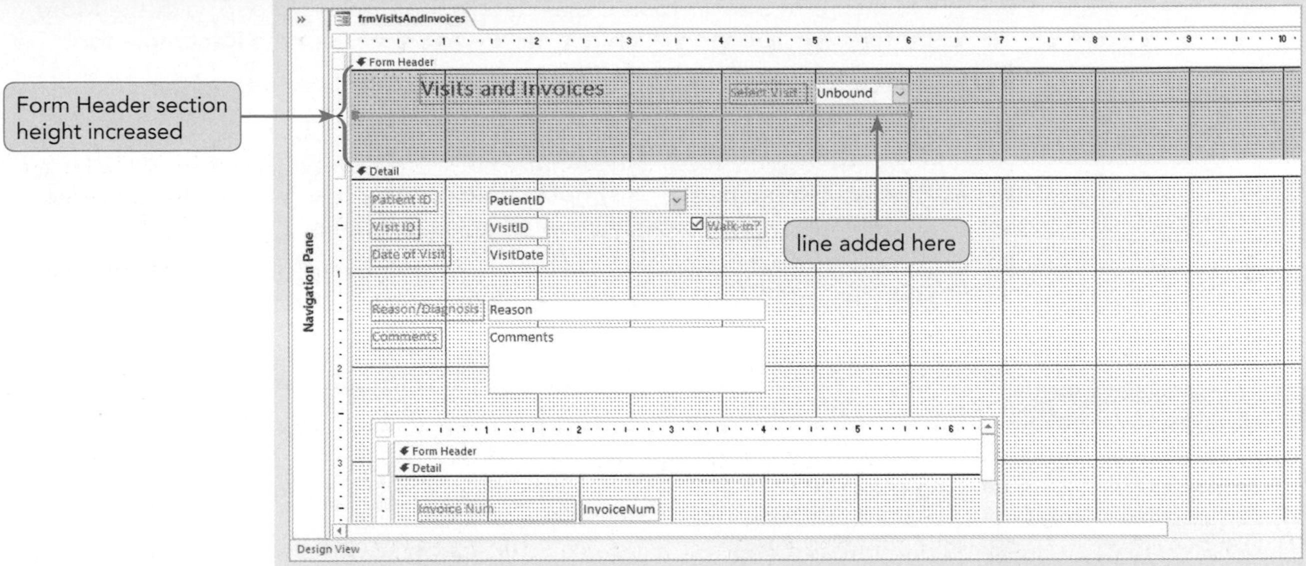

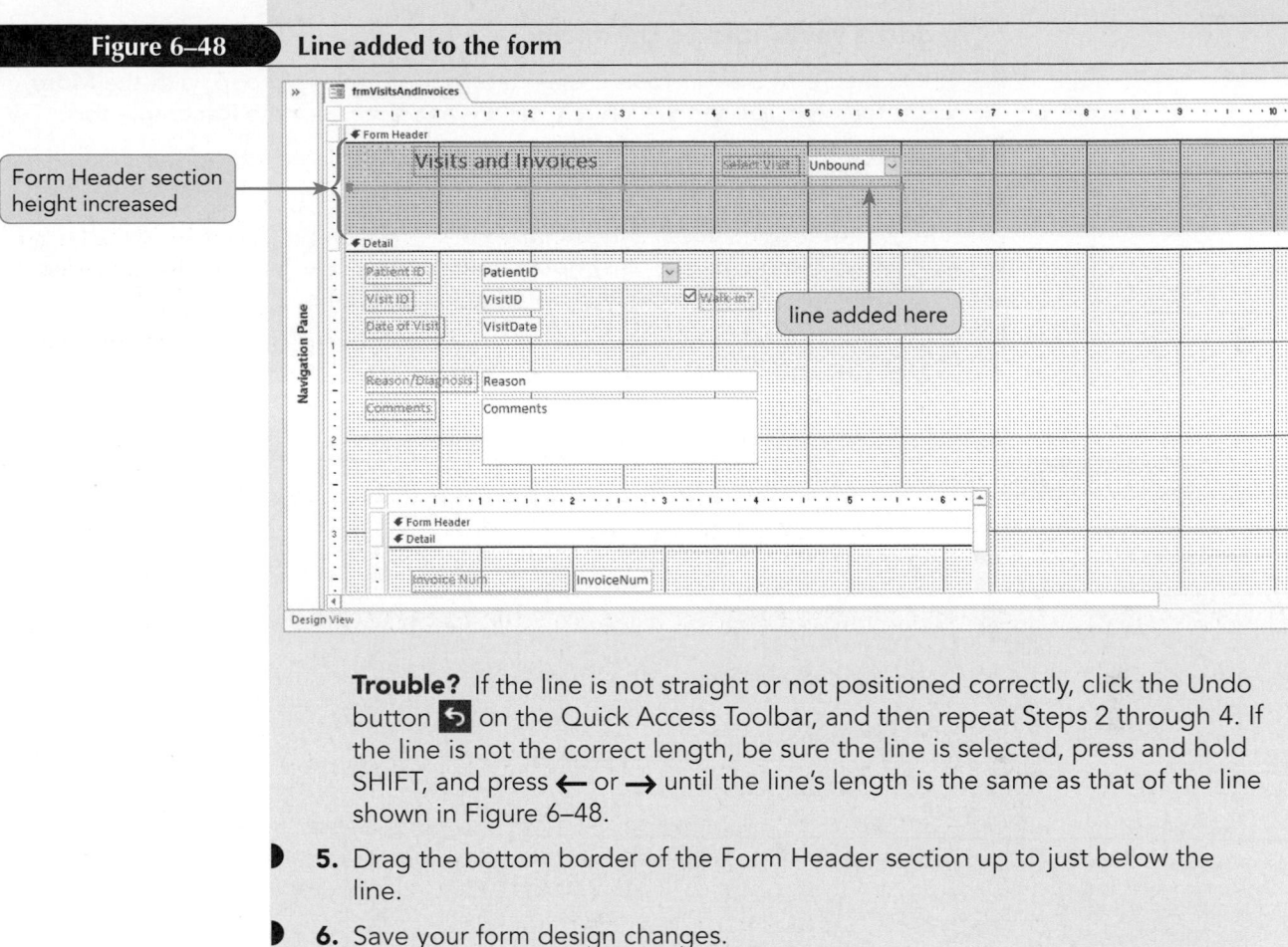

Form Header section height increased
line added here
frmVisitsAndInvoices
Form Header
Visits and Invoices
Unbound
Detail
Patient ID
PatientID
Visit ID
VisitID
Date of Visit
VisitDate
Walk-in?
Reason/Diagnosis
Reason
Comments
Comments
Form Header
Detail
Invoice Num
InvoiceNum
Navigation Pane
Design View

Trouble? If the line is not straight or not positioned correctly, click the Undo button on the Quick Access Toolbar, and then repeat Steps 2 through 4. If the line is not the correct length, be sure the line is selected, press and hold SHIFT, and press ← or → until the line's length is the same as that of the line shown in Figure 6–48.

5. Drag the bottom border of the Form Header section up to just below the line.
6. Save your form design changes.

Next, you'll add a rectangle around the calculated controls in the Detail section.

Adding a Rectangle to a Form

You can use a rectangle in a form to group related controls and to visually separate the group from other controls. You use the Rectangle tool in Design view to add a rectangle to a form or report.

REFERENCE

Adding a Rectangle to a Form or Report

- Display the form or report in Design view.
- On the Form Design Tools Design tab, in the Controls group, click the More button, and then click the Rectangle tool.
- Click in the form or report to create a default-sized rectangle, or drag a rectangle in the position and size you want.

You will add a rectangle around the calculated controls and their labels to separate them from the subform and from the other controls in the Detail section.

To add a rectangle to the form:

1. On the Form Design Tools Design tab, in the Controls group, click the **More** button to open the Controls gallery, and then click the **Rectangle** tool.
2. If necessary, scroll down the form so the two calculated controls and their labels are fully visible, with at least one grid dot between the bottom of the controls and the scroll bar.
3. Position the pointer's plus symbol approximately one grid dot above and one grid dot to the left of the Number of Invoices label.
4. Drag the pointer down and to the right to create a rectangle that that has all four sides approximately one grid dot from the two calculated controls and their labels. See Figure 6–49.

Figure 6–49 Rectangle added to the form

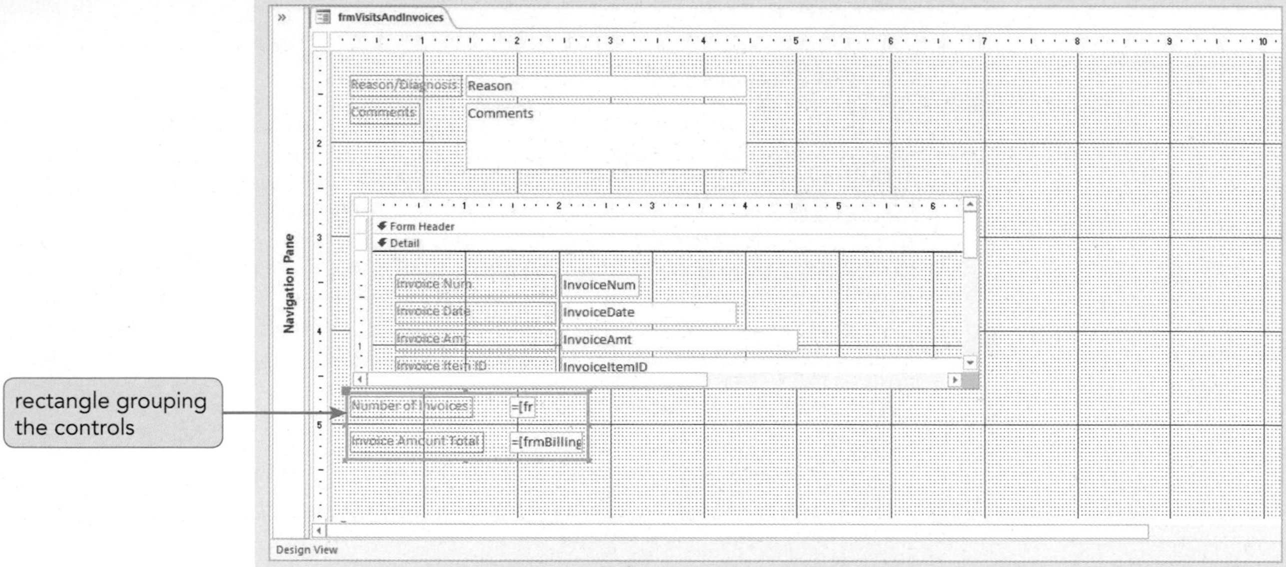
rectangle grouping the controls
frmVisitsAndInvoices
Reason/Diagnosis
Reason
Comments
Comments
Form Header
Detail
InvoiceNum
InvoiceDate
InvoiceAmt
InvoiceItemID
=[fr
=[frmBilling
Navigation Pane
Design View

Trouble? If the rectangle is not sized or positioned correctly, use the sizing handles on its selection border to adjust its size and the move handle to adjust its position.

Next, you'll set the thickness of the rectangle's lines.

5. Click the **Form Design Tools Format** tab.
6. In the Control Formatting group, click the **Shape Outline button**, point to **Line Thickness** at the bottom of the gallery, and then click **1 pt** line (second line from the top).
7. Click a blank area of the Form window to deselect the control.

TIP

Using a theme can improve a form's appearance, but a theme doesn't provide the control you can achieve by setting individual properties in Design or Layout view.

Next, you'll add color and visual effects to the form's controls.

Modifying the Visual Effects of the Controls in a Form

Distinguishing one group of controls in a form from other groups is an important visual cue to the users of the form. For example, users should be able to distinguish the bound controls in the form from the calculated controls and from the Select Visit control in the Form Header section. You can modify the visual effects of a control in either Form

Design View or Form Layout View. You'll now use Form Design View to modify the controls in Reginald's form to provide these visual cues. You'll start by setting font properties for the calculated control's labels.

To modify the format of the controls in the form:

1. Select the **Number of Invoices** label and the **Invoice Amount Total** label, using SHIFT to select multiple controls.
2. On the Form Design Tools Format tab, in the Font group, click the **Font Color button arrow** [A], click the **Blue** color (row 7, column 8 in the Standard Colors palette), and then in the Font group, click the **Bold** button [B]. The labels' captions now appear in bold, blue font.

   Next, you'll set properties for the Select Visit label in the Form Header section.
3. If necessary, scroll up so the entire Form Header section is visible.
4. Select the **Select Visit** label in the Form Header section, change the label's font color to **Red** (row 7, column 2 in the Standard Colors palette), and then apply bold formatting.

   Next, you'll set the label's Special Effect property to a shadowed effect. The **Special Effect property** specifies the type of special effect applied to a control in a form or report. The choices for this property are Flat, Raised, Sunken, Etched, Shadowed, and Chiseled.
5. Open the Property Sheet for the Select Visit label, click the **All** tab (if necessary), set the Special Effect property to **Shadowed**, and then deselect the label. The label now has a shadowed special effect, and the label's caption appears in a red, bold font.

   Next, you'll set the Special Effect property for the bound control text boxes to a sunken effect.
6. Select the **VisitID** text box, the **VisitDate** text box, the **Reason** text box, and the **Comments** text box, set the controls' Special Effect property to **Sunken**, close the Property Sheet, and then deselect the controls.

   Finally, you'll set the background color of the Form Header section, the Detail section, the Select Visit combo box, and the two calculated controls. You can use the **Background Color button** in the Font group on the Form Design Tools Format tab to change the background color of a control, section, or object (form or report).
7. Click the **Form Header** section bar.
8. On the Form Design Tools Format tab, in the Font group, click the **Background Color button arrow** [icon], and then click the **Light Blue 2** color (row 3, column 5 in the Standard Colors palette). The Form Header's background color changes to the Light Blue 2 color.
9. Click the **Detail** section bar, and then in the Font Group, click the **Background Color** button to change the Detail section's background color to the **Light Blue 2** color.
10. Select the **Select Visit** combo box, **Number of Invoices** calculated control box, and the **Invoice Amount Total** calculated control box, set the selected controls' background color to the **Light Blue 2** color, and then deselect all controls by clicking to the right of the Detail section's grid.
11. Save your form design changes, switch to Form view, hide the ribbon, click the **Select Visit** arrow, and then click **1451** in the list to display this visit record in the form. See Figure 6–50.

TIP

To set a background image instead of a background color, click the Background Image button in the Background group on the Form Design Tools Format tab.

Figure 6–50 **Completed custom form in Design view**

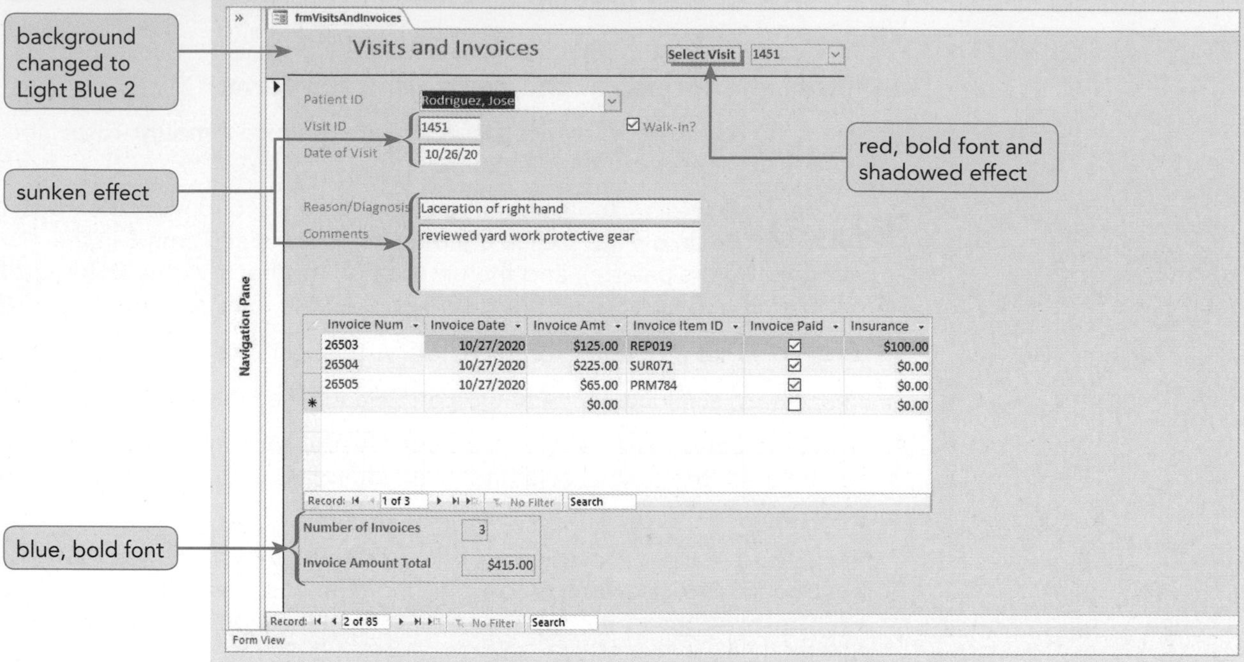
background changed to Light Blue 2
sunken effect
blue, bold font
red, bold font and shadowed effect
frmVisitsAndInvoices
Visits and Invoices
Select Visit
1451
Patient ID
Rodriguez, Jose
Visit ID
1451
Walk-in?
Date of Visit
10/26/20
Reason/Diagnosis
Laceration of right hand
Comments
reviewed yard work protective gear
Navigation Pane
Invoice Num
Invoice Date
Invoice Amt
Invoice Item ID
Invoice Paid
Insurance
26503
10/27/2020
$125.00
REP019
$100.00
26504
10/27/2020
$225.00
SUR071
$0.00
26505
10/27/2020
$65.00
PRM784
$0.00
$0.00
$0.00
Record: 1 of 3
No Filter
Search
Number of Invoices
3
Invoice Amount Total
$415.00
Record: 2 of 85
No Filter
Search
Form View

12. Test the form by tabbing between fields, navigating between records, and using the Select Visit combo box to find records, making sure you don't change any field values and observing that the calculated controls display the correct values.

13. **sam** Close the form, pin the ribbon, make a backup copy of the database, compact and repair the database, and then close the database.

INSIGHT

Applying Styles to Form and Report Controls

You can use the Quick Styles gallery to apply a built-in style reflecting a combination of several formatting options to a control in a form or report. To do this, select the control in either Layout or Design view, and then, on the Form or Report Design Tools Format tab, click the Quick Styles button in the Control Formatting group to display the Quick Styles gallery. Click a style in the gallery to apply it to the selected control.

You can also change the shape of a control in a form or report by clicking the Change Shape button in the Control Formatting group to display the Change Shape gallery, and then clicking a shape to apply it to the selected control.

Donna is pleased with the forms you have created. She will show these to her staff, and determine which of the forms will be most effective for using and managing the Clinic database.

REVIEW

Session 6.3 Quick Check

1. To create a combo box to find records in a form with the Combo Box Wizard, the form's record source must be a(n) ________.
2. You use the ________ tool to add a subform to a form.
3. To calculate subtotals and overall totals in a form or report, you use the ______ function.
4. The Control Source property setting can be either a(n) ________ or a(n) ________.
5. Explain the difference between the Tab Stop property and tab order.
6. What is focus?
7. The ________ property has settings such as Raised and Sunken.

PRACTICE

Review Assignments

Data File needed for the Review Assignments: Supplier.accdb (*cont. from Module 5*)

Donna wants you to create several forms, including a custom form that displays and updates companies and the products they offer. Complete the following steps:

1. Open the **Supplier** database you worked with in the previous module.
2. In the **tblProduct** table, remove the lookup feature from the SupplierID field, and then resize the Supplier ID column in the datasheet to its best fit. Save and close the table.
3. Edit the relationship between the primary tblSupplier and related tblProduct tables to enforce referential integrity and to cascade-update related fields. Create the relationship report, save the report as **rptRelationshipsForSupplier**, and then close it.
4. Use the Documenter to document the qryCompanyContacts query. Select all query options; use the Names, Data Types, and Sizes option for fields; and use the Names and Fields option for indexes. Export the report produced by the Documenter as a PDF file with the filename **NP_AC_6_SupplierDocumenter.pdf** and without saving the export steps, and then close the report.
5. Use the Datasheet tool to create a form based on the tblProduct table, save the form as **frmProductDatasheet**, and then close it.
6. Use the Multiple Items tool to create a form based on the qryDuplicateProductTypes query, save the form as **frmProductTypeMultipleItems**, and then close it.
7. Use the Split Form tool to create a split form based on the tblProduct table, and then make the following changes to the form in Layout view:
   a. Remove the two Units controls from the stacked layout and then reduce the width of the Units field value box by about half. Move the controls to the bottom left, and then anchor the two Units controls to the bottom left.
   b. Remove the four control pairs in the right column from the stacked layout, and then anchor the group to the bottom right. You may see a dotted border outlining the location of the previously removed controls. This may be automatically selected as well.
   c. Remove the ProductName control pair from the stacked layout, move them to the top right, and then anchor them to the top right.
   d. Reduce the widths of the ProductID and SupplierID field value boxes to a reasonable size.
   e. Change the title to **Product**, save the modified form as **frmProductSplitForm**, and then close it.
8. Use Figure 6–51 and the following steps to create a custom form named **frmSuppliersWithProducts** based on the tblSupplier and tblProduct tables.

Figure 6–51 **Supplier database custom form design**

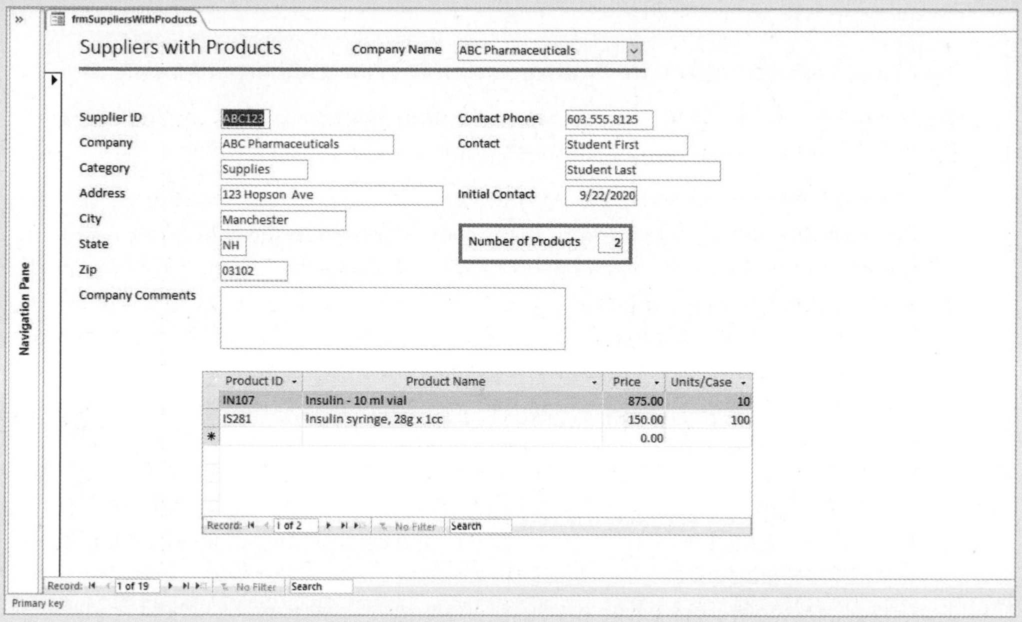
frmSuppliersWithProducts
Suppliers with Products
Company Name
ABC Pharmaceuticals
Supplier ID
ABC123
Company
ABC Pharmaceuticals
Category
Supplies
Address
123 Hopson Ave
City
Manchester
State
NH
Zip
03102
Company Comments
Contact Phone
603.555.8125
Contact
Student First
Student Last
Initial Contact
9/22/2020
Number of Products
2
Product ID
Product Name
Price
Units/Case
IN107
Insulin - 10 ml vial
875.00
10
IS281
Insulin syringe, 28g x 1cc
150.00
100
0.00
Record: 1 of 2
No Filter
Search
Record: 1 of 19
No Filter
Search
Navigation Pane
Primary key

a. Place the 12 fields from the tblSupplier table shown in Figure 6–51 at the top of the Detail section. Delete the Contact Last Name label, and change the caption for the Contact First Name label to **Contact**.

b. Move the fields into two columns in the Detail section, as shown in Figure 6–51, resizing and aligning controls, as necessary, and increasing the width of the form.

c. Add the title in the Form Header section.

d. Make sure the form's Record Source property is set to tblSupplier, and then add a combo box in the Form Header section to find Company field values. In the Combo Box Wizard steps, select the Company and SupplierID fields, and hide the key column. Resize and move the control. Ensure the label displays the text "Company Name". Make sure the size of the Company Name field value box can accommodate the largest company name.

e. Add a subform based on the tblProduct table, include only the fields shown in Figure 6–51, link with SupplierID, name the subform **frmPartialProductSubform**, delete the subform label, resize the columns in the subform to their best fit, and resize and position the subform.

f. Create a calculated control in the subform that totals the number of products displayed, and then add a control to the main form that displays this calculated value. Set the main form control's Tab Stop property to No, and specify the text **Calculated number of products** for the ControlTip Text property.

g. Add a line in the Form Header section, and add a rectangle around the calculated control and its label, setting the line thickness of both controls to 3 pt. Set the rectangle's color the same as the line's color.

h. In the main form, use the Green 1 fill color (row 2, column 7 in the Standard Colors palette) for all form sections, and use the Black font color (row 1, column 2 in the Standard Colors palette) for all the label text, the calculated control, Company Name combo box, and the Title.

i. Make sure the tab order is top-to-bottom, left-to-right for the main form text boxes.

9. Make a backup copy of the database, compact and repair the database, and then close the database.

APPLY

Case Problem 1

Data File needed for this Case Problem: School.accdb (*cont. from Module 5*)

Great Giraffe Jeremiah Garver wants you to create several forms, including two custom forms that display and update data in the database. Complete the following steps:

1. Open the **School** database you worked with in the previous module.
2. Remove the lookup feature from the InstanceID field in the tblRegistration table, and then resize the Instance ID column to its best fit. Save and close the table.
3. Define a one-to-many relationship between the primary tblCourse table and the related tblRegistration table. Select the referential integrity option and the cascade updates option for this relationship.
4. Use the Documenter to document the qryStudentData query. Select all query options; use the Names, Data Types, and Sizes option for fields; and use the Names and Fields option for indexes. Export the report produced by the Documenter as a PDF file with the filename **NP_AC_6_StudentDataDocumenter.pdf** and without saving the export steps.
5. Use the Datasheet tool to create a form based on the tblCourse table, and then save the form as **frmCourseDatasheet**.
6. Create a custom form based on the qryBalanceContacts query. Display all fields from the query in the form. Create your own design for the form. Add a label to the bottom of the Detail section that contains your first and last names. Change the label's font so that your name appears in bold, blue font. Change the BalanceDue text box format so that the field value is displayed in bold, red font. Save the form as **frmBalanceContacts**.
7. Use Figure 6–52 and the following steps to create a custom form named **frmCoursesWithRegistrations** based on the tblCourse and tblRegistration tables.

Figure 6–52 School database custom form design

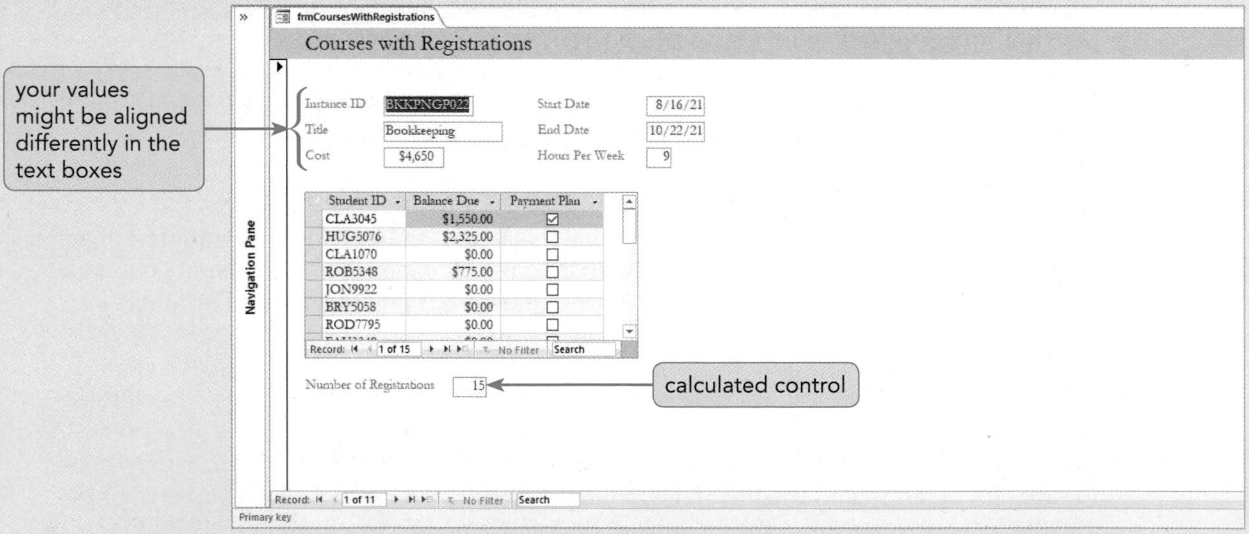
your values might be aligned differently in the text boxes
frmCoursesWithRegistrations
Courses with Registrations
Instance ID
BKKPNGP022
Title
Bookkeeping
Cost
$4,650
Start Date
8/16/21
End Date
10/22/21
Hours Per Week
9
Student ID
Balance Due
Payment Plan
CLA3045 $1,550.00
HUG5076 $2,325.00
CLA1070 $0.00
ROB5348 $775.00
JON9922 $0.00
BRY5058 $0.00
ROD7795 $0.00
Record: 1 of 15
No Filter
Search
Number of Registrations
15
calculated control
Navigation Pane
Record: 1 of 11
No Filter
Search
Primary key

   a. Place the fields from the tblCourse table shown in Figure 6–52 at the top of the Detail section, and edit the captions in the associated label controls as shown.
   b. Selected fields from the tblRegistration table appear in a subform named **frmCoursesWithRegistrationsSubform**.
   c. The calculated control displays the total number of records that appear in the subform. Set the text **Total number of students registered for this course** as the value of the calculated control's ControlTip Text property. Set the calculated control's Tab Stop property to **No**.

d. Apply the Organic theme to the frmCoursesWithRegistrations form only.
e. Save and close the form.

8. Make a backup copy of the database, compact and repair the database, and then close the database.

CREATE

Case Problem 2

Data File needed for this Case Problem: Storm.accdb (*cont. from Module 5*)

Drain Adopter Tandrea Austin wants you to create several forms, including a custom form that displays and updates the location and information of drains that volunteers have signed up for. Complete the following steps:

1. Open the **Storm** database you worked with in the previous module.
2. Remove the lookup feature from the VolunteerID field in the tblDrain table, and then resize the Volunteer ID column to its best fit. Save and close the table.
3. Define a one-to-many relationship between the primary tblVolunteer table and the related tblDrain table. Select the referential integrity option and the cascade updates option for this relationship.
4. Use the Documenter to document the tblDrain table. Select all table options; use the Names, Data Types, and Sizes option for fields; and use the Names and Fields option for indexes. Export the report produced by the Documenter as a PDF file with the filename **NP_AC_6_DrainDocumenter.pdf** and without saving the export steps.
5. Create a query called **qryDrainsByVolunteer** that uses the tblVolunteer and tblDrain tables and includes the fields FirstName and LastName from the tblVolunteer table, and the fields DrainID, MainStreet, CrossStreet, and Direction from the tblDrain table.
6. Use the Multiple Items tool to create a form based on the qryDrainsByVolunteer query, change the title to **Drains by Volunteer**, and then save the form as **frmDrainsByVolunteerMultipleItems**.
7. Use the Split Form tool to create a split form based on the qryDrainsByVolunteer query, and then make the following changes to the form in Layout view.
   a. Size each field value box as necessary to fit a reasonable amount of data.
   b. Remove the MainStreet, CrossStreet, and Direction controls and their labels from the stacked layout, move these six controls to the right and then to the top of the form, and then anchor them to the top right.
   c. Remove the DrainID control and its label from the stacked layout, and then anchor the pair of controls to the bottom left.
   d. Change the title to **Drains by Volunteer**, and then save the modified form as **frmDrainsByVolunteerSplitForm**.
8. Use Figure 6–53 and the following steps to create a custom form named **frmSupply** based on the tblSupply table.
   a. Make sure the form's Record Source property is set to tblSupply, and then add a combo box in the Form Header section to find SupplyID field values.
   b. Add a calculated control that displays the total value of current inventory (cost multiplied by number on hand). *Hint*: Use the * symbol for multiplication. Set the calculated control's Tab Stop property to No, set the format to Currency, and use **Calculated value of stock on hand** as the ControlTip text value.
   c. Add a line in the Form Header section, add a second line below it, and then add a second pair of lines near the bottom of the Detail section. Set the line thickness of all lines to 1 pt.
   d. Use the Label tool to add your name below the pair of lines at the bottom of the Detail section.
   e. For the labels in the Detail section, except for the Total Hours label and the label displaying your name, use the Aqua Blue 5 font color (row 6, column 9 in the Standard Colors palette) and make the text bold.

f. For the background fill color of the sections, the calculated control, and the Supply ID combo box, apply the Brown 2 color (row 3, column 10 in the Standard Colors palette).
g. Make sure the tab order is top-to-bottom, left-to-right for the main form field value boxes.

9. Make a backup copy of the database, compact and repair the database, and then close the database.

Figure 6–53 **Storm database custom form design**

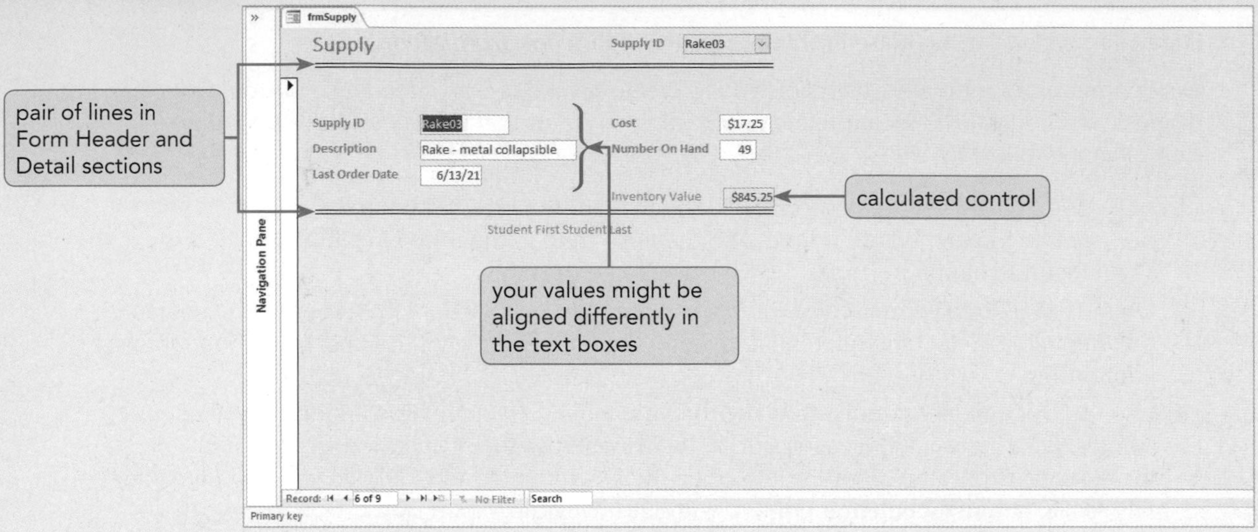
frmSupply
Supply
Supply ID
Rake03
pair of lines in Form Header and Detail sections
Supply ID
Rake03
Description
Rake - metal collapsible
Last Order Date
6/13/21
Cost
$17.25
Number On Hand
49
Inventory Value
$845.25
calculated control
Student First Student Last
your values might be aligned differently in the text boxes
Navigation Pane
Record: 6 of 9
No Filter
Search
Primary key

MODULE 7

Creating Custom Reports

Creating Custom Reports for Lakewood Community Health Services

OBJECTIVES

Session 7.1
- View and filter a report in Report view
- Copy information from a report into a Word document
- Modify a report in Layout view
- Modify a report in Design view

Session 7.2
- Design and create a custom report
- Sort and group data in a report
- Add, move, resize, and align controls in a report
- Hide duplicate values in a report

Session 7.3
- Add the date and page numbers to a report's Footer section
- Add and format report titles
- Create and modify mailing labels

Case | ***Lakewood Community Health Services***

At a recent staff meeting, Donna Taylor, the office manager, indicated that she would like to make some changes to an existing report in the database. She also requested a new report that she can use to produce a printed list of all invoices for all visits.

In this module, you will modify an existing report and create the new report for Donna. In modifying and building these reports, you will use many Access features for customizing reports, including grouping data, calculating totals, and adding lines to separate report sections. These features will enhance the reports and make them easier for Donna and her staff to work with.

STARTING DATA FILES

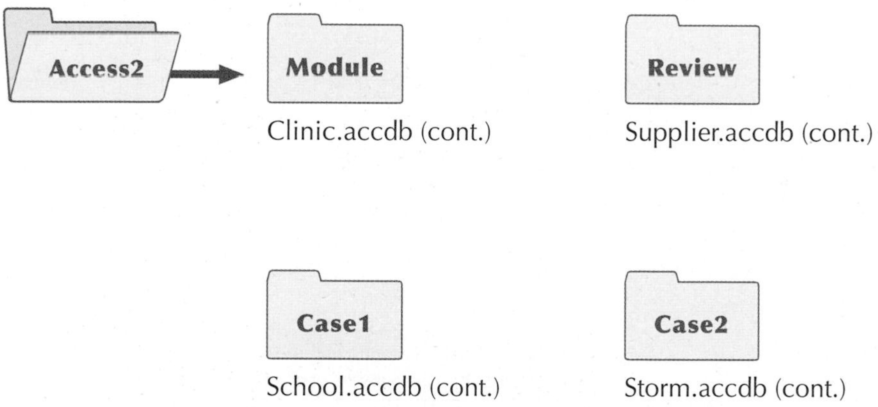
Access2
Module
Clinic.accdb (cont.)
Review
Supplier.accdb (cont.)
Case1
School.accdb (cont.)
Case2
Storm.accdb (cont.)

Session 7.1 Visual Overview:

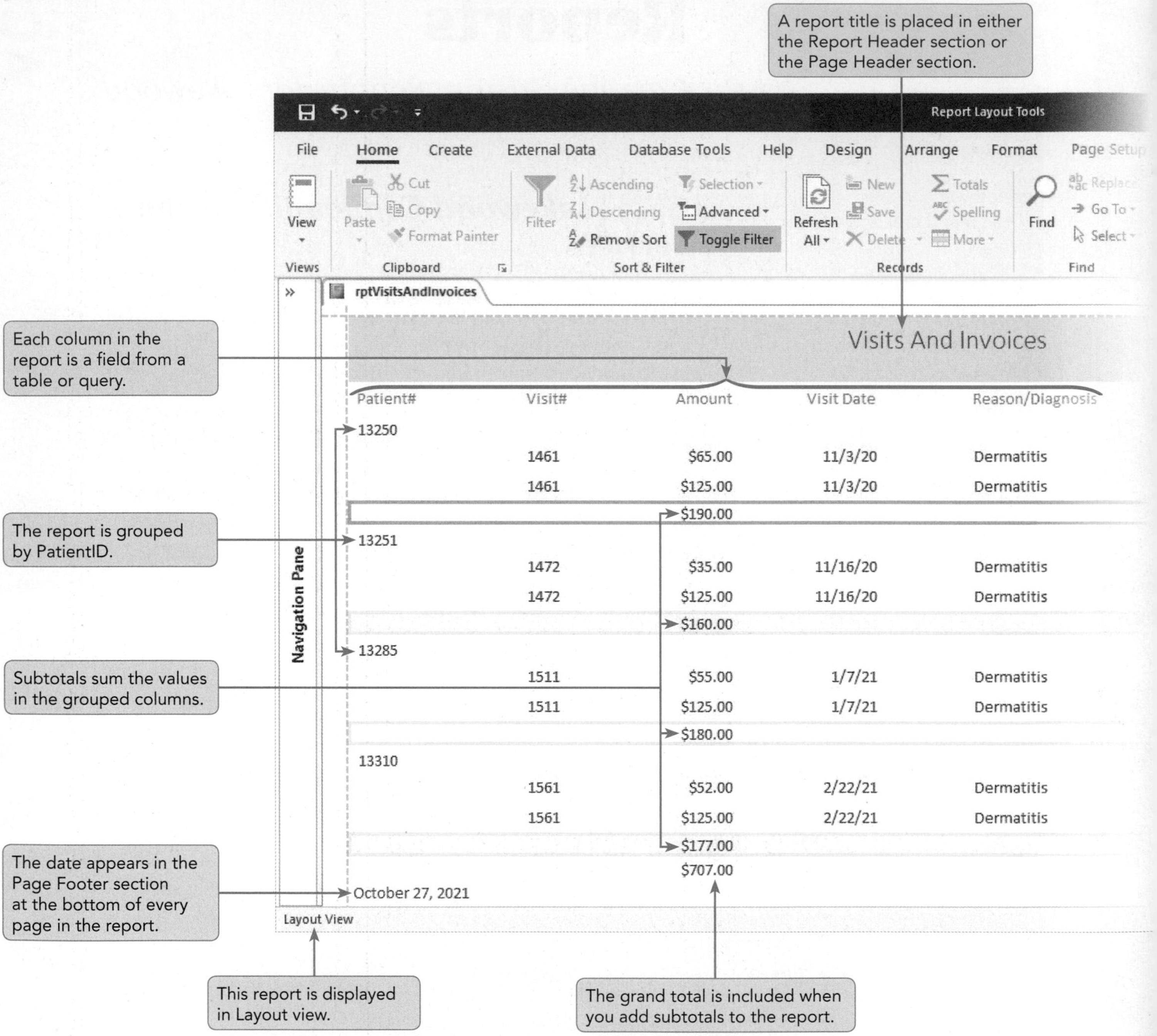
A report title is placed in either the Report Header section or the Page Header section.
Report Layout Tools
File
Home
Create
External Data
Database Tools
Help
Design
Arrange
Format
Page Setup
View
Paste
Cut
Copy
Format Painter
Filter
Ascending
Descending
Remove Sort
Selection
Advanced
Toggle Filter
Refresh All
New
Save
Delete
Totals
Spelling
More
Find
Replace
Go To
Select
Views
Clipboard
Sort & Filter
Records
Find
rptVisitsAndInvoices
Visits And Invoices
Each column in the report is a field from a table or query.
Patient#
Visit#
Amount
Visit Date
Reason/Diagnosis
13250
1461 $65.00 11/3/20 Dermatitis
1461 $125.00 11/3/20 Dermatitis
$190.00
The report is grouped by PatientID.
13251
1472 $35.00 11/16/20 Dermatitis
1472 $125.00 11/16/20 Dermatitis
$160.00
Navigation Pane
13285
Subtotals sum the values in the grouped columns.
1511 $55.00 1/7/21 Dermatitis
1511 $125.00 1/7/21 Dermatitis
$180.00
13310
1561 $52.00 2/22/21 Dermatitis
1561 $125.00 2/22/21 Dermatitis
$177.00
$707.00
The date appears in the Page Footer section at the bottom of every page in the report.
October 27, 2021
Layout View
This report is displayed in Layout view.
The grand total is included when you add subtotals to the report.

Report Sections

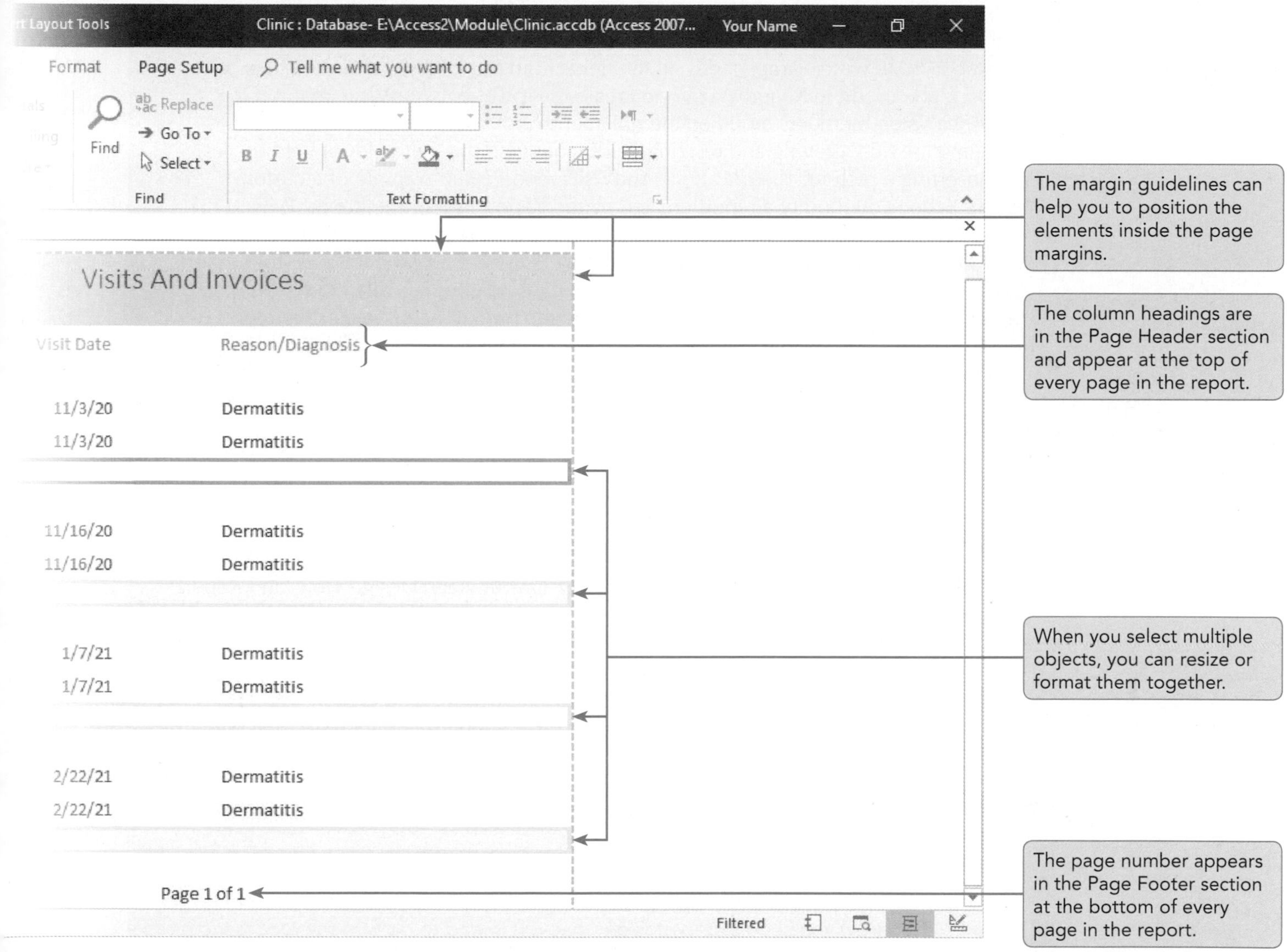
Layout Tools
Clinic : Database- E:\Access2\Module\Clinic.accdb (Access 2007...
Your Name
Format
Page Setup
Tell me what you want to do
Replace
Go To
Select
Find
Find
Text Formatting
Visits And Invoices
Visit Date
Reason/Diagnosis
11/3/20
Dermatitis
11/3/20
Dermatitis
11/16/20
Dermatitis
11/16/20
Dermatitis
1/7/21
Dermatitis
1/7/21
Dermatitis
2/22/21
Dermatitis
2/22/21
Dermatitis
Page 1 of 1
Filtered
The margin guidelines can help you to position the elements inside the page margins.
The column headings are in the Page Header section and appear at the top of every page in the report.
When you select multiple objects, you can resize or format them together.
The page number appears in the Page Footer section at the bottom of every page in the report.

Customizing Existing Reports

As you know, a report is a formatted output (screen display or printout) of the contents of one or more tables in a database. Although you can format and print data using datasheets, queries, and forms, reports offer greater flexibility and provide a more professional, readable appearance. For example, a billing statement created using a datasheet would not look professional, but the staff at Lakewood Community Health Services can easily create professional-looking billing statements from the database using reports.

Before Reginald Morales was tasked with enhancing the Clinic database, Donna and her staff created two reports. Donna created the rptVisitsAndInvoices report using the Report tool, which simply adds all the fields from the selected table or query to a report. She used the Report Wizard to create the rptPatientsAndVisits report. One of Donna's staff members modified the rptPatientsAndVisits report in Layout view by changing the title, moving and resizing fields, changing the font color of field names, and inserting a picture. The rptPatientsAndVisits report is an example of a custom report. When you modify a report created by the Report tool or the Report Wizard in Layout view or in Design view, or when you create a report from scratch in Layout view or in Design view, you produce a **custom report**. You need to produce a custom report whenever the Report tool or the Report Wizard cannot automatically create the specific report you need, or when you need to fine-tune the formatting of an existing report or to add controls and special features.

The rptVisitsAndInvoices report is included in the Clinic database. Donna asks Reginald to review the rptVisitsAndInvoices report and suggest improvements to make it more user friendly. You will make the changes Reginald suggests, but first, you will view and work with the report in Report view.

Viewing a Report in Report View

You can view reports on screen in Print Preview, Layout view, Design view, and Report view. You've already viewed and worked with reports in Print Preview and Layout view. Making modifications to reports in Design view is similar to making changes to forms in Design view. **Report view** provides an interactive view of a report. You can use Report view to view the contents of a report and to apply a filter to its data. You can also copy selected portions of the report to the Clipboard and then use that data in another program.

INSIGHT

Choosing the View to Use for a Report

You can view a report on screen using Report view, Print Preview, Layout view, or Design view. Which view you choose depends on what you intend to do with the report and its data.

- Use Report view when you want to filter the report data before printing a report or when you want to copy a selected portion of a report.
- Use Print Preview when you want to see what a report will look like when it is printed. Print Preview is the only view in which you can navigate the pages of a report, zoom in or out, or view a **multiple-column report**, which is a report that prints the same collection of field values in two or more sets across the page.
- Use Layout view when you want to modify a report while seeing actual report data.
- Use Design view when you want to fine-tune a report's design or when you want to add lines, rectangles, and other controls that are available only in Design view.

You'll open the rptVisitsAndInvoices report in Report view, and then you'll interact with its data in this view.

To view and filter the rptVisitsAndInvoices report in Report view:

1. **sam** Start Access, and then open the **Clinic** database you worked with in the previous two modules.

   Trouble? If the security warning is displayed below the ribbon, click the Enable Content button.

2. Open the Navigation Pane if necessary, double-click **rptVisitsAndInvoices**, and then close the Navigation Pane. The rptVisitsAndInvoices report opens in Report view.

   In Report view, you can view the report prior to printing it, just as you can do in Print Preview. Report view also lets you apply filters to the report before printing it. You'll apply a text filter to the rptVisitsAndInvoices report.

3. Scroll down to Patient ID 13252, which has four report detail lines for Visit ID 1585, right-click **Annual wellness visit** in the Reason column to open the shortcut menu, and then point to **Text Filters**. A submenu of filter options for the Text field opens. See Figure 7–1.

Figure 7–1 Filter options for a Text field in Report view

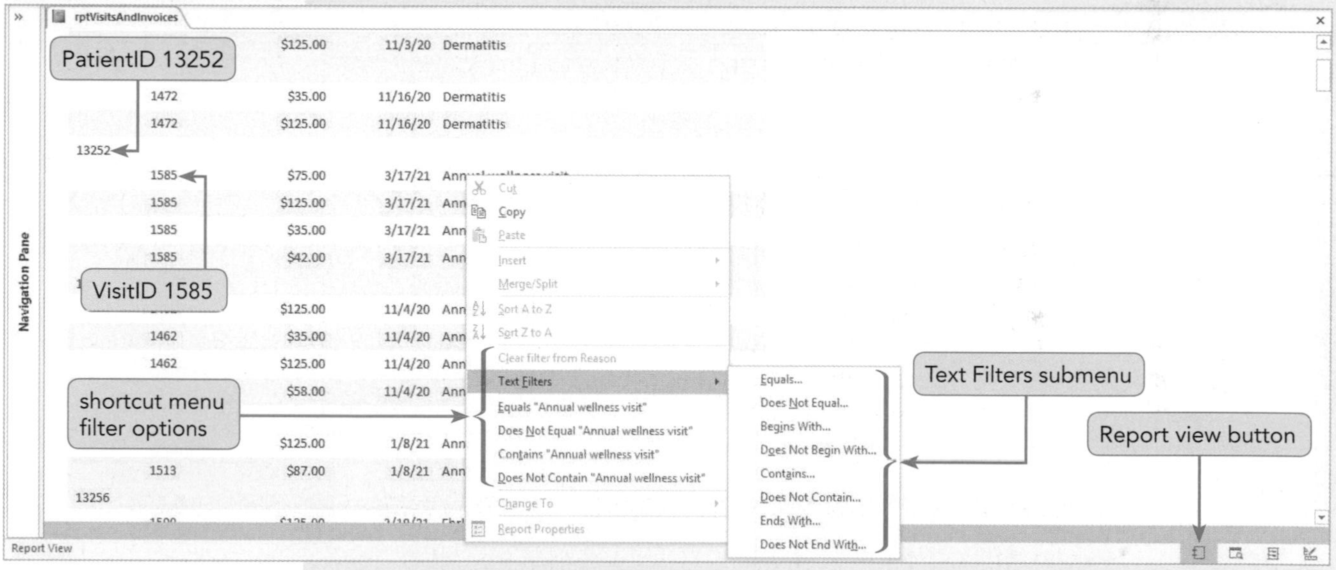
PatientID 13252
VisitID 1585
shortcut menu filter options
Text Filters submenu
Report view button

   The filter options that appear on the shortcut menu depend on the selected field's data type and the selected value. Because you clicked the Reason field value without selecting a portion of the value, the shortcut menu displays filter options—various conditions using the value "Annual wellness visit"—for the entire Reason field value. You'll close the menus and select a portion of the Reason field value to explore a different way of filtering the report.

4. Click a blank area of the screen to close the menus.

5. For Patient ID 13252: Visit ID 1585, double-click **visit** in the Reason/Diagnosis column to select it, and then right-click **visit**. The filter options on the shortcut menu now apply to the selected text, "visit." Notice that the filter options on the shortcut menu include options such as "Ends With" and "Does Not End With" because the text you selected is at the end of the field value in the Reason/Diagnosis column.

6. On the shortcut menu, click **Contains "visit"**. The report content changes to display only those visits that contain the word "visit" anywhere in the Reason/Diagnosis column.
7. In the Reason/Diagnosis column, double-click the word **Annual** for the Visit ID 1585 report detail line for Patient ID 13252, right-click **Annual** to open the shortcut menu, and then point to **Text Filters**. The filter options now include the "Begins With" and "Does Not Begin With" options because the text you selected is at the beginning of the field value in the Reason/Diagnosis column.

   Donna wants to view only those visits that contain the phrase "Annual wellness visit" in the Reason/Diagnosis column.
8. Click a blank area of the screen to close the menus, and then click in a blank area again to deselect the text.
9. In the report detail line for Visit ID 1585, right-click **Annual wellness visit** in the Reason/Diagnosis column, and then click **Equals "Annual wellness visit"** on the shortcut menu. Only the 15 invoices that contain the selected phrase are displayed in the report. See Figure 7–2.

Figure 7–2 **Filter applied to the report in Report View**

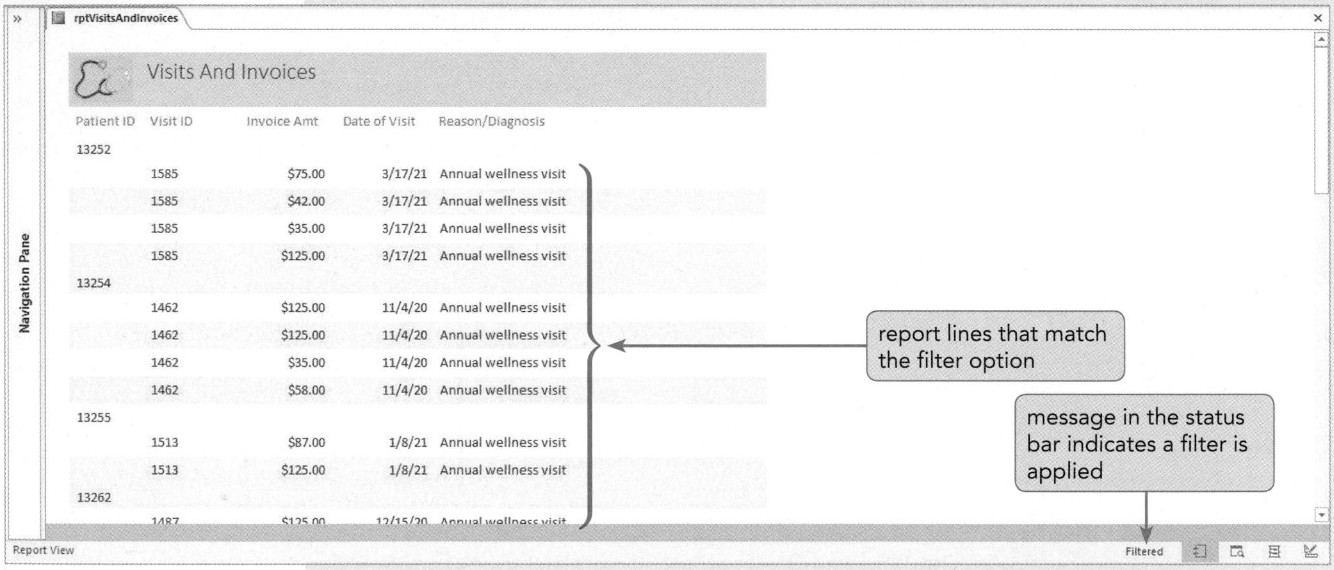
rptVisitsAndInvoices
Visits And Invoices
Patient ID Visit ID Invoice Amt Date of Visit Reason/Diagnosis
13252
1585 $75.00 3/17/21 Annual wellness visit
1585 $42.00 3/17/21 Annual wellness visit
1585 $35.00 3/17/21 Annual wellness visit
1585 $125.00 3/17/21 Annual wellness visit
13254
1462 $125.00 11/4/20 Annual wellness visit
1462 $125.00 11/4/20 Annual wellness visit
1462 $35.00 11/4/20 Annual wellness visit
1462 $58.00 11/4/20 Annual wellness visit
13255
1513 $87.00 1/8/21 Annual wellness visit
1513 $125.00 1/8/21 Annual wellness visit
13262
Navigation Pane
Report View
Filtered
report lines that match the filter option
message in the status bar indicates a filter is applied

You can print the filtered report, or you can select the entire filtered report or a portion of it and copy it into another file so you can work with it in a different program.

Copying and Pasting a Report into Word

Sometimes it is helpful to copy a filtered report or a portion of a filtered report into another file, such as a Word document or an Excel spreadsheet. This allows you to distribute the report electronically in a format that others can easily access, or you can print the filtered report to distribute on paper. When you copy information contained in an Access object such as a report, it is placed on the Clipboard. The Clipboard is a temporary storage area on your computer on which text or objects are stored when you cut or copy them, and its contents are available to all Windows programs. You can then paste the text or objects stored on the Clipboard into another file, such as a Word document or an Excel spreadsheet.

Donna would like you to create a Word document that contains the records from the Annual wellness visit filter so she can provide this information to the nurse who will follow up with these patients. Next, you'll copy the entire filtered report to the Clipboard.

TIP

You can press CTRL+A to select all items in the report.

To copy the filtered report and paste it into a Word document:

1. Click to the left of the title graphic at the top of the report to select the report title control, drag down to the end of the last record in the report, and then release the mouse button to select the report title, field titles, and all of the records in the report. See Figure 7–3.

   Trouble? If you selected nothing, you clicked above the title graphic. Make sure the mouse pointer is to the left of the title graphic, but not above it, and then repeat Step 1.

   Trouble? If you selected only a portion of the report, press ESC to deselect your selection, and then repeat Step 1.

Figure 7–3 Selected filtered report in Report view

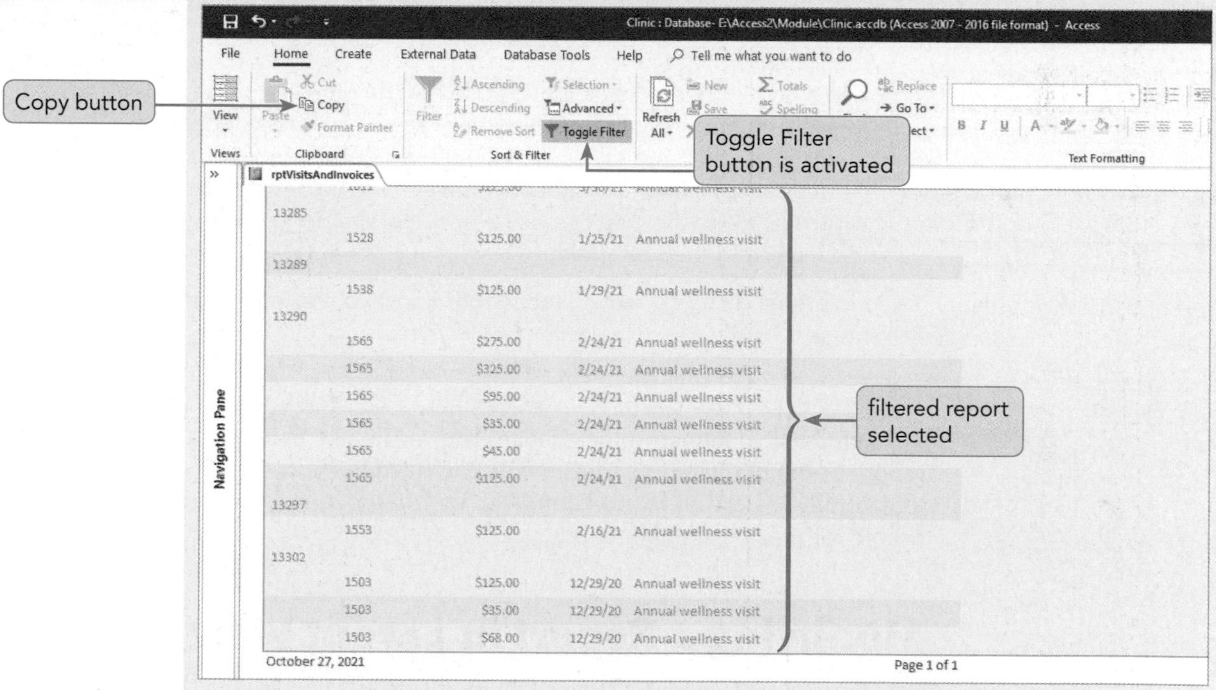
Copy button
Toggle Filter button is activated
filtered report selected

2. On the Home tab, in the Clipboard group, click the **Copy** button.

   You'll copy this report data into a Word document.

3. Open Word, and then in Backstage view, click **Blank document**. A blank Word document opens.
4. On the Home tab, in the Clipboard group, click the **Paste** button to paste the report data into the document.
5. Save the Word document with the filename **NP_AC_7_AnnualWellnessVisit** in the location where you are saving your files, and then close the NP_AC_7_AnnualWellnessVisit.docx document and exit Word. You return to Access with the rptVisitsAndInvoices filtered report in Report view.
6. To the right of the records, click a blank area of the window to deselect the report records, and then, in the Sort & Filter group, click the **Toggle Filter** button. The filters are removed from the report.

Viewing and working with a report in Report view often helps you to identify adjustments and modifications you can make to the report to enhance its readability. You can make modifications to a report in Layout view and Design view.

PROSKILLS

Written Communication: Enhancing Reports Created by the Report Tool and the Report Wizard

Creating a report using the Report tool or the Report Wizard can save time, but you should review the report to determine if you need to make any of the following types of common enhancements and corrections:

- Change the report title from the report object name (with an rpt prefix and no spaces) to one that has meaning to the users.
- Reduce the widths of the date and page number controls, and move the controls so that they are not printed on a separate page.
- Review the report in Print Preview, and, if the report displays excess pages, adjust the page margins and the placement of controls.
- Verify that all controls are large enough to fully display their values.
- Use page margins and field widths that display equal margins to the left and right of the data.
- Use a layout for the fields that distributes the data in a balanced way across the report, and use the same spacing between all columns of data.
- The report and page titles can be centered on the page, but do not center the report data. Instead, use spacing between the columns and reasonable column widths to make the best use of the width of the page, extending the data from the left margin to the right margin.

By fine-tuning and correcting the format and layout of your reports, you ensure the report's information is clearly conveyed to users.

Donna has identified some changes she would like made to the rptVisitsAndInvoices report. Some of the report adjustments you need to make are subtle ones, so you need to carefully review all report controls to ensure the report is completely readable and usable for those using the report.

Modifying a Report in Layout View

You can make the report changes Donna wants in Layout view. Modifying a report in Layout view is similar to modifying a form in Layout view. When you open a report in Layout view, the Report Layout Tools Design, Arrange, Format, and Page Setup contextual tabs appear on the ribbon. You use the commands on these tabs to modify and format the elements of the report.

Donna wants you to decrease the width of columns and adjust the page margins in the report. She also wants you to rename some of the column headings, format the InvoiceAmt field values using the Standard format, resize the column headings, delete the picture from the Report Header section, remove the alternate row color from the detail and group header lines, and add a grand total of the InvoiceAmt field values. These changes will make the report more useful for Donna and her staff.

First, you will view the report in Layout view and observe how the information in the report is grouped and sorted.

To view the report in Layout view:

1. On the status bar, click the **Layout View** button, and then scroll to the top of the report (if necessary).
2. On the Report Layout Tools Design tab, in the Grouping & Totals group, click the **Group & Sort** button to open the Group, Sort, and Total pane at the bottom of the window. The Group & Sort button is a toggle button; you click this button to open and close this pane as needed. See Figure 7–4.

Figure 7–4 Viewing the report in Layout view

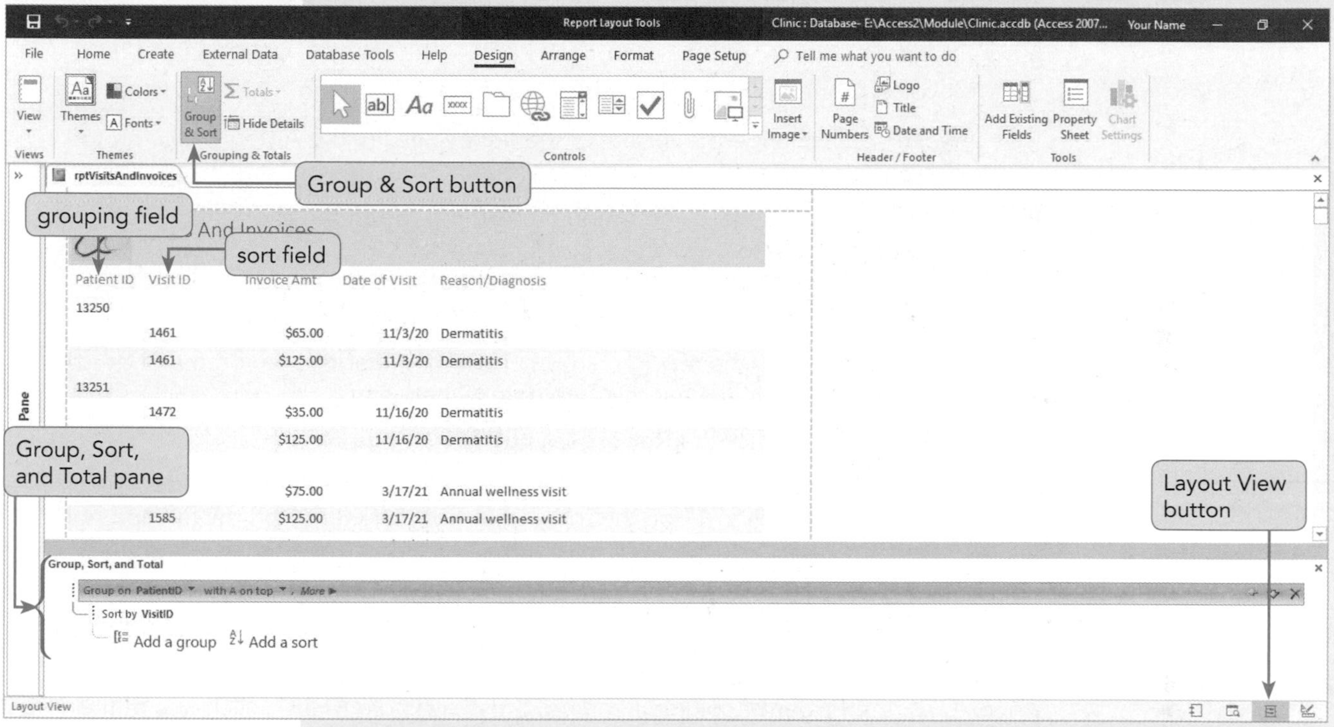
Group & Sort button
grouping field
sort field
Group, Sort, and Total pane
Layout View button
Patient ID
Visit ID
Invoice Amt
Date of Visit
Reason/Diagnosis
Group, Sort, and Total
Group on PatientID with A on top, More
Sort by VisitID
Add a group
Add a sort

The rptVisitsAndInvoices report has a grouping field (the PatientID field) and a sort field (the VisitID field). At the bottom of the window, the **Group, Sort, and Total pane** provides you with the options to modify the report's grouping fields and sort fields and the report calculations for the groups. A **grouping field** is a report sort field that includes a Group Header section before a group of records having the same sort field value and a Group Footer section after the group of records. These sections are defined with section bars in Design view. A Group Header section usually displays the group name and the sort field value for the group. A Group Footer section usually displays subtotals or counts for the records in that group. The rptVisitsAndInvoices report's grouping field is the PatientID field, which is displayed in a Group Header section that precedes the set of visits for the Patient; the grouping field does not have a Group Footer section. The VisitID field is a secondary sort key, as shown in the Group, Sort, and Total pane.

Because you don't need to change the grouping or sort fields for the report, you'll close the pane and then make Donna's modifications to the report.

3. In the Grouping & Totals group, click the **Group & Sort** button to close the Group, Sort, and Total pane.

Now that you have an understanding of how the information in the report is grouped and sorted, you are ready to make the modifications to the report Donna has requested. First, you'll change the column headings for the first three columns to Patient#, Visit#, and Amount. Donna prefers to see all the detail data on one line, even when it means abbreviating column headings for columns whose headings are wider than the data. After reducing the column headings, you'll reduce the column widths, freeing up space on the detail lines to widen the Reason/Diagnosis column.

To modify the columns in the report in Layout view:

1. Double-click the **Patient ID** column heading to change to editing mode, change it to **Patient#**, and then press **ENTER**.
2. Repeat Step 1 to change the Visit ID column heading to **Visit#** and the Invoice Amt heading to **Amount**.

   Next, you'll change the format of the field values in the Amount column to Standard.
3. Right-click any value in the Amount column to open the shortcut menu, click **Properties** to open the Property Sheet, set the Format property to **Standard**, and then close the Property Sheet. The Standard format uses comma separators and two decimal places, but no dollar signs.

   Now you'll widen the report margins. This will provide room on the printed page for staff to make handwritten notes if necessary.
4. On the ribbon, click the **Report Layout Tools Page Setup** tab.
5. In the Page Size group, click the **Margins** button, and then click **Wide**. This sets page margins to 1" on the top and bottom and 0.75" on the left and right.

   Sometimes when margins are decreased, some elements appear outside the margins, and this causes additional pages to be created in the report. This has occurred with the page number, and you'll fix that later. Now you'll adjust the widths of the columns to fit the data better.
6. Click the **Patient#** column heading, press and hold **SHIFT**, click one of the PatientID values in the column, and then release **SHIFT**. The Patient# column heading and all the values in this column are selected.
7. Position the pointer on the right border of the Patient# column heading selection box, and then when the pointer changes to the horizontal resize pointer ↔, drag the right border of the Patient# heading to the left until the border is just to the right of the # symbol in the column heading text. Now, you'll move the VisitID column to the left, closer to the Patient# column.
8. Click the **Visit#** column heading, press and hold **SHIFT**, click one of the VisitID values in the column, and then release **SHIFT**. The Visit# column heading and all the VisitID values in this column are selected.
9. Using the move pointer ✥, drag the **Visit#** column to the left, until it is positioned such that the left border of the Visit# column heading selection box aligns with the right edge of the image in the report header. The column does not appear to move until you release the mouse button.

   Trouble? If the window scrolls to the bottom of the report after you release the mouse button in the drag operation, scroll back to the top of the report.
10. Drag the right edge of the Visit# column to the left to fit the column heading and the VisitID values.

Now you'll resize and move the Amount heading and InvoiceAmt values to the left, closer to the VisitID column, and then you'll move the Date of Visit and Reason/Diagnosis columns to the left, closer to the Amount column.

11. Select the **Amount** column heading and the **InvoiceAmt** values in the column, and then drag the right border of the Amount column heading selection box to the left until it is positioned just to the right of the "t" in the column heading "Amount." The Amount column is resized to better fit the values in the column.

12. With the Amount column heading and the InvoiceAmt values still selected, drag the column heading to the left until the left border of its selection box aligns with the letter "A" in the word "And" in the report's title.

13. Select the **Date of Visit** column heading and the **VisitDate** values, and then resize and reposition the selected column heading and column of values as shown in Figure 7–5.

Figure 7–5 **Resized columns in Layout view**

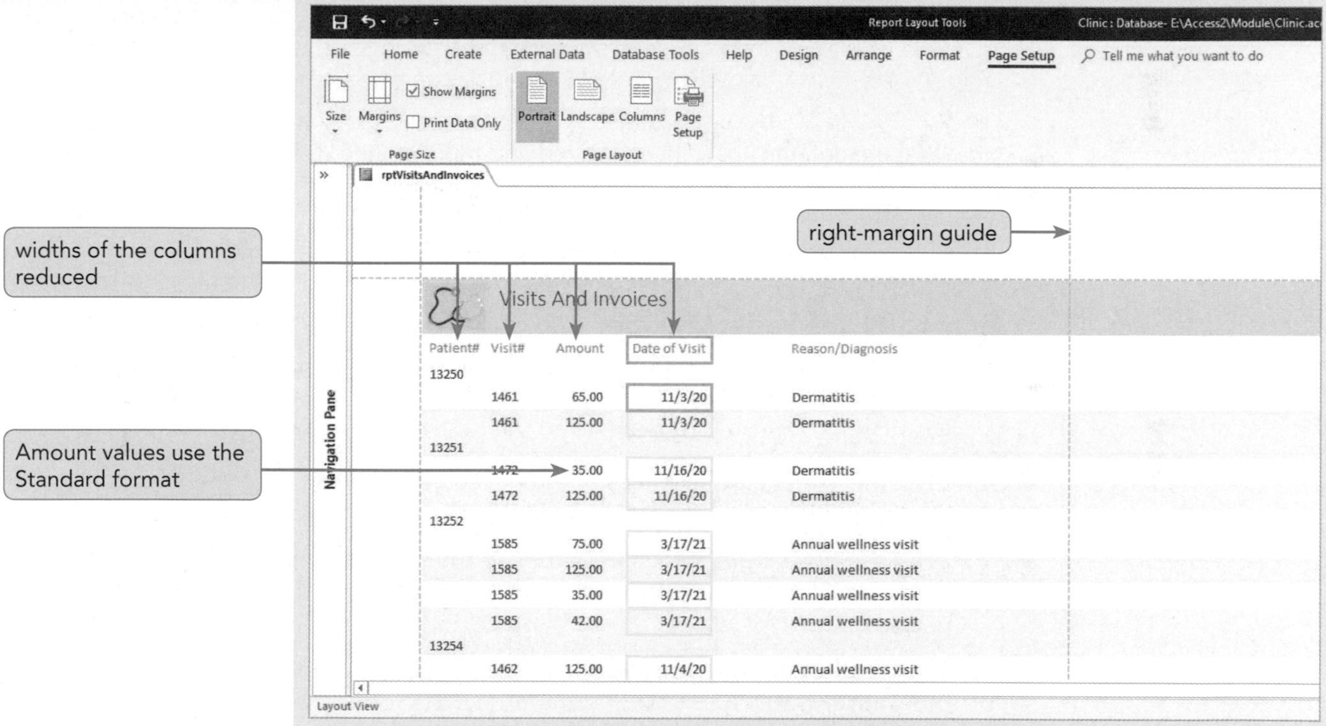
widths of the columns reduced
Amount values use the Standard format
right-margin guide
Report Layout Tools
File
Home
Create
External Data
Database Tools
Help
Design
Arrange
Format
Page Setup
Tell me what you want to do
Show Margins
Print Data Only
Size
Margins
Portrait
Landscape
Columns
Page Setup
Page Size
Page Layout
rptVisitsAndInvoices
Visits And Invoices
Patient#
Visit#
Amount
Date of Visit
Reason/Diagnosis
13250
1461
65.00
11/3/20
Dermatitis
1461
125.00
11/3/20
Dermatitis
13251
1472
35.00
11/16/20
Dermatitis
1472
125.00
11/16/20
Dermatitis
13252
1585
75.00
3/17/21
Annual wellness visit
1585
125.00
3/17/21
Annual wellness visit
1585
35.00
3/17/21
Annual wellness visit
1585
42.00
3/17/21
Annual wellness visit
13254
1462
125.00
11/4/20
Annual wellness visit
Navigation Pane
Layout View

Now you'll move the column for the Reason field to the left and resize it to better fit the data, aligning it with the page's right margin.

14. Select the **Reason/Diagnosis** column heading and field values, move them to the left, closer to the Date of Visit column, then resize the column heading and the column of values by dragging the right border of the selected items to the right margin of the report, as shown in Figure 7–6.

Figure 7–6 **Adjusted Reason/Diagnosis column width**

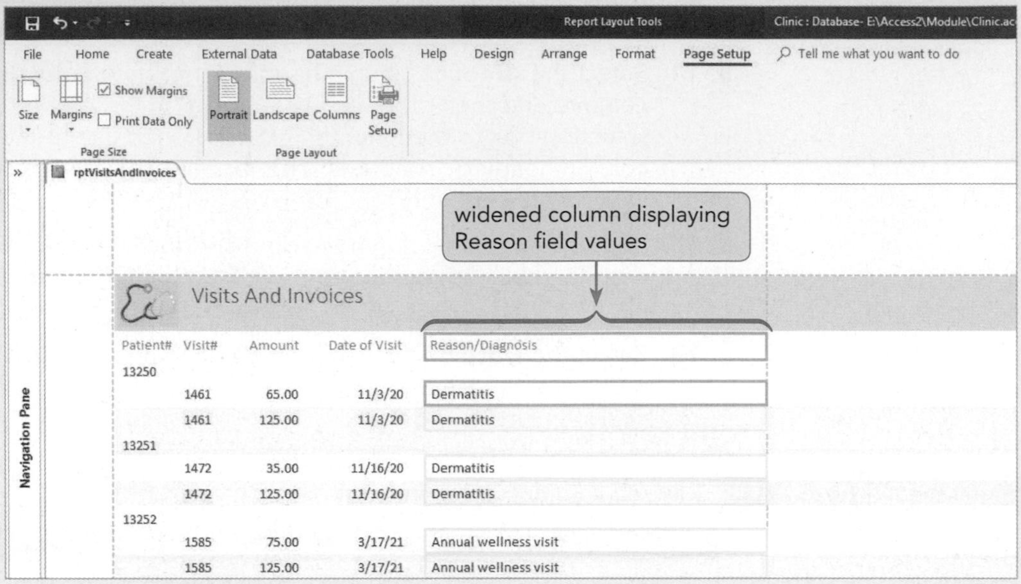
Report Layout Tools
Clinic : Database- E:\Access2\Module\Clinic.ac
File
Home
Create
External Data
Database Tools
Help
Design
Arrange
Format
Page Setup
Tell me what you want to do
Show Margins
Print Data Only
Size
Margins
Portrait
Landscape
Columns
Page Setup
Page Size
Page Layout
rptVisitsAndInvoices
Navigation Pane
widened column displaying Reason field values
Visits And Invoices
Patient#
Visit#
Amount
Date of Visit
Reason/Diagnosis
13250
1461
65.00
11/3/20
Dermatitis
1461
125.00
11/3/20
Dermatitis
13251
1472
35.00
11/16/20
Dermatitis
1472
125.00
11/16/20
Dermatitis
13252
1585
75.00
3/17/21
Annual wellness visit
1585
125.00
3/17/21
Annual wellness visit

Now that the columns have been resized and repositioned, Donna asks you to make adjustments to the report header, which contains a picture and the report's title. You'll also remove the alternate row color.

To modify the report header and row color:

1. If necessary, scroll to the top of the report, right-click the picture to the left of the report title to open the shortcut menu, and then click **Delete** to remove the picture.
2. Click the **Visits And Invoices** title to select it, and then drag the title to the left to position its left selection border at the left-margin guide.
3. Drag the title's right selection border to the right to position it at the right-margin guide to increase the width of the title box to the full width of the page.
4. Click the **Report Layout Tools Format** tab, and then in the Font group, click the **Center** button to center the title in the report header.

   Donna finds the alternate row color setting in the group header and detail lines distracting, and asks you to remove this formatting.
5. To the left of the first PatientID value in the first column, click to the left of the left-margin guide to select the group headers.
6. In the Background group, click the **Alternate Row Color** arrow to display the gallery of available colors, and then at the bottom of the gallery, click **No Color**. The alternate row color is removed from the PatientID group header rows.

   You've removed the alternate row color from the PatientID values in the report, and next you'll remove the alternate row color from the detail lines. Because the Alternate Row Color button is now set to "No Color," you can just click the button to remove the color.

7. Next to the first VisitID in the first PatientID record detail line, click to the left of the left-margin guide and then in the Background group, click the **Alternate Row Color** button to remove the alternate row color from the detail lines.

Donna's last change to the report is to add a grand total for the Amount field values. First, you must select the Amount column or one of the values in the column.

To add a grand total to the report in Layout view:

1. In the first detail line for VisitID 1461, click **65.00** in the Amount column. The values in this column are all selected.

2. Click the **Report Layout Tools Design** tab, and then in the Grouping & Totals group, click the **Totals** button to display the Totals menu. See Figure 7–7.

Figure 7–7 The Totals menu

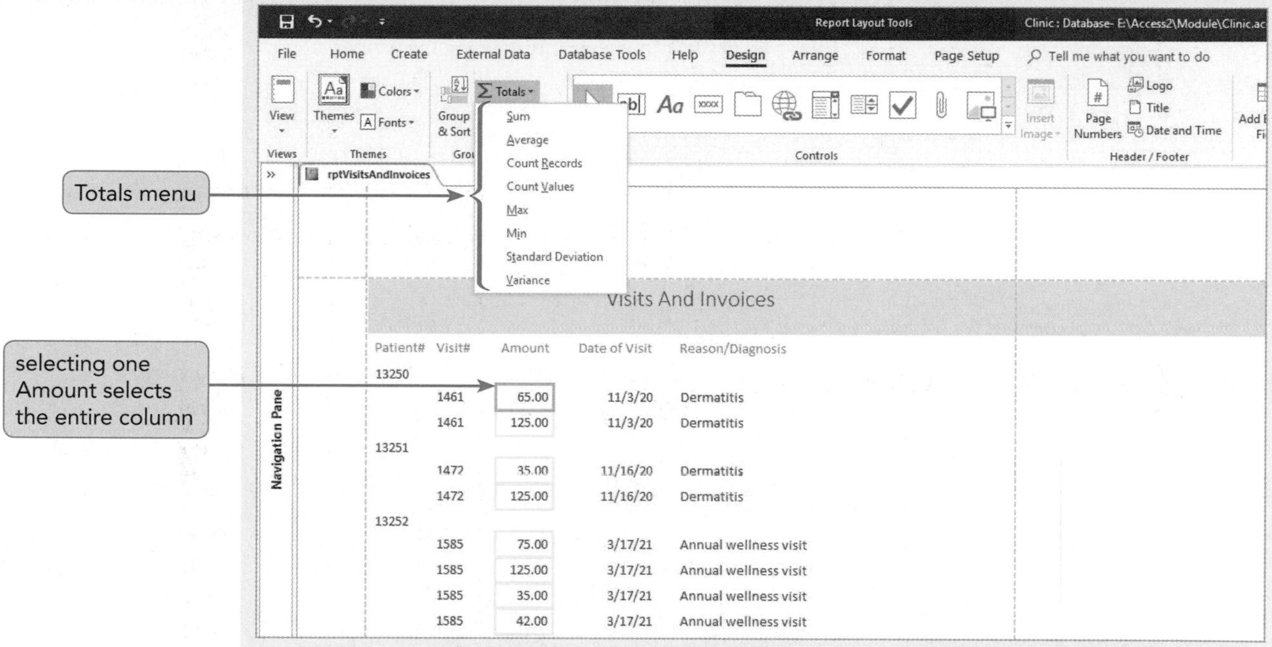
Totals menu
selecting one Amount selects the entire column
Report Layout Tools
Clinic : Database- E:\Access2\Module\Clinic.ac
File
Home
Create
External Data
Database Tools
Help
Design
Arrange
Format
Page Setup
Tell me what you want to do
Totals
Sum
Average
Count Records
Count Values
Max
Min
Standard Deviation
Variance
rptVisitsAndInvoices
Visits And Invoices
Patient# Visit# Amount Date of Visit Reason/Diagnosis
13250
1461 65.00 11/3/20 Dermatitis
1461 125.00 11/3/20 Dermatitis
13251
1472 35.00 11/16/20 Dermatitis
1472 125.00 11/16/20 Dermatitis
13252
1585 75.00 3/17/21 Annual wellness visit
1585 125.00 3/17/21 Annual wellness visit
1585 35.00 3/17/21 Annual wellness visit
1585 42.00 3/17/21 Annual wellness visit
Navigation Pane

You can select one of the eight aggregate functions on the Totals menu to summarize values in the selected column. To calculate and display the grand total visit amount, you'll select the Sum aggregate function.

3. Click **Sum** in the Totals menu, scroll to the bottom of the report, and then if the last value in the Amount column displays as ######## instead of numbers, click **########** to select it, then drag the left selection border of the selected value to the left until the grand total of 22,223.00 is displayed.

Notice subtotals for each group of visits are displayed for each PatientID field value (355.00 for the last patient). See Figure 7–8.

Trouble? If the field value box still contains ###### after you resize it, increase the width again until the grand total value of 22,223.00 is visible.

Figure 7–8 **Report showing subtotals and a grand total of the InvoiceAmt field values**

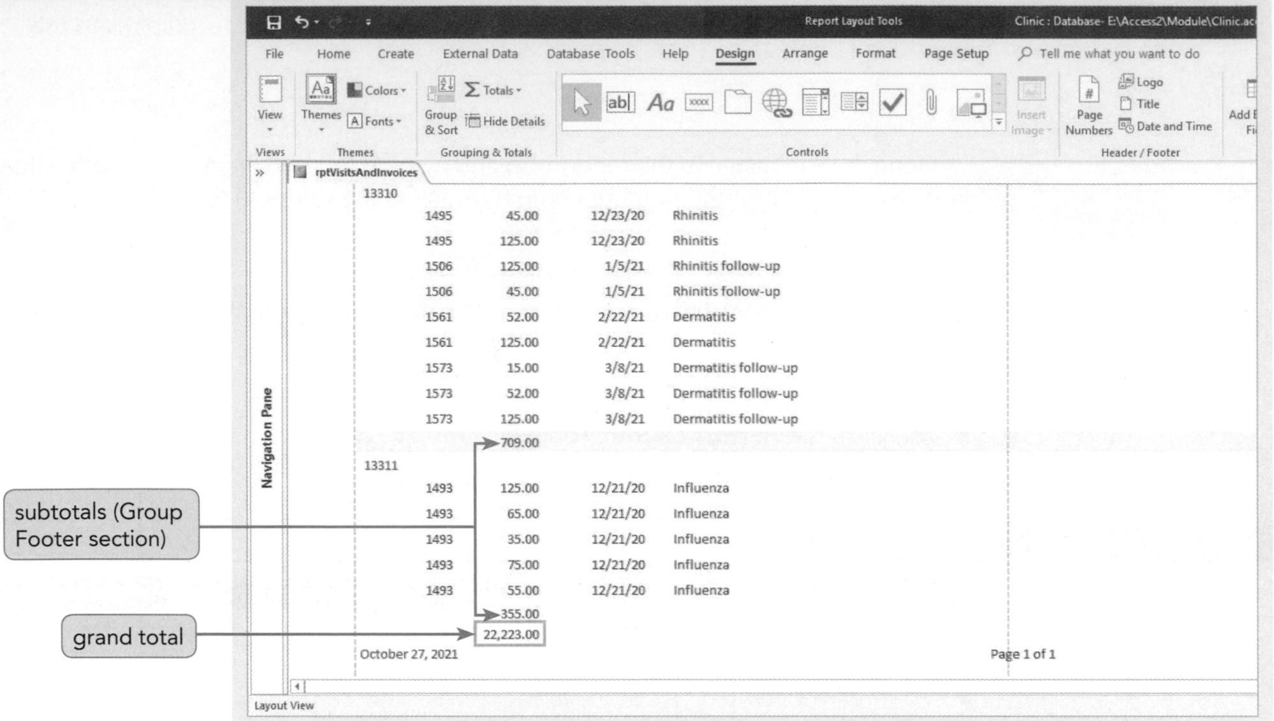

Report Layout Tools
Clinic : Database- E:\Access2\Module\Clinic.ac
File
Home
Create
External Data
Database Tools
Help
Design
Arrange
Format
Page Setup
Tell me what you want to do
View
Themes
Colors
Fonts
Group & Sort
Totals
Hide Details
Logo
Title
Date and Time
Insert Image
Page Numbers
Views
Themes
Grouping & Totals
Controls
Header / Footer
rptVisitsAndInvoices
Navigation Pane
13310
1495 45.00 12/23/20 Rhinitis
1495 125.00 12/23/20 Rhinitis
1506 125.00 1/5/21 Rhinitis follow-up
1506 45.00 1/5/21 Rhinitis follow-up
1561 52.00 2/22/21 Dermatitis
1561 125.00 2/22/21 Dermatitis
1573 15.00 3/8/21 Dermatitis follow-up
1573 52.00 3/8/21 Dermatitis follow-up
1573 125.00 3/8/21 Dermatitis follow-up
709.00
13311
1493 125.00 12/21/20 Influenza
1493 65.00 12/21/20 Influenza
1493 35.00 12/21/20 Influenza
1493 75.00 12/21/20 Influenza
1493 55.00 12/21/20 Influenza
355.00
22,223.00
October 27, 2021
Page 1 of 1
Layout View
subtotals (Group Footer section)
grand total

When you select an aggregate function in Layout view, the results of the function are added to the end of the report, and subtotals for each grouping field are also added. Because some patients have few visits, Donna asks you to remove the subtotals from the report.

4. Right-click the **355.00** subtotal for the last record to open the shortcut menu, click **Delete** to remove the subtotals, and then scroll to the end of the report. You deleted the subtotals, but the grand total still appears at the end of the report.

   Donna wants to review the rptVisitsAndInvoices report in Print Preview.

5. Save your report changes, switch to Print Preview, and then use the navigation buttons to page through the report. Viewing the report in Print Preview allows you to identify possible problems that might occur when you print the report. For example, as you navigate through the report, notice that every other page is blank, with just the page number appearing in the footer.

6. Navigate to the second to last page of the report that shows the grand total line, and then click the **Zoom In** button [+] on the status bar to increase the zoom percentage to 110%. See Figure 7–9.

Figure 7–9 **The rptVisitsAndInvoices report in Print Preview**

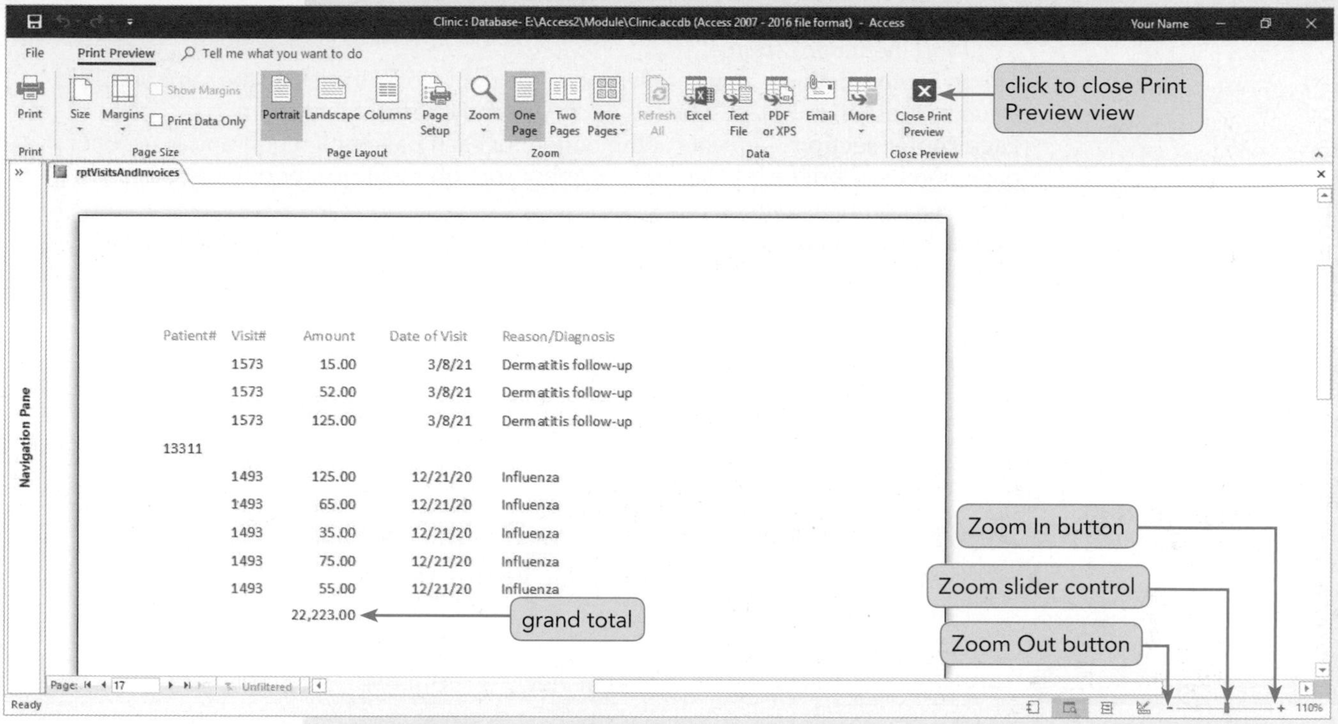
click to close Print Preview view
Zoom In button
Zoom slider control
Zoom Out button
grand total

Trouble? Depending on the printer you are using, the last page of your report might differ. If so, don't worry. Different printers format reports in different ways, sometimes affecting the total number of pages and the number of records printed per page.

7. On the status bar, click the **Zoom Out** button [−] to decrease the zoom percentage to 100%, and close the Print Preview view and display the report in Layout view.

As you saw in Print Preview, the page numbers are outside the right margin and are causing extra pages in the report. Therefore, you need to reposition the page number that appears at the bottom of each page. Donna suggests you move the page number box to the left so that its right edge is aligned with the right edge of Reason field value box in the Detail section, thereby eliminating the extra pages in the report. She also wants you to add a line below the column heading labels. Although you can make Donna's modifications in Layout view, you'll make them in Design view so you can work more precisely.

Modifying a Report in Design View

Design view for reports is similar to Design view for forms, which you used in the previous module to customize forms. When you open a report in Design view, the Report Design Tools contextual tabs—Design, Arrange, Format, and Page Setup—appear on the ribbon,

A report in Design view is divided into seven sections:

- **Report Header section**—appears once at the beginning of a report and is used for report titles, company logos, report introductions, dates, visual elements such as lines, and cover pages.
- **Page Header section**—appears at the top of each page of a report and is used for page numbers, column headings, report titles, and report dates.

- **Group Header section**—appears before each group of records that share the same sort field value, and usually displays the group name and the sort field value for the group.
- **Detail section**—contains the bound controls to display the field values for each record in the record source.
- **Group Footer section**—appears after each group of records that share the same sort field value, and usually displays subtotals or counts for the records in that group.
- **Page Footer section**—appears at the bottom of each page of a report and is used for page numbers, brief explanations of symbols or abbreviations, or other information such as a company name.
- **Report Footer section**—appears once at the end of a report and is used for report totals and other summary information.

As Donna requested, you need to move the page number in the report, and you need to insert a line below the column headings. To do this, you will work in Design view to move the page number control in the Page Footer section to the left and then create a line control below the column headings in the Page Header.

To view and modify the report in Design view:

1. Switch to Design view, and click the **Report Design Tools Design** tab, if necessary. See Figure 7–10.

Figure 7–10 rptVisitsAndInvoices report in Design view

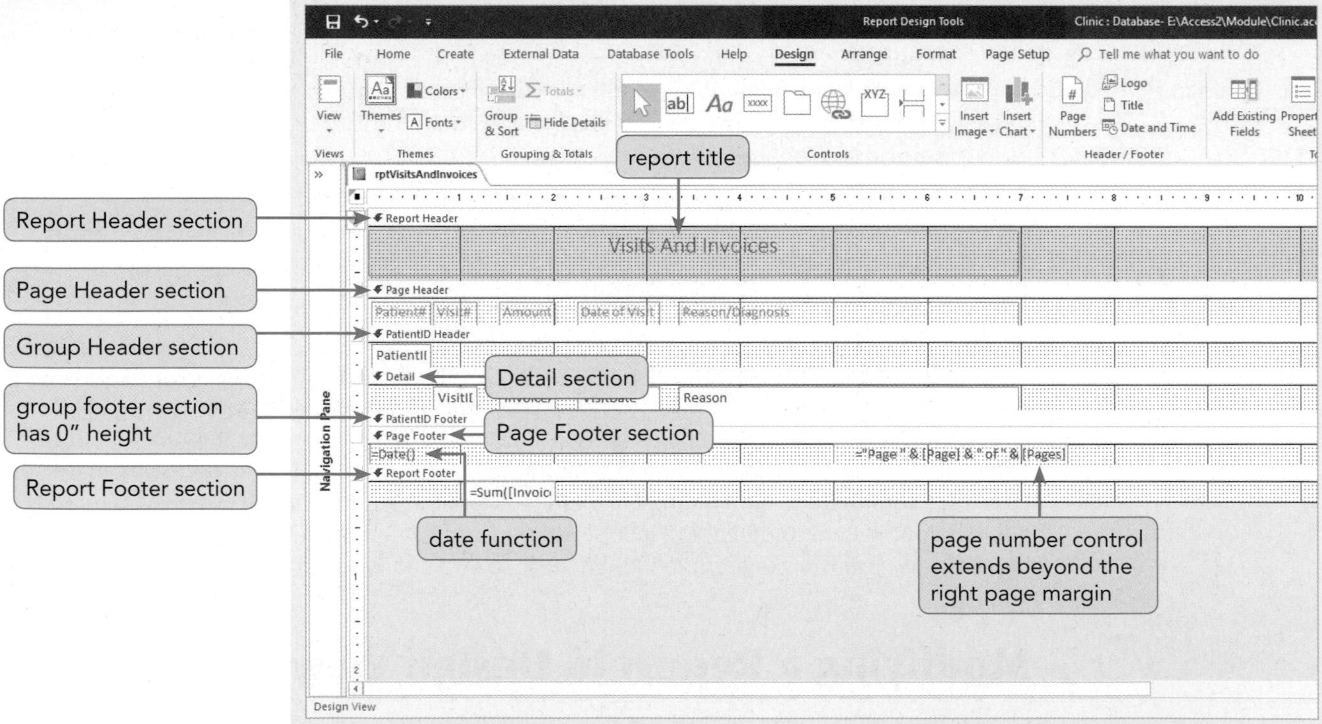
report title
Report Header section
Page Header section
Group Header section
Detail section
group footer section has 0" height
Page Footer section
Report Footer section
date function
page number control extends beyond the right page margin
Visits And Invoices
=Date()
="Page " & [Page] & " of " & [Pages]
=Sum([Invoic

Notice that Design view for a report has most of the same components as Design view for a form. For example, Design view for forms and reports includes horizontal and vertical rulers, grids in each section, and similar buttons in the groups on the Report Design Tools Design tab.

Design view for the rptVisitsAndInvoices report displays seven sections: the Report Header section contains the report title; the Page Header section contains the column heading labels; the Group Header section (PatientID Header) contains the PatientID grouping field; the Detail section contains the bound controls to display the field values for each record in the record source (tblVisit); the Group Footer section (PatientID Footer) isn't displayed in the report; the Page Footer section contains the current date and the page number; and the Report Footer section contains the Sum function, which calculates the grand total of the InvoiceAmt field values.

You will now move the page number control in the Page Footer section so that it is within the report's right page margin. To guide you in this, recall you earlier resized and repositioned the Reason/Diagnosis column in Layout view so it aligned to the right margin of the page. Therefore, you will right-align the page number control to the Reason field value box in the Detail section.

2. Click the **Page Number** control to select it (the control on the right side of the Page Footer section), and then press ← to move the control to the left until the right border of its selection box is roughly aligned with the right edge of the Reason field value control box in the Detail section.

   Trouble? If the page number control overlaps the date control in the Report Footer section, don't worry about it. The contents of both will still be displayed.

3. With the Page Number control still selected, press and hold **SHIFT**, click the **Reason** field value control box in the Detail section, and then release **SHIFT**. Both controls are now selected.

4. Right-click one of the selected controls, point to **Align** on the shortcut menu, and then click **Right**. Both controls are now right-aligned.

   Finally, you'll create the line in the Page Header section.

5. Drag the bottom border of the Page Header section down to increase the height approximately half an inch. You'll resize this again after the line is created.

6. On the Report Design Tools Design tab, in the Controls group, click the **More** button, and then click the **Line** tool.

7. In the Page Header section, position the plus symbol of the Line tool pointer approximately two grid dots below the column header boxes, press and hold **SHIFT**, drag to the right page margin, and then release **SHIFT** to create a horizontal line that spans the width of the page. Holding SHIFT while drawing or extending a line snaps the line to either horizontal or vertical—whichever is nearest to the angle at which the line is drawn.

8. If necessary, drag the lower edge of the Page Header section up so it is approximately two grid dots below the line. See Figure 7–11.

Figure 7–11 **Modified report in Design view**

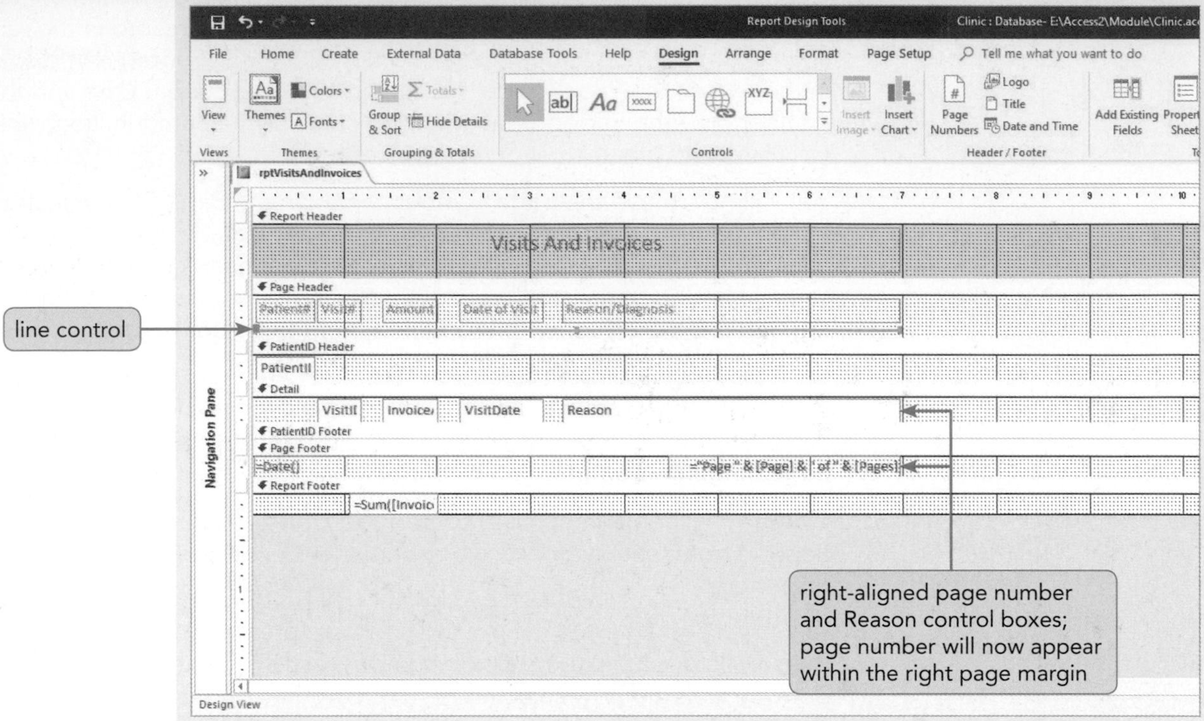
line control
right-aligned page number and Reason control boxes; page number will now appear within the right page margin

9. Save your report changes, switch to Print Preview, and then scroll and use the navigation buttons to page through the report, paying particular attention to the placement of the line in the Page Header section and the page number in the Page Footer section. The page number is right-aligned in the control box, so the text appears flush with the right margin. The data in the Reason field value text boxes are left-aligned, so this data does not appear flush with the right margin.

   Trouble? If you resize a field to position it outside the current margin, the report may widen to accommodate it, triggering a dialog box about the section width being greater than the page width. If this dialog box opens, click OK, manually move form elements as necessary so that no elements extend past 7 inches, and then adjust the report width to 7 inches.

   Trouble? If you position all report elements within the margins and still receive a message about the section width being greater than the page width, click OK, then click the Form Selector button where the rulers intersect, click the Error Checking Options button, and then on the menu, click Remove Extra Report Space.

10. Save and close the report.
11. If you are not continuing on to the next session, close the Clinic database.

Donna is happy with the changes you've made to the rptVisitsAndInvoices report. In the next session, you create a new custom report for her based on queries instead of tables.

REVIEW

Session 7.1 Quick Check

1. What is a custom report?
2. Can a report be modified in Layout view?
3. Besides viewing a report, what other actions can you perform in Report view?
4. What is a grouping field?
5. List and describe the seven sections of an Access report.

Session 7.2 Visual Overview:

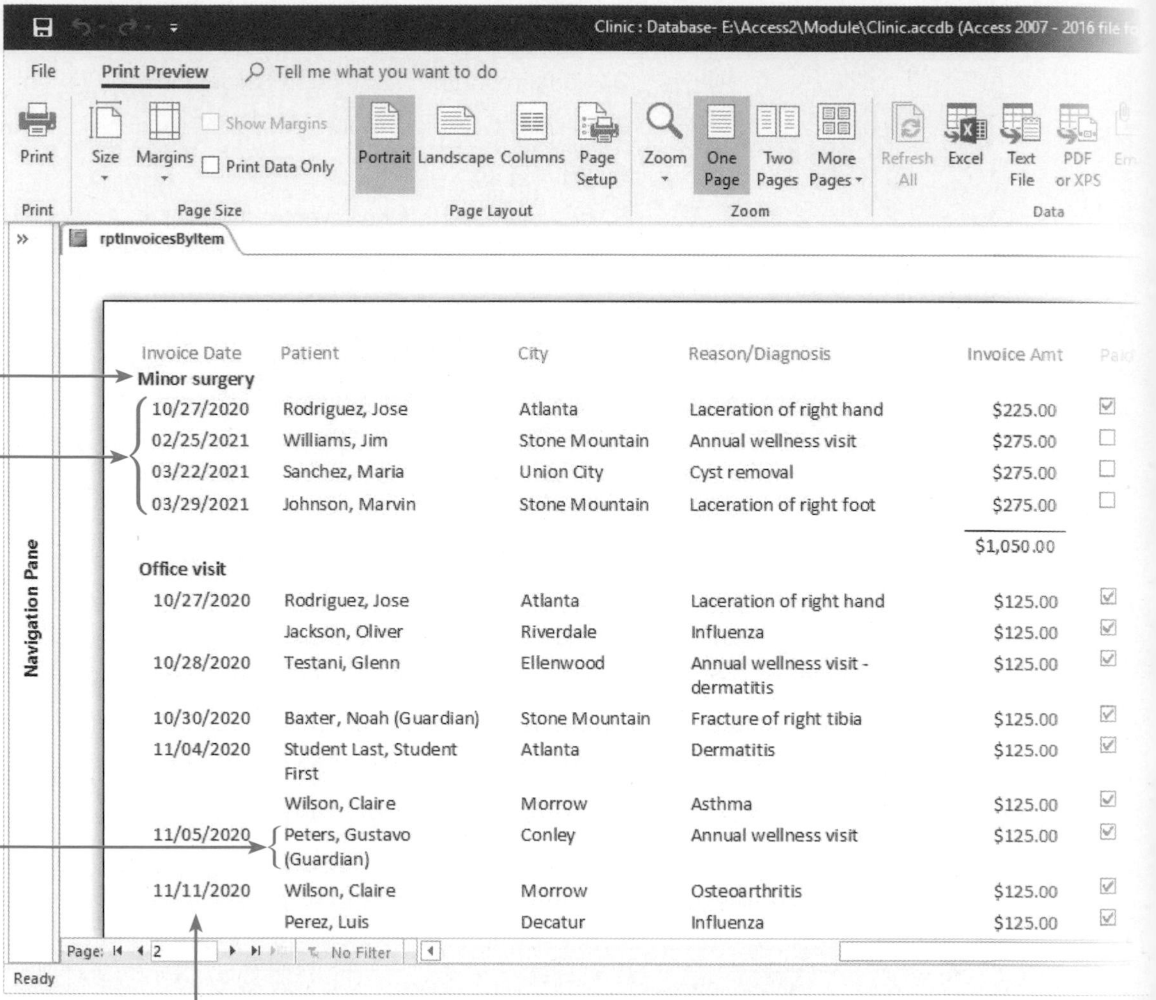
Clinic : Database- E:\Access2\Module\Clinic.accdb (Access 2007 - 2016 file
File
Print Preview
Tell me what you want to do
Print
Size
Margins
Show Margins
Print Data Only
Portrait
Landscape
Columns
Page Setup
Zoom
One Page
Two Pages
More Pages
Refresh All
Excel
Text File
PDF or XPS
Print
Page Size
Page Layout
Zoom
Data
rptInvoicesByItem
Navigation Pane
Invoice Date
Patient
City
Reason/Diagnosis
Invoice Amt
Minor surgery
10/27/2020 Rodriguez, Jose Atlanta Laceration of right hand $225.00
02/25/2021 Williams, Jim Stone Mountain Annual wellness visit $275.00
03/22/2021 Sanchez, Maria Union City Cyst removal $275.00
03/29/2021 Johnson, Marvin Stone Mountain Laceration of right foot $275.00
$1,050.00
Office visit
10/27/2020 Rodriguez, Jose Atlanta Laceration of right hand $125.00
Jackson, Oliver Riverdale Influenza $125.00
10/28/2020 Testani, Glenn Ellenwood Annual wellness visit - dermatitis $125.00
10/30/2020 Baxter, Noah (Guardian) Stone Mountain Fracture of right tibia $125.00
11/04/2020 Student Last, Student First Atlanta Dermatitis $125.00
Wilson, Claire Morrow Asthma $125.00
11/05/2020 Peters, Gustavo (Guardian) Conley Annual wellness visit $125.00
11/11/2020 Wilson, Claire Morrow Osteoarthritis $125.00
Perez, Luis Decatur Influenza $125.00
Page: 2
No Filter
Ready

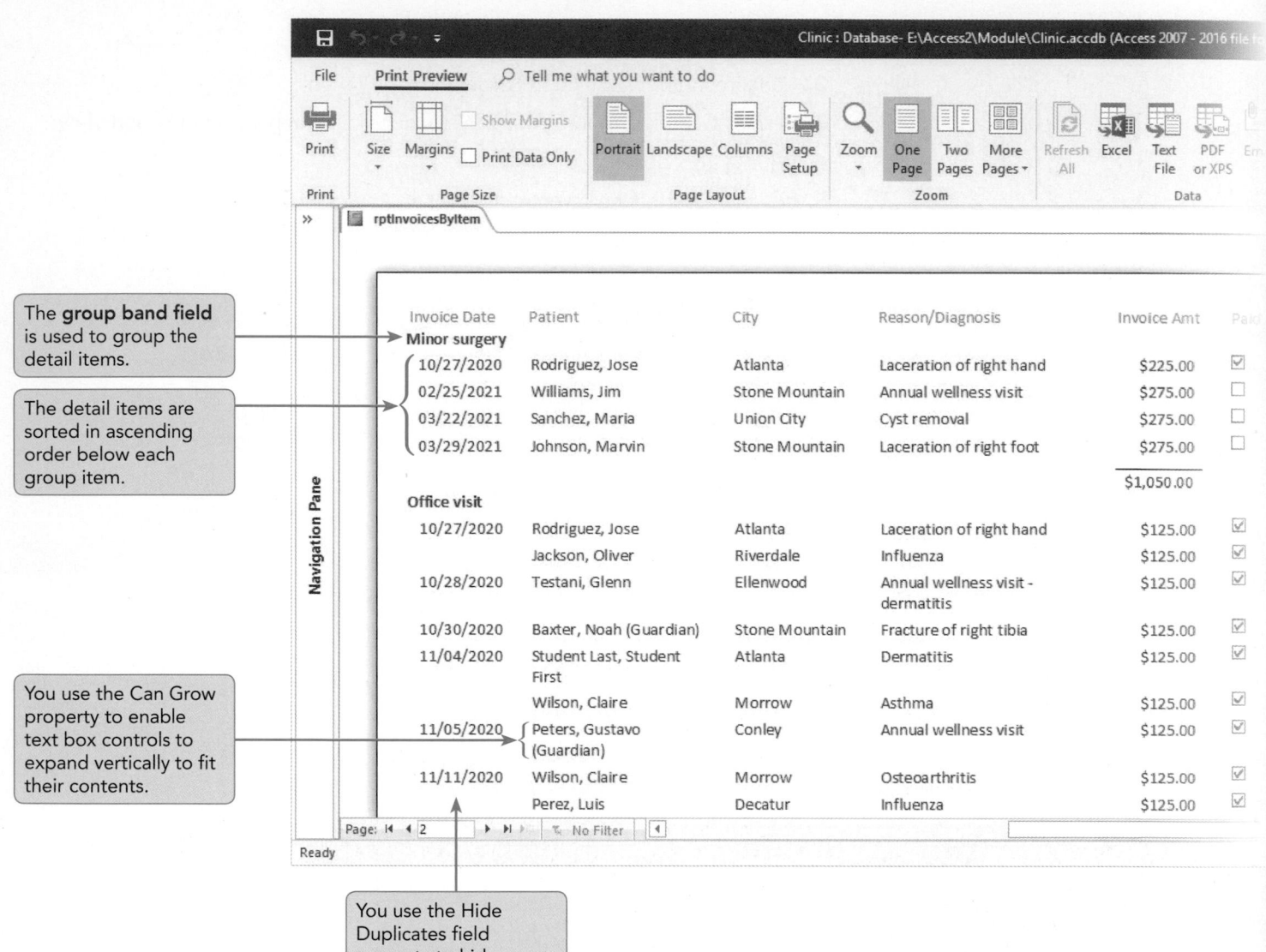

The **group band field** is used to group the detail items.

The detail items are sorted in ascending order below each group item.

You use the Can Grow property to enable text box controls to expand vertically to fit their contents.

You use the Hide Duplicates field property to hide duplicate field values.

Form in Design View and Print Preview

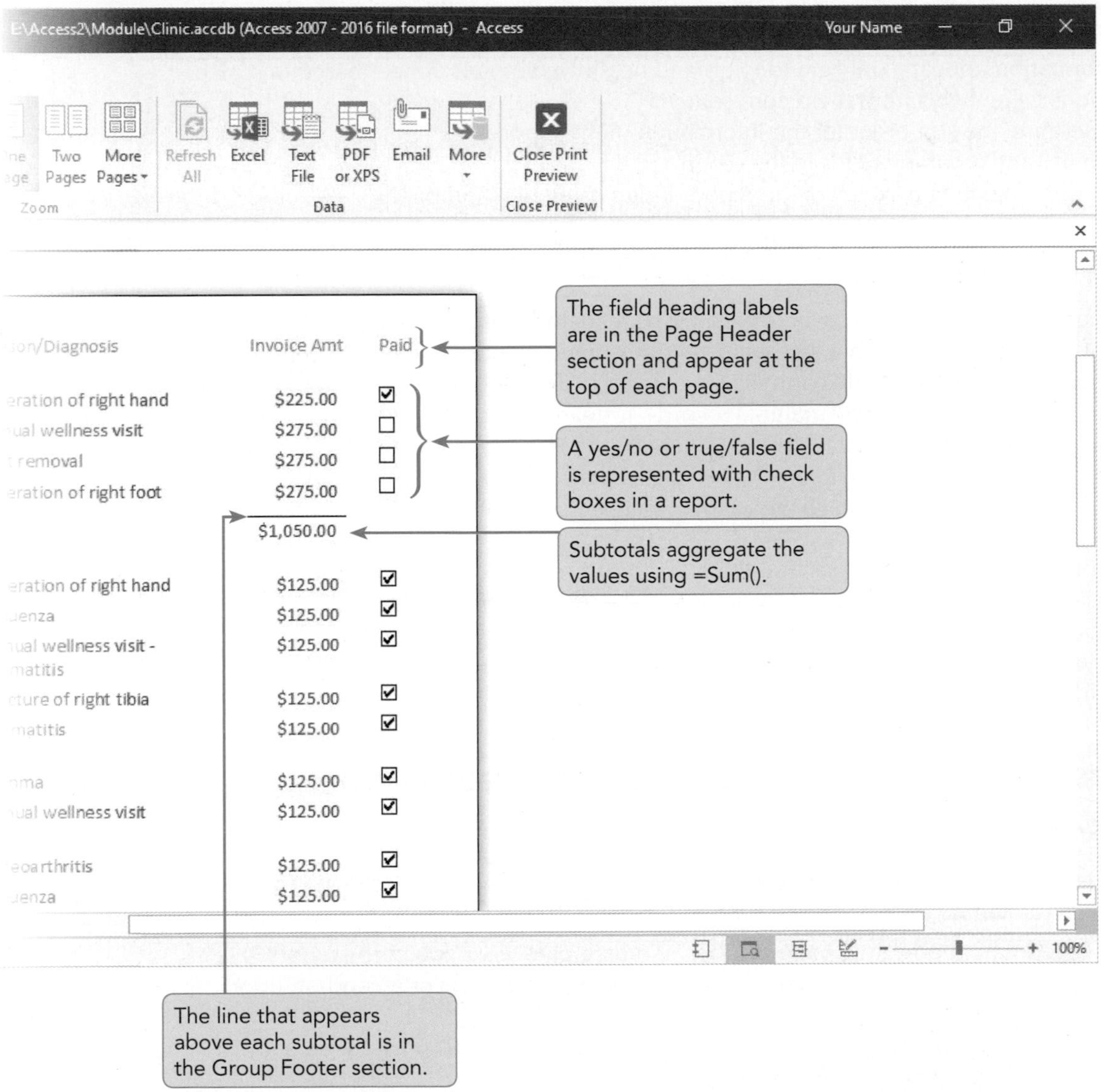
E:\Access2\Module\Clinic.accdb (Access 2007 - 2016 file format) - Access
Your Name
Two Pages
More Pages
Refresh All
Excel
Text File
PDF or XPS
Email
More
Close Print Preview
Zoom
Data
Close Preview
Invoice Amt
Paid
$225.00
$275.00
$275.00
$275.00
$1,050.00
$125.00
100%
The field heading labels are in the Page Header section and appear at the top of each page.
A yes/no or true/false field is represented with check boxes in a report.
Subtotals aggregate the values using =Sum().
The line that appears above each subtotal is in the Group Footer section.

Planning and Designing a Custom Report

Before you create a custom report, you should first plan the report's contents and its layout. When you plan a report, you should follow this general process:

- Determine the purpose of the report and its record source. Recall that the record source is a table or query that provides the fields for a report. If the report displays detailed information (a **detail report**), such as a list of all visits, then the report will display fields from the record source in the Detail section. If the report displays only summary information (a **summary report**), such as total visits by city, then no detailed information appears; only grand totals and possibly subtotals appear based on calculations using fields from the record source.
- Determine the sort order for the information in the report.
- Identify any grouping fields in the report.
- Consider creating a sketch of the report design using pen and paper.

At the same time you are planning a report, you should keep in mind the following layout guidelines:

- Balance the report's attractiveness against its readability and economy. Keep in mind that an attractive, readable, two-page report is more economical than a report of three pages or more. Unlike forms, which usually display one record at a time in the main form, reports display multiple records. Instead of arranging fields vertically as you do in a form, you usually position fields horizontally across the page in a report. Typically, you set the detail lines to be single-spaced in a report. At the same time, make sure to include enough white space between columns so the values do not overlap or run together.
- Group related fields and position them in a meaningful, logical order. For example, position identifying fields, such as names and codes, on the left. Group together all location fields, such as street and city, and position them in their customary order.
- Identify each column of field values with a column heading label that names the field.

PROSKILLS

Written Communication: Formatting a Report

The formatting of a report impacts its readability. Keep in mind the following guidelines when formatting a report:

- Include the report title, page number, and date on every page of the report.
- Identify the end of a report either by displaying grand totals or an end-of-report message.
- Use only a few colors, fonts, and graphics to keep the report uncluttered and to keep the focus on the information.
- Use a consistent style for all reports in a database.

By following these report-formatting guidelines, you'll create reports that make it easier for users to conduct their daily business and to make better decisions.

After working with Donna and her staff to determine their requirements for a new report, Reginald prepared a design for a custom report to display invoices grouped by invoice item. Refer to the Session 7.2 Visual Overview, which details Reginald's custom report design in Print Preview.

The custom report will list the records for all invoices and will contain five sections:

- The Page Header section will contain the report title ("Invoices by Item") centered between the current date on the left and the page number on the right. A horizontal line will separate the column heading labels from the rest of the report page. From your work with the Report Wizard, you know that, by default, Access places the report title in the Report Header section and the date and page number in the Page Footer section. Donna prefers that the date, report title, and page number appear at the top of each page, so you need to place this information in the custom report's Page Header section.

- The InvoiceItem field value from the tblInvoiceItem table will be displayed in a Group Header section.
- The Detail section will contain the InvoiceDate, InvoiceAmt, and InvoicePaid field values from the tblBilling table; the Reason field value from the tblVisit table; the PatientName field value from the tblPatient table; and the Patient calculated field value from the qryPatientsByName query. The detail records will be sorted in ascending order by the InvoiceDate field.
- A subtotal of the InvoiceAmt field values will be displayed below a line in the Group Footer section.
- The grand total of the InvoiceAmt field values will be displayed below a double line in the Report Footer section.

Before you start creating the custom report, you need to create a query that will serve as the record source for the report.

Creating a Query for a Custom Report

TIP

Create queries to serve as the record source for forms and reports. As requirements change, you can easily add fields, including calculated fields, to the queries.

As you know, the data for a report can come from a single table, from a single query based on one or more tables, or from multiple tables and/or queries. Donna's report will contain data from the tblInvoiceItem, tblBilling, tblVisit, and tblPatient tables, and from the qryPatientsByName query. You'll use the Simple Query Wizard to create a query to retrieve all the data required for the custom report and to serve as the report's record source. A query filters data from one or more tables using criteria that can be quite complex. Creating a report based on a query allows you to display and distribute the results of the query in a readable, professional format, rather than only in a datasheet view.

To create the query to serve as the custom report's record source:

1. If you took a break after the previous session, make sure that the Clinic database is open and the Navigation Pane is closed.
2. On the ribbon, click the **Create** tab.
3. In the Queries group, click the **Query Wizard** button to open the New Query dialog box, make sure **Simple Query Wizard** is selected, and then click the **OK** button. The first Simple Query Wizard dialog box opens.

   You need to select fields from the tblInvoiceItem, tblBilling, tblVisit, and tblPatient tables and from the qryPatientsByName query, in that order.
4. In the Tables/Queries box, select **Table: tblInvoiceItem**, and then move the **InvoiceItem** field from the Available Fields box to the Selected Fields box.
5. In the Tables/Queries box, select **Table: tblBilling**, and then move the **InvoiceItemID**, **InvoiceDate**, **InvoiceAmt**, and **InvoicePaid** fields, in that order, from the Available Fields box to the Selected Fields box.
6. In the Tables/Queries box, select **Table: tblVisit**, and then move the **Reason** field from the Available Fields box to the Selected Fields box.
7. In the Tables/Queries box, select **Table: tblPatient**, and then move the **City** field from the Available Fields box to the Selected Fields box.
8. In the Tables/Queries box, select **Query: qryPatientsByName**, move the **Patient** calculated field from the Available Fields box to the Selected Fields box, and then click the **Next** button.

9. Make sure the **Detail (shows every field of every record)** option button is selected, and then click the **Next** button to open the final Simple Query Wizard dialog box.

10. Change the query name to **qryInvoicesByItem**, click the **Modify the query design** option button, and then click the **Finish** button. The query is displayed in Design view.

Next you need to set the sort fields for the query. The InvoiceItem field will be a grouping field, which means it's the primary sort field, and the InvoiceDate field is the secondary sort field.

To set the sort fields for the query:

1. In the design grid, set the value in the InvoiceItem Sort box to **Ascending** and then set the value in the InvoiceDate Sort box to **Ascending**.

2. Lengthen the query and table field lists as necessary to view all fields, drag the tables if necessary to position them so the join lines between them are visible, and then save your query changes. The completed query contains eight fields from four tables and one query, and the query includes two sort fields, the InvoiceItem primary sort field and the InvoiceDate secondary sort field. See Figure 7–12.

Figure 7–12 Completed qryInvoicesByItem query in Design View

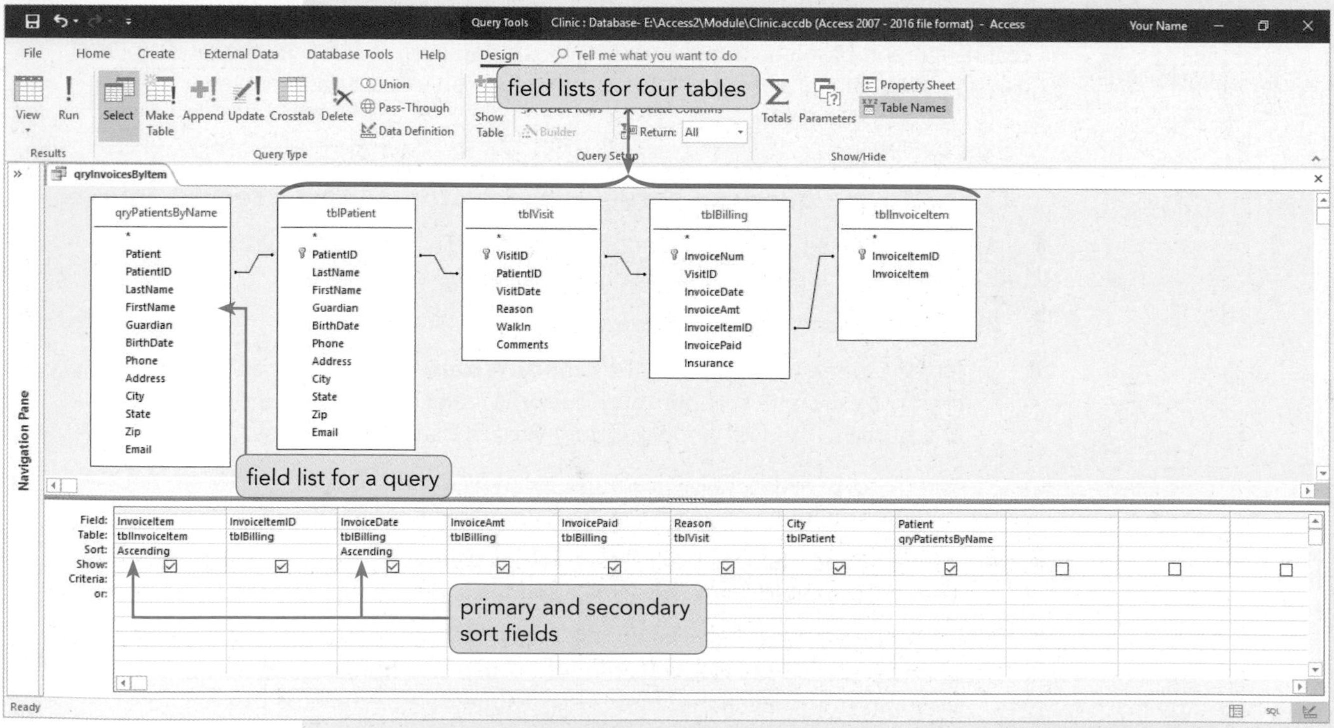
field lists for four tables
field list for a query
primary and secondary sort fields
qryPatientsByName
tblPatient
tblVisit
tblBilling
tblInvoiceItem

3. If necessary, click the **Query Tools Design** tab, run the query, verify that it returns 204 records, and then save and close the query.

You'll use the qryInvoicesByItem query as the record source for the custom report.

Creating a Custom Report

Now that you've created the record source for the custom report, you could use the Report Wizard to create the report and then modify it to match the report design. However, because you need to customize several components of the report, you will create a custom report in Layout view and then switch between Layout and Design view to fine-tune the report.

INSIGHT

Making Report Design Modifications

You perform operations in Layout and Design views for reports in the same way that you perform operations in these views for forms. These operations become easier with practice. Remember to use the Undo button when necessary, back up your database frequently, save your report changes frequently, work from a copy of the report for complicated design changes, and compact and repair the database on a regular basis. You can also display the report in Print Preview at any time to view your progress on the report.

You'll create a blank report in Layout view, set the record source, and then add controls to the custom report.

To create a blank report and add bound controls in Layout view:

1. Click the **Create** tab, and then in the Reports group, click the **Blank Report** button. A new report opens in Layout view, with the Field List pane open, and the Report Layout Tools Design tab active on the ribbon. See Figure 7–13.

Figure 7–13 **Blank report in Layout view**

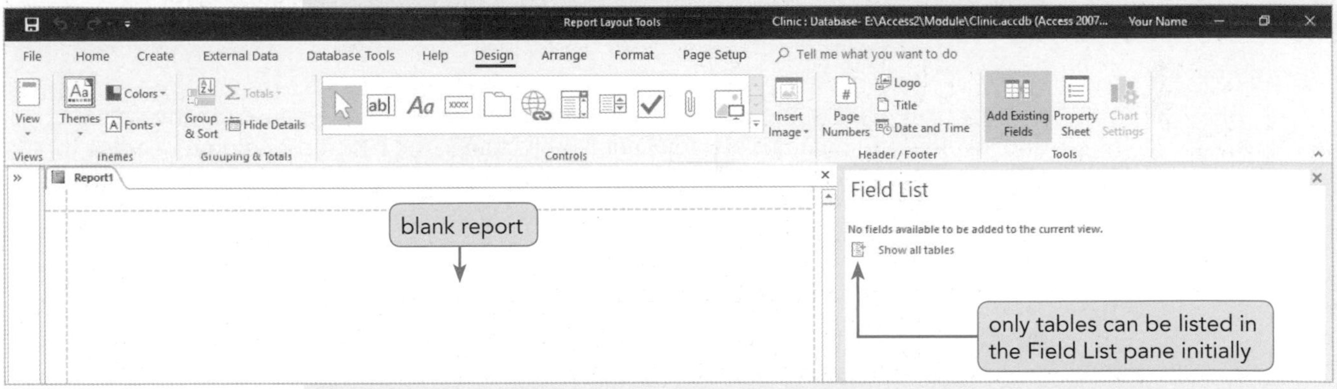
blank report
only tables can be listed in the Field List pane initially
Field List
No fields available to be added to the current view.
Show all tables

2. In the Tools group, click the **Property Sheet** button to open the Property Sheet for the report.
3. In the Property Sheet, click the **All** tab (if necessary), click the **Record Source** arrow, click **qryInvoicesByItem**, and then close the Property Sheet.
4. In the Tools group, click the **Add Existing Fields** button to open the Field List pane. The Field List pane displays the eight fields in the qryInvoicesByItem query, which is the record source for the report.

   Referring to Reginald's report design, you'll add six of the eight fields to the report in a tabular layout, which is the default control layout when you add fields to a report in Layout view.

5. In the Field List pane, double-click **InvoiceItem**, and then, in order, double-click **InvoiceDate**, **Patient**, **City**, **Reason**, **InvoiceAmt**, and **InvoicePaid** in the Field List pane. The six bound controls are displayed in a tabular layout in the report. See Figure 7–14.

Figure 7–14 After adding fields to the report in Layout view

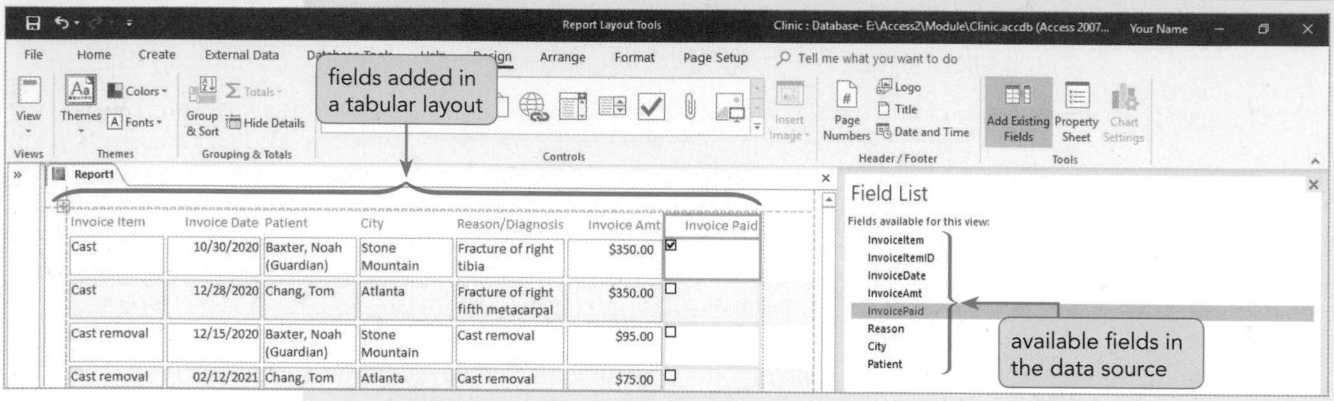
fields added in a tabular layout
available fields in the data source

Trouble? If you add the wrong field to the report, click the field's column heading, press and hold SHIFT, click one of the field values in the column to select the column, release SHIFT, click the Home tab on the ribbon, and then in the Records group, click the Delete button to delete the field. If you add a field in the wrong order, click the column heading in the tabular layout, press and hold SHIFT, click one of the field values in the column, release SHIFT, and then drag the column to its correct position.

You are done working with the Field List pane.

6. Close the Field List pane, and then save the report as **rptInvoicesByItem**.

Next, you'll adjust the column widths in Layout view. Also, because the Invoice Amt and Invoice Paid columns are adjacent, you'll change the rightmost column heading to "Paid" to save space.

To resize and rename columns in Layout view:

1. In the rightmost column, double-click **Invoice Paid**, delete **Invoice** and the following space, and then press **ENTER**.
2. Drag the right border of the Paid column heading selection box to the left to decrease the column's width so it just fits the column heading.
3. Repeat Step 2 to resize the InvoiceDate and InvoiceAmt columns.
4. Click the **Patient** column heading to select the column, and then drag the right edge of the selection box to the right to increase its width, until it accommodates the contents of all data in the column. (You might need to scroll through the report to ensure all Patient field values are visible.)
5. Repeat Step 4 to resize the Invoice Item, City, and Reason columns, if necessary, as shown in Figure 7–15. You'll fine-tune the adjustments and the spacing between columns later in Design view.

Figure 7–15 **Resized and renamed columns in Layout view**

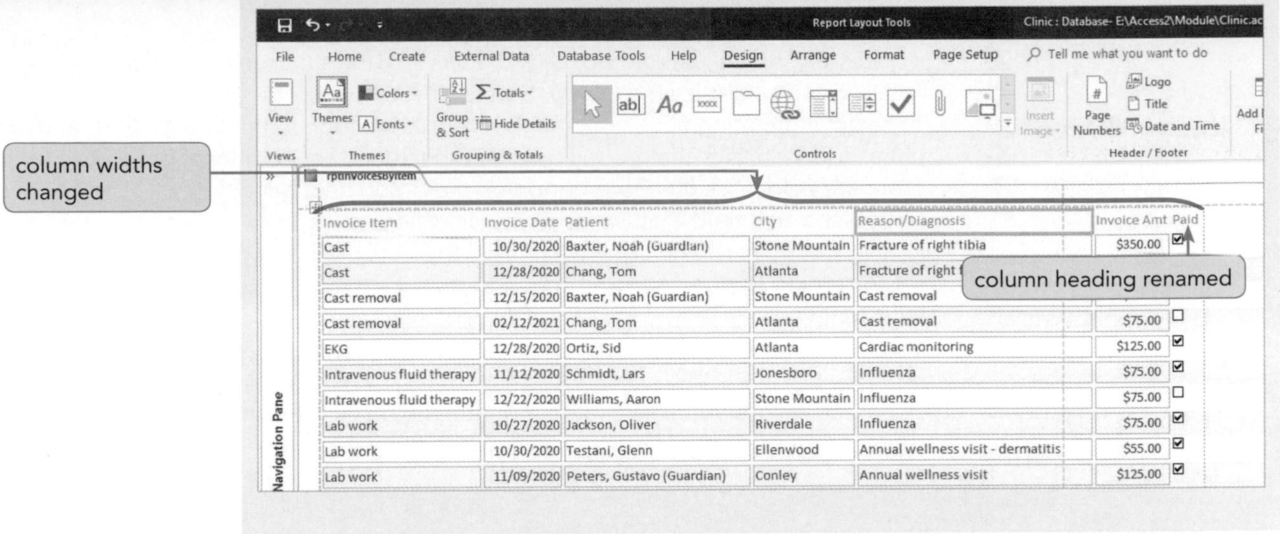
column widths changed
column heading renamed

Next you need to add the sorting and grouping data to the report.

Sorting and Grouping Data in a Report

In Access, you can organize records in a report by sorting them using one or more sort fields. Each sort field can also be a grouping field. If you specify a sort field as a grouping field, you can include a Group Header section and a Group Footer section for the group. A Group Header section typically includes the name of the group, and a Group Footer section typically includes a count or subtotal for records in that group. Some reports have a Group Header section but not a Group Footer section, some reports have a Group Footer section but not a Group Header section, and some reports have both sections or have neither section.

You use the Group, Sort, and Total pane to select sort fields and grouping fields for a report. Each report can have up to 10 sort fields, and any of its sort fields can also be grouping fields.

In Reginald's report design, the InvoiceItem field is a grouping field, and the InvoiceDate field is a sort field. The InvoiceItem field value is displayed in a Group Header section, but the InvoiceItem field label is not displayed. The sum of the InvoiceAmt field values is displayed in the Group Footer section for the InvoiceItem grouping field.

REFERENCE

Sorting and Grouping Data in a Report

- Display the report in Layout view or Design view.
- If necessary, on the Design tab, click the Group & Sort button in the Grouping & Totals group to display the Group, Sort, and Total pane.
- To select a grouping field, click the Add a group button in the Group, Sort, and Total pane, and then click the grouping field in the list. To set additional properties for the grouping field, click the More button on the group field band.
- To select a sort field that is not a grouping field, click the Add a sort button in the Group, Sort, and Total pane, and then click the sort field in the list. To set additional properties for the sort field, click the More button on the sort field band.

Next, in the report, you'll select the grouping field and the sort field and set their properties.

To select and set the properties for the grouping field and the sort field:

1. Switch to Design view, and then click the **Report Design Tools Design** tab, if necessary.
2. In the Grouping & Totals group, click the **Group & Sort** button to open the Group, Sort, and Total pane at the bottom of the Report window.
3. In the Group, Sort, and Total pane, click the **Add a group** button, and then click **InvoiceItem** in the list. An empty Group Header section is added to the report, and group band options appear in the Group, Sort, and Total pane for this section.

Be sure to click the Add a group button and not the Add a sort button.

4. In the Detail section, right-click the **InvoiceItem** text box control, point to **Layout**, then click **Remove Layout**.
5. With the InvoiceItem control still selected, press **CTRL+X** to cut the control and move it to the Clipboard, click the **InvoiceItem Header** bar, then press **CTRL+V** to paste the control into the Group Header. InvoiceItem is now a bound control in the report in a Group Header section that displays a field value box.
6. In the Page Header section, right-click the **InvoiceItem** label control, then click **Delete** on the shortcut menu. See Figure 7–16.

Figure 7–16 InvoiceItem set as a grouping field in Design view

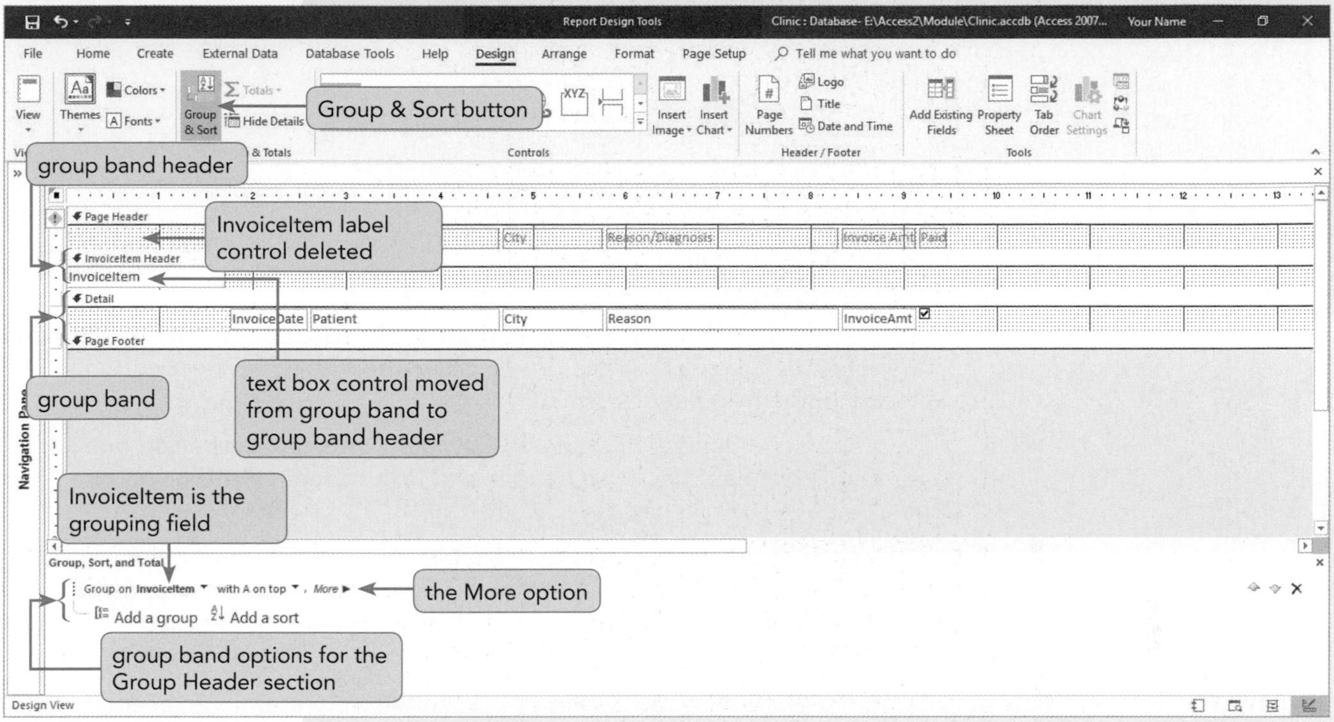
Group & Sort button
group band header
InvoiceItem label control deleted
group band
text box control moved from group band to group band header
InvoiceItem is the grouping field
the More option
group band options for the Group Header section

7. In the Group, Sort, and Total pane, click the **Group on InvoiceItem** group band to select it.

   The group band options in the Group, Sort, and Total pane contain the name of the grouping field (InvoiceItem), the sort order ("with A on top" to indicate ascending), and the More button, which you click to display more options for the grouping field. You can click the "with A on top" arrow to change to descending sort order ("with Z on top").

   Reginald's design specifies an additional ascending sort on the InvoiceDate field. Next, you'll select this field as a secondary sort field; the InvoiceItem grouping field is the primary sort field.

8. In the Group, Sort, and Total pane, click the **Add a sort** button, and then click **InvoiceDate** in the list. A sort band is added for the InvoiceDate field in the Group, Sort, and Total pane.

   Next, you'll display all the options for the InvoiceItem group band field and set group band options as shown in Reginald's report design.

9. In the Group, Sort, and Total pane, click **Group on InvoiceItem**, and then click the **More** button to display all group band options in an orange bar at the top of the Group, Sort, and Total pane. See Figure 7–17.

Figure 7–17 Expanded group band

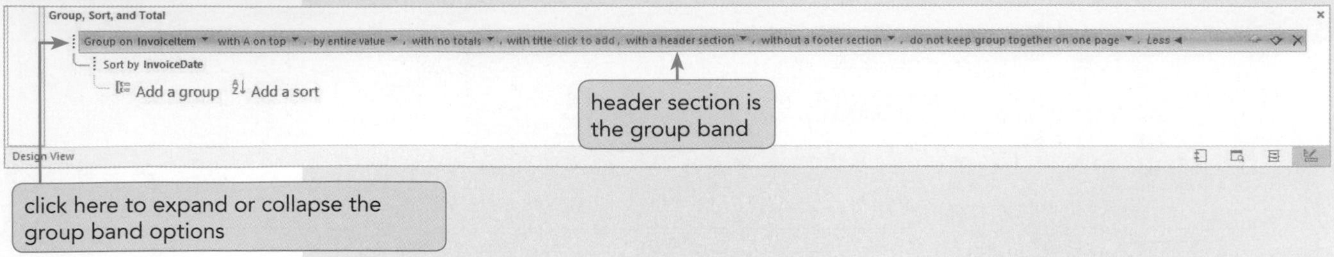
Group, Sort, and Total
Group on InvoiceItem with A on top, by entire value, with no totals, with title click to add, with a header section, without a footer section, do not keep group together on one page, Less
Sort by InvoiceDate
Add a group
Add a sort
header section is the group band
Design View
click here to expand or collapse the group band options

Next you'll set the Keep Together property. The **Keep Together property** prints a group header on a page only if there is enough room on the page to print the first detail record for the group; otherwise, the group header prints at the top of the next page.

10. In the group band options, click the **do not keep group together on one page** arrow, and then click **keep header and first record together on one page**.
11. In the group band options, click the **More** button to expand the options (if necessary), click the **without a footer section** arrow, and then click **with a footer section**. A Group Footer section is added to the report for the InvoiceItem grouping band field, but the report will not display this new section until you add controls to it.
12. In the group band options, click the **More** button to expand the options (if necessary), click the **with no totals** arrow to open the Totals menu, click the **Total On** arrow, click **InvoiceAmt**, make sure **Sum** is selected in the Type box, click the **Show Grand Total** check box, click the **Show subtotal in group footer** check box, and then click a blank area of the report window to close the menu. This adds subtotals in the Amount column, at the bottom of each group.
13. In the group band options, click the **More** button to expand the options (if necessary). The group band options show the InvoiceAmt subtotals and a grand total added to the report. See Figure 7–18.

Figure 7–18 Completed properties in the group band

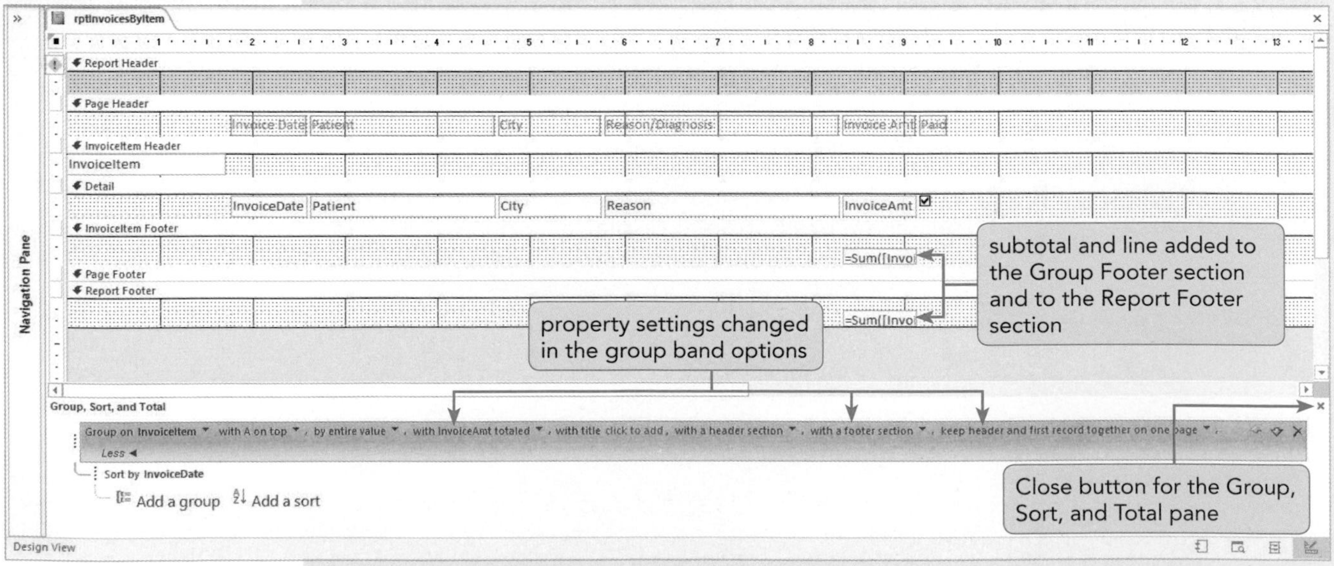
rptInvoicesByItem
Report Header
Page Header
Invoice Date Patient City Reason/Diagnosis Invoice Amt Paid
InvoiceItem Header
InvoiceItem
Detail
InvoiceDate Patient City Reason InvoiceAmt
InvoiceItem Footer
=Sum([Invo
Page Footer
Report Footer
=Sum([Invo
subtotal and line added to the Group Footer section and to the Report Footer section
property settings changed in the group band options
Navigation Pane
Group, Sort, and Total
Group on InvoiceItem with A on top, by entire value, with InvoiceAmt totaled, with title click to add, with a header section, with a footer section, keep header and first record together on one page, Less
Sort by InvoiceDate
Add a group
Add a sort
Close button for the Group, Sort, and Total pane
Design View

14. Save your report changes, switch to Print Preview, and then use the navigation buttons to review each page until you reach the end of the report—noticing in particular the details of the report format and the effects of the Keep Together property. Also, notice that because of the space left by the grouping field after you moved it, the current report design prints the detail values across two pages.

Before you can move the detail values to the left onto one page, you need to remove all controls from the control layout.

To remove controls from a control layout in Design view:

1. Switch to Design view.
2. Click the layout selector [icon], which is located at the upper-left corner of the Page Header section, to select the entire control layout. An orange selection border, which identifies the controls that you've selected, appears around the labels and field value boxes in the report.
3. Right-click one of the selected controls to open the shortcut menu, point to **Layout**, and then click **Remove Layout**. This removes the selected controls from the layout so they can be moved individually without affecting the other controls.

   Next you'll move all the controls to the left except for the InvoiceItem field value box. You have to be careful when you move the remaining controls to the left. If you try to select all the column headings and the field value boxes, you're likely to miss the subtotal and grand total controls. The safest technique is to select all controls in the report, and then remove the InvoiceItem field value box from the selection.
4. Click the **Report Design Tools Format** tab, and then in the Selection group click the **Select All** button. All controls in the report are now selected.
5. Press and hold **SHIFT**, click the **InvoiceItem** control box in the InvoiceItem Header section to remove this control from the selection, and then release **SHIFT**.
6. Press and hold ← to move the selected controls rapidly to the left edge of the report, and then release ←. See Figure 7–19.

Figure 7–19 Controls repositioned in the report

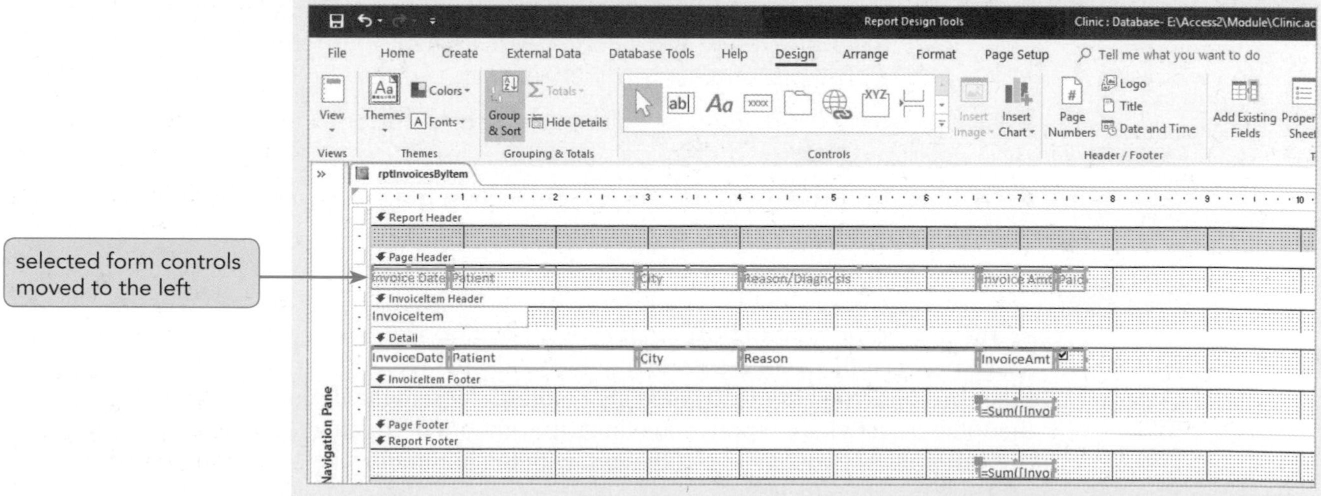
selected form controls moved to the left
Report Design Tools
rptInvoicesByItem
Report Header
Page Header
Invoice Date
Patient
City
Reason/Diagnosis
Invoice Amt
Paid
InvoiceItem Header
InvoiceItem
Detail
InvoiceDate
Patient
City
Reason
InvoiceAmt
InvoiceItem Footer
=Sum([Invo
Page Footer
Report Footer
=Sum([Invo
Navigation Pane

The grand total of the InvoiceAmt field values is displayed at the end of the report, and subtotals are displayed for each unique InvoiceItem field value in the Group Footer section. It's possible for subtotals to appear in an orphaned footer section.

An **orphaned footer section** appears by itself at the top of a page, and the detail lines for the section appear on the previous page. When you set the Keep Together property for the grouping field, you set it to keep the group and the first detail record together on one page to prevent an **orphaned header section**, which is a section that appears by itself at the bottom of a page. To prevent both types of orphaned sections, you'll set the Keep Together property to keep the whole group together on one page.

In addition, you need to fine-tune the sizes of the field value boxes in the Detail section, adjust the spacing between columns, and make other adjustments to the current content of the report design before adding a report title, the date, and page number to the Page Header section. You'll make most of these report design changes in Design view.

Working with Controls in Design View

As you learned when working with forms, Design view gives you greater control over the placement and sizing of controls than you have in Layout view and lets you add and manipulate many more controls; however, this power comes at the expense of not being able to see live data in the controls to guide you as you make changes.

The rptInvoicesByItem report has five sections that contain controls: the Page Header section contains the six column heading labels; the InvoiceItem Header section (a Group Header section) contains the InvoiceItem field value box; the Detail section contains the six bound controls; the InvoiceItem Footer section (a Group Footer section) contains a line and the subtotal control; and the Report Footer section contains a line and the grand total control.

You'll format, move, and resize controls in the report in Design view. The Group, Sort, and Total pane is still open, so first you'll change the Keep Together property setting.

To set the report size:

1. In the Group, Sort, and Total pane, click the **More** button to display all group options, click the **keep header and first record together on one page** arrow, click **keep whole group together on one page**, and then click the **Close** button [X] in the upper-right corner of the Group, Sort, and Total pane to close it.

   You'll start improving the report by setting the InvoiceItem label control to bold.

2. Select the **InvoiceItem** text box in the InvoiceItem Header section, and then on the Report Design Tools Format tab, in the Font group, click the **Bold** button. The placeholder text in the InvoiceItem text box is displayed in bold.
3. Select the Page Setup tab, click the **Margins** button, and then if necessary click the **Narrow** button.
4. If the report area is wider than eight inches, drag the right border of any report section to the 8-inch mark on the horizontal ruler.

TIP

To copy formatting from one control to another, select the control whose format you want to copy, click the Format Painter tool on the Form Design Tools Format tab, and then click another control to apply the copied formatting.

The field value control boxes in the Detail section are crowded together with little space between them. Your reports shouldn't have too much space between columns, but reports are easier to read when the columns are separated more than they are in the rptInvoicesByItem report. Sometimes the amount of spacing is dictated by the users of the report, but you also need to work with the minimum size of the form controls as well. To design this report to fit on a page with narrow margins, the report width will have to be 8.5 inches minus the left and right margins of 0.25 inches each, which results in a maximum report width of 8 inches (8.5″–0.25″–0.25″). This is the size you already applied to your report. Next you'll add some space between the columns while ensuring they still fit in the 8-inch report width. First, you'll resize the Invoice Date, Patient, and Reason columns, and then you'll arrange the columns. You'll size the corresponding heading and field value boxes for each column to be the same width.

To move and resize controls in the report:

1. In the Page Header section, click the **Invoice Date** column heading, press and hold **SHIFT**, and then in the Detail section, click the **Invoice Date** control.
2. Drag the right side of the controls to the left to approximately the 3/4-inch mark on the ruler.
3. Switch to Layout view. The date values are displayed as a series of # symbols because the controls are too narrow to display them. It's often more efficient to resize controls to fit data in Layout view because you can instantly see whether the new size is appropriate for the data.
4. Click the **Invoice Date** column heading, press and hold **SHIFT**, and then click one of the **Invoice Date** field values to select all of the Invoice Date field values boxes.
5. Drag the right side of the controls to the right to increase the size of the field value boxes to fit the values and the heading text.
6. Click the Group Header text **Cast** at the top of the first page of the report to select all of the group header controls, then if necessary drag the right side of the control to the right until the text of the fourth group header, Intravenous fluid therapy, is fully visible. Intravenous fluid therapy is the longest group header in the report.
7. Switch to Design view, then Repeat Steps 1 and 2 to resize the Patient column heading and field values so the right edge is at the 2.5-inch mark on the ruler, and to resize the Reason column heading and field values so the right edge is at the 6-inch mark on the ruler. Reginald's design calls for the widths of these two items to be set to sizes that are narrower than their longest values, but you'll adjust formatting later to ensure that all contents are visible. See Figure 7–20.

TIP

You can resize labels and controls added with the Label tool using the To Fit command, but you can't resize field value boxes using the To Fit method.

Figure 7–20 Labels and controls resized in Design View

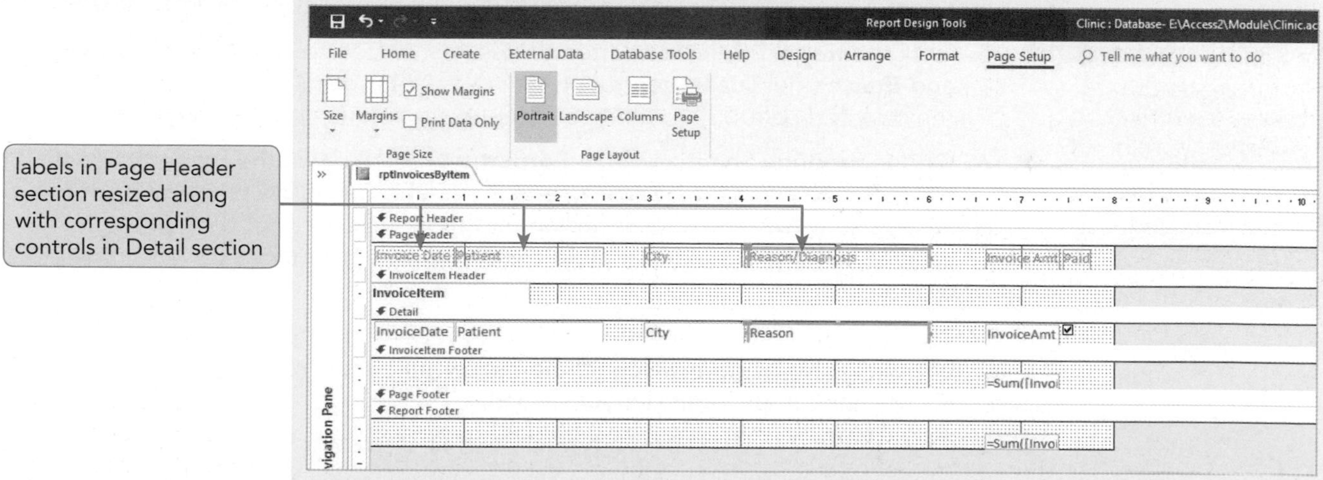
labels in Page Header section resized along with corresponding controls in Detail section
Report Design Tools
File
Home
Create
External Data
Database Tools
Help
Design
Arrange
Format
Page Setup
Tell me what you want to do
Show Margins
Print Data Only
Size
Margins
Portrait
Landscape
Columns
Page Setup
Page Size
Page Layout
rptInvoicesByItem
Report Header
Page Header
Invoice Date
Patient
City
Reason/Diagnosis
Invoice Amt
Paid
InvoiceItem Header
InvoiceItem
Detail
InvoiceDate
Patient
City
Reason
InvoiceAmt
InvoiceItem Footer
=Sum([Invoi
Page Footer
Report Footer
=Sum([Invoi

Next you'll adjust the spacing between the controls to distribute them evenly across the page.

To redistribute controls in the report:

TIP

To delete a control in Report Design view, right-click the control, and then click Delete from the menu.

1. Click the **Report Design Tools Format** tab, and then in the Selection group, click the **Select All** button to select all controls.
2. Press and hold **SHIFT**, and click the **InvoiceItem** control in the Group Header to deselect it.
3. On the ribbon, click the **Report Design Tools Arrange** tab
4. In the Sizing & Ordering group, click the **Size/Space** button, and then click **Equal Horizontal**. The form controls are shifted horizontally so the spacing between them is equal. See Figure 7–21.

Figure 7–21 Equal horizontal spacing applied to form controls in Design view

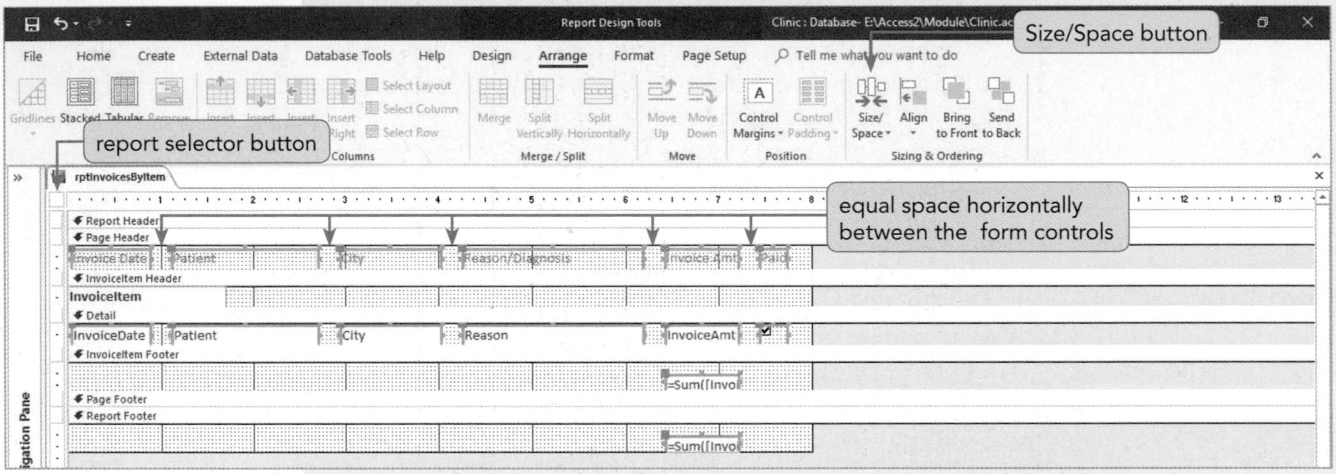
Size/Space button
report selector button
equal space horizontally between the form controls
Report Design Tools
rptInvoicesByItem
Report Header
Page Header
Invoice Date
Patient
City
Reason/Diagnosis
Invoice Amt
Paid
InvoiceItem Header
InvoiceItem
Detail
InvoiceDate
Reason
InvoiceAmt
InvoiceItem Footer
Page Footer
Report Footer

Because of the changes you made to the widths of the Patient and Reason field value boxes, they may not be wide enough to display the entire field value in all cases. For the Patient and Reason field value boxes, you'll set their Can Grow property to Yes. The **Can Grow property**, when set to Yes, expands a field value box vertically to fit the field value when the report is printed, previewed, or viewed in Layout and Report views.

TIP

You can select two or more controls, and then set common properties for the selected controls, instead of setting them one control at a time.

5. Click the **Report Selector** button to deselect all controls, select the **Patient** and **Reason** field value control boxes in the Detail section, right-click one of the selected controls, and then on the shortcut menu click **Properties**.
6. On the Property Sheet, click the **Format** tab, scroll down the Property Sheet to locate the Can Grow property, and then if the Can Grow property is set to Yes, set it to **No**. The default setting for this feature may not work properly, so to ensure the setting is applied correctly, you must make sure it is first set to No.

   Trouble? If you don't see the Can Grow property on the Format tab, double-check to ensure you've selected the Patient and Reason controls in the Detail section, not in the Page Header section.
7. Change the Can Grow property value to **Yes**, close the Property Sheet, and then save your report changes.

8. Switch to Print Preview, and then review every page of the report, ending on the last page. See Figure 7–22.

Figure 7–22 Effect of setting the Can Grow property

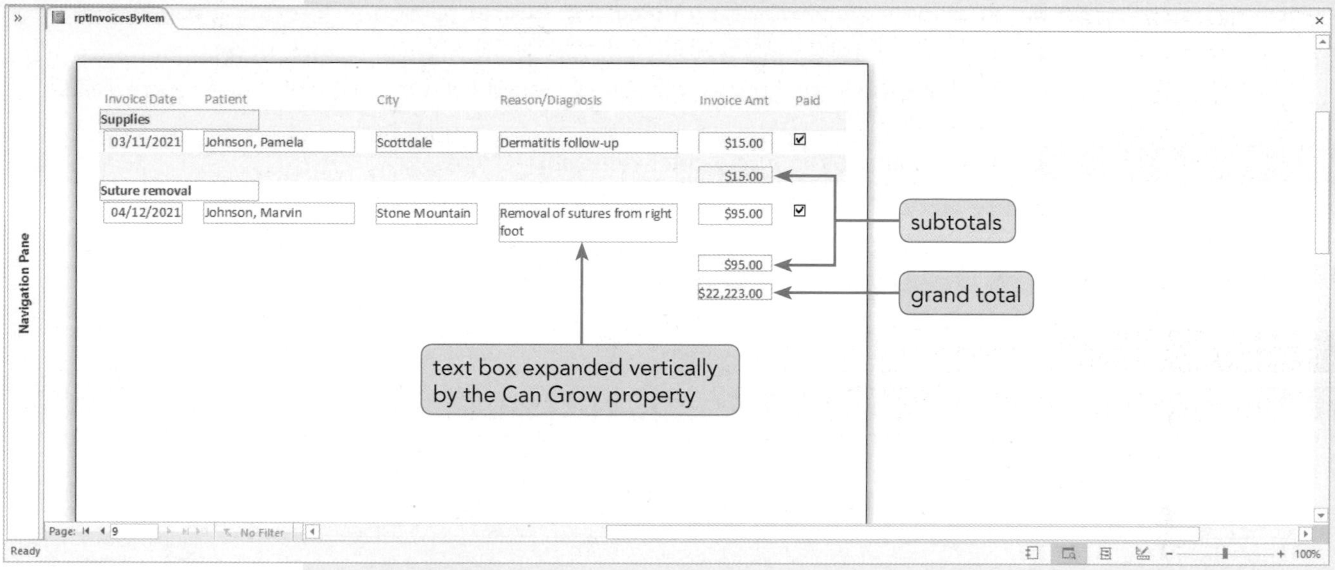
rptInvoicesByItem
Invoice Date
Patient
City
Reason/Diagnosis
Invoice Amt
Paid
Supplies
03/11/2021
Johnson, Pamela
Scottdale
Dermatitis follow-up
$15.00
$15.00
Suture removal
04/12/2021
Johnson, Marvin
Stone Mountain
Removal of sutures from right foot
$95.00
$95.00
$22,223.00
subtotals
grand total
text box expanded vertically by the Can Grow property
Navigation Pane
Page: 9
No Filter
Ready
100%

The groups stay together on one page, except for the groups that have too many detail lines to fit on one page. Where necessary, the Can Grow property expands the height of the Patient and Reason field value boxes.

Also, the lines that were displayed above the subtotals and grand total are no longer displayed, and the commas in the values are not fully visible. You'll add the totals lines back in the report and resize the field value boxes for the totals. First, Reginald thinks the borders around the field value boxes and the alternate row color are too distracting, so you'll remove them from the report.

To remove the borders and alternate row color:

1. Switch to Design view.
2. Click the **Report Design Tools Format tab**, and then in the Selection group, click the **Select All** button.
3. Right-click one of the selected controls, and then click **Properties** on the shortcut menu to open the Property Sheet.
4. Click the **Format** tab (if necessary) in the Property Sheet, click the right side of the Border Style box, and then click **Transparent**. The transparent setting removes the borders from the report by making them transparent.
5. Click the **InvoiceItem Header** section bar, click the right side of the **Alternate Back Color** box in the Property Sheet, and then click **No Color** at the bottom of the gallery. This setting removes the alternate row color from the InvoiceItem Header section. You can also control the Alternate Back Color property using the Alternate Row Color button in the Background group on the Format tab, because the two options set the same property.

6. Click the **Detail** section bar, and then on the **Report Design Tools Format** tab, in the Background group, click the **Alternate Row Color button arrow**, and then click **No Color** at the bottom of the gallery. The Alternate Back Color property setting in the Property Sheet is now set to No Color.
7. Repeat Step 6 for the **InvoiceItem Footer** section.
8. Close the Property Sheet, save your report changes, switch to Print Preview, and review each page of the report, ending on the last page. See Figure 7–23.

Figure 7–23 Borders and alternate row color removed

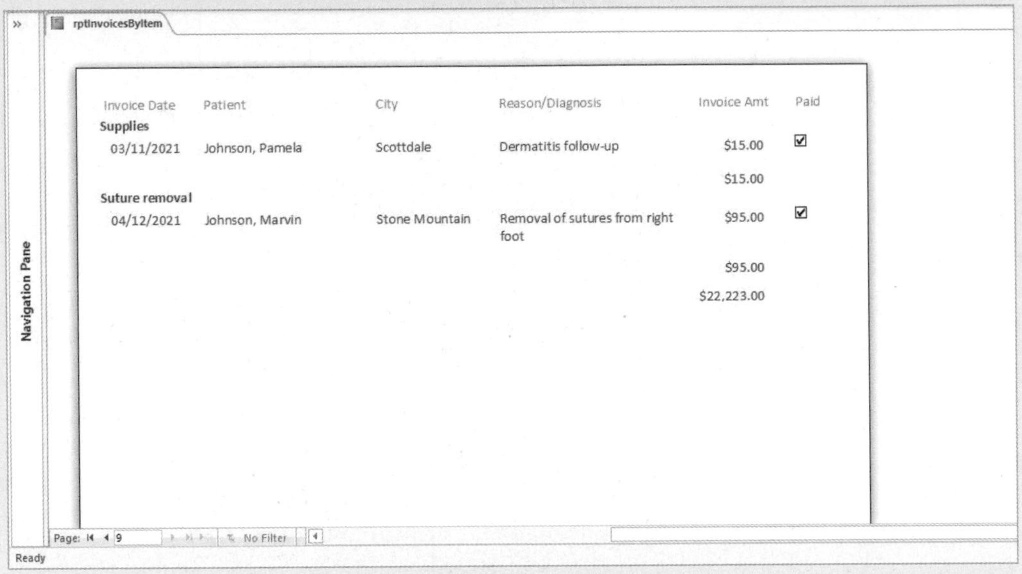
rptInvoicesByItem
Navigation Pane
Invoice Date
Patient
City
Reason/Diagnosis
Invoice Amt
Paid
Supplies
03/11/2021
Johnson, Pamela
Scottdale
Dermatitis follow-up
$15.00
$15.00
Suture removal
04/12/2021
Johnson, Marvin
Stone Mountain
Removal of sutures from right foot
$95.00
$95.00
$22,223.00
Page: 9
No Filter
Ready

You still need to resize the subtotal and grand total field value boxes so that the comma separators are fully displayed. In addition, you'll add lines to separate the values from the subtotals and grand total.

To resize the subtotals and grand totals field value boxes and add totals lines to the report:

1. Switch to Design view.
2. In the InvoiceItem Footer section, click the calculated control box to select it, and then drag the upper-middle sizing handle up to increase its height by one row of grid dots.
3. Repeat Step 2 to resize the calculated control box in the Report Footer section.
4. On the Report Design Tools Design tab, in the Controls group, click the **More** button to open the Controls gallery.
5. Click the **Line** tool, position the Line tool pointer's plus symbol in the InvoiceItem Footer section in the upper-left corner of the calculated control box, press and hold **SHIFT**, drag from left to right so the line aligns with the top border of the calculated control box and ends at the upper-right corner of the calculated control box, release the mouse button, and then release **SHIFT**.

6. In the Report Footer section, click the calculated control box, press ↓ two times to move the control down slightly in the section, and then deselect all controls.
7. In the Controls group, click the **More** button, click the **Line** tool, position the pointer's plus symbol in the Report Footer section in the upper-left corner of the calculated control box, press and hold **SHIFT**, drag left to right so the line aligns with the top border of the calculated control box and ends at the upper-right corner of the calculated control box, release the mouse button, and then release **SHIFT**.

   The grand total line should have two lines separating it from the rest of the report. Next, you'll copy and paste the line you just created in the Report Footer section, and then align the copied line into position.
8. Right-click the selected line in the Report Footer section, and then click **Copy** on the shortcut menu.
9. Right-click the **Report Footer** section bar, and then click **Paste** on the shortcut menu. A copy of the line is pasted in the upper-left corner of the Report Footer section.
10. Press ↓ two times to move the copied line down in the section, press and hold **SHIFT**, click the first line in the Report Footer section to select both lines, and then release **SHIFT**.
11. Right-click the selected lines to open the shortcut menu, point to **Align**, and then click **Right**. A double line is now positioned above the grand total box.
12. Save your report changes, switch to Print Preview, and then navigate to the last page of the report. See Figure 7–24.

Figure 7–24 Total lines added to the report

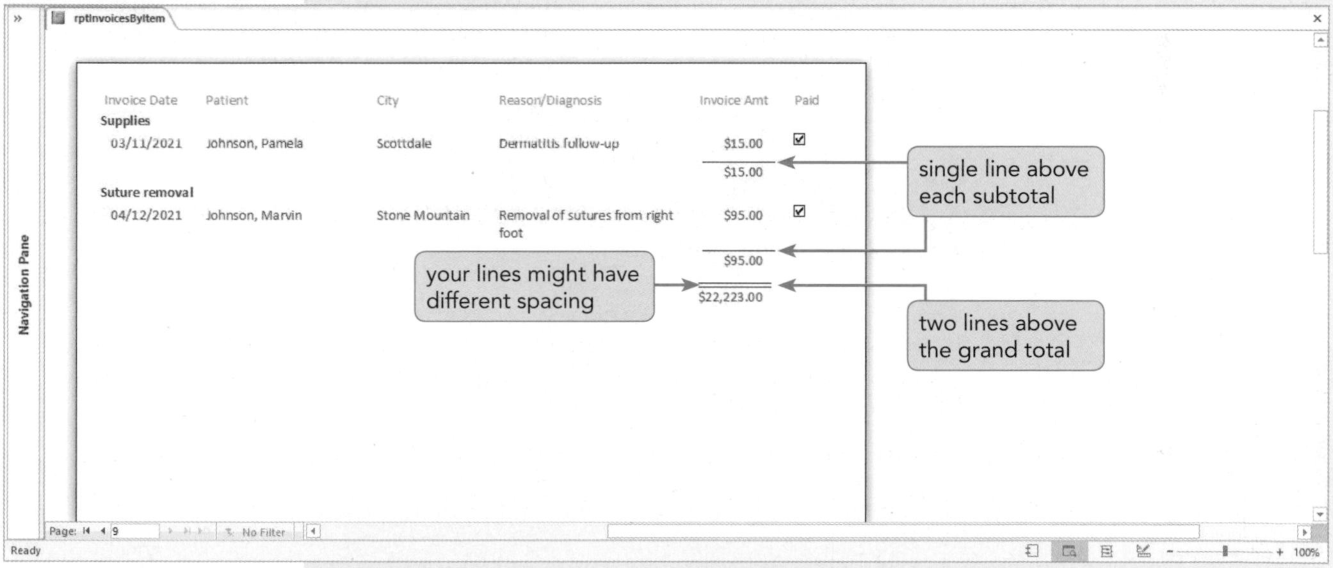

rptInvoicesByItem
Invoice Date
Patient
City
Reason/Diagnosis
Invoice Amt
Paid
Supplies
03/11/2021
Johnson, Pamela
Scottdale
Dermatitis follow-up
$15.00
$15.00
Suture removal
04/12/2021
Johnson, Marvin
Stone Mountain
Removal of sutures from right foot
$95.00
$95.00
$22,223.00
single line above each subtotal
your lines might have different spacing
two lines above the grand total
Navigation Pane
Page: 9
No Filter
Ready
100%

Your next design change to the report is to hide duplicate InvoiceDate field values in the Detail section. This change will make the report easier to read.

Hiding Duplicate Values in a Report

You use the **Hide Duplicates property** to hide a control in a report when the control's value is the same as that of the preceding record in the group. You should use the Hide Duplicates property only on fields that are sorted. Otherwise it may look as if data is missing.

For the rptInvoicesByItem report, the InvoiceDate field is a sort field. Two or more consecutive detail report lines can have the same InvoiceDate field value. In these cases, Reginald wants the InvoiceDate field value to appear for the first detail line but not for subsequent detail lines because he believes it makes the printed information easier to read.

To hide the duplicate InvoiceDate field values:

1. Switch to Design view, and then click a blank area of the window to deselect all controls.
2. Open the Property Sheet for the InvoiceDate field value box in the Detail section.
3. Click the **Format** tab (if necessary), scroll down the Property Sheet, click the right side of the **Hide Duplicates** box, and then click **Yes**.
4. Close the Property Sheet, save your report changes, switch to Print Preview, navigate to page 1 (the actual page you view might vary, depending on your printer) to the Lab work group to see the two invoice records for 01/27/2021. The InvoiceDate field value does not display for the second of the two consecutive records with a 01/27/2021 date. See Figure 7–25.

TIP

For properties offering a list of choices, you can double-click the property name repeatedly to cycle through the option in the list.

Figure 7–25 Report in Print Preview with hidden duplicate values

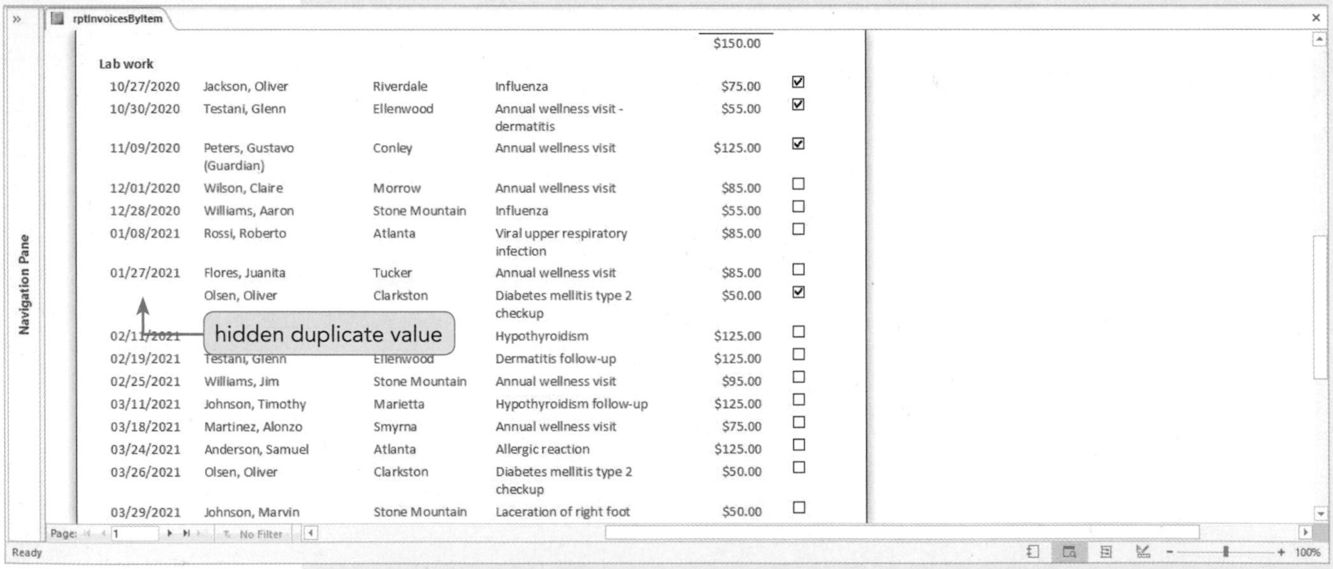
rptInvoicesByItem
$150.00
Lab work
10/27/2020 Jackson, Oliver Riverdale Influenza $75.00
10/30/2020 Testani, Glenn Ellenwood Annual wellness visit - dermatitis $55.00
11/09/2020 Peters, Gustavo (Guardian) Conley Annual wellness visit $125.00
12/01/2020 Wilson, Claire Morrow Annual wellness visit $85.00
12/28/2020 Williams, Aaron Stone Mountain Influenza $55.00
01/08/2021 Rossi, Roberto Atlanta Viral upper respiratory infection $85.00
01/27/2021 Flores, Juanita Tucker Annual wellness visit $85.00
Olsen, Oliver Clarkston Diabetes mellitis type 2 checkup $50.00
hidden duplicate value
Hypothyroidism $125.00
02/19/2021 Dermatitis follow-up $125.00
02/25/2021 Williams, Jim Stone Mountain Annual wellness visit $95.00
03/11/2021 Johnson, Timothy Marietta Hypothyroidism follow-up $125.00
03/18/2021 Martinez, Alonzo Smyrna Annual wellness visit $75.00
03/24/2021 Anderson, Samuel Atlanta Allergic reaction $125.00
03/26/2021 Olsen, Oliver Clarkston Diabetes mellitis type 2 checkup $50.00
03/29/2021 Johnson, Marvin Stone Mountain Laceration of right foot $50.00
Navigation Pane
Page: 1
No Filter
Ready
100%

5. If you are not continuing on to the next session, close the Clinic database.

You have completed the Detail section, the Group Header section, and the Group Footer section of the custom report. In the next session, you will complete the custom report according to Reginald's design by adding controls to the Page Header section.

REVIEW

Session 7.2 Quick Check

1. What is a detail report? A summary report?
2. The _______ property prints a group header on a page only if there is enough room on the page to print the first detail record for the group; otherwise, the group header prints at the top of the next page.
3. A(n) ______ section appears by itself at the top of a page, and the detail lines for the section appear on the previous page.
4. The ______ property, when set to Yes, expands a field value box vertically to fit the field value when a report is printed, previewed, or viewed in Layout and Report views.
5. Why might you want to hide duplicate values in a report?

Session 7.3 Visual Overview:

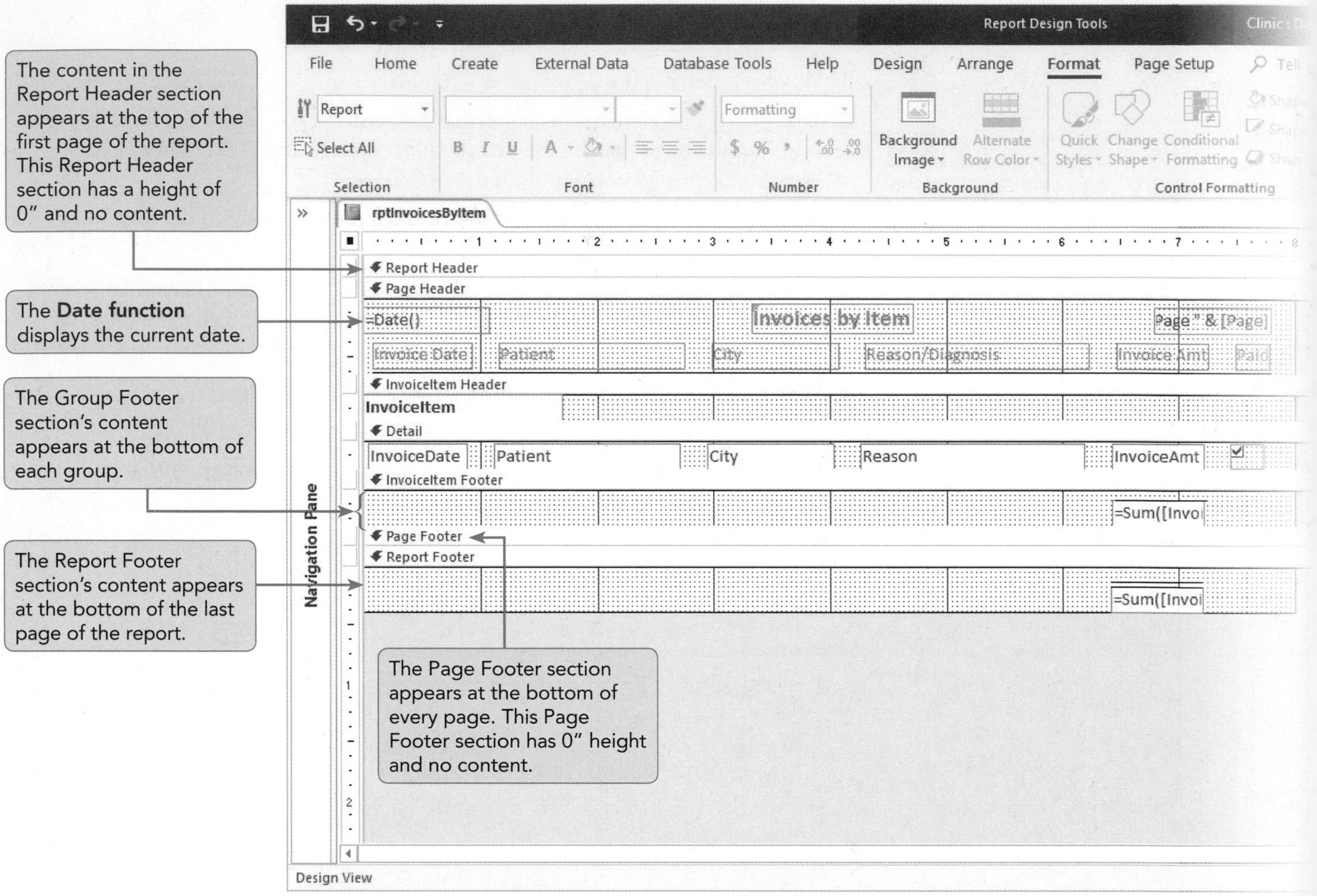
The content in the Report Header section appears at the top of the first page of the report. This Report Header section has a height of 0" and no content.
The **Date function** displays the current date.
The Group Footer section's content appears at the bottom of each group.
The Report Footer section's content appears at the bottom of the last page of the report.
The Page Footer section appears at the bottom of every page. This Page Footer section has 0" height and no content.
Report Design Tools
File
Home
Create
External Data
Database Tools
Help
Design
Arrange
Format
Page Setup
Report
Select All
Selection
Font
Formatting
Number
Background Image
Alternate Row Color
Background
Quick Styles
Change Shape
Conditional Formatting
Control Formatting
rptInvoicesByItem
Report Header
Page Header
=Date()
Invoices by Item
Invoice Date
Patient
City
Reason/Diagnosis
Invoice Amt
Paid
InvoiceItem Header
InvoiceItem
Detail
InvoiceDate
Patient
City
Reason
InvoiceAmt
InvoiceItem Footer
=Sum([Invoi
Page Footer
Report Footer
=Sum([Invoi
Navigation Pane
Design View

Custom Form in Design View

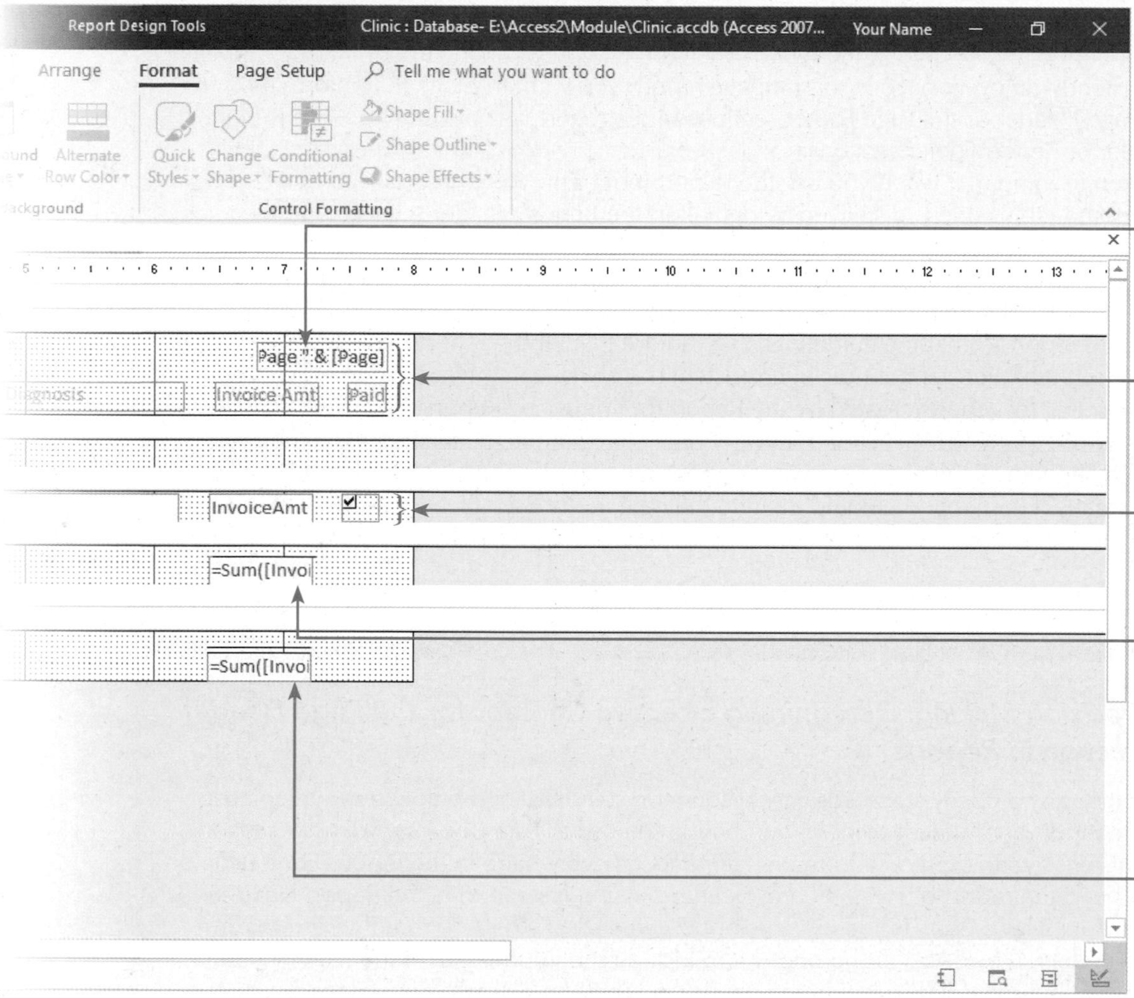
Report Design Tools
Clinic : Database- E:\Access2\Module\Clinic.accdb (Access 2007...
Your Name
Arrange
Format
Page Setup
Tell me what you want to do
Alternate Row Color
Quick Styles
Change Shape
Conditional Formatting
Shape Fill
Shape Outline
Shape Effects
Control Formatting
="Page " & [Page]
Invoice Amt
Paid
InvoiceAmt
=Sum([Invoi
=Sum([Invoi

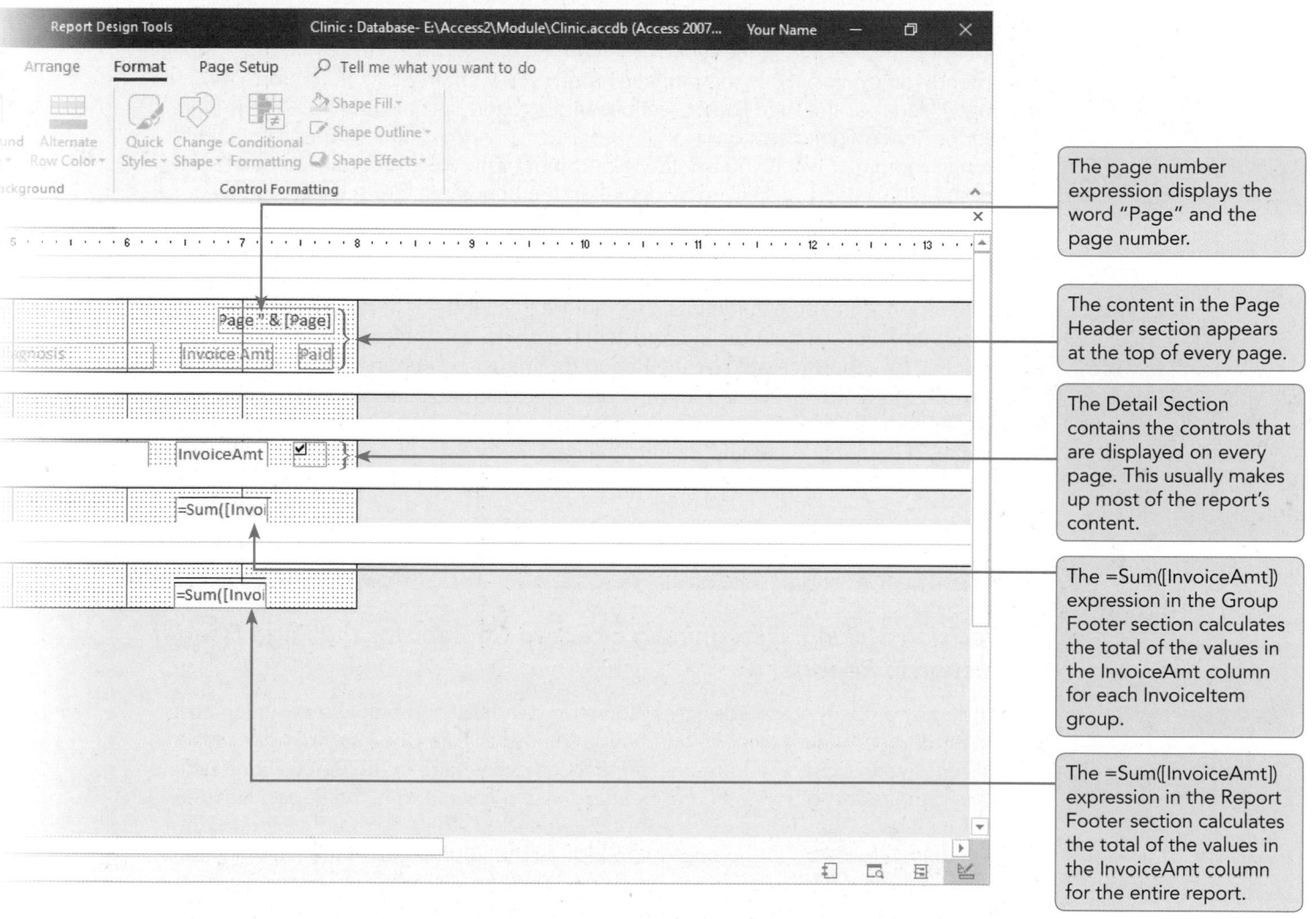

The page number expression displays the word "Page" and the page number.

The content in the Page Header section appears at the top of every page.

The Detail Section contains the controls that are displayed on every page. This usually makes up most of the report's content.

The =Sum([InvoiceAmt]) expression in the Group Footer section calculates the total of the values in the InvoiceAmt column for each InvoiceItem group.

The =Sum([InvoiceAmt]) expression in the Report Footer section calculates the total of the values in the InvoiceAmt column for the entire report.

Understanding Page Header and Page Footer Sections

Recall that in Access reports, the Report Header and Footer sections appear only once, at the top and bottom of the report, respectively. In contrast, the Page Header Section appears at the top of every page in the report, and the Page Footer Section appears at the bottom of every page in the report. Therefore, if you want any information to appear consistently on every page in a multipage report, you want to place that information in the Page Header or the Page Footer sections of the report, as opposed to in the Report Header or Report Footer sections.

Keep in mind that when you use the Report tool or the Report Wizard to create a report, the report title is displayed by default in the Report Header section, and the page number is displayed in the Page Footer section. The date and time are displayed in the Report Header section when you use the Report tool and in the Page Footer section when you use the Report Wizard. Therefore, because most companies implement standard report-formatting guidelines that require that all the reports in a database display certain types of controls in consistent positions, you might have to move the date control for reports created by the Report tool or by the Report Wizard so the date is displayed in the same section for all reports. For example, at Lakewood Community Health Services, Reginald's recommendations are that all reports, including the rptInvoicesByItem report, should include the date in the Page Header section, along with the report title, the page number, the column heading labels, and a line below the labels.

PROSKILLS

Decision Making: Determining Effective Content for the Page Header Section in Reports

Although company standards vary, a common standard for multipage reports places the report title, date, and page number on the same line in the Page Header section. This ensures this critical information appears on every page in the report. For example, placing the report title in the Page Header section, instead of in the Report Header section, allows users to identify the report name on any page without having to turn to the first page. Also, using one line to include this information in the Page Header section saves vertical space in the report compared to placing some of these controls in the Page Header section and others in the Page Footer section.

When you develop reports with a consistent format, the report users become more productive and more confident working with the information in the reports.

Adding the Date to a Report

To add the date to a report, you can click the Date and Time button in the Header/Footer group on the Report Layout Tools or Report Design Tools Design tab. Doing so inserts the Date function in a control (without a corresponding label control) in the Report Header section. The Date function returns the current date. The format of the Date function is *=Date()*. The equal sign (=) indicates that what follows it is an expression; *Date* is the name of the function; the empty set of parentheses indicates a function rather than simple text.

REFERENCE

Adding the Date and Time to a Report

- Display the report in Layout or Design view.
- In Design view or in Layout view, on the Design tab, in the Header/Footer group, click the Date and Time button to open the Date and Time dialog box.
- To display the date, click the Include Date check box, and then click one of the three date option buttons.
- To display the time, click the Include Time check box, and then click one of the three time option buttons.
- Click the OK button.

In Reginald's design for the report, the date appears on the left side of the Page Header section. You'll add the date to the report and then cut the date from its default location in the Report Header section and paste it into the Page Header section. You can add the current date in Layout view or Design view. However, because you can't cut and paste controls between sections in Layout view, you'll add the date in Design view.

To add the date to the report:

1. If you took a break after the previous session, make sure that the Clinic database is open, that the rptInvoicesByItem report is open in Design view, and that the Navigation Pane is closed.

   First, you'll move the column heading labels down in the Page Header section to make room for the controls you'll be adding above them.

2. Increase the height of the Page Header section by dragging the Page Header's bottom border down until the 1-inch mark on the vertical ruler appears.
3. Select all six label controls in the Page Header section, and then move the controls down until the tops of the label controls are at the 3/8-inch mark on the vertical ruler. You may find it easier to use the arrow keys, rather than the mouse, to position the label controls.

   Reginald's report design calls for a horizontal line below the labels. You'll add this line next.

4. On the Report Design Tools Design tab, in the Controls group, click the **More** button, click the **Line** tool, and then drag to create a horizontal line positioned one grid dot below the bottom border of the six label controls and spanning from the left edge of the Invoice Date label control and the right edge of the Paid label control.
5. Reduce the height of the Page Header section by dragging the bottom border of the section up until it touches the bottom of the line you just added.
6. In the Header/Footer group, click the **Date and Time** button to open the Date and Time dialog box, make sure the **Include Date** check box is checked and the **Include Time** check box is unchecked, and then click the third date format option button. See Figure 7–26.

TIP

To add the time to a report, check the Include Time check box in the Date and Time dialog box, and select one of the three time formats.

Figure 7–26 **Completed Date and Time dialog box**

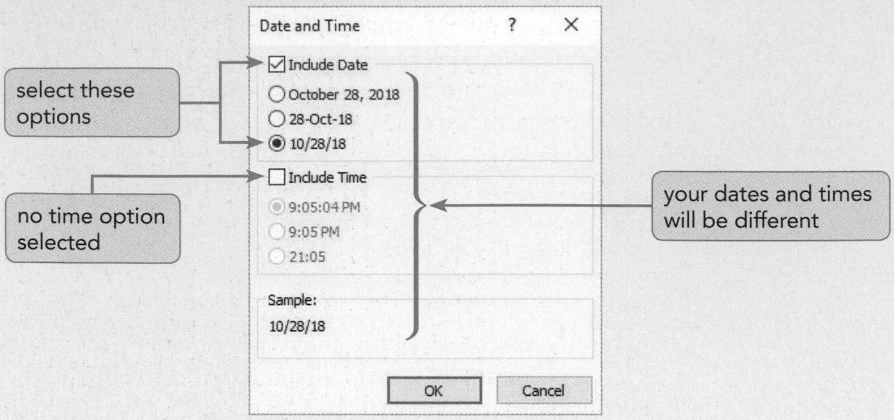
Date and Time
Include Date
October 28, 2018
28-Oct-18
10/28/18
Include Time
9:05:04 PM
9:05 PM
21:05
Sample:
10/28/18
OK
Cancel
select these options
no time option selected
your dates and times will be different

7. Click the **OK** button. The Date function control is added to the right side of the Report Header section.

Next you'll move the Date function control to the Page Header section to match Reginald's design.

To add the date to the Page Header section:

1. Click the **Date function** control box, and then click the **layout selector** in the upper-left corner of the Report Header section. The Date function control box is part of a control layout with three additional empty control boxes. See Figure 7–27.

Figure 7–27 **Date function added to the Report Header section**

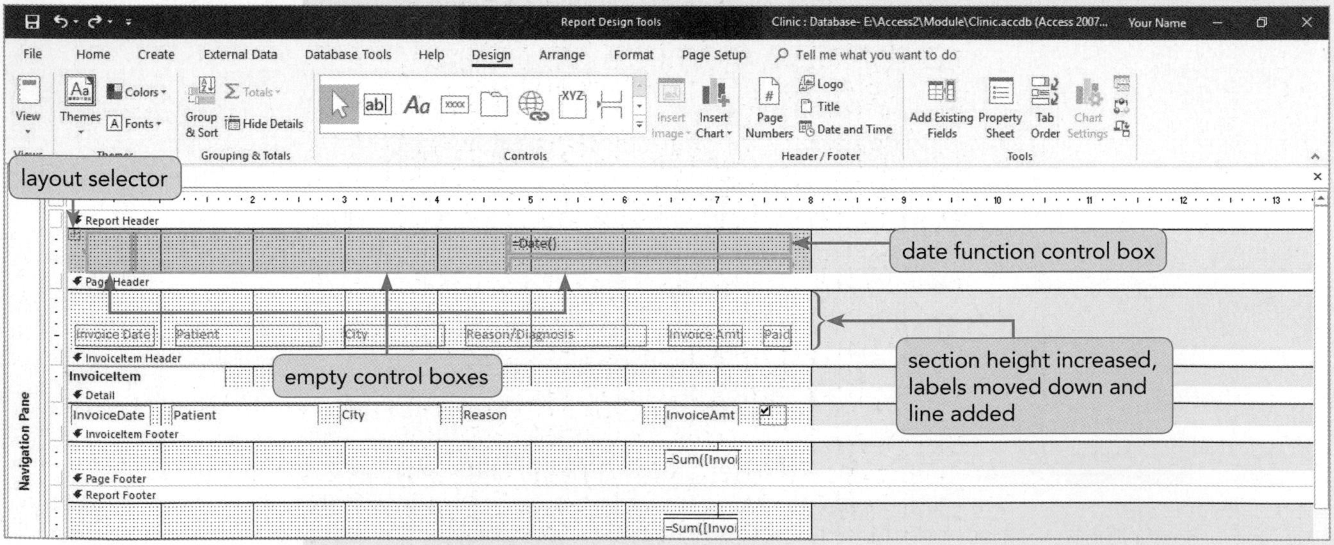
layout selector
date function control box
empty control boxes
section height increased, labels moved down and line added
Report Header
=Date()
Page Header
Invoice Date
Patient
City
Reason/Diagnosis
Invoice Amt
Paid
InvoiceItem Header
InvoiceItem
Detail
InvoiceDate
Patient
City
Reason
InvoiceAmt
InvoiceItem Footer
=Sum([Invoi
Page Footer
Report Footer
=Sum([Invoi
Navigation Pane

You need to remove these controls from the control layout before you work further with the Date function control box.

2. Right-click one of the selected control boxes, point to **Layout** on the shortcut menu, and then click **Remove Layout**. The three empty cells are deleted, and the Date function control box remains selected.

   The default size for the Date function control box accommodates long dates and long times, so the control box is much wider than needed for the date that will appear in the custom report. You'll decrease its width and move it to the Page Header section.

3. Drag the left border of the Date function control box to the right until it is 1 inch wide.

4. Right-click the selected **Date function** control box to open the shortcut menu, click **Cut** to delete the control, right-click the **Page Header** section bar to select that section and open the shortcut menu, and then click **Paste**. The Date function control box is pasted in the upper-left corner of the Page Header section.

Be sure to paste the Date function control box in the Page Header section and not in the Report Header section.

5. Save your report changes, and then switch to Print Preview to view the date in the Page Header section. See Figure 7–28.

Figure 7–28 **Date in page header section in Print Preview**

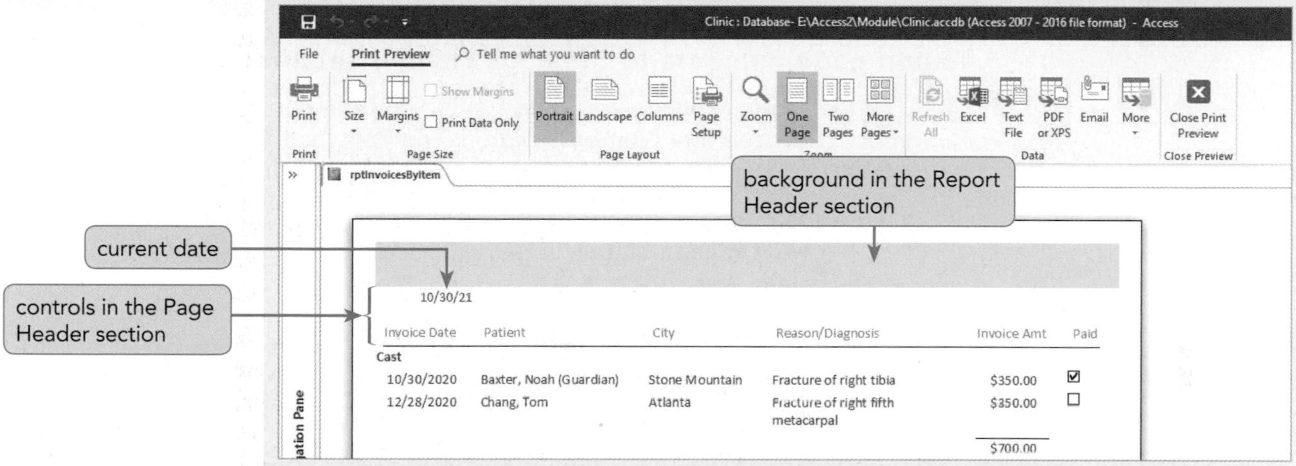

current date
controls in the Page Header section
background in the Report Header section
Clinic : Database- E:\Access2\Module\Clinic.accdb (Access 2007 - 2016 file format) - Access
File
Print Preview
Tell me what you want to do
Print
Size
Margins
Show Margins
Print Data Only
Portrait
Landscape
Columns
Page Setup
Zoom
One Page
Two Pages
More Pages
Refresh All
Excel
Text File
PDF or XPS
Email
More
Close Print Preview
Page Size
Page Layout
Data
Close Preview
rptInvoicesByItem
10/30/21
Invoice Date
Patient
City
Reason/Diagnosis
Invoice Amt
Paid
Cast
10/30/2020
Baxter, Noah (Guardian)
Stone Mountain
Fracture of right tibia
$350.00
12/28/2020
Chang, Tom
Atlanta
Fracture of right fifth metacarpal
$350.00
$700.00

Trouble? Your year might appear with four digits instead of two digits as shown in Figure 7–28. Your date format might also differ, depending on your computer's date settings. These differences do not cause any problems.

Now that the date has been added to the Page Header section, you need to format and position it appropriately.

6. Switch to Design view, make sure the **Date function** control box is still selected, click the **Report Design Tools Format** tab, and then in the Font group, click the **Align Left** button.

7. In the Report Header section, drag the bottom border up to the top of the section so the section's height is reduced to zero.

If a report includes a control with the Date function, the current date will be displayed each time the report is run. If you instead want a specific date to appear each time the report is run, use a label control that contains the date, rather than the Date function.

You are now ready to add page numbers to the Page Header section.

Adding Page Numbers to a Report

You can display page numbers in a report by including an expression in the Page Header or Page Footer section. On the Report Layout Tools or Report Design Tools Design tab, you can click the Page Numbers button in the Header/Footer group to add a page number expression. The inserted page number expression automatically displays the correct page number on each page of a report.

REFERENCE

Adding Page Numbers to a Report

- Display the report in Layout or Design view.
- On the Design tab, click the Page Numbers button in the Header/Footer group to open the Page Numbers dialog box.
- Select the format, position, and alignment options you want.
- Select whether you want to display the page number on the first page.
- Click the OK button to place the page number expression in the report.

Reginald's design shows the page number displayed on the right side of the Page Header section, bottom-aligned with the date.

To add page numbers to the Page Header section:

1. Click the **Report Design Tools Design** tab, and then in the Header/Footer group, click the **Page Numbers** button. The Page Numbers dialog box opens.

   You use the Format options to specify the format of the page number. Reginald wants page numbers to appear as Page 1, Page 2, and so on. This is the "Page N" format option. You use the Position options to place the page numbers at the top of the page in the Page Header section or at the bottom of the page in the Page Footer section. Reginald's design shows page numbers at the top of the page.

2. In the Format section, make sure that the **Page N** option button is selected, and then in the Position section, make sure that the **Top of Page [Header]** option button is selected.

   The report design shows page numbers at the right side of the page. You can specify this placement in the Alignment box.

3. Click the **Alignment** arrow, and then click **Right**.
4. Make sure the **Show Number on First Page** check box is checked, so the page number prints on the first page and all other pages as well. See Figure 7–29.

Figure 7–29 **Completed Page Numbers dialog box**

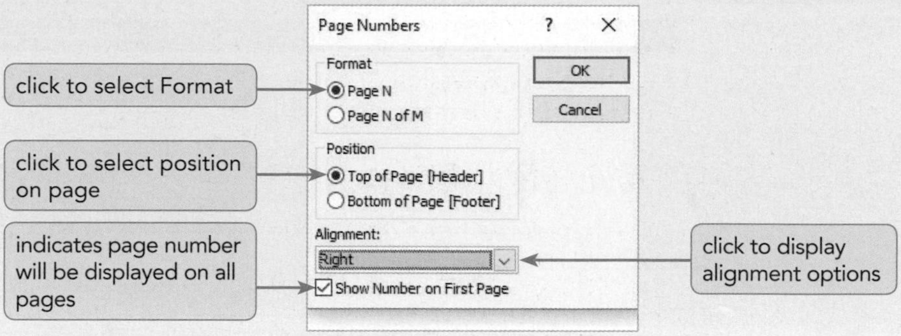
Page Numbers
Format
Page N
Page N of M
OK
Cancel
Position
Top of Page [Header]
Bottom of Page [Footer]
Alignment:
Right
Show Number on First Page
click to select Format
click to select position on page
indicates page number will be displayed on all pages
click to display alignment options

5. Click the **OK** button. A control box containing the expression =*"Page " & [Page]* appears in the upper-right corner of the Page Header section. The expression=*"Page " & [Page]* in the control box means that the printed report will show the word "Page" followed by a space and the page number. The page number control box is much wider than needed for the page number expression that will appear in the custom report. You'll decrease its width.
6. Click the **Page Number** control box, decrease its width from the left until it is 1 inch wide, and then move it to the left so its right edge aligns with the right edge of the Paid field value box. See Figure 7–30.

Figure 7–30 **Page number expression added to the Page Header section**

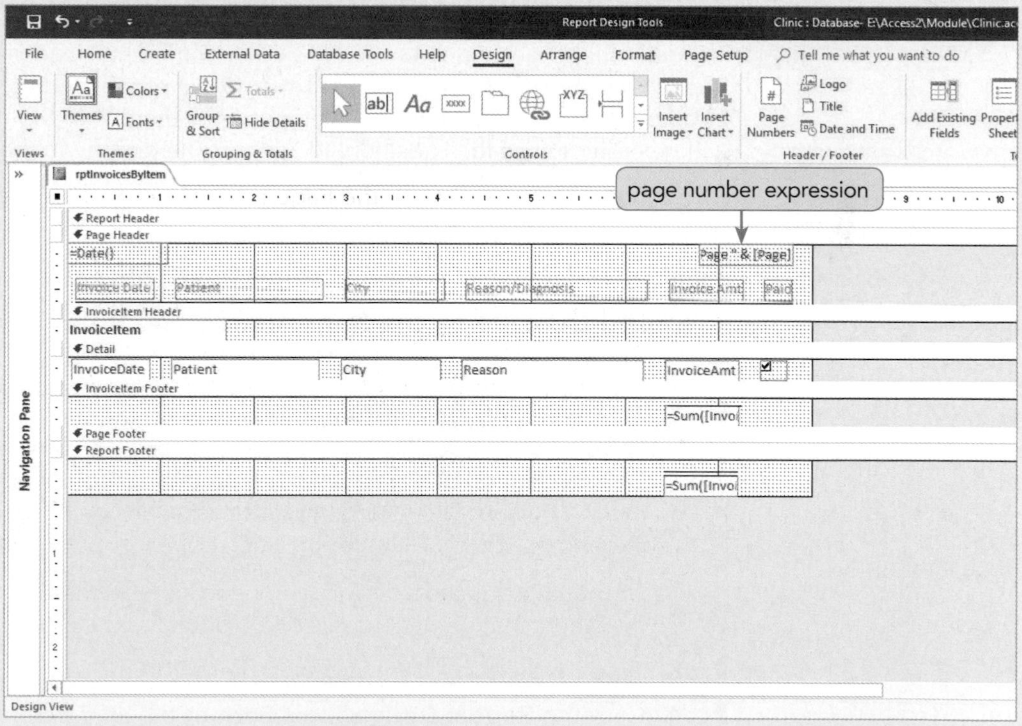
page number expression
Report Design Tools
rptInvoicesByItem
Report Header
Page Header
=Date()
="Page " & [Page]
InvoiceItem Header
InvoiceItem
Detail
InvoiceDate
Patient
City
Reason
InvoiceAmt
InvoiceItem Footer
Page Footer
Report Footer
Navigation Pane
Design View

7. Save your report changes, and then switch to Print Preview. See Figure 7–31.

Figure 7–31 Date and page number in the Page Header section

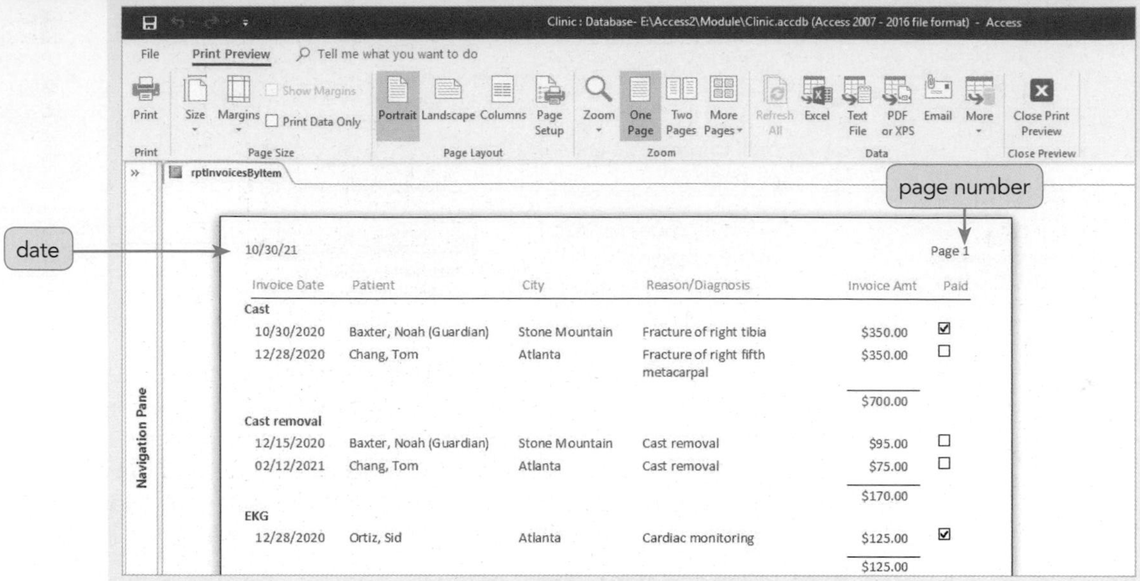

page number
date
10/30/21
Page 1
Invoice Date
Patient
City
Reason/Diagnosis
Invoice Amt
Paid
Cast
10/30/2020 Baxter, Noah (Guardian) Stone Mountain Fracture of right tibia $350.00
12/28/2020 Chang, Tom Atlanta Fracture of right fifth metacarpal $350.00
$700.00
Cast removal
12/15/2020 Baxter, Noah (Guardian) Stone Mountain Cast removal $95.00
02/12/2021 Chang, Tom Atlanta Cast removal $75.00
$170.00
EKG
12/28/2020 Ortiz, Sid Atlanta Cardiac monitoring $125.00
$125.00

Now you are ready to add the title to the Page Header section.

Adding a Report Title to a Page Header Section

TIP

All reports should contain a title, either in the Report Header section to display only on the first page or in the Page Header section to display on all pages.

To add a title to a report, you use the Title button in the Header/Footer group on the Report Design Tools Design tab. However, doing so will add the title to the Report Header section, and Reginald's design positions the title in the Page Header section. It will be easier to use the Label tool to add the title directly in the Page Header section.

Reginald's report design includes the title "Invoices by Item" in the Page Header section, centered between the date and the page number.

To add the title to the Page Header section:

1. Switch to Design view.
2. On the Report Design Tools Design tab, in the Controls group, click the **Label** tool [Aa], position the Label pointer's plus symbol at the top of the Page Header section at the 3-inch mark on the horizontal ruler, and then click the mouse button. The insertion point flashes inside a narrow box, which will expand as you type the report title.

   To match Reginald's design, you need to type the title as "Invoices by Item" and then change its font size to 14 points and its style to bold.
3. Type **Invoices by Item** and then press **ENTER**.
4. Click the **Report Design Tools Format** tab, in the Font group, click the **Font Size** arrow, click **14**, and then click the **Bold** button [B].
5. Resize the label control box to display the full title, increase the height of the label control box by one grid dot, and move the label control box to the right so it is centered at the 4-inch mark. See Figure 7–32.

Figure 7–32 **Report title in the Page Header section**

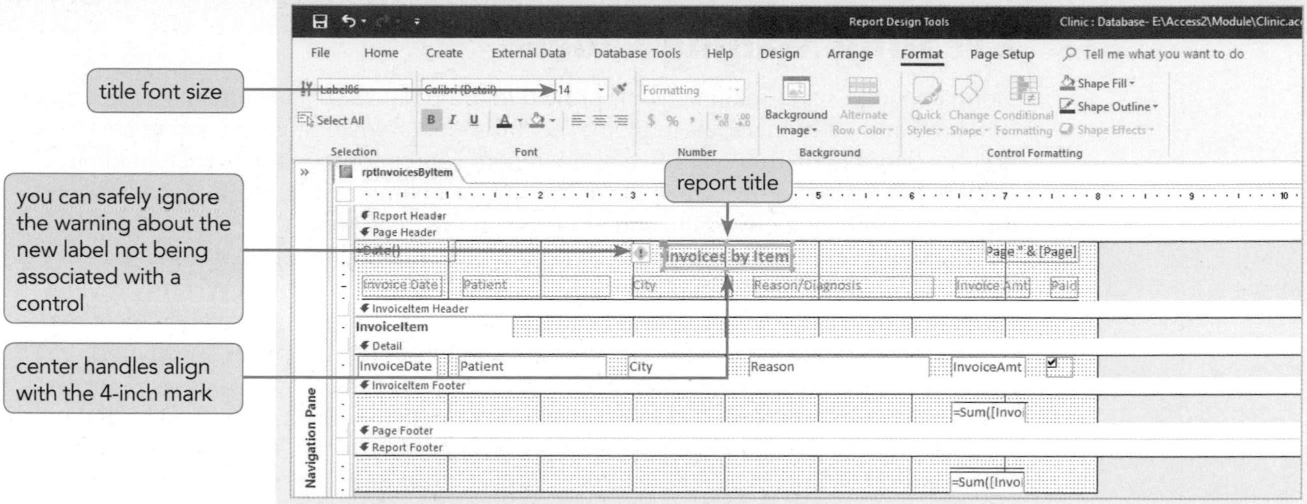
title font size
you can safely ignore the warning about the new label not being associated with a control
center handles align with the 4-inch mark
report title
Invoices by Item

Trouble? If a warning icon is displayed with ScreenTip text "This is a new label and is not associated with a control.", you can safely ignore it. A page heading does not need to be associated with a control.

Finally, you'll bottom-align the date, report title, and page number controls boxes. Yours might appear aligned already, but if not, this step will align the controls.

6. Select the **date**, **report title**, and **page number** control boxes in the Page Header section, right-click one of the selected controls, point to **Align,** and then click **Bottom**.

7. Save your report changes, and then switch to Print Preview to review the completed report. See Figure 7–33.

Figure 7–33 **Completed rptInvoicesByItem report in Print Preview**

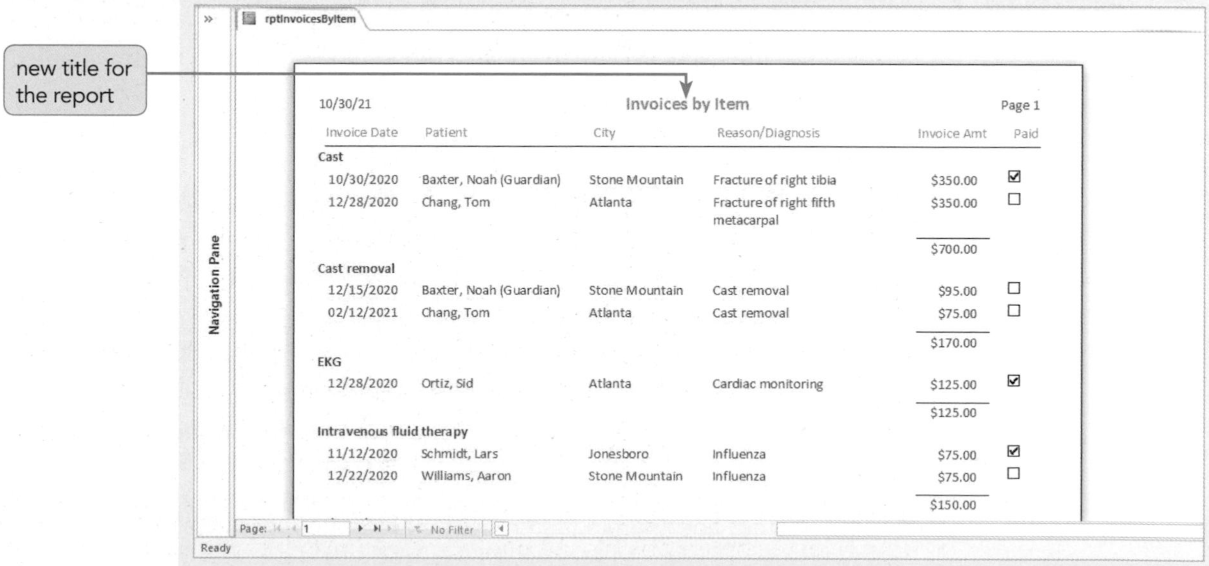
new title for the report
Invoices by Item

8. Close the report.

Next, Donna wants you to create mailing labels that she can use to address materials to the patients seen by the Lakewood Community Health Services.

Creating Mailing Labels

Donna needs a set of mailing labels printed for all patients so she can mail a marketing brochure and other materials to them. The tblPatient table contains the name and address information that will serve as the record source for the labels. Each mailing label will have the same format: first name and last name on the first line; address on the second line; and city, state, and zip code on the third line.

You could create a custom report to produce the mailing labels, but using the Label Wizard is an easier and faster way to produce them. The **Label Wizard** provides templates for hundreds of standard label formats, each of which is uniquely identified by a label manufacturer's name and product number. These templates specify the dimensions and arrangement of labels on each page. Standard label formats can have between one and five labels across a page; the number of labels printed on a single page also varies. Donna's mailing labels are manufactured by Avery and their product number is C2163. Each sheet contains 12 labels; each label is 1.5 inches by 3.9 inches, and the labels are arranged in two columns and six rows on the page.

REFERENCE

Creating Mailing Labels and Other Labels

- In the Navigation Pane, click the table or query that will serve as the record source for the labels.
- On the Create tab, click the Labels button in the Reports group to start the Label Wizard and open its first dialog box.
- Select the label manufacturer and product number, and then click the Next button.
- Select the label font, color, and style, and then click the Next button.
- Construct the label content by selecting the fields from the record source and specifying their placement and spacing on the label, and then click the Next button.
- Select one or more optional sort fields, click the Next button, specify the report name, and then click the Finish button.

You'll use the Label Wizard to create a report Donna can use to print mailing labels for all patients.

To use the Label Wizard to create the mailing label report:

1. Open the Navigation Pane, click **tblPatient** to make it the current object that will serve as the record source for the labels, close the Navigation Pane, and then click the **Create** tab.
2. In the Reports group, click the **Labels** button. The first Label Wizard dialog box opens and asks you to select the standard or custom label you'll use.
3. In the Unit of Measure section make sure that the **English** option button is selected, in the Label Type section make sure that the **Sheet feed** option button is selected, in the Filter by manufacturer box make sure that **Avery** is selected, and then in the Product number box, click **C2163**. See Figure 7–34.

Figure 7–34 Label wizard dialog box

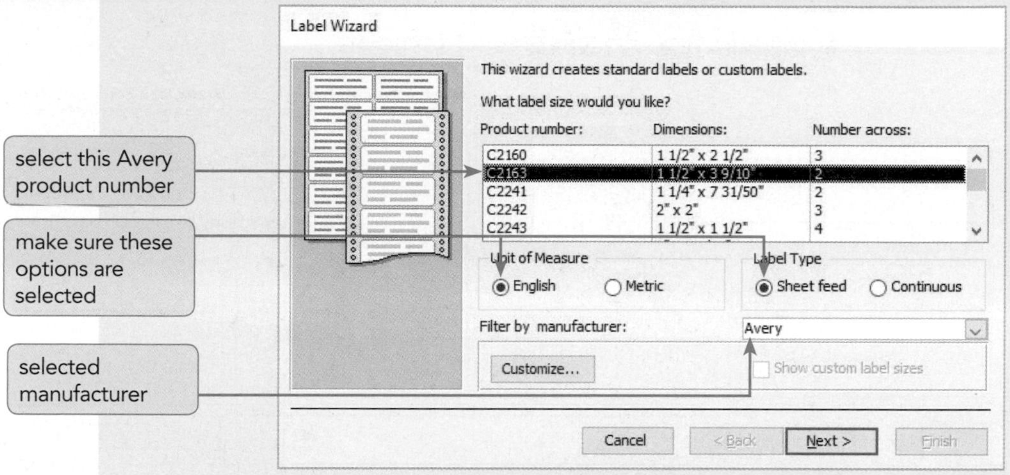
Label Wizard
This wizard creates standard labels or custom labels.
What label size would you like?
Product number:
Dimensions:
Number across:
C2160
1 1/2" x 2 1/2"
3
C2163
1 1/2" x 3 9/10
2
C2241
1 1/4" x 7 31/50"
2
C2242
2" x 2"
3
C2243
1 1/2" x 1 1/2"
4
Unit of Measure
English
Metric
Label Type
Sheet feed
Continuous
Filter by manufacturer:
Avery
Customize...
Show custom label sizes
Cancel
< Back
Next >
Finish
select this Avery product number
make sure these options are selected
selected manufacturer

TIP

If your label manufacturer or its labels do not appear in the box, you can create your own custom format for them.

The top box shows the Avery product number, dimensions, and number of labels across the page for each of its standard label formats. You can display the dimensions in the list in either inches or millimeters by choosing the appropriate option in the Unit of Measure section. You specify in the Label Type section whether the labels are on individual sheets or are continuous forms.

4. Click the **Next** button to open the second Label Wizard dialog box, in which you choose font specifications for the labels.

   Donna wants the labels to use 10-point Arial with a medium font weight and without italics or underlines. The font weight determines how light or dark the characters will print; you can choose from nine values ranging from thin to heavy.

5. If necessary, select **Arial** in the Font name box, **10** in the Font size box, and **Medium** in the Font weight box, make sure the Italic and the Underline check boxes are not checked and that black is the text color (bottom left in the Basic Colors gallery), and then click the **Next** button. The third Label Wizard dialog box opens, in which you select the data to appear on the labels.

   Donna wants the mailing labels to print the FirstName and LastName fields on the first line, the Address field on the second line, and the City, State, and Zip fields on the third line. A single space will separate the FirstName and LastName fields, the City and State fields, and the State and Zip fields.

6. In the Available fields box, click **FirstName**, click the **Select Single Field** > button to move the field to the Prototype label box, press **SPACEBAR**, in the Available fields box click **LastName** (if necessary), and then click the **Select Single Field** > button. As you select fields from the Available fields box or type text for the label, the Prototype label box shows the format for the label. The braces around the field names in the Prototype label box indicate that the name represents a field rather than text that you entered.

   Trouble? If you select the wrong field or type the wrong text, click the incorrect item in the Prototype label box, press the Delete key to remove the item, and then select the correct field or type the correct text.

7. Press **ENTER** to move to the next line in the Prototype label box, and then use Figure 7–35 to complete the entries in the Prototype label box. Make sure you type a comma and press SPACEBAR after selecting the City field, and then press SPACEBAR after selecting the State field.

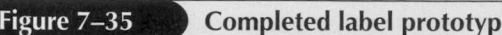

Figure 7–35 Completed label prototype

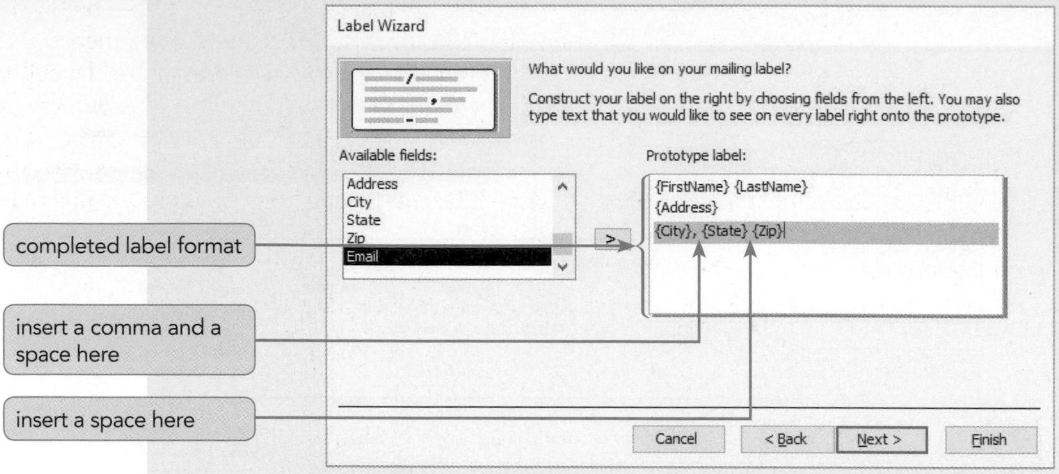
Label Wizard
What would you like on your mailing label?
Construct your label on the right by choosing fields from the left. You may also type text that you would like to see on every label right onto the prototype.
Available fields:
Address
City
State
Zip
Email
Prototype label:
{FirstName} {LastName}
{Address}
{City}, {State} {Zip}
completed label format
insert a comma and a space here
insert a space here
Cancel
< Back
Next >
Finish

8. Click the **Next** button to open the fourth Label Wizard dialog box, in which you choose the sort fields for the labels.

   Donna wants Zip to be the primary sort field and LastName to be the secondary sort field.

9. In the Available fields list, click the **Zip** field, click the **Select Single Field** > button to select Zip as the primary sort field, click the **LastName** field, click the **Select Single Field** > button to select LastName as the secondary sort field, and then click the **Next** button to open the last Label Wizard dialog box, in which you enter a name for the report.

10. Change the report name to **rptPatientMailingLabels**, and then click the **Finish** button. The report is saved, and the first page of the report appears in Print Preview. Note that two columns of labels appear across the page. See Figure 7–36.

Figure 7–36 Print Preview of mailing labels

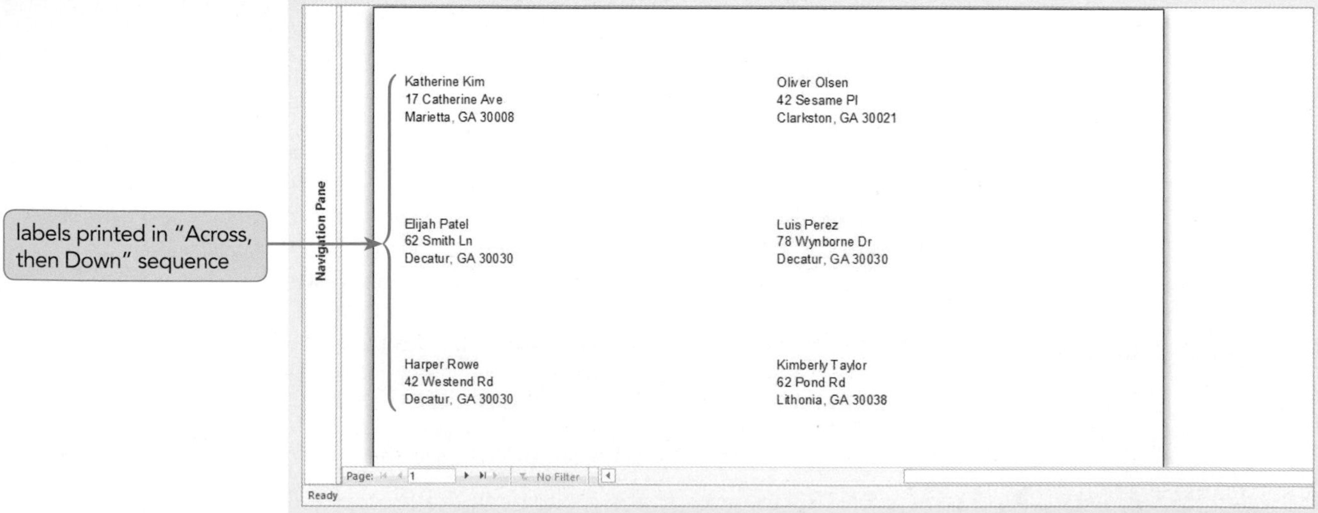
labels printed in "Across, then Down" sequence
Navigation Pane
Katherine Kim
17 Catherine Ave
Marietta, GA 30008
Oliver Olsen
42 Sesame Pl
Clarkston, GA 30021
Elijah Patel
62 Smith Ln
Decatur, GA 30030
Luis Perez
78 Wynborne Dr
Decatur, GA 30030
Harper Rowe
42 Westend Rd
Decatur, GA 30030
Kimberly Taylor
62 Pond Rd
Lithonia, GA 30038
Page: 1
No Filter
Ready

The rptPatientMailingLabels report is a multiple-column report. The labels will be printed in ascending order by zip code and, within each zip code, in ascending order by last name. The first label will be printed in the upper-left corner on the first page, the second label will be printed to its right, the third label will be printed below the first label, and so on. This style of multiple-column report is the "across, then down" layout. Instead, Donna wants the labels to print with the "down, then across" layout because she prefers to pull the labels from the sheet in this manner. In this layout, the first label is printed, the second label is printed below the first, and so on. After the bottom label in the first column is printed, the next label is printed at the top of the second column. The "down, then across" layout is also called **newspaper-style columns** or **snaking columns**.

To change the layout of the mailing label report:

1. Switch to Design view. The Detail section, the only section in the report, is sized for a single label.

   First, you'll change the layout to snaking columns.

2. On the ribbon, click the **Report Design Tools Page Setup** tab.
3. In the Page Layout group, click the **Page Setup** button to open the Page Setup dialog box, and then click the **Columns** tab. The Page Setup dialog box displays the column options for the report. See Figure 7–37.

   The options in the Page Setup dialog box let you change the properties of a multiple-column report. In the Grid Settings section, you specify the number of columns and the row and column spacing. In the Column Size section, you specify the width and height of each column set. In the Column Layout section, you specify the direction the information flows in the columns.

Figure 7–37 Columns tab in the Page Setup dialog box

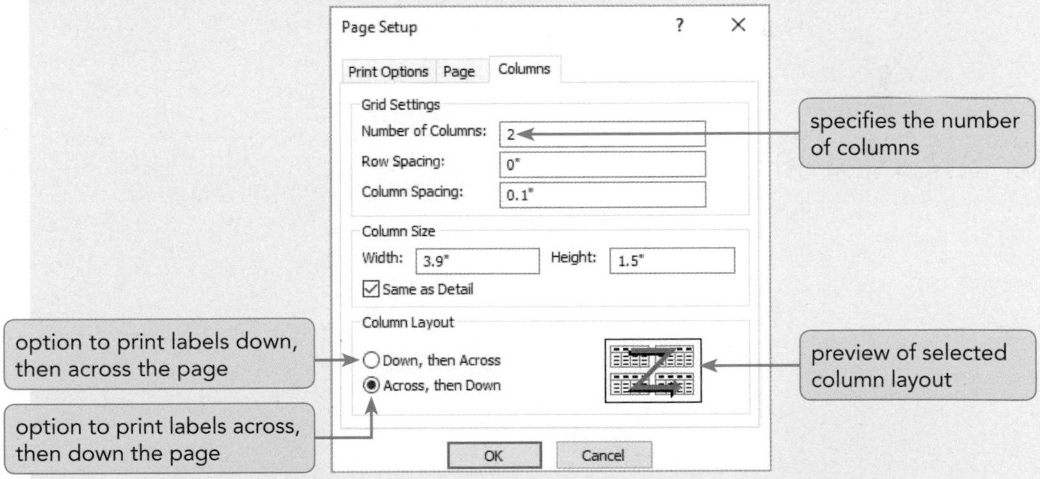
Page Setup
?
Print Options
Page
Columns
Grid Settings
Number of Columns:
2
Row Spacing:
0"
Column Spacing:
0.1"
Column Size
Width:
3.9"
Height:
1.5"
Same as Detail
Column Layout
Down, then Across
Across, then Down
OK
Cancel
specifies the number of columns
option to print labels down, then across the page
option to print labels across, then down the page
preview of selected column layout

TIP

When you select a label using a manufacturer's name and product code, the options in the dialog box are set automatically.

4. Click the **Down, then Across** option button, and then click the **OK** button. You've finished the report changes, so you can now save and preview the report.
5. Save your report design changes, and then switch to Print Preview. The labels appear in the snaking columns layout.

   You've finished all work on Donna's reports.

6. **sam** Close the report, make a backup copy of the database, compact and repair the database, and then close it.

Donna is very pleased with the modified report and the two new reports, which will provide her with improved information and expedite her written communications with patients.

REVIEW

Session 7.3 Quick Check

1. What is the function and syntax to print the current date in a report?
2. How do you insert a page number in the Page Header section?
3. Must the page number reside only in the Page Header section?
4. Clicking the Title button in the Header/Footer group on the Report Design Tools Design tab adds a report title to the _______ section.
5. What is a multiple-column report?

PRACTICE

Review Assignments

Data File needed for the Review Assignments: Supplier.accdb ***(cont. from Module 6)***

Donna wants you to create a custom report for the Supplier database that prints all companies and the products they offer. She also wants you to customize an existing report. Complete the following steps:

1. Open the **Supplier** database you worked with in the previous two modules.
2. Modify the **rptSupplierDetails** report by completing the following steps:
   a. Change the report title to **Lakewood Suppliers**.
   b. Remove the alternate row color from the detail lines in the report.
   c. Change the first column heading to **Supplier ID**. Change the fourth column heading to **First Name** and the fifth column heading to **Last Name**.
   d. In the Report Footer section, add a grand total count of the number of suppliers that appear in the report, make sure the calculated control box has a transparent border, and left-align the control with the left edge of the Company field value box. Left-align the count value in the calculated control box.
   e. Add a label that contains the text **Suppliers:** to the left of the count of the total number of suppliers, aligned to the left margin, and aligned with the bottom of the count calculated control box.
   f. Set the margins to Normal, and adjust the width of the grid to 7.5 inches. Adjust the width of the label control in the Report Header to span the width of the page, ending up one grid dot to the left of the width of the right margin.
   g. Move the page number control to the right until it is one grid dot to the left of the right margin. Right-align the page number value in the control box.
3. After you've completed and saved your modifications to the rptSupplierDetails report, filter the report in Report view, selecting all records that contain the word "supplies" in the Company field. Copy the headings and detail lines of the filtered report, and paste it into a new Word document. Save the document as **NP_AC_7_Supplies** in the location where you are storing your files. Close Word, save your changes to the Access report, and then close it.
4. Create a query that displays the Company and Category fields from the tblSupplier table and the ProductName, Price, and Units fields from the tblProduct table. Save the query as **qrySupplierProducts**, modify it to sort in ascending order by the first three fields in the query, and then save your changes.
5. Create a custom report based on the qrySupplierProducts query. Figure 7–38 shows a sample of the completed report. Refer to the figure as you create the report. Distribute the fields horizontally to produce a visually balanced report.

Figure 7–38 Supplier database custom report

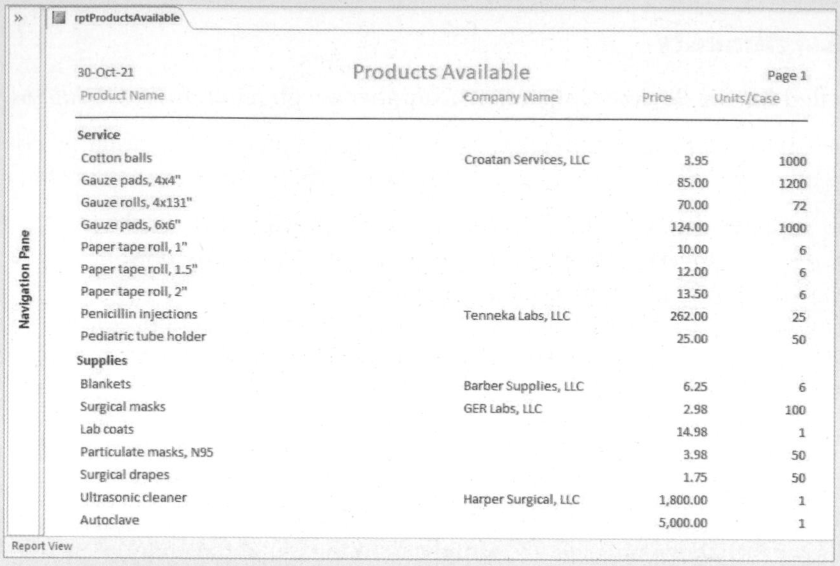
rptProductsAvailable
Navigation Pane
Report View

30-Oct-21 Products Available Page 1

Product Name	Company Name	Price	Units/Case
Service			
Cotton balls	Croatan Services, LLC	3.95	1000
Gauze pads, 4x4"		85.00	1200
Gauze rolls, 4x131"		70.00	72
Gauze pads, 6x6"		124.00	1000
Paper tape roll, 1"		10.00	6
Paper tape roll, 1.5"		12.00	6
Paper tape roll, 2"		13.50	6
Penicillin injections	Tenneka Labs, LLC	262.00	25
Pediatric tube holder		25.00	50
Supplies			
Blankets	Barber Supplies, LLC	6.25	6
Surgical masks	GER Labs, LLC	2.98	100
Lab coats		14.98	1
Particulate masks, N95		3.98	50
Surgical drapes		1.75	50
Ultrasonic cleaner	Harper Surgical, LLC	1,800.00	1
Autoclave		5,000.00	1

a. Save the report as **rptProductsAvailable**.
b. Use the Category field (from the tblSupplier table) as a grouping field, and use the Company field (from the tblSupplier table) as a sort field.
c. Hide duplicate values for the Company field.
d. Keep the whole group together on one page.
e. Remove the borders from the field value boxes.
f. Remove the alternate row color from the group header and detail line.
g. Add the Page title **Products Available** using an 18-point Calibri font, centered horizontally.
h. Apply a text filter for companies that contain "LLC" in the Company Name.

6. Create a mailing label report according to the following instructions:
   a. Use the tblSupplier table as the record source.
   b. Use Avery C2160 labels, and use the default font, size, weight, and color.
   c. For the prototype label, add the ContactFirst, a space, and ContactLast on the first line; the Company on the second line; the Address on the third line; and the City, a comma and a space, State, a space, and Zip on the fourth line.
   d. Sort by Zip and then by Company, and then name the report **rptCompanyMailingLabels**.
   e. Format the report with a down, then across page layout.
7. Make a backup copy of the database, compact and repair, and then close the Supplier database.

APPLY

Case Problem 1

Data File needed for this Case Problem: School.accdb *(cont. from Module 6)*

Great Giraffe Jeremiah Garver wants you to create a custom report and mailing labels for the School database. The custom report will be based on the results of a query you will create. Complete the following steps:

1. Open the **School** database you worked with in the previous two modules.
2. Create a query that displays the Title and StartDate fields from the tblCourse table, and the SignupID, TotalCost, BalanceDue, and PaymentPlan fields from the tblRegistration table. Sort in ascending order by the Title and StartDate fields, and then save the query as **qryRegistrationPayments**.
3. Create a custom report based on the qryRegistrationPayments query. Figure 7–39 shows a sample of the first page of the completed report. Refer to the figure as you create the report.

Figure 7–39 School database custom report

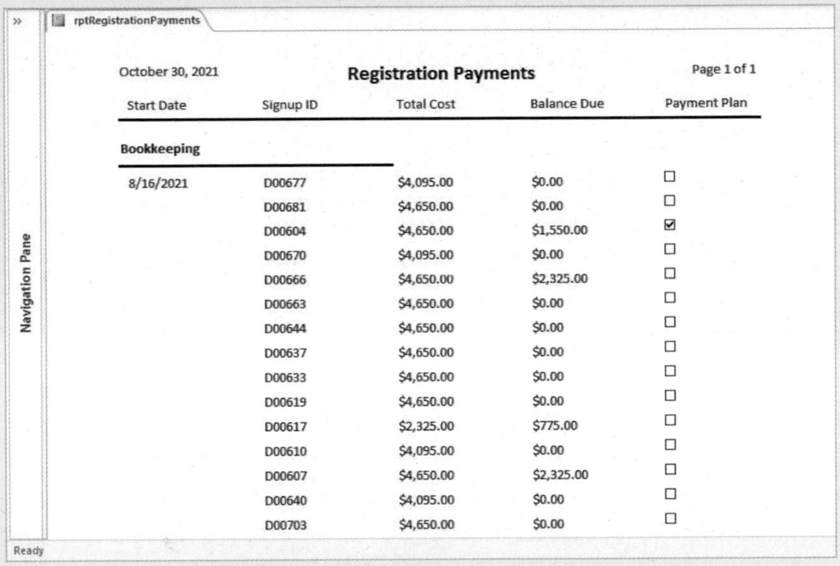
rptRegistrationPayments

October 30, 2021 — **Registration Payments** — Page 1 of 1

Start Date	Signup ID	Total Cost	Balance Due	Payment Plan
Bookkeeping				
8/16/2021	D00677	$4,095.00	$0.00	☐
	D00681	$4,650.00	$0.00	☐
	D00604	$4,650.00	$1,550.00	☑
	D00670	$4,095.00	$0.00	☐
	D00666	$4,650.00	$2,325.00	☐
	D00663	$4,650.00	$0.00	☐
	D00644	$4,650.00	$0.00	☐
	D00637	$4,650.00	$0.00	☐
	D00633	$4,650.00	$0.00	☐
	D00619	$4,650.00	$0.00	☐
	D00617	$2,325.00	$775.00	☐
	D00610	$4,095.00	$0.00	☐
	D00607	$4,650.00	$2,325.00	☐
	D00640	$4,095.00	$0.00	☐
	D00703	$4,650.00	$0.00	☐

Navigation Pane
Ready

a. Save the report as **rptRegistrationPayments**.
b. Use the Title field as a grouping field.
c. Hide duplicate values for the StartDate field.
d. Keep the whole group together on one page.
e. Use Wide margins and spacing to distribute the columns evenly across the page.
f. Remove the alternate row color for all sections.
g. Use black font for all the controls and a 2-point thickness for the lines.

4. Use the following instructions to create the mailing labels:
   a. Use the tblStudent table as the record source for the mailing labels.
   b. Use Avery C2160 labels, and use the default font, size, weight, and color.
   c. For the prototype label, place FirstName, a space, and LastName on the first line; Address on the second line; and City, a comma and space, State, a space, and Zip on the third line.
   d. Sort by Zip and then by LastName, and then name the report **rptStudentLabels**.
   e. Format the report with a three-column, down, then across page layout.
5. Make a backup copy of the database, compact and repair it, and then close the School database.

CREATE

Case Problem 2

Data File needed for this Case Problem: Storm.accdb *(cont. from Module 6)*

Drain Adopter Tandrea Austin wants you to modify an existing report and to create a custom report and mailing labels for the Storm database. Complete the following steps:

1. Open the **Storm** database you worked with in the previous two modules.
2. Modify the **rptVolunteersAndDrains** report. Figure 7–40 shows a sample of the first page of the completed report. Refer to the figure as you modify the report.

Figure 7–40 **Storm database enhanced report**

rptVolunteersAndDrains
Navigation Pane
Volunteers
10/30/21
Page 1
Volunteer ID ABE2300 City Bellingham Email student@example.com
First Name Student First State WA Signup Date 3/12/21
Last Name Student Last Zip 98226 Trained
Street 503 Veterans Boulevard Phone 3605556202
Drain ID Main Street Cross Street Direction Maint Req
CAR13SE Carvell Boulevard 13th Street SE
Volunteer ID ADA1006 City Bellingham Email k.adams13@example.com
First Name Kathryn State WA Signup Date 2/8/22
Last Name Adams Zip 98225 Trained
Street 322 Emerald Avenue Phone 3605555225
Drain ID Main Street Cross Street Direction Maint Req
TRO20SE Troy Boulevard 20th Street SE
Volunteer ID ALL8993 City Bellingham Email r.allen70@example.com
Report View

a. Delete the picture at the top of the report.
b. Set Narrow margins and a grid width of 10.5 inches.
c. Center the report title at the 5.25-inch mark on the ruler, and ensure the text is "Volunteers", formatted in bold and 22-point font.
d. Move the Maint Req column to the right margin, and use horizontal spacing to evenly distribute the columns.
e. Remove the alternate row color from the detail lines in the report.
f. Change the page number format from "Page n of m" to "Page n."
g. Move the date and page number to the Page Header section.
h. Change the date format to short date.
i. Add a grand total control that calculates the total number of volunteers, and add a label with the text **Total volunteers**.

3. Create a query that displays, in order, the DrainID, MainStreet, CrossStreet, and Direction fields from the tblDrain table, the FirstName and LastName fields from the tblVolunteer table. Sort in ascending order by the DrainID and LastName fields, and then save the query as **qryDrainsWithVolunteers**.
4. Create a custom report based on the qryDrainsWithVolunteers query. Figure 7–41 shows a sample of the first page of the completed report. Refer to the figure as you create the report.

Figure 7–41 **Storm database custom report**

rptDrainsWithVolunteers
11/11/18
Adopted Drains
Page 1
Drain ID Main Street Cross Street First Name Last Name
12-point bold text
NE
34 adopted drains
count of records for each direction
ARC39NE Arcade Avenue 39th Street Kevin Johnson
BES11NE Best Way 11th Street James Rainey
BIR22NE Birchwood Way 22nd Street Brian Anderson
CAN7NE Canalport Street 7th Street Sharon Wilson
CAR17NE Carvell Boulevard 17th Street Anna Erickson
COU3NE Court Street 3rd Street Willie Anderson
COU19NE 19th Street Deborah Tyrell
EME44NE Emerald Way 44th Street Gloria Bertrand
FRO2NE Frontenac Way 2nd Street Sarah Buck
HAS26NE Haskins Court 26th Street Robert Medlock
HUR23NE Huron Court 23rd Street Patricia Hacker
ING36NE Ingleside Way 36th Street Carl Ben
KER42NE Kerfoot Street 42nd Street Sergio Curry
KIN34NE Kint Lane 34th Street Clarence McCrary
LAV33NE Lavergne Avenue 33rd Street Calvin Mclemore
LLO40NE Lloyd Street 40th Street Jeanette Peterson
LOT41NE Lotus Court 41st Street Marc Long
Loyola Avenue 32nd Street Teresa Haynes
Navigation Pane
Report View

a. Save the report as **rptDrainsWithVolunteers**.
b. The Direction field (from the tblDrain table) is a grouping field.
c. The MainStreet field is a sort field.
d. Hide duplicate values for the MainStreet field.
e. Use Wide margins, and set the grid width to 7 inches. Size fields as shown, and distribute them horizontally using spacing to create a balanced look.
f. Set the background color for the group header and its controls to Blue, Accent 5, Lighter 80% (row 2, column 9 in the Theme Colors palette).
g. In addition to the total for each direction, give a grand total for all drains with the label **Total adopted drains:**.

5. Create a mailing label report according to the following instructions:
   a. Use the tblVolunteer table as the record source.
   b. Use Avery C2160 labels, use a 12-point font size, and use the other default font and color options.
   c. For the prototype label, place FirstName, a space, and LastName on the first line; Street on the second line; and City, a comma and a space, State, a space, and Zip on the third line.
   d. Sort by Zip and then by LastName, and then enter the report name **rptVolunteerMailingLabels**.
   e. Change the page layout of the rptVolunteerMailingLabels report to three snaking columns.
6. Make a backup copy of the database, compact and repair it, and then close the Storm database.

MODULE 8

Sharing, Integrating, and Analyzing Data

Importing, Exporting, Linking, and Analyzing Data in the Clinic Database

ACCESS

OBJECTIVES

Session 8.1

- Export an Access query to an HTML document and view the document
- Import a CSV file as an Access table
- Use the Table Analyzer
- Import and export XML files
- Save and run import and export specifications

Session 8.2

- Create a tabbed subform using a tab control
- Create a chart in a tab control using the Chart Wizard
- Create and use an application part
- Export a PDF file
- Describe the difference between importing, embedding, and linking external objects
- Link data from an Excel workbook

Case | *Lakewood Community Health Services*

Donna Taylor is pleased with the design and contents of the Clinic database. Donna feels that other employees would benefit from gaining access to the Clinic database and sharing data among the different applications employees use. Donna would also like to be able to analyze the data in the database.

In this module, you will import, export, and link data, and you will create application parts. You will also explore the charting features of Access.

STARTING DATA FILES

Access2 → **Module**

Clinic.accdb (*cont.*)
Support_AC_8_NewPatientReferrals.accdb
Support_AC_8_NewPatients.csv
Support_AC_8_Referral.xml
Support_AC_8_Volunteer.xlsx

Review

Supplier.accdb (*cont.*)
Support_AC_8_Ads.xlsx
Support_AC_8_Partners.accdb
Support_AC_8_Payables.csv
Support_AC_8_Payments.xml

Case1

School.accdb (*cont.*)
Support_AC_8_Company.xml
Support_AC_8_Instructor.csv
Support_AC_8_NewStudentReferrals.accdb
Support_AC_8_Room.xlsx

Case2

Storm.accdb (*cont.*)
Support_AC_8_Maintenance.xml
Support_AC_8_Suppliers.xlsx
Support_AC_8_Volunteers.csv

Session 8.1 Visual Overview:

The field names from the table are used as XML tags to identify data.

Each piece of data is encapsulated in paired tags.

```
<tblReferral>
<PatientID>20001</PatientID>
<LastName>Santos</LastName>
<FirstName>Betty</FirstName>
<Guardian>Santos, Lee</Guardian>
<BirthDate>5/25/1920</BirthDate>
<Phone>4045552265</Phone>
<Street>643 Wellington Street</Street>
<City>Atlanta</City>
<State>GA</State>
<Zip>30303</Zip>
<Email>b.santos20@example.com</Email>
</tblReferral>
<tblReferral>
<PatientID>20002</PatientID>
<LastName>Fernandez</LastName>
<FirstName>Amy</FirstName>
<BirthDate>9/18/1943</BirthDate>
<Phone>4045551929</Phone>
<Street>935 Berteau Court</Street>
<City>Atlanta</City>
<State>GA</State>
<Zip>30303</Zip>
<Email>a.fernandez43@example.com</Email>
</tblReferral>
<tblReferral>
<PatientID>20003</PatientID>
<LastName>Brown</LastName>
<FirstName>William</FirstName>
<BirthDate>8/12/1966</BirthDate>
<Phone>4045555871</Phone>
<Street>104 North Greenleaf Court</Street
<City>Atlanta</City>
<State>GA</State>
```

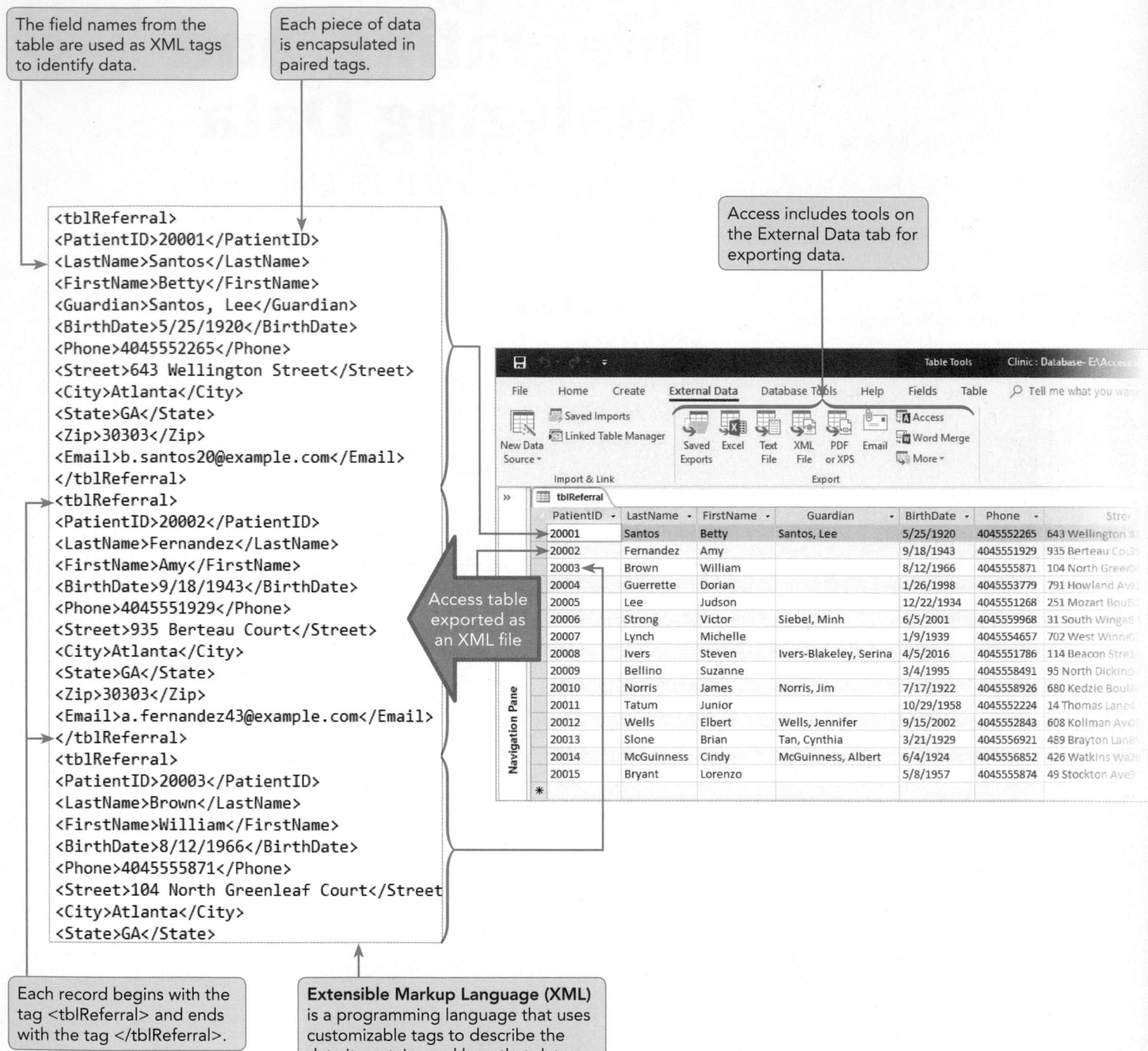

Access table exported as an XML file

Access includes tools on the External Data tab for exporting data.

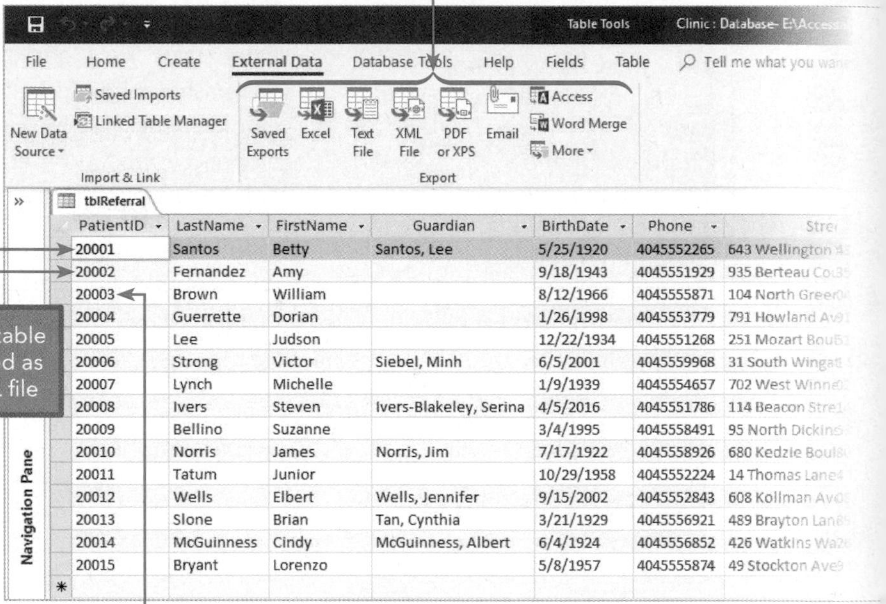

Table Tools
File
Home
Create
External Data
Database Tools
Help
Fields
Table
Tell me what you want
New Data Source
Saved Imports
Linked Table Manager
Import & Link
Saved Exports
Excel
Text File
XML File
PDF or XPS
Email
Access
Word Merge
More
Export
tblReferral
Navigation Pane
PatientID LastName FirstName Guardian BirthDate Phone
20001 Santos Betty Santos, Lee 5/25/1920 4045552265
20002 Fernandez Amy 9/18/1943 4045551929
20003 Brown William 8/12/1966 4045555871
20004 Guerrette Dorian 1/26/1998 4045553779
20005 Lee Judson 12/22/1934 4045551268
20006 Strong Victor Siebel, Minh 6/5/2001 4045559968
20007 Lynch Michelle 1/9/1939 4045554657
20008 Ivers Steven Ivers-Blakeley, Serina 4/5/2016 4045551786
20009 Bellino Suzanne 3/4/1995 4045558491
20010 Norris James Norris, Jim 7/17/1922 4045558926
20011 Tatum Junior 10/29/1958 4045552224
20012 Wells Elbert Wells, Jennifer 9/15/2002 4045552843
20013 Slone Brian Tan, Cynthia 3/21/1929 4045556921
20014 McGuinness Cindy McGuinness, Albert 6/4/1924 4045556852
20015 Bryant Lorenzo 5/8/1957 4045555874

Each record begins with the tag <tblReferral> and ends with the tag </tblReferral>.

Extensible Markup Language (XML) is a programming language that uses customizable tags to describe the data it contains and how that data should be structured.

Exporting Data to XML and HTML

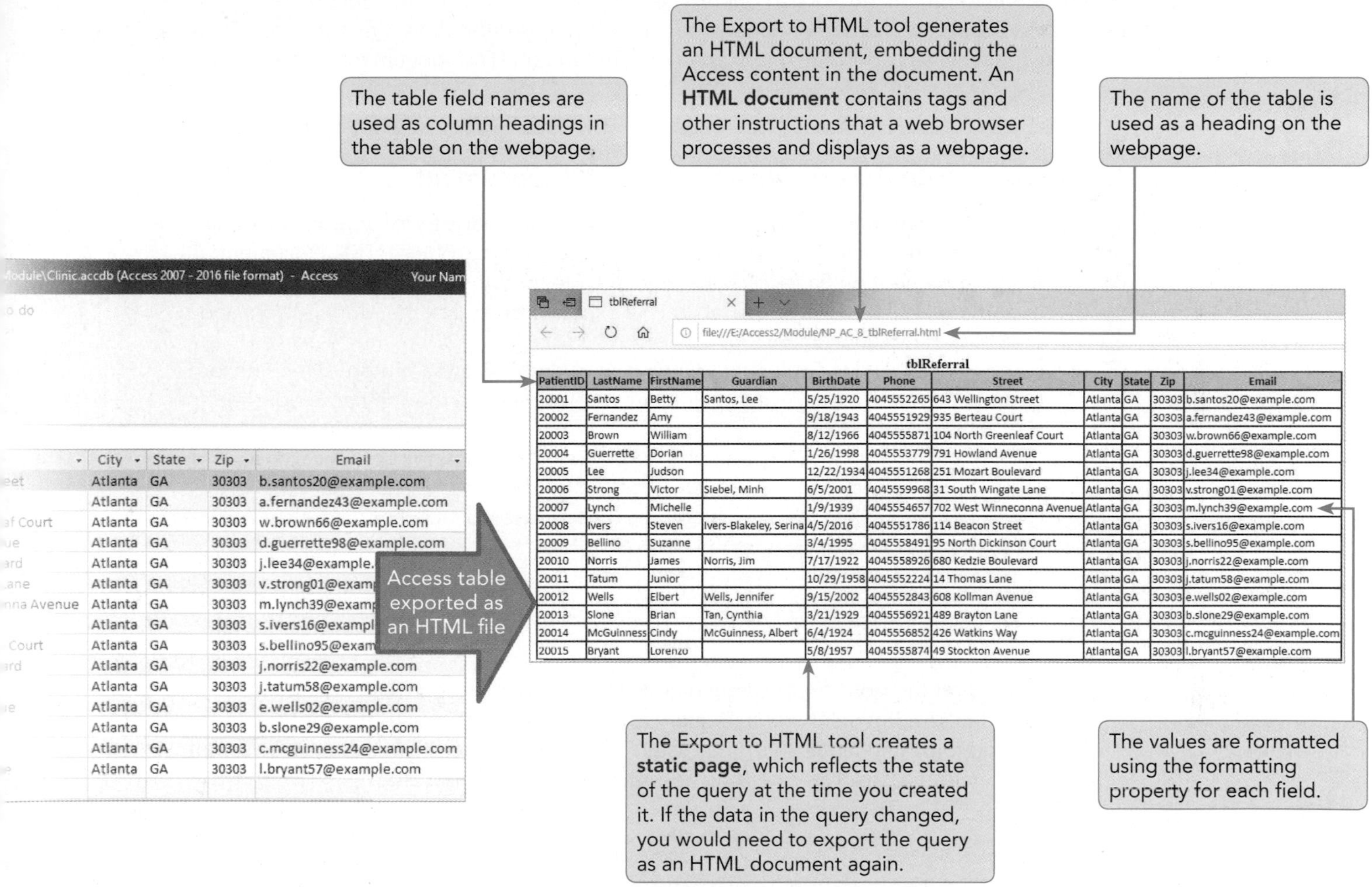
The Export to HTML tool generates an HTML document, embedding the Access content in the document. An HTML document contains tags and other instructions that a web browser processes and displays as a webpage.
The table field names are used as column headings in the table on the webpage.
The name of the table is used as a heading on the webpage.
Access table exported as an HTML file
tblReferral
file:///E:/Access2/Module/NP_AC_8_tblReferral.html
The Export to HTML tool creates a static page, which reflects the state of the query at the time you created it. If the data in the query changed, you would need to export the query as an HTML document again.
The values are formatted using the formatting property for each field.

Exporting an Access Query to an HTML Document

An HTML document contains tags and other instructions that a web browser, such as Google Chrome, Microsoft Edge, or Apple Safari, processes and displays as a webpage.

Donna wants to display the summary data in the qryPatientsAndInvoicesCrosstab query on the clinic's intranet so that all employees working in the office can view it. To store the data on the clinic's intranet, you'll create a webpage version of the qryPatientsAndInvoicesCrosstab query. Creating the necessary HTML document to provide Donna with the information she wants is not as difficult as it might appear. You can use Access to export the query and convert it to an HTML document automatically.

REFERENCE

Exporting an Access Object to an HTML Document

- In the Navigation Pane, right-click the object (table, query, form, or report) you want to export, point to Export on the shortcut menu, and then click HTML Document; or in the Navigation Pane, click the object (table, query, form, or report) you want to export, click the External Data tab, in the Export group, click the More button, and then click HTML Document.
- In the Export - HTML Document dialog box, click the Browse button, select the location where you want to save the file, enter the filename in the File name box, and then click the Save button.
- Click the Export data with formatting and layout check box to retain most formatting and layout information, and then click the OK button.
- In the HTML Output Options dialog box, if using a template, click the Select a HTML Template check box, click the Browse button, select the location for the template, click the template filename, and then click the OK button.
- Click the OK button, and then click the Close button.

You'll export the qryPatientsAndInvoicesCrosstab query as an HTML document. The qryPatientsAndInvoicesCrosstab query is a select query that joins the tblPatient, tblVisit, and tblBilling tables to display selected data associated with those tables for all invoices. The query displays one row for each unique City field value.

To export the qryPatientsAndInvoicesCrosstab query as an HTML document:

1. Start Access, and then open the **Clinic** database you worked with in the previous three modules.

   Trouble? If the security warning is displayed below the ribbon, click the Enable Content button.

2. Open the Navigation Pane (if necessary), right-click **qryPatientsAndInvoicesCrosstab** to display the shortcut menu, point to **Export**, and then click **HTML Document**. The Export - HTML Document dialog box opens.

3. Click the **Browse** button to open the File Save dialog box, navigate to the location where your Data Files are stored, select the text in the File name box, type **NP_AC_8_Crosstab**, make sure HTML Documents appears in the Save as type box, and then click the **Save** button. The File Save dialog box closes, and you return to the Export - HTML Document dialog box. See Figure 8–1.

Figure 8–1 Export - HTML Document dialog box

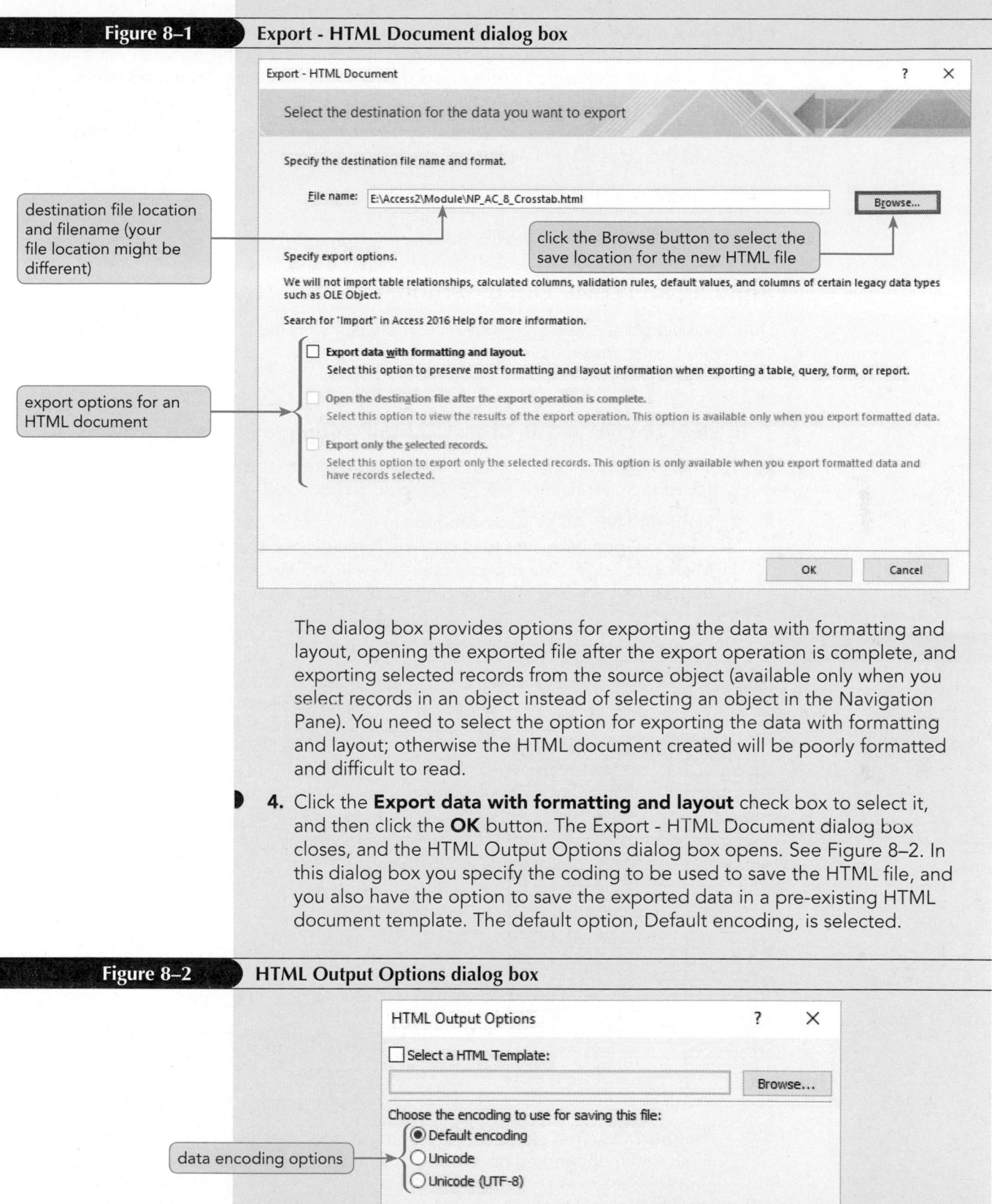

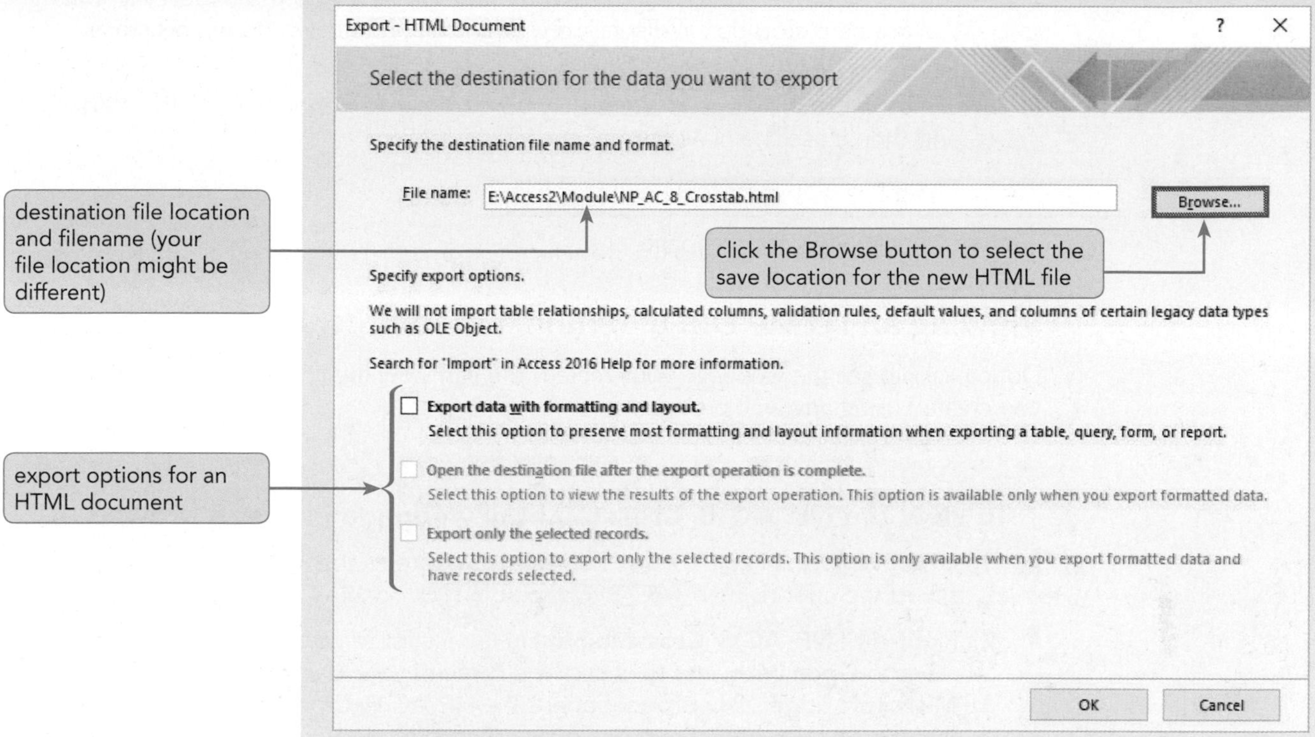
Export - HTML Document
Select the destination for the data you want to export
Specify the destination file name and format.
File name: E:\Access2\Module\NP_AC_8_Crosstab.html
Browse...
Specify export options.
We will not import table relationships, calculated columns, validation rules, default values, and columns of certain legacy data types such as OLE Object.
Search for "Import" in Access 2016 Help for more information.
Export data with formatting and layout.
Select this option to preserve most formatting and layout information when exporting a table, query, form, or report.
Open the destination file after the export operation is complete.
Select this option to view the results of the export operation. This option is available only when you export formatted data.
Export only the selected records.
Select this option to export only the selected records. This option is only available when you export formatted data and have records selected.
OK
Cancel
destination file location and filename (your file location might be different)
click the Browse button to select the save location for the new HTML file
export options for an HTML document

The dialog box provides options for exporting the data with formatting and layout, opening the exported file after the export operation is complete, and exporting selected records from the source object (available only when you select records in an object instead of selecting an object in the Navigation Pane). You need to select the option for exporting the data with formatting and layout; otherwise the HTML document created will be poorly formatted and difficult to read.

4. Click the **Export data with formatting and layout** check box to select it, and then click the **OK** button. The Export - HTML Document dialog box closes, and the HTML Output Options dialog box opens. See Figure 8–2. In this dialog box you specify the coding to be used to save the HTML file, and you also have the option to save the exported data in a pre-existing HTML document template. The default option, Default encoding, is selected.

Figure 8–2 HTML Output Options dialog box

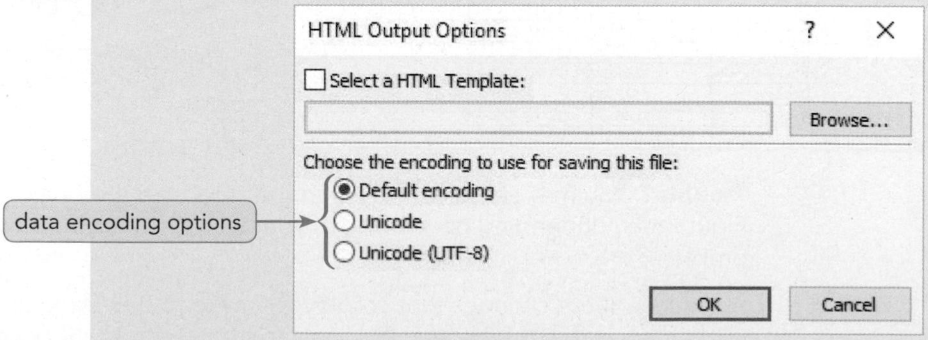
HTML Output Options
Select a HTML Template:
Browse...
Choose the encoding to use for saving this file:
Default encoding
Unicode
Unicode (UTF-8)
OK
Cancel
data encoding options

5. Click the **OK** button. The HTML Output Options dialog box closes, the HTML document named NP_AC_8_Crosstab.html is saved, and the Export - HTML Document dialog box is displayed with an option to save the export steps. You won't save these export steps.
6. Click the **Close** button in the dialog box to close it without saving the steps, and then close the Navigation Pane.

Now you can view the webpage.

Viewing an HTML Document in a Web Browser

Donna asks to see the webpage you created. You can view the HTML document that you created using any web browser.

To view the NP_AC_8_Crosstab.html webpage in a web browser:

1. Open Windows File Explorer, and then navigate to the location where you saved the exported NP_AC_8_Crosstab HTML document.
2. Right-click **NP_AC_8_Crosstab.html** in the file list to open the shortcut menu, point to **Open with**, and then click the name of your web browser, such as **Microsoft Edge**. Your browser opens the NP_AC_8_Crosstab.html webpage that displays the qryPatientsAndInvoicesCrosstab query results. See Figure 8–3.

Figure 8–3 qryPatientsAndInvoicesCrosstab query displayed in Edge

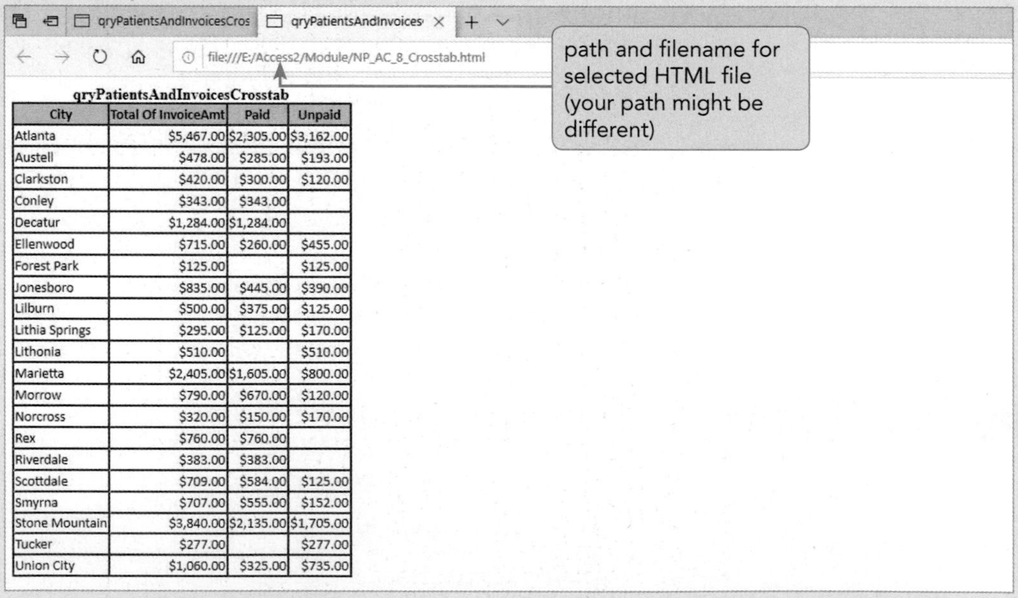
qryPatientsAndInvoicesCros
qryPatientsAndInvoices
file:///E:/Access2/Module/NP_AC_8_Crosstab.html
path and filename for selected HTML file (your path might be different)
qryPatientsAndInvoicesCrosstab

City	Total Of InvoiceAmt	Paid	Unpaid
Atlanta	$5,467.00	$2,305.00	$3,162.00
Austell	$478.00	$285.00	$193.00
Clarkston	$420.00	$300.00	$120.00
Conley	$343.00	$343.00	
Decatur	$1,284.00	$1,284.00	
Ellenwood	$715.00	$260.00	$455.00
Forest Park	$125.00		$125.00
Jonesboro	$835.00	$445.00	$390.00
Lilburn	$500.00	$375.00	$125.00
Lithia Springs	$295.00	$125.00	$170.00
Lithonia	$510.00		$510.00
Marietta	$2,405.00	$1,605.00	$800.00
Morrow	$790.00	$670.00	$120.00
Norcross	$320.00	$150.00	$170.00
Rex	$760.00	$760.00	
Riverdale	$383.00	$383.00	
Scottdale	$709.00	$584.00	$125.00
Smyrna	$707.00	$555.00	$152.00
Stone Mountain	$3,840.00	$2,135.00	$1,705.00
Tucker	$277.00		$277.00
Union City	$1,060.00	$325.00	$735.00

Trouble? You may see different column widths than the ones shown in Figure 8–3, depending on the size of your web browser window. This is not a problem.

Any subsequent changes that employees make to the Clinic database will not appear in the NP_AC_8_Crosstab.html webpage that you created because it is a static webpage—that is, it reflects the state of the qryPatientsAndInvoicesCrosstab query in the Clinic database at the time you created it. If data in the qryPatientsAndInvoicesCrosstab query changes, Donna would need to export the query as an HTML document again.

3. Close your browser, and then click the **Close** button [X] on the Windows File Explorer window title bar to close it and to return to Access.

Trouble? If the Access window is not active on your screen, click the Microsoft Access program button on the taskbar.

Now that you've completed your work creating the webpage, Donna has a file containing information for new patients that she needs to add to the Clinic database. Instead of typing the information into new records, she asks you to import the data into the Clinic database.

Importing a CSV File as an Access Table

Many people use Excel to manage a simple table, such as a table of contact information or product information. Donna has been maintaining an Excel workbook containing basic information for people who have signed up with the Lakewood Community Health Services clinic as patients but have not yet booked appointments. Recall that she could use the Excel button on the External Data tab to access the Import Spreadsheet Wizard and import the Excel worksheet data. However, in this case, Donna has already exported the Excel data to a CSV file. A **CSV (comma-separated values) file** is a text file in which commas separate values, and each line is a record containing the same number of values in the same positions. This is a common format for representing data in a table and is used by spreadsheet applications such as Excel as well as database applications. A CSV file can easily be imported into the Clinic database as a table. To do so, you use the Import Text Wizard, which you open by clicking the Text File button on the External Data Tab.

REFERENCE

Importing a CSV File into an Access Table

- On the External Data tab, in the Import & Link group, click the Text File button to open the Get External Data - Text File dialog box.
- Click the Browse button in the dialog box, navigate to the location where the file to import is stored, click the filename, and then click the Open button.
- Click the "Import the source data into a new table in the current database" option button, and then click the OK button.
- In the Import Text Wizard dialog box, click the Delimited option button, and then click the Next button.
- Make sure the Comma option button is selected. If appropriate, click the First Row Contains Field Names check box to select it, and then click the Next button.
- For each field, if necessary, select the column, type its field name and select its data type, and then click the Next button.
- Choose the appropriate option button to let Access create a primary key, to choose your own primary key, or to avoid setting a primary key, and then click the Next button.
- Type the table name in the Import to Table box, and then click the Finish button.

Donna's CSV file is named Support_AC_8_NewPatients.csv, and you'll import the data as a new table in the Clinic database.

To view and import the CSV file as an Access table:

1. Open Windows File Explorer, navigate to the **Access2 > Module** folder included with your Data Files, right-click **Support_AC_8_NewPatients.csv** in the file list to open the shortcut menu, click **Open with**, and then click **Notepad**.

   Trouble? If Notepad isn't an option when you click Open with, click Choose another app, click Notepad in the How do you want to open this file dialog box that opens, and then click the OK button.

2. Examine the contents of the Support_AC_8_NewPatients.csv file. The file contains rows of data, with commas separating the individual pieces of data.

3. Close the Notepad window, and then close the File Explorer window. You return to the Access window.

   Trouble? If a dialog box appears prompting you to save the file, click Don't Save. You may have accidentally added or deleted a character, and you don't want to save this change to the file.

4. On the ribbon, click the **External Data** tab, and then in the Import & Link group, click **New Data Source**, point to **From File**, and then click the **Text File** button to open the Get External Data - Text File dialog box.

   Trouble? If the Export - Text File dialog box opens, you clicked the Text File button in the Export group. Click the Cancel button, and then repeat Step 4, being sure to select the New Data Source button in the Import & Link group.

5. Click the **Browse** button, navigate to the **Access2 > Module** folder included with your Data Files, click **Support_AC_8_NewPatients.csv**, and then click the **Open** button.

6. In the Get External Data - Text File dialog box, click the **Import the source data into a new table in the current database** option button (if necessary). The selected path and filename appear in the File name box. See Figure 8–4.

Figure 8–4 Get External Data - Text File dialog box

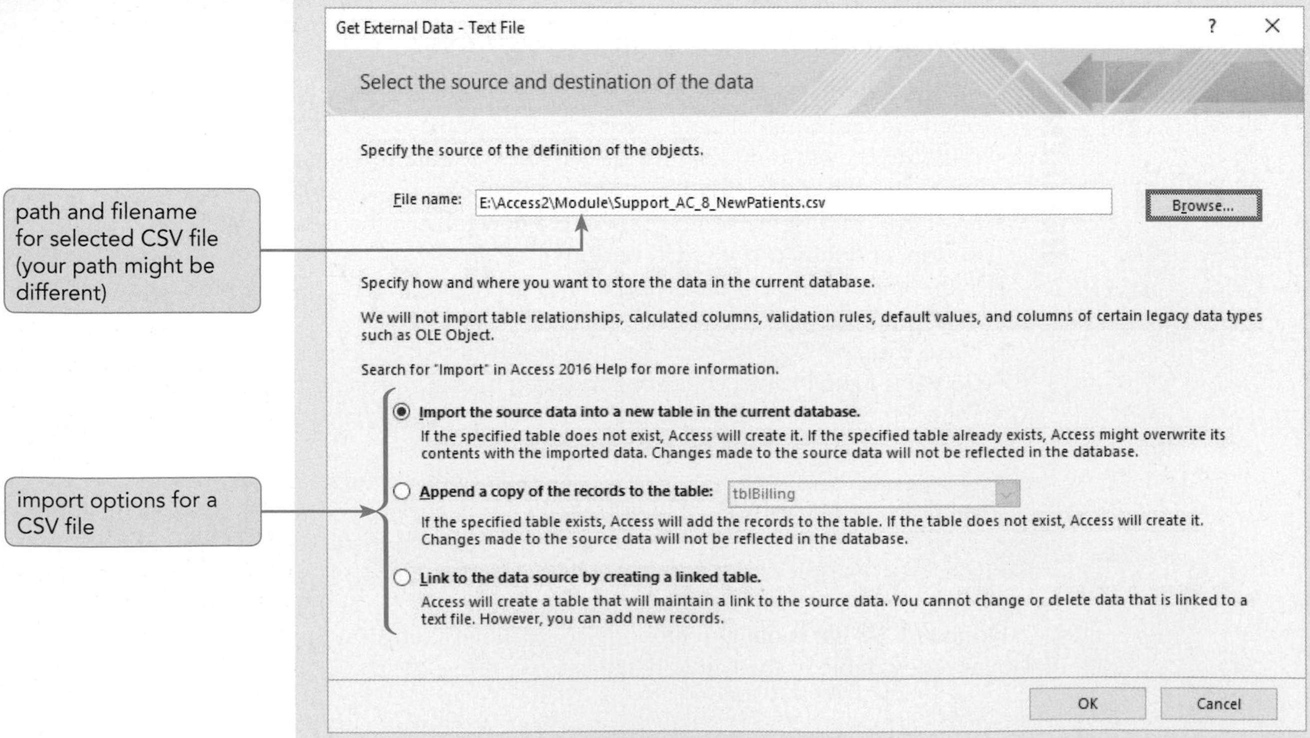
Get External Data - Text File
Select the source and destination of the data
Specify the source of the definition of the objects.
File name: E:\Access2\Module\Support_AC_8_NewPatients.csv
Browse...
Specify how and where you want to store the data in the current database.
We will not import table relationships, calculated columns, validation rules, default values, and columns of certain legacy data types such as OLE Object.
Search for "Import" in Access 2016 Help for more information.
Import the source data into a new table in the current database.
If the specified table does not exist, Access will create it. If the specified table already exists, Access might overwrite its contents with the imported data. Changes made to the source data will not be reflected in the database.
Append a copy of the records to the table: tblBilling
If the specified table exists, Access will add the records to the table. If the table does not exist, Access will create it. Changes made to the source data will not be reflected in the database.
Link to the data source by creating a linked table.
Access will create a table that will maintain a link to the source data. You cannot change or delete data that is linked to a text file. However, you can add new records.
OK
Cancel
path and filename for selected CSV file (your path might be different)
import options for a CSV file

The dialog box provides options for importing the data into a new table in the database, appending a copy of the data to an existing table in the database, and linking to the source data. In the future, Donna wants to maintain the potential new patient data in the Clinic database, instead of using her Excel workbook, so you'll import the data into a new table.

7. Click the **OK** button to open the first Import Text Wizard dialog box, in which you designate how to identify the separation between field values in each line in the source data. The choices are the use of characters to separate, or delimit, the values, or the use of fixed-width columns with spaces between each column. The wizard has identified your file as delimited, which is correct.

8. Click the **Next** button to open the second Import Text Wizard dialog box, in which you specify the delimiter character. The choices are tab, semicolon, comma, space, or another character. The wizard has correctly identified that values are delimited by commas. See Figure 8–5.

Figure 8–5 **Import Text Wizard dialog box specifying the delimiter for values in the CSV file**

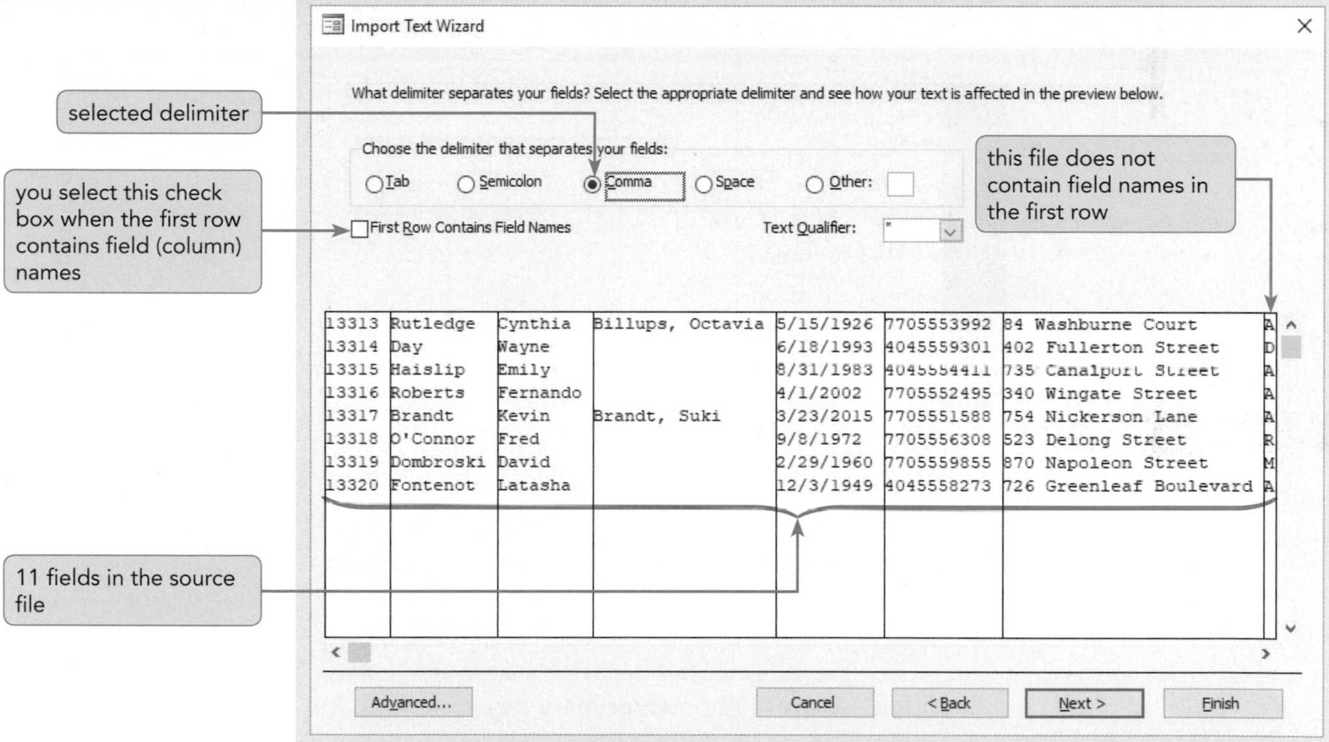
selected delimiter
you select this check box when the first row contains field (column) names
11 fields in the source file
this file does not contain field names in the first row
Import Text Wizard
What delimiter separates your fields? Select the appropriate delimiter and see how your text is affected in the preview below.
Choose the delimiter that separates your fields:
Tab
Semicolon
Comma
Space
Other:
First Row Contains Field Names
Text Qualifier:
13313 Rutledge Cynthia Billups, Octavia 5/15/1926 7705553992 84 Washburne Court
13314 Day Wayne 6/18/1993 4045559301 402 Fullerton Street
13315 Haislip Emily 8/31/1983 4045554411 735 Canalport Street
13316 Roberts Fernando 4/1/2002 7705552495 340 Wingate Street
13317 Brandt Kevin Brandt, Suki 3/23/2015 7705551588 754 Nickerson Lane
13318 O'Connor Fred 9/8/1972 7705556308 523 Delong Street
13319 Dombroski David 2/29/1960 7705559855 870 Napoleon Street
13320 Fontenot Latasha 12/3/1949 4045558273 726 Greenleaf Boulevard
Advanced...
Cancel
< Back
Next >
Finish

The CSV source file contains eight records with 11 fields in each record. A comma serves as the delimiter for values in each line (record), so the Comma option button is selected. The first row in the source file contains the first record, not field names, so the "First Row Contains Field Names" check box is not checked.

9. Click the **Next** button to open the third Import Text Wizard dialog box, in which you enter the field names and set other properties for the imported fields. You will import all fields from the source file and use the Short Text data type and default indexed settings for most fields, except for the data type of the BirthDate field.

10. In the Field Name box, type **PatientID**, click the **Data Type** arrow, click **Short Text**, and then click **Field2** in the table list. The heading for the first column changes to PatientID (partially hidden) in the table list, and the second column is selected.

Be sure the data type for BirthDate is Date With Time, and the data type for Phone and Zip is Short Text.

11. Repeat Step 10 for the remaining 10 columns, making sure Short Text is the data type for all fields, except for BirthDate, which should be Date With Time, typing **LastName**, **FirstName**, **Guardian**, **BirthDate**, **Phone**, **Address**, **City**, **State**, **Zip**, and **Email** in the Field Name box. See Figure 8–6.

Figure 8–6 Field names and options as specified in the Import Text Wizard

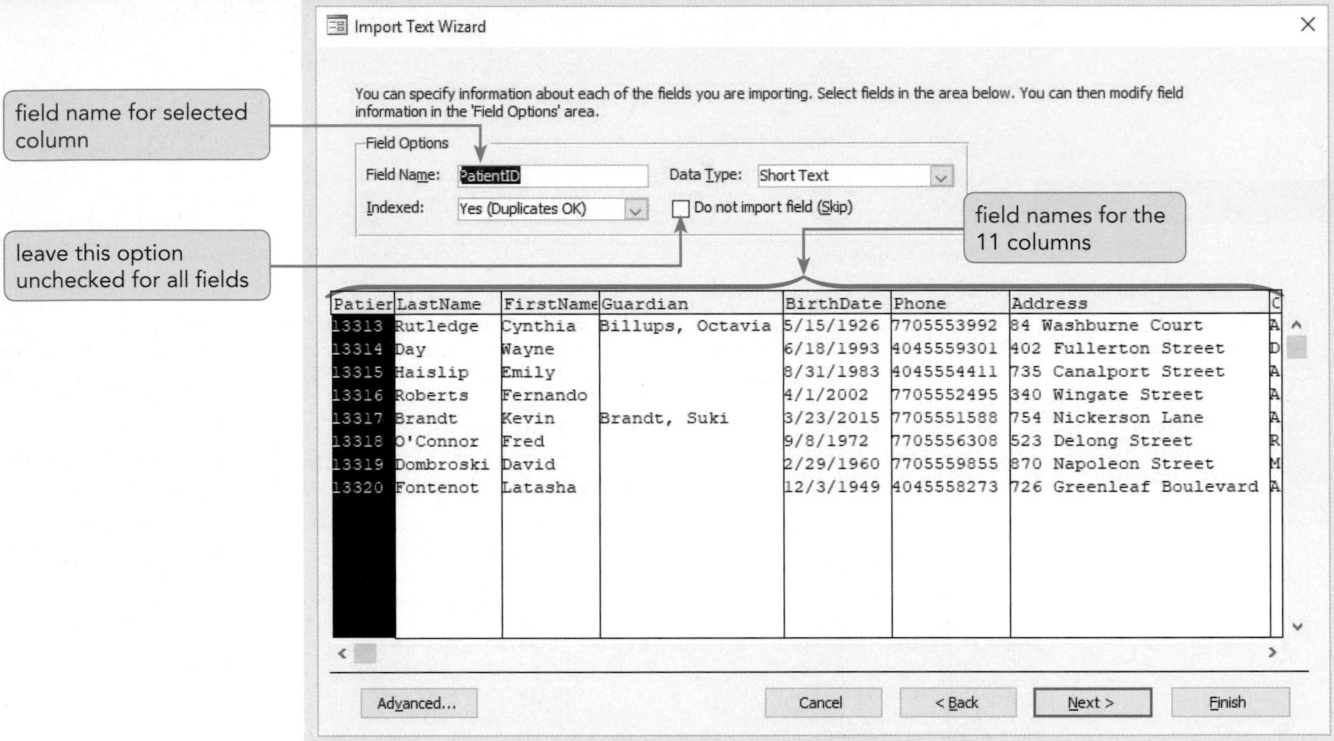
Import Text Wizard
You can specify information about each of the fields you are importing. Select fields in the area below. You can then modify field information in the 'Field Options' area.
Field Options
Field Name: PatientID
Data Type: Short Text
Indexed: Yes (Duplicates OK)
Do not import field (Skip)
field name for selected column
leave this option unchecked for all fields
field names for the 11 columns
Patier LastName FirstName Guardian BirthDate Phone Address C
13313 Rutledge Cynthia Billups, Octavia 5/15/1926 7705553992 84 Washburne Court A
13314 Day Wayne 6/18/1993 4045559301 402 Fullerton Street D
13315 Haislip Emily 8/31/1983 4045554411 735 Canalport Street A
13316 Roberts Fernando 4/1/2002 7705552495 340 Wingate Street A
13317 Brandt Kevin Brandt, Suki 3/23/2015 7705551588 754 Nickerson Lane A
13318 O'Connor Fred 9/8/1972 7705556308 523 Delong Street R
13319 Dombroski David 2/29/1960 7705559855 870 Napoleon Street M
13320 Fontenot Latasha 12/3/1949 4045558273 726 Greenleaf Boulevard A
Advanced...
Cancel
< Back
Next >
Finish

12. Click the **Next** button to open the fourth Import Text Wizard dialog box, in which you select the primary key for the imported table. PatientID, the first column, will be the primary key. When you select this column as the table's primary key, the ID column created by the wizard will be deleted.

13. Click the **Choose my own primary key** option button, make sure **PatientID** appears in the box for the option, click the **Next** button, type **tblNewPatients** as the table name in the Import to Table box, click the **I would like a wizard to analyze my table after importing the data** check box to select it, and then click the **Finish** button. An Import Text Wizard dialog box opens, asking if you want to analyze the table.

14. Click the **Yes** button to close the dialog box and start the Table Analyzer Wizard. You will continue working with this wizard in the next set of steps.

TIP

You can start the Table Analyzer Wizard directly by clicking the Database Tools tab and then clicking the Analyze Table button in the Analyze group.

After importing data and creating a new table, you can use the Table Analyzer Wizard to analyze the imported table. The wizard identifies duplicate data in your table and displays a diagram and explanation in the dialog box describing the potential problem.

Analyzing a Table with the Table Analyzer

Normalizing is the process of identifying and eliminating anomalies, or inconsistencies, from a collection of tables in the database. The **Table Analyzer** analyzes a single table and, if necessary, splits it into two or more tables that are in third normal form. The Table Analyzer looks for redundant data in the table. When the Table Analyzer encounters redundant data, it removes redundant fields from the table and then places them in new tables. The database designer must always review the analyzer results carefully to determine if the suggestions are appropriate.

To use the Table Analyzer Wizard to analyze the imported table:

1. In the first Table Analyzer Wizard dialog box, click the first **Show me an example** button [»], read the explanation, close the example box, click the second **Show me an example** button [»], read the explanation, close the example box, and then click the **Next** button to open the second Table Analyzer Wizard dialog box. The diagram and explanation in this dialog box describe how the Table Analyzer solves the duplicate data problem.
2. Again, click the first **Show me an example button** [»], read the explanation, close the example box, click the second **Show me an example** button [»], read the explanation, close the example box, and then click the **Next** button to open the third Table Analyzer Wizard dialog box. In this dialog box, you choose whether to let the wizard decide the appropriate table placement for the fields, if the table is not already normalized. You'll let the wizard decide.
3. Make sure the **Yes, let the wizard decide** option button is selected, and then click the **Next** button. The wizard indicates that the City and State fields should be split into separate tables. Although this data is redundant, it is an industry practice to keep the city, state, and zip information with the address information in a table, so you'll cancel the wizard rather than split the table.
4. Click the **Cancel** button to close the Table Analyzer Wizard. You return to the final Get External Data - Text File dialog box, in which you specify if you want to save the import steps. You don't need to save these steps because you're importing the data only this one time.
5. Click the **Close** button to close the dialog box.

The tblNewPatients table is now listed in the Tables section in the Navigation Pane. You'll open the table to verify the import results.

To open the imported tblNewPatients table:

1. Open the Navigation Pane, if necessary.
2. Double-click **tblNewPatients** to open the table datasheet, and then close the Navigation Pane.
3. Resize all columns to their best fit, and then click **13313** in the first row in the PatientID column to deselect all values. See Figure 8–7.

Figure 8–7 **Imported tblNewPatients table datasheet**

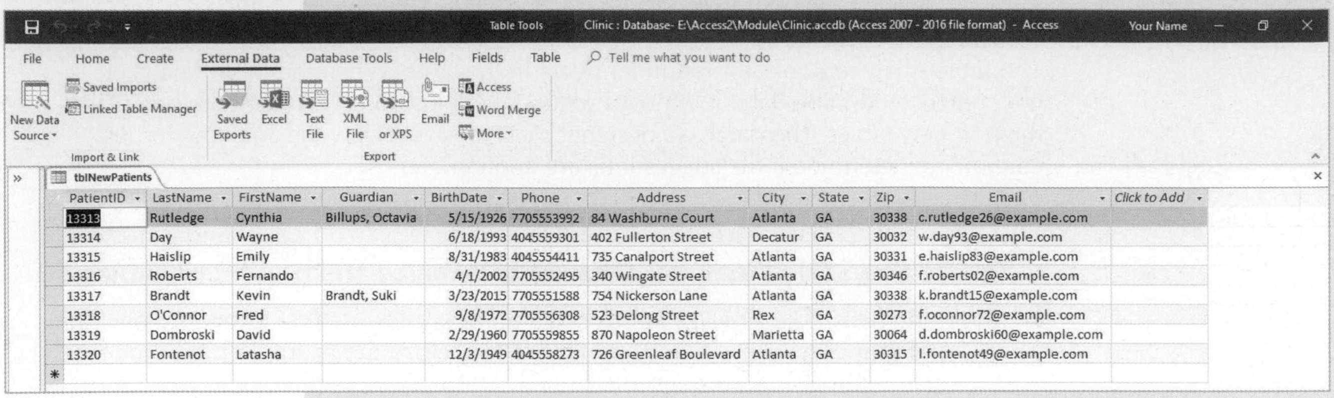
Table Tools
Clinic : Database- E:\Access2\Module\Clinic.accdb (Access 2007 - 2016 file format) - Access
Your Name
File
Home
Create
External Data
Database Tools
Help
Fields
Table
Tell me what you want to do
New Data Source
Saved Imports
Linked Table Manager
Import & Link
Saved Exports
Excel
Text File
XML File
PDF or XPS
Email
Access
Word Merge
More
Export
tblNewPatients
PatientID | LastName | FirstName | Guardian | BirthDate | Phone | Address | City | State | Zip | Email | Click to Add
13313 | Rutledge | Cynthia | Billups, Octavia | 5/15/1926 | 7705553992 | 84 Washburne Court | Atlanta | GA | 30338 | c.rutledge26@example.com
13314 | Day | Wayne | | 6/18/1993 | 4045559301 | 402 Fullerton Street | Decatur | GA | 30032 | w.day93@example.com
13315 | Haislip | Emily | | 8/31/1983 | 4045554411 | 735 Canalport Street | Atlanta | GA | 30331 | e.haislip83@example.com
13316 | Roberts | Fernando | | 4/1/2002 | 7705552495 | 340 Wingate Street | Atlanta | GA | 30346 | f.roberts02@example.com
13317 | Brandt | Kevin | Brandt, Suki | 3/23/2015 | 7705551588 | 754 Nickerson Lane | Atlanta | GA | 30338 | k.brandt15@example.com
13318 | O'Connor | Fred | | 9/8/1972 | 7705556308 | 523 Delong Street | Rex | GA | 30273 | f.oconnor72@example.com
13319 | Dombroski | David | | 2/29/1960 | 7705559855 | 870 Napoleon Street | Marietta | GA | 30064 | d.dombroski60@example.com
13320 | Fontenot | Latasha | | 12/3/1949 | 4045558273 | 726 Greenleaf Boulevard | Atlanta | GA | 30315 | l.fontenot49@example.com

4. Save and close the table.

Next, Donna would like you to import data from another file containing new patient referrals from another health clinic. However, this data is not in an Access table; instead, it's stored in XML format.

Working with XML Files

Lakewood Community Health Services occasionally receives patient referrals from other clinics. Donna was provided an XML document that contains patient contact information from another clinic, which she wants to add to the Clinic database. XML (Extensible Markup Language) is a programming language that is similar in format to HTML but is more customizable and is suited to the exchange of data between different programs. Unlike HTML, which uses a fixed set of tags to describe the appearance of a webpage, developers can customize XML to describe the data it contains and how that data should be structured.

PROSKILLS

Teamwork: Exchanging Data Between Programs

If all companies used Access, you could easily exchange data between any two databases. However, not all companies use Access. One universal and widely used method for transferring data between different database systems is to export data to XML files and import data from XML files. XML files are used to exchange data between companies, and they are also used to exchange data between programs within a company. For example, you can store data either in an Excel workbook or in an Access table or query, depending on which program is best suited to the personnel working with the data and the business requirements of the company. Because the XML file format is a common format for both Excel and Access—as well as many other programs—whenever the data is needed in another program, you can export the data from one program as an XML file and then import the file into the other program. When collaborating with a team of users or sharing database information with other organizations, always consider the characteristics of the programs being used and the best format for exchanging data between programs.

Importing Data from an XML File

In Access, you can import data from an XML file directly into a database table. Donna's XML file is named Support_AC_8_Referral.xml, and you'll import it into a table called tblReferral in the Clinic database.

REFERENCE

Importing an XML File as an Access Table

- On the External Data tab, in the Import & Link group, click the New Data Source button, point to From File, and then click the XML File button to open the Get External Data - XML File dialog box; or right-click the table name in the Navigation Pane, point to Import, and then click XML File.
- Click the Browse button, navigate to the location of the XML file, click the XML filename, and then click the Open button.
- Click the OK button in the Get External Data - XML File dialog box, click the table name in the Import XML dialog box, click the appropriate option button in the Import Options section, and then click the OK button.
- Click the Close button; or if you need to save the import steps, click the Save import steps check box, enter a name for the saved steps in the Save as box, and then click the Save Import button.

Now you will import the Support_AC_8_Referral.xml XML document as an Access table.

To import the contents of the XML document:

1. On the ribbon, click the **External Data** tab if necessary, and then in the Import & Link Group, click the **New Data Source** button, point to **From File**, and then click the **XML File** button. The Get External Data - XML File dialog box opens.
2. Click the **Browse** button to open the File Open dialog box, navigate to the **Access2 > Module** folder included with your Data Files, click **Support_AC_8_Referral.xml**, and then click the **Open** button. The selected path and filename now appear in the File name box.
3. Click the **OK** button. The Import XML dialog box opens. See Figure 8–8.

Figure 8–8 **Import XML dialog box**

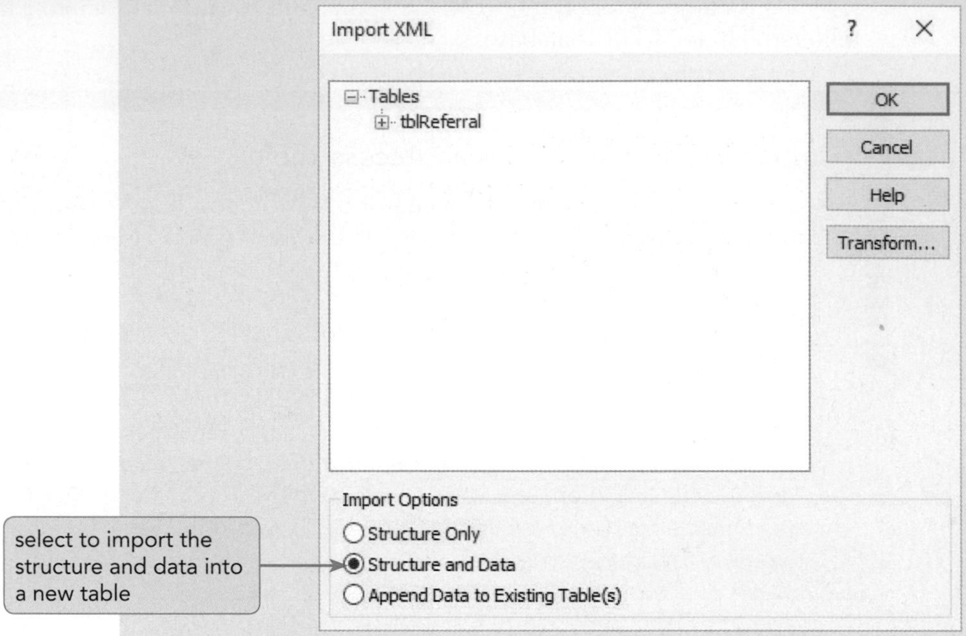
Import XML
Tables
tblReferral
OK
Cancel
Help
Transform...
Import Options
Structure Only
Structure and Data
Append Data to Existing Table(s)
select to import the structure and data into a new table

From the XML file, you can import only the table structure to a new table, import the table structure and data to a new table, or append the data in the XML file to an existing table. You'll choose to import the data and structure to a new table.

4. Make sure the **Structure and Data** option button is selected, click **tblReferral** in the box, and then click the **OK** button. The Import XML dialog box closes, and the last Get External Data - XML File Wizard dialog box is displayed. You'll continue to work with this dialog box in the next set of steps.

Saving and Running Import Specifications

If you need to repeat the same import procedure many times, you can save the steps for the procedure and expedite future imports by running the saved import steps without using a wizard. Because Donna will receive additional lists of patient referrals in the future, you'll save the import steps so she can reuse them whenever she receives a new list.

To save the XML file import steps:

1. In the Get External Data - XML File dialog box, click the **Save import steps** check box to select it. The dialog box displays additional options for the save operation. See Figure 8–9.

Figure 8–9 Save Import Steps dialog box in the Get External Data - XML File Wizard

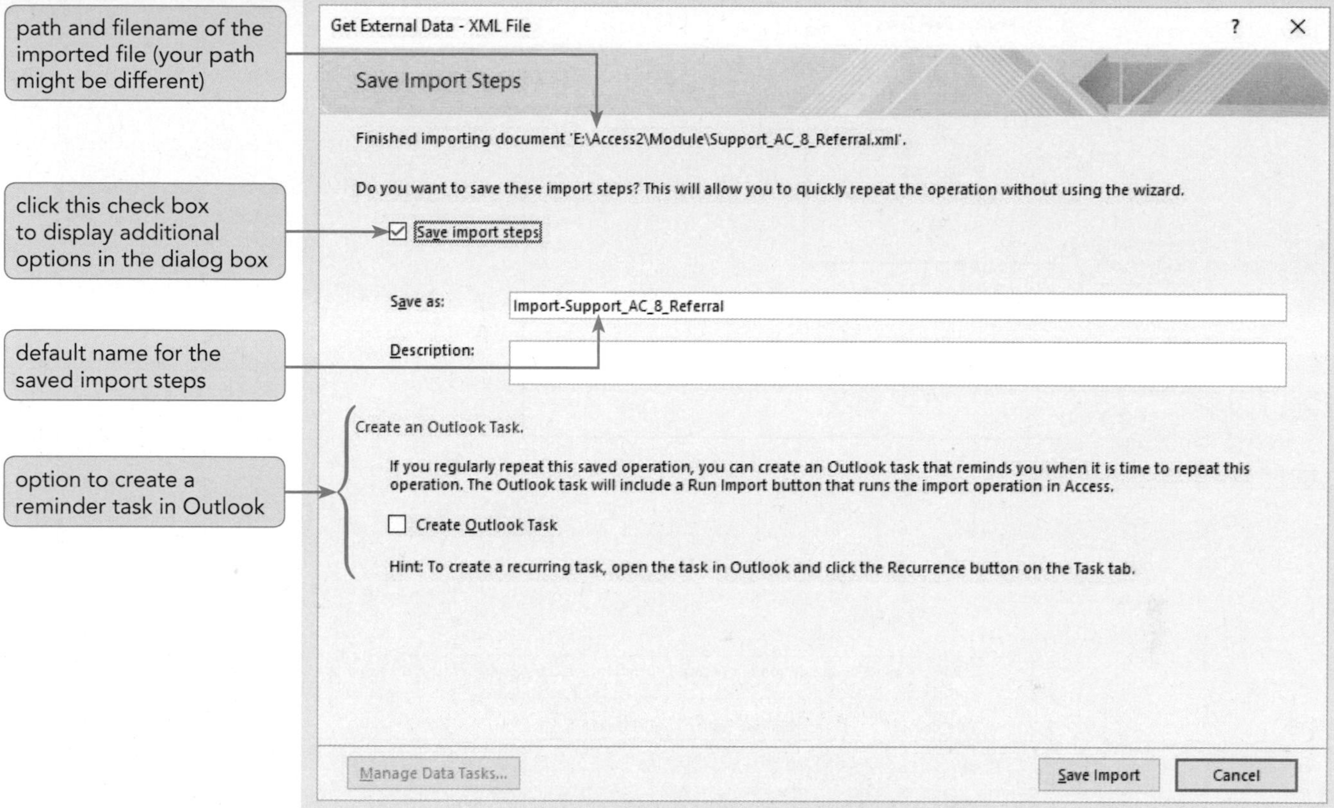
path and filename of the imported file (your path might be different)
click this check box to display additional options in the dialog box
default name for the saved import steps
option to create a reminder task in Outlook
Get External Data - XML File
Save Import Steps
Finished importing document 'E:\Access2\Module\Support_AC_8_Referral.xml'.
Do you want to save these import steps? This will allow you to quickly repeat the operation without using the wizard.
Save import steps
Save as:
Import-Support_AC_8_Referral
Description:
Create an Outlook Task.
If you regularly repeat this saved operation, you can create an Outlook task that reminds you when it is time to repeat this operation. The Outlook task will include a Run Import button that runs the import operation in Access.
Create Outlook Task
Hint: To create a recurring task, open the task in Outlook and click the Recurrence button on the Task tab.
Manage Data Tasks...
Save Import
Cancel

You can accept the default name for the saved import steps or specify a different name, and you can enter an optional description. If the import will occur on a set schedule, you can also create a reminder task in Microsoft Outlook. You'll accept the default name for the saved steps, and you won't enter a description or schedule an Outlook task.

2. Click the **Save Import** button. The import steps are saved as Import-Support_AC_8_Referral, the Get External Data - XML File dialog box closes, and the data from the Support_AC_8_Referral.xml file has been imported into the Clinic database with the name tblReferral. Before reviewing the imported table, you'll add a description to the saved import steps.

3. On the External Data tab, in the Import & Link group, click the **Saved Imports** button to open the Manage Data Tasks dialog box. See Figure 8–10.

Trouble? If the Saved Exports tab is displayed in the Manage Data Tasks dialog box, then you selected the Saved Exports button instead of the Saved Imports button. Click the Saved Imports tab in the dialog box.

Figure 8–10 Saved Imports tab in the Manage Data Tasks dialog box

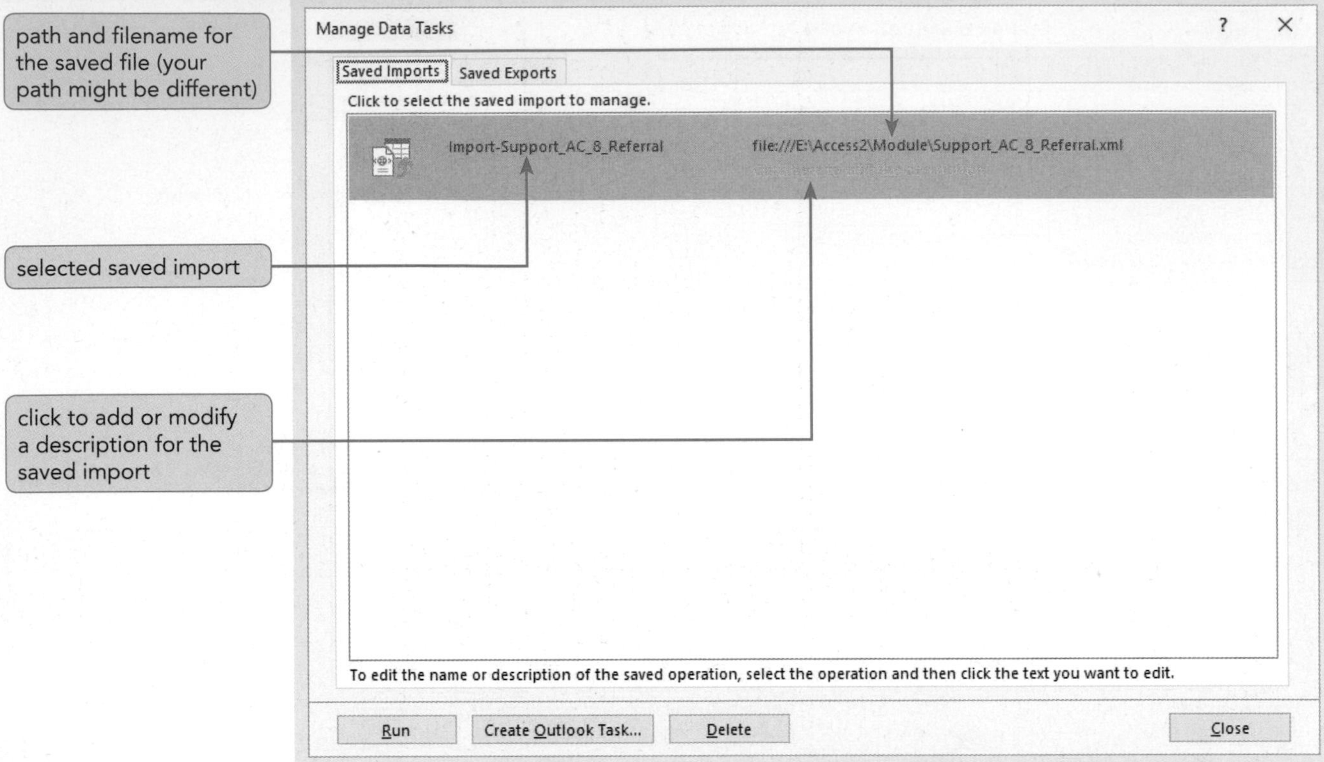
path and filename for the saved file (your path might be different)
selected saved import
click to add or modify a description for the saved import
Manage Data Tasks
Saved Imports
Saved Exports
Click to select the saved import to manage.
Import-Support_AC_8_Referral
file:///E:\Access2\Module\Support_AC_8_Referral.xml
To edit the name or description of the saved operation, select the operation and then click the text you want to edit.
Run
Create Outlook Task...
Delete
Close

In this dialog box, you can change the name of a saved import, add or change its description, create an Outlook task for it, run it, or delete it. You can also manage any saved export by clicking the Saved Exports tab. You'll add a description for the saved import procedure.

4. Click the **Click here to edit the description** link to open a box that contains an insertion point, type **XML file containing patient referrals from another clinic**, click an unused portion of the highlighted selection band to close the box and accept the typed description, and then click the **Saved Exports** tab. You have not saved any export steps, so no saved exports are displayed.

5. Click the **Close** button to close the Manage Data Tasks dialog box.

6. Open the Navigation Pane, double-click the **tblReferral** table to open the table datasheet, close the Navigation Pane, resize all columns to their best fit if necessary, and then click **20001** in the first row in the Patient ID column to deselect all values. See Figure 8–11.

Figure 8–11 Imported XML records in new tblReferral table

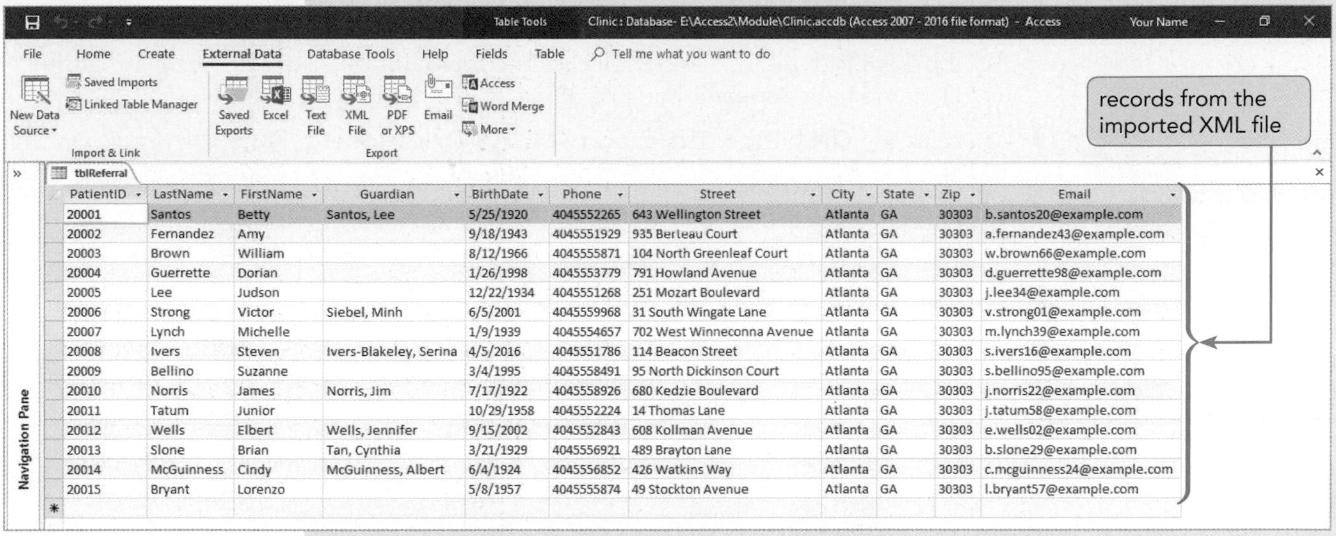
Table Tools
Clinic : Database- E:\Access2\Module\Clinic.accdb (Access 2007 - 2016 file format) - Access
Your Name
File
Home
Create
External Data
Database Tools
Help
Fields
Table
Tell me what you want to do
New Data Source
Saved Imports
Linked Table Manager
Import & Link
Saved Exports
Excel
Text File
XML File
PDF or XPS
Email
Access
Word Merge
More
Export
records from the imported XML file
tblReferral
Navigation Pane
PatientID | LastName | FirstName | Guardian | BirthDate | Phone | Street | City | State | Zip | Email
20001 | Santos | Betty | Santos, Lee | 5/25/1920 | 4045552265 | 643 Wellington Street | Atlanta | GA | 30303 | b.santos20@example.com
20002 | Fernandez | Amy | | 9/18/1943 | 4045551929 | 935 Berleau Court | Atlanta | GA | 30303 | a.fernandez43@example.com
20003 | Brown | William | | 8/12/1966 | 4045555871 | 104 North Greenleaf Court | Atlanta | GA | 30303 | w.brown66@example.com
20004 | Guerrette | Dorian | | 1/26/1998 | 4045553779 | 791 Howland Avenue | Atlanta | GA | 30303 | d.guerrette98@example.com
20005 | Lee | Judson | | 12/22/1934 | 4045551268 | 251 Mozart Boulevard | Atlanta | GA | 30303 | j.lee34@example.com
20006 | Strong | Victor | Siebel, Minh | 6/5/2001 | 4045559968 | 31 South Wingate Lane | Atlanta | GA | 30303 | v.strong01@example.com
20007 | Lynch | Michelle | | 1/9/1939 | 4045554657 | 702 West Winneconna Avenue | Atlanta | GA | 30303 | m.lynch39@example.com
20008 | Ivers | Steven | Ivers-Blakeley, Serina | 4/5/2016 | 4045551786 | 114 Beacon Street | Atlanta | GA | 30303 | s.ivers16@example.com
20009 | Bellino | Suzanne | | 3/4/1995 | 4045558491 | 95 North Dickinson Court | Atlanta | GA | 30303 | s.bellino95@example.com
20010 | Norris | James | Norris, Jim | 7/17/1922 | 4045558926 | 680 Kedzie Boulevard | Atlanta | GA | 30303 | j.norris22@example.com
20011 | Tatum | Junior | | 10/29/1958 | 4045552224 | 14 Thomas Lane | Atlanta | GA | 30303 | j.tatum58@example.com
20012 | Wells | Elbert | Wells, Jennifer | 9/15/2002 | 4045552843 | 608 Kollman Avenue | Atlanta | GA | 30303 | e.wells02@example.com
20013 | Slone | Brian | Tan, Cynthia | 3/21/1929 | 4045556921 | 489 Brayton Lane | Atlanta | GA | 30303 | b.slone29@example.com
20014 | McGuinness | Cindy | McGuinness, Albert | 6/4/1924 | 4045556852 | 426 Watkins Way | Atlanta | GA | 30303 | c.mcguinness24@example.com
20015 | Bryant | Lorenzo | | 5/8/1957 | 4045555874 | 49 Stockton Avenue | Atlanta | GA | 30303 | l.bryant57@example.com

7. Save and close the table.

Next, Donna asks you to export the tblBilling table as an XML file.

Exporting an Access Table as an XML File

Lakewood Community Health Services uses an accounting system that accepts data in XML files. Donna wants to export the tblBilling table as an XML file so it can be tested with the accounting system.

REFERENCE

Exporting an Access Object as an XML File

- Right-click the object (table, query, form, or report) in the Navigation Pane, point to Export, and then click XML File; or click the object (table, query, form, or report) in the Navigation Pane, and then on the External Data tab, click the XML File button in the Export group.
- Click the Browse button in the Export - XML File dialog box, navigate to the location where you will save the XML file, and then click the Save button.
- Click the OK button in the dialog box, select the options in the Export XML dialog box, or click the More Options button and select the options in the expanded Export XML dialog box, and then click the OK button.
- Click the Close button; or if you need to save the export steps, click the Save export steps check box, enter a name for the saved steps in the Save as box, and then click the Save Export button.

You'll export the tblBilling table as an XML file now.

To export the tblBilling table as an XML file:

1. Open the Navigation Pane (if necessary), right-click **tblBilling**, point to **Export** on the shortcut menu, and then click **XML File**. The Export - XML File dialog box opens.

2. Click the **Browse** button to open the File Save dialog box, navigate to the **Access2 > Module** folder included with your Data Files, change the name in the File name box to **NP_AC_8_Billing**, make sure **XML** is specified in the Save as type box, and then click the **Save** button. The selected path and filename now appear in the File name box in the Export-XML File dialog box.

3. Click the **OK** button. The Export XML dialog box opens.

   Clicking the More Options button in the Export XML dialog box expands the dialog box and lets you view and select additional options for exporting a database object to an XML file.

4. Click the **More Options** button to display detailed export options in the Export XML dialog box. See Figure 8–12.

Figure 8–12 Data tab in the Export XML dialog box

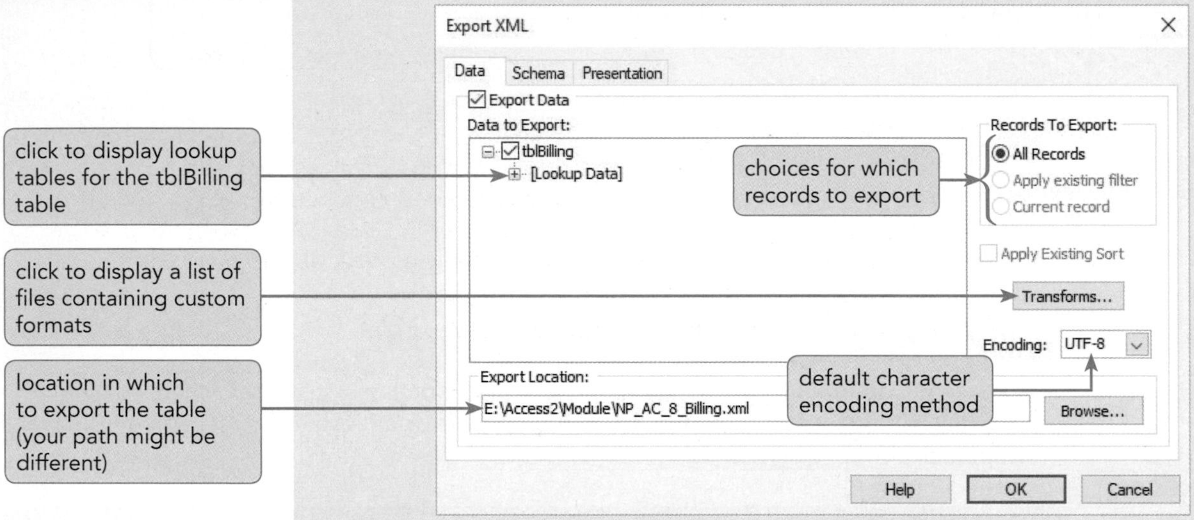
click to display lookup tables for the tblBilling table
click to display a list of files containing custom formats
location in which to export the table (your path might be different)
choices for which records to export
default character encoding method
Export XML
Data
Schema
Presentation
Export Data
Data to Export:
tblBilling
[Lookup Data]
Records To Export:
All Records
Apply existing filter
Current record
Apply Existing Sort
Transforms...
Encoding:
UTF-8
Export Location:
E:\Access2\Module\NP_AC_8_Billing.xml
Browse...
Help
OK
Cancel

The Export Data check box, the Export Location box, and the Records To Export option group display the selections you made in the previous steps. You're exporting all records from the tblBilling table, including the data in the records and the structure of the table, to the NP_AC_8_Billing.xml file in the Access2 > Module folder. The encoding option determines how characters will be represented in the exported XML file. The encoding choices are UTF-8, which uses 8 bits to represent each character, and UTF-16, which uses 16 bits to represent each character. You can also click the Transforms button if you have a special file that contains instructions for changing the exported data.

The accounting software used by the center doesn't have a transform file and requires the default encoding, but Donna wants to review the tables that contain lookup data.

5. In the Data to Export box, click the **expand** icon [+] to the left of [Lookup Data], and then verify that the tblInvoiceItem check box and the tblVisit check box are not checked. Both the tblInvoiceItem table and tblVisit tables contain lookup data because they are in a one-to-many relationship with the tblBilling table. The accounting program requirements don't include any lookup data from the tblInvoiceItem table or tblVisit table, so you don't want the tblInvoiceItem check box or the tblVisit check box to be checked.

   The Data tab settings are correct, so next you'll verify the Schema tab settings.

6. Click the **Schema** tab. See Figure 8–13.

Figure 8–13 **Schema tab in the Export XML dialog box**

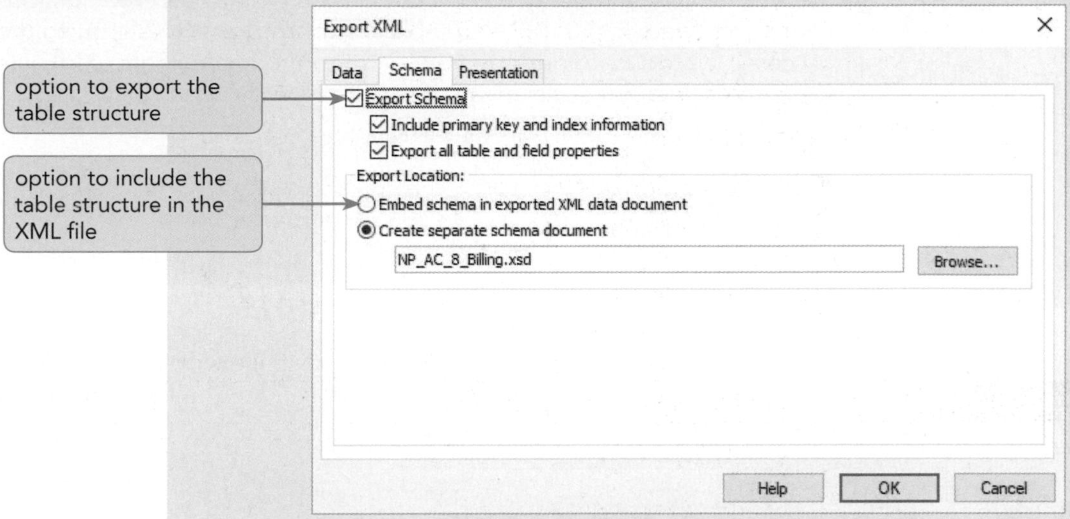
option to export the table structure
option to include the table structure in the XML file
Export XML
Data
Schema
Presentation
Export Schema
Include primary key and index information
Export all table and field properties
Export Location:
Embed schema in exported XML data document
Create separate schema document
NP_AC_8_Billing.xsd
Browse...
Help
OK
Cancel

Along with the data from the tblBilling table, you'll be exporting its table structure, including information about the table's primary key, indexes, and table and field properties. An **XSD (XML Structure Definition) file** is a file that defines the structure of the XML file, much like the Design view of a table defines the fields and their data types. You can include this structure information in a separate XSD file, or you can embed the information in the XML file. The accounting software accepts a single XML file, so you'll embed the structure information in the XML file.

7. Click the **Embed schema in exported XML data document** option button. The Create separate schema document option button is now grayed out.
8. Click the **Presentation** tab. See Figure 8–14.

Figure 8–14 **Presentation tab in the Export XML dialog box**

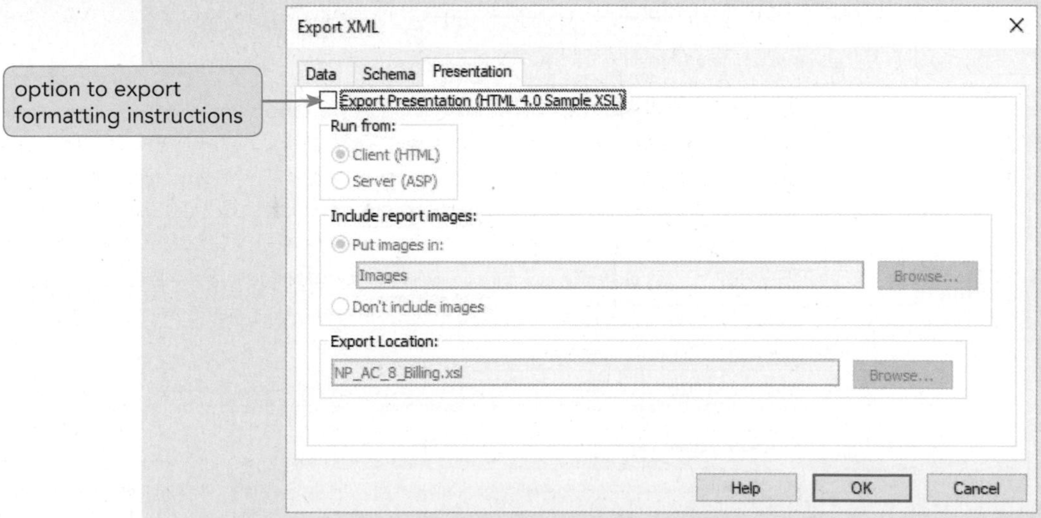
option to export formatting instructions
Export XML
Data
Schema
Presentation
Export Presentation (HTML 4.0 Sample XSL)
Run from:
Client (HTML)
Server (ASP)
Include report images:
Put images in:
Images
Browse...
Don't include images
Export Location:
NP_AC_8_Billing.xsl
Browse...
Help
OK
Cancel

The Presentation tab options let you export a separate **XSL (Extensible Stylesheet Language) file** containing the format specifications for the tblBilling table data. The accounting software contains its own formatting instructions for any imported data, so you will not export an XSL file.

9. Make sure that the Export Presentation (HTML 4.0 Sample XSL) check box is not checked, and then click the **OK** button. The Export XML dialog box closes, the data in the tblBilling table is exported as an XML file to the Access2 > Module folder, and you return to the final Export - XML File dialog box. You'll see the results of creating this file in the next set of steps.

Donna plans to make further tests exporting the tblBilling table as an XML file, so you'll save the export steps.

Saving and Running Export Specifications

Saving the steps to export the tblBilling table as an XML file will save time and eliminate errors when Donna repeats the export procedure. You'll save the export steps and then run the saved steps.

To save and run the XML file export steps:

1. In the Export - XML File Wizard dialog box, click the **Save export steps** check box. The dialog box displays additional options for the save operation.

   The dialog box has the same options you saw earlier when you saved the XML import steps. You'll enter a description, and you won't create an Outlook task because Donna will be running the saved export steps only on an as-needed basis.

2. In the Description box, type **XML file containing accounting entries from the tblBilling table**. See Figure 8–15.

Figure 8–15 Saving the export steps

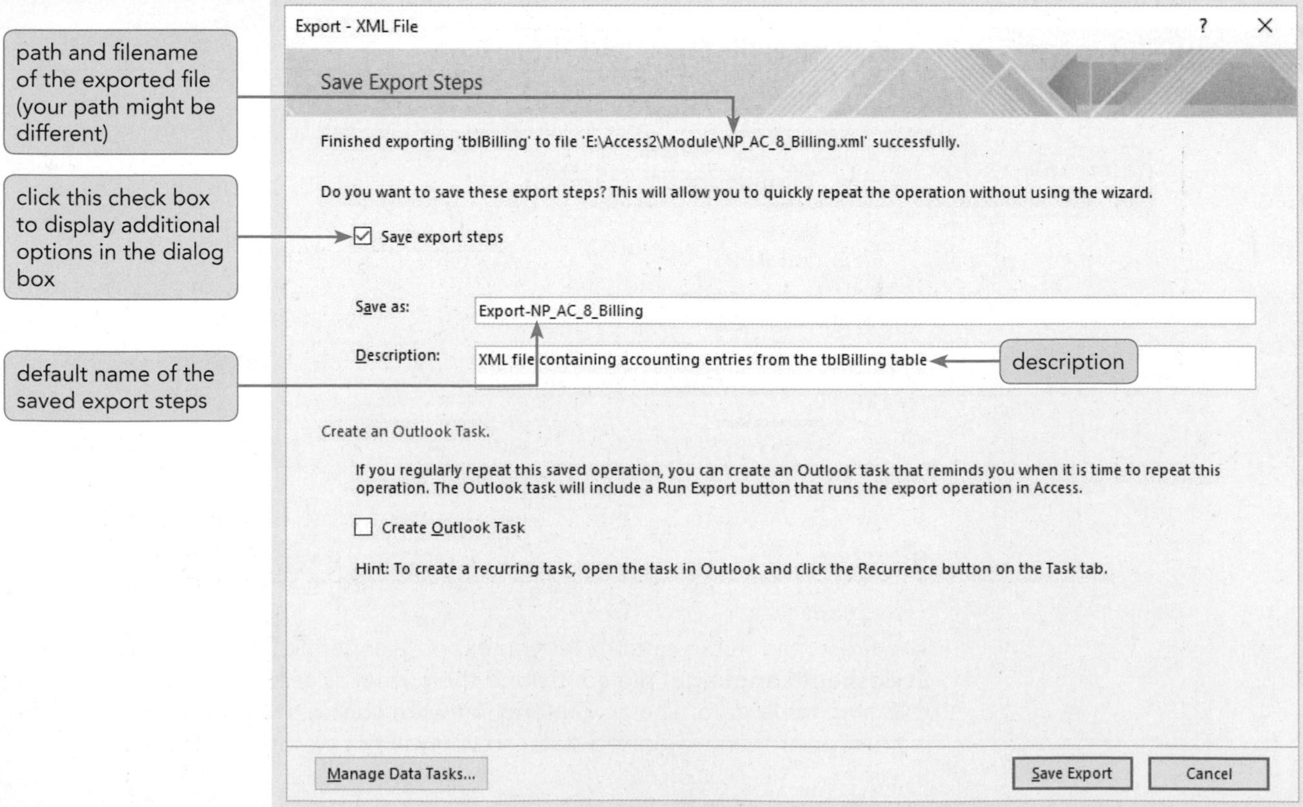
path and filename of the exported file (your path might be different)
click this check box to display additional options in the dialog box
default name of the saved export steps
description
Export - XML File
Save Export Steps
Finished exporting 'tblBilling' to file 'E:\Access2\Module\NP_AC_8_Billing.xml' successfully.
Do you want to save these export steps? This will allow you to quickly repeat the operation without using the wizard.
Save export steps
Save as:
Export-NP_AC_8_Billing
Description:
XML file containing accounting entries from the tblBilling table
Create an Outlook Task.
If you regularly repeat this saved operation, you can create an Outlook task that reminds you when it is time to repeat this operation. The Outlook task will include a Run Export button that runs the export operation in Access.
Create Outlook Task
Hint: To create a recurring task, open the task in Outlook and click the Recurrence button on the Task tab.
Manage Data Tasks...
Save Export
Cancel

3. Click the **Save Export** button. The export steps are saved as Export-NP_AC_8_Billing and the Export - XML File dialog box closes.

   Now you'll run the saved steps.

4. Click the **External Data** tab (if necessary), and then in the Export group, click the **Saved Exports** button. The Manage Data Tasks dialog box opens with the Saved Exports tab selected. See Figure 8–16.

   Trouble? If the Saved Imports tab is displayed in the Manage Data Tasks dialog box, then you selected the Saved Imports button instead of the Saved Exports button. Click the Save Exports tab in the dialog box.

Figure 8–16 Saved Exports tab in the Manage Data Tasks dialog box

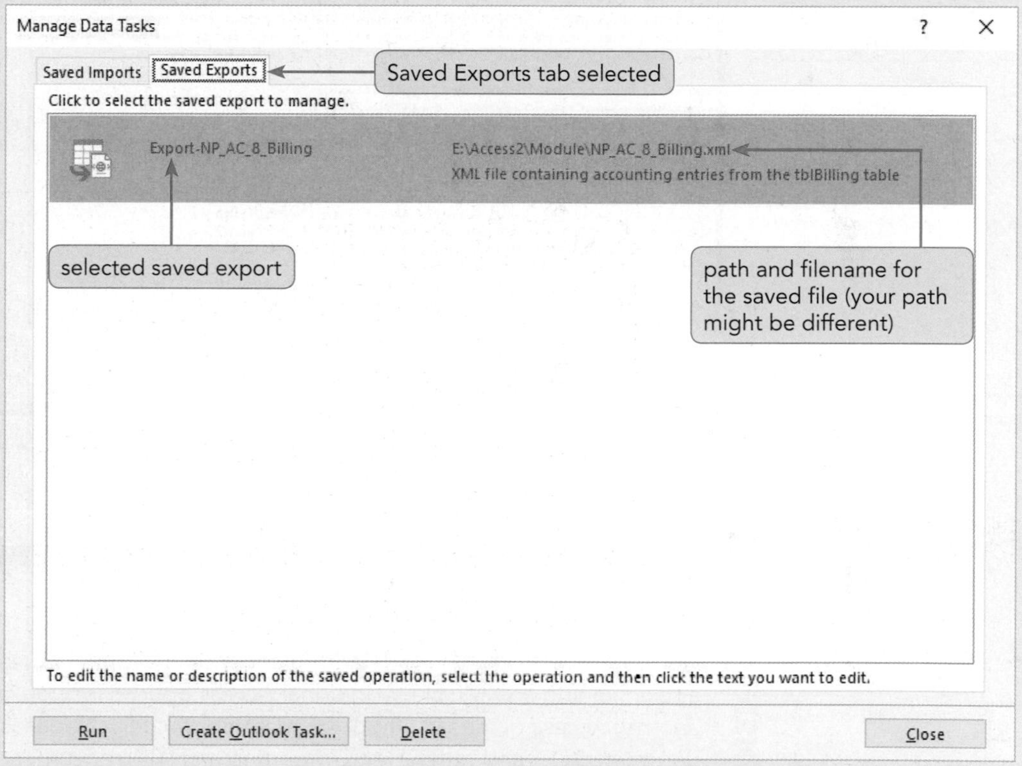
Manage Data Tasks
Saved Imports
Saved Exports
Saved Exports tab selected
Click to select the saved export to manage.
Export-NP_AC_8_Billing
E:\Access2\Module\NP_AC_8_Billing.xml
XML file containing accounting entries from the tblBilling table
selected saved export
path and filename for the saved file (your path might be different)
To edit the name or description of the saved operation, select the operation and then click the text you want to edit.
Run
Create Outlook Task...
Delete
Close

5. Verify that the Export-NP_AC_8_Billing export is selected, and then click the **Run** button. The saved procedure runs, and a message box opens, asking if you want to replace the existing XML file you created earlier.
6. Click the **Yes** button to replace the existing XML file. A message box informs you that the export was completed successfully.
7. Click the **OK** button to close the message box, and then click the **Close** button to close the Manage Data Tasks dialog box.
8. Open Windows File Explorer, navigate to the **Access2 > Module** folder included with your Data Files, right-click the **NP_AC_8_Billing.xml** XML file in the file list to open the shortcut menu, click **Open with**, and then click **Notepad**. See Figure 8–17.

Figure 8–17 NP_AC_8_Billing XML file in Notepad

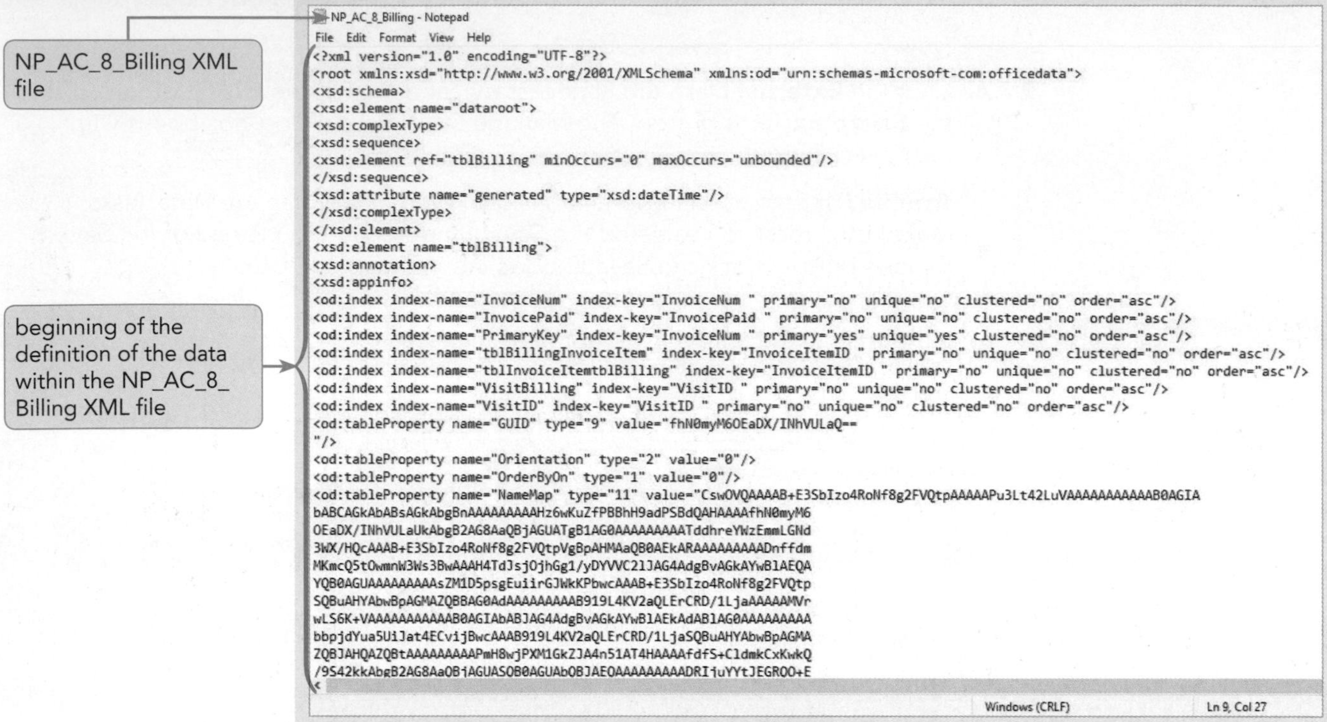
NP_AC_8_Billing XML file
beginning of the definition of the data within the NP_AC_8_ Billing XML file
NP_AC_8_Billing - Notepad
File Edit Format View Help
<?xml version="1.0" encoding="UTF-8"?>
<root xmlns:xsd="http://www.w3.org/2001/XMLSchema" xmlns:od="urn:schemas-microsoft-com:officedata">
<xsd:schema>
<xsd:element name="dataroot">
<xsd:complexType>
<xsd:sequence>
<xsd:element ref="tblBilling" minOccurs="0" maxOccurs="unbounded"/>
</xsd:sequence>
<xsd:attribute name="generated" type="xsd:dateTime"/>
</xsd:complexType>
</xsd:element>
<xsd:element name="tblBilling">
<xsd:annotation>
<xsd:appinfo>
<od:index index-name="InvoiceNum" index-key="InvoiceNum " primary="no" unique="no" clustered="no" order="asc"/>
<od:index index-name="InvoicePaid" index-key="InvoicePaid " primary="no" unique="no" clustered="no" order="asc"/>
<od:index index-name="PrimaryKey" index-key="InvoiceNum " primary="yes" unique="yes" clustered="no" order="asc"/>
<od:index index-name="tblBillingInvoiceItem" index-key="InvoiceItemID " primary="no" unique="no" clustered="no" order="asc"/>
<od:index index-name="tblInvoiceItemtblBilling" index-key="InvoiceItemID " primary="no" unique="no" clustered="no" order="asc"/>
<od:index index-name="VisitBilling" index-key="VisitID " primary="no" unique="no" clustered="no" order="asc"/>
<od:index index-name="VisitID" index-key="VisitID " primary="no" unique="no" clustered="no" order="asc"/>
<od:tableProperty name="GUID" type="9" value="fhN0myM6OEaDX/INhVULaQ==
"/>
<od:tableProperty name="Orientation" type="2" value="0"/>
<od:tableProperty name="OrderByOn" type="1" value="0"/>
<od:tableProperty name="NameMap" type="11" value="CswOVQAAAAB+E3SbIzo4RoNf8g2FVQtpAAAAAPu3Lt42LuVAAAAAAAAAAAB0AGIA
bABCAGkAbABsAGkAbgBnAAAAAAAAAHz6wKuZfPBBhH9adPSBdQAHAAAAfhN0myM6
OEaDX/INhVULaUkAbgB2AG8AaQBjAGUATgB1AG0AAAAAAAAATddhreYWzEmmLGNd
3WX/HQcAAAB+E3SbIzo4RoNf8g2FVQtpVgBpAHMAaQB0AEkARAAAAAAAAAADnffdm
MKmcQ5tOwmnW3Ws3BwAAAH4TdJsjOjhGg1/yDYVVC21JAG4AdgBvAGkAYwBlAEQA
YQB0AGUAAAAAAAAAsZM1D5psgEuiirGJWkKPbwcAAAB+E3SbIzo4RoNf8g2FVQtp
SQBuAHYAbwBpAGMAZQBBAG0AdAAAAAAAAAB919L4KV2aQLErCRD/1LjaAAAAAMVr
wLS6K+VAAAAAAAAAAAB0AGIAbABJAG4AdgBvAGkAYwBlAEkAdAB1AG0AAAAAAAAA
bbpjdYua5UiJat4ECvijBwcAAAB919L4KV2aQLErCRD/1LjaSQBuAHYAbwBpAGMA
ZQBJAHQAZQBtAAAAAAAAAPmH8wjPXM1GkZJA4n51AT4HAAAAfdfS+CldmkCxKwkQ
/9S42kkAbgB2AG8AaQBjAGUASQB0AGUAbQBJAEQAAAAAAAAAADRIjuYYtJEGROO+E
Windows (CRLF)
Ln 9, Col 27

- **9.** Close the Notepad window, and then close the File Explorer window.
- **10.** If you are not continuing on to the next session, close the Clinic database.

INSIGHT

Importing and Exporting Data

Access supports importing data from common file formats such as an Excel workbook, a text file, and an XML file. Additional Access options include importing an object from another Access database, importing data from other databases (such as Microsoft SQL Server, mySQL, and others), and importing an HTML document, an Outlook folder, or a SharePoint list.

In addition to exporting an Access object as an XML file or an HTML document, Access includes options for exporting data to another Access database, other databases (Microsoft SQL Server, mySQL), an Excel workbook, a text file, a Word document, a SharePoint list, or a PDF or XPS file. You can also export table or query data directly to Word's mail merge feature or export an object to an email message.

The steps you follow for other import and export options work similarly to the import and export steps you've already used.

You've imported and exported data, analyzed a table's design, and saved and run import and export specifications. In the next session, you will analyze data by working with a chart, creating and using an application part, linking external data, and adding a tab control to a form.

REVIEW

Session 8.1 Quick Check

1. What is HTML?
2. What is an HTML template?
3. What is a static webpage?
4. What is a CSV file?
5. What is the Table Analyzer?
6. ___________ is a programming language that describes data and its structure.

Session 8.2 Visual Overview:

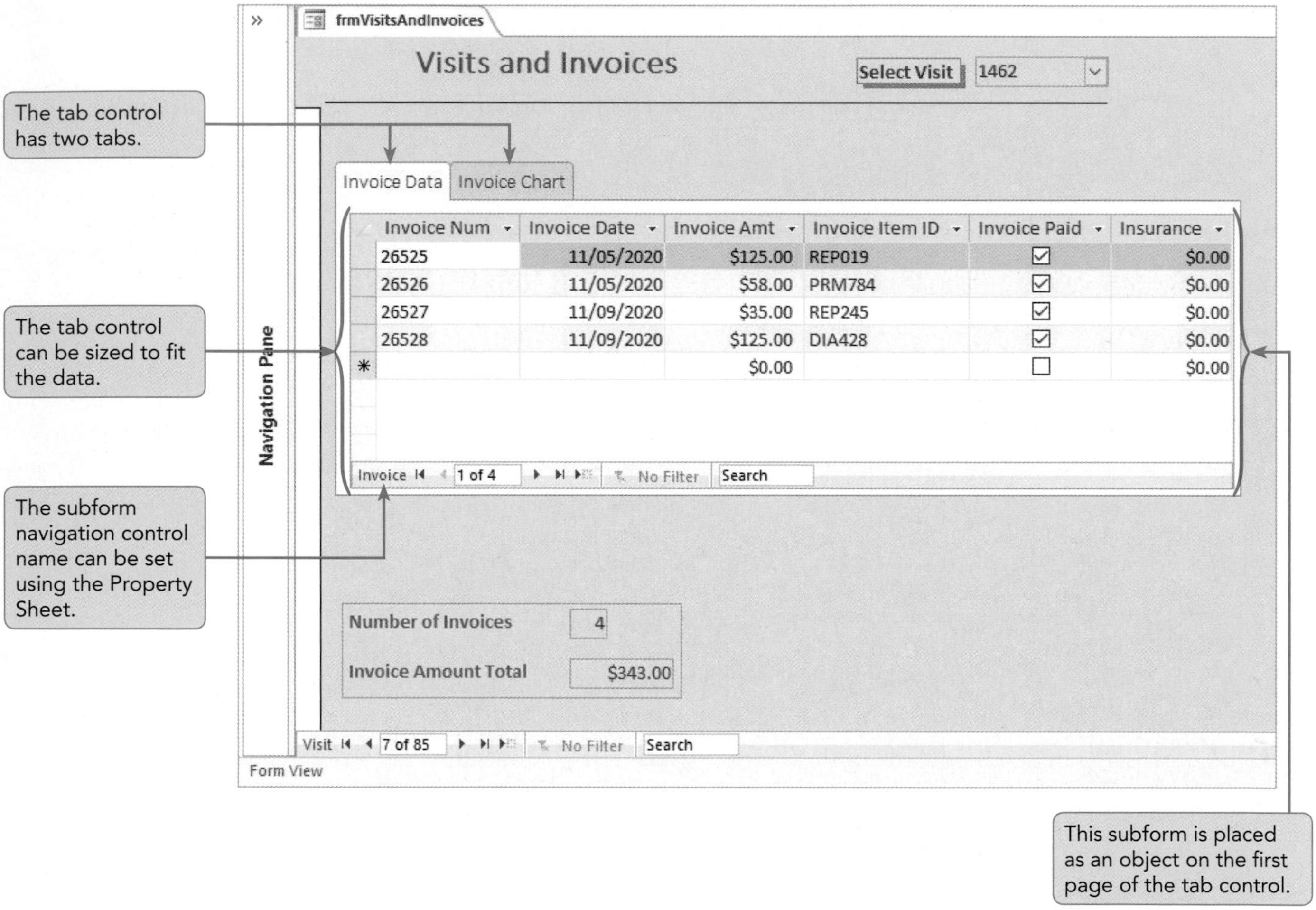
The tab control has two tabs.
The tab control can be sized to fit the data.
The subform navigation control name can be set using the Property Sheet.
This subform is placed as an object on the first page of the tab control.
frmVisitsAndInvoices
Visits and Invoices
Select Visit
1462
Navigation Pane
Invoice Data
Invoice Chart
Invoice Num
Invoice Date
Invoice Amt
Invoice Item ID
Invoice Paid
Insurance
26525 11/05/2020 $125.00 REP019 $0.00
26526 11/05/2020 $58.00 PRM784 $0.00
26527 11/09/2020 $35.00 REP245 $0.00
26528 11/09/2020 $125.00 DIA428 $0.00
$0.00 $0.00
Invoice 1 of 4 No Filter Search
Number of Invoices 4
Invoice Amount Total $343.00
Visit 7 of 85 No Filter Search
Form View

Tabbed Control with a Chart

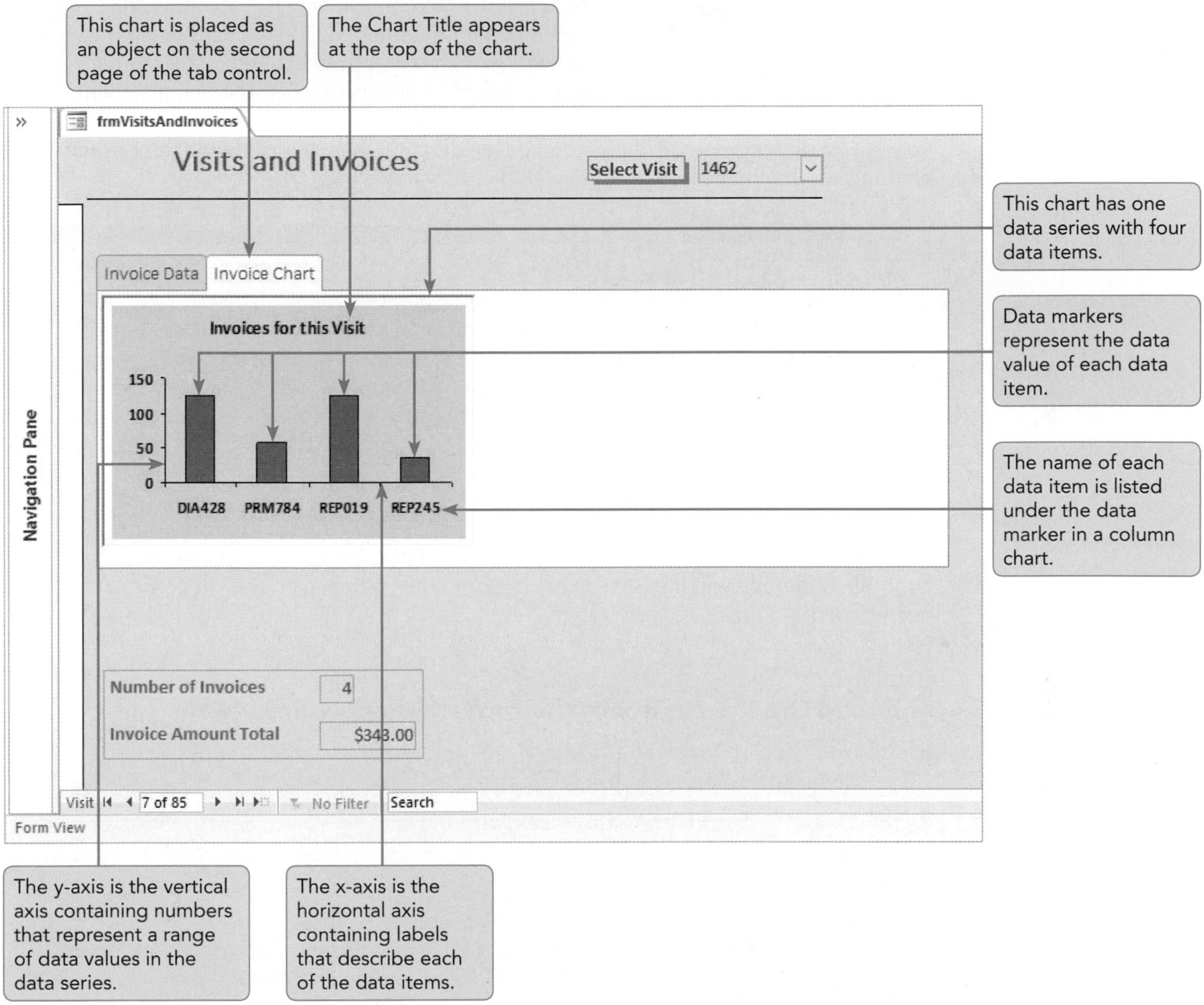

This chart is placed as an object on the second page of the tab control.
The Chart Title appears at the top of the chart.
frmVisitsAndInvoices
Visits and Invoices
Select Visit
1462
This chart has one data series with four data items.
Invoice Data
Invoice Chart
Invoices for this Visit
150
100
50
0
DIA428
PRM784
REP019
REP245
Data markers represent the data value of each data item.
The name of each data item is listed under the data marker in a column chart.
Navigation Pane
Number of Invoices
4
Invoice Amount Total
$343.00
Visit
7 of 85
No Filter
Search
Form View
The y-axis is the vertical axis containing numbers that represent a range of data values in the data series.
The x-axis is the horizontal axis containing labels that describe each of the data items.

Using a Tab Control in a Form

Donna wants you to enhance the frmVisitsAndInvoices form in the Clinic database to enable users to switch between different content. Recall the frmVisitsAndInvoices form currently contains a main form displaying Visit data and the frmBillingSubform subform displaying the information for the billed invoices related to a displayed visit. Specifically, Donna wants users to be able to choose between viewing the frmBillingSubform subform or viewing a chart showing the invoices associated with the displayed visit.

You can use the **Tab Control tool** to insert a tab control, which is a control that appears with tabs at the top. Each tab is commonly referred to as a page, or tab page, within the tab control. Users can switch between pages by clicking the tabs. You'll use a tab control to implement Donna's requested enhancements. The first page will contain the frmBillingSubform subform that is currently positioned at the bottom of the frmVisitsAndInvoices form. The second page will contain a chart showing the invoice amounts for the invoices associated with the displayed visit.

INSIGHT

Working with Large Forms

When you want to work with a form that is too large to display in the Access window, one way to help you navigate the form is to manually add page breaks, where it makes sense to do so. You can use the Page Break tool to insert a page break control in the form, which lets users move between the form pages by pressing the Page Up and Page Down keys.

To expedite placing the subform in the first page within the tab control, you'll first cut the subform from the form, placing it on the Clipboard. You'll then add the tab control, and finally you'll paste the subform into the first page on the tab control. You need to perform these steps in Design view.

To add the tab control to the frmVisitsAndInvoices form:

1. If you took a break after the previous session, make sure that the Clinic database is open with the Navigation Pane displayed.
2. Open the **frmVisitsAndInvoices** form in Form view to review the form and the frmBillingSubform, switch to Design view, and then close the Navigation Pane.
3. Scroll down until the subform is fully visible (if necessary), right-click the top-left corner of the subform control to open the shortcut menu, and then click **Cut** to remove the subform control from the form and place it on the Clipboard.

   Trouble? If you do not see Cut as one of the options on the shortcut menu, you did not click the top edge of the subform control correctly. Right-click the top edge of the subform control until you see this option on the shortcut menu, and then click Cut.
4. Increase the length of the Detail section to **7.0** inches.
5. Select the **Number of Invoices** label and control, the **Invoice Amount Total** label and control, and the rectangle control surrounding them, and then move the selected controls below the 6-inch horizontal line in the grid.
6. On the Form Design Tools Design tab, in the Controls group, click the **Tab Control** tool.

7. Position the + portion of the Tab Control tool pointer in the Detail section at the 2.75-inch mark on the vertical ruler and three grid dots from the left edge of the form, and then click the mouse button. A tab control with two tabs is inserted in the form.
8. Right-click in the middle of the tab control, and then when an orange outline appears inside the tab control, click **Paste** on the shortcut menu. The subform is pasted in the tab control on the leftmost tab. See Figure 8–18.

Figure 8–18 Subform in the tab control

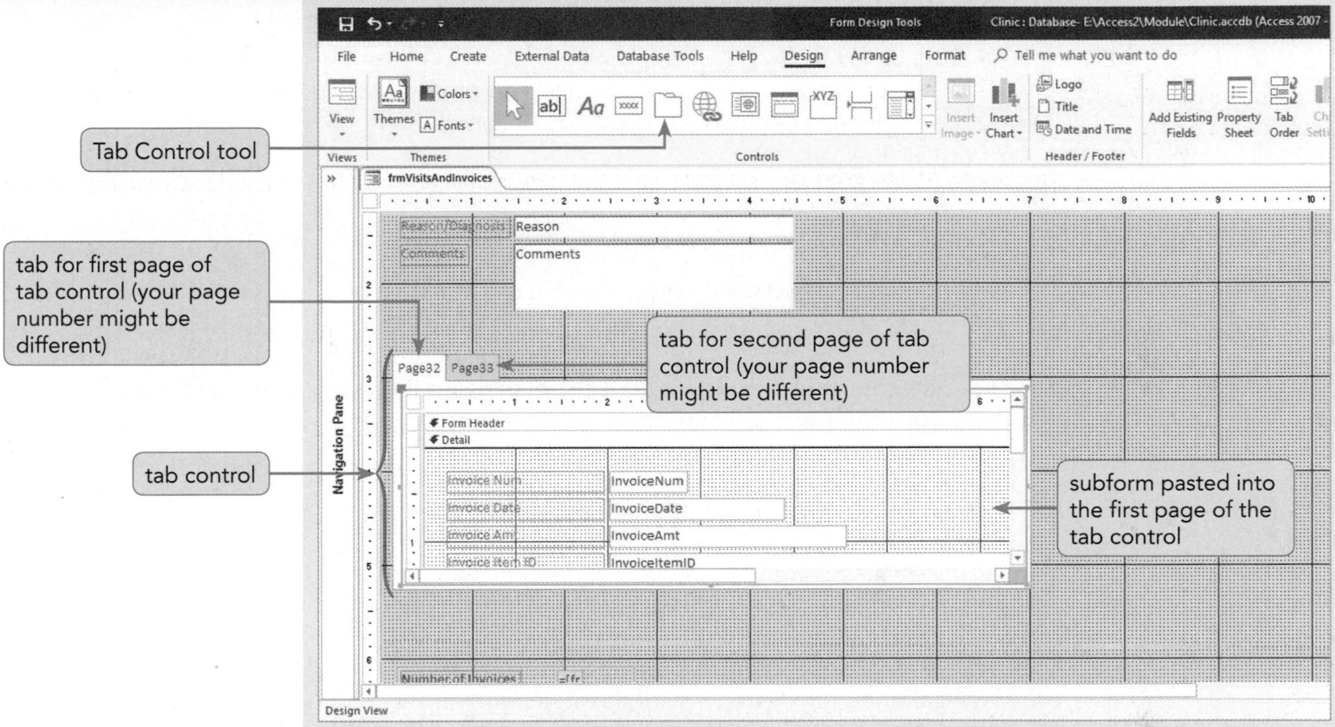

Tab Control tool
tab for first page of tab control (your page number might be different)
tab for second page of tab control (your page number might be different)
tab control
subform pasted into the first page of the tab control
Form Design Tools
Clinic : Database- E:\Access2\Module\Clinic.accdb (Access 2007 -
File
Home
Create
External Data
Database Tools
Help
Design
Arrange
Format
Tell me what you want to do
frmVisitsAndInvoices
Reason
Comments
Page32
Page33
Form Header
Detail
InvoiceNum
InvoiceDate
InvoiceAmt
InvoiceItemID
Navigation Pane
Design View

9. Switch to Form view, click the **Select Visit** arrow, click **1462** in the list, and then click **1462** in the Visit ID box to deselect all controls.
10. Scroll down to the bottom of the form. The left tab, which is labeled Page32 (yours might differ), is the active tab. See Figure 8–19.

Figure 8–19 Subform in the tab control in Form view

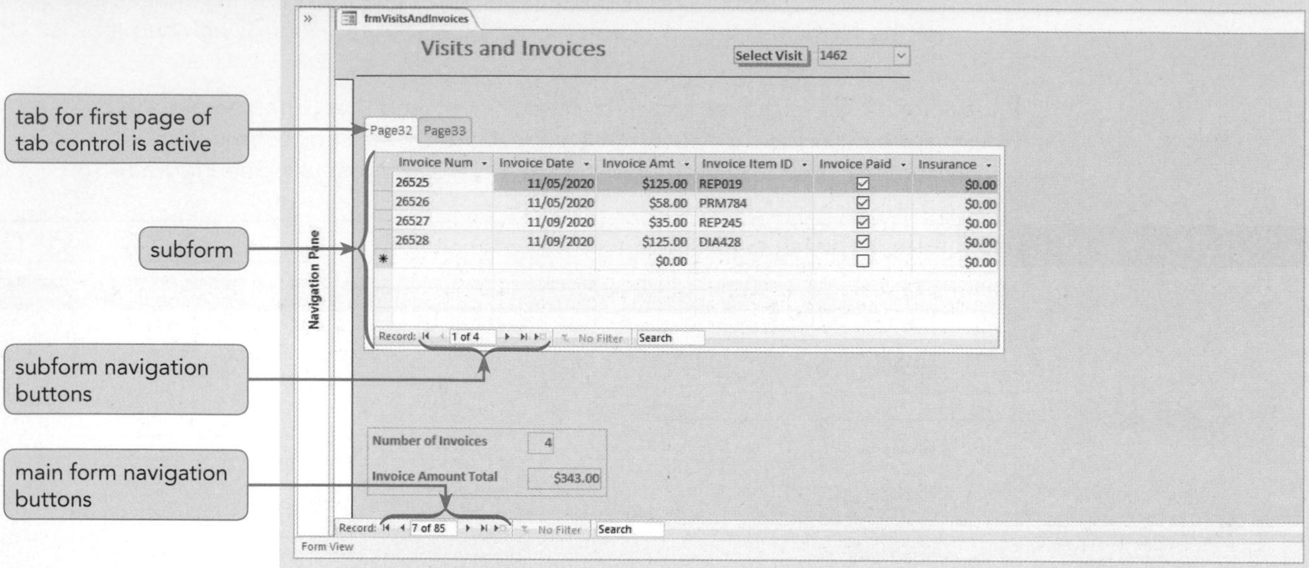

tab for first page of tab control is active
subform
subform navigation buttons
main form navigation buttons
frmVisitsAndInvoices
Visits and Invoices
Select Visit
1462
Page32
Page33
Invoice Num
Invoice Date
Invoice Amt
Invoice Item ID
Invoice Paid
Insurance
26525
11/05/2020
$125.00
REP019
$0.00
26526
11/05/2020
$58.00
PRM784
$0.00
26527
11/09/2020
$35.00
REP245
$0.00
26528
11/09/2020
$125.00
DIA428
$0.00
$0.00
$0.00
Record: 1 of 4
No Filter
Search
Number of Invoices
4
Invoice Amount Total
$343.00
Record: 7 of 85
No Filter
Search
Navigation Pane
Form View

The subform is now displayed on the first page of the tab control.

11. Click the **right tab** of the tab control (labeled Page33) to display the second page. The page is empty because you haven't added any controls to it yet.

12. Click the **left tab** of the tab control again to display the frmBillingSubform subform.

After viewing the form and subform in Form view, Donna's staff finds the two sets of navigation buttons confusing—they waste time determining which set of navigation buttons applies to the subform and which to the main form. To clarify this, you'll set the Navigation Caption property for the main form and the subform. The **Navigation Caption property** lets you change the navigation label from the word "Record" to another value. Because the main form displays data about visits and the subform displays data about invoices, you'll change the Navigation Caption property for the main form to "Visit" and for the subform to "Invoice."

You'll also set the Caption property for the tabs in the tab control, so they identify the contents of each page.

To change the captions for the navigation buttons and the tabs:

1. Switch to Design view, and then click the main form's form selector to select the form control in the main form, open the Property Sheet to display the properties for the selected form control, click the **All** tab (if necessary), click the **Navigation Caption** box, and then type **Visit**. See Figure 8–20.

Figure 8–20 **Navigation Caption property set for the main form**

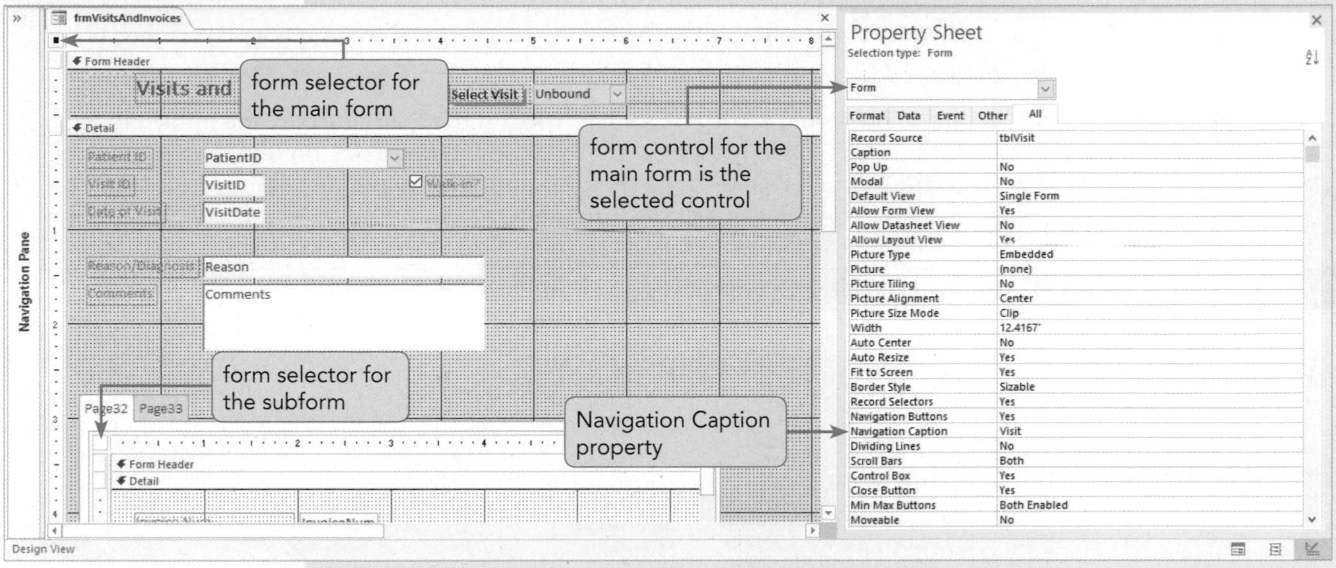
form selector for the main form
form control for the main form is the selected control
form selector for the subform
Navigation Caption property
Property Sheet
Selection type: Form

2. Click the **form selector** for the subform on the leftmost tab to select the subform, click the **form selector** for the subform again to select the form control in the subform and to display the Property Sheet for the selected form control, click the **Navigation Caption** box, and then type **Invoice**. Navigation buttons don't appear in Design view, so you won't see the effects of the Navigation Caption property settings until you switch to Form view. Before you do that, you will set the Caption property for the two tabs in the tab control.
3. Click the **left tab** in the tab control, and then click the **left tab** in the tab control again to select it.
4. In the Property Sheet, in the Caption box, type **Invoice Data** and then press **TAB**. The Caption property value now appears on the left tab in the tab control. See Figure 8–21.

Figure 8–21 **Caption property set for the left tab of a tab control**

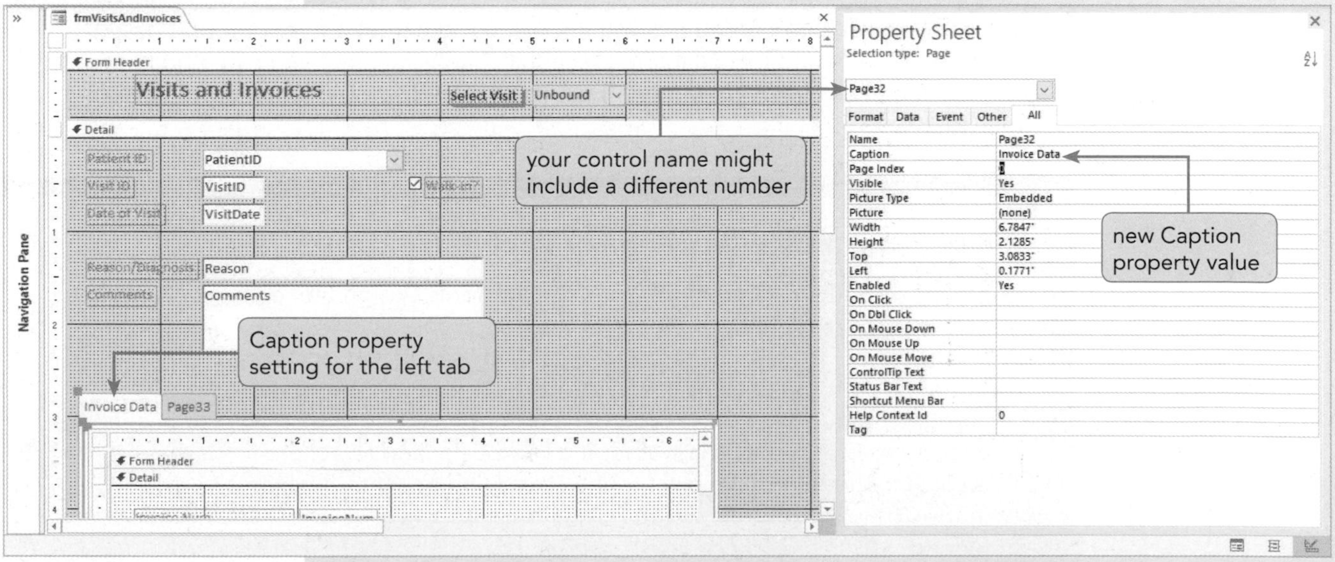
your control name might include a different number
new Caption property value
Caption property setting for the left tab
Property Sheet
Selection type: Page

5. Click the **right tab** in the subform to select it, in the Property Sheet, in the Caption box, type **Invoice Chart**, press **TAB**, and then close the Property Sheet.
6. Save your form design changes, and then switch to Form view.
7. Click the **Select Visit** arrow, click **1462** in the list to display the information for this visit, click **1462** in the Visit ID box to deselect the text, and then scroll to the bottom of the form. The tabs and the navigation buttons now display the new caption values. See Figure 8–22.

Figure 8–22 Modified report with tab control in Form view

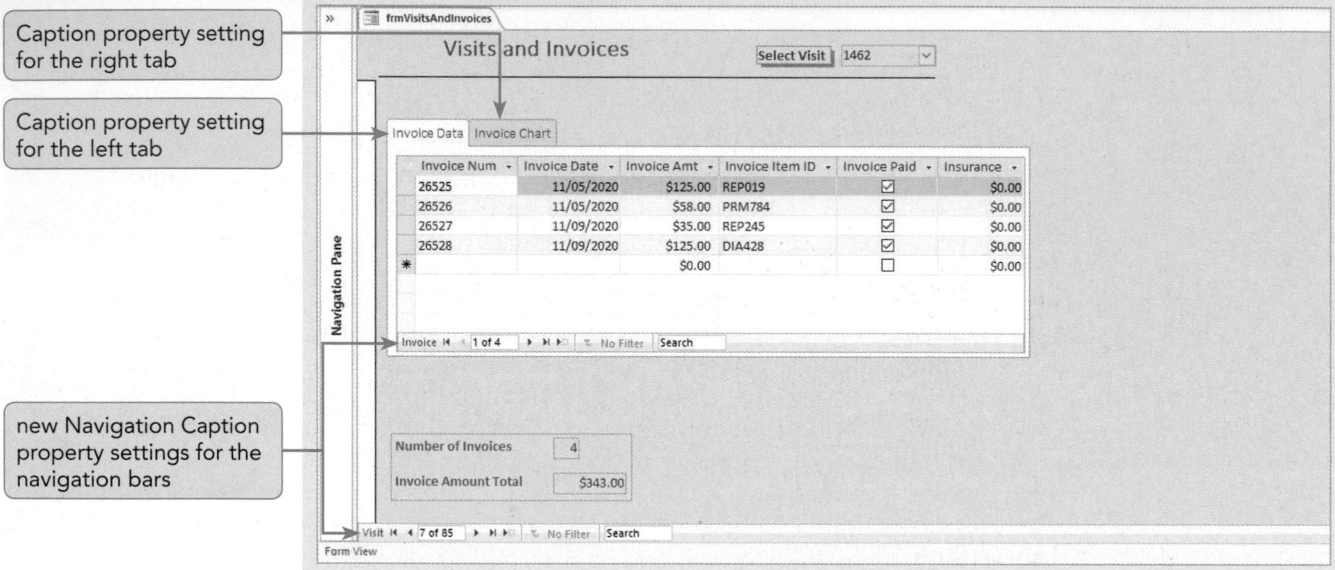
Caption property setting for the right tab
Caption property setting for the left tab
new Navigation Caption property settings for the navigation bars
frmVisitsAndInvoices
Visits and Invoices
Select Visit
1462
Invoice Data
Invoice Chart
Navigation Pane
Invoice Num
Invoice Date
Invoice Amt
Invoice Item ID
Invoice Paid
Insurance
26525 11/05/2020 $125.00 REP019 $0.00
26526 11/05/2020 $58.00 PRM784 $0.00
26527 11/09/2020 $35.00 REP245 $0.00
26528 11/09/2020 $125.00 DIA428 $0.00
$0.00 $0.00
Invoice 1 of 4 No Filter Search
Number of Invoices 4
Invoice Amount Total $343.00
Visit 7 of 85 No Filter Search
Form View

Next, Donna wants you to add a simple chart to the second page of the tab control. You will create the chart using the Chart Wizard.

Creating a Chart Using the Chart Wizard

The Chart Wizard in Access guides you in creating a chart in a form or report based upon data contained in the database. Once the chart is created, you can modify and format the chart using Microsoft Graph, a simple graphing tool included in Microsoft Office 365.

REFERENCE

Embedding a Chart in a Form or Report

- On the Report Design Tools or Form Design Tools Design tab, click the More button in the Controls group, and then click the Chart tool.
- Position the + portion of the pointer in the form or report, and then click the mouse button to start the Chart Wizard.
- Navigate through the Chart Wizard dialog boxes to select the record source, fields, and chart type; specify a layout for the chart data; and select the fields that link the records in the database object to the chart's components, if necessary.
- In the Chart Wizard's last dialog box, enter a chart title, select whether to include a legend, and then click the Finish button.

The tblBilling table contains the information Donna wants displayed in chart form on the right tab in the tab control.

To create a chart in the tab control using the Chart Wizard:

1. Switch to Design view, click the **Invoice Chart** tab in the tab control, then click the **Invoice Chart** tab again to select it, as indicated by the orange selection border.
2. On the Form Design Tools Design tab, in the Controls group, click the **Chart** tool, and then position the pointer in the tab control. When the pointer is inside the tab control, the rectangular portion of the tab control you can use to place controls is filled with the color black.
3. Position the + portion of the pointer in the upper-left corner of the black tab control, and then click the mouse button. A chart control appears in the tab control, and the first Chart Wizard dialog box opens, in which you select the source record for the chart.

   Donna wants the chart to provide a simple visual display of the relative proportions of the invoice amounts for the invoice items for the currently displayed patient visit. You'll use the tblBilling table as the record source for the chart and select the InvoiceAmt and InvoiceItemID fields as the fields to use in the chart.
4. Click **Table: tblBilling** in the box listing the available tables, and then click the **Next** button to display the second Chart Wizard dialog box, in which you select the fields from the tblBilling table that contain the data to be used to create the chart.
5. From the Available Fields box, add the **InvoiceItemID** and **InvoiceAmt** fields to the Fields for Chart box, in that order, and then click the **Next** button to display the third Chart Wizard dialog box, in which you choose the chart type.

   The order of the items is important. Be sure to add InvoiceItemID first, then InvoiceAmt.
6. Click the **Pie Chart** button (column 1, row 4) to select the pie chart as the chart type to use for Donna's chart. The box on the right displays a brief description of the selected chart type. See Figure 8–23.

Figure 8–23 Chart Wizard showing selected chart type

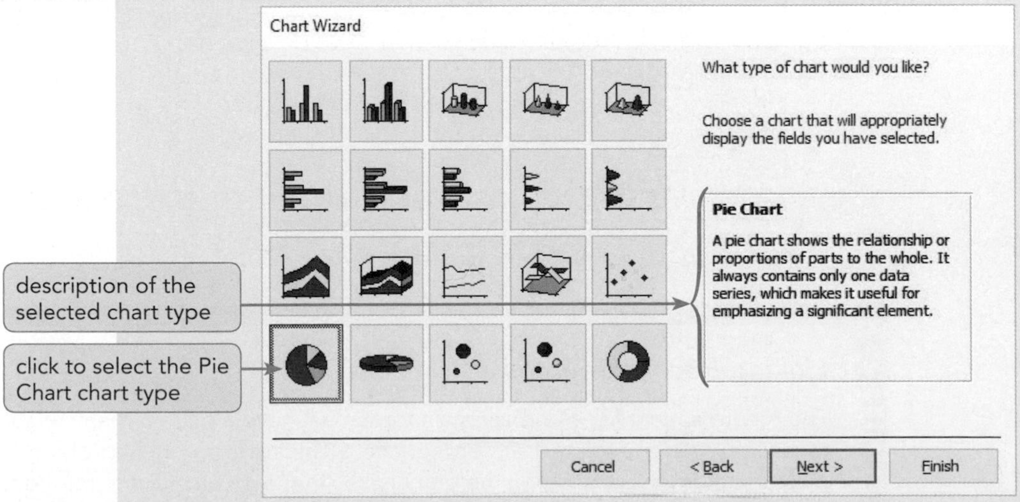
Chart Wizard
What type of chart would you like?
Choose a chart that will appropriately display the fields you have selected.
Pie Chart
A pie chart shows the relationship or proportions of parts to the whole. It always contains only one data series, which makes it useful for emphasizing a significant element.
Cancel
< Back
Next >
Finish
description of the selected chart type
click to select the Pie Chart chart type

7. Click the **Next** button to display the next Chart Wizard dialog box, which displays a preview of the chart and options to modify the layout of the data in the chart. You'll use the default layout based on the two selected fields.
8. Click the **Next** button to display the next Chart Wizard dialog box, which lets you choose the fields that link records in the main form (which uses the tblVisit table as its record source) to records in the chart (which uses the tblBilling table as its record source). You don't need to make any changes in this dialog box because the wizard has already identified VisitID as the common field linking these two tables. You can use the VisitID field as the linking field even though you didn't select it as a field for the chart.
9. Click the **Next** button to display the final Chart Wizard dialog box, in which you enter the title that will appear at the top of the chart and choose whether to include a legend in the chart.
10. Type **Invoices for this Visit**, make sure the **Yes, display a legend** option button is selected, and then click the **Finish** button. The completed chart appears in the tab control.

    You'll view the form in Form view, where it's easier to assess the chart's appearance.
11. Save your form design changes, switch to Form view, display Visit ID **1462** in the main form, click the **Invoice Chart** tab to display the chart, and then scroll down to the bottom of the form (if necessary). See Figure 8–24.

Figure 8–24 Pie chart in the tab control

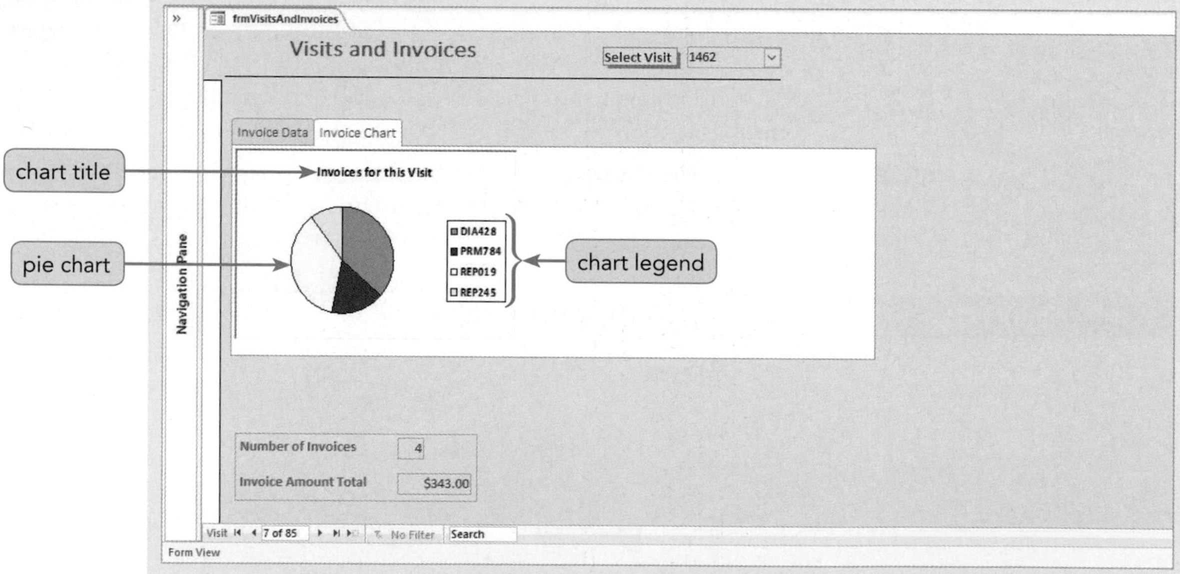

frmVisitsAndInvoices
Visits and Invoices
Select Visit
1462
Invoice Data
Invoice Chart
Invoices for this Visit
DIA428
PRM784
REP019
REP245
Number of Invoices
4
Invoice Amount Total
$343.00
Visit 7 of 85
No Filter
Search
Form View
Navigation Pane
chart title
pie chart
chart legend

INSIGHT

Linking Record Sources

The record source for a primary main form must have a one-to-many relationship to the record source for a related subform or chart. The subform or chart object has its Link Master Fields property set to the primary key in the record source for the main form and its Link Child Fields property set to the foreign key in the record source for the subform or chart.

After viewing the chart, Donna decides it needs some modifications. She wants you to change the chart type from a pie chart to a bar chart, remove the legend, and modify the chart's background color. To make these formatting changes, you'll switch to Design view. To modify the chart, you need to access the Microsoft Graph tools. You can double-click the chart to display the Microsoft Graph menu bar and toolbar on the ribbon and open the datasheet for the chart, or you can right-click the chart and use the shortcut menu to open the chart in a separate Microsoft Graph window.

To edit the chart using Microsoft Graph tools:

1. Switch to Design view, right-click an edge of the chart object to open the shortcut menu, point to **Chart Object**, and then click **Open**. Microsoft Graph starts and displays the chart and datasheet in a separate window on top of the Access window. See Figure 8–25.

Figure 8–25 Chart in the Microsoft Graph window

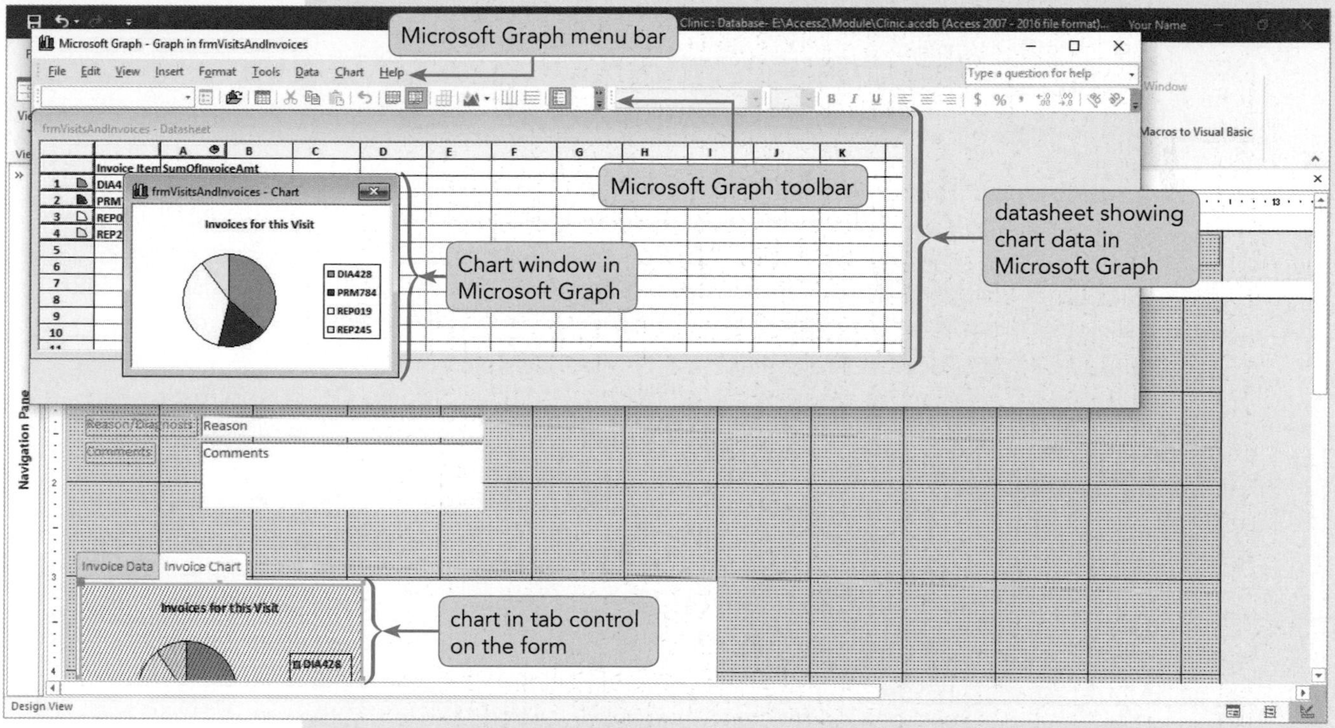
Microsoft Graph menu bar
Microsoft Graph toolbar
datasheet showing chart data in Microsoft Graph
Chart window in Microsoft Graph
chart in tab control on the form
Microsoft Graph - Graph in frmVisitsAndInvoices
frmVisitsAndInvoices - Chart
Invoices for this Visit
DIA428
PRM784
REP019
REP245
Design View

2. On the Microsoft Graph menu bar, click **Chart**, click **Chart Type** to open the Chart Type dialog box, and then click **Column** in the Chart type box to display the types of column charts. See Figure 8–26.

Figure 8–26 Microsoft Graph Chart Type dialog box

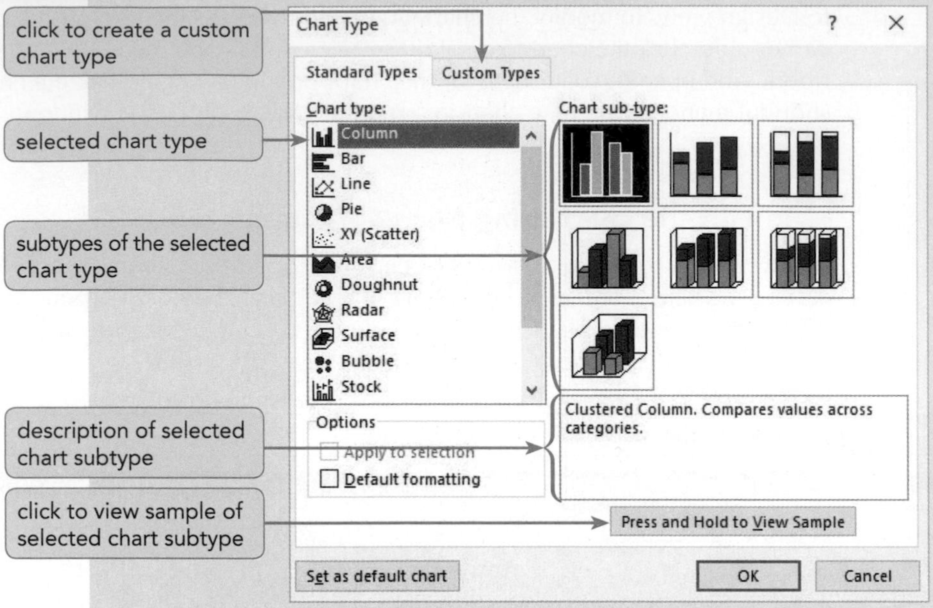
click to create a custom chart type
selected chart type
subtypes of the selected chart type
description of selected chart subtype
click to view sample of selected chart subtype
Chart Type
Standard Types
Custom Types
Chart type:
Column
Bar
Line
Pie
XY (Scatter)
Area
Doughnut
Radar
Surface
Bubble
Stock
Chart sub-type:
Options
Apply to selection
Default formatting
Clustered Column. Compares values across categories.
Press and Hold to View Sample
Set as default chart
OK
Cancel

The column chart is the selected chart type, and the clustered column chart is the default chart subtype (row 1, column 1). A description of the selected chart subtype appears below the chart subtypes. You can create a custom chart by clicking the Custom Types tab. You can also use the Press and Hold to View Sample button to display a sample of the selected subtype.

3. Click the **Press and Hold to View Sample** button to view a sample of the chart, release the mouse button, and then click the **OK** button to close the dialog box and change the chart to a column chart in the Microsoft Graph window and in the tab control on the form.

4. On the Microsoft Graph menu bar, click **Chart**, click **Chart Options** to open the Chart Options dialog box, click the **Legend** tab to display the chart's legend options, click the **Show legend** check box to uncheck it, and then click the **OK** button. The legend is removed from the chart object in the Microsoft Graph window and in the tab control on the form.

To change the color or other properties of a chart's elements—the chart background (or chart area), axes, labels to the left of the y-axis, labels below the x-axis, or data markers (columnar bars for a column chart)—you need to double-click the chart element.

TIP

A data marker is a bar, dot, segment, or other symbol that represents a single data value.

5. In the Microsoft Graph Chart window, double-click one of the column data markers in the chart to open the Format Data Series dialog box, and then in the Area section, click the **orange** color (row 2, column 2) in the color palette. The sample color in the dialog box changes to orange to match the selected color. See Figure 8–27.

Figure 8–27 **Format Data Series dialog box in Microsoft Graph**

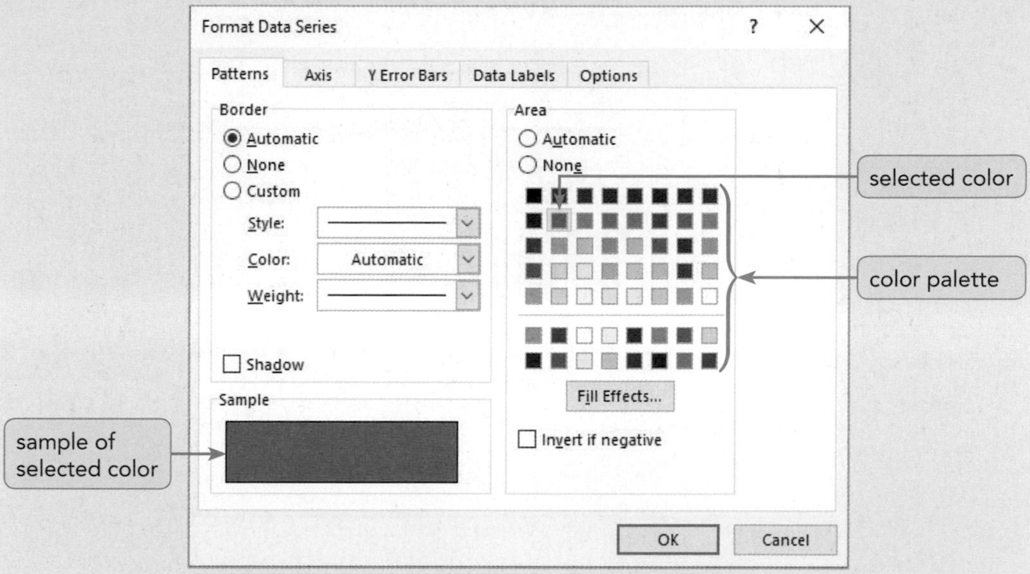
Format Data Series
Patterns
Axis
Y Error Bars
Data Labels
Options
Border
Automatic
None
Custom
Style:
Color:
Automatic
Weight:
Shadow
Sample
Area
Automatic
None
Fill Effects...
Invert if negative
OK
Cancel
selected color
color palette
sample of selected color

6. Click the **OK** button to close the dialog box. The color of the data markers in the chart in the Microsoft Graph window and in the form's tab control changes to orange.

   Trouble? If only one of the bars changed color, you selected one bar instead of the entire series. Click Edit, click Undo, and then repeat Steps 5 and 6.

7. In the Chart window, double-click the white chart background to the left of the title to open the Format Chart Area dialog box, in the Area section, click the **light orange** color (row 5, column 2) in the color palette, and then click the **OK** button. The chart's background color changes from white to light orange in the chart in the Microsoft Graph window and in the form's tab control.

8. Click **File** on the Microsoft Graph menu bar, and then click **Exit & Return to frmVisitsAndInvoices** to close the Microsoft Graph window and return to the form.

9. Save your form design changes, switch to Form view, display Visit ID **1462** in the main form, and then click the **Invoice Chart** tab to display the chart. Scroll down to the bottom of the form. See Figure 8–28.

Figure 8–28 Completed chart in Form view

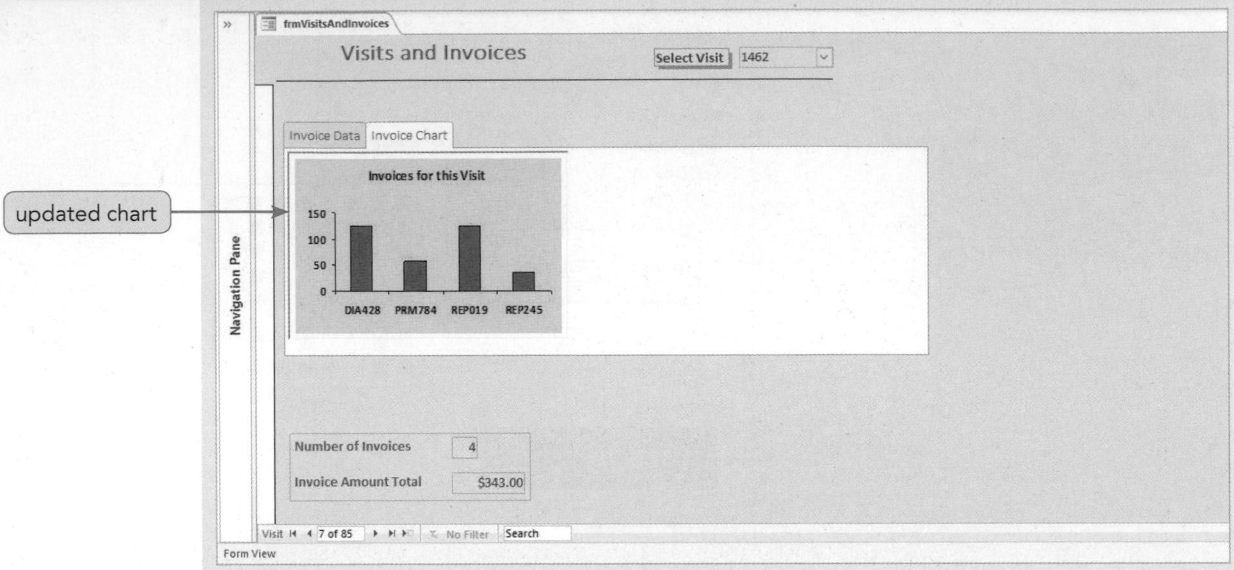
updated chart
frmVisitsAndInvoices
Visits and Invoices
Select Visit
1462
Invoice Data
Invoice Chart
Invoices for this Visit
150
100
50
0
DIA428
PRM784
REP019
REP245
Navigation Pane
Number of Invoices
4
Invoice Amount Total
$343.00
Visit
7 of 85
No Filter
Search
Form View

10. Close the form.

Sometimes it is useful to use a table structure from one database in other databases. One option would be to import the table structure only from the database file into each subsequent database, a method you used in an earlier module. Another option is to create an application part in one database, which can then easily be included in any Access database file on your computer.

Using Templates and Application Parts

A template is a predefined database that can include tables, relationships, queries, forms, reports, and other database objects and is used to create a new database file. On the New tab in Backstage view, a list of predefined templates is displayed. You can also create your own template from an existing database file. In addition to creating a database template, you can also create templates for objects using an **application part**, which is a specialized template for a specific database object that can be imported into an existing database. There are predefined application parts included with Access, and you can also create your own user-defined application part. Once you create a user-defined application part in one database, it is available to all Access databases created and stored on your computer.

You can use an application part to insert a predefined object from another database or template into an existing database. Like a template, an application part can contain tables, relationships, queries, forms, reports, and other database objects.

Donna would like to reuse a table structure from another database to create a new table in the Clinic database. You'll use the NewPatientReferrals.accdb database file to create an application part for the table structure, and then you'll import the new application part into the Clinic database to use to create a table of referrals from local pharmacies.

To create an application part from a database file:

1. Click the **Create** tab, and then in the Templates group, click the **Application Parts** button to open the gallery of predefined application parts. See Figure 8–29.

Figure 8–29 Predefined application parts

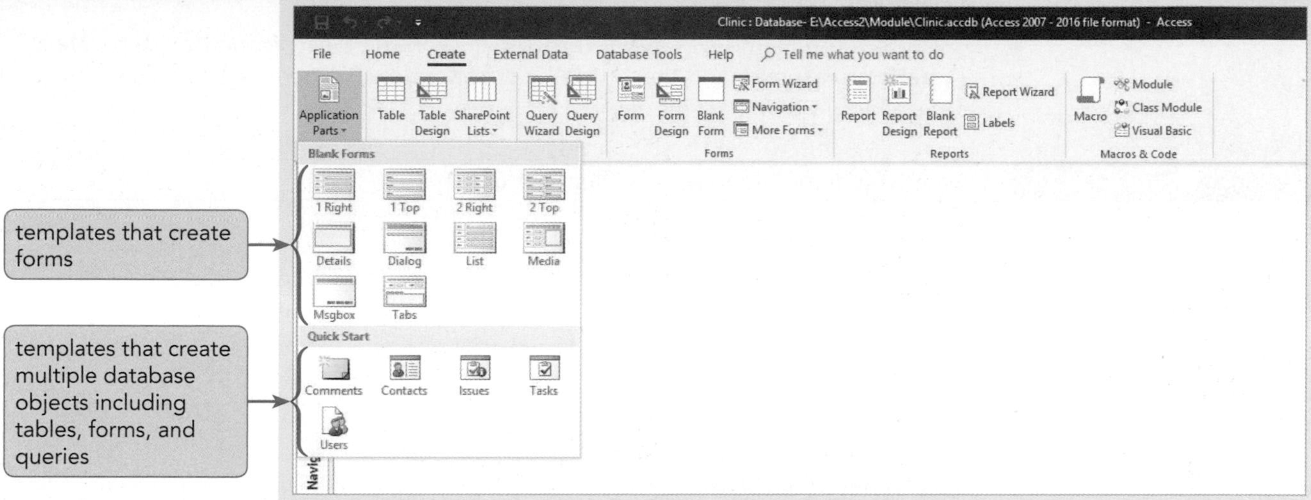
templates that create forms
templates that create multiple database objects including tables, forms, and queries
Clinic : Database- E:\Access2\Module\Clinic.accdb (Access 2007 - 2016 file format) - Access
File
Home
Create
External Data
Database Tools
Help
Tell me what you want to do
Application Parts
Table
Table Design
SharePoint Lists
Query Wizard
Query Design
Form
Form Design
Blank Form
Form Wizard
Navigation
More Forms
Forms
Report
Report Design
Blank Report
Report Wizard
Labels
Reports
Macro
Module
Class Module
Visual Basic
Macros & Code
Blank Forms
1 Right
1 Top
2 Right
2 Top
Details
Dialog
List
Media
Msgbox
Tabs
Quick Start
Comments
Contacts
Issues
Tasks
Users

Note that there are Blank Forms and Quick Start Application Parts. If you or another user of your computer has created user-defined application parts, they also will appear in the gallery.

2. Close the Clinic database file.
3. Open the **Support_AC_8_NewPatientReferrals.accdb** database file from the **Access2 > Module** folder included with your Data Files, enabling the content if necessary.

   When you save this file as a template, all database objects that are in the file will be included in the template file. This file contains only the tblReferral table.
4. Click the **File** tab to open Backstage view, and then in the navigation bar, click **Save As**.
5. In Database File Types section of the Save Database As list, click **Template**. See Figure 8–30.

Figure 8–30 Save As options in Backstage View

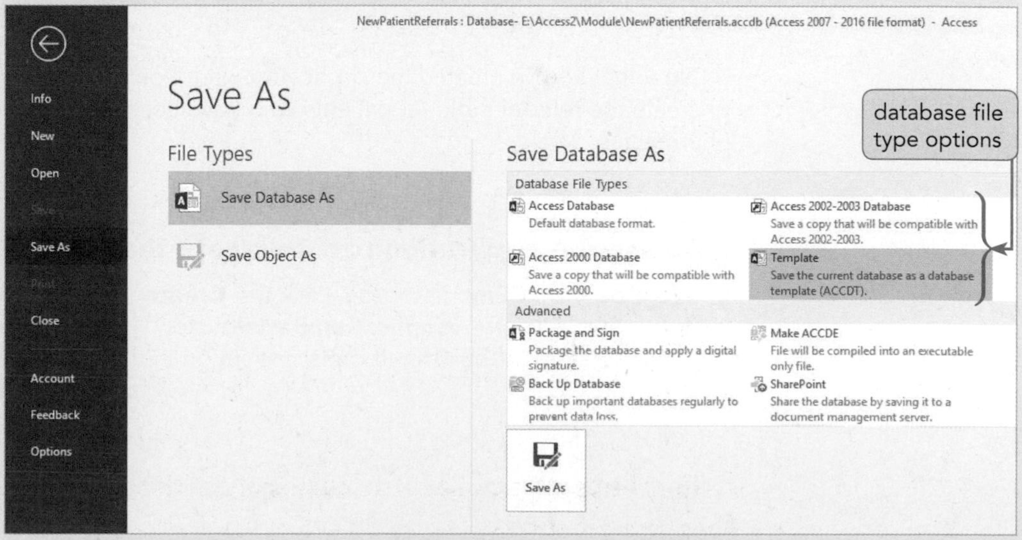
database file type options
NewPatientReferrals : Database- E:\Access2\Module\NewPatientReferrals.accdb (Access 2007 - 2016 file format) - Access
Info
New
Open
Save
Save As
Print
Close
Account
Feedback
Options
Save As
File Types
Save Database As
Save Object As
Save Database As
Database File Types
Access Database
Default database format.
Access 2002-2003 Database
Save a copy that will be compatible with Access 2002-2003.
Access 2000 Database
Save a copy that will be compatible with Access 2000.
Template
Save the current database as a database template (ACCDT).
Advanced
Package and Sign
Package the database and apply a digital signature.
Make ACCDE
File will be compiled into an executable only file.
Back Up Database
Back up important databases regularly to prevent data loss.
SharePoint
Share the database by saving it to a document management server.
Save As

6. Click the **Save As** button. The Create New Template from This Database dialog box opens.
7. Click in the Name box, type **Referral**, click in the Description box, type **New patient referral**, and then click the **Application Part** check box to select it. See Figure 8–31.

Figure 8–31 Create New Template from This Database dialog box

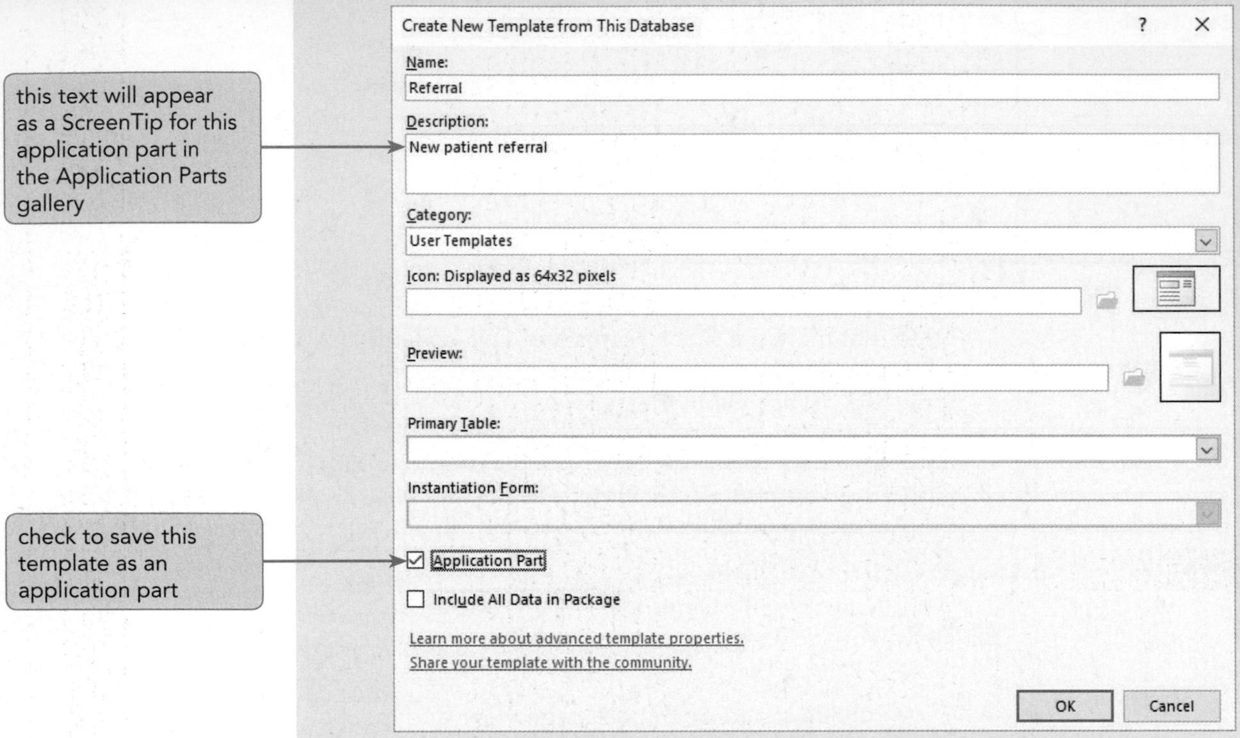
this text will appear as a ScreenTip for this application part in the Application Parts gallery
check to save this template as an application part
Create New Template from This Database
Name:
Referral
Description:
New patient referral
Category:
User Templates
Icon: Displayed as 64x32 pixels
Preview:
Primary Table:
Instantiation Form:
Application Part
Include All Data in Package
Learn more about advanced template properties.
Share your template with the community.
OK
Cancel

8. Click the **OK** button to close the dialog box. An alert box opens, indicating that the application part, as a template, has been saved.
9. Click the **OK** button to close the message box, and then close the Support_AC_8_NewPatientReferrals.accdb database.

Now that you've created the application part, you'll use it in the Clinic database to create the referral table for patients who have been referred to the clinic from local pharmacies.

To use the application part to create the referral table:

1. Open the **Clinic** database, click the **Create** tab, and then in the Templates group, click the **Application Parts** button. The Referral template is displayed in the User Templates section in the Application Parts gallery. See Figure 8–32.

Figure 8–32 Referral template in Application Parts Gallery

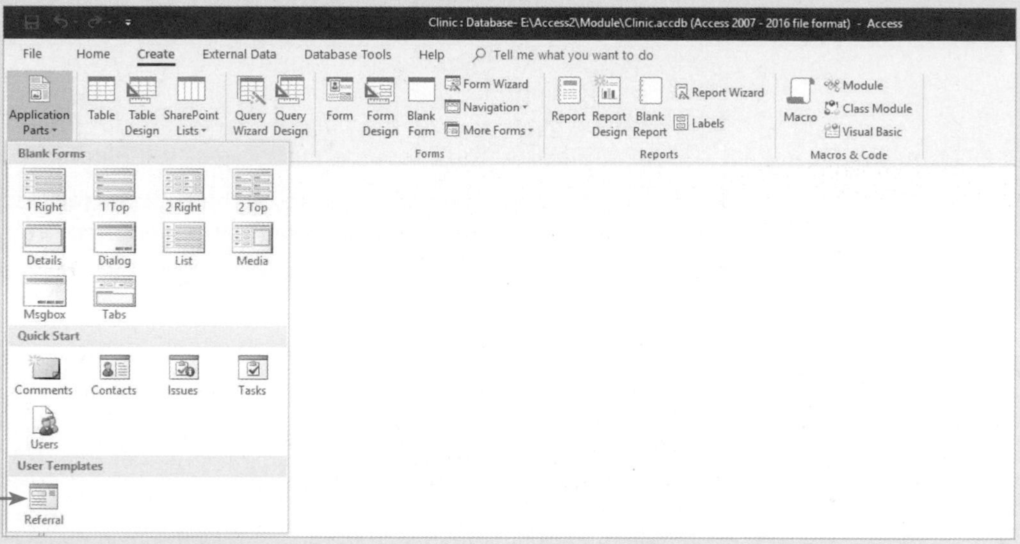
Clinic : Database- E:\Access2\Module\Clinic.accdb (Access 2007 - 2016 file format) - Access
File
Home
Create
External Data
Database Tools
Help
Tell me what you want to do
Application Parts
Table
Table Design
SharePoint Lists
Query Wizard
Query Design
Form
Form Design
Blank Form
Form Wizard
Navigation
More Forms
Forms
Report
Report Design
Blank Report
Report Wizard
Labels
Reports
Macro
Module
Class Module
Visual Basic
Macros & Code
Blank Forms
1 Right
1 Top
2 Right
2 Top
Details
Dialog
List
Media
Msgbox
Tabs
Quick Start
Comments
Contacts
Issues
Tasks
Users
User Templates
Referral

user-defined template added as an application part

2. Click **Referral**. The Create Relationship dialog box opens because the application part includes a table.

3. Click the **There is no relationship** option button. This indicates that the new table is not related to other tables in the current database. See Figure 8–33.

Figure 8–33 Create Relationship dialog box

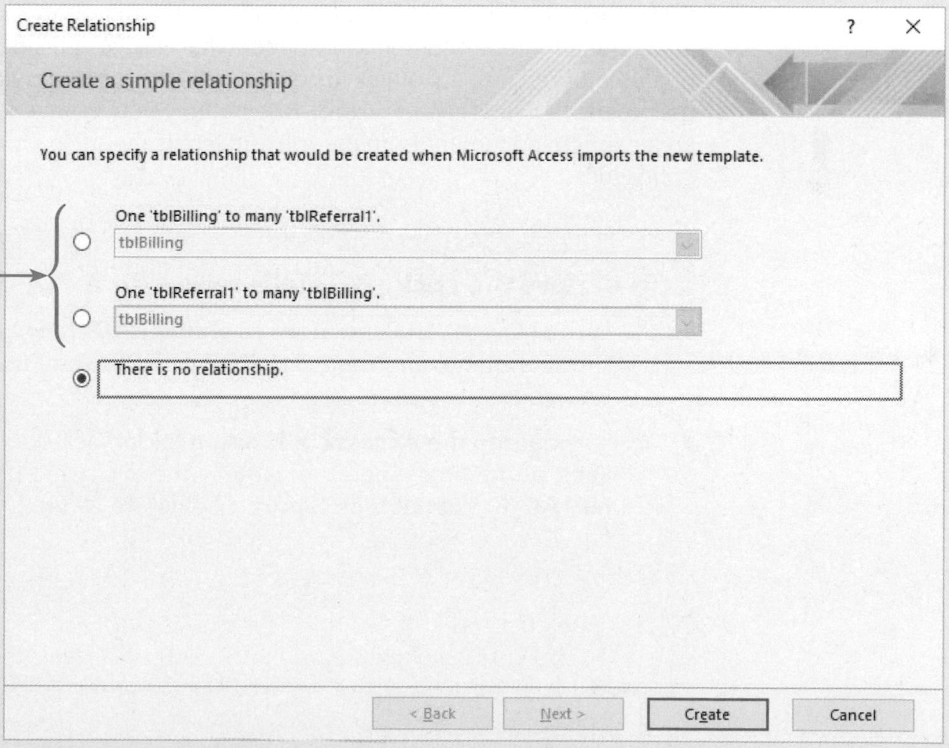
Create Relationship
?
Create a simple relationship
You can specify a relationship that would be created when Microsoft Access imports the new template.
One 'tblBilling' to many 'tblReferral1'.
tblBilling
One 'tblReferral1' to many 'tblBilling'.
tblBilling
There is no relationship.
< Back
Next >
Create
Cancel

use these options to create a relationship between the table in the application part and a table in the current database

4. Click the **Create** button to insert the Referral database object into the current database, and then open the Navigation Pane.

Only the tblReferral table will be inserted into the current database because the Referral template contains only one database object, which is the tblReferral table. Because the Clinic database already contains a table called tblReferral, the newly inserted table is named tblReferral1, to avoid overwriting the table that already exists. The newly inserted tblReferral1 will be used to store the patient information for patients referred by local pharmacists. You'll rename this table as tblReferralPharm.

5. In the Navigation Pane, right-click the **tblReferral1** table, click **Rename**, change the name to **tblReferralPharm**, and then press **ENTER**.
6. In the Navigation Pane, double-click **tblReferralPharm** to open it in Datasheet view.

   Note that the tblReferralPharm table contains the same fields as the tblReferral table but does not contain any records.
7. Close the tblReferralPharm table.

Donna would like to be able to send an electronic copy of the rptVisitDetails report that other people can view on their computers, rather than distributing printed reports. You can export tables, queries, reports, and other database objects as files that can be opened in other programs such as Excel and PDF readers. Donna would like to distribute rptVisitDetails as a PDF and asks you to export the report in this format.

Exporting a Report to a PDF File

PDF (portable document format) is a file format that preserves the original formatting and pagination of its contents no matter what device is used to view it. Current versions of all major operating systems for computers and handheld devices include software that opens PDF files. Most web browsers allow you to view PDF files as well. You'll create a PDF document from the rptVisitDetails report so Donna can send this report to colleagues.

To export the rptVisitDetails report to a PDF file:

1. In the Navigation Pane, right-click **rptVisitDetails**, point to **Export** on the shortcut menu, and then click **PDF or XPS**. The Publish as PDF or XPS dialog box opens.
2. Navigate to the **Access2 > Module** folder included with your Data Files, and then change the name in the File name box to **NP_AC_8_VisitDetailsReport**. See Figure 8–34.

Figure 8–34 Publish as PDF or XPS file dialog box

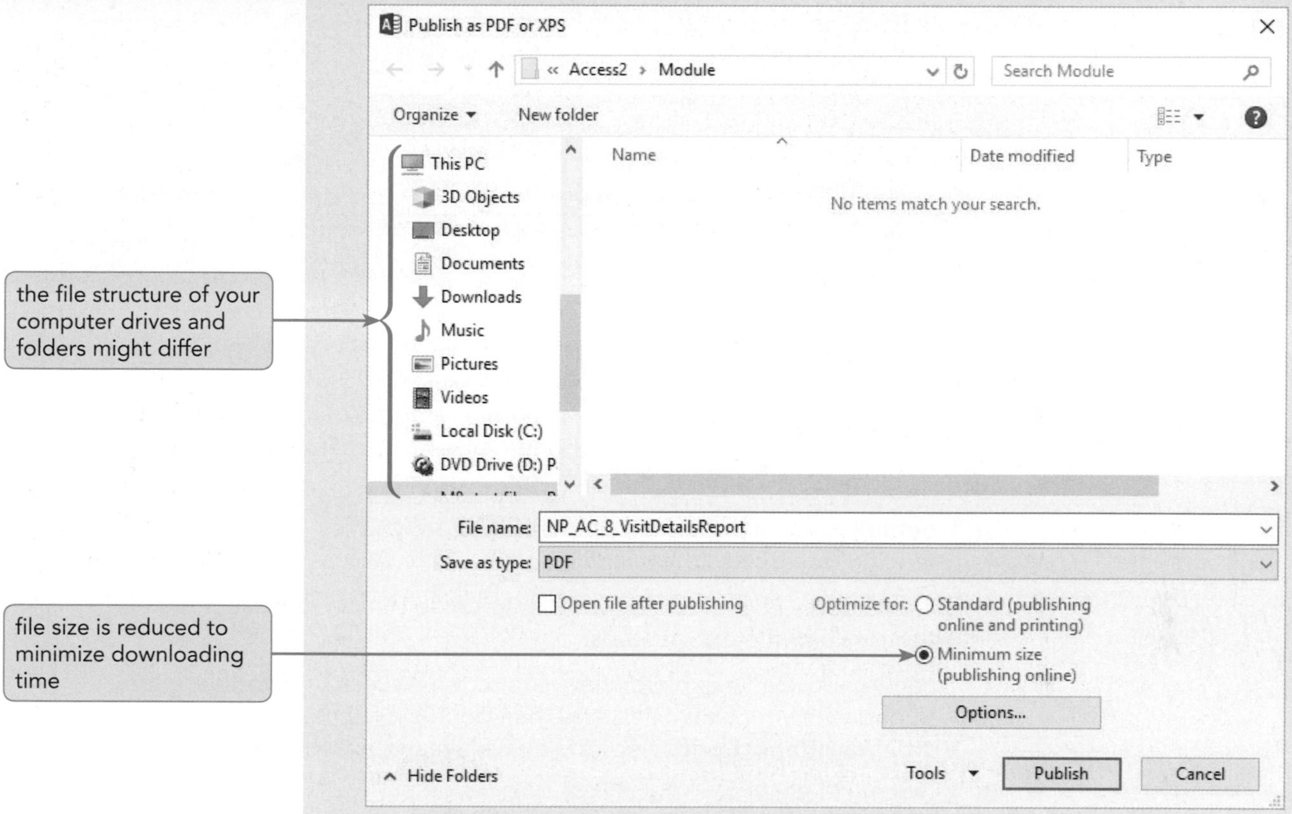
Publish as PDF or XPS
« Access2 › Module
Search Module
Organize
New folder
This PC
3D Objects
Desktop
Documents
Downloads
Music
Pictures
Videos
Local Disk (C:)
Name
Date modified
Type
No items match your search.
File name: NP_AC_8_VisitDetailsReport
Save as type: PDF
Open file after publishing
Optimize for: Standard (publishing online and printing)
Minimum size (publishing online)
Options...
Hide Folders
Tools
Publish
Cancel
the file structure of your computer drives and folders might differ
file size is reduced to minimize downloading time

Donna would like people who are visually impaired to be able to use the PDF document with their screen readers. When a PDF file is saved using the minimum size option, there is no additional functionality for screen readers. You can include document structure tags that allow people using screen readers to navigate the document easily. Screen reader software voices the structure tags, such as a tag that provides a description of an image. Structure tags also reflow text so that screen readers understand the flow of information and can read it in a logical order. For instance, a page with a sidebar shouldn't be read as two columns; the main column needs to be read as a continuation of the previous page.

In order to add this functionality, you'll specify that document structure tags should be included.

3. Click the **Options** button. The Options dialog box opens.
4. Click the **Document structure tags for accessibility** check box to select it. See Figure 8–35.

Figure 8–35 Options dialog box for PDF file export

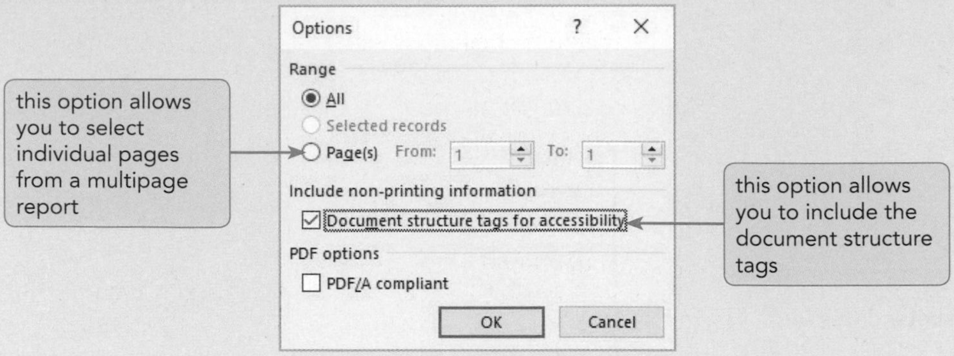
Options
Range
All
Selected records
Page(s) From: 1 To: 1
Include non-printing information
Document structure tags for accessibility
PDF options
PDF/A compliant
OK
Cancel
this option allows you to select individual pages from a multipage report
this option allows you to include the document structure tags

5. Click the **OK** button to close the Options dialog box, and then click the **Publish** button to close the Publish as PDF or XPS dialog box and to create the PDF file. The Export - PDF dialog box opens.

   Trouble? Depending on the operating system you're using, the PDF file may open. If it does, close the PDF file and return to Access.

6. In the Export - PDF dialog box, click the **Close** button to close the dialog box without saving the export steps.
7. Open Windows File Explorer, navigate to the **Access2 > Module** folder included with your Data Files, and then double-click the **NP_AC_8_VisitDetailsReport.pdf** to open the PDF file and examine the results.
8. Close the PDF file, and then close Windows File Explorer.

Donna is pleased to know that she can export database objects as PDF files. Now she would like your help with one additional external data issue. Her staff maintains an Excel workbook that contains contact information for people who volunteer at Lakewood Community Health Services. Donna wants to be able to use this data in the Clinic database.

Integrating Access with Other Applications

As you know, when you create a form or report in Access, you include more than just the data from the record source table or query. You've added controls such as lines, rectangles, tab controls, and graphics in your forms and reports to improve their appearance and usability. You can also add charts, drawings, and other objects to your forms and reports, but Access doesn't have the capability to create them. Instead, you create these objects using other applications and then place them in a form or report using the appropriate integration method.

When you integrate information between two files created using different software applications, the file containing the original information, or object, is called the **source file**, and the file in which you place the information from the source file is called the **destination file**. In Access there are three ways for you to integrate objects created by other applications—importing, embedding, and linking.

When you import an object, you include the contents of a file in a new table or append it to an existing table, or you include the contents of the file in a form, report, or field. In this module you imported CSV and XML files as new tables in the Clinic database, and the CSV and XML files you imported were created by other applications.

After importing an object into a destination file, it no longer has a connection to the original object in the source file or the application used to create it. Any subsequent changes you make to the object in the source file using the source application are not reflected in the imported object in the destination file.

When you **embed** an object from the source file into a form, report, or field in the destination file, you preserve its connection to the application used to create it in the source file, enabling you to edit the object, if necessary, using the features of the source application. However, any changes you make to the object are reflected only in the destination file in which it is embedded; the changes do not affect the original object in the source file from which it was embedded. Likewise, if you make any changes to the original object in the source file, these changes are not reflected in the embedded object in the destination file.

When you **link** an object to a form, report, or field in a destination file, you maintain a connection between the object in the destination file and the original object in the source file. You can make changes to a linked object only in the source file. Any changes you make to the original object in the source file using the source application are then reflected in the linked object in the destination file. To view or use the linked object in a form, report, or field in the destination file, you must first open the source file in the source application.

PROSKILLS

Decision Making: Importing, Embedding, and Linking Data

How do you decide which integration method to use when you need to include in an Access database data that is stored in another file created in a different application?

- You should choose to import an object when you want to copy an object from a file created using a different application into a table, form, or report in the Access database, *and* you want to be able to manipulate and work with that object using Access tools, *and* you do not need these changes to the imported object to be reflected in the original object in the source file.
- Conversely, you should choose to embed or link the object when you want to be able to edit the copied object in the table, form, or report using the application with which the source object was created. You should embed the object when you *do not* want your changes to the embedded object in the destination file to affect the original object in the source file. You should choose to link the object when you want the object in the destination file to always match the original object in the source file.

The decision to import, embed, or link to an object containing data depends on how you will use the data in your database and what connection is required to the original data. You should carefully consider the effect of changes to the original data and to the copied data before choosing which method to use.

Linking Data from an Excel Worksheet

Donna's staff has extensive experience working with Excel, and one of her staff members prefers to use an Excel file named Support_AC_8_Volunteer.xlsx to maintain the data for people who volunteer at the clinic. However, Donna needs to reference the volunteer data in the Clinic database on occasion, and the data she's referencing must always be the current version of the data in the Support_AC_8_Volunteer.xlsx Excel file. Importing the Excel workbook data as an Access table would provide Donna with data that's quickly out of date unless she repeats the import steps each time the data in the Excel workbook changes. Therefore, you'll link the data in the Excel file to a table in the Clinic database. When the staff changes data in the Support_AC_8_Volunteer.xlsx Excel workbook, the changes will be reflected automatically in the linked version in the database table. In addition, Donna won't be able to update the volunteer data from the Clinic database, which ensures that only the staff members responsible for maintaining the Support_AC_8_Volunteer.xlsx Excel workbook can update the data.

To link table data to an Excel file:

1. Click the **External Data** tab, and then in the Import & Link group, click **New Data Source**, point to **From File**, and then click the **Excel** button. The Get External Data - Excel Spreadsheet dialog box opens.

   Trouble? If the Export - Excel File dialog box opens, you clicked the Excel button in the Export group. Click the Cancel button and then repeat Step 1, being sure to select the Excel button from the Import & Link group.

2. Click the **Browse** button to open the File Open dialog box, navigate to the **Access2 > Module** folder included with your Data Files, click **Support_AC_8_Volunteer.xlsx**, click the **Open** button, and then click the **Link to the data source by creating a linked table** option button. This option links to the data instead of importing or appending it. The selected path and filename are displayed in the File name box. See Figure 8–36.

Figure 8–36 **Linking to data in an Excel workbook**

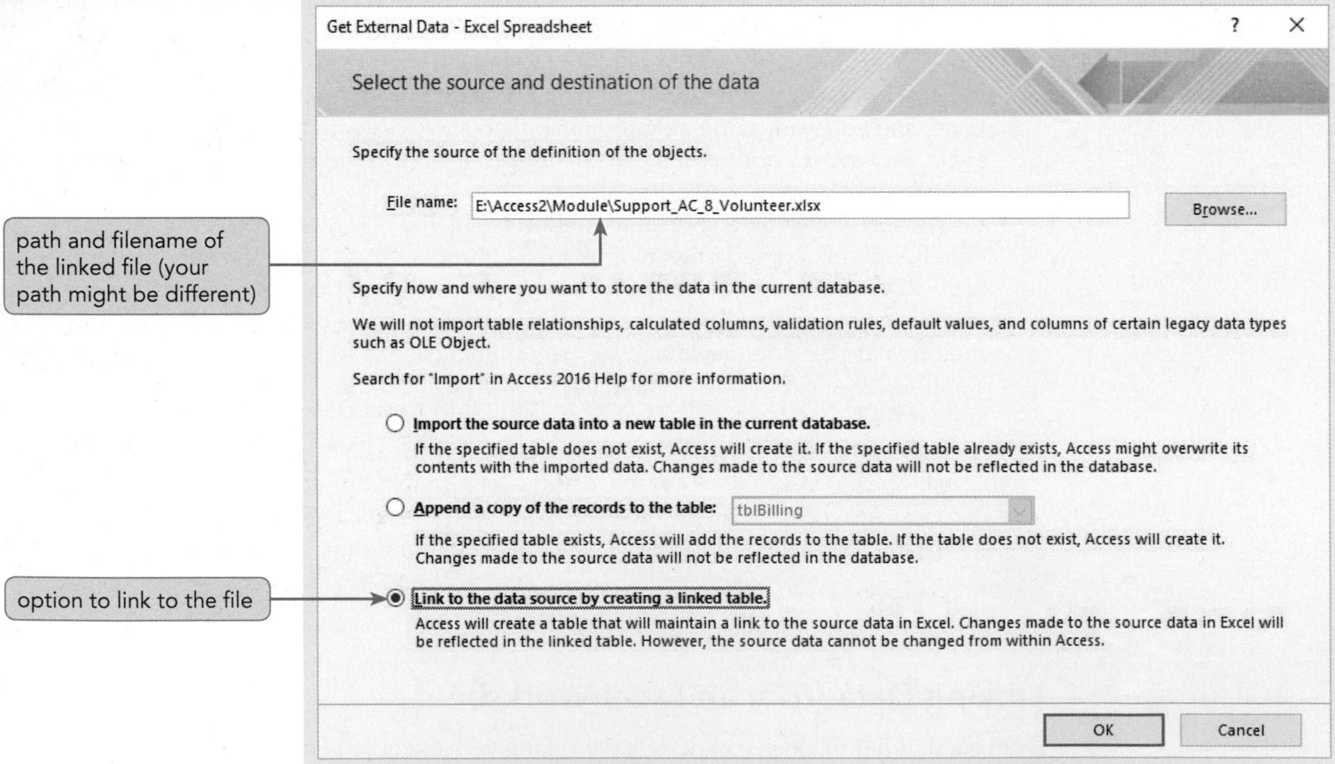
Get External Data - Excel Spreadsheet
Select the source and destination of the data
Specify the source of the definition of the objects.
File name: E:\Access2\Module\Support_AC_8_Volunteer.xlsx
Browse...
path and filename of the linked file (your path might be different)
Specify how and where you want to store the data in the current database.
We will not import table relationships, calculated columns, validation rules, default values, and columns of certain legacy data types such as OLE Object.
Search for "Import" in Access 2016 Help for more information.
Import the source data into a new table in the current database.
If the specified table does not exist, Access will create it. If the specified table already exists, Access might overwrite its contents with the imported data. Changes made to the source data will not be reflected in the database.
Append a copy of the records to the table: tblBilling
If the specified table exists, Access will add the records to the table. If the table does not exist, Access will create it. Changes made to the source data will not be reflected in the database.
option to link to the file
Link to the data source by creating a linked table.
Access will create a table that will maintain a link to the source data in Excel. Changes made to the source data in Excel will be reflected in the linked table. However, the source data cannot be changed from within Access.
OK
Cancel

3. Click the **OK** button. The first Link Spreadsheet Wizard dialog box opens.

   The first row in the worksheet contains column heading names, and each row in the worksheet represents the data about a single volunteer.

4. Click the **First Row Contains Column Headings** check box to select it. See Figure 8–37.

Figure 8–37 Link Spreadsheet Wizard dialog box

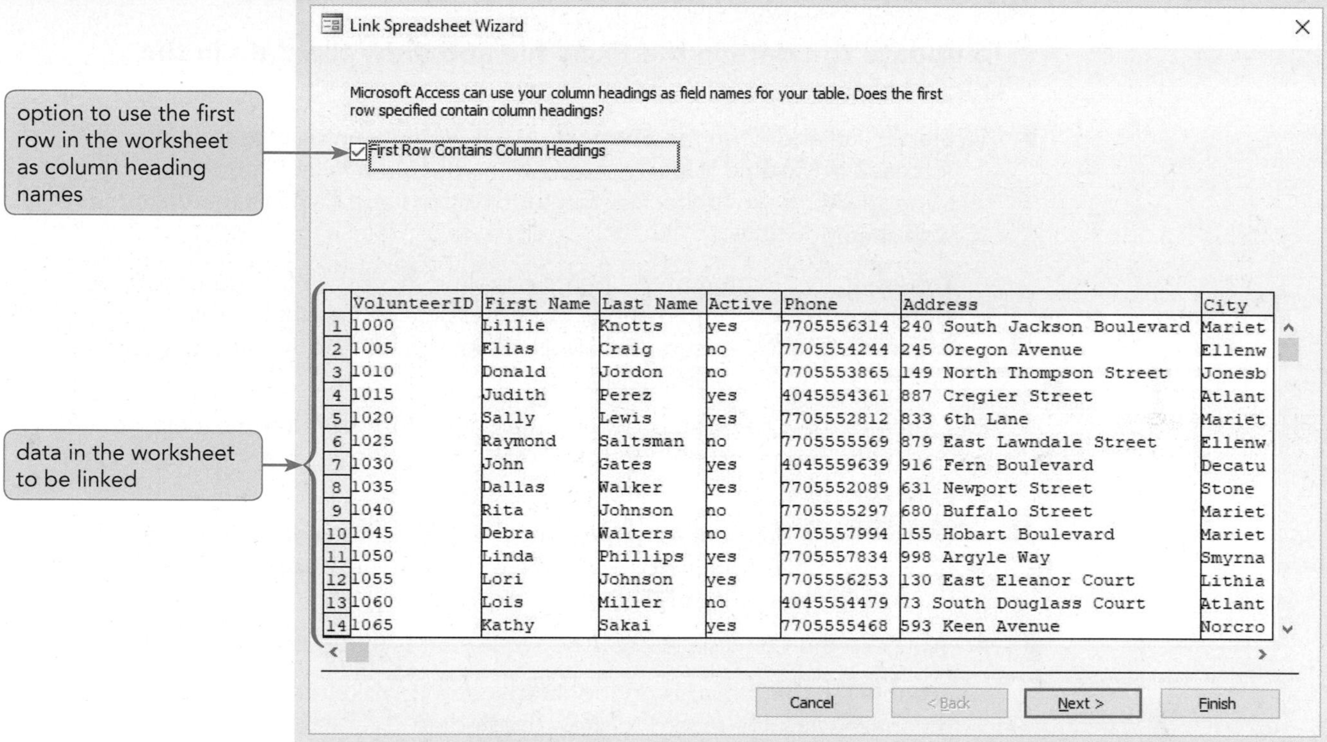
Link Spreadsheet Wizard
Microsoft Access can use your column headings as field names for your table. Does the first row specified contain column headings?
First Row Contains Column Headings
option to use the first row in the worksheet as column heading names
data in the worksheet to be linked

	VolunteerID	First Name	Last Name	Active	Phone	Address	City
1	1000	Lillie	Knotts	yes	7705556314	240 South Jackson Boulevard	Mariet
2	1005	Elias	Craig	no	7705554244	245 Oregon Avenue	Ellenw
3	1010	Donald	Jordon	no	7705553865	149 North Thompson Street	Jonesb
4	1015	Judith	Perez	yes	4045554361	887 Cregier Street	Atlant
5	1020	Sally	Lewis	yes	7705552812	833 6th Lane	Mariet
6	1025	Raymond	Saltsman	no	7705555569	879 East Lawndale Street	Ellenw
7	1030	John	Gates	yes	4045559639	916 Fern Boulevard	Decatu
8	1035	Dallas	Walker	yes	7705552089	631 Newport Street	Stone
9	1040	Rita	Johnson	no	7705555297	680 Buffalo Street	Mariet
10	1045	Debra	Walters	no	7705557994	155 Hobart Boulevard	Mariet
11	1050	Linda	Phillips	yes	7705557834	998 Argyle Way	Smyrna
12	1055	Lori	Johnson	yes	7705556253	130 East Eleanor Court	Lithia
13	1060	Lois	Miller	no	4045554479	73 South Douglass Court	Atlant
14	1065	Kathy	Sakai	yes	7705555468	593 Keen Avenue	Norcro

Cancel
< Back
Next >
Finish

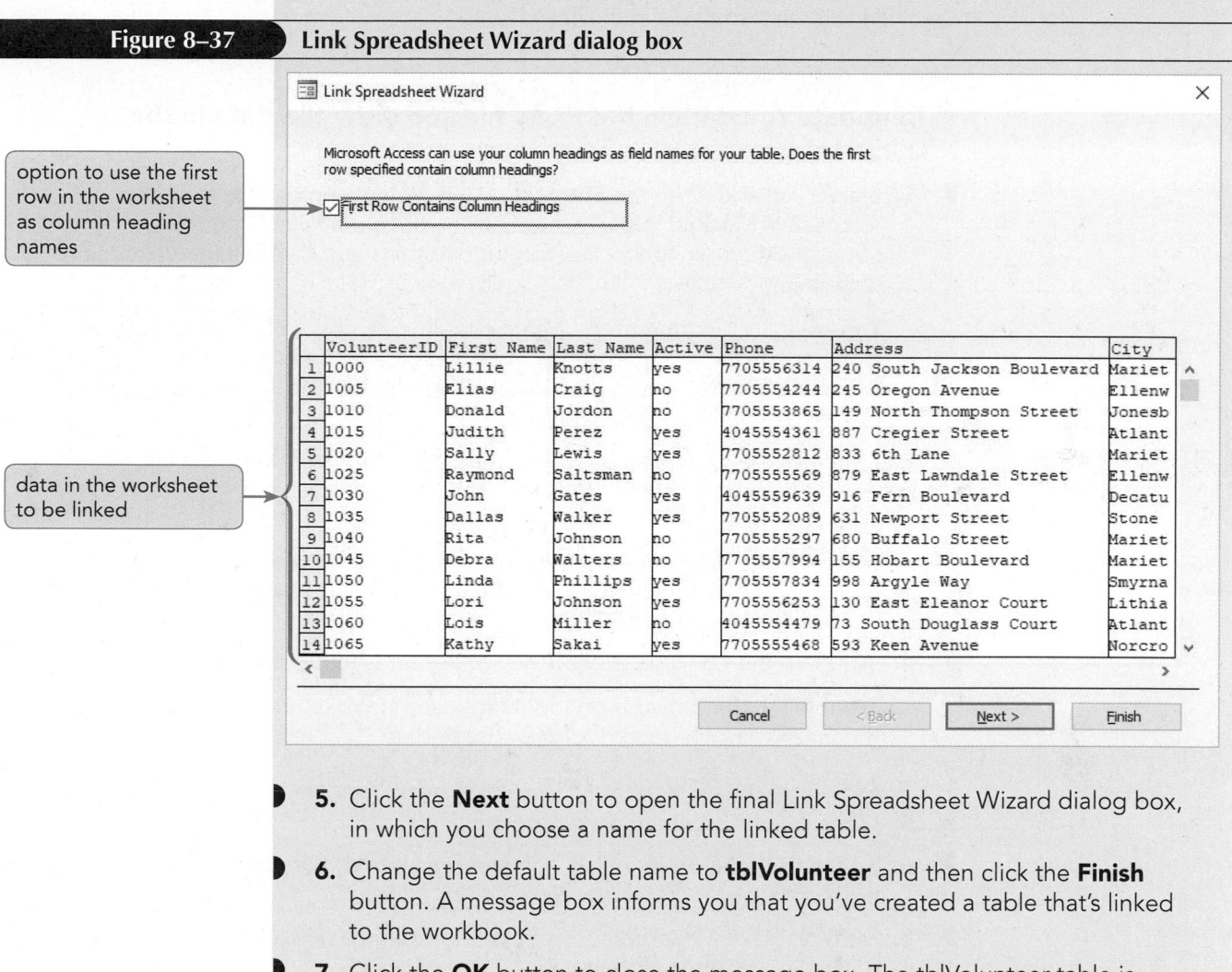

5. Click the **Next** button to open the final Link Spreadsheet Wizard dialog box, in which you choose a name for the linked table.

6. Change the default table name to **tblVolunteer** and then click the **Finish** button. A message box informs you that you've created a table that's linked to the workbook.

7. Click the **OK** button to close the message box. The tblVolunteer table is listed in the Navigation Pane, with an icon to its left indicating it is a linked table.

You can open and view the tblVolunteer table and use fields from the linked table in queries, forms, and reports, but you cannot update the data using the Clinic database. You can only update the data from the Excel workbook file. To open and view the tblVolunteer table in the Clinic database, you must first open and leave open the Excel file to which the table is linked.

Donna tells you that the volunteer Judith Perez had not been able to volunteer for a while, so her Active status was "no". She's now able to volunteer, and Donna would like to change her Active status to "yes". Next, you'll make a change to data in the Excel file and see the update in the linked table.

To update the data in the Excel file and view the data in the linked table:

1. Start Excel and open the **Support_AC_8_Volunteer.xlsx** file from the **Access2 > Module** folder included with your Data Files. The Support_AC_8_Volunteer.xlsx workbook opens and displays the Volunteer worksheet.

   Trouble? If you attempt to open the table in Access before you open the workbook in Excel, you'll get an error message and won't be able to open the workbook. Make sure you always open the workbook or other source file before you open a linked table.

2. Switch to the Clinic database, and then open the **tblVolunteer** datasheet. The fields and records in the tblVolunteer table display the same data as the Volunteer worksheet.
3. Switch to the Support_AC_8_Volunteer.xlsx Excel workbook, select the value **no** in the Active column for Judith Perez (row 5), type **yes** to replace the value, and then press **ENTER**.
4. Switch to the Clinic database. The Active status for Judith Perez is now yes.

   Trouble? If the record is not updated in the tblVolunteer table in the Clinic database, click the record to show the update.

   You've completed your work for Donna and her staff.

5. Close the tblVolunteer table in Access.
6. Switch to the Support_AC_8_Volunteer.xlsx workbook, save your changes to the workbook, and then exit Excel.
7. **sam** Make a backup copy of the Clinic database, compact and repair the database, and then close it.

Knowing how to create tab controls and application parts, export data to PDF documents, and link to data maintained by other applications will make it easier for Donna and her staff to efficiently manage their data.

REVIEW

Session 8.2 Quick Check

1. The _______ property lets you change the default navigation label from the word "Record" to another value.
2. What is the Microsoft Graph program?
3. What is a PDF file?
4. What is an application part?
5. What is the difference between an application part and a template?
6. How can you edit data in a table that has been linked to an Excel file?

PRACTICE

Review Assignments

Data Files needed for the Review Assignments: Supplier.accdb (*cont. from previous module*), Support_AC_8_Ads.xlsx, Support_AC_8_Partners.accdb, Support_AC_8_Payables.csv, and Support_AC_8_Payments.xml

Donna wants you to integrate data in other files created with other applications with the data in the Supplier database, and she wants to be able to analyze the data in the database. Complete the following steps:

1. Open the **Supplier** database you worked with in the previous three modules.
2. Export the qrySupplierProducts query as an HTML document to the Access2 > Review folder provided with your Data Files, saving the file as **NP_AC_8_qrySupplierProducts** and exporting the data with formatting and layout. Save the export steps with the name **Export-NP_AC_8_qrySupplierProducts**. Once saved, modify the description to be **HTML file containing the qrySupplierProducts query**.
3. Import the CSV file named Support_AC_8_Payables.csv, which is located in the Access2 > Review folder, as a new table in the database. Use the names in the first row as field names, use Currency as the data type for the numeric fields, choose your own primary key, name the table **tblPayables**, run the Table Analyzer, record the Table Analyzer's recommendation, and then cancel out of the Table Analyzer Wizard without making the recommended changes. Do not save the import steps.
4. Import the data and structure from the XML file named **Support_AC_8_Payments.xml**, which is located in the Access2 > Review folder included with your Data Files, as a new table named **tblPayments** in the database. Do not save the import steps, and then rename the table **tblPayment** (with no "s" on the end of the name).
5. Export the tblSupplier table as an XML file named **NP_AC_8_Supplier** to the Access2 > Review folder; do not create a separate XSD file. Save the export steps, and use the default name given.
6. Lakewood Community Health Services also pays for advertisements, and information on this activity is contained in an Excel file named Support_AC_8_Ads.xlsx. Create a table named **tblAds** in the Supplier database that links to the Support_AC_8_Ads.xlsx Excel file, which is located in the Access2 > Review folder included with your Data Files. Change the cost of the flyer for Ad 6 to **$89**, and save the workbook.
7. Modify the frmSuppliersWithProducts form in the following ways:
   a. Add a tab control to the bottom of the Detail section, so the left edge is aligned with the left edge of the Company Comments label, and then place the existing subform on the first page of the tab control.
   b. Change the caption for the left tab to **Product Data** and for the right tab to **Product Chart**.
   c. Change the caption for the main form's navigation buttons to **Supplier**.
   d. Add a chart to the second page of the tab control. Use the tblProduct table as the record source, select the ProductName and Price, use the 3-D Column Chart type (row 1, column 2), do not include a legend, and use **Products Offered** as the chart title.
   e. Change the chart to a 3-D Clustered Bar chart, and change the purple colored data markers to pink.
8. Export the tblPayment table as a PDF file called **NP_AC_8_Payments**, using document structure tags for accessibility. Do not save the export steps.
9. Open the Support_AC_8_Partners.accdb database from the Access2 > Review folder, and then create and implement an application part as follows:
   a. Create an application part called **Vendor** with the description **New Vendor**, and do not include the data.
   b. Close the Support_AC_8_Partners.accdb database.
   c. Open the **Supplier** database and import the Vendor application part, which has no relationship to any of the other tables. Open the tblNewVendor table to verify the structure has been imported, but does not contain any records.
10. Make a backup copy of the database, compact and repair the database, and then close it.

APPLY

Case Problem 1

Data Files needed for this Case Problem: School.accdb (*cont. from previous module*), Support_AC_8_AddSubject.xml, Support_AC_8_NewStudentReferrals.accdb, Support_AC_8_Room.xlsx, and Support_AC_8_Subject.csv

Great Giraffe Jeremiah Garver wants you to integrate data from other files created with different applications with the data in the School database, and he wants to be able to analyze the data in the database. Complete the following steps:

1. Open the **School** database you worked with in the previous three modules.
2. Export the rptCourseRosters report as a PDF document with a filename of **NP_AC_8_CourseRosters** to the Access2 > Case1 folder provided with your Data Files. Include the document structure tags for accessibility, and do not save the export steps.
3. Import the CSV file named Support_AC_8_Instructor.csv, which is located in the Access2 > Case1 folder, as a new table in the database. Use the names in the first row as field names, set the data type for the first two columns to Short Text and for the third and fourth columns to Yes/No, choose your own primary key, name the table **tblInstructor**, run the Table Analyzer, and record the Table Analyzer's recommendation, but do not accept the recommendation. Do not save the import steps.
4. Export the tblCourse table as an XML file named **NP_AC_8_Course** to the Access2 > Case1 folder; do not create a separate XSD file. Save the export steps.
5. Create a new table named **tblRoom** that is linked to the Support_AC_8_Room.xlsx Excel file, which is located in the Access2 > Case1 folder provided with your Data Files. Add the following new record to the Room workbook: Room Num **6**, Rental Cost **$275**, and Type **Private**.
6. Import the XML file named Support_AC_8_Company.xml file, which is located in the Access2 > Case1 folder included with your Data Files, adding the records to a new table named tblCompany. Do not save any import steps.
7. Modify the frmStudentsByCourse form in the following ways:
   a. At the bottom of the Detail section, delete the Student label, then move the Student subform onto the first page of a new tab control. Align the tab control with the left edge of the Cost label and at the 2-inch mark on the vertical ruler.
   b. Change the caption for the left tab to **Student Data** and for the right tab to **Student Chart**.
   c. Change the caption for the main form's navigation buttons to **Course**.
   d. Add a chart to the second page of the tab control. Use the tblRegistration table as the record source, select the BalanceDue and StudentID fields, use the Column Chart type (row 1, column 1), do not include a legend, and use **Outstanding Balances** as the chart title.
8. Open the **Support_AC_8_NewStudentReferrals.accdb** database from the Access2 > Case1 folder provided with your Data Files, and then create and work with an application part as follows:
   a. Create an application part called **NewStudentContact** with the description **New student referrals**.
   b. Close the Support_AC_8_NewStudentReferrals.accdb database.
   c. Open the **School** database and import the **NewStudentContact** application part, which has no relationship to any of the other tables. Verify that the tblContact table is created and contains no data.
9. Make a backup copy of the database, compact and repair the database, and then close it.

CREATE

Case Problem 2

Data Files needed for this Case Problem: Storm.accdb (*cont. from previous module*), Support_AC_8_CreditCard.xml, Support_AC_8_Maintenance.xml, Support_AC_8_Schedule.xlsx, Support_AC_8_Suppliers.xlsx, and Support_AC_8_Volunteers.csv.

Drain Adopter Tandrea Austin wants you to integrate data from files created with other applications with the data in the Storm database, and she wants to be able to analyze the data in the database. Complete the following steps:

1. Open the **Storm** database you worked with in the previous three modules.
2. Export the qryVolunteersWithoutDrains query as an HTML document to the Access2 > Case2 folder using a filename of **NP_AC_8_UnmatchedVolunteers**. Save the export steps.
3. Export the rptDrainsWithVolunteers report as a PDF document with a filename of **NP_AC_8_Drains** to the Access2 > Case2 folder. Include the document structure tags for accessibility, and do not save the export steps.
4. Import the CSV file named Support_AC_8_Volunteers.csv, which is located in the Access2 > Case2 folder, as a new table in the database. Use the names in the first row as field names, set the data type for the first nine columns to Short Text, set the data type for the SignupDate column to Date With Time, set the data type for the Trained column to Yes/No, choose your own primary key, name the table **tblNewVolunteers**, run the Table Analyzer, and record the Table Analyzer's recommendation, but do not accept the recommendation. Do not save the import steps.
5. Import the data and structure from the XML file named Support_AC_8_Maintenance.xml, which is located in the Access2 > Case2 folder provided with your Data Files, as a new table. Save the import steps.
6. Export the tblSupply table as an XML file named **NP_AC_8_Supplies** to the Access2 > Case2 folder; do not create a separate XSD file. Save the export steps.
7. Create a new table named **tblSupplier** by linking to the Support_AC_8_Suppliers.xlsx Excel file, which is located in the Access2 > Case2 folder provided with your Data Files. For SupplierID 1004, change the ShippingCost value to **Free**.
8. Modify the frmVolunteersAndDrains form to include a tab control and named navigation tools as shown in Figure 8–38.
   a. At the bottom of the Detail section, delete the Drain label.
   b. Add a tab control to the bottom of the Detail section, and place the existing subform on the first page tab of the tab control.
   c. Change the caption for the left tab to **Drain Details** and for the right tab to **Status Summary**. Leave the main section of the right tab empty.
   d. Change the caption for the main form's navigation buttons to **Volunteer** and for the subform's navigation buttons to **Drain**.

Figure 8–38 **Customized frmVolunteersAndDrains form**

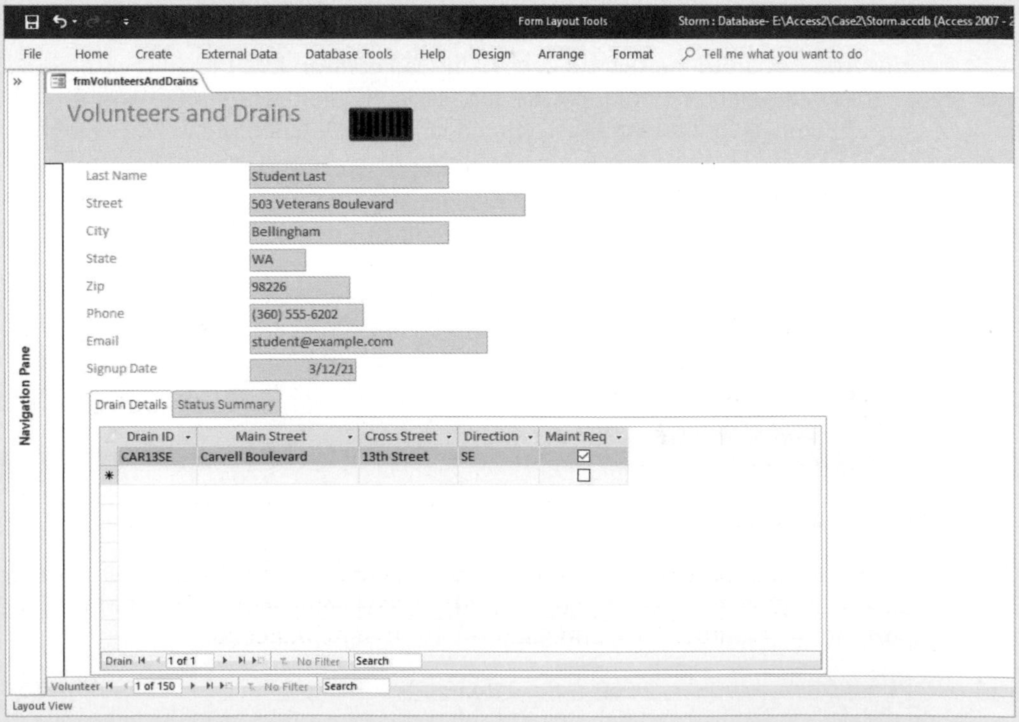
Form Layout Tools
Storm : Database- E:\Access2\Case2\Storm.accdb (Access 2007 -
File Home Create External Data Database Tools Help Design Arrange Format Tell me what you want to do
frmVolunteersAndDrains
Volunteers and Drains
Last Name
Student Last
Street
503 Veterans Boulevard
City
Bellingham
State
WA
Zip
98226
Phone
(360) 555-6202
Email
student@example.com
Signup Date
3/12/21
Drain Details
Status Summary
Drain ID
Main Street
Cross Street
Direction
Maint Req
CAR13SE
Carvell Boulevard
13th Street
SE
Drain 1 of 1 No Filter Search
Volunteer 1 of 150 No Filter Search
Navigation Pane
Layout View

9. Make a backup copy of the database, compact and repair the database, and then close it.

MODULE 9

Using Action Queries and Advanced Table Relationships

Enhancing User Interaction with the Health Database

OBJECTIVES

Session 9.1
- Create an action query to create a table
- Create an action query to append data
- Construct an action query to delete data
- Build an action query to update data

Session 9.2
- Define many-to-many relationships between tables
- Define one-to-one relationships between tables
- Understand join types
- Create a query using a self-join
- View and create indexes for tables

Case | *Lakewood Community Health Services*

Lakewood Community Health Services is a nonprofit health clinic located in Atlanta, Georgia. It provides a range of medical services to patients of all ages. The clinic specializes in chronic disease management, cardiac care, and geriatrics. Donna Taylor, the office manager for Lakewood Community Health Services, oversees a small staff and is responsible for maintaining records for the clinic's patients.

The Lakewood staff developed the Health database of patient, visit, billing, employee, and treatment data, and the employees use **Microsoft Access 2019** (or simply **Access**), to manage it. Donna has been enhancing the Health database containing tables, queries, forms, and reports that she and other staff members use to track patients and their visits. Donna has asked you to continue enhancing the database by creating some advanced queries and integrating more tables into the database.

STARTING DATA FILES

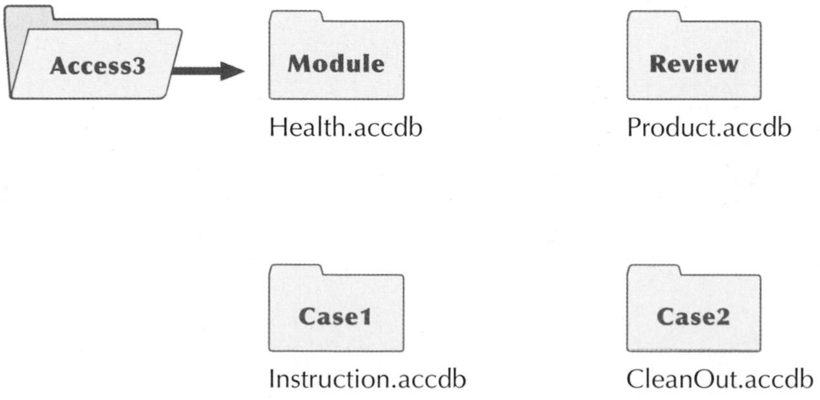
Access3
Module
Health.accdb
Review
Product.accdb
Case1
Instruction.accdb
Case2
CleanOut.accdb

Session 9.1 Visual Overview:

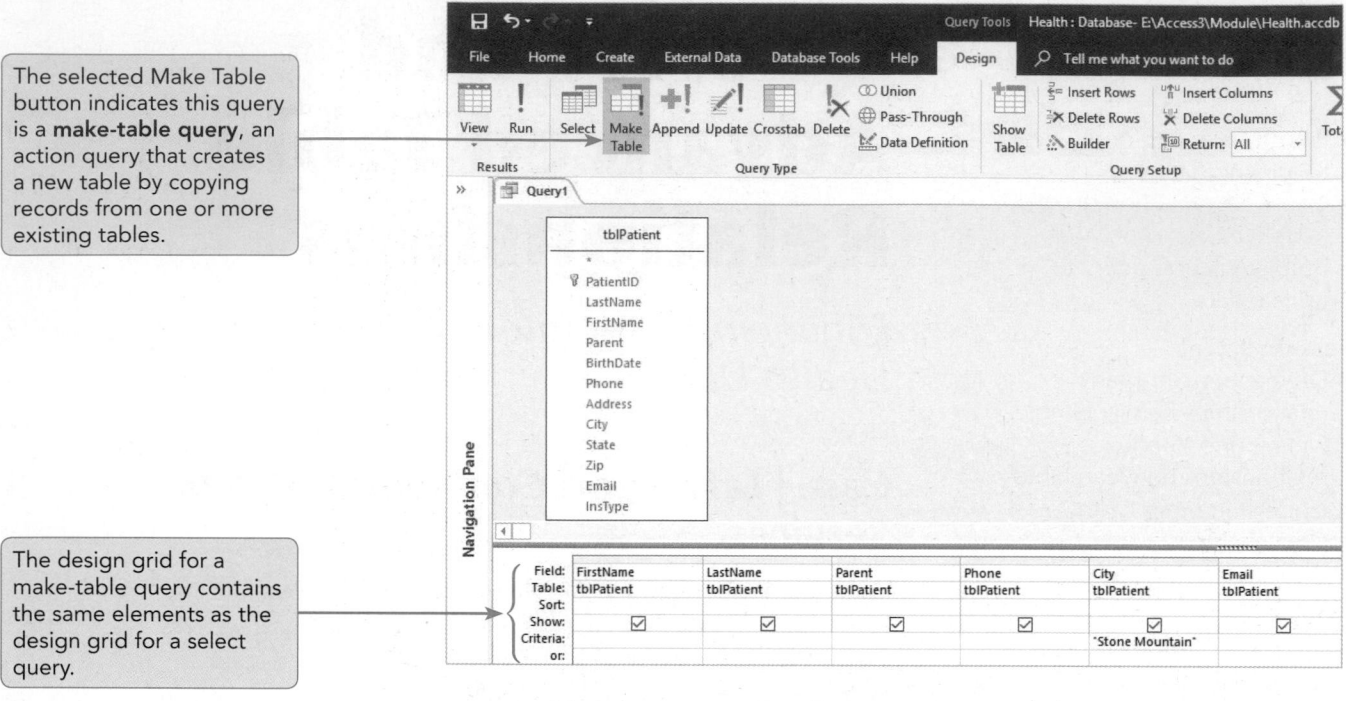

The selected Make Table button indicates this query is a **make-table query**, an action query that creates a new table by copying records from one or more existing tables.

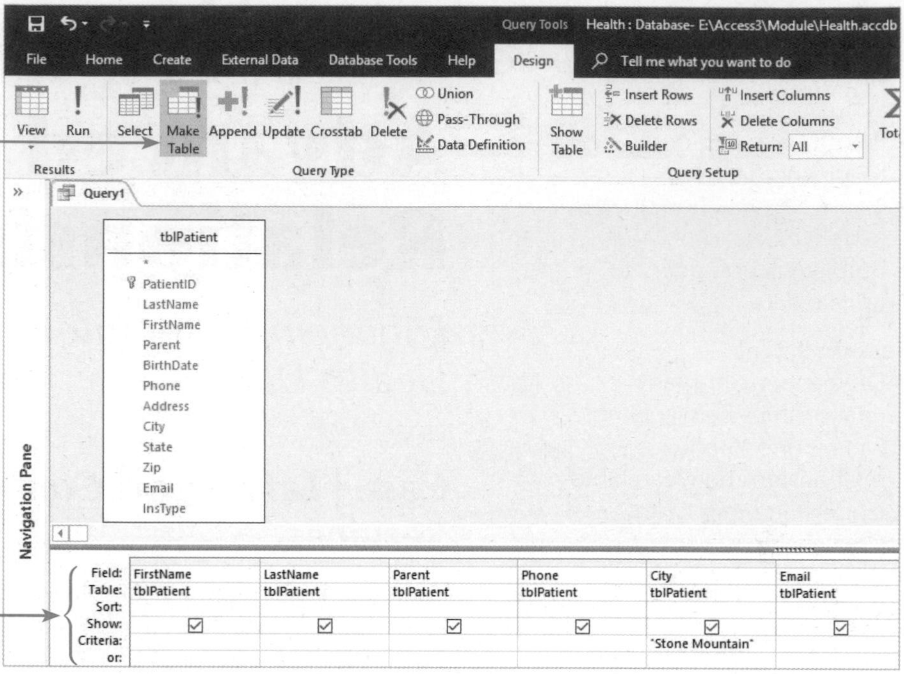
Query Tools
Health : Database- E:\Access3\Module\Health.accdb
File
Home
Create
External Data
Database Tools
Help
Design
Tell me what you want to do
View
Run
Select
Make Table
Append
Update
Crosstab
Delete
Union
Pass-Through
Data Definition
Show Table
Insert Rows
Delete Rows
Builder
Insert Columns
Delete Columns
Return: All
Results
Query Type
Query Setup
Query1
tblPatient
PatientID
LastName
FirstName
Parent
BirthDate
Phone
Address
City
State
Zip
Email
InsType
Navigation Pane
Field:
Table:
Sort:
Show:
Criteria:
or:
FirstName
LastName
Parent
Phone
City
Email
tblPatient
"Stone Mountain"

The design grid for a make-table query contains the same elements as the design grid for a select query.

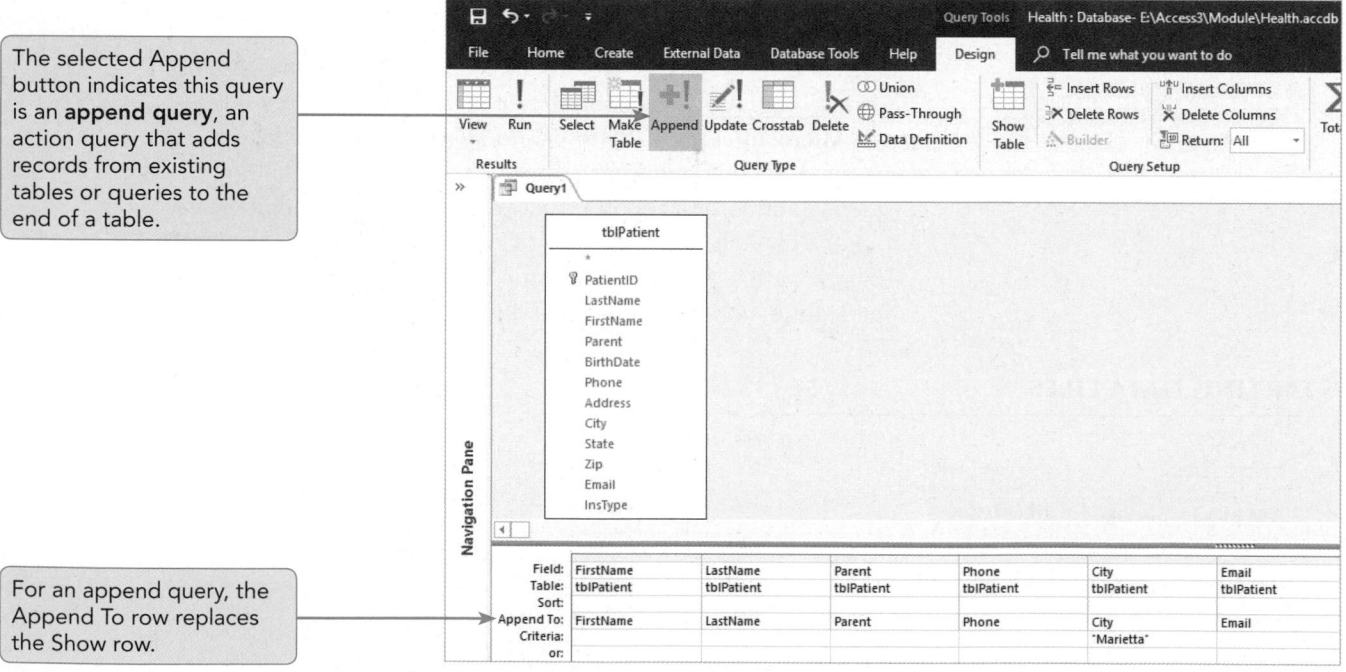

The selected Append button indicates this query is an **append query**, an action query that adds records from existing tables or queries to the end of a table.

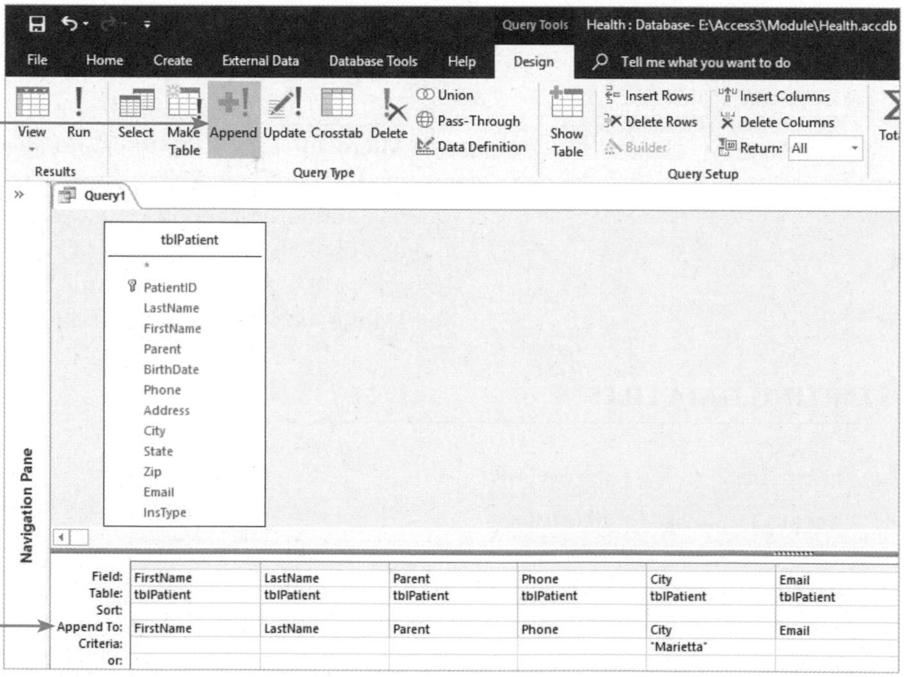
Query Tools
Health : Database- E:\Access3\Module\Health.accdb
File
Home
Create
External Data
Database Tools
Help
Design
Tell me what you want to do
View
Run
Select
Make Table
Append
Update
Crosstab
Delete
Union
Pass-Through
Data Definition
Show Table
Insert Rows
Delete Rows
Builder
Insert Columns
Delete Columns
Return: All
Results
Query Type
Query Setup
Query1
tblPatient
PatientID
LastName
FirstName
Parent
BirthDate
Phone
Address
City
State
Zip
Email
InsType
Navigation Pane
Field:
Table:
Sort:
Append To:
Criteria:
or:
FirstName
LastName
Parent
Phone
City
Email
tblPatient
"Marietta"

For an append query, the Append To row replaces the Show row.

Action Queries

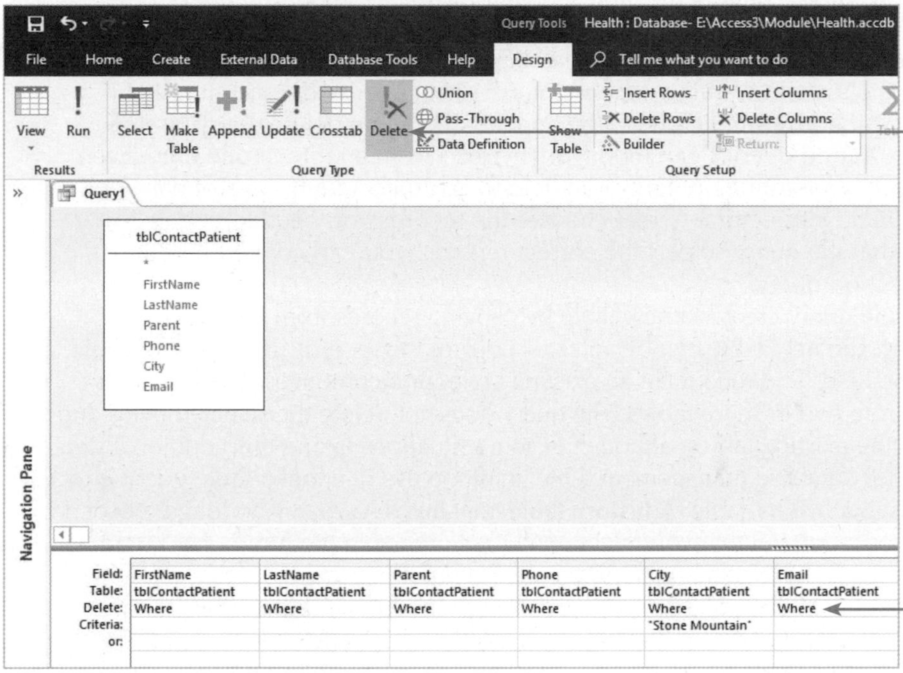
Query Tools
Health : Database- E:\Access3\Module\Health.accdb
File
Home
Create
External Data
Database Tools
Help
Design
Tell me what you want to do
View
Run
Select
Make Table
Append
Update
Crosstab
Delete
Union
Pass-Through
Data Definition
Show Table
Insert Rows
Delete Rows
Builder
Insert Columns
Delete Columns
Return:
Results
Query Type
Query Setup
Query1
tblContactPatient
*
FirstName
LastName
Parent
Phone
City
Email
Navigation Pane
Field: FirstName | LastName | Parent | Phone | City | Email
Table: tblContactPatient | tblContactPatient | tblContactPatient | tblContactPatient | tblContactPatient | tblContactPatient
Delete: Where | Where | Where | Where | Where | Where
Criteria: "Stone Mountain"
or:

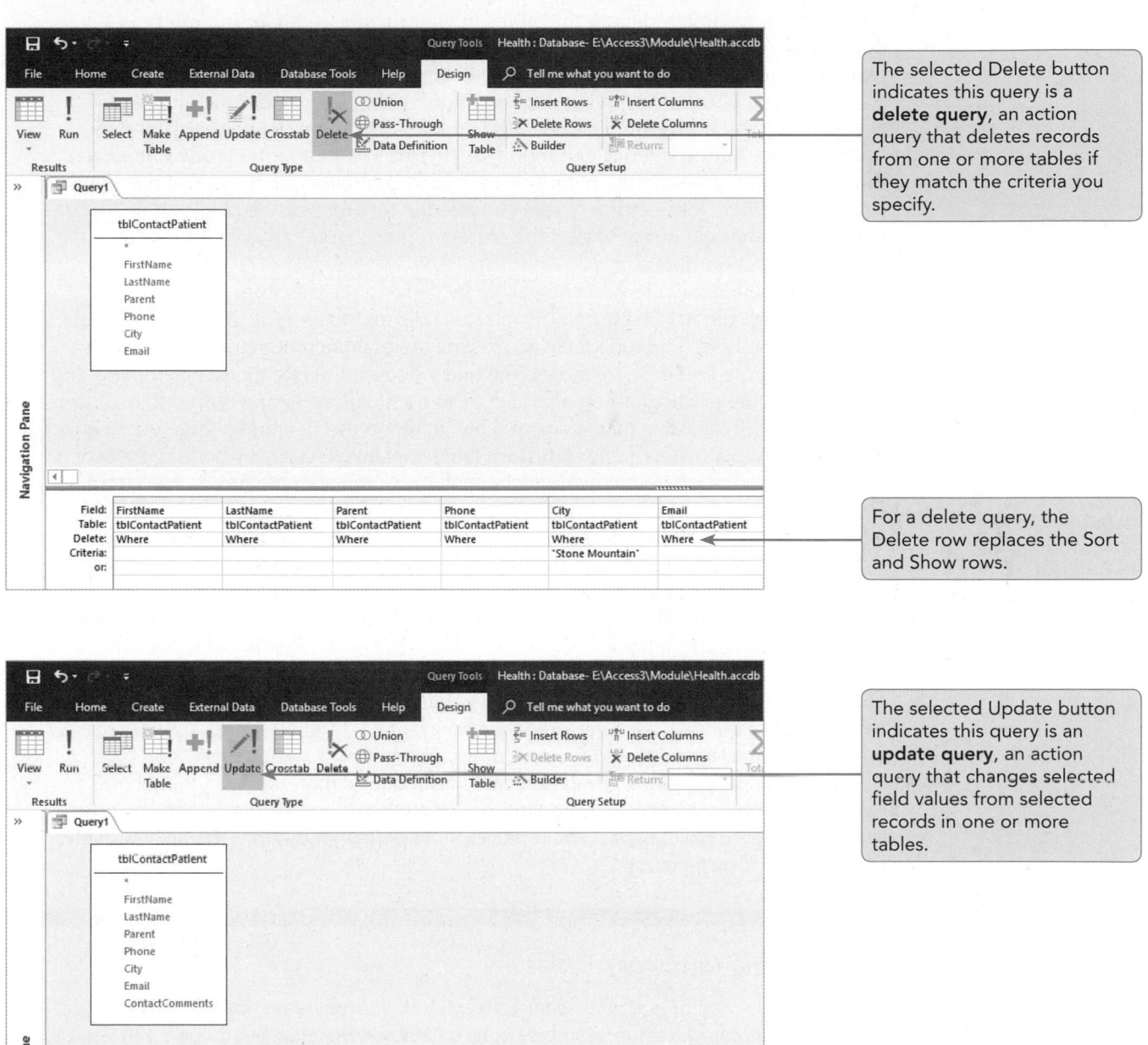

The selected Delete button indicates this query is a **delete query**, an action query that deletes records from one or more tables if they match the criteria you specify.

For a delete query, the Delete row replaces the Sort and Show rows.

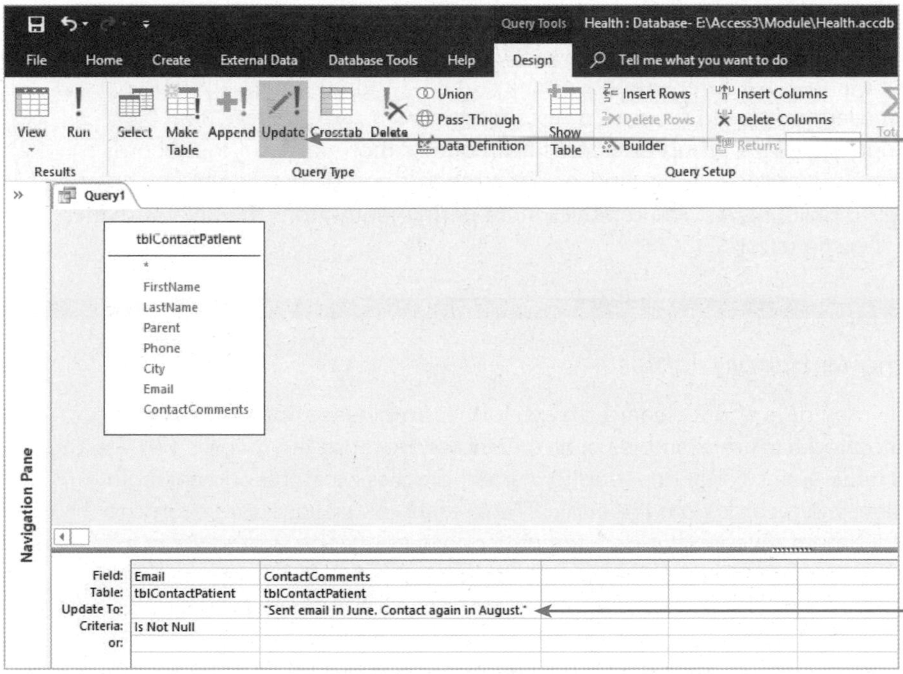
Query Tools
Health : Database- E:\Access3\Module\Health.accdb
File
Home
Create
External Data
Database Tools
Help
Design
Tell me what you want to do
View
Run
Select
Make Table
Append
Update
Crosstab
Delete
Union
Pass-Through
Data Definition
Show Table
Insert Rows
Delete Rows
Builder
Insert Columns
Delete Columns
Return:
Results
Query Type
Query Setup
Query1
tblContactPatient
*
FirstName
LastName
Parent
Phone
City
Email
ContactComments
Navigation Pane
Field: Email | ContactComments
Table: tblContactPatient | tblContactPatient
Update To: "Sent email in June. Contact again in August."
Criteria: Is Not Null
or:

The selected Update button indicates this query is an **update query**, an action query that changes selected field values from selected records in one or more tables.

For an update query, the Update To row replaces the Sort and Show rows.

Action Queries

Queries can do more than display answers to the questions you ask; they can also perform actions on the data in the tables in your database. An **action query** is a query that adds, changes, or deletes multiple table records at a time. For example, Donna could use an action query to delete all paid invoices from the previous year. As shown in the Visual Overview for Session 9.1, Access provides four types of action queries: the make-table query, the append query, the delete query, and the update query. Action queries can modify many records in a table at one time. Even though enforcing referential integrity can help to avoid accidental loss of data, you should first create a select query that chooses the records you need to update. After you confirm that the query selects the correct records, you can convert it to the appropriate action query.

A make-table query creates a new table by copying records from one or more existing tables. The new table can be an exact copy of the records in an existing table, a subset of the fields and records in an existing table, or a combination of the fields and records from two or more tables. The query does not delete the selected fields and records from the existing tables, although in some situations taking this additional step makes sense for database management. One common use of a make-table query is to move records to a history table. A **history table** contains data that is no longer needed for current processing but that you might need to reference in the future. For instance, Donna could use a make-table query to create a table of records for patients that have not visited the clinic for more than five years, and then remove those records from the source tables. The new table created by a make-table query reflects data at a point in time; future changes made to the original (existing) tables are not reflected in the new table. You need to run the make-table query periodically if you want the newly created table to contain current data.

An append query adds records from existing tables or queries to the end of another table. For an append query, you choose the fields you want to append from one or more tables or queries; the selected data remains in the original tables. Append queries are most often used to append records to history tables.

A delete query deletes a group of records from one or more tables if the records match the criteria you specify. You choose which records you want to delete by entering selection criteria. Deleting records removes them permanently from the database after the database is compacted.

INSIGHT

Appending to History Tables

Tables containing data about cleared checks, former employees, inactive customers, and obsolete products are examples of history tables. Because the records you append to a history table are no longer needed for current processing in the original table, you can delete the records from the original table after you append the records to the history table. Before deleting the data from the original table, be sure to verify that you appended the correct records. When you delete data, the deletion is permanent.

An update query changes selected field values from selected records in one or more tables. You choose the fields and records you want to change by entering the selection criteria and the update rules. Donna could use an update query to add text in the comment field of every patient record that contains an email address to note that an email message had been sent to these patients. Update queries are particularly valuable in performing multiple updates to large tables.

Creating a Make-Table Query

Donna wants to contact all patients who live in Stone Mountain to remind them about the importance of annual flu vaccinations. She asks you to create a new temporary table containing the FirstName, LastName, Parent, Phone, City, and Email fields from the tblPatient table for all patients whose City field value is Stone Mountain. She only wants to keep this table for this phone call campaign. After the campaign, she will not need the table anymore. She wants to create a temporary table instead of a query so she can modify it by adding notes that she will take when she calls the patients who live in Stone Mountain. By creating a new temporary table, Donna doesn't need to worry about disrupting or changing the data in any existing tables or in any objects based on the tables. After Donna is satisfied that all patients have been called and she's gathered their feedback, she can delete the temporary table.

INSIGHT

Making Temporary Tables

Duplicating data in a database is frowned upon. When a database has multiple copies of data and a change is made, the data could have errors if some instances of the data are changed and others are not changed. However, sometimes it is useful to create a temporary table for a specific purpose. When the table is no longer needed, it is deleted. For instance, the manager of a small appliance store might want to notify all customers who purchased a toaster more than two years ago that a new model is now available. The manager could create a temporary table containing the First Name, Last Name, and Phone Number for each of these customers, and add a field for comments so the staff can indicate when they called each customer and whether they left a message or spoke to the customer directly. It would not make sense to track this information in the database because it does not directly relate to the customers' purchases. When the telephone campaign is finished, the table could be deleted.

You can create the new temporary table for Donna by using a make-table query that uses fields from the tblPatient table in the Health database. When you run a make-table query, you create a new table. The records in the new table are based on the records in the query's underlying tables. The fields in the new table will have the data type and field size of the fields in the query's underlying tables. The new table will not preserve the primary key designation or field properties such as the format or lookup properties.

REFERENCE

Creating a Make-Table Query

- Create a select query with the necessary fields and selection criteria.
- On the Query Tools Design tab, click the Run button in the Results group to preview the results.
- Switch to Design view to make any necessary changes to the query, and then, when the query is correct, click the Make Table button located in the Query Type group on the Query Tools Design tab.
- In the Make Table dialog box, type the new table name in the Table Name box, making sure the Current Database option button is selected to include the new table in the current database; or, click the Another Database option button, enter the database name in the File Name box, and then click the OK button.
- Click the Run button, and then click the Yes button to confirm the creation of the new table.

You'll create the new temporary table now using a make-table query. You'll base the make-table query on the tblPatient table.

To create and run the select query based on the tblPatient table:

1. **sam** Start Access, and then open the **Health** database from the **Access3 > Module** folder included with your Data Files.

   Trouble? If you don't have the starting Data Files, you need to get them before you can proceed. Your instructor will either give you the Data Files or ask you to obtain them from a specified location (such as a network drive). If you have any questions about the Data Files, see your instructor or technical support person for assistance.

   Trouble? If the security warning is displayed below the ribbon, click the Enable Content button.

2. Make sure the Navigation Pane is closed, click the **Create** tab, and then, in the Queries group, click the **Query Design** button. The Show Table dialog box opens on top of the Query window in Design view.
3. Add the **tblPatient** field list to the Query window, and then close the Show Table dialog box.
4. Resize the tblPatient field list to display all its fields, and then add the **FirstName**, **LastName**, **Parent**, **Phone**, **City**, and **Email** fields to the design grid in that order.

   Next, you'll enter the City field's selection criterion of Stone Mountain.

5. In the design grid, click the **City Criteria** box, type **Stone Mountain**, and then press **TAB**. The condition changes to "Stone Mountain". See Figure 9–1.

Figure 9–1 Select query on which make-table query will be based

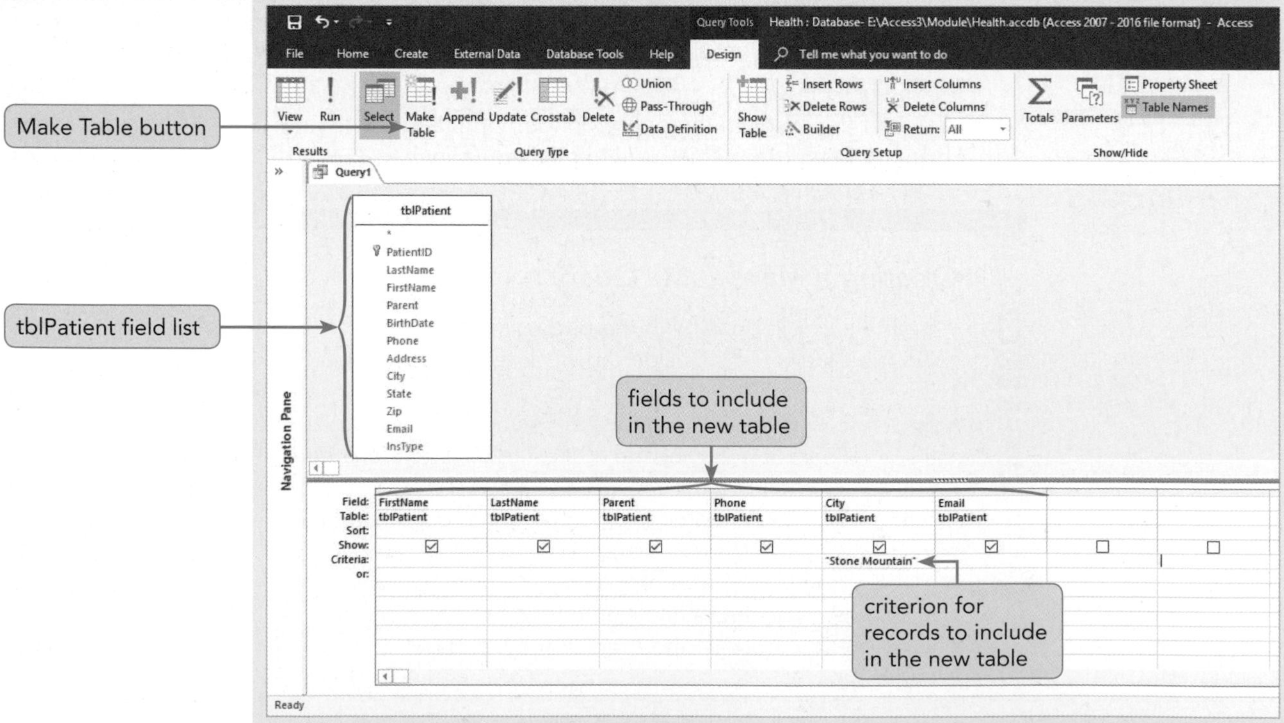
Make Table button
tblPatient field list
fields to include in the new table
criterion for records to include in the new table
tblPatient
PatientID
LastName
FirstName
Parent
BirthDate
Phone
Address
City
State
Zip
Email
InsType
Field: FirstName LastName Parent Phone City Email
Table: tblPatient
Criteria: "Stone Mountain"
Ready

You've completed the select query, so now you can run it to make sure the recordset contains the data Donna needs.

6. Run the query. The query recordset shows the seven records for Stone Mountain patients.

Now that you have verified that the records selected contain the city Stone Mountain, you can be confident these are the same records that the make-table query will select. Next, you'll change the query to a make-table query.

To change the query type, and then run and save the make-table query:

1. Switch to Design view, and then on the Query Tools Design tab, in the Query Type group, click the **Make Table** button. The Make Table dialog box opens. You use the dialog box to enter a name for the new table and designate the database to be used to store the table. See Figure 9–2.

Figure 9–2 Make Table dialog box

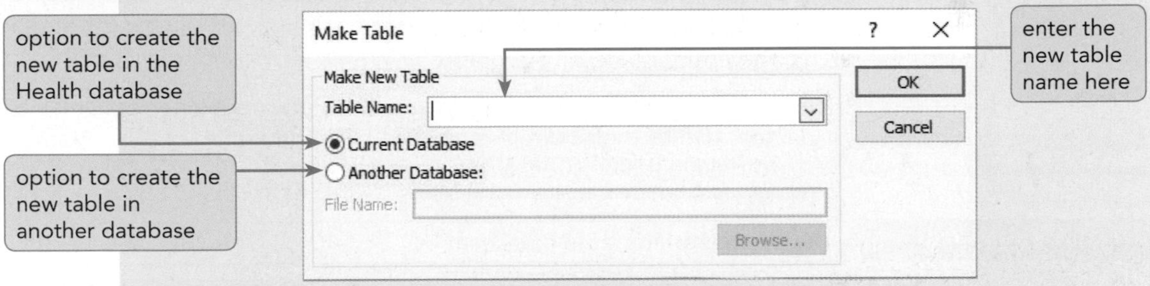
option to create the new table in the Health database
option to create the new table in another database
enter the new table name here
Make Table
Make New Table
Table Name:
Current Database
Another Database:
File Name:
OK
Cancel
Browse...

Be sure to select the Current Database option button; otherwise, Access will require you to specify the name of another data file in which to place the table.

2. In the Table Name box, type **tblContactPatient**, make sure the **Current Database** option button is selected, ensuring the new table will be added to the Health database, and then click **OK**.

   Now that you have created and tested the query, you can run it to create the tblContactPatient table. After you run the query, you can save it, and then view the new table. Because you have not saved the query yet, the name on the tab is Query1.

3. Run the query. A dialog box opens, indicating that you are about to paste seven rows into a new table. Because you are running an action query that alters the contents of the database, you have the opportunity to cancel the operation, if necessary, or to confirm it.
4. Click **Yes**. The dialog box closes, and the make-table query creates the tblContactPatient table. The query is still displayed in Design view.
5. Save the query as **qryContactPatientMakeTable**, close the query, and then open the Navigation Pane. The qryContactPatientMakeTable query appears in the Queries list with a special icon indicating that it is a make-table query. See Figure 9–3.

Figure 9–3 **Query type icons in the Navigation Pane**

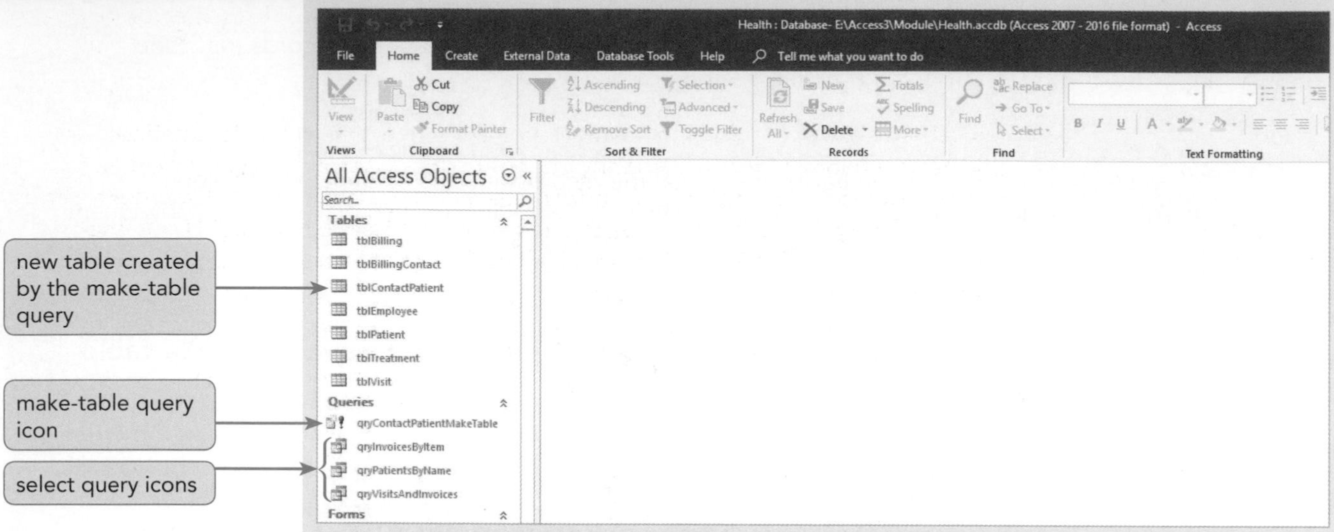
new table created by the make-table query
make-table query icon
select query icons
All Access Objects
Tables
tblBilling
tblBillingContact
tblContactPatient
tblEmployee
tblPatient
tblTreatment
tblVisit
Queries
qryContactPatientMakeTable
qryInvoicesByItem
qryPatientsByName
qryVisitsAndInvoices
Forms

You can now open the tblContactPatient table to view the results of the make-table query.

Trouble? You may have to increase the width of the Navigation Pane to see the entire name of the query.

6. Open the **tblContactPatient** table in Datasheet view, resize all datasheet columns to their best fit, and then click the first row's **FirstName** field value to deselect all values. See Figure 9–4.

Figure 9–4 **tblContactPatient table datasheet**

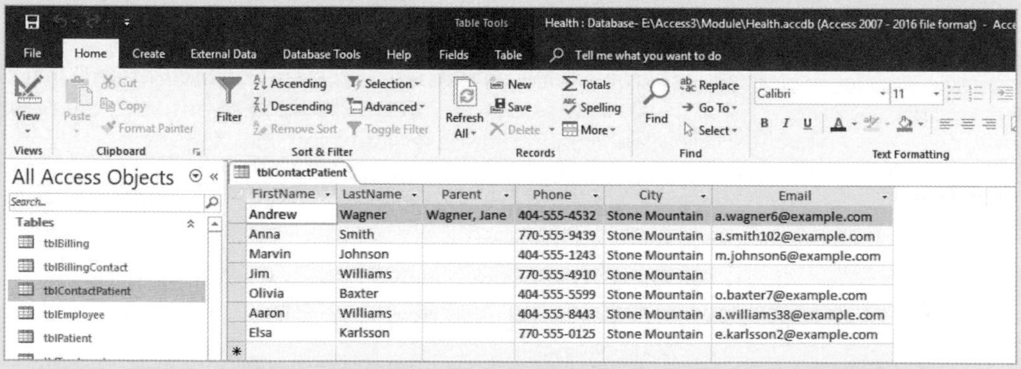
tblContactPatient
FirstName LastName Parent Phone City Email
Andrew Wagner Wagner, Jane 404-555-4532 Stone Mountain a.wagner6@example.com
Anna Smith 770-555-9439 Stone Mountain a.smith102@example.com
Marvin Johnson 404-555-1243 Stone Mountain m.johnson6@example.com
Jim Williams 770-555-4910 Stone Mountain
Olivia Baxter 404-555-5599 Stone Mountain o.baxter7@example.com
Aaron Williams 404-555-8443 Stone Mountain a.williams38@example.com
Elsa Karlsson 770-555-0125 Stone Mountain e.karlsson2@example.com

The tblContactPatient table includes the FirstName, LastName, Parent, Phone, City, and Email fields for patients who live in Stone Mountain. Make-table queries do not transfer Caption property settings to the created tables, so the FirstName and LastName column headings do not contain spaces. The tblContactPatient table also does not include formatting for the phone number. Other field properties that do not transfer include Decimal Places, Default Value, Format, Input Mask, Validation Rule, and Validation Text.

7. Save your datasheet changes, close the table, and then close the Navigation Pane.

Donna can now make any necessary changes to the tblContactPatient table records when she contacts patients without affecting the tblPatient table in the Health database.

PROSKILLS

Decision Making: Determining When to Delete Objects

A database evolves to meet the needs of its users, and eventually some database objects are no longer needed. A table, query, or report created for a special event, for instance, would no longer be useful after that event is over. Likewise, a database might contain a form created to enter data that is no longer relevant. Periodically, you should evaluate the objects in your database and consider whether they are still providing useful information. If some are not, you may want to delete such tables, queries, forms, and reports. If the database is a large one and serves a large user base, you will want to gain input from all users before deciding to delete objects.

Creating an Append Query

Donna has decided to expand the list of patients that she will contact to include the patients who live in Marietta. She asks you to add these new records to the tblContactPatient table. You could make this change by modifying the selection criterion in the qryContactPatientMakeTable query to select owners with City field values of Marietta. If you ran this modified query, however, you would overwrite the existing tblContactPatient table with a new table. If Donna had made any changes to the existing tblContactPatient table records, creating a new table would overwrite these changes as well.

Instead, you will create the qryContactPatientAppend query as a select query to select only owners whose city is Marietta, and then you'll change the query to an append query. An append query adds records from existing tables or queries to the end of another table. When you run this new query, the selected records will be appended to (added to the bottom of) the records in the existing tblContactPatient table.

REFERENCE

Creating an Append Query

- Create a select query with the necessary fields and selection criteria.
- On the Query Tools Design tab, click the Run button in the Results group to preview the results.
- Switch to Design view to make any necessary changes to the query, and then, when the query is correct, click the Append button located in the Query Type group on the Query Tools Design tab.
- In the Append dialog box, select the table name in the Table Name box, making sure the Current Database option button is selected to include the new table in the current database; or click the Another Database option button, enter the database name in the File Name box, and then click the OK button.
- Click the Run button, and then click the Yes button to confirm appending the records to the table.

You can now create the append query you'll use to include the additional patient data Donna wants in the tblContactPatient table.

To create the append query:

1. Click the **Create** tab, and then, in the Queries group, click the **Query Design** button. The Show Table dialog box opens on top of the Query window in Design view.
2. Add the **tblPatient** field list to the Query window, and then close the Show Tables dialog box.
3. Resize the tblPatient field list to display all its fields, then add the **FirstName**, **LastName**, **Parent**, **Phone**, **City**, and **Email** fields to the design grid in that order. The selected fields match the fields in the table to which the records will be appended.

   Next, you'll enter the selection criterion of Marietta for the City field.

4. In the design grid, click the **City Criteria** box, type **Marietta**, and then press **TAB**. See Figure 9–5.

Figure 9–5 Changing the selection criterion

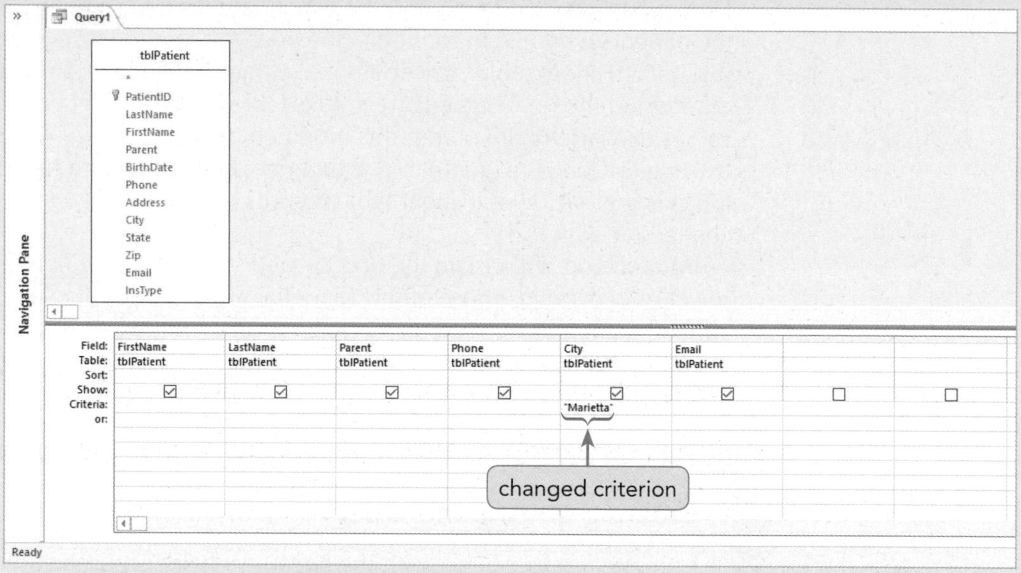
Query1
tblPatient
PatientID
LastName
FirstName
Parent
BirthDate
Phone
Address
City
State
Zip
Email
InsType
Navigation Pane
Field: FirstName LastName Parent Phone City Email
Table: tblPatient tblPatient tblPatient tblPatient tblPatient tblPatient
Sort:
Show:
Criteria: "Marietta"
or:
changed criterion
Ready

Before you can run the query to append the records to the tblContactPatient table, you have to change the query type to an append query. It is always a good idea to test an action query before you run it, so you will first run this select query to make sure it selects the correct records. Then you will change the query type to an append query and run it to append the new records to the tblContactPatient table.

5. On the Query Tools Design tab, in the Query Type group, click the **Select** button to select it (if necessary).
6. Run the query. The query recordset shows the five records for patients who live in Marietta.

   These five records are the additional records you will append to the tblContactPatient table. Now that you've verified that the results shown in the query are correct, you can change the query type to an append query.

7. Switch to Design view, and then on the Query Tools Design tab, in the Query Type group, click the **Append** button. The Append dialog box opens. You use this dialog box to select the name of the table to which you want to append the data and to designate the database to be used to store the table.
8. In the Table Name box, click the arrow, click **tblContactPatient**, ensure that the **Current Database** option button is selected, and then click **OK**. The Append To row replaces the Show row in the design grid.

The Append To row in the design grid identifies the fields that the query will append to the designated table. The FirstName, LastName, Parent, Phone, City, and Email fields are selected and will be appended to the tblContactPatient table, which already contains these same six fields for patients.

You'll run and save the append query now.

To run and save the append query:

1. Run the query. A dialog box opens, warning that you are about to append five rows.
2. Click **Yes** to acknowledge the warning. The dialog box closes, and the append query adds the five records to the tblContactPatient table. The Query window is still displayed in Design view.
3. Save the query as **qryContactPatientAppend**, and then close the query.

   Next, you'll open the tblContactPatient table to make sure that the five records were appended to the table.
4. Open the Navigation Pane, open the **tblContactPatient** table datasheet, resize the fields to their best fit, and then click the first row's **FirstName** field value to deselect all values. See Figure 9–6.

Figure 9–6 tblContactPatient table datasheet after appending records

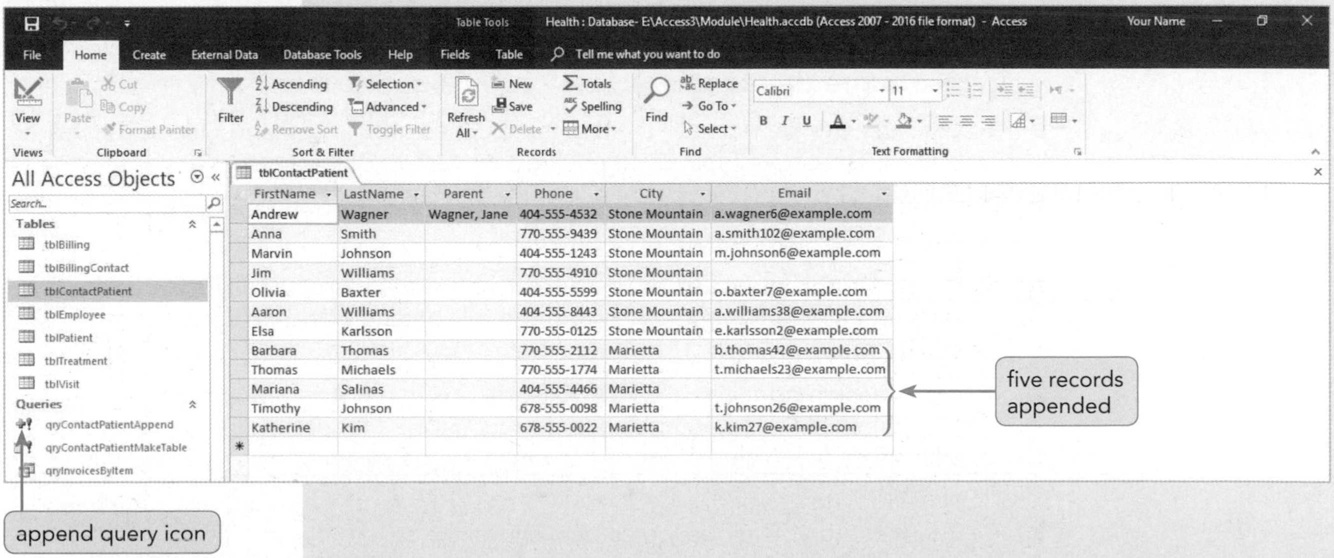
Table Tools
Health : Database- E:\Access3\Module\Health.accdb (Access 2007 - 2016 file format) - Access
All Access Objects
Tables
tblBilling
tblBillingContact
tblContactPatient
tblEmployee
tblPatient
tblTreatment
tblVisit
Queries
qryContactPatientAppend
qryContactPatientMakeTable
qryInvoicesByItem
FirstName LastName Parent Phone City Email
Andrew Wagner Wagner, Jane 404-555-4532 Stone Mountain a.wagner6@example.com
Anna Smith 770-555-9439 Stone Mountain a.smith102@example.com
Marvin Johnson 404-555-1243 Stone Mountain m.johnson6@example.com
Jim Williams 770-555-4910 Stone Mountain
Olivia Baxter 404-555-5599 Stone Mountain o.baxter7@example.com
Aaron Williams 404-555-8443 Stone Mountain a.williams38@example.com
Elsa Karlsson 770-555-0125 Stone Mountain e.karlsson2@example.com
Barbara Thomas 770-555-2112 Marietta b.thomas42@example.com
Thomas Michaels 770-555-1774 Marietta t.michaels23@example.com
Mariana Salinas 404-555-4466 Marietta
Timothy Johnson 678-555-0098 Marietta t.johnson26@example.com
Katherine Kim 678-555-0022 Marietta k.kim27@example.com
five records appended
append query icon

The new records have been added to the tblContactPatient table. Because the tblContactPatient table does not have a primary key, the new records appear at the end of the table.

5. Save your datasheet changes, close the table, and then close the Navigation Pane.

Donna has contacted all the patients in the tblContactPatient table who are located in the city of Stone Mountain. She asks you to delete these records from the tblContactPatient table so that it contains only those records for patients she has not yet contacted.

Creating a Delete Query

You can either delete records in a table individually or create a delete query to remove a group of them all at once. When using a delete query, you specify one or more criteria that identify the records you want to delete. For example, to delete the records Donna no longer needs from the tblContactPatient table, you can create a delete query to delete the patient records in the table whose city is Stone Mountain.

REFERENCE

Creating a Delete Query

- Create a select query with the necessary fields and selection criteria.
- On the Query Tools Design tab, click the Run button in the Results group to preview the results.
- Switch to Design view to make any necessary changes to the query, and then, when the query is correct, click the Delete button located in the Query Type group on the Query Tools Design tab.
- Click the Run button, and then click the Yes button to confirm deleting the records.

You will create the delete query next.

To create the delete query:

1. Click the **Create** tab, and then, in the Queries group, click the **Query Design** button. The Show Table dialog box opens on top of the Query window.
2. Add the **tblContactPatient** field list to the Query window, and then close the Show Table dialog box.
3. Resize the tblContactPatient field list if necessary to display all its fields, and then add all the fields in order from the tblContactPatient field list to the design grid.
4. In the design grid, click the **City Criteria** box, type **Stone Mountain**, and then press **TAB**. The criterion changes to "Stone Mountain". Only the records with a City field value of Stone Mountain will be selected when you run the query.
5. Run the query. The query recordset shows the seven records with City field values of Stone Mountain. The select query is correct. See Figure 9–7.

Figure 9–7 **Seven records to be deleted**

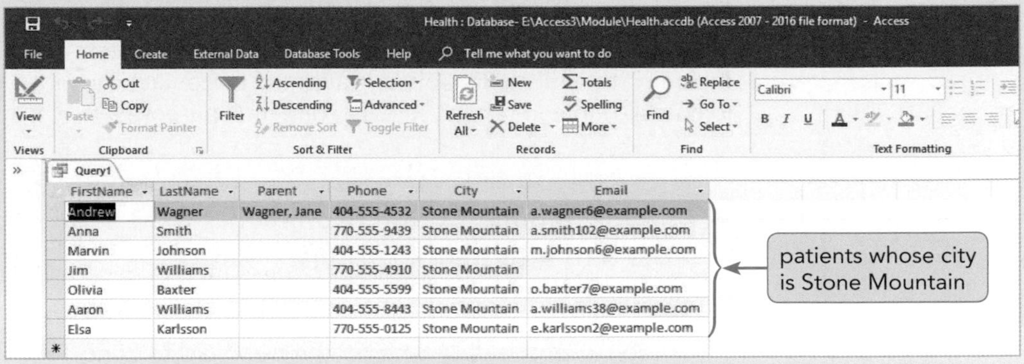
Query1
FirstName LastName Parent Phone City Email
Andrew Wagner Wagner, Jane 404-555-4532 Stone Mountain a.wagner6@example.com
Anna Smith 770-555-9439 Stone Mountain a.smith102@example.com
Marvin Johnson 404-555-1243 Stone Mountain m.johnson6@example.com
Jim Williams 770-555-4910 Stone Mountain
Olivia Baxter 404-555-5599 Stone Mountain o.baxter7@example.com
Aaron Williams 404-555-8443 Stone Mountain a.williams38@example.com
Elsa Karlsson 770-555-0125 Stone Mountain e.karlsson2@example.com
patients whose city is Stone Mountain

Trouble? If your query did not select the correct seven records, switch to Design view, correct the selection criterion, and then run the query again.

Now that you have verified that the query selects the correct records, you can change the query to a delete query.

6. Switch to Design view, and then on the Query Tools Design tab, in the Query Type group, click the **Delete** button. In the design grid, the Delete row replaces the Sort and Show rows.
7. Run the query. A dialog box opens, warning that you are about to delete seven rows from the table.
8. Click **Yes** to acknowledge the warning. The dialog box closes, and the seven records are deleted from the tblContactPatient table. The Query window is still displayed in Design view.
9. Save the query as **qryContactPatientDelete**, and then close the query. Next, you'll open the tblContactPatient table to verify that the records have been deleted.
10. Open the Navigation Pane, and then open the **tblContactPatient** table in Datasheet view. The table contains five records, and the Stone Mountain records were correctly deleted. See Figure 9–8.

TIP

Once records have been deleted from a table using a delete query, they cannot be restored using the Undo command.

Figure 9–8 **tblContactPatient table after deleting seven records**

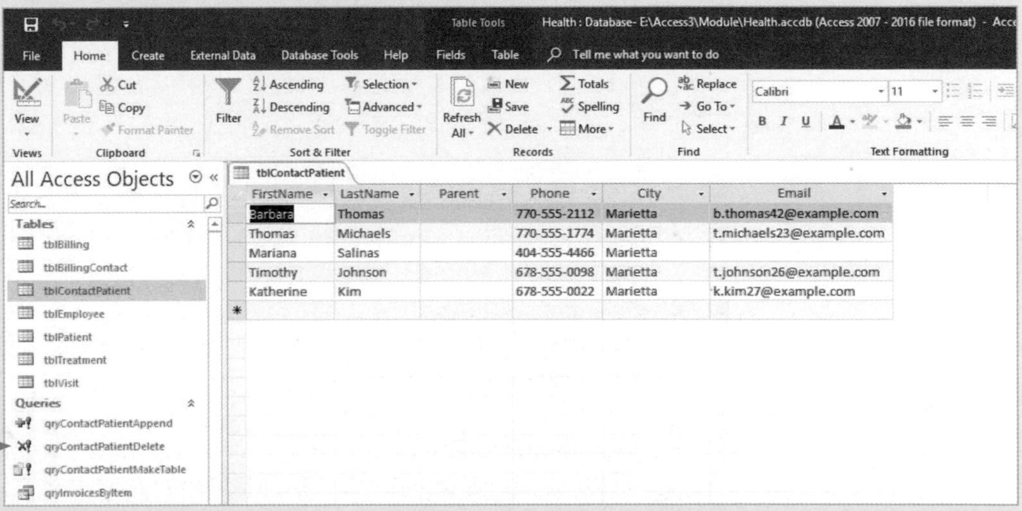
All Access Objects
Tables
tblBilling
tblBillingContact
tblContactPatient
tblEmployee
tblPatient
tblTreatment
tblVisit
Queries
qryContactPatientAppend
qryContactPatientDelete
qryContactPatientMakeTable
qryInvoicesByItem
FirstName LastName Parent Phone City Email
Barbara Thomas 770-555-2112 Marietta b.thomas42@example.com
Thomas Michaels 770-555-1774 Marietta t.michaels23@example.com
Mariana Salinas 404-555-4466 Marietta
Timothy Johnson 678-555-0098 Marietta t.johnson26@example.com
Katherine Kim 678-555-0022 Marietta k.kim27@example.com
delete query icon

Donna wants you to make some structural changes to the tblContactPatient table. First she wants you to add a field named ContactComments where she can keep notes about the calls she makes. She also wants you to add appropriate captions to the FirstName and LastName fields. You can add the field and captions to the tblContactPatient table without affecting the other objects in the Health database, including the tblPatient table, because the tblContactPatient table was created as a temporary table to serve a specific, one-time purpose.

To add the new ContactComments field to the tblContactPatient table and add field captions:

1. Switch to Design view.

   You'll set the data type for the new field to Long Text, so that Donna is not limited to 255 characters of data in the field, as she would when using the Short Text data type.

2. Click the **Field Name** box below the Email field, type **ContactComments**, press **TAB**, type the letter **l**, and then press **TAB** to select the Long Text data type.

3. Press **F6** to position the insertion point in the Format box in the Field Properties pane, press **TAB**, and then type **Contact Comments** in the Caption box. You've completed adding the ContactComments field to the table. See Figure 9–9.

Figure 9–9 ContactComments field added to the tblContactPatient table

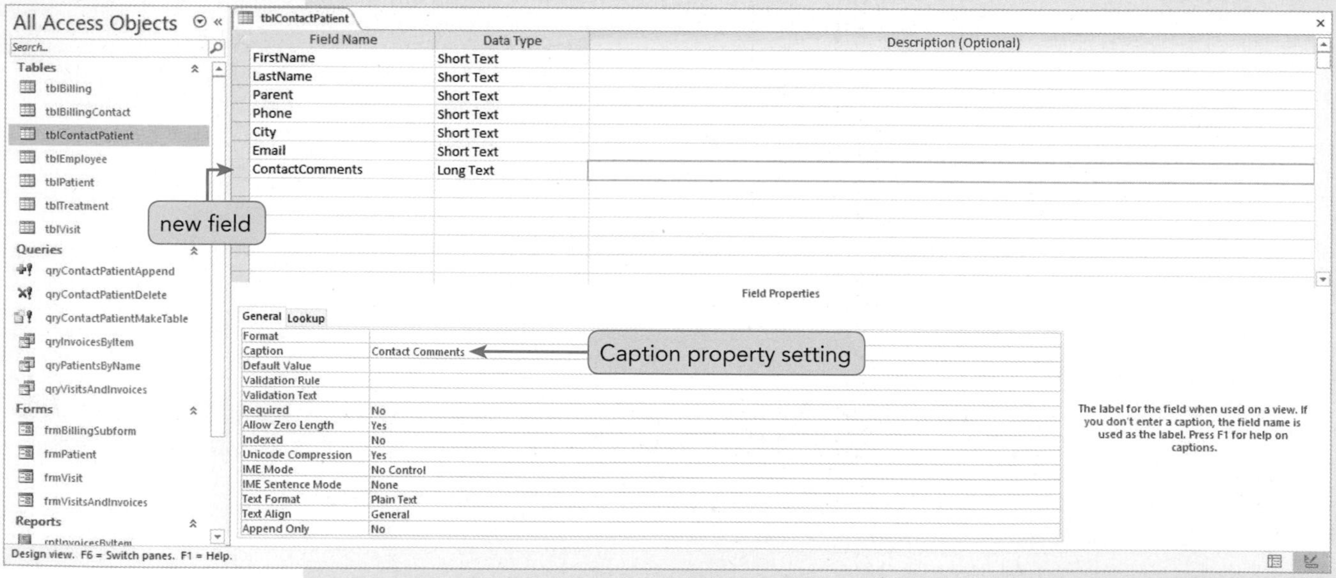

All Access Objects
tblContactPatient
Field Name
Data Type
Description (Optional)
FirstName Short Text
LastName Short Text
Parent Short Text
Phone Short Text
City Short Text
Email Short Text
ContactComments Long Text
new field
Field Properties
Caption property setting
Caption Contact Comments

4. Add the caption **First Name** to the FirstName field, and then add the caption **Last Name** to the LastName field.

5. Save your changes to the table structure, switch to Datasheet view, and then resize the columns to their best fit. Notice that the captions and new field are displayed.

6. Save your changes to the table layout, close the table, and then close the Navigation Pane.

Donna has sent an email message to each patient who has an email address in the Email field, and she wants to update the ContactComments field in the tblContactPatient table with the same comments for all records with an email address in the Email field. To accomplish this for Donna, you'll create an update query.

Creating an Update Query

Recall that an update query changes selected field values and records in one or more tables. An update query is useful when a group of records in a table all require the same change to data in the same field. For example, in the tblContactPatient table, Donna wants to enter the same comment in the ContactComments field for those patients who have an email address. She could type the comments in the ContactComments field for one of the records and then copy and paste the comments to the other records. However, performing these steps takes time and could result in incorrectly updating a record or neglecting to update one of the records. Instead, using an update query allows Donna to make this change to the table records quickly and accurately.

REFERENCE

Creating an Update Query

- Create a select query with the necessary fields and selection criteria.
- On the Query Tools Design tab, click the Run button in the Results group to preview the results.
- Switch to Design view to make any necessary changes to the query, and then, when the query is correct, click the Update button located in the Query Type group on the Query Tools Design tab.
- Type the updated values in the Update To boxes for the fields you want to update.
- Click the Run button, and then click the Yes button to confirm changing the records.

Now you can create an update query to update the ContactComments field in the tblContactPatient table for records that contain an email address in the Email field.

To create the update query:

1. Click the **Create** tab, and then in the Queries group, click the **Query Design** button to open the Show Table dialog box on top of the Query window.
2. Add the **tblContactPatient** field list to the Query window, close the Show Table dialog box, and then resize the tblContactPatient field list to display all its fields.

   You will select the Email and ContactComments fields for the query results. The Email field lets you select records for patients who have an email address listed in this field. The ContactComments field is the field Donna needs to update.
3. Add the **Email** and **ContactComments** fields, in that order, to the design grid.
4. In the design grid, click the **Email Criteria** box, type **Is Not Null**, and then press **TAB**. The query will select a record only if the Email field contains a value—in other words, if the field is not null.
5. Run the query. The query recordset displays four records, each containing an Email value. The select query is correct.

   Now that you have verified that the query selects the correct records, you can change it to an update query.

6. Switch to Design view, and then on the Query Tools Design tab, in the Query Type group, click the **Update** button. In the design grid, the Update To row replaces the Sort and Show rows.

   You specify how you want to change a field value for the selected records by entering an expression in the field's Update To box. An expression is a calculation resulting in a single value. You can type a simple expression directly into the Update To box.

7. In the design grid, click the **ContactComments Update To** box, type **"Sent email in June. Contact again in August."** (be sure to type the quotation marks), and then drag the right border of the ContactComments column to the right to display the entire expression value. See Figure 9–10.

Figure 9–10 **Update query for the tblContactPatient table**

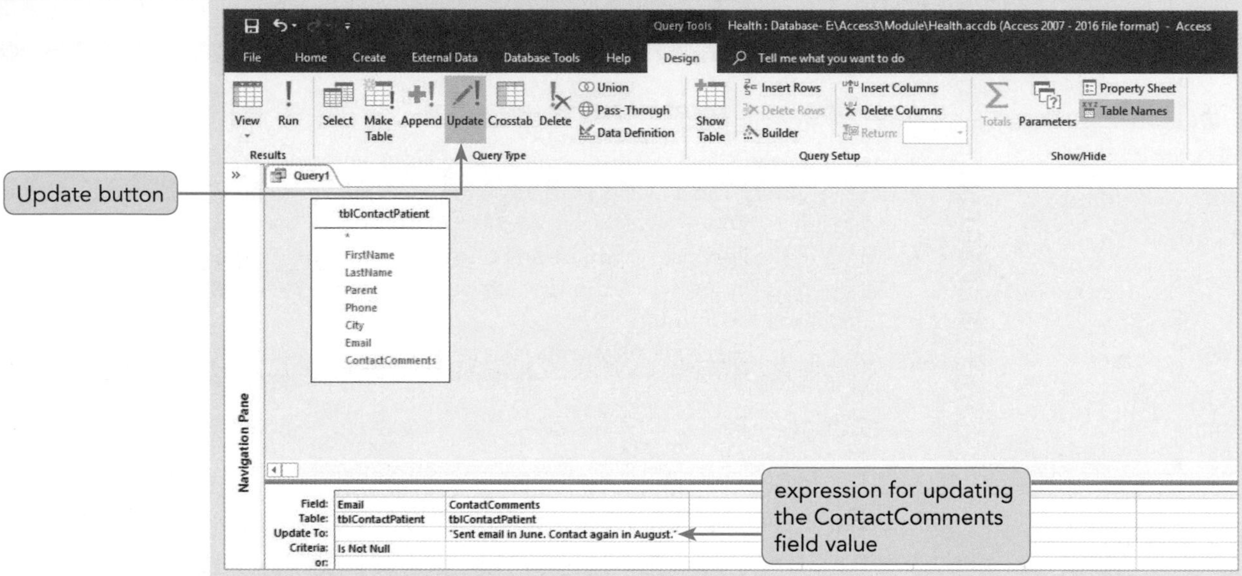
Update button
expression for updating the ContactComments field value
tblContactPatient
FirstName
LastName
Parent
Phone
City
Email
ContactComments
Field: Email ContactComments
Table: tblContactPatient tblContactPatient
Update To: "Sent email in June. Contact again in August."
Criteria: Is Not Null

8. Run the query. A dialog box opens, warning that you are about to update four rows in the tblContactPatient table.

9. Click the **Yes** button. The dialog box closes, and the query updates the ContactComments field values for patients who have an email address in the Email field. The Query window is still displayed in Design view.

   You are finished updating the tblContactPatient table, so you'll save and close the query.

10. Save the query as **qryContactPatientUpdate** and then close the query.

TIP

For text expressions that contain quotation marks, you need to type the quotation marks twice. For example, to enter the expression *A "text" expression*, type "A ""text"" expression".

Now you can view the tblContactPatient table to see the results of the update operation.

To view the updated tblContactPatient table:

1. Open the Navigation Pane, open the **tblContactPatient** table in Datasheet view, and then resize the Contact Comments column to its best fit. The ContactComments field values for patients who have email addresses have been updated correctly. See Figure 9–11.

Figure 9–11 **tblContactPatient table with updated ContactComments field values**

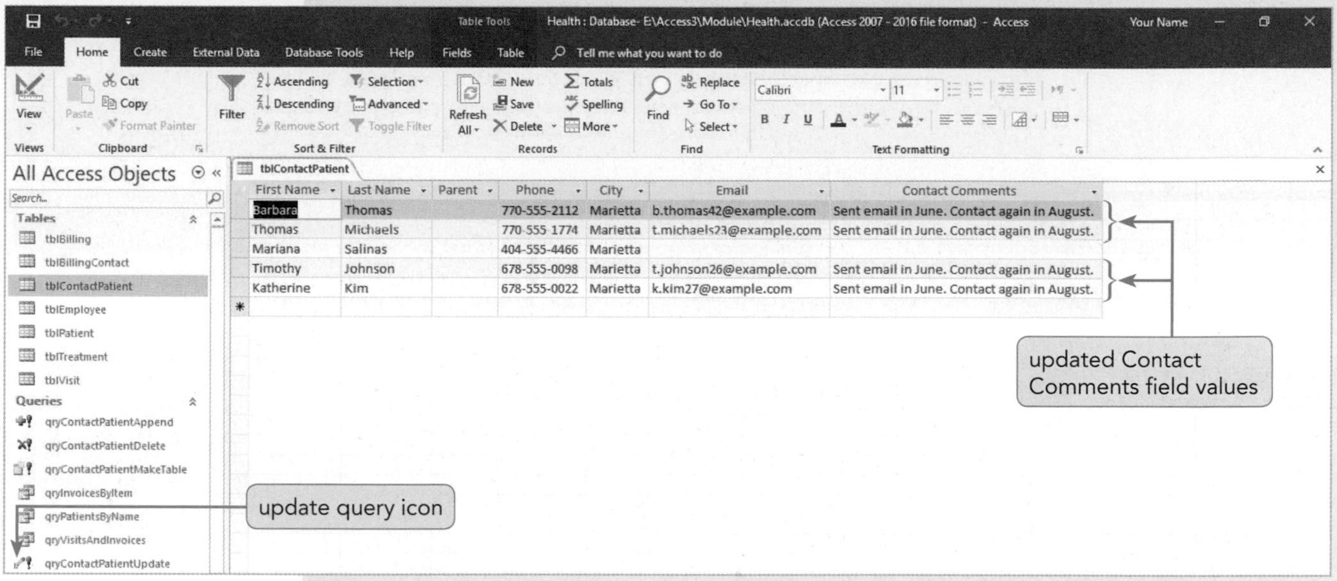
updated Contact Comments field values
update query icon

2. Save the table datasheet changes and close the table.
3. If you are not continuing on to the next session, close the Health database.

INSIGHT

Deleting Action Queries

You usually create an action query and run it for a special purpose. In most cases, you need to run the query only once. If you create and run an action query and then save it, you might accidentally run it again. Doing so would update tables in unintended ways. Therefore, after you've run an action query, you shouldn't save it in your database. Deleting an action query at this point prevents users from running it by mistake.

Donna can now use action queries in her future work with the Health database. In the next session, you'll learn about the different types of relationships you can create between tables, and you'll view and create indexes to increase a database's efficiency.

REVIEW

Session 9.1 Quick Check

1. What is an action query?
2. What precautions should you take before running an action query?
3. What is the difference between a make-table query and an append query?
4. What does a delete query do?
5. What does an update query do?
6. How does the design grid change when you create an update query?

Session 9.2 Visual Overview:

For a many-to-many relationship, you must create a third table, known as a **relationship table**, and form one-to-many relationships between the two original primary tables and the relationship table. The tblTreatment table exists only because the tblBilling and tblEmployee tables have a many-to-many relationship.

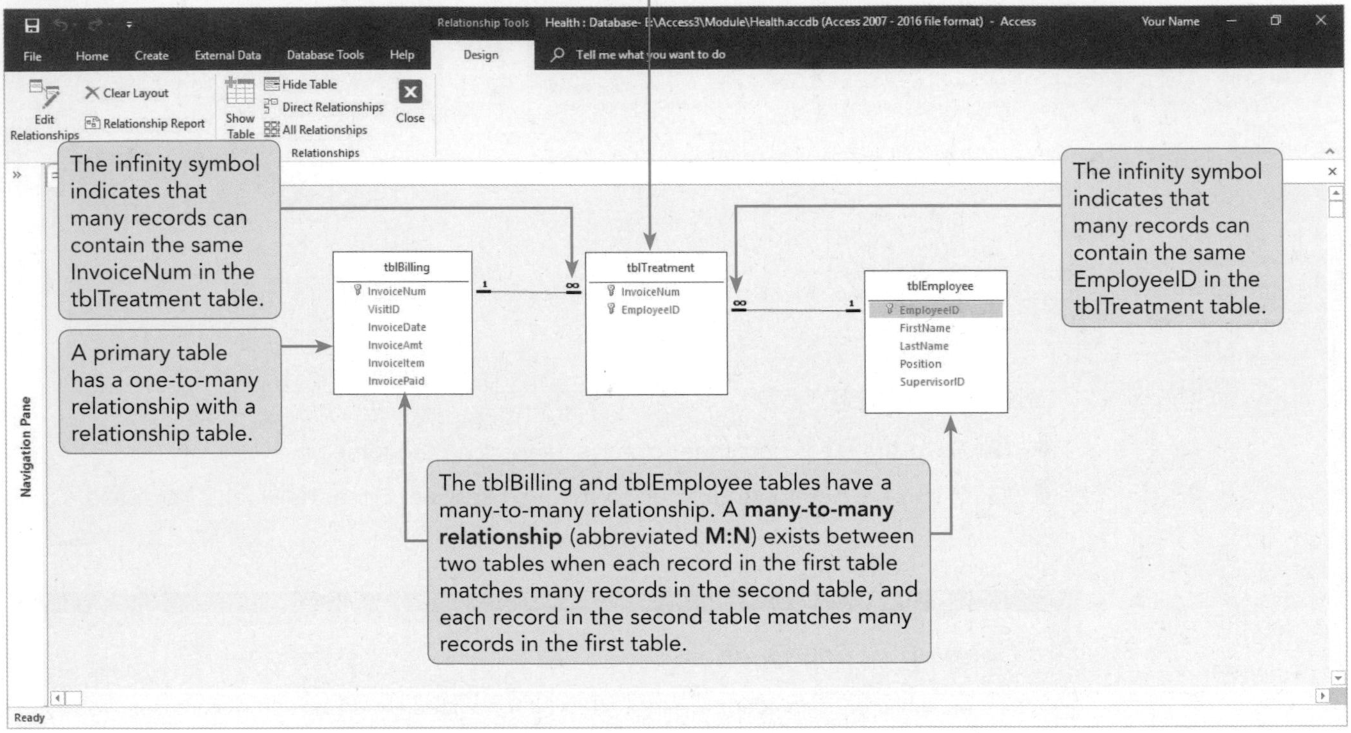

Relationship Tools
Health : Database- E:\Access3\Module\Health.accdb (Access 2007 - 2016 file format) - Access
Your Name
File
Home
Create
External Data
Database Tools
Help
Design
Tell me what you want to do
Edit Relationships
Clear Layout
Relationship Report
Show Table
Hide Table
Direct Relationships
All Relationships
Close
Relationships
Navigation Pane
tblBilling
InvoiceNum
VisitID
InvoiceDate
InvoiceAmt
InvoiceItem
InvoicePaid
tblTreatment
InvoiceNum
EmployeeID
tblEmployee
EmployeeID
FirstName
LastName
Position
SupervisorID
Ready

The infinity symbol indicates that many records can contain the same InvoiceNum in the tblTreatment table.

A primary table has a one-to-many relationship with a relationship table.

The infinity symbol indicates that many records can contain the same EmployeeID in the tblTreatment table.

The tblBilling and tblEmployee tables have a many-to-many relationship. A **many-to-many relationship** (abbreviated **M:N**) exists between two tables when each record in the first table matches many records in the second table, and each record in the second table matches many records in the first table.

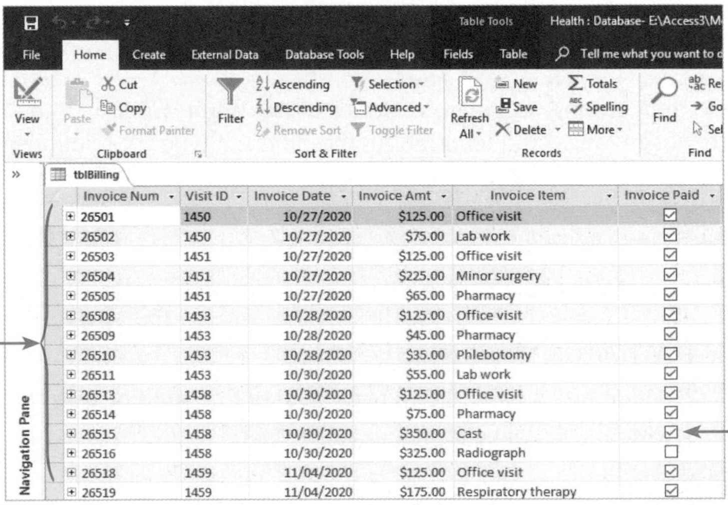

Table Tools
Health : Database- E:\Access3\M
File
Home
Create
External Data
Database Tools
Help
Fields
Table
Tell me what you want to
View
Paste
Cut
Copy
Format Painter
Filter
Ascending
Descending
Remove Sort
Selection
Advanced
Toggle Filter
Refresh All
New
Save
Delete
Totals
Spelling
More
Find
Views
Clipboard
Sort & Filter
Records
Find
tblBilling
Navigation Pane
Invoice Num
Visit ID
Invoice Date
Invoice Amt
Invoice Item
Invoice Paid
26501 1450 10/27/2020 $125.00 Office visit
26502 1450 10/27/2020 $75.00 Lab work
26503 1451 10/27/2020 $125.00 Office visit
26504 1451 10/27/2020 $225.00 Minor surgery
26505 1451 10/27/2020 $65.00 Pharmacy
26508 1453 10/28/2020 $125.00 Office visit
26509 1453 10/28/2020 $45.00 Pharmacy
26510 1453 10/28/2020 $35.00 Phlebotomy
26511 1453 10/30/2020 $55.00 Lab work
26513 1458 10/30/2020 $125.00 Office visit
26514 1458 10/30/2020 $75.00 Pharmacy
26515 1458 10/30/2020 $350.00 Cast
26516 1458 10/30/2020 $325.00 Radiograph
26518 1459 11/04/2020 $125.00 Office visit
26519 1459 11/04/2020 $175.00 Respiratory therapy

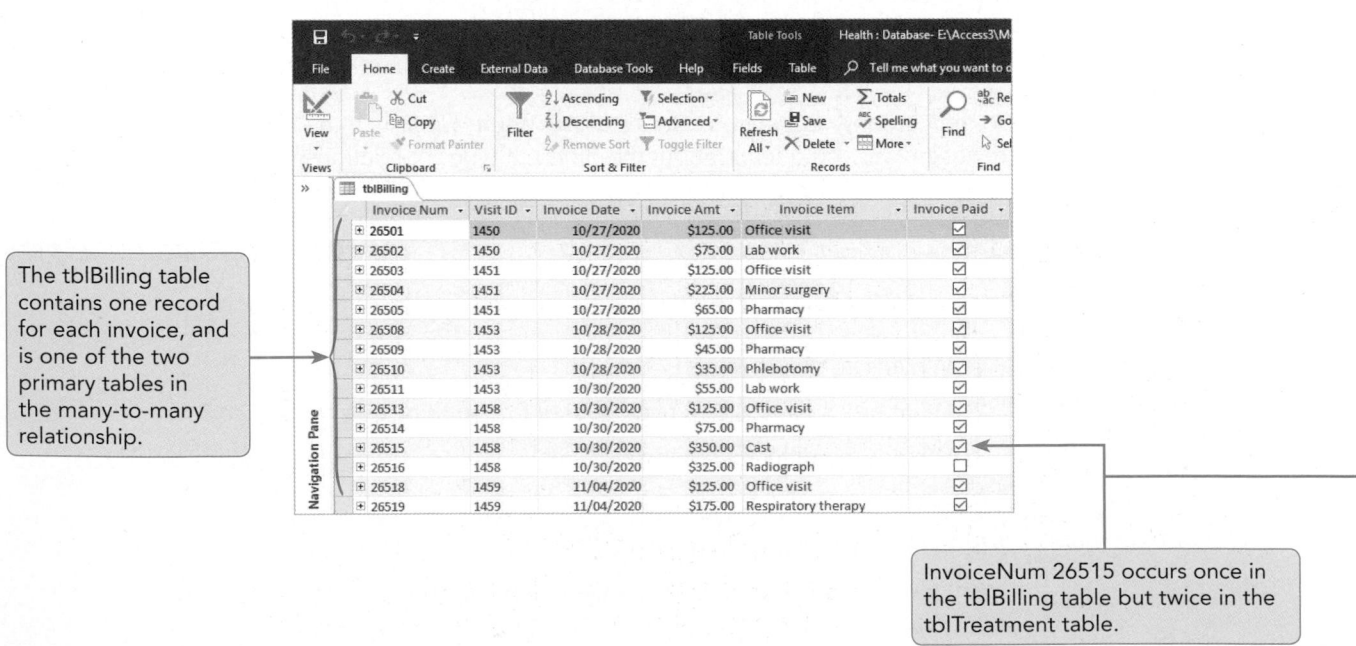

The tblBilling table contains one record for each invoice, and is one of the two primary tables in the many-to-many relationship.

InvoiceNum 26515 occurs once in the tblBilling table but twice in the tblTreatment table.

Many-to-Many Relationship

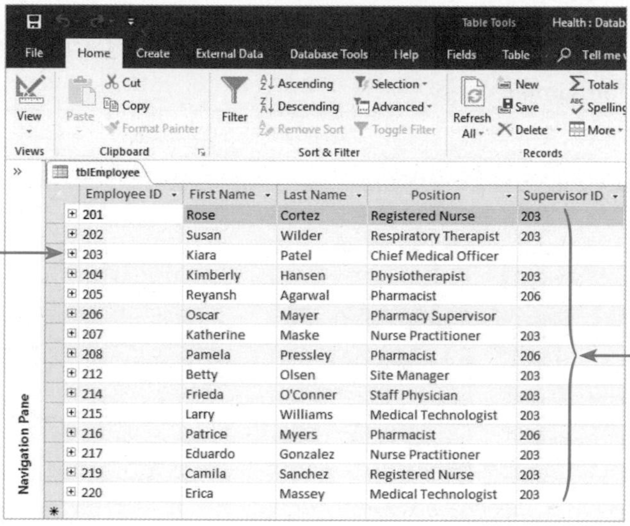
Table Tools
Health : Datab
File
Home
Create
External Data
Database Tools
Help
Fields
Table
Tell me
View
Paste
Cut
Copy
Format Painter
Filter
Ascending
Descending
Remove Sort
Selection
Advanced
Toggle Filter
Refresh All
New
Save
Delete
Totals
Spelling
More
Views
Clipboard
Sort & Filter
Records
tblEmployee
Navigation Pane
Employee ID | First Name | Last Name | Position | Supervisor ID
201 | Rose | Cortez | Registered Nurse | 203
202 | Susan | Wilder | Respiratory Therapist | 203
203 | Kiara | Patel | Chief Medical Officer |
204 | Kimberly | Hansen | Physiotherapist | 203
205 | Reyansh | Agarwal | Pharmacist | 206
206 | Oscar | Mayer | Pharmacy Supervisor |
207 | Katherine | Maske | Nurse Practitioner | 203
208 | Pamela | Pressley | Pharmacist | 206
212 | Betty | Olsen | Site Manager | 203
214 | Frieda | O'Conner | Staff Physician | 203
215 | Larry | Williams | Medical Technologist | 203
216 | Patrice | Myers | Pharmacist | 206
217 | Eduardo | Gonzalez | Nurse Practitioner | 203
219 | Camila | Sanchez | Registered Nurse | 203
220 | Erica | Massey | Medical Technologist | 203

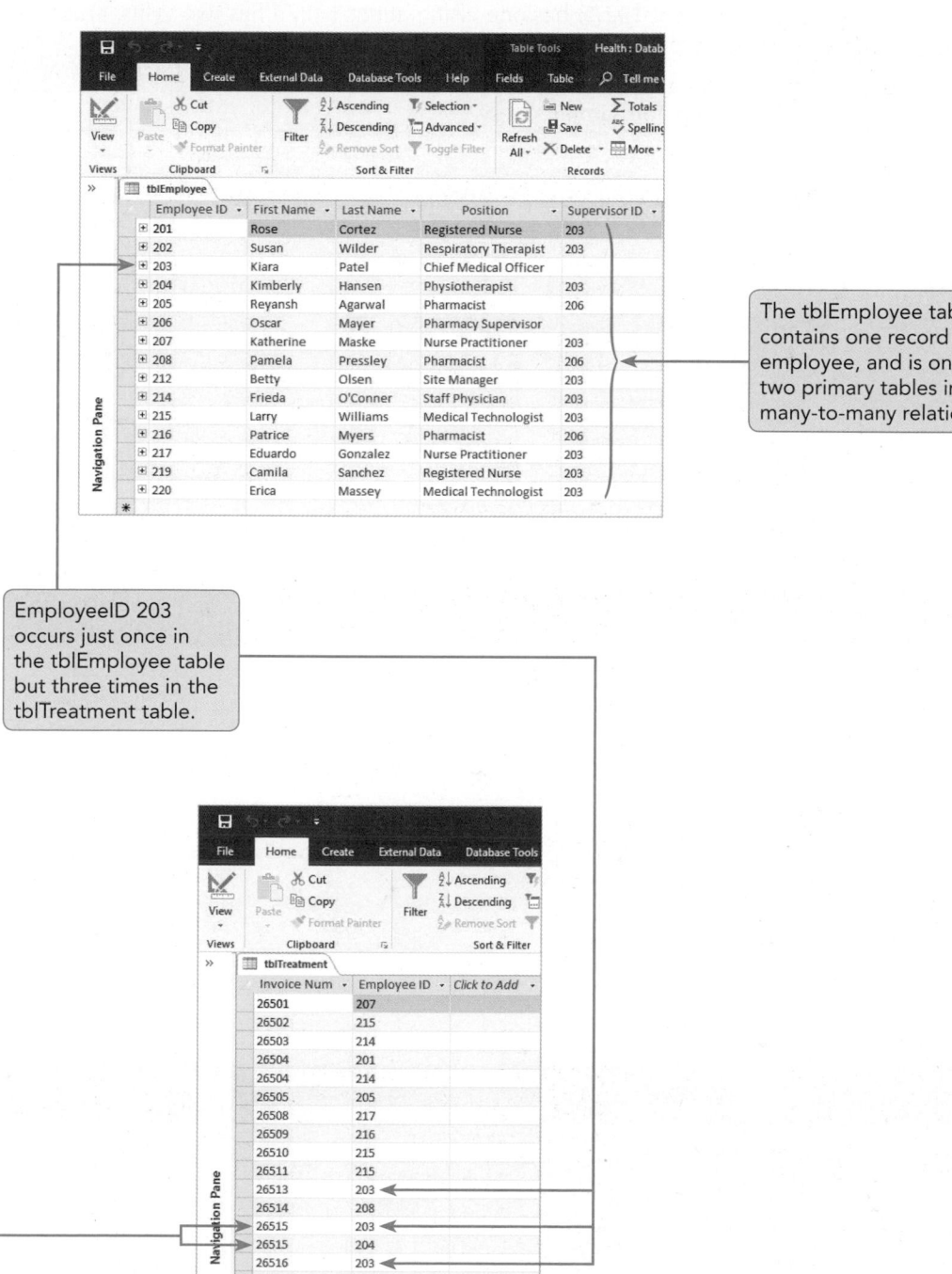

The tblEmployee table contains one record for each employee, and is one of the two primary tables in the many-to-many relationship.

EmployeeID 203 occurs just once in the tblEmployee table but three times in the tblTreatment table.

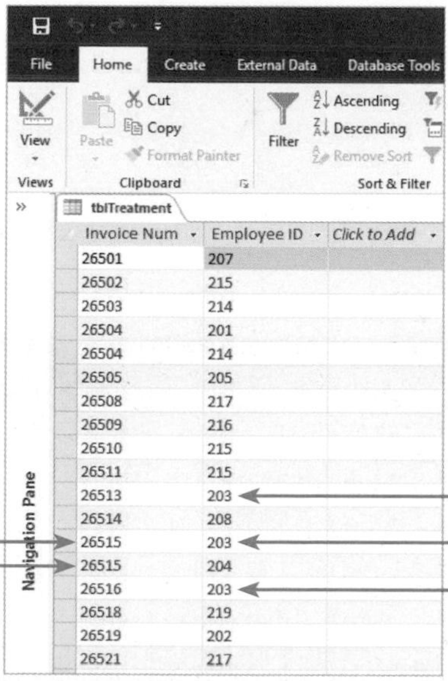
File
Home
Create
External Data
Database Tools
View
Paste
Cut
Copy
Format Painter
Filter
Ascending
Descending
Remove Sort
Views
Clipboard
Sort & Filter
tblTreatment
Navigation Pane
Invoice Num | Employee ID | Click to Add
26501 | 207
26502 | 215
26503 | 214
26504 | 201
26504 | 214
26505 | 205
26508 | 217
26509 | 216
26510 | 215
26511 | 215
26513 | 203
26514 | 208
26515 | 203
26515 | 204
26516 | 203
26518 | 219
26519 | 202
26521 | 217

Understanding Types of Table Relationships

As you know, a one-to-many relationship (abbreviated as 1:M) exists between two tables when each record in the primary table matches zero, one, or more records in the related table, and when each record in the related table matches at most one record in the primary table. For example, Figure 9–12 shows a one-to-many relationship between portions of the tblPatient and tblVisit tables. It also shows a sample query based on the two tables. (Most examples in this session use portions of tables for illustrative purposes.) For instance, patient 13273 has one visit, patient 13275 has two visits, and patient 13276 has three visits.

Figure 9–12 One-to-many relationship and sample query

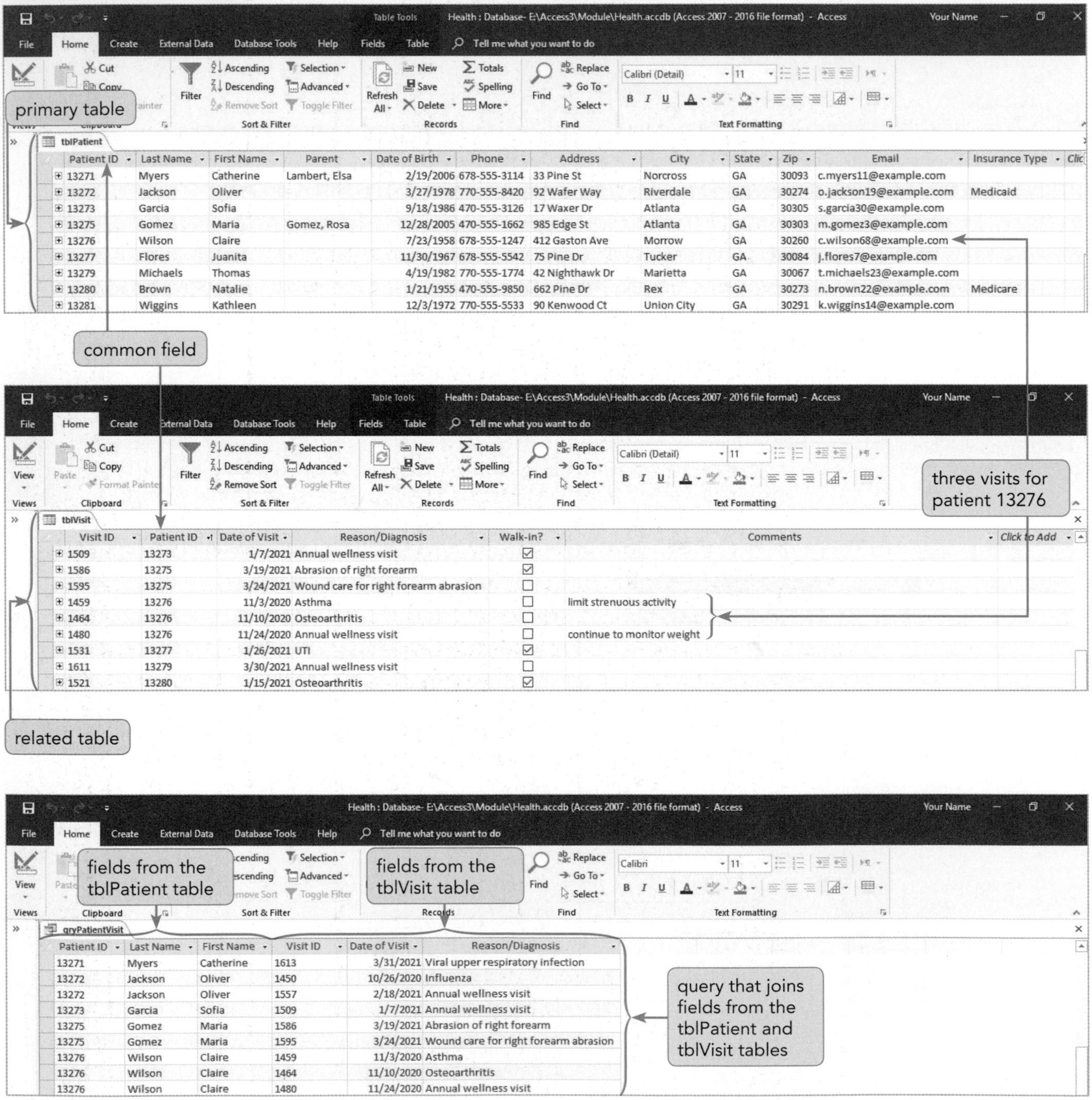
primary table
common field
three visits for patient 13276
related table
fields from the tblPatient table
fields from the tblVisit table
query that joins fields from the tblPatient and tblVisit tables

You use the common field—the PatientID field—to form the one-to-many relationship between the tblPatient and tblVisit tables. When you join the two tables based on PatientID field values, you can extract data from them as if they were one larger table. For example, you can join the tblPatient and tblVisit tables to create the qryPatientVisit query shown in Figure 9–12. In the qryPatientVisit query, the Patient ID, Last Name, and First Name columns are from the tblPatient table, and the Visit ID, Date of Visit, and Reason/Diagnosis columns are from the tblVisit table.

In addition to one-to-many relationships between tables, you can also relate tables through many-to-many and one-to-one relationships.

Many-to-Many Relationships

In the Health database, an invoice can represent treatment performed by many employees, and each employee can provide treatment on many invoiced patients, so the tblBilling and tblEmployee tables have a many-to-many relationship, as shown in the Session 9.2 Visual Overview.

When you have a many-to-many relationship (abbreviated as M:N) between two tables, you must create a third table, known as a relationship table, and form one-to-many relationships between the two original primary tables and the relationship table. For instance, the tblTreatment table, shown in the Session 9.2 Visual Overview, exists only because the tblBilling and tblEmployee tables have a many-to-many relationship. Each record in the tblTreatment table contains two foreign keys. The EmployeeID field is a foreign key that allows you to join the tblEmployee table to the tblTreatment table. The InvoiceNum field is a foreign key that allows you to join the tblBilling table to the tblTreatment table. The primary key of the tblTreatment table is a composite key, consisting of the combination of the EmployeeID and InvoiceNum fields. Each pair of values in this primary key is unique.

Unlike a one-to-many or one-to-one relationship, a many-to-many relationship is not represented by a single line between two tables in the Relationships window. Rather, a many-to-many relationship is represented by the two one-to-many relationships between the primary tables and the relationship table. For instance, Visual Overview 9.2 shows a one-to-many relationship line between the tblBilling and tblTreatment tables and another one-to-many relationship line between the tblEmployee and tblTreatment tables. Because the tblTreatment table is a relationship table, these two relationships together represent a many-to-many relationship.

You can see the one-to-many relationship between each primary table and the relationship table by examining the records. For example, the thirteenth record in the tblTreatment table represents a surgery for InvoiceNum 26515 that was performed by Kiara Patel, who has EmployeeID 203. EmployeeID 203 appears in many records in the tblTreatment table that represent treatment Kiara Patel billed on many other invoices including 26513 and 26516. Also, InvoiceNum 26515 appears in two tblTreatment table records, each for a different employee: Kimberly Hansen and Kiara Patel.

PROSKILLS

Decision Making: Identifying Many-to-Many Relationships

Although one-to-many relationships are the most common type of table relationship, many-to-many relationships occur frequently, and most databases have one or more many-to-many relationships. When developing a database, you need to decide when the relationship between two tables should be many-to-many rather than one-to-many. You can recognize when this relationship is appropriate by thinking about how all the pieces of data interrelate, as demonstrated by the following examples:

- In a college database, a student takes more than one class, and each class has more than one student enrolled; a course has many prerequisites and can be the prerequisite to many courses.
- In a pharmacy database, a medication is prescribed to many customers, and a customer can take many medications.
- In an airline database, a flight has many passengers, and a passenger can take many flights.
- In a publisher database, an author can write many books, and a book can have multiple authors.
- In a manufacturing database, a manufactured product consists of many parts, and a part can be a component in many manufactured products.
- In a film database, a movie has many actors, and each actor appears in many movies.

Common one-to-many relationships can turn into many-to-many relationships when circumstances change. For example, a department in an organization has many employees, and an employee usually works in a single department. However, an instructor can have a joint appointment to two college departments, and some companies hire employees and split their time between two departments. You must carefully analyze each situation and design your table relationships to handle the specific requirements for today and for the future.

When you join tables that have a many-to-many relationship, you can extract data from them as if they were one larger table. For example, you can join the tblBilling and tblEmployee tables to create a qryTreatment query. As shown in the Session 9.2 Visual Overview, in the tblTreatment table, the EmployeeID field joins the tblEmployee and tblTreatment tables, and the InvoiceNum field joins the tblBilling and tblTreatment tables.

One-to-One Relationships

A **one-to-one relationship** (abbreviated as **1:1**) exists between two tables when each record in the first table matches at most one record in the second table, and each record in the second table matches at most one record in the first table. Most relationships between tables are either one-to-many or many-to-many; the primary use for one-to-one relationships is as entity subtypes. An **entity subtype** is a table whose primary key is a foreign key to a second table and whose fields are additional fields for the second table.

For most patients, the Address, City, State, and Zip fields in the tblPatient table identify both the patient's location and billing address, which is where Lakewood Community Health Services sends the patient's invoices. In a few cases, however, a friend or relative pays the medical bills, so the billing name and address are different from the patient's name and address. You can handle these two sets of names and addresses in two ways. One way is to add the BillingCompany, BillingAddress, BillingCity, BillingState, and BillingZip fields to the tblPatient table. For each patient with an additional billing name and address, you store the appropriate values in these billing fields. For those patients who do not have additional billing information, you leave these billing fields null.

Another way to handle the two sets of addresses is to create an entity subtype, which in this case could be a table named tblBillingContact. In the tblBillingContact table, the PatientID field, which is the primary key, is also a foreign key to the tblPatient table. A record appears in the tblBillingContact table only for those patients who have different mailing and billing names and addresses. All billing data appears only in the tblBillingContact table. The tblPatient table and the tblBillingContact table, which is an entity subtype, have a one-to-one relationship, as shown in Figure 9–13.

Figure 9–13 **tblPatient and tblBillingContact tables with a 1:1 relationship**

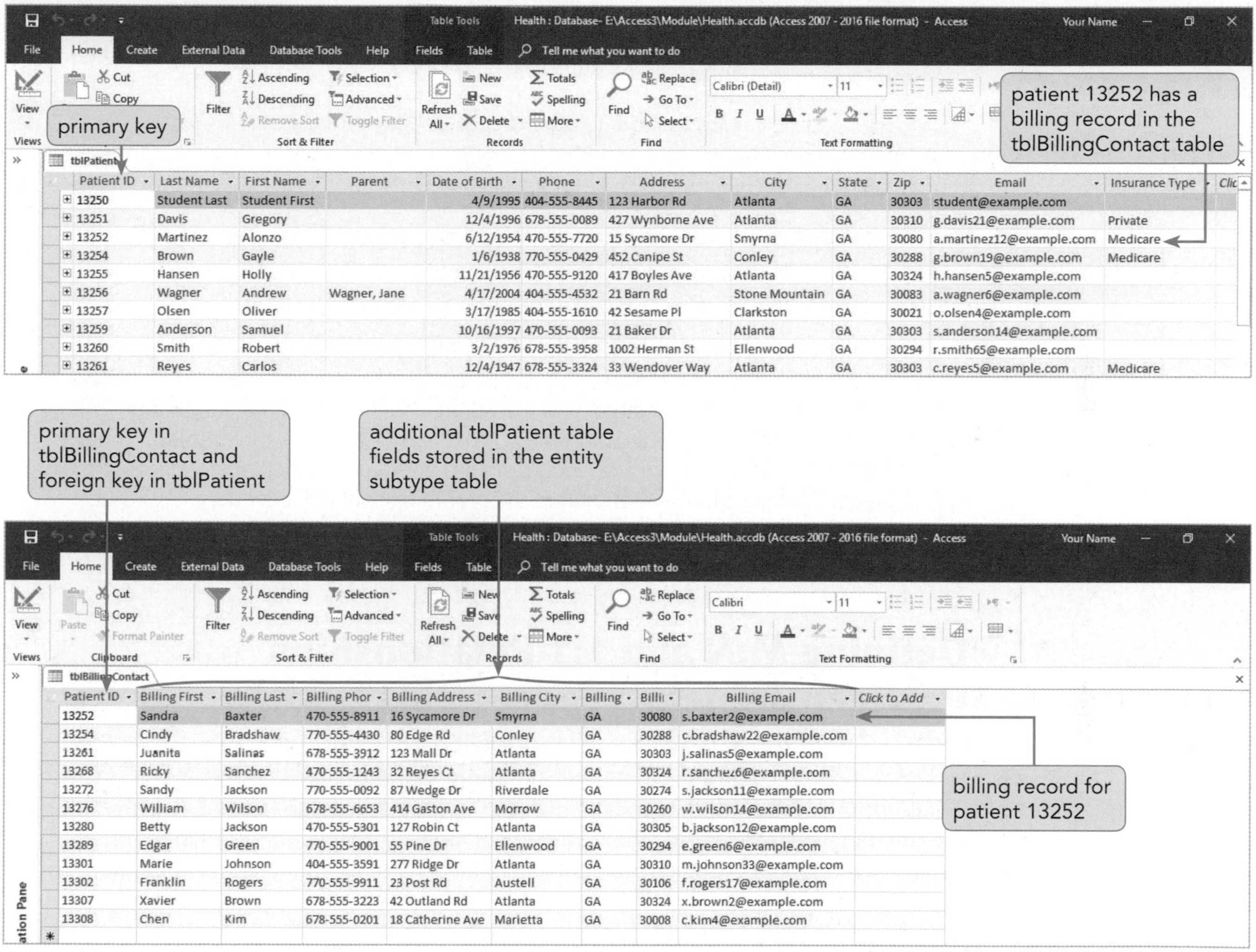
primary key
patient 13252 has a billing record in the tblBillingContact table
primary key in tblBillingContact and foreign key in tblPatient
additional tblPatient table fields stored in the entity subtype table
billing record for patient 13252

When you define a one-to-one relationship between tables, you can extract data from them as if they were one larger table. For example, you can define a relationship between the tblPatient and tblBillingContact tables to create the qryBillingContactData query shown in Figure 9–14.

Figure 9–14 Query results produced by joining tables having a 1:1 relationship

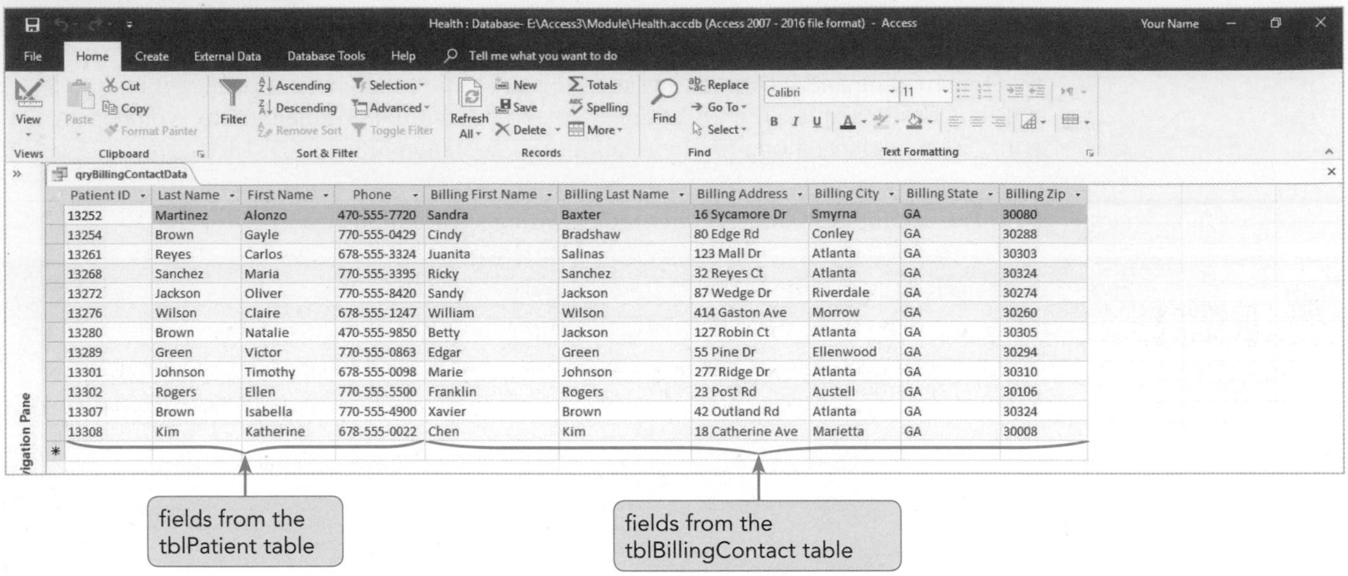
qryBillingContactData
fields from the tblPatient table
fields from the tblBillingContact table

Patient ID	Last Name	First Name	Phone	Billing First Name	Billing Last Name	Billing Address	Billing City	Billing State	Billing Zip
13252	Martinez	Alonzo	470-555-7720	Sandra	Baxter	16 Sycamore Dr	Smyrna	GA	30080
13254	Brown	Gayle	770-555-0429	Cindy	Bradshaw	80 Edge Rd	Conley	GA	30288
13261	Reyes	Carlos	678-555-3324	Juanita	Salinas	123 Mall Dr	Atlanta	GA	30303
13268	Sanchez	Maria	770-555-3395	Ricky	Sanchez	32 Reyes Ct	Atlanta	GA	30324
13272	Jackson	Oliver	770-555-8420	Sandy	Jackson	87 Wedge Dr	Riverdale	GA	30274
13276	Wilson	Claire	678-555-1247	William	Wilson	414 Gaston Ave	Morrow	GA	30260
13280	Brown	Natalie	470-555-9850	Betty	Jackson	127 Robin Ct	Atlanta	GA	30305
13289	Green	Victor	770-555-0863	Edgar	Green	55 Pine Dr	Ellenwood	GA	30294
13301	Johnson	Timothy	678-555-0098	Marie	Johnson	277 Ridge Dr	Atlanta	GA	30310
13302	Rogers	Ellen	770-555-5500	Franklin	Rogers	23 Post Rd	Austell	GA	30106
13307	Brown	Isabella	770-555-4900	Xavier	Brown	42 Outland Rd	Atlanta	GA	30324
13308	Kim	Katherine	678-555-0022	Chen	Kim	18 Catherine Ave	Marietta	GA	30008

The relationship between the tblPatient and tblBillingContact tables is based upon the common PatientID field. In the query, the Patient ID, Last Name, First Name, and Phone columns are from the tblPatient table; and the Billing First Name, Billing Last Name, Billing Address, Billing City, Billing State, and Billing Zip columns are from the tblBillingContact table. Only the 12 patients who have records in the tblBillingContact table—because they have different billing addresses—appear in the qryBillingContactData query recordset.

Next, you'll define a many-to-many relationship between the tblBilling and tblEmployee tables and a one-to-one relationship between the tblPatient and tblBillingContact tables.

Defining M:N and 1:1 Relationships Between Tables

Similar to the way you define one-to-many relationships, you define many-to-many and one-to-one relationships in the Relationships window. First, you'll open the Relationships window and define the many-to-many relationship between the tblBilling and tblEmployee tables, using the tblTreatment table as the relationship table. You'll start by defining a one-to-many relationship between the tblBilling and tblTreatment tables, with tblBilling as the primary table, tblTreatment as the related table, and InvoiceNum as the common field (the primary key in the tblBilling table and a foreign key in the tblTreatment table). Next, you'll define a one-to-many relationship between the tblEmployee and tblTreatment tables, with tblEmployee as the primary table, tblTreatment as the related table, and EmployeeID as the common field (the primary key in the tblEmployee table and a foreign key in the tblTreatment table).

To define a many-to-many relationship between the tblBilling and tblEmployee tables:

1. If you took a break after the previous session, make sure that the Health database is open.
2. Close the Navigation Pane (if necessary), click the **Database Tools** tab, and then in the Relationships group, click the **Relationships** button to open the Relationships window.

3. On the Relationship Tools Design tab, in the Relationships group, click the **Show Table** button to open the Show Table dialog box.
4. Add the **tblTreatment**, **tblBillingContact**, and **tblEmployee** field lists to the Relationships window, and then close the Show Table dialog box.
5. Resize the tblBillingContact field list and the tblPatient field list, so that all field names are visible, and then drag the field list title bars of the field lists for the tblBillingContact, tblBilling, tblEmployee, and tblTreatment tables to arrange them as shown in Figure 9–15.

Figure 9–15 **After adding three table field lists to the Relationships window**

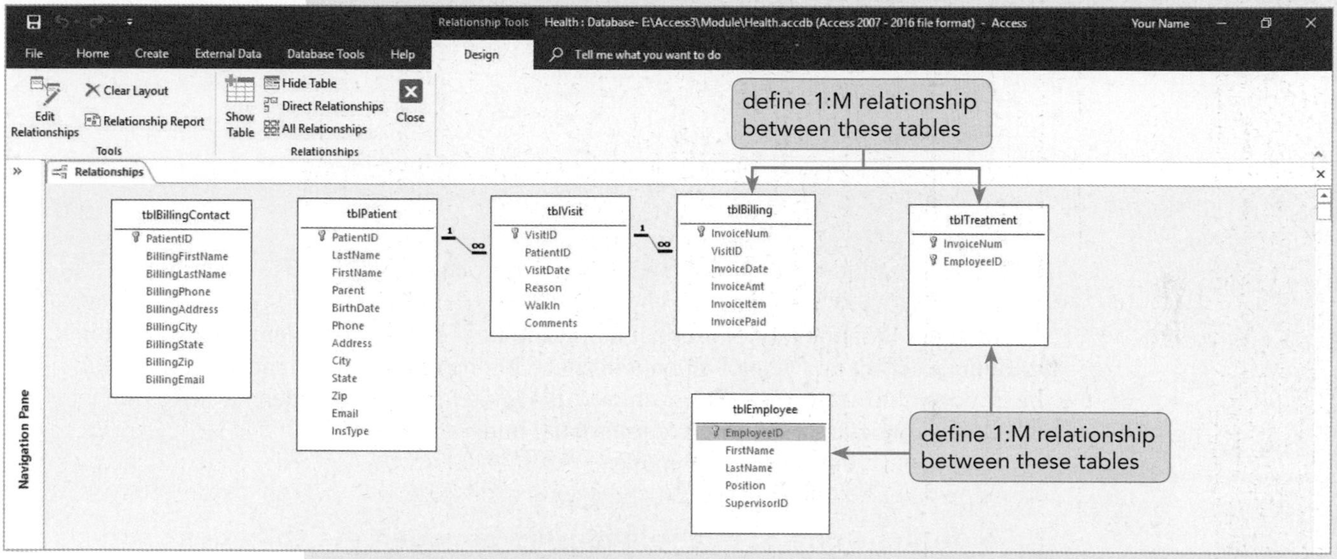
Relationship Tools
Health : Database- E:\Access3\Module\Health.accdb (Access 2007 - 2016 file format) - Access
Your Name
File
Home
Create
External Data
Database Tools
Help
Design
Tell me what you want to do
Clear Layout
Edit Relationships
Relationship Report
Tools
Show Table
Hide Table
Direct Relationships
All Relationships
Close
Relationships
define 1:M relationship between these tables
Relationships
tblBillingContact
PatientID
BillingFirstName
BillingLastName
BillingPhone
BillingAddress
BillingCity
BillingState
BillingZip
BillingEmail
tblPatient
PatientID
LastName
FirstName
Parent
BirthDate
Phone
Address
City
State
Zip
Email
InsType
tblVisit
VisitID
PatientID
VisitDate
Reason
WalkIn
Comments
tblBilling
InvoiceNum
VisitID
InvoiceDate
InvoiceAmt
InvoiceItem
InvoicePaid
tblTreatment
InvoiceNum
EmployeeID
tblEmployee
EmployeeID
FirstName
LastName
Position
SupervisorID
define 1:M relationship between these tables
Navigation Pane

First, you'll define the one-to-many relationship between the tblBilling and tblTreatment tables.

6. In the tblBilling field list, click **InvoiceNum**, and then drag it to **InvoiceNum** in the tblTreatment field list. When you release the mouse button, the Edit Relationships dialog box opens.

   The primary table, related table, and common field appear at the top of the dialog box. The Relationship Type box at the bottom of the dialog box lists One-To-Many. You'll enforce referential integrity and cascade updates to related fields, but you won't cascade deletions to related records because you want to preserve the Billing contact information in case it will be used again later.

7. Click the **Enforce Referential Integrity** check box, and then click the **Cascade Update Related Fields** check box. You have now selected all the necessary relationship options.
8. Click the **Create** button to close the dialog box and define the one-to-many relationship between the two tables. The completed relationship appears in the Relationships window.
9. Repeat Steps 6 through 8 to define the one-to-many relationship between the primary tblEmployee table and the related tblTreatment table, using EmployeeID as the common field. See Figure 9–16.

Figure 9–16 M:N relationship defined between the tblBilling and tblEmployee tables

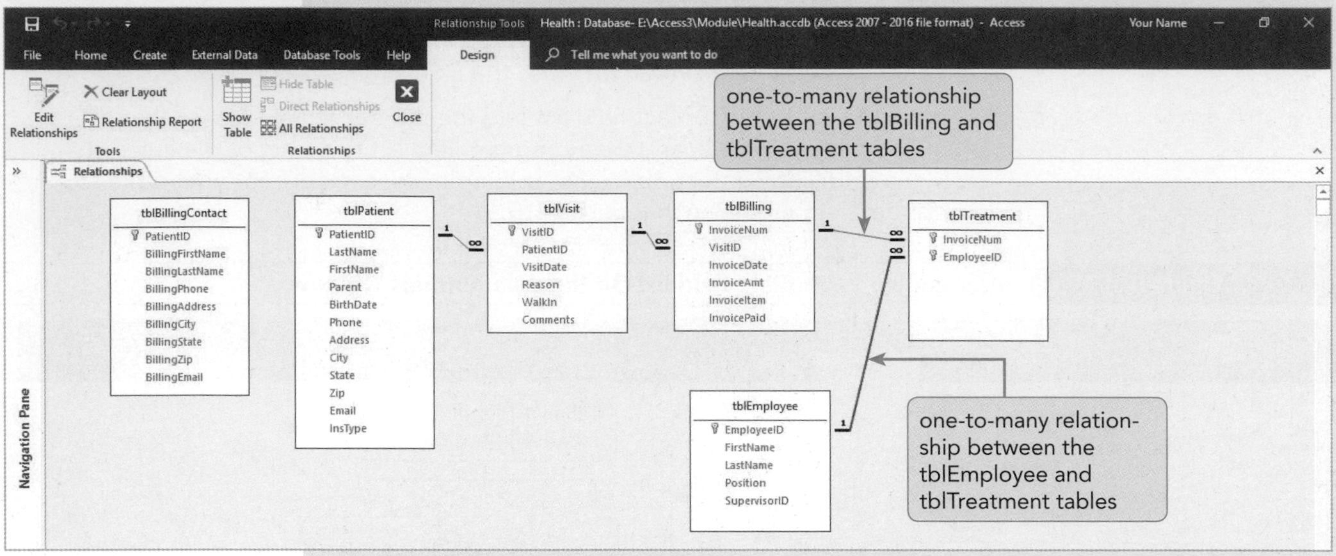
one-to-many relationship between the tblBilling and tblTreatment tables
one-to-many relation-ship between the tblEmployee and tblTreatment tables
tblBillingContact
PatientID
BillingFirstName
BillingLastName
BillingPhone
BillingAddress
BillingCity
BillingState
BillingZip
BillingEmail
tblPatient
PatientID
LastName
FirstName
Parent
BirthDate
Phone
Address
City
State
Zip
Email
InsType
tblVisit
VisitID
PatientID
VisitDate
Reason
WalkIn
Comments
tblBilling
InvoiceNum
VisitID
InvoiceDate
InvoiceAmt
InvoiceItem
InvoicePaid
tblTreatment
InvoiceNum
EmployeeID
tblEmployee
EmployeeID
FirstName
LastName
Position
SupervisorID

Now you'll define a one-to-one relationship between the tblPatient and tblBillingContact tables. Not all patients have billing contact information, so it will be important to create the relationship by dragging from the tblPatient table to the tblBillingContact table to preserve referential integrity.

To define a one-to-one relationship between the tblPatient and tblBillingContact tables:

Be sure to drag from the tblPatient to the tblBillingContact table and not the reverse.

1. In the tblPatient field list, click **PatientID**, and then drag it to **PatientID** in the tblBillingContact field list. When you release the mouse button, the Edit Relationships dialog box opens.

   The primary table, related table, and common field appear at the top of the dialog box. The Relationship Type box at the bottom of the dialog box lists One-To-One.

   Trouble? If an error message appears indicating a violation of referential integrity, you mistakenly dragged the PatientID field from the tblBillingContact table to the tblPatient table. Click the Cancel button and try again, dragging from the tblPatient table to the tblBillingContact table.

2. Click the **Enforce Referential Integrity** check box, click the **Cascade Update Related Fields** check box, and then click the **Create** button to define the one-to-one relationship between the two tables and close the dialog box. The completed relationship appears in the Relationships window. See Figure 9–17.

Figure 9–17 1:1 relationship defined between the tblPatient and tblBillingContact tables

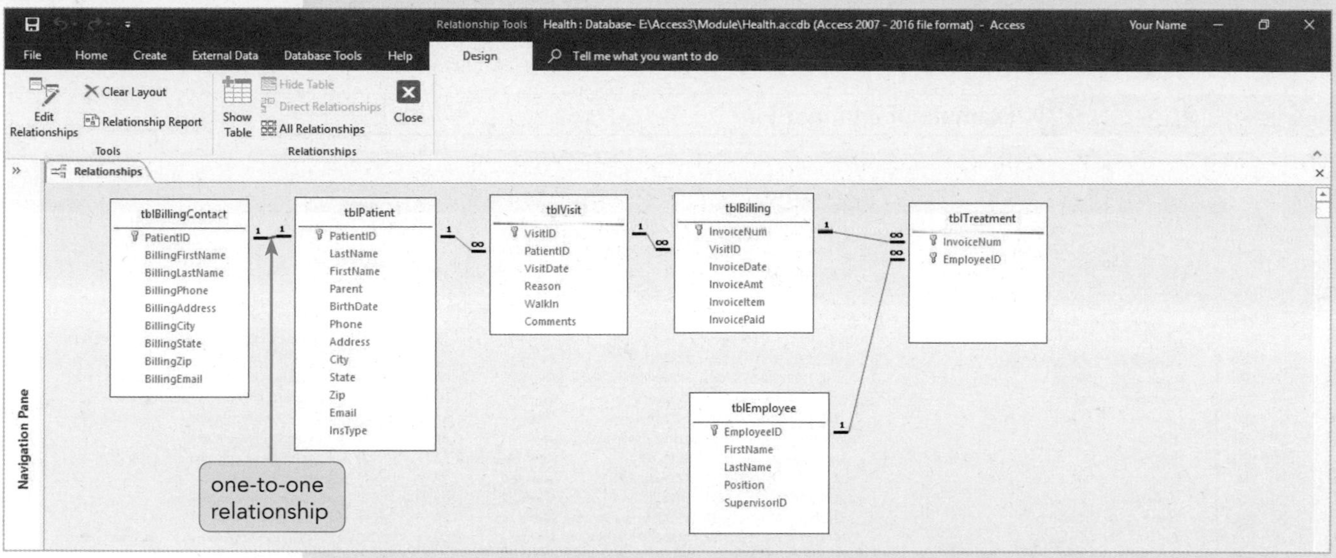

tblBillingContact
PatientID
BillingFirstName
BillingLastName
BillingPhone
BillingAddress
BillingCity
BillingState
BillingZip
BillingEmail
tblPatient
PatientID
LastName
FirstName
Parent
BirthDate
Phone
Address
City
State
Zip
Email
InsType
tblVisit
VisitID
PatientID
VisitDate
Reason
WalkIn
Comments
tblBilling
InvoiceNum
VisitID
InvoiceDate
InvoiceAmt
InvoiceItem
InvoicePaid
tblTreatment
InvoiceNum
EmployeeID
tblEmployee
EmployeeID
FirstName
LastName
Position
SupervisorID
one-to-one relationship

Each side of the relationship has the digit 1 at its end of the join line to indicate a one-to-one relationship between the two tables.

3. Save your relationship changes.

The tblEmployee table contains data about the employees at Lakewood Community Health Services who provide patient care. Donna asks you to create a select query to display the employees in the tblEmployee table and their supervisors. The select query you'll create will require a special join using the tblEmployee table.

Understanding Join Types

The design of the Health database includes a one-to-many relationship between the tblPatient and tblVisit tables using PatientID as the common field, which allows you to join the two tables to create a query based on data from both tables. While the term *join* is sometimes used to refer to any relationship between tables in a database, **join** is also a technical database term that describes how data from the tables in a relationship is selected and returned. The most common type of join is referred to as an inner join, which is the type of join you have used in your work with the database for Lakewood Community Health Services thus far. Two other types of joins are the outer join and the self-join.

Inner and Outer Joins

An **inner join** selects records from two tables only when the records have the same value in the common field that links the tables. For example, in a database containing a table of student information and a table of class information, an inner join would return all student records that have a matching class record and all class records that have a matching student record. In the Health database, PatientID is the common field for the tblPatient and tblBillingContact tables. As shown in Figure 9–18, the results of a query based on an inner join of these two tables would return only those records that have a matching ID value. The record in the tblPatient table with a Patient ID column value of 13250 is not included in the query recordset because it fails to match a record with the same Patient ID column value in the tblBillingContact table.

(That patient does not have a different billing address.) Because primary key values can't be null, records with null foreign key values do not appear in a query recordset based on an inner join. You usually use an inner join whenever you perform a query based on more than one table; it is the default join you have used to this point. You can specify or change the join type of a relationship in the Join Properties dialog box.

Figure 9–18 Example of an inner join

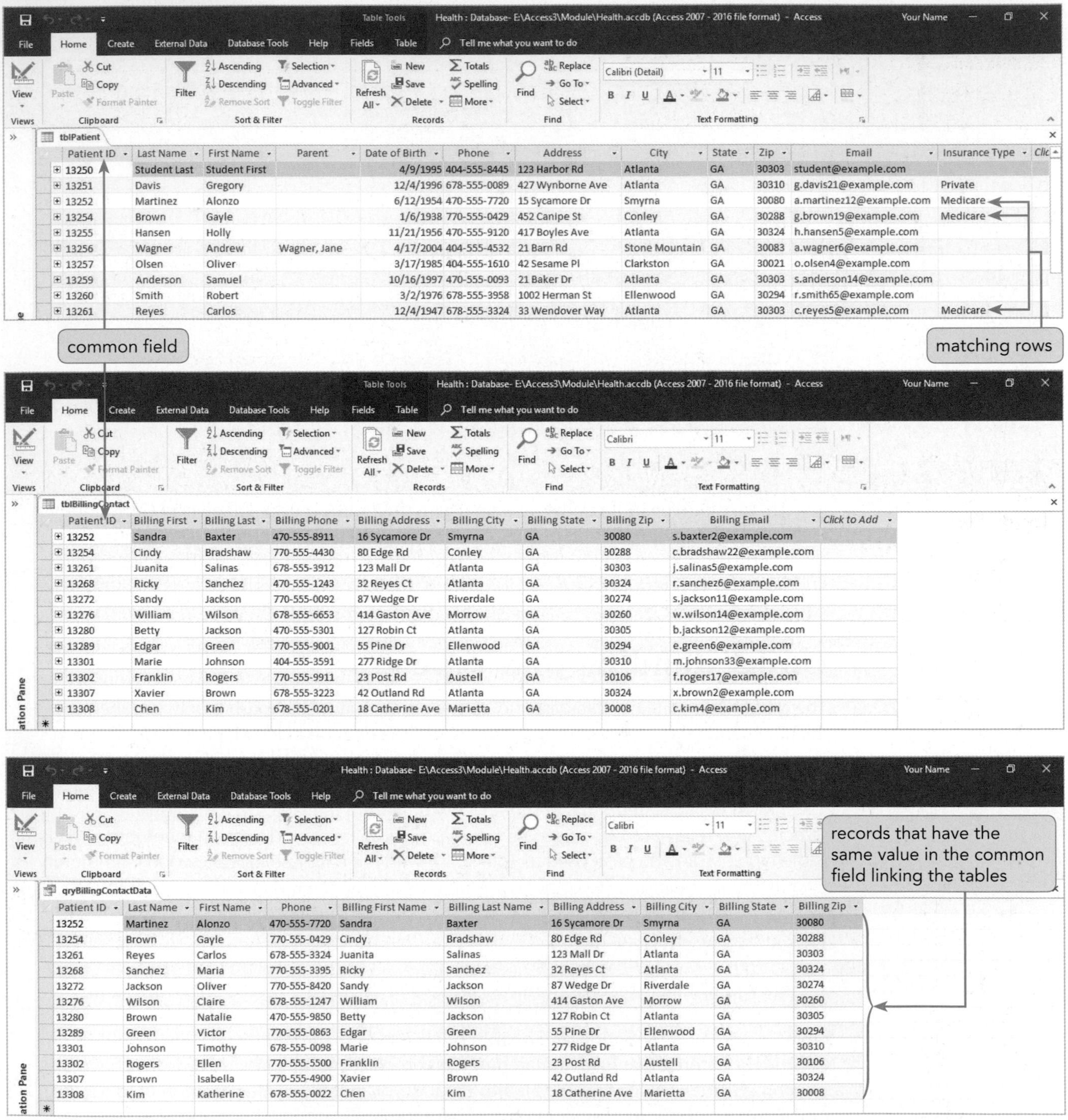
common field
matching rows
records that have the same value in the common field linking the tables
tblPatient
tblBillingContact
qryBillingContactData

Patient ID	Last Name	First Name	Parent	Date of Birth	Phone	Address	City	State	Zip	Email	Insurance Type
13250	Student Last	Student First		4/9/1995	404-555-8445	123 Harbor Rd	Atlanta	GA	30303	student@example.com	
13251	Davis	Gregory		12/4/1996	678-555-0089	427 Wynborne Ave	Atlanta	GA	30310	g.davis21@example.com	Private
13252	Martinez	Alonzo		6/12/1954	470-555-7720	15 Sycamore Dr	Smyrna	GA	30080	a.martinez12@example.com	Medicare
13254	Brown	Gayle		1/6/1938	770-555-0429	452 Canipe St	Conley	GA	30288	g.brown19@example.com	Medicare
13255	Hansen	Holly		11/21/1956	470-555-9120	417 Boyles Ave	Atlanta	GA	30324	h.hansen5@example.com	
13256	Wagner	Andrew	Wagner, Jane	4/17/2004	404-555-4532	21 Barn Rd	Stone Mountain	GA	30083	a.wagner6@example.com	
13257	Olsen	Oliver		3/17/1985	404-555-1610	42 Sesame Pl	Clarkston	GA	30021	o.olsen4@example.com	
13259	Anderson	Samuel		10/16/1997	470-555-0093	21 Baker Dr	Atlanta	GA	30303	s.anderson14@example.com	
13260	Smith	Robert		3/2/1976	678-555-3958	1002 Herman St	Ellenwood	GA	30294	r.smith65@example.com	
13261	Reyes	Carlos		12/4/1947	678-555-3324	33 Wendover Way	Atlanta	GA	30303	c.reyes5@example.com	Medicare

Patient ID	Billing First	Billing Last	Billing Phone	Billing Address	Billing City	Billing State	Billing Zip	Billing Email
13252	Sandra	Baxter	470-555-8911	16 Sycamore Dr	Smyrna	GA	30080	s.baxter2@example.com
13254	Cindy	Bradshaw	770-555-4430	80 Edge Rd	Conley	GA	30288	c.bradshaw22@example.com
13261	Juanita	Salinas	678-555-3912	123 Mall Dr	Atlanta	GA	30303	j.salinas5@example.com
13268	Ricky	Sanchez	470-555-1243	32 Reyes Ct	Atlanta	GA	30324	r.sanchez6@example.com
13272	Sandy	Jackson	770-555-0092	87 Wedge Dr	Riverdale	GA	30274	s.jackson11@example.com
13276	William	Wilson	678-555-6653	414 Gaston Ave	Morrow	GA	30260	w.wilson14@example.com
13280	Betty	Jackson	470-555-5301	127 Robin Ct	Atlanta	GA	30305	b.jackson12@example.com
13289	Edgar	Green	770-555-9001	55 Pine Dr	Ellenwood	GA	30294	e.green6@example.com
13301	Marie	Johnson	404-555-3591	277 Ridge Dr	Atlanta	GA	30310	m.johnson33@example.com
13302	Franklin	Rogers	770-555-9911	23 Post Rd	Austell	GA	30106	f.rogers17@example.com
13307	Xavier	Brown	678-555-3223	42 Outland Rd	Atlanta	GA	30324	x.brown2@example.com
13308	Chen	Kim	678-555-0201	18 Catherine Ave	Marietta	GA	30008	c.kim4@example.com

Patient ID	Last Name	First Name	Phone	Billing First Name	Billing Last Name	Billing Address	Billing City	Billing State	Billing Zip
13252	Martinez	Alonzo	470-555-7720	Sandra	Baxter	16 Sycamore Dr	Smyrna	GA	30080
13254	Brown	Gayle	770-555-0429	Cindy	Bradshaw	80 Edge Rd	Conley	GA	30288
13261	Reyes	Carlos	678-555-3324	Juanita	Salinas	123 Mall Dr	Atlanta	GA	30303
13268	Sanchez	Maria	770-555-3395	Ricky	Sanchez	32 Reyes Ct	Atlanta	GA	30324
13272	Jackson	Oliver	770-555-8420	Sandy	Jackson	87 Wedge Dr	Riverdale	GA	30274
13276	Wilson	Claire	678-555-1247	William	Wilson	414 Gaston Ave	Morrow	GA	30260
13280	Brown	Natalie	470-555-9850	Betty	Jackson	127 Robin Ct	Atlanta	GA	30305
13289	Green	Victor	770-555-0863	Edgar	Green	55 Pine Dr	Ellenwood	GA	30294
13301	Johnson	Timothy	678-555-0098	Marie	Johnson	277 Ridge Dr	Atlanta	GA	30310
13302	Rogers	Ellen	770-555-5500	Franklin	Rogers	23 Post Rd	Austell	GA	30106
13307	Brown	Isabella	770-555-4900	Xavier	Brown	42 Outland Rd	Atlanta	GA	30324
13308	Kim	Katherine	678-555-0022	Chen	Kim	18 Catherine Ave	Marietta	GA	30008

An **outer join** selects *all* records from one table along with only those records from a second table that have matching common field values. For example, in a database containing a student table and a class table, you could create two different outer joins between these two tables. One outer join would return the records for all students whether or not the students are enrolled in classes, and another outer join between these two tables would return all classes whether or not any students are enrolled in them. In the Health database, you would use this kind of join if you wanted to see, for example, all records from the tblPatient table and any matching records from the tblBillingContact table. Figure 9–19 shows an outer join for the tblPatient and tblBillingContact tables. All records from the tblPatient table appear in the query recordset, along with only matching records from the tblBillingContact table. Notice that the record from the tblPatient table for Patient ID 13250 appears in the query recordset even though it does not match a record in the tblBillingContact table.

Figure 9–19 **Example of an outer join**

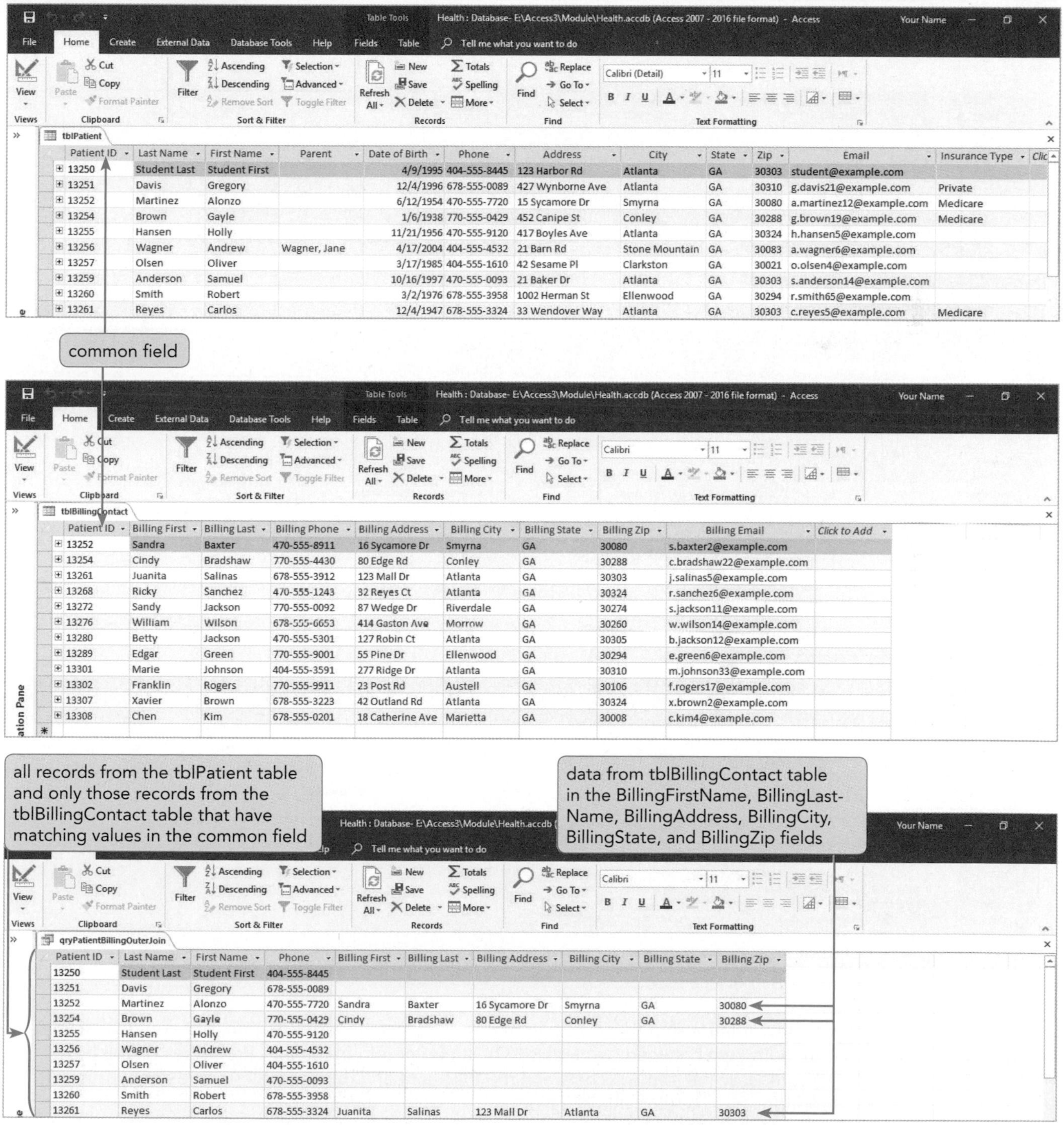
tblPatient
Patient ID | Last Name | First Name | Parent | Date of Birth | Phone | Address | City | State | Zip | Email | Insurance Type
13250 Student Last Student First 4/9/1995 404-555-8445 123 Harbor Rd Atlanta GA 30303 student@example.com
13251 Davis Gregory 12/4/1996 678-555-0089 427 Wynborne Ave Atlanta GA 30310 g.davis21@example.com Private
13252 Martinez Alonzo 6/12/1954 470-555-7720 15 Sycamore Dr Smyrna GA 30080 a.martinez12@example.com Medicare
13254 Brown Gayle 1/6/1938 770-555-0429 452 Canipe St Conley GA 30288 g.brown19@example.com Medicare
13255 Hansen Holly 11/21/1956 470-555-9120 417 Boyles Ave Atlanta GA 30324 h.hansen5@example.com
13256 Wagner Andrew Wagner, Jane 4/17/2004 404-555-4532 21 Barn Rd Stone Mountain GA 30083 a.wagner6@example.com
13257 Olsen Oliver 3/17/1985 404-555-1610 42 Sesame Pl Clarkston GA 30021 o.olsen4@example.com
13259 Anderson Samuel 10/16/1997 470-555-0093 21 Baker Dr Atlanta GA 30303 s.anderson14@example.com
13260 Smith Robert 3/2/1976 678-555-3958 1002 Herman St Ellenwood GA 30294 r.smith65@example.com
13261 Reyes Carlos 12/4/1947 678-555-3324 33 Wendover Way Atlanta GA 30303 c.reyes5@example.com Medicare
common field
tblBillingContact
Patient ID | Billing First | Billing Last | Billing Phone | Billing Address | Billing City | Billing State | Billing Zip | Billing Email
13252 Sandra Baxter 470-555-8911 16 Sycamore Dr Smyrna GA 30080 s.baxter2@example.com
13254 Cindy Bradshaw 770-555-4430 80 Edge Rd Conley GA 30288 c.bradshaw22@example.com
13261 Juanita Salinas 678-555-3912 123 Mall Dr Atlanta GA 30303 j.salinas5@example.com
13268 Ricky Sanchez 470-555-1243 32 Reyes Ct Atlanta GA 30324 r.sanchez6@example.com
13272 Sandy Jackson 770-555-0092 87 Wedge Dr Riverdale GA 30274 s.jackson11@example.com
13276 William Wilson 678-555-6653 414 Gaston Ave Morrow GA 30260 w.wilson14@example.com
13280 Betty Jackson 470-555-5301 127 Robin Ct Atlanta GA 30305 b.jackson12@example.com
13289 Edgar Green 770-555-9001 55 Pine Dr Ellenwood GA 30294 e.green6@example.com
13301 Marie Johnson 404-555-3591 277 Ridge Dr Atlanta GA 30310 m.johnson33@example.com
13302 Franklin Rogers 770-555-9911 23 Post Rd Austell GA 30106 f.rogers17@example.com
13307 Xavier Brown 678-555-3223 42 Outland Rd Atlanta GA 30324 x.brown2@example.com
13308 Chen Kim 678-555-0201 18 Catherine Ave Marietta GA 30008 c.kim4@example.com
all records from the tblPatient table and only those records from the tblBillingContact table that have matching values in the common field
data from tblBillingContact table in the BillingFirstName, BillingLast-Name, BillingAddress, BillingCity, BillingState, and BillingZip fields
qryPatientBillingOuterJoin
Patient ID | Last Name | First Name | Phone | Billing First | Billing Last | Billing Address | Billing City | Billing State | Billing Zip
13250 Student Last Student First 404-555-8445
13251 Davis Gregory 678-555-0089
13252 Martinez Alonzo 470-555-7720 Sandra Baxter 16 Sycamore Dr Smyrna GA 30080
13254 Brown Gayle 770-555-0429 Cindy Bradshaw 80 Edge Rd Conley GA 30288
13255 Hansen Holly 470-555-9120
13256 Wagner Andrew 404-555-4532
13257 Olsen Oliver 404-555-1610
13259 Anderson Samuel 470-555-0093
13260 Smith Robert 678-555-3958
13261 Reyes Carlos 678-555-3324 Juanita Salinas 123 Mall Dr Atlanta GA 30303

Another example of an outer join using the tblPatient and tblVisit tables is shown in Figure 9–20. All records from the tblVisit table appear in the query recordset. If any tblVisit records had a Patient ID that did not match a Patient ID in the tblPatient table, these records would not be in the query recordset. For example, the Patient ID 13313 record from the tblPatient table does not appear in the query recordset because it does not match a record in the tblVisit table.

Figure 9–20 Another example of an outer join

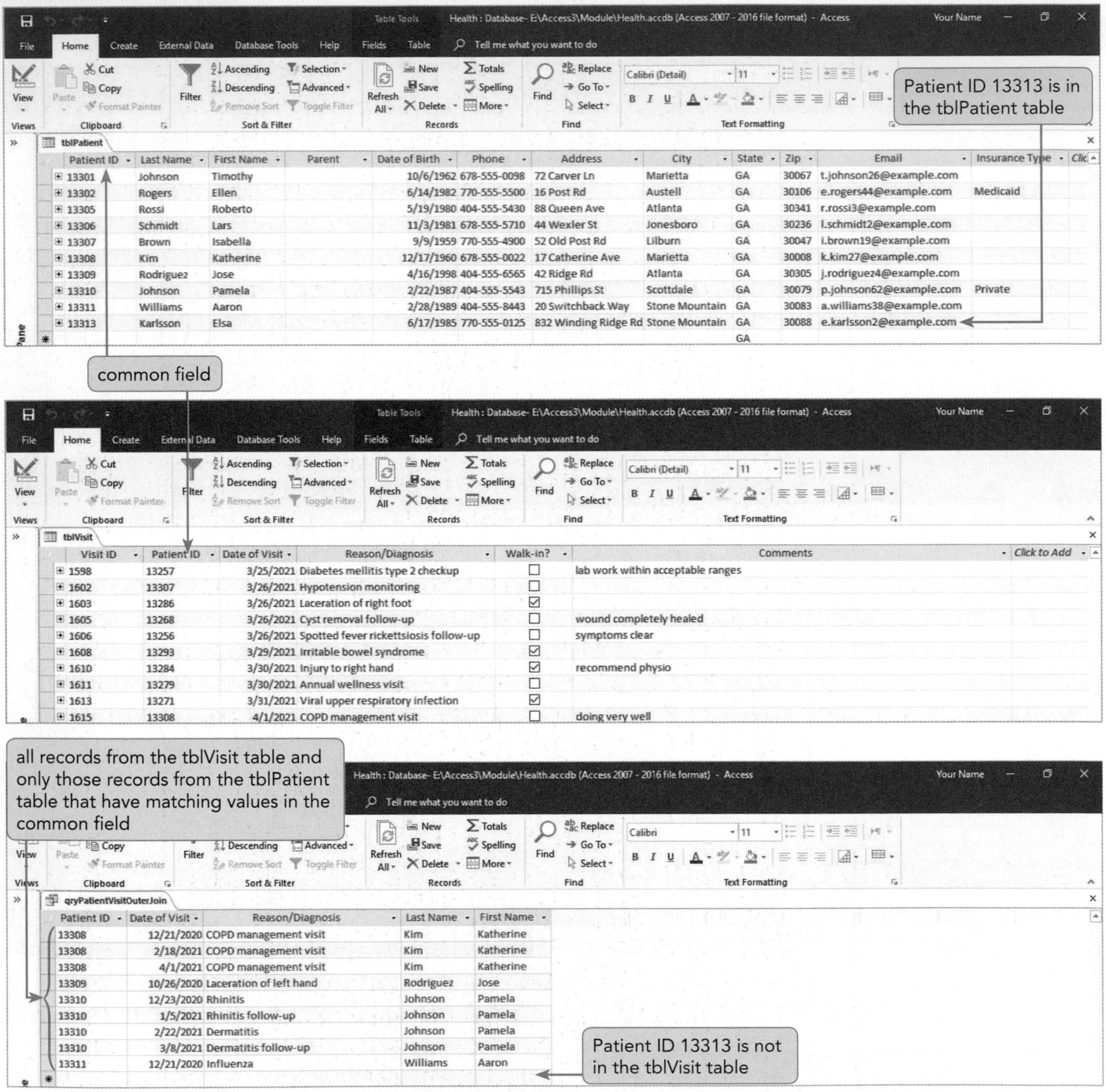
Patient ID 13313 is in the tblPatient table
tblPatient
common field
tblVisit
all records from the tblVisit table and only those records from the tblPatient table that have matching values in the common field
qryPatientVisitOuterJoin
Patient ID 13313 is not in the tblVisit table

Any relationship you create in Access is by default an inner join, but you can change the join type between two tables to be an outer join in the Join Properties dialog box. You'll view the join type between the tblPatient and tblVisit tables and examine the options for changing the join type.

To view the join type between the tblPatient and tblVisit tables:

1. Right-click the **join line** between the tblPatient and tblVisit tables, and then click **Edit Relationship** on the shortcut menu to open the Edit Relationships dialog box.

   Trouble? If the Edit Relationship dialog box does not open, click the join line, and then on the Relationship Tools Design tab, in the Tools group, click the Edit Relationships button.

2. Click the **Join Type** button in the dialog box to open the Join Properties dialog box. See Figure 9–21.

Figure 9–21 Join Properties dialog box

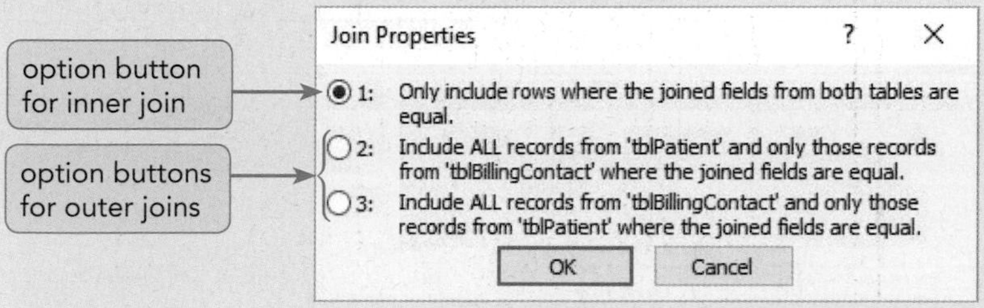
option button for inner join
option buttons for outer joins
Join Properties
?
1: Only include rows where the joined fields from both tables are equal.
2: Include ALL records from 'tblPatient' and only those records from 'tblBillingContact' where the joined fields are equal.
3: Include ALL records from 'tblBillingContact' and only those records from 'tblPatient' where the joined fields are equal.
OK
Cancel

In the Join Properties dialog box, the first option button is selected, indicating that the join type between the tblPatient and tblVisit tables is an inner join. You would click the second or third option button to establish an outer join between the two tables. You'd select the second option if you wanted to select all records from the tblPatient table and any matching records from the tblVisit table based on the PatientID common field. You'd select the third option if you wanted to select all records from the tblVisit table and any matching records from the tblPatient table based on the PatientID common field.

When you change the join type for a relationship between two tables in the Relationships window, every new object created based on the two related tables uses the join type you selected in the Join Properties dialog box. Existing queries, reports, or forms based on the two related tables continue to use the join type that was in effect at the time you created these items.

Donna wants to continue to use an inner join for all queries based on the related tblPatient and tblVisit tables.

3. Click the **Cancel** button to close the Join Properties dialog box without making any changes, and then click the **Cancel** button to close the Edit Relationships dialog box without making any changes.
4. Close the Relationships window, and then if you are prompted to save changes, click **No** to ensure that you don't change the relationship type.

Self-Joins

A table can also be joined with itself; this join is called a **self-join**. A self-join can be either an inner or outer join. For example, the tblEmployee table lists all employees, and for each employee who has a supervisor, the SupervisorID is included. The SupervisorID is the EmployeeID of the supervisor. It doesn't make sense to have separate SupervisorID and Employee ID fields. Imagine a situation with multiple supervisors, and each supervisor also has a supervisor. Separate tables for supervisors would be very confusing. The supervisors are also employees, and thus the EmployeeID for a supervisor is entered in the SupervisorID field. This is a case where a self-join would be used. The tblEmployee table would be joined to itself so the SupervisorID field could be related to the EmployeeID field to display the name of the supervisor for each employee. You would use a self-join to relate the SupervisorID field to the EmployeeID field to determine the name of the supervisor if you wanted to see records from the tblEmployee table together with information about each employee's supervisor. Figure 9–22 shows a self-join for the tblEmployee table. In this case, the self-join is an inner join because records appear in the query results only if the SupervisorID field value matches an EmployeeID field value. To create this self-join, you would add two copies of the tblEmployee field list to the Query window in Design view and then join the SupervisorID field of one tblEmployee field list to the EmployeeID field of the other tblEmployee field list.

Figure 9–22 Example of self-join

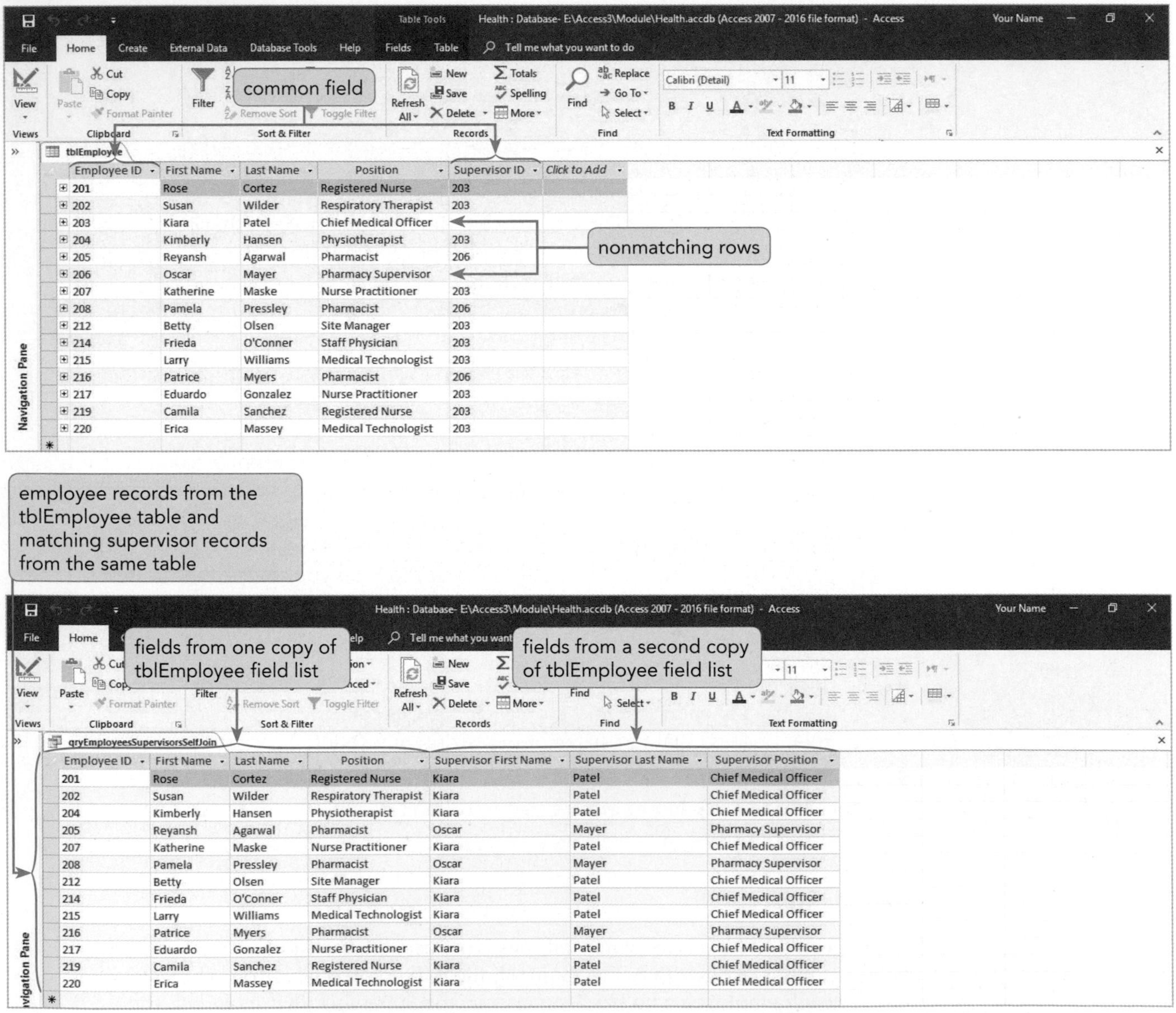
common field
nonmatching rows
tblEmployee
Employee ID | First Name | Last Name | Position | Supervisor ID | Click to Add
201 Rose Cortez Registered Nurse 203
202 Susan Wilder Respiratory Therapist 203
203 Kiara Patel Chief Medical Officer
204 Kimberly Hansen Physiotherapist 203
205 Reyansh Agarwal Pharmacist 206
206 Oscar Mayer Pharmacy Supervisor
207 Katherine Maske Nurse Practitioner 203
208 Pamela Pressley Pharmacist 206
212 Betty Olsen Site Manager 203
214 Frieda O'Conner Staff Physician 203
215 Larry Williams Medical Technologist 203
216 Patrice Myers Pharmacist 206
217 Eduardo Gonzalez Nurse Practitioner 203
219 Camila Sanchez Registered Nurse 203
220 Erica Massey Medical Technologist 203
employee records from the tblEmployee table and matching supervisor records from the same table
fields from one copy of tblEmployee field list
fields from a second copy of tblEmployee field list
qryEmployeesSupervisorsSelfJoin
Employee ID | First Name | Last Name | Position | Supervisor First Name | Supervisor Last Name | Supervisor Position
201 Rose Cortez Registered Nurse Kiara Patel Chief Medical Officer
202 Susan Wilder Respiratory Therapist Kiara Patel Chief Medical Officer
204 Kimberly Hansen Physiotherapist Kiara Patel Chief Medical Officer
205 Reyansh Agarwal Pharmacist Oscar Mayer Pharmacy Supervisor
207 Katherine Maske Nurse Practitioner Kiara Patel Chief Medical Officer
208 Pamela Pressley Pharmacist Oscar Mayer Pharmacy Supervisor
212 Betty Olsen Site Manager Kiara Patel Chief Medical Officer
214 Frieda O'Conner Staff Physician Kiara Patel Chief Medical Officer
215 Larry Williams Medical Technologist Kiara Patel Chief Medical Officer
216 Patrice Myers Pharmacist Oscar Mayer Pharmacy Supervisor
217 Eduardo Gonzalez Nurse Practitioner Kiara Patel Chief Medical Officer
219 Camila Sanchez Registered Nurse Kiara Patel Chief Medical Officer
220 Erica Massey Medical Technologist Kiara Patel Chief Medical Officer

In Figure 9–22, the query results show the record for each employee in the tblEmployee table with a value in the SupervisorID field, and the detail for each record includes information about the supervisor for that employee. The supervisor information also comes from the tblEmployee table through the SupervisorID field. The join for the query is an inner join, so only employees with nonnull SupervisorID field values appear in the query recordset.

TIP

You can work with relationships and join properties in the Query window just as you do in the Relationship window, but any relationships you make in the Query window apply only to that query.

You need to create a query to display the employees and their supervisors in the tblEmployee table. This query requires a self-join. To create the self-join, you need to add two copies of the tblEmployee field list to the Query window in Design view and then add a join line from the EmployeeID field in one field list to the SupervisorID field in the other. The SupervisorID field is a foreign key that matches the primary key field EmployeeID. You can then create a query to display employee information with the related supervisor information.

REFERENCE

Creating a Query Using a Self-Join

- Click the Create tab on the ribbon.
- In the Queries group, click the Query Design button.
- In the Show Table dialog box, double-click the table for the self-join, double-click the table a second time, and then click the Close button.
- Click and drag the primary key field from one field list to the foreign key field in the other field list.
- Right-click the join line between the two tables, and then click Join Properties to open the Join Properties dialog box.
- Click the first option button to select an inner join, or click the second option button or the third option button to select an outer join, and then click the OK button.
- Select the fields, specify the selection criteria, select the sort options, and set other properties as appropriate for the query.

Now you'll create the query using a self-join to display supervisor information with the relevant employee records.

To create the query using a self-join:

1. Click the **Create** tab, and then in the Queries group, click the **Query Design** button. The Show Table dialog box opens on top of the Query window in Design view.

TIP

To remove a table's field list from the Query window, right-click the field list, and then click Remove Table on the shortcut menu.

2. Double-click **tblEmployee** to add the tblEmployee field list to the Query window.
3. Double-click **tblEmployee** again to add a second copy of the tblEmployee field list to the Query window, and then close the Show Table dialog box. The left field list is identified as tblEmployee, and the right field list is identified as tblEmployee_1 to distinguish the two copies of the table.

   You will now create a join between the two copies of the tblEmployee field list by linking the EmployeeID field in the tblEmployee field list to the SupervisorID field in the tblEmployee_1 field list. The SupervisorID field is a foreign key that matches the primary key field, EmployeeID.
4. In the tblEmployee field list, click the **EmployeeID** field, and then drag it to the **SupervisorID** field in the tblEmployee_1 field list. A join line is created between the two fields. You can verify that this is an inner join query by opening the Join Properties dialog box.
5. Right-click the join line between the two field lists, and then click **Join Properties** on the shortcut menu to open the Join Properties dialog box. See Figure 9–23.

Figure 9–23 **Join Properties dialog box**

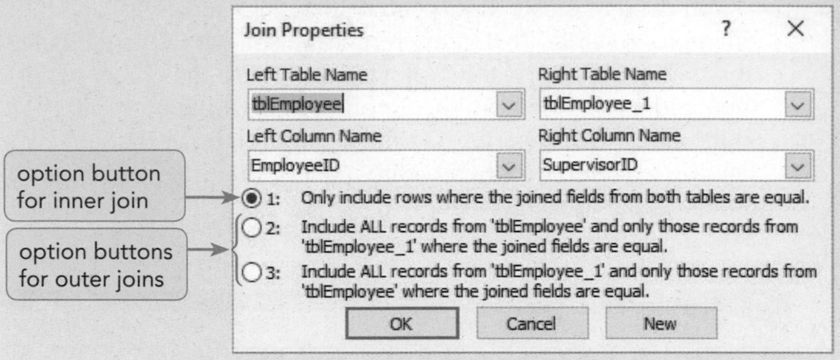
Join Properties
Left Table Name
tblEmployee
Right Table Name
tblEmployee_1
Left Column Name
EmployeeID
Right Column Name
SupervisorID
option button for inner join
option buttons for outer joins
1: Only include rows where the joined fields from both tables are equal.
2: Include ALL records from 'tblEmployee' and only those records from 'tblEmployee_1' where the joined fields are equal.
3: Include ALL records from 'tblEmployee_1' and only those records from 'tblEmployee' where the joined fields are equal.
OK
Cancel
New

The first option button is selected, indicating that this is an inner join. Because the inner join is correct, you can close the dialog box and then add the necessary fields in the design grid.

Your query will use each employee's SupervisorID value to retrieve data associated with the supervisor's corresponding EmployeeID value. To accomplish this, you choose the employee-related records from the tblEmployee_1 field list, which is connected to the other field list using the SupervisorID field.

6. Click the **Cancel** button, and then from the tblEmployee_1 field list, add the **EmployeeID**, **FirstName**, **LastName**, and **Position** fields to the design grid.
7. From the tblEmployee field list, add the **FirstName** and **LastName** fields to the design grid.

   The tblEmployee field list is connected to the other field list using the EmployeeID field, so the FirstName and LastName fields will display the first and last names of the supervisor for each record in the tblEmployee_1 field list.
8. Run the query. The query recordset displays six fields and 13 records. See Figure 9–24.

Figure 9–24 **Initial self-join on the tblEmployee table**

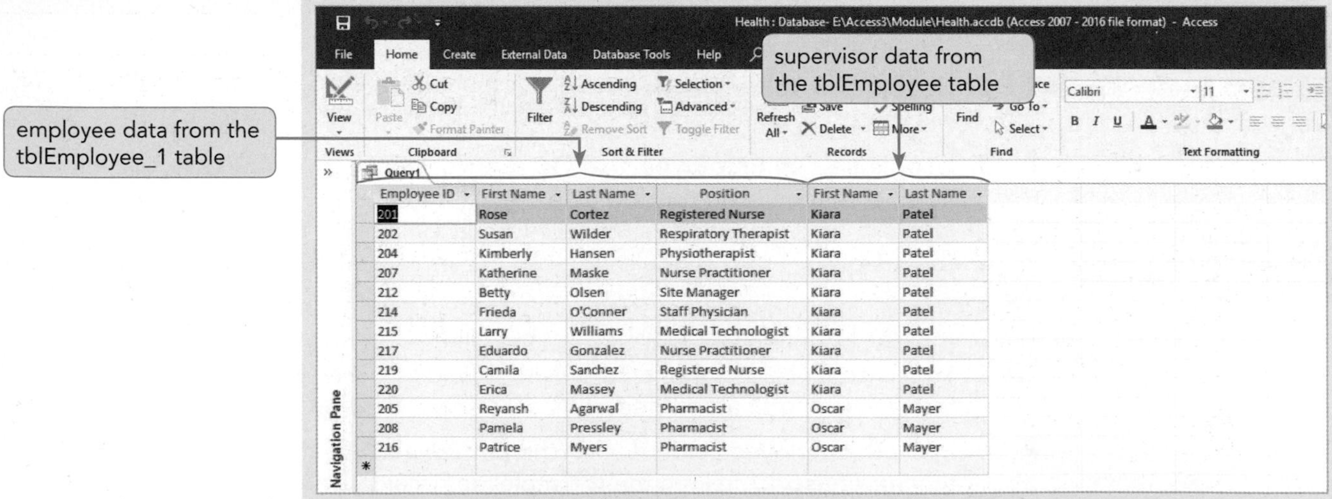
Health : Database- E:\Access3\Module\Health.accdb (Access 2007 - 2016 file format) - Access
supervisor data from the tblEmployee table
employee data from the tblEmployee_1 table
Query1
Employee ID | First Name | Last Name | Position | First Name | Last Name
201 | Rose | Cortez | Registered Nurse | Kiara | Patel
202 | Susan | Wilder | Respiratory Therapist | Kiara | Patel
204 | Kimberly | Hansen | Physiotherapist | Kiara | Patel
207 | Katherine | Maske | Nurse Practitioner | Kiara | Patel
212 | Betty | Olsen | Site Manager | Kiara | Patel
214 | Frieda | O'Conner | Staff Physician | Kiara | Patel
215 | Larry | Williams | Medical Technologist | Kiara | Patel
217 | Eduardo | Gonzalez | Nurse Practitioner | Kiara | Patel
219 | Camila | Sanchez | Registered Nurse | Kiara | Patel
220 | Erica | Massey | Medical Technologist | Kiara | Patel
205 | Reyansh | Agarwal | Pharmacist | Oscar | Mayer
208 | Pamela | Pressley | Pharmacist | Oscar | Mayer
216 | Patrice | Myers | Pharmacist | Oscar | Mayer
Navigation Pane

The query recordset displays all employees and their supervisors with the exception of the records for Kiara Patel and Oscar Mayer because their records contain null SupervisorID field values. (They are supervisors of the other employees and do not have assigned supervisors.) Remember that an inner join doesn't display records from the second table unless it contains a matching value in the common field. In the tblEmployee_1 table, the SupervisorID field values for Kiara Patel and Oscar Mayer are null, so the inner join doesn't select their records in the tblEmployee table.

Trouble? If your query results do not match Figure 9–24, switch to Design view and review the preceding steps to make any necessary corrections to your query design. Then run the query again.

Two columns in the query recordset are titled "First Name," and two columns are titled "Last Name." Donna asks you to rename the two rightmost columns so that the contents of the query recordset will be more clear. After you set the Caption property for the two rightmost fields, the column names in the query recordset will be, from left to right, Employee ID, First Name, Last Name, Position, Supervisor First Name, and Supervisor Last Name. You'll also sort the query in ascending order by EmployeeID.

To set the Caption property for two query fields and sort the query:

1. Switch to Design view.
2. Click the **Field** box for the fifth column.
3. On the Query Tools Design tab, in the Show/Hide group, click the **Property Sheet** button, and then set the Caption property to **Supervisor First Name**.
4. Click the **Field** box for the sixth column, and then set the Caption property to **Supervisor Last Name**.
5. Close the Property Sheet, click the right side of the EmployeeID Sort box to display the sort order options, and then click **Ascending**.
6. Save the query as **qryEmployeesSupervisors**, run the query, resize all columns to their best fit, and then click the first row's Employee ID field value to deselect all values. The query recordset displays the new captions for the fifth and sixth columns. See Figure 9–25.

Figure 9–25 Final self-join on the tblEmployee table

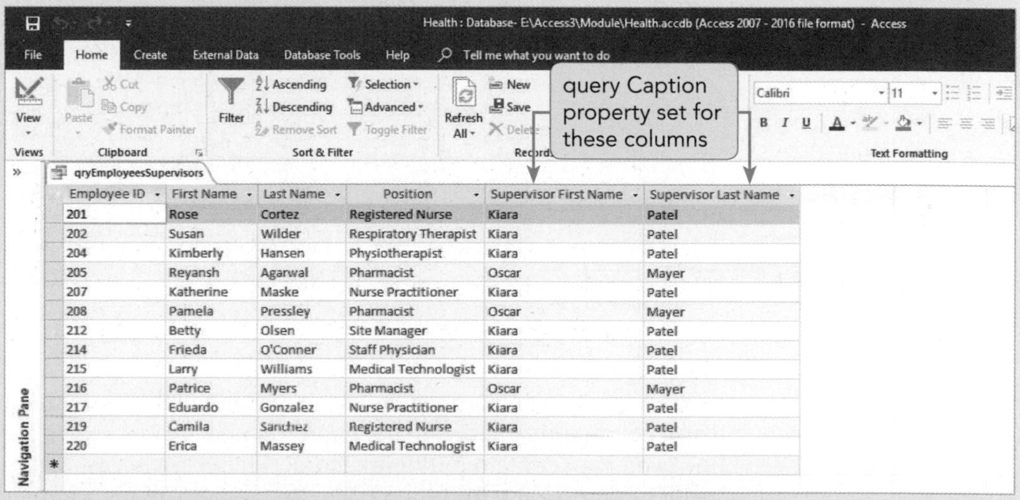
Health : Database- E:\Access3\Module\Health.accdb (Access 2007 - 2016 file format) - Access
query Caption property set for these columns
qryEmployeesSupervisors
Employee ID | First Name | Last Name | Position | Supervisor First Name | Supervisor Last Name
201 Rose Cortez Registered Nurse Kiara Patel
202 Susan Wilder Respiratory Therapist Kiara Patel
204 Kimberly Hansen Physiotherapist Kiara Patel
205 Reyansh Agarwal Pharmacist Oscar Mayer
207 Katherine Maske Nurse Practitioner Kiara Patel
208 Pamela Pressley Pharmacist Oscar Mayer
212 Betty Olsen Site Manager Kiara Patel
214 Frieda O'Conner Staff Physician Kiara Patel
215 Larry Williams Medical Technologist Kiara Patel
216 Patrice Myers Pharmacist Oscar Mayer
217 Eduardo Gonzalez Nurse Practitioner Kiara Patel
219 Camila Sanchez Registered Nurse Kiara Patel
220 Erica Massey Medical Technologist Kiara Patel
Navigation Pane

7. Save and close the query.

Donna wonders if her staff's work will take longer as the Health database grows with the addition of more table records. Specifically, she wants to know if queries will take longer to run. Using indexes will help make her queries run faster.

Using Indexes for Table Fields

Suppose you need to find all the pages in a book that discuss a specific topic. The fastest, most accurate way to perform your search is to look up the topic in the book's index. In a similar fashion, you can create indexes for fields in a table, so that Access can quickly locate all the records in a table that contain specific values for one or more fields. An **index** is a list that relates field values to the records that contain those field values.

In Access, an index is automatically created for a table's primary key. When you view a table in datasheet view, the records are always in primary key order, even though they may not have been entered in that order. This is due to the automatically created index for the primary key. For example, the tblBilling table in the Health database includes an index for the InvoiceNum field, which is the table's primary key. Conceptually, as shown in Figure 9–26, each record in the tblBilling table is identified by its record number, and the InvoiceNum index has two columns. The first column contains a record number in the tblBilling table, and the second column contains the InvoiceNum value for that record number. For instance, InvoiceNum 26503 in the index has a record number value of 3; and record number 3 in the tblBilling table contains the data for InvoiceNum 26503.

Figure 9–26 **tblBilling table with the index set for the InvoiceNum field**

Index Value (Record Number)	Invoice Num
1	26501
2	26502
3	26503
4	26504

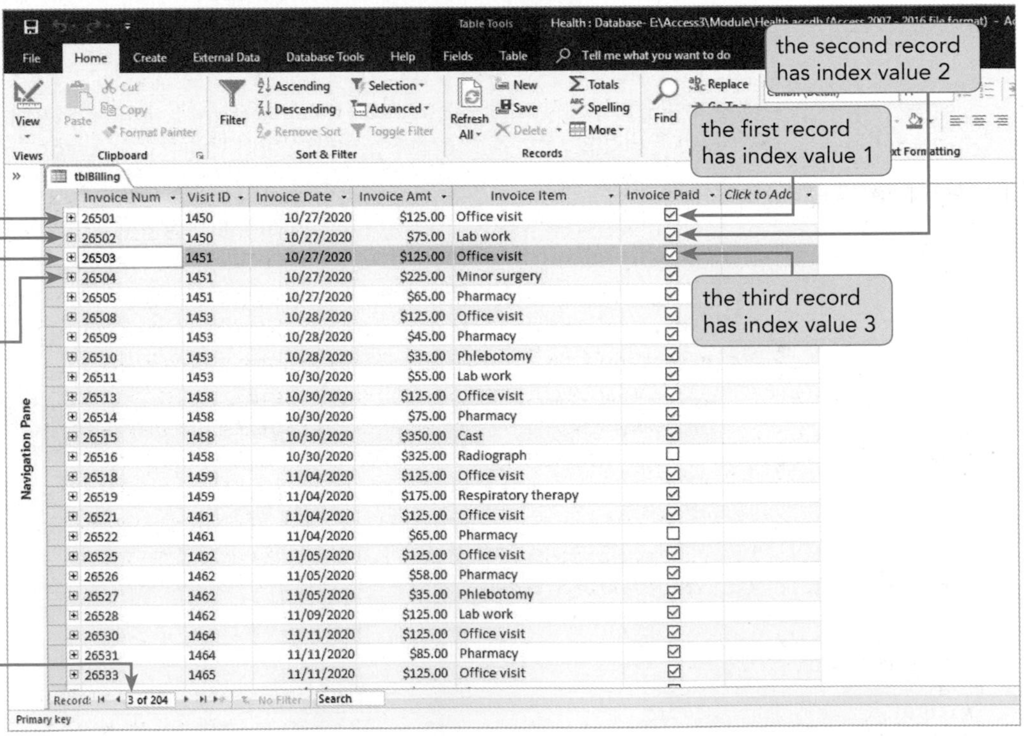
the second record has index value 2
the first record has index value 1
the third record has index value 3
the record number is the index number
tblBilling
Invoice Num
Visit ID
Invoice Date
Invoice Amt
Invoice Item
Invoice Paid
Click to Add
26501 1450 10/27/2020 $125.00 Office visit
26502 1450 10/27/2020 $75.00 Lab work
26503 1451 10/27/2020 $125.00 Office visit
26504 1451 10/27/2020 $225.00 Minor surgery
26505 1451 10/27/2020 $65.00 Pharmacy
26508 1453 10/28/2020 $125.00 Office visit
26509 1453 10/28/2020 $45.00 Pharmacy
26510 1453 10/28/2020 $35.00 Phlebotomy
26511 1453 10/30/2020 $55.00 Lab work
26513 1458 10/30/2020 $125.00 Office visit
26514 1458 10/30/2020 $75.00 Pharmacy
26515 1458 10/30/2020 $350.00 Cast
26516 1458 10/30/2020 $325.00 Radiograph
26518 1459 11/04/2020 $125.00 Office visit
26519 1459 11/04/2020 $175.00 Respiratory therapy
26521 1461 11/04/2020 $125.00 Office visit
26522 1461 11/04/2020 $65.00 Pharmacy
26525 1462 11/05/2020 $125.00 Office visit
26526 1462 11/05/2020 $58.00 Pharmacy
26527 1462 11/05/2020 $35.00 Phlebotomy
26528 1462 11/09/2020 $125.00 Lab work
26530 1464 11/11/2020 $125.00 Office visit
26531 1464 11/11/2020 $85.00 Pharmacy
26533 1465 11/11/2020 $125.00 Office visit
Record: 3 of 204
Primary key

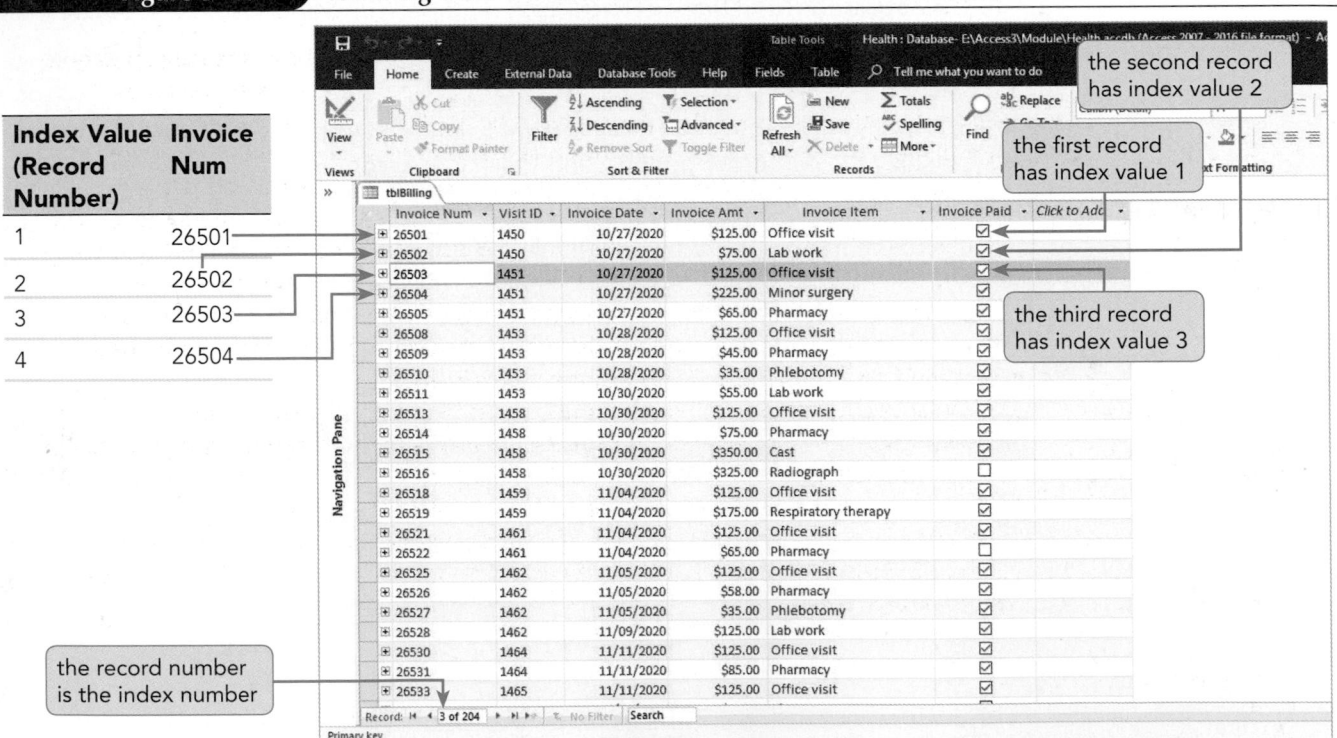

Because InvoiceNum values in the tblBilling table are unique, each row in the InvoiceNum index has a single record number. An index for a non-primary-key field, however, may contain multiple record numbers in a row. Figure 9–27 illustrates a VisitID index for the tblBilling table. Because VisitID is a foreign key in the tblBilling table (a visit can have many invoices), each VisitID entry in the index can be associated with many record numbers in the tblBilling table. For instance, VisitID 1450 in the index has record number values of 1 and 2, and record numbers 3, 4, and 5 in the tblBilling table contain the invoice data for VisitID 1451.

Figure 9–27 tblBilling table with index for the VisitID field

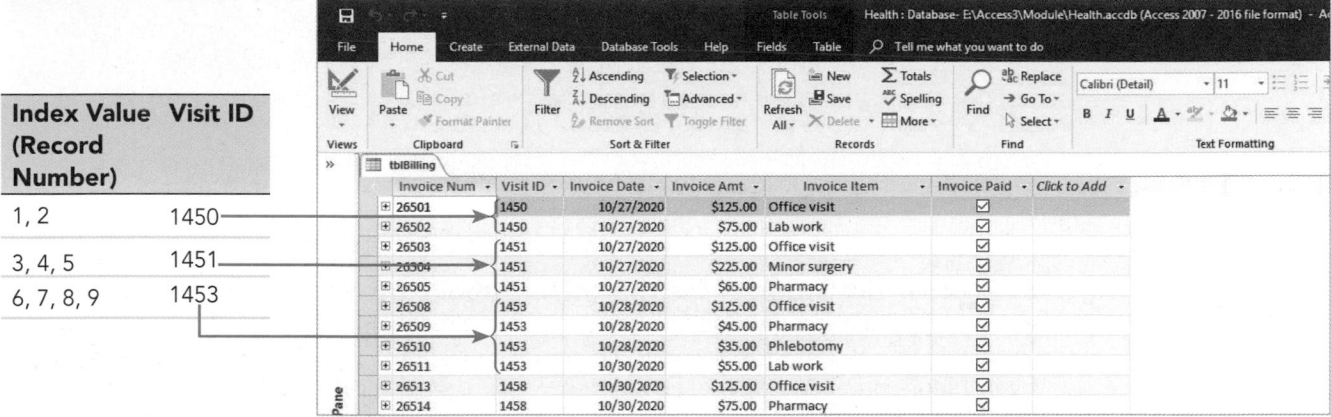

Index Value (Record Number)	Visit ID
1, 2	1450
3, 4, 5	1451
6, 7, 8, 9	1453

Table Tools
Health : Database- E:\Access3\Module\Health.accdb (Access 2007 - 2016 file format)
File
Home
Create
External Data
Database Tools
Help
Fields
Table
Tell me what you want to do
View
Paste
Cut
Copy
Format Painter
Filter
Ascending
Descending
Remove Sort
Selection
Advanced
Toggle Filter
Refresh All
New
Save
Delete
Totals
Spelling
More
Find
Replace
Go To
Select
Calibri (Detail)
11
Views
Clipboard
Sort & Filter
Records
Find
Text Formatting
tblBilling
Invoice Num | Visit ID | Invoice Date | Invoice Amt | Invoice Item | Invoice Paid | Click to Add
26501 | 1450 | 10/27/2020 | $125.00 | Office visit
26502 | 1450 | 10/27/2020 | $75.00 | Lab work
26503 | 1451 | 10/27/2020 | $125.00 | Office visit
26504 | 1451 | 10/27/2020 | $225.00 | Minor surgery
26505 | 1451 | 10/27/2020 | $65.00 | Pharmacy
26508 | 1453 | 10/28/2020 | $125.00 | Office visit
26509 | 1453 | 10/28/2020 | $45.00 | Pharmacy
26510 | 1453 | 10/28/2020 | $35.00 | Phlebotomy
26511 | 1453 | 10/30/2020 | $55.00 | Lab work
26513 | 1458 | 10/30/2020 | $125.00 | Office visit
26514 | 1458 | 10/30/2020 | $75.00 | Pharmacy
Pane

If you were to create an index for the VisitID field in the tblBilling table, queries that use VisitID as a sort field or as a selection criterion would run faster.

INSIGHT

Benefits and Limitations of Indexes

With small tables, the increased speed associated with indexes is not readily apparent. In practice, tables with hundreds of thousands or millions of records are common. In such cases, the increase in speed is dramatic. In fact, without indexes, many database operations in large tables would not be practical because they would take too long to complete. Why the speed difference in these cases? Sorting or selecting records from a large table without an index requires numerous accesses to storage media to retrieve table records because the entire table can't fit in computer memory. In contrast, indexes are usually small enough to fit completely in computer memory, and records can be sorted and selected based on indexes with minimal need to access storage media. Because accessing storage media is generally slower than performing operations in computer memory, using indexes in large tables is faster.

The speed advantage of using an index must be weighed against two disadvantages: The index adds storage requirements to the database, and it takes time to update the index as you add and delete records. Except for primary key indexes, you can add and delete indexes at any time. Thus, you can add an index if you think searching and querying would be faster as the number of records in the database increases. You can also delete an existing index if you later deem it to be unnecessary.

You can view the existing indexes for a table by opening the table in Design view.

REFERENCE

View a Table's Indexes

- Open the table in Design view.
- To view an index for a single field, click the field, and then view the Indexed property in the Field Properties pane.
- To view all the indexes for a table or to view an index consisting of multiple fields, click the Indexes button in the Show/Hide group on the Table Tools Design tab.

You'll view the indexes for the tblTreatment table.

To view the indexes for the tblTreatment table:

1. Open the Navigation Pane, and then open the **tblTreatment** table in Design view.
2. On the Table Tools Design tab, in the Show/Hide group, click the **Indexes** button to open the Indexes: tblTreatment dialog box. Click **PrimaryKey** in the Index Name column, and then drag the dialog box to the position shown in Figure 9–28.

Figure 9–28 Indexes for the tblTreatment table

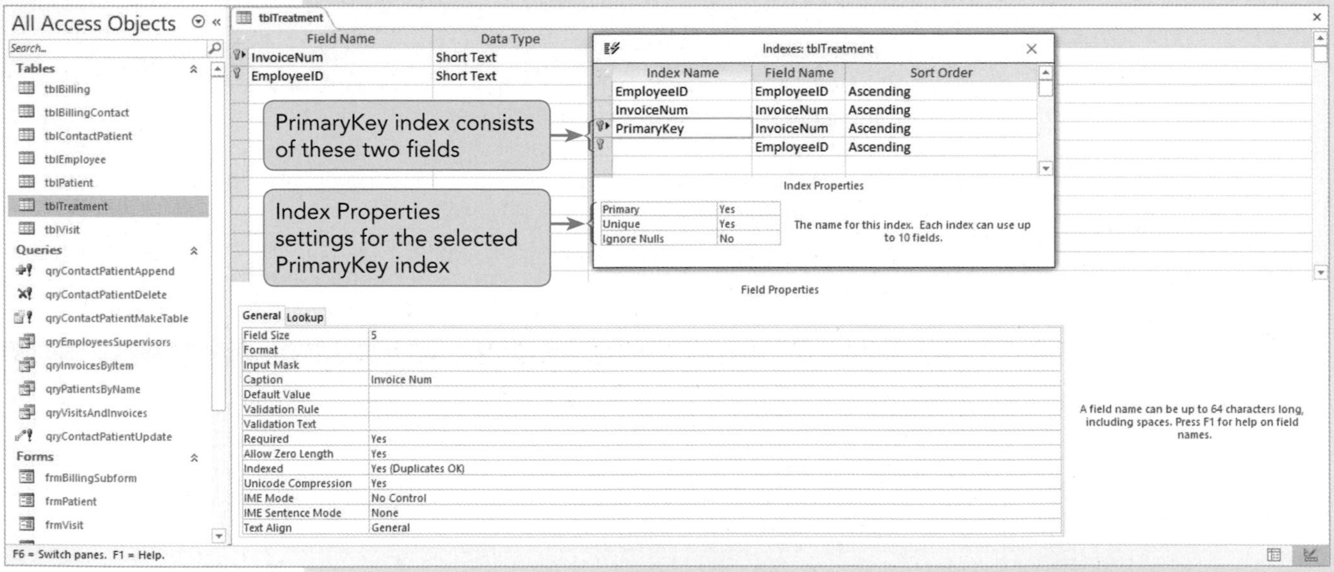
PrimaryKey index consists of these two fields
Index Properties settings for the selected PrimaryKey index
Indexes: tblTreatment
Index Name
Field Name
Sort Order
EmployeeID
EmployeeID
Ascending
InvoiceNum
InvoiceNum
Ascending
PrimaryKey
InvoiceNum
Ascending
EmployeeID
Ascending
Index Properties
Primary
Yes
Unique
Yes
Ignore Nulls
No
The name for this index. Each index can use up to 10 fields.

In the Indexes: tblTreatment dialog box, the properties in the Index Properties section apply to the selected PrimaryKey index, which consists of the table's composite key of the InvoiceNum and EmployeeID fields. Because EmployeeID in the fourth row of the dialog box does not have an Index Name property value, both InvoiceNum and EmployeeID make up the PrimaryKey index. The PrimaryKey index was generated automatically when the table was created, and the InvoiceNum and EmployeeID fields were designated as the table's composite key. The properties for the PrimaryKey index indicate that this index is the primary key index (Primary property setting of Yes) and that values in this index must be unique (Unique property setting of Yes)—that is, each InvoiceNum and EmployeeID pair of field values must be unique. The Ignore Nulls property setting of No means that records with null values for the InvoiceNum field or EmployeeID field are included in the index, but this setting is ignored because the Yes setting for the Primary property doesn't allow either field to have a null value.

3. Close the Indexes: tblTreatment dialog box, and then close the table.

INSIGHT

Default Automatic Indexes

In addition to the automatically created primary key index, an index is also automatically created for any field name that contains the following letter sequences: "code", "ID", "key", or "num". You can add, change, and delete from this list of letter sequences to manage the automatic indexes created in a database. To do so, click the File tab to open Backstage view, click Options in the navigation bar to open the Access Options dialog box, and then click Object Designers in the left pane. In the Table design view section, the AutoIndex on Import/Create box displays, by default, ID;key;code;num. Modify the entries in the AutoIndex on Import/Create box if you want a different list of letter sequences to be used in automatically created indexes for the fields in your tables.

Over the past few weeks, Donna's staff has been monitoring the performance of the Health database by timing how long it takes to run queries. She wants her staff to let her know if the performance changes over the next several days as a result of creating an index for the City field in the tblPatient table. Many queries use the City field as a sort field or selection criterion, and adding an index might speed up those queries.

Creating an Index

You can create an index for a single field using the Indexes dialog box or by setting the Indexed property for the field in Design view. However, for a multiple-field index, you must create the index in the Indexes dialog box.

REFERENCE

Creating an Index

- Open the table in Design view.
- To create an index for a single field, click the field, and then set the Indexed property in the Field Properties pane.
- To create an index consisting of multiple fields, click the Indexes button located on the Table Tools Design tab in the Show/Hide group to open the Indexes dialog box.
- Enter a name for the index in the first Index Name box, and select the first field in the Field Name box.
- In the second Index Name box, leave the name blank, and select the second field in the Field Name box.
- Set additional field names in each row as needed, leaving the Index Name box blank for each row except the first one, set other properties as necessary for the index, and then close the Indexes dialog box.

Next, you'll create an index for the City field in the tblPatient table by setting the field's Indexed property.

To create an index for the City field in the tblPatient table:

1. Open the **tblPatient** table in Design view, and then close the Navigation Pane.
2. On the Table Tools Design tab, in the Show/Hide group, click the Indexes button to open the Indexes: tblPatient dialog box, and then position the dialog box as shown in Figure 9–29.

Figure 9–29 Indexes list for the tblPatient table

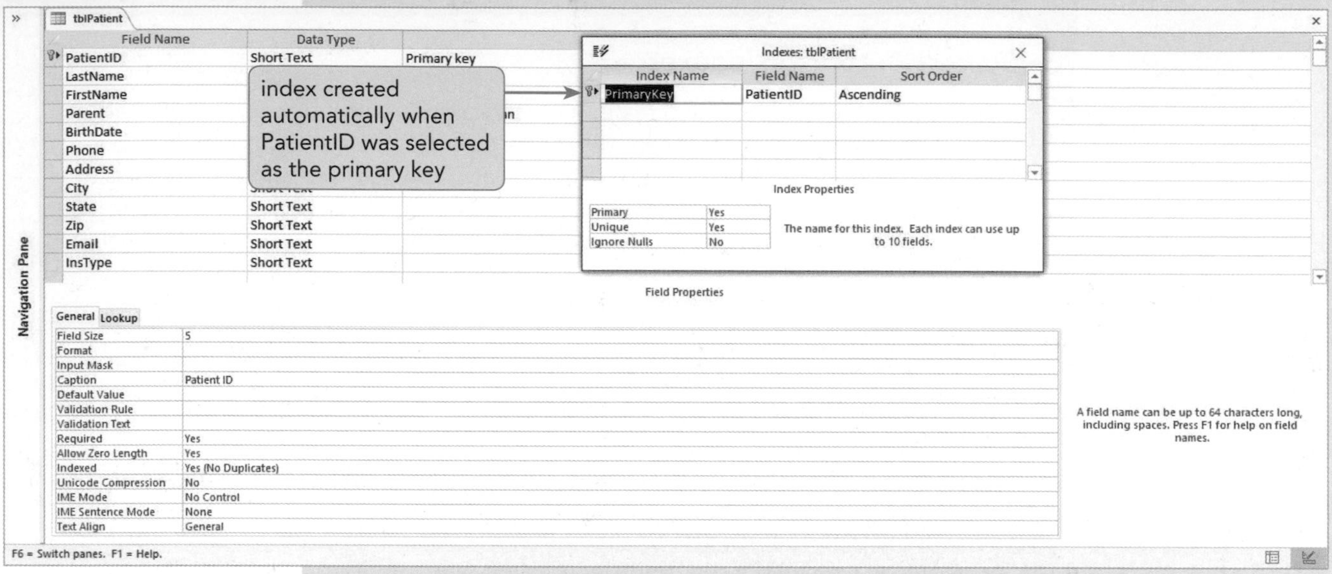
index created automatically when PatientID was selected as the primary key
Indexes: tblPatient
Index Name
Field Name
Sort Order
PrimaryKey
PatientID
Ascending
Index Properties
The name for this index. Each index can use up to 10 fields.
Field Properties
A field name can be up to 64 characters long, including spaces. Press F1 for help on field names.
F6 = Switch panes. F1 = Help.

An index was created for the PatientID field because it is the primary key. The PatientID index would have been created even if the field wasn't the primary key because the field name has an ID suffix. No other indexes exist for the tblPatient table. You'll create an index for the City field that allows duplicates because the same City field value can appear in many records in the tblPatient table.

3. Click **City** in the Field Name column to make it the current field.

   The Indexed property in the Field Properties pane for the City field is currently set to No, indicating there is not an index on the City field.

4. Click the right side of the **Indexed** box in the Field Properties pane, and then click **Yes (Duplicates OK)**. An index for the City field is created with duplicate values allowed. Setting the Indexed property automatically created the City index in the Indexes: tblPatient dialog box. See Figure 9–30.

Figure 9–30 City index added to the tblPatient table

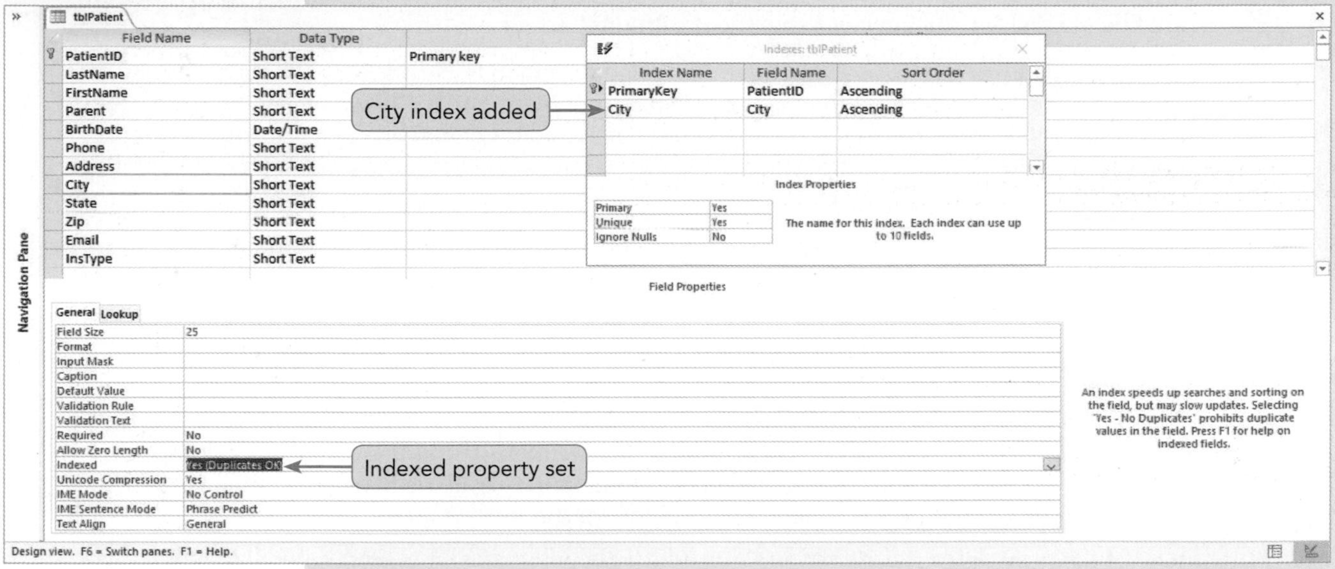
tblPatient
City index added
Indexes: tblPatient
Index Name
Field Name
Sort Order
PrimaryKey
PatientID
Ascending
City
City
Ascending
Indexed property set
Yes (Duplicates OK)
Design view. F6 = Switch panes. F1 = Help.

5. Close the dialog box, save your table design changes, and then switch to Datasheet view.
6. Change the first record in the table so the Last Name and First Name columns contain your last and first names, respectively.
7. sam Close the table, make a backup copy of the Health database, compact and repair the database, and then close it.

The work you completed with table relationships, table and query joins, and indexes will make it much easier for Donna and her staff to enter, retrieve, and view information in the Health database.

REVIEW

Session 9.2 Quick Check

1. What are the three types of relationships you can define between tables?
2. What is an entity subtype?
3. What is the difference between an inner join and an outer join?
4. Describe the results of two different outer joins that you could create between a members table and a classes table in a database for a fitness club.
5. What is a self-join?
6. What is an index?
7. In Access, an index is generated automatically for a table's ___ key.

PRACTICE

Review Assignments

Data File needed for the Review Assignments: Product.accdb

The Product database contains data about Lakewood Community Health Services suppliers and their products, as well as data about the invoices from the suppliers and the payments made by Lakewood Community Health Services to the suppliers. The database also contains queries, forms, and reports. Donna wants you to define relationships between the tables and to create some new queries for her. Complete the following steps:

1. Open the **Product** database located in the Access3 > Review folder provided with your Data Files, and then click the Enable Content button next to the security warning, if necessary.
2. Modify the first record in the tblSupplier table datasheet so the Contact First Name and Contact Last Name columns contain your first and last names, and the Company Comments field contains your city and state. Close the table.
3. Define a many-to-many relationship between the tblInvoice and tblPayment tables, using the tblInvoicePayment table as the relationship table. Define a one-to-one relationship between the primary tblSupplier table and the related tblSupplierCreditLine table. Select the referential integrity option and the cascade updates option for the relationships.
4. Create a make-table query based on the tblProduct table, selecting the ProductID, SupplierID, ProductName, Price, TempControl, and Sterile fields, and selecting only those records for products that require a temperature-controlled environment. Use **tblProductSpecialEnviron** as the new table name, store the table in the current database, and then run the query. Save this query as **qryMakeSpecialEnviron** and close the query.
5. Open the tblProductSpecialEnviron table, and then adjust the column widths to their best fit. Format the TempControlled and Sterile fields to Yes/No. (*Hint*: In Design View, select the field name, and then select the Format property to Yes/No.) Save and close the tblProductSpecialEnviron table.
6. Create an append query based on the tblProduct table, selecting the ProductID, SupplierID, ProductName, Price, TempControl, and Sterile fields, and selecting only those records for products that are sterile and do not require a temperature-controlled environment. Append the records to the tblProductSpecialEnviron table, run the query, save it as **qryAppendSterile**, and then close the query. Open the tblProductSpecialEnviron table, and then verify that the records have been added. Close the table.
7. Create a delete query that deletes all records in the tblProductSpecialEnviron table in which the Price is less than $20.00. Run the query, save it as **qryDeletePriceLess20**, and then close the query. Open the tblProductSpecialEnviron table, verify that the table now contains 30 records, and then close the table.
8. Create a query using a self-join that selects all products in the tblProduct table that are included in another product. To do so, add two copies of the tblProduct field list to the query design window, and then create a relationship between the ProductID field in the first list and the IncludedIn field in the second list. The query results should display the ProductID and ProductName fields for the included items. (*Hint*: These should come from the second field list.) The query should also assign the captions **Collection Product ID** and **Collection Product Name** as appropriate to the fields. In Design view, sort the records in ascending order by the Collection Product ID column. Resize all columns in the datasheet to best fit, save the query as **qryProductCollection**, and then close the query
9. Open the tblProductSpecialEnviron table in Design view, specify the primary key, add an index that allows duplicates for the SupplierID field, and then save and close the table.
10. Make a backup copy of the database, compact and repair the database, and then close it.

APPLY

Case Problem 1

Data File needed for this Case Problem: Instruction.accdb

Great Giraffe Jeremiah Garver is the operations manager at Great Giraffe, a career school in Denver, Colorado. Great Giraffe offers part-time and full-time courses in areas of study that are in high demand by industries in the area, including data science, digital marketing, and bookkeeping. Jeremiah created the Instruction database to track and view information about the students, faculty, and courses his business offers. The database also contains queries, forms, and reports. Jeremiah wants you to define relationships between the tables and to create some new queries for him. Complete the following steps:

1. Open the **Instruction** database located in the Access3 > Case1 folder provided with your Data Files, and then click the Enable Content button next to the security warning, if necessary.
2. Modify the first record in the tblFaculty table datasheet so the First Name and Last Name columns contain your first and last names. Close the table.
3. Define a many-to-many relationship between the tblCourse and tblFaculty tables, using the tblTeaching table as the relationship table. Define a one-to-one relationship between the primary tblStudent table and the related tblScholarship table. Select the referential integrity option and the cascade updates option for the relationships.
4. Create a make-table query based on the qryAllPaymentPlanStudents query, selecting all fields from the query and only those records where the City field value is **Denver**. Use **tblCityPaymentPlan** as the new table name, store the table in the current database, and then run the query. Save the query as **qryMakeCityPaymentPlan**, and close the query. Open the tblCityPaymentPlan table and verify the City value is Denver for all records. Close the tblCityPaymentPlan table.
5. Create an append query based on the qryAllPaymentPlanStudents query that selects all fields for only those records where the City field value is **Littleton**. Append the records to the tblCityPaymentPlan table and run the query. Save the query as **qryAppendLittleton**, and then close the query. Open the tblCityPaymentPlan table and verify that the City column includes values of both Denver and Littleton. Close the tblCityPaymentPlan table.
6. Create an update query to select all records in the tblCityPaymentPlan table where the value in the City field value is **Littleton**, and set the remaining balance to 0. Run the query, save it as **qryUpdateLittletonToZero**, and then close the query. Open the tblCityPaymentPlan table and verify balances for the Littleton students have been reduced to $0. Close the tblCityPaymentPlan table.
7. Create a delete query that deletes all records in the tblCityPaymentPlan table in which the BalanceDue field value is greater **$1500**. Run the query, save it as **qryDeleteMoreThan1500**, and then close the query. Open the tblCityPaymentPlan table, resize all columns to their best fit, and then verify there are no records whose BalanceDue field is greater than $1500. Save your layout changes, and then close the tblCityPaymentPlan table.
8. Create a query using a self-join that lists all faculty that have supervisors. To do so, add two copies of the tblFaculty field list to the query design window, and then create a relationship between the FacultyID field in the first list and the SupervisorID field in the second list. The query results should display the FacultyID, FacultyFirst, and FacultyLast fields. (*Hint*: These should come from the second field list.) The query should also assign the captions **Faculty ID**, **Faculty First Name**, and **Faculty Last Name**, respectively, to these fields. The query results should also include the following fields for the supervisor of each faculty member: FacultyFirst, FacultyLast, and Position. (*Hint*: These should come from the first field list.) The query should also assign the captions **Supervisor First Name**, **Supervisor Last Name**, and **Supervisor Position**, respectively, to these fields. Sort the records in ascending order by the Faculty ID column. Resize all columns in the datasheet to best fit, save the query as **qryFacultySupervisors**, and then close the query.
9. Open the tblCityPaymentPlan table in Design view, add an index that allows duplicates for the City field, and then save and close the table.
10. Make a backup copy of the database, compact and repair the database, and then close it.

CHALLENGE

Case Problem 2

Data File needed for this Case Problem: CleanOut.accdb

Drain Adopter Tandrea Austin manages the Drain Adopter program for the Department of Water and Power in Bellingham, Washington. The program recruits volunteers to regularly monitor and clear storm drains near their homes to ensure the drains are clear and unobstructed when large rainstorms are predicted. Tandrea created the CleanUp database to track, maintain, and analyze data about the drains and volunteers in the Drain Adopter program. Tandrea asks you to define table relationships and create some new queries for her. Complete the following steps:

1. Open the **CleanOut** database located in the Access3 > Case2 folder provided with your Data Files, and then click the Enable Content button next to the security warning, if necessary.
2. Change the first record in the tblEmployee table datasheet so the First Name and Last Name columns contain your first and last names. Close the table.
3. Define a many-to-many relationship between the tblDrain and tblEmployee tables, using the tblSpotCheck table as the related table. Define a one-to-one relationship between the primary tblVolunteer table and the related tblAlternateVolunteer table. Select the referential integrity option and the cascade updates option for the relationships.
4. Create a make-table query based on the qryFirstVolunteers query, selecting all fields from the query and only those records where the Trained field value is **Yes**. Use **tblSpecialVolunteers** as the new table name, store the table in the current database, and then run the query. Save the query as **qryMakeSpecialVolunteers**, and close the query. Open the tblSpecialVolunteers table, and verify the records are all from the first three months of 2021 and the value for the Trained field is Yes (-1) for all records. Close the tblSpecialVolunteers table.

Explore 5. Create an append query based on the tblVolunteer table that selects the VolunteerID, FirstName, Zip, Email, SignupDate, and Trained fields for only those records where the value of the SignupDate field is between April 1, 2021 and May 31, 2021. Append the records to the tblSpecialVolunteers table and run the query. (*Note*: You are pulling data from one table and appending it to another table.) Save the query as **qryAppendAprilMay**, and then close the query. Open the tblSpecialVolunteers table and verify that the SignupDate column now contains only dates for the first five months of 2021. Close the tblSpecialVolunteers table.

6. Create an update query to select all records in the tblSpecialVolunteers table where the value of the Trained field is **No** and update it to **Yes**. Run the query, save it as **qryUpdateTrained**, and then close the query.

Explore 7. Open the tblSpecialVolunteers table and change the format of the Trained field to a Yes/No display format. Verify the Trained field for all records is now set to Yes. Resize all columns to their best fit, and then close and save the tblSpecialVolunteers table.

8. Create a delete query that deletes all records in the tblSpecialVolunteers table in which the SignupDate field is between March 1, 2021 and May 31, 2021. Run the query, save it as **qryDeleteMarchAprilMay**, and then close the query. Open the tblSpecialVolunteers table, resize all columns to their best fit (if necessary), and then verify that all records have SignupDate field value in either January 2021 or February 2021. Save your layout changes, and then close the tblSpecialVolunteers table.

Explore 9. Create a select query with an outer join between the tblVolunteer and tblAlternateVolunteer tables, selecting all records from the tblVolunteer table and any matching records from the tblAlternateVolunteer table. Display the VolunteerID, FirstName and LastName fields from the tblVolunteer table and the AltFirstName and AltLastName fields from the tblAlternateVolunteer table. (*Hint*: You will need to modify the Join Properties for the relationship between the tblVolunteer and tblAlternateVolunteer tables.) Save the query as **qryVolunteerAltOuterJoin**, and then run and close the query. Your output of the query should consist of all records from the tblVolunteer table, and only those records from the tblAlternateVolunteer table that have a match in the tblVolunteer table.

10. Make a backup copy of the database, compact and repair the database, and then close it.

MODULE **10**

Automating Tasks with Macros

Creating a User Interface for the Health Database

OBJECTIVES

Session 10.1

- View macros in the Macro Designer
- Run and add actions to macros
- Single step a macro
- Create a submacro
- Add a command button to a form
- Attach a submacro to a command button

Session 10.2

- Create an unbound form
- Add a list box control to a form
- Use a SQL statement to fill a list box control with object names
- Create multiple macros for a form
- Create a navigation form

Case | *Lakewood Community Health Services*

Donna Taylor recently hired new staff at Lakewood Community Health Services. The new staff members have limited experience working with databases, so Donna consults with Mista Kristiansen, the database developer for the clinic, about providing training to the new staff. In addition, Mista suggests implementing some advanced Access features to automate and control how users interact with the Health database. One of these features helps to create a custom user interface that will make it easier for inexperienced users to access the database and minimize the chance that an unauthorized user could change the design of any database object.

To meet the needs of the less experienced users, she would like the interface to display specific forms and reports and all the queries in the database, so that users can select objects they want to work with from the interface. For more advanced users, Mista would like a form with buttons users can click to perform common tasks. In this module, you will automate tasks in the Health database by creating and editing macros. You will also modify the user interface for the database by creating buttons that are linked to macros and by creating a navigation form.

STARTING DATA FILES

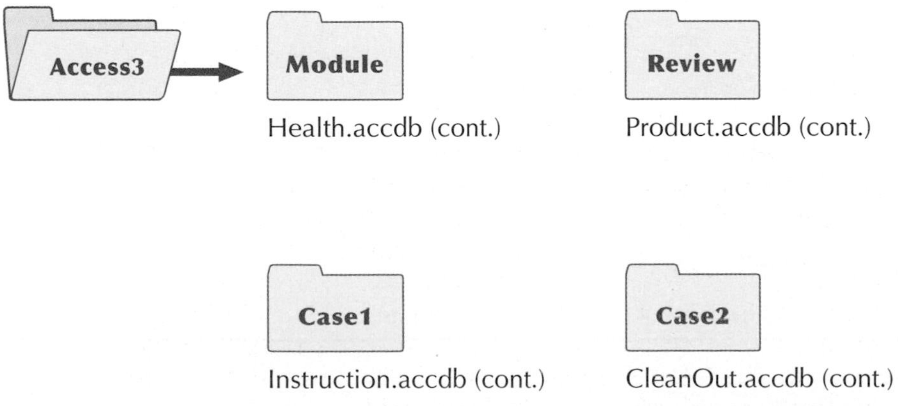
Access3
Module
Health.accdb (cont.)
Review
Product.accdb (cont.)
Case1
Instruction.accdb (cont.)
Case2
CleanOut.accdb (cont.)

Session 10.1 Visual Overview:

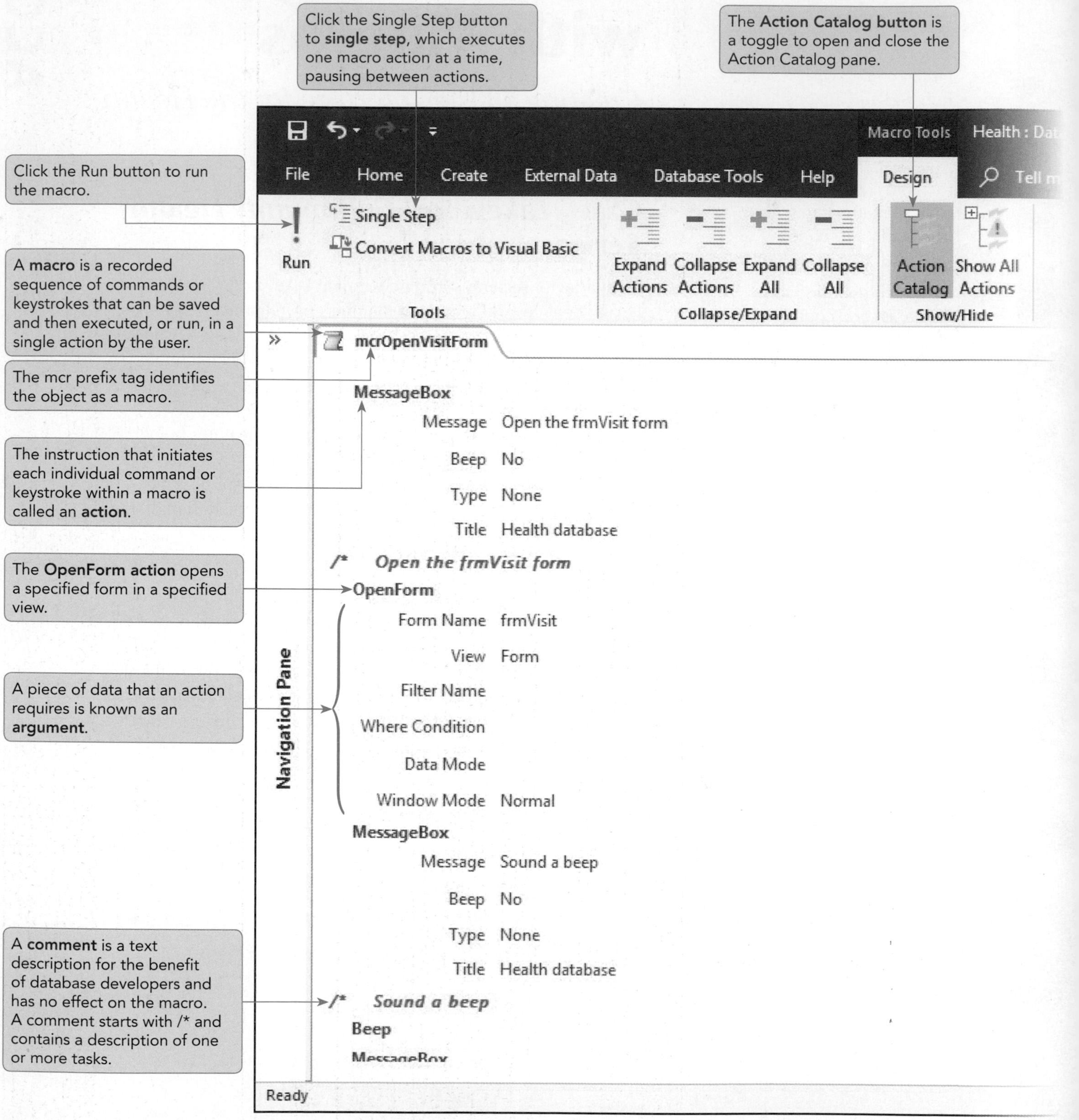
Click the Single Step button to **single step**, which executes one macro action at a time, pausing between actions.
The **Action Catalog button** is a toggle to open and close the Action Catalog pane.
Click the Run button to run the macro.
A **macro** is a recorded sequence of commands or keystrokes that can be saved and then executed, or run, in a single action by the user.
The mcr prefix tag identifies the object as a macro.
The instruction that initiates each individual command or keystroke within a macro is called an **action**.
The **OpenForm action** opens a specified form in a specified view.
A piece of data that an action requires is known as an **argument**.
A **comment** is a text description for the benefit of database developers and has no effect on the macro. A comment starts with /* and contains a description of one or more tasks.
Macro Tools
File
Home
Create
External Data
Database Tools
Help
Design
Run
Single Step
Convert Macros to Visual Basic
Tools
Expand Actions
Collapse Actions
Expand All
Collapse All
Collapse/Expand
Action Catalog
Show All Actions
Show/Hide
mcrOpenVisitForm
MessageBox
Message Open the frmVisit form
Beep No
Type None
Title Health database
/* Open the frmVisit form
OpenForm
Form Name frmVisit
View Form
Filter Name
Where Condition
Data Mode
Window Mode Normal
MessageBox
Message Sound a beep
Beep No
Type None
Title Health database
/* Sound a beep
Beep
Navigation Pane
Ready

The Macro Designer Window

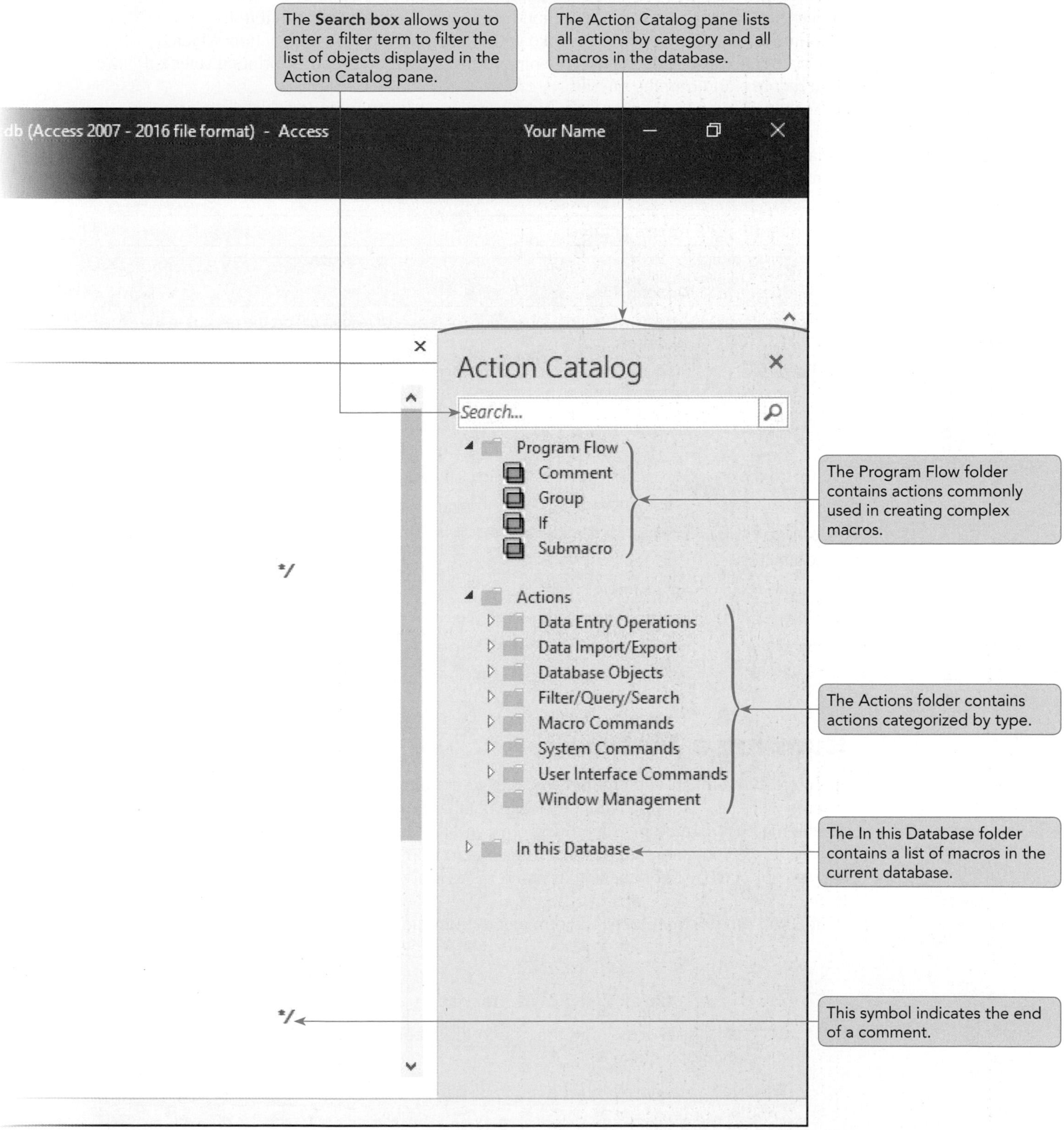
The **Search box** allows you to enter a filter term to filter the list of objects displayed in the Action Catalog pane.
The Action Catalog pane lists all actions by category and all macros in the database.
db (Access 2007 - 2016 file format) - Access
Your Name
Action Catalog
Search...
Program Flow
Comment
Group
If
Submacro
Actions
Data Entry Operations
Data Import/Export
Database Objects
Filter/Query/Search
Macro Commands
System Commands
User Interface Commands
Window Management
In this Database
*/
*/
The Program Flow folder contains actions commonly used in creating complex macros.
The Actions folder contains actions categorized by type.
The In this Database folder contains a list of macros in the current database.
This symbol indicates the end of a comment.

Introduction to Macros

Mista plans to automate some tasks in the Health database, initially by using macros. A **macro** is a recorded sequence of commands or keystrokes that can be saved and then executed, or run, in a single action by the user. The instruction that initiates each individual command or keystroke within the macro is called an action. Macros automate repetitive tasks, such as opening forms, tables, and reports; printing selected form records; and running queries.

Access provides more than 80 common actions you can include in database macros. Each of these actions has a designated name you reference to include its instruction in a macro. Figure 10–1 lists the names and corresponding instructions for Access actions commonly used in macro development.

Figure 10–1 **Frequently used Access actions**

Action	Description
ApplyFilter	Applies a filter to a table, form, or report to restrict or sort the records in the recordset
Beep	Produces a beep tone through the computer's speakers
CloseWindow	Closes the specified window, or the active window if none is specified
FindRecord	Finds the first record (or the next record, if the action is used again) that meets the specified criteria
GoToControl	Moves the focus to a specified field or control on the active datasheet or form
MessageBox	Displays a message box containing a warning or informational message
OpenForm	Opens a form in the specified view
QuitAccess	Exits Microsoft Access
RunMacro	Runs a macro
SelectObject	Selects a specified object so you can run an action that applies to the object
SendKeys	Sends keystrokes to Microsoft Access or another active program

Running a Macro

Mista created a macro with multiple actions to demonstrate to Donna how using macros will make working with the Health database easier for the newer staff members. Mista's macro is named mcrOpenVisitForm, and it performs multiple actions using the frmVisit form. You can reference and run a macro from within a form or report, or you can run a macro by right-clicking its name in the Macros section of the Navigation Pane.

You will run the mcrOpenVisitForm macro from the Navigation Pane.

To run the mcrOpenVisitForm macro:

1. sam Start Access, and then open the **Health** database you worked with in the previous module.

   Trouble? If the security warning is displayed below the ribbon, click the Enable Content button.

2. Make sure the Navigation Pane is open, scroll down the Navigation Pane (if necessary) to view the Macros section, right-click **mcrOpenVisitForm**, and then click **Run** on the shortcut menu. A message box opens. See Figure 10–2.

Figure 10–2 **Message box opened by the first action in the mcrOpenVisitForm macro**

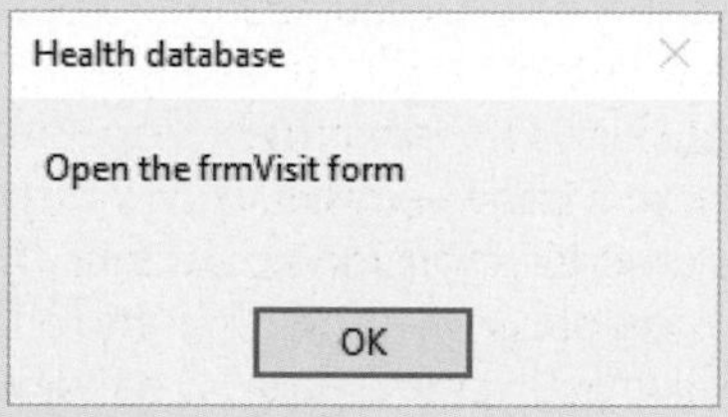
Health database
Open the frmVisit form
OK

Opening the message box is the first action Mista added to the mcrOpenVisitForm macro. As in other computer applications, a **message box** in Access is a special dialog box that contains a message and a **command button**, but no options. A command button is a button that performs an action when a user clicks it. The message box that Mista created specifies that the next macro action will open the frmVisit form. When the user clicks the OK button, the message box will close, and the macro will resume with the next action. Mista added this message box and other message boxes to the macro so that she could demonstrate to Donna how macros can execute multiple actions to complete multistep tasks. With macros you create for working databases, you don't include message boxes between steps as Mista did in her macro.

3. Click **OK**. The next two actions in the mcrOpenVisitForm macro are performed: the frmVisit form opens, and the second message box opens. See Figure 10–3.

Figure 10–3 **Second and third actions in the mcrOpenVisitForm macro**

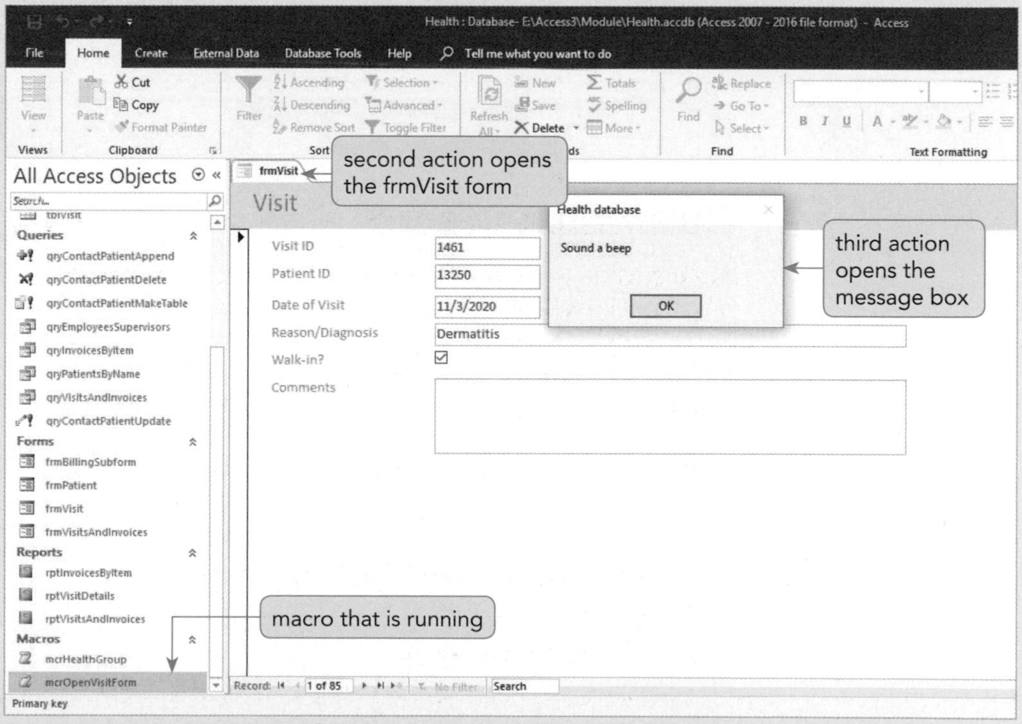
second action opens the frmVisit form
third action opens the message box
macro that is running
Health database
Sound a beep
OK
All Access Objects
Visit
Visit ID
Patient ID
Date of Visit
Reason/Diagnosis
Walk-in?
Comments
1461
13250
11/3/2020
Dermatitis
mcrHealthGroup
mcrOpenVisitForm

4. Click **OK**. A beep sounds, and the third message box opens. These are the fourth and fifth actions in the mcrOpenVisitForm macro.

Trouble? If your computer doesn't have speakers or if your audio is turned down or muted, you won't hear the beep. If you do hear the beep, it might not sound like a beep at all, depending on your computer and its settings.

5. Click **OK**, and then drag the message box from its title bar to the right so you can view the values displayed in the form. The frmVisit form now displays record 17 for VisitID 1549. The sixth action in the mcrOpenVisitForm is displaying record 17, and the seventh action is displaying the message box with the message "Close the form."
6. Click **OK**. The frmVisit form closes, and the mcrOpenVisitForm macro ends.

Now that you have run Mista's sample macro to view it as a user would, you will view the code, or instructions, for the macro and examine its components.

Viewing a Macro in the Macro Designer

You create, view, and edit a macro using the **Macro Designer**, which is a development environment built into Access. To open the Macro Designer, you'll open the macro in Design view.

To open Macro Designer and view the mcrOpenVisitForm macro:

1. Right-click **mcrOpenVisitForm** in the Navigation Pane, click **Design View** on the shortcut menu, and then close the Navigation Pane. The Macro Designer displays the mcrOpenVisitForm macro. See Figure 10–4.

Figure 10–4 Macro Designer showing the mcrOpenVisitForm macro

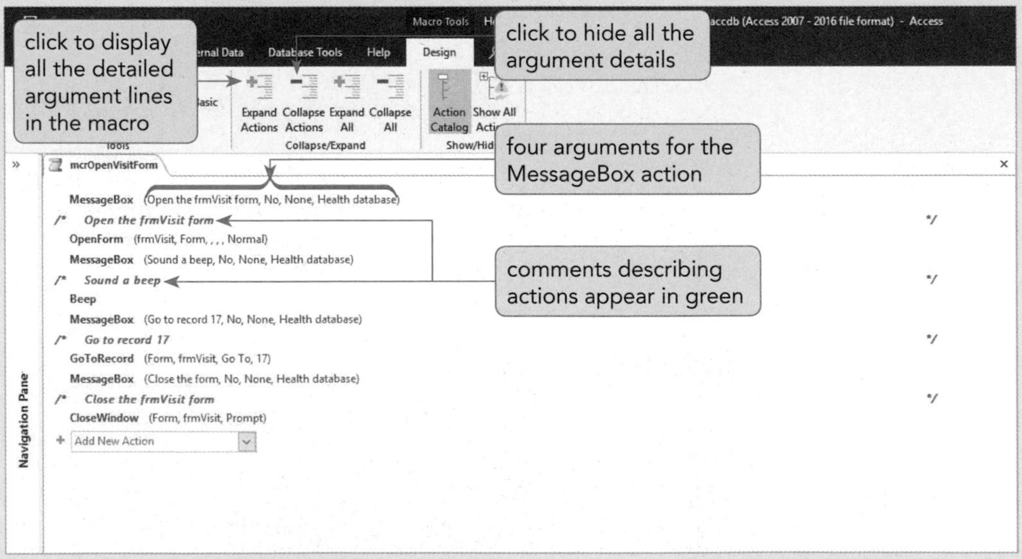
click to display all the detailed argument lines in the macro
click to hide all the argument details
four arguments for the MessageBox action
comments describing actions appear in green
Expand Actions
Collapse Actions
Expand All
Collapse All
Action Catalog
Collapse/Expand
mcrOpenVisitForm
MessageBox (Open the frmVisit form, No, None, Health database)
/* Open the frmVisit form */
OpenForm (frmVisit, Form, , , , Normal)
MessageBox (Sound a beep, No, None, Health database)
/* Sound a beep */
Beep
MessageBox (Go to record 17, No, None, Health database)
/* Go to record 17 */
GoToRecord (Form, frmVisit, Go To, 17)
MessageBox (Close the form, No, None, Health database)
/* Close the frmVisit form */
CloseWindow (Form, frmVisit, Prompt)
Add New Action
Navigation Pane

The Macro Designer lists the actions included in the macro. In addition to actions, a macro can also include arguments and comments, as described in the Session 10.1 Visual Overview. You can change the view of the Macro Designer to display more detail.

2. On the Macro Tools Design tab, in the Collapse/Expand group, click the **Expand All** button to display all the details for the actions, arguments, and comments that make up the mcrOpenVisitForm macro.

   If you rest the mouse pointer on the MessageBox action or on any argument line, a ScreenTip displays a brief explanation of the action or argument. You can also use Help to learn about specific actions and their arguments and about macros in general.

3. Move the mouse pointer over the **MessageBox** action at the top of the Macro Designer. The mouse pointer changes to the hand pointer, and a ScreenTip appears, describing the action and common ways to use the action.

4. Click **MessageBox**. The arguments for the message are displayed in a shaded box.

After a macro has been created, you can modify it in the Macro Designer. You can add or delete actions, and modify the arguments for an action. Mista asks you to add actions to the mcrOpenVisitForm macro. Before doing so, you need to understand how arguments are used in macros.

Using Arguments in a Macro

Some actions require information. For instance, if an action is going to open a form, the action needs to know the name of the form to open. A piece of data that is required by an action is known as an argument. An action can have more than one argument; multiple arguments are separated by commas.

TIP

When a macro contains a MessageBox action, the macro doesn't proceed to the next action until users click the OK button, so they have as much time as they need to read and react to the message box.

The mcrOpenVisitForm macro contains a MessageBox action as the first action. The name of the MessageBox action is followed by the four arguments needed by the action—Message, Beep, Type, and Title:

- The Message argument contains the text that appears in the message box when it is displayed.
- The Beep argument is either Yes or No to specify whether a beep sounds when the message box opens.
- The Type argument determines which icon, if any, appears in the message box to signify the critical level of the message. The icon choices are None (no icon), Critical, Warning?, Warning!, and Information.
- The Title argument contains the word(s) that will appear in the message box title bar.

Adding Actions to a Macro

You can modify a macro by adding or deleting actions in the Macro Designer. When you add an action, you use the Add New Action box at the bottom of the Macro Designer window. After entering the appropriate arguments, you use the Move up and Move down buttons for the action to position it within the macro.

You'll add two actions, the MessageBox and FindRecord actions, to the mcrOpenVisitForm macro between the GoToRecord action and the last MessageBox action. You'll start by adding the MessageBox action and then moving it up to the correct position within the macro.

To add the MessageBox action to the mcrOpenVisitForm macro and position it in the macro:

1. On the Macro Tools Design tab, in the Collapse/Expand group, click the **Collapse Actions** button to hide all the detailed argument lines in the macro. Only the lines for the actions and comments are now displayed in the Macro Designer.

   Below the last action in the macro is the Add New Action box, which you use to add actions to the end of the macro.

2. Click the **Add New Action** arrow to display the list of actions, scroll down the list (if necessary), and then click **MessageBox**. The list closes, a new MessageBox action is added to the end of the macro with its four arguments displayed, and two arguments are set with default values. See Figure 10–5.

Figure 10–5 MessageBox action added to mcrOpenVisitForm

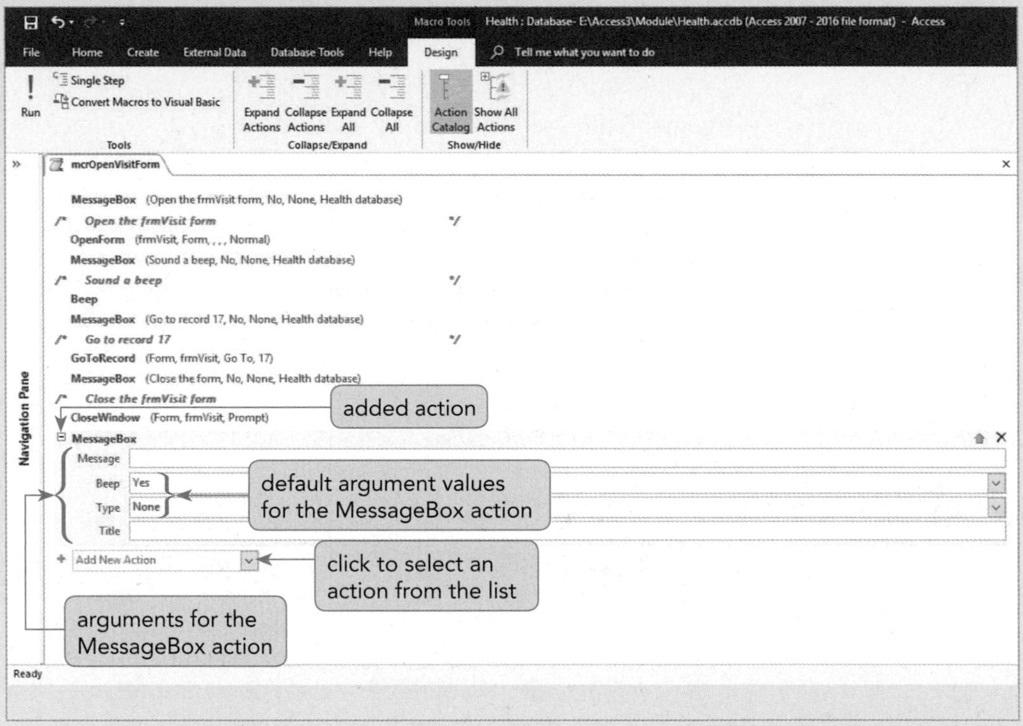
added action
default argument values for the MessageBox action
click to select an action from the list
arguments for the MessageBox action

You'll enter values for the Message and Title arguments, change the Beep argument value from Yes to No, and retain the default Type argument value of None.

3. Click in the **Message** box, type **Find visit 1586**, and then press **TAB**. The contents of the Beep box are now selected.

4. Click the **Beep** arrow, click **No** in the list, press **TAB** twice, and then type **Health database** in the Title box. See Figure 10–6.

Figure 10–6 Argument values added to MessageBox action

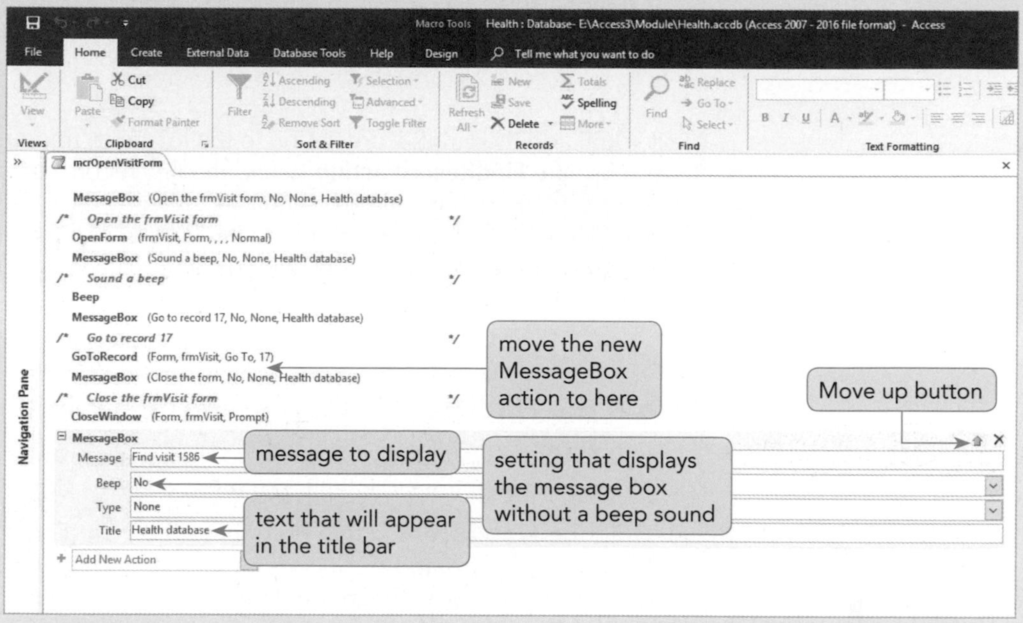
mcrOpenVisitForm
MessageBox (Open the frmVisit form, No, None, Health database)
/* Open the frmVisit form */
OpenForm (frmVisit, Form, , , , Normal)
MessageBox (Sound a beep, No, None, Health database)
/* Sound a beep */
Beep
MessageBox (Go to record 17, No, None, Health database)
/* Go to record 17 */
GoToRecord (Form, frmVisit, Go To, 17)
MessageBox (Close the form, No, None, Health database)
/* Close the frmVisit form */
CloseWindow (Form, frmVisit, Prompt)
MessageBox
Message Find visit 1586
Beep No
Type None
Title Health database
Add New Action
move the new MessageBox action to here
Move up button
message to display
setting that displays the message box without a beep sound
text that will appear in the title bar

This MessageBox action is currently the last action in the mcrOpenVisitForm macro. However, it should be the seventh action in the macro, so that it takes place after the GoToRecord action that moves to record 17 and before the MessageBox action with the message "Close the form." You need to move the new MessageBox action three positions up in the macro.

5. In the upper-right corner of the shaded MessageBox action box, click the **Move up** button three times to move the action to its correct position below the GoToRecord action. See Figure 10–7.

Figure 10–7 New MessageBox action after being moved up

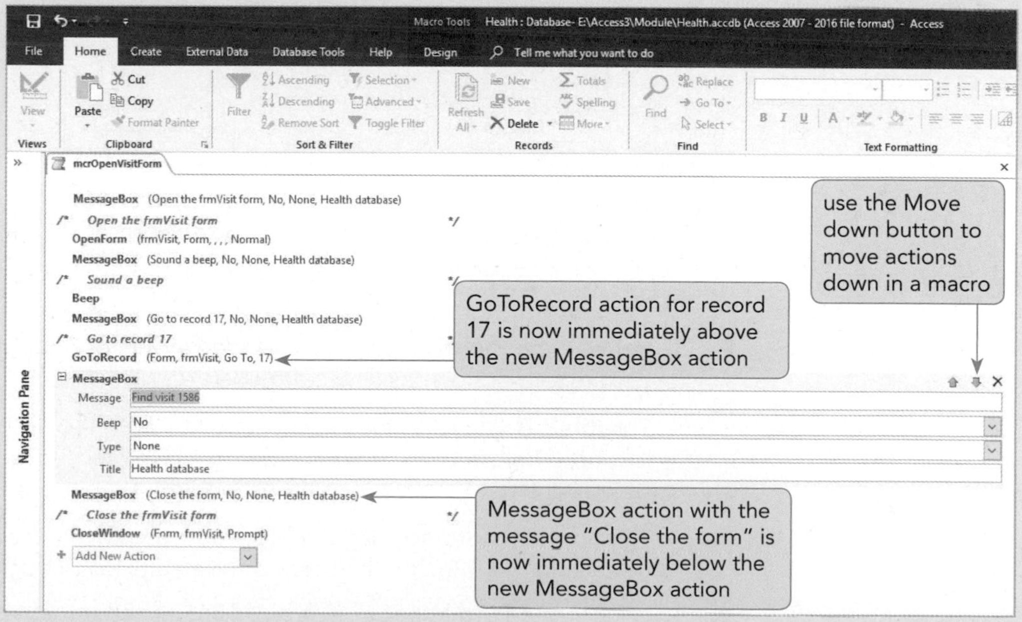
mcrOpenVisitForm
MessageBox (Open the frmVisit form, No, None, Health database)
/* Open the frmVisit form */
OpenForm (frmVisit, Form, , , , Normal)
MessageBox (Sound a beep, No, None, Health database)
/* Sound a beep */
Beep
MessageBox (Go to record 17, No, None, Health database)
/* Go to record 17 */
GoToRecord (Form, frmVisit, Go To, 17)
MessageBox
Message Find visit 1586
Beep No
Type None
Title Health database
MessageBox (Close the form, No, None, Health database)
/* Close the frmVisit form */
CloseWindow (Form, frmVisit, Prompt)
Add New Action
use the Move down button to move actions down in a macro
GoToRecord action for record 17 is now immediately above the new MessageBox action
MessageBox action with the message "Close the form" is now immediately below the new MessageBox action

6. On the Macro Tools Design tab, in the Collapse/Expand group, click the **Collapse Actions** button to hide all the argument lines in the MessageBox action.

Next you'll add the FindRecord action to the macro to find the record for VisitID 1586. You use the **FindRecord action** to find the first record, or the next record if the action is used again, that meets the criteria specified by the FindRecord arguments.

You could add the FindRecord action to the bottom of the macro and move it up three positions as you did for the MessageBox action. Instead, you'll search for the action in the Action Catalog pane and then drag it to its correct position in the macro.

To add the FindRecord action to the mcrOpenVisitForm macro:

1. In the Action Catalog pane, click the **Search** box, and then type **find**. A filtered list of actions containing the search term "find" is displayed.
2. Drag the **FindRecord** action from the Action Catalog pane to the Macro Designer window and position it immediately below the newly added MessageBox action until a red line appears just below the MessageBox action. See Figure 10–8.

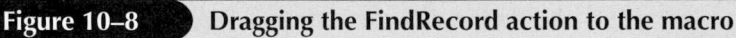

Figure 10–8 **Dragging the FindRecord action to the macro**

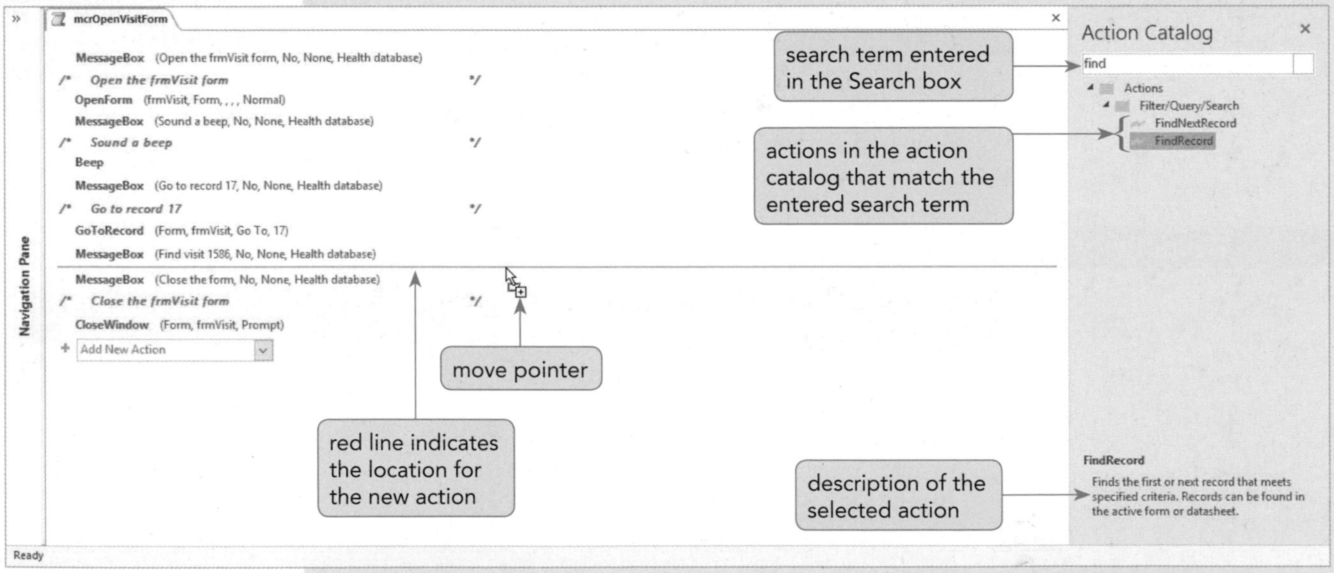
mcrOpenVisitForm
MessageBox (Open the frmVisit form, No, None, Health database)
/* Open the frmVisit form */
OpenForm (frmVisit, Form, , , , Normal)
MessageBox (Sound a beep, No, None, Health database)
/* Sound a beep */
Beep
MessageBox (Go to record 17, No, None, Health database)
/* Go to record 17 */
GoToRecord (Form, frmVisit, Go To, 17)
MessageBox (Find visit 1586, No, None, Health database)
MessageBox (Close the form, No, None, Health database)
/* Close the frmVisit form */
CloseWindow (Form, frmVisit, Prompt)
Add New Action
Navigation Pane
Ready
Action Catalog
find
Actions
Filter/Query/Search
FindNextRecord
FindRecord
FindRecord
Finds the first or next record that meets specified criteria. Records can be found in the active form or datasheet.
search term entered in the Search box
actions in the action catalog that match the entered search term
move pointer
red line indicates the location for the new action
description of the selected action

3. Release the mouse button to add the FindRecord action to the macro. The FindRecord action has seven arguments.

   Trouble? If you drag the wrong action or drag the action to the wrong location, delete the action by clicking its Delete button [X] to the right of the Move up and Move down buttons, and then repeat Steps 2 and 3.

   To find the record for VisitID 1586, you need to set the Find What argument to a value of 1586. You'll accept the defaults for the other action arguments.

4. Click in the **Find What** box, type **1586**, and then next to FindRecord, click the **Collapse** button [⊟] to hide all the argument boxes for the action.

Finally, you'll add a comment above the FindRecord action to document the FindRecord action.

5. In the Action Catalog pane, click the **blank square** on the right end of the Search box to clear the contents of the Search box. The Action Catalog pane again displays the categories of available actions.
6. In the Program Flow section of the Action Catalog pane, drag **Comment** to the macro, and position it immediately above the FindRecord action. A Comment box is displayed, with move buttons and a Delete button to its right.
7. Click in the **Comment** box, type **Find visit 1586**, and then click a blank area of the Macro Designer to close the Comment box. See Figure 10–9.

Figure 10–9 Actions and comment added to the mcrOpenVisitForm macro

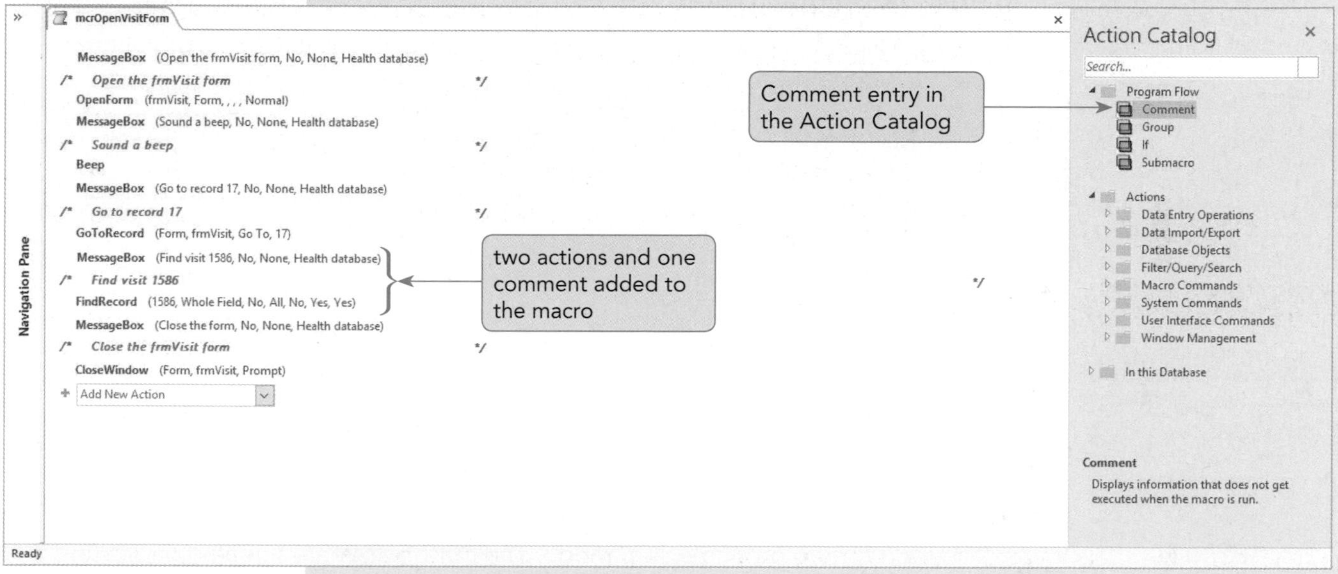
mcrOpenVisitForm
MessageBox (Open the frmVisit form, No, None, Health database)
/* Open the frmVisit form */
OpenForm (frmVisit, Form, , , , Normal)
MessageBox (Sound a beep, No, None, Health database)
/* Sound a beep */
Beep
MessageBox (Go to record 17, No, None, Health database)
/* Go to record 17 */
GoToRecord (Form, frmVisit, Go To, 17)
MessageBox (Find visit 1586, No, None, Health database)
/* Find visit 1586 */
FindRecord (1586, Whole Field, No, All, No, Yes, Yes)
MessageBox (Close the form, No, None, Health database)
/* Close the frmVisit form */
CloseWindow (Form, frmVisit, Prompt)
Add New Action
Navigation Pane
Ready
Comment entry in the Action Catalog
two actions and one comment added to the macro
Action Catalog
Search...
Program Flow
Comment
Group
If
Submacro
Actions
Data Entry Operations
Data Import/Export
Database Objects
Filter/Query/Search
Macro Commands
System Commands
User Interface Commands
Window Management
In this Database
Comment
Displays information that does not get executed when the macro is run.

8. On the Quick Access Toolbar, click the **Save** button to save your macro design changes.

After you create or change a macro, you should test it. You can use single step mode to make sure the individual actions in a macro are executed in the proper order and that the arguments for a given action are correctly set.

PROSKILLS

Teamwork: Using Comments to Share Information

When working with a team to develop and maintain a database, you'll be regularly reading and making changes to macros that other team members wrote; in addition, other team members will be changing and extending macros that you created. Therefore, it's important to use comments to document the macros you write. Including a comment before each related set of actions to explain its purpose can help other team members understand the structure of your macro. In addition, including comments makes it easier for everyone on the team to find and fix any errors, because they can compare the explanation of what a section of a macro should do, as given in the comment, with the actions that follow.

Single Stepping a Macro

When you create a complicated macro with many actions, you'll often find it useful to run through the macro one step at a time. In Access, you can do this using single step mode. In **single step mode**, a macro is executed one action at a time, with a pause between actions. Using single step mode is also referred to as single stepping, and allows you to confirm you have listed actions in the right order and with the correct arguments. If you have problems with a macro, you can use single step mode to find the causes of the problems and to determine appropriate corrections. The Single Step button in the Tools group on the Macro Tools Design tab is a toggle you use to turn single step mode on and off. Once you turn on single step mode, it stays on for all macros until you turn it off.

REFERENCE

Single Stepping a Macro

- On the Macro Tools Design tab in the Macro Designer, click the Single Step button in the Tools group.
- In the Tools group, click the Run button.
- In the Macro Single Step dialog box, click the Step button to execute the next action.
- To stop the macro, click the Stop All Macros button.
- To execute all remaining actions in the macro and turn off single step mode, click the Continue button.

Now that you have added actions to the mcrOpenVisitForm macro, you'll single step through it to ensure the actions are in the correct order and the arguments are correctly set.

To single step through the macro:

1. On the Macro Tools Design tab, in the Tools group, click the **Single Step** button to turn on single step mode. The button appears selected, indicating that single step mode is on.
2. In the Tools group, click the **Run** button. The Macro Single Step dialog box opens. See Figure 10–10.

Figure 10–10 Macro Single Step dialog box

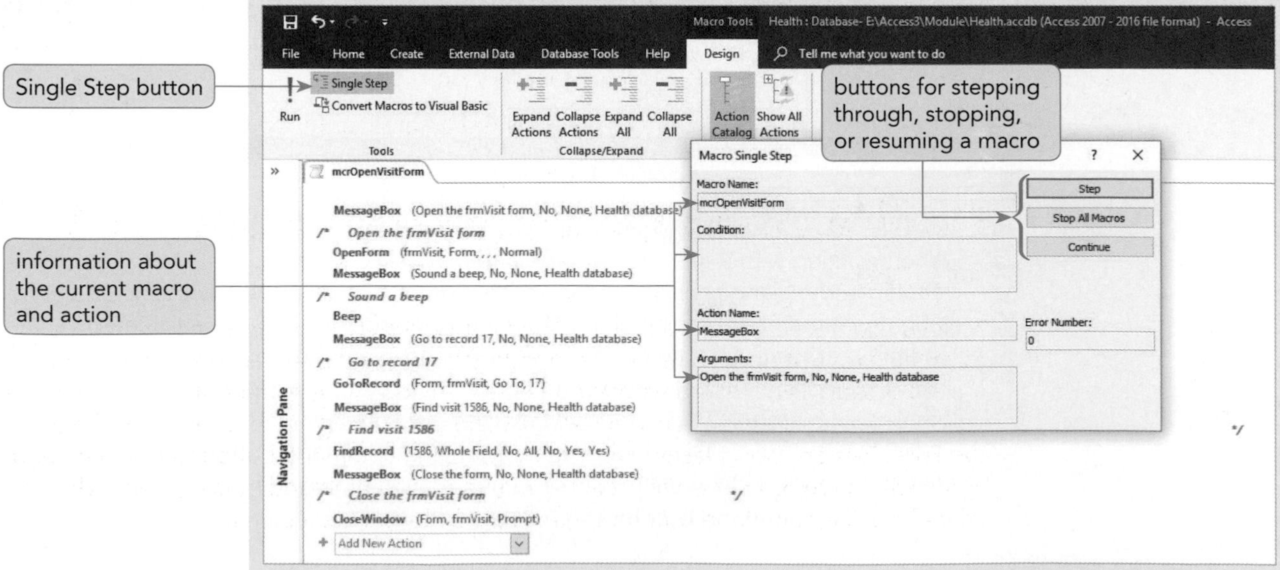
Single Step button
information about the current macro and action
buttons for stepping through, stopping, or resuming a macro

Trouble? If the first message box opens instead of the Macro Single Step dialog box, you turned off single stepping in Step 1 when you clicked the Single Step button. Click the OK button to run the complete macro, and then repeat Steps 1 and 2.

When you single step through a macro, the Macro Single Step dialog box opens before performing each action. This dialog box shows the macro's name and the action's condition, name, and arguments. The action will be executed or not executed, depending on whether the condition is true or false. From this dialog box, you can step through the macro one action at a time, stop the macro and return to the Macro Designer, or continue by executing all remaining actions without pausing. If you click the Continue button, you also turn off single step mode.

3. Click **Step**. The first action in the macro (MessageBox) runs. Because the MessageBox action pauses the macro, the Macro Single Step dialog box remains hidden until you click the OK button in the message box.
4. Click **OK** to close the message box. The Macro Single Step dialog box shows the macro's second action (OpenForm).
5. Click **Step**. The second action in the macro runs, opening the frmVisit form, and shows the macro's third action (MessageBox) in the Macro Single Step dialog box.
6. Continue clicking **Step** and **OK** until the "Find visit 1586" message box opens, making sure you read the Macro Single Step dialog box carefully and observe the actions that occur. At this point, record 17 is the current record in the frmVisit form.
7. Click **OK**, and then click **Step**. The FindRecord action runs, record 33 for VisitID 1586 is now the current record in the frmVisit form, and the Macro Single Step dialog box shows the macro's last MessageBox action.
8. Click **Step**, click **OK**, and then click **Step**. The Macro Single Step dialog box closes automatically after the last macro action is completed; the last macro action closes the frmVisit form.

   You've finished checking Mista's macro and can turn off the single step feature.

9. Click the **Macro Tools Design** tab, in the Tools group, click the **Single Step** button to turn off single step feature, and then click the **Close 'mcrOpenVisitForm'** button ☒ to close the macro.

Next, you will review another macro Mista created for the frmVisit form.

Using a Command Button with an Attached Macro

Mista created a macro that she associated with a command button on the frmVisit form that you just opened using the mcrOpenVisitForm macro. A command button is a control that runs a macro when you click it. To add a command button to a form, you open the form in Design view and use the Button tool in the Controls group on the Form Design Tools Design tab. After adding the command button to the form, and while still in Design view, you attach a macro to the command button. Then, when a user clicks the command button, the macro's actions are executed.

You'll use the Open Patient Table command button on the frmVisit form to see how a command button works.

To use the Open Patient Table command button:

1. Open the Navigation Pane, open the **frmVisit** form in Form view, click **1461** in the Visit ID box to deselect all values, and then close the Navigation Pane. The first visit with VisitID 1461 and PatientID 13250 is displayed. See Figure 10–11.

Figure 10–11 Open Patient Table command button on the frmVisit form

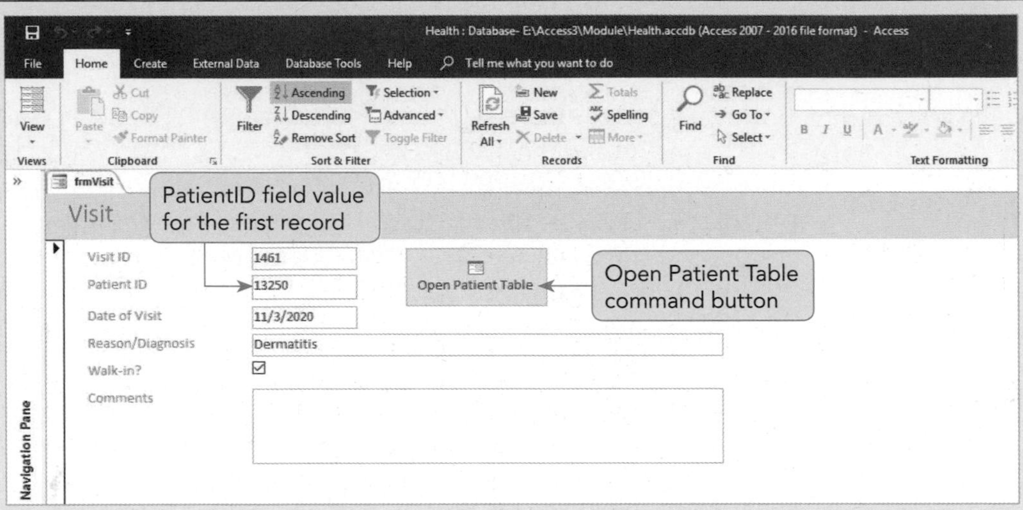
PatientID field value for the first record
Open Patient Table command button
Visit
Visit ID
Patient ID
Date of Visit
Reason/Diagnosis
Walk-in?
Comments
1461
13250
11/3/2020
Dermatitis
Open Patient Table

2. Click the **Open Patient Table** command button. The frmVisit form remains open, and the tblPatient table opens. The tblPatient table is the active object. See Figure 10–12.

Figure 10–12 tblPatient table opened with the Open Patient Table command button

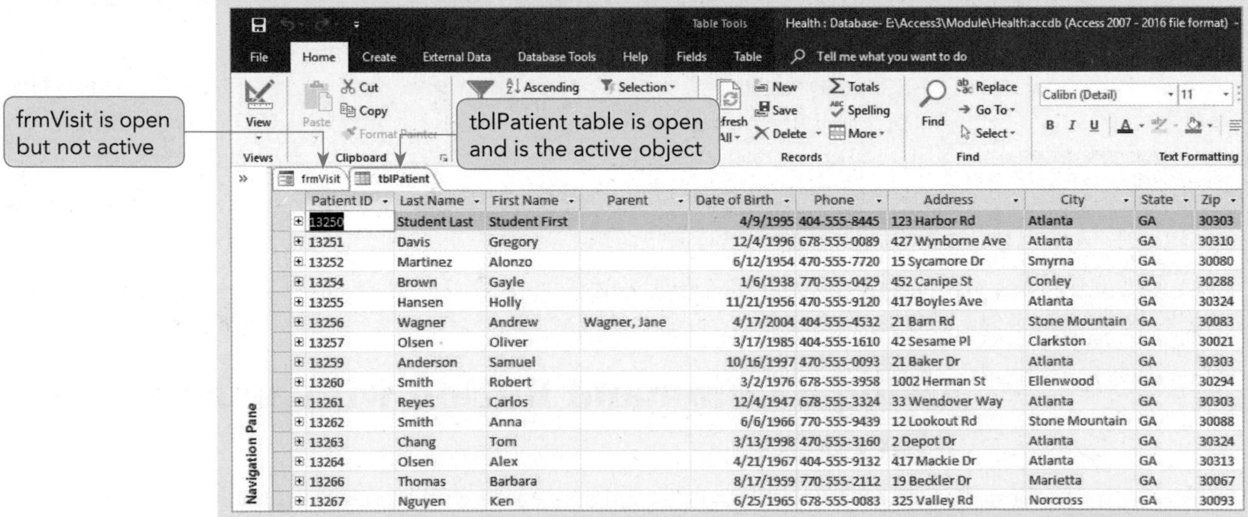
frmVisit is open but not active
tblPatient table is open and is the active object

Clicking the Open Patient Table command button triggered an attached macro that opened the tblPatient table. The tblPatient table will remain open until it is closed manually or by another macro.

3. Close the **tblPatient** table. The frmVisit form is now the active object.

Understanding Events

Clicking the Open Patient Table command button is an event, and the opening of the tblPatient table is controlled by setting an event property. An **event** is something that happens to a database object, such as a user clicking a check box or a form being loaded. You can connect an action to a specific event so the action occurs in response to that event. For example, an event occurs when you click a command button on a form, when you use the mouse to position the pointer on a form, or when you press a key to choose an option. In your work with Access, you've initiated hundreds of events on forms, controls, records, and reports without any special effort. For example, events you've triggered in forms include Open, which occurs when you open a form; Activate, which occurs when the form becomes the active window; and Close, which occurs when you close a form and the form is removed from the screen. Each event has an associated event property. An **event property** specifies how an object responds when an event occurs. For example, each form has OnOpen, OnActivate, and OnClose event properties associated with the Open, Activate, and Close events, respectively.

Event properties appear in the Property Sheet when you create forms and reports. Unlike most properties you've used previously in the Property Sheet, event properties do not have an initial value. If an event property contains no value, it means the event property has not been set. In this case, no special action results when the associated event occurs. For example, if the OnOpen event property of a form is not set and you open the form, then the Open event occurs (the form opens), and no special action occurs beyond the opening of the form. You can set an event property value to a macro name, and the named macro will run when the event occurs. For example, you could write a macro that automatically selects a particular field in a form when you open it. You can also create a group of statements using Visual Basic for Applications (VBA) code and set the event property value to the name of that group of statements. The group of statements, or **procedure**, is then executed when the event occurs. Such a procedure is called an **event procedure**. You will learn more about VBA code and procedures in the next module.

When you clicked the Open Patient Table command button on the frmVisit form, the Click event occurred and triggered an attached macro. This happened because the Open Patient Table command button contains an OnClick event property setting, which you will examine next.

To view the OnClick event property setting for the Open Patient Table command button:

TIP

The Event tab in the Property Sheet lists the names of the event properties with spaces, even though you type each event property name without a space.

1. Switch to Design view, right-click the **Open Patient Table** command button control, click **Properties** on the shortcut menu to open the Property Sheet (if necessary), and then click the **Event** tab (if necessary).
2. Right-click the **On Click** box, click **Zoom** on the shortcut menu to open the Zoom dialog box, and then click to the right of the selected text to deselect it. See Figure 10–13.

   Event property values are often longer than the boxes in the Property Sheet can display at once. Working with them in the Zoom dialog box ensures you can always see the entire value.

Figure 10–13 Macro attached to the OnClick event property

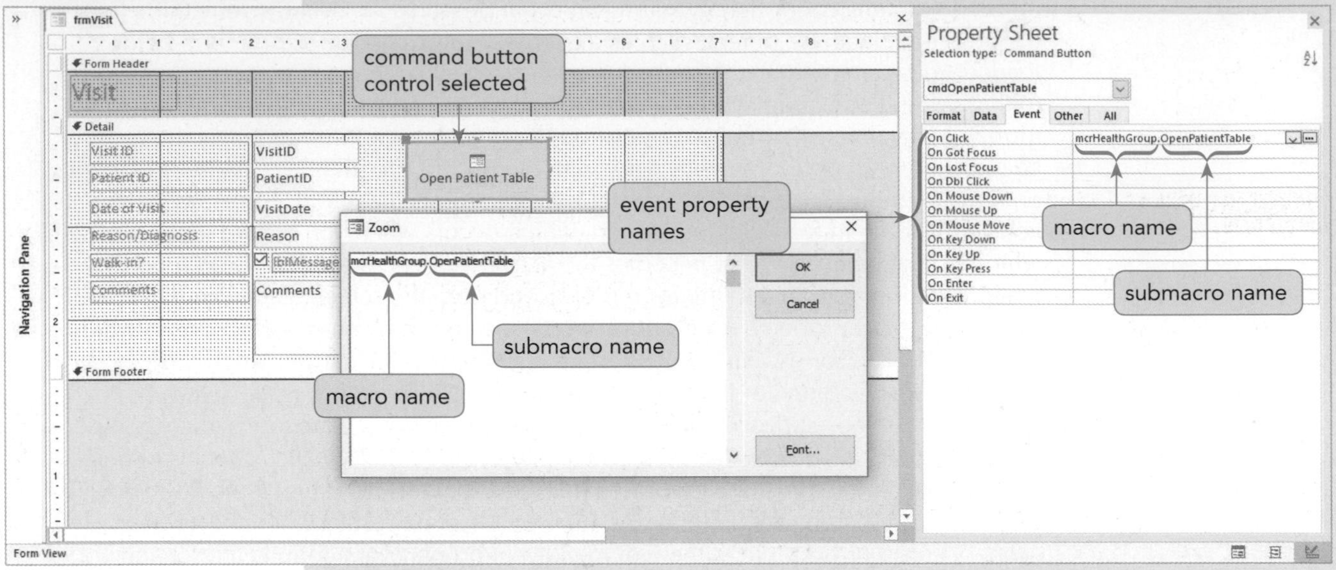
command button
control selected
event property
names
macro name
submacro name
submacro name
macro name
Open Patient Table
mcrHealthGroup.OpenPatientTable
Property Sheet
Selection type: Command Button
cmdOpenPatientTable
Format
Data
Event
Other
All
On Click
On Got Focus
On Lost Focus
On Dbl Click
On Mouse Down
On Mouse Up
On Mouse Move
On Key Down
On Key Up
On Key Press
On Enter
On Exit
Zoom
OK
Cancel
Font...
frmVisit
Form Header
Detail
Form Footer
Visit ID
Patient ID
Date of Visit
Reason/Diagnosis
Walk-in?
Comments
VisitID
PatientID
VisitDate
Reason
Comments
Navigation Pane
Form View

Trouble? The position of the Zoom dialog box may be slightly different from the figure. You may move the Zoom dialog box to align with the figure for clarity.

The OnClick event property value shown in the Zoom dialog box is mcrHealthGroup. OpenPatientTable. This is an example of a reference to a submacro in a macro.

Understanding Submacros

If you need to create several related macros, you can create them as submacros in a single macro instead of creating them as separate macros. A **submacro** is a complete macro with a Submacro header within a macro. Submacros are especially useful in a large database that contains many objects as they allow you to limit the number of objects by consolidating related macros. Because you can specify a submacro to run in response to an event, using submacros gives you more options than simply creating a large macro that performs many actions. For example, if a form's design uses command buttons to open a form with a related record and to print the related record displayed in the form, you can create one macro for the form that contains two submacros—one submacro to open the form, and a second submacro to print the related record. Because you created the macro specifically for the form object, you can store all the submacros you need in a single macro.

When you reference a submacro in an event property value, a period separates the macro name from the submacro name. For the OnClick event property value shown in Figure 10–13, for example, mcrHealthGroup is the macro name and OpenPatientTable is the submacro name. When you click the Open Patient Table command button on the frmVisit form, the actions contained in the OpenPatientTable submacro are processed. This submacro is located in the mcrHealthGroup macro.

You'll now close the Zoom dialog box, and then you'll open the Macro Designer from the Property Sheet.

To open the mcrHealthGroup macro in the Macro Designer:

1. Click **Cancel** in the Zoom dialog box to close it. In the Property Sheet for the selected Open Patient Table command button, the On Click box contains an arrow and a Build button. The command button is named cmdOpenPatientTable; *cmd* is a prefix tag to identify a command button control. See Figure 10–14.

Figure 10–14 Property Sheet Event tab for the Open Patient Table command button

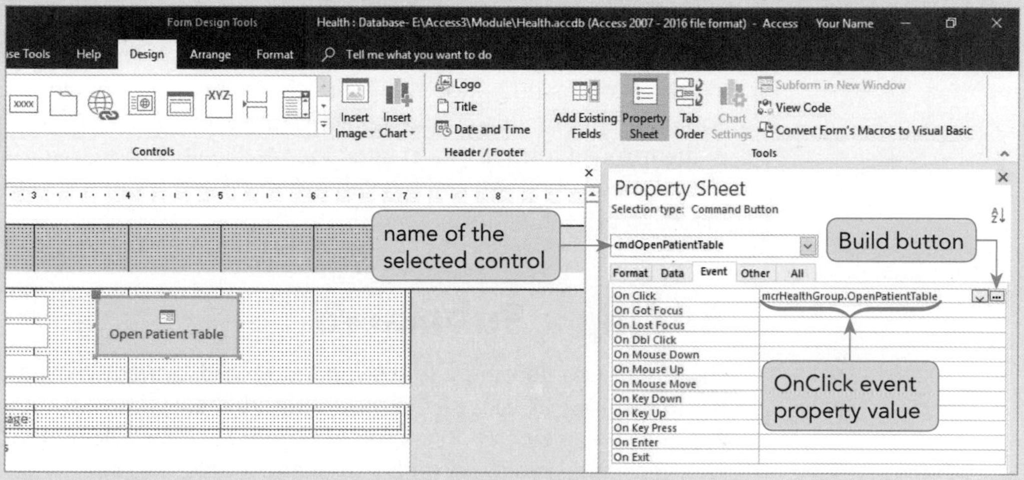

name of the selected control
Build button
OnClick event property value
Property Sheet
Selection type: Command Button
cmdOpenPatientTable
Format
Data
Event
Other
All
On Click
mcrHealthGroup.OpenPatientTable
On Got Focus
On Lost Focus
On Dbl Click
On Mouse Down
On Mouse Up
On Mouse Move
On Key Down
On Key Up
On Key Press
On Enter
On Exit
Open Patient Table

You click the On Click arrow if you want to change the current macro to a different macro, and you click the Build button if you want to use the Macro Designer to view or change the existing macro. The Build button is also called the **Macro Builder** when you use it to work with macros.

2. Click the **Build** button on the right end of the On Click box. The Macro Designer opens and displays the mcrHealthGroup macro and the OpenPatientTable submacro. See Figure 10–15.

Figure 10–15 Macro Designer displaying the mcrHealthGroup macro and its submacro

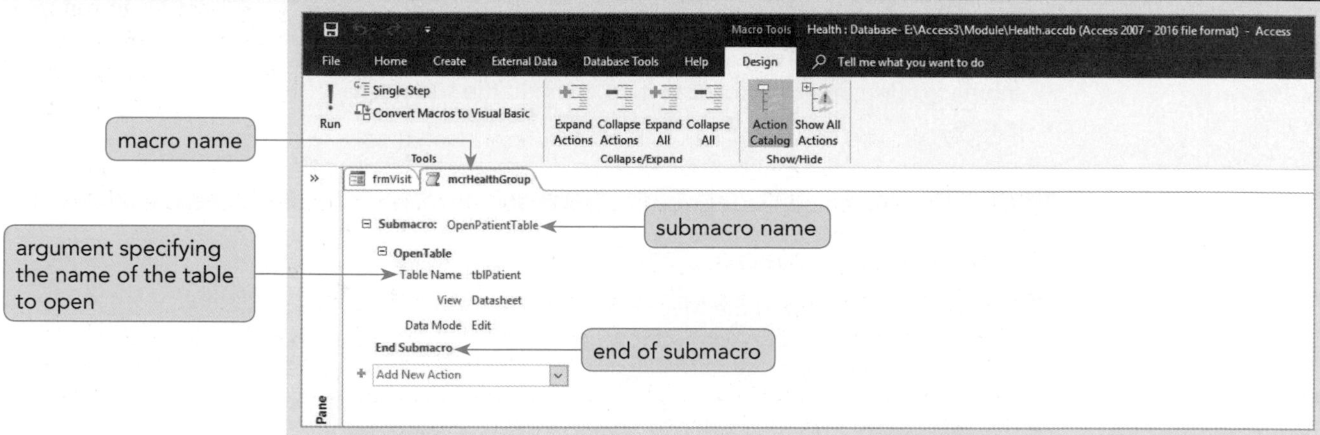

macro name
argument specifying the name of the table to open
submacro name
end of submacro
frmVisit
mcrHealthGroup
Submacro: OpenPatientTable
OpenTable
Table Name tblPatient
View Datasheet
Data Mode Edit
End Submacro
Add New Action

The mcrHealthGroup macro consists of one submacro that starts with the Submacro statement and ends with the End Submacro statement. These statements are not actions; they are control statements to identify the beginning and end of a submacro. If a macro contains several submacros, each submacro starts with a Submacro statement and ends with an End Submacro statement.

The OpenPatientTable submacro consists of a single action, OpenTable, which opens the tblPatient table. The OpenTable action arguments are as follows:

- The **Table Name argument** specifies the name of a table that will open when the macro is run.
- The **View argument** specifies the view in which the object will open. For tables, you can specify Datasheet, Design, Print Preview, PivotTable, or PivotChart.
- The **Data Mode argument** specifies the table's data entry options. Allowable settings for this argument are Add (users can add new records but can't change or delete existing records), Edit (users can change and delete existing records and can add new records), and Read Only (users can only view records). If you don't select an argument value, Edit is the default setting.

Now that you've seen a macro attached to a command button, Mista asks you to add a command button to the frmVisit form and then attach a new macro to the command button. Users can then click the command button to print the current record in the frmVisit form. Mista created the mcrHealthGroup macro to group together all the submacros in the Health database. You'll add a submacro to the mcrHealthGroup macro to print the current record.

Adding a Submacro

To print the contents of a form's current record, normally you have to click the File tab to display Backstage view, click Print in the navigation bar, click Print in the list of options, click Selected Record(s), and then click the OK button—a process that takes five steps and several seconds. As an alternative, you can create a command button on the form, create a macro that prints the contents of a form's current record, and then attach the macro to the command button on the form. Instead of following multiple steps to print the form's current record, a user could simply click the command button.

First, you'll add a submacro to the mcrHealthGroup macro. You'll use the SelectObject and RunMenuCommand actions for the new submacro. The **SelectObject action** selects a specified object so that you can run an action that applies to the object. The **RunMenuCommand action** selects and runs a command on the ribbon. The specific argument you'll use with the RunMenuCommand action is the **PrintSelection argument**, which prints the selected form record. Because macros and submacros are database objects, you'll follow the naming conventions for database objects when naming macros and submacros. These naming conventions include using descriptive object names so that the object's function is obvious, capitalizing the first letter of each word in the name, and excluding spaces from the name. Therefore, you'll name the submacro PrintSelectedRecord when you add the submacro to the mcrHealthGroup macro.

REFERENCE

Adding a Submacro

- Open the macro in the Macro Designer.
- Click the Add New Action arrow, click Submacro, and then type the submacro name in the Submacro box.
- Click the Add New Action arrow above the End Submacro statement, click the action you want to use, and then set the action's arguments.
- If the submacro consists of more than one action, repeat the previous step for each action.
- Add comments as needed to the submacro to document the submacro's function or provide other information.
- Save the macro.

You'll now add the PrintSelectedRecord submacro to the mcrHealthGroup macro.

To add the PrintSelectedRecord submacro to the mcrHealthGroup macro:

1. Click the **Collapse** icon ⊟ to the left of Submacro OpenPatientTable to collapse the actions and arguments for the submacro.
2. Click the **Add New Action** arrow to display the list of actions and control statements, and then click **Submacro**. A submacro box appears with the default name selected in it, which is Sub followed by one or more numbers. You will replace the default name with a more appropriate name for the submacro.
3. Type **PrintSelectedRecord** in the Submacro box. The Submacro and End Submacro statements are added to the macro, and another Add New Action box is displayed between these two statements. See Figure 10–16.

TIP

You can also type the first few letters of the action until the full action name appears and then press TAB to select the action.

Figure 10–16 New submacro added

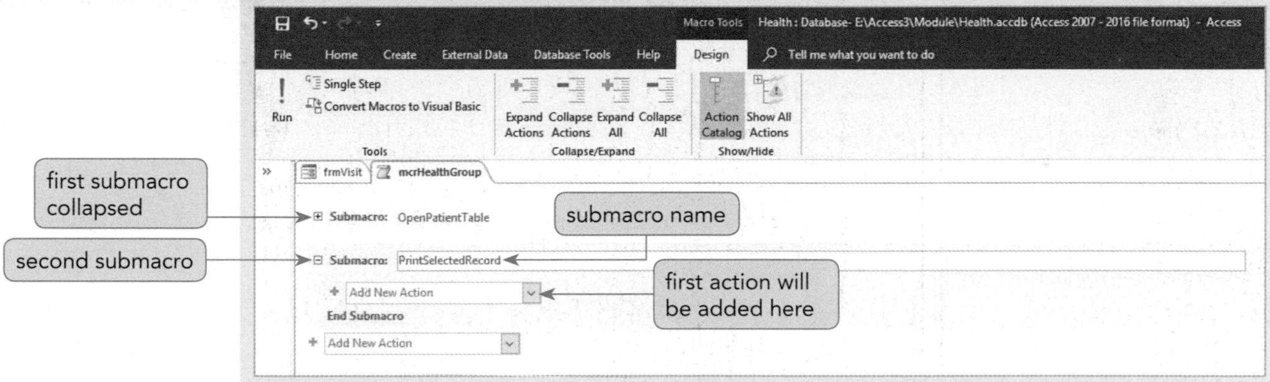
Macro Tools
Health : Database- E:\Access3\Module\Health.accdb (Access 2007 - 2016 file format) - Access
File
Home
Create
External Data
Database Tools
Help
Design
Tell me what you want to do
Single Step
Convert Macros to Visual Basic
Run
Tools
Expand Actions
Collapse Actions
Expand All
Collapse All
Collapse/Expand
Action Catalog
Show All Actions
Show/Hide
frmVisit
mcrHealthGroup
first submacro collapsed
Submacro: OpenPatientTable
submacro name
second submacro
Submacro: PrintSelectedRecord
Add New Action
first action will be added here
End Submacro
Add New Action

You need to select the SelectObject action and set its arguments.

4. Between the Submacro and End Submacro statements, click the **Add New Action** arrow, scroll down the list, and then click **SelectObject**. The **SelectObject action** is added to the PrintSelectedRecord submacro. This action has three arguments. The first argument, Object Type, specifies the type of database object to select. The second argument, Object Name, specifies the name of the object to open. The third argument, In Database Window, specifies whether to open the object in the database window (Yes) or not (No). You would open a table, form, or report in the database window if it is not already open. If the table, form, or report is already open, you would select No as the value for the Database Window argument.

   You need to open a form named frmVisit, so you'll set these arguments first.

5. Click the **Object Type** arrow, click **Form**, click the **Object Name** arrow, and then click **frmVisit**. Because the form will be open when you run the macro, you'll leave the In Database Window argument set to No.

   You'll next select the RunMenuCommand action and set its arguments. The RunMenuCommand action lets you add a command available on the ribbon to a submacro. The Command argument in this submacro lets you select the command. In this case, the Command argument is named PrintSelection.

6. Below the SelectObject action, click the **Add New Action** arrow, scroll down the list, and then click **RunMenuCommand**. The RunMenuCommand action

box appears with the Command box, in which you specify the Command argument.

7. Click the **Command** arrow, scroll down the list, and then click **PrintSelection**. You've completed the second action. You'll add another SelectObject action to the submacro to make the frmVisit form the active object after the selected record prints.

8. Below the RunMenuCommand action, click the **Add New Action** arrow, scroll down the list, click **SelectObject**, set the Object Type argument to **Form**, and then set the Object Name argument to **frmVisit**. You've finished adding the three actions to the PrintSelectedRecord submacro. See Figure 10–17.

Figure 10–17 **Three actions added to the PrintSelectedRecord submacro**

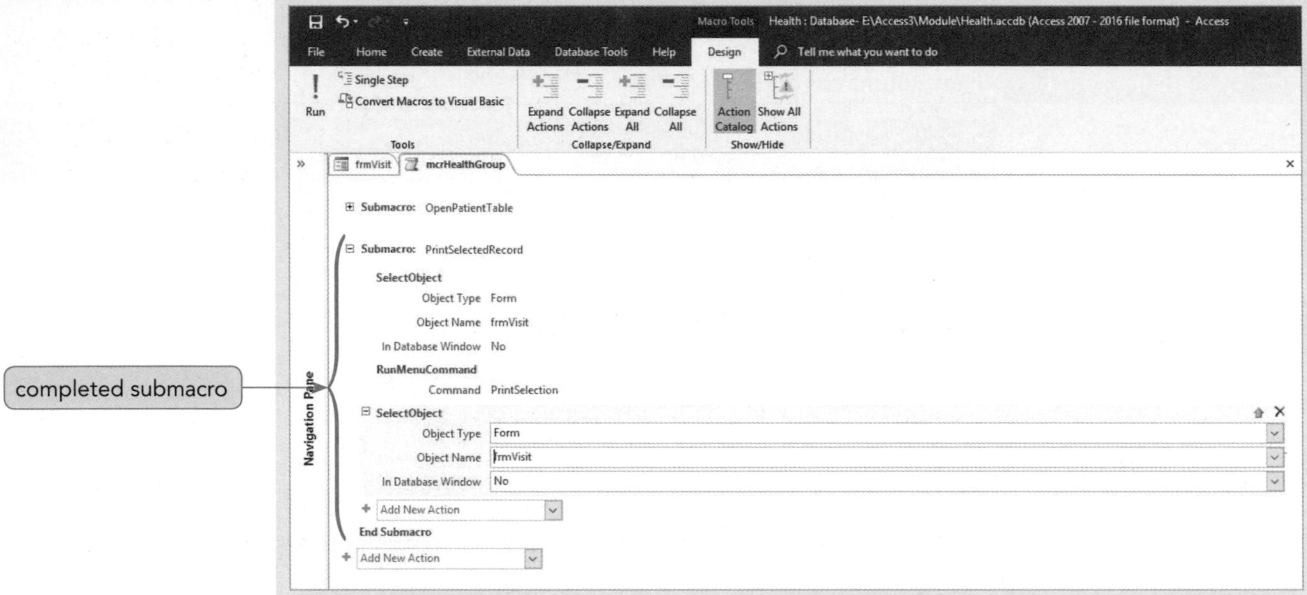
completed submacro
Submacro: OpenPatientTable
Submacro: PrintSelectedRecord
SelectObject
Object Type Form
Object Name frmVisit
In Database Window No
RunMenuCommand
Command PrintSelection
SelectObject
Object Type Form
Object Name frmVisit
In Database Window No
Add New Action
End Submacro
Add New Action

9. Save your macro design changes, and then close the mcrHealthGroup macro. The frmVisit form is the active object.

Next, you'll add a command button to the frmVisit form. After you attach the PrintSelectedRecord macro to the command button control, you'll be able to click the command button to print the current frmVisit form record.

INSIGHT

Using Submacros, Subforms, Subqueries, and Subreports

You can create a small macro and embed it in another macro as a submacro. Likewise, you can create a small form and embed it in another form as a subform, create a small query and embed it in another query as a subquery, and create a small report and embed it in another report as a subreport. The techniques for each of these object types are quite different.

- To embed a macro as a submacro, you use the Macro Designer and add a submacro as a new action.
- To embed a subform, you view the main form in Design view and add the subform using the wizard, or you drag the subform to the main form.
- To embed a query as a subquery, you use SQL view to copy the SQL for the subquery, and then you paste it in the SQL statement for the main query.
- To embed a report as a subreport, you use the Subreport Wizard, or you drag the report to the main report in Design view.

Although the techniques are different, the underlying logic is the same. An embedded object works with the data that is used by the main object. That is, a subform uses the related data from the main form, a subreport uses the related data from the main report, a subquery uses the related data from the main query, and a submacro is executed as an action of the main macro.

Adding a Command Button to a Form

In Design view for a form, you use the Button tool in the Controls group on the Form Design Tools Design tab to add a command button control to a form. If the Use Control Wizards tool is selected when you click the Button tool, the Command Button Wizard guides you through the process of adding the command button control. You'll explore adding the command button control directly to the frmVisit form without using the wizard, and then you'll set the command button control's properties using its Property Sheet.

To add a command button control to the frmVisit form:

1. Close the Property Sheet, and then click the **Form Design Tools Design** tab.
2. In the Controls group, click the **More** button, and then make sure the **Use Control Wizards** tool is not selected.

   Trouble? If the Use Control Wizards tool has an orange background, click it to disable the control wizards, and then continue with Step 3.
3. In the Controls group, click the **Button** tool.
4. Position the pointer's plus symbol (+) to the right of the Open Patient Table button in the Details section, and then click the mouse button. A second command button is added to the form. See Figure 10–18.

Figure 10–18 New command button added to the frmVisit form

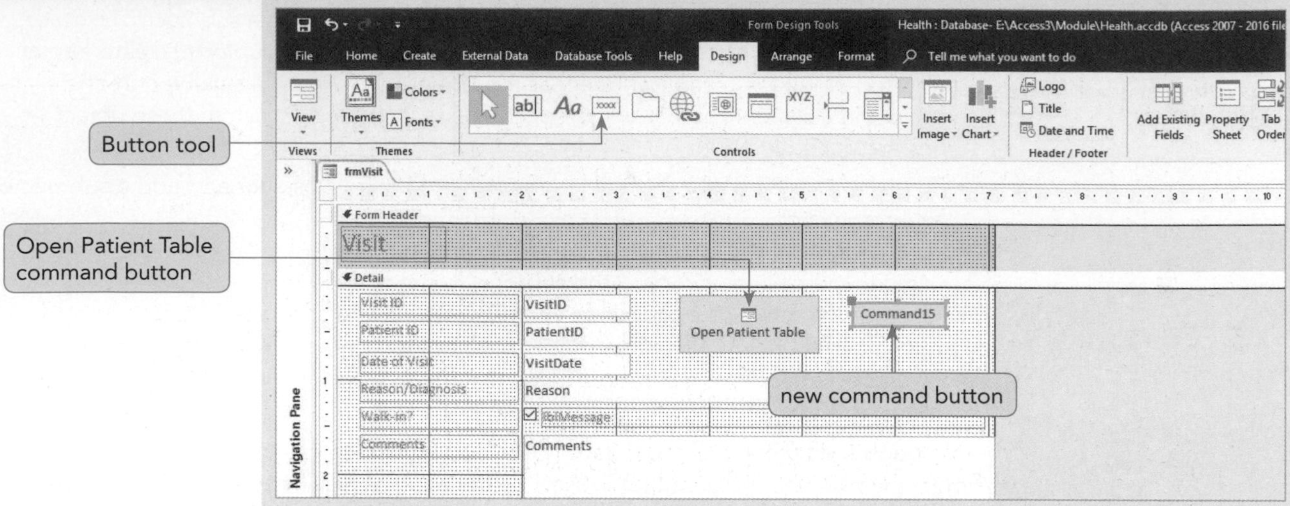
Button tool
Open Patient Table command button
new command button
Open Patient Table
Command15

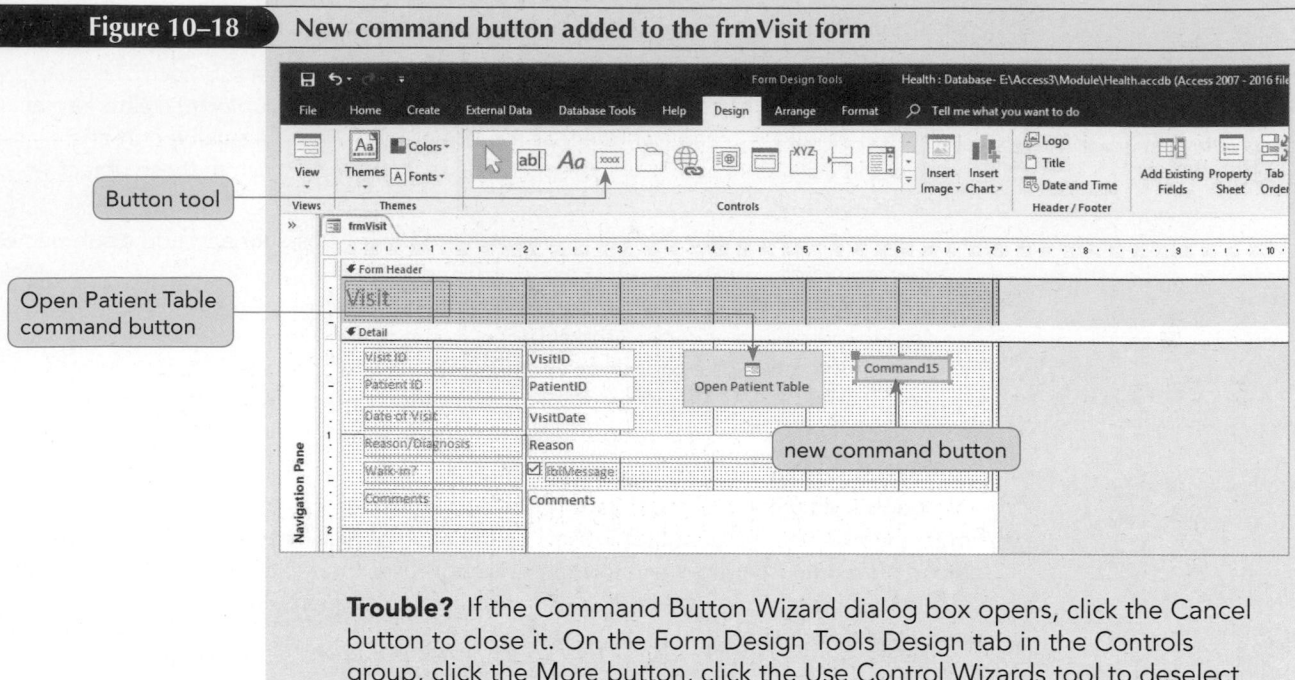

Trouble? If the Command Button Wizard dialog box opens, click the Cancel button to close it. On the Form Design Tools Design tab in the Controls group, click the More button, click the Use Control Wizards tool to deselect it, and then repeat Steps 3 and 4.

Trouble? The command button on your screen might show a different number in its label, depending on how you completed the previous steps. This difference will not affect the command button or macro.

You can now attach the PrintSelectedRecord submacro to the command button.

Attaching a Submacro to a Command Button

So far you've created the PrintSelectedRecord submacro and added the command button to the frmVisit form. Now you'll attach the submacro to the command button control's OnClick property so that the submacro is executed when the command button is clicked.

To attach the PrintSelectedRecord submacro to the command button control:

1. Make sure the new command button control is selected.
2. Open the **Property Sheet**, and then, if necessary, click the **Event** tab in the Property Sheet.
3. Click the **On Click** arrow to display the macros list, and then click **mcrHealthGroup.PrintSelectedRecord**.

TIP

You can drag the left edge of the Property Sheet to the left to display more of the macro and submacro names if needed.

You can change the text that appears on the command button (also known as the command button's label or caption) by changing its Caption property. You can also replace the text with a picture by setting its Picture property, or you can include both text and a picture. Mista wants you to place a picture of a printer on the command button and to display text on the command button.

4. In the Property Sheet, click the **Format** tab, click the **Picture** box, and then click the **Build** button that appears on the right side of the Picture box. The Picture Builder dialog box opens. See Figure 10–19.

Figure 10–19 Picture Builder dialog box

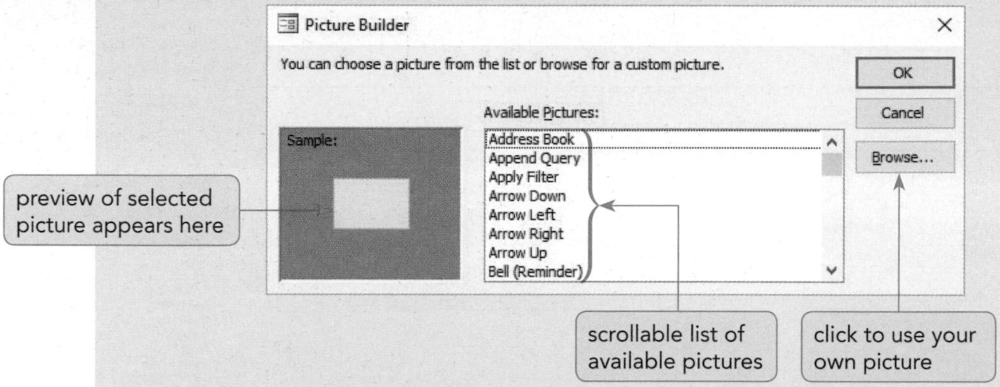
Picture Builder
You can choose a picture from the list or browse for a custom picture.
OK
Cancel
Browse...
Available Pictures:
Sample:
Address Book
Append Query
Apply Filter
Arrow Down
Arrow Left
Arrow Right
Arrow Up
Bell (Reminder)
preview of selected picture appears here
scrollable list of available pictures
click to use your own picture

The Picture Builder dialog box contains an alphabetical list of pictures supplied with Access. You can scroll the list and select one of the pictures, or you can click the Browse button to select your own picture. When you select a picture, a sample is displayed on the command button in the Sample box.

5. Scroll the Available Pictures box, and then click **Printer**. A picture of a printer is displayed on the command button in the Sample box.
6. Click **OK**. The Picture Builder dialog box closes, and the printer picture is displayed on the command button in the form.
7. Change the Caption property to **Print Selected Record**, and then press **TAB**.

   The **Picture Caption Arrangement property** specifies how a command button's Caption property value is arranged in relation to the picture placed on the command button. The choices are No Picture Caption, General, Top, Bottom, Left, and Right.

8. Click the **Picture Caption Arrangement** arrow, and then click **Bottom**. The caption will appear below the printer picture. However, the command button is not tall enough or wide enough to display the picture and caption, so you'll resize it.
9. Use the middle-bottom sizing handle and the middle-right sizing handle to increase the width and height of the command button so it is approximately the same size as the Open Patient Table button and looks like the one shown in Figure 10–20.

Figure 10–20 Command button with picture and caption

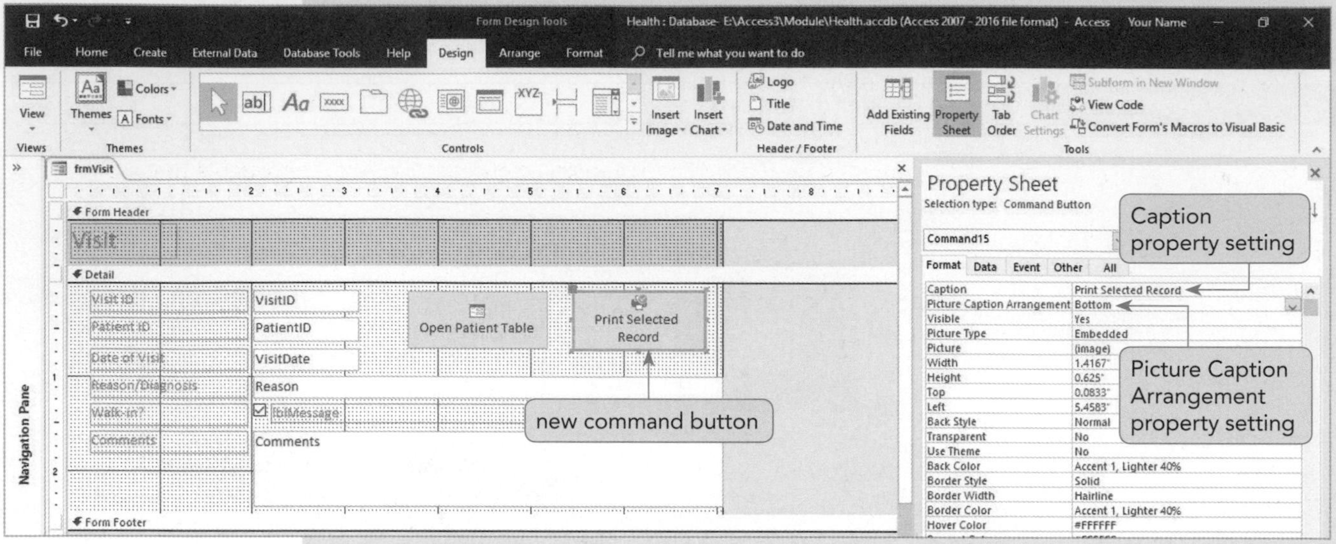
Caption property setting
Picture Caption Arrangement property setting
new command button
Print Selected Record
Open Patient Table

Trouble? If the background color of your button does not match the Open Patient Table button, in the Property Sheet, on the Format tab, click the Use Theme box, click the Use Theme arrow, and then click No.

Next, you'll save the frmVisit form and test the command button.

In this session, you have learned how to create and use macros in a form to automate tasks. In the next session, you'll create a navigation system that will limit access to the database objects while still allowing users to run queries and view forms and reports. You'll create a form that contains a list box to display specific forms, reports, and queries in the Health database, use a SQL statement to select the values for the list box, and then add command buttons to the form.

To save the form and test the command button:

1. Close the Property Sheet, save your form design changes, and then switch to Form view.
2. Navigate to the last visit record, for VisitID 1493.
3. Click the **Print Selected Record** command button on the form to open the Print dialog box. Notice that the submacro correctly set the print range to print the selected record.
4. Click **OK** to print the last visit record. The submacro returns control to the frmVisit form after the record is printed.
5. Close the form.
6. If you are not continuing on to the next session, close the Health database.

TIP

If the Print dialog box contains a Print to File check box, you can print to a file instead of printing on paper.

REVIEW

Session 10.1 Quick Check

1. What is a macro?
2. What is the Macro Designer?
3. What does the MessageBox action do?
4. What are you trying to accomplish when you single step through a macro?
5. What is an event property?
6. How do you add a picture to a command button?

Session 10.2 Visual Overview:

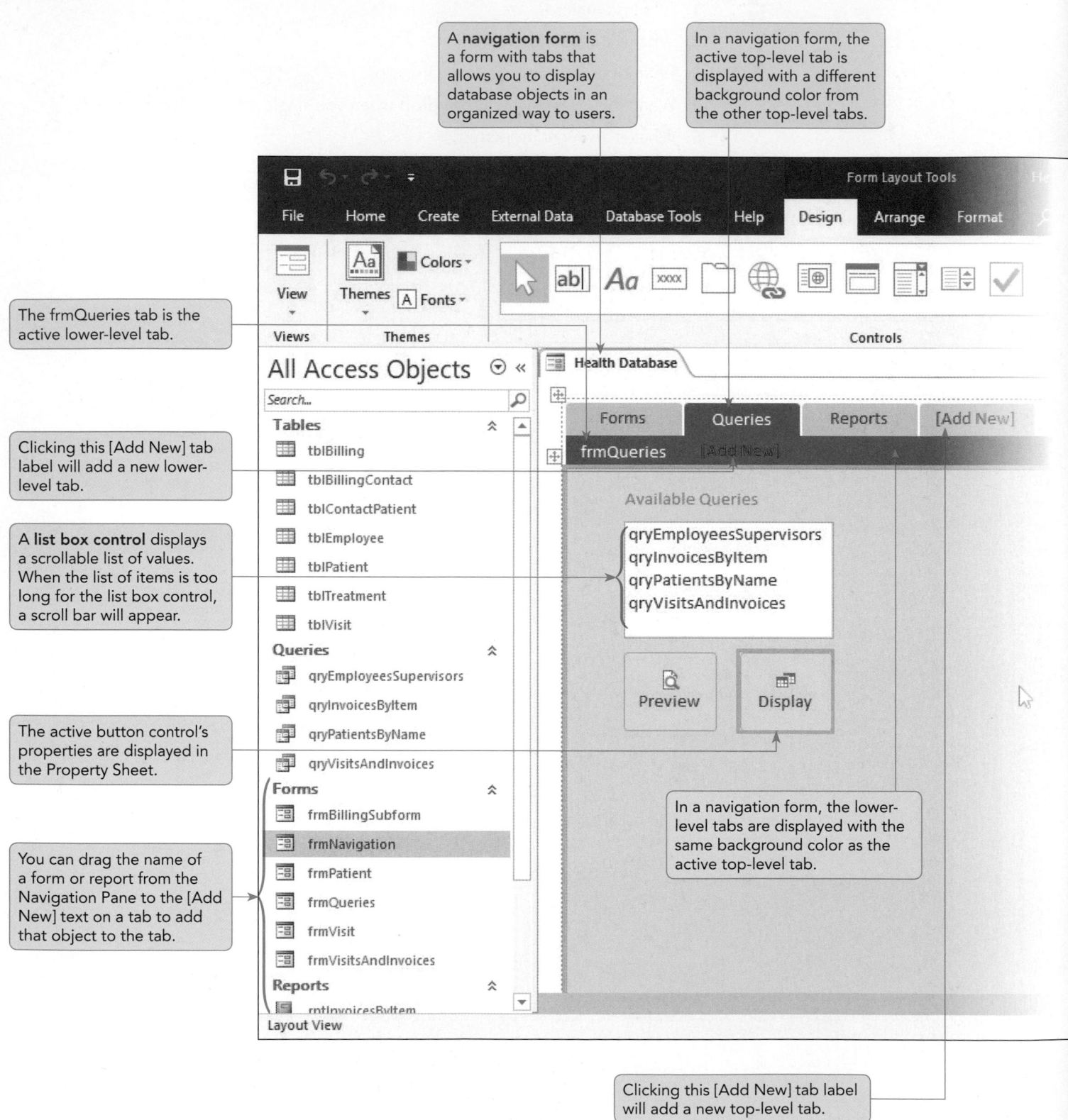

A **navigation form** is a form with tabs that allows you to display database objects in an organized way to users.

In a navigation form, the active top-level tab is displayed with a different background color from the other top-level tabs.

The frmQueries tab is the active lower-level tab.

Clicking this [Add New] tab label will add a new lower-level tab.

A **list box control** displays a scrollable list of values. When the list of items is too long for the list box control, a scroll bar will appear.

The active button control's properties are displayed in the Property Sheet.

You can drag the name of a form or report from the Navigation Pane to the [Add New] text on a tab to add that object to the tab.

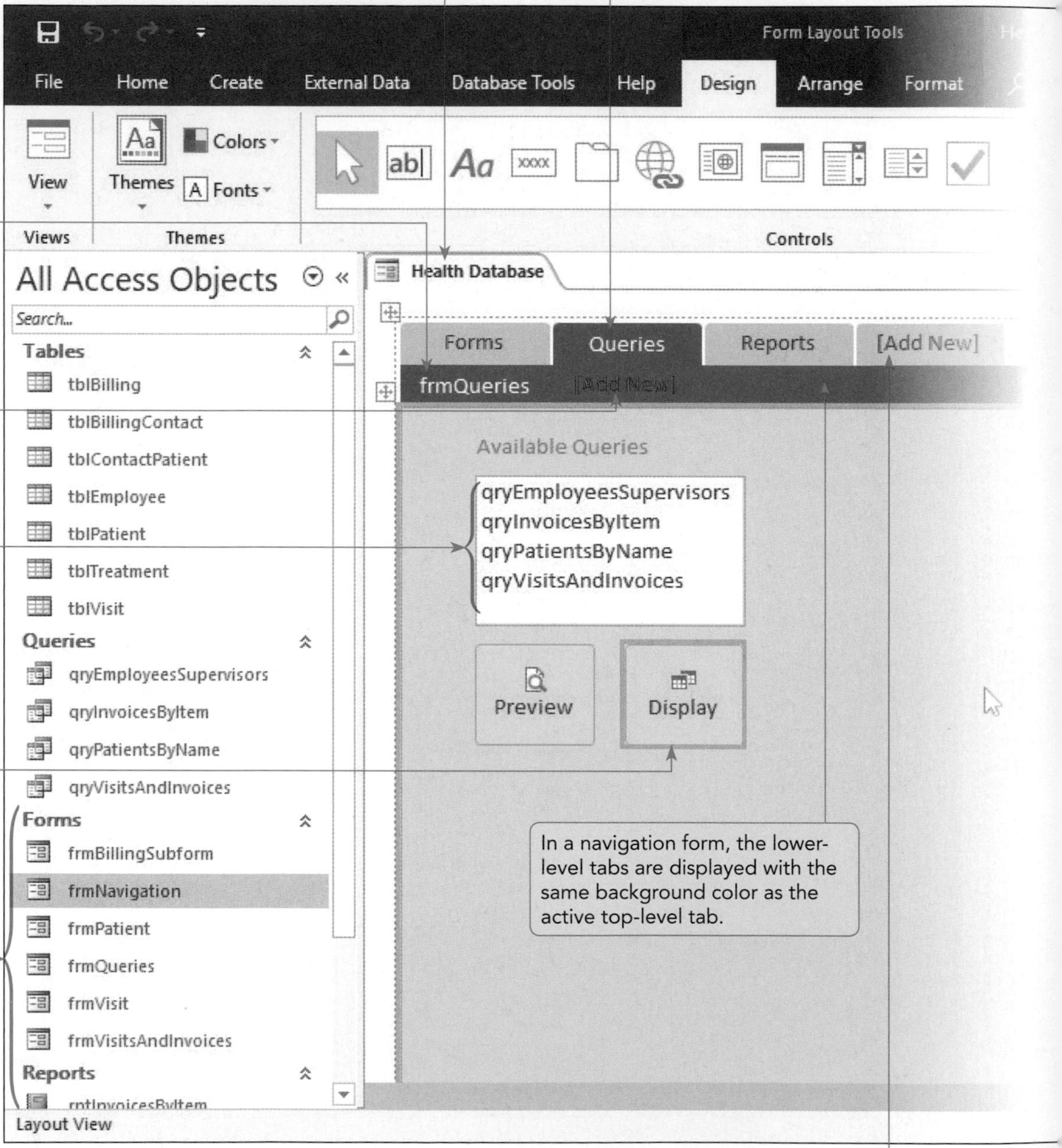

Form Layout Tools
File
Home
Create
External Data
Database Tools
Help
Design
Arrange
Format
View
Themes
Colors
Fonts
Views
Themes
Controls
All Access Objects
Search...
Tables
tblBilling
tblBillingContact
tblContactPatient
tblEmployee
tblPatient
tblTreatment
tblVisit
Queries
qryEmployeesSupervisors
qryInvoicesByItem
qryPatientsByName
qryVisitsAndInvoices
Forms
frmBillingSubform
frmNavigation
frmPatient
frmQueries
frmVisit
frmVisitsAndInvoices
Reports
Layout View
Health Database
Forms
Queries
Reports
[Add New]
frmQueries
[Add New]
Available Queries
qryEmployeesSupervisors
qryInvoicesByItem
qryPatientsByName
qryVisitsAndInvoices
Preview
Display

In a navigation form, the lower-level tabs are displayed with the same background color as the active top-level tab.

Clicking this [Add New] tab label will add a new top-level tab.

A Navigation Form

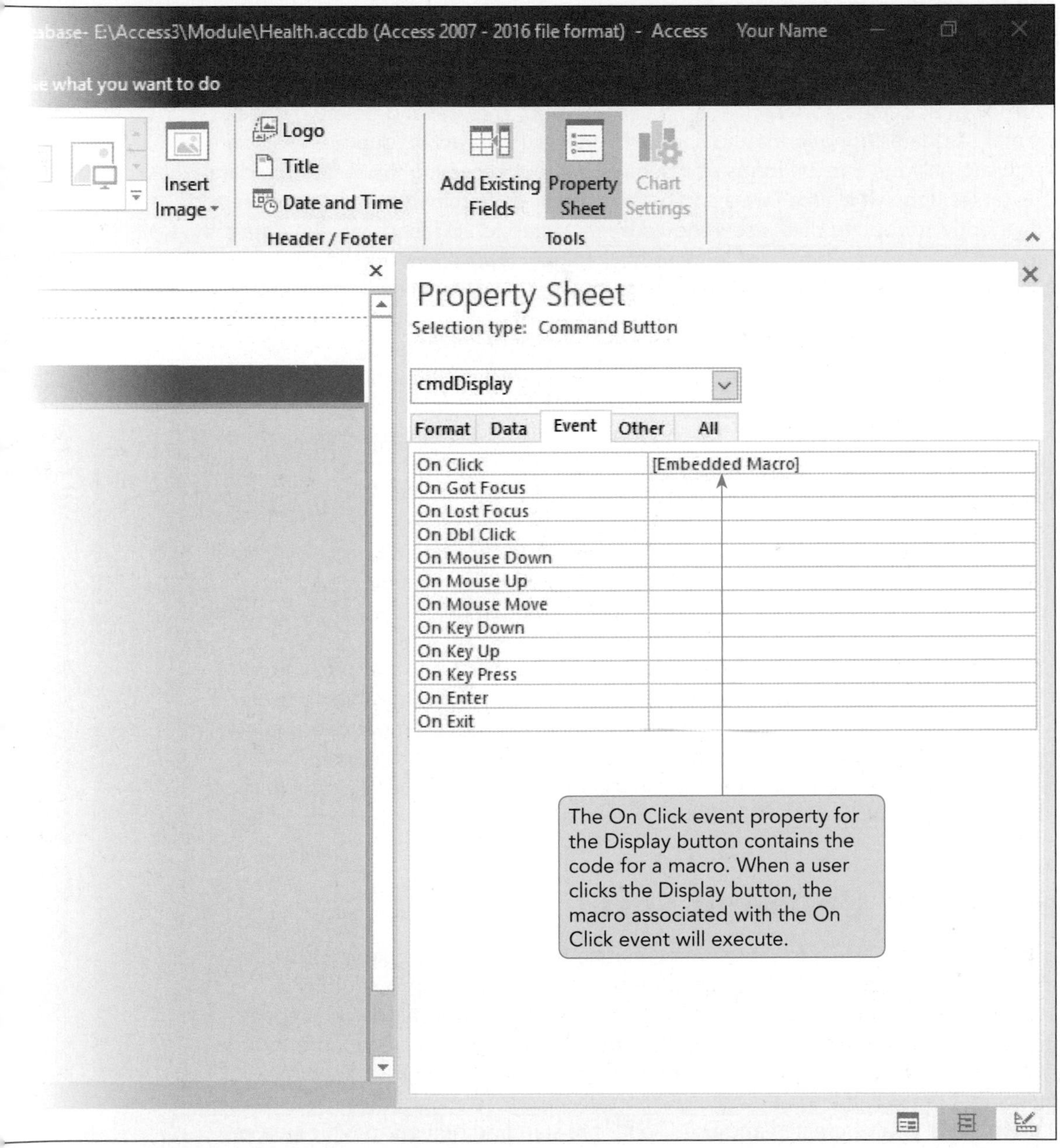
abase- E:\Access3\Module\Health.accdb (Access 2007 - 2016 file format) - Access Your Name
e what you want to do
Insert Image
Logo
Title
Date and Time
Header / Footer
Add Existing Fields
Property Sheet
Chart Settings
Tools
Property Sheet
Selection type: Command Button
cmdDisplay
Format
Data
Event
Other
All
On Click
[Embedded Macro]
On Got Focus
On Lost Focus
On Dbl Click
On Mouse Down
On Mouse Up
On Mouse Move
On Key Down
On Key Up
On Key Press
On Enter
On Exit
The On Click event property for the Display button contains the code for a macro. When a user clicks the Display button, the macro associated with the On Click event will execute.

Designing a User Interface

A **user interface** is what you see and use when you communicate with a computer application. Mista wants to provide a simple user interface for the Health database to assist beginning users as they become familiar with and start using the database objects.

PROSKILLS

Problem Solving: Restricting Access to Database Objects and Prohibiting Design Changes

It's important to ensure that data is as accurate as possible. Many database users do not have much experience with database applications and could inadvertently corrupt data. However, database users need to be able to add, change, and delete data. If they make updates using forms and special queries, such as action queries, users can manipulate only the data on forms and queries, without accessing the rest of the data in the tables upon which the forms and queries are built. To minimize the risk of users inadvertently corrupting data, users should be restricted to updating only the data they need. For this reason, a database administrator might create forms and special queries for the purpose of restricting the users' ability to access only authorized data. Users also need to review and print information from a database using reports, forms, and queries. Similarly, users should not be allowed to change the design of any database object or the design of the user interface. You can create a user interface that meets all these needs and restrictions. When users open a database, you can present them with a form that allows them to choose among the available forms, reports, and queries and to navigate from one object to another object as they perform their work. At the same time, you can limit users to this controlled user interface, thereby preventing them from changing any aspect of the design of the database. By considering the needs of users and by using the features and tools provided by the DBMS, you can enable users to work productively with a database and ensure the integrity of the stored data.

Before she creates the user interface for the Health database, Mista wants you to create a form to display a list of the database queries in a list box, from which users can select and run a query. The list will include only select queries, not action queries, because you want to prevent inexperienced users from selecting and running action queries. Mista's technique enables users to choose and run select queries, which select records from tables but do not affect the records in a table.

Creating an Unbound Form

When the form controls in a form do not need data from a table or query, you create an unbound form. The data displayed in an unbound form can be provided by a Structured Query Language (SQL) statement. Recall that SQL is a standard language used in querying, updating, and managing relational databases. To create an unbound form, you create a blank form, add one or more form controls, and then specify SQL statements that provide the form data.

All the objects you've created and used so far are standard objects in which users need to navigate from record to record, or from page to page in the case of reports, and to perform other operations such as copying data and closing the object. For unbound forms, users do not need to perform any of these operations, so when you create an unbound form, you can remove these features from the form.

The Health database contains several queries, and more queries might be added in the future. To allow users to choose from the available queries, Mista wants you to create a form that will display the queries in a list box. The Session 10.2 Visual Overview shows a preview of the frmQueries form you'll create as part of a navigation form. To create the frmQueries form, you'll begin by creating a blank form. You'll add a list box control and two command buttons to the form, and you'll enter a SQL statement that will provide the contents of the list box.

The Health database contains a few action queries. First, you'll delete any action queries that are in the Health database, then you'll create the frmQueries form.

Next, you'll create the frmQueries form.

To delete the action queries in the Health database:

1. If you took a break after the previous session, make sure that the Health database is open and the Navigation Pane is displayed.
2. If you want to keep the action queries you created, make a copy of the Health database.
3. In the Navigation Pane, right-click **qryContactPatientAppend**, and then click **Delete** on the shortcut menu. A dialog box opens that prompts you to confirm that you want to delete the query.
4. In the dialog box, click the **Yes** button to confirm that you want to delete the query. The qryContactPatientAppend query is deleted from the database.
5. Repeat Steps 3 and 4 to delete the following queries from the database: **qryContactPatientDelete**, **qryContactPatientMakeTable**, and **qryContactPatientUpdate**.
6. Close the Navigation Pane.

TIP

You can also use this shortcut menu to delete a table, form, report, or macro from the database.

Next, you'll create the frmQueries form.

To create and save the frmQueries form:

1. Click the **Create** tab, and then in the Forms group, click the **Blank Form** button. A blank form opens in the Form window in Layout view, and the Field List pane is displayed.
2. Close the Field List pane, and then switch to Design view.
3. Save the form with the name **frmQueries**.

TIP

Some developers prefer to set form properties after they've created all the form controls.

Some Access form properties are especially helpful in designing a user interface; for Mista's form, you'll use properties that let you disable the display of the Close button, the navigation buttons, the record selector, and the right-click shortcut menu. In addition, to match Mista's design, you need to set the Caption property to "Queries," which is the value that appears on the object tab when you open the form. Figure 10–21 shows the form property settings you will use to create the frmQueries form for Mista.

Figure 10–21 Frequently used Access actions

Property	Setting	Function
Caption	Queries	Value that appears on the form's object tab when the form is open
Close Button	No	Disables the display of the Close button on the form's object tab
Navigation Buttons	No	Disables the display of navigation buttons at the bottom of the form
Record Selectors	No	Disables the display of a record selector on the left side of the form
Shortcut Menu	No	Disables the display of the shortcut menu when a user right-clicks the form

Next you'll use the Property Sheet to set the form properties shown in Figure 10–21.

To set the properties for the unbound frmQueries form:

1. Right-click the form selector, ▪ and then click **Properties** on the shortcut menu to open the form's Property Sheet.
2. If necessary, click the **Format** tab in the Property Sheet to display the format properties for the form.

   You can now set the Caption property for the form. As you know, the Caption property value will appear on the tab when the form is displayed.
3. Click the **Caption** box, and then type **Queries**.

   Next, you'll set the Record Selectors property. Because the form does not display any records, there's no need to include a record selector.
4. In the Record Selectors box, double-click **Yes** to change the property setting from Yes to No.

   Next you'll set the remaining form properties.
5. Scrolling as necessary, set the Navigation Buttons property to **No**, and set the Close Button property to **No**.
6. Click the **Other** tab in the Property Sheet to display the Other page of the Property Sheet, and then set the Shortcut Menu property to **No**.
7. Close the Property Sheet, and then save your form design changes.

Now that you have set the form's properties, you can add a list box control to the form.

Adding a List Box Control to a Form

You can add a list box control to a form using the Control Wizards tool, or you can set the properties for the list box control individually in the control's Property Sheet.

The label associated with the list box control that you will add to the frmQueries form will identify the list box for the user. The list box control will include queries in the Health database that users can preview or view. A user will be able to click the name of a query to select it and then click one of the command buttons to preview or view the query. Double-clicking a query name in the list box will also open the query datasheet.

You will not use the Control Wizards tool to create the list box control because you'll be using a SQL statement to provide the query names for the list box control.

REFERENCE

Adding a List Box Control to a Form

- Switch to Design view, if necessary.
- If necessary, on the Form Design Tools Design tab, in the Controls group, click the More button, and then click the Use Control Wizards tool to select or deselect it, depending on whether you want to use the wizard.
- On the Form Design Tools Design tab, in the Controls group, click the More button, and then click the List Box tool.
- Position the pointer's plus symbol (+) where you want to place the upper-left corner of the list box control, and then click the mouse button.
- If you use the List Box Control Wizard, complete the dialog boxes to choose the source of the list, select the fields to appear in the list box, select a sort order, size the columns, and select the label; or if you do not use the List Box Wizard, set the Row Source property and size the list box control.

Now you'll add the list box control to the form.

To add the list box control to the form and position its label:

1. Click the **Form Design Tools Design** tab, in the Controls group, click the **More** button, and then make sure the **Use Control Wizards** tool is not selected.
2. In the Controls gallery, click the **List Box** tool. You may have to scroll to locate it.
3. Position the pointer's plus symbol (+) approximately 0.5 inches from the top and 0.5 inches from the left edge of the Details section, and then click the mouse button. A list box control and attached label control appear in the form. See Figure 10–22.

   Trouble? If your list box control is sized or positioned differently, resize it or move it until it matches the list box control shown in Figure 10–22.

Figure 10–22 Form with the list box control and label control

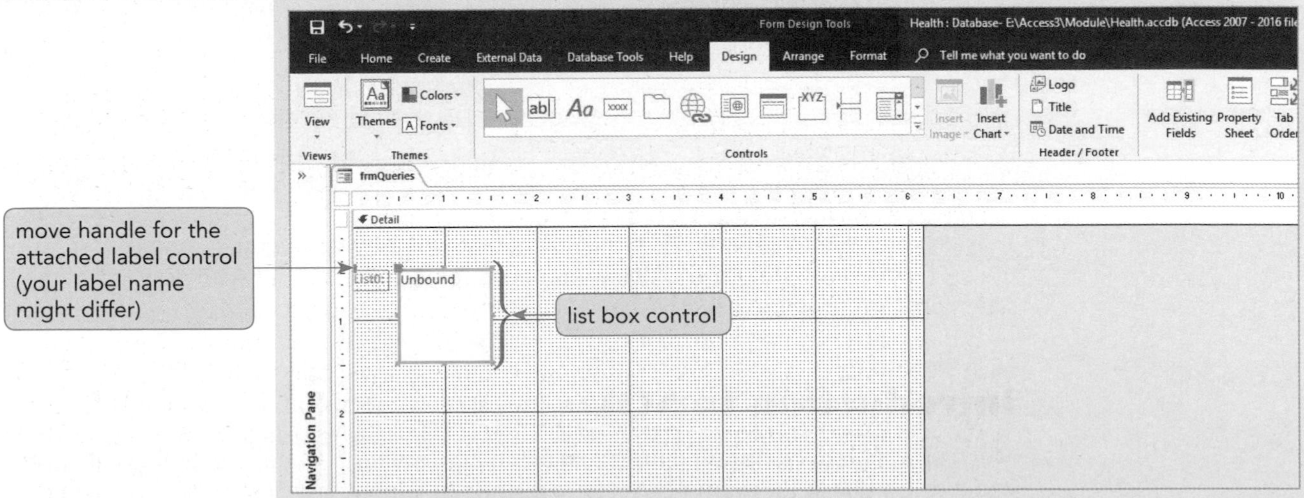
move handle for the attached label control (your label name might differ)
list box control
Form Design Tools
Health : Database- E:\Access3\Module\Health.accdb (Access 2007 - 2016 file
File
Home
Create
External Data
Database Tools
Help
Design
Arrange
Format
Tell me what you want to do
View
Themes
Colors
Fonts
Insert Image
Insert Chart
Logo
Title
Date and Time
Add Existing Fields
Property Sheet
Tab Order
Views
Themes
Controls
Header / Footer
frmQueries
Detail
List0:
Unbound
Navigation Pane

Next you'll move the attached label control from its current position to above the list box control.

4. Click the label control to select it, position the mouse pointer on the move handle in the upper-left corner of the label control, and then drag it to position it two grid dots above the list box control and aligned with the left edge of the list box control.

You can now set the Caption property for the label control.

5. Open the Property Sheet, and then click the **Format** tab, if necessary.
6. Set the label control's Caption property value to **Available Queries**.
7. Resize the label control by dragging its right border to the right until it is wide enough to display all of the caption text.
8. Close the Property Sheet. Now you'll save the form and check your progress by switching to Form view.
9. Save your form design changes, and then switch to Form view. See Figure 10–23.

Figure 10–23 frmQueries form displayed in Form view

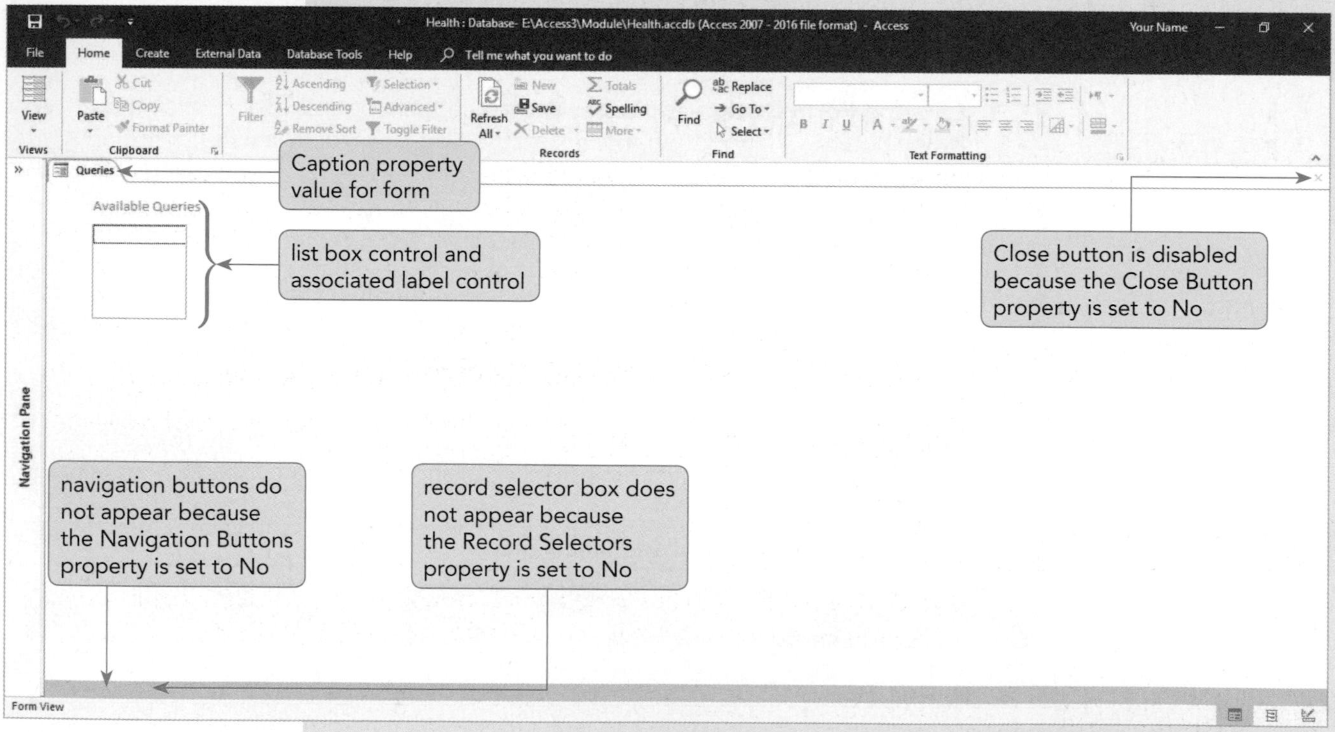
Caption property value for form
list box control and associated label control
Close button is disabled because the Close Button property is set to No
navigation buttons do not appear because the Navigation Buttons property is set to No
record selector box does not appear because the Record Selectors property is set to No
Queries
Available Queries
Form View

Next you need to enter the SQL statement that will provide the query names for the list box control. Before you do so, you need to become familiar with how SQL statements are structured.

Introduction to SQL

Much of what is accomplished in Access behind the scenes is done with SQL. Whenever you create a query, for example, Access constructs an equivalent SQL statement. When you save a query, Access also saves the SQL statement version of the query.

In viewing the SQL statements, you'll recognize some of the query statement names. This is not a coincidence. SQL has five statement types: select, update, delete, insert, and create. These correspond with the Access queries Select, Update, Delete, Append, and Make Table. For example, the following SQL statement selects records in the tblPatient table, selecting the fields PatientID, LastName, FirstName, and City where the city is Atlanta:

SELECT tblPatient.PatientID, tblPatient.LastName, tblPatient.FirstName, tblPatient.City FROM tblPatient

WHERE (((tblPatient.City)="Atlanta"));

INSIGHT

Using SQL

Instead of using an application with a graphical user interface like Access, which allows you to perform database tasks by clicking buttons and completing dialog boxes, a database administrator in a large organization uses a relational DBMS such as mySQL or Oracle and uses SQL statements to query, update, delete, and make tables. Every full-featured relational DBMS has its own version of the current standard SQL. If you learn SQL for one relational DBMS, it's a relatively easy task to begin using SQL for other relational DBMSs. When you work with two or more relational DBMSs, which is the case in most companies, you'll learn that few differences exist among the various SQL versions.

Viewing a SQL Statement for a Query

When you are working in Design view or viewing a query recordset, you can see the SQL statement that is equivalent to your query by switching to SQL view.

You'll start learning about SQL by examining the SQL statements that are equivalent to two existing queries: qryPatientsByName and qryVisitsAndInvoices.

To view the SQL statement for the qryPatientsByName query:

1. Open the Navigation Pane, open the **qryPatientsByName** query datasheet, and then close the Navigation Pane. The query displays 52 records from the tblPatient table. The columns displayed are Patient, Patient ID, Last Name, First Name, Parent, Date of Birth, Phone, Address, City, State, Zip, and Email.
2. Right-click the **qryPatientsByName** object tab to open the shortcut menu, click **SQL View** to display the query in SQL view, and then click a blank area of the window to deselect the SQL statement. See Figure 10–24.

Figure 10–24 **SQL view for the qryPatientsByName query**

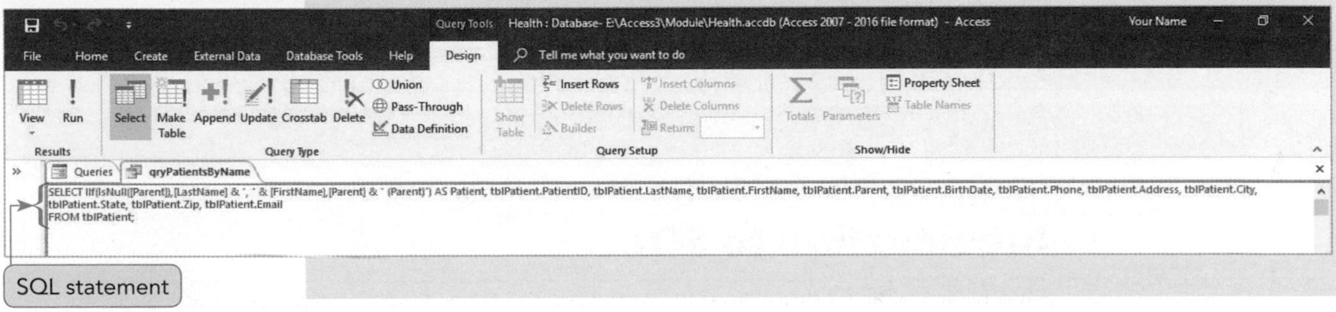
SELECT IIf(IsNull([Parent]),[LastName] & ", " & [FirstName],[Parent] & " (Parent)") AS Patient, tblPatient.PatientID, tblPatient.LastName, tblPatient.FirstName, tblPatient.Parent, tblPatient.BirthDate, tblPatient.Phone, tblPatient.Address, tblPatient.City, tblPatient.State, tblPatient.Zip, tblPatient.Email
FROM tblPatient;
SQL statement

Thus far, you have been able to complete all Access database tasks using the options on the ribbon, in dialog boxes, and in the Property Sheet. If you learn SQL so you can use it efficiently, you will be able to enter your own SQL statements in SQL view. If you work with more complicated databases, you might find that you need the extra power of the SQL language to implement your database strategies fully.

TIP

The first clause of a SQL statement begins with SELECT, CREATE, UPDATE, DELETE, or INSERT.

SQL uses the **SELECT statement** to define what data it retrieves from a database and how it presents the data. A SELECT statement like the one shown in Figure 10–24 must follow these rules:

- The basic form of a SQL SELECT statement includes four sections, known as clauses. Each clause starts with a different keyword: SELECT, FROM, WHERE, and ORDER BY. After the SELECT keyword, you list the fields you want to display. After FROM, you list the tables used in the query. After WHERE, you list the selection criteria. After ORDER BY, you list the sort fields.
- If a field name includes a space or a special symbol, you enclose the field name in brackets. Because the Health database does not use field names with spaces or special symbols, you don't have to enclose its field names in brackets. However, if your database had a field name such as *Contract Type*, then you would use [Contract Type] in a SQL statement. Some database administrators prefer to enclose every field name in square brackets to make it easier to identify field names in SQL statements.
- You precede a field name with the name of its table by connecting the table name to the field name with a period. For example, you would enter the PatientID field in the tblVisit table as *tblVisit.PatientID*.
- You use commas to separate values in a list of field names or a list of table names, and you end the SELECT statement with a semicolon.

The SQL statement shown in Figure 10–24 selects the Patient, Patient ID, Last Name, First Name, Parent, Date of Birth, Phone, Address, City, State, Zip, and Email fields from the tblPatient table; the records are sorted in ascending order by the Patient ID field. The SQL statement does not contain a WHERE clause, so the recordset includes all records from the tblPatient table when the query is run.

You can enter or change SQL statements directly in SQL view. If you enter a SQL statement and then switch to Design view, you will see its equivalent in the design grid.

Next, you'll examine the SQL statement for the qryVisitsAndInvoices query.

To view the SQL statement for the qryVisitsAndInvoices query:

1. Close the qryPatientsByName query, open the Navigation Pane, open the **qryVisitsAndInvoices** query in Design view, and then close the Navigation Pane. The query selects data from the tblVisit and tblBilling tables and does not sort the records. The fields included in the query design are PatientID, VisitID, InvoiceAmt, VisitDate, and Reason.
2. On the Query Tools Design tab, in the Results group, click the **View** button arrow, click **SQL View** to change to SQL view, and then click a blank area of the window to deselect the SQL statement. See Figure 10–25.

Figure 10–25 SQL view for the qryVisitsAndInvoices query

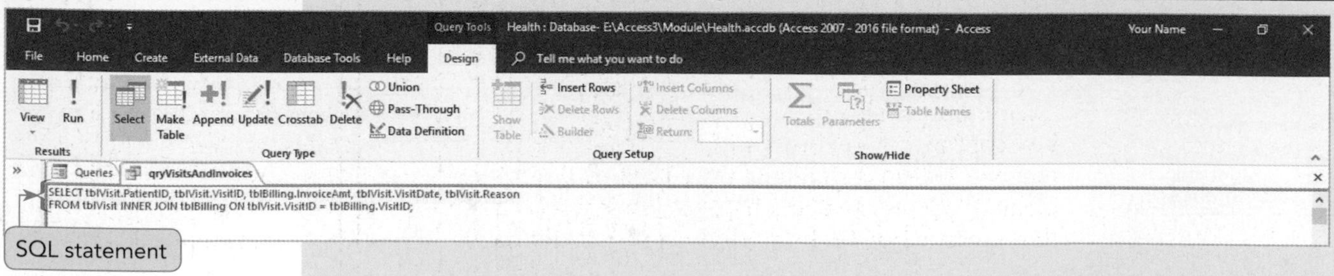
Query Tools
Health : Database- E:\Access3\Module\Health.accdb (Access 2007 - 2016 file format) - Access
Your Name
File
Home
Create
External Data
Database Tools
Help
Design
Tell me what you want to do
View
Run
Select
Make Table
Append
Update
Crosstab
Delete
Union
Pass-Through
Data Definition
Show Table
Insert Rows
Delete Rows
Builder
Insert Columns
Delete Columns
Return:
Totals
Parameters
Property Sheet
Table Names
Results
Query Type
Query Setup
Show/Hide
Queries
qryVisitsAndInvoices
SELECT tblVisit.PatientID, tblVisit.VisitID, tblBilling.InvoiceAmt, tblVisit.VisitDate, tblVisit.Reason
FROM tblVisit INNER JOIN tblBilling ON tblVisit.VisitID = tblBilling.VisitID;
SQL statement

The SELECT statement for this query is similar to the one shown in Figure 10–24, except that it includes an INNER JOIN clause. The INNER JOIN clause selects records from the two tables only when the records have the same value in the common fields that link the tables. The general syntax for a SQL statement with an inner join is the following:

SELECT *field list* FROM *Table1* INNER JOIN *Table2* ON *Table1.Field1* = *Table2.Field2*;

Access uses the ON clause instead of the standard SQL WHERE clause.

3. Close the query. The frmQueries form in Form view is now the active object.

The SQL SELECT statements mirror the query options you viewed in Design view. In effect, every choice you make in Design view is reflected as part of the SQL SELECT statement. Viewing the SQL statements generated from queries that you design is an effective way to begin learning SQL.

You now can enter the SQL statement that will provide the query names for the list box control.

Using a SQL Statement for a List Box Control

You'll use a SQL SELECT statement to retrieve the list of query names from one of the Access system tables. **System tables** are special tables maintained by Access that store information about the characteristics of a database and about the structure of the objects in the database. Although system tables do not appear in the Navigation Pane, you can retrieve information from them using SELECT statements. One of the system tables, the **MSysObjects table**, keeps track of the names, types, and other characteristics of every object in a database. The Name and Type fields are the two MSysObjects table fields you'll use in the SELECT statement. The Type field value contains a numeric value that corresponds to an object type. Figure 10–26 shows the numbers that correspond to some commonly used objects. For instance, a table is a type 1 object, and a query is a type 5 object. If the Type value of an MSObject is 5, then the MSObject referred to must be a query. The values may seem cryptic, but think of them as values that Microsoft developers have assigned to these objects so they can use a number instead of a name.

Figure 10–26 **MSysObjects table Type field values**

Object Type	Type Field Value in MSysObjects Table
Table	1
Query	5
Form	–32768
Report	–32764
Macro	–32766
Module	–32761

TIP

SQL is not case sensitive, but typing SQL keywords in uppercase is an industry convention and makes the statements more readable.

Access creates special system queries to handle many tasks for you; each of these queries has a name that begins with the tilde (~) character. When a form contains a list box control, combo box control, or subform control, Access creates a system query to manage the functionality of these controls. For instance, when the frmVisit form was created, Access created a hidden system query called ~sq_ffrmVisit. You cannot see these system queries because users should not be able to run them or manipulate them.

The purpose of the system queries is to manage the functionality of the form controls. You want to exclude the special system queries from the list box control you've created for the user interface. Because every system query name begins with the ~ character, you'll use the Left function in your SELECT statement to identify the query names that begin with ~ and exclude those from the list of queries to appear in the list box control. The **Left function** provides the first character(s) in a text string. The format of the Left function is *Left*(text string, number of characters). You'll test the first character of the name of each query to determine if it is the ~ character. If the first character is not the ~ character, you'll include the query name in the list box control. You'll use *Left([Name],1)* to retrieve the first character of the Name field, and you'll use the not equal operator (<>). To include only those queries whose names do not begin with the ~ character, you'll use the expression *Left([Name],1)<>"~"*. Access interprets this expression as "the first character of the Name field does not equal the ~ character." The complete SELECT statement that you will use to select the list of query names is as follows:

SELECT [Name] FROM MSysObjects WHERE [Type]=5 And Left([Name],1)<>"~" ORDER BY [Name];

Recall that the Row Source property for a control specifies the data source, such as a table, a query, or a SQL statement. You'll enter the SELECT statement as the value for the Row Source property for the list box control you created.

To set the Row Source property for the list box control:

1. Switch to Design view, right-click the **list box** control to open the shortcut menu, click **Properties** to open the Property Sheet, and then click the **Data** tab (if necessary).
2. Right-click the **Row Source** box to open the shortcut menu, and then click **Zoom**. The Zoom dialog box opens.
3. In the Zoom dialog box, type **SELECT [Name] FROM MSysObjects WHERE [Type]=5 And Left([Name],1)<>"~" ORDER BY [Name];** as shown in Figure 10–27.

Be sure to type the semicolon at the end of the SELECT statement.

Figure 10–27 SELECT statement for the list box control

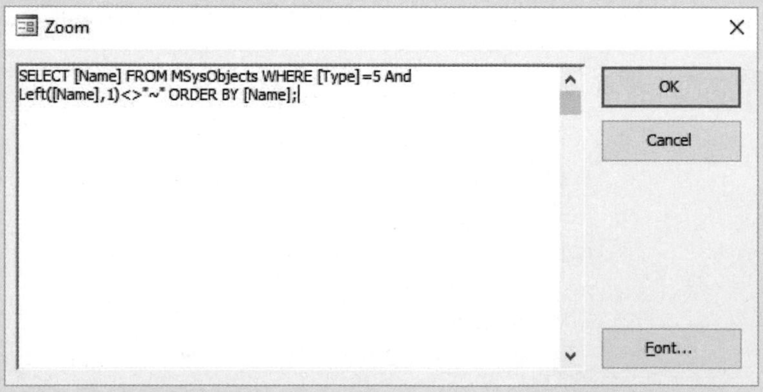
Zoom
SELECT [Name] FROM MSysObjects WHERE [Type]=5 And Left([Name],1)<>"~" ORDER BY [Name];
OK
Cancel
Font...

4. Click the **OK** button to close the Zoom dialog box.
5. Close the Property Sheet, save your form design changes, and then switch to Form view. The queries in the database (excluding system queries) now appear in alphabetical order in the list box control. See Figure 10–28.

Figure 10–28 List box control displaying query names

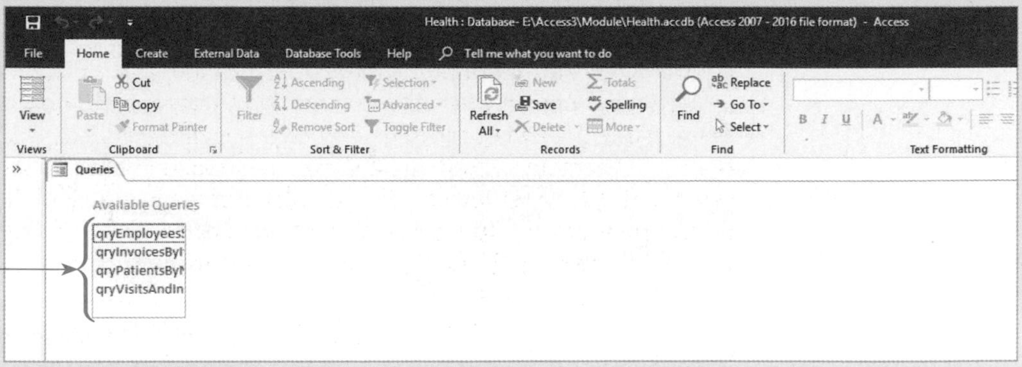
query names retrieved by a SQL statement from the MSysObjects table
Health : Database- E:\Access3\Module\Health.accdb (Access 2007 - 2016 file format) - Access
Queries
Available Queries
qryEmployees
qryInvoicesBy
qryPatientsBy
qryVisitsAndIn

Trouble? If a syntax error message appears, click the OK button, switch to Design view, right-click the list box control, click Properties, right-click the Row Source box, and then click Zoom. Correct the SELECT statement so it's the same as the statement shown in Step 3, click the OK button, and then repeat Step 5.

6. Switch to Layout view, and then resize the list box by dragging its right border to the right until the query names are fully displayed.

TIP

If you use the Use Control Wizards tool to add a command button control, you can attach a standard Access action (such as opening a specific query or closing a window) or a macro to the button.

Next you will add the two command button controls to the form that are specified in Mista's design: Preview and Display. The Preview command button will allow users to view the query in Print Preview, and the Display command button will allow users to view the query as a datasheet. When a user clicks either command button, the query that opens is the query the user has selected in the list box. For the Print Preview button, you'll attach a macro to the command button's On Click property that will display the selected query in Print Preview. Similarly, you'll attach a macro to the Display command button that will display the selected query as a datasheet. You'll add both command button controls and appropriate macros to the form. First, you'll add the Preview command button to the form.

To add the Preview command button control to the form:

1. Switch to Design view, click the **Form Design Tools Design** tab, and then increase the width of the form to 4" and the length of the form to 4" (if necessary).
2. In the Controls group, click the **More** button, make sure the Use Control Wizards tool is deselected, and then in the Controls group, click the **Button** tool.
3. Position the pointer's plus symbol (+) below and aligned with the left edge of the list box control in the Details section, and then click the mouse button.

   A command button control is added to the form.
4. If necessary, open the Property Sheet for the command button control.

   You can now change the default text that appears on the command button to the word "Preview" and add the Print Preview picture. When you add the picture, the button will be too small to display both the picture and the caption. You'll fix that in subsequent steps.

5. In the Property Sheet, click the **Format** tab (if necessary), set the Caption property to **Preview**, click the **Picture** box, and then click the **Build** button ... on the right end of the Picture box. The Picture Builder dialog box opens.
6. Scroll the Available Pictures box, and then click **Preview**. A Print Preview picture appears on the command button in the Sample box.
7. Click **OK** to close the Picture Builder dialog box and to place the Print Preview picture on the command button.
8. Click the **Picture Caption Arrangement** box, click its **arrow**, and then click **Bottom**.

   Mista wants you to change the background color of the command button. You'll change the color and then resize the button control to display the caption as well.

9. On the Property Sheet, click the **Back Color** box, click its **Build** button ..., in the Theme Colors section, click **Green, Accent 6, Lighter 60%** (third color down in the last column), and then close the Property Sheet.
10. Use the bottom-right sizing handle and the middle-right sizing handle to change the size of the command button control to match the size shown in Figure 10–29. The width of the button should be less than half the width of the list box control because you'll be adding another button control of the same size to the right. See Figure 10–29.

Figure 10–29 Preview command button added to the form

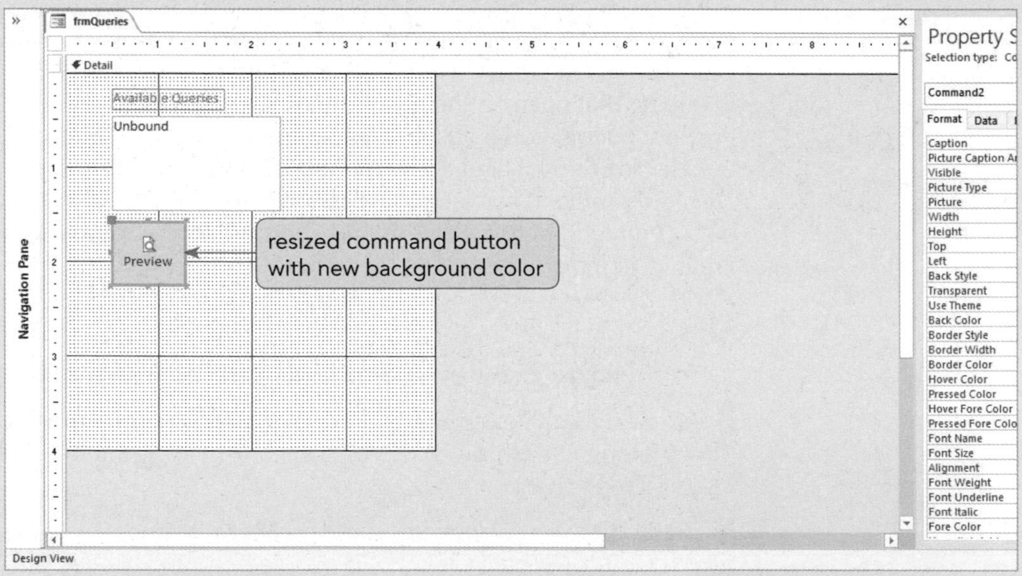
frmQueries
Detail
Available Queries
Unbound
Preview
resized command button with new background color
Navigation Pane
Design View
Property S
Selection type: Co
Command2
Format
Data
Caption
Picture Caption Ar
Visible
Picture Type
Picture
Width
Height
Top
Left
Back Style
Transparent
Use Theme
Back Color
Border Style
Border Width
Border Color
Hover Color
Pressed Color
Hover Fore Color
Pressed Fore Colo
Font Name
Font Size
Alignment
Font Weight
Font Underline
Font Italic
Fore Color

Instead of repeating the steps to add the command button control for viewing a query recordset, you'll copy the Preview command button control and paste it in the Detail section. This will also ensure the button controls are the same dimensions. After moving the copied button control into position, you can change its properties to control the text and picture that will appear on it.

To add the Display command button control to the form:

1. Right-click the **Preview** command button control, and then click **Copy** on the shortcut menu.
2. Right-click a blank area of the grid, and then click **Paste** on the shortcut menu. A copy of the command button is added in the upper-left corner of the Detail section.
3. Move the new command button into position to the right of the original command button, aligning the bottom edges of the two buttons and aligning the right edge of the new button with the right edge of the list box. See Figure 10–30.

Figure 10–30 **Command button control duplicated and repositioned**

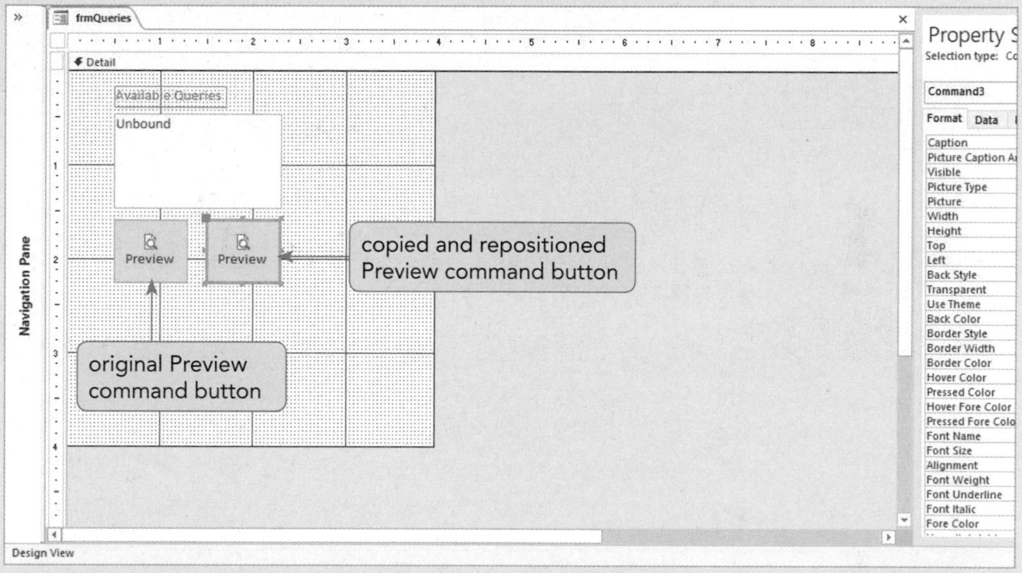
copied and repositioned Preview command button
original Preview command button

4. Open the Property Sheet for the new command button (if necessary), set the Caption property to **Display**, click the **Picture property Build button** [...], and then in the Picture Builder dialog box, set the Picture property to **MS Access Query**.
5. Save your form design changes.

Before creating the macros for the form and for the command button controls to open the query selected by the user, you'll set the Name property for the list box control. The naming convention for a list box control is to use the three-letter prefix LST in lowercase (lst). You'll enter the name lstQueryList for the list box control. You'll also set the background color of the Detail section and the list box control.

To set the Name property for the list box and to set background colors:

Be sure to type the first character as a lowercase L, not as a number 1.

1. Click the list box control to make it the active control.
2. In the Property Sheet, click the **All** tab, select the value in the **Name** box, and then type **lstQueryList**.

3. Click the **Back Color** box, click its **Build** button, and then in the Theme Colors section of the color palette, click the **White, Background 1** color (row 1, column 1).
4. Click the **Detail** section bar, and then set the section's Back Color property to **White, Background 1, Darker 15%** (row 3, column 1 in the Theme Colors section of the color palette).
5. Save your form design changes, and then switch to Form view to display the completed frmQueries form. See Figure 10–31.

Figure 10–31 Completed list box control

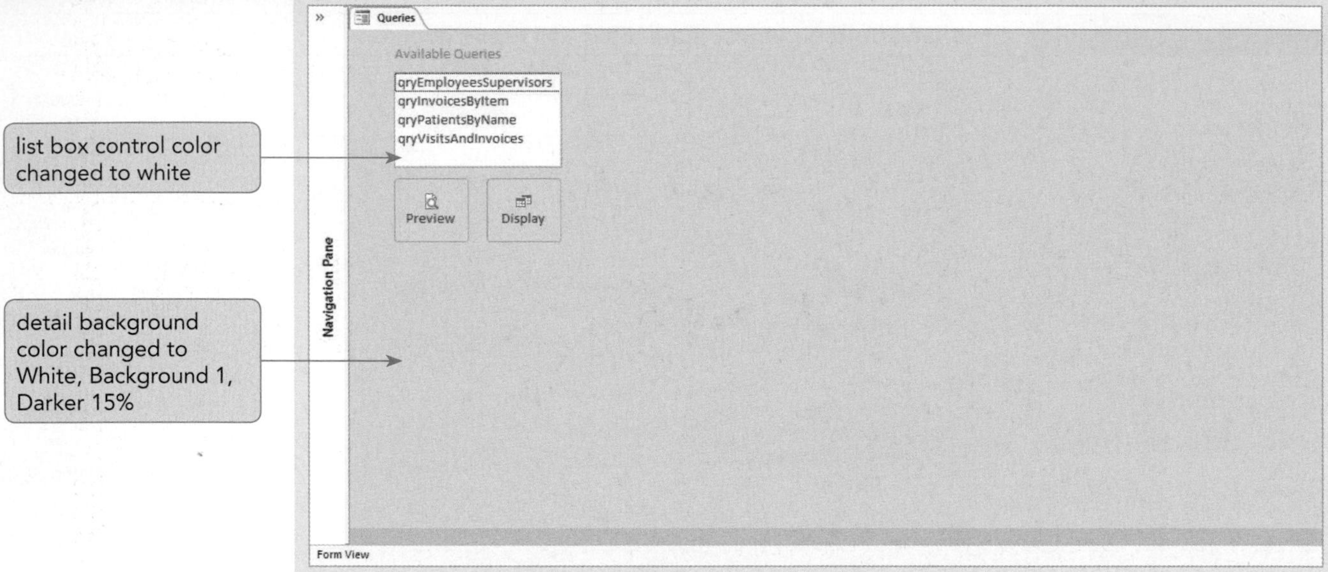
list box control color changed to white
detail background color changed to White, Background 1, Darker 15%
Queries
Available Queries
qryEmployeesSupervisors
qryInvoicesByItem
qryPatientsByName
qryVisitsAndInvoices
Preview
Display
Navigation Pane
Form View

You now can create the macros for the frmQueries form.

Creating Multiple Macros for a Form

Mista wants to highlight the first query name in the list box control when the frmQueries form first opens. You can accomplish this by placing the focus on the first query name. When an item has the focus, it may be selected and appear highlighted, or a flashing insertion point may be visible in the control. In general, it is a good practice to ensure a form element has the focus when the form opens so that if a user presses ENTER, the default behavior of the element with the focus is executed. If no form controls have the focus when a form opens and a user presses ENTER, an error message might be displayed, which could confuse or frustrate users. To avoid this situation, you'll place the focus on the first query name in the lstQueryList list box control when the form opens.

When a user double-clicks a query name in the list box or selects a query name and then clicks the Display command button, the selected query should open in Datasheet view. When a user selects a query name in the list box and then clicks the Preview command button, the selected query should open in Print Preview. You'll create and attach four different macros to the objects on your form to enable these behaviors. You'll start by creating and attaching a macro to the On Load property for the form to place the focus on the first query name in the list box control and highlight it when the form opens.

The **Load event** occurs when a form or report opens. When you attach a macro to the Load event through the On Load property for the form, the actions in the macro are processed each time the form opens. You'll create a macro containing two actions. First, you'll use the GoToControl action to move the focus to the list box control. This action does not set the focus to any specific query name in the list box control, so you'll use the SendKeys action to send the DOWN ARROW keystroke to the list box control. The SendKeys action will result in the first query name in the list box being highlighted. The end result of these two actions will be that when a user opens the frmQueries form, the first query name will have the focus.

To create the macro for the On Load property:

1. Switch to Design view, and then, in the Property Sheet, click the **Event** tab.
2. Click the **On Load** box, and then click its **Build** button [...]. The Choose Builder dialog box opens and includes three options for setting the property value. See Figure 10–32.

Figure 10–32 **Choose Builder dialog box**

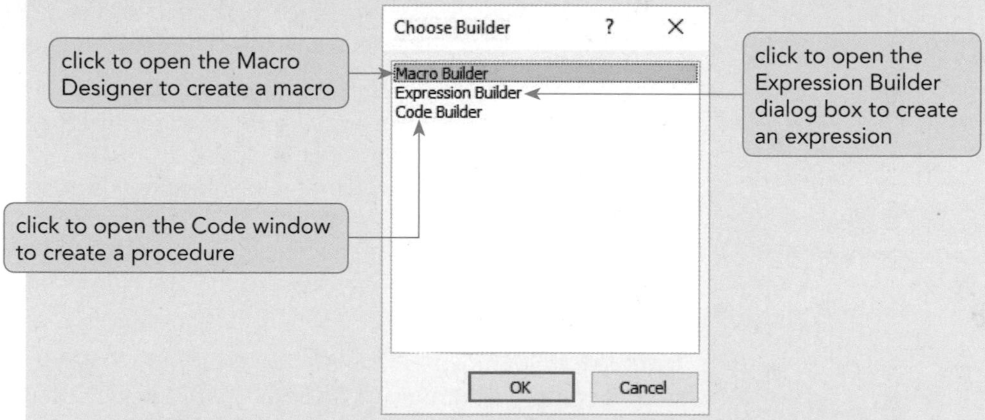
Choose Builder
?
Macro Builder
Expression Builder
Code Builder
OK
Cancel
click to open the Macro Designer to create a macro
click to open the Expression Builder dialog box to create an expression
click to open the Code window to create a procedure

You'll attach a macro to the event property.

3. Make sure **Macro Builder** is selected, and then click **OK** to open the Macro Designer.
4. Click the **Add New Action** arrow to display the list of actions, and then click **GoToControl**. The list closes, and a new GoToControl action is added with one argument.
5. In the Control Name box, type **lst** and then double-click the **lstQueryList** AutoComplete option. This is the Name property setting for the list box control.

   Trouble? If you do not see the lstQueryList AutoComplete value, you most likely typed the number 1 as the first character instead of a lowercase L. Delete the characters you have typed and retype the correct beginning characters.

   The second and final action you need to add is the SendKeys action. The SendKeys action doesn't appear in the Add New Action list. You'll verify this and then use the Show All Actions button to display the SendKeys action.
6. Click the **Add New Action** arrow, scroll down the list, notice that the SendKeys action doesn't appear in the list, and then click the **Add New Action** arrow to close the list.
7. On the Macro Tools Design tab, in the Show/Hide group, position the mouse pointer over the **Show All Actions** button to display the button's ScreenTip. See Figure 10–33.

Figure 10–33 Macro for the On Load property of the form

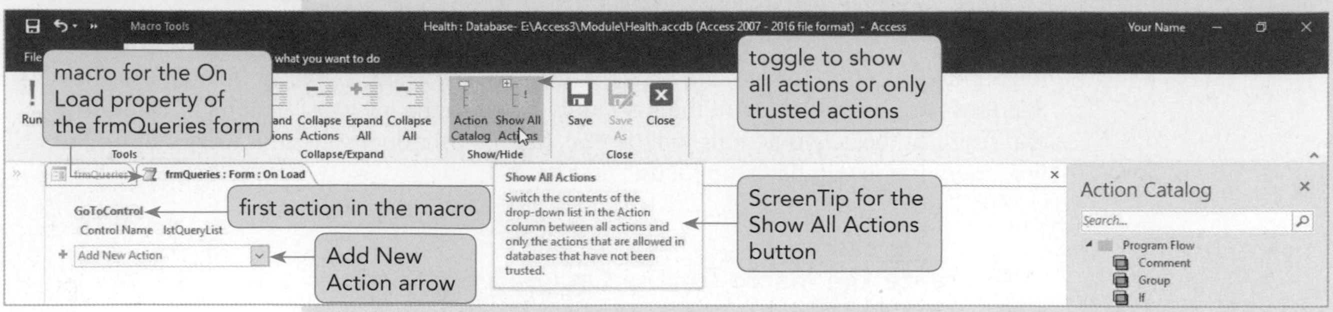

macro for the On Load property of the frmQueries form
toggle to show all actions or only trusted actions
first action in the macro
ScreenTip for the Show All Actions button
Add New Action arrow

By default, only trusted actions are displayed in the Add New Action list, but you can display all actions by clicking the Show All Actions button. The actions that are categorized as unsafe actions (not trusted) are not displayed in the list by default; this includes the SendKeys action. This action is considered unsafe because an inexperienced developer could use the SendKeys action to send keystrokes to the database application that could delete data, for instance. Because you need to use the SendKeys action and you understand the risks, you'll display all actions so you can select it from the menu.

8. In the Show/Hide group, click the **Show All Actions** button to toggle it on, click the **Add New Action** arrow, scroll the list, and then click **SendKeys**. The list closes, and a SendKeys action is added to the macro with two arguments. You'll use the Keystrokes value of {Down}, which represents the DOWN ARROW keystroke, and a Wait value of No, which prevents the macro from pausing when it runs. (If the macro pauses, the DOWN ARROW keystroke might not be received right away, and the first query in the list box control may not receive the focus.)

   Trouble? If SendKeys isn't in the list, check the Show All Actions button; if it has a white background, it is toggled off. Click it again, click the Add New Action arrow, and then select the SendKeys action.

9. In the Keystrokes box, type **{Down}** to complete the macro. See Figure 10–34.

Figure 10–34 Completed macro for the On Load property of the form

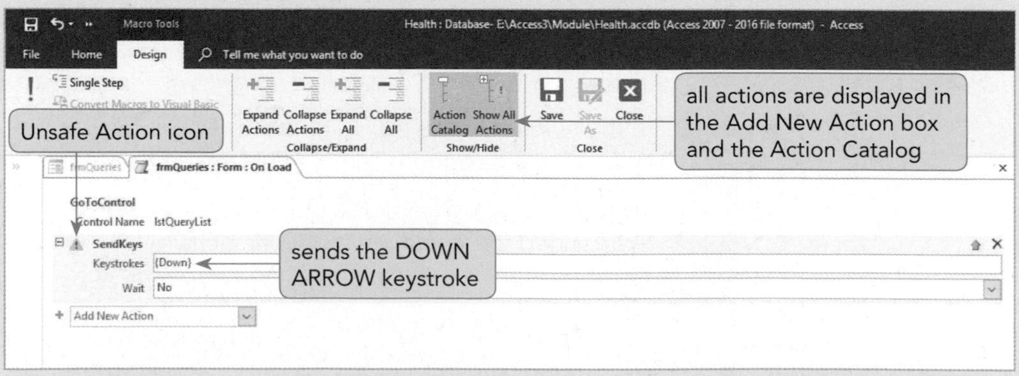

Unsafe Action icon
all actions are displayed in the Add New Action box and the Action Catalog
sends the DOWN ARROW keystroke

10. Position the mouse pointer over the icon to the left of the SendKeys action. The icon's ScreenTip of "Unsafe Action" identifies that the action isn't a trusted action.

11. Save the macro, and then close the Macro Designer to return to the frmQueries form in Design view.

Now you'll create the macros for the Preview and Display command button controls.

To create the macros for the command button controls:

1. Click the **Preview** command button control.
2. In the Property Sheet, click the **On Click** box (if necessary), click its **Build** button [...] to open the Choose Builder dialog box, and then click the **OK** button to open the Macro Designer.

   When users click the Preview command button, the query selected in the list box control should open in Print Preview.
3. Click the **Add New Action** arrow, scroll the list, and then click **OpenQuery**. The list closes, and a new OpenQuery action is added with three arguments.

   You'll enter the expression *=[lstQueryList]* in the Query Name box to indicate the query to open is equal to the name of the query selected in the lstQueryList list box control.
4. In the Query Name box, type an equal sign (**=**). The Query Name arrow to the right of the Query Name box changes to the Expression Builder button.
5. Click the **Expression Builder** button to open the Expression Builder dialog box, double-click **lstQueryList** in the Expression Categories list, and then click **OK** to close the dialog box. The expression *= [lstQueryList]* is now displayed in the Query Name box.
6. Click the **View** arrow, and then click **Print Preview** to complete the macro. See Figure 10–35.

Figure 10–35 Completed macro for the Preview command button

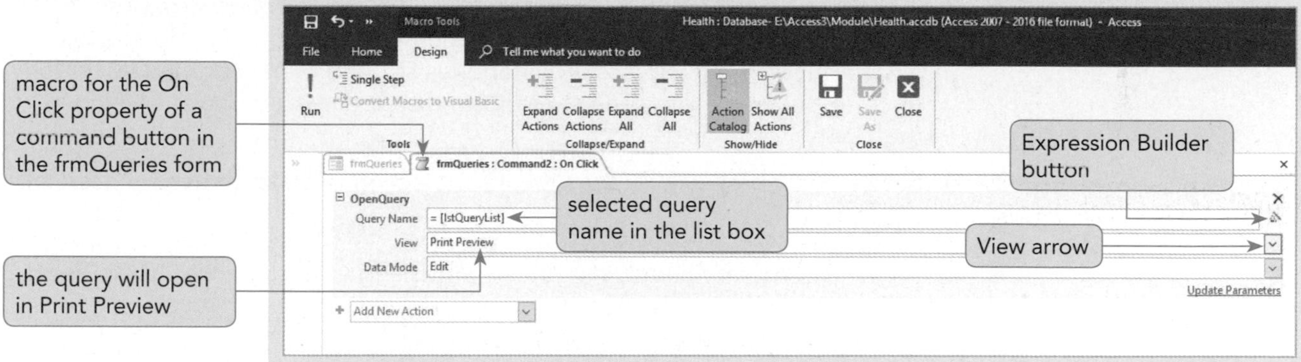
macro for the On Click property of a command button in the frmQueries form
the query will open in Print Preview
Expression Builder button
selected query name in the list box
View arrow
Macro Tools
Health : Database- E:\Access3\Module\Health.accdb (Access 2007 - 2016 file format) - Access
File
Home
Design
Tell me what you want to do
Single Step
Convert Macros to Visual Basic
Run
Tools
Expand Actions
Collapse Actions
Expand All
Collapse All
Collapse/Expand
Action Catalog
Show All Actions
Show/Hide
Save
Save As
Close
frmQueries
frmQueries : Command2 : On Click
OpenQuery
Query Name
= [lstQueryList]
View
Print Preview
Data Mode
Edit
Add New Action
Update Parameters

   Because you did not set the Name property for the command buttons, the object tab displays the default name of Command2 (your name might be different).
7. Save the macro, and then close the Macro Designer.

   Next you'll create the macro for the Display command button.
8. Repeat Steps 2 to 5 for the Display command button.
9. Set the View property for the OpenQuery action to **Datasheet** (if necessary). See Figure 10–36.

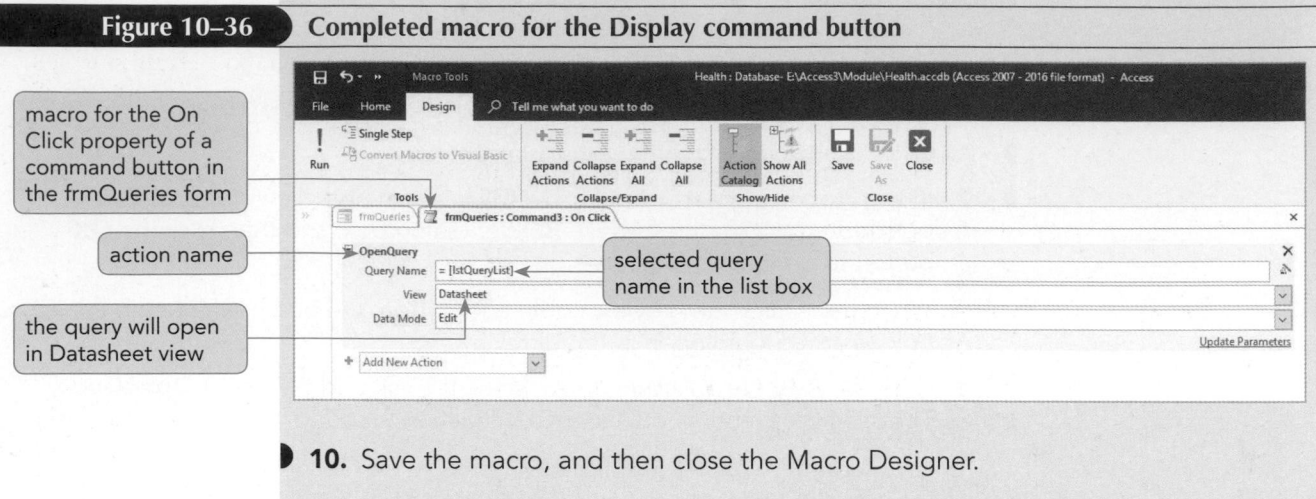

Figure 10–36 Completed macro for the Display command button

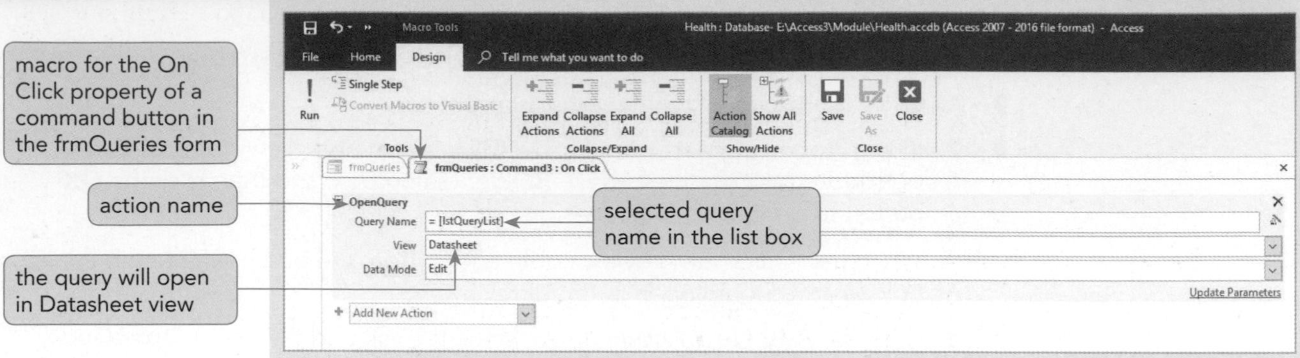
macro for the On Click property of a command button in the frmQueries form
action name
the query will open in Datasheet view
selected query name in the list box
Macro Tools
Health : Database- E:\Access3\Module\Health.accdb (Access 2007 - 2016 file format) - Access
File
Home
Design
Tell me what you want to do
Single Step
Convert Macros to Visual Basic
Run
Expand Actions
Collapse Actions
Expand All
Collapse All
Action Catalog
Show All Actions
Save
Save As
Close
Tools
Collapse/Expand
Show/Hide
Close
frmQueries
frmQueries : Command3 : On Click
OpenQuery
Query Name
= [lstQueryList]
View
Datasheet
Data Mode
Edit
Update Parameters
Add New Action

10. Save the macro, and then close the Macro Designer.

Next you'll add a macro that will open a query in Datasheet view if the user double-clicks a query name in the list box control.

To create the macro for the list box control:

1. Click the **list box** control, in the Property Sheet, click the **On Dbl Click** box, click its **Build** button [...] to open the Choose Builder dialog box, and then click the **OK** button to open the Macro Designer.
2. Click the **Add New Action** arrow, scroll the list, and then click **OpenQuery**. The list closes, and a new OpenQuery action is added with three arguments.
3. In the Query Name box, type an equal sign (**=**), click the **Expression Builder** button to open the Expression Builder dialog box, double-click **lstQueryList** in the Expression Categories list, and then click the **OK** button to close the dialog box. The expression *=[lstQueryList]* is now displayed in the Query Name box.
4. Set the View property for the OpenQuery action to **Datasheet** (if necessary).
5. Save the macro, and then close the Macro Designer.
6. Close the Property Sheet, save your form changes, and then switch to Form view.

You have finished creating the macros for the form. Next, you will test the list box control and the command button controls.

After creating a custom form, you should test the form in Form view. For the frmQueries form, you need to double-click a query name in the list box to make sure the query datasheet opens. You also need to scroll the list box, click a query name, and then click the Display command button to make sure the query datasheet opens and click the Preview command button to make sure the query opens in Print Preview.

To test the form's controls:

1. Double-click the first query name in the list box to verify that the correct query datasheet opens, and then close the query to make the frmQueries form the active object.

2. Repeat Step 1 for each of the other query names in the list box.
3. Click a query name in the list box, click the **Preview** command button to verify that the correct query opens in Print Preview, and then close the Print Preview window to make the frmQueries form the active object.

   Note that the Preview command button turns blue when the mouse pointer is positioned on it and when it is clicked. This formatting is applied to the button automatically.
4. Repeat Step 3 for the other query names in the list box.
5. Click a query name in the list box, click the **Display** command button to verify that the correct query datasheet opens, and then close the query to make the frmQueries form the active object.
6. Repeat Step 5 for the other query names in the list box.

   Because the frmQueries form's Close button is disabled, you need to switch to Design view, which still has an enabled Close button, to close the form, or you can close the form by using the shortcut menu for the form object's tab.
7. Right-click the **Queries** tab, and then click **Close** on the shortcut menu.

You've completed the custom frmQueries form. The frmQueries form is an example of a form designed to allow a user to easily choose a select query and view the records, without having to know how to run a query from the Navigation Pane. Next, Mista wants you to create the navigation form for the Health database. You'll incorporate the frmQueries form into this overall navigation system.

Creating a Navigation Form

The frmVisit form is a great example of navigation using a single form. You can set properties in Access to display only a single form if that's sufficient to provide the functionality users need and to restrict them from being able to accidentally use other database objects or to corrupt data. If users need access to several queries, forms, reports, or other database objects, though, another option is to build a separate navigation form. A navigation form is a form with tabs that allows you to present database objects in an organized way to users.

A database generally uses either one or more single, independent forms or a navigation form. The choice to use one or the other generally depends on the designer's assessment of the abilities of people using the database. If the users have little experience with databases, a navigation form approach might be better. If they have more experience, a few well-designed forms that the users can select themselves might be a better approach.

Mista wants to restrict the access users have to the Health database to just the queries that will be displayed in the frmQueries form and to selected forms and reports. To control how users interact with the database, she wants you to create a navigation form that provides users access to only those database objects. Six predefined layouts for a navigation form are available in Access, with the layouts differing in the placement of tabs and subtabs. Of the several navigation form styles available, Mista wants you to use the Horizontal Tabs, 2 Levels layout.

To create the navigation form:

1. On the ribbon, click the **Create** tab.
2. In the Forms group, click the **Navigation** button. The Navigation gallery opens. See Figure 10–37.

Figure 10–37 The Navigation gallery

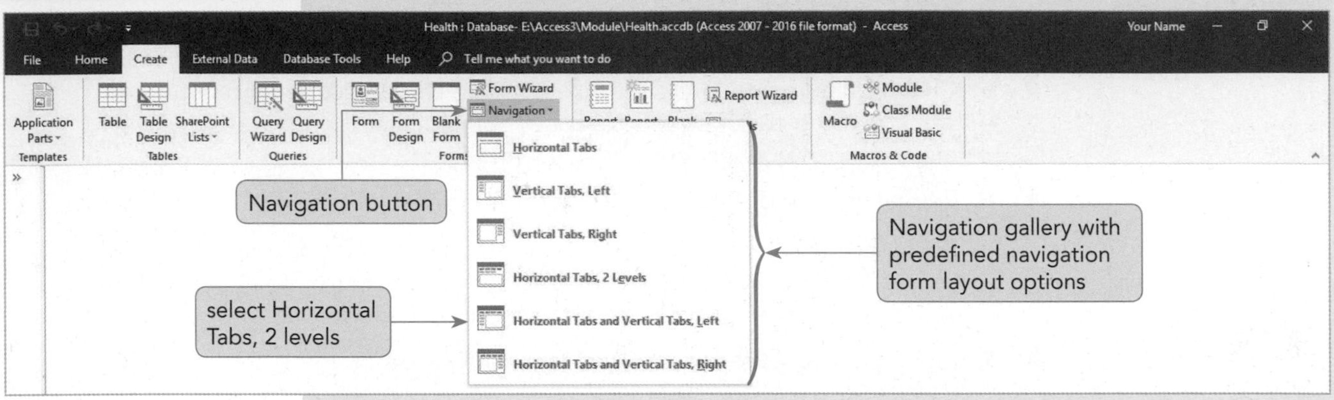
Health : Database- E:\Access3\Module\Health.accdb (Access 2007 - 2016 file format) - Access
Your Name
File
Home
Create
External Data
Database Tools
Help
Tell me what you want to do
Application Parts
Table
Table Design
SharePoint Lists
Query Wizard
Query Design
Form
Form Design
Blank Form
Form Wizard
Navigation
Report Wizard
Macro
Module
Class Module
Visual Basic
Templates
Tables
Queries
Macros & Code
Horizontal Tabs
Vertical Tabs, Left
Vertical Tabs, Right
Horizontal Tabs, 2 Levels
Horizontal Tabs and Vertical Tabs, Left
Horizontal Tabs and Vertical Tabs, Right
Navigation button
Navigation gallery with predefined navigation form layout options
select Horizontal Tabs, 2 levels

3. Click **Horizontal Tabs, 2 Levels** in the gallery, and then close the Field List pane. The navigation form with the default title of Navigation Form opens in Layout view. See Figure 10–38.

Figure 10–38 Initial navigation form

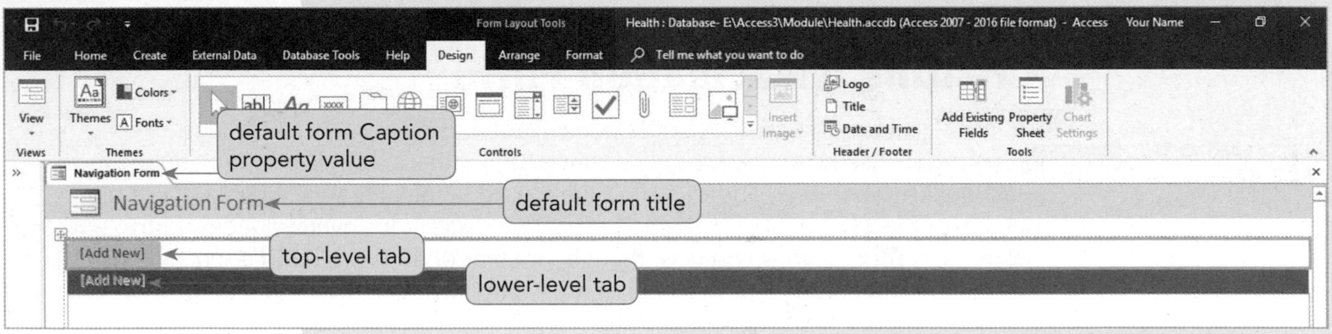
Form Layout Tools
Health : Database- E:\Access3\Module\Health.accdb (Access 2007 - 2016 file format) - Access
Your Name
File
Home
Create
External Data
Database Tools
Help
Design
Arrange
Format
Tell me what you want to do
View
Themes
Colors
Fonts
Logo
Title
Date and Time
Insert Image
Add Existing Fields
Property Sheet
Chart Settings
Views
Themes
Controls
Header / Footer
Tools
Navigation Form
default form Caption property value
default form title
[Add New]
top-level tab
lower-level tab

Because the navigation form won't display data from the database, it will be an unbound form. You'll enter the labels "Forms," "Reports," and "Queries" for the top-level tabs. You'll then drag the forms and reports that Mista wants to include in the navigation form from the Navigation Pane to the lower-level tabs. The Session 10.2 Visual Overview shows a preview of the completed top-level tabs as well as a lower-level tab. You won't add the frmVisit form to the navigation form because the frmVisit form was created as a manual navigation form for a more advanced user. The macros for previewing and displaying the records would not function in the navigation form because they become submacros of the frmVisit subform of the frmNavigation form. The macros would have to be rewritten to work in a navigation form. If you wanted to have this functionality in a navigation form, you would create a new version of the frmVisit form that is designed to work as a subform of a navigation form. The frmVisit form you created is designed to work as a stand-alone form, not as a subform. However, the simple select queries, simple forms, and reports all work well as subforms in a navigation form.

To add names and objects to the navigation form:

1. Click the top **[Add New]** tab, type **Forms**, and then press **ENTER**. The name on the first tab changes to Forms, and a second tab appears to its right.

   Trouble? If you type the first letter and it does not appear in the tab, click the tab again to switch to editing mode.

   Trouble? If you need to correct or change a tab name, click the name, edit the name, and then press ENTER.

2. Click the **[Add New]** tab to the right of the Forms tab, type **Queries**, and then press **ENTER**.

3. Click the **[Add New]** tab to the right of the Queries tab, type **Reports**, and then press **ENTER**. You have created the top-level tabs and named them Forms, Queries, and Reports. To create the lower-level tabs that will display these respective objects, you will drag some form and report objects from the Navigation Pane to the lower-level tabs. As you drag the objects, their names are added to the tabs.

TIP

You can drag only forms and reports, not queries, to tabs in a navigation form.

4. Open the Navigation Pane, click the **Forms** tab in the navigation form, and then drag the **frmVisitsAndInvoices** form from the Navigation Pane to the lower-level [Add New] tab. The frmVisitsAndInvoices form opens in the first tab below the Forms tab, and the tab displays the form's name.

   Trouble? If you drag the wrong object to a tab, right-click the tab, click Delete on the shortcut menu, and then drag the correct object to the tab.

   Trouble? You can rearrange the order of objects on the lower-level tabs by dragging the name of an object from its current tab to a new tab.

5. Drag the **frmPatient** form from the Navigation Pane to the next [Add New] tab to the right of the frmVisitsAndInvoices tab. You've added the two forms Mista wants users to work with in the Health database. See Figure 10–39.

Figure 10–39 Navigation form after adding two forms to lower-level tabs

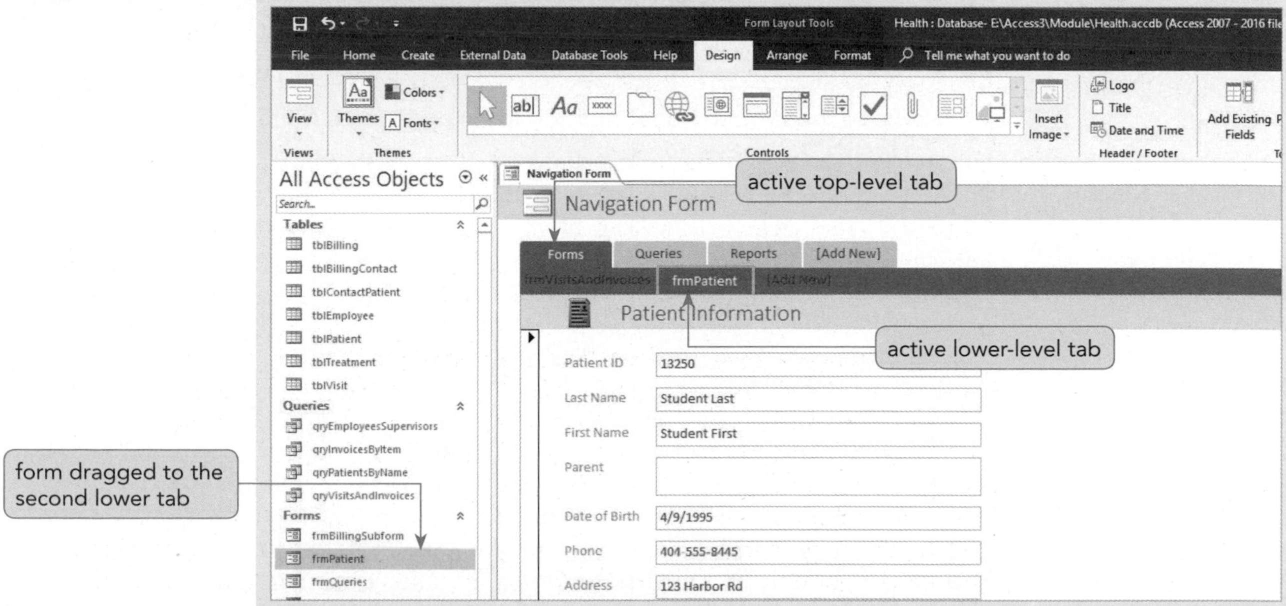

active top-level tab
active lower-level tab
form dragged to the second lower tab
Navigation Form
Forms
Queries
Reports
[Add New]
frmVisitsAndInvoices
frmPatient
Patient Information
Patient ID
13250
Last Name
Student Last
First Name
Student First
Parent
Date of Birth
4/9/1995
Phone
404-555-8445
Address
123 Harbor Rd
All Access Objects
Tables
tblBilling
tblBillingContact
tblContactPatient
tblEmployee
tblPatient
tblTreatment
tblVisit
Queries
qryEmployeesSupervisors
qryInvoicesByItem
qryPatientsByName
qryVisitsAndInvoices
Forms
frmBillingSubform
frmPatient
frmQueries

6. Click the Queries tab at the top of the navigation form, and then drag the **frmQueries** form from the Navigation Pane to the [Add New] tab below the Queries tab. Although you can't drag queries to a navigation form, in this case you're instead dragging the form you created that users can use to view and print queries.
7. Click the **Reports** tab at the top of the navigation form, and then drag from the Navigation Pane to the lower-level tabs, in order, the **rptVisitDetails** report, the **rptVisitsAndInvoices** report, and the **rptInvoicesByItem** report. Notice that each report opens as you drag it to the form.
8. Close the Navigation Pane. You've finished adding objects to the navigation form. See Figure 10–40.

Figure 10–40 Reports added to the navigation form

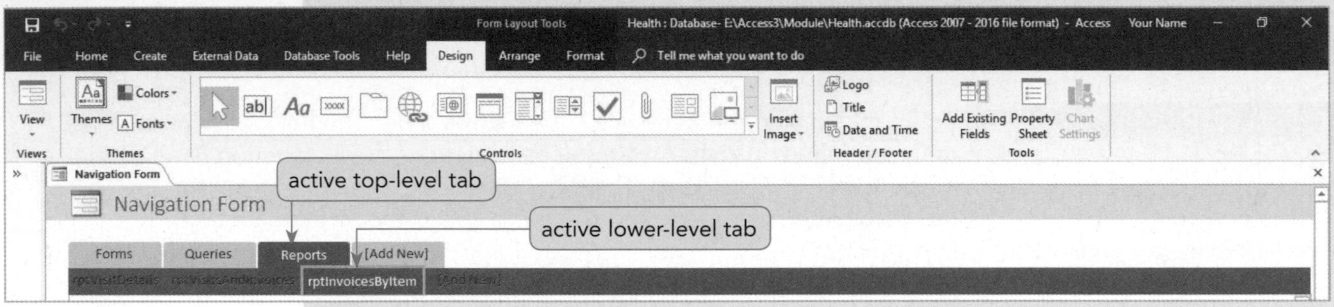
Form Layout Tools
Health : Database- E:\Access3\Module\Health.accdb (Access 2007 - 2016 file format) - Access
Your Name
File
Home
Create
External Data
Database Tools
Help
Design
Arrange
Format
Tell me what you want to do
View
Themes
Colors
Fonts
Insert Image
Logo
Title
Date and Time
Add Existing Fields
Property Sheet
Chart Settings
Views
Themes
Controls
Header / Footer
Tools
Navigation Form
Navigation Form
active top-level tab
active lower-level tab
Forms
Queries
Reports
[Add New]
rptInvoicesByItem

Mista asks you to delete the picture at the top of the navigation form, delete the form title, set the form's Caption property to "Health Database," and then save the form.

To finalize the navigation form:

1. Right-click the **picture** at the top of the form, click **Delete** on the shortcut menu, right-click the **form title**, and then click **Delete** on the shortcut menu.
2. Save the form as **frmNavigation**, and then switch to Design view.
3. Open the Property Sheet for the form, and then set the Caption property to **Health Database**.
4. Switch to Form view. See Figure 10–41.

Figure 10–41 Completed navigation form

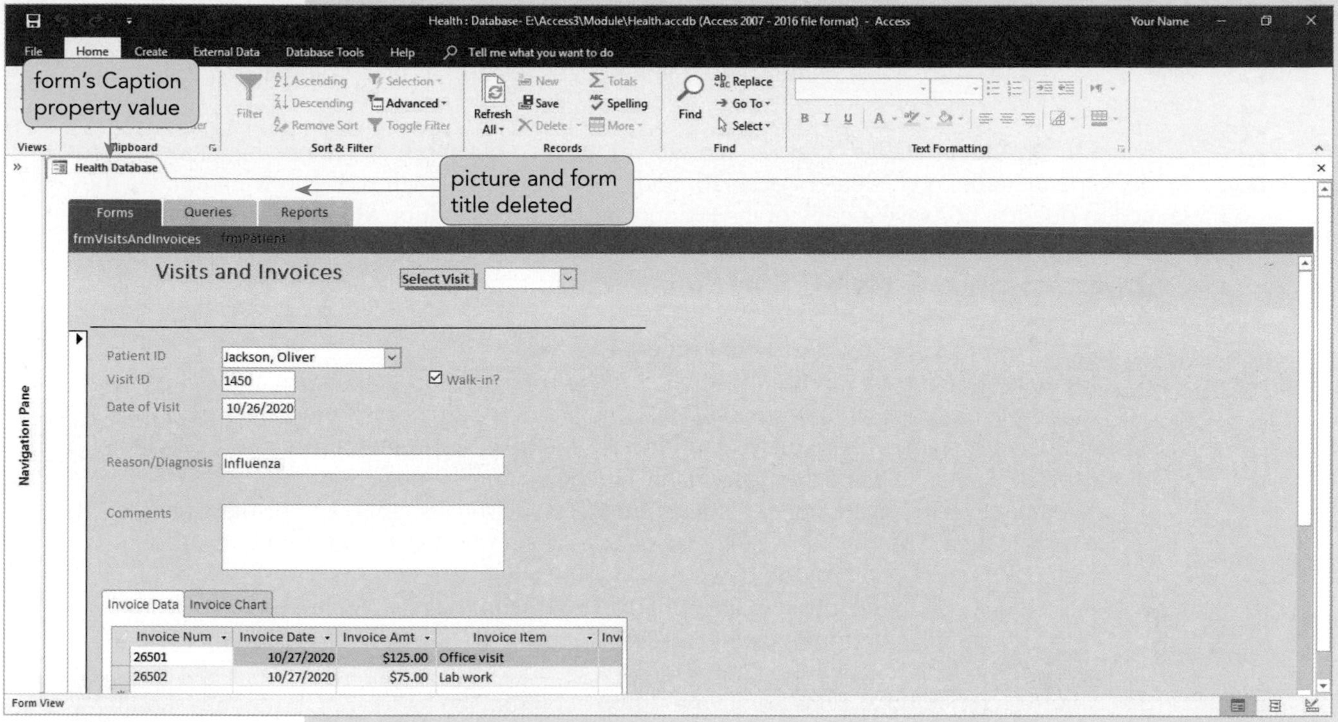
form's Caption property value
picture and form title deleted
Health Database
Forms
Queries
Reports
frmVisitsAndInvoices
Visits and Invoices
Select Visit
Patient ID
Jackson, Oliver
Visit ID
1450
Walk-in?
Date of Visit
10/26/2020
Reason/Diagnosis
Influenza
Comments
Invoice Data
Invoice Chart
Form View

> **TIP**
>
> When you click the Forms tab's lower-level tabs, you need to click a blank area of the form to place the focus in the first field in the record.

5. Navigate through the navigation form by clicking each top-level tab and its lower-level tabs.

   When you click the Queries tab, you may notice that the first query is not selected. This is because the frmQueries form is a subform of the frmNavigation form, and the Load event occurs on the frmNavigation form but does not occur on its subforms. When you load the frmQueries form itself, the Load event occurs on the frmQueries form. You'll need to click a query in the Available Queries list box before you click one of the command buttons on the form.

6. **sam** Save and close the form, make a backup copy of the database, compact and repair the database, and then close it.

Mista is happy with the two user interfaces you created for the Health database. She can direct experienced users to the database objects, including the frmVisit form that has some advanced features. She can load the frmNavigation form for users who are less experienced.

REVIEW

Session 10.2 Quick Check

1. What is a list box control?
2. What are system tables?
3. What are the five SQL statement types, and which query types do they correspond to?
4. When does the Load event occur?
5. What is a navigation form?

PRACTICE

Review Assignments

Data File needed for the Review Assignments: Product.accdb *(cont. from Module 9)*

Mista wants you to create a user interface for the Product database. To help with this request, complete the following steps:

1. Open the **Product** database you worked with in the previous module. Delete the action queries qryAppendSterile, qryDeletePriceLess20, and qryMakeSpecialEnviron. If you want to keep the action queries, first save a copy of the Product database as **Product_M9**, and then delete the action queries from the Product database.
2. Design and create a blank form named **frmQueries** that has the following components and characteristics:
   a. Set the form's Caption property to **Product Queries**.
   b. Add a list box control (approximately 0.5 inches from the top of the form and 0.5 inches from the left border of the form) with a Name property value of **lstQueryList** that displays all the query names contained in the Product database, excluding those that start with a "~" character. To place the query names in the list box control, use a SQL SELECT statement to retrieve the query names from the MSysObjects table, and display the queries in alphabetical order. (*Hint*: Use the same SQL select query that you used in the module.) Widen the list box control to approximately 2.5 inches.
   c. In the attached label control, change the caption to **Queries Available**, formatted with a 12-point, bold Calibri font, position the label above the list box control, and increase the width of the label control to fit the text.
   d. Add two command buttons below the list box control. The left command button should display the Preview icon above the word **Preview**, and the right command button should display the MS Access Query icon above the word **Display**. Resize the buttons to the same size so that they both show their icon and text.
   e. Create a macro for the form that moves the focus to the first query name in the list box control when the form loads.
   f. Create a macro that causes the query datasheet to display the selected query, and then configure the form so the macro runs when a user double-clicks a query name in the list box.
   g. Create a macro that causes the query datasheet to display the selected query, and then configure the form so the macro runs when a user selects a query name in the list box and clicks the right command button (the Display button).
   h. Create a macro for the left command button (Preview button) that opens the selected query in Print Preview.
   i. Set the background color of the Detail section to Green 3 in the Standard Colors section. Set the background color of the list box and the two command buttons to Green 2.
   j. Disable the form's shortcut menu, record selectors, Close button, and navigation buttons.
   k. Test the form.
3. Create a navigation form named **frmNavigation**, using the Horizontal Tabs, 2 Levels layout that includes the following tab names and objects:
   a. Use **Forms** as the name for the far left, top-level tab and place the following forms below it as lower-level tabs, in order: frmSupplier and frmSuppliersWithProducts. Expand the second lower-level tabs to show each entire form name.
   b. Use **Queries** as the name for the second tab, and place the frmQueries form below it on a lower-level tab.
   c. Use **Reports** as the name for the third tab, and place the following reports below it as lower-level tabs, in order: rptSupplier and rptSupplierProducts. Expand the second lower-level tabs to show each entire report name.
   d. Delete the navigation form's picture and title and set the form's caption to **Product**.
   e. Test the navigation form, remembering to first select a query in the list on the Queries tab before testing the command buttons.
4. Make a backup copy of the database, compact and repair the database, and then close it.

APPLY

Case Problem 1

Data File needed for this Case Problem: Instruction.accdb ***(cont. from Module 9)***

Great Giraffe Jeremiah wants you to create a user interface for the Instruction database. To help with this request, complete the following steps:

1. Open the **Instruction** database you worked with in the previous module. Delete the action queries qryAppendLittleton, qryDeleteMoreThan1500, qryMakeCityPaymentPlan, and qryUpdateLittletonToZero. If you want to keep the action queries, first save a copy of the Instruction database as **Instruction_M9**, and then delete the action queries from the Instruction database.
2. Design and create a form named **frmQueries** that has the following components and characteristics:
   a. Set the form's Caption property to **Instruction Queries**.
   b. Add a list box control (approximately 1 inch from the top of the form and 1 inch from the left border of the form) with a Name property value of **lstQueryList** that displays all the query names contained in the Instruction database, excluding those that start with a "~" character. To place the query names in the list box control, use a SQL SELECT statement to retrieve the query names from the MSysObjects table, and display the queries in reverse alphabetical order (descending order). (*Hint*: Use the same SQL select query that you used in the module.) Widen the list box control to approximately 2.25 inches.
   c. In the attached label control, change the caption to **Available Queries**, formatted with a 12-point, bold, italic Calibri font, position the label above the list box control, and increase the width of the label control to fit the text.
   d. Add two command buttons below the list box control. The left command button should display the Preview icon *below* the word **Preview**, and the right command button should display the MS Access Query icon *below* the word **Display**.
   e. Create a macro for the form that moves the focus to the first query name in the list box control when the form loads.
   f. Create a macro that causes the query datasheet to display the selected query, and then configure the form so the macro runs when a user double-clicks a query name in the list box.
   g. Create a macro that causes the query datasheet to display the selected query, and then configure the form so the macro runs when a user selects a query name in the list box and clicks the right command button (the Display button).
   h. Create a macro for the left command button (Preview button) that opens the selected query in Print Preview.
   i. Set the background color of the Detail section to Light Blue 3 in the Standard Colors section. Set the background color of the list box and the two command buttons to Light Blue 2.
   j. Disable the form's shortcut menu, record selectors, and navigation buttons, but do not disable the Close button.
   k. Test the form.
3. Create a navigation form named **frmNavigation** using the Horizontal Tabs, 2 Levels layout that includes the following tab names and objects:
   a. Use **Forms** as the name for the far left, top-level tab and place the following forms below it as lower-level tabs, in order: frmCourseData, frmStudentInfo, and frmStudentsByCourse. Expand the second lower-level tabs to show each entire form name.
   b. Use **Queries** as the name for the second tab, and place the frmQueries form below it on a lower-level tab.
   c. Use **Reports** as the name for the third tab, and place the following reports below it as lower-level tabs, in order: rptCourseRosters and rptStudentList. Expand the second lower-level tabs to show each entire report name.

d. Delete the navigation form's picture and title and set the form's caption to **Instruction Information**.
e. Test the navigation form, remembering to first select a query in the list on the Queries tab before testing the command buttons.

4. Make a backup copy of the database, compact and repair the database, and then close it.

CHALLENGE

Case Problem 2

Data File needed for this Case Problem: CleanOut.accdb ***(cont. from Module 9)***

Drain Adopter Tandrea wants you to create a user interface for the CleanOut database. To help with this request, complete the following steps:

1. Open the **CleanOut** database you worked with in the previous module. Delete the action queries qryAppendAprilMay, qryDeleteMarchAprilMay, qryMakeSpecialVolunteers, and qryUpdateTrained. If you want to keep the action queries, first save a copy of the Instruction database as **CleanOut_M9**, and then delete the action queries from the CleanOut database.
2. Design and create a form named **frmQueries** that has the following components and characteristics:
   a. Set the form's Caption property to **CleanOut Queries**.
   Explore b. Add a list box control (approximately 0.75 inches from the top of the form and 0.75 inches from the left border of the form) with a Name property value of **lstQueryList** that displays all the query names contained in the CleanOut database, excluding those that start with a "~" character. To place the query names in the list box control, use a SQL SELECT statement to retrieve the query names from the MSysObjects table, and display the queries in reverse alphabetical order (descending order). (*Hint*: By default SQL sorts data in ascending order. To sort the data in descending order you would place the keyword DESC at the end of the ORDER BY clause just prior to the semicolon in the SQL statement.) Widen the list box control to approximately 2.25 inches.
   In the attached label control, change the caption to **Available Queries**, formatted with a 12-point, bold, italic, underlined Calibri font, position the label above the list box control, and increase the width of the label control to fit the text.
   Explore c. Add two command buttons below the list box control. The left command button should display the Preview icon to the left of the word **Preview**, and the right command button should display the MS Access Query icon to the left of the word **Display**.
   Explore d. Create a macro for the form that moves the focus to the third query name in the list box control when the form loads, not the first entry. (*Hint*: You used the SendKeys action once to give the focus to the first name in the list box, so performing the action twice more should move the focus down two additional entries).
   e. Create a macro that causes the query datasheet to display the selected query, and then configure the form so the macro runs when a user double-clicks a query name in the list box.
   f. Create a macro that causes the query datasheet to display the selected query, and then configure the form so the macro runs when a user selects a query name in the list box and clicks the right command button (the Display button).
   g. Create a macro for the left command button (Preview button) that opens the selected query in Print Preview.
   h. Set the background color of the Detail section to Aqua Blue 3 in the Standard Colors section. Set the background color of the list box to Aqua Blue 2.
   i. Disable the form's shortcut menu, record selectors, and navigation buttons, but do not disable the Close button.
   j. Test the form.

Explore 3. Create a navigation form named **frmNavigation** using the Horizontal Tabs and Vertical Tabs, Left layout that includes the following tab names and objects. (*Hint*: The categories of Forms, Queries, and Reports are the horizontal values across the top of the form, with lower-level values beginning in the vertical slots.)

a. Use **Forms** as the name for the far left, top-level horizontal tab and place the following forms below it as lower-level vertical tabs, in order: frmVolunteerData, frmVolunteerMasterData, and frmVolunteersAndDrains. Expand the vertical lower-level tabs to show each entire form name.
b. Use **Queries** as the name for the second horizontal tab, and place the frmQueries form below it on a vertical lower-level tab.
c. Use **Reports** as the name for the third horizontal tab, and place the following reports below it as vertical lower-level tabs, in order: rptVolunteerList and rptVolunteersAndDrains. Expand the vertical lower-level tabs to show each entire report name.
d. Delete the navigation form's picture and title and set the form's caption to **CleanOut Information**.
e. Test the navigation form, remembering to first select a query in the list on the Queries tab before testing the command buttons.

4. Make a backup copy of the database, compact and repair the database, and then close it.

MODULE **11**

Using and Writing Visual Basic for Applications Code

Creating VBA Code for the Health Database

OBJECTIVES

Session 11.1

- Describe user-defined functions, Sub procedures, and modules
- Review and modify an existing Sub procedure in an event procedure
- Create a function in a standard module
- Test a procedure in the Immediate window

Session 11.2

- Create event procedures
- Compile and test functions, Sub procedures, and event procedures
- Create a field validation procedure

Case | *Lakewood Community Health Services*

Donna Taylor is pleased with your progress in developing the user interface for the Health database. She realizes that many different people will be entering information in the Health database. Whenever users enter data manually, they introduce the potential for typographical errors. Donna wants you to modify the frmVisit, frmPatient, and frmVisitsAndInvoices forms to make data entry easier and to highlight important information on them. To make these modifications, you will write Visual Basic for Applications code.

STARTING DATA FILES

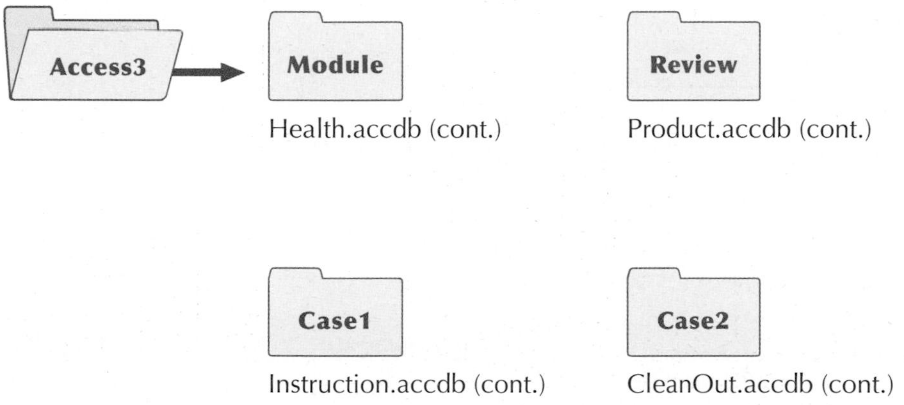
Access3
Module
Health.accdb (cont.)
Review
Product.accdb (cont.)
Case1
Instruction.accdb (cont.)
Case2
CleanOut.accdb (cont.)

Session 11.1 Visual Overview:

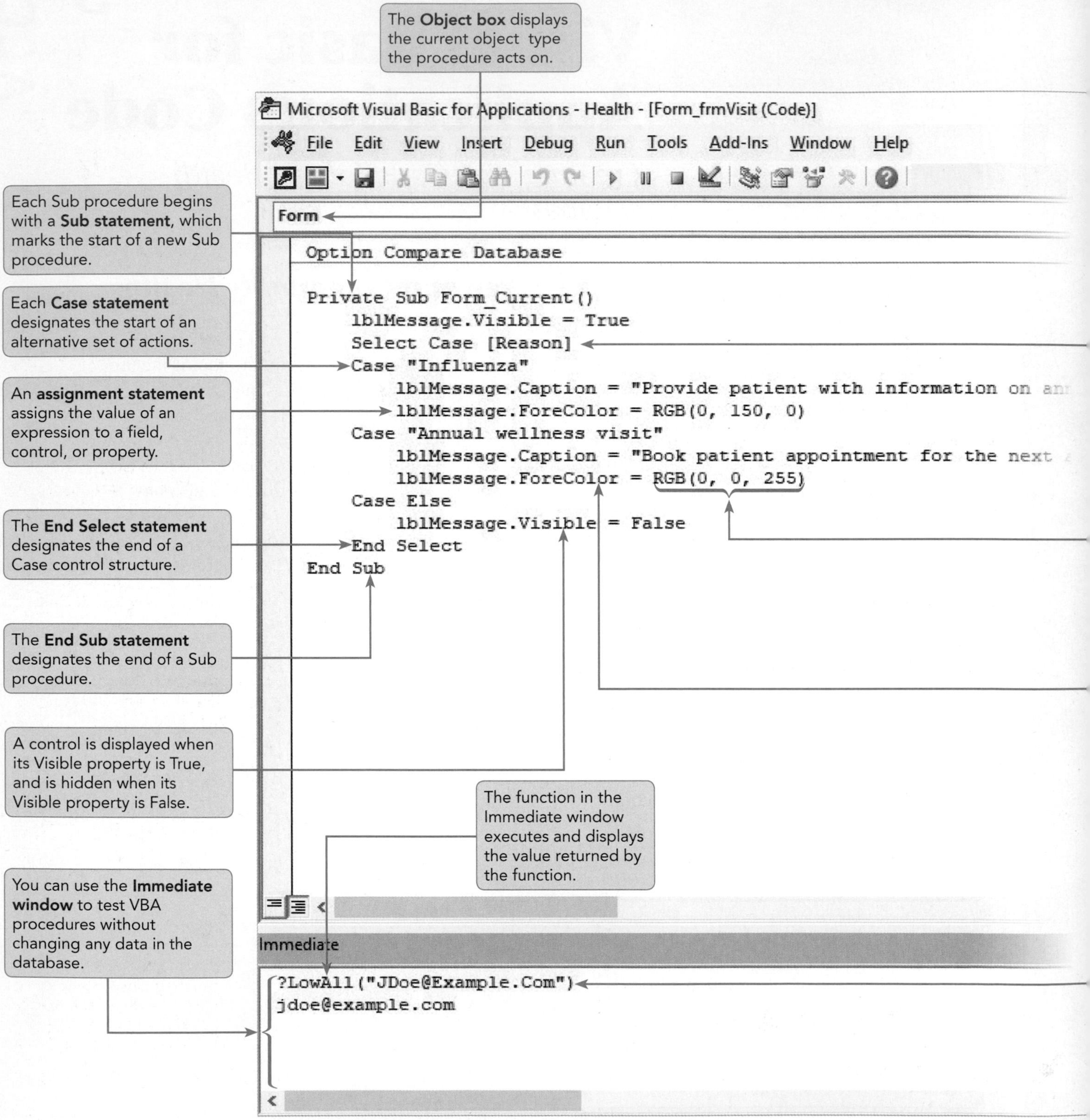
The **Object box** displays the current object type the procedure acts on.
Microsoft Visual Basic for Applications - Health - [Form_frmVisit (Code)]
File Edit View Insert Debug Run Tools Add-Ins Window Help
Form
Option Compare Database
Private Sub Form_Current()
lblMessage.Visible = True
Select Case [Reason]
Case "Influenza"
lblMessage.Caption = "Provide patient with information on an
lblMessage.ForeColor = RGB(0, 150, 0)
Case "Annual wellness visit"
lblMessage.Caption = "Book patient appointment for the next
lblMessage.ForeColor = RGB(0, 0, 255)
Case Else
lblMessage.Visible = False
End Select
End Sub
Each Sub procedure begins with a **Sub statement**, which marks the start of a new Sub procedure.
Each **Case statement** designates the start of an alternative set of actions.
An **assignment statement** assigns the value of an expression to a field, control, or property.
The **End Select statement** designates the end of a Case control structure.
The **End Sub statement** designates the end of a Sub procedure.
A control is displayed when its Visible property is True, and is hidden when its Visible property is False.
The function in the Immediate window executes and displays the value returned by the function.
You can use the **Immediate window** to test VBA procedures without changing any data in the database.
Immediate
?LowAll("JDoe@Example.Com")
jdoe@example.com

VBA Code Window

Current
vaccines"
ellness visit"

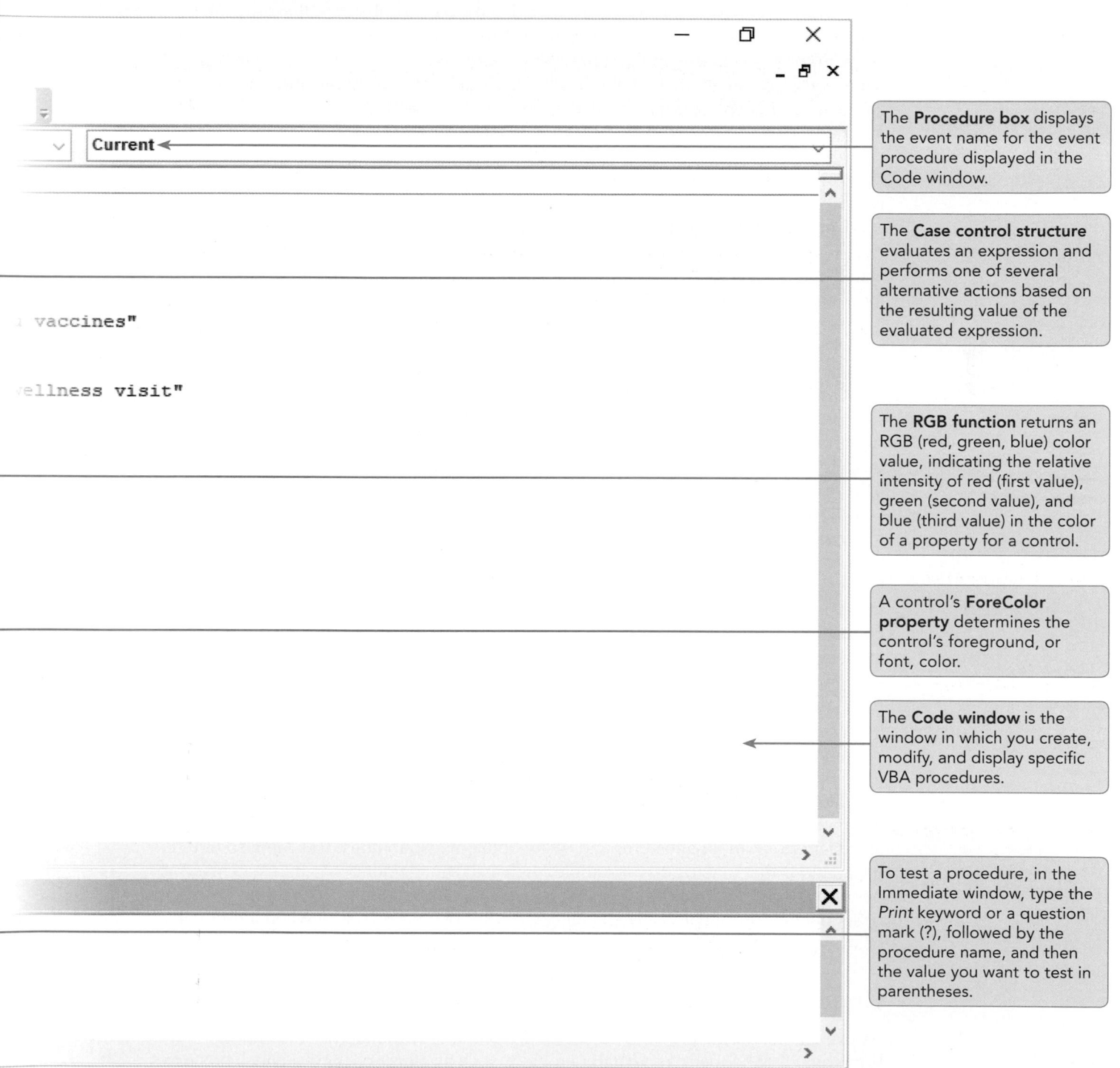

The **Procedure box** displays the event name for the event procedure displayed in the Code window.

The **Case control structure** evaluates an expression and performs one of several alternative actions based on the resulting value of the evaluated expression.

The **RGB function** returns an RGB (red, green, blue) color value, indicating the relative intensity of red (first value), green (second value), and blue (third value) in the color of a property for a control.

A control's **ForeColor property** determines the control's foreground, or font, color.

The **Code window** is the window in which you create, modify, and display specific VBA procedures.

To test a procedure, in the Immediate window, type the *Print* keyword or a question mark (?), followed by the procedure name, and then the value you want to test in parentheses.

Introduction to Visual Basic for Applications

Your next task in developing the Health database is to add a procedure to ensure proper capitalization of data entered using the frmPatient form. Donna wants the email addresses in the database to have a uniform case rather than the inconsistency that inevitably happens when users type their own data. She wants to make sure that all values entered in this form's Email field will be stored in the tblPatient table using lowercase letters. She asks you to modify the form so that it will automatically convert any uppercase letters entered in the Email field to lowercase. One method to accomplish this is to use an input mask to convert all letters to lowercase when the data is entered. An alternate method is to use Visual Basic for Applications to convert the letters to lowercase when the data is entered. This method could be used as the foundation for a more complex method to validate an email address. An input mask can restrict characters during data entry, but Visual Basic for Applications could also check to see if the email address contains the @ symbol and a valid suffix such as .com, which an input mask cannot do.

Visual Basic for Applications (VBA) is the programming language provided with Access and other Office programs. VBA has a common syntax and a set of common features for all Microsoft Office programs, but it also has features that are unique for each Microsoft Office program due to each program's distinct structure and components. For example, because Access has fields, tables, queries, forms, other objects, tab controls, subforms, and other controls that are unique to it, VBA for Access includes features that support these particular components. In contrast, because Microsoft Excel does not have these same Access components, VBA for Excel does not support them, but it does support cells, ranges, and worksheets—three of the basic structures of Excel. The fundamental VBA skills you learn for one of the Microsoft Office programs transfer to any other Microsoft Office program, but to become proficient with VBA in another program, you first need to master its unique aspects.

When you use a programming language, such as VBA, you write a set of instructions to direct the computer to perform specific operations in a specific order, similar to writing a set of instructions for a recipe or an instruction manual. The Visual Overview for Session 11.1 shows the VBA Code window with instructions for Access to use in the frmVisit form. The process of writing instructions in a programming language is called **coding**. You write the VBA instructions, each of which is called a **statement**, to respond to an event that occurs with an object or a form control in a database. A language such as VBA is, therefore, is called an **event-driven language**, because an event in the database triggers a set of instructions. It is also called an **object-oriented language**, because each set of instructions operates on objects in the database. Your experience with macros, which are also event-driven and object-oriented, should facilitate your learning of VBA. Although you must use macros if you need to assign actions to a specific keyboard key or key combination, you can use VBA for everything else you normally accomplish with macros. VBA provides advantages over using macros, such as better error-handling features and easier updating capabilities. You can also use VBA in situations that macros do not handle, such as creating your own set of statements to perform special calculations, verifying a field value based on the value of another field or set of fields, or dynamically changing the color of a form control when a user enters or views a specific field value.

Understanding Procedures

As you learned in the previous module when working with macros, an event is something that happens to a database object, such as a user clicking a check box or a form being loaded. You can connect an action to a specific event so the action occurs in response to that event. Each event has an associated event property, which specifies how an object responds when an event occurs. In the previous module, you set event property values to macro names, and Access executed the macros when those events occurred. You can also create a group of statements, known as a procedure, using VBA code and set an event property value to the name of that procedure. Access then executes the procedure when the event occurs. As you know, such a procedure is called an event procedure. Access has over 60 events and associated event properties. Figure 11–1 describes some frequently used Access events. Each event (such as the AfterUpdate event) has an associated event property (AfterUpdate) and event procedure (ContractNum_AfterUpdate for the AfterUpdate event procedure for the ContractNum control).

Figure 11–1 **Frequently used Access events**

Event	Description
AfterUpdate	Occurs after changed data in a control or a record is updated
BeforeUpdate	Occurs before changed data in a control or a record is updated
Click	Occurs when a user presses and then releases a mouse button over a control in a form
Current	Occurs when the focus moves to a record, making it the current record, or when a form is refreshed or requeried
DblClick	Occurs when a user presses and releases the left mouse button twice over a control in a form within the double-click time limit
Delete	Occurs when a user performs some action, such as pressing the Delete key, to delete a record, but before the record is actually deleted
GotFocus	Occurs when a form or a form control receives the focus
Load	Occurs when a form is opened and its records are displayed
MouseDown	Occurs when a user presses a mouse button
NoData	Occurs after Access formats a report for printing that has no data (the report is bound to an empty recordset), but before the report is printed; you use this event to cancel the printing of a blank report
Open	Occurs when a form is opened, but before the first record is displayed; for reports, the event occurs before a report is previewed or printed

The two types of VBA procedures are Function procedures and Sub procedures. A **user-defined function**, or **function procedure**, performs operations, returns a value, accepts input values, and can be used in expressions (recall that an expression is a calculation resulting in a single value). For example, some of the Health database queries use built-in Access functions, such as Sum, Count, and Avg, to calculate a sum, a record count, or an average. To meet Donna's request, you will create a function named LowAll by entering the appropriate VBA statements. The LowAll function will accept the value entered in a field value box—in this case, the Email field—as an input value, convert all characters in the field value to lowercase, and then return the changed field value to be stored in the database and displayed in the field value box.

A **Sub procedure** executes instructions and accepts input values but does not return a value and cannot be used in expressions. Most Access procedures are Sub procedures because you need the procedures to perform a series of actions or operations in response to an event. Later in this module, you will create a Sub procedure that displays a message in the frmVisitsAndInvoices form only when the visit date is earlier than a specified date.

Understanding Modules

You store a group of related procedures together in an object called a **module**. Figure 11–2 shows the structure of a typical module.

Figure 11–2 Structure of a VBA module and its procedures

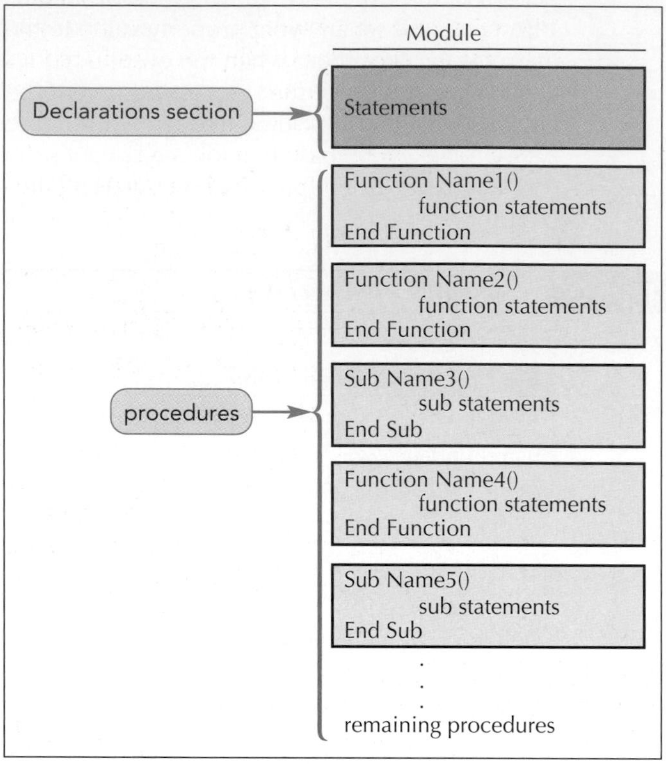
Module
Declarations section
Statements
Function Name1()
function statements
End Function
Function Name2()
function statements
End Function
procedures
Sub Name3()
sub statements
End Sub
Function Name4()
function statements
End Function
Sub Name5()
sub statements
End Sub
remaining procedures

Each module starts with a **Declarations section**, which contains statements that apply to all procedures in the module. One or more procedures, which follow the Declarations section and which can be a mixture of functions and Sub procedures, constitute the rest of the module. The two basic types of modules are standard modules and class modules.

A **standard module** is a database object that is stored in memory with other database objects (queries, forms, and so on) when you open the database. You can use the procedures in a database's standard modules from anywhere in the database—even from procedures in other modules. All standard modules are listed in the Modules section of the Navigation Pane. A procedure that more than one object can use is called a **public procedure**. For example, the LowAll procedure that you will create converts all letters in the value passed to it to lowercase. Although you are creating this procedure specifically to work with Email field values, you will place it in a standard module and make it public. You could then use the LowAll procedure for any object in the database.

A **class module** is usually associated with a particular form or report. When you create the first event procedure for a form or report, an associated form or report class module is also created. When you add additional event procedures to the form or report, they are automatically added to the class module for that form or report. Each event procedure in a class module is a **local procedure**, or a **private procedure**, which means that only the form or report for which the class module was created can use the event procedure.

Using an Existing VBA Procedure

Before creating the LowAll procedure for Donna, you'll use an existing procedure that Donna created in the class module for the frmVisit form. The Lakewood Community Health Services team would like to provide information about annual flu vaccines for patients who come to the clinic for influenza. They would also like to book the next annual wellness visit for all patients who come to the clinic for an annual wellness visit. To remind the staff to provide information and book the next wellness visit, Donna created a local procedure stored in the class module of the frmVisit form that displays the message about annual flu vaccines in red text in a box to the right of the Walk-in? check box, and displays the message reminding the user to book the next annual wellness visit in blue text. For patients with any other reason for visiting the clinic, the class module makes the box invisible.

You'll navigate through the records using the frmVisit form to observe the effects of the procedure.

To navigate a form that uses a VBA procedure:

1. **sam** Start Access, and then open the **Health** database you worked with in the previous two modules.
2. Open the Navigation Pane (if necessary), open the **frmVisit** form in Form view, and then close the Navigation Pane. Navigate to the third record, VisitID 1585, by clicking the **Next record** button twice. The value "Book patient appointment for the next annual wellness visit" is displayed in a blue font to the right of the Walk-in? check box because the Reason field value is "Annual wellness visit." See Figure 11–3.

Figure 11–3 Using an existing VBA procedure

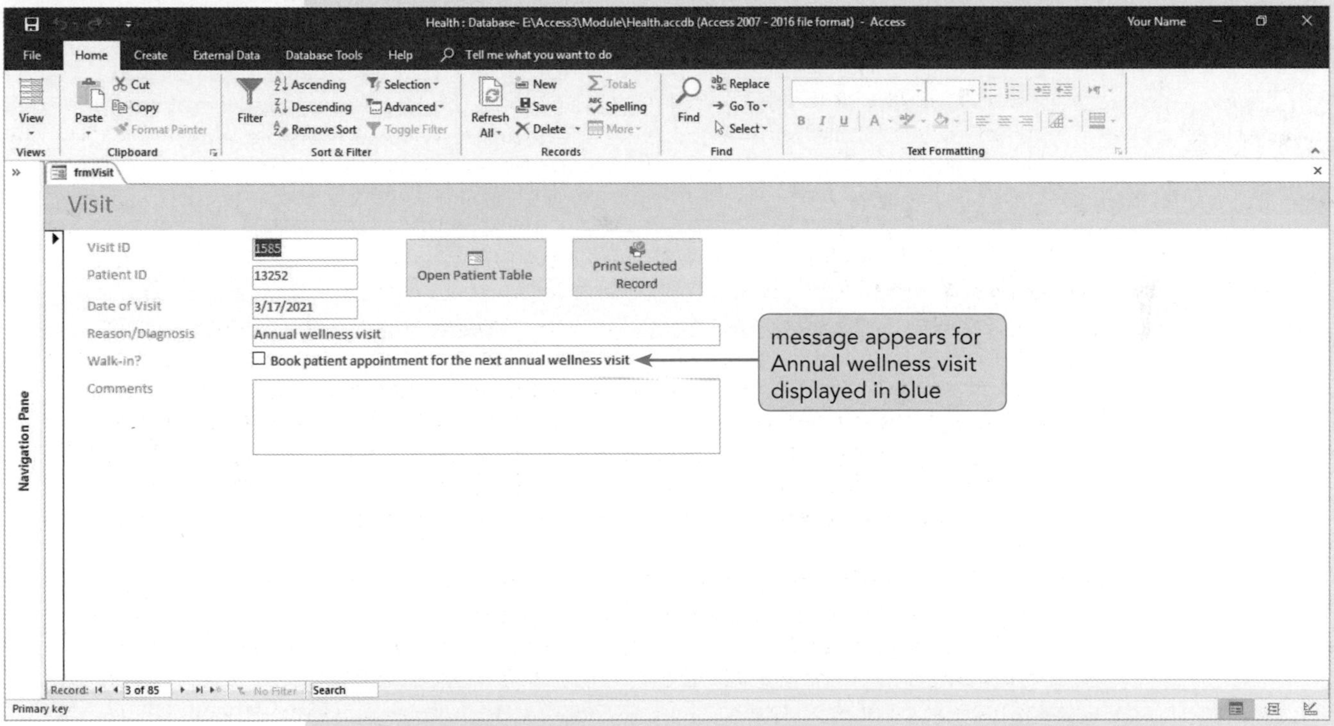
Health : Database- E:\Access3\Module\Health.accdb (Access 2007 - 2016 file format) - Access
Visit
Visit ID
1585
Patient ID
13252
Date of Visit
3/17/2021
Reason/Diagnosis
Annual wellness visit
Walk-in?
Book patient appointment for the next annual wellness visit
Comments
Open Patient Table
Print Selected Record
message appears for Annual wellness visit displayed in blue
Record: 3 of 85

3. Click the **Next record** button three times to move to the sixth record. The frmVisit form displays record 6 for VisitID 1590. There is no value displayed to the right of the Walk-in? check box because the Reason field is neither "Annual wellness visit" nor "Influenza."
4. Navigate to record 18 for VisitID 1483. Because the Reason value for this visit is "Influenza," the text "Provide patient with information on annual flu vaccines" is displayed in a red font to the right of the Walk-in? check box.

Donna asks you to change the red color for the display of "Provide patient with information on annual flu vaccines" to green so that it doesn't appear to be an urgent warning.

Examining a VBA Event Procedure

The VBA procedure that controls the display of the message and its color for each record is in the class module for the frmVisit form. The statements in the procedure are processed when you open the frmVisit form and also when the focus leaves one record and moves to another. The event called the **Current event** occurs when the focus shifts to the next record loaded in a form, making it the current record. This also happens when the form loads and when the form is refreshed. The **Current property** contains a reference to a macro, VBA code, or some other expression that runs when the Current event occurs.

TIP

Pay attention to the property names as you move from the Property Sheet to VBA. The names are interrelated, yet the syntax is different in each environment.

To change the color of the text "Provide patient with information on annual flu vaccines" from red to green, you'll modify the event procedure for the form's OnCurrent property. First, you'll switch to Design view, and then you'll display the event procedure.

To display the event procedure for the form's OnCurrent property:

1. Switch to Design view.
2. Right-click the **form selector** ■ to display the shortcut menu, and then (if necessary) click **Properties** to open the Property Sheet for the form.
3. Click the **Event** tab (if necessary) to display the Event page, click the **On Current** box, and then (if necessary) drag the left border of the Property Sheet to the left until the On Current property value is visible. See Figure 11–4.

Figure 11–4 Event properties for the frmVisit form

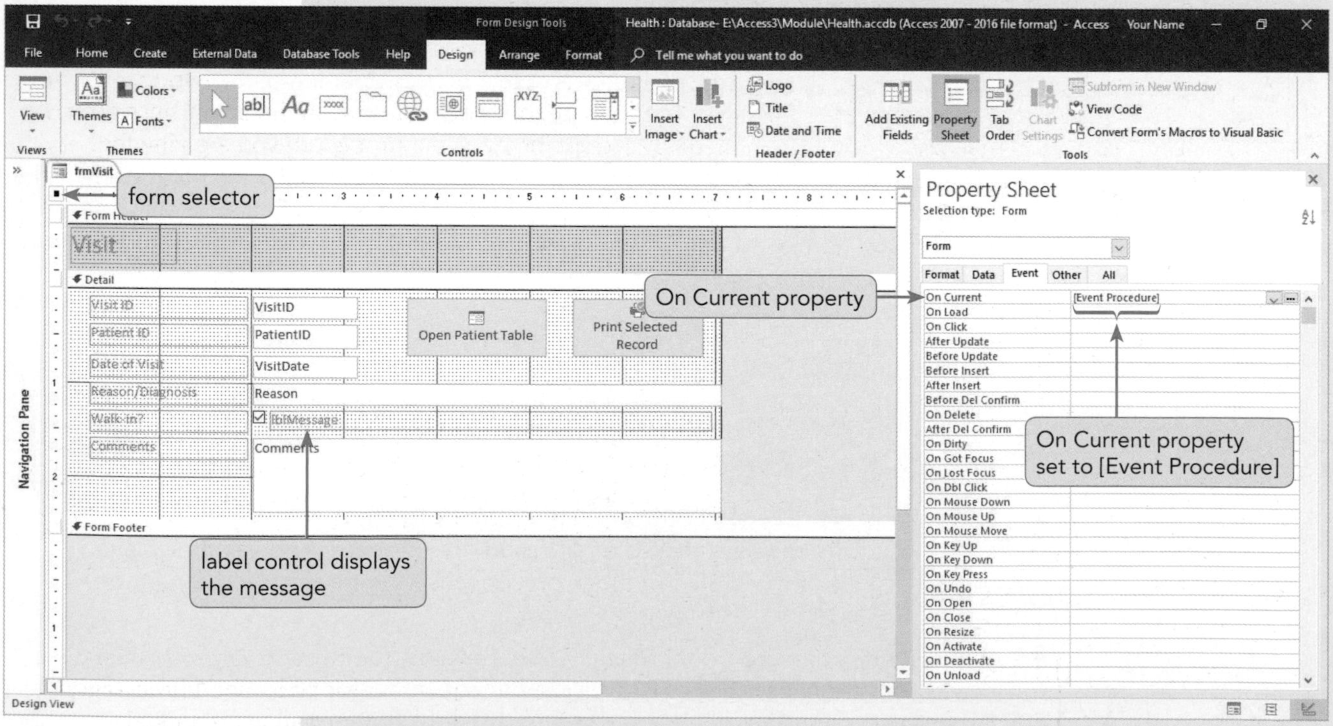
form selector
On Current property
On Current property set to [Event Procedure]
label control displays the message

The On Current property is set to [Event Procedure], indicating that a VBA procedure is called when the Current event occurs. You'll click the Build button to display the procedure.

4. In the On Current box, click the **Build** button [...]. The Code window opens in the Visual Basic window. See Figure 11–5.

Figure 11–5 **Code window in the Visual Basic window**

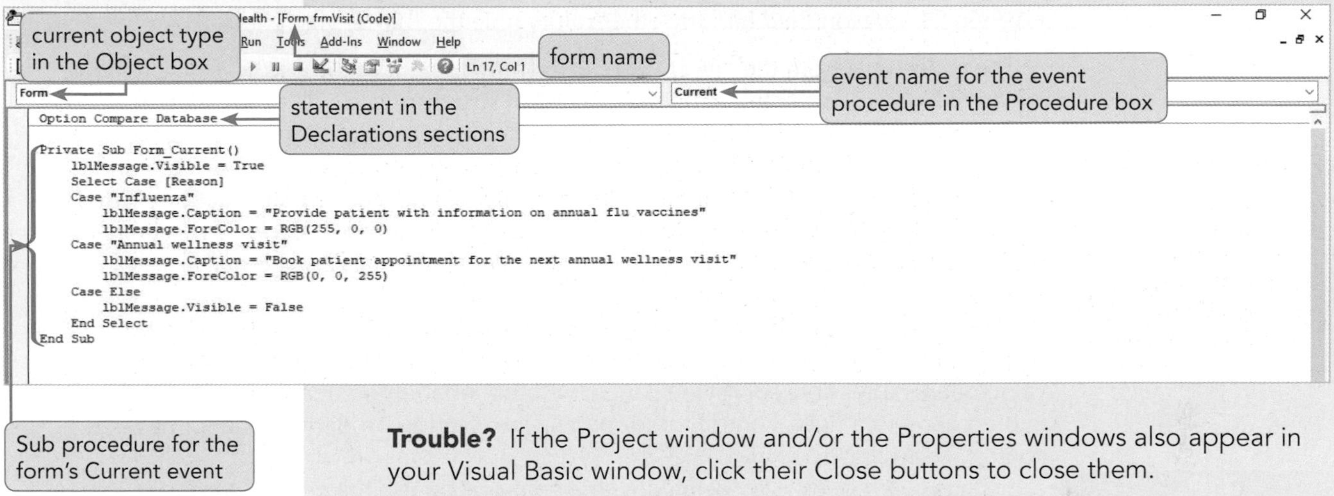
current object type in the Object box
form name
event name for the event procedure in the Procedure box
statement in the Declarations sections
Sub procedure for the form's Current event
Form
Current
Option Compare Database
Private Sub Form_Current()
lblMessage.Visible = True
Select Case [Reason]
Case "Influenza"
lblMessage.Caption = "Provide patient with information on annual flu vaccines"
lblMessage.ForeColor = RGB(255, 0, 0)
Case "Annual wellness visit"
lblMessage.Caption = "Book patient appointment for the next annual wellness visit"
lblMessage.ForeColor = RGB(0, 0, 255)
Case Else
lblMessage.Visible = False
End Select
End Sub

Trouble? If the Project window and/or the Properties windows also appear in your Visual Basic window, click their Close buttons to close them.

Trouble? If the Code window isn't maximized within the VBA window, click the Maximize button.

The program you use to create and modify VBA code is called the **Visual Basic Editor** (**VBE** or **editor** for short), and the **Visual Basic window** is the program window that opens when you use VBE. As shown in the Session 11.1 Visual Overview, the Code window is the window in which you create, modify, and display specific VBA procedures. You can have as many Code windows open as you have modules in the database. In the Code window, the Object box in the upper-left of the window indicates the current object type (Form), and the Procedure box in the upper-right of the window indicates the event name (Current) for the event procedure you are viewing.

All event procedures are Sub procedures. A horizontal line visually separates each procedure in the Code window. Each Sub procedure begins with a Sub statement and ends with an End Sub statement. The Sub statement includes the scope of the procedure (private or public), the name of the procedure (for example, Form_Current, which means the Current event for the form control), and opening and closing parentheses. The **scope** of a procedure indicates where the procedure is available. If its scope is public, the procedure is available in all objects in the database. If its scope is private, the procedure is available only in the object in which it is created. Event procedures are private by default. For instance, the event procedure in the OnCurrent property in the frmVisit form is private, and other forms do not have access to this procedure code.

Notice the Option Compare statement in the Declarations section above the horizontal line. The Option Compare statement designates the technique used to compare and sort text data. The default method "Database," as shown in Figure 11–5, means letters are compared and sorted in alphabetical order, using the language settings specified for Access on your computer.

The remaining statements in the Form_Current procedure shown in Figure 11–5 use only two controls in the form: The Reason field from the tblVisit table; and lblMessage, which is a label control that displays "Provide patient with information on annual flu vaccines" or "Book patient appointment for the next annual wellness visit" when it's visible. Based on the Reason field value, the statements in the procedure do the following:

- When the Reason field value is "Influenza," set the Caption property for the lblMessage control to "Provide patient with information on annual flu vaccines" and set its font color to red.
- When the Reason field value is "Annual wellness visit," set the Caption property for the lblMessage control to "Book patient appointment for the next annual wellness visit" and set its font color to blue.
- When the Reason field has any other value, hide the lblMessage control.

The statements from the *Select Case [Reason]* statement to the *End Select* statement are an example of a control structure. A **control structure** is a set of VBA statements that work together as a unit. The Case control structure is a conditional control structure. A **conditional control structure** evaluates an expression—the value of the Reason field, in this case—and then performs one of several alternative actions based on the resulting value (or condition) of the evaluated expression. Each Case statement, such as *Case "Influenza"* and *Case Else*, designates the start of an alternative set of actions.

Statements such as *lblMessage.Caption = "Provide patient with information on annual flu vaccines"* are assignment statements. An assignment statement assigns the value of an expression—"Provide patient with information on annual flu vaccines", in this case—to a field, control, or property—the Caption property of the lblMessage control, in this case.

TIP

The RGB color model is commonly used by graphic designers and enables you to specify over 16 million different colors.

Because a property is associated with a control, you use the general form of *ControlName.PropertyName* to specify a property for a control. An assignment statement such as *lblMessage.ForeColor = RGB(255, 0, 0)*, for example, assigns a value to the ForeColor property of the lblMessage control. A control's ForeColor property determines the control's foreground, or font, color. The expression in this assignment statement uses a built-in VBA function named RGB. The RGB function returns an RGB (red, green, blue) color value, indicating the relative intensity of red (first value), green (second value), and blue (third value) in the color of a property for a control. Figure 11–6 displays a list of some common colors and the red, green, and blue values for the RGB function that produces those colors. Each color component value must be in the range 0 through 255. Instead of using the RGB function for the eight colors shown in Figure 11–6, you can use one of the VBA constants (vbBlack, vbBlue, vbCyan, vbGreen, vbMagenta, vbRed, vbWhite, or vbYellow). A **VBA constant** is a predefined memory location that is initialized to a value that doesn't change. For example, *lblMessage.ForeColor = vbRed* and *lblMessage.ForeColor = RGB(255, 0, 0)* would set the color of the lblMessage control to red. You must use the RGB function when you want colors that differ from the eight colors shown in Figure 11–6.

Figure 11–6 **RGB function values for some common colors**

Color	Red Value	Green Value	Blue Value	VBA Constant
Black	0	0	0	vbBlack
Blue	0	0	255	vbBlue
Cyan	0	255	255	vbCyan
Green	0	255	0	vbGreen
Magenta	255	0	255	vbMagenta
Red	255	0	0	vbRed
White	255	255	255	vbWhite
Yellow	255	255	0	vbYellow

INSIGHT

Assigning a Color Value

A color value can be assigned to a control property using a variety of methods. A color value could be one of the following:

- A built-in VB constant such as vbRed, vbWhite, or vbBlack.
- A set of red, green, and blue values, each ranging from 0 to 255, specified in the RGB function. For instance, RGB(0,255,0) represents the color green.
- A hexadecimal value that represents color intensities of red, green, and blue. For instance, 00FF00 represents the color green. The first two characters represent red, the second two characters represent green, and the last two characters represent blue. Similar to the RGB function, these triplets represent the intensity of each color, mixed to form the resulting color.
- A ColorIndex property value, which uses a color code specific to VBA. For instance, the color green has a ColorIndex value of 4.
- A Microsoft Access color code, which is a code specific to Access. For instance, the color green has the Microsoft Access color code 32768.

With all those choices, which one should you use? The most common are the built-in VB constants, RGB function, and hexadecimal values. The RGB function and hexadecimal values are also used in web design and VB.NET programming, so you may find these techniques especially useful if you modify webpage code as well.

The Visible property determines whether or not a control is displayed. A control is displayed when its Visible property is True, and the control is hidden when its Visible property is False. The *lblMessage.Visible = True* statement, which is processed before the *Select Case [Reason]* statement, displays the lblMessage control. Because Donna doesn't want the lblMessage control to appear for reasons other than Influenza and Annual wellness visit, the *lblMessage.Visible = False* statement hides the lblMessage control when the Reason field value doesn't equal one of the two reasons.

Modifying an Event Procedure

Donna wants you to change the red color for the display of the message "Provide patient with information on annual flu vaccines" to green. This requires changing the red RGB function value of (255, 0, 0) to the green value (0, 150, 0). To make this change, you'll modify the first set of RGB function values in the event procedure. Then you'll close the Visual Basic window and save and test your modifications.

To modify, save, and test the event procedure:

1. In the line lblMessage.Forecolor = RGB(255, 0, 0), double-click **255** to select it, and then type **0** to replace the selected value. The RGB function is now RGB(0, 0, 0).
2. In the same line of code, double-click the next **0**, and then type **150**. The RGB function is now RGB(0, 150, 0), which is a value that will produce a medium shade of green. See Figure 11–7.

Figure 11–7 Modified RGB values

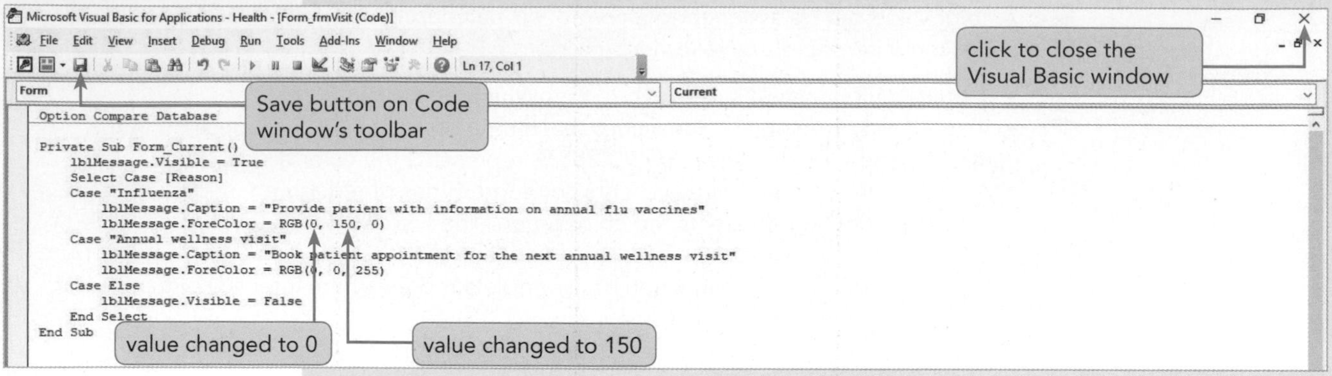
Microsoft Visual Basic for Applications - Health - [Form_frmVisit (Code)]
click to close the Visual Basic window
Save button on Code window's toolbar
Option Compare Database
Private Sub Form_Current()
lblMessage.Visible = True
Select Case [Reason]
Case "Influenza"
lblMessage.Caption = "Provide patient with information on annual flu vaccines"
lblMessage.ForeColor = RGB(0, 150, 0)
Case "Annual wellness visit"
lblMessage.Caption = "Book patient appointment for the next annual wellness visit"
lblMessage.ForeColor = RGB(0, 0, 255)
Case Else
lblMessage.Visible = False
End Select
End Sub
value changed to 0
value changed to 150

3. On the Code window's toolbar, click the **Save** button to save your changes.
4. On the Visual Basic window's title bar, click the **Close** button to close it and return to the Form window in Design view.
5. Close the Property Sheet, save your form design changes, and then switch to Form view.
6. Navigate to record 18 for the VisitID 1483. The text "Provide patient with information on annual flu vaccines" is displayed in green to the right of the Walk-in? check box. Your modification to the event procedure was completed successfully. See Figure 11–8.

Figure 11–8 Forecolor changed in frmVisit form

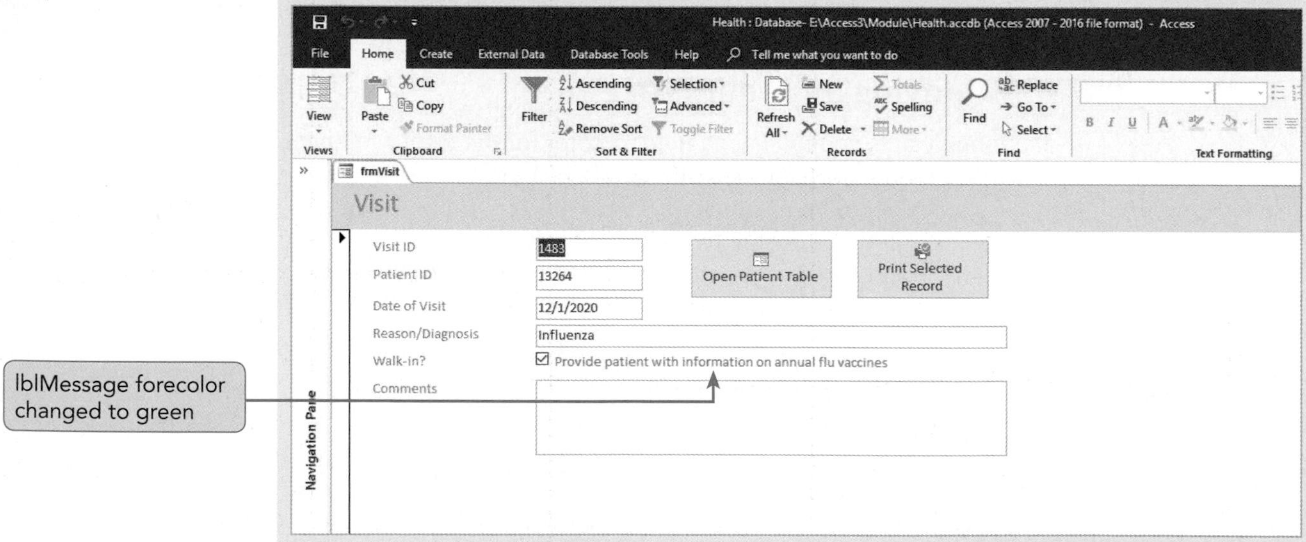
lblMessage forecolor changed to green
Visit
Visit ID
Patient ID
Date of Visit
Reason/Diagnosis
Walk-in?
Comments
1483
13264
12/1/2020
Influenza
Provide patient with information on annual flu vaccines
Open Patient Table
Print Selected Record

7. Close the frmVisit form.

Now that you have viewed and modified an event procedure, you'll create a function in a standard module.

Creating Functions in a Standard Module

Donna wants you to create a VBA procedure for the frmPatient form that will automatically convert the values entered in the Email field to lowercase. For example, if a user enters "JDoe@Example.Com" as the email address, the procedure will automatically convert it to "jdoe@example.com". Donna feels that this function will make data more uniform in the database. Additionally, she might want to add code later that ensures the entry is a valid email address, and this VBA procedure could serve as a foundation for further validation code.

Any user input in the Email field is a **string**, which is one or more characters that could include alphabetic characters, numbers, spaces, and punctuation. To accomplish the change Donna wants, you will first create a simple function, named LowAll, that accepts a string input value and converts that string to lowercase. You will create the function by typing the required statements in the Code window. Then you will create an event procedure that calls the LowAll function whenever a user enters a value in the Email field using the frmPatient form.

Whenever a user enters or changes a field value in a control or in a form and then changes the focus to another control or record, the **AfterUpdate event** is automatically triggered, which, by default, simply accepts the new or changed entry. However, you can set the AfterUpdate event property of a control to a specific event procedure in order to have something else happen when a user enters or changes the field value. In this case, you need to set the Email field's AfterUpdate event property to [Event Procedure] and then code an event procedure to call the LowAll function. Calling the LowAll function will cause the entry in the Email field to be converted to lowercase letters before storing it in the database.

You could add the LowAll function to the class module for the frmPatient form. However, adding the function to the class module for the frmPatient form would make it a private function; that is, you could not use it in other forms or database objects. Because Donna and her staff might use the LowAll function in other forms in the Health database, you'll instead place the LowAll function in a new standard module named basHealthProcedures (*bas* is a standard prefix for modules). Generally, when you enter a procedure in a standard module, it is public, and you can use it in event procedures for any object in the database.

To create a new standard module, you'll begin by opening the Code window.

To create a new standard module:

1. On the ribbon, click the **Create** tab.
2. In the Macros & Code group, click the **Module** button. A new Code window opens in the Visual Basic window. See Figure 11–9.

Figure 11–9 **New standard module in the Code window**

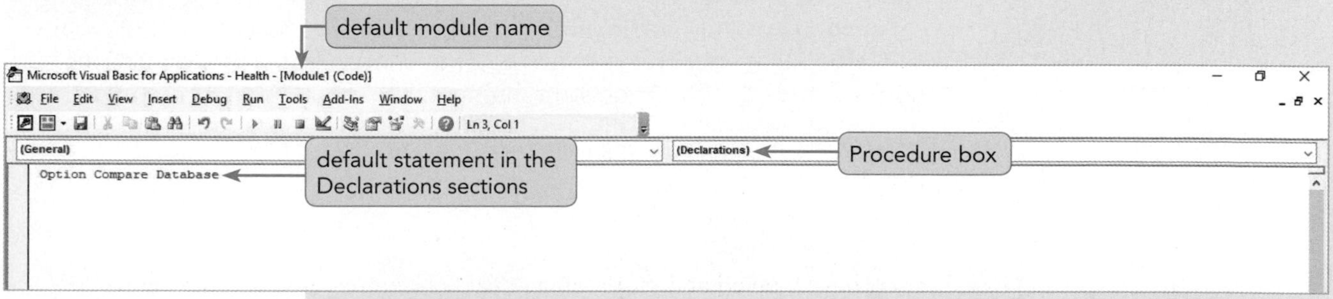
default module name
Microsoft Visual Basic for Applications - Health - [Module1 (Code)]
File Edit View Insert Debug Run Tools Add-Ins Window Help
Ln 3, Col 1
(General)
(Declarations)
Procedure box
Option Compare Database
default statement in the Declarations sections

Trouble? If other windows appear in your Visual Basic window, click their Close buttons to close them.

In the Code window for the new standard module, the Procedure box indicates the Declarations section as the current procedure in the module. The Option Compare statement is automatically included in the Declarations section of a new module. The LowAll function is a simple function that does not require additional statements in the Declarations section.

Creating a Function

Each function begins with a **Function statement** and ends with an **End Function statement**. Each procedure in the Code window is separated by a horizontal line. You can view a procedure's statements by selecting the procedure name from the Procedure box.

You'll start the LowAll function with the statement *Function LowAll(FValue)*. LowAll is the function name, and FValue is used as a placeholder for the input value in the function definition. When a user enters a value for the Email field in the frmPatient form, that value will be passed to the LowAll function and substituted for FValue in the function definition. A placeholder like FValue is called a **parameter**. The value passed to the function and used in place of the parameter when the function is executed is called an **argument**. In other words, the value passed to the function is the argument, which is assigned to the parameter named FValue.

INSIGHT

VBA Naming Rules

Each VBA function name, Sub procedure name, argument name, and any other name you create must conform to the following rules:

- It must begin with a letter.
- It cannot exceed 255 characters.
- It can include letters, numbers, and the underscore character (_). You cannot use a space or any punctuation characters.
- It cannot contain keywords—such as Function, Sub, Case, and Option—that VBA uses as part of its language.
- It must be unique, that is, you can't declare the same name twice within the same procedure.

Next you'll enter the LowAll function in the Code window.

To enter the LowAll function in the Code window:

1. If necessary, position the insertion point two lines below the Option Compare statement.
2. Type **Function LowAll(FValue)** and then press **ENTER**. The editor displays a horizontal line that visually separates the new function from the Declarations section and adds the End Function statement. See Figure 11–10.

Figure 11–10 **Function entered in the Code window**

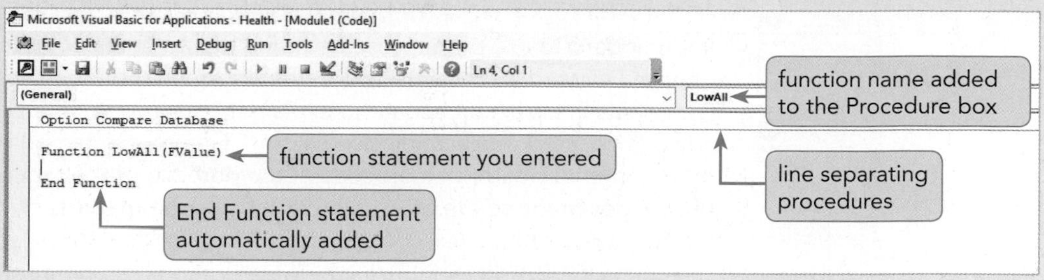
Microsoft Visual Basic for Applications - Health - [Module1 (Code)]
File Edit View Insert Debug Run Tools Add-Ins Window Help
Ln 4, Col 1
(General)
LowAll
Option Compare Database
Function LowAll(FValue)
End Function
function name added to the Procedure box
function statement you entered
line separating procedures
End Function statement automatically added

The LowAll function will consist of a single executable assignment statement that you will place between the Function and End Function statements. The assignment statement you'll enter is *LowAll = LCase(FValue)*. The value of the expression, which is LCase(FValue), will be assigned to the function, which is LowAll.

The expression in the assignment statement uses a built-in Access function named LCase. The **LCase function** accepts a single string argument as input, converts the value of the argument to lowercase letters, and then returns the converted value. The assignment statement assigns the converted value to the LowAll function. Figure 11–11 illustrates this process.

Figure 11–11 **Evaluation of the assignment statement**

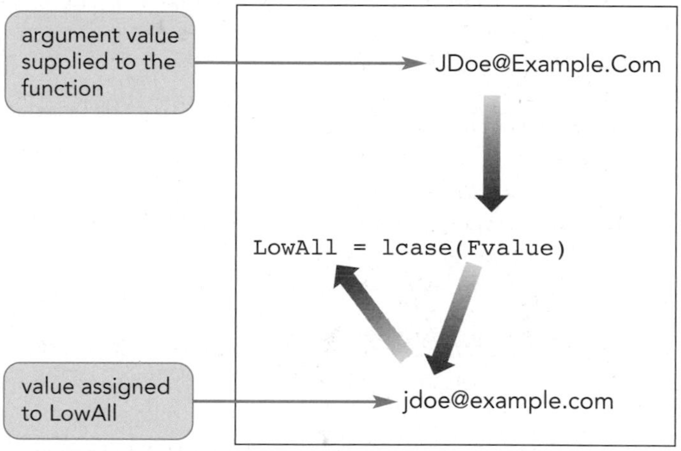
argument value supplied to the function
JDoe@Example.Com
LowAll = lcase(Fvalue)
value assigned to LowAll
jdoe@example.com

TIP

Because VBA ignores the contents of comments, you can include spaces, special characters, and mixed-case strings in your comments.

Before entering the assignment statement, you will add a comment line to explain the procedure's purpose. You can include comments anywhere in a VBA procedure to describe what the procedure does or what a statement does. You begin a comment with the word Rem (for "Remark") or with a single quotation mark ('). VBA ignores anything following the word Rem or the single quotation mark on a single line.

PROSKILLS

Written Communication: Guidelines for Writing VBA Code

It is standard to use proper case in writing VB statements, that is, the first character of each keyword is capitalized, as in the statement End If. In addition, you should use comments in a VBA procedure to explain the purpose of the procedure and to clarify any complicated programming logic used. Comments can be used to identify the name of the original creator of a procedure, the purpose of the procedure, and a history of changes made to the procedure, including who made each change and for what purpose.

Although VBA does not require statements to be indented in procedures, experienced programmers indent statements to make procedures easier to read and maintain. Pressing TAB once indents a line four spaces to the right, and pressing SHIFT+TAB or BACKSPACE once moves the insertion point four spaces to the left. Commenting and indenting your procedures will help you recall the logic of the procedures you created months or years ago and will help others understand your work.

To add a comment and statement to the LowAll function:

1. Click in the blank line between the Function and End Function statements (if necessary) to position the insertion point, and then press **TAB**.

   You will add the comment in this blank line. The single quotation mark is a comment marker, and it indicates that the text that follows is a comment and will not be executed.

2. Type **'Convert all letters of a field value to lowercase**, and then press **ENTER**.

   Notice that the editor displays the comment in green and moves the insertion point to a new indented line. After entering the comment line, you can enter the assignment statement, which is the executable statement in the function that performs the actual conversion of the argument to lowercase.

3. Type **LowAll = LCase(**

   The editor displays a Quick Info banner with a reminder that LCase accepts a single string argument. See Figure 11–12.

Figure 11–12 LowAll function entered in the Code window

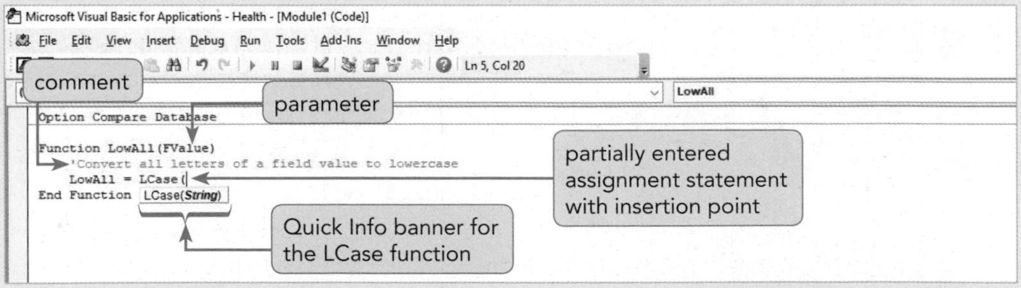
Microsoft Visual Basic for Applications - Health - [Module1 (Code)]
File Edit View Insert Debug Run Tools Add-Ins Window Help
Ln 5, Col 20
LowAll
comment
parameter
Option Compare Database
Function LowAll(FValue)
'Convert all letters of a field value to lowercase
LowAll = LCase(
End Function
LCase(String)
partially entered assignment statement with insertion point
Quick Info banner for the LCase function

Trouble? If the Quick Info banner is not displayed, click Tools on the menu bar, click Options, click the Editor tab (if necessary), click the Auto Quick Info check box to select it, and then click the OK button.

You'll now finish typing the assignment statement.

4. Type **FValue)** to finish the assignment statement. The editor scans each statement for errors when you press ENTER or move the insertion point to another line. Because the function is complete and you want the editor to scan the line you just entered for errors, you must move the insertion point to another line.
5. Press **DOWN ARROW** to move the insertion point to the next line. See Figure 11–13.

Figure 11–13 Complete LowAll statement in the Code window

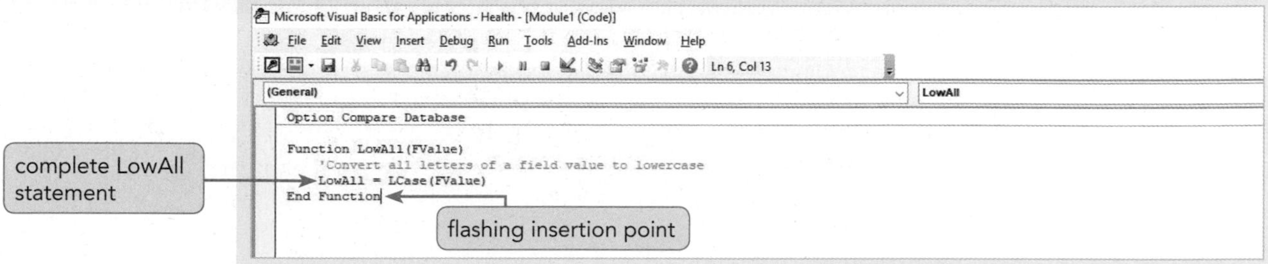
Microsoft Visual Basic for Applications - Health - [Module1 (Code)]
File Edit View Insert Debug Run Tools Add-Ins Window Help
Ln 6, Col 13
(General)
LowAll
Option Compare Database
Function LowAll(FValue)
'Convert all letters of a field value to lowercase
LowAll = LCase(FValue)
End Function
complete LowAll statement
flashing insertion point

You have finished entering the function in the module, so you'll save it before continuing with your work. When you click the Save button in the Visual Basic window, the editor saves the module and its procedures. If you are entering a long procedure, it's a good idea to save your work periodically.

To save the module:

1. On the Code window toolbar, click the **Save** button to open the Save As dialog box.
2. In the Module Name box, type **basHealthProcedures**, and then press **ENTER**. The Save As dialog box closes, the editor saves the module, and the new module name appears in editor the title bar.

After creating a module, you should test its procedures.

Testing a Procedure in the Immediate Window

TIP

VBA functions that you create won't run if the database is not trusted. You must click the Enable Content button that appears below the ribbon when you first open a database that is not stored in a trusted folder.

When you finish entering a VBA statement, the editor checks the statement to make sure its syntax is correct. Even though you may have entered all procedure statements with the correct syntax, however, the procedure may still contain logic errors. A **logic error** occurs when a procedure produces incorrect results. For example, the LowAll function would have a logic error if you typed JDoe@Example.Com and the function changed it to JDOE@EXAMPLE.COM or anything other than the correct result of jdoe@example.com. Even the simplest procedure can contain logic errors. Be sure to test each procedure thoroughly to ensure that it does exactly what you expect it to do in all situations.

When working in the Code window, you can use the **Immediate window** to test VBA procedures without changing any data in the database. The Immediate window allows you to run individual lines of VBA code for **debugging**, or testing. In the Immediate window, you can enter different values to test the procedure you just entered. To test a procedure, you type the *Print* keyword or a question mark (?), followed by the procedure name, and then the value you want to test in parentheses. For example, to test the LowAll function in the Immediate window using the test word JDoe@Example.Com, you type *?LowAll("JDoe@Example.Com")* and then press ENTER. The editor executes the function and displays the value returned by the function (you expect it to return jdoe@example.com). Note that you must enclose a string of characters within quotation marks in the test statement.

REFERENCE

Testing a Procedure in the Immediate Window

- In the Code window, click View on the menu bar, and then click Immediate Window to open the Immediate window.
- Type a question mark (?), the procedure name, and the procedure's arguments in parentheses. If an argument contains a string of characters, enclose the argument in quotation marks.
- Press ENTER, and verify that the result displayed is the expected output.

Now you'll use the Immediate window to test the LowAll function.

To test the LowAll function in the Immediate window:

1. Click **View** on the menu bar, and then click **Immediate Window**. The editor opens the Immediate window below the Code window and places the insertion point inside the window.
2. Type **?LowAll("JDoe@Example.Com")** and then press **ENTER**. The editor executes the function and displays the function result, jdoe@example.com, on the next line. See Figure 11–14.

Figure 11–14 **LowAll function executed in the Immediate window**

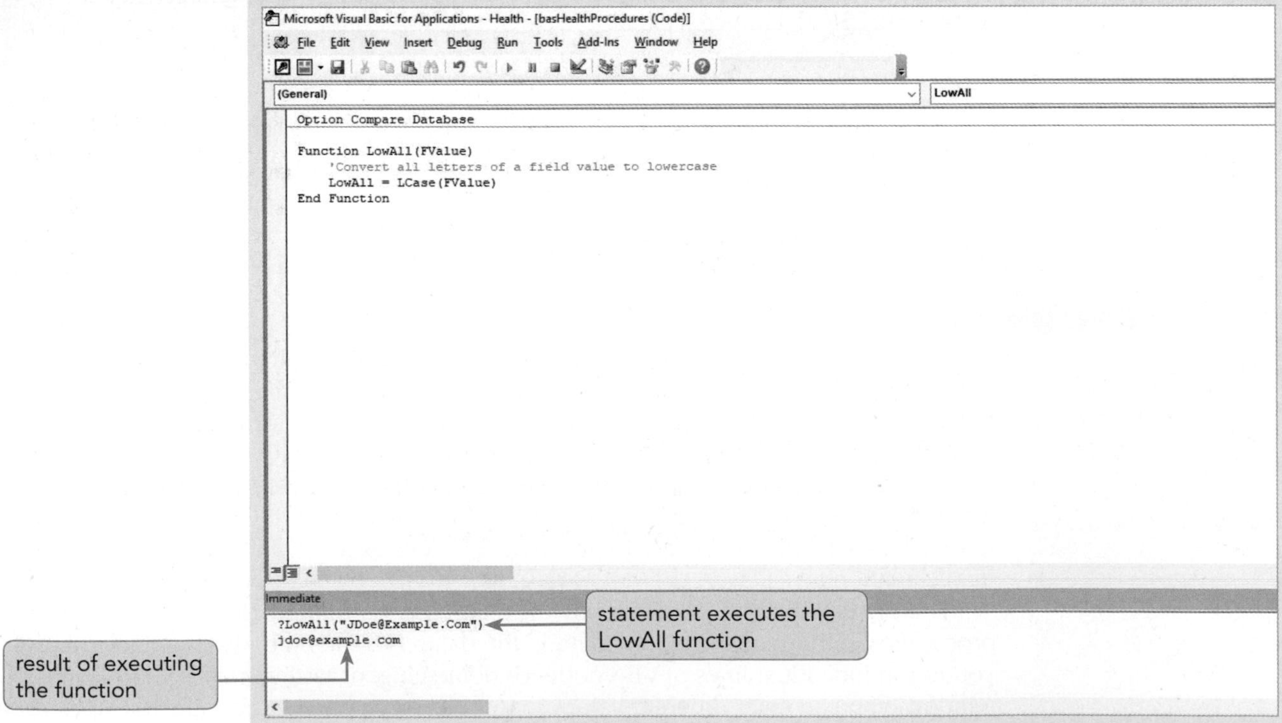
Microsoft Visual Basic for Applications - Health - [basHealthProcedures (Code)]
File Edit View Insert Debug Run Tools Add-Ins Window Help
(General)
LowAll
Option Compare Database
Function LowAll(FValue)
'Convert all letters of a field value to lowercase
LowAll = LCase(FValue)
End Function
Immediate
?LowAll("JDoe@Example.Com")
jdoe@example.com
statement executes the LowAll function
result of executing the function

Trouble? If a dialog box displays an error message, click the OK button in the dialog box, correct the error in the Immediate window, and then press ENTER. If the function does not produce the correct output (jdoe@example.com), compare your code to Figure 11–13, correct the LowAll function statements in the Code window as necessary, save your changes, click a blank line in the Immediate window, and then repeat Step 2.

To test the LowAll function further, you could enter several other test values, retyping the entire statement each time. Instead, you'll select the current test value, type another value, and then press ENTER.

3. Delete the email address **JDoe@Example.Com** in the first line of the Immediate window.
4. Type **JDOE@EXAMPLE.COM**, move the insertion point to the end of the line, and then press **ENTER**. The editor executes the function and displays the function result, jdoe@example.com, on a new line.
5. On the Immediate window's title bar, click the **Close** button ☒.
6. On the Visual Basic window's title bar, click the **Close** button ☒.
7. If you are not continuing on to the next session, close the Health database.

INSIGHT

Converting a Macro to Visual Basic

Creating a macro can be a bit more user-friendly than learning VBA code. Some people may find it easier to create a macro and then convert it to VBA. They may find that they have a database with several macros but have learned some VBA and would like to convert the macros to VBA so they can copy them and use them in other databases, or keep as much code as possible in a standard module.

To convert a macro to VBA, you open the macro you'd like to convert, then use the Convert Macros to Visual Basic button in the Tools group on the Macro Tools Design tab.

Your initial test of the LowAll function in the standard module is successful. In the next session, you'll modify the frmPatient form to execute the LowAll function for the Email field in that form.

REVIEW

Session 11.1 Quick Check

1. Why is Visual Basic for Applications called an event-driven, object-oriented language?
2. What is an event procedure?
3. What are the differences between a user-defined function and a Sub procedure?
4. Describe the two different types of modules.
5. The ______________ of a procedure is either private or public.
6. What is the Immediate window used for?

Session 11.2 Visual Overview:

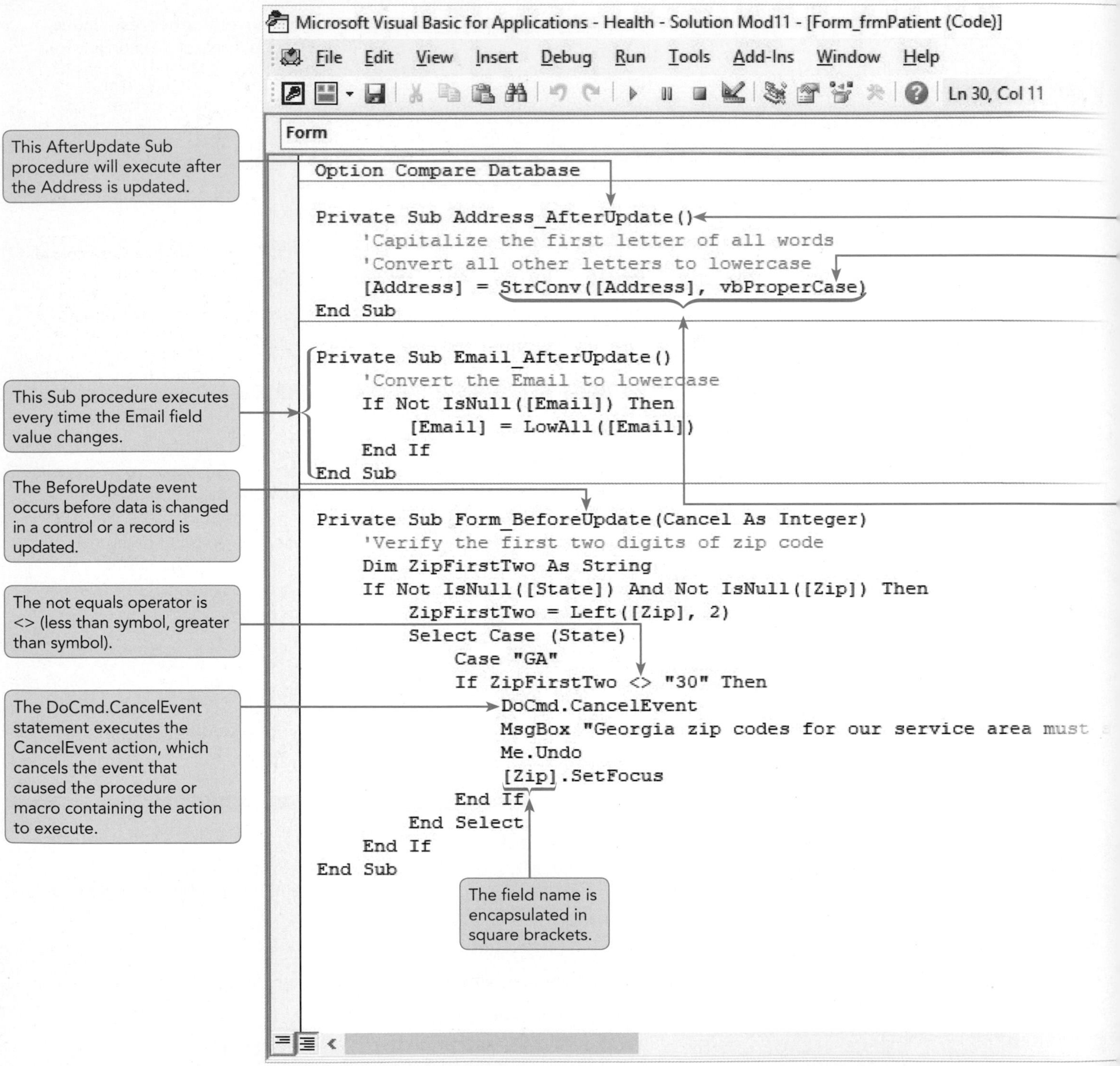
Microsoft Visual Basic for Applications - Health - Solution Mod11 - [Form_frmPatient (Code)]
File Edit View Insert Debug Run Tools Add-Ins Window Help
Ln 30, Col 11
Form
Option Compare Database
Private Sub Address_AfterUpdate()
'Capitalize the first letter of all words
'Convert all other letters to lowercase
[Address] = StrConv([Address], vbProperCase)
End Sub
Private Sub Email_AfterUpdate()
'Convert the Email to lowercase
If Not IsNull([Email]) Then
[Email] = LowAll([Email])
End If
End Sub
Private Sub Form_BeforeUpdate(Cancel As Integer)
'Verify the first two digits of zip code
Dim ZipFirstTwo As String
If Not IsNull([State]) And Not IsNull([Zip]) Then
ZipFirstTwo = Left([Zip], 2)
Select Case (State)
Case "GA"
If ZipFirstTwo <> "30" Then
DoCmd.CancelEvent
MsgBox "Georgia zip codes for our service area must
Me.Undo
[Zip].SetFocus
End If
End Select
End If
End Sub
This AfterUpdate Sub procedure will execute after the Address is updated.
This Sub procedure executes every time the Email field value changes.
The BeforeUpdate event occurs before data is changed in a control or a record is updated.
The not equals operator is <> (less than symbol, greater than symbol).
The DoCmd.CancelEvent statement executes the CancelEvent action, which cancels the event that caused the procedure or macro containing the action to execute.
The field name is encapsulated in square brackets.

Example of an Event Procedure

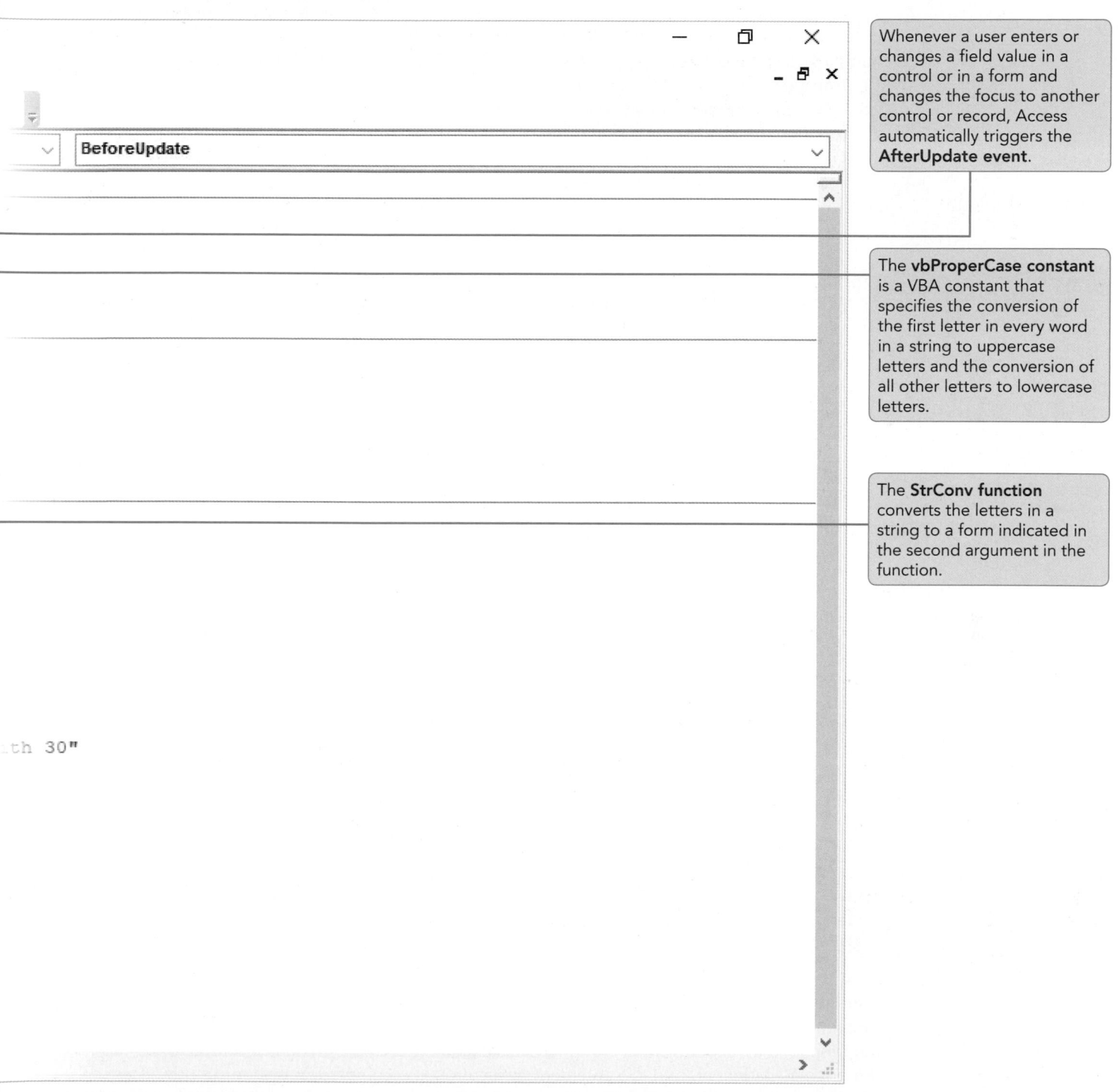

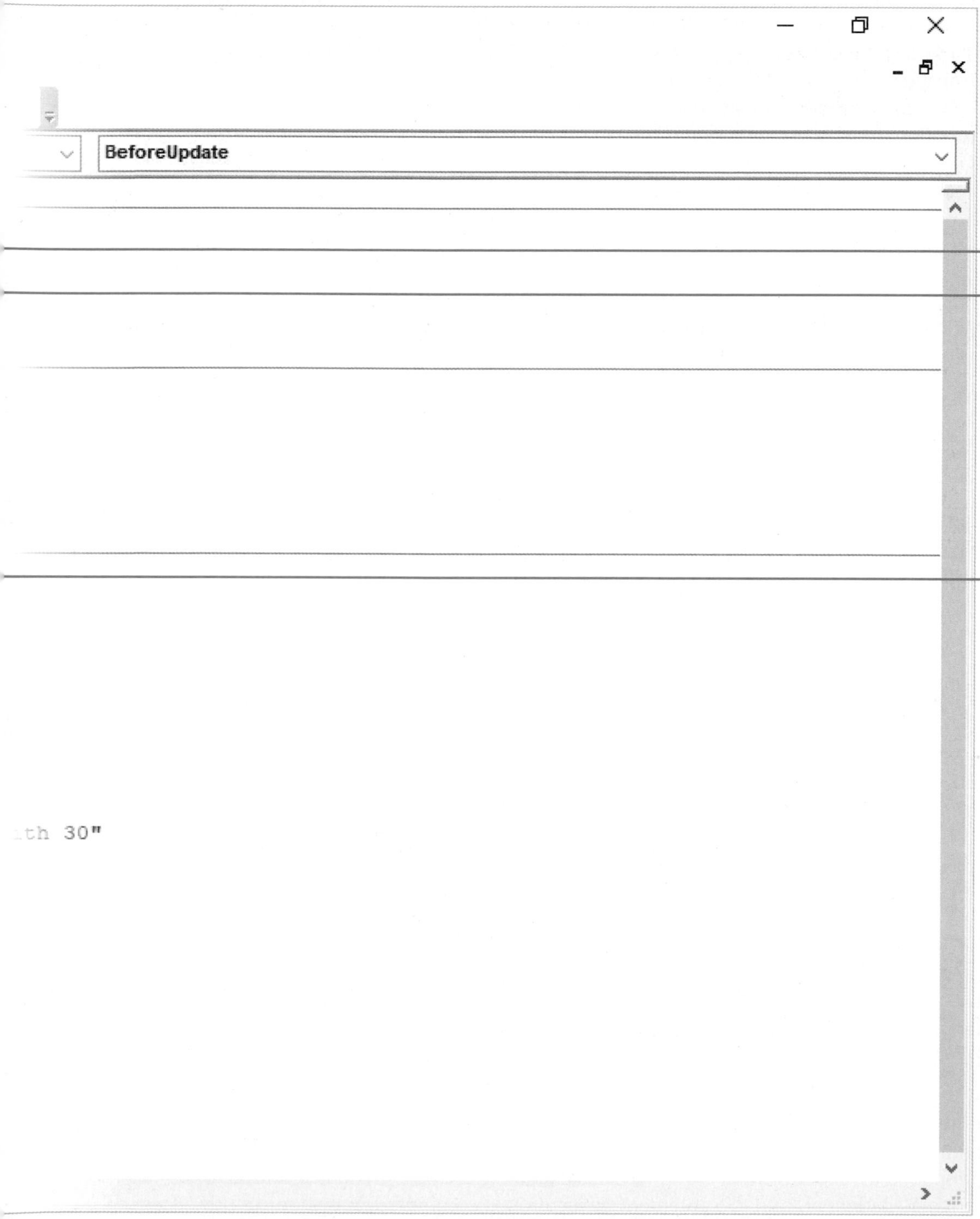
BeforeUpdate
th 30"

Whenever a user enters or changes a field value in a control or in a form and changes the focus to another control or record, Access automatically triggers the **AfterUpdate event**.

The **vbProperCase constant** is a VBA constant that specifies the conversion of the first letter in every word in a string to uppercase letters and the conversion of all other letters to lowercase letters.

The **StrConv function** converts the letters in a string to a form indicated in the second argument in the function.

Understanding How an Event Procedure Processes Commands

As stated in the previous session, when you add a procedure to a form or report, a class module for that form or report is created automatically, and the procedure is added to that class module. When you create an event procedure, the procedure runs only when a specific event occurs.

Now that you have created the LowAll function as a public procedure in the standard module named basHealthProcedures, you can create an event procedure for the frmPatient form to call the LowAll function for the Email field's AfterUpdate event. Whenever a user enters or changes an Email field value, the AfterUpdate event occurs, so by calling the LowAll function for the Email field's AfterUpdate event, you'll ensure that your event procedure will run whenever this field has a new or changed value.

What exactly happens when a procedure is called? There is an interaction between the calling statement and the function statements. Figure 11–15 shows the process for the LowAll procedure.

Figure 11–15 Process of executing a function

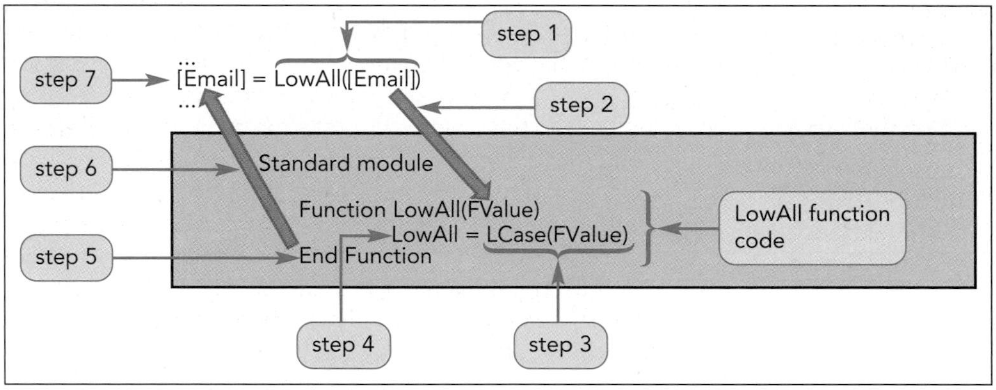
step 1
step 7
...
[Email] = LowAll([Email])
...
step 2
step 6
Standard module
Function LowAll(FValue)
LowAll = LCase(FValue)
End Function
LowAll function code
step 5
step 4
step 3

The steps in Figure 11–15 are numbered in the order in which they occur as the statement and the function are processed. These steps are as follows:

- **Step 1:** The call to the function LowAll passes the value of the argument [Email] to the function. This is the value of the Email field that is entered or changed by the user.
- **Step 2:** The function LowAll begins, and the parameter FValue receives the value of [Email].
- **Step 3:** FValue is changed to lowercase.
- **Step 4:** The result of the function is assigned to the name of the function (LowAll). This is how the result will be returned from the function when the function completes.
- **Step 5:** The function LowAll ends.
- **Step 6:** The value of LowAll is returned to the point of the call to the function.
- **Step 7:** The value of [Email] is set equal to the returned value of LowAll.

Although it might look complicated, the general function process is simple. The statement contains a **function call**, which is a statement that contains the name of the function plus any parameters required by the function. When the statement is executed, the function call is performed, the function is executed, a single value is returned to the original statement, and the statement's execution is completed. You should study the steps in Figure 11–15 and trace their sequence until you understand the complete process.

Once you understand the steps in which the event procedure will process, you should consider how to construct the event procedure in the Visual Basic (VB) Editor.

All event procedures are Sub procedures. The VB editor automatically adds the Sub and End Sub statements to an event procedure. All you need to do is place the statements between the Sub and End Sub statements. Figure 11–16 shows the completed event procedure in the Code window.

Figure 11–16 **AfterUpdate event procedure for the Email field**

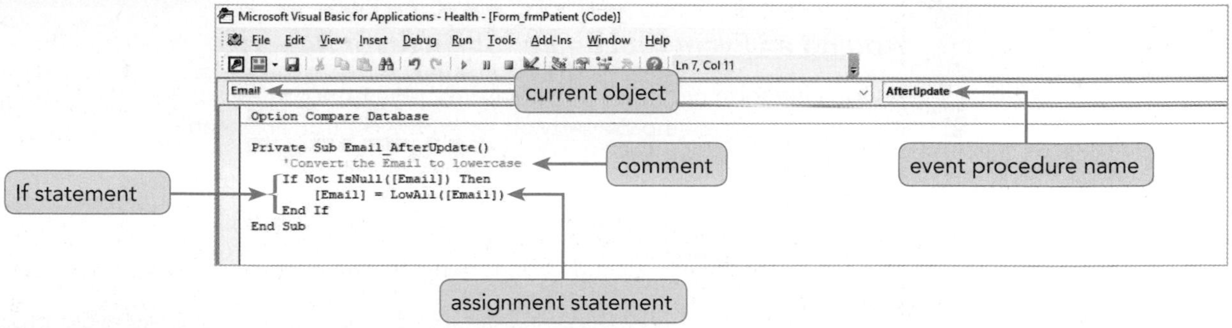

Microsoft Visual Basic for Applications - Health - [Form_frmPatient (Code)]
File Edit View Insert Debug Run Tools Add-Ins Window Help
Ln 7, Col 11
Email
current object
AfterUpdate
Option Compare Database
Private Sub Email_AfterUpdate()
'Convert the Email to lowercase
If Not IsNull([Email]) Then
[Email] = LowAll([Email])
End If
End Sub
comment
event procedure name
If statement
assignment statement

TIP

If the name of a control contains spaces or special characters, the underscores are substituted for them in the event procedure name.

In reviewing the completed event procedure in Figure 11–16, notice the following. Each event procedure is named in a standard way, using the name of the control, an underscore (_), and the event name. No parameters are passed to an event procedure, so nothing is placed in the parentheses following the name of the Sub procedure.

A user might delete an existing Email field value so that it contains no value, or becomes null. In this case, calling the function accomplishes nothing. The procedure is designed to call the LowAll function only when a user changes the Email field to a value that is not null. The If statement screens out the null values. In its simplest form, an **If statement** executes one of two groups of statements based on a condition, similar to common English usage. For example, consider the English statements, "If the door is unlocked, I'll open it and walk through it. Otherwise, I'll knock on the door and wait until someone unlocks it." In these sentences, the two groups of statements come before and after the "otherwise," depending on the condition, "if the door is unlocked." The first group of statements consists of the clause "I'll open it and walk through it." This clause is called the **true-statement group** because it's what happens if the condition ("the door is unlocked") is true. The second group of statements contains "I'll knock on the door and wait until someone unlocks it." This clause is called the **false-statement group** because it is what happens if the condition is false. VBA uses the keyword *If* to precede the condition. The keyword *Then* precedes the true-statement group, and the keyword *Else* precedes the false-statement group. The general syntax of a VBA If statement is:

```
If condition Then
    true-statement group
[Else
    false-statement group]
End If
```

The true-statement group executes when the condition is true, and the false-statement group when the condition is false. In this statement's syntax, the bracketed portions are optional. Therefore, you must omit the *Else* and its related false-statement group when you want a group of statements to execute only when the condition is true.

TIP

Notice that the Email field name is enclosed in brackets, even though brackets are optional for field names and control names that do not contain spaces and special characters.

In Figure 11–16, the If statement uses the VBA **IsNull function**, which returns a value of True when the Email field value is null and False when it is not null. The *Not* in the If statement is the same logical operator you've used previously to negate an expression. So, the statement *[Email] = LowAll([Email])* executes only when the Email field value is not null.

Adding an Event Procedure

To add an event procedure to a control in a form or report, you need to open the form or report in Design view. In this case, you need to add an event procedure to the frmPatient form, specifically to the Email field's AfterUpdate event property.

REFERENCE

Adding an Event Procedure to a Form or Report

- Open the form or report in Design view, select the control whose event property you want to set, open the Property Sheet for the control, and then click the Event tab in the Property Sheet.
- Click the appropriate event property box, click its Build button, click Code Builder in the Choose Builder dialog box, and then click the OK button to open the Code window in the VB editor.
- Enter the Sub procedure statements in the Code window.
- Compile the procedure, fix any statement errors, and then save the event procedure.

Next you'll add the event procedure to the frmPatient form.

To add the event procedure to the frmPatient form:

1. If you took a break after the previous session, make sure that the Health database is open.
2. Open the Navigation Pane (if necessary), open the **frmPatient** form in Design view, and then close the Navigation Pane.
3. Right-click the **Email** field value box to select it and to display the shortcut menu, click **Properties** to open the Property Sheet, and then, if necessary, click the **Event** tab in the Property Sheet. You need to set the AfterUpdate property for the Email field value box.

   Trouble? If you do not see any events on the Event tab, you might have clicked the Email label control instead of the field value box. Right-click the Email field value box.
4. Click the **After Update** box, click its **Build** button [...] to open the Choose Builder dialog box, click **Code Builder**, and then click **OK**. The Code window opens in the Visual Basic window. See Figure 11–17.

Figure 11–17 Starting a new event procedure in the Code window

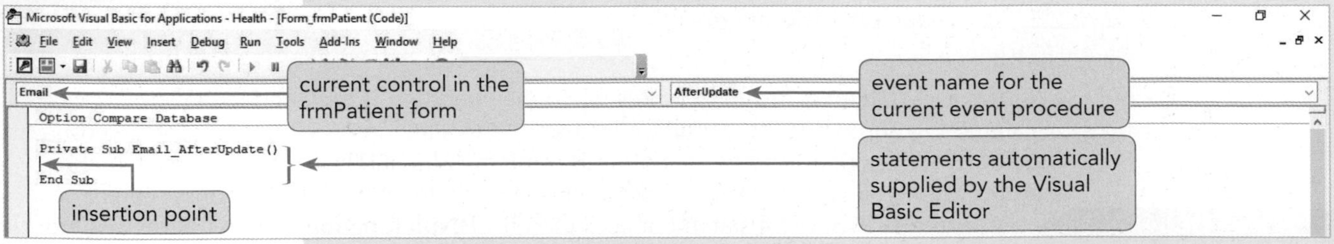
Microsoft Visual Basic for Applications - Health - [Form_frmPatient (Code)]
File Edit View Insert Debug Run Tools Add-Ins Window Help
Email
AfterUpdate
current control in the frmPatient form
event name for the current event procedure
Option Compare Database
Private Sub Email_AfterUpdate()
End Sub
statements automatically supplied by the Visual Basic Editor
insertion point

5. Enter the statements shown in Figure 11–18, using TAB to indent the lines as shown in the figure (if necessary), pressing ENTER at the end of each line, and pressing BACKSPACE to move one tab stop to the left.
6. Compare your screen with Figure 11–18, and make any necessary corrections by selecting the errors and typing the corrections.

Figure 11–18 **Completed event procedure**

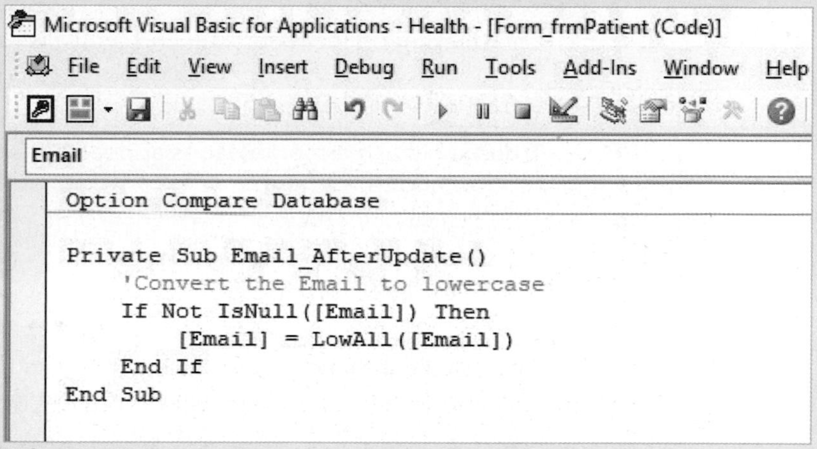
Microsoft Visual Basic for Applications - Health - [Form_frmPatient (Code)]
File Edit View Insert Debug Run Tools Add-Ins Window Help
Email
Option Compare Database
Private Sub Email_AfterUpdate()
'Convert the Email to lowercase
If Not IsNull([Email]) Then
[Email] = LowAll([Email])
End If
End Sub

Trouble? If your event procedure contains errors, correct them by selecting the errors and typing the corrections. Press BACKSPACE or DELETE to delete characters.

Before saving the event procedure, you'll compile the module.

Compiling Modules

The VBA programming language is not the computer's native language. Although you can learn VBA and become fluent in it, computers cannot understand or learn VBA. For a computer to understand the statements in your VBA modules, the statements must be translated into a form that the computer processor can use. The process of translating modules from VBA to a form your computer processor understands is called **compilation**; you say that you **compile** the module when you translate it.

You can compile a procedure at any time as you enter it by clicking the Compile command on the Debug menu in the Visual Basic window. The procedure and all other procedures in all modules in the database are then compiled. Also, when you run a procedure for the first time, the procedure is compiled automatically, and a dialog box will open if any syntax errors exist in the procedure, in which case the computer cannot translate the procedure statements. If no errors are detected, the procedure translates.

INSIGHT

The Importance of Compiling Procedures

It's best to compile and save your modules after you've made changes to them, to make sure they don't contain syntax errors. If you don't compile a procedure when you first create it or after you've changed it, the procedure will be compiled when the first user opens the form or report that uses the procedure. The user could encounter a syntax error and be unable to use the form or report. You don't want users to experience these types of problems, so you should compile and fully test all procedures as you create them.

You'll now compile the procedures in the Health database and save the class module for the frmPatient form.

To compile the procedures in the Health database and save the class module:

1. Click **Debug** on the menu bar, and then click **Compile Health**. The modules in the database are compiled. Because you have no syntax errors, the VBA statements translate.

   Trouble? If any error messages appear, correct the errors in the Code window and repeat Step 1.

2. Save your module changes, close the Visual Basic window, and then close the Property Sheet.

You have created the function and the event procedure and have set the event property. Next, you'll test the event procedure in the frmPatient form to make sure it works correctly.

Testing an Event Procedure

You need to display the frmPatient form in Form view to test the Email field's event procedure by entering a few different test Email field values in the first record of the form. Moving the focus to another control in the form or to another record triggers the AfterUpdate event for the Email field and executes the attached event procedure. Because the LowAll function is attached only to the frmPatient form, the automatic conversion to lowercase of Email field values is not in effect when you enter them in the tblPatient table or in any other object in the Health database.

To test the event procedure:

1. Switch to Form view, and navigate to record 2, Patient ID 13251.
2. Select the **Email** field value (g.davis21@example.com), type **G.DAVIS21@ EXAMPLE.COM** in the Email text box, and click the Zip text box control to enter the data. Access executes the AfterUpdate event procedure for the Email field and changes the Email field value to "g.davis21@example.com." See Figure 11–19.

Figure 11–19 frmPatient form after executing the event procedure

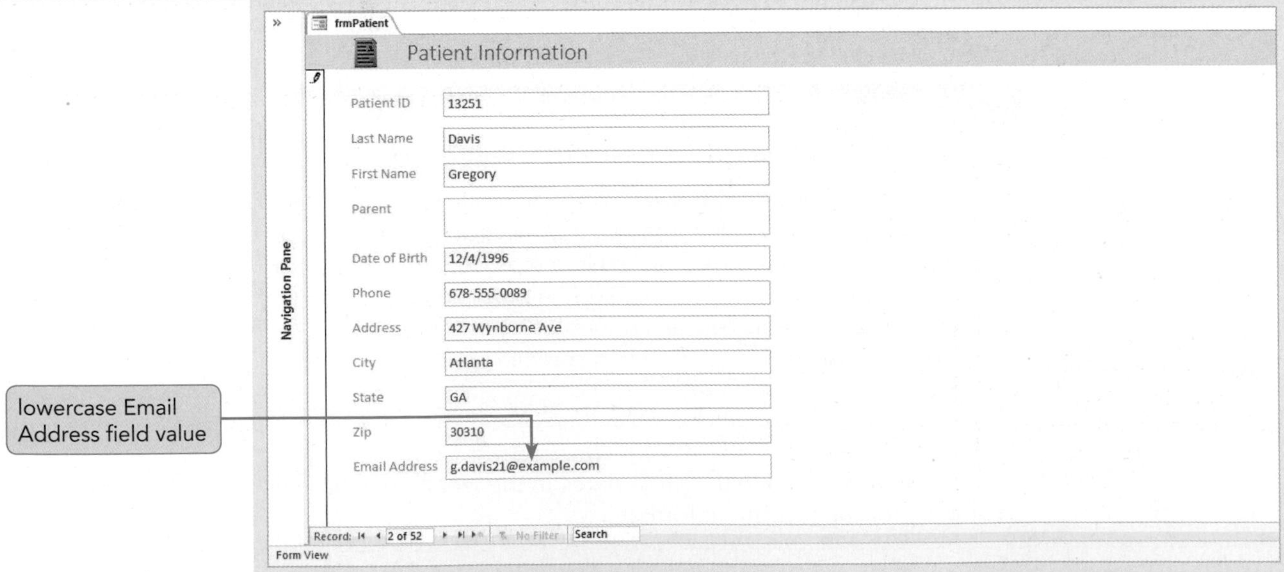

frmPatient
Patient Information
Patient ID
13251
Last Name
Davis
First Name
Gregory
Parent
Date of Birth
12/4/1996
Phone
678-555-0089
Address
427 Wynborne Ave
City
Atlanta
State
GA
Zip
30310
Email Address
g.davis21@example.com
Navigation Pane
Record: 2 of 52
No Filter
Search
Form View
lowercase Email Address field value

3. Repeat Step 2 again, this time entering **G.Davis21@Example.com** in the Email box. The correct value of g.davis21@example.com is displayed in the Email box.

Donna is happy with the functionality you've added to the Email box. Next she wants you to create a more complex function for the Zip field in the frmPatient form.

Adding a Second Procedure to a Class Module

Donna has found her staff makes frequent errors when entering Georgia zip codes, whose first two digits are always 30 in the primary area that Lakewood Community Health Services serves. She asks you to create a procedure that will verify that Georgia zip codes are in the correct range (beginning with 30) when her staff updates the Zip field in the frmPatient form. One option is to use a form validation rule, but Donna would like to be able to add complexity later, to validate other zip codes because patients from other areas in Georgia and other states may visit the clinic. Also, Donna would like to be able to use this VBA code in other databases. If the validation property is used in the tblPatient table instead of using VBA, then this validation rule would have to be re-created in another database. Instead, by creating an event procedure, Donna will be able to copy the VBA code and paste it into another VBA window in another database.

You'll build a simple procedure that can be modified later to add more complexity. For this procedure, you will use an event procedure attached to the BeforeUpdate event for the frmPatient form. The BeforeUpdate event occurs before changed data in a control or a record is updated. You'll use the form's BeforeUpdate event for this new procedure because you want to find data-entry errors for Georgia zip codes and alert users to the errors before the database is updated.

Designing the Field Validation Procedure

Figure 11–20 shows the procedure that you will create to verify Georgia zip codes for the area that the Lakewood Community Health Services primarily serves. You've already seen several of the statements in this procedure in your work with the LowAll function and with the form's Current event.

Figure 11–20 **Zip validation procedure**

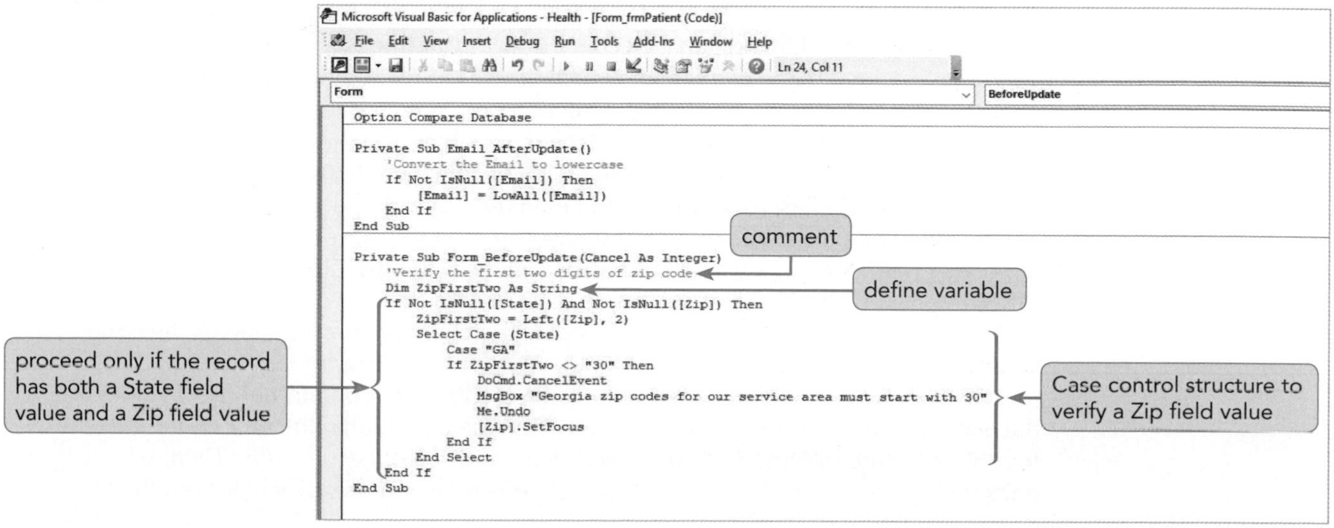
Microsoft Visual Basic for Applications - Health - [Form_frmPatient (Code)]
File Edit View Insert Debug Run Tools Add-Ins Window Help
Ln 24, Col 11
Form
BeforeUpdate
Option Compare Database
Private Sub Email_AfterUpdate()
'Convert the Email to lowercase
If Not IsNull([Email]) Then
[Email] = LowAll([Email])
End If
End Sub
Private Sub Form_BeforeUpdate(Cancel As Integer)
'Verify the first two digits of zip code
Dim ZipFirstTwo As String
If Not IsNull([State]) And Not IsNull([Zip]) Then
ZipFirstTwo = Left([Zip], 2)
Select Case (State)
Case "GA"
If ZipFirstTwo <> "30" Then
DoCmd.CancelEvent
MsgBox "Georgia zip codes for our service area must start with 30"
Me.Undo
[Zip].SetFocus
End If
End Select
End If
End Sub
comment
define variable
proceed only if the record has both a State field value and a Zip field value
Case control structure to verify a Zip field value

The Sub and End Sub statements begin and end the Sub procedure. As specified in the Sub statement, the Sub procedure executes when the form's BeforeUpdate event occurs. Within parentheses in the Sub statement, *Cancel As Integer* defines Cancel as a parameter with the Integer data type. VBA has data types that are different from the Access data types you've used to define table fields, but each Access data type is equivalent to one of the VBA data types. For example, the Access Number data type with an Integer field size is the same as the VBA Integer data type, and the Access Short Text data type is the same as the VBA String data type. Figure 11–21 shows the primary VBA data types.

Figure 11–21 Primary VBA data types

Data Type	Stores
Boolean	True/False values
Byte	Integer values from 0 to 255
Currency	Currency values from –922,337,203,685,477.5808 to 922,337,203,685,477.5807
Date	Date and time values from 1 January 100 to 31 December 9999
Decimal	Non-integer values with 0 to 28 decimal places
Double	Non-integer values from $-1.79769313486231*10^{308}$ to $-4.94065645841247*11^{-324}$ for negative values, from $4.94065645841247*11^{-324}$ to $1.79769313486232*10^{308}$ for positive values, and 0
Integer	Integer values from –32,768 to 32,767
Long	Integer values from –2,147,483,648 to 2,147,483,647
Object	Any object reference
Single	Non-integer values from $-3.402823*10^{38}$ to $-1.401298*11^{-45}$ for negative values, from $1.401298*11^{-45}$ to $3.402823*10^{38}$ for positive values, and 0
String	Text values up to 2 billion characters in length
Variant	Any numeric or string data type

When an event occurs, the default behavior for the event is performed. For some events, such as the BeforeUpdate event, the event procedure or macro executes before performing the default behavior. Thus, if something is wrong and the default behavior should not occur, you can cancel the default behavior in the event procedure or macro. For this reason, the Cancel parameter is automatically included for the BeforeUpdate event.

The second procedure statement, which starts with a single quotation mark, is a comment. The third statement, *Dim ZipFirstTwo As String*, declares the String variable named ZipFirstTwo that the Sub procedure uses. A **variable** is a named location in computer memory that can contain a value. If you use a variable in a module, you must explicitly declare it in the Declarations section or in the procedure where the variable is used. You use the **Dim statement** to declare variables and their associated data types in a procedure. The Sub procedure will assign the first two digits of a zip code (the Zip field) to the ZipFirstTwo variable and then use the variable when verifying that a Georgia zip code the clinic primarily serves begins in the correct range. Because the zip code could contain a value that begins with zero (0), the ZipFirstTwo variable uses the String data type instead of a numeric data type. The first two characters of any zip code for the Georgia area primarily served by the clinic are represented as the string value "30".

The procedure should not attempt to verify records that contain null field values for the State field and the Zip field. To screen out these conditions, the procedure uses the fourth procedure statement, *If Not IsNull([State]) And Not IsNull([Zip]) Then*, which pairs with the last *End If* statement. The *If* statement determines whether both the State and Zip fields are nonnull. If both conditions are true (both fields contain values), then the next statement in the procedure executes. If either condition is false, then the paired End If statement executes, and the following End Sub statement ends the procedure without the execution of any other statement.

The fifth procedure statement, *ZipFirstTwo = Left([Zip], 2)*, uses a built-in VBA function, the Left function, to assign the first two characters of the Zip field value to the ZipFirstTwo variable. The Left function returns a string containing a specified number of characters from the left side of a specified string. In this case, the Left function returns the leftmost two characters of the Zip field value.

You encountered the Case control structure previously in the frmVisit form's Current event procedure. For the BeforeUpdate event procedure, the *Select Case [State]* statement evaluates the State field value. For a State field value equal to GA (indicating the record should have a GA zip code), the next If statement is executed. For all other State field values, nothing further in the procedure is executed; the default behavior is performed, and control returns back to the form for further processing. The procedure uses the Case control structure because although Donna wants the procedure to verify the first two characters of only Georgia zip codes for now, she might want to expand the procedure in the future to verify the first two digits of zip codes for other areas of Georgia and other states as Lakewood Community Health Services expands its services.

Because valid Georgia zip codes in the area the clinic serves begin with "30", invalid values for the Zip field will not be equal to "30". The not equals operator in VBA is <> (less than symbol followed by the greater than symbol). The next VBA statement, *If ZipFirstTwo <> "30" Then*, is true only for invalid Georgia zip codes. When the If statement is true, the next four statements are executed. When the If statement is false, nothing further in the procedure is executed, the default behavior performs, and control returns back to the form for further processing.

The first of the four VBA statements that executes for invalid Georgia zip codes is the DoCmd statement. The DoCmd statement executes an action in a procedure. The *DoCmd.CancelEvent* statement executes the CancelEvent action. The CancelEvent action cancels the event that caused the procedure or macro containing the action to execute. In this case, the BeforeUpdate event cancels and does not update the database with the changes to the current record. In addition, subsequent events—those that would have occurred if the BeforeUpdate event had been executed—are canceled. For example, in addition to the form's BeforeUpdate event being triggered when you move to a different record, the following events are also triggered when you move to a different record, in the order listed: BeforeUpdate event for the form, AfterUpdate event for the form, Exit event for the control with the focus, LostFocus event for the control with the focus, RecordExit event for the form, and Current event for the form. When the CancelEvent action is executed, all these events are canceled, and the focus remains with the record being edited.

TIP

The macro MessageBox action is the same as the VBA MsgBox statement.

The second of the four VBA statements that are executed for invalid Georgia zip codes is the MsgBox statement. The *MsgBox "Georgia zip codes for our service area must start with 30"* statement displays its message in a message box that remains on the screen until the user clicks the OK button. The message box appears on top of the frmPatient form so the user can view the changed field values in the current record.

For invalid Georgia zip codes, after the user clicks the OK button in the message box, the *Me.Undo* statement is executed. The Me keyword refers to the current object—in this case, the frmPatient form. Undo is a method that clears all changes made to the current record in the frmPatient form, so that the field values in the record return to the way they were before the user made the current changes. A **method** is an action that operates on specific objects or controls.

Finally, for invalid Georgia zip codes, the *[Zip].SetFocus* statement is executed. SetFocus is a method that moves the focus to the specified object or control. In this case, the focus is moved to the Zip field in the current record in the frmPatient form.

Adding a Field Value Event Procedure

You can now add an event procedure for the frmPatient form's BeforeUpdate event property that will execute whenever field values in a record are entered or updated.

When entering "30", be sure to enter the number zero, not the letter O.

To add the event procedure for the frmPatient form's BeforeUpdate event property:

1. Switch to Design view, open the **Property Sheet** for the frmPatient form, and then if necessary, click the **Event** tab in the Property Sheet.
2. Click the **Before Update** box, click the **Before Update** arrow, click [**Event Procedure**], and then click the **Build** button [...]. The Code window, which contains new Private Sub and End Sub statements, opens in the Visual Basic window. Horizontal lines separate the Option Compare statement from the new procedure and from the AfterUpdate event procedure you entered earlier.
3. Press **TAB**, and then type the Sub procedure statements exactly as shown in Figure 11–22. Press **ENTER** after you enter each statement, press **TAB** to indent lines as necessary, and press **BACKSPACE** to move the insertion point one tab stop to the left. When you are finished, your screen should look like Figure 11–22.

Figure 11–22 Event procedure for the frmOwner form's BeforeUpdate event

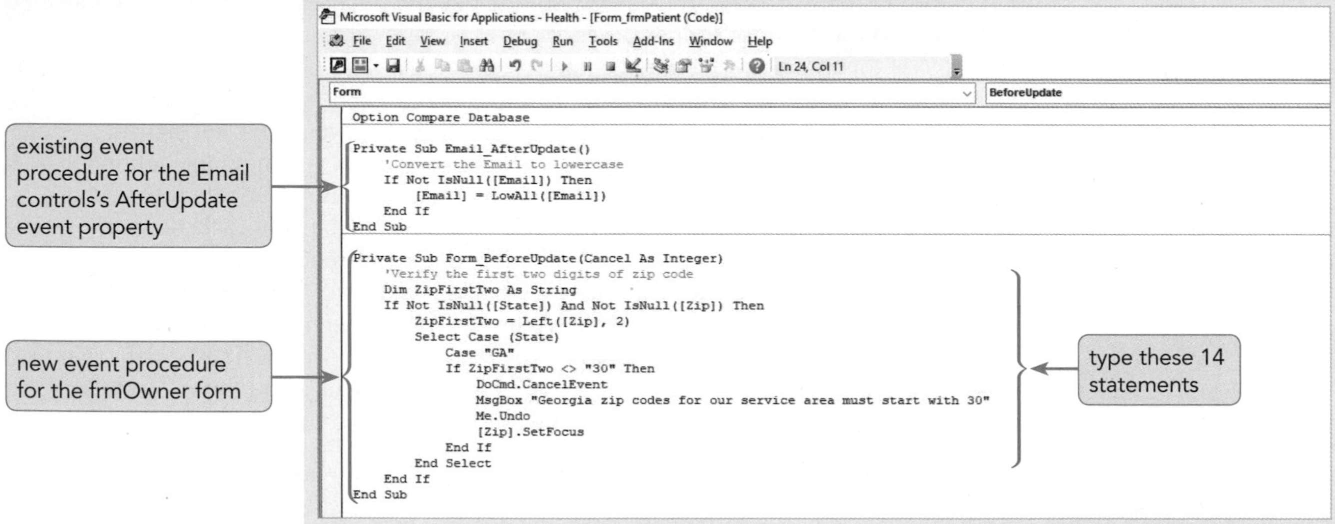
Microsoft Visual Basic for Applications - Health - [Form_frmPatient (Code)]
File Edit View Insert Debug Run Tools Add-Ins Window Help
Ln 24, Col 11
Form
BeforeUpdate
Option Compare Database
Private Sub Email_AfterUpdate()
'Convert the Email to lowercase
If Not IsNull([Email]) Then
[Email] = LowAll([Email])
End If
End Sub
Private Sub Form_BeforeUpdate(Cancel As Integer)
'Verify the first two digits of zip code
Dim ZipFirstTwo As String
If Not IsNull([State]) And Not IsNull([Zip]) Then
ZipFirstTwo = Left([Zip], 2)
Select Case (State)
Case "GA"
If ZipFirstTwo <> "30" Then
DoCmd.CancelEvent
MsgBox "Georgia zip codes for our service area must start with 30"
Me.Undo
[Zip].SetFocus
End If
End Select
End If
End Sub
existing event procedure for the Email controls's AfterUpdate event property
new event procedure for the frmOwner form
type these 14 statements

4. On the menu bar, click **Debug**, and then click **Compile Health** to compile all the modules in the Health database.

   Trouble? If a message box appears identifying an error, click the OK button in the message box, compare your Code window with the one shown in Figure 11–22, make any necessary corrections, and then repeat Step 4 to scan the statements for errors again and to compile the module.
5. Save your class module changes.
6. Close the Visual Basic window to return to the Form window, and then close the Property Sheet.

You can now test the BeforeUpdate event procedure. To do so, you'll switch to Form view and enter valid and invalid Zip field values in the frmPatient form.

To test the form's BeforeUpdate event procedure:

1. Switch to Form view with the form displaying record 1. The first two digits of the Zip field value, 30, represent a valid Georgia zip code for the service area.
2. Select **30303** in the Zip box, type **12345**, press **TAB** to move to the Email box, and then click the **Next record** button ▶ to move to the next record. The BeforeUpdate event procedure for the frmPatient form executes and determines that the Georgia zip code's first two digits are incorrect and displays the message box you included in the procedure. See Figure 11–23.

TIP

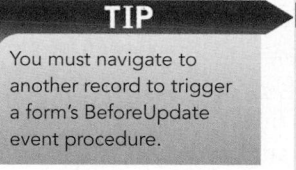

You must navigate to another record to trigger a form's BeforeUpdate event procedure.

Figure 11–23 After the frmPatient form's BeforeUpdate event procedure detects an error

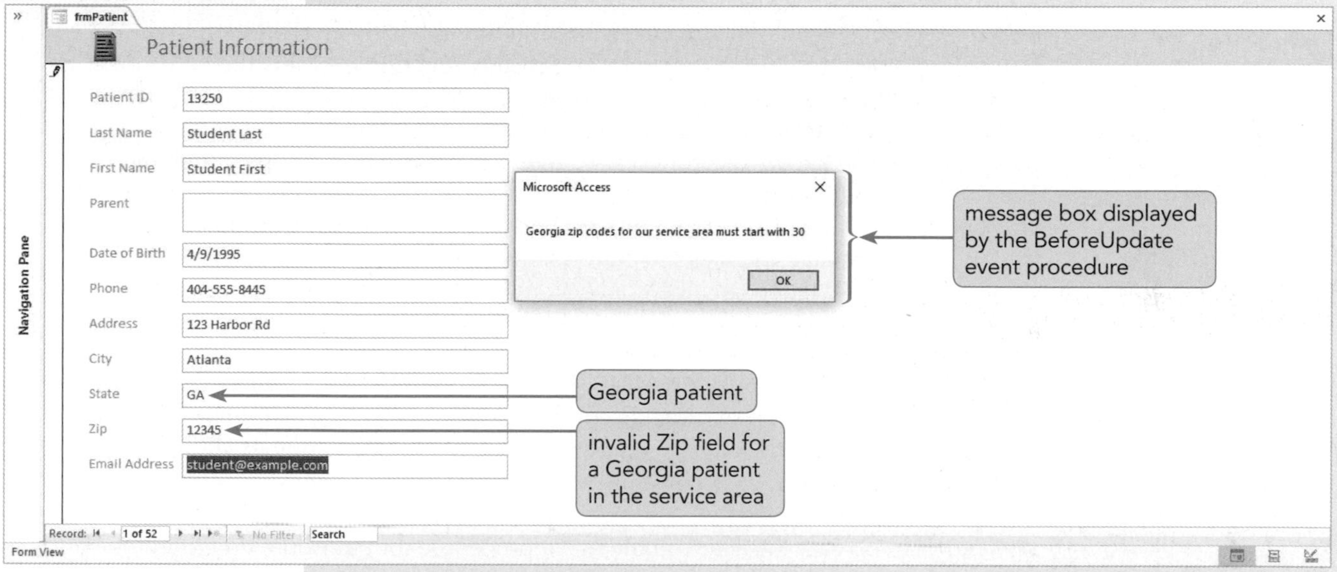

frmPatient
Patient Information
Patient ID
13250
Last Name
Student Last
First Name
Student First
Parent
Date of Birth
4/9/1995
Phone
404-555-8445
Address
123 Harbor Rd
City
Atlanta
State
GA
Zip
12345
Email Address
student@example.com
Microsoft Access
Georgia zip codes for our service area must start with 30
OK
message box displayed by the BeforeUpdate event procedure
Georgia patient
invalid Zip field for a Georgia patient in the service area
Navigation Pane
Record: 1 of 52
No Filter
Search
Form View

While the message box is displayed, the updated Zip field value of 12345 remains on screen for you to review.

3. Click **OK**. The message box closes, the Undo method changes the Zip field value to 30303 (its original value), and the SetFocus method moves the focus to the Zip box.
4. With the Zip field value set to **30303**, navigate to the next record. The form's BeforeUpdate event procedure verifies that the zip code is a valid value for a Georgia patient in the service area, and the focus moves to the Zip box for the next record.
5. Navigate back to record 1, change the State field value to **SC**, change the Zip field value to **12345**, and then click the **Next record** button ▶ to move to the next record. The form's BeforeUpdate event procedure checks zip codes only when the State field value is "GA" (Georgia), so even though the zip code 12345 is not valid for South Carolina (abbreviated SC), the focus moves to the Zip box in the next record anyway.

   Next, you'll change the first record's State field value to GA and the Zip field value to 30303, which are the original values for the record.

6. Navigate to the first record, change the State field value to **GA**, and then change the Zip field value to **30303**.

Donna is impressed with the zip code validation you've added to the frmPatient form. She has one additional procedure she wants you to create for the form.

Adding an Event Procedure to Change the Case of a Field Value

Donna wants to make it quicker for users to enter an address when using the frmPatient form, so she asks you to create a procedure that will automatically convert the case of letters entered in the Address field. This procedure will capitalize the first letter of each word in the field and change all other letters to lowercase. For example, if a user enters "12 mAin sT" as the Address field value, the event procedure will correct the field value to "12 Main St".

You'll use an event procedure attached to the AfterUpdate event for the Address field to perform this automatic conversion. You'll use the StrConv function in the event procedure to perform the conversion. The **StrConv function** converts the letters in a string to all uppercase letters or to all lowercase letters, or converts the first letter of every word in the string to uppercase letters and all other letters to lowercase letters, which is a pattern known as proper case. The StrConv function ignores numbers. The statement you'll use in the event procedure is *[Address] = StrConv([Address], vbProperCase)*. The StrConv function's second argument, the **vbProperCase constant**, is a VBA constant that specifies the conversion of the first letter in every word in a string to uppercase letters and the conversion of all other letters to lowercase letters. Recall that the LowAll function you created earlier in this tutorial used the statement *LowAll = LCase(FValue)* to convert every character in a string to lowercase. You could also have used the statement *LowAll = StrConv(FValue, vbLowerCase)* to accomplish the same result. Other VBA constants you can use with the StrConv function are the **vbUpperCase constant**, which specifies the conversion of the string to all uppercase letters, and the **vbLowerCase constant**, which specifies the conversion of the string to all lowercase letters.

Next, you'll create the AfterUpdate event procedure for the Address field in the frmPatient form to perform the automatic conversion of entered and updated Address field values.

To add the event procedure for the Address field's AfterUpdate event:

1. Switch to Design view.
2. Right-click the **Address** field value box to display the shortcut menu, and then click **Properties** to open the Property Sheet for the control.
3. If necessary, click the **Event** tab in the Property Sheet.
4. Click the **After Update** box, click the **After Update** arrow, click **[Event Procedure]**, and then click the **Build** button [...]. The Code window, which contains new Private Sub and End Sub statements, opens in the Visual Basic window. The Code window also contains two other event procedures defined in the form's class module: one event procedure for the form's BeforeUpdate event, and another event procedure for the Email field's AfterUpdate event.
5. Press **TAB**, and then type the Sub procedure statements exactly as shown in Figure 11–24.

Figure 11–24 **Event procedure for the Address control's AfterUpdate event**

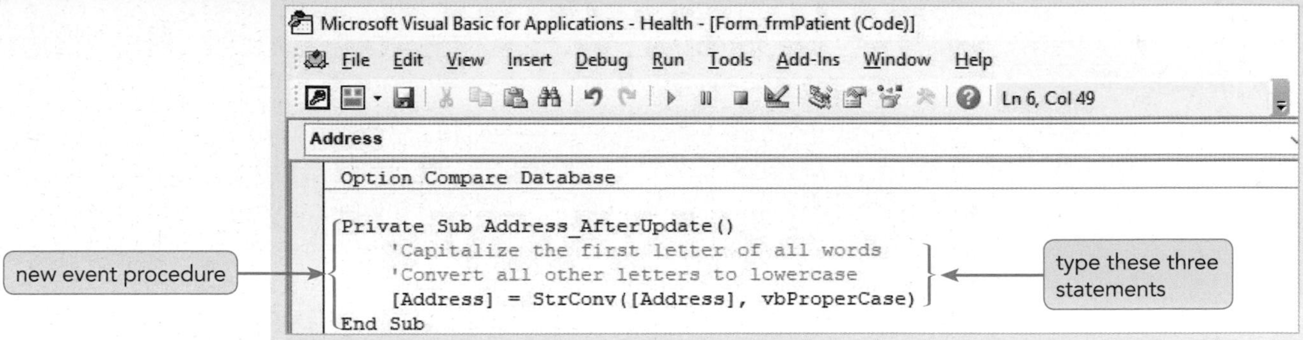
Microsoft Visual Basic for Applications - Health - [Form_frmPatient (Code)]
File Edit View Insert Debug Run Tools Add-Ins Window Help
Ln 6, Col 49
Address
Option Compare Database
Private Sub Address_AfterUpdate()
'Capitalize the first letter of all words
'Convert all other letters to lowercase
[Address] = StrConv([Address], vbProperCase)
End Sub
new event procedure
type these three statements

6. Click **Debug** on the menu bar, click **Compile Health**, save your class module changes, close the Visual Basic window, and then close the Property Sheet.

You can now test the event procedure. To do so, you'll view the frmPatient form in Form view and test the Address field's event procedure by entering different Address field values.

To test the new event procedure for the Address field:

1. Switch to Form view. You'll test the new event procedure by entering Address field values in record 1.
2. Select the current value in Address box, type **123 harbor rd** and then press **ENTER**. The AfterUpdate event procedure for the Address field executes and changes the Address field value to "123 Harbor Rd".
3. Repeat Step 2 two more times, entering **123 harBOR rD** (correctly changed to "12 Harbor Rd"), and then entering **123 HARBOR RD** (correctly changed to "123 Harbor Rd").
4. Close the form.

Hiding a Control and Changing a Control's Color

Donna wants you to add a message to the frmVisitsAndInvoices form that will remind her staff when a visit record should be considered for archiving from the tblVisit table. Specifically, when the visit date is prior to the year 2021, Donna wants the VisitDate field value displayed in red; all other VisitDate field values should be displayed in black. She also wants to display a message to the right of the VisitDate box in red only when the visit is a candidate for archiving. The red font will help to draw attention to these visit records. Figure 11–25 shows a preview of the formatting she's requesting.

Figure 11–25 Archive message and red VisitDate field value in frmVisitsAndInvoices form

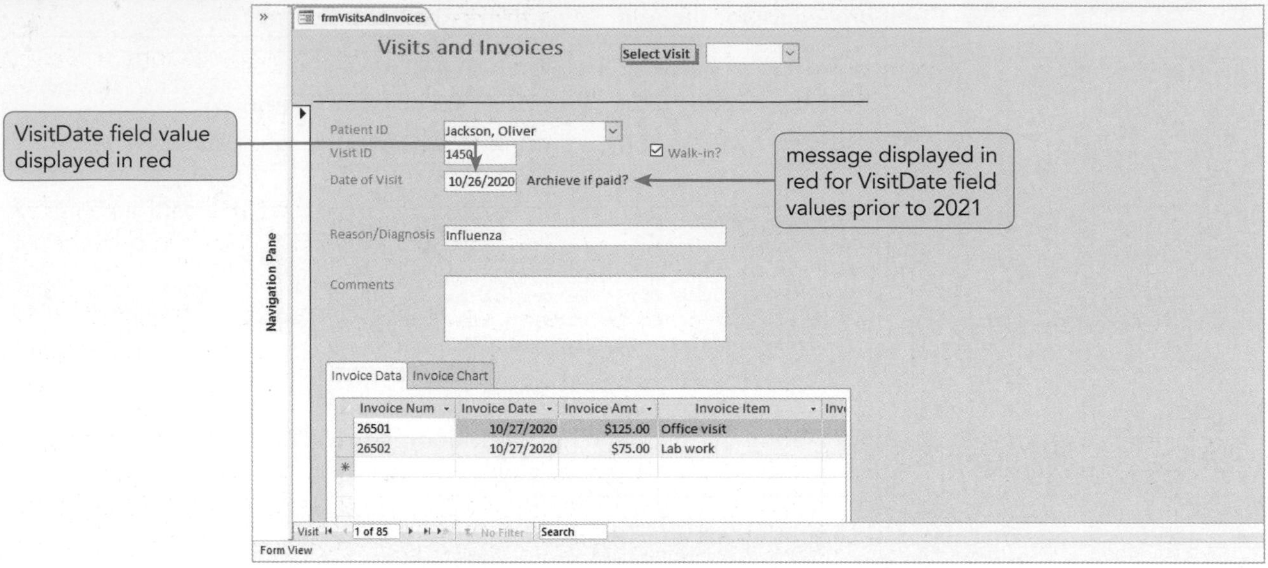
VisitDate field value displayed in red
message displayed in red for VisitDate field values prior to 2021
frmVisitsAndInvoices
Visits and Invoices
Select Visit
Patient ID
Jackson, Oliver
Visit ID
1450
Walk-in?
Date of Visit
10/26/2020
Archieve if paid?
Reason/Diagnosis
Influenza
Comments
Navigation Pane
Invoice Data
Invoice Chart
Invoice Num
Invoice Date
Invoice Amt
Invoice Item
26501
10/27/2020
$125.00
Office visit
26502
10/27/2020
$75.00
Lab work
Visit
1 of 85
No Filter
Search
Form View

In the frmVisitsAndInvoices form, you will add a label to the right of the VisitDate field value box that will display the text "Archive if paid?" in red. Because Donna wants the text to appear only when the VisitDate field has a value earlier than 1/1/2021, you will change the label's Visible property during execution. You will also change the foreground color of the value in the VisitDate field value box to red when the VisitDate field value is earlier than 1/1/2021 and to black for all other dates.

Because the change to the Visible property takes place during execution, you will add code to the Current event procedure in the frmVisitsAndInvoices form. To set a property in a VBA statement, you enter the object name followed by a period and the property name. For example, if the label name for the message is lblArchiveMsg, then the statement *lblArchiveMsg.Visible = False* hides the label on the form.

PROSKILLS

Problem Solving: Using Sample Code from Other Sources

Creating your first few VBA procedures from scratch can be a daunting task. To get started, you should take advantage of the available resources that discuss various ways of designing and programming commonly encountered situations. These resources include the sample databases available from Microsoft, Access VBA books, periodicals, websites that provide sample code, and Access Help. These resources contain sample procedures and code segments, often with commentary about what the procedures and statements accomplish and why. However, when you create a procedure, you are responsible for knowing what it does, how it does it, when to use it, how to enhance it in the future, and how to fix it when problems occur. If you simply copy statements from another source without thoroughly understanding them, you won't be able to enhance or fix the procedure in the future. In addition, you might overlook better ways to accomplish the same thing—better because the procedure would run faster or would be easier to enhance. In some cases, the samples you find might be flawed, so that they won't work properly for you. The time you spend researching and completely understanding sample code will pay dividends in your learning experience to create VBA procedures.

First, you'll add a label to the frmVisitsAndInvoices form that will display a message in red for each value that has a VisitDate field value earlier than 1/1/2021. For all other dates, the label will be hidden.

To add the label to the frmVisitsAndInvoices form:

1. Open the Navigation Pane, open the **frmVisitsAndInvoices** form in Design view, and then close the Navigation Pane.
2. On the Form Design Tools Design tab, in the Controls group, click the **Label** tool [Aa].
3. In the Detail section, position the plus symbol of the Label tool pointer two grid dots to the right of the VisitDate field value box, and then click the mouse button.
4. Type **Archive if paid?** and then press **ENTER**. The new label control appears in the form and displays the Error Checking Options button. See Figure 11–26.

Figure 11–26 Label control added to the form

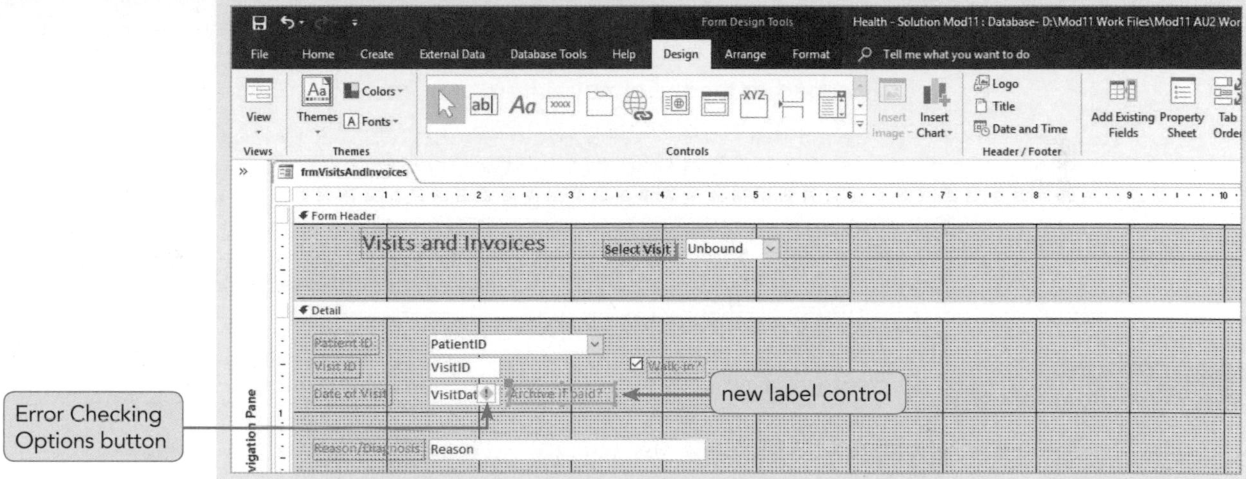
Error Checking Options button
new label control
Visits and Invoices
Select Visit
Unbound
Form Header
Detail
PatientID
VisitID
VisitDat
Reason

Trouble? If you do not see the Error Checking Options button, error checking is disabled in Access. Click the File tab, click Options in the navigation bar, click Object Designers, scroll down the page, click the Enable error checking check box to add a checkmark to it, click the OK button, click a blank area in the form, and then click the "Archive if paid?" label control. Continue with Step 5.

5. Position the pointer on the **Error Checking Options** button [!]. The message "This is a new label and is not associated with a control" appears. Because the new label should not be associated with a control, you'll choose to ignore this error.
6. Click the **Error Checking Options** arrow [!], and then click **Ignore Error**. The Error Checking Options button disappears.
7. Press and hold **SHIFT**, click the **VisitDate** field value box to select this control and its label control, release **SHIFT**, right-click one of the selected controls, point to **Align**, and then click **Top** to top-align the selected controls.

   Trouble? If the Error Checking Options button appears, click the Error Checking Options button arrow, and then click Dismiss Error.

You'll now set the label control's Name and ForeColor properties, and you'll add the Current event procedure to the frmVisitsAndInvoices form.

To set the label's properties and add the Current event procedure to the form:

1. Deselect all controls, right-click the **Archive if paid?** label control to display the shortcut menu, and then click **Properties** to open the Property Sheet.
2. Click the **All** tab (if necessary), and then set the Name property for the Archive if paid? label control to **lblArchiveMsg**.

   You can now set the ForeColor property for the label so that the message is displayed in red.
3. Click the **Fore Color** box, and then click its **Build** button [...] to display the color gallery.
4. Click the **Red** color (row 7, column 2 in the Standard Colors palette), and then press **ENTER**. The ForeColor property value is set to the code for red (#ED1C24), and in the form it now appears in red.

   Next you will enter the event procedure for the form's Current event. This event procedure will execute whenever the frmVisitsAndInvoices form is opened or the focus moves from one record to another.
5. Select the form, scroll down the Property Sheet to the On Current box, click the **On Current** box, click the **On Current** arrow, click [**Event Procedure**], and then click the **Build** button [...] to open the Code window in the Visual Basic window, displaying the Sub and End Sub statements.
6. Press **TAB**, and then type the Sub procedure statements exactly as shown in Figure 11–27.

Figure 11–27 **Current event procedure for the frmVisitsAndInvoices form**

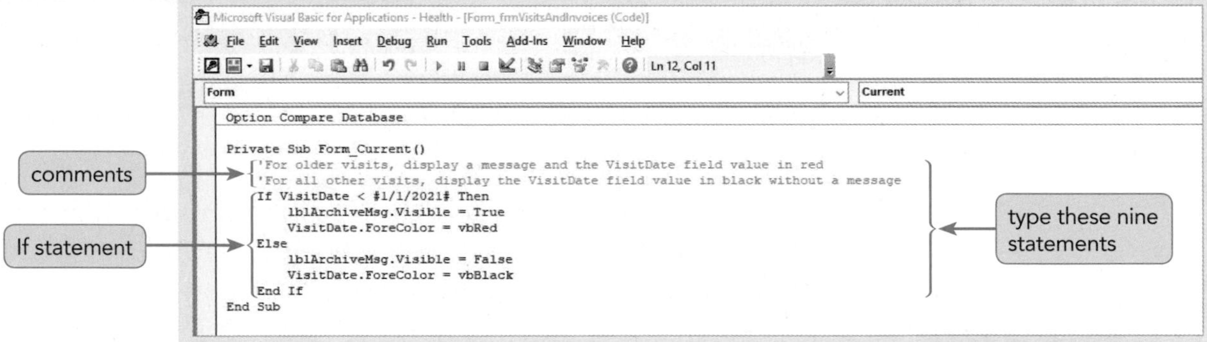
Microsoft Visual Basic for Applications - Health - [Form_frmVisitsAndInvoices (Code)]
File Edit View Insert Debug Run Tools Add-Ins Window Help
Ln 12, Col 11
Form
Current
Option Compare Database
Private Sub Form_Current()
'For older visits, display a message and the VisitDate field value in red
'For all other visits, display the VisitDate field value in black without a message
If VisitDate < #1/1/2021# Then
lblArchiveMsg.Visible = True
VisitDate.ForeColor = vbRed
Else
lblArchiveMsg.Visible = False
VisitDate.ForeColor = vbBlack
End If
End Sub
comments
If statement
type these nine statements

The form's Current procedure uses an If statement to determine whether the current value of the VisitDate field is less than 1/1/2021. If the current value of the VisitDate field is less than 1/1/2021, the procedure sets the lblArchiveMsg control's Visible property to True (which means the "Archive if paid?" message will appear in the frmVisitsAndInvoices form), and it sets the VisitDate control's ForeColor property to vbRed (red). If the current value of the VisitDate field is greater than or equal to 1/1/2021, the procedure sets the lblArchiveMsg control's Visible property to False, hiding the message in the form, and sets the VisitDate control's ForeColor property to vbBlack.

7. Click **Debug** on the menu bar, and then click **Compile Health** to compile all the modules in the Health database.
8. Save your class module changes, close the Visual Basic window, and then close the Property Sheet.

You'll now test the frmVisitsAndInvoices form's Current event procedure.

To test the Current event procedure for the frmVisitsAndInvoices form:

1. Switch to Form view. The first record for VisitID 1450 is displayed in the form with the Date of Visit date prior to 1/1/2021. The "Archive if paid?" message appears in red, as does the VisitDate field value of 10/26/2020.

   Trouble? If a dialog box is displayed indicating a runtime error, the event procedure could not execute. Click the Debug button in the dialog box to open the event procedure in the Code window with the line containing the error highlighted. Check the statements carefully against those shown in Figure 11–27. Make the necessary changes so they match the figure exactly, compile the module, save the module, and then close the Code window. Then repeat Step 1.

2. Navigate to the last record to display record 85 for Visit ID 1623, for which the visit date is 4/5/2021. The "Archive if paid?" message is not displayed, and the VisitDate field value is displayed in black.

3. sam Close the form, make a backup copy of the database, compact and repair the database, and then close it.

Donna is pleased with the modifications you have made to the forms using Visual Basic code. The forms will be easier for her staff to use and help to minimize errors.

REVIEW

Session 11.2 Quick Check

1. The VBA ___ statement executes one of two groups of statements based on a condition.
2. What happens when you compile a module?
3. What is the purpose of the Dim statement?
4. The ___ function returns a value of true if the field value is empty and false if the field value is not empty.
5. What is the purpose of the DoCmd statement?
6. What is a method?
7. What is a VBA constant?
8. You can use the UCase function or the ___ function to convert a string to all uppercase letters.
9. What does the Visible property determine?
10. What does the ForeColor property determine?

PRACTICE

Review Assignments

Data File needed for the Review Assignments: Product.accdb *(cont. from Module 10)*

Donna asks you to continue your work on the Product database by enhancing the usability of the frmSuppliersWithProducts form and the frmSupplier form. To help with this request, complete the following steps:

1. Open the **Product** database you worked with in the previous two modules.
2. In the frmSuppliersWithProducts form, create an event procedure on the AfterUpdate event for the Address field to convert Address field values to proper case—capitalize the first letter of each word, and convert all other letters to lowercase. When adding event procedures or user-defined functions, remember to always document your code as you did in the main module. Test the procedure, and then close the form.
3. Create an event procedure on the Current event for the frmSuppliersWithProducts form to do the following:
   a. Display the InitialContact field value in red when the date is December 1, 2020, or later, and in black for earlier dates.
   b. Display the message **Newer Supplier** below the InitialContact box in red text. Display the message only when the InitialContact field value is December 1, 2020, or later. Use **lblSupplierMsg** as the name of the new label control to contain the message.
   c. Test the procedure, and then save and close the form.
4. Create a user-defined function called **CapAll** that will accept one argument called **FValue**, convert it to uppercase, and return the uppercase value back to the instruction that called it. (*Hint*: Use the UCase function to convert characters to uppercase.) Store this user-defined function in a standard module called **basProductProcedures**.
5. In the frmSupplier form, create an event procedure on the AfterUpdate event for the State field that will convert the characters to uppercase only if the field value box is not empty. Call the CapAll function to perform the character conversion. Test the procedure, and then close the form.
6. Make a backup copy of the database, compact and repair the Product database, and then close the database.

APPLY

Case Problem 1

Data File needed for this Case Problem: Instruction.accdb *(cont. from Module 10)*

Great Giraffe Jeremiah asks you to continue your work on the Instruction database by enhancing the usability of some of the forms. To help with this request, complete the following steps:

1. Open the **Instruction** database you worked with in the previous two modules.
2. Create a user-defined function called **CapAll** that will accept one argument called **FValue**, convert it to uppercase, and return the uppercase value back to the instruction that called it. (*Hint*: Use the UCase function to convert characters to uppercase.) When adding event procedures or user-defined functions, remember to always document your code as you did in the main module. Store this user-defined function in a standard module called **basInstructionProcedures**.
3. In the frmStudentsByCourse form, create an event procedure on the AfterUpdate event for the InstanceID field that will convert the characters to uppercase only if the field value box is not empty. Call the CapAll function to perform the character conversion. Test the procedure, and then close the form.
4. In the frmStudentsByCourse form, create an event procedure on the AfterUpdate event for the Title field to convert Title field values to proper case—capitalize the first letter of each word, and convert all other letters to lowercase. Test the procedure, and then close the form.

5. Create an event procedure on the Current event for the frmCourseData form to do the following:
   a. Display the HoursPerWeek field value in red when the value equals 40, and in black otherwise.
   b. Display the message **Full Week** to the right of the HoursPerWeek box in red text. Display the message only when the HoursPerWeek field value equals 40. Use **lblFullWeekMsg** as the name of the new label control to contain the message.
   c. Test the procedure, and then save and close the form.
6. Make a backup copy of the database, compact and repair the database, and then close it.

CHALLENGE

Case Problem 2

Data File needed for this Case Problem: CleanOut.accdb ***(cont. from Module 10)***

Drain Adopter Tandrea asks you to continue your work on the CleanOut database by enhancing the usability of some of the forms. To help with this request, complete the following steps:

1. Open the **CleanOut** database you worked with in the previous two modules.
2. In the frmVolunteerMasterData form, create an event procedure for the AfterUpdate event on the Street field to convert Street field values to proper case—capitalize the first letter of each word, and convert all other letters to lowercase. Test the procedure, and then close the form. When adding event procedures or user-defined functions, remember to always document your code as you did in the main module.

Explore 3. In the frmVolunteerMasterData form, create an event procedure for the form's BeforeUpdate event to verify the Zip field values by doing the following:
   a. For a State field value of WA in the city of Bellingham, WA, the first four digits of the Zip field value must equal 9822. If the Zip field value is invalid, display an appropriate message, cancel the event, undo the change, and move the focus to the Zip field.
   b. No special action is required for other Zip field values.
   c. Test the procedure, and then save your form changes.

Explore 4. In the frmVolunteerData form, create an event procedure for the form's Current event to do the following:
   a. Display the SignupDate field value in a bold, blue text when the value is in the first three months of the year 2021, and in normal, black text for all other values. (*Hint*: Use the FontBold property set with the value True for bold or False for not bold, and use the color vbBlue for blue.)
   b. Display the message **First Adopters** to the right of the SignupDate box in a label control called **lblFirstAdoptersMsg**, in bold, blue text only when the SignupDate field value is in the first three months of the year 2021. (*Hint*: Use the Font Weight property to make the label bold, and use the Blue from the standard colors.)
   c. Test the procedure, and then save your form changes.

5. Make a backup copy of the database, compact and repair the database, and then close it.

MODULE 12

Managing and Securing a Database

Administering the Health Database

ACCESS

OBJECTIVES

Session 12.1
- Filter By Form and apply an advanced filter/sort
- Save a filter as a query and apply the saved query as a filter
- Create a subquery
- Create a multivalued field

Session 12.2
- Create an Attachment field
- Use an AutoNumber field
- Save a database as a previous version
- Analyze a database's performance
- Link a database to a table in another database
- Update linked tables
- Split a database
- Encrypt a database with a password
- Set database properties and startup options

Case | *Lakewood Community Health Services*

Donna Taylor will be offering training sessions for staff members to learn how to use the Health database. Before she begins these training sessions, she asks for your help in finalizing the database. Your remaining work will apply advanced Access features for filtering, creating subqueries, and using advanced field types in tables, such as multivalued fields and Attachment fields. In addition, you will learn about database management, database security, and maximizing the database's overall performance. You'll also set database startup options as a final step in the development of the Health database.

STARTING DATA FILES

Access3 → Module

Health.accdb (cont.)
Support_AC_12_KimberlyHansen-BachelorDegree.docx
Support_AC_12_KimberlyHansen-Expenses.xlsx
Support_AC_12_KimberlyHansen-MasterDegree.docx
Support_AC_12_Referral.accdb

Review

Product.accdb (cont.)
Support_AC_12_Ads.accdb
Support_AC_12_Autoclave.xlsx
Support_AC_12_Autoclave_Specification_Sheet.pdf

Case1

Instruction.accdb (cont.)
Support_AC_12_Allen.txt
Support_AC_12_RoomOptions.accdb

Case2

CleanOut.accdb (cont.)
Support_AC_12_BEN36NE_111820.txt
Support_AC_12_Trucks.accdb

Session 12.1 Visual Overview:

The Degree field is defined as a multivalued field. A **multivalued field** is a lookup field that allows you to store more than one value in a field in each record.

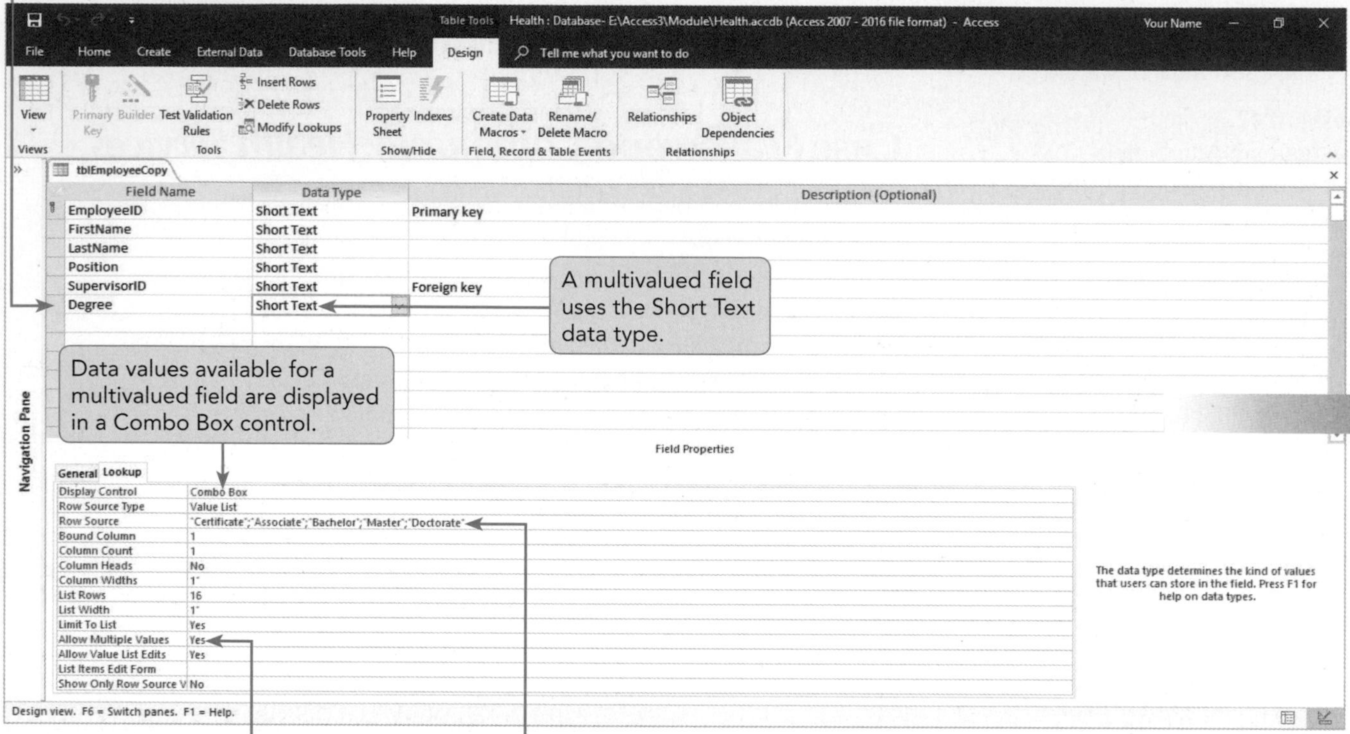
Table Tools Health : Database- E:\Access3\Module\Health.accdb (Access 2007 - 2016 file format) - Access
Your Name
File Home Create External Data Database Tools Help Design Tell me what you want to do
View Primary Key Builder Test Validation Rules Insert Rows Delete Rows Modify Lookups Property Sheet Indexes Create Data Macros Rename/ Delete Macro Relationships Object Dependencies
Views Tools Show/Hide Field, Record & Table Events Relationships
tblEmployeeCopy
Field Name Data Type Description (Optional)
EmployeeID Short Text Primary key
FirstName Short Text
LastName Short Text
Position Short Text
SupervisorID Short Text Foreign key
Degree Short Text
Navigation Pane
Field Properties
General Lookup
Display Control Combo Box
Row Source Type Value List
Row Source "Certificate";"Associate";"Bachelor";"Master";"Doctorate"
Bound Column 1
Column Count 1
Column Heads No
Column Widths 1"
List Rows 16
List Width 1"
Limit To List Yes
Allow Multiple Values Yes
Allow Value List Edits Yes
List Items Edit Form
Show Only Row Source V No
The data type determines the kind of values that users can store in the field. Press F1 for help on data types.
Design view. F6 = Switch panes. F1 = Help.

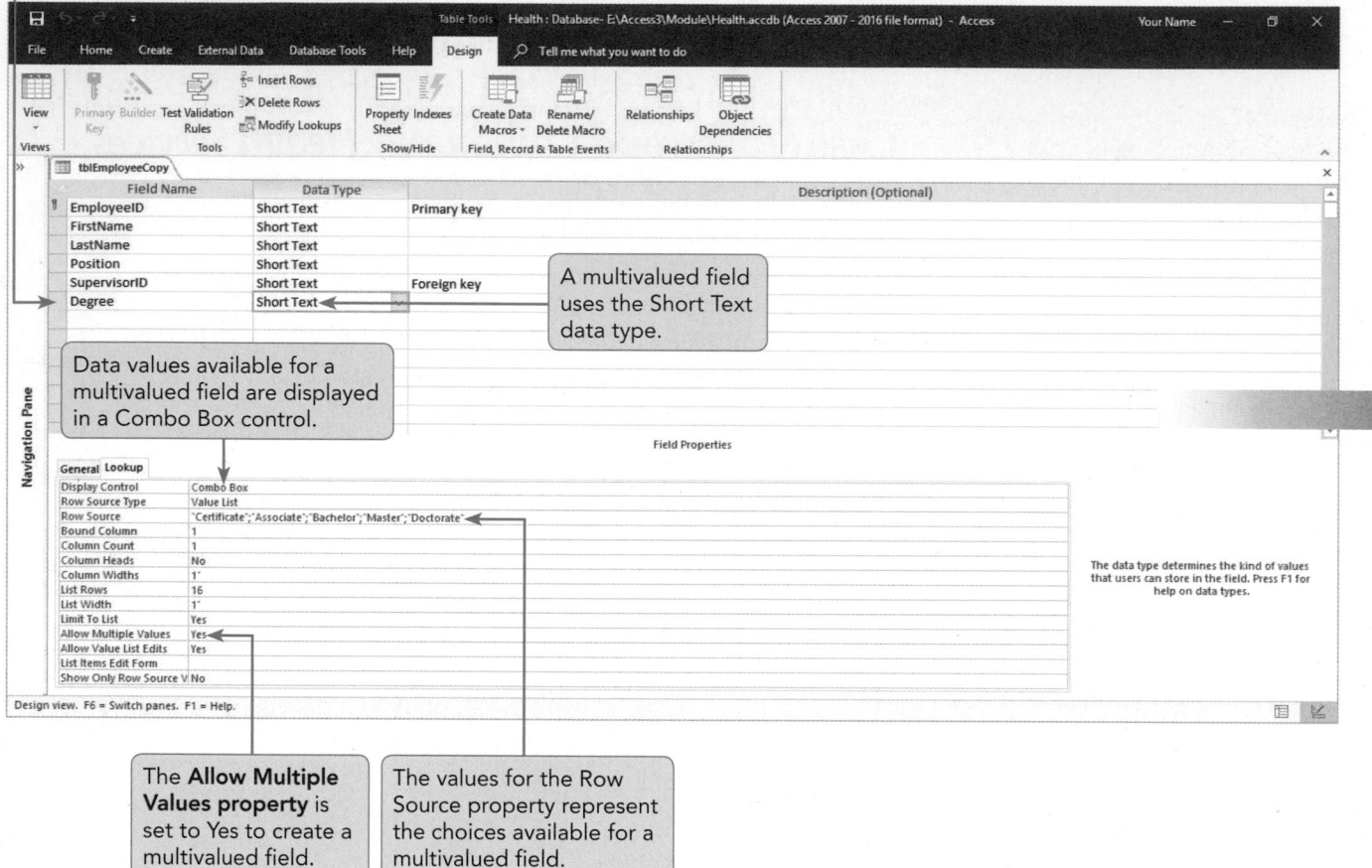

A multivalued field uses the Short Text data type.

Data values available for a multivalued field are displayed in a Combo Box control.

The **Allow Multiple Values property** is set to Yes to create a multivalued field.

The values for the Row Source property represent the choices available for a multivalued field.

Multivalued Fields and Subqueries

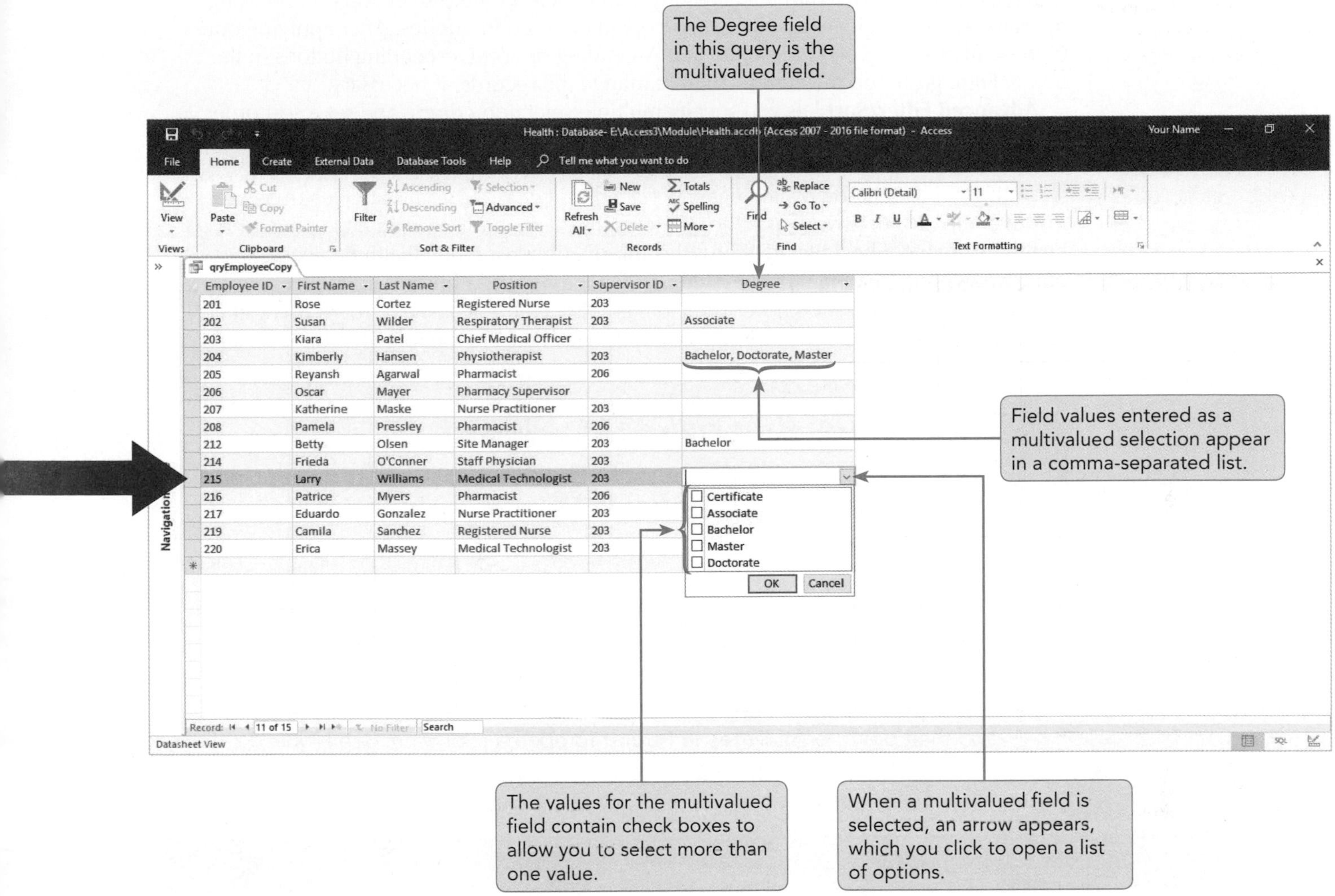
The Degree field in this query is the multivalued field.
Field values entered as a multivalued selection appear in a comma-separated list.
The values for the multivalued field contain check boxes to allow you to select more than one value.
When a multivalued field is selected, an arrow appears, which you click to open a list of options.
Health : Database- E:\Access3\Module\Health.accdb (Access 2007 - 2016 file format) - Access
qryEmployeeCopy
Employee ID
First Name
Last Name
Position
Supervisor ID
Degree
Associate
Bachelor, Doctorate, Master
Bachelor
Certificate
Associate
Bachelor
Master
Doctorate
OK
Cancel
Record: 11 of 15
Datasheet View

Additional Filtering Options

As you know, you can use a filter to temporarily display specified records from a table or form. In previous modules, you used AutoFilter and Filter By Selection. Two additional filtering features in Access are Filter By Form and Advanced Filter/Sort.

Recall that Filter By Form filters records that match multiple selection criteria using the same Access logical and comparison operators used in queries. After applying one of these filter tools, you can use the Sort Ascending or Sort Descending buttons in the Sort & Filter group on the Home tab to rearrange the records, if necessary.

Advanced Filter/Sort lets you specify multiple selection criteria and set a sort order for selected records in the Filter window, in the same way you specify record selection criteria and sort orders for a query in Design view.

Donna needs to know which patients visited Lakewood Community Health Services in November 2020, as well as which patients in Atlanta and Marietta have private health insurance. She'd like to access this information from the Health database quickly, without creating a query. Although Donna has used filters with a query datasheet and a form, she's never used a filter with a table datasheet. You'll use a filter to display all clinic visits with November 2020 visit dates in the tblVisit table datasheet.

To filter records in the tblVisit table datasheet:

1. **sam** Start Access, and then open the Health.accdb database you worked with in the previous three modules.

   Trouble? If the security warning is displayed below the ribbon, click the Enable Content button.

2. Open the Navigation Pane (if necessary), open the **tblVisit** table in Datasheet view, and then close the Navigation Pane.
3. Click the **arrow** on the Date of Visit column heading to open the AutoFilter menu, point to **Date Filters** to open a submenu of context-sensitive options, and then point to **All Dates In Period** to open a submenu. See Figure 12–1.

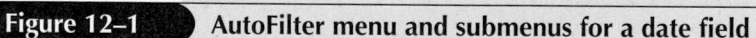

Figure 12–1 AutoFilter menu and submenus for a date field

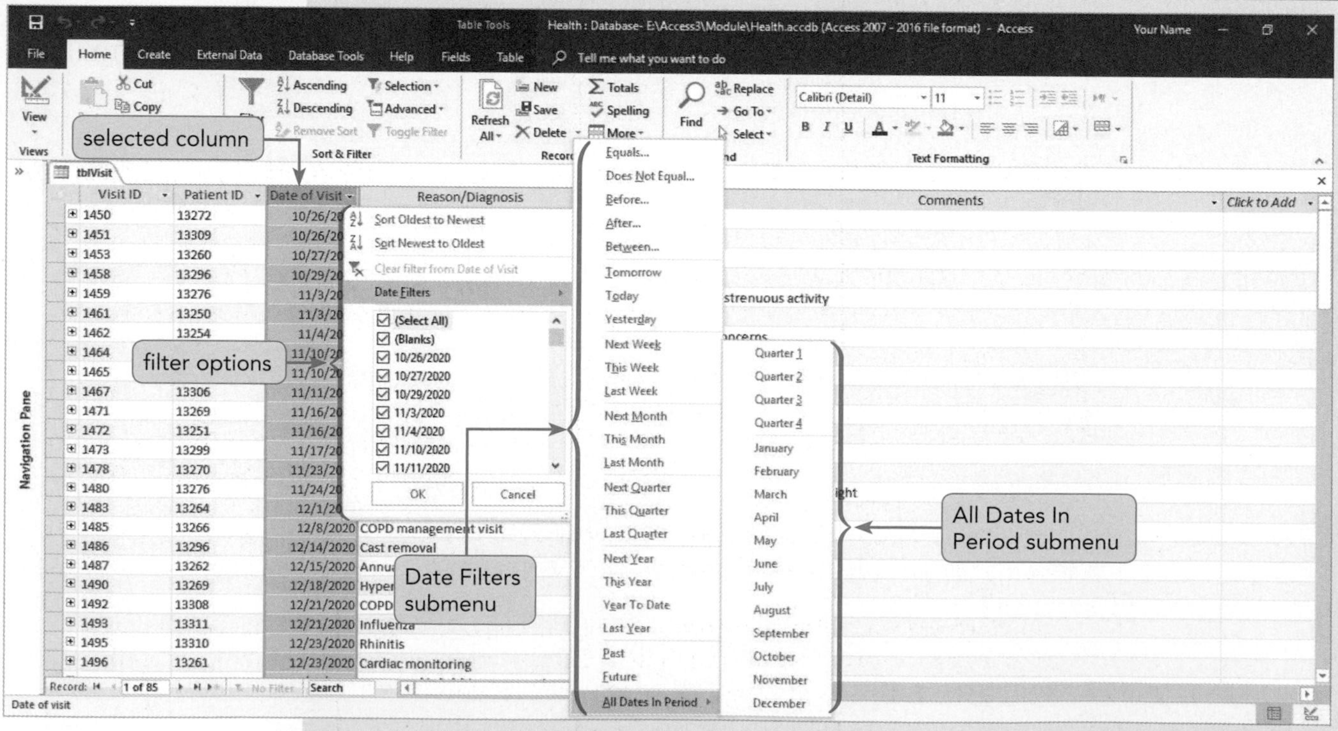

selected column
filter options
Date Filters submenu
All Dates In Period submenu

The Date of Visit menu displays all the values that appear in the Date of Visit column; you use the Date of Visit menu when you want to select specific values for the filter. The Date Filters submenu displays filter options that apply to a Date field, and the All Dates In Period submenu displays additional filter options for a Date field.

4. In the All Dates In Period submenu, click **November**. Only the 11 records with November visit dates are displayed in the datasheet. If you save a table with an applied filter, the filter is saved, and you can reapply the filter anytime you open the table datasheet.
5. Save and close the tblVisit table.
6. Open the Navigation Pane, open the **tblVisit** table datasheet to display all 85 records, and then on the Home tab, in the Sort & Filter group, click the **Toggle Filter** button. The VisitDate filter is applied, displaying the 11 records with November visit dates.
7. Close the tblVisit table.

Next, you'll use Filter By Form to produce the other results Donna wants—the list of patients from Atlanta or Marietta who have private health insurance.

Filter By Form

You use the Filter By Form filter option when you need to filter data in a table or form on multiple criteria. When you select the Filter By Form option from the Advanced button menu in the Sort & Filter group, a blank datasheet opens that includes all the fields in the table, and this blank datasheet has two tabs—the Look for tab and the Or tab. In the blank datasheet on the Look for tab, you specify multiple selection criteria by entering conditions in the appropriate field value boxes. If you enter criteria in more than one field, you create the equivalent of an And condition—any record that matches all criteria will be selected. To create an Or condition, you enter the criteria for the first part of the condition in the field on the Look for tab's datasheet and then click the Or tab at the bottom of the datasheet window to display a new blank datasheet. You enter the criteria for the second part of the condition on the Or tab's blank datasheet. Any record that matches all criteria on the Look for datasheet or all criteria on the Or datasheet will be selected.

REFERENCE

Selecting Records Using Filter By Form

- Open the table or query datasheet or the form in Form view.
- On the Home tab, in the Sort & Filter group, click the Advanced button, and then click Filter By Form.
- Enter a simple selection criterion or an And condition in the Look for tab or form, using the boxes for the appropriate fields.
- If you need to specify an Or condition, click the Or tab, and then enter the Or condition in the second datasheet or form. Continue to enter Or conditions on separate datasheets or forms by using the Or tab.
- On the Home tab, in the Sort & Filter group, click the Toggle Filter button.

Donna wants to display records for only those patients in Atlanta and Marietta with private health insurance. To accomplish this, the multiple selection criteria you will enter are: Atlanta *and* Private *or* Marietta *and* Private.

To select the records using Filter By Form:

1. Open the **tblPatient** table to display the 52 records in the recordset, and then close the Navigation Pane.
2. On the Home tab, in the Sort & Filter group, click the **Advanced** button, click **Filter By Form** to display a blank datasheet that has two tabs: the Look for tab and the Or tab. The Look for tab is the active tab. See Figure 12–2.

Figure 12–2 Blank form for Filter By Form option

tblPatient: Filter by Form
Patient ID
Last Name
First Name
Parent
Date of Birth
Phone
Address
City
State
Zip
Email
Insurance Type
Filter by Form tab
Navigation Pane
Look for tab
Or tab
Look for
Or
Form View

For a criterion, you can select a value from the list of values in a field value box, or you can use a comparison operator (such as <, >=, <>, and Like) and a value, similar to conditions you enter in the query design grid.

3. Click the **City** box, click the **City** arrow, and then click **Atlanta**. The criterion "Atlanta" appears in the City box.
4. Click the **Insurance Type** box, click the **Insurance Type** arrow, and then click **Private**. Access adds the criterion "Private" to the Insurance Type box.

   Before you add other options to the filter, you'll verify that the filter is working.

5. In the Sort & Filter group, click the **Toggle Filter** button. The records that contain Atlanta for the city and Private for the Insurance Type are displayed.

   The results contain three records. Now you'll return to the Filter by Form window to continue creating the filter.

6. On the Home tab, in the Sort & Filter group, click the **Advanced** button, and then click **Filter By Form** to return to the filter.

   You've specified the logical operator (And) for the condition "Atlanta" And "Private". To add the rest of the criteria, you need to display the Or blank datasheet.

TIP

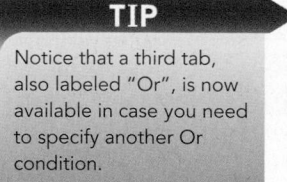

Notice that a third tab, also labeled "Or", is now available in case you need to specify another Or condition.

7. Click the **Or** tab to display a second blank datasheet. The insertion point is in the City box.
8. Click the **City** arrow to display the list, and then click **Marietta**.
9. Click the **Insurance Type** box, click the **Insurance Type** arrow, and then click **Private**. The filter is now set for the second And condition of "Marietta" And "Private". See Figure 12–3.

Figure 12–3 Completed filter using Filter By Form option

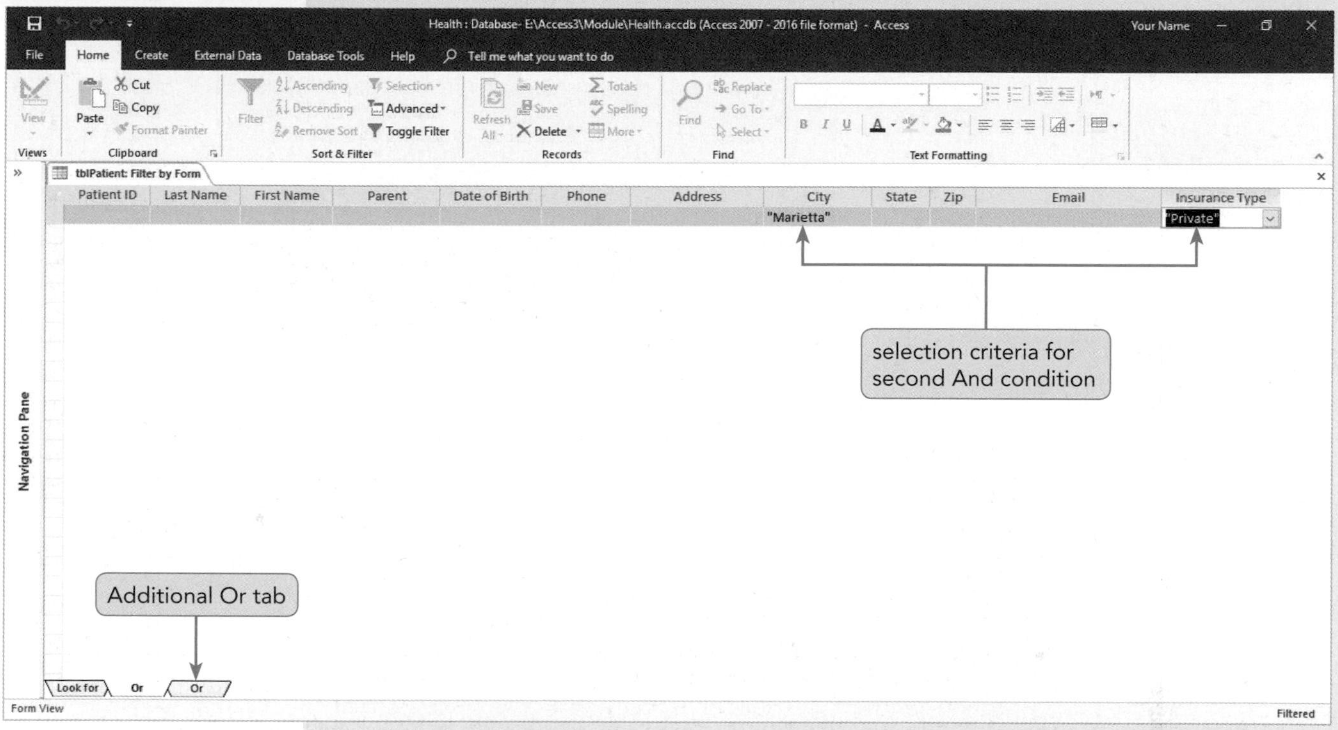
selection criteria for second And condition
Additional Or tab

Combined with the Look for conditions, you now have the Or conditions and the complete Filter By Form conditions. Much like building queries, all data that is on the same line in the criteria must be satisfied in order for the record to satisfy the criteria.

10. In the Sort & Filter group, click the **Toggle Filter** button, and then scroll to the right until both the City and Insurance Type columns are visible (if necessary). The filter displays the five records that match the selection criteria and displays "Filtered" in the navigation bar. See Figure 12–4.

Figure 12–4 Records that match the Filter By Form criteria

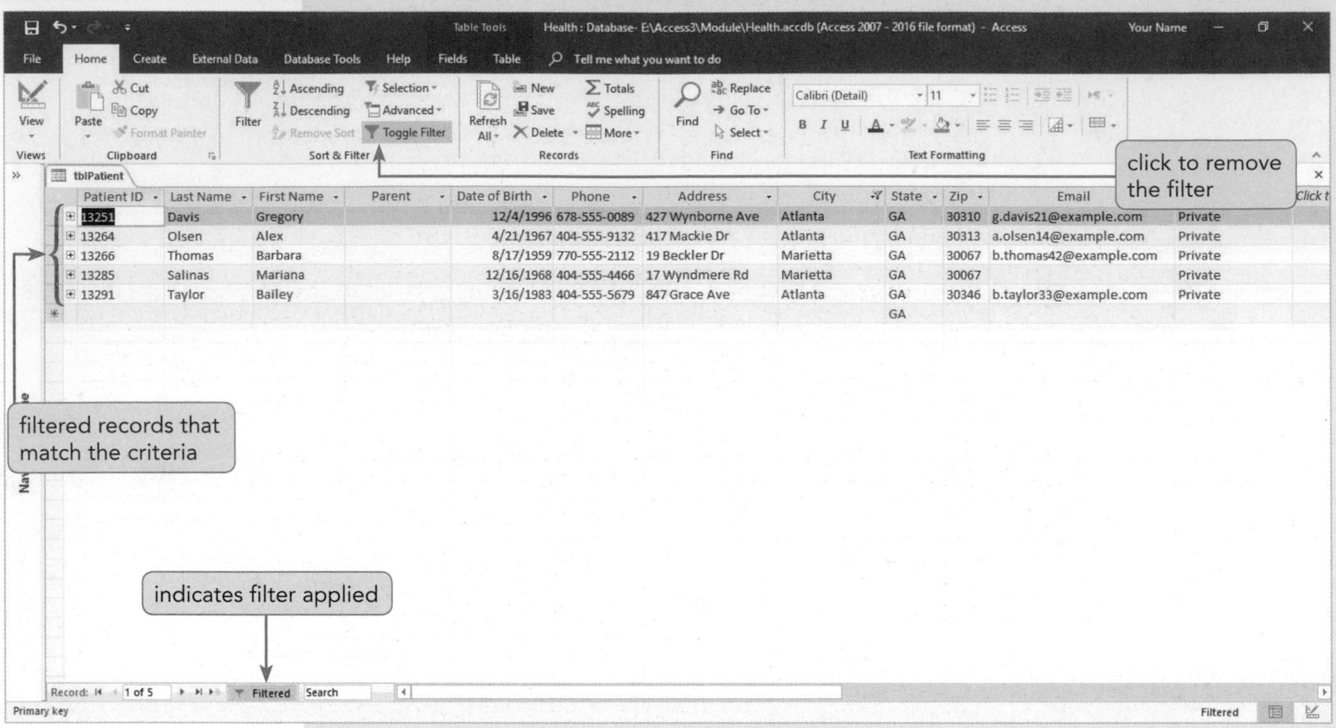
click to remove the filter
filtered records that match the criteria
indicates filter applied

Now that you have defined the filter, you can save it as a query so that Donna can easily view the information in the future.

Saving a Filter as a Query

When you save a filter as a query, you can reuse the filter by opening the saved query.

REFERENCE

Saving a Filter as a Query

- Create a filter using Filter By Selection, Filter By Form, or Advanced Filter/Sort.
- If you applied the filter using Filter By Form, click the Advanced button, and then click Filter By Form.
- On the Home tab, in the Sort & Filter group, click the Advanced button, and then click Save As Query.
- Type the name for the query, and then press ENTER.

Next, you'll save the filter as a query named qryAtlantaMariettaPrivateFilter.

To save the filter as a query:

1. On the Home tab, in the Sort & Filter group, click the **Advanced** button, and then click **Filter By Form**. The datasheet displays the selection criteria.
2. In the Sort & Filter group, click the **Advanced** button, and then click **Save As Query**. The Save As Query dialog box opens.

3. Type **qryAtlantaMariettaPrivateFilter** in the Query Name box, and then click **OK**. The filter is saved as a query in the Health database.

   Now you can clear the selection criteria, close the Filter by Form tab, and return to Datasheet view.

4. In the Sort & Filter group, click the **Advanced** button, and then click **Clear Grid** to remove the selection criteria from the filter datasheet.

5. Close the tblPatient: Filter by Form tab to return to Datasheet view for the tblPatient table. The five filtered records are still displayed in the datasheet, and the filter is still applied.

6. In the Sort & Filter group, click the **Toggle Filter** button, click the **Advanced** button, and then click **Clear All Filters**. Because no filters are applied, the table displays 52 records. Next, you'll leave the tblPatient table open while you open the qryAtlantaMariettaPrivateFilter query in Design view.

7. Open the Navigation Pane, open the **qryAtlantaMariettaPrivateFilter** query, switch to Design view, and then close the Navigation Pane. In the design grid, the first And condition ("Atlanta" And "Private") appears in the Criteria row, and the second And condition ("Marietta" And "Marietta") appears in the or row. You can interpret these criteria as "the records that contain Atlanta and Private, or that contain Marietta and Private." See Figure 12–5.

Figure 12–5 **Filter saved as a query in Design view**

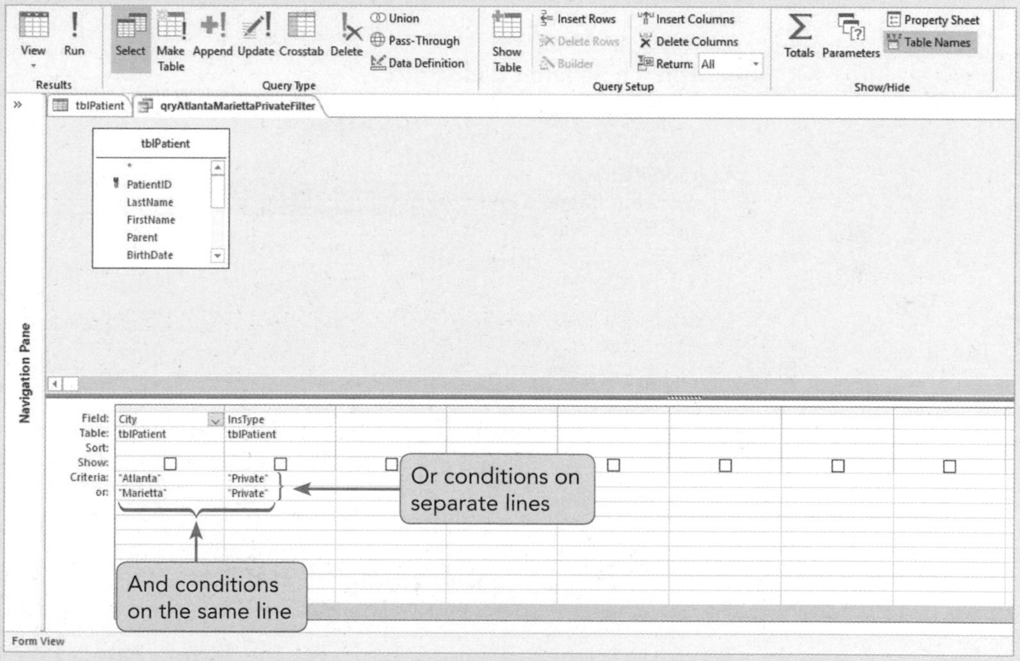
Or conditions on separate lines
And conditions on the same line

8. Run the query to display the five records that satisfy the selection criteria, close the query, close the tblPatient table, and then click **No** in the dialog box that prompts you to save the table design changes. You don't want to save the filter with the table because you've already saved the filter as a separate query.

The next time Donna wants to view the records selected by the filter, she can run the qryAtlantaMariettaPrivateFilter query. She could also open the tblPatient table and apply the qryAtlantaMariettaPrivateFilter query as a filter.

REFERENCE

Applying a Query as a Filter

- Open the table to which you want to apply the filter in Datasheet view.
- On the Home tab, in the Sort & Filter group, click the Advanced button, and then click Filter By Form.
- In the Sort & Filter group, click the Advanced button, and then click Load from Query.
- In the Applicable Filter dialog box, click the query you want to apply as a filter, and then click the OK button.
- On the Home tab, in the Sort & Filter group, click the Toggle Filter button to apply the filter.

To apply the qryAtlantaMariettaPrivateFilter query as a filter, you first need to open the tblPatient table.

To apply the query as a filter:

1. Open the Navigation Pane, open the **tblPatient** table, and then close the Navigation Pane.
2. In the Sort & Filter group, click the **Advanced** button, and then click **Filter By Form**. The blank Look for tab in the Filter By Form datasheet is displayed.
3. In the Sort & Filter group, click the **Advanced** button, and then click **Load from Query**. The Applicable Filter dialog box opens. See Figure 12–6.

Figure 12–6 **Applicable Filter dialog box**

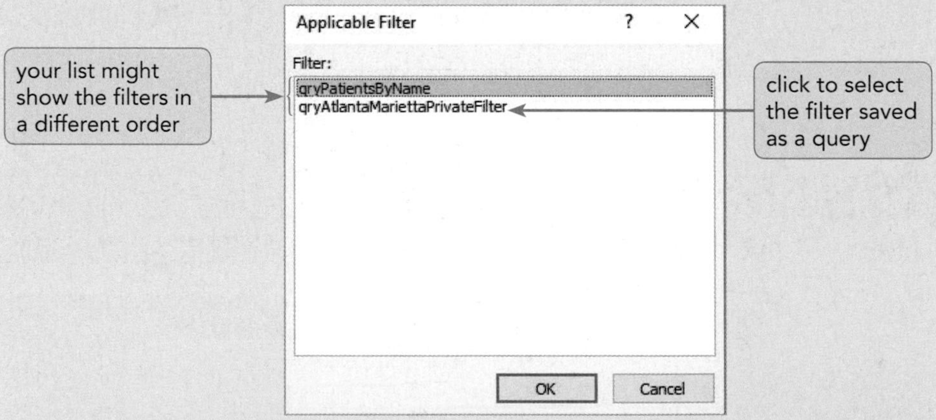
Applicable Filter
?
Filter:
qryPatientsByName
qryAtlantaMariettaPrivateFilter
OK
Cancel
your list might show the filters in a different order
click to select the filter saved as a query

4. Click **qryAtlantaMariettaPrivateFilter** in the Filter box if necessary to select it, and then click **OK**. The query is displayed in the Filter by Form window.
5. In the Sort & Filter group, click the **Toggle Filter** button. The five filtered records are displayed in the datasheet.
6. Click the **Advanced** button, click **Clear All Filters**, and then close the tblPatient table without saving your design changes.

Donna finds the qryAtlantaMariettaPrivateFilter useful, but she'd also like a list of the patients who have visited the clinic, and their visit information, for patients who live in either Atlanta or Marietta, and who have private health insurance. To generate this list, you can use the qryAtlantaMariettaPrivateFilter as a subquery within a query that searches for these patient visit records in the tblVisit table. You'll modify the qryAtlantaMariettaPrivateFilter query to use a subquery.

Creating a Subquery

When you create a query using a SQL SELECT statement, you can place a second SELECT statement inside it; this second query is called a **subquery**. The subquery is run first, and then the results of the subquery are used to run the outer query. A subquery is also known as an **inner query**. It runs inside another query, referred to as a **parent query**, which is simply a query that contains a subquery. A parent query can also be referred to as an **outer query**.

The records that result from the parent query are the only records that will be used as the dataset for the subquery. You can think of this arrangement as a query within a query. For instance, you might have a query that finds all patients from Atlanta and then use a subquery to find all patients within those records who visited the clinic in November. The subquery would be patients who visited in November, and the parent query would be patients whose city is Atlanta. This is a simple example, and you could certainly create one query that contains both the tblVisit and tblPatient tables, with criteria that set the city and visit date appropriately. However, in other situations you may be dealing with much more complex parent queries and subqueries. In these cases, rather than dealing with troubleshooting one very complex query, you could build two simpler queries and combine them in this manner. This can be a time-saving technique because you can create a very complex query by combining queries that are easier to understand.

To view the qryAtlantaMariettaPrivateFilter query in SQL view:

1. Open the Navigation Pane, open the **qryAtlantaMariettaPrivateFilter** query in Design view, and then close the Navigation Pane. In the design grid, the first And condition ("Atlanta" And "Private") appears in the Criteria row, the second And condition ("Marietta" And "Private") appears in the or row, and the Or condition combines the first And condition with the second And condition.
2. On the Query Tools Design tab, in the Results group, click the **View** arrow, click **SQL View**, and then click a blank area of the window to deselect the SQL SELECT statement. See Figure 12–7.

Figure 12–7 SQL statement for the qryAtlantaMariettaPrivateFilter query

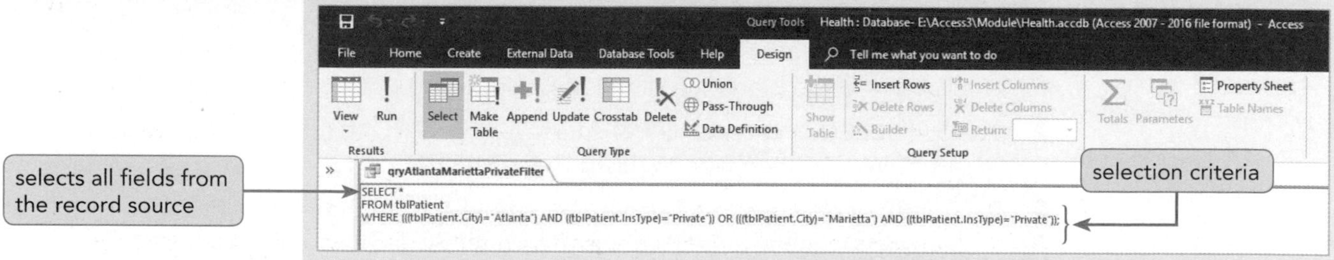
selects all fields from the record source
selection criteria
SELECT *
FROM tblPatient
WHERE (((tblPatient.City)="Atlanta") AND ((tblPatient.InsType)="Private")) OR (((tblPatient.City)="Marietta") AND ((tblPatient.InsType)="Private"));

*SELECT * FROM tblPatient* selects all fields from the tblPatient table in the order in which they appear in the table. The WHERE clause specifies the selection criteria: records with a City field value of Atlanta and an InsType field value of Private, or records with a City field value of Marietta and an InsType field value of Private.

In the next set of steps, you'll add the following outer query to modify the query to use it as a subquery:

SELECT * FROM tblVisit WHERE PatientID IN (

This will perform a SELECT query to find all fields (*) in the tblVisit table. The IN function will contain the SQL code for the qryAtlantaMariettaPrivateFilter query, which becomes the subquery. You'll need to add a right parenthesis) before the final semicolon to end the subquery. The finished SQL statement is shown in Figure 12–8.

Figure 12–8 SQL SELECT statement using a subquery

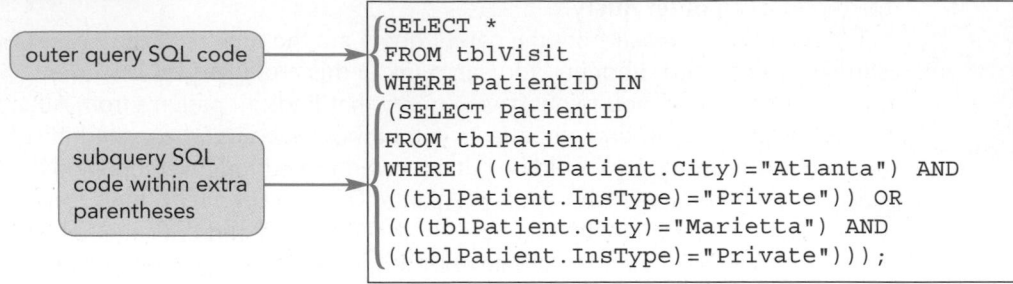

outer query SQL code

subquery SQL code within extra parentheses

```
SELECT *
FROM tblVisit
WHERE PatientID IN
(SELECT PatientID
FROM tblPatient
WHERE (((tblPatient.City)="Atlanta") AND
((tblPatient.InsType)="Private")) OR
(((tblPatient.City)="Marietta") AND
((tblPatient.InsType)="Private")));
```

To create this query, you'll copy the qryAtlantaMariettaPrivateFilter query and then add to this SQL code to form the query that uses this as a subquery.

To create the query that contains a subquery:

1. Close the qryAtlantaMariettaPrivateFilter query, and then open the Navigation Pane.
2. Right-click **qryAtlantaMariettaPrivateFilter**, and then on the shortcut menu, click **Copy**.
3. On the Home tab, in the Clipboard group, click **Paste** to open the Paste As dialog box, and then save as the copy with the name **qryAtlantaMariettaPrivateFilterVisit**.
4. Open the **qryAtlantaMariettaPrivateFilterVisit** query in Design view, and then close the Navigation Pane.
5. On the Query Tools Design tab, in the Results group, click the **View arrow**, click **SQL View**, and then click a blank area of the window to deselect the SQL SELECT statement.
6. Click to the left of the SELECT statement, press **ENTER** three times, and then click in the top blank line of the SQL window to position the insertion point.
7. Type **SELECT ***, press **DOWN ARROW**, type **FROM tblVisit**, press **DOWN ARROW**, and then type **WHERE PatientID IN**
8. Edit the next line to add **(** (an open parenthesis) to the left of SELECT, and then delete the asterisk (*) that comes after SELECT and replace it with **PatientID** so the statement is:

   (SELECT PatientID
9. Click to the left of the semicolon at the end of the SQL statement and type **)** (close parenthesis). See Figure 12–9.

Figure 12–9 Modified SQL statement

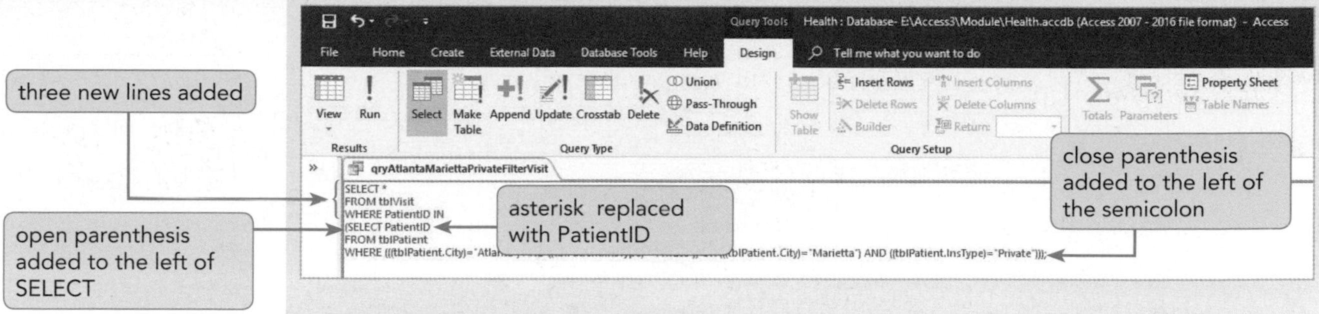
three new lines added
open parenthesis added to the left of SELECT
asterisk replaced with PatientID
close parenthesis added to the left of the semicolon
SELECT *
FROM tblVisit
WHERE PatientID IN
(SELECT PatientID
FROM tblPatient
qryAtlantaMariettaPrivateFilterVisit

10. Save your query design changes, and then run the query. The query returns eight records from the tblVisit table whose PatientID values are in the qryAtlantaMariettaPrivateFilter.
11. Switch to Design view, and then click the first column's **Field** box to deselect all values. The value in the PatientID Criteria box is a subquery that selects Atlanta and Marietta patients who have Private health insurance. See Figure 12–10.

Figure 12–10 Query using a subquery in the Design window

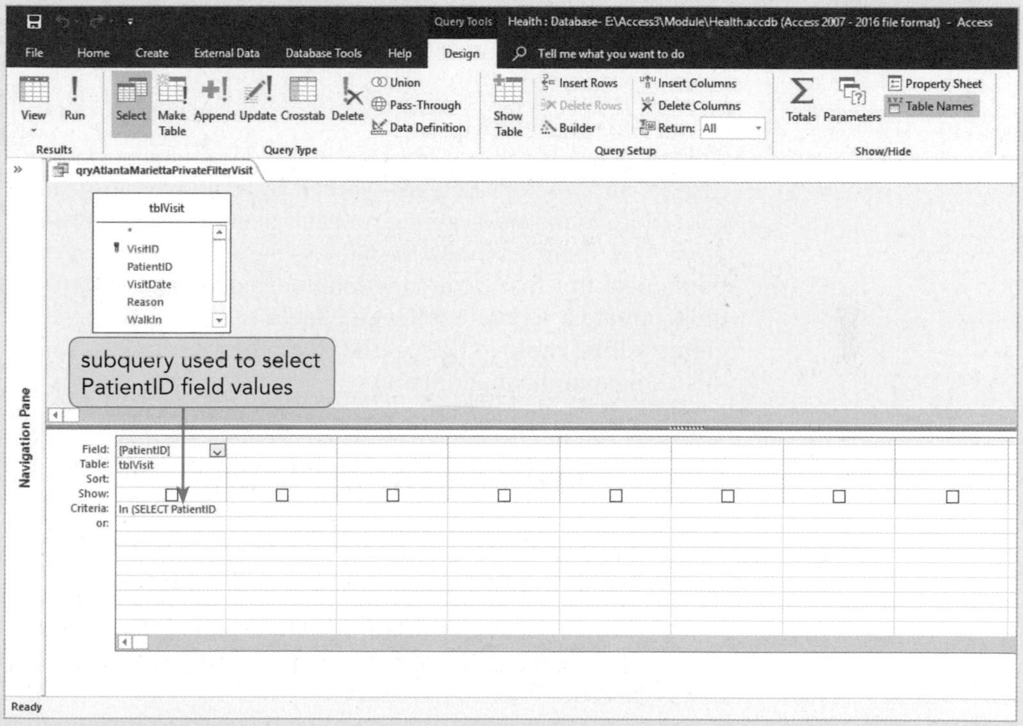
subquery used to select PatientID field values
qryAtlantaMariettaPrivateFilterVisit
tblVisit
Field: [PatientID]
Table: tblVisit
Criteria: In (SELECT PatientID

It's unclear from looking at the column in the design grid that all fields are displayed from the tblVisit table.

12. On the Query Tools Design tab, in the Show/Hide group, click the **Property Sheet** button to display the properties for the query. See Figure 12–11.

Figure 12–11 **Properties for the query**

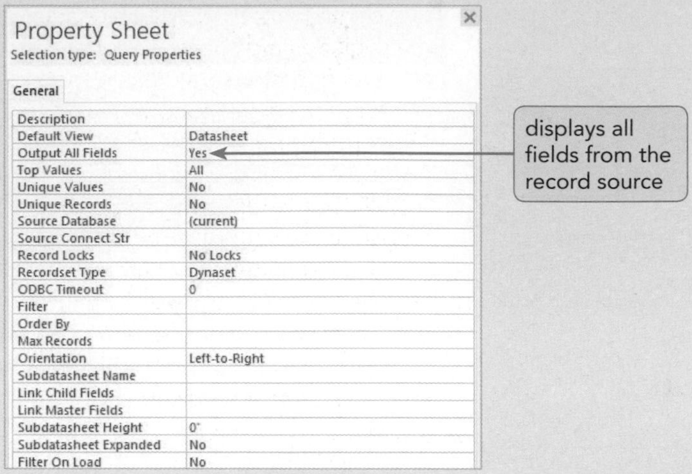
Property Sheet
Selection type: Query Properties
General
Description
Default View Datasheet
Output All Fields Yes
Top Values All
Unique Values No
Unique Records No
Source Database (current)
Source Connect Str
Record Locks No Locks
Recordset Type Dynaset
ODBC Timeout 0
Filter
Order By
Max Records
Orientation Left-to-Right
Subdatasheet Name
Link Child Fields
Link Master Fields
Subdatasheet Height 0"
Subdatasheet Expanded No
Filter On Load No
displays all fields from the record source

The Output All Fields property setting of Yes specifies that the query displays all fields from the record source, the tblVisit table, without these fields being added to the design grid.

13. Close the Property Sheet, close the query, and then click **Yes** when prompted to save changes to the query design.

Donna wants to keep track of the degrees—such as associate's degree, bachelor's degree, and master's degree—earned by employees. Because each employee can earn more than one degree, and each degree can be earned by more than one employee, there's a many-to-many relationship between employees and degrees. To implement this many-to-many relationship, you could use the existing tblEmployee table, create a separate tblDegree table to store the Degree field values, and then create a third table to tie together the other two tables. You could also accomplish this using a multivalued field.

Using Multivalued Fields

A multivalued field is a lookup field that allows you to store more than one value. When you define a multivalued field in a table, the values are not actually stored in the field in that table. Instead, they are stored as hidden values in system tables that have a many-to-many relationship with the table. The values in these system tables are managed, manipulated, and displayed as if the data were stored in the multivalued field in the table.

Using a multivalued field, you can add a Degree field to the tblEmployee table and use the Lookup Wizard to enter the Degree field values and specify that you want to store multiple values in the Degree field. Donna and her staff can then select one or more Degree field values from the list of degrees.

INSIGHT

Using Multivalued Fields

Users with limited Access and database experience are the intended audience for multivalued fields because understanding the concepts of many-to-many relationships and creating them are difficult for beginning or casual database users. Experienced database users generally avoid multivalued fields and instead implement many-to-many relationships because that method provides total control over the data, rather than limiting options as working with multivalued fields does. One of the limitations of multivalued fields is that except in special circumstances, you can't sort records based on the values stored in a multivalued field in queries, forms, and reports. Also, multivalued fields do not convert properly to a database managed by a DBMS such as SQL Server or Oracle. If you need to convert an Access database using a multivalued field to another DBMS in the future, you'd have to change the multivalued field to many-to-many relationships, which is a change that's much more difficult at that point than if you had avoided using a multivalued field from the beginning. As a precaution, you should save a copy of the database file before you create a multivalued field.

You'll use the multivalued field feature without modifying the existing tables and relationships in the Health database, so Donna can decide whether you should keep the multivalued field or use a traditional many-to-many implementation. You'll make a copy of the tblEmployee table, and then you will add the multivalued field to the copied version of the table. This way, you can delete the copy of the tblEmployee table if Donna decides not to use a multivalued field. If Donna decides to keep it, she has the option to delete the original tblEmployee table and rename this new table as the tblEmployee table.

To create a copy of the tblEmployee table:

1. Open the Navigation Pane, right-click **tblEmployee**, and then on the shortcut menu, click **Copy**.
2. In the Clipboard group, on the Home tab, click the **Paste** button to open the Paste Table As dialog box, and then click the **Table Name** box to deselect the current name. See Figure 12–12.

Figure 12–12 Paste Table As dialog box

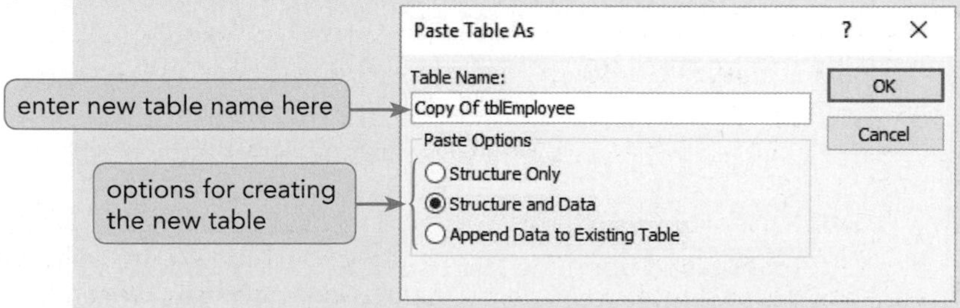
enter new table name here
options for creating the new table
Paste Table As
?
Table Name:
Copy Of tblEmployee
OK
Cancel
Paste Options
Structure Only
Structure and Data
Append Data to Existing Table

When you copy a table to create a new table, you can use the design of the table without copying its data (Structure Only), use the design and copy the data from the table (Structure and Data), or add the data to an existing table (Append Data to Existing Table).

You'll create the new table using the design and data from the tblEmployee table.

3. Change the name in the Table Name box to **tblEmployeeCopy**, make sure the **Structure and Data** option button is selected, and then click **OK**. A new table named tblEmployeeCopy is created, and it contains the same structure and data as the tblEmployee table.

Now you can add the multivalued field to the tblEmployeeCopy table.

To add the multivalued field to the tblEmployeeCopy table:

1. Open the **tblEmployeeCopy** table in Design view, and then close the Navigation Pane.
2. In the blank row below the SupervisorID field, click the **Field Name** box, type **Degree**, press **TAB**, click the **Data Type** arrow, and then click **Lookup Wizard**. The first Lookup Wizard dialog box opens. You'll type the Degree field values instead of obtaining them from a table or query.
3. Click the **I will type in the values that I want** option button, and then click **Next** to open the second Lookup Wizard dialog box, in which you'll type the Degree field values.
4. Click the **Col1** box in the first row, type **Certificate**, press **TAB**, type **Associate**, press **TAB**, type **Bachelor**, press **TAB**, type **Master**, press **TAB**, and then type **Doctorate**. These are the five values that users can choose among for the Degree multivalued field. See Figure 12–13.

Figure 12–13 Values for the Degree multivalued field

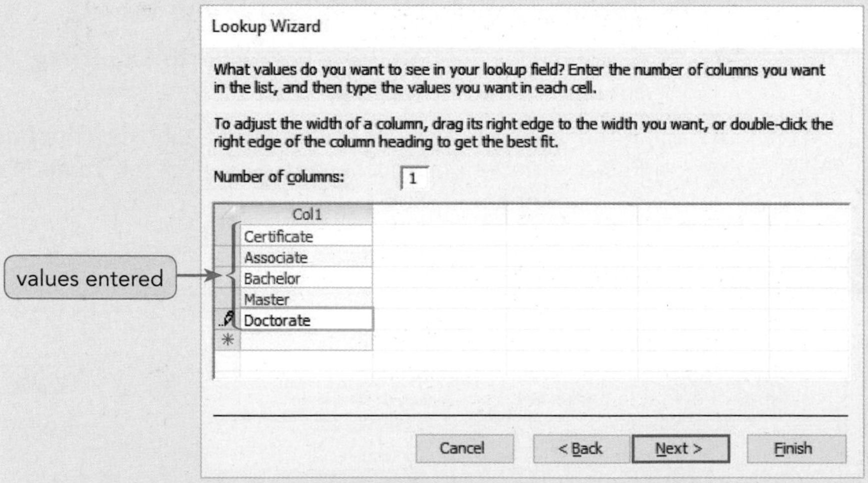
Lookup Wizard
What values do you want to see in your lookup field? Enter the number of columns you want in the list, and then type the values you want in each cell.
To adjust the width of a column, drag its right edge to the width you want, or double-click the right edge of the column heading to get the best fit.
Number of columns:
1
Col1
Certificate
Associate
Bachelor
Master
Doctorate
values entered
Cancel
< Back
Next >
Finish

5. Click **Next** to open the last Lookup Wizard dialog box, and then click the **Allow Multiple Values** check box to add a checkmark to it, specifying that you want the Degree field to be a multivalued field. See Figure 12–14.

Figure 12–14 Specifying a multivalued field

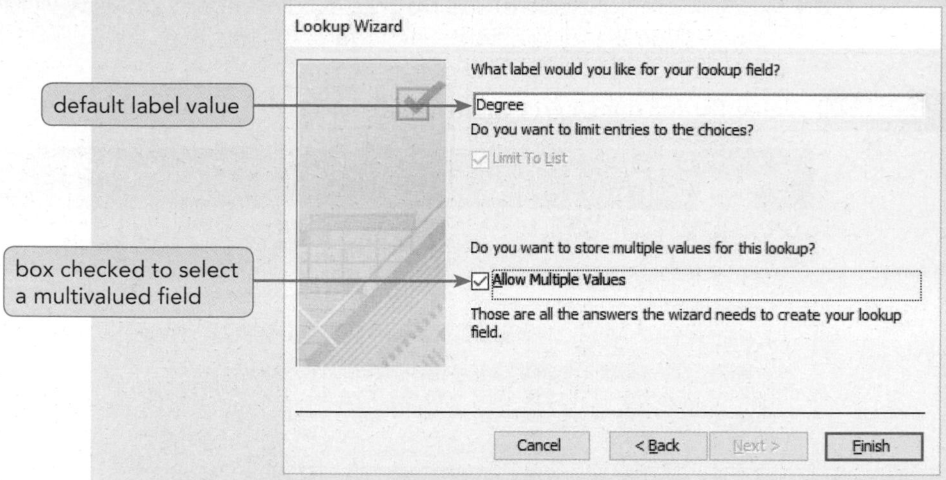
Lookup Wizard
What label would you like for your lookup field?
Degree
Do you want to limit entries to the choices?
Limit To List
Do you want to store multiple values for this lookup?
Allow Multiple Values
Those are all the answers the wizard needs to create your lookup field.
Cancel
< Back
Next >
Finish
default label value
box checked to select a multivalued field

You'll accept the default label name of Degree for the field.

6. Click **Finish** to complete the definition of the Degree field as a lookup field that allows multiple values, or a multivalued field.
7. In the Field Properties pane, click the **Lookup** tab. The Degree field has its Row Source property set to the five values you typed in one of the Lookup Wizard dialog boxes, and the Allow Multiple Values property is set to Yes. See Figure 12–15.

Figure 12–15 Degree field as a multivalued field

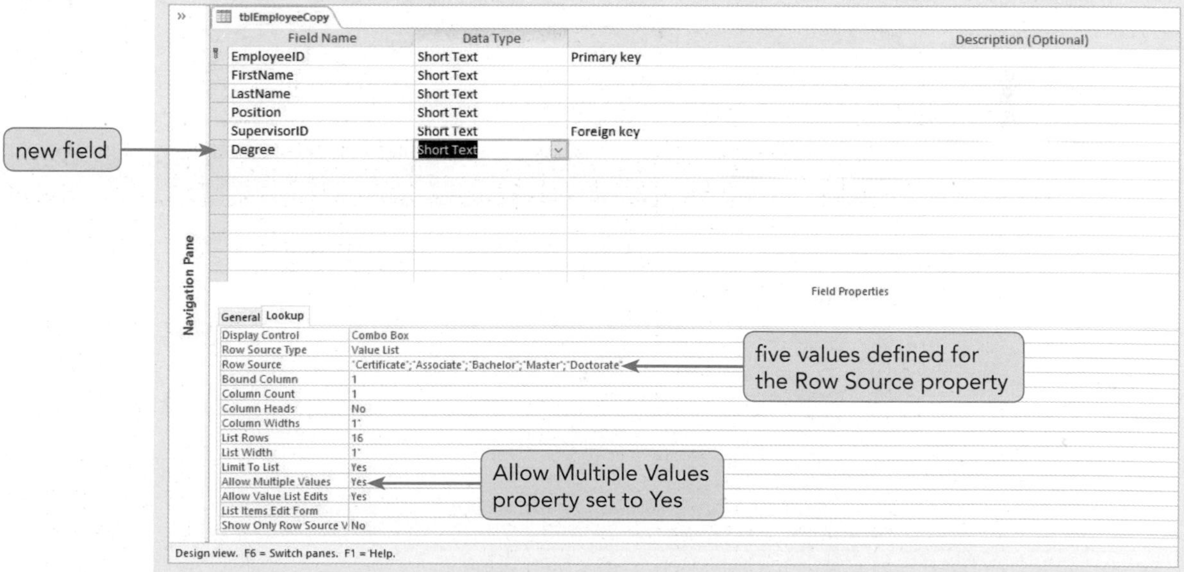
tblEmployeeCopy
Field Name
Data Type
Description (Optional)
EmployeeID Short Text Primary key
FirstName Short Text
LastName Short Text
Position Short Text
SupervisorID Short Text Foreign key
Degree Short Text
Navigation Pane
Field Properties
General Lookup
Display Control Combo Box
Row Source Type Value List
Row Source "Certificate";"Associate";"Bachelor";"Master";"Doctorate"
Bound Column 1
Column Count 1
Column Heads No
Column Widths 1"
List Rows 16
List Width 1"
Limit To List Yes
Allow Multiple Values Yes
Allow Value List Edits Yes
List Items Edit Form
Show Only Row Source V No
Design view. F6 = Switch panes. F1 = Help.
new field
five values defined for the Row Source property
Allow Multiple Values property set to Yes

If you forget to select the Allow Multiple Values check box when you use the Lookup Wizard, you can switch to Design view and set the Allow Multiple Values property for the field to Yes to change a field to a multivalued field. If you need to add values in the future to the multivalued field, you can add them to the Row Source property.

8. Save your table design changes, and then switch to Datasheet view.
9. Click the right side of the **Degree** box for record 2 (Susan Wilder) to open the value list for the field. See Figure 12–16.

Figure 12–16 Value list for the Degree multivalued field

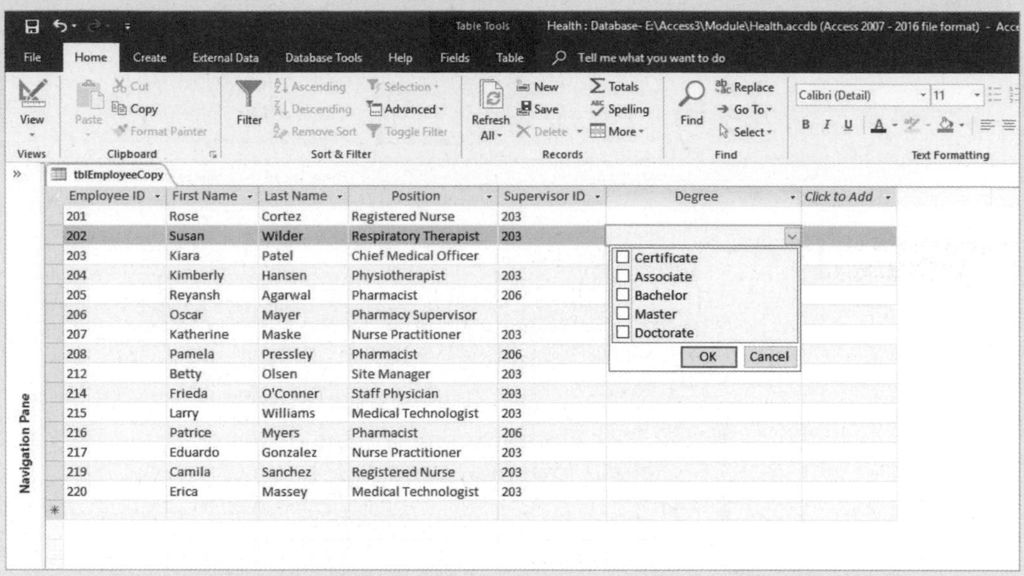
tblEmployeeCopy
Certificate
Associate
Bachelor
Master
Doctorate
OK
Cancel

10. Click the **Associate** check box, and then click **OK**.
11. For record 4 (Kimberly Hansen), select **Bachelor**, **Master**, and **Doctorate**, and for record 9 (Betty Olsen), select **Bachelor**.
12. Resize the Degree column to its best fit. See Figure 12–17.

Figure 12–17 Values selected for the multivalued field

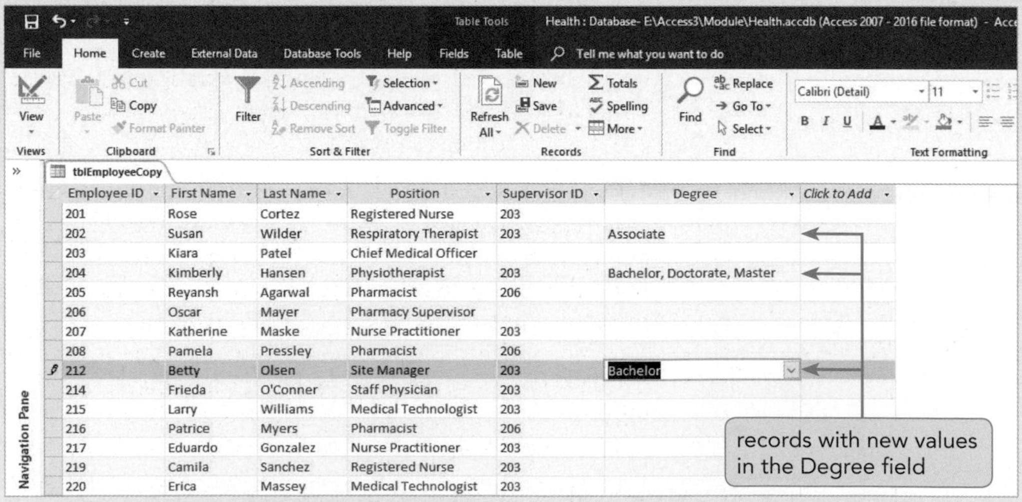
tblEmployeeCopy
Associate
Bachelor, Doctorate, Master
Bachelor
records with new values in the Degree field

Next, you'll create queries to display all field values from the tblEmployeeCopy table to display the multivalued field values.

To create queries to display the Degree multivalued field:

1. Save and close the tblEmployeeCopy table, click the **Create** tab, and then in the Queries group, click the **Query Wizard** button to open the New Query dialog box.
2. Make sure the Simple Query Wizard option is selected, click **OK** to open the Simple Query Wizard dialog box, from the tblEmployeeCopy table select all fields, click the **Next** button, change the query title to **qryEmployeeCopy**, and then click **Finish**.
3. Click the first row's **Employee ID** column value to deselect all values (if necessary), and then resize the Degree.Value column to best fit. The query results include 17 records. See Figure 12–18.

Figure 12–18 Query that displays the Degree multivalued field

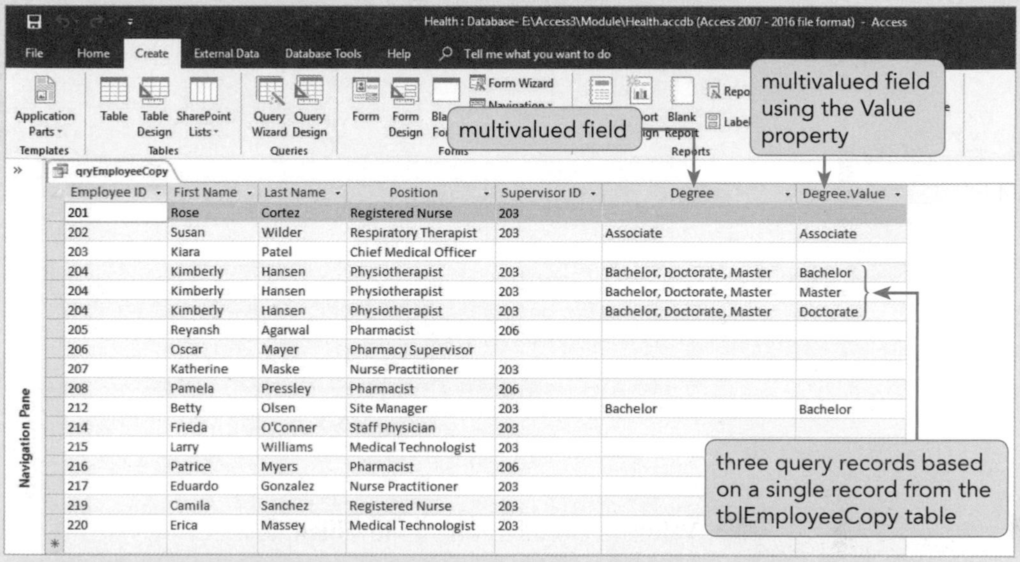
multivalued field
multivalued field using the Value property
three query records based on a single record from the tblEmployeeCopy table

Trouble? The rightmost column heading on your screen might be the equivalent of tblEmployee-Copy.Degree.Value instead of Degree.Value, indicating the Degree field in the tblEmployeeCopy table. This difference does not affect the contents of the column.

The six fields from the tblEmployeeCopy table are displayed in seven columns in the query recordset because the Degree field is displayed in two columns: the Degree column and the Degree.Value column. The Degree column displays field values exactly as they appear in the tblEmployeeCopy table; all values for the Degree multivalued field, such as those for Kimberly Hansen, are displayed in one row in the query. The Degree.Value column displays the Degree multivalued field in expanded form so that each value appears in a separate row in the query. "Degree.Value" identifies the Degree field and the Value property for the Degree field.

In queries that contain a multivalued field, you should display the field in a single column, not in two columns, with values appearing as they are in the table or in expanded form. You can eliminate the extra column by deleting it, by clearing its Show check box in Design view, or by selecting just one of the two fields in the Simple Query Wizard when you select the fields for the query.

4. Click the **Home** tab, notice that the Ascending and Descending buttons in the Sort & Filter group are active, click the first row's **Degree** box, notice that the Ascending and Descending buttons are grayed out, and then click the first row's **Degree.Value** box. The Ascending and Descending buttons are active, and you can sort records in the query based on the values in the Degree.Value column.

   Next, you'll review the query design.

5. Switch to Design view, and then resize the tblEmployeeCopy field list to display all the values in the list. See Figure 12–19.

Figure 12–19 Design of the query containing the Degree multivalued field

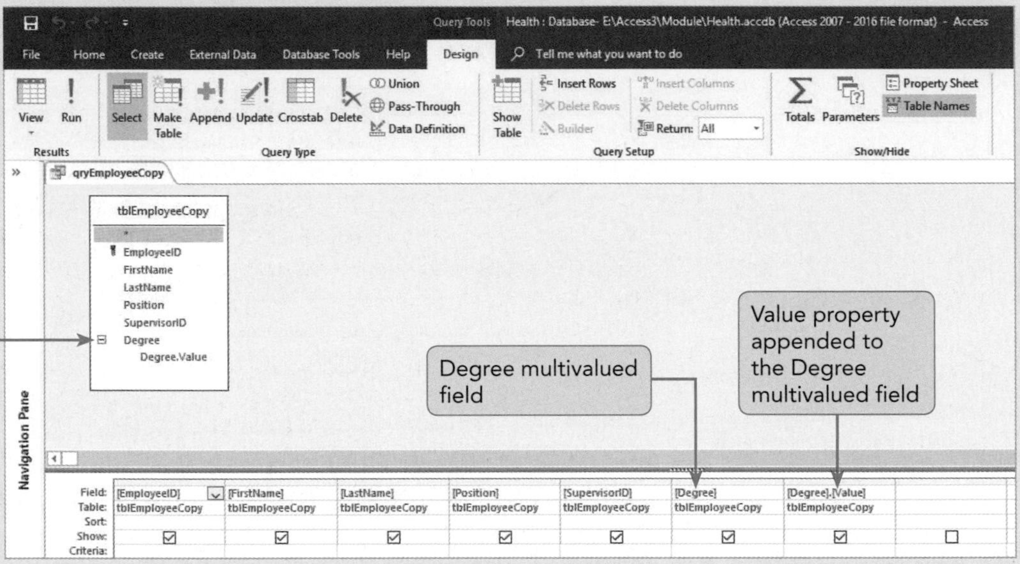
collapse indicator for the multivalued field
Degree multivalued field
Value property appended to the Degree multivalued field
tblEmployeeCopy
EmployeeID
FirstName
LastName
Position
SupervisorID
Degree
Degree.Value
qryEmployeeCopy
Navigation Pane

The Degree field in the tblEmployeeCopy field list has a collapse indicator to its left that you can click to hide the Degree.Value entry below it. The rightmost column in the design grid, [Degree].[Value], uses the Value property for the Degree field. Using the Value property with a multivalued field displays the multivalued field in expanded form so that each value is displayed in a separate row.

You'll delete the [Degree] column from the query design, retaining the [Degree].[Value] column and setting its Caption property, and then you'll save the query with a new name.

6. Right-click the **column selector bar** for the [Degree] column to select the column and open the shortcut menu, and then click **Cut**.
7. Click the **column selector bar** for the [Degree].[Value] column to select it, open the Property Sheet for the [Degree].[Value] column, set the Caption property to **Degree**, and then close the Property Sheet.
8. Click the **File** tab to open Backstage view, in the navigation bar, click **Save As**, click **Save Object As**, and then click the **Save As** button to open the Save As dialog box.
9. Change the query name to **qryEmployeeCopyValue**, click **OK**, click the **Home** tab, and then switch to Datasheet view. The datasheet appears, displaying 17 records in the query recordset.

10. Close the query, open the Navigation Pane, open the **qryEmployeeCopy** query in Design view, and then close the Navigation Pane.
11. Delete the **Degree.Value** column, save the query, and then run the query. The query returns 15 records from the tblEmployeeCopy table and displays the Degree multivalued field values in one row.
12. Close the query, and then, if you are not continuing on to the next session, close the Health database.

Donna is pleased with your work and will review it as she decides whether to use the multivalued Degree field or a many-to-many relationship. In the next session, you'll add Attachment fields using the tblEmployeeCopy table and evaluate database performance and management options.

REVIEW

Session 12.1 Quick Check

1. Filter By ___ filters records that match multiple selection criteria using the same Access comparison operators used in queries.
2. You can save a filter as a(n) ___ and reuse the filter by opening the saved object.
3. What is a subquery?
4. What is a multivalued field?
5. You use the ___ property to display a multivalued field in expanded form so that each value is displayed in a separate row in a query.

Session 12.2 Visual Overview:

The **Current Database option** displays options that apply only to the currently open database.

The **Application Title option** value appears in the Access window title bar.

The **Use Access Special Keys option** enables or disables the F11 key (show/hide the Navigation Pane), CTRL+G (show/hide the Immediate window in VB editor), and ALT+F1 (start VB Editor).

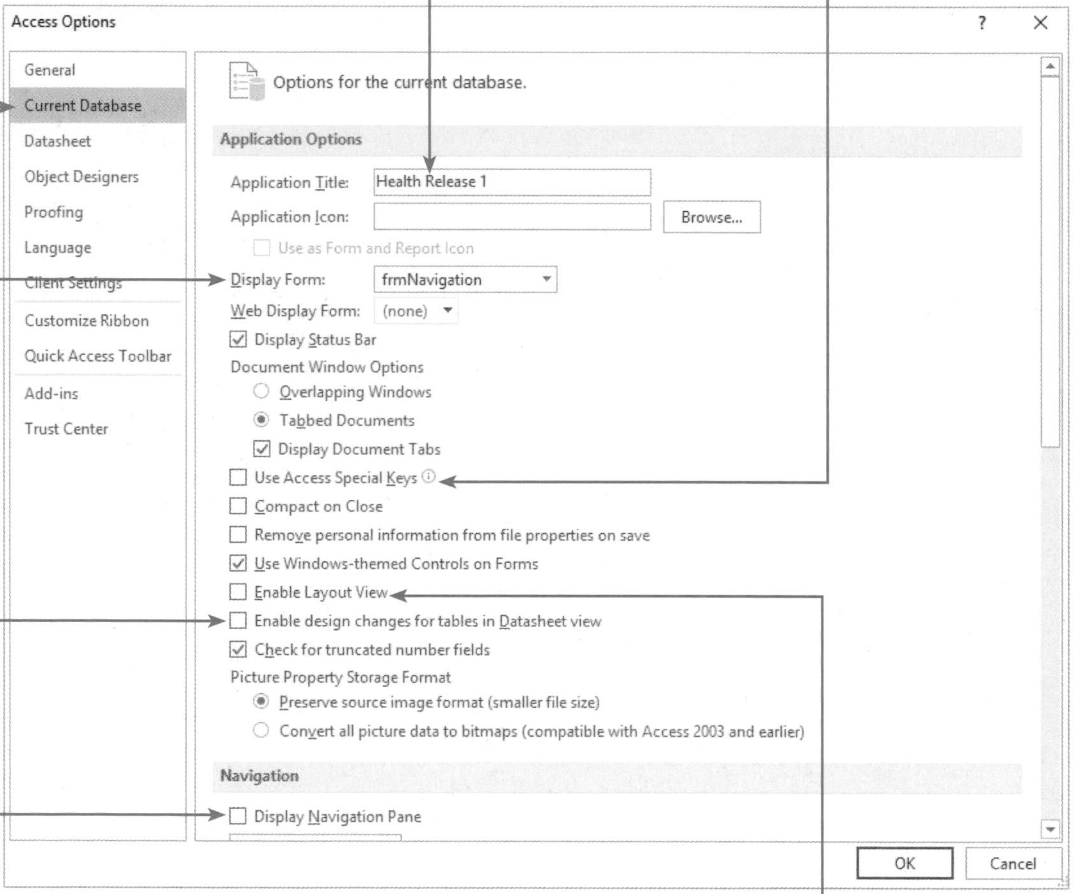
Access Options
General
Current Database
Datasheet
Object Designers
Proofing
Language
Client Settings
Customize Ribbon
Quick Access Toolbar
Add-ins
Trust Center
Options for the current database.
Application Options
Application Title: Health Release 1
Application Icon:
Browse...
Use as Form and Report Icon
Display Form: frmNavigation
Web Display Form: (none)
Display Status Bar
Document Window Options
Overlapping Windows
Tabbed Documents
Display Document Tabs
Use Access Special Keys
Compact on Close
Remove personal information from file properties on save
Use Windows-themed Controls on Forms
Enable Layout View
Enable design changes for tables in Datasheet view
Check for truncated number fields
Picture Property Storage Format
Preserve source image format (smaller file size)
Convert all picture data to bitmaps (compatible with Access 2003 and earlier)
Navigation
Display Navigation Pane
OK
Cancel

The **Display Form option** specifies the form that opens automatically when you open the database.

The **Enable design changes for tables in Datasheet view option** allows you to change a table's design in Datasheet view.

The **Display Navigation Pane option** controls whether the Navigation Pane is available in the Access window.

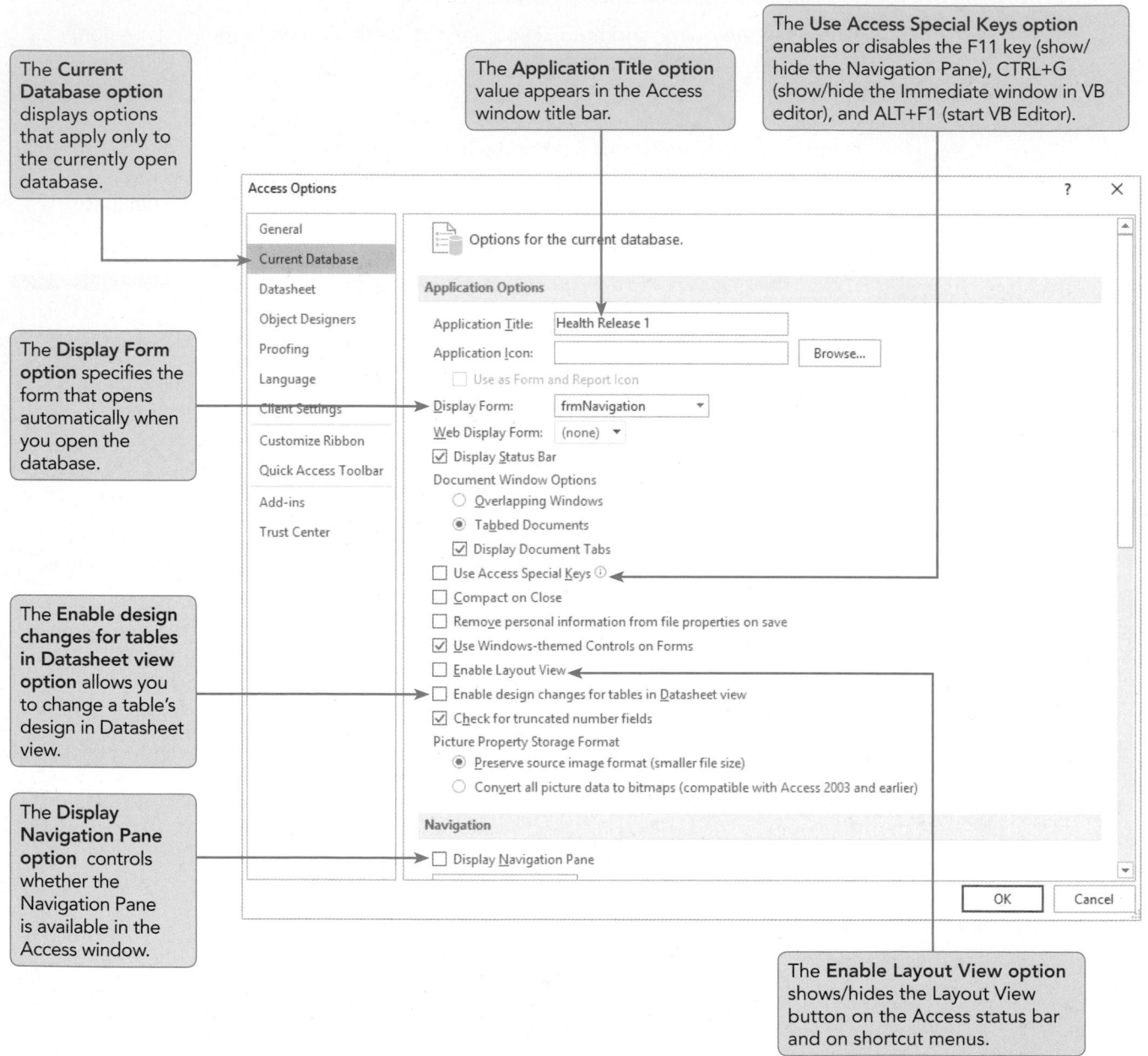

The **Enable Layout View option** shows/hides the Layout View button on the Access status bar and on shortcut menus.

Database Options

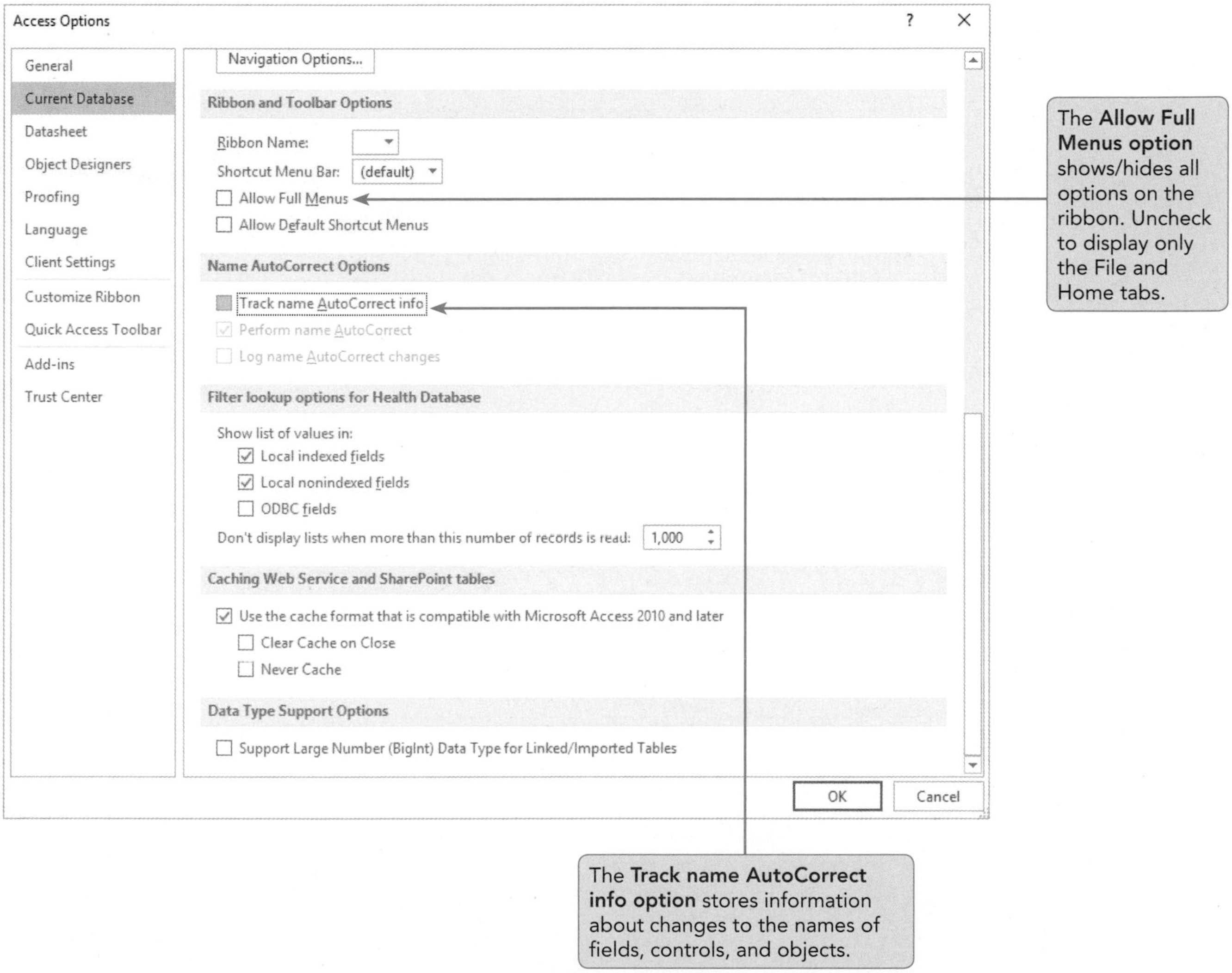
Access Options
General
Current Database
Datasheet
Object Designers
Proofing
Language
Client Settings
Customize Ribbon
Quick Access Toolbar
Add-ins
Trust Center
Navigation Options...
Ribbon and Toolbar Options
Ribbon Name:
Shortcut Menu Bar: (default)
Allow Full Menus
Allow Default Shortcut Menus
Name AutoCorrect Options
Track name AutoCorrect info
Perform name AutoCorrect
Log name AutoCorrect changes
Filter lookup options for Health Database
Show list of values in:
Local indexed fields
Local nonindexed fields
ODBC fields
Don't display lists when more than this number of records is read: 1,000
Caching Web Service and SharePoint tables
Use the cache format that is compatible with Microsoft Access 2010 and later
Clear Cache on Close
Never Cache
Data Type Support Options
Support Large Number (BigInt) Data Type for Linked/Imported Tables
OK
Cancel
The **Allow Full Menus option** shows/hides all options on the ribbon. Uncheck to display only the File and Home tabs.
The **Track name AutoCorrect info option** stores information about changes to the names of fields, controls, and objects.

Creating an Attachment Field

In addition to storing data such as text, numbers, and dates in a database, you can attach external files such as Excel workbooks, Word documents, and images, similar to how you attach external files to email messages. You use the **Attachment data type** to attach one or more files to a table record. The attachments are stored as part of the database. An attachment data field can contain one or more file attachments in a table record.

TIP

After you change a field type to Attachment, you can't change the field type again. Instead, you have to delete the field and re-create it with a new field type.

Donna wants to be able to attach documents to the tblEmployeeCopy table that contain information about Kimberly Hansen's degrees and expenses. You'll add a field with the Attachment data type and use it to attach the documents to the table.

To add a new field with the Attachment data type to the tblEmployeeCopy table:

1. If you took a break after the previous session, make sure that the Health database is open.
2. Open the Navigation Pane (if necessary), open the **tblEmployeeCopy** table in Design view, and then close the Navigation Pane.
3. Click the **Field Name** box for the blank row below the Degree field, type **AddedDocuments**, press **TAB**, type **at**, press **TAB** to select Attachment as the data type, press **F6** to navigate to the Caption box in the Field Properties pane, and then type **Added Documents**. The AddedDocuments field is added to the table. See Figure 12–20.

Figure 12–20 New AddedDocuments field with the Attachment data type

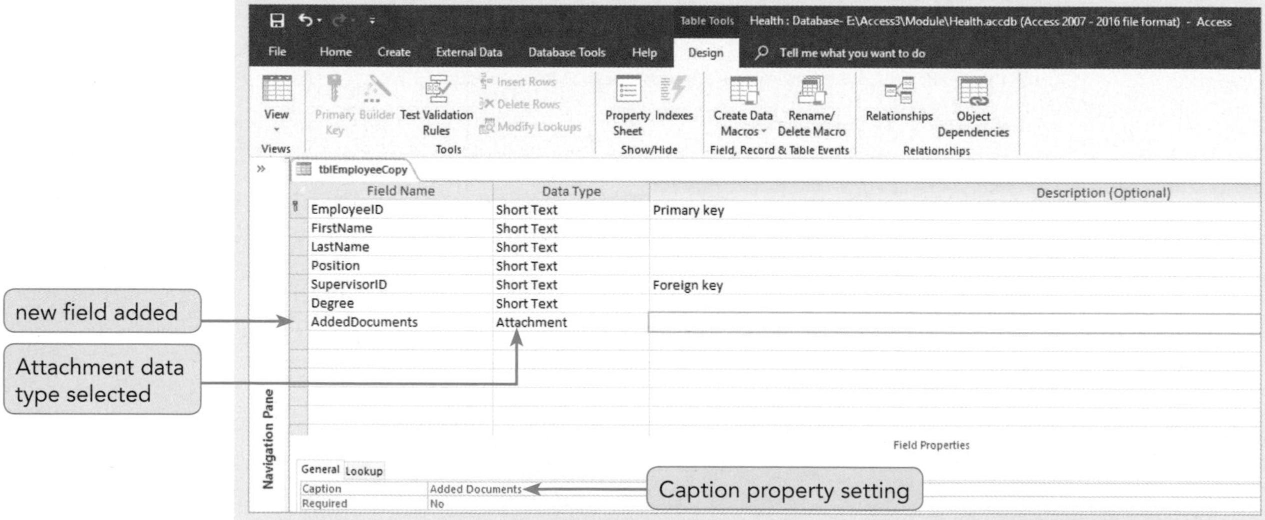

new field added
Attachment data type selected
Caption property setting
Field Name
Data Type
Description (Optional)
EmployeeID
FirstName
LastName
Position
SupervisorID
Degree
AddedDocuments
Short Text
Attachment
Primary key
Foreign key
Caption
Added Documents
Required
No

4. Save your table design changes, switch to Datasheet view, resize the Added Documents column to its best fit, click the first row's **Employee ID** box to deselect all values, and then save your datasheet format changes. See Figure 12–21.

Figure 12–21 Attachment field displayed in the table datasheet

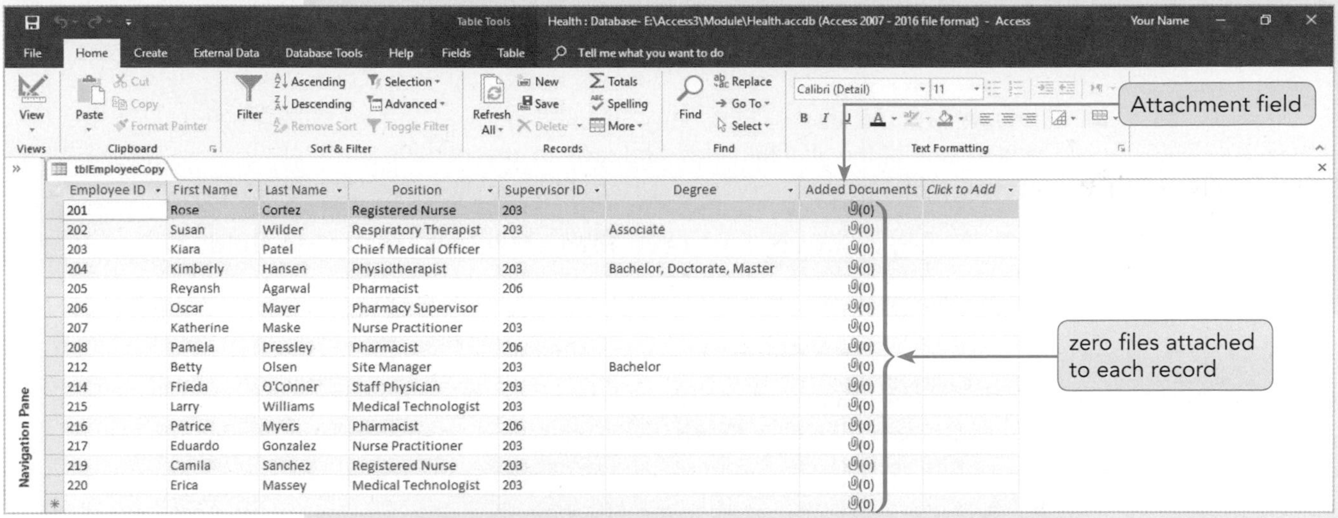
Attachment field
zero files attached to each record
tblEmployeeCopy
Employee ID
First Name
Last Name
Position
Supervisor ID
Degree
Added Documents
Click to Add
201 Rose Cortez Registered Nurse 203
202 Susan Wilder Respiratory Therapist 203 Associate
203 Kiara Patel Chief Medical Officer
204 Kimberly Hansen Physiotherapist 203 Bachelor, Doctorate, Master
205 Reyansh Agarwal Pharmacist 206
206 Oscar Mayer Pharmacy Supervisor
207 Katherine Maske Nurse Practitioner 203
208 Pamela Pressley Pharmacist 206
212 Betty Olsen Site Manager 203 Bachelor
214 Frieda O'Conner Staff Physician 203
215 Larry Williams Medical Technologist 203
216 Patrice Myers Pharmacist 206
217 Eduardo Gonzalez Nurse Practitioner 203
219 Camila Sanchez Registered Nurse 203
220 Erica Massey Medical Technologist 203

Each AddedDocuments field value displays an attachment icon in the shape of a paper clip followed by a number in parentheses that indicates the number of files attached in that field for the record. You haven't attached any files, so each record displays zero file attachments. Donna has some files from Kimberly Hansen that she would like you to attach to her record in the Added Documents column.

5. In the row for Kimberly Hansen, right-click the **Added Documents** box to open the shortcut menu, and then click **Manage Attachments** to open the Attachments dialog box. You'll add all three of Kimberly's files as attachments to the AddedDocuments field for Kimberly Hansen.
6. Click **Add** to open the Choose File dialog box, navigate to the **Access3 > Module** folder included with your Data Files, click **Support_AC_12_KimberlyHansenBachelorDegree.docx**, and then click **Open** to add the Support_AC_12_KimberlyHansenBachelorDegree.docx file to the Attachments dialog box.
7. Click **Add** to open the Choose File dialog box, click **Support_AC_12_KimberlyHansenMasterDegree.pdf**, press and hold **CTRL**, click **Support_AC_12_KimberlyHansenExpenses.xlsx**, release **CTRL**, and then click **Open**. The three files you've added now appear in the Attachments dialog box. See Figure 12–22.

Figure 12–22 Attachments dialog box

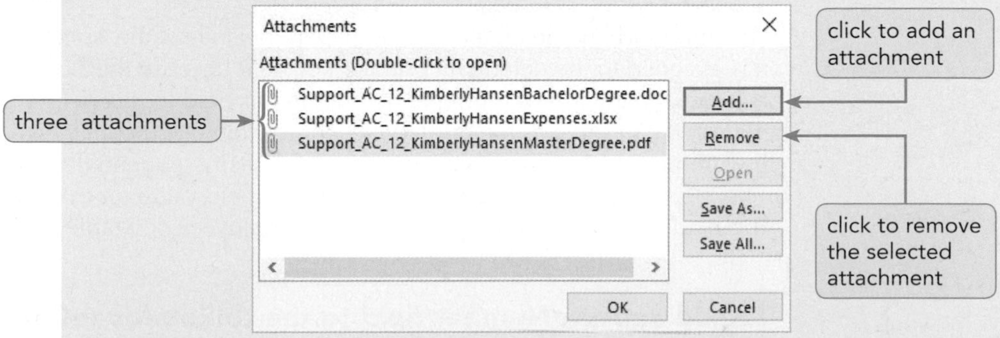
Attachments
Attachments (Double-click to open)
Support_AC_12_KimberlyHansenBachelorDegree.doc
Support_AC_12_KimberlyHansenExpenses.xlsx
Support_AC_12_KimberlyHansenMasterDegree.pdf
Add...
Remove
Open
Save As...
Save All...
OK
Cancel
three attachments
click to add an attachment
click to remove the selected attachment

8. Click **OK** to close the dialog box. The table datasheet now indicates that three files (as noted by the 3 in parentheses) are attached to the AddedDocuments field in the record for Kimberly Hansen.

Next, you'll open one of the files attached in the record for Kimberly Hansen, remove one of the attached files, and save an attached file.

To open, remove, and save files attached in a table field:

1. In the row for Kimberly Hansen, right-click the **Added Documents** box, and then on the shortcut menu, click **Manage Attachments** to open the Attachments dialog box.
2. Click **Support_AC_12_KimberlyHansenExpenses.xlsx** in the Attachments list, and then click **Open**. Excel starts and opens the Support_AC_12_KimberlyHansenExpenses.xlsx workbook.
3. Close Excel. You return to the Attachments dialog box open in the Access window.
4. Click **Support_AC_12_KimberlyHansenBachelorDegree.docx** in the Attachments list, and then click **Remove**. The Support_AC_12_KimberlyHansenBachelorDegree.docx document is removed from the Attachments list, and it no longer is attached to the AddedDocuments field for the Kimberly Hansen record.
5. Click **Support_AC_12_KimberlyHansenMasterDegree.pdf** in the Attachments list, click **Save As** to open the Save Attachment dialog box, if necessary, navigate to the location where you are storing your Data Files, type **NP_AC_12_KimberlyHansenMasterDegreeDetach** in the File name box, and then click **Save**.
6. Click **OK** to close the Attachments dialog box. Because you removed the Support_AC_12_KimberlyHansenBachelorDegree.docx file as an attachment, the AddedDocuments field for the Kimberly Hansen record now shows that it has two attachments.

TIP

The Support_AC_12_KimberlyHansenBachelor-Degree.docx document remains in the Access3 > Module folder because detaching a file doesn't delete it.

Donna is considering adding an employee number for each employee that could be automatically generated when a new employee record is added. You can do this by adding an AutoNumber field to the tblEmployeeCopy table.

Using an AutoNumber Field

As you know, when you create a table in Datasheet view, the AutoNumber data type is assigned to the default ID primary key field because the AutoNumber data type automatically inserts a unique number in this field for every record in the table. Therefore, it can serve as the primary key for any table you create. When defining a field with the AutoNumber data type, you can specify sequential numbering or random numbering, either of which guarantees a unique field value for every record in the table.

You'll add an AutoNumber field to the tblEmployeeCopy table.

To add an AutoNumber field to the tblEmployeeCopy table:

1. Switch to Design view, right-click the **row selector** for the EmployeeID field to open the shortcut menu, and then click **Insert Rows**. A blank row is inserted above the EmployeeID row. Next, you'll add the AutoNumber field to this new first row in the table design.

2. Click the first row's **Field Name** box, type **EmployeeNum**, press **TAB**, type **a**, press **TAB** to accept AutoNumber as the data type, press **F6** to navigate to the Field Properties pane, press **TAB** three times to navigate to the Caption box, and then enter **Employee Num** in the Caption box. You've finished adding the EmployeeNum field to the table. See Figure 12–23.

Figure 12–23 EmployeeNum field added with the AutoNumber data type

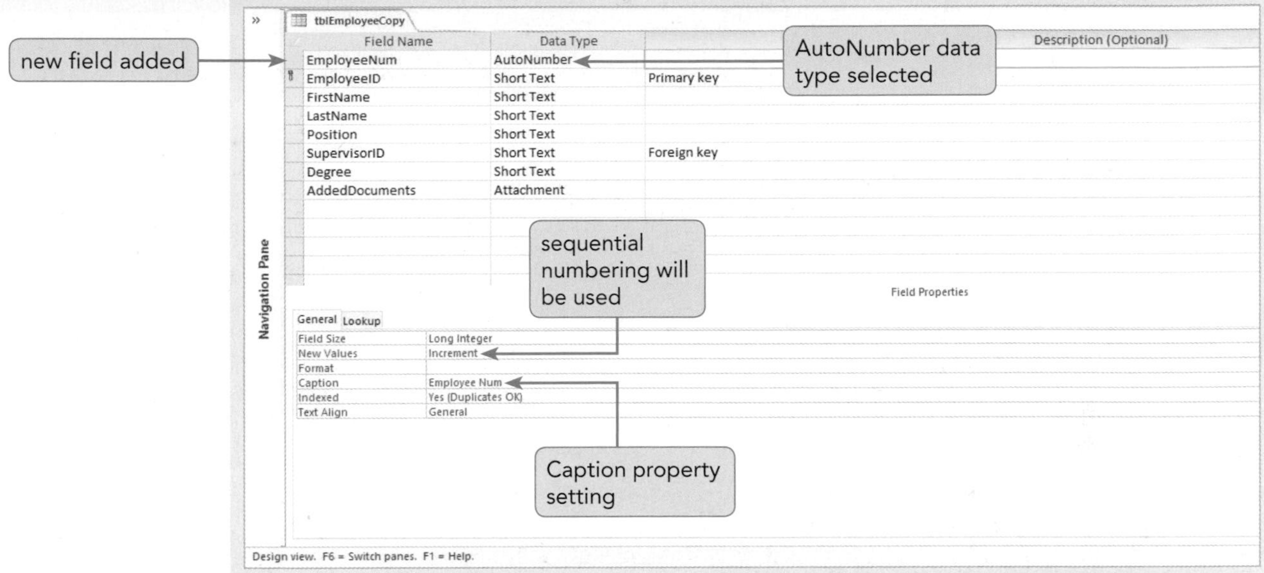
new field added
AutoNumber data type selected
sequential numbering will be used
Caption property setting

3. Save your table design changes, switch to Datasheet view, resize the Employee Num column to its best fit, and then click the first row's **Employee Num** box to deselect all values. The new EmployeeNum field is displayed as the first column in the table, and unique incremental (sequential) numbers appear in the EmployeeNum field for the 15 records in the table. See Figure 12–24.

Figure 12–24 AutoNumber field displayed in the table datasheet

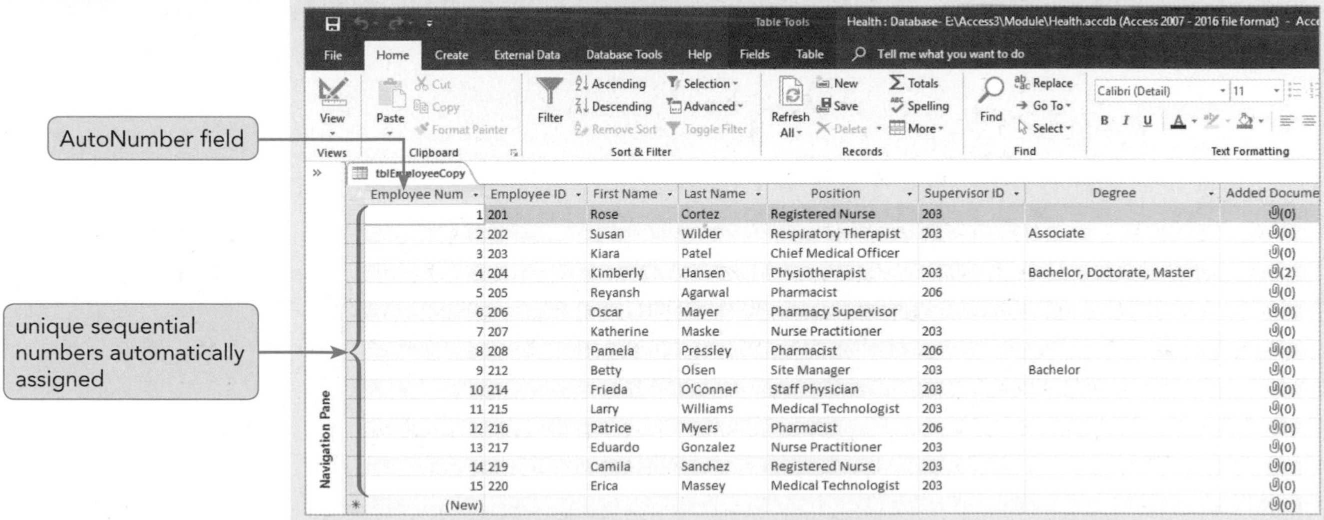
AutoNumber field
unique sequential numbers automatically assigned

Next, you'll review the property settings for the Position field in the tblEmployeeCopy table to verify they are correct.

To view the property settings for the Position field:

1. Switch to Design view, and then click the Field Name box for the Position field to display its properties. See Figure 12–25.

Figure 12–25 Property settings for the Position field

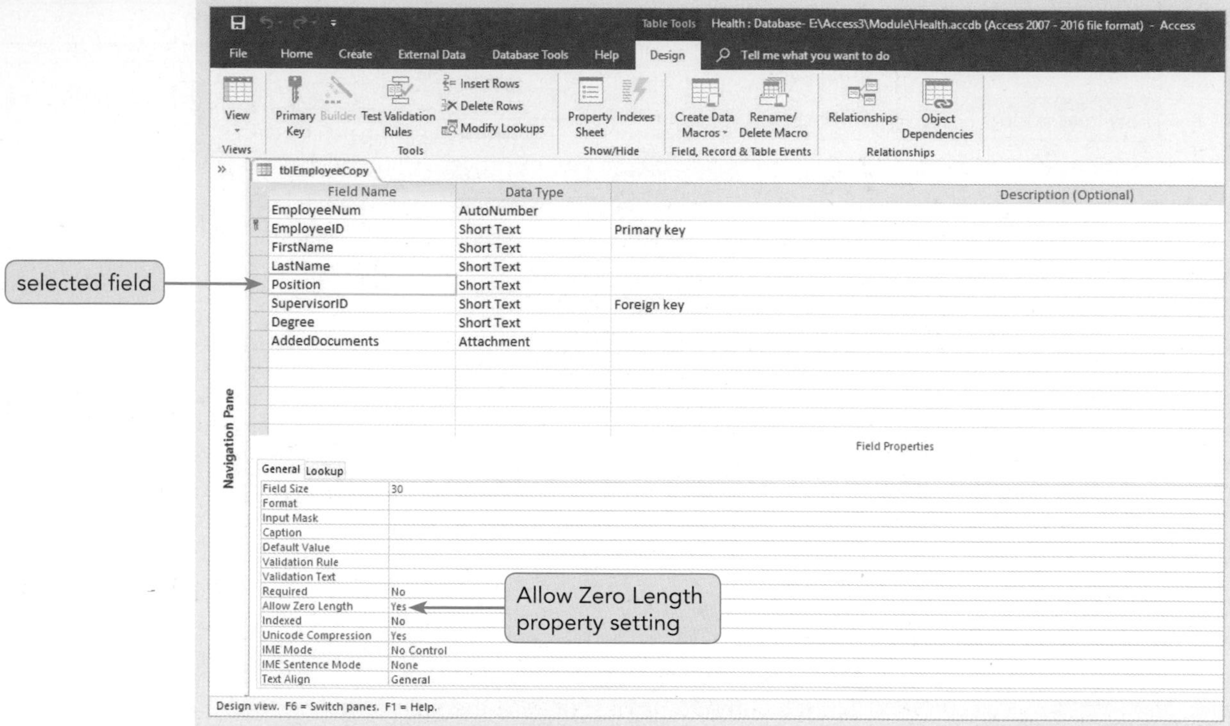
selected field
Allow Zero Length property setting
Table Tools Health : Database- E:\Access3\Module\Health.accdb (Access 2007 - 2016 file format) - Access
File
Home
Create
External Data
Database Tools
Help
Design
Tell me what you want to do
View
Primary Key
Builder
Test Validation Rules
Insert Rows
Delete Rows
Modify Lookups
Property Sheet
Indexes
Create Data Macros
Rename/ Delete Macro
Relationships
Object Dependencies
Views
Tools
Show/Hide
Field, Record & Table Events
Relationships
tblEmployeeCopy
Field Name
Data Type
Description (Optional)
EmployeeNum
AutoNumber
EmployeeID
Short Text
Primary key
FirstName
Short Text
LastName
Short Text
Position
Short Text
SupervisorID
Short Text
Foreign key
Degree
Short Text
AddedDocuments
Attachment
Navigation Pane
Field Properties
General
Lookup
Field Size
30
Format
Input Mask
Caption
Default Value
Validation Rule
Validation Text
Required
No
Allow Zero Length
Yes
Indexed
No
Unicode Compression
Yes
IME Mode
No Control
IME Sentence Mode
None
Text Align
General
Design view. F6 = Switch panes. F1 = Help.

The Position field's Required property is set to No, which means field value entries are optional. The Allow Zero Length property is set to Yes, which is the default setting for Text fields and Memo fields. When a field's **Allow Zero Length property** is set to Yes, the field can store a zero length string value.

2. Save and close the tblEmployeeCopy table.

INSIGHT

Setting the Allow Zero Length Property to No

For a Text or Memo field, there is a difference between how you specify a null field value and a zero length value and how the two values are interpreted. Recall that null means that the field does not contain any value at all and describes a text field or a numeric field that is empty. A numeric field that contains the number zero is not empty. Similarly, a text field that contains a zero length value is not empty. You specify a zero length value in a Text or a Memo field by typing two consecutive double quotation marks (""). (You used this method in the previous session.) You specify a null value in a Text or Memo field by entering a No value in the Allow Zero Length property. When you view a value for a Text or Memo field that has its Allow Zero Length property set to Yes, you can't determine if the field value has been set to null or has a zero length value because both field values look the same—the absence of a visible value.

However, the two values are treated differently. If you run a query to display all records in the table that have a null value in the field using the IsNull function, only the records with null field values appear in the query recordset; the records with zero length values in the field do not appear. And if you change the query to display all records that have a nonnull value, the records with zero length values in the field appear in the query recordset, which often raises questions from users about why those records are displayed. A typical user doesn't understand the distinction between a null value and a zero length value and doesn't need to make this distinction, so you should set the Allow Zero Length property to No for Text and Memo fields.

Donna has a previous version of Access on her home computer and wonders if she can open the Health database on that computer.

Saving an Access Database as a Previous Version

The default file format for databases you create in Access 2019 uses the .accdb filename extension and is referred to as the Access 2007 file format because it was introduced with Access 2007. None of the versions of Access prior to Access 2007 can open a database that has the .accdb filename extension. However, you can save an .accdb database to a format that is compatible with previous versions of Access—specifically, to a format compatible with Access 2000 or to a format compatible with Access 2002-2003; both have the .mdb filename extension. For people who don't have Access 2019, Access 2016, Access 2013, Access 2010, or Access 2007 but do have one of the previous versions of Access, saving the database to a previous version allows them to use the database. Unfortunately, when an Access 2007 file format database uses features such as multivalued and Attachment fields, you cannot save the database in a previous version.

To save an Access 2007 file format database as a previous version, you would complete the following steps (note that you will not actually save the database now):

1. Make sure that the database you want to save is open and all database objects are closed, and that the database does not contain any multivalued fields, Attachment fields, or any other features that are included only in Access 2007 file-formatted databases.
2. Click the File tab to open Backstage view, click Save As in the navigation bar, click Save Database As, and then click Access 2002-2003 Database or click Access 2000 Database, depending on which file format you want to use.
3. Click the Save As button. In the Save As dialog box, navigate to the folder where you want to save the file, enter a name for the database in the File name box, and then click the Save button.

Donna is glad to know it's possible for her to open the database on her home computer. Because the Health database currently uses multivalued and Attachment fields, she'll continue to work on the database only at the office, so you don't need to save it as a previous version now.

Next, Donna asks you to analyze the performance of the Health database.

Analyzing Database Performance with the Performance Analyzer

Donna wants the Health database to respond as quickly as possible to user requests, such as running queries and opening reports. You'll use the Performance Analyzer to check the performance of the Health database. The **Performance Analyzer** is an Access tool that you can use to optimize the performance of an Access database. You select the database objects you want to analyze for performance and then run the Performance Analyzer. You can select tables, queries, forms, reports, and macros either as a group or individually. The Performance Analyzer lists three types of analysis results: Recommendation, Suggestion, and Idea. You can use Access to perform the Recommendation and Suggestion optimizations for you, but you must implement the Idea optimizations. Analysis results include changes such as those related to the storage of fields and the creation of indexes and relationships.

REFERENCE

Using the Performance Analyzer

- Start Access, and open the database you want to analyze.
- On the Database Tools tab, in the Analyze group, click the Analyze Performance button.
- Select the object(s) you want to analyze, and then click OK.
- Select the analysis result(s) you want the Performance Analyzer to complete for you, and then click the Optimize button.
- Note the Idea optimizations, and perform those optimizations, as appropriate.
- Click Close.

You'll use the Performance Analyzer to optimize the performance of the Health database.

To use the Performance Analyzer to optimize the performance of the Health database:

1. Click the **Database Tools** tab, and then in the Analyze group, click the **Analyze Performance** button. The Performance Analyzer dialog box opens. See Figure 12–26.

Figure 12–26 **Performance Analyzer dialog box**

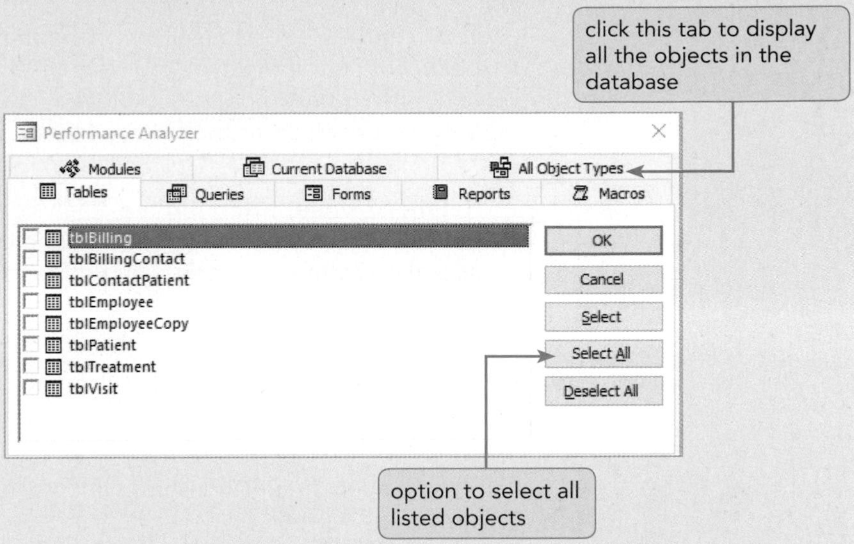
click this tab to display all the objects in the database
Performance Analyzer
Modules
Current Database
All Object Types
Tables
Queries
Forms
Reports
Macros
tblBilling
tblBillingContact
tblContactPatient
tblEmployee
tblEmployeeCopy
tblPatient
tblTreatment
tblVisit
OK
Cancel
Select
Select All
Deselect All
option to select all listed objects

You'll analyze every object in the Health database.

2. Click the **All Object Types** tab, and then click **Select All**. All objects in the Health database are listed on this tab, and all of them are now selected.

3. Click **OK**. The Performance Analyzer analyzes all the objects in the Health database and, after a few moments, displays the analysis results. See Figure 12–27.

Figure 12–27 **Performance Analyzer analysis results**

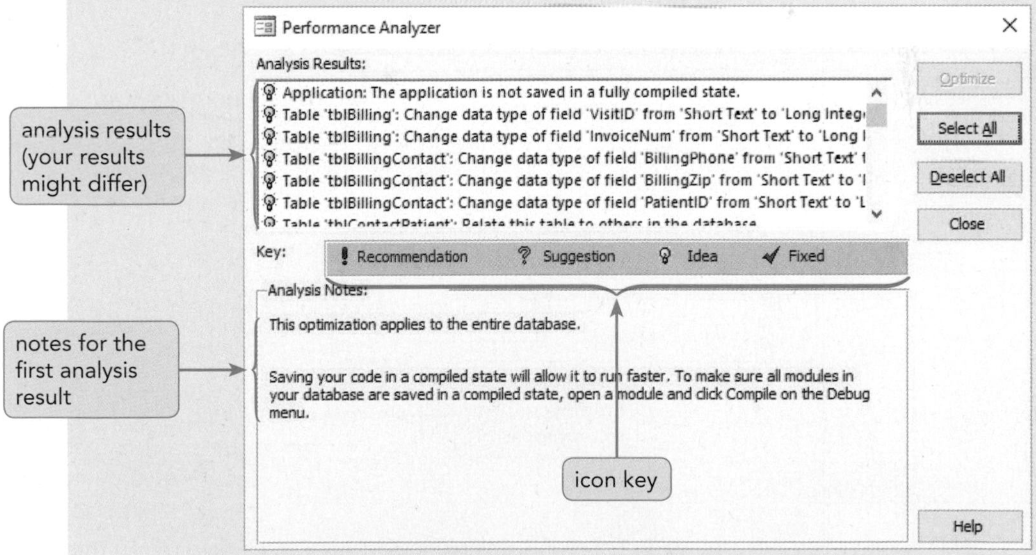
Performance Analyzer
Analysis Results:
Application: The application is not saved in a fully compiled state.
Table 'tblBilling': Change data type of field 'VisitID' from 'Short Text' to 'Long Integ
Table 'tblBilling': Change data type of field 'InvoiceNum' from 'Short Text' to 'Long I
Table 'tblBillingContact': Change data type of field 'BillingPhone' from 'Short Text'
Table 'tblBillingContact': Change data type of field 'BillingZip' from 'Short Text' to 'I
Table 'tblBillingContact': Change data type of field 'PatientID' from 'Short Text' to 'L
Optimize
Select All
Deselect All
Close
Key:
Recommendation
Suggestion
Idea
Fixed
Analysis Notes:
This optimization applies to the entire database.
Saving your code in a compiled state will allow it to run faster. To make sure all modules in your database are saved in a compiled state, open a module and click Compile on the Debug menu.
Help
analysis results (your results might differ)
notes for the first analysis result
icon key

Trouble? The contents of the Analysis Results box on your screen might be different from those shown in Figure 12–27, depending on how you've completed the steps in the previous modules.

The icons that appear to the left of each result indicate the type of analysis result. Most of the analysis results are of the Idea type, which means that you have to implement them yourself. You should consider all the Idea type of analysis results, but more important now are the Recommendation and Suggestion types of analysis results, which the Performance Analyzer can complete for you automatically.

4. Click several entries in the Analysis Results box, and read each entry and its analysis notes.

   You'll let the Performance Analyzer automatically create a relationship between the tblEmployee table and itself because the table has a one-to-many relationship based on the EmployeeID field as the primary key and the SupervisorID field as the foreign key.

5. Scroll the Analysis Results box as necessary, click the **Table 'tblEmployee': Relate to table 'tblEmployee'** analysis result (its icon is a green question mark, indicating it is a Suggestion type of analysis result) to select it, and then click the **Optimize** button. The Performance Analyzer creates a relationship between the tblEmployee table and itself, and the icon for the selected analysis result changes to a checkmark to indicate a "Fixed" status.

6. Click **Close** to close the dialog box.

Next, you'll open the Relationships window to view the new relationship created by the Performance Analyzer.

To view the relationship created by the Performance Analyzer:

1. Click the **Database Tools** tab, and then in the Relationships group, click the **Relationships** button to open the Relationships window. See Figure 12–28.

Figure 12–28 tblEmployee table one-to-many relationship

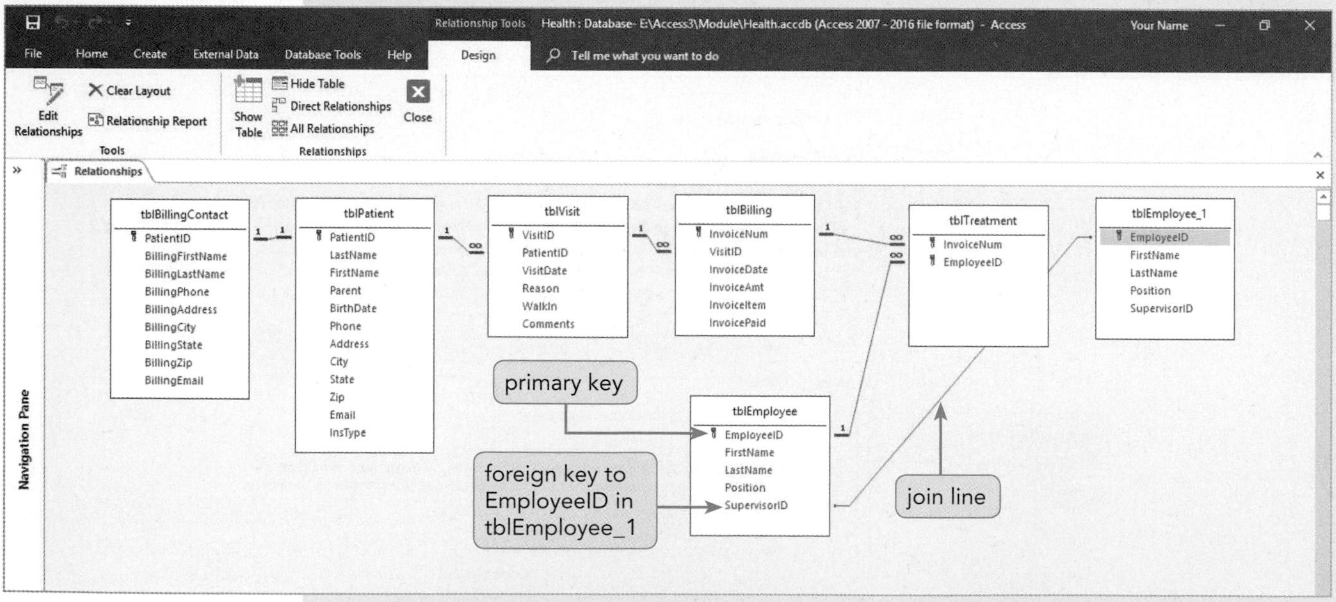
primary key
foreign key to EmployeeID in tblEmployee_1
join line
tblBillingContact
tblPatient
tblVisit
tblBilling
tblTreatment
tblEmployee_1
tblEmployee
Relationships
Navigation Pane

Trouble? The field lists in the Relationships window might be in different positions from those shown in Figure 12–28. This difference causes no problems.

The Performance Analyzer added a second copy of the tblEmployee table (named tblEmployee_1) and a join line between the tblEmployee and tblEmployee_1 tables to the Relationships window. The join line connects the primary table (tblEmployee_1) to the related table (tblEmployee) using the

EmployeeID field as the primary key and the SupervisorID field as the foreign key. You'll use the Edit Relationships dialog box to view the join properties for the relationship.

2. Right-click the join line between the tblEmployee_1 and tblEmployee tables, and then click **Edit Relationship** on the shortcut menu to open the Edit Relationships dialog box. See Figure 12–29.

Figure 12–29 **Edit Relationships dialog box for the new relationship**

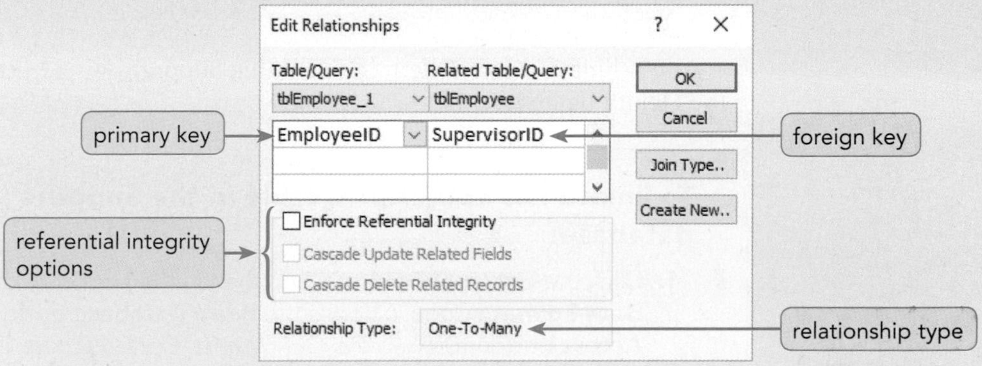
Edit Relationships
Table/Query:
Related Table/Query:
tblEmployee_1
tblEmployee
EmployeeID
SupervisorID
OK
Cancel
Join Type..
Create New..
Enforce Referential Integrity
Cascade Update Related Fields
Cascade Delete Related Records
Relationship Type:
One-To-Many
primary key
foreign key
referential integrity options
relationship type

The referential integrity options are not selected, so you'll select them now for the new one-to-many relationship to show this as a one-to-many relationship in the Relationship window.

3. Click the **Enforce Referential Integrity** check box, click the **Cascade Update Related Fields** check box, and then click **OK** to close the dialog box.

4. Close the Relationships window, and then click **Yes**, if necessary, to save your changes.

Donna also has the responsibility at Lakewood Community Health Services for maintaining a separate database named Support_AC_12_Referral.accdb in which she stores information about patients who have been referred by other physicians but who have not yet contacted the Community Health Services. Donna wants to be able to retrieve the data in the tblReferral table in the Support_AC_12_Referral database from within the Health database. To provide Donna with access to this table, you'll create a link to the tblReferral table in the Health database.

Linking Tables between Databases

A **linked table** is a table that is stored in a separate database file from the open database and that can be updated from the open database. You can retrieve and update (add, change, and delete) records in a linked table, but you can't change its structure.

You'll provide Donna and other users of the Health database with access to the tblReferral table by using a linked table in the Health database. From the Health database, you'll be able to update the tblReferral table as a linked table, but you won't be able to change its structure. However, from the Support_AC_12_Referral database, Donna will be able to update the tblReferral table *and* change its structure.

REFERENCE

Linking to a Table in Another Access Database

- Click the External Data tab.
- In the Import & Link group, click the Access button to open the Get External Data - Access Database dialog box.
- Click the "Link to the data source by creating a linked table" option button.
- Click Browse to open the File Open dialog box, select the folder and file containing the linked data, and then click Open.
- Click OK, select the table(s) in the Link Tables dialog box, and then click OK.

You'll link to the tblReferral table in the Support_AC_12_Referral database from the Health database.

To link to the tblReferral table in the Support_AC_12_Referral database:

1. Click the **External Data** tab, and then in the Import & Link group click the **New Data Source** button. Choose the **From Database** option, and then click the **Access** button to open the Get External Data - Access Database dialog box.
2. Click the **Link to the data source by creating a linked table** option button, and then click the **Browse** button to open the File Open dialog box.
3. Navigate to the **Access3 > Module** folder, click **Support_AC_12_Referral .accdb**, and then click **Open** to close the File Open dialog box and return to the Get External Data - Access Database dialog box. The path and file you selected now appear in the File name box.
4. Click **OK**. The Link Tables dialog box opens. See Figure 12–30.

Figure 12–30 Link Tables dialog box

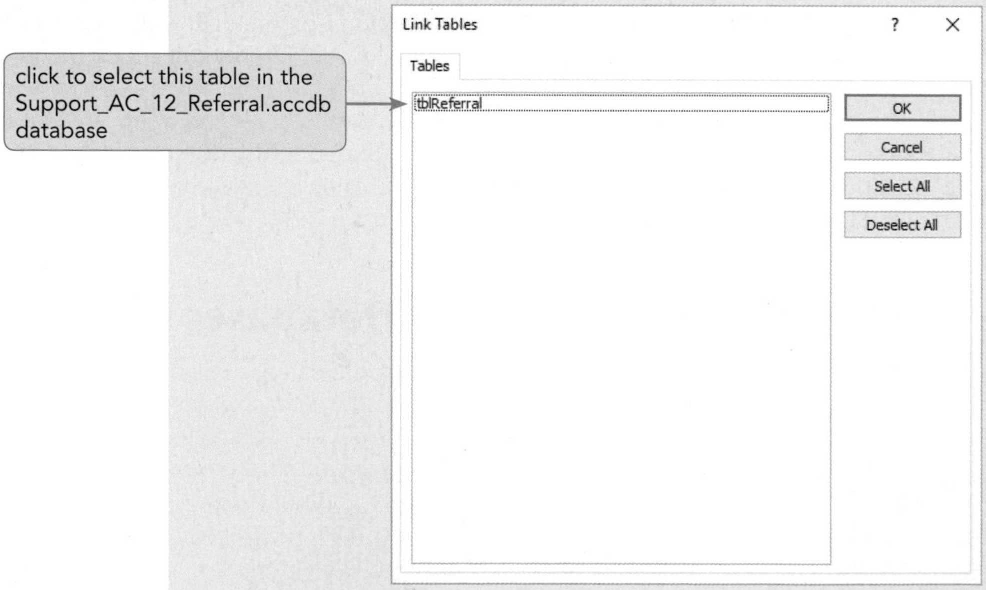
click to select this table in the Support_AC_12_Referral.accdb database
Link Tables
?
Tables
tblReferral
OK
Cancel
Select All
Deselect All

5. Click **tblReferral** in the Tables box, and then click **OK**. The Link Tables dialog box closes, and you return to the Access window. A small blue arrow appears to the left of the tblReferral table icon in the Navigation Pane, identifying the tblReferral table as a linked table.

Donna will be reorganizing the company network folders soon and might move the Support_AC_12_Referral database to a different folder. She asks if moving the Support_AC_12_Referral database would cause a problem for the linked tblReferral table. You'll use the Linked Table Manager to handle this situation. The **Linked Table Manager** is an Access tool you use to change the filename or drive location for linked tables in an Access database. When you use Access to link to data in another file, the file's location (drive, folder, and filename) is stored in the database, and this stored location is used to connect to the linked data. If you change the file's location, you can use the Linked Table Manager to update the stored file location.

REFERENCE

Updating Linked Tables

- In the Navigation Pane, right-click the linked table name, and then click Linked Table Manager on the shortcut menu; or on the External Data tab, in the Import & Link group, click the Linked Table Manager button.
- In the Linked Table Manager dialog box, click the check box(es) for the linked table(s) you want to update, and then click OK.
- In the Select New Location dialog box, navigate to the linked table location, click the filename, and then click Open.
- Click OK, and then close the Linked Table Manager dialog box.

Next, you'll move the Support_AC_12_Referral database to a different folder, and then you'll use the Linked Table Manager to update the link to the tblReferral table in the Health database.

To move the Support_AC_12_Referral database and update the link to the tblReferral table:

1. Use Windows File Explorer to move the Support_AC_12_Referral.accdb database from the Access3 > Module folder to the Access3 folder, and then switch back to Access.
2. In the Navigation Pane, right-click **tblReferral** to open the shortcut menu, and then click **Linked Table Manager**. The Linked Table Manager dialog box opens. See Figure 12–31.

Figure 12–31 **Linked Table Manager dialog box**

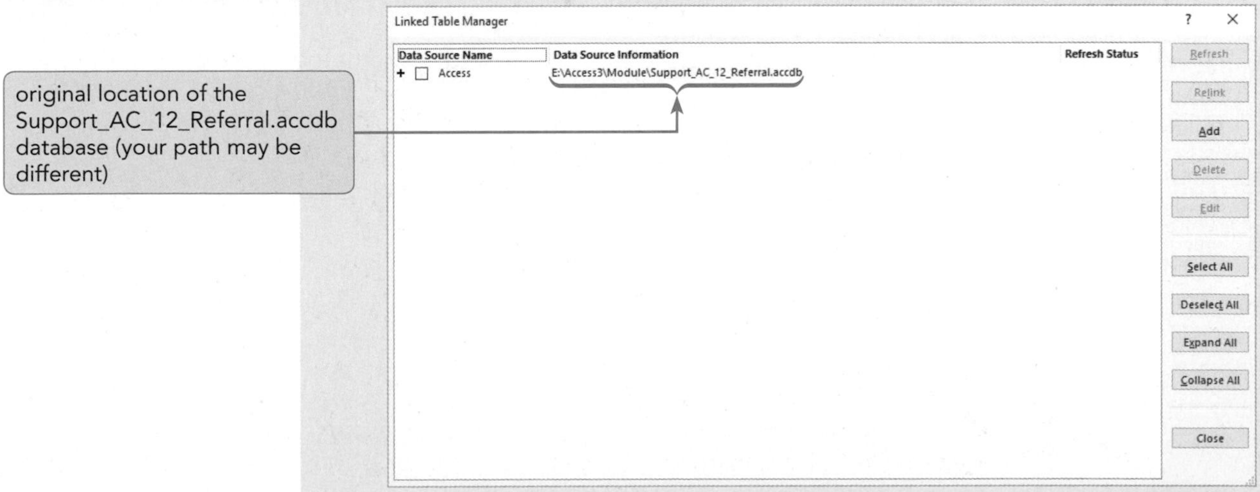
original location of the Support_AC_12_Referral.accdb database (your path may be different)
Linked Table Manager
? X
Data Source Name
Data Source Information
Refresh Status
+ Access
E:\Access3\Module\Support_AC_12_Referral.accdb
Refresh
Relink
Add
Delete
Edit
Select All
Deselect All
Expand All
Collapse All
Close

The tblReferral table is the only linked table, so it's the only table listed. The Access3 > Module folder provided with your Data Files, which is the original location of the Support_AC_12_Referral.accdb database, is listed as the current location for the tblReferral table.

3. Click **Select All**, and then click **Relink**. The Select New Location of Access dialog box opens.
4. Navigate to the **Access3** folder, click **Support_AC_12_Referral.accdb** in the file list, and then click **OK**.
5. A Relink tblReferral dialog box appears and asks for the name of the table you want to link. Since tblReferral is already highlighted, as it is the only table, click **OK** to close the dialog box. The Linked Table Manager dialog box now displays the Access3 folder as the current location of the linked tblReferral table.
6. Close the Linked Table Manager dialog box.

Next, you'll open the tblReferral table to update it as a linked table from the new location.

To update the tblReferral table and view its design in the Health database:

1. Open the **tblReferral** table in Datasheet view, and then close the Navigation Pane. The tblReferral table datasheet displays four records. First, you'll add a new record to the tblReferral table.
2. Click the **New (blank) record** button, type **15005** in the Patient ID column, press **TAB**, type **Suzanne** in the First Name column, press **TAB**, type **Miller** in the Last Name column, press **TAB**, type **470-555-1907** in the Phone column, press **TAB**, type **1234 Jasper Ct** in the Address column, press **TAB**, type **Atlanta** in the City column, press **TAB**, type **GA** in the State column, press **TAB**, type **30305** in the Zip column, press **TAB**, type **s.miller21@ example.com** in the Email Address column, and then press **TAB**.

   Next, you'll switch to Design view to verify that you can't change the design of the tblReferral table from the Health database.

3. Switch to Design view. A dialog box appears informing you that the tblReferral table is a linked table whose design cannot be modified here, only from the source database. Click **Yes** to open the database anyway. The PatientID field is the current field, and the Help message in the Field Properties section indicates that you can't change the Field Name property value for linked tables. See Figure 12–32.

Figure 12–32 Linked table in Design view

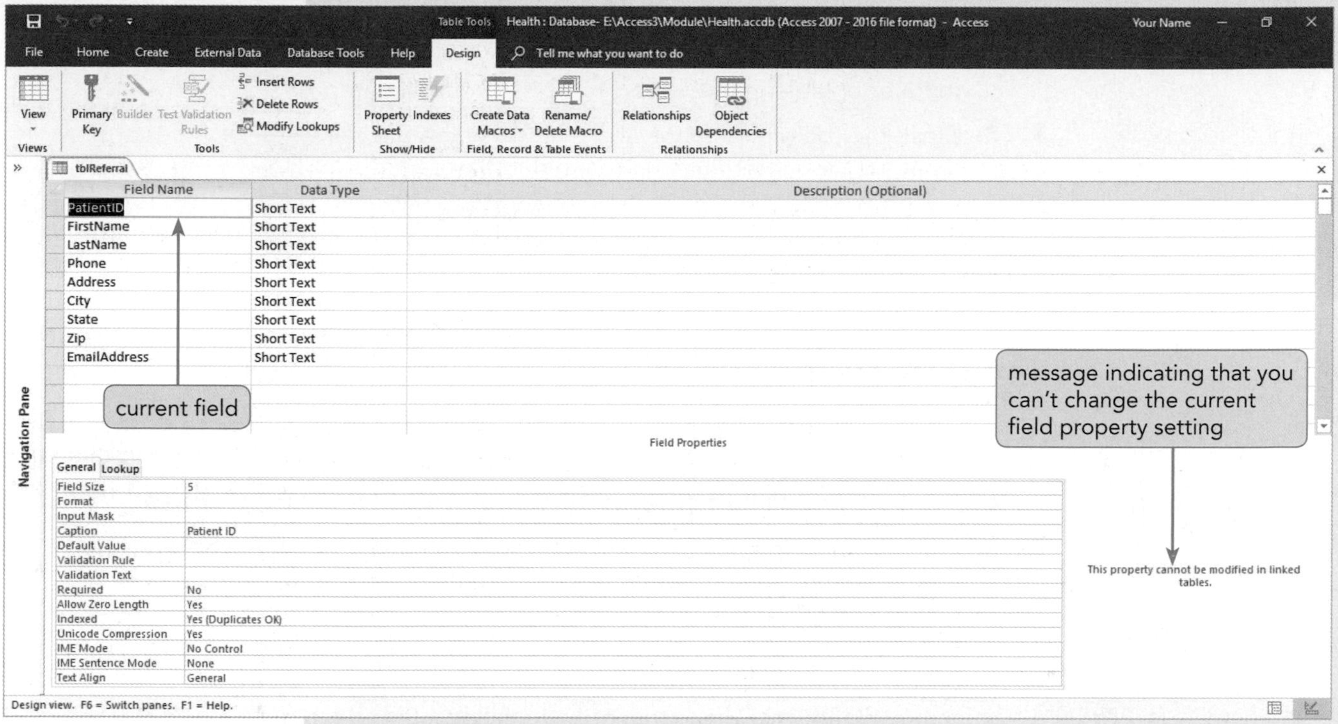
current field
message indicating that you can't change the current field property setting
This property cannot be modified in linked tables.

4. Press **F6** to select the Field Size property in the Field Properties pane. The Help message indicates that you can't change the Field Size property.
5. Press **TAB** to position the insertion point in the Format box. The standard Help message for the Format property appears, which means you can change this field property.
6. Close the table.

Now you'll open the Support_AC_12_Referral database to see the new record in the tblReferral table that you added from the Health database. Then you'll delete that record and view the table in Design view.

To update the tblReferral table and view its design in the Support_AC_12_Referral database:

1. Start another instance of Access, keeping the Health database open as well, and then open the Support_AC_12_Referral.accdb database located in the Access3 > Module folder provided with your Data Files.

   Trouble? If the security warning is displayed below the ribbon, click the Enable Content button.

2. Open the Navigation Pane (if necessary), open the **tblReferral** table in Datasheet view, and then click the **row selector** for record 5. The record for Suzanne Miller, which you added to the tblReferral linked table in the Health database, appears as record 5 in the tblReferral table in the Referral database.
3. On the Home tab, in the Records group, click **Delete**, and then click **Yes** in the message box that opens to delete record 5.

4. Switch to Design view. Because the tblReferral table is not a linked table in the Support_AC_12_Referral database (its own database), the Help message in the Field Properties pane does not warn you that you can't change the Field Name property. You can make any design changes you want to the tblReferral table in the Support_AC_12_Referral database.
5. Close the tblReferral table, and then close the Support_AC_12_Referral database. You return to the Health database.

Donna decides that she'd like to maintain the Support_AC_12_Referral database separately and asks you to delete the linked tblReferral table in the Health database. When you delete the linked tblReferral table in the Health database, you are deleting the *link* to the tblReferral table that exists in the Support_AC_12_Referral database; the tblReferral table will remain in the Support_AC_12_Referral database.

To delete the linked tblReferral table in the Health database:

1. In the Health database, open the Navigation Pane, right-click **tblReferral** in the Navigation Pane to open the shortcut menu, and then click **Delete**. A dialog box asks if you want to remove the link to the tblReferral table. See Figure 12–33.

Figure 12–33 **Dialog box that opens when attempting to delete a linked table**

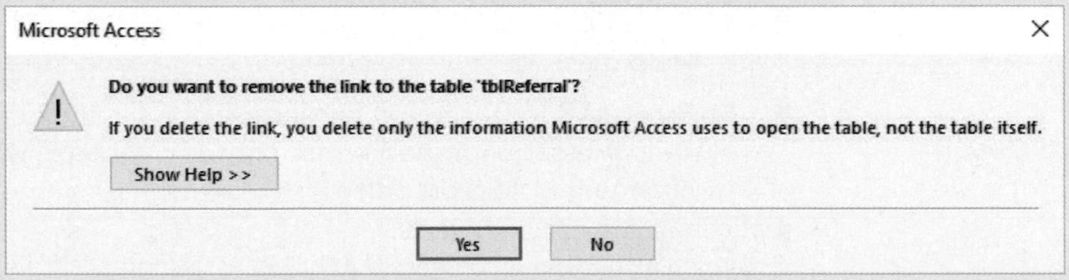
Microsoft Access
Do you want to remove the link to the table 'tblReferral'?
If you delete the link, you delete only the information Microsoft Access uses to open the table, not the table itself.
Show Help >>
Yes
No

The dialog box confirms that you'll delete only the link to the tblReferral table but not the tblReferral table itself in the Referral database.

2. Click **Yes**. The link to the tblReferral table is deleted, and the tblReferral table no longer appears in the Navigation Pane for the Health database.

Next, Donna wants to create several queries for the Health database, but she doesn't want the user interface for other users to be cluttered with queries they won't need to use. She asks if she can have a special user interface to access the data in the Health database. You can accomplish this by splitting the database.

Using the Database Splitter

TIP

Be sure to make a backup before splitting a database.

Users of a particular database might want to customize the user interface to create their own custom versions of the interface, while accessing the same central table data. The **Database Splitter** is an Access tool that splits an Access database into two files: one file contains the tables, and the other file contains the queries, forms, reports, and other database objects. Although a single master copy of the file containing the tables is stored and accessed, users can have their own copies of the other file and add their own queries, reports, and other objects to handle their unique processing needs. Each file created by the Database Splitter is an Access database. The database that contains the tables is called the **back-end database**, and the database that contains the other objects, including the user interface, is called the **front-end database**.

After you split a database, when users open a front-end database, the objects they open use data in the tables in the back-end database. Because the tables in the front-end database are linked tables that are stored in the back-end database, the front-end database contains the physical drive locations of the tables in the back-end database. You can move the front-end database to a different drive location without affecting the physical connections to the back-end database. However, if you move the back-end database to a different drive location, you'll need to use the Linked Table Manager to change the physical drive locations of the back-end database's tables in the front-end database.

People who develop databases and sell them to multiple companies usually split their databases. When a developer delivers a split database, the initial back-end database does not include the company's data, and the initial front-end database is complete as created by the developer. Companies use the front-end database to update their data in the back-end database, but they do not modify the front-end database in any way. Periodically, the database developer improves the front-end database by modifying and adding queries, reports, and other objects without changing the structure of the tables. In other words, the developer changes the front-end database but does not change the back-end database. The developer gives its client companies replacement front-end databases, which continue to work with the back-end database that contains the company's data.

Splitting a database also lets you place the files on different computers. You can place a copy of the front-end database on each user's computer and place the back-end database on a network server that users access through their front-end databases; this arrangement distributes the workload across the network. Finally, as a company grows, it might need a more powerful DBMS such as Oracle, SQL Server, DB2, or MySQL. You could retain the original Access front-end database and replace the Access back-end database with a new non-Access back-end database, which is an easier task than replacing all database objects.

Because splitting an Access database causes minimal disruption to a company's database processing as you periodically enhance the user interface, and because splitting provides greater flexibility for future growth, you should always develop your databases with splitting in mind. The entire process of splitting a database is illustrated in Figure 12–34.

Figure 12–34 Split Access database

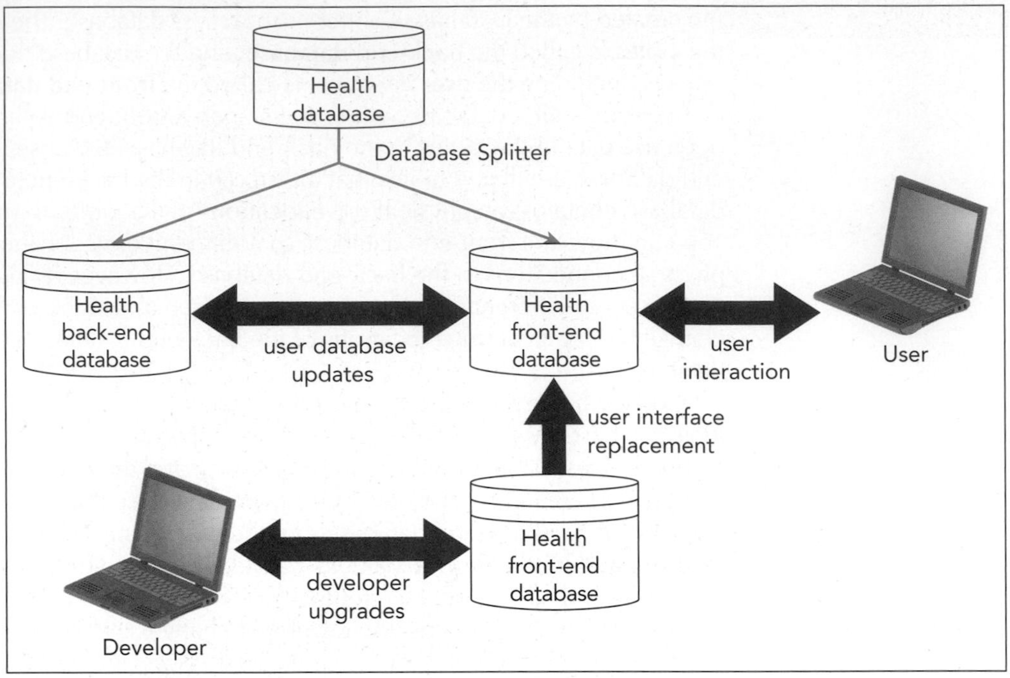
Health
database
Database Splitter
Health
back-end
database
user database
updates
Health
front-end
database
user
interaction
User
user interface
replacement
Health
front-end
database
developer
upgrades
Developer

REFERENCE

Using the Database Splitter

- Make a backup copy of the database that you want to split.
- Start Access and open the database you want to split.
- Click the Database Tools tab, and then in the Move Data group, click the Access Database button to start the Database Splitter Wizard.
- Click the Split Database button, select the drive and folder for the back-end database, type a name for the database in the File name box, and then click the Split button.
- Click OK.

You'll use the Database Splitter to split the Health database into two files. You will make a backup copy of the database before you split the database.

To use the Database Splitter:

1. Make a backup copy of the Health database.
2. Click the **Database Tools** tab, and then in the Move Data group, click **Access Database**. The Database Splitter Wizard opens. See Figure 12–35.

Figure 12–35 Database Splitter Wizard

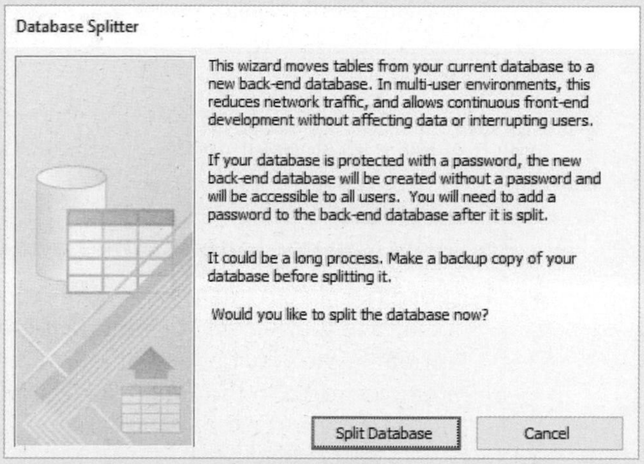
Database Splitter
This wizard moves tables from your current database to a new back-end database. In multi-user environments, this reduces network traffic, and allows continuous front-end development without affecting data or interrupting users.
If your database is protected with a password, the new back-end database will be created without a password and will be accessible to all users. You will need to add a password to the back-end database after it is split.
It could be a long process. Make a backup copy of your database before splitting it.
Would you like to split the database now?
Split Database
Cancel

3. Click **Split Database**. The Create Back-end Database dialog box opens. The back-end database will contain the tables from the Health database. You'll use the default filename (Health_be with the .accdb extension) for the back-end database.
4. Navigate to the **Access3 > Module** folder (if necessary), and then click **Split**. After a few moments, a dialog box informs you that the database was successfully split.
5. Click **OK** to close the dialog boxes, and then scroll up to the top of the Navigation Pane, if necessary. See Figure 12–36.

Figure 12–36 Linked tables in the Health database

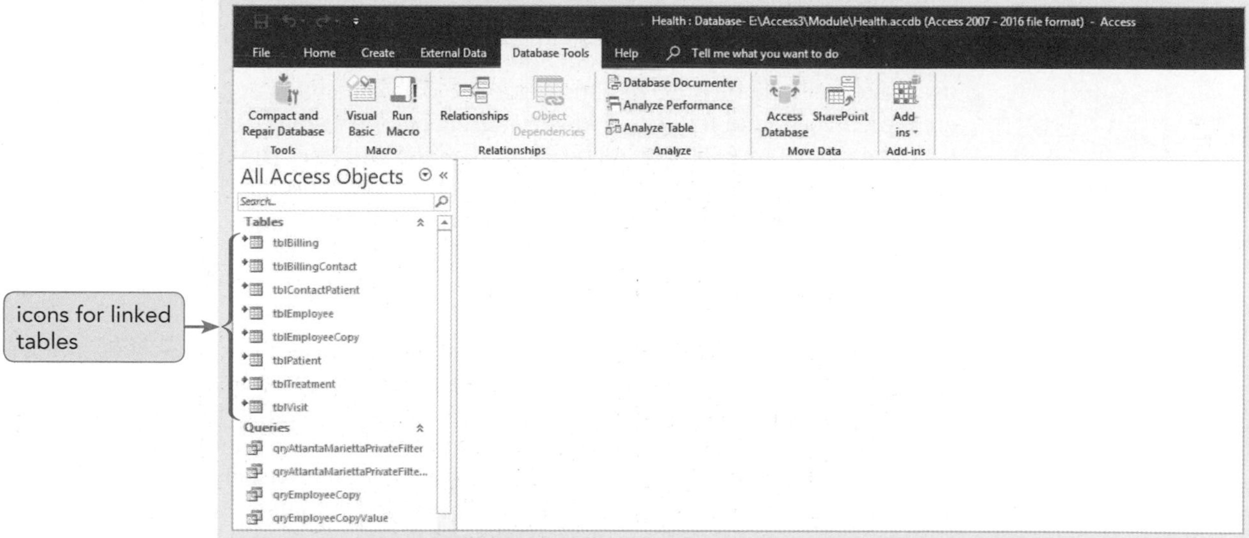
icons for linked tables
Health : Database- E:\Access3\Module\Health.accdb (Access 2007 - 2016 file format) - Access
File
Home
Create
External Data
Database Tools
Help
Tell me what you want to do
Compact and Repair Database
Visual Basic
Run Macro
Relationships
Object Dependencies
Database Documenter
Analyze Performance
Analyze Table
Access Database
SharePoint
Add-ins
Tools
Macro
Relationships
Analyze
Move Data
Add-ins
All Access Objects
Search...
Tables
tblBilling
tblBillingContact
tblContactPatient
tblEmployee
tblEmployeeCopy
tblPatient
tblTreatment
tblVisit
Queries
qryAtlantaMariettaPrivateFilter
qryAtlantaMariettaPrivateFilte...
qryEmployeeCopy
qryEmployeeCopyValue

Each table in the Health database has a blue arrow next to its name indicating that it links to that table in another file. The tables are no longer stored in the Health database; they are stored in the Health_be database file you just created with the Database Splitter. You can use the linked tables as if they were stored in the Health database, except that you cannot change a table's design from the Health database. You have to close the Health database and open the Health_be database to change a table's design.

6. Scroll down the Navigation Pane. The queries, forms, reports, macros, and modules you've created appear in the Navigation Pane and are still stored in the Health database.

You'll close the Health database and then open the Health_be database to verify which objects are stored in the back-end database.

To verify the contents of the back-end database:

1. Close the Health database, and then open the **Health_be.accdb** database located in the Access3 > Module folder. The tables from the Health database appear in the Navigation Pane with their usual icons, indicating the tables are now stored in the Health_be database. No other objects exist in the Health_be database.
2. Open the **tblBilling** table in Design view. You can modify the design of the tables in the Health_be database because they are stored in that database; they are not linked from another database as they are in the Health database.
3. Close the tblBilling table, close the Health_be database, and then open the Health database.

Securing an Access Database

Security refers to the protection of a database against unauthorized access, either intentional or accidental. Access provides a unique approach to securing a database by allowing the user to set a password that is used as a key to encrypt the database.

Encryption translates the data in a database to a scrambled format that's indecipherable to another program and stores it in an encrypted format. If unauthorized users attempt to bypass Access and get to the data directly, they will see only the encrypted version of the data. However, users accessing the data using Access and who have the password will have no problem working with the data. When a user stores or modifies data in an encrypted database, Access encrypts the data before updating the database. Once you've encrypted a database, you can use Access to decrypt it. **Decrypting** a database reverses the encryption. Before a user retrieves encrypted data using Access, the data will be decrypted and presented to the user in the normal format.

To prevent access to a database by an unauthorized user through Access, you can assign a password to the database. A **password** is a string of characters assigned to a database that users must enter before they can open the database. As long as the password is known only to authorized users of the database, unauthorized access to the database is prevented. You should use a password that's easily remembered by authorized users but is not obvious or easily guessed by others.

Access provides a single method to encrypt a database and set a password at the same time.

PROSKILLS

Decision Making: Determining When to Encrypt Data Using a Password

You probably are familiar with setting a password and using it to unlock a cell phone or to sign into your email or another device or software application. In these cases, the password acts as an authorization for you to use the device or software. Some software applications use a password for more than simply opening a file. Access uses the password to actually encrypt the data. The password itself isn't stored anywhere. Instead, the password is used as part of a mathematical formula to encrypt the data. When a user tries to open an encrypted file, the user is prompted to provide a password, and attempts to open the file. If the entered password is correct, the password is used to decrypt the data and open the file. If the password is incorrect, the data is not readable, and, therefore, the file will not open.

Because the password itself isn't stored anywhere and the data is actually encrypted, the contents of the database cannot be recovered if a user forgets a password. This is a security feature and also a potential problem if you are concerned about losing the password. Unlike your cell phone, which can be reset and still used if the password is lost, an encrypted Access file cannot be used if the password is lost.

If the data isn't sensitive, it's not as important to encrypt the data with a password. An encrypted Access database provides security for data and should be considered when the data it contains is sensitive, such as credit card information or private health record information. If the database is accessible only from a desktop computer in a secured, locked office, that may be enough security, and it may not be necessary to add encryption.

If you've decided to set a password, therefore encrypting your database, keep in mind that passwords are more secure when they consist of a mixture of numbers, symbols, and both lowercase and uppercase letters.

Access has some built-in security so that users cannot accidentally change data. When you open a database from the Open dialog box in Access, the default setting is for **shared access**; that is, two or more users can open and use the same database at the same time. However, if you want to set a password for encrypting the database, you first need to open the database with exclusive access. You do this by clicking the Open arrow in the Open dialog box and selecting Open Exclusive on the menu that opens. When you open an Access database with **exclusive access**, you prevent multiple users from opening and using the database at the same time. You must open the database with exclusive access in order to set a password, so that you can guarantee that only one copy of the database is open when you set the password.

If you want someone to be able to view the data without changing it, you can open a database as a read-only file, by selecting the Open Read-Only option from the Open menu in the Open dialog box. **Open Read-Only** includes any database action that does not involve updating the database, such as running queries (but not action queries) and viewing table records. Actions that are prohibited when you open a database as read-only (because they involve updating the database) include changing the database design and updating table records. The other two open options on the Open menu open the selected database with exclusive access for reading and updating (Open Exclusive) or for reading only (Open Exclusive Read-Only).

When multiple users update the database at the same time, row-level locking is enabled so that one user can't change the row content while another user is viewing it. **Locking** denies access by other users to data while one user's updates are processed in the database. **Row-level locking** denies access by other users to the table rows one user is in the process of updating; other users can update the database simultaneously as long as the rows they need to update are not being updated by other users at the same time.

INSIGHT

Setting and Removing Password Encryption

In order to set a password, you first open an Access database file with exclusive access to ensure no other users are viewing or manipulating the data when you add or remove the password. After you open the file with exclusive access, you can open Backstage view to access the Encrypt with Password button. If you decide to apply encryption, you are prompted to type the password twice. This is a security feature to ensure that you did not make a mistake the first time you type the password. Both password entries must be identical in order to set the password encryption. To remove password encryption, you click the Decrypt Database button in Backstage view. Doing so cancels the password protection for the database and also decrypts the database.

Donna is pleased with the changes you have made. As a final enhancement to the user interface, she asks you to set Access to open the navigation form you created in a previous module automatically when a user opens the Health database.

Setting the Database Startup Options

TIP

To bypass the startup options that you set, press and hold SHIFT when you open the database or after entering the password in an encrypted database.

In Access you can specify certain actions, called **startup options**, that take place when a database opens. For example, you can specify the name that appears in the Access window title bar, prevent users from using the Navigation Pane, or specify a form that is automatically opened when a user opens a database.

Donna wants Access to automatically display the navigation form you created in a previous module when users open the Health database. Users can then avoid having to use the Navigation Pane to access the navigation form.

REFERENCE

Setting the Database Startup Options

- Open the database, and then click the File tab to open Backstage view.
- Click Options in the navigation bar to open the Access Options dialog box.
- In the left pane, click Current Database.
- Set the database startup options in the right pane, and then click OK to have these options take effect the next time the database is opened.

The Session 12.2 Visual Overview identifies the database startup options Donna wants you to set for the Health database. In addition, you'll disable the **Enable error checking option**, which checks for design errors in forms and reports and alerts you to errors by displaying the Error Checking Options button. Disabling the Enable error checking option will suppress the display of the triangle-shaped error indicators that appear in the upper-right or upper-left corner of a control when a potential error occurs. Unlike all the other options, which appear on the Current Database page in the Access Options dialog box, the Enable error checking option appears on the Object Designers page in the Access Options dialog box, and disabling this option will affect all databases you open.

You'll finish developing the Health database by setting the database startup options.

To set the database startup options in the Health database:

1. Click the **File** tab to open Backstage view, and then in the navigation bar, click **Options** to open the Access Options dialog box.
2. In the left pane of the dialog box, click **Current Database** to display the list of options for the current database.
3. In the Application Title box, type **Health Release 1**, click the **Display Form** arrow, and then click **frmNavigation**. This sets the title in the Access title bar and sets the frmNavigation form as the initial form that loads when the Health database is opened.
4. Scrolling as necessary, click the following check boxes to disable (uncheck) the options:

   Use Access Special Keys

   Enable Layout View

   Enable design changes for tables in Datasheet view

   Display Navigation Pane

   Allow Full Menus

   Allow Default Shortcut Menus

   Track name AutoCorrect info
5. Compare your Access Options dialog box to the Session 12.2 Visual Overview.
6. In the left pane of the Access Options dialog box, click **Object Designers** to display the list of options for creating and modifying database objects, and then scroll to the bottom of the dialog box.
7. If necessary, click the **Enable error checking** check box to clear it and disable all error checking options. See Figure 12–37.

   Trouble? If the Error checking check box does not contain a checkmark, skip Step 7.

Figure 12–37 Error checking options in the Access Options dialog box

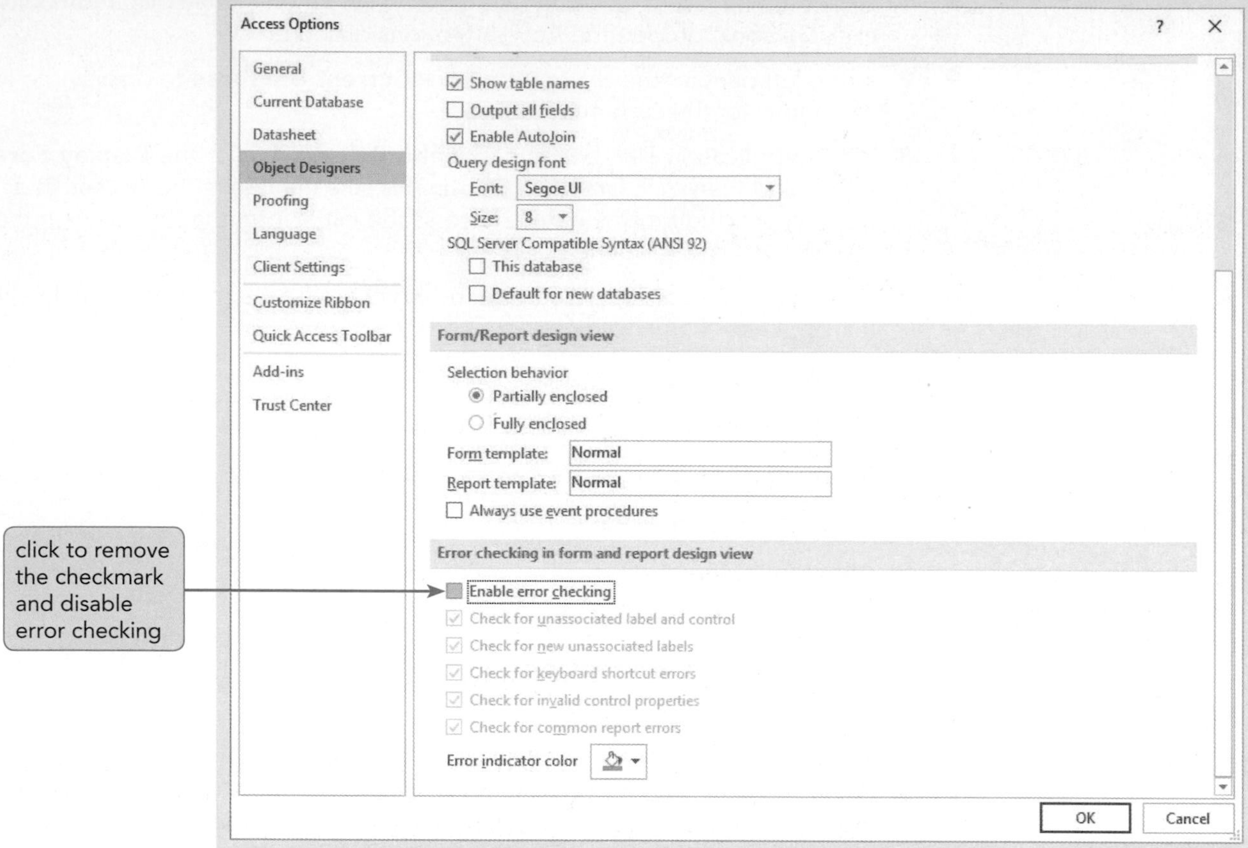
Access Options
General
Current Database
Datasheet
Object Designers
Proofing
Language
Client Settings
Customize Ribbon
Quick Access Toolbar
Add-ins
Trust Center
Show table names
Output all fields
Enable AutoJoin
Query design font
Font: Segoe UI
Size: 8
SQL Server Compatible Syntax (ANSI 92)
This database
Default for new databases
Form/Report design view
Selection behavior
Partially enclosed
Fully enclosed
Form template: Normal
Report template: Normal
Always use event procedures
Error checking in form and report design view
Enable error checking
Check for unassociated label and control
Check for new unassociated labels
Check for keyboard shortcut errors
Check for invalid control properties
Check for common report errors
Error indicator color
OK
Cancel
click to remove the checkmark and disable error checking

8. Click **OK** to close the Access Options dialog box. A dialog box informs you that you must close and reopen the Health database for the options you selected to take effect.
9. Click **OK** to close the dialog box.

To test the database startup options you have set, you need to close and reopen the Health database.

To test the database startup options:

1. Click the **File** tab to open Backstage view, and then click **Close** in the navigation bar to close the Health database without exiting Access.
2. Click the **File** tab to open Backstage view again, click **Open** in the navigation bar, and then in the Recent list, click **Health.accdb** to open the Health database. See Figure 12–38.

Figure 12–38 Health database user interface

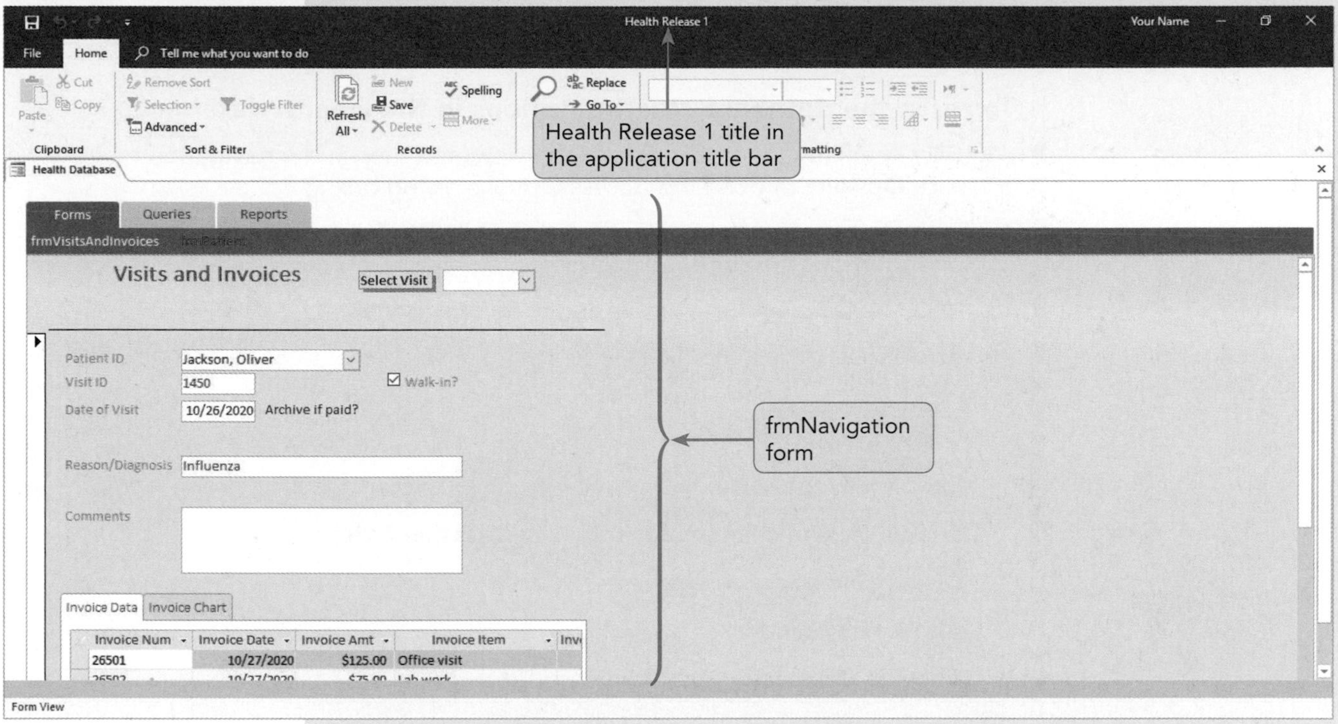
Health Release 1
Health Release 1 title in the application title bar
Health Database
Forms
Queries
Reports
Visits and Invoices
Select Visit
Patient ID
Jackson, Oliver
Visit ID
1450
Walk-in?
Date of Visit
10/26/2020
Archive if paid?
Reason/Diagnosis
Influenza
Comments
Invoice Data
Invoice Chart
Invoice Num
Invoice Date
Invoice Amt
Invoice Item
26501
10/27/2020
$125.00
Office visit
frmNavigation form
Form View

The Health database opens and displays the frmNavigation form. Notice the Navigation Pane is not available on the left side of the window, and the ribbon displays only the File and Home tabs. The name "Health Release 1" appears in the Access window title bar.

3. Click each of the tabs in the navigation form to verify that all features work properly on the Health database user interface.

Donna likes the navigation startup setting but realizes that some of her staff will need access to the ribbon and database objects. One method her staff could use is to press and hold SHIFT when they open the database. You'll open the database using this method to bypass the startup options now.

To bypass the startup options when opening the database:

1. Close the Health database. Doing so also closes Access.
2. Start Access, and then press and hold **SHIFT** while you click **Health.accdb** in the Recent list.

   The Health database opens without the startup options you set. For instance, the Navigation Pane is now accessible on the left side of the window, and you can now use the shortcut keys to close a table, which had been disabled previously in the startup options when Allow Default Shortcut Menus was disabled.
3. Open the Navigation Pane, open the **tblEmployee** table in Datasheet view, and then right-click the **tblEmployee** tab to display the shortcut menu.
4. Click **Close** on the shortcut menu to close the tblEmployee table.

Using SHIFT to open the file bypasses the startup options, but Donna thinks this method also defeats the purpose of having startup options. Instead, she would like you to change the database options to fully display the ribbon and enable the database objects again. You'll reset the database startup options.

To reset the database startup options in the Health database:

1. Click the **File** tab to open Backstage view, and then in the navigation bar, click **Options** to open the Access Options dialog box.
2. In the left pane of the dialog box, click **Current Database** to display the list of options for the current database.
3. Click the **Display Form** arrow, and then click **(none)**.
4. Scrolling as necessary, click the following check boxes to enable (check) the properties:

   Use Access Special Keys

   Enable Layout View

   Enable design changes for tables in Datasheet view

   Display Navigation Pane

   Allow Full Menus

   Allow Default Shortcut Menus

   Track name AutoCorrect info

   A dialog box opens that indicates the Track name AutoCorrect info option generates name maps for the database objects and may take several minutes.
5. Click **OK** to accept and close the dialog box.
6. In the left pane of the Access Options dialog box, click **Object Designers** to display the list of options for creating and modifying database objects, and then scroll to the bottom of the dialog box.
7. Click the **Enable error checking** check box to select it and enable all error checking options.
8. Click **OK** to close the Access Options dialog box. A dialog box may inform you that the Health database must close all objects and update dependency Information.
9. Click **Yes** to close the dialog box (if necessary). A dialog box informs you that you must close and reopen the Health database for the changes to take effect.
10. Click **OK** to close the dialog box, and then exit Access.
11. Open the **Health.accdb** database again to verify the ribbon and database objects are displayed.
12. **sam** Close the Health database and exit Access.

INSIGHT

Saving a Database as an ACCDE File

If a database contains VBA code, you can save an ACCDE file version of the database to prevent people from viewing or changing the VBA code. Saving an Access database as an **ACCDE file**, which has the .accde extension instead of the .accdb extension, compiles all VBA modules, removes all editable VBA source code, and compacts the resulting database. The database and its VBA code continue to run as normal, but users cannot view or edit the VBA code. Also, users can't view, modify, or create forms, reports, or modules in Design view, nor can they import or export forms, reports, or modules. Because an ACCDE file limits database design changes to tables and queries, saving a database as an ACCDE file is best suited to a front-end database. You should keep a backup copy of the complete front-end database in case you need to modify the database design. To save a database as an ACCDE file, follow these steps:

1. Open the database you want to save as an ACCDE file.
2. Click the File tab to open Backstage view, click Save As in the navigation bar, and then click Make ACCDE.
3. Click the Save As button to open the Save As dialog box.
4. Type the name for the file in the File name box, navigate to the location where you want to store the file, and then click the Save button.

Your work with the Health database is now complete. Donna is happy with your work and believes the database will fully satisfy the requirements of the clinic.

REVIEW

Session 12.2 Quick Check

1. You can specify sequential numbering or random numbering for a(n) ___ field.
2. What is the Performance Analyzer?
3. When do you use the Linked Table Manager?
4. What is the Database Splitter?
5. ___ refers to the protection of a database against unauthorized access, either intentional or accidental.
6. What is a startup option?

PRACTICE

Review Assignments

Data Files needed for the Review Assignments: Product.accdb *(cont. from previous module)*, Support_AC_12_Ads.accdb, Support_AC_12_Autoclave_Specification_Sheet.pdf, and Support_AC_12_Autoclave.xlsx

Donna asks you to complete your work with the user interface for the Product database. To meet this request, complete the following steps:

1. Open the **Product** database you worked with in the previous three modules.
2. Open the **tblProduct** table datasheet, use an AutoFilter to filter records using the TempControlled field for values of Yes and Sterile field for values of Yes, and then save and close the table.
3. Use Filter By Form with the tblSupplier table to select all records in which the state is FL or SC and the category is Supplies. Apply the filter, save the filter as a query named **qryStateSuppliesFilter**, clear all filters, and then close the table.
4. Create a query named **qryProductSubquery** that selects the SupplierID field from the tblProduct table for all products that weigh 50 pounds or more. (*Hint*: Do not show the Weight field.) Switch to SQL view, copy the SQL code, and save the qryProductSubquery query.
5. Create a new query in SQL view. Paste the SQL code that you copied in the previous step from qryProductSubquery, and add code that uses the existing code as a subquery and selects all fields from the tblInvoice table where the SupplierID is in the tblInvoice table. Run the query, save the query as **qryProductSubqueryInvoice**, and then close the query.
6. Add a multivalued field to the end of the **tblInvoice** table, defining permitted values of **Courier**, **Email**, **Fax**, and **USPS**, and naming the field **Transmitted**. Save the table, and then add the following values to the field in the table datasheet: for record 4—Email and USPS, for record 8—Courier, and for record 12—Fax and USPS. Close the table.
7. Use the Simple Query Wizard to create a query named **qryInvoiceValue** that displays all fields from the tblInvoice table; for the Transmitted field, display only the version of the field that uses the Value property, and change its Caption property setting to **Transmitted**. Save and close the query.
8. Add an Attachment field named **ProductFiles** to the end of the tblProduct table, using a Caption property setting of **Product Files**. Attach the files **Support_AC_12_Autoclave_Specification_Sheet.pdf** and **Support_AC_12_Autoclave.xlsx** to the ProductFiles field for record 3 (Product ID AU490 - Autoclave) in the tblProduct table, and then close the table.
9. Add an AutoNumber field named **ProductNum** to the beginning of the tblProductSpecialEnviron table, using a Caption property setting of **Product Num** and a New Values property setting of Random. View the table in Datasheet view to see the random numbers. Resize the Product Num column to its best fit. Save and close the table.
10. Use the Performance Analyzer to analyze the entire Product database, but do not implement any of the analysis results. How many analysis results of the Recommendation type did the Performance Analyzer find? Of the Suggestion type? Of the Idea type? If requested, record the answers in a Word document, and submit it to your instructor. Close the Performance Analyzer dialog box.
11. Use Windows File Explorer to move the **Support_AC_12_Ads.accdb** database from the Access3 > Review folder to the Access3 folder. In the Product database, link to the tblAd table, and then move the **Support_AC_12_Ads.accdb** database to the Access3 > Review folder. Use the Linked Table Manager to update the link to the tblAd table. Open the tblAd table in Datasheet view, and then add a new record to the table: Ad Num **7**, Ad Date **07/12/2020**, Ad Cost **$250.00**, and Placed **Web ad.**
12. Close the Product database without exiting Access, create a copy of the Product database in the Access3 > Review folder, and then rename the copy as **NP_AC_12_Sellers**. Open the **Product** database in the Access3 > Review folder, and then use the Database Splitter to split the Product database. Use the default name for the back-end database, and store it in the Access3 > Review folder.
13. Set the same database startup options for the Product database that you set in Module 12 for the Health database, using a value of **Vendor for Lakewood Community Health Services** for the Application Title option. Test the new startup options and then reset them as you did with the Health database; however, keep the new Application Title.
14. Compact and repair the database, exit Access, open the **Product** database, test all the navigation options, and then close the database.

APPLY

Case Problem 1

Data Files needed for this Case Problem: Instruction.accdb *(cont. from previous module)*, Support_AC_12_Allen.txt, and Support_AC_12_RoomOptions.accdb

Great Giraffe Jeremiah asks you to complete your work with the user interface for the Instruction database. To meet his request, complete the following steps:

1. Open the **Instruction** database you worked with in the previous three modules.
2. Open the tblStudent table datasheet, use an AutoFilter to filter records using the City field for values of Englewood and Littleton, and then save and close the table.
3. Use Filter By Form with the **qryStudentData** query to select all records in which the Last Name is Bailey or Brown. Apply the filter, save the filter as a query named **qryBaileyBrownFilter**, and then close the query.
4. Create a query named **qry40HoursSubquery** that selects the InstanceID field from the tblCourse table for all records that have a value of 40 for HoursPerWeek. (*Hint*: Do not show the HoursPerWeek field.) Switch to SQL view, copy the SQL code, and then save and close the qry40HoursSubquery query.
5. Create a new query in SQL view. Paste the SQL code you copied in the previous step from qry40HoursSubquery, add code that uses the current code as a subquery and selects all fields from the tblRegistration table where the InstanceID is in the tblRegistration table, and then run the query. Save the query as **qry40HoursSubquerySignupID**, and then save and close the query.
6. Add an Attachment field named **StudentAttachment** to the end of the tblStudent table, using a Caption property setting of **Student Attachment**. Cody Allen, one of the students at Great Giraffe, has written a note thanking them for their excellent instruction. The document is stored in the **Support_AC_12_Allen.txt** text file and is located in the Access3 > Case1 folder. Attach the document to the StudentAttachment field for record 2 (Cody Allen record) in the tblStudent table, resize the Student Attachment column to its best fit, and then save and close the table.
7. Add an AutoNumber field named **PlanNum** to the beginning of the tblCityPaymentPlan table, using a Caption property setting of **Plan Num** and a New Values property setting of Random. Specify the PlanNum field as the primary key. Resize the Plan Num column to its best fit in the datasheet, and then save and close the table.
8. Use the Performance Analyzer to analyze the entire Instruction database, but do not implement any of the analysis results. How many analysis results of the Recommendation type did the Performance Analyzer find? Of the Suggestion type? Of the Idea type? If requested, record the answers in a Word document, and submit it to your instructor. Close the Performance Analyzer dialog box.
9. Use Windows File Explorer to move the **Support_AC_12_RoomOptions.accdb** database from the Access3 > Case1 folder to the Access3 folder. Link to the tblRoomOptions table in the Support_AC_12_RoomOptions database located in the Access3 folder. Use Windows File Explorer to move the **Support_AC_12_RoomOptions.accdb** database to the Access3 > Case1 folder, and then use the Linked Table Manager to update the link to the tblRoomOptions table. Open the tblRoomOptions table in Datasheet view, and then add a new record to the table: Room ID **BIT 123A** and Capacity **35**. Save and close the tblRoomOptions table.
10. Close the Instruction database without exiting Access, create a copy of the Instruction database in the Access3 > Case1 folder, and then rename the copy as **NP_AC_12_InProgress**. Open the **Instruction** database in the Access3 > Case1 folder, and then use the Database Splitter to split the Instruction database. Use the default name for the back-end database, and store it in the Access3 > Case1 folder.
11. Set the same database startup options for the Instruction database that you set in Module 12 for the Health database, using a value of **Great Giraffe** for the Application Title option. Test the new startup options and then reset them as you did with the Health database; however, keep the new Application Title.
12. Compact and repair the database, exit Access, open the **Instruction** database, test all the navigation options, and then close the database.

CHALLENGE

Case Problem 2

Data Files needed for this Case Problem: CleanOut.accdb *(cont. from previous module)*, Support_AC_12_BEN36NE_111820.txt, and Support_AC_12_Trucks.accdb

Drain Adopter Tandrea wants you to complete your work with the user interface for the CleanOut database. To meet her request, complete the following steps:

1. Open the **CleanOut** database you worked with in the previous three modules.
2. **Explore** Open the tblSupply table datasheet, and then use an AutoFilter to filter records using the LastOrderDate field for values in the second quarter of a year. (*Hint*: In the Health database in the module, you filtered for November; here you will be filtering for Quarter 2 in the same fashion). Save and close the table.
3. **Explore** Use Filter By Form with the **frmVolunteerMasterData** form to select all records in which the zip is 98225 and the volunteer has not been trained. (*Hint*: Review your options on how to select those volunteers that have not been trained since you do not have a list to choose from.) Apply the filter, save the filter as a query named **qry98225NotTrainedFilter**, and then close the form.
4. **Explore** Create a query named **qrySpecialVolunteersSubquery** that selects the VolunteerID from the tblSpecialVolunteers table. Create a query named **qrySpecialVolunteersData** that contains all fields from the tblVolunteer table for records whose VolunteerID is in the subquery qrySpecialVolunteersSubquery. Use SQL view to create the qrySpecialVolunteersData query. The results should be sorted in descending order by VolunteerID. Save and close the query. (*Hint*: Create the qrySpecialVolunteersSubquery first, copy the SQL code from the subquery to create the new query qrySpecialVolunteersData, and then open the new qrySpecialVolunteersData in Design view to apply the sort order.)
5. Add a multivalued field to the end of the tblSupply table, defining permitted values of **Grounds**, **Roads**, and **Technician**, and naming the field **Areas**. Allow the user to choose more than one area. Save the table, and then add the following values to the field in the table datasheet: for record 1 (Broom01)—Grounds and Roads; for record 2 (Broom04)—Roads; and for record 4 (Gloves01)—Grounds, Roads, and Technician; for record 6 (Rake03)—Grounds. Resize the Areas column to its best fit, and then save and close the table.
6. Use the Simple Query Wizard to create a query named **qrySupplyMultivalued** that displays the SupplyID, Description, Cost, NumberOnHand, LastOrderDate, and Areas from the tblSupply table; for the Areas field, display only the version of the field that displays multiple values in a text box. Resize the Areas column to its best fit, and then save and close the query.
7. Add an Attachment field named **Notes** to the end of the tblDrain table, using a Caption property setting of **Special Notes**. This will be used to supply volunteers with extra information about drains. Attach a file named **Support_AC_12_BEN36NE_111820.txt** to the Notes field in the third record (BEN36NE). This document gives information about the cleaning of the BEN36NE drain on 11/18/2020. Resize the Special Notes column to its best fit, and then save and close the table.
8. **Explore** Add an AutoNumber field named **SpecialNum** to the top of the tblSpecialVolunteers table, using a Caption property setting of **Special Num** and a New Values property setting of Increment. Specify the SpecialNum field as the primary key. Resize the Special Num column to its best fit in the datasheet, and then save and close the table.
9. Use the Performance Analyzer to analyze the entire CleanOut database. How many analysis results of the Recommendation type did the Performance Analyzer find? Of the Suggestion type? Of the Idea type? If requested, record the answers in a Word document, and submit it to your instructor. Notice the analyzer gives ideas that would have you change data types in various tables from the Short Text to Long Integer data type. Think about the consequences of performing this change, noting that when you created the relationships previously, you were careful to associate similar data types with each other. If changed now, you would have to ensure all the necessary data types would be updated to ensure integrity. You will not attempt any modifications at this juncture, so close the Performance Analyzer dialog box.

10. Use Windows File Explorer to move the **Support_AC_12_Trucks.accdb** database from the Access3 > Case2 folder to the Access3 folder. Link to the tblTrucks table in the Support_AC_12_Trucks database located in the Access3 folder. Use Windows File Explorer to move the **Support_AC_12_Trucks.accdb** database to the Access3 > Case2 folder, and then use the Linked Table Manager to update the link to the tblTrucks table. Open the tblTrucks table in Datasheet view, and then add a new record to the table: Truck ID **Truck05**, Type **Standard pickup**, Year **2019**, and Color **Green**. Close the table.

Explore 11. Close the CleanOut database without exiting Access, create a copy of the CleanOut database in the Access3 > Case2 folder, and then rename the copy as **NP_AC_12_CleanStreets**. Open the **CleanOut** database in the Access3 > Case2 folder, and then use the Database Splitter to split the CleanOut database. Use the default name for the back-end database, and store it in the Access3 > Case2 folder.

Explore 12. Set the same database startup options for the CleanOut database that you set in Module 12 for the Health database, using a value of **Drain Adopter Program** for the Application Title property. Test the new startup options; however, do not reset the startup options as you did with the Health database. Close the CleanOut database and open it once again pressing and holding SHIFT to disable the startup options.

13. Compact and repair the database. Notice that once the database is compacted and repaired, the database is opened again and the startup options are again implemented. This will occur each time the database is opened unless you press and hold SHIFT when the database is being opened, or you change the startup options. Close the database.

APPENDIX A

Relational Databases and Database Design

ACCESS

OBJECTIVES

- Learn the characteristics of a table
- Learn about primary, candidate, alternate, composite, and foreign keys
- Study one-to-one, one-to-many, and many-to-many relationships
- Learn to describe tables and relationships with entity-relationship diagrams and with a shorthand method
- Study database integrity constraints for primary keys, referential integrity, and domains
- Learn about determinants, functional dependencies, anomalies, and normalization
- Understand the differences among natural, artificial, and surrogate keys
- Learn about naming conventions

This appendix introduces you to the basics of database design. Before trying to master this material, be sure you understand the following concepts: data, information, field, field value, record, table, relational database, common field, database management system (DBMS), and relational database management system (RDBMS).

STARTING DATA FILES

There are no starting Data Files needed for this appendix.

Tables

A relational database stores its data in tables. A **table** is a two-dimensional structure made up of rows and columns. The terms table, **record** (row), and **field** (column) are the popular names for the more formal terms **relation** (table), **tuple** (row), and **attribute** (column), as shown in Figure A–1.

Figure A–1 **A table (relation) consisting of records and fields**

table name → Employee

field names

EmployeeNum	FirstName	LastName	DeptNum
2173	Barbara	Hennessey	27
4519	Lee	Noordsy	31
8005	Pat	Amidon	27
8112	Chris	Wandzell	24

records (rows or tuples)

fields (columns or attributes)

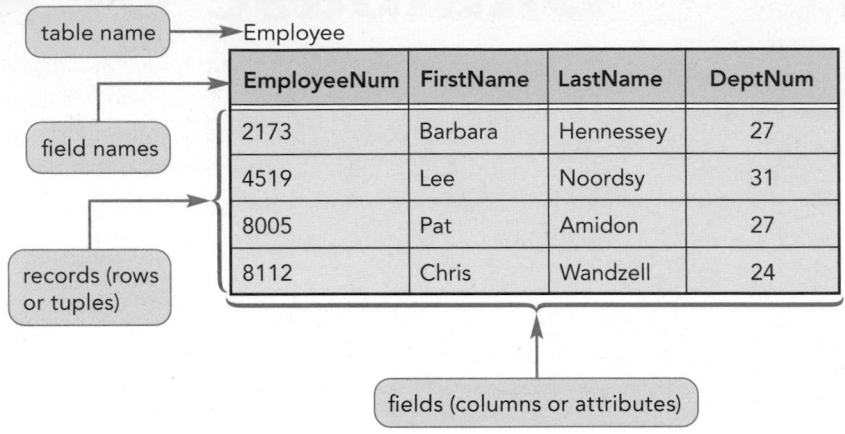

The Employee table shown in Figure A–1 is an example of a relational database table, a two-dimensional structure with the following characteristics:

- Each row is unique. Because no two rows are the same, you can easily locate and update specific data. For example, you can locate the row for EmployeeNum 8005 and change the FirstName value, Pat, the LastName value, Amidon, or the DeptNum value, 27.
- The order of the rows is unimportant. You can add or view rows in any order. For example, you can view the rows in LastName order instead of EmployeeNum order.
- Each table entry contains a single value. At the intersection of each row and column, you cannot have more than one value. For example, each row in Figure A–1 contains one EmployeeNum value, one FirstName value, one LastName value, and one DeptNum value.
- The order of the columns is unimportant. You can add or view columns in any order.
- Each column has a unique name called the **field name**. The field name allows you to access a specific column without needing to know its position within the table.
- Each row in a table describes, or shows the characteristics of, an entity. An **entity** is a person, place, object, event, or idea for which you want to store and process data. For example, EmployeeNum, FirstName, LastName, and DeptNum are characteristics of the employees of a company. The Employee table represents all the employee entities and their characteristics. That is, each row of the Employee table describes a different employee of the company using the characteristics of EmployeeNum, FirstName, LastName, and DeptNum. The Employee table includes only characteristics of employees. Other tables would exist for the company's other entities. For example, a Department table would describe the company's departments and a Position table would describe the company's job positions.

Knowing the characteristics of a table leads directly to a definition of a relational database. A **relational database** is a collection of tables (relations).

Note that this book uses singular table names, such as Employee and Department, but some people use plural table names, such as Employees and Departments. You can use either singular table names or plural table names, as long as you consistently use the style you choose.

Keys

Primary keys ensure that each row in a table is unique. A **primary key** is a column, or a collection of columns, whose values uniquely identify each row in a table. In addition to being *unique*, a primary key must be *minimal* (that is, contain no unnecessary extra columns) and must not change in value. For example, in Figure A–2 the State table contains one record per state and uses the StateAbbrev column as its primary key.

Figure A–2 A table and its keys

alternate keys

primary key

State

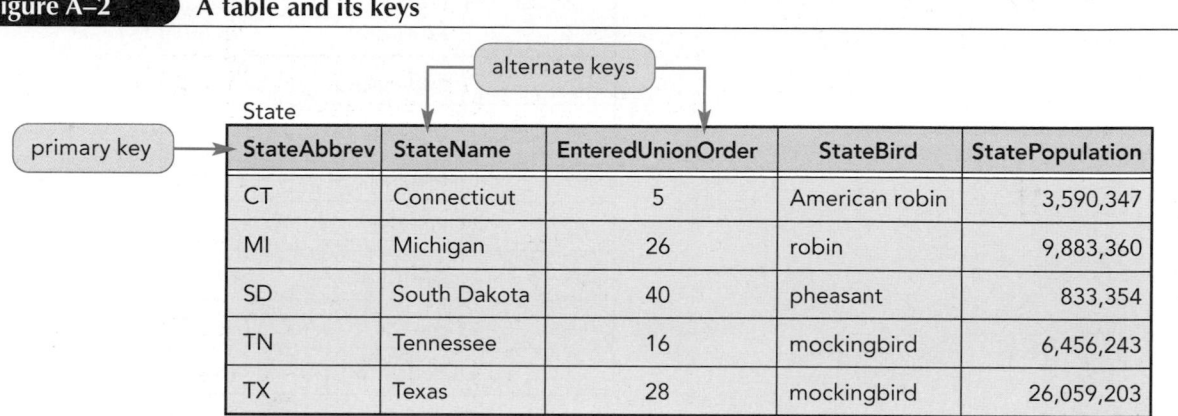

StateAbbrev	StateName	EnteredUnionOrder	StateBird	StatePopulation
CT	Connecticut	5	American robin	3,590,347
MI	Michigan	26	robin	9,883,360
SD	South Dakota	40	pheasant	833,354
TN	Tennessee	16	mockingbird	6,456,243
TX	Texas	28	mockingbird	26,059,203

Could any other column, or collection of columns, be the primary key of the State table?

- Could the StateBird column serve as the primary key? No, because the StateBird column does not have unique values (for example, the mockingbird is the state bird of more than one state).
- Could the StatePopulation column serve as the primary key? No, because the StatePopulation column values change periodically and are not guaranteed to be unique.
- Could the StateAbbrev and StateName columns together serve as the primary key? No, because the combination of these two columns is not minimal. Something less, such as the StateAbbrev column by itself, can serve as the primary key.
- Could the StateName column serve as the primary key? Yes, because the StateName column has unique values. In a similar way, you could select the EnteredUnionOrder column as the primary key for the State table. One column, or a collection of columns, that can serve as a primary key is called a **candidate key**. The candidate keys for the State table are the StateAbbrev column, the StateName column, and the EnteredUnionOrder column. You choose one of the candidate keys to be the primary key, and each remaining candidate key is called an **alternate key**. The StateAbbrev column is the State table's primary key in Figure A–2, so the StateName and EnteredUnionOrder columns become alternate keys in the table.

Figure A–3 shows a City table containing the fields StateAbbrev, CityName, and CityPopulation.

Figure A–3 A table with a composite key

composite primary key

City

StateAbbrev	CityName	CityPopulation
CT	Hartford	124,062
CT	Madison	18,803
CT	Portland	9,551
MI	Lansing	119,128
SD	Madison	6,482
SD	Pierre	13,899
TN	Nashville	569,462
TX	Austin	757,688
TX	Portland	16,490

What is the primary key for the City table? The values for the CityPopulation column periodically change and are not guaranteed to be unique, so the CityPopulation column cannot be the primary key. Because the values for each of the other two columns are not unique, the StateAbbrev column alone cannot be the primary key and neither can the CityName column (for example, there are two cities named Madison and two cities named Portland). The primary key is the combination of the StateAbbrev and CityName columns. Both columns together are needed to identify—uniquely and minimally—each row in the City table. A multiple-column key is called a **composite key** or a **concatenated key**. A multiple-column primary key is called a **composite primary key**.

The StateAbbrev column in the City table is also a foreign key. A **foreign key** is a column, or a collection of columns, in one table in which each column value must match the value of the primary key of some table or must be null. A **null** is the absence of a value in a particular table entry. A null value is not blank, nor zero, nor any other value. You give a null value to a column value when you do not know its value or when a value does not apply. As shown in Figure A–4, the values in the City table's StateAbbrev column match the values in the State table's StateAbbrev column. Thus, the StateAbbrev column, the primary key of the State table, is a foreign key in the City table. Although the field name StateAbbrev is the same in both tables, the names could be different. As a rule, experts use the same name for a field stored in two or more tables to broadcast clearly that they store similar values; however, some exceptions exist.

Figure A–4 **StateAbbrev as a primary key (State table) and a foreign key (City table)**

primary key (State table)

State

StateAbbrev	StateName	EnteredUnionOrder	StateBird	StatePopulation
CT	Connecticut	5	American robin	3,518,288
MI	Michigan	26	robin	9,969,727
SD	South Dakota	40	pheasant	812,383
TN	Tennessee	16	mockingbird	6,296,254
TX	Texas	28	mockingbird	24,782,302

composite primary key (City table)

foreign key

City

StateAbbrev	CityName	CityPopulation
CT	Hartford	124,062
CT	Madison	18,803
CT	Portland	9,551
MI	Lansing	119,128
SD	Madison	6,482
SD	Pierre	13,899
TN	Nashville	596,462
TX	Austin	757,688
TX	Portland	16,490

A **nonkey field** is a field that is not part of the primary key. In the two tables shown in Figure A–4, all fields are nonkey fields except the StateAbbrev field in the State and City tables and the CityName field in the City table. "Key" is an ambiguous word because it can refer to a primary, candidate, alternate, or foreign key. When the word "key" appears alone, however, it means primary key and the definition for a nonkey field consequently makes sense.

Relationships

In a database, a table can be associated with another table in one of three ways: a one-to-many relationship, a many-to-many relationship, or a one-to-one relationship.

One-to-Many Relationship

The Department and Employee tables, shown in Figure A–5, have a one-to-many relationship. A **one-to-many relationship** (abbreviated **1:M** or **1:N**) exists between two tables when each row in the first table (sometimes called the **primary table**) matches many rows in the second table and each row in the second table (sometimes called the **related table**) matches at most one row in the first table. "Many" can mean zero rows, one row, or two or more rows. As Figure A–5 shows, the DeptNum field, which is a foreign key in the Employee table and the primary key in the Department table, is the common field that ties together the rows of the two tables. Each department has many employees; and each employee works in exactly one department or hasn't been assigned to a department, if the DeptNum field value for that employee is null.

Figure A–5 **A one-to-many relationship**

Department

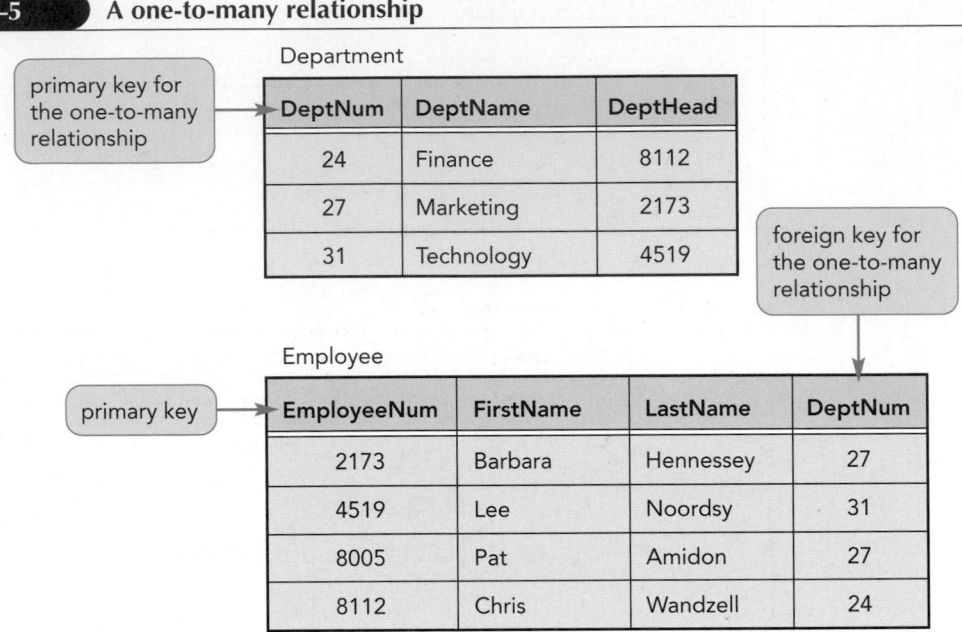

primary key for the one-to-many relationship → DeptNum

DeptNum	DeptName	DeptHead
24	Finance	8112
27	Marketing	2173
31	Technology	4519

foreign key for the one-to-many relationship → DeptNum (Employee)

Employee

primary key → EmployeeNum

EmployeeNum	FirstName	LastName	DeptNum
2173	Barbara	Hennessey	27
4519	Lee	Noordsy	31
8005	Pat	Amidon	27
8112	Chris	Wandzell	24

Many-to-Many Relationship

In Figure A–6, the Employee table (with the EmployeeNum field as its primary key) and the Position table (with the PositionID field as its primary key) have a many-to-many relationship. A **many-to-many relationship** (abbreviated as **M:N**) exists between two tables when each row in the first table matches many rows in the second table and each row in the second table matches many rows in the first table. In a relational database, you must use a third table (often called an **intersection table**, **junction table**, or **link table**) to serve as a bridge between the two many-to-many tables; the third table has the primary keys of the two many-to-many tables as its primary key. The original tables now each have a one-to-many relationship with the new table. The EmployeeNum and PositionID fields represent the primary key of the Employment table that is shown in Figure A–6. The EmployeeNum field, which is a foreign key in the Employment table and the primary key in the Employee table, is the common field that ties together the rows of the Employee and Employment tables. Likewise, the PositionID field is the common field for the Position and Employment tables. Each employee may serve in many different positions within the company over time, and each position in the company will be filled by different employees over time.

Figure A–6 A many-to-many relationship

primary key (Employee table)

Employee

EmployeeNum	FirstName	LastName	DeptNum
2173	Barbara	Hennessey	27
4519	Lee	Noordsy	31
8005	Pat	Amidon	27
8112	Chris	Wandzell	24

primary key (Position table)

Position

PositionID	PositionDesc	PayGrade
1	Director	45
2	Manager	40
3	Analyst	30
4	Clerk	20

composite primary key of the intersection table

foreign keys related to the Employee and Position tables

Employment

EmployeeNum	PositionID	StartDate	EndDate
2173	2	12/14/2016	
4519	1	04/23/2018	
4519	3	11/11/2012	04/22/2018
8005	3	06/05/2017	08/25/2018
8005	4	07/02/2015	06/04/2017
8112	1	12/15/2017	
8112	2	10/04/2016	12/14/2017

One-to-One Relationship

In Figure A–5, recall that there's a one-to-many relationship between the Department table (the primary table) and the Employee table (the related table). Each department has many employees, and each employee works in one department. The DeptNum field in the Employee table serves as a foreign key to connect records in that table to records with matching DeptNum field values in the Department table.

Furthermore, each department has a single employee who serves as the head of the department, and each employee either serves as the head of a department or simply works in a department without being the department head. Therefore, the Department and Employee tables not only have a one-to-many relationship, but these two tables also have a second relationship, a one-to-one relationship. A **one-to-one relationship** (abbreviated **1:1**) exists between two tables when each row in each table has at most one matching row in the other table. As shown in Figure A–7, each DeptHead field value in the Department table represents the employee number in the Employee table of the employee who heads the department. In other words, each DeptHead field value in the Department table matches exactly one EmployeeNum field value in the Employee table. At the same time, each EmployeeNum field value in the Employee table matches at most one DeptHead field value in the Department table—matching one DeptHead field value if the employee is a department head, or matching zero DeptHead field values if the employee is not a department head. For this one-to-one relationship, the EmployeeNum field in the Employee table and the DeptHead field in the Department table are the fields that link the two tables, with the DeptHead field serving as a foreign key in the Department table and the EmployeeNum field serving as a primary key in the Employee table.

Some database designers might use EmployeeNum instead of DeptHead as the field name for the foreign key in the Department table because they both represent the employee number for the employees of the company. However, DeptHead better identifies the purpose of the field and would more commonly be used as the field name.

Figure A–7 **A one-to-one relationship**

primary key (Department table)

foreign key for the one-to-one relationship

Department

DeptNum	DeptName	DeptHead
24	Finance	8112
27	Marketing	2173
31	Technology	4519

primary key for the one-to-one relationship

Employee

EmployeeNum	FirstName	LastName	DeptNum
2173	Barbara	Hennessey	27
4519	Lee	Noordsy	31
8005	Pat	Amidon	27
8112	Chris	Wandzell	24

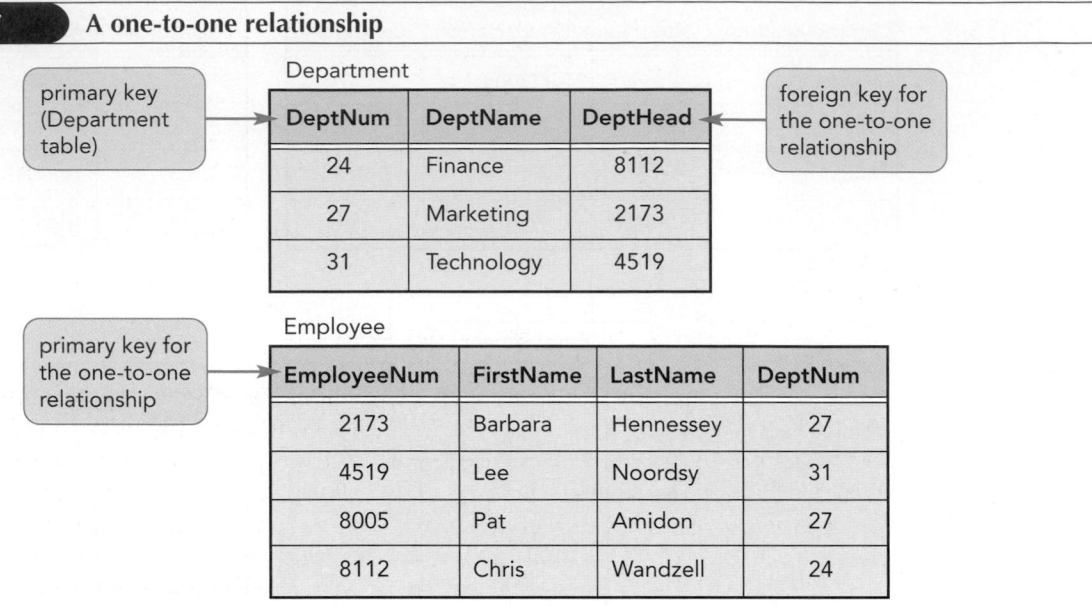

Entity Subtype

Suppose the company awards annual bonuses to a small number of employees who fill director positions in selected departments. As shown in Figure A–8, you could store the Bonus field in the Employee table because a bonus is an attribute associated with employees. The Bonus field would contain either the amount of the employee's bonus (record 4 in the Employee table) or a null value for employees without bonuses (records 1 through 3 in the Employee table).

Figure A–8 **Bonus field added to the Employee table**

Employee

EmployeeNum	FirstName	LastName	DeptNum	Bonus
2173	Barbara	Hennessey	27	
4519	Lee	Noordsy	31	
8005	Pat	Amidon	27	
8112	Chris	Wandzell	24	$20,000

nulls for these Bonus field values

Bonus field value for the fourth record

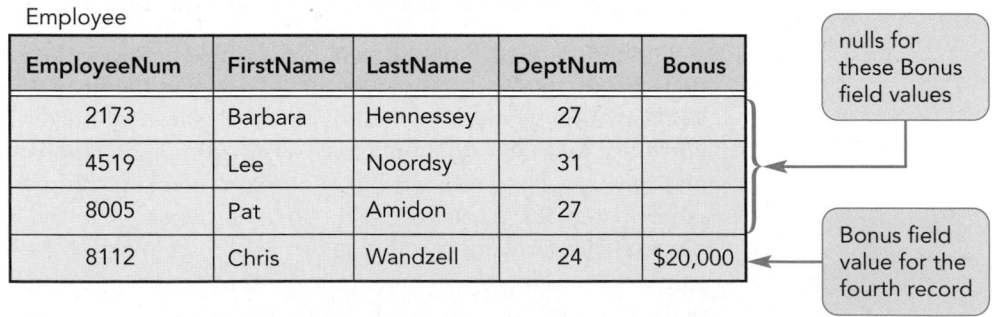

Figure A–9 shows an alternative approach, in which the Bonus field is placed in a separate table, the EmployeeBonus table. The EmployeeBonus table's primary key is the EmployeeNum field, and the table contains one row for each employee earning a bonus. Because some employees do not earn a bonus, the EmployeeBonus table has fewer rows than the Employee table. However, each row in the EmployeeBonus table has a matching row in the Employee table, with the EmployeeNum field serving as the common field; the EmployeeNum field is the primary key in the Employee table and is a foreign key in the EmployeeBonus table.

Figure A–9 **Bonus values stored in a separate table, an entity subtype**

primary key (Employee table)

Employee

EmployeeNum	FirstName	LastName	DeptNum
2173	Barbara	Hennessey	27
4519	Lee	Noordsy	31
8005	Pat	Amidon	27
8112	Chris	Wandzell	24

primary key (EmployeeBonus table)

EmployeeBonus

EmployeeNum	Bonus
8112	$20,000

foreign key

entity subtype

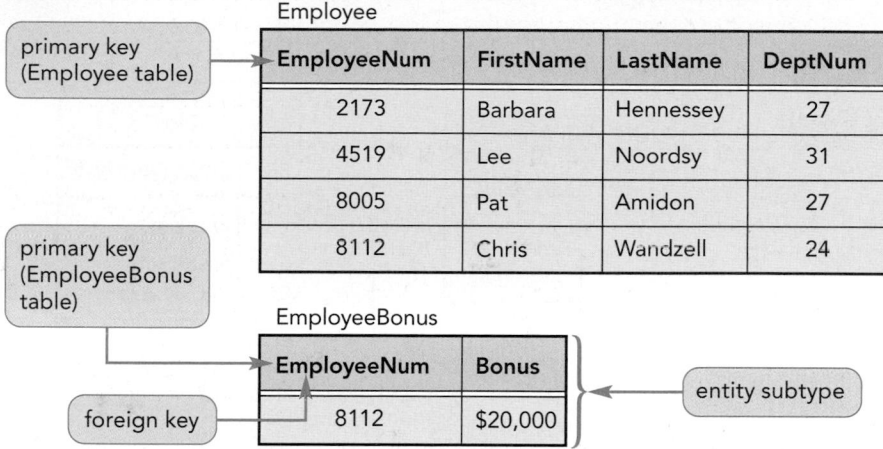

The EmployeeBonus table, in this situation, is called an **entity subtype**, a table whose primary key is a foreign key to a second table and whose fields are additional fields for the second table. Database designers create an entity subtype in two situations. In the first situation, some users might need access to all employee fields, including employee bonuses, while other employees might need access to all employee fields except bonuses. Because most DBMSs allow you to control which tables a user can access, you can specify that some users can access both tables and that other users can access the Employee table but not the EmployeeBonus table, keeping the employee bonus information hidden from the latter group. In the second situation, you can create an entity subtype when a table has fields that could have nulls, as was the case for the Bonus field stored in the Employee table in Figure A–8. You should be aware that database experts debate the validity of the use of nulls in relational databases, and many experts insist that you should never use nulls. This warning against nulls is partly based on the inconsistent way different RDBMSs treat nulls and partly due to the lack of a firm theoretical foundation for how to use nulls. In any case, entity subtypes are an alternative to the use of nulls.

Entity-Relationship Diagrams

A common shorthand method for describing tables is to write the table name followed by its fields in parentheses, underlining the fields that represent the primary key and identifying the foreign keys for a table immediately after the table. Using this method, the tables that appear in Figures A-5 through A-7 and Figure A–9 are described in the following way:

Department (<u>DeptNum</u>, DeptName, DeptHead)
  Foreign key: DeptHead to Employee table
Employee (<u>EmployeeNum</u>, FirstName, LastName, DeptNum)
  Foreign key: DeptNum to Department table
Position (<u>PositionID</u>, PositionDesc, PayGrade)
Employment (<u>EmployeeNum</u>, <u>PositionID</u>, StartDate, EndDate)
  Foreign key: EmployeeNum to Employee table
  Foreign key: PositionID to Position table
EmployeeBonus (<u>EmployeeNum</u>, Bonus)
  Foreign key: EmployeeNum to Employee table

Another popular way to describe tables *and their relationships* is with entity-relationship diagrams. An **entity-relationship diagram (ERD)** shows a database's entities and the relationships among the entities in a symbolic, visual way. In an ERD, an entity and a table are equivalent. Figure A–10 shows an entity-relationship diagram for the tables that appear in Figures A–5 through A–7 and Figure A–9.

Figure A–10 An entity-relationship diagram (ERD)

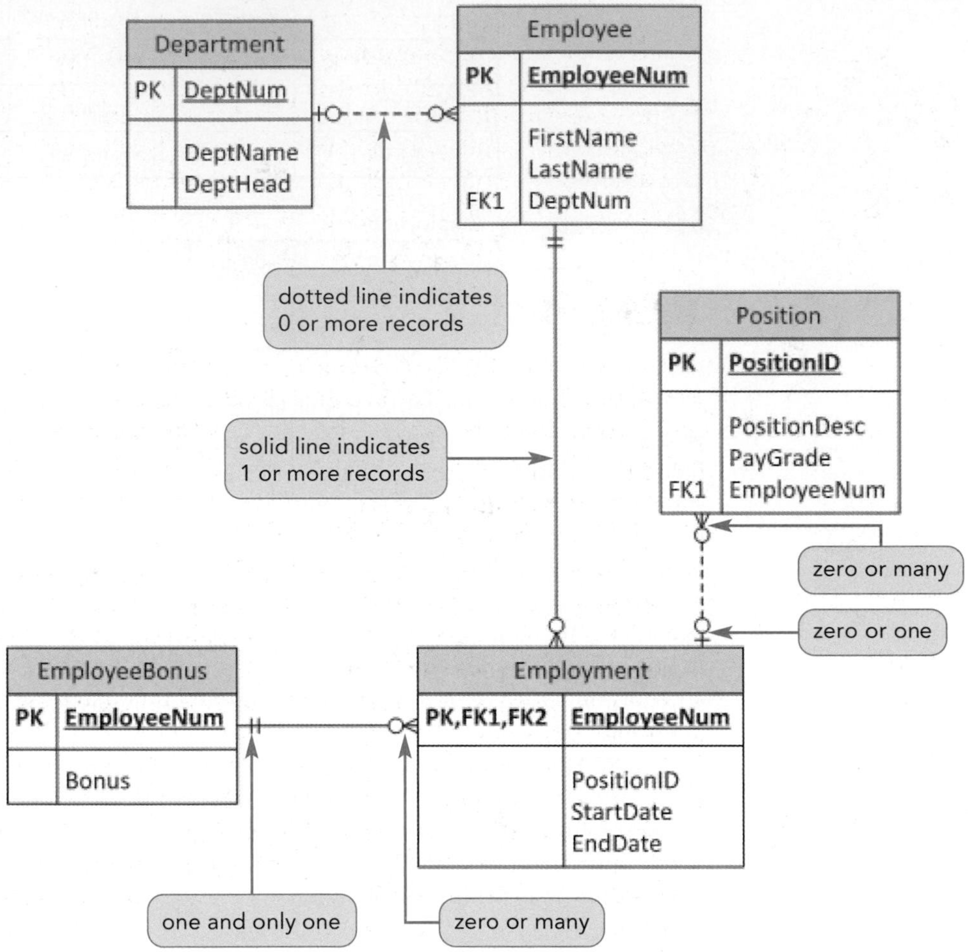
Department
PK DeptNum
DeptName
DeptHead
Employee
PK EmployeeNum
FirstName
LastName
FK1 DeptNum
dotted line indicates 0 or more records
Position
PK PositionID
PositionDesc
PayGrade
FK1 EmployeeNum
solid line indicates 1 or more records
zero or many
zero or one
EmployeeBonus
PK EmployeeNum
Bonus
Employment
PK,FK1,FK2 EmployeeNum
PositionID
StartDate
EndDate
one and only one
zero or many

ERDs have the following characteristics:

- A table is represented by a rectangle that contains the table name and lists the field names. Within each rectangle, the primary key is identified with the abbreviation PK, and any foreign keys are designated with FK. Required fields are formatted in bold.
- Relationships are identified by lines joining the tables. A solid relationship line between two tables indicates there could be 1 or more related records. A dotted relationship line between two tables indicates there could be 0 or more related records.

- At the ends of each relationship line, symbols identify the minimum and maximum possible number of related records from each entity in the relationship. A single perpendicular line represents 1 record, a circle represents 0 records, and a group of three branching lines—known as a crow's foot—represents many records. A one-to-many relationship is represented by a 1 at one end of the relationship line and a crow's foot at the opposite end of the relationship line. For example, the Department and Employee tables have a one-to-many relationship. In a similar manner, a many-to-many relationship exists between the Employee and Position entities and one-to-one relationships exist between the Department and Employee entities and between the Employee and EmployeeBonus entities. The relationships in Figure A–10 illustrate all the possible designations for the ends of lines except for "one or many," which is represented by a single perpendicular line with a crow's foot.

Integrity Constraints

A database has **integrity** if its data follows certain rules; each rule is called an **integrity constraint**. The ideal is to have the DBMS enforce all integrity constraints. If a DBMS can enforce some integrity constraints but not others, the other integrity constraints must be enforced by other programs or by the people who use the DBMS. Integrity constraints can be divided into three groups: primary key constraints, foreign key constraints, and domain integrity constraints.

- One primary key constraint is inherent in the definition of a primary key, which says that the primary key must be unique. The **entity integrity constraint** says that the primary key cannot be null. For a composite key, none of the individual fields can be null. The uniqueness and nonnull properties of a primary key ensure that you can reference any data value in a database by supplying its table name, field name, and primary key value.
- Foreign keys provide the mechanism for forming a relationship between two tables, and referential integrity ensures that only valid relationships exist. **Referential integrity** is the constraint specifying that each nonnull foreign key value must match a primary key value in the primary table. Specifically, referential integrity means that you cannot add a row containing an unmatched foreign key value. Referential integrity also means that you cannot change or delete the related primary key value and leave the foreign key orphaned. In some RDBMSs, when you create a relationship, you can specify one of these options: restricted, cascades, or nullifies. If you specify **restricted** and then change or delete a primary key, the DBMS updates or deletes the value only if there are no matching foreign key values. If you choose **cascades** and then change a primary key value, the DBMS changes the matching foreign key values to the new primary key value, or, if you delete a primary key value, the DBMS also deletes the matching foreign key rows. If you choose **nullifies** and then change or delete a primary key value, the DBMS sets all matching foreign key values to null.
- A **domain** is a set of values from which one or more fields draw their actual values. A **domain integrity constraint** is a rule you specify for a field. By choosing a data type for a field, you impose a constraint on the set of values allowed for the field. You can create specific validation rules for a field to limit its domain further. As you make a field's domain definition more precise, you exclude more and more unacceptable values for the field. For example, in the State table, shown in Figures A–2 and A–4, you could define the domain for the EnteredUnionOrder field to be a unique integer between 1 and 50 and the domain for the StateBird field to be any text string containing 25 or fewer characters.

Dependencies and Determinants

Just as tables are related to other tables, fields are also related to other fields. Consider the modified Employee table shown in Figure A–11. Its description is:

Employee (EmployeeNum, PositionID, LastName, PositionDesc, StartDate, HealthPlan, PlanDesc)

Figure A–11 **A table combining fields from three tables**

composite primary key

Employee

EmployeeNum	PositionID	LastName	PositionDesc	StartDate	HealthPlan	PlanDesc
2173	2	Hennessey	Manager	12/14/2016	B	Managed HMO
4519	1	Noordsy	Director	04/23/2018	A	Managed PPO
4519	3	Noordsy	Analyst	11/11/2012	A	Managed PPO
8005	3	Amidon	Analyst	06/05/2017	C	Health Savings
8005	4	Amidon	Clerk	07/02/2015	C	Health Savings
8112	1	Wandzell	Director	12/15/2017	A	Managed PPO
8112	2	Wandzell	Manager	10/04/2016	A	Managed PPO

The modified Employee table combines several fields from the Employee, Position, and Employment tables that appeared in Figure A–6. The EmployeeNum and LastName fields are from the Employee table. The PositionID and PositionDesc fields are from the Position table. The EmployeeNum, PositionID, and StartDate fields are from the Employment table. The HealthPlan and PlanDesc fields are new fields for the Employee table, whose primary key is now the combination of the EmployeeNum and PositionID fields.

In the Employee table, each field is related to other fields. To determine field relationships, you ask "Does a value for a particular field give me a single value for another field?" If the answer is Yes, then the two fields are **functionally** related. For example, a value for the EmployeeNum field determines a single value for the LastName field, and a value for the LastName field depends on the value of the EmployeeNum field. In other words, EmployeeNum functionally determines LastName, and LastName is functionally dependent on EmployeeNum. In this case, EmployeeNum is called a determinant. A **determinant** is a field, or a collection of fields, whose values determine the values of another field. A field is functionally dependent on another field (or a collection of fields) if that other field is a determinant for it.

You can graphically show a table's functional dependencies and determinants in a **bubble diagram**; a bubble diagram is also called a **data model diagram** or a **functional dependency diagram**. Figure A–12 shows the bubble diagram for the Employee table shown in Figure A–11.

Figure A–12 A bubble diagram for the modified Employee table

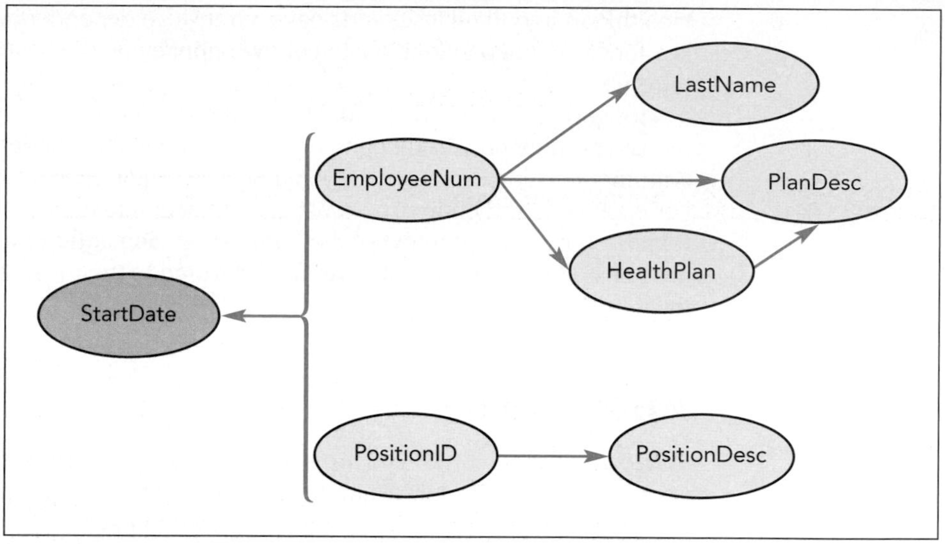
LastName
EmployeeNum
PlanDesc
HealthPlan
StartDate
PositionID
PositionDesc

You can read the bubble diagram in Figure A–12 as follows:

- The EmployeeNum field is a determinant for the LastName, HealthPlan, and PlanDesc fields.
- The PositionID field is a determinant for the PositionDesc field.
- The StartDate field is functionally dependent on the EmployeeNum and PositionID fields together.
- The HealthPlan field is a determinant for the PlanDesc field.

Note that EmployeeNum and PositionID together serve as a determinant for the StartDate field and for all fields that depend on the EmployeeNum field alone and the PositionID field alone. Some experts include these additional fields and some don't. The previous list of determinants does not include these additional fields.

An alternative way to show determinants is to list the determinant, a right arrow, and then the dependent fields, separated by commas. Using this alternative, the determinants shown in Figure A–12 are:

EmployeeNum → LastName, HealthPlan, PlanDesc
PositionID → PositionDesc
EmployeeNum, PositionID → StartDate
HealthPlan → PlanDesc

Only the StartDate field is functionally dependent on the table's full primary key, the EmployeeNum and PositionID fields. The LastName, HealthPlan, and PlanDesc fields have partial dependencies because they are functionally dependent on the EmployeeNum field, which is part of the primary key. A **partial dependency** is a functional dependency on part of the primary key, instead of the entire primary key. Does another partial dependency exist in the Employee table? Yes, the PositionDesc field has a partial dependency on the PositionID field.

Because the EmployeeNum field is a determinant of both the HealthPlan and PlanDesc fields, and the HealthPlan field is a determinant of the PlanDesc field, the HealthPlan and PlanDesc fields have a transitive dependency. A **transitive dependency** is a functional dependency between two nonkey fields, which are both dependent on a third field.

How do you know which functional dependencies exist among a collection of fields, and how do you recognize partial and transitive dependencies? The answers lie with the questions you ask as you gather the requirements for a database application. For each field and entity, you must gain an accurate understanding of its meaning and relationships in the context of the application. **Semantic object modeling** is an entire area of study within the database field devoted to the meanings and relationships of data.

Anomalies

When you use a DBMS, you are more likely to get results you can trust if you create your tables carefully. For example, problems might occur with tables that have partial and transitive dependencies, whereas you won't have as much trouble if you ensure that your tables include only fields that are directly related to each other. Also, when you remove data redundancy from a table, you improve that table. **Data redundancy** occurs when you store the same data in more than one place.

The problems caused by data redundancy and by partial and transitive dependencies are called **anomalies** because they are undesirable irregularities of tables. Anomalies are of three types: insertion, deletion, and update.

To examine the effects of these anomalies, consider the modified Employee table that is shown again in Figure A–13.

Figure A–13 **A table with insertion, deletion, and update anomalies**

composite primary key

Employee

EmployeeNum	PositionID	LastName	PositionDesc	StartDate	HealthPlan	PlanDesc
2173	2	Hennessey	Manager	12/14/2016	B	Managed HMO
4519	1	Noordsy	Director	04/23/2018	A	Managed PPO
4519	3	Noordsy	Analyst	11/11/2012	A	Managed PPO
8005	3	Amidon	Analyst	06/05/2017	C	Health Savings
8005	4	Amidon	Clerk	07/02/2015	C	Health Savings
8112	1	Wandzell	Director	12/15/2017	A	Managed PPO
8112	2	Wandzell	Manager	10/04/2016	A	Managed PPO

- An **insertion anomaly** occurs when you cannot add a record to a table because you do not know the entire primary key value. For example, you cannot add the new employee Cathy Corbett with an EmployeeNum of 3322 to the Employee table if you do not know her position in the company. Entity integrity prevents you from leaving any part of a primary key null. Because the PositionID field is part of the primary key, you cannot leave it null. To add the new employee, your only option is to make up a PositionID field value, until you determine the correct position. This solution misrepresents the facts and is unacceptable, if a better approach is available.

- A **deletion anomaly** occurs when you delete data from a table and unintentionally lose other critical data. For example, if you delete EmployeeNum 2173 because Hennessey is no longer an employee, you also lose the only instance of HealthPlan B in the database. Thus, you no longer know that HealthPlan B is the "Managed HMO" plan.
- An **update anomaly** occurs when a change to one field value requires the DBMS to make more than one change to the database, and a failure by the database to make all the changes results in inconsistent data. For example, if you change a LastName, HealthPlan, or PlanDesc field value for EmployeeNum 8005, the DBMS must change multiple rows of the Employee table. If the DBMS fails to change all the rows, the LastName, HealthPlan, or PlanDesc field now has different values in the database and is inconsistent.

Normalization

Database design is the process of determining the content and structure of data in a database in order to support some activity on behalf of a user or group of users. After you have determined the collection of fields users need to support an activity, you need to determine the precise tables needed for the collection of fields and then place those fields into the correct tables. Understanding the functional dependencies of all fields; recognizing the anomalies caused by data redundancy, partial dependencies, and transitive dependencies when they exist; and knowing how to eliminate the anomalies are all crucial to good database design. Failure to eliminate anomalies leads to data redundancy and can cause data integrity and other problems as your database grows in size.

The process of identifying and eliminating anomalies is called **normalization**. Using normalization, you start with a collection of tables, apply sets of rules to eliminate anomalies, and produce a new collection of problem-free tables. The sets of rules are called **normal forms**. Of special interest for our purposes are the first three normal forms: first normal form, second normal form, and third normal form. First normal form improves the design of your tables, second normal form improves the first normal form design, and third normal form applies even more stringent rules to produce an even better design. Note that normal forms beyond third normal form exist; these higher normal forms can improve a database design in some situations but won't be covered in this section.

First Normal Form

Consider the Employee table shown in Figure A–14. For each employee, the table contains EmployeeNum, which is the primary key; the employee's first name, last name, health plan code and description; and the ID, description, pay grade, and start date of each position held by the employee. For example, Barbara Hennessey has held one position, while the other three employees have held two positions. Because each entry in a table must contain a single value, the structure shown in Figure A–14 does not meet the requirements for a table, or relation; therefore, it is called an **unnormalized relation**. The set of fields that includes the PositionID, PositionDesc, PayGrade, and StartDate fields, which can have more than one value, is called a **repeating group**.

Figure A–14 Repeating groups of data in an unnormalized Employee table

repeating group

Employee

EmployeeNum	PositionID	FirstName	LastName	PositionDesc	PayGrade	StartDate	HealthPlan	PlanDesc
2173	2	Barbara	Hennessey	Manager	40	12/14/2016	B	Managed HMO
4519	1 3	Lee	Noordsy	Director Analyst	45 30	04/23/2018 11/11/2012	A	Managed PPO
8005	3 4	Pat	Amidon	Analyst Clerk	30 20	06/05/2017 07/02/2015	C	Health Savings
8112	1 2	Chris	Wandzell	Director Manager	45 40	12/15/2017 10/04/2016	A	Managed PPO

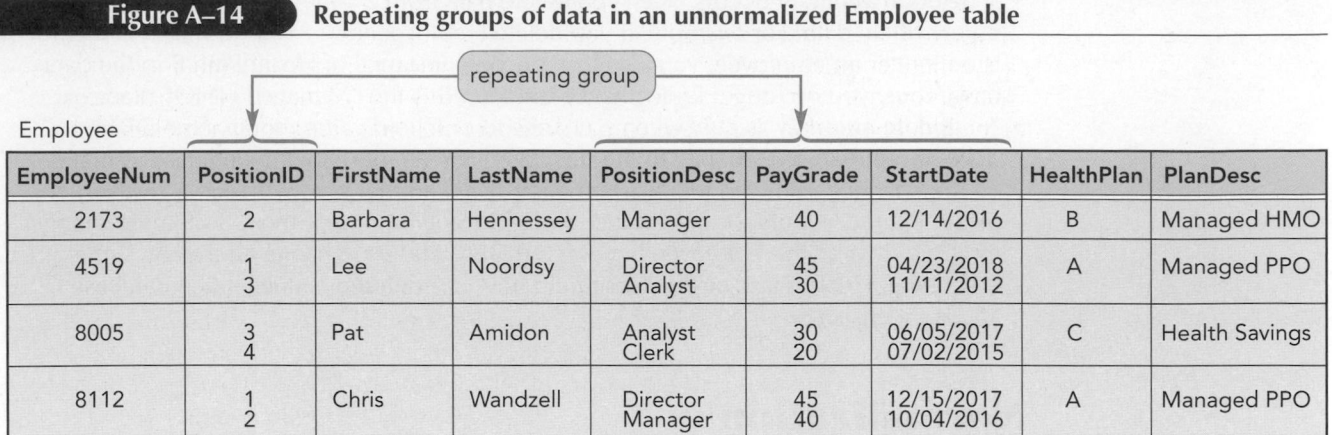

First normal form addresses this repeating-group situation. A table is in **first normal form (1NF)** if it does not contain repeating groups. To remove a repeating group and convert to first normal form, you expand the primary key to include the primary key of the repeating group, forming a composite key. Performing the conversion step produces the 1NF table shown in Figure A–15.

Figure A–15 After conversion to 1NF

composite primary key

Employee

EmployeeNum	PositionID	FirstName	LastName	PositionDesc	PayGrade	StartDate	HealthPlan	PlanDesc
2173	2	Barbara	Hennessey	Manager	40	12/14/2016	B	Managed HMO
4519	1	Lee	Noordsy	Director	45	04/23/2018	A	Managed PPO
4519	3	Lee	Noordsy	Analyst	30	11/11/2012	A	Managed PPO
8005	3	Pat	Amidon	Analyst	30	06/05/2017	C	Health Savings
8005	4	Pat	Amidon	Clerk	20	07/02/2015	C	Health Savings
8112	1	Chris	Wandzell	Director	45	12/15/2017	A	Managed PPO
8112	2	Chris	Wandzell	Manager	40	10/04/2016	A	Managed PPO

The alternative way to describe the 1NF table is:

Employee (<u>EmployeeNum</u>, <u>PositionID</u>, FirstName, LastName, PositionDesc, PayGrade, StartDate, HealthPlan, PlanDesc)

The Employee table is now a true table and has a composite key. The table, however, suffers from insertion, deletion, and update anomalies. (As an exercise, find examples of the three anomalies in the table.) The EmployeeNum field is a determinant for the FirstName, LastName, HealthPlan, and PlanDesc fields, so partial dependencies exist in the Employee table. It is these partial dependencies that cause the anomalies in the Employee table, and second normal form addresses the partial-dependency problem.

Second Normal Form

A table in 1NF is in **second normal form (2NF)** if it does not contain any partial dependencies. To remove partial dependencies from a table and convert it to second normal form, you perform two steps. First, identify the functional dependencies for every field in the table. Second, if necessary, create new tables and place each field in a table such that the field is functionally dependent on the entire primary key, not part of the primary key. If you need to create new tables, restrict them to tables with a primary key that is a subset of the original composite key. Note that partial dependencies occur only when you have a composite key; a table in first normal form with a single-field primary key is automatically in second normal form.

First, identifying the functional dependencies leads to the following determinants for the Employee table:

EmployeeNum → FirstName, LastName, HealthPlan, PlanDesc
PositionID → PositionDesc, PayGrade
EmployeeNum, PositionID → StartDate
HealthPlan → PlanDesc

The EmployeeNum field is a determinant for the FirstName, LastName, HealthPlan, and PlanDesc fields. The PositionID field is a determinant for the PositionDesc and PayGrade fields. The composite key EmployeeNum and PositionID is a determinant for the StartDate field. The HealthPlan field is a determinant for the PlanDesc field. Performing the second step in the conversion from first normal form to second form produces the three 2NF tables shown in Figure A–16.

Figure A–16 After conversion to 2NF

Employee

primary key → EmployeeNum

EmployeeNum	FirstName	LastName	HealthPlan	PlanDesc
2173	Barbara	Hennessey	B	Managed HMO
4519	Lee	Noordsy	A	Managed PPO
8005	Pat	Amidon	C	Health Savings
8112	Chris	Wandzell	A	Managed PPO

Position

primary key → PositionID

PositionID	PositionDesc	PayGrade
1	Director	45
2	Manager	40
3	Analyst	30
4	Clerk	20

Employment

composite primary key → EmployeeNum, PositionID

EmployeeNum	PositionID	StartDate
2173	2	12/14/2016
4519	1	04/23/2018
4519	3	11/11/2012
8005	3	06/05/2017
8005	4	07/02/2015
8112	1	12/15/2017
8112	2	10/04/2016

The alternative way to describe the 2NF tables is:

Employee (<u>EmployeeNum</u>, FirstName, LastName, HealthPlan, PlanDesc)
Position (<u>PositionID</u>, PositionDesc, PayGrade)
Employment (<u>EmployeeNum</u>, <u>PositionID</u>, StartDate)
  Foreign key: EmployeeNum to Employee table
  Foreign key: PositionID to Position table

All three tables are in second normal form. Do anomalies still exist? The Position and Employment tables show no anomalies, but the Employee table suffers from anomalies caused by the transitive dependency between the HealthPlan and PlanDesc fields. (As an exercise, find examples of the three anomalies caused by the transitive dependency.) That is, the HealthPlan field is a determinant for the PlanDesc field, and the EmployeeNum field is a determinant for the HealthPlan and PlanDesc fields. Third normal form addresses the transitive-dependency problem.

Third Normal Form

A table in 2NF is in **third normal form (3NF)** if every determinant is a candidate key. This definition for 3NF is referred to as **Boyce-Codd normal form (BCNF)** and is an improvement over the original version of 3NF. What are the determinants in the Employee table? The EmployeeNum and HealthPlan fields are the determinants; however, the EmployeeNum field is a candidate key because it's the table's primary key, and the HealthPlan field is not a candidate key. Therefore, the Employee table is in second normal form, but it is not in third normal form.

To convert a table to third normal form, remove the fields that depend on the non-candidate-key determinant and place them into a new table with the determinant as the primary key. For the Employee table, the PlanDesc field depends on the HealthPlan field, which is a non-candidate-key determinant. Thus, you remove the PlanDesc field from the table, create a new HealthBenefits table, place the PlanDesc field in the HealthBenefits table, and then make the HealthPlan field the primary key of the HealthBenefits table. Note that only the PlanDesc field is removed from the Employee table; the HealthPlan field remains as a foreign key in the Employee table. Figure A–17 shows the database design for the four 3NF tables.

Figure A–17 After conversion to 3NF

Employee

primary key

EmployeeNum	FirstName	LastName	HealthPlan
2173	Barbara	Hennessey	B
4519	Lee	Noordsy	A
8005	Pat	Amidon	C
8112	Chris	Wandzell	A

HealthBenefits

primary key

HealthPlan	PlanDesc
A	Managed PPO
B	Managed HMO
C	Health Savings

Position

primary key

PositionID	PositionDesc	PayGrade
1	Director	45
2	Manager	40
3	Analyst	30
4	Clerk	20

Employment

composite primary key

EmployeeNum	PositionID	StartDate
2173	2	12/14/2016
4519	1	04/23/2018
4519	3	11/11/2012
8005	3	06/05/2017
8005	4	07/02/2015
8112	1	12/15/2017
8112	2	10/04/2016

The alternative way to describe the 3NF relations is:

Employee (EmployeeNum, FirstName, LastName, HealthPlan)
  Foreign key: HealthPlan to HealthBenefits table
HealthBenefits (HealthPlan, PlanDesc)
Position (PositionID, PositionDesc, PayGrade)
Employment (EmployeeNum, PositionID, StartDate)
  Foreign key: EmployeeNum to Employee table
  Foreign key: PositionID to Position table

The four tables have no anomalies because you have eliminated all the data redundancy, partial dependencies, and transitive dependencies. Normalization provides the framework for eliminating anomalies and delivering an optimal database design, which you should always strive to achieve. You should be aware, however, that experts sometimes denormalize tables to improve database performance—specifically, to decrease the time it takes the database to respond to a user's commands and requests. Typically, when you denormalize tables, you combine separate tables into one table to reduce the need for the DBMS to join the separate tables to process queries and other informational requests. When you denormalize a table, you reintroduce redundancy to the table. At the same time, you reintroduce anomalies. Thus, improving performance exposes a database to potential integrity problems. Only database experts should denormalize tables, but even experts first complete the normalization of their tables.

Natural, Artificial, and Surrogate Keys

When you complete the design of a database, your tables should be in third normal form, free of anomalies and redundancy. Some tables, such as the State table (see Figure A–2), have obvious third normal form designs with obvious primary keys. The State table's description is:

State (StateAbbrev, StateName, EnteredUnionOrder, StateBird, StatePopulation)

Recall that the candidate keys for the State table are StateAbbrev, StateName, and EnteredUnionOrder. Choosing the StateAbbrev field as the State table's primary key makes the StateName and EnteredUnionOrder fields alternate keys. Primary keys such as the StateAbbrev field are sometimes called natural keys. A **natural key** (also called a **logical key** or an **intelligent key**) is a primary key that consists of a field, or a collection of fields, that is an inherent characteristic of the entity described by the table and that is visible to users. Other examples of natural keys are the ISBN (International Standard Book Number) for a book, the SSN (Social Security number) for a U.S. individual, the UPC (Universal Product Code) for a product, and the VIN (vehicle identification number) for a vehicle.

Is the PositionID field, which is the primary key for the Position table (see Figure A–17), a natural key? No, the PositionID field is not an inherent characteristic of a position. Instead, the PositionID field has been added to the Position table only as a way to identify each position uniquely. The PositionID field is an **artificial key**, which is a field that you add to a table to serve solely as the primary key and that is visible to users.

Another reason for using an artificial key arises in tables that allow duplicate records. Although relational database theory and most experts do not allow duplicate records in a table, consider a database that tracks donors and their donations. Figure A–18 shows a Donor table with an artificial key of DonorID and with the DonorFirstName and DonorLastName fields. Some cash donations are anonymous, which accounts for the fourth record in the Donor table. Figure A–18 also shows the Donation table with the DonorID field, a foreign key to the Donor table, and the DonationDate and DonationAmt fields.

Figure A–18 Donor and Donation tables

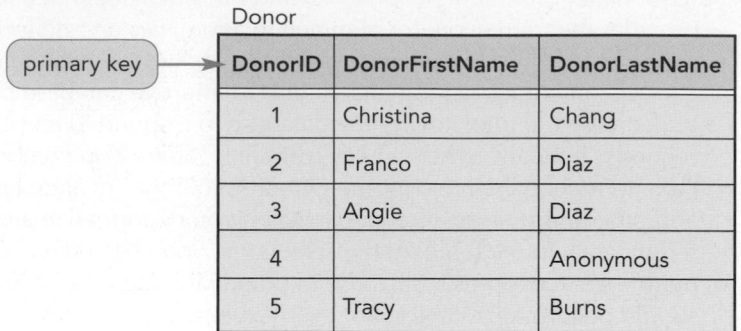

Donor

primary key → DonorID

DonorID	DonorFirstName	DonorLastName
1	Christina	Chang
2	Franco	Diaz
3	Angie	Diaz
4		Anonymous
5	Tracy	Burns

Donation

DonorID	DonationDate	DonationAmt
1	10/12/2020	$50.00
1	09/30/2021	$50.00
2	10/03/2021	$75.00
4	10/10/2021	$50.00
4	10/10/2021	$50.00
4	10/11/2021	$25.00
5	10/13/2021	$50.00

duplicate records (the two rows for DonorID 4 on 10/10/2021)

What is the primary key of the Donation table? No single field is unique, and neither is any combination of fields. For example, on 10/10/2021, two anonymous donors (DonorID value of 4) donated $50 each. You need to add an artificial key, DonationID for example, to the Donation table. The addition of the artificial key makes every record in the Donation table unique, as shown in Figure A–19.

Figure A–19 Donation table after adding DonationID, an artificial key

Donation

artificial key → DonationID

DonationID	DonorID	DonationDate	DonationAmt
1	1	10/12/2020	$50.00
2	1	09/30/2021	$50.00
3	2	10/03/2021	$75.00
4	4	10/10/2021	$50.00
5	4	10/10/2021	$50.00
6	4	10/11/2021	$25.00
7	5	10/13/2021	$50.00

The descriptions of the Donor and Donation tables now are:

Donor (DonorID, DonorFirstName, DonorLastName)
Donation (DonationID, DonorID, DonationDate, DonationAmt)
    Foreign key: DonorID to Donor table

For another common situation, consider the 3NF tables you reviewed in the previous section (see Figure A–17) that have the following descriptions:

Employee (EmployeeNum, FirstName, LastName, HealthPlan)
    Foreign key: HealthPlan to HealthBenefits table
HealthBenefits (HealthPlan, PlanDesc)
Position (PositionID, PositionDesc, PayGrade)
Employment (EmployeeNum, PositionID, StartDate)
    Foreign key: EmployeeNum to Employee table
    Foreign key: PositionID to Position table

Recall that a primary key must be unique, must be minimal, and must not change in value. In theory, primary keys don't change in value. However, in practice, you might have to change EmployeeNum field values that you incorrectly entered in the Employment table. Further, if you need to change an EmployeeNum field value in the Employee table, the change must cascade to the EmployeeNum field values in the Employment table. Also, changes to a PositionID field value in the Position table must cascade to the Employment table. For these and other reasons, many experts add surrogate keys to their tables. A **surrogate key** (also called a **synthetic key**) is a system-generated primary key that is hidden from users. Usually you can use an automatic numbering data type, such as the Access AutoNumber data type, for a surrogate key. Figure A–20 shows the four tables with surrogate keys added to each table.

Figure A–20 Using surrogate keys

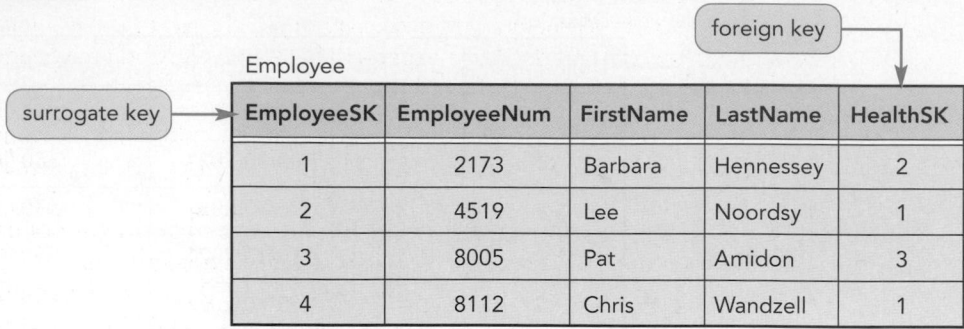

Employee (surrogate key: EmployeeSK; foreign key: HealthSK)

EmployeeSK	EmployeeNum	FirstName	LastName	HealthSK
1	2173	Barbara	Hennessey	2
2	4519	Lee	Noordsy	1
3	8005	Pat	Amidon	3
4	8112	Chris	Wandzell	1

HealthBenefits (surrogate key: HealthSK)

HealthSK	HealthPlan	PlanDesc
1	A	Managed PPO
2	B	Managed HMO
3	C	Health Savings

Position (artificial key: PositionID)

PositionID	PositionDesc	PayGrade
1	Director	45
2	Manager	40
3	Analyst	30
4	Clerk	20

Employment (surrogate key: EmploymentSK; foreign key: EmployeeSK; foreign key: PositionID)

EmploymentSK	EmployeeSK	PositionID	StartDate
1	1	2	12/14/2016
2	2	1	04/23/2018
3	2	3	11/11/2012
4	3	3	06/05/2017
5	3	4	07/02/2015
6	4	1	12/15/2017
7	4	2	10/04/2016

The HealthSK field replaces the HealthPlan field as a foreign key in the Employee table, and the EmployeeSK field replaces the EmployeeNum field in the Employment table. Now when you change an incorrectly entered EmployeeNum field value in the Employee table, you don't need to cascade the change to the Employment table. Likewise, when you change an incorrectly entered HealthPlan field value in the HealthBenefits table, you don't need to cascade the change to the Employee table.

As you design a database, you should *not* consider the use of surrogate keys, and you should use an artificial key only for the rare table that has duplicate records. At the point when you implement a database, you might choose to use artificial and surrogate keys, but be aware that database experts debate their use and effectiveness. You need to consider the following tradeoffs between natural and surrogate keys:

- You use surrogate keys to avoid cascading updates to foreign key values. Surrogate keys can also replace lengthier foreign keys when those foreign keys reference composite fields.
- You don't need a surrogate key for a table whose primary key is not used as a foreign key in another table because cascading updates is not an issue.
- Tables with surrogate keys require more joins than do tables with natural keys. For example, if you need to know all employees with a HealthPlan field value of A, the surrogate key in Figure A–20 requires that you join the Employee and HealthBenefits tables to answer the question. Using natural keys as shown in Figure A–17, the HealthPlan field appears in the Employee table, so no join is necessary.
- Although surrogate keys are meant to be hidden from users, they cannot be hidden from users who create SQL statements and use other ad hoc tools.
- Because you need a unique index for the natural key and a unique index for the surrogate key, your database size is larger and index maintenance takes more time when you use a surrogate key. On the other hand, a foreign key using a surrogate key is usually smaller than a foreign key using a natural key, especially when the natural key is a composite key, so those indexes are smaller and faster to access for lookups and joins.

Microsoft Access Naming Conventions

In the early 1980s, Microsoft's Charles Simonyi introduced an identifier naming convention that became known as Hungarian notation. Microsoft and other companies use this naming convention for variable, control, and other object naming in Basic, Visual Basic, and other programming languages. When Access was introduced in the early 1990s, Stan Leszynski and Greg Reddick adapted Hungarian notation for Microsoft Access databases; their guidelines became known as the Leszynski/Reddick naming conventions. In recent years, the Leszynski naming conventions, the Reddick naming conventions, and other naming conventions have been published. Individuals and companies have created their own Access naming conventions, but many are based on the Leszynski/Reddick naming conventions, as are the naming conventions covered in this section.

An Access database can contain thousands of objects, fields, controls, and other items, and keeping track of their names and what they represent is a difficult task. Consequently, you should use naming conventions that identify the type and purpose of each item in an Access database. You can use naming conventions that identify items generally or very specifically.

For an object, include a prefix tag to identify the type of object, as shown in Figure A–21. In each example in Figure A–21, the final object name consists of a three-character tag prefixed to the base object name. For example, the form name of frmEmployeesAndPositions consists of the frm tag and the EmployeesAndPositions base form name.

Figure A–21 Object naming tags

Object type	Tag	Example
Form	frm	frmEmployeesAndPositions
Macro	mcr	mcrSwitchboard
Module	bas	basCalculations
Query	qry	qryEmployee
Report	rpt	rptEmployeesAndPositions
Table	tbl	tblEmployee

The tags in Figure A–21 identify each object type in general. If you want to identify object types more specifically, you could expand Figure A–21 to include tags such as fsub for a subform, qxtb for a crosstab query, tlkp for a lookup table, rsub for a subreport, and so on.

For controls in forms and reports, a general naming convention uses lbl as a prefix tag for labels and ctl as a prefix tag for other types of controls. For more specific naming conventions for controls, you'd use a specific prefix tag for each type of control. Figure A-22 shows the prefix tags for some common controls in forms and reports.

Figure A–22 Control naming tags

Control type	Tag
Check box	chk
Combo box	cbo
Command button	cmd
Image	img
Label	lbl
Line	lin
List box	lst
Option button	opt
Rectangle	shp
Subform/Subreport	sub
Text box	txt

Some database developers use a prefix tag for each field name to identify the field's data type (for example, dtm for Date/Time, num for Number, and chr for Text or Character), others use a prefix tag for each field name to identify in which table the field is located (for example, emp for the Employee table and pos for the Position table), and still others don't use a prefix tag for field names.

You might use suffix tags for controls that might otherwise have identical names. For example, if you have two text boxes in a form for calculated controls that display the average and the sum of the OrderAmt field, both could legitimately be named txtOrderAmt unless you used suffix tags to name them txtOrderAmtAvg and txtOrderAmtSum.

You should ensure that any name you use does not duplicate a property name or any keyword Access reserves for special purposes. In general, you can avoid property and keyword name conflicts by using two-word field, control, and object names. For example, use StudentName instead of Name, and use OrderDate instead of Date to avoid name conflicts.

All database developers avoid spaces in names, mainly because spaces are not allowed in server DBMSs, such as SQL Server, Oracle, and DB2. If you are prototyping a Microsoft Access database that you'll migrate to one of these server DBMSs, or if future requirements might force a migration, you should restrict your Access identifier names so that they conform to the rules common to them all. Figure A–23 shows the identifier naming rules for Access, SQL Server, Oracle, and DB2.

Figure A–23 **Identifier naming rules for common database management systems**

Identifier naming rule	Access	SQL Server	Oracle	DB2
Maximum character length	64	30	30	30
Allowable characters	Letters, digits, space, and special characters, except for period (.), exclamation point (!), grave accent (`), and square brackets ([ ])	Letters, digits, dollar sign ($), underscore (_), number symbol (#), and at symbol (@)	Letters, digits, dollar sign ($), underscore (_), and number symbol (#)	Letters, digits, at symbol (@), dollar sign ($), underscore (_), and number symbol (#)
Special rules		No spaces; first character must be a letter or at symbol (@)	No spaces; first character must be a letter; stored in the database in uppercase	No spaces; first character must be a letter, at symbol (@), dollar sign ($), or number symbol (#); stored in the database in uppercase

PRACTICE

Review Assignments

1. What are the formal names for a table, for a row, and for a column? What are the popular names for a row and for a column?
2. What is a domain?
3. What is an entity?
4. What is the relationship between a primary key and a candidate key?
5. What is a composite key?
6. What is a foreign key?
7. Look for and describe an example of a one-to-one relationship, an example of a one-to-many relationship, and an example of a many-to-many relationship in a newspaper, magazine, book, or everyday situation you encounter.
8. When do you use an entity subtype?
9. What is the entity integrity constraint?
10. What is referential integrity?
11. What does the cascades option, which is used with referential integrity, accomplish?
12. What are partial and transitive dependencies?
13. What three types of anomalies can be exhibited by a table, and what problems do they cause?
14. Figure A–24 displays an Employee table where the EmployeeID and PositionID form a composite primary key. The table contains insertion, deletion, and update anomalies. Identify at least one of each type of anomaly contained within the table.

Figure A–24 **Table with update anomalies**

Employee

EmployeeID	PositionID	LastName	HealthPlan	PlanDesc
1426	C	Sanders	3	80/20
2817	A	Pollack	2	90/10
3480	B	Brown	1	100
3480	B	Brown	1	100
4416	D	Edwards	4	70/30
5128	A	Martin	3	80/20
5128	C	Martin	3	80/20

15. Figure A–25 shows the Faculty, Title, and Personnel tables with the primary keys FacultyNum for the Faculty table, TitleID for the Title table, and both FacultyNum and TitleID for the Personnel table. Which two integrity constraints do these tables violate and why?

Figure A–25 Integrity constraint violations

Faculty

FacultyNum	FirstName	LastName	Department
1324	Leslie	Jenkins	Business
3855	Jimmy	Cantrell	Technology
5721	Roberto	Sanchez	Languages
5947	Samantha	Roberts	Science

Title

TitleID	TitleDesc	Months
101	Chair	12
102	Professor	12
103	Lecturer	5
104	Teaching assistant	5

Personnel

FacultyNum	TitleID	StartDate
1324	101	12/01/2010
3855		08/01/2015
3855	102	05/01/2016
5721	103	08/12/2014
5721	102	01/02/2018
5815	103	08/10/2017
5947	104	01/02/2019

16. Suppose you have a table for a tutoring service. The fields are the student's identification number, student's name, student's telephone number, student's email address, tutoring session identification number, tutoring session meeting day, tutoring session meeting time, name of tutor, and tutor identification number. Assume that each student has one tutoring session, each tutoring session meets only once a week and has one tutor, and each tutor can teach more than one class. In what normal form is the table, given the following alternative description?

    Student (StudentID, StudentName, StudentPhone, StudentEmail, SessionID, SessionDay, SessionTime, TutorName, TutorID)

    Convert this relation to 3NF and represent the design using the alternative description method.
17. In the database shown in Figure A–26, which consists of the Majors and Students tables, add one record to the end of the Students table that violates both the entity integrity constraint and the referential integrity constraint.

Figure A–26 Creating integrity constraint violations

Majors

MajorID	MajorName
ACC	Accounting
BUS	Business
CSC	Computer Science
EGR	Engineering

Students

StudentID	StudentName	MajorID
123	Smith	CSC
234	Jones	EGR
345	Williams	ACC
456	Cortez	CSC
567	Hansen	BUS
678	Adams	EGR

18. Consider the following table:

    Auction (AuctionID, AuctionDate, AuctionMinPrice, DonationID, DonationDate, DonationDesc, DonationValue, PatronID, PatronName, PatronPhone, PatronEmail)

    This table contains data about an auction house that conducts auctions with donations provided by patrons. The Auction table has the following dependencies:

    AuctionID → AuctionDate, AuctionMinPrice

    DonationID → DonationDate, DonationDesc, DonationValue

    PatronID → PatronName, PatronPhone, PatronEmail

    a. Based on the dependencies, convert the table to first normal form.
    b. Next, convert the Auction table to third normal form.

19. Consider the following table:

    Customer (CustID, CustName, CustBal, CustCredit, RepID, RepName, RepDateHired)

    This table contains data about customers and the sales representatives that call on them from a company. The Customer table has the following dependencies:

    CustID → CustName, CustBal, CustCredit

    RepID → RepName, RepDateHired

    a. Based on the dependencies, convert the Customer table to first normal form.
    b. Next, convert the Customer table to third normal form.

20. Suppose you need to track data for a veterinary office. The veterinary office treats various types of animals. Each animal has one owner; however, one owner may own multiple animals. Each animal may visit the veterinary office multiple times and each visit will generate an invoice. The data you need to collect on each owner is as follows:

    OwnerID, OwnerName, OwnerPhone, OwnerEmail

    The data you need to collect on each animal is as follows:

    AnimalID, OwnerID, AnimalName, AnimalType, AnimalBreed

    The data you need to collect on each visit is as follows:

    VisitID, AnimalID, VisitDate, Reason

    Finally, the data you need to collect for each invoice is as follows:

    InvoiceID, VisitID, InvoiceDate, InvoiceAmount

    a. Create the tables for the veterinary database and describe them using the alternative method. Be sure the tables are in third normal form.
    b. Draw an entity-relationship diagram for the veterinary database.
21. What is the difference among natural, artificial, and surrogate keys?
22. Why should you use naming conventions for the identifiers in a database?

INDEX

A

E

G

H

I

M

N

Q

R